D1441878

# MACROECONOMICS

## FIFTH CANADIAN EDITION

### OLIVIER BLANCHARD
Massachusetts Institute of Technology

### DAVID JOHNSON
Wilfrid Laurier University

**PEARSON**

Toronto

À Noelle
O.B.

To Susan
D.J.

**Managing Editor:** Claudine O'Donnell
**Senior Marketing Manager:** Leigh-Anne Graham
**Developmental Editor:** Paul Donnelly
**Project Manager:** Jessica Hellen
**Production Services:** Rashmi Tickyani, Aptara®, Inc.
**Permissions Project Manager:** Joanne Tang
**Photo Permissions Researcher:** Q2a/Bill Smith/Luke Malone
**Text Permissions Research:** Anna Waluk, Electronic Publishing Services Inc.
**Interior Designer:** Aptara®, Inc.
**Cover Designer:** Suzanne Duda
**Cover Image:** © r-o-x-o-r/Fotolia

Credits and acknowledgments of material borrowed from other sources and reproduced, with permission, in this textbook appear on the appropriate page within the text.

Original edition published by Pearson Education, Inc., Upper Saddle River, New Jersey, USA. Copyright © 2013 Pearson Education, Inc. This edition is authorized for sale only in Canada.

If you purchased this book outside the United States or Canada, you should be aware that it has been imported without the approval of the publisher or author.

**Copyright © 2015, 2010, 2007, 2003, 1998 Pearson Canada Inc.** All rights reserved. Manufactured in the United States of America. This publication is protected by copyright and permission should be obtained from the publisher prior to any prohibited reproduction, storage in a retrieval system, or transmission in any form or by any means, electronic, mechanical, photocopying, recording, or likewise. To obtain permission(s) to use material from this work, please submit a written request to Pearson Canada Inc., Permissions Department, 26 Prince Andrew Place, Don Mills, Ontario, M3C 2T8, or fax your request to 416-447-3126, or submit a request to Permissions Requests at www.pearsoncanada.ca.

10 9 8 7 6 5 4 3 2 1 [EB]

**Library and Archives Canada Cataloguing in Publication**

Blanchard, Olivier (Olivier J.), author
    Macroeconomics / Olivier Blanchard, David Johnson. -- Fifth
Canadian edition.
Includes index.
ISBN 978-0-13-216436-8 (bound)
    1. Macroeconomics--Textbooks.  I. Johnson, David R., 1956-, author
II. Title.
HB172.5.B556 2014                 339              C2013-904778-6

PEARSON

ISBN 978-0-13-216436-8

# ABOUT THE AUTHORS

## Olivier Blanchard

**Olivier Blanchard** is the Robert M. Solow Professor of Economics at the Massachusetts Institute of Technology. He did his undergraduate work in France and received a Ph.D. in economics from MIT in 1977. He taught at Harvard from 1977 to 1982 and has taught at MIT since 1983. He has frequently received the award for best teacher in the department of economics. He is currently on leave from MIT and serves as the Chief Economist at the International Monetary Fund.

He has done research on many macroeconomic issues, including the effects of fiscal policy, the role of expectations, price rigidities, speculative bubbles, unemployment in Western Europe, transition in Eastern Europe, the role of labour market institutions, and the various aspects of the current crisis. He has done work for many governments and many international organizations, including the *World Bank*, the *IMF*, the *OECD*, the *EU Commission*, and the *EBRD*. He has published over 150 articles and edited or written over 20 books, including *Lectures on Macroeconomics* with Stanley Fischer.

He is a research associate of the National Bureau of Economic Research, a fellow of the Econometric Society, a member of the American Academy of Arts and Sciences, and a past Vice President of the American Economic Association.

He currently lives in Washington, D.C. with his wife, Noelle. He has three daughters: Marie, Serena, and Giulia.

## David Johnson

David Johnson is Professor of Economics at Wilfrid Laurier University, and Education Policy Scholar at the C. D. Howe Institute.

Professor Johnson's areas of specialty are macroeconomics, international finance, and, more recently, the economics of education. His published work in macroeconomics includes studies of Canada's international debt, the influence of American interest rates on Canadian interest rates, and the determination of the exchange rate between Canada and the United States. His 2005 book *Signposts of Success*, a comprehensive analysis of elementary school test scores in Ontario, was selected as a finalist in 2006 for both the Donner Prize and the Purvis Prize. He has also written extensively on inflation targets as part of monetary policy in Canada and around the world. His primary teaching area is macroeconomics. He is coauthor with Olivier Blanchard of *Macroeconomics* the sixth U.S. edition.

Professor Johnson received his undergraduate degree from the University of Toronto, his Master's degree from the University of Western Ontario, and his Ph.D. in 1983 from Harvard University, where Olivier Blanchard served as one of his supervisors. He has worked at the Bank of Canada and visited at the National Bureau of Economic Research, Cambridge University, and most recently at the University of California, Santa Barbara as Canada–U.S. Fulbright Scholar and Visiting Chair.

Professor Johnson lives in Waterloo, Ontario, with his wife Susan, who is also an economics professor. They have shared the raising of two children, Sarah and Daniel. When not studying or teaching economics, David plays Oldtimers' Hockey and enjoys cross-country skiing in the winter and sculling in the summer. For a complete change of pace, Professor Johnson has been heavily involved in the Logos program, an after-school program for children and youth at First Mennonite Church in Kitchener, Ontario.

# BRIEF CONTENTS

# C O N T E N T S

# FOCUS BOXES

# P R E F A C E

We had two main goals in writing this book:

- To make close contact with current macroeconomic events: What makes macroeconomics exciting is the light it sheds on what is happening around the world, from the major economic crisis that has engulfed the world since 2008, to the budget deficits of the United States, to the problems of the euro area, to high growth in China. The Canadian policy response to world events is a significant part of the story in this book. These events and responses—and many more—are described in the book, not in footnotes, but in the text or in detailed Focus boxes. Each box shows how you can use what you have learned to get an understanding of these events. Our belief is that these boxes not only convey the "life" of macroeconomics, but also reinforce the lessons from the models, making them more concrete and easier to grasp.
- To provide an integrated view of macroeconomics: The book is built on one underlying model, a model that draws the implications of equilibrium conditions in three sets of markets: the goods market, the financial markets, and the labour market. Depending on the issue at hand, the parts of the model relevant to the issue are developed in more detail while the other parts are simplified or lurk in the background. But the underlying model is always the same. This way, you will see macroeconomics as a coherent whole, not a collection of models. And you will be able to make sense not only of past macroeconomic events, but also of those that unfold in the future.

## New to this Edition

- Chapter 1 starts with a history of the crisis, giving a sense of the world of macroeconomics, and setting up the issues to be dealt with throughout the book.
- Chapter 2 and the appendix on national income accounting uses the new presentation of Canada's national accounts announced in the fall of 2012.
- Chapter 4, the initial chapter on monetary policy and the *LM* curve, includes a treatment of the case where the central bank sets the interest rate.
- Chapters 6, 7, and 8 include the new presentation of Canada's international payments, also revised in 2012.
- A new Chapter 11, which comes after the short- and medium-run architecture have been put in place, presents an extensive analysis of the world economic crisis. It shows how one can use and extend the short-run and medium-run analysis to understand the various aspects of the crisis, from the role of the financial system to the constraints on macroeconomic policy.
- Material on depressions and slumps has been relocated from later chapters to Chapter 11 and the material on very high inflation has been reduced and included in Chapter 24.
- A rewritten Chapter 25, on fiscal policy, is an extensive analysis of recent fiscal policy in Canada.

- Chapters 23, 24, and 25 draw the implications of the crisis for the conduct of fiscal and monetary policy in particular, and for macroeconomics in general.
- Many new Focus boxes have been introduced. Most are necessary to consider the macroeconomic events related to the crisis. The new boxes include: "The Lehman Bankruptcy, Fears of Another Great Depression, and Shifts in the Consumption Function" and "Recessions in Canada since 1981" in Chapter 3; "Bank Runs and Bank Collapses" in Chapter 4; "The U.S. Economy and the *IS-LM* Model from 2000 to 2012" in Chapter 5; "The G20 and the 2009 Fiscal Stimulus" in Chapter 7; "Sudden Stops, Safe Havens, and the Limits to the Interest-Parity Condition" in Chapter 8; "Canada's Macroeconomic Policy Response to the World Economic Crisis" in Chapter 10; "The Great Depression in North America," "Increasing Bank Leverage in the United States—the SIV," "Japan, the Liquidity Trap, and Fiscal Policy," in Chapter 11; "The Release of GDP Growth Measures in Canada and the United States: Numbers to Watch" in Chapter 13; "Labour Productivity in Canada and the United States, 1961–2011" in Chapter 17; "Temporary Foreign Workers in Canada" in Chapter 18; "Why Deflation Can Be Very Bad: Deflation and the Real Interest Rate in America During the Great Depression" in Chapter 19; "The Yield Curve in Canada and the United States in 2013" and "Are Canadian Houses Overpriced in 2013?" in Chapter 20; "LTV Ratios and Housing Price Increases from 2000 to 2007" in Chapter 24; "What is Canada's Cyclically Adjusted Budget Balance?" and "How Countries Decreased Their Debt Ratios after World War II" and "Is Fiscal Policy Neutral in the Short Run?" in Chapter 25.
- Figures and tables have been updated using the latest data available. The presentation of the national accounts and the balance in payments has been updated to the new conventions recently adopted by Statistics Canada.

## Organization

The book has two central components, a core and two additional sections. An introduction precedes the core. The two sections that extend the core are followed by a review of the role of policy. The book ends with an epilogue on the history of macroeconomics.

- Chapters 1 and 2 introduce the basic facts and issues of macroeconomics.

  Chapter 1 offers a tour of the world, from Canada, to the United States, to Europe, to Japan. Some instructors may prefer to cover Chapter 1 later, perhaps after Chapter 2, which introduces basic concepts, articulates the notions of short run, medium run, and long run, and gives a quick tour of the book.

  While Chapter 2 gives the basics of national income accounting, we have put a detailed treatment of national income accounts in Appendix 1 at the end of the book. This both decreases the burden on the beginning reader and allows for a more thorough treatment in the appendix.

- Chapters 3 to 18 constitute the **core**.

  Chapters 3 to 8 focus on the **short run**. They characterize equilibrium in the goods market and in the financial markets, and they derive the basic model used to study short-run movements in output, the *IS-LM* model. The open economy material appears in Chapters 6, 7, and 8.

  Chapters 9 to 14 focus on the **medium run**. Chapter 9 focuses on equilibrium in the labour market and introduces the natural rate of unemployment. Chapter 10 develops a model based on aggregate demand and aggregate supply and show how that model can be used to understand movements in activity that come from shifts in demand. Chapter 11 adds shifts in aggregate supply and, more importantly, extends the model to look at the crisis. To understand the crisis there is a discussion of financial markets and the liquidity trap. Chapter 12 introduces the Phillips Curve and a basic tradeoff between the change in inflation and a higher level of unemployment. Chapter 13, which looks at the dynamic relation between inflation and economic activity, is a bit harder and is structured to allow an instructor to delete the chapter without loss of continuity. Chapter 14 looks at open economy issues in the medium run. In particular, there is an analysis of fixed and flexible exchange rates. Chapter 14 is also a bit harder and can also be dropped without loss of continuity.

  Chapters 15 to 18 focus on the **long run**. Chapter 15 describes the facts, showing the evolution of output over countries and over long periods of time. Chapters 16 and 17 develop a model of growth, focusing on the determinants of capital accumulation and technological progress and the role of each in growth. Chapter 18 looks at growth in the open economy. It stresses the role of net immigration and foreign capital in creating economic growth. An appendix to Chapter 18 deals with the concept of an optimal current account deficit.

- There are two sections outside the **core**.

  Chapters 19 to 22 focus on **expectations**. Expectations play a major role in most economic decisions and, by implication, in the determination of output. Chapter 19 introduces the basic tools. Chapter 20 focuses on expectations in financial markets. There is a extensive discussion of housing and the housing bubble as part of the crisis. Chapter 21 looks at investment and consumption. Chapter 22 presents complications in monetary and fiscal policy when expectations matter.

  Chapters 23, 24, and 25 return to **macroeconomic policy**. While most of the first 22 chapters discuss macroeconomic policy in one form or another, the purpose of Chapters 23 to 25 is to tie the threads together. Chapter 23 looks at the role and the limits of macroeconomic policy in general. Chapters 24 and 25 review monetary and fiscal policy. Some teachers may want to use parts or all of these chapters earlier. For example, it is easy to move forward the discussion of the government budget constraint in Chapter 25.

- Chapter 26 is a short history of the development of macroeconomic thought. It includes a section asking what we have learned from the crisis.

## Alternative Course Outlines

Intermediate macroeconomics is typically taught as a single two-semester course with one instructor or as two one-semester courses, often with different instructors. The book's organization assumes two 12- or 13-week terms with some time used for evaluation and perhaps review. Some chapters are more difficult than others and would require more time in class.

If an instructor had a group of intermediate macroeconomics students for two consecutive semesters, it would make sense to use the book in the order it is written.

A first one-semester course could cover Chapters 1 through 14. This would bring the course to the end of the medium-run analysis. You could leave out Chapters 13 and 14 without loss of continuity and include some material in Chapters 23 to 25 if that were your preference.

The second one-semester course often reviews the core material, particularly if students have been away from macroeconomics for a period of time. It then covers the long run, the material on expectations and the material on policy.

## Features

We have made sure never to present a theoretical result without relating it to the real world. For this purpose, in addition to discussions of facts in the text itself, we have included **Focus** boxes, which expand on a point made in the text.

The margin notes running parallel to the text create a dialogue with the reader, smoothing out the more difficult passages and allowing for a deeper understanding of the concepts and the results derived along the way.

For students who want to explore macroeconomics further, there are two features present in some chapters:

- **Short appendices** to some chapters, which show how a proposition in the text can be derived more rigorously or expanded.
- A **Further Readings** section at the end of the some chapters, as appropriate, indicates where to find more information.

Each chapter ends with three ways of making sure that the material in the chapter has been thoroughly understood:

- A **summary** of the chapter's main points.
- A list of **key terms**.
- A series of **end-of-chapter exercises**, some of them requiring access to the Internet, some of them requiring the use of a spreadsheet program.

## The Teaching and Learning Package

The book comes with a number of supplements to help both students and instructors.

## For Instructors:

- **Instructor's Solutions Manual.** This manual includes solutions to all end-of-chapter questions and exercises. It can be downloaded from the Pearson Canada Catalogue.
- **Test Item File.** The test bank is completely revised with additional new multiple-choice questions for each chapter.
- **TestGen.** The printed Test Item File is designed for use with the computerized TestGen package, which allows

instructors to customize, save, and generate classroom tests. The test program permits instructors to edit, add, or delete questions from the test bank; edit existing graphics and create new graphics; analyze test results; and organize a database of tests and student results. This software allows for extensive flexibility and ease of use. It provides many options for organizing and displaying tests, along with search and sort features. The software and the Test Item File can be downloaded from the Pearson Canada Catalogue.

- **Digital Image Library.** We have digitized the complete set of figures, graphs, and charts from the book. These files can be downloaded from the Pearson Canada Catalogue.

- **PowerPoint Lecture Slides.** These electronic slides provide section titles, tables, equations, and graphs for each chapter and can be downloaded from the Pearson Canada Catalogue.

- **Technology Specialists.** Pearson's Technology Specialists work with faculty and campus course designers to ensure that Pearson technology products, assessment tools, and online course materials are tailored to meet your specific needs. This highly qualified team is dedicated to helping schools take full advantage of a wide range of educational resources, by assisting in the integration of a variety of instructional materials and media formats. Your local Pearson Education sales representative can provide you with more details on this service program.

- **CourseSmart.** CourseSmart goes beyond traditional expectations, providing instant, online access to the textbooks and course materials you need at a lower cost for students. And even as students save money, you can save time and hassle with a digital eTextbook that allows you to search for the most relevant content at the very moment you need it. Whether it's evaluating textbooks or creating lecture notes to help students with difficult concepts, CourseSmart can make life a little easier. See how when you visit **www.coursesmart.com/**instructors.

- **Pearson Custom Library.** For enrollments of at least 25 students, you can create your own textbook by choosing the chapters that best suit your own course needs. To begin building your custom text, visit **www.pearsoncustomlibrary.com.** You may also work with a dedicated Pearson Custom editor to create your ideal text—publishing your own original content or mixing and matching Pearson content. Contact your local Pearson Representative to get started.

- **peerScholar.** Firmly grounded in published research, peerScholar is a powerful online pedagogical tool that helps develop your students' critical and creative thinking skills. peerScholar facilitates this through the process of creation, evaluation, and reflection. Working in stages, students begin by submitting a written assignment. peerScholar then circulates their work for others to review, a process that can be anonymous or not, depending on your preference. Students receive peer feedback and evaluations immediately, reinforcing their learning and driving the development of higher-order thinking skills. Students can then resubmit revised work, again depending on your preference. Contact your Pearson Representative to learn more about peerScholar and the research behind it.

## For Students:

- **Spreadsheets.** Most of the chapters have one or more spreadsheets associated with the material in the chapter. These spreadsheets allow the student to work through a large number of calculations related to the chapter material. These spreadsheets can be downloaded by instructors from the Pearson Canada Catalogue.

- **CourseSmart.** CourseSmart goes beyond traditional expectations, providing instant, online access to the textbooks and course materials you need at an average savings of 60%. With instant access from any computer and the ability to search your text, you'll quickly find the content you need, no matter where you are. And with online tools like highlighting and note-taking, you can save time and study efficiently. See all the benefits at **www.coursesmart.com/students.**

## Acknowledgments and Thanks

Any book owes much to many. A fifth edition begins with all those who worked on the previous Canadian editions and then on the numerous American editions. There are two students who require special thanks: Ewelina Sinkiewicz, who prepared the data for many of the figures in the fourth edition, and Greg Lang, who undertook the same task for the third edition. Greg Lang put a great deal of effort into the spreadsheet exercises that supplement the book. A group of students who need to be thanked are the many students who have taken Economics 290 and 390 at Wilfrid Laurier University over many years. They are the testers for many of my ideas on macroeconomics.

I was blessed with four excellent instructors in macroeconomics at the graduate level: David Laidler, Michael Parkin, Benjamin Friedman, and Olivier Blanchard. These professors taught macroeconomics in a way that made it engaging and exciting. I hope I have passed on some of their enthusiasm and knowledge.

Alastair Robertson, who was a superb colleague for many years in teaching intermediate macroeconomics at WLU, taught me a lot about teaching this subject.

In addition to those already listed, a number of persons at Pearson Canada worked hard on this edition. They are: Managing Editor, Claudine O'Donnell; Developmental Editor, Paul Donnelly; Project Manager, Jessica Hellen; Senior Marketing Manager, Leigh-Anne Graham; Copy Editor, Susan Bindernagel; Proofreader, Julie Fletcher; and Technical Checker, Marcelo Arbex.

We have also benefited from the comments and suggestions of reviewers. They include:

Masoud Anjomshoa, University of Toronto

Marcelo Arbex, University of Windsor

Ajit Dayanandan, University of Northern British Columbia

Xavier de Vanssay, York University

Robert Gateman, University of British Columbia

Jean-François Tremblay, University of Ottawa

Finally I would like to thank my wife Susan. I benefit so much from her love and support.

David Johnson,
Wilfrid Laurier University
Waterloo, Ontario

# The Core: Introduction

The first two chapters of this book introduce you to the issues and the approach of macroeconomics.

## Chapter 1

Chapter 1 takes you on a macroeconomic tour of the world. It starts with a look at the economic crisis and its aftermath, which have dominated the world economy since the late 2000s. The tour includes Canada, and stops at three of the world's major economic powers: the United States, the euro area, and China.

## Chapter 2

Chapter 2 takes you on a tour of the book. It defines the three central variables of macroeconomics: output, unemployment, and inflation. It then introduces the three time periods around which the book is organized: the short run, the medium run, and the long run.

# A Tour of the World

What is macroeconomics? The best way to answer is not to give you a formal definition, but rather to take you on an economic tour of the world, to describe both the main economic event since 2000 and the issues that keep macroeconomists and macroeconomic policy makers awake at night.

At the time of this writing (in 2013), macroeconomic policy makers are not sleeping well and have not slept well in a long time. In 2008, the world economy entered a major macroeconomic crisis, the largest one since the Great Depression. World output growth, which typically runs at 4 to 5% a year, was actually negative in 2009. Since then, growth has turned positive, and the world economy is slowly recovering. But the crisis has left scars, and many worries remain.

Our goal in this chapter is to give you a sense of these events and of some of the macroeconomic issues confronting different countries today. There is no way we can take you on a full tour. We begin with an overview of the crisis and its aftermath. Then we stop to look at details in Canada, the United States, and Europe. The tour ends in China, which was not much affected by the crisis. The ever-increasing development of China and the integration of its billion-plus people into the world economy is the other major story of the world economy in the last 25 years.

**Section 1-1** looks at the crisis.

**Section 1-2** looks at Canada.

**Section 1-3** looks at the United States.

**Section 1-4** looks at the euro area.

**Section 1-5** looks at China.

**Section 1-6** concludes and looks ahead.

Read this chapter as you would read an article in a newspaper or magazine. Do not worry about the exact meaning of the words or about understanding all the arguments in detail: The words will be defined and the arguments further developed in later chapters. Regard this chapter as background, intended to introduce you to the issues of macroeconomics. If you enjoy reading this chapter, you will probably enjoy reading this book. Indeed, once you have read the book, come back to this chapter; see where you stand on the issues, and judge how much progress you have made in your study of macroeconomics.

# 1-1 | The World Economic Crisis in 2008 and 2009

Table 1–1 gives you output growth rates for the world economy, for advanced economies, and for other countries separately, since 2000 and ending with the forecasts from the International Monetary Fund for 2012, 2013, and 2014.* As you can see, from 2000 to 2007 the world economy had a sustained expansion. Annual average world output growth was 4.0%, with advanced economies (the group of 30 or so richest countries in the world) growing at 2.6% per year, and emerging and developing economies (the other 150 or so other countries in the world) growing at a much faster 6.6% per year.

In 2007, however, signs that the expansion might be coming to an end started to appear. U.S. housing prices, which had doubled since 2000, started declining. In mid-2007, as we wrote the previous edition of this book, we described how economists were divided as to whether this might lead to a recession—a decrease in output. Optimists believed that, while lower housing prices might lead to lower housing construction and to lower spending by consumers, the Fed (the short name for the U.S. central bank, formally known as the *Federal Reserve Board*) could lower interest rates to stimulate demand and avoid a recession. Pessimists believed that the decrease in interest rates might not be enough to sustain demand, and that the United States might go through a short recession.

Even the pessimists turned out not to be pessimistic enough. As housing prices continued to decline, falling by about 30% in total, it became clear that many of the mortgage loans that had been given out during the earlier expansion were of poor quality. Many of the borrowers had taken too large a loan and were increasingly unable to make mortgage payments. And, with declining housing prices, the value of their mortgage often exceeded the price of the house, giving them an incentive to default. This was not the worst of it: The banks that had issued the mortgages had often bundled and packaged them together into new securities and then sold these securities to other banks and investors. These securities had often been repackaged into more new securities, and so on. The result is that many banks, instead of holding the mortgages themselves, held these securities, which were so complex that their value was nearly impossible to assess.

> "Banks" here actually means "banks and other financial institutions." But ◄ this is too long to write and we do not want to go into these complications in this chapter.

This complexity and opaqueness turned a housing price decline into a major financial crisis, a development that very few economists had anticipated. Not knowing the quality of the assets that other banks had on their balance sheets, banks became very reluctant to lend to each other for fear that the bank to which they lent might not be able to repay. Unable to borrow, and with assets of uncertain value, many banks found themselves in trouble. On September 15, 2008, a major bank, Lehman Brothers, went bankrupt. The effects were dramatic. Because the links between Lehman and other banks were so opaque, many other banks appeared at risk

| TABLE 1–1 | World Output Growth since 2000 | | | | | | | |
|---|---|---|---|---|---|---|---|---|
| Percent | 2000–2007 (average) | 2008 | 2009 | 2010 | 2011 | 2012 | 2013 | 2014 |
| World | 4.0 | 2.8 | −0.6 | 5.2 | 3.9 | 3.1 | 3.3 | 4.0 |
| Advanced economies | 2.6 | 0.1 | −3.5 | 3.0 | 1.6 | 1.2 | 1.2 | 2.3 |
| Emerging and developing economies | 6.6 | 6.0 | 2.7 | 7.6 | 6.4 | 5.0 | 5.3 | 5.7 |

*Source:* Data from International Monetary Fund, World Economic Outlook Database, April 2013. The numbers for 2012, 2013, and 2014 are estimates or forecasts as of 2013.

---

*Where data were not yet available at the time of writing, throughout this chapter numbers for 2012, 2013, and 2014 are estimates or forecasts as of spring 2013.

FIGURE 1–1

Stock Prices in Canada, the United States, the Euro Area, and Emerging Economies, 2007–2010

*Source:* Data from USA, Haver Analytics S11ACD; Euro area, Haver Analytics S023ACD; Emerging economies, Haver Analytics S200ACD; Canada, CANSIM II Variable V122620

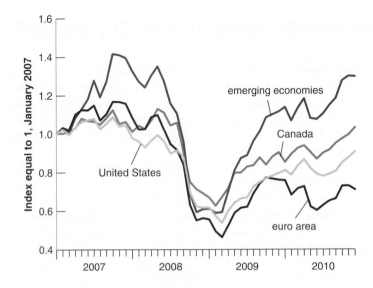

of going bankrupt as well. For a few weeks, it looked as if the whole financial system might collapse.

This financial crisis quickly turned into a major economic crisis. Stock prices collapsed. Figure 1–1 plots the evolution of four stock price indexes, for the United States, for Canada, for the euro area, and for emerging economies, from the beginning of 2007 over the crisis period. The indexes are set equal to 1 in January 2007. Note how, by the end of 2008, stock prices had lost half or more of their value from their previous peak. Note also that, despite the fact that the crisis originated in the United States, stock market prices in the rest of the world had decreased by as much as their U.S. counterparts.

The Great Depression in the United States saw four years of negative output growth ▶ from 1929 to 1932. The unemployment rate peaked at 24.9%. Canada had a very similar experience.

Hit by the decrease in housing prices and the collapse in stock prices, and worried that this might be the beginning of another Great Depression, Americans sharply cut their consumption. Auto sales plummeted. Worried about sales and uncertain about the future, firms sharply cut back investment. With house prices dropping and many vacant homes on the market, very few new homes were built in the United States. In the third quarter of 2008, U.S. output growth turned negative and remained so in 2009.

One might have hoped that the crisis and the accompanying unemployment would remain largely contained in the United States. As Table 1–1 and Figure 1–1 both show, this was not the case. The U.S. crisis quickly became a world crisis. Other countries were affected through two channels. The first channel was trade. As U.S. consumers and firms cut spending, part of the decrease fell on imports of foreign goods. Looking at it from the viewpoint of countries exporting to the United States, their exports went down, and so, in turn, did their output. The second channel was financial. U.S. banks, badly needing funds in the United States, repatriated funds from other countries, creating problems for banks in those countries as well. As stock prices fell all over the world, consumers lost confidence and firms reduced investment. The result was not just a U.S. but a world recession. By 2009, average growth in advanced economies was –3.5%, by far the lowest annual growth rate since the Great Depression. Growth in emerging and developing economies remained positive but was about 3 percentage points lower than the 2000–2007 average.

Since then, thanks to strong monetary and fiscal policies and to the slow repair of the financial system, the two North American economies have returned to positive, if much slower, growth. The euro area continues to struggle. What do we mean by strong monetary and fiscal policy?

One policy response to the crisis was an immediate reduction in interest rates. Figure 1–2 shows interest rates on the U.S. dollar, euro, and Canadian dollar 3-month bank deposits since 2000. Interest rate reductions began in 2008. These interest rate reductions were designed to

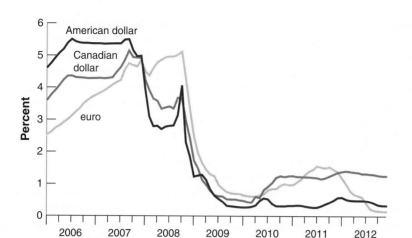

FIGURE 1-2

Interest Rates in Three Currencies since the Crisis

*Source:* Data from LIBOR interbank 3-month rates: Canadian dollar, CAD3MT-D156N; American dollar, USD3MTD156N; euro, EUR-3MTD156N. Federal Reserve Economic Database (FRED). http://research.stlouisfed.org.fred2/

increase demand and prevent an even larger fall in GDP. The changes in monetary policy were implemented swiftly.

There was a decisive fiscal policy response in 2009. In the United States, in Europe, and in Canada, taxes were cut and government spending was increased. This was partly a result of international agreements in 2008 that all the advanced economics would increase government spending or reduce taxes together. Figure 1–3 shows the magnitude of the increase in the budget deficits.

The figure shows the budget deficit as a percentage of GDP so that it is easy to compare across the different economies. It is also the budget deficit for all governments put together, not just federal or central governments. This is important because many countries, like Canada, have a federal structure, and provincial or state governments are very important. The United States started the crisis with the biggest deficit and increased the biggest deficit by the largest amount. Before the crisis, Canadian governments were running a small budget surplus, which is the meaning of a negative budget deficit. The euro area countries were also near a surplus. Then, in 2009 and 2010 all three economies used expansionary fiscal policy to maintain demand and prevent an even more severe recession.

Figure 1–3 highlights one of the important issues facing almost all advanced economy countries in 2013. How quickly should the budget deficit be reduced? You may have realized that, as output recovers further and unemployment gradually decreases, revenues will increase and some of the spending will be phased out. This is indeed likely to be the case, and Figure 1–3 shows a reduction in deficits. However, all three deficits are large and positive even in 2014. A 5% deficit in the United States is still too large a number and creates a steadily

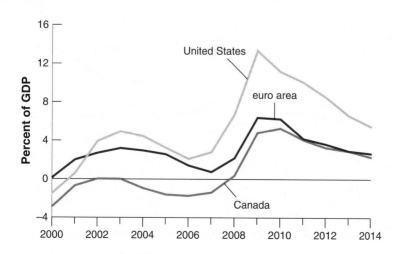

FIGURE 1-3

Budget Deficits in the United States, Canada, and the Euro Area since 2000

*Source:* Data from Variable GGXCNL_NGDP from the International Monetary Fund, World Economic Outlook database, April 2013.

increasing debt. In all of these countries, budget forecasts for the more distant future are even gloomier. In every country, the population is aging and benefits to the elderly are increasing. As populations age, health expenditures grow quickly. In all these countries, governments provide significant public health care. Many believe that the United States does not have public health care. This is incorrect. The U.S. federal government provides health care to those over 65, and U.S. federal and state governments contribute to health care for lower-income citizens. So there is wide agreement in all countries that budget deficits must be reduced further. But there is disagreement as to both when and how to do so.

- Some economists argue that deficit reduction should start now and proceed rapidly. They argue that the credibility of governments is at stake, and that only a strong reduction will convince people that the government will do what is needed to stabilize the debt. Other economists argue, however, that too fast a reduction in the deficit would be dangerous. A reduction in the deficit can be achieved by a combination of an increase in taxes and a decrease in spending. Either one, they argue, will decrease demand and slow down growth at a time when unemployment is still very high. Their recommendation is thus to reduce the deficit, but to do it slowly and steadily. In Europe, unemployment has remained high even as the budget deficits have gradually come down. Some blame the high unemployment on over-aggressive reductions in budget deficits, often called **austerity**.

- Even if there is agreement on the need for deficit reduction, there is much less agreement on how it should be achieved. The disagreement in all countries is along political lines. Small "c" conservatives believe that it should be done primarily through decreases in spending. Small "l" liberals believe that most existing spending programs are justified, and they are more inclined to want to do the adjustment through an increase in taxes. In all countries, these positions are hard to reconcile, and, as a result, large deficits may continue for a long time to come. These problems seem most intractable in the United States with its divided government structure. In the United States, the House of Representatives has been controlled by the conservative Republican party and the Senate and presidency controlled by the more liberal Democratic party. No agreement on how to reduce the budget deficit has been achieved.

Although the worst of the crisis would appear to be over, Table 1–1 shows that growth in output has not returned to its pre-crisis level. The consequence of that slow growth is that unemployment has remained high in all three economies. Figure 1–4 shows unemployment rates in Canada, the euro area countries, and the United States. It is a depressing figure! The increase in the unemployment rate in the United States during the crisis is particularly striking, increasing from 4.6% in 2007 to 9.6% in 2010. The more recent increase in Europe is equally disturbing. Forecasts show a further increase in 2013 and 2014. In each economy

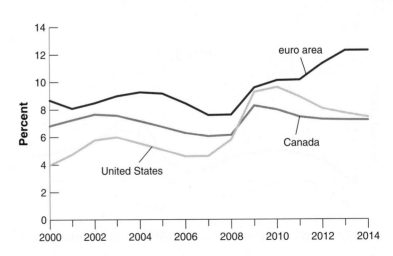

**FIGURE 1–4**

Unemployment Rates in the United States, Canada, and the Euro Area since 2000

*Source:* Data from Variable LUR from the International Monetary Fund, World Economic Outlook database, April 2013.

shown, the unemployment rate remains above the pre-crisis level. What is behind persistently high unemployment is low output growth.

The cost of high unemployment is not equally spread across society. In periods of high unemployment, it is the young and the less educated that have the most difficulty finding jobs. Persistent high unemployment is the most serious consequence of the crisis and the most difficult problem to solve.

In short, while the worst of the crisis is probably over, it has left three clear problems in its aftermath, which will keep macroeconomists and policy makers busy for many years to come. The problems are high unemployment, low output growth, and large budget deficits. We shall return to these issues in more detail at many points in the text. In the rest of this chapter, we take a closer look at recent macroeconomic events in Canada and then at events in three of the main economic powers of the world: the United States, the euro area, and China.

# 1-2 | Canada

When economists first look at a country, the first two questions they ask are: How big is the country, from an economic point of view? And what is its standard of living? To answer the first, they look at output—the level of production of the country as a whole. To answer the second, they look at output per person. The answers, for Canada and the United States, are given in Figure 1–5. We will look further at the United States in section 1-3.

Canada is a tiny portion of the world economy, accounting for a mere 2.5% of world output. The standard of living in Canada is very high; US$51,400 per person per year of output was produced in Canada in 2012. In the measure used in Figure 1–5, the standard of living in Canada is actually slightly higher than that in the United States. We will learn later that measuring and making exact comparisons of the standard of living between countries are not quite that straightforward. By most other measures, output per person in Canada is slightly lower than that in the United States. However, compared to nearly every other country in the world,

*Can you guess which countries have a higher standard of living than Canada or the United States?* Hint: *Think of oil producers and financial centres. For answers, go to www.imf.org/external/pubs/ft/weo/2011/01/weodata/weoselgr.aspx and look for "Gross Domestic Product per capita, in current prices."*

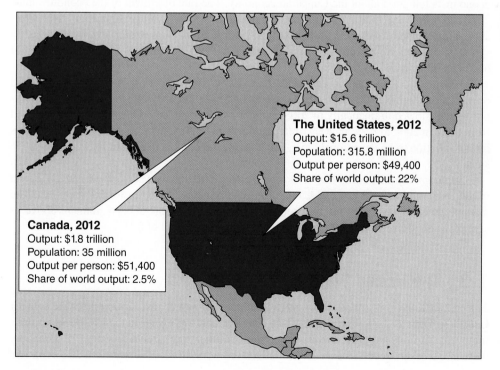

FIGURE 1-5

**Canada and the United States**

*Source:* Various tables on the OECD Web site: www.oecd.org

**The United States, 2012**
Output: $15.6 trillion
Population: 315.8 million
Output per person: $49,400
Share of world output: 22%

**Canada, 2012**
Output: $1.8 trillion
Population: 35 million
Output per person: $51,400
Share of world output: 2.5%

| TABLE 1–2 | Growth, Unemployment, and Inflation in Canada, 1980–2014 | | | | | | | | |
|---|---|---|---|---|---|---|---|---|---|
| Percent | 1980–1999 (average) | 2000–2007 (average) | 2008 | 2009 | 2010 | 2011 | 2012 | 2013 | 2014 |
| Output growth rate | 2.7 | 2.8 | 1.0 | −2.8 | 3.1 | 2.6 | 1.8 | 1.4 | 2.4 |
| Unemployment rate | 9.4 | 7.0 | 6.1 | 8.9 | 8.0 | 7.5 | 7.3 | 7.3 | 7.2 |
| Inflation rate | 4.3 | 2.3 | 2.3 | 0.3 | 1.8 | 2.9 | 1.5 | 1.5 | 1.8 |

*Source:* Data from International Monetary Fund, World Economic Outlook Database, April 2013. Figures for 2013 and 2014 are forecasts.

output per person in Canada and in the United States is very high. Very few countries in the world have a higher standard of living than Canada and the United States.

When economists want to dig deeper and look further at the state of health of the country's economy, they look at three other basic variables:

- *Output growth*—the rate of change of output
- The *unemployment rate*—the proportion of workers in the economy who are not employed and are looking for a job
- The *inflation rate*—the rate at which the average price of the goods in the economy is increasing over time

Numbers for the three variables for the Canadian economy are given in Table 1–2. To put current numbers in perspective, the first column gives the average value of the rate of growth of output, the unemployment rate, and the inflation rate in Canada for the period 1980 to 1999. The next columns look at the more recent years, giving you first average numbers for the period 2000 to 2007, and then numbers for each year from 2008 to 2014. The numbers for 2012 to 2014 are estimates and forecasts as of 2013.

By looking at the first two columns, you can see why, in 2007, just before the crisis, economists felt good about the Canadian economy. The rate of growth of the economy since 2000 had been 2.8%, slightly higher than the previous 20-year average. Importantly, the average unemployment rate since 2000 was 7.0%, substantially lower than in the previous 20 years. And inflation was low, 2.3% on average since 2000, again substantially lower than it had been in the past 20 years.

Then the world economic crisis came, and you can see it in the numbers from 2008 onward. Although Canada did not cause the crisis, it was severely affected by the crisis. Output growth slowed dramatically in 2008 and was negative in 2009. Unemployment increased from 6.1% in 2008 to 8.9% in 2009. Inflation declined in 2009 to 0.3%. Many considered this rate of inflation to be dangerously low. Inflation has rebounded to remain between 1 and 3% since 2010.

Output growth in Canada has been positive since 2010; however, in 2011 and 2012, and in the forecasts for 2013 and 2014, output growth remains low by historical standards. The unemployment rate, while it has dropped well below its 2009 peak of 8.9%, remains above its average value from 2000 to 2007 and well above the 2006 level of 6.1%.

## 1-3 | The United States

The data in Table 1–3 that describe the United States economy since 2000 mirror the data for Canada in Table 1–2. However, you can be certain that it was events in the United States driving events in Canada during the crisis and not the other way around! As the U.S. economy went into a severe recession, the Canadian economy followed. Much of Canada's economy

In fact, with Canada at only 2.5% of the world economy, it is unlikely Canada could cause a world economic crisis.

| TABLE 1-3 | Growth, Unemployment, and Inflation in the United States, 1980–2014 | | | | | | | | | |
| --- | --- | --- | --- | --- | --- | --- | --- | --- | --- | --- |
| Percent | 1980–1999 (average) | 2000–2007 (average) | 2008 | 2009 | 2010 | 2011 | 2012 | 2013 | 2014 |
| Output growth rate | 3.1 | 2.6 | −0.3 | −3.0 | 2.4 | 1.8 | 2.2 | 1.8 | 3.0 |
| Unemployment rate | 6.5 | 5.0 | 5.8 | 9.3 | 9.6 | 8.9 | 8.0 | 7.7 | 7.4 |
| Inflation rate | 4.3 | 2.8 | 3.8 | −0.3 | 1.6 | 3.1 | 2.0 | 1.8 | 1.7 |

*Source:* Data from International Monetary Fund, World Economic Outlook Database, April 2013. Figures for 2013 and 2014 are forecasts.

depends on sales of exports to the United States, and the automobile industries in the two countries are highly integrated.

You can see that, although Tables 1–2 and 1–3 are similar in many respects, the recession in the United States was more severe than the recession in Canada. There were two years of negative output growth, 2008 and 2009. The total percentage fall in U.S. output was larger. The increase in the unemployment rate in the United States was larger. From 2006, where unemployment was 5.8%, unemployment peaked at 9.6% in 2009. Unemployment had already risen to 9.3% in 2008. Unemployment has been very slow to fall in the United States and is expected to remain well above its pre-crisis level into 2014.

Finally, inflation in the United States was actually negative in 2009. As we shall see later in the course, negative inflation can create particular problems. However, inflation has remained low and positive after 2010 and the danger of a long period of negative inflation appears to have passed.

In the Great Depression, inflation was negative for 5 years from 1929 to 1934. In Japan, prices fell slightly over many years beginning in 1999. Negative inflation has been accompanied by very slow growth in Japan.

# 1-4 | The Euro Area

In 1957, six European countries decided to form a common European market—an economic zone where people and goods could move freely. Since then, 21 more countries have joined, bringing the total to 27. This group is now known as the **European Union**, or EU for short.

In 1999, the European Union decided to go one step further and started the process of replacing national currencies with one common currency, called the *euro*. Only eleven countries participated at the start; since then, six more have joined. Some countries, in particular the United Kingdom, have decided not to join, at least for the time being. The official name for the group of member countries is the **euro area**. The transition took place in steps. On January 1, 1999, each of the 11 countries fixed the value of its currency to the euro. For example, 1 euro was set equal to 6.56 French francs, to 166 Spanish pesetas, and so on. From 1999 to 2002, prices were quoted both in national currency units and in euros, but the euro was not yet used as currency. This happened in 2002, when euro notes and coins replaced national currencies. Seventeen countries now belong to this *common currency* area.

The area also goes by the names of "euro zone" or "euroland." The first sounds too technocratic, and the second reminds one of Disneyland. We shall avoid them.

As you can see from Figure 1–6, the euro area is a strong economic power. Its output is nearly equal to that of the United States, and its standard of living is not far behind. (The European Union as a whole has an output that exceeds that of the United States.)

Table 1–4 presents the recent economic data from the euro area, the 17 countries currently using the euro as their currency. Look at the first two columns of Table 1–4. Even during the pre-crisis period, from 2000 to 2007, the euro area was not doing as well as the United States or Canada. Output growth was lower than in the United States or Canada over the same period. Unemployment was substantially higher than in the United States or Canada.

Until a few years ago, the official name was the European Community, or EC. You may still encounter that name.

**euro** the common currency used by euro area member countries.

**euro area** the 17 countries, as of 2013, that replaced national currencies with the euro.

**European Union** the 27 countries, as of 2013, that form an economic zone where people and goods move freely.

The euro area has existed only since 1999 and membership has increased; numbers for 1980 to 1999 are constructed by adding national numbers for each of the 17 current member countries.

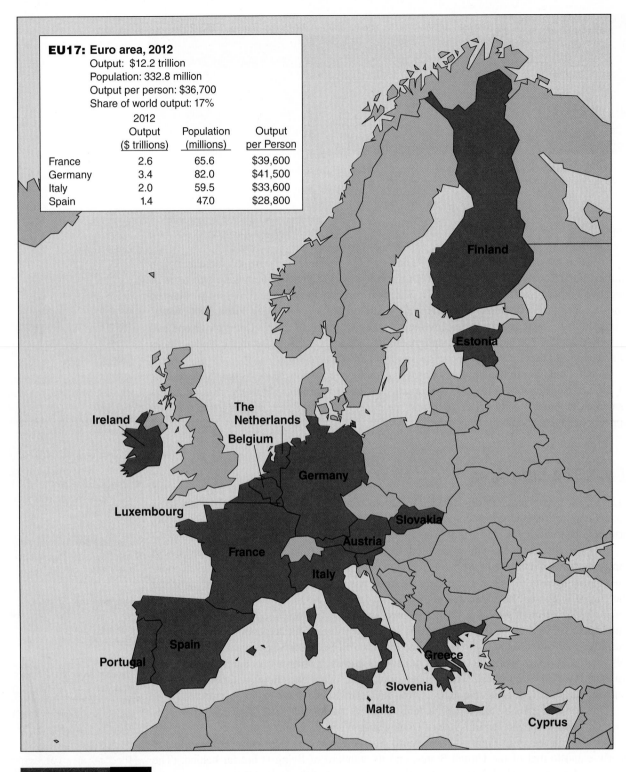

**EU17: Euro area, 2012**
Output: $12.2 trillion
Population: 332.8 million
Output per person: $36,700
Share of world output: 17%

| | 2012 Output ($ trillions) | Population (millions) | Output per Person |
|---|---|---|---|
| France | 2.6 | 65.6 | $39,600 |
| Germany | 3.4 | 82.0 | $41,500 |
| Italy | 2.0 | 59.5 | $33,600 |
| Spain | 1.4 | 47.0 | $28,800 |

**FIGURE 1-6**

The euro area

*Source:* Data from HVPVOB measure of real GDP per capita, OECD, www.oecd.org.

| Percent | 1980–1999 (average) | 2000–2007 (average) | 2008 | 2009 | 2010 | 2011 | 2012 | 2013 | 2014 |
|---|---|---|---|---|---|---|---|---|---|
| Output growth rate | 2.2 | 2.2 | 0.4 | −4.4 | 2.0 | 1.4 | −0.6 | −0.3 | 1.0 |
| Unemployment rate | 9.6 | 8.5 | 7.6 | 9.6 | 10.1 | 10.1 | 11.4 | 12.3 | 12.3 |
| Inflation rate | 5.2 | 2.3 | 1.6 | 1.0 | 2.2 | 2.7 | 2.2 | 1.6 | 1.4 |

**TABLE 1–4  Growth, Unemployment, and Inflation in the Euro Area, 1980–2014**

*Source:* Data from International Monetary Fund, World Economic Outlook Database, April 2013. Figures for 2013 and 2014 are forecasts.

Admittedly, inflation was low. The overall picture was of a slowly growing economy with high unemployment. Not surprisingly, the crisis made things worse. Growth was negative in 2009, and then turned positive only briefly in 2010 and 2011. Forecasts are for negative growth in the euro area in 2012 and 2013. Unemployment has increased to beyond 10% and, because of the expected recession in Europe in 2012 and 2013, is forecast to increase rapidly.

The euro area thus faces two main issues today. First (and this is a problem it shares with the rest of Europe and much of the rest of the world) is how to reduce unemployment. Second is how to function efficiently as a **common currency area**. We consider these two issues in turn. There are some interconnections.

## How Can European Unemployment Be Reduced?

The increase in European unemployment since 2007 is primarily due to the crisis, and it is reasonable to expect that the unemployment rate will eventually return to its pre-crisis level. But this pre-crisis level was already high, 8.5% for the euro area over the period 2000–2007. Why is this? Despite a large amount of research, there is still no full agreement on the answers.

Some politicians blame macroeconomic policy. They argue that the monetary policy followed by the European Central Bank has kept interest rates too high, leading to low demand and high unemployment. According to them, the central bank should decrease interest rates and allow an increase in demand, and unemployment would decrease. Others blame austerity policies where taxes are raised and government spending is reduced.

Most economists believe, however, that the source of the problem is not macroeconomic policy, but *labour market institutions*. Too tight a monetary policy or too much austerity, they concede, can indeed lead to high unemployment for some time, but surely not for 20 years. The fact that unemployment has been so high for so long points to problems in the labour market. The challenge is then to identify exactly what these problems are.

Some economists believe the main problem is that European states protect workers too much. To prevent workers from losing their jobs, they make it expensive for firms to lay off workers. One of the unintended results of this policy is to deter firms from hiring workers in the first place, and this increases unemployment. To protect workers who become unemployed, European governments provide generous unemployment insurance. But, by doing so, they decrease the incentives for the unemployed to look for jobs; this also increases unemployment. The solution, they argue, is to be less protective, to eliminate these *labour market rigidities*, and to adopt U.S.-style labour-market institutions. This is what the United Kingdom has largely done, and, until the crisis, its unemployment rate was low.

Others are more skeptical. They point to the fact that, before the crisis, unemployment was not high everywhere in Europe. It was low in a number of smaller countries—for example, the Netherlands or Denmark, where the unemployment rate was under 4%. Yet these countries are very different from the United States and provide generous social insurance to workers. This suggests that the problem may lie not so much with the degree of protection but with the way it is implemented. The challenge, these economists argue, is to understand what the Netherlands or Denmark have done right. Resolving these questions is one of the major tasks facing European macroeconomists and policy makers today.

### What Has the Euro Done for Its Members?

Supporters of the euro point first to its enormous symbolic importance. In light of the many past wars among European countries, what better proof of the permanent end to military conflict than the adoption of a common currency? They also point to the economic advantages of having a common currency: no more changes in the relative price of currencies for European firms to worry about, no more need to change currencies when crossing borders. Together with the removal of other obstacles to trade among European countries, the euro contributes, they argue, to the creation of a large economic power in the world. There is little question that the move to the euro was indeed one of the main economic events of the start of the twenty-first century.

Others worry, however, that the symbolism of the euro may come with substantial economic costs. They point out that a common currency means a common monetary policy, which means the same interest rate across the euro countries. What if, they argue, one country plunges into recession while another is in the middle of an economic boom? The first country needs lower interest rates to increase spending and output; the second country needs higher interest rates to slow down its economy. If interest rates have to be the same in both countries, what will happen? Isn't there the risk that one country will remain in recession for a long time or that the other will not be able to slow down its booming economy?

Until recently, the debate was somewhat abstract. It no longer is. A number of euro area members, from Ireland, to Portugal, to Greece, are going through deep recessions. Recessions have begun in larger euro members in 2013: France, Italy, and Spain. If these countries had their own currency, they likely would have decreased their interest rate or depreciated their currency vis-à-vis other euro area members to increase the demand for their exports. Because they share a currency with their neighbours, this is not possible. Thus, some economists argue that they should drop out of the euro area. Others argue that such an exit would be both unwise, as it would give up the other advantages of being in the euro area, and extremely disruptive, leading to even deeper problems for the country that has exited. This issue is likely to remain a hot one for some time to come.

# 1-5 | China

China is in the economic news almost every day. It is increasingly seen as one of the major economic powers in the world. Is the attention justified? A first look at the numbers in Figure 1–7 suggests it may not be. True, the population of China is enormous, more than four times that of the United States. But its output, expressed in dollars by multiplying output measured in yuans (the Chinese currency) by the dollar–yuan exchange rate, is only $8.2 trillion, about half that of the United States. Output per person is only $6100, roughly one-eighth of output per person in the United States.

So why is so much attention paid to China? There are two reasons. To understand the first, we need to go back to the number for output per person. When comparing output per person in a rich country like the United States and a relatively poor country like China, one must be careful. The reason is that many goods are cheaper in poor countries. For example, the price of an average restaurant meal in New York City is about $20; the price of an average restaurant meal in Beijing is about 25 yuans, or, at the current exchange rate, about $4. Put another way, the same income (expressed in dollars) buys you much more in Beijing than in New York City. If we want to compare standards of living, we have to correct for these differences; measures which do so are called PPP (for *purchasing power parity*) measures. Using such a measure, output per person in China is estimated to be about $7500, roughly one-sixth of the output per person in the United States. This gives a more accurate picture of the standard of

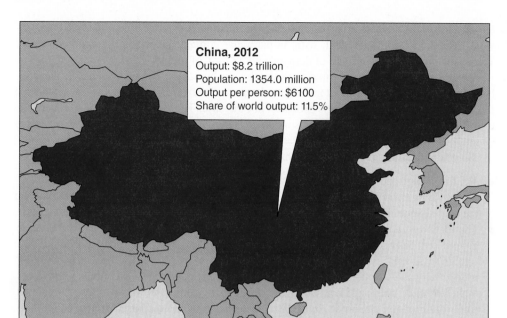

FIGURE 1–7

**China**

*Source:* Map of China

China, 2012
Output: $8.2 trillion
Population: 1354.0 million
Output per person: $6100
Share of world output: 11.5%

living in China. It is obviously still much lower than that of the United States or other rich countries. But it is higher than suggested by the number in Figure 1–7.

Second, and more importantly, China has been growing rapidly for more than three decades. This is shown in Table 1–5, which gives output growth, unemployment, and inflation for the periods 1980–1999 and 2000–2007, and for each of the years 2008 to 2012. The numbers for 2012, 2013, and 2014 are estimates or forecasts as of 2013.

Look at the first two columns of Table 1–5. The most impressive numbers are those for output growth. Since 1980, China's output has grown at roughly 10% a year. This represents a doubling of output every seven years. Compare this number to the numbers for the United States and for Europe we saw earlier, and you understand why the importance of the emerging economies in the world economy, China being the main one, is increasing so rapidly. Turn to unemployment. Numbers for unemployment are typically less reliable in poorer countries, so you should take those numbers with a grain of salt. Nevertheless, the numbers suggest consistently low unemployment. And inflation, which was high before 2000, is now relatively low.

Another striking aspect of Table 1–5 is how difficult it is to see the effects of the crisis in the data. Growth has barely decreased and unemployment has barely increased since 2007. The reason is not that China is closed to the rest of the world. Chinese exports slowed during

The issue is less important when comparing two rich countries. Thus, this was not a major issue when comparing standards of living in the United States and the euro area earlier. Exchange rate movements in 2012 partly account for the higher standard of living in Canada than the United States as shown in Figure 1–5. PPP adjusted measures show Canada has a slightly lower average standard of living than the United States.

| **TABLE 1–5** Growth, Unemployment, and Inflation in China, 1980–2014 | | | | | | | | | |
|---|---|---|---|---|---|---|---|---|---|
| Percent | 1980–1999 (average) | 2000–2007 (average) | 2008 | 2009 | 2010 | 2011 | 2012 | 2013 | 2014 |
| Output growth rate | 9.9 | 10.5 | 9.6 | 9.2 | 10.4 | 9.3 | 7.8 | 8.0 | 8.2 |
| Unemployment rate | 2.7 | 3.9 | 4.2 | 4.3 | 4.1 | 4.1 | 4.1 | 4.1 | 4.1 |
| Inflation rate | 7.7* | 1.6 | 5.9 | −0.7 | 3.3 | 5.4 | 2.7 | 3.0 | 3.0 |

*1990–1999 average

*Source:* Data from International Monetary Fund, World Economic Outlook Database, April 2013. Figures for 2012 are estimates; those for 2013 and 2014 are forecasts.

the crisis. But the adverse effect on demand was nearly fully offset by a major fiscal expansion by the Chinese government, with, in particular, a major increase in public investment. The result was sustained growth of demand and, in turn, of output.

This sustained growth performance raises obvious questions. The first is whether the numbers are accurate. Could it be that growth has been overstated? Economists who have looked at this carefully conclude that this is probably not the case. The statistics are not as reliable as they are in richer countries, but there is no obvious bias. Output growth is indeed very high in China.

So where does the growth come from? It clearly comes from two sources:

- The first is high accumulation of capital. The investment rate (the ratio of investment to output) in China exceeds 40% of output, a high number. For comparison, the investment rate in the United States is about 17%. More capital means higher productivity and higher output.
- The second is rapid technological progress. One of the strategies followed by the Chinese government has been to encourage foreign firms to relocate to and produce in China. As foreign firms are typically much more productive than Chinese firms, this has increased productivity and output. Another aspect of the strategy has been to encourage joint ventures between foreign and Chinese firms. As Chinese firms have worked with and learned from foreign firms, the productivity of the Chinese firms has increased dramatically.

When described in this way, achieving high productivity and high output growth appears easy; this is a recipe that every poor country could and should follow. In fact, things are less obvious. China is one of a number of countries that has made a successful transition from central planning to a market economy. Some other countries, often former Soviet republics like Bulgaria and Romania, experienced a large decrease in output at the time of transition. Most still have growth rates far below that of China. So why has China fared so much better? Some economists believe that this is the result of a slower transition: The first Chinese reforms took place in agriculture as early as 1980, and even today, many firms remain owned by the state. Others argue that the fact that the communist party has remained in control has actually helped the economic transition; tight political control has allowed a better protection of property rights, at least for new firms, giving them incentives to invest. Getting the answers to these questions, and thus learning what other poor countries can take from the Chinese experience, can clearly make a huge difference, not only for China but for the rest of the world.

## 1-6 | Looking Ahead

This concludes our world tour. There are many other regions of the world we could have looked at:

- India, another poor and large country, with a population of 1.2 billion people, like China, could grow in output per person very quickly in the future. There have been some bursts of growth in India in the last 20 years.
- Japan, whose growth performance for the 40 years following World War II was so impressive that it was referred to as an economic miracle, has done very poorly in the last two decades. Since a stock market crash in the early 1990s, Japan has been in a prolonged slump, with average output growth under 1% per year. Inflation has often been negative.
- Latin America went from very high inflation to low inflation in the 1990s. Many countries, such as Chile and Brazil, appear to be in good economic shape and have done relatively well in the crisis.
- Central and Eastern Europe shifted from central planning to a market system in the early 1990s. In most countries, the shift was characterized by a sharp decline in output at the start of transition. Some countries, such as Poland, now have high growth rates; others,

such as Bulgaria or Romania, are still struggling. Many of these countries are working toward joining the euro area.

- Africa has suffered decades of economic stagnation, but contrary to common perceptions, growth has been high since 2000, averaging 5.5% per year during the decade and reflecting growth in most of the countries of the continent.

## SUMMARY

There is a limit to how much you can absorb in this first chapter. Think about the questions to which you have been exposed:

- The big issues triggered by the crisis: What caused the crisis? Why did it transmit so fast from the United States to the rest of the world? In retrospect, what could and should have been done to prevent it? Were the monetary and fiscal responses around the world appropriate? Why is the recovery so slow in advanced countries? How was China able to maintain high growth?

- Can monetary and fiscal policies be used to avoid recessions? At what rate should the United States, Canada, and other countries reduce the budget deficits that resulted from the crisis? What are the pros and cons of joining a common currency area such as the euro area? What measures could be taken in Europe to reduce persistently high unemployment?

- Why do growth rates differ so much across countries, even over long periods of time? Can other countries emulate China and grow at the same rapid rate?

The purpose of this book is to give you a way of thinking about these questions. As we develop the tools you need, we shall show you how to use them by returning to these questions and showing you the answers the tools suggest.

## KEY TERMS

- austerity, 6
- European Union (EU), 9
- euro area, 9
- common currency area, 11
- Organisation for Economic Co-operation and Development (OECD), 17
- International Monetary Fund (IMF), 18

## QUESTIONS AND PROBLEMS

### 1. TRUE/FALSE/UNCERTAIN

Using the information in this chapter, label each of the following statements true, false, or uncertain. Explain briefly.

a. Output growth was negative both in advanced and in emerging and developing countries in 2009.

b. Stock prices fell between 2007 and 2010 around the world.

c. In the 1960s and early 1970s, the United States had a higher rate of unemployment than Canada, but today the United States has a much lower rate of unemployment.

d. The high rate of unemployment in Europe started when a group of major European countries adopted a common currency.

e. Central banks lower interest rates to avoid recessions and raise interest rates to slow the rate of growth in the economy.

f. Output per person is very different in the euro area, the United States, Canada, and China.

g. Governments in the United States, as a group, have not operated with a budget surplus since the year 2000.

### 2. MACROECONOMIC POLICY IN EUROPE

Beware of simplistic answers to complicated macroeconomic questions. Consider each of the following statements and comment on whether there is another side to the story.

a. There is a simple solution to the problem of high European unemployment: Reduce labour market rigidities.

b. What can be wrong about joining forces and adopting a common currency? The euro is obviously good for Europe.

### 3. CHINESE ECONOMIC GROWTH

Chinese economic growth is the outstanding feature of the world economic scene over the past two decades.

**a.** In 2012, U.S. output was $15.6 trillion, and Chinese output was $8.2 trillion. Suppose that from now on, the output of China grows at an annual rate of 10.5% per year, while the output of the United States grows at an annual rate of 2.6% per year. These are the values in each country for the period 2000–2007 as stated in the text. Using these assumptions and a spreadsheet, calculate and plot U.S. and Chinese output from 2012 over the next 100 years. How many years will it take for China to have a total level of output equal to that of the United States?

**b.** When China catches up with the United States in total output, will residents of China have the same standard of living as U.S. residents? Explain.

**c.** Another term for standard of living is output per person. How has China raised its output per person in the last two decades? Are these methods applicable to the United States?

**d.** Do you think China's experience in raising its standard of living (output per person) provides a model for developing countries to follow?

### 4. DEFICIT REDUCTION

Deficit reduction, often called an austerity program, is identified as a major issue facing the developed world as of the writing of this chapter.

Go to the most recent issue of Fiscal Reference Tables published by the federal Department of Finance (www.fin.gc.ca). There should be a table entitled "General Government Financial Balances: National Accounts Basis." This lists all government surpluses (deficits are negative surpluses) by country in the G7. Nearby will be tables on outlays and revenue as a percent of GDP.

**a.** Has Canada reduced its budget deficit as a percentage of GDP since 2009? In the last 3 years?

**b.** Has the United States reduced its budget deficit as a percentage of GDP since 2009? In the last 3 years?

**c.** Which country has the smallest deficit (or largest surplus) in the most recent year of data?

**d.** Find the country with the largest deficit reduction in the last two years of data. There should be tables preceding the Financial Balances table that show both outlays and revenue as a percentage of GDP. What proportion of the largest deficit reduction came from revenue increases? What proportion of deficit reduction came from outlay reduction?

**e.** Use the data entitled Economic and Financial Indicators found in *The Economist* to find the country with largest budget deficit and largest budget surplus. In this list the budget deficit is called the "Budget Balance."

### 5. HIGH UNEMPLOYMENT

High unemployment rates were also identified as a major issue facing the developed world as of the writing of this chapter.

Go to the most recent issue of the *Economic Report of the President*. Table B-109 contains information about unemployment rates in major industrial countries similar to the United States. Find the row with the most recent year of data for all countries.

**a.** Which country has the highest unemployment rate? Which has the lowest?

**b.** In what countries has the unemployment rate increased in the past three years? Decreased?

---

### FURTHER READING

The best way to follow current economic events and issues is to read *The Economist*, a weekly magazine published in the United Kingdom. The articles are well informed, well written, witty, and opinionated. Make sure to read the magazine regularly.

---

### APPENDIX

# WHERE TO FIND THE NUMBERS

This appendix will help you find the numbers you are looking for, be it inflation in Malaysia last year, or consumption in the United States in 1959, or unemployment in Ireland in the 1980s. In most cases, the data can be downloaded to spreadsheets for further treatment.

### For a Quick Look at Current Numbers

● The easiest and best source for the most recent numbers on production, unemployment, inflation, exchange rates, interest rates, and stock prices for a large number of countries is in the last pages of *The Economist*, published each week (web address: www.economist.com).

This website, like most of the websites listed below, contains both information available free of charge and information available only to subscribers.

## For More Detail about the Canadian Economy

- Statistics Canada provides a number of sources. Its webpage (www.statcan.gc.ca) provides free access to most economic data it produces. The most recent measures of GDP growth, inflation, and the unemployment rate are usually right on the front page.

  The main database of economic time series available from Statistics Canada is called CANSIM II. CANSIM II gives yearly data as far back as 1926 and quarterly data as far back as 1947 on hundreds of thousands of economic time series. Finding what you want in CANSIM II is not always easy. The Statistics Canada webpage now leads you directly to most of the data in CANSIM. The access is then organized by topic but there are still many choices within the same topic.

- Statistics Canada publishes a daily electronic release called The Daily. Whatever new information released that day by Statistics Canada appears in that issue. Using the "search" feature in "Search The Daily" is often an efficient way to find specific information about Canada. The article in The Daily often makes references to specific tables in CANSIM II.

- The Department of Finance publishes *Economic Reference Tables*, which give annual data on the main economic and financial aggregates over the past few years. Its website (www.fin.gc.ca) has a number of other useful (and free) publications, including a detailed description of the federal budget and monthly statements about federal government revenues and expenditures (*The Fiscal Monitor*). The various provincial ministries also make similar information available online. You should be warned that budgets are often political statements and may contain misleading analysis and information about the economy.

- On a quarterly basis, the Bank of Canada publishes the *Bank of Canada Review*. There is also a publication titled *Banking and Financial Statistics,* which is described well by its title. The *Monetary Policy Report* is likely the most important publication of the Bank of Canada. Each quarter, the *Monetary Policy Report* summarizes recent economic events and outlines the expected path for monetary policy.

- Several of the large chartered banks have economics departments that provide daily and weekly summaries of developments in financial markets, including various interest rates for Canada and the United States. A few also provide current values of the main economic aggregates. Read their explanations of what is currently

happening and what they expect will occur in the near future in financial markets. Ask yourself how it compares with what you have learned in this class.

- Recent data are much easier to obtain than earlier data. A good source for the latter is F. H. Leacy (ed.), *Historical Statistics of Canada*, 1983. This is available online from Statistics Canada.

## For More Detail about the U.S. Economy

- A convenient database, with numbers often going back to the 1960s for both the United States and other countries, is the *Federal Reserve Economic Database* (called *FRED*), maintained by the Federal Reserve Bank of St. Louis. Access is free, and some of the data used in this book comes from that database (www.research.stlouisfed.org/fred2/).

- Once a year, the *Economic Report of the President*, written by the Council of Economic Advisers and published by the U.S. Government Printing Office in Washington, D.C., gives a description of current evolutions, as well as numbers for most major macroeconomic variables, often going back to the 1950s. It contains two parts, a report on the economy, and a set of statistical tables. The statistical tables download directly as spreadsheets.

- A detailed presentation of the most recent numbers for national income accounts is given in the *Survey of Current Business*, published monthly by the U.S. Department of Commerce, Bureau of Economic Analysis (www.bea.gov). A user's guide to the statistics published by the Bureau of Economic Analysis is given in the *Survey of Current Business*, April 1996.

- The standard reference for national income accounts is the *National Income and Product Accounts of the United States.* Volume 1, 1929–1958, and Volume 2, 1959–1994, are published by the U.S. Department of Commerce, Bureau of Economic Analysis (www.bea.gov).

- For long-term historical statistics for the United States, the basic reference is *Historical Statistics of the United States, Colonial Times to 1970*, Parts 1 and 2, published by the U.S. Department of Commerce, Bureau of the Census.

## Numbers for Other Countries

The **Organisation for Economic Co-operation and Development**, OECD for short, located in Paris, France (www.oecd.org), is an organization that includes most of the richer countries in the world (Australia, Austria, Belgium, Canada, Chile, the Czech Republic, Denmark, Estonia, Finland, France, Germany, Greece, Hungary, Iceland, Ireland, Israel, Italy, Japan, Korea, Luxembourg, Mexico, the Netherlands, New Zealand, Norway, Poland, Portugal, the Slovak Republic, Slovenia, Spain, Sweden, Switzerland, Turkey, the United Kingdom, and the United States). Together, these countries account for about 70% of the world's output. One strength of the OECD data is that, for many variables, the OECD tries to make the variables comparable across member countries (or tells you when they are not comparable). The OECD puts out two particularly useful publications:

- The first is the *OECD Economic Outlook*, published twice a year. In addition to describing current macroeconomic issues and evolutions, it includes a data appendix, with data for many macroeconomic variables. The data typically go back to the 1980s and are reported consistently, both across time and across countries.
- The second is the *OECD Employment Outlook*, published annually. It focuses more specifically on labour-market issues and numbers.

The main strength of the publications of the **International Monetary Fund (IMF)**, located in Washington, D.C., is that they cover nearly all of the countries of the world. The IMF has 187 member countries and provides data on each of them (www.imf.org).

- A particularly useful IMF publication is the *World Economic Outlook* (WEO for short), which is published twice a year and which describes major economic events in the world and in specific member countries. Selected series associated with the *Outlook* are available in the WEO database, on the IMF site (www.imf.org/external/data.htm). Most of the data shown in this chapter come from this database.
- Two other useful IMF publications are the *Global Financial Stability Report* (GFSR for short), which focuses on financial developments, and the *Fiscal Monitor*, which focuses on fiscal developments. All three publications are available on the IMF Website (www.imf.org/external/index.htm).
- For long-term historical statistics for several countries, an invaluable data source is Angus Maddison's *Monitoring the World Economy, 1820–1992*, Development Centre Studies, OECD, Paris, 1995. This study gives data going back to 1820 for 56 countries. Two even longer and broader sources are *The World Economy: A Millennial Perspective*, Development Studies, OECD, 2001, and *The World Economy: Historical Statistics*, Development Studies, OECD 2004, both also by Angus Maddison.

# A Tour of the Book

## Introduction

The words *output, unemployment,* and *inflation* appear daily in newspapers and on the evening news, so when we used them in Chapter 1, you were familiar with them, at least to the extent that you knew roughly what they meant. Now they need to be defined precisely, and this is done in the first two sections of this chapter. In section 2-1, we focus on aggregate output and show how we can look at aggregate output both from the production side and from the income side. In section 2-2, we look at the unemployment rate and at the inflation rate. Section 2-3 is a very brief introduction to the goals of macroeconomic policy and the need to make choices. Having defined the major macroeconomic variables, we then take you, in section 2-4, on a tour of the book. On that tour, we introduce the three central concepts around which the book is organized:

- The *short run*—what happens to the economy from year to year.
- The *medium run*—what happens to the economy over a decade or so.
- The *long run*—what happens to the economy over a half century or more.

Building on these three concepts, we then give you a road map to the rest of the book.

# 2-1 | Aggregate Output

Economists studying economic activity in the nineteenth century or during the Great Depression had no reliable measure of aggregate activity (*aggregate* is the word macroeconomists use for *total*). They had to put together bits and pieces of information, such as the production of iron or sales at department stores, to infer what was happening to the economy as a whole.

Putting the national income accounts together was a gigantic intellectual achievement. The Nobel Prize was awarded in 1971 to Simon Kuznets, from Harvard University, and in 1984 to Richard Stone, from Oxford University, for their contributions to the development of the national income and product accounts.

It was not until the end of World War II that **national income and expenditure accounts** (or national income accounts, for short) were put together in major countries. Measures of aggregate output have been published on a regular basis in Canada since 1947. (You will find measures of aggregate output for earlier times, but these have been constructed retrospectively.)

Like any accounting system, the national income accounts define concepts and then construct measures corresponding to these concepts. One needs only to look at statistics from countries that have not yet developed such accounts to realize how crucial such precision and consistency are. Without them, numbers that should add up do not; trying to understand what is going on often feels like trying to balance someone else's chequebook. We shall not burden you with the details of national income accounting here. But because you will occasionally need to know the definition of a variable and how variables relate to each other, Appendix 1 at the end of the book gives you the basic accounting framework used in Canada (and, with minor variations, in most other countries). You will find it useful whenever you want to look at economic data on your own.

## GDP, Value Added, and Income

You may encounter another term, **gross national product** (**GNP**). There is a subtle difference between "domestic" and "national," and thus between GDP and GNP. We shall examine it in Chapters 6 and 18. For the moment, you can ignore the difference between the two.

The measure of **aggregate output** in the national income accounts is **gross domestic product** (**GDP**). There are three ways of thinking about an economy's GDP. Let us examine each one:

**1. GDP Is the Value of the Final Goods and Services Produced in the Economy during a Given Period.** The important word is *final*. To see why, consider the following example. Suppose that the economy is composed of just two firms.

- Firm 1 produces steel, employing workers and using machines. It sells the steel for $100 to Firm 2, which produces cars. Firm 1 pays its workers $80 and keeps what remains, $20, as profit.
- Firm 2 buys the steel and uses it, together with workers and machines, to produce cars. Revenues from car sales are $210. Of the $210, $100 goes to pay for steel and $70 goes to workers in the firm, leaving $40 in profit.

We can summarize this information in a table:

| Steel Company | | |
|---|---|---|
| Revenues from sales | | $100 |
| Expenses (wages) | | $80 |
| Profit | | $20 |
| **Car Company** | | |
| Revenues from sales | | $210 |
| Expenses | | $170 |
| Wages | $70 | |
| Steel purchases | $100 | |
| Profit | | $40 |

What is GDP in this economy? Is it the sum of the values of all production in the economy—the sum of $100 from the production of steel and $210 from the production of cars, $310? Or is it the value of the production of final goods, here cars, $210?

Some thought suggests that the right answer must be $210. Why? Because steel is an **intermediate good**, a good used in the production of the final goods, cars, and thus should not be counted in GDP—the value of *final* output. We can look at this example in another way. Suppose the two firms merged so that the sale of steel took place inside the new firm and was no longer recorded. All we would see would be one firm selling cars for $210, paying workers $80 + $70 = $150, and making $20 + $40 = $60 in profits. The $210 measure would remain unchanged—as it should.

This example suggests constructing GDP by recording and adding up the production of final goods—and this is indeed roughly the way actual GDP numbers are put together. But the example also suggests another way of thinking about and constructing GDP.

> An intermediate good is a good used in the production of another good. Some goods can be both final goods and intermediate goods. When sold directly to consumers, potatoes are final goods. When used to produce chips, they are intermediate goods.

**2. GDP Is the Sum of Value Added in the Economy during a Given Period.** The term *value added* means exactly what it suggests. The value added by a firm in the production process is defined as the value of its production minus the value of the intermediate goods it uses in production.

In our two-firm example, the steel company does not use intermediate goods. Its value added is simply equal to the value of its production, $100. The car company, however, uses steel as an intermediate good. Thus, value added by the car company is equal to the value of the cars it produces minus the value of the steel it uses in production, $210 − $100 = $110. Total value added in the economy, or GDP, equals $100 + $110 = $210. Note that aggregate value added would remain the same if the steel and car firms merged and became one firm.

This definition gives us a second way of thinking about GDP. Put together, the two definitions imply that the value of final goods and services—the first definition of GDP—can also be thought of as the sum of the value added by all firms along the chain of production of those final goods—the second definition of GDP.

**3. GDP Is the Sum of Incomes in the Economy during a Given Period.** We have looked so far at GDP from the *production side*. A third way of looking at GDP is from the *income side*. Think about the revenues left to a firm after it has paid for intermediate goods.

- Some of the revenues are collected by government in the form of taxes on sales—such taxes are called *indirect taxes*.
- Some of the revenues go to pay workers—this component is called *labour income*.
- The rest goes to the firm—that component is called *capital income*.

In short, looking at it from the income side, value added is the sum of indirect taxes, labour income, and capital income.

Let us return to our example. There are no indirect taxes. Of the $100 of value added by the steel manufacturer, $80 goes to workers (labour income) and the remaining $20 goes to firms as profit (capital income). Of the $110 of value added by the car manufacturer, $70 goes to labour income and $40 to capital income. For the economy as a whole, value added is $210, of which $150 ($80 + $70) goes to labour income and $60 ($20 + $40) to capital income.

In this example, labour income accounts for 71% of GDP, capital income for 29%, indirect taxes for 0%. Table 2–1 shows the breakdown of value added among the different types of income in Canada in 1981 and 2012. The table shows that except for indirect taxes (which are equal to zero in our example), the proportions we have been using in our example are comparable with those of the Canadian economy. Labour income accounted for about 63% of Canadian GDP in 1981 and slightly less, 60%, in 2012. Capital income, which includes depreciation, that portion of capital used up in production, totals either 27% in 1981 or 30% in 2012. Indirect taxes account for the remaining 10%. In 2012, corporate profits were relatively high by historical standards. To summarize: You can think about aggregate output—about *GDP*—in three different but equivalent ways.

- From the output side: GDP is equal to the value of the final goods and services produced in the economy during a given period.

| TABLE | 2–1 | The Composition of Canadian GDP by Type of Income, 1981 and 2012. | |
|---|---|---|---|
| | | **1981** | **2012** |
| Labour income | | 63% | 60% |
| Capital income | | 14% | 16% |
| Depreciation | | 13% | 14% |
| Indirect taxes | | 10% | 10% |

*Source*: Data from Gross domestic product, chained 2002 dollars, using CANSIM II variable V3850085; gross domestic product, 1997 constant prices, using CANSIM II variable V3862685; gross domestic product, 1992, constant prices, using CANSIM II variable V646962.

- Also from the output side: GDP is the sum of value added in the economy during a given period.
- From the income side: GDP is the sum of incomes in the economy during a given period.

## Nominal and Real GDP

Canadian GDP was $1.817 trillion in 2012, compared with $366 billion in 1981. Was output 5 times higher in 2012 than in 1981? No. This leads us to the distinction between nominal GDP and real GDP.

**Nominal GDP** is the sum of the quantities of final goods produced times their current price. This definition makes it clear that nominal GDP increases over time for two reasons. First, the production of most goods increases over time. Second, the prices of most goods also increase over time. We produce more and more cars and their prices increase each year as well. If our intention is to measure production and its change over time, we need to eliminate the effect of increasing prices. That is why **real GDP** is constructed as the sum of the quantities of final goods times *constant* (rather than current) prices.

Let us look more closely at the construction of real GDP. If the economy produced only one final good, say, a particular car model, constructing real GDP would be easy. We could merely count the number of cars produced each year and call that number real GDP. Or, if we wanted to have a measure in dollars rather than cars, we could use the price of cars in a given year and then use it to multiply quantities in all years.

Suppose, for example, that the quantity produced and the price of cars in three successive years was as shown here:

| Year | Quantity of Cars | Price of Cars | Nominal GDP |
|---|---|---|---|
| 2006 | 10 | $10,000 | $100,000 |
| 2007 | 12 | $12,000 | $144,000 |
| 2008 | 13 | $13,000 | $169,000 |

Nominal GDP, which is equal to quantity of cars times their price, goes up from $100,000 in 2006 to $144,000 in 2007, a 44% increase, and from $144,000 in 2007 to $169,000 in 2008, a 16% increase.

How should we define real GDP, and by how much does it go up? We can define it as the number of cars: 10 in 2006, 12 in 2007, 13 in 2008. This implies a 20% increase in real GDP from 2006 to 2007 and an 8% increase from 2007 to 2008. Or we can define it by multiplying the number of cars in each year by a *common* price, say, the price of a car in 2007 (base year). This approach gives us, in effect, *real GDP in 2007 dollars*.

Using this approach, real GDP in 2006 (in 2007 dollars) is equal to $10 \times \$12,000 = \$120,000$. Real GDP in 2007 (in 2007 dollars) is equal to $12 \times \$12,000 = \$144,000$, the same as nominal GDP in 2007. Real GDP in 2008 (in 2007 dollars) is equal to $13 \times \$12,000 = \$156,000$. Note that because we multiply the number of cars in each year by the *same* price,

Warning! People often use ▶ "nominal" to denote small amounts. Economists use nominal for variables expressed in current prices. And economists surely do not refer to small amounts. The numbers you will see in this book are typically expressed in billions or millions of dollars.

the increase in real GDP, when measured in 2007 dollars, is the same as when measured in cars: Real GDP in 2007 dollars increases by 20% from 2006 to 2007 and by 8% from 2007 to 2008. If we had decided to measure real GDP in 2008 prices, the level of real GDP would be different (because the prices are not the same in 2008 as in 2007), but its increase from year to year would be the same as above.

Just to be sure: Compute real GDP in 2008 prices, and compute the rate of growth from 2006 to 2007 and from 2007 to 2008.

The main problem in constructing real GDP in practice is that there is more than one final good. Real GDP must be defined as a weighted average of the output of all final goods, which brings the question of what the weights should be. Relative prices of the goods would appear to be the natural weights. If a good costs twice as much per unit as another one, then it should clearly count twice as much in the construction of real output. But this raises other questions: What if, as is often the case, relative prices change over time? Should we choose the relative prices in a given year as weights, or should we change the weights over time? More discussion of these issues and of the way real GDP is constructed in Canada is left to an appendix to this chapter. What you should know is that the best measure of real GDP in the national income accounts is called **real GDP in chained (2007) dollars** ("2007" because, as in our example, 2007 is the year when, by construction, real GDP is equal to nominal GDP). It is a measure of the output of the Canadian economy, and its evolution shows how Canadian output has increased over time.

Figure 2–1 plots the evolution of both nominal and real GDP since 1981. By construction, the two are equal in 2007. The figure shows that real GDP in 2012 was 2.1 times its level of 1981—a considerable increase, but clearly much less than the 5-fold increase in nominal GDP over the same years. The difference between the two results from the increase in prices over the period.

Suppose that real GDP were measured in 1990 dollars rather than 2007 dollars. Where would the two graphs intersect?

The terms *nominal GDP* and *real GDP* each have many synonyms, and you are likely to encounter them in your readings:

- *Nominal GDP* is also called **dollar GDP** or **GDP in current dollars**.
- *Real GDP* is also called **GDP in terms of goods**, **GDP in constant dollars**, **GDP adjusted for inflation**, or **GDP in 2007 dollars**—if the year in which real GDP is set equal to nominal GDP is 2007, as is the case in Canada at this point.

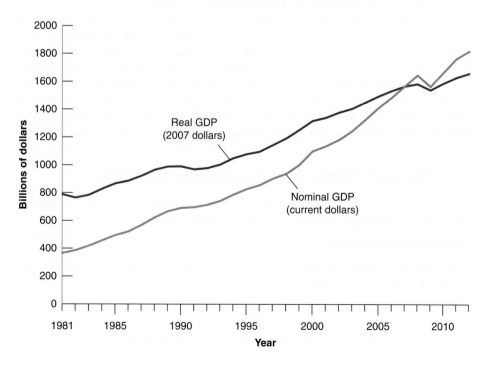

**FIGURE 2–1**

**Nominal and Real GDP in Canada, 1981–2012**

From 1981 to 2012, nominal GDP increased by a factor of 5. Real GDP increased by a factor of 2.1.

*Source*: Data from Real GDP, CANSIM II variable; nominal GDP, CANSIM II variable.

A tough problem when it comes to computing real GDP is how to deal with changes in the quality of existing goods. One of the most difficult cases is computers. It would clearly be absurd to assume that the quality of a personal computer in 2012 is the same as the quality of a personal computer produced in 1981 (the year IBM first introduced the PC). The same amount of money clearly buys much more computing power in 2012 than it did in 1981. But how much more? Does a 2012 computer provide 10 times, 100 times, or 1000 times the computing services of a 1981 computer? How should we take into account the improvements in internal speed, RAM, and hard drive sizes, and the fact that 2012 computers can access the Internet, and so on? Computers in 2012 are often portable; computers in 1981 were many, many times larger and heavier.

The approach used by economists to adjust for these improvements is to look at the market for computers and how it values computers with different characteristics in a given year. Example: Suppose the evidence from prices of different models on the market shows that people are willing to pay 10% more for a computer with a speed of 4 GHz (4000 megahertz) rather than 3 GHz. (The first edition of this book, published in 1996, compared two computers, with speeds of 50 and 16 megahertz, respectively. A good example of technological progress.) Suppose all new computers this year have a speed of 4 GHz compared with 3 GHz last year. And suppose the

dollar price of new computers this year is the same as the dollar price of new computers last year. In this case, the economists in charge of computing the adjusted price of computers will conclude that new computers this year are, in fact, 10% cheaper than they were last year.

This approach, called **hedonic pricing**, puts an implicit price on each of a good's characteristics—in the case of a computer, its speed, memory, and so forth. ("Hedone" means "pleasure" in Greek.) Hedonic pricing is used by the Department of Commerce, which constructs real GDP, to estimate changes in the price of complex and fast-changing goods, such as automobiles and computers. Using this approach, the Department of Commerce estimates that for a given price, the quality of new computers has increased, on average, by 18% a year since 1981. Put another way, a typical personal computer in 2012 delivers $1.18^{31} = 169$ times the computing services a typical personal computer delivered in 1981.

Not only do computers deliver more services, they have become cheaper as well. Their dollar price has declined by about 10% a year since 1981. Putting this together with the information in the previous paragraph, it means that their quality-adjusted price has fallen at an average rate of 18% + 10% = 28% per year. Put another way, a dollar spent on a computer today buys $1.28^{31} = 2106$ times more computing services than did a dollar spent on a computer in 1981.

This concludes your introduction to the main macroeconomic variable, GDP. In the chapters that follow, unless indicated otherwise, GDP will refer to real GDP, and $Y_t$ will denote *real* GDP in year $t$. Nominal GDP and variables measured in current dollars will be denoted by a dollar sign in front—for example, $\$Y_t$ for nominal GDP in year $t$.

Similarly, **GDP growth** in year $t$ will refer to the rate of change of real GDP in year $t$. GDP growth equals $(Y_t - Y_{t-1})/Y_{t-1}$. Periods of positive GDP growth are called **expansions**. Periods of negative GDP growth are called **recessions**. To avoid calling just one quarter of negative growth a recession, macroeconomists usually use the word only if the economy goes through at least two consecutive quarters of negative growth. The Canadian recession of 1990 to 1991, for example, was characterized by five consecutive quarters of negative growth, including all four quarters of 1990 and the first quarter of 1991. There were recessions in 1982 and in 2009. The most recent recession saw negative growth in quarter 4 of 2008 and quarters 1 and 2 of 2009.

> Rate of output growth:
> $(Y_t - Y_{t-1})/Y_{t-1}$
>
> rate of growth > 0: expansion
>
> rate of growth < 0: recession

## 2-2 | The Other Major Macroeconomic Variables

GDP is the main macroeconomic variable. Two others, unemployment and inflation, tell us about other important aspects of how an economy is performing.

### The Unemployment Rate

The **unemployment rate** is defined from the ratio of the number of unemployed to the labour force and then expressed as a percentage:

$$u = \frac{U}{L} \times 100$$

Unemployment rate = Unemployed/Labour force

The **labour force** is defined as the sum of those employed and those unemployed:

$$L \quad = \quad N \quad + \quad U$$
$$\text{Labour force} = \text{Employed} + \text{Unemployed}$$

What determines whether a worker is counted as unemployed? Until 1945, in Canada, and more recently in other countries, the number of people registered at unemployment offices was the only available data on unemployment, and only those workers who were registered in unemployment offices were counted as unemployed. This system led to a poor measure of unemployment. How many of the truly unemployed actually registered varied both across countries and across time. Those who had no incentive to register—for example, those who had exhausted their unemployment benefits—were unlikely to take the time to come to the unemployment office, so they were not counted. Countries with less generous benefit systems were likely to have fewer unemployed registering and therefore smaller measured unemployment rates.

Today, most countries rely on large surveys of households to compute the unemployment rate. In Canada, this survey is called the **Labour Force Survey (LFS)**. It relies on interviews of 60,000 households every month. The survey classifies a person as employed if he or she has a job at the time of the interview; it classifies a person as unemployed if he or she does not have a job and has been looking for work in the last four weeks. Most other countries use a similar definition of unemployment. In Canada, estimates based on the LFS survey show that in 2012, on average, 17.3 million people were employed and 1.4 million people were unemployed, so the unemployment rate was $1.4/(17.3 + 1.4) = 7.5\%$.

Note that only those *looking for work* are counted as unemployed; those not working and not looking for work are counted as **not in the labour force**. When unemployment is high, some of those without jobs give up looking for work and therefore are no longer counted as unemployed. These people are known as **discouraged workers**. Take an extreme case: If all workers without a job gave up looking, the unemployment rate would equal zero. This would make the unemployment rate a very poor indicator of what is happening in the labour market. More typically, high unemployment is associated with more workers dropping out of the labour force. Equivalently, a higher unemployment rate is typically associated with a lower **participation rate**, defined as the ratio of the labour force to the total population of working-age persons. In 2012, the participation rate was 66.7%, a full percentage point lower than it was in 2008. People have dropped out of the labour force as a consequence of the 2009 recession and have yet to return.

Macroeconomists care about unemployment for two main reasons: The unemployment rate tells them something about whether an economy is operating above or below its normal level. And unemployment has important social consequences. Let us look at each in turn.

### Unemployment and Activity.

In most countries, there is a clear relation between the change in unemployment and GDP growth. This relation is known as **Okun's law**, after the economist Arthur Okun, who first identified and interpreted it in the 1960s. The relation between these two variables in Canada since 1982 is plotted in Figure 2–2, which shows the change in the unemployment rate on the vertical axis and the rate of GDP growth on the horizontal axis. Each point in the figure shows the growth rate and the change in the unemployment rate for a given year. (Figures that plot one variable against another over time, such as Figure 2–2, are called **scatter diagrams**.)

The figure shows that high output growth is typically associated with a decrease in the unemployment rate and low output growth associated with an increase in the unemployment rate. This makes sense: High output growth leads to high employment growth, as firms hire more workers to produce more. High employment growth leads to a decrease in unemployment.

The relation has a simple implication. If the current unemployment rate is too high (what constitutes *too high* or *too low* will be the topic many chapters later; we can leave this discussion until then), it will take a period of higher growth to reduce it. The high levels of the unemployment rate that followed the world economic crisis have remained high precisely because growth in output and demand has been low.

Okun's law:

High output growth $\Rightarrow$
Unemployment rate $\downarrow$

Low output growth $\Rightarrow$
Unemployment rate $\uparrow$

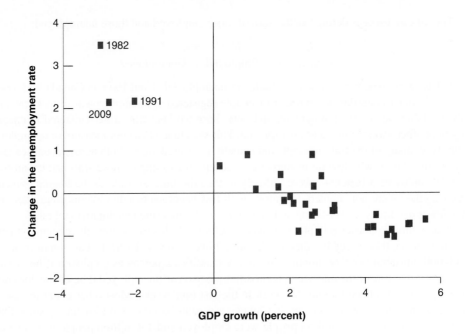

FIGURE 2-2

**Change in the Unemployment Rate versus GDP Growth, 1982–2012**

High output growth is typically associated with a decrease in the unemployment rate. Conversely, low output growth is typically associated with an increase in the unemployment rate. The recessions in 1982, 1991, and 2009 are labelled.

*Source*: Data from GDP growth is percent change in real GDP using CANSIM II variable.

From Figure 2–2, what is the rate of growth of output associated with ▶ roughly no change in the unemployment rate?

**Social Implications of Unemployment.** Macroeconomists also care about unemployment because of its direct effects on the welfare of the unemployed. Although unemployment benefits are greater today than they were during the Great Depression, unemployment is still associated with financial and psychological suffering. How much depends on the nature of the unemployment. One image of the unemployed is that of a stagnant pool, of people remaining unemployed for long periods of time. As we shall see later in the book, this image does not reflect what happens in Canada or other Western economies. In reality, each month, many people become unemployed, and many of the unemployed (on average, 30% of them) find jobs. But even in this setting, some groups (often the young, ethnic minorities, and the unskilled) suffer disproportionately from unemployment, remaining chronically unemployed and being most vulnerable to becoming unemployed when the unemployment rate increases.

Figure 1–4 in the previous chapter showed the variation in Canada's unemployment rate since 2000. Table 1–2 presented numbers showing a decline in the unemployment rate in Canada, on average, since 1980. Virtually everyone would agree that when the unemployment rate is at 9, 10, 11, or 12%, it is too high. Everyone is adversely affected when unemployment is too high. You may be unemployed. Your neighbour or your relative may be unemployed.

## The Inflation Rate

**Inflation** is a sustained rise in the general level of prices, the **price level**. The **inflation rate** is the rate at which the price level increases.

The practical issue is how to define this price level. Macroeconomists typically look at two measures of the price level, at two *price indexes*: the GDP deflator and the consumer price index.

Index numbers are often set to 100 rather than 1 in the base year. 100 is short for 100%, which, in decimal terms, is equal to ▶ 1. In Canada, the base year choice for GDP is 2007. The choice of base year is arbitrary; the rate of change is far more important.

**The GDP Deflator.** Suppose nominal GDP, $\$Y_t$, increases but real GDP, $Y_t$, remains unchanged. Then, the increase in nominal GDP must result from the increase in prices. This motivates the definition of the GDP deflator. The **GDP deflator** in year $t$, $P_t$, is defined as the ratio of nominal GDP to real GDP in year $t$:

$$P_t = \frac{\text{nominal GDP}_t}{\text{real GDP}_t} = \frac{\$Y_t}{Y_t}$$

Note that in the year in which, by construction, real GDP is equal to nominal GDP (2007 at this point in Canada), this definition implies that the price level is equal to 1. This is worth emphasizing: The GDP deflator is what is called an **index number**. Its level is chosen arbitrarily—here it is equal to 1 in 2007—and has no economic interpretation. In other words, the GDP is equal to 1 in the base year—in this case it is equal to 1 in the year 2007. But its rate of change has a clear economic interpretation: It gives the rate at which the general level of prices goes up over time—the rate of inflation.

Rate of inflation:
$$(P_t - P_{t-1})/P_{t-1}$$

One advantage to defining the price level as the GDP deflator is that it implies that a simple relation holds among nominal GDP, real GDP, and the price level. To see this, reorganize the previous equation to get:

$$\$Y_t = P_t Y_t$$

Nominal GDP is equal to the GDP deflator times real GDP.

**The Consumer Price Index.** The GDP deflator gives the average price of the goods included in GDP—the final goods *produced* in the economy. But consumers care about the average price of the goods they *consume*. The two prices need not be the same: The set of goods produced in the economy is not the same as the set of goods bought by consumers. This is true for two reasons. Some of the goods in GDP are sold not to consumers but to firms (machine tools, for example), to government, or to foreigners. And some of the goods bought by consumers are not produced at home but rather imported from abroad.

To measure the average price of consumption, or equivalently the **cost of living index**, macroeconomists look at another index, the **consumer price index (CPI)**. The CPI has been in existence since 1914 and is published monthly (in contrast, GDP numbers and the GDP deflator are published quarterly).

The CPI gives the cost in dollars of a specific list of goods and services over time. The list, which is based on a detailed study of consumer spending, attempts to represent the consumption basket of a typical urban consumer. It is revised approximately every five years. Each month, Statistics Canada employees shop to find out what has happened to the price of the goods on the list. Each month, about 60,000 price quotations are collected. These prices are then used to construct the price index.

Like the GDP deflator, the CPI is an index. It is set equal to 100 in the period chosen as the base period and thus does not have a natural level. The current base period is 2002 so that the average for the year 2002 is equal to 100. In 2012, the CPI stood at 121.6; thus, it cost 21.6% more in dollars to purchase the same consumption basket than in 2002.

You may wonder how the rate of inflation differs depending on whether the GDP deflator or the CPI is used to measure it. The answer is given in Figure 2–3, which plots the two inflation rates since 1982 for Canada.

Like the GDP deflator, the CPI is also typically set to 100 rather than to 1 in the base period (so, for example, equal to 121.6 rather than to 1.216 for 2012). It is conventional to add one, not two, decimal points to measures of both prices indexes and inflation rates.

The plots on the graph yield two conclusions:

● The CPI and the GDP deflator move together most of the time. In most years, the two inflation rates differ by less than 1%.

● There are a few exceptions. The GDP deflator is the price of goods produced in Canada. The CPI is the price of goods consumed. These can be different goods. As an obvious example, Canada produces a lot more energy products than it consumes. Energy prices rose in the early 2000s and the GDP deflator rate of inflation was larger than the CPI rate of inflation. A sharp decline in energy prices in 2009 saw GDP deflator inflation become negative while CPI inflation was zero. In 1991, when Canada switched from a manufacturers' sales tax, which was hidden, to the Goods and Services Tax, which consumers paid directly, CPI inflation was considerably higher than GDP inflation.

In what follows, we shall make no distinction between the two indexes unless the discussion requires us to focus on their difference. Thus, we shall simply talk about the *price level* and denote it by $P_t$, without indicating whether we have the CPI or the GDP deflator in mind. You infer whether the base value for the index is 100 or 1 by its context.

FIGURE    2–3

**Canadian Inflation Rate, Using the CPI and the GDP Deflator, 1982–2012**

The inflation rates, computed using either the CPI or the GDP deflator, are largely similar.

*Source*: Data from GDP deflator using CANSIM II variable; and consumer price index using CANSIM II variable.

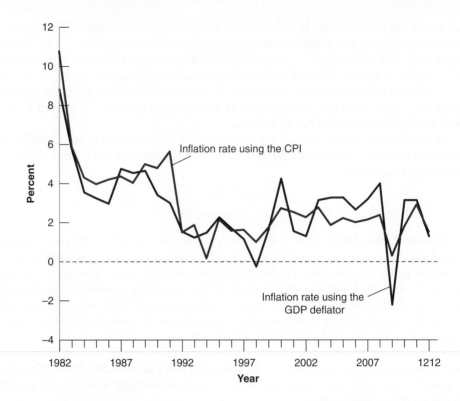

The Phillips curve:

Low unemployment ⇒ Inflation ↑

High unemployment ⇒ Inflation ↓

**Inflation and Unemployment.** Is there a relation between inflation and either output or unemployment? Or does inflation have a life of its own? The answer: There is a relation, but it is far from mechanical—it varies across time and countries.

The relation between unemployment and inflation in Canada since 1976 is shown in Figure 2–4. The change in the inflation rate (using the CPI)—that is, the inflation rate this year minus the inflation rate last year—is plotted on the vertical axis. The unemployment rate is

FIGURE    2–4

**Change in the Canadian Inflation Rate versus the Canadian Unemployment Rate, 1976–2012**

When the unemployment rate is low, inflation tends to increase. When the unemployment rate is high, inflation tends to decrease.

*Source*: Data from Inflation is the percent change in the CPI using CANSIM II variable; unemployment rate 1976 using CANSIM II variable.

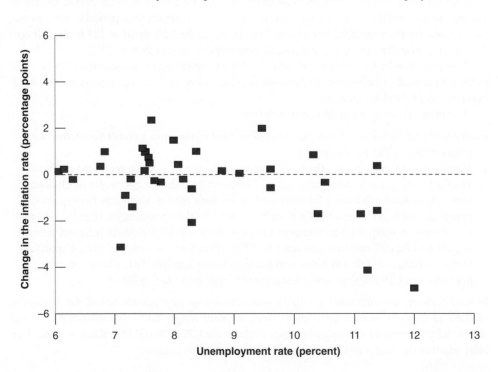

plotted on the horizontal axis. The figure gives the combinations of unemployment rates and changes in inflation rates for each year since 1976.

Figure 2–4 shows a negative relation between the unemployment rate and the change in inflation. When the unemployment rate is low, inflation tends to increase. When the unemployment rate is high, inflation tends to decrease. This negative relation is called the Phillips relation, and the curve that fits the set of points best is called the **Phillips curve**, named for the economist who first documented the relation between unemployment and inflation. Where this relation comes from, why it changes through time and place, and what it implies, will be the focus of many later chapters.

◀ We will see in Chapter 12 that the nature of the Phillips curve has changed since Phillips first documented it in 1958, but the name is still used.

## 2-3 | Macroeconomic Policy

Large increases in unemployment and large declines in output are severe problems. People do not like recessions. There is very interesting work being done in economics on the measurement of life satisfaction (sometimes called happiness). One example of such work is found in Figure 2–5. For a sample of European countries in 2003, the Eurobarometer Survey asked, "On the whole, are you very satisfied, not very satisfied, or not at all satisfied with the life you lead?" To look directly at the effect of unemployment on life satisfaction requires that citizens in a number of countries be asked the same question about life satisfaction and that the countries use a similar measure of unemployment. The Eurobarometer Survey meets this requirement. The graph (and other research) shows that as unemployment rises, all else equal, life satisfaction is much lower. High levels of unemployment matter to citizens on average, whether they are unemployed themselves or not. This suggests that much of macroeconomic policy should be oriented to keeping unemployment as low as possible.

Figure 2–4, the Phillips curve, suggests one constraint on policy makers. When the unemployment rate is too low, inflation tends to increase. Economists and central banks seem to care about inflation and whether inflation gets either too high or too low. What is a good rate of inflation? Once again we can turn to the measures of the relation between life satisfaction and inflation using the Eurobarometer Survey. Figure 2–6 (and other research) shows that if inflation is too high, all else equal, life satisfaction is lower.

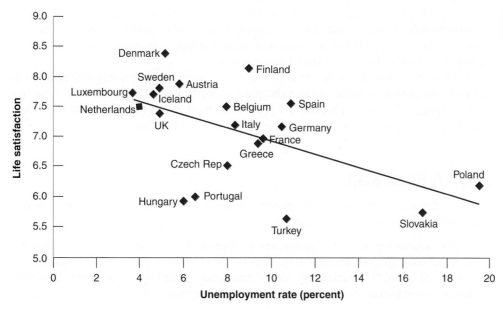

### FIGURE 2–5

**Unemployment and Life Satisfaction**

The graph shows that there is a negative relationship between unemployment and life satisfaction for a sample of European countries in 2003. Life satisfaction and unemployment are measured in the same way across these countries.

*Source:* David G. Blanchflower, Figure 3 in "Is unemployment more costly than inflation?" National Bureau of Economic Research, Working Paper 13505, October 2007.

FIGURE 2-6

**Inflation and Life Satisfaction**

The graph shows that there is a negative relationship between inflation and life satisfaction for a sample of European countries in 2003. Life satisfaction and inflation are measured in the same way across these countries.

*Source*: David G. Blanchflower, Figure 4 in "Is unemployment more costly than inflation?" National Bureau of Economic Research, Working Paper 13505, October 2007.

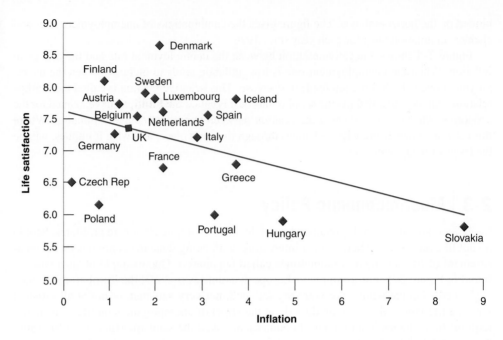

Canada's central bank, the Bank of Canada, in conjunction with the federal government, sets a target for inflation of between 1% and 3% per year. If inflation is higher than this target, then the Bank of Canada is to take action to reduce inflation. If inflation were to fall below this target, the Bank of Canada should take action to increase inflation. Figure 2–3 shows that, since 1992, inflation in Canada has been between 1% and 3% in most years. This part of macroeconomic policy seems to have been very successful in the past two decades.

A look back at Figure 1–4 and Table 1–2 suggests that there have been large fluctuations in the unemployment rate in Canada. Unemployment was very high in Canada in 2009 and 2010. But unemployment was also very high in the rest of the world in 2009 and 2010. The federal government takes some responsibility for managing the economy so that unemployment does not get too high. The initial "Economic Action Plan" in 2009 was designed to minimize the increase in unemployment in Canada in 2009 and 2010 even as the rest of the world underwent a severe recession. An "Economic Action Plan" has followed in each year since 2009. The Conservative government claims that Canada has recovered better from the world economic crisis than other countries, partly because of its policy actions. The government also claims that its policy decisions will encourage higher growth in GDP over a longer period of time and thus help to reduce unemployment.

Much of the rest of the book asks how to operate macroeconomic policy with three goals in mind. One goal is, as noted above, to keep unemployment from being too high. A second goal is to keep inflation from becoming a problem. A third goal is to create conditions where output, and more particularly output per person, grow in the long run.

## 2-4 | A Road Map

Having defined the main variables, let us now turn to the central question of macroeconomics. What determines the level of aggregate output?

● Hearing and seeing the way economic news is presented suggests one answer: Movements in output come from movements in the demand for goods. You probably have seen news stories that begin, "Production and sales of automobiles were higher last month, apparently due to a surge in consumer confidence, which drove consumers to showrooms in record numbers." Such explanations point to the role of demand in determining aggregate output, as well as to factors ranging from consumer confidence to tax rates to interest rates.

- But, surely, no amount of consumers rushing to showrooms will increase India's output to the level of output in North America. This suggests a second answer. What must matter is the supply side: how advanced the technology of the country is, how much capital it is using, and the size and the skills of its labour force. These factors, not consumer confidence, must be the fundamental determinants of the level of output.

- One may want to push this argument one step further: Neither technology and skills nor capital is a given. The technological sophistication of a country depends on its ability to innovate and introduce new technologies. The skills of workers depend on the quality of the education system. The size of its capital stock depends on how much people save. Other factors may also be important. If firms are to operate efficiently, they need a clear system of laws under which to operate and an honest government to enforce them. This suggests a third answer: The true determinants of output are such factors as the education system, the saving rate, and the quality of government. It is there that we must look if we want to understand what determines output.

Which of the three answers is the correct one? The answer is all three. But each of them applies over a different time period.

- In the **short run**, say a few years or so, the first answer is the correct one. Year-to-year movements in output are primarily driven by movements in demand. Changes in demand, which can arise from changes in consumer confidence or from any other source, can lead to a decrease in output (a recession) or an increase in output (an expansion).

- In the **medium run**, say, a decade or two, the second answer is the correct one. Over the medium run, the economy tends to return to the level of output determined by supply factors: the capital stock, technology, and the size of the labour force. These factors move slowly over time. For 5 to 10 years, we take these factors as given.

- In the **long run**, say, periods from as short as a decade to as long as a century, the third answer is the correct one. To understand why some countries, such as China, are growing very quickly, we need to look at changes in the level of capital and the level of technology. We need to look at the saving rate, the education system, and the role of government. We also need to consider demographic factors: birth rates, death rates, and immigration policy. All these factors are important in the long run.

This way of thinking about the determinants of output underlies macroeconomics, and it underlies the organization of this book.

## A Tour of the Book

The book is organized into six sections. Let us describe each section in more detail:

**The Introduction.**  You have just finished the first two chapters. They described recent events in the world and introduced the major macroeconomic variables.

**The Core.**  The core is composed of three parts—the short run, the medium run, and the long run.

- Chapters 3 to 8 look at the determination of output in the short run.
    The focus is on the determination of the demand for goods. To focus on the role of demand, we assume that firms are willing to supply any quantity at a given price; in other words, we ignore supply constraints. Chapter 3 looks at the goods market. Chapter 4 focuses on financial markets. Chapter 5 puts goods and financial markets together. The resulting framework is known as the *IS-LM* model. Developed in the late 1930s, the *IS-LM* model still provides a simple way of thinking about the determination of output in the short run, and it remains a basic building block of macroeconomics. It also allows a first pass at studying the role of fiscal policy and monetary policy in affecting output.

Chapters 6 to 8 add the open economy into the short-run analysis. Chapter 6 looks at openness in goods and in financial markets. Chapter 7 looks at the effects of the open economy on the demand for goods. Chapter 8 looks at the *IS-LM* model in an open economy.

- Chapters 9 to 14 reintroduce the supply side and look at the determination of output in the medium run.

  Chapter 9 focuses on the labour market. Chapter 10 puts together goods, and financial and labour markets, and shows how one can think about the determination of output both in the short run and in the medium run. The model developed in that chapter is called the aggregate supply–aggregate demand (*AS-AD*) model of output. Chapter 11 takes the *AS-AD* model and uses it to understand the operation of macroeconomic policy when interest rates are close to zero. This has been the context of macroeconomic policy for most of the world since 2009. Chapters 12 and 13 show how the model can be used to think about several issues, such as the relation between output and inflation and the role of monetary and fiscal policy both in the short run and in the medium run. Chapter 14 analyzes the medium run in the open economy setting. When countries have different inflation rates there are important implications for exchange rate policy.

- Chapters 15 to 18 focus on the long run.

  Chapter 15 introduces the facts and looks at the growth of output both across countries and across long periods of time. Chapters 16 and 17 then discuss the role and the determinants of both capital accumulation and technological progress in growth. Chapter 18 recognizes the role of the rest of the world in the process of growth. There are significant movements of people, capital, and technology across national borders.

**Expectations.** The core chapters give you a way of thinking about the determination of output (and unemployment and inflation) over the short, medium, and long runs. But they leave out one important element.

- The core chapters do not include an explicit role for *expectations.* But expectations play an essential role in macroeconomics. Nearly all the economic decisions people and firms make—to buy bonds or stocks, whether or not to buy a machine—depend on their expectations of future profits, future interest rates, and so on. Fiscal and monetary policies affect activity not only through their direct effects but also through their effects on expectations. Chapters 19 to 22 focus on the role of expectations and their implications for fiscal and monetary policies. There is a discussion of the recent events in North American housing markets.

**Back to Policy.** Monetary and fiscal policies are discussed in every chapter of the book. But once the core and the extensions have been covered, it is worth going back and assessing the role of policy.

- Chapter 23 focuses on general issues of policy, such as whether macroeconomists know enough to use policy at all and whether policy makers can be trusted to do what is right.

- Chapters 24 and 25 then assess the role of monetary and fiscal policies respectively.

**Epilogue.** The final chapter, Chapter 26, looks at the recent history of macroeconomics and how macroeconomists have come to believe what they believe today. From the outside, macroeconomics often looks like a field divided, with different schools—Keynesians, monetarists, new classicals, supply-siders, and so on—hurling arguments at each other. The actual process of research is more orderly and more productive than this image suggests. We identify what we see as the main differences among macroeconomists and the set of propositions that define the core of macroeconomics today. We ask what lessons have been learned from the world macroeconomic crisis that started in 2008.

- We can think of GDP, the measure of aggregate activity, in three equivalent ways: (1) GDP is the value of the final goods and services produced in the economy during a given period; (2) GDP is the sum of value added in the economy during a given period; and (3) GDP is the sum of incomes in the economy during a given period.

- Nominal GDP is equal to the sum of the quantities of final goods produced times their current prices. This implies that changes in nominal GDP reflect both changes in quantities and changes in prices. Real GDP is a measure of output. Changes in real GDP reflect changes in quantities only.

- The labour force is defined as the sum of those employed and those unemployed. The unemployment rate is defined as the ratio of the number of unemployed to the labour force. A person is classified as unemployed if he or she does not have a job and has been looking for work in the last four weeks.

- The empirical relation between GDP growth and the change in the unemployment rate is called Okun's law. The relation shows that high output growth is associated with a decrease in the unemployment rate and, conversely, that low growth is associated with an increase in the unemployment rate.

- Inflation is a rise in the general level of prices, in the price level. The inflation rate is the rate at which the price level increases. Macroeconomists look at two measures of the price level. The first is the GDP deflator, which gives the average price of goods produced in the economy. The second is the consumer price index (CPI), which gives the average price of goods consumed in the economy.

- The empirical relation between the change in the inflation rate and the unemployment rate is called the Phillips curve. This relation has changed over time and also varies across countries. In Canada today, it takes the following form: When the unemployment rate is low, inflation tends to increase. When the unemployment rate is high, inflation tends to decrease.

- Inflation leads to changes in income distribution and increases distortions and uncertainty.

- There are costs to society associated with both inflation and unemployment. Good macroeconomic policy is conducted to minimize these costs.

- Macroeconomists distinguish among the short run (a few years), the medium run (a decade or two), and the long run (a half century or more.) They think of output as being determined by demand in the short run, by the level of technology, the capital stock, and the labour force in the medium run, and by such factors as education, research, saving, and the quality of government in the long run.

- aggregate output, 20
- base year, 36
- consumer price index (CPI), 27
- cost of living index, 27
- discouraged worker, 25
- dollar GDP, GDP in current dollars, 23
- GDP growth, expansions, recessions, 24
- GDP in terms of goods, GDP in constant dollars, GDP adjusted for inflation, GDP in 2007 dollars, 23
- gross domestic product (GDP), 20
- gross national product (GNP), 20
- hedonic pricing, 24
- index number, 27
- inflation, 26
- inflation rate, 26

- intermediate good, 21
- labour force, 25
- Labour Force Survey (LFS), 25
- national income and expenditure accounts, 20
- nominal GDP, 22
- not in the labour force, 25
- Okun's law, 25
- participation rate, 25
- Phillips curve, 29
- price level, 26
- real GDP, 22
- real GDP in chained (2007) dollars, 23
- scatter diagram, 25
- short run, medium run, and long run, 31
- unemployment rate, 24

## 1. TRUE/FALSE/UNCERTAIN

**a.** The share of labour income in GDP is much smaller than the share of capital income.

**b.** Canadian GDP in 2012 was 5 times higher than Canadian GDP in 1981.

**c.** If a high unemployment rate discourages workers from looking for work, then the unemployment rate can be a poor indicator of labour market conditions. To assess the situation, one must also look at the participation rate.

**d.** In the usual case, when output growth is high, the rate of unemployment will fall.

**e.** If the Japanese CPI is currently at 108 and the U.S. CPI is at 104, then the Japanese rate of inflation is higher than the U.S. rate of inflation.

**f.** The rate of inflation computed using the CPI is a better index of inflation than the rate of inflation computed using the GDP deflator.

## 2. GDP AND ITS COMPONENTS

Suppose you are measuring annual GDP by adding up the final value of all goods and services produced in the economy. Determine the effect of each of the following transactions on the level of GDP. You may have to consult Appendix 1.

**a.** You buy from a fisherman $100 worth of fish, which you cook and eat at home.

**b.** A seafood restaurant buys $100 worth of fish from a fisherman.

**c.** CN Rail buys new railcars from Bombardier for $200 million.

**d.** The French national railway buys new railcars from Bombardier for $200 million.

**e.** WestJet sells one of its jets to Air Canada for $80 million.

## 3. MEASURED VERSUS TRUE GDP

Suppose that instead of cooking dinner for an hour, you decide to work an extra hour, earning an additional $12. You then buy some Chinese food for $10.

**a.** By how much does measured GDP increase?

**b.** Does true GDP increase or decrease? Explain.

## 4. MEASURING GDP

During a given year, the following activities occur:

**i.** A silver mining company pays its workers $200,000 to mine 75 kilograms of silver. The silver is then sold to a jewellery manufacturer for $300,000.

**ii.** The jewellery manufacturer pays its workers $250,000 to make silver necklaces, which it sells directly to consumers for $1,000,000.

    **a.** Using the "production of final goods" approach, what is GDP in this economy?

    **b.** What is the value added at each stage of production? Using the "value added" approach, what is GDP?

    **c.** What are the total wages and profits earned? Using the income approach, what is GDP?

## 5. NOMINAL AND REAL GDP

An economy produces three goods: cars, computers, and oranges. Production units and prices per unit for years 1998 and 1999 are as follows:

|  | 1998 | | 1999 | |
| --- | --- | --- | --- | --- |
|  | Quantity | Price | Quantity | Price |
| Cars | 10 | $2000 | 12 | $3000 |
| Computers | 4 | $1000 | 6 | $500 |
| Oranges | 1000 | $1 | 1000 | $1 |

**a.** What is nominal GDP in 1998 and in 1999?

**b.** Using 1998 as the base year (i.e., using 1998 prices), what is real GDP in 1998 and 1999? By what percentage does real GDP increase from 1998 to 1999?

**c.** Using 1999 as the base year (i.e., using 1999 prices), what is real GDP in 1998 and 1999? By what percentage does real GDP increase from 1998 to 1999?

**d.** True or false: "The growth rate of real GDP depends on which year is used as the base year."

## 6. THE GDP DEFLATOR

Use the data from problem 5 to answer the following:

**a.** Using 1998 as the base year, what is the GDP deflator for 1998 and 1999? What is the rate of inflation over this period?

**b.** Using 1999 as the base year, what is the GDP deflator for 1998 and 1999? What is the rate of inflation over this period?

**c.** Does the choice of base year affect the rate of inflation computed using the GDP deflator?

## 7. THE UNEMPLOYMENT RATE

Suppose that in a given month in Canada, there are 18 million working-age people. Of these, only 14 million have jobs. Of the remainder, 2 million are looking for work. 1.5 million have given up looking for work, and 0.5 million do not want to work.

**a.** What is the labour force?

**b.** What is the labour-force participation rate?

**c.** What is the official unemployment rate?

**d.** If all discouraged workers were counted as unemployed, what would be the unemployment rate?

## 8. CHAIN-TYPE INDEXES

As can be seen from problems 5 and 6, the use of base year prices to compute the rate of change of real GDP and the rate of inflation has some very unattractive properties. Every time a new base year is selected (e.g., to reflect the growing share of services in GDP), all past growth rates of real GDP and all past rates of inflation based on the GDP deflator have to be revised. To avoid these problems, virtually all statistical agencies around the world, including Statistics Canada, started using chain-type indexes in

1995. In this problem, we shall see, using the economy described in problem 5, how chain-type indexes are constructed. Further discussion of this method can be found in the appendix to this chapter.

**a.** Construct real GDP for years 1998 and 1999 for the economy described in problem 5 by using the average price of each good over the two years.

**b.** By what percentage does real GDP increase from 1998 to 1999?

**c.** What is the GDP deflator in 1998 and 1999? What is the rate of inflation using the chain-type deflator?

**d.** Do you find this method of construction of real GDP growth and of the inflation rate attractive? Why, or why not?

## 9. USING THE WEB TO GET THE MOST RECENT GDP INFORMATION

Look up the value of "real gross domestic product" on the Statistics Canada website www.statcan.gc.ca.

**a.** Do the changes over the most recent four quarters suggest that the economy was in a recession? An expansion? Neither? Explain briefly.

**b.** For each of the most recent two years, compute the percentage of total GDP consisting of consumption, investment, exports, and imports.

---

### FURTHER READING

If you want to know more about the many economic indicators that are regularly reported on the news—from the help-wanted index to the retail sales index—a good reference is:

John Grant, *A Handbook of Economic Indicators* (Toronto: University of Toronto Press, 1992).

For more about the LFS or the CPI, see:

- Statistics Canada, *Guide to the Labour Force Survey*, Catalogue no: 71-543-GWE.
- Statistics Canada, *Your Guide to the Consumer Price Index*, No. 62-557-XPB, December 1996.

Both publications can be found and downloaded from the Statistics Canada website www.statcan.gc.ca.

---

### APPENDIX

# THE CONSTRUCTION OF REAL GDP AND CHAIN-TYPE INDEXES

The example we used in the chapter had only one final good—cars—so constructing real GDP was easy. But how should one construct real GDP when there are two or more final goods? This is the question taken up in this appendix.

All that is needed to make the relevant points is an economy where there are two goods. So, suppose that an economy produces cars and potatoes.

- In year 0, it produces 100,000 kilograms of potatoes, at $1 a kilogram, and 10 cars, at $10,000 a car.
- One year later, in year 1, it produces 100,000 kilograms of potatoes, at $1.20 a kilogram, and 11 cars, at $10,000 a car.

- Nominal GDP in year 0 is therefore equal to $200,000; nominal GDP in year 1 is equal to $230,000. This information is summarized in the following table:

**Nominal GDP in Year 0 and in Year 1**

| | Quantity | Year 0 $ Price | $ Value |
|---|---|---|---|
| Potatoes (kg) | 100,000 | 1.00 | 100,000 |
| Cars (units) | 10 | 10,000.00 | 100,000 |
| Nominal GDP | | | 200,000 |

| | Quantity | Year 1 $ Price | $ Value |
|---|---|---|---|
| Potatoes (kg) | 100,000 | 1.20 | 120,000 |
| Cars (units) | 11 | 10,000.00 | 110,000 |
| Nominal GDP | | | 230,000 |

The increase in nominal GDP from year 0 to year 1 is equal to $30,000/$200,000 × 100 = 15%. But what is the increase in real GDP?

The basic idea in constructing real GDP is to evaluate quantities in both years using the same set of prices. Suppose we choose, for example, the prices of year 0; year 0 is then called the **base year**. The computation is then as follows:

- Real GDP in year 0 is the sum of quantities in year 0 times prices in year 0:
  (100,000 × $1) + (10 × $10,000) = $200,000.
- Real GDP in year 1 is the sum of quantities in year 1 times prices in year 0:
  (100,000 × $1) + (11 × $10,000) = $210,000.
- The rate of change of real GDP from year 0 to year 1 is:
  ($210,000 − $200,000)/$200,000 × $100 = 5%.

However, this answer raises an important issue: Instead of using year 0 as the base year, we could have used year 1, or any other year for that matter. If, for example, we had used year 1 as the base year, then:

- Real GDP in year 0 would be:
  (100,000 × $1.2 + 10 × $10,000) = $220,000.
- Real GDP in year 1 would be:
  (100,000 × $1.2 + 11 × $10,000) = $230,000.
- The rate of change of real GDP from year 0 to year 1 would be:
  $10,000/$220,000 × $100 = 4.5%.

The answer using year 1 as the base year would therefore be different from the answer using year 0 as the base year. So, if the choice of the base year affects the con-

structed rate of change of output, what base year should one choose?

Until 2001, in Canada the practice was to choose a base year and change it infrequently, say, every five years or so. This practice was logically unappealing. Every time the base year was changed and a new set of prices was used, all past real GDP numbers—and all past rates of change of real GDP—were recomputed: History was, in effect, rewritten every five years! Starting in 2001, Statistics Canada (the government office that produces the GDP numbers) shifted to a new method, which does not suffer from this problem. The method requires three steps.

1. The rate of change of real GDP from each year to the next is computed using as the common set of prices the average of the prices for the two years. For example, the rate of change of real GDP from 2007 to 2008 is computed by constructing real GDP for 2008 and real GDP for 2008, using as the common set of prices the average of the prices for 2007 and 2008 and then computing the rate of change from 2007 to 2008.

2. An index for the level of real GDP is then constructed by linking—or chaining—the constructed rates of change for each year. The index is set equal to 1 in some arbitrary year. Right now, the year is 2007. Given that the constructed rate of growth for 2007 by Statistics Canada is 1.0%, the index for 2008 equals (1 + 1.0%) = 1.010. The index for 2008 is obtained by multiplying the index for 2007 by the rate of growth from 2007 to 2008, and so on.

3. Finally, this index is multiplied by nominal GDP in 2007 to give real GDP in chained (2007) dollars. As the index is 1 in 2007, this implies that real GDP in 2007 equals nominal GDP in 2007. *Chained* refers to the chaining of rates of change described above. (*2007*) refers to the year where, by construction, real GDP is equal to nominal GDP.

This index is more complicated to construct than the simpler measure of real GDP described in the text. But it is clearly better. The prices used to evaluate real GDP in two adjacent years are the right prices, namely, the average prices for those two years. And because the rate of growth from one year to the next is constructed using the average prices in those two years rather than the set of prices in an arbitrary base year, history will not be rewritten every five years or so, as it used to be under the previous method for constructing real GDP: when the base year was changed all past growth rates were recomputed.

Figure 2A–1 presents growth rates of real GDP from 1962 to 2007, using three measures of real GDP over that time period. One set of growth rates, available for all years, is calculated using chained measures of real GDP. Statistics Canada has chained real GDP back to 1961. Real

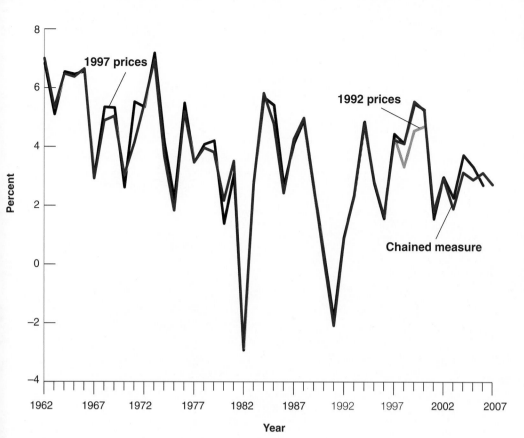

**Comparing the Growth Rate of Real GDP: Chained and Nonchained Measures**

The figure shows that the growth rate of real GDP is very similar whether a chained measure of real GDP is used or the more traditional base-year measure is used. The further back in time the base year, the greater is the variation. Growth in real GDP using 1992 prices is slower than growth in real GDP using 1997 prices after 1997.

*Source:* Gross domestic product, chained 2002 dollars, using CANSIM II variable V3860085; gross domestic product, 1997 constant prices, using CANSIM II variable V3862685; gross domestic product, 1992, constant prices, using CANSIM II variable V646962.

GDP measured in 1997 dollars is available up to 2006. Real GDP measured in 1992 dollars is available up to 2000. The three measures of the growth of real GDP are very similar but they are not identical. The more there are large swings in prices of items from the 1992 or 1997 base years, the more the measures diverge.

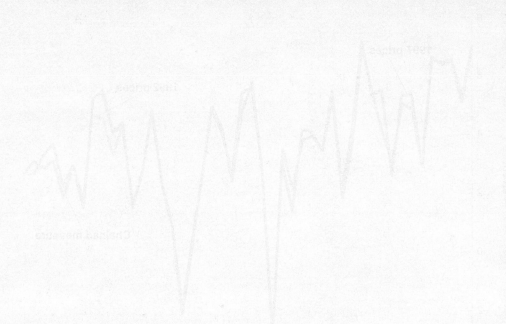

# The Core: The Short Run

In the short run, demand determines output. Many factors affect demand, from consumer confidence to fiscal and monetary policies.

## Chapter 3

Chapter 3 looks at equilibrium in the goods market and the determination of output. It focuses on the interaction among demand, production, and income. It shows how fiscal policy can be used to affect output.

## Chapter 4

Chapter 4 looks at equilibrium in financial markets and the determination of the interest rate. Monetary policy affects the interest rate.

## Chapter 5

Chapter 5 looks at the goods and financial markets together. It shows what determines output and the interest rate in the short run. The model developed in Chapter 5 is called the *IS-LM* model and is one of the workhorses of macroeconomics.

## Chapter 6

Chapter 6 discusses the implications of openness in goods and financial markets. An important determinant of the choice between domestic and foreign goods is the real exchange rate—the relative price of foreign goods in terms of domestic goods. Openness in financial markets allows people to choose between domestic and foreign assets. This imposes a tight relation, the interest parity condition, among the exchange rates, current and expected, and domestic and foreign interest rates.

## Chapter 7

Chapter 7 focuses on goods market equilibrium in an open economy. It shows how fiscal policy affects both output and the trade balance and discusses conditions under which a real depreciation improves the trade balance.

## Chapter 8

Chapter 8 characterizes goods and financial market equilibrium in an open economy, the open economy version of the *IS-LM* model from Chapter 5. Under flexible exchange rates, monetary policy affects output not only through its effect on the interest rate but also through the exchange rate. Fixing the exchange rate implies giving up the ability to change the interest rate.

# The Goods Market

## The Core: The Short Run

When economists think about year-to-year movements in economic activity, they focus on the interaction among *production*, *income*, and *demand*. Changes in the demand for goods lead to changes in production. Changes in production lead to changes in income. And changes in income lead to changes in the demand for goods. This interaction is summarized in Figure 3–1.

This chapter looks at this interaction and its implications.

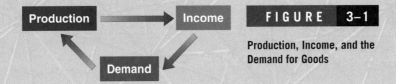

**FIGURE 3–1**

Production, Income, and the Demand for Goods

# 3-1 | The Composition of GDP

Purchases of machines by firms, food by consumers, or new executive jets by the federal government depend on different factors. If we are to think about what determines the demand for goods, it makes sense to decompose aggregate production (GDP) from the point of view of the different goods being produced and the different buyers for these goods. The decomposition of GDP typically used by macroeconomists is given in Table 3–1. Appendix 1 presents details on the national accounts, using 2012 as an example. The values below rearrange the national accounts to separate spending by household consumers, business investors, governments, and the foreign sector.

◀ "Output" and "production" are synonymous. There is no rule for using one or the other; use the one that sounds better.

- The first component of GDP is **consumption** (*C*). These are the goods and services purchased by consumers, ranging from food to airline tickets, to vacations, to new cars, and so on. Consumption is by far the largest component of GDP, accounting for 56% of GDP in 2012.
- **Investment** (*I*) is sometimes called **fixed investment** to distinguish it from inventory investment. Investment is the sum of **nonresidential investment**, the purchases by firms of new plants or new machines (from turbines to computers), and **residential investment**, the purchases of new houses, usually by households, as well as the building of rental housing, usually by firms.

  The two types of investment (residential and nonresidential) and the decisions behind them have more in common than might first appear. Firms buy machines or plants to be able to produce more output in the future. Houses or apartments are built to get *housing services* in the future. This is the justification for lumping both under "investment." Total investment accounted for 20% of GDP in 2012.

◀ Warning! To the person on the street or the financial press, "investment" refers to the purchase of any asset, such as gold or shares of General Motors. Economists use "investment" to refer to the purchase of *new capital goods*, such as machines, buildings, or houses. When referring to the purchase of financial assets, economists say "financial investment."

- **Government spending** (*G*) represents the purchases of goods and services by the federal, provincial, and local governments. The goods range from airplanes to office equipment. The services include services provided by government employees. In effect, the national income accounts treat government as buying the services provided by government employees—and then providing these services to the public, free of charge.

  Note that *G* does not include **government transfers**, such as Employment Insurance or Old Age Security, or interest payments on the government debt. Although these are clearly government expenditures, they are not purchases of goods and services. That is why the figure for government spending on goods and services in Table 3–1, 26% of GDP, is smaller than the figure for total government spending, including transfers and interest payments. That figure is about 40% of GDP.

| TABLE 3–1 | The Composition of Canadian GDP, 2012 | | | |
|---|---|---|---|---|
| | | **Billions of dollars** | | **Percent of GDP** |
| | GDP (*Y*) | 1817 | | 100 |
| 1 | Consumption (*C*) | 1014 | | 56 |
| 2 | Investment (*I*) | 362 | | 20 |
| | Nonresidential | | 236 | 13 |
| | Residential | | 126 | 7 |
| 3 | Government spending (*G*) | | | 26 |
| 4 | Net Exports | −36 | | −2 |
| | Exports (*X*) | | 546 | 30 |
| | Imports (*Q*) | | −582 | −32 |
| 5 | Inventory investment (*I_S*) | +8 | | 0 |

*Source:* Statistics Canada, CANSIM Table 380-0064.

- The sum of lines 1, 2, and 3 gives the purchases of goods and services by consumers, firms, and government. To get to the production of goods and services, we must take two more steps.

  First, we must subtract **imports** ($Q$), the purchases of foreign goods and services by consumers, firms, and government. Second, we must add **exports** ($X$), the purchases of Canadian goods and services by foreigners.

  The difference between exports and imports, ($X - Q$), is called **net exports**, or the **trade balance**. If exports exceed imports, a country is said to run a **trade surplus**. If exports are less than imports, the country is said to run a **trade deficit**. In 2012, exports accounted for 30% of GDP. Imports were equal to 32% of GDP, so Canada was running a trade surplus of $-2\%$ of GDP. A negative trade surplus is also called a trade deficit. The trade deficit would be $+2\%$ of GDP.

- The sum of lines 1 through 4 gives the purchases (equivalently, the sales) of Canadian goods and services in 2012. To get to production in 2012, we need one last step. Some of the goods produced in a given year are not sold in that year but sold in later years. And some of the goods sold in a given year may have been produced in an earlier year. The difference between goods produced and goods sold in a given year—equivalently, between production and sales—is called **inventory investment** and is denoted $I_S$ (subscript $S$ for **stocks** of goods, another term for inventories). If production exceeds sales, firms accumulate inventories. Inventory investment is positive. If production is less than sales, firms decrease inventories. Inventory investment is negative. Inventory investment is typically small—positive in some years, negative in others. In 2012, inventory investment was positive, but not even one full percent of GDP.

  With this decomposition of GDP, we can now turn to our first model of output determination. The first step is to think about what determines the demand for goods.

Exports − Imports ≡ Net exports ≡ Trade balance

Exports > Imports ⇔ Trade surplus

Exports < Imports ⇔ Trade deficit

Production − Sales = Inventory investment

## 3-2 | The Demand for Goods

Denote the total demand for goods by $Z$. Using the decomposition of GDP we just saw in section 3-1, we can write $Z$ as:

$$Z \equiv C + I + G + X - Q$$

Note that this equation is an **identity** (which is why it is written using the symbol "$\equiv$" rather than an equal sign). It defines $Z$ as the the sum of consumption, plus investment, plus government spending, plus exports, minus imports.

Assume now that all firms produce the same good, which can be used by consumers for consumption, by firms for investment, or by government. With this simplification, we need to look at only one market—the market for "the" good (thus the title of the chapter, "The Goods Market" rather than "The Goods Market*s*")—and think about what determines supply and demand in that market.

Assume further that firms are willing to supply any amount of the good at a given price, $P$. In other words, assume that the supply of goods is completely elastic at price $P$. This assumption will allow us to focus on the role of demand in the determination of output. As we shall see later in the book, this assumption is valid only in the short run. When we move to the study of the medium run (starting in Chapter 9), we will need to give up this assumption.

Assume finally that the economy is *closed*, that it does not trade with the rest of the world: Both exports and imports are equal to zero. The assumption is clearly counterfactual: Modern economies do trade with the rest of the world. Later (starting in Chapter 6), we will abandon this assumption and look at what happens when the economy is open. But, for the moment, this assumption will simplify things: We will not have to think about what determines exports and imports.

A model nearly always starts with the word "assume" (or "suppose"). This is an indication that reality is about to be simplified in order to focus on the issue at hand.

Under this last assumption, $X = Q = 0$, and the demand for goods $Z$ is the sum of consumption, investment, and government spending:

$$Z \equiv C + I + G$$

Let us discuss each of these three components in turn.

## Consumption (*C*)

The main determinant of consumption is surely income, or more precisely **disposable income**, the income that remains once consumers have received transfers from government and paid their taxes. When their disposable income goes up, people buy more goods; when it goes down, they buy fewer goods. Other variables, for instance, interest rates, affect consumption, but for the moment we will ignore them.

Let $C$ denote consumption, and $Y_D$ denote disposable income. We can write:

$$C = C(Y_D)$$
$$(+)$$

This is just a formal way of stating that consumption is a function of disposable income. The function $C(Y_D)$ is called the **consumption function**. The positive sign below $Y_D$ reflects the fact that when disposable income increases, so does consumption. Economists call such an equation a **behavioural equation**, to indicate that the equation reflects some aspect of behaviour—in this case, the behaviour of consumers.

We will use functions in this book as a simple but formal way of representing relations between variables. What you need to know about functions—which is very little—is described in Appendix 2 at the end of the book. This appendix develops the mathematics you need to go through this book. Do not worry: We will always describe a function in words when we introduce it for the first time.

It is often useful to be more specific about the form of the function. Here is such a case. It is reasonable to assume that the relation between consumption and disposable income is given by:

$$C = c_0 + c_1 Y_D \qquad (3.1)$$

In words: It is reasonable to assume that the function is a **linear relation**. The relation between consumption and disposable income is then characterized by two **parameters**, $c_0$ and $c_1$.

The parameter $c_1$ is called the **propensity to consume**. (It is also called the *marginal propensity to consume*. We will drop "marginal" for simplicity.) It gives the effect of an additional dollar of disposable income on consumption. If $c_1$ is equal to 0.6, then an additional dollar of income increases consumption by $\$1 \times 0.6 = 60$ cents. A natural restriction on $c_1$ is that it be positive: An increase in disposable income is likely to lead to an increase in consumption. Another natural restriction is that $c_1$ be less than 1: People are likely to consume only part of any increase in income and to save the rest.

The parameter $c_0$ has a simple, literal interpretation. It is what people would consume if their disposable income in the current year were equal to zero: If $Y_D$ equals zero in equation (3.1), $C = c_0$. A natural restriction is that if current income is equal to zero, consumption is still positive: People must eat! This implies that $c_0$ is positive. How can people have positive consumption if their income is equal to zero? The answer is by dissaving—by selling some of their assets or by borrowing.

A second interpretation of the parameter $c_0$ is that if this value is larger, then consumers increase their consumption (decrease their saving) at the same level of disposable income. It is equally possible that consumption could fall (savings increase) at the same level of disposable income. This would be represented by a smaller value of $c_0$. In Chapter 21, there is a more extensive discussion of changes in consumption at the same level of disposable income.

FIGURE 3-2

**Consumption and Disposable Income**

Consumption increases with disposable income, but less than one for one.

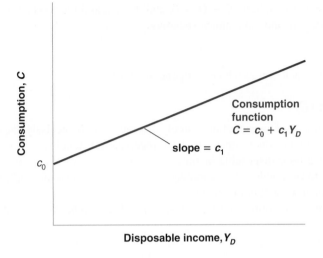

Consumption function
$C = c_0 + c_1 Y_D$

slope $= c_1$

$c_0$

In Canada, the two major taxes of this type are income taxes and payroll taxes. Income taxes are paid federally and provincially. Payroll taxes are contributions to the Employment Insurance Plan and the Canada (Quebec) Pension Plan. The main sources of government transfers are payments to the elderly and the unemployed, a federal responsibility, and welfare payments, a provincial responsibility.

The Focus box "The Lehman Bankruptcy, Fears of Another Great Depression, and Shifts in the Consumption Function" shows a clear example of a downward shift in the American consumption function over 2008 and 2009.

The relation between consumption and disposable income implied by equation (3.1) is drawn in Figure 3–2. Because it is a linear relation, it is represented by a straight line. Its intercept with the vertical axis is $c_0$; its slope is $c_1$. Because $c_1$ is less than 1, the slope of the line is less than 1: The line is flatter than a 45-degree line. (Appendix 3 shows how $c_1$ might be estimated.)

Next, we need to define disposable income. Disposable income is given by:

$$Y_D \equiv Y - T$$

where $Y$ is income and $T$ is taxes paid minus government transfers received by consumers. This equation is an identity; thus the use of the symbol "$\equiv$". For short, we will refer to $T$ simply as taxes—but remember that it is equal to taxes minus transfers.

Replacing $Y_D$ in equation (3.1) gives:

$$C = c_0 + c_1(Y - T) \tag{3.2}$$

Why would consumers decrease consumption if their disposable income has not changed? Or, in terms of equation (3.2), why might $c_0$ decrease—leading in turn to a decrease in demand, output, and so on? There is some direct evidence from the United States on this issue from the last recession.

One of the first reasons that comes to mind is that, even if their current income has not changed, consumers could start worrying about the future and decide to save more. This is precisely what happened in the United States at the start of the world economic crisis in late 2008 and early 2009. The basic facts are shown in Figure 1 below. The figure plots, from the first quarter of 2008 to the last quarter of 2009, the behaviour of three American variables: disposable income, total consumption, and consumption of durables—the part of consumption that falls on goods such as cars, computers, and so

on. All three variables are normalized to equal 1 in the first quarter of 2008. During the crisis, consumption, especially consumption of durables, fell much more than disposable income. Why?

A number of factors were at play, but an important factor was the psychological fallout from the collapse on September 15, 2008, of Lehman Brothers, a very large bank in New York City with worldwide operations. There was much fear in the ensuing weeks that other banks might follow suit and the financial system might collapse entirely. For most people, the main sign of trouble was what they read in newspapers: Even though they still had their jobs and received their monthly income cheques, the events reminded them of the stories of the **Great Depression** of the 1930s when U.S. output fell by more than 20% and unemployment peaked at 25%. People

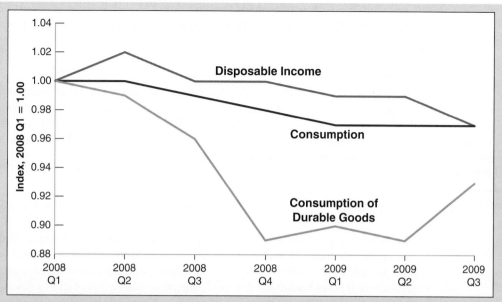

**FIGURE 1**   Disposable income, consumption, and consumption of durables in the United States, 2008:1 to 2009:3

*Source*: Calculated using series DPIC96, PCECC96, PCDGCC96: Federal Reserve Economic Data (FRED) http://research.stlouisfed.org/fred2/

would know of the Great Depression through history classes at school, as well as from books and movies.

Google Trends reports the number of searches for "Great Depression" from January 2008 to September 2009. The series, plotted in Figure 2, is normalized so its average value is 1 over the two years. The series shows a sharp peak in October 2008 and then slowly decreases over the course of 2009. This series is used to measure how much people feared the onset of another Great Depression.

If you felt that the economy might go into another Great Depression, what would you do? Worried that you might become unemployed or that your income might decline in the future, you would probably cut consumption, even if your disposable income had not changed yet. And, given the uncertainty about what was going on, you might also delay the purchases you could afford to delay; for example, the purchase of a new car or a new TV. This is exactly what consumers did in late 2008: Total consumption decreased, and consumption of durables collapsed. In terms of our model, the value of $c_0$ fell in the United States in 2008. As consumption fell in the United States, exports from Canada to American consumers, especially of cars, fell.

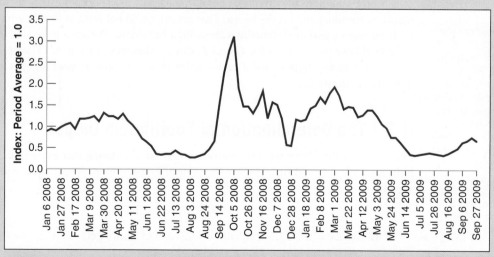

**FIGURE 2**   Google search volume for "Great Depression," January 2008 to September 2009

*Source*: Google Trends, "Great Depression." p. 56: Copyright © 2012 Google Inc.

Consumption is a function of income and taxes. Higher income increases consumption, although less than one for one. Higher taxes decrease consumption, also less than one for one.

### Investment (*I*)

Two types of variables:

Endogenous variables—
explained by the model

Exogenous variables—
taken as a given

Models have two types of variables. Some variables depend on other variables in the model and are therefore explained within the model. Such variables are called **endogenous**. This is the case for consumption here. Other variables are not explained within the model but are instead taken as a given. Such variables are called **exogenous**. This is how we will treat investment here. We will take investment as a given, and write:

$$I = \bar{I} \tag{3.3}$$

Putting a bar on investment is a simple typographical way to remind us that we take investment as a given.

The reason for taking investment as a given is to keep our model simple. But the assumption is not innocuous. It implies that when we look at the effects of changes in production later, we will do so under the assumption that investment does not respond to such changes in production. It is not hard to see that this implication may be quite bad as a description of reality: Firms that experience an increase in production may decide that they need more machines and increase their investment. We will leave this mechanism out of the model here, but we will introduce a more realistic treatment of investment in Chapter 5.

### Government Spending (*G*)

Recall that "taxes" stands for taxes minus government transfers.

The third component of demand in our model is government spending, *G*. Together with taxes *T*, *G* describes **fiscal policy**—the choice of taxes and spending by government. Just as we just did for investment, we will take *G* and *T* as exogenous. But the rationale for this assumption is different from that for investment. It is based on two considerations.

First, governments do not behave with the same regularity as do consumers or firms, and so there is no reliable rule we could write for *G* or *T* corresponding to the rule we wrote for consumption. This consideration is not fully convincing, however. Even if governments do not follow simple behavioural rules as consumers do, a good part of their behaviour is predictable. We will look at these issues later, in particular in Chapter 23, but we leave them aside until then.

Because we will (nearly always) take *G* and *T* as exogenous, we will not use a bar to denote their value. This will keep the notation lighter.

Second, and more importantly, one of the tasks of macroeconomists is to advise governments on spending and tax decisions. That means we do not want to look at a model in which we have already assumed something about their behaviour. We want to be able to say, "If you were to choose these values for *G* and *T*, this is what would happen." The approach in this book will typically treat *G* and *T* as variables chosen by government and not try to explain them within the model.

If firms hold inventories, then the supply of goods need not equal production all the time: Firms can supply more than they produce by decreasing their inventories. Conversely, firms can increase inventories by producing more than they supply. It is easier to start thinking about the equilibrium by ignoring this possibility. (Think of an economy that produces only haircuts. There cannot be inventories of haircuts— haircuts produced but not sold. Equilibrium requires that production of haircuts be equal to demand for haircuts.)

## 3-3 | The Determination of Equilibrium Output

Let us collect the pieces we have introduced so far. Assuming that exports and imports are both zero, the demand for goods is the sum of consumption, investment, and government spending:

$$Z \equiv C + I + G$$

If we replace *C* and *I* from equations (3.2) and (3.3), we get:

$$Z = c_0 + c_1(Y - T) + \bar{I} + G \tag{3.4}$$

The demand for goods (*Z*) depends on income (*Y*), taxes (*T*), investment ($\bar{I}$), and government spending (*G*).

Let us now turn to **equilibrium** in the goods market. Assume that firms do not hold inventories so that the supply of goods is equal to production $Y$. Then, **equilibrium in the goods market** requires that the supply of goods ($Y$) equals the demand for goods ($Z$):

$$Y = Z \tag{3.5}$$

This equation is called an **equilibrium condition**. Models include three types of equations: identities, behavioural equations, and equilibrium conditions. We now have seen examples of each: The equation defining disposable income is an identity, the consumption function is a behavioural equation, and the condition that supply equals demand is an equilibrium condition.

◀ Three types of equations:
  identities
  behavioural equations
  equilibrium conditions

Replacing demand ($Z$) using equation (3.4) gives:

$$Y = c_0 + c_1(Y - T) + \bar{I} + G \tag{3.6}$$

Equation (3.6) represents algebraically what we described informally at the beginning of this chapter. Production, $Y$, (the left side of the equation) must be equal to demand (the right side). And demand, in turn, depends on income, $Y$. Note that we are using the same symbol $Y$ for production and income. This is no accident! As we saw in Chapter 2, production and income are identically equal: They are the two ways of looking at GDP—one from the production side, the other from the income side.

See Figure 3–1: Demand
◀ determines production
(the equilibrium condition).
Production is equal to
income. And income
determines demand
(equation [3.4]).

Having constructed a model, we can solve it to look at what determines the level of output, how output changes in response to, say, a change in government spending. Solving a model means not only solving it algebraically but also understanding why the results are what they are. In this book, solving a model will also mean characterizing the results using graphs—sometimes skipping the algebra altogether—and describing the results and the mechanisms in words. Macroeconomists always use these three tools:

1. Algebra to make sure that the logic is right
2. Graphs to build the intuition
3. Words to explain the results

Make it a habit to do the same.

## Using Algebra

Rewrite the equilibrium equation (3.6):

$$Y = c_0 + c_1Y - c_1T + \bar{I} + G$$

Move $c_1Y$ to the left side and reorganize the right and the left sides:

$$(1 - c_1)Y = c_0 + \bar{I} + G - c_1T$$

Divide both sides by $(1 - c_1)$:

$$Y = \frac{1}{1 - c_1}(c_0 + \bar{I} + G - c_1T) \tag{3.7}$$

Equation (3.7) characterizes equilibrium output, the level of output such that supply equals demand. Let us look at both terms on the right, beginning with the second one.

The second term, $(c_0 + \bar{I} + G - c_1T)$, is that part of the demand for goods that does not depend on output. This term is called **autonomous spending**. Can we be sure that autonomous spending is positive? We cannot, but it is very likely to be. The first two terms in brackets, $c_0$ and $\bar{I}$, are positive. What about the last two, $G - c_1T$? Suppose that government is running a **balanced budget**—taxes equal government spending. If $T = G$, and the propensity to consume ($c_1$) is less than 1 (as we have assumed), then $(G - c_1T)$ is positive and so is autonomous spending. Only if government ran a very large budget surplus—if taxes were much larger than government spending—could autonomous spending be negative. We can safely ignore that case here.

*Autonomous* means independent—in this
◀ case, independent of output.

◀ If $T = G$

$$G - c_1T = G - c_1G$$
$$= G(1 - c_1)$$
$$> 0 \text{ if } c_1 < 1$$

Turn to the first term, $1/(1 - c_1)$. Because the propensity to consume ($c_1$) is between 0 and 1, $1/(1 - c_1)$ is a number greater than 1. This number, which multiplies autonomous spending, is called the **multiplier**. The closer $c_1$ is to 1, the larger the multiplier.

What does the multiplier imply? Suppose that for a given level of income, consumers decide to consume more. More precisely, assume that $c_0$ in equation (3.2) increases by \$1 billion. Equation (3.7) tells us that output will increase by more than \$1 billion. For example, if $c_1$ equals 0.6, the multiplier equals $1/(1 - 0.6) = 2.5$ so that output increases by $2.5 \times \$1$ billion = \$2.5 billion. We have looked here at an increase in consumption, but clearly, any increase in autonomous spending—from an increase in investment to an increase in government spending to a reduction in taxes—will have the same qualitative effect: It will increase output by more than its direct effect on autonomous spending.

Where does the multiplier effect come from? Looking back at equation (3.6) gives the beginning of a clue. An increase in $c_0$ increases demand. The increase in demand then leads to an increase in production and income. But the increase in income further increases consumption, which further increases demand, and so on. The best way to strengthen this intuition is to use a graphical approach.

## Using a Graph

Equilibrium requires that the production of goods ($Y$) equals the demand for goods ($Z$). Figure 3–3 plots both production and demand as functions of income; the equilibrium is the point at which production and demand are equal.

First, look at the plot of production as a function of income. Production is measured on the vertical axis, and income is measured on the horizontal axis. Plotting production as a function of income is straightforward, as production and income are always equal. Thus, the relation between the two is simply the 45-degree line, the line with a slope equal to 1, in Figure 3–3.

Second, look at the plot of demand as a function of income. The relation between demand and income is given by equation (3.4). Let us rewrite it here for convenience, regrouping the terms for autonomous spending together in the term in parentheses:

$$Z = (c_0 + \bar{I} + G - c_1 T) + c_1 Y$$

FIGURE    3-3

**Equilibrium in the Goods Market**

Equilibrium output is determined by the condition that production be equal to demand.

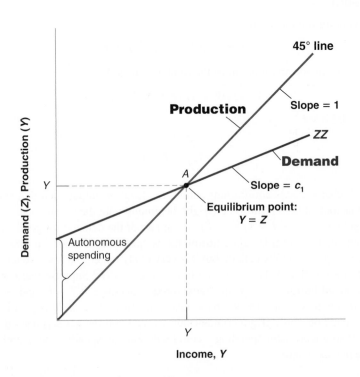

45° line

**Production**

Slope = 1

ZZ

**Demand**

Demand (Z), Production (Y)

$Y$

$A$

Slope = $c_1$

**Equilibrium point:**
$Y = Z$

Autonomous spending

$Y$

Income, $Y$

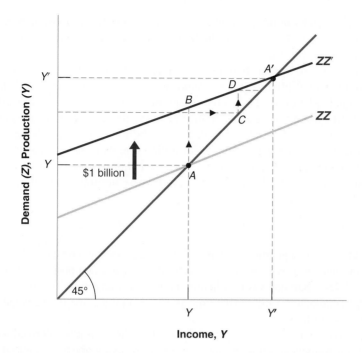

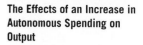

FIGURE    3–4

**The Effects of an Increase in Autonomous Spending on Output**

An increase in autonomous spending has a more than one-for-one effect on equilibrium output.

Demand depends on autonomous spending and on income—through its effect on consumption. The relation between demand and income is drawn as ZZ in the figure. The intercept with the vertical axis—the value of demand when income is equal to zero—equals autonomous spending. The slope of the line is the propensity to consume, $c_1$: When income increases by 1, demand increases by $c_1$. Under the restriction that $c_1$ is positive but less than 1, the line is upward sloping but with slope less than 1.

Equilibrium holds when production equals demand. Thus, equilibrium output, $Y$, is given by the intersection, at point $A$, of the 45-degree line and the demand relation, ZZ. To the left of $A$, demand exceeds production; to the right, production exceeds demand. Only at $A$ are the two equal.

Now, return to the example we looked at earlier. Suppose that $c_0$ increases by $1 billion. At the initial level of income (the level of income associated with point $A$), consumers increase their consumption by $1 billion. What happens then is shown in Figure 3–4, which builds on Figure 3–3.

For any value of income, demand is higher by $1 billion. Before the increase in $c_0$, the relation between demand and income was given by the line ZZ. After the increase in $c_0$ by $1 billion, the relation between demand and income is given by the line ZZ′, which is parallel to ZZ but higher by $1 billion. In other words, the demand relation shifts up by $1 billion. The new equilibrium is at the intersection of the 45-degree line and the new demand relation, at point $A′$. Equilibrium output increases from $Y$ to $Y′$. It is clear that the increase in output, $(Y′ - Y)$, which we can measure either on the horizontal or the vertical axis, is larger than the initial increase in consumption of $1 billion. This is the multiplier effect.

With the help of the graph, it becomes easier to tell how and why the economy moves from $A$ to $A′$. The initial increase in consumption leads to an increase in demand of $1 billion. At the initial level of income, $Y$, the level of demand is now given by point $B$: Demand is $1 billion higher. To satisfy this higher level of demand, firms increase production by $1 billion. The economy moves to point $C$, with both demand and production higher by $1 billion. But this is not the end of the story. The higher level of production leads to an increase in income of $1 billion and to a further increase in demand so that

The distance between $Y$ and $Y′$ on the horizontal axis is larger than the distance between $A$ and $B$—which is equal to $1 billion.

demand is now given by point $D$. Point $D$ leads to a higher level of production, and so on, until the economy is at $A'$, where production and demand are again equal, and which is therefore the new equilibrium.

We can pursue this line of thought a bit more, and this will give us another way of thinking about the multiplier. The first-round increase in production (the distance $AB$ in Figure 3–4) equals \$1 billion. The second-round increase in production (the distance $CD$), in turn, equals \$1 billion (the increase in income in the first round) times the marginal propensity to consume out of income, $c_1$—hence, $\$c_1$ billion. Following the same logic, the third-round increase in production equals $\$c_1$ billion (the increase in income in the second round), times $c_1$, the marginal propensity to consume out of income; it is thus equal to $\$c_1 \times c_1 = \$c_1^2$ billion. Following this logic, the total increase in production after, say, $n$ rounds equals \$1 billion times the sum:

$$1 + c_1 + c_1^2 + \cdots + c_1^n$$

Such a sum is called a **geometric series**. Geometric series will come up often in this book. A refresher on their properties is given in Appendix 2. The main property of such series is that when $c_1$ is less than one (as it is here) and as $n$ gets larger and larger, the sum keeps increasing but approaches a limit. That limit is $1/(1 - c_1)$, making the eventual increase in output $\$1/(1 - c_1)$ billion.

The expression $1/(1 - c_1)$ should be familiar: It is the multiplier, derived another way. This gives us an equivalent but more intuitive way of thinking about the multiplier. We can think of the original increase in spending as triggering successive increases in production, with each increase in production implying an increase in income, which leads to an increase in demand, which leads to a further increase in production, which leads . . . and so on. The multiplier is the sum of all these successive increases in production.

A trick question: Think about the multiplier as the result of these successive rounds. What would happen in each successive round if $c_1$, the propensity to consume, were larger than one?

## Using Words

How can we summarize our findings in words?

Production depends on demand, which depends on income, which is itself equal to production. An increase in demand, such as an increase in government or in consumer spending, leads to an increase in production and a corresponding increase in income. This increase in income leads to a further increase in demand, which leads to a further increase in production, and so on. The end result is an increase in output that is larger than the initial shift in demand, by a factor equal to the multiplier.

The size of the multiplier is directly related to the value of the propensity to consume: The higher the propensity to consume, the higher is the multiplier. What is the value of the propensity to consume in Canada today? To answer this question, and more generally to estimate behavioural equations and their parameters, economists use **econometrics**, the set of statistical methods used in economics. To give you a sense of what econometrics is and how it is used, Appendix 3 at the end of the book gives you a quick introduction, using as an application

[1] **Digging deeper.** In reality, the multiplier is smaller than 2.5, for two reasons.

We have assumed that taxes, $T$, are a given. But in reality, when income increases, taxes increase. This means disposable income increases less than one for one with income, and this implies that consumption increases less than we have assumed here. (This is explored in more detail in problem 6 at the end of the chapter.)

We have assumed that imports and exports were equal to zero. But in reality, when income increases, some of the increase in demand falls not on domestic goods but on foreign goods. In other words, the demand for domestic goods increases by less than we have assumed here. We will explore this in more detail in Chapter 7.

the estimation of the propensity to consume. The conclusion from the appendix is that in Canada today, the propensity to consume is around 0.6. An additional dollar of disposable income leads on average to an increase in consumption of 60 cents. This implies a multiplier equal to $1/(1 - c_1) = 1/(1 - 0.6) = 2.5$.[1]

## How Long Does It Take for Output to Adjust?

Let us return to our example one last time. Suppose that $c_0$ increases by \$1 billion. We know that output will increase by an amount equal to the multiplier $1/(1 - c_1)$ times \$1 billion. But how long will it take for output to reach this new higher level?

Under the assumptions we have made so far, the answer is: Right away! In writing the equilibrium condition (3.5), we have assumed that production is always equal to demand—in other words, production responds to demand instantaneously. In writing the consumption function (3.1), we have assumed that consumption responds to disposable income instantaneously. Under these two assumptions, the economy goes instantaneously from point $A$ to point $A'$: The increase in demand leads to an increase in production right away, the increase in income associated with the increase in production leads to an increase in demand right away, and so on. We can think of the adjustment in terms of successive rounds as we did earlier, but all these rounds happen at once.

This instantaneous adjustment does not seem very plausible. And, indeed, it is not. A firm that faces an increase in demand may decide to wait before adjusting its production, drawing down its inventories to satisfy demand. A consumer who gets a raise at work may not adjust her consumption right away. And these delays imply that the adjustment of output will take time.

Formally describing this adjustment of output over time—what economists call the **dynamics** of adjustment—would take us too far. But it is easy to do it in words.

Suppose that firms make decisions about their production level at the beginning of each quarter; once the decision is made, production cannot be adjusted for the rest of the quarter. If purchases are higher than production, firms draw down inventories to satisfy purchases. If purchases are lower than production, firms accumulate inventories.

Now, let us return to our example and suppose that consumers decide to spend more, that they increase $c_0$. During the quarter in which this happens, demand increases, but—because of our assumption that production was set at the beginning of the quarter—production does not yet change. Therefore, income does not change either. In the following quarter, firms having observed an increase in demand in the previous quarter are likely to set a higher level of production. This increase in production leads to a corresponding increase in income and a further increase in demand. If purchases still exceed production, firms further increase production in the following quarter, and so on. In short, in response to an increase in consumer spending, output does not jump to the new equilibrium but rather increases over time from $Y$ to $Y'$. How long this adjustment takes depends on how and how often firms revise their production schedule. The more often firms adjust their production schedule and the larger the response of production to past increases in purchases, the faster is the adjustment.

We will often do in the book what we just did in the last two paragraphs. Having looked at changes in equilibrium output, we will then describe informally how the economy moves from one equilibrium to the other. This will not only make the description of what happens in the economy feel more realistic, but it will often reinforce our intuition about why the equilibrium changed in the first place.

We have focused in this section on *increases* in demand. But the mechanism is symmetrical: Decreases in demand lead to decreases in output. The Focus Box compares the last three recessions in Canada. It is clear that recessions are costly to Canadians and it is important to understand the causes of recessions.

Since 1981, Canada has had three severe recessions. As we saw in Chapter 2, a recession is sometimes defined as two consecutive quarterly decreases in real GDP. Each of the three shaded periods in Figure 1 in this box contains at least two consecutive quarters of declining GDP followed by a recovery. Which of the three recessions was the worst?

Table 1 in this box lists the quarter just before the decline in output, the quarter where output reached its lowest level and the percentage decline in output from the pre-recesssion peak to the trough. By this measure, the recession that began in 1981Q1 had the largest percent decline in output, 5.1% expressed at an annual rate. Reporting monthly or quarterly values at an annual rate may at first appear confusing. But reporting all variables (whether daily, monthly, or quarterly) at an annual rate—and thus at a common rate—makes comparison among them easier. We see that the other two recessions, starting in 1990Q1 and 2008Q3 had total declines in output expressed at an annual rate of 3.4% and 4.2% respectively. By this measure, the 1981 recession was the worst recession.

The three recessions lasted a similar length of time. The table measures the number of quarters when output was below its pre-recession peak. Using this measure, the recessions were 9, 12, and 8 quarters long. The 1990 recession was, in this sense, a year longer than the other two recessions. By this measure, the 1990 recession was the worst recession. However, all recessions are bad.

How bad? In the most recent recession, output fell from $1,594 B in 2008 Q3 to $1,528 B in 2009 Q2 (all values in 2007 chained dollars). In 2008, the population of Canada was about 33 million. Thus income per Canadian fell by about $2,000. This is a substantial amount of money for most individuals. You could also think of this as $8000 for a household of 4 people. It is equally important to note that losses in the recession would not have been equally distributed. For many in Canada, recessions do not reduce incomes at all. If you were among the group of people unfortunate enough to have lost your job, your loss would have been much larger.

## FURTHER READING

Phillip Cross and Phillipe Bergevin in *Turning Points: Business Cycles in Canada since 1926,* C.D. Howe Policy Commentary No. 366, October 2012, offer a much broader and longer comparison of recessions in Canada. http://www.cdhowe.org/pdf/Commentary_366.pdf

**FIGURE 1   Real GDP in Canada 1981–2012**

*Source*: CANSIM II Variable V62305752.

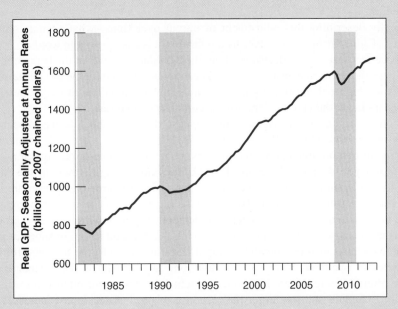

| TABLE | 1 | A comparison of three recessions | | |
|---|---|---|---|---|
| Quarter of peak output preceding recession | Quarter of lowest level of output in recession—the trough | Percentage decline in output from peak to trough at annual rate | Quarter when output returned to pre-recession peak | Number of quarters where output is below previous peak |
| 1981Q2 | 1982Q4 | −5.1 | 1983Q4 | 9 |
| 1990Q1 | 1991Q1 | −3.4 | 1993Q2 | 12 |
| 2008Q3 | 2009Q2 | −4.2 | 2010Q4 | 8 |

*Source*: Data from Cansim II variable V6230575.

As we grow up, we are told of the virtues of thrift. Those who spend all their income are doomed to end up poor. Those who save are promised a happy life. Similarly, governments tell us, an economy that saves is an economy that will grow strong and prosper! Equation (3.7), however, tells a different and quite surprising story.

Suppose that at a given level of disposable income, consumers decide to save more. In terms of equation (3.2), the equation describing consumption, they decrease $c_0$, therefore decreasing consumption and increasing saving at a given level of disposable income. What happens to output and to saving?

Equation (3.7) makes it clear that equilibrium output decreases when $c_0$ decreases. As people save more at their initial level of income, they decrease their consumption. But this decreased consumption decreases demand, which decreases production.

Can we tell what happens to saving? Return to the equation for private saving (by assumption, there is no change in public saving, and so saving and private saving move together):

$$S = -c_0 + (1 - c_1)(Y - T)$$

On the one hand, $-c_0$ is higher: Consumers are saving more at any level of income; this tends to increase saving. But,

on the other hand, $Y$ is lower: This decreases saving. The net effect would seem to be ambiguous. In fact, we can tell which way it goes. Remember that we can think of the equilibrium condition as the condition that saving equals investment, equation (3.8). By assumption, investment does not change. So, the equilibrium condition tells us that in equilibrium, saving does not change either. Although people want to save more at a given level of income, income decreases by an amount such that saving is unchanged. This means that attempts by people to save more lead both to a decline in output and to unchanged saving. This surprising pair of results is known as the **paradox of saving**.

So should you abandon the old wisdom? Should government tell people to be less thrifty? No. The results of this simple model are of much relevance in the *short run*. But—as we shall see later in this book when we look at the *medium run* and the *long run*—other mechanisms come into play over time and an increase in the saving rate is likely to lead to higher saving and higher income. An important warning remains, however: Policies that encourage saving may be good in the medium and the long runs, but may lead to a recession in the short run.

# 3-4 | Investment Equals Saving: An Alternative Way of Thinking about Goods–Market Equilibrium

Thus far, we have thought about equilibrium in terms of equality between the supply and the demand for goods. An alternative—but equivalent—way of thinking about equilibrium focuses on *investment* and *saving* instead. This is how John Maynard Keynes first articulated this model in 1936, in *The General Theory of Employment, Interest and Money*.

By definition, **private saving** ($S$), saving by consumers, is equal to their disposable income minus their consumption:

$$S \equiv Y_D - C$$

Using the definition of disposable income, we can rewrite private savings as income minus taxes minus consumption:

$$S \equiv Y - T - C$$

Now, return to the equation for equilibrium in the goods market. Production must be equal to demand, which, in turn, is the sum of consumption, investment, and government spending:

$$Y = C + I + G$$

Subtract taxes ($T$) from both sides and move consumption to the left side:

$$Y - T - C = I + G - T$$

The left side of this equation is simply private saving ($S$) so that:

$$S = I + G - T$$

Or equivalently,

$$I = S + (T - G) \tag{3.8}$$

The term on the left is investment. The first term on the right is *private saving*. The second term is **public saving**—taxes minus government spending.

If taxes exceed government spending, the government is running a budget surplus—public saving is positive. If taxes are less than government spending, the government is running a budget deficit—public saving is negative.

Equation (3.8) thus gives us another way of looking at equilibrium in the goods market. Equilibrium in the goods market requires that investment equals **saving**—the sum of private and public saving. This way of looking at equilibrium explains why the equilibrium condition for the goods market introduced in Chapter 5 is called the *IS relation*, for "**I**nvestment equals **S**aving." What firms want to invest must be equal to what people and the government want to save.

To strengthen your intuition for equation (3.8), think of an economy where there is only one person who has to decide how much to consume, invest, and save—a "Robinson Crusoe" economy. For Robinson Crusoe, the saving and the investment decisions are one and the same: What he invests (say, by keeping rabbits for reproduction rather than eating them), he automatically saves. In a modern economy, however, investment decisions are made by firms, whereas saving decisions are made by consumers and the government. In equilibrium, equation (3.8) tells us all those decisions have to be consistent: Investment must be equal to saving.

The two equivalent ways of stating the condition for equilibrium in the goods market:

Supply of goods
    = Demand for goods
Investment = Saving

We can study the characteristics of the equilibrium using equation (3.8) and the behavioural equations for saving and investment. Note first that *consumption and saving decisions are one and the same*: Given their disposable income, once consumers have chosen consumption, their saving is determined, and vice versa. The way we specified consumption behaviour implies that private saving is given by:

$$S = Y - T - C$$
$$= Y - T - c_0 - c_1(Y - T)$$

Rearranging, we get:

$$S = -c_0 + (1 - c_1)(Y - T)$$

In the same way that we called $c_1$ the propensity to consume, we can call $(1 - c_1)$ the **propensity to save**. The propensity to save tells us how much people save out of an additional unit of income. The assumption we made earlier that the propensity to consume ($c_1$) is between zero and one implies that the propensity to save $(1 - c_1)$ is also between zero and one. Private saving increases with disposable income but by less than one dollar for each additional dollar of disposable income.

In equilibrium, investment must be equal to savings, the sum of private and public saving. Replacing private saving in equation (3.8) by its expression from above,

$$I = -c_0 + (1 - c_1)(Y - T) + (T - G)$$

Solving for output,

$$Y = \frac{1}{1 - c_1}(c_0 + \bar{I} + G - c_1 T)$$

This is exactly the same expression as equation (3.7) earlier. This should come as no surprise. We are looking at the same model, just in a different way. This alternative way will prove useful in various applications later in the book. Such an application is given in the Focus box, "The Paradox of Saving" on page 53.

## 3-5 | Is Government Omnipotent? A Warning

Equation (3.7) implies that government, by choosing the level of spending ($G$) or the level of taxes ($T$), can choose the level of output it wants. If it wants output to increase by, say, $1 billion, all it needs to do is to increase $G$ by $$(1 - c_1)$ billion; this increase in government spending, in theory, will lead to an output increase of $(1 - c_1)$ billion times the multiplier $1/(1 - c_1)$, thus $1 billion.

Can governments really choose the level of output they want? The existence of recessions makes it clear that the answer is no. Both Canada and the United States engaged in expansionary fiscal policy during the 2008–2009 recession. But these recessions still occurred. While fiscal policy may have reduced the size of the recession, the recessions did occur and were severe. The governments were not omnipotent. There are many aspects of reality that we have not yet incorporated in our model. We will do so in due time. But it is useful to list them in brief here:

- The effects of spending and taxes on demand are much less mechanical than equation (3.7) makes them appear. They may happen slowly, consumers and firms may be scared of the budget deficit and change their behaviour, and so on (Chapters 5 and 22).
- Maintaining a desired level of output may come with unpleasant side effects. Trying to achieve too high a level of output may, for example, lead to accelerating inflation and may become unsustainable in the medium run (Chapters 12 and 13).
- Cutting taxes or increasing government spending may lead to large budget deficits and an accumulation of public debt. Such debt will have adverse implications in the long run (Chapters 23 and 25).

◄ Section 25-1 presents a summary of what we know about fiscal policy.

As we refine our analysis, the role of government in general and the successful use of fiscal policy in particular will become increasingly difficult. Governments will never again have it so good as in this chapter.

## SUMMARY

What you should remember about the components of GDP:

- GDP is the sum of consumption, plus investment, plus government spending, plus exports, minus imports, plus inventory investment.
- Consumption (C) is the purchase of goods and services by consumers. Consumption is the largest component of demand.
- Investment (I) is the sum of nonresidential investment—the purchase of new plants and new machines by firms; and of residential investment—the purchase of new houses or apartments by people.
- Government spending (G) is the purchase of goods and services by federal, provincial, and local governments.
- Exports (X) are purchases of Canadian goods by foreigners. Imports (Q) are purchases of foreign goods by Canadian consumers, Canadian firms, and the Canadian government.
- Inventory investment ($I_S$) is the difference between production and purchases. It can be positive or negative.

What you should remember about our first model of output determination:

- In the short run, demand determines production. Production is equal to income. And income determines demand.

- The consumption function shows how consumption depends on disposable income. The propensity to consume describes how much consumption increases for a given increase in disposable income.
- Equilibrium output is the point at which supply (production) equals demand. In equilibrium, output equals autonomous spending times the multiplier. Autonomous spending is that part of demand that does not depend on income. The multiplier is equal to $1/(1 - c_1)$, where $c_1$ is the propensity to consume.
- Increases in consumer confidence, in investment demand, or in government spending, or decreases in taxes all increase equilibrium output in the short run.
- An alternative way of stating the goods-market equilibrium condition is that investment must be equal to saving, the sum of private and public saving. For this reason, the equilibrium condition in goods markets is also called the IS relation (I for investment, S for saving). We use this term extensively in Chapter 5.

## QUESTIONS AND PROBLEMS

### 1. TRUE/FALSE/UNCERTAIN

a. The largest component of GDP is consumption.

b. Government spending, including transfers, was equal to 22% of GDP in 2012.

c. The propensity to consume has to be positive, but beyond that it can take on any positive value.

d. Fiscal policy describes the choice of government spending and taxes and is treated as exogenous in our goods-market model.

e. The equilibrium condition for the goods market states that consumption equals output.

f. An increase of one unit in government spending leads to an increase of one unit in equilibrium output.

### 2. A SIMPLE ECONOMY

Suppose that the economy is characterized by the following behavioural equations:

$$C = 160 + 0.6Y_D$$
$$\bar{I} = 150$$
$$G = 150$$
$$T = 100$$

Solve for

a. equilibrium GDP ($Y$).

b. disposable income ($Y_D$).

c. consumption spending ($C$).

### 3. THE CONCEPT OF EQUILIBRIUM

For the economy in question 2,

a. Assume output is equal to 900. Compute total demand. Is it equal to production? Explain.

b. Assume output is equal to 1000. Compute total demand. Is it equal to production? Explain.

c. Assume output is equal to 1000. Compute private saving. Is it equal to investment? Explain.

### 4. USING THE MULTIPLIER

a. Consider a decline in real GDP of 2%. For the simple economy in question 2, how many units of real GDP equal 2% of equilibrium GDP?

b. If the 2% decline in real GDP were caused by a reduction in $\bar{I}$, how many units would $\bar{I}$ fall?

c. If the government wanted to return real GDP to its equilibrium level after the fall in $\bar{I}$, would it increase or decrease $G$? By how many units would it increase or decrease $G$?

## 5. THE BALANCED BUDGET MULTIPLIER

For both political and macroeconomic reasons, governments are often reluctant to run budget deficits. Here, we examine whether policy changes in $G$ and $T$ that maintain a balanced budget are macroeconomically neutral. Put another way, we examine whether it is possible to affect output through changes in $G$ and $T$ so that the government budget remains balanced. Start with equation (3.7).

**a.** By how much does $Y$ increase when $G$ increases by one unit?

**b.** By how much does $Y$ decrease when $T$ increases by one unit?

**c.** Why are your answers to (a) and (b) different?

Suppose that the economy starts with a balanced budget: $T = G$. If the increase in $G$ is equal to the increase in $T$, then the budget remains in balance. Let us now compute the balanced budget multiplier.

**d.** Suppose that both $G$ and $T$ increase by exactly one unit. Using your answers to parts (a) and (b), what is the change in equilibrium GDP? Are balanced budget changes in $G$ and $T$ macroeconomically neutral?

**e.** How does the value of the propensity to consume affect your answer? Why?

## 6. AUTOMATIC STABILIZERS

So far in this chapter, we have been assuming that the fiscal policy variable $T$ is independent of the level of income. In the real world, however, this is not the case. Taxes typically depend on the level of income, so tax revenue tends to be higher when income is higher. In this problem, we examine how this automatic response of taxes can help reduce the impact of changes in autonomous spending on output.

Consider the following model of the economy:

$$C = c_0 + c_1 Y_D$$
$$T = t_0 + t_1 Y$$
$$Y_D = Y - T$$

$G$ and $\bar{I}$ are both constant.

**a.** Is $t_1$ greater or less than one? Explain.

**b.** Solve for equilibrium output.

**c.** What is the multiplier? Does the economy respond more to changes in autonomous spending when $t_1$ is zero or when $t_1$ is positive? Explain.

**d.** Why is fiscal policy in this case called an "automatic stabilizer"?

## 7. BALANCED BUDGET VERSUS AUTOMATIC STABILIZERS

It is often argued that a balanced budget amendment would actually be destabilizing. To understand this argument, consider the economy of question 6.

**a.** Solve for equilibrium output.

**b.** Solve for taxes in equilibrium.

Suppose that the government starts with a balanced budget and that there is a drop in $c_0$.

**c.** What happens to $Y$? What happens to taxes?

**d.** Suppose that government cuts spending in order to keep the budget balanced. What will be the effect on $Y$? Does the cut in spending required to balance the budget counteract or reinforce the effect of the drop in $c_0$ on output? (*Do not do* the algebra. Give the answer in words.)

# Financial Markets

## The Core: The Short Run

The **Bank of Canada**, the Canadian central bank, operates monetary policy. About every six weeks, the Bank announces whether interest rates will increase, decrease, or stay the same. The model of economic activity we developed in Chapter 3 did not include interest rates. This was a strong simplification, and it is time to relax it. This requires that we take two steps. First, we must look at what determines interest rates and the role of the Bank of Canada in this determination. This is the topic of this chapter. Second, we must look at how interest rates affect economic activity. That is the topic of the next chapter.

To understand what determines interest rates, we must look at **financial markets**. The task appears daunting: In modern economies, there are thousands of financial assets and thousands of interest rates—interest rates on short-term bonds, on long-term bonds, on government bonds, on corporate bonds, and so on. To make progress, we must simplify. Just as we assumed, in looking at the goods market in Chapter 3, that there was only one type of good, we assume in this chapter that there is just one type of bond, and therefore just one interest rate. We can then think about the determinants of *the* interest rate. As we shall see, one way to solve this problem is to have the interest rate determined by the condition that the demand for money is equal to the supply of money. Because the central bank can change the supply of money, monetary policy has a direct effect on the interest rate. A second, equivalent analysis, shows that if a central bank directly announces a target interest rate, it must then act in financial markets to change the supply of money and achieve that interest rate.

The chapter has five sections. Section 4-1 looks at the demand for money. Section 4-2 looks at the determination of the interest rate under the assumption that the supply of money is directly under the control of the central bank. Section 4-3 (which is optional) introduces banks as suppliers of money and revisits the determination of the interest rate and the role of the central bank. Section 4-4 considers how the analysis of central bank behaviour changes when the central bank announces a target for the interest rate. Section 4-5 provides a summary.

Before we start, a warning: Discussions of financial markets and financial issues are fraught with semantic traps. Such words as "money" or "wealth" have very specific meanings in economics, and these are often not the same meanings as in everyday conversations. The purpose of the Focus box "Semantic Traps: Money, Income, and Wealth" is to help you avoid some of these traps. Read it carefully, and come back to it once in a while.

In everyday life, we use the word "money" to denote many things. We use it as a synonym for income: "making money." We use it as a synonym for wealth: "She has a lot of money." In economics, you must be more careful. Here is a basic guide to some terms and their precise meanings.

**Income** is what you earn from working plus what you receive in interest and dividends. It is a **flow**—that is, it is expressed per unit of time: weekly income, monthly income, or yearly income. J. Paul Getty was once asked what his income was. Getty answered, "$1000." He meant but did not say: per minute.

*Saving* is that part of after-tax income that is not spent. It is also a flow. If you save 10% of income and your income is $3000 per month, then you save $300 per month. **Savings** (plural) is sometimes used as a synonym for wealth—the value of what you have accumulated over time. To avoid potential confusion, we will not use it in the book.

Your **financial wealth**, or simply **wealth**, is the value of all your financial assets minus all your financial liabilities. In contrast to income or saving, which are flow variables, financial wealth is a **stock** variable. It is the value of wealth at a given moment of time. At a given moment of time, you cannot change the total amount of your financial wealth. You can do this only over time, as you save or dissave, or as the value of your assets change. But you can change the composition of your wealth; you can, for example, decide to pay back part of your mortgage by writing a cheque on your chequing account. This leads to a decrease in your liabilities (a smaller mortgage) and a corresponding decrease in your assets (a smaller chequing account balance); but it does not change your wealth.

Financial assets that can be used directly to buy goods are called money. Money includes currency and chequable deposits, deposits against which you can write cheques. Money is also a stock. Someone can have a large wealth but small money holdings, for example, $1,000,000 worth of stocks but only $500 in his chequing account. Or someone can have a large income but small money holdings, for example, be paid $10,000 a month but have a very small positive balance in her chequing account.

*Investment* is a term economists reserve for the purchase of new capital goods, from machines to manufacturing plants to office buildings. When you want to talk about the purchase of shares or other financial assets, you should refer to **financial investment**.

Learn how to be economically correct: Do not say, "Mary is making a lot of money"; say, "Mary receives a high income." Do not say, "Joe has a lot of money"; say, "Joe is very wealthy."

# 4-1 | The Demand for Money

Assume that you have the choice between only two financial assets:

- **Money**, which can be used for transactions but pays zero interest. In reality, there are two types of money: **currency**, the coins and bills issued by the central bank, and **chequable deposits**, the bank deposits on which you can write cheques. The distinction between the two will be important later when we look at the supply of money. But for the moment, it does not matter.

  > Chequable deposits often pay a small interest rate. We ignore this here.

- **Bonds**, which cannot be used for transactions but pay a positive interest rate, *i*. In reality, there are many assets other than money and, in particular, many types of bonds, each associated with a specific interest rate. As discussed earlier, we shall also ignore this aspect of reality for the moment.

Suppose that, as a result of having steadily saved part of your income in the past, your financial wealth today is $50,000. You may intend to keep saving in the future and to increase your wealth further, but its value today is a given. The choice you have to make today is how to allocate this $50,000 between money and bonds.

> Make sure you see the difference between the decision about how much to save (a decision that determines how wealth changes over time) and the decision about how to allocate a given stock of wealth between money and bonds.

Think of buying or selling bonds as implying some cost, for example, a phone call to a broker and the payment of a transaction fee. How much of your $50,000 should you hold in money and how much in bonds?

Holding all your wealth in the form of money is clearly very convenient. You will never have to call a broker or pay transaction fees. But it also means you will not receive interest income. Holding all your wealth in the form of bonds implies receiving income as interest on all your wealth. But having to call your broker whenever you need money to take the subway or pay for a cup of coffee is a rather inconvenient way of living. Therefore, it is clear that you should hold both money and bonds. In what proportions? This depends mainly on two variables:

- Your *level of transactions.* You want to have enough money on average to avoid having to sell bonds to get money too often. Say that you typically spend $5000 a month. You may want to have, on average, say, two months' worth of spending on hand, or $10,000 in money, and the rest, $50,000 − $10,000 = $40,000, in bonds. If, instead, you typically spend $6000 a month, you may want to have $12,000 in money and thus only $38,000 in bonds.

- The *interest rate on bonds.* The only reason to hold any of your wealth in bonds is that they pay interest. If bonds paid no interest, you would hold all of your wealth in money: Bonds and money would pay the same interest rate (namely, zero), and money, which can be used for transactions, would therefore be more convenient.

  The higher the interest rate, the more you will be willing to incur the hassle and the costs associated with buying and selling bonds. If the interest rate is very high, you may decide to squeeze your money holdings to an average of only two weeks' worth of spending, or $2500 (assuming your monthly spending is $5000). This means you will be able to keep, on average, $47,500 in bonds, getting more interest as a result.

Let us make this last point more concrete. Most of you probably do not hold bonds directly; few of you have a broker. But you or your parents may hold bonds indirectly, through a money market account. **Money market funds** receive funds from people and firms and use these funds to buy bonds, typically government bonds. Money market funds pay an interest rate close to the interest rate on the bonds that they hold—the difference coming from the administrative costs of running the funds and from their profit margin.

In the early 1980s, with the interest rate on money market funds reaching 14% per year, people who had previously kept all their financial wealth in their chequing accounts (which paid no interest) realized how much interest they could earn by holding part of those funds in a money market account instead. Money market funds became the rage. Since then, however, the interest rate has decreased. In 2001, the interest rate paid by money market funds was down to about 2%. This is better than zero—the rate paid on many chequing accounts—but much less attractive than the rate in 1981. As a result, most people put less in their money market fund and more in their chequing account than they did in 1981.

Let us formalize this discussion. Denote the amount of money people want to hold— their *demand for money*—by $M^d$ (the superscript $d$ stands for *demand*). We just argued that an individual's money demand depends on two variables: his level of transactions and the interest rate. The demand for money for the economy as a whole is just the sum of all individual demands for money. Thus, money demand for the economy as a whole depends on the overall level of transactions in the economy and on the interest rate. The overall level of transactions in the economy is hard to measure. But it is reasonable to assume that it is roughly proportional to nominal income: If nominal income increases by 10%, it is reasonable to think that the amount of transactions in the economy also increases by roughly 10%. So, we write the relation between the demand for money, nominal income, and the interest rate as:

$$M^d = \$Y\,L(i) \qquad\qquad (4.1)$$
$$(-)$$

where $\$Y$ denotes nominal income. This equation says that the demand for money is equal to nominal income times a function of the interest rate, denoted $L(i)$. The minus sign under $i$ in $L(i)$ captures the fact that the interest rate has a negative effect on money demand: An increase in the interest rate *decreases* the demand for money.

This equation summarizes what we have learned so far:

- The demand for money increases in proportion to nominal income. If income doubles, increasing from $\$Y$ to $\$2Y$, then the demand for money increases from $\$Y\,L(i)$ to $\$2Y\,L(i)$; it also doubles.

Revisit Chapter 2's example of an economy composed of a steel company and a car company. Calculate the total volume of transactions in that economy and its relation to GDP. If the steel company and the car company double in size, what happens to transactions and to GDP?

What matters here is nominal income—income in dollars, not real income. If real income does not change but prices double, leading to a doubling of nominal income, people will need to hold twice as much money to buy the same consumption basket.

FIGURE 4-1

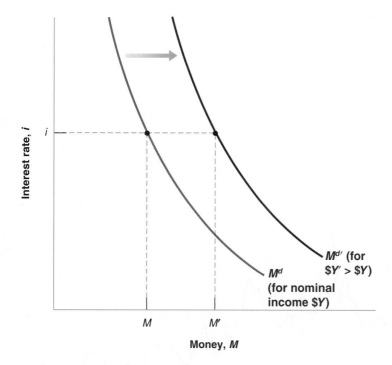

**The Demand for Money**

For a given level of nominal income, a lower interest rate increases the demand for money. For a given interest rate, an increase in nominal income increases the demand for money.

- The demand for money depends negatively on the interest rate. This is captured by the function $L(i)$ and the negative sign underneath: An increase in the interest rate decreases the demand for money.

The relation between the demand for money, nominal income, and the interest rate implied by equation (4.1) is represented graphically in Figure 4–1. The interest rate, $i$, is measured on the vertical axis. Money, $M$, is measured on the horizontal axis.

The relation between the demand for money and the interest rate, for a given level of nominal income, is represented by the $M^d$ curve. The curve is downward sloping: The lower the interest rate (the lower $i$), the higher the amount of money people want to hold (the higher $M$).

At any interest rate, an increase in nominal income increases the demand for money. In other words, an increase in nominal income shifts the demand for money to the right, from $M^d$ to $M^{d'}$. For example, at interest rate $i$, an increase in nominal income from $\$Y$ to $\$Y'$ increases the demand for money from $M$ to $M'$.

## Money Demand and the Interest Rate: The Evidence

How well does equation (4.1) fit the facts? In particular, how much does the demand for money respond to changes in the interest rate?

To get at the answer, first divide both sides of equation (4.1) by $\$Y$:

$$\frac{M^d}{\$Y} = L(i) \qquad (4.2)$$

The term on the left side of the equation is the ratio of money demand to nominal income—in other words, how much money people want to hold in relation to their incomes. Thus, if equation (4.1)—and by implication equation (4.2)—is a good description of reality, we should observe an inverse relation between the ratio of money to nominal income and the interest rate. This provides the motivation for Figure 4–2, which plots the ratio of money to nominal income and the interest rate against time, for the period 1975 to 2012.

> $L(i)$ is a decreasing function of the interest rate, $i$. Equation (4.2) predicts that when the interest rate is high, the ratio of money to nominal income should be low. When the interest rate is low, the ratio of money to nominal income should be high.

| FIGURE | 4-2 |
| --- | --- |

**The Ratio of Money to Nominal Income and the Interest Rate, 1975–2012**

The interest rate and the ratio of money to nominal income typically move in opposite directions.

*Source:* Data from Nominal income (nominal GDP using CANSIM II variable V498086); Money supply (gross M1+ using CANSIM variable V37258); Interest rate (three-month Treasury bill using CANSIM II variable V122484).

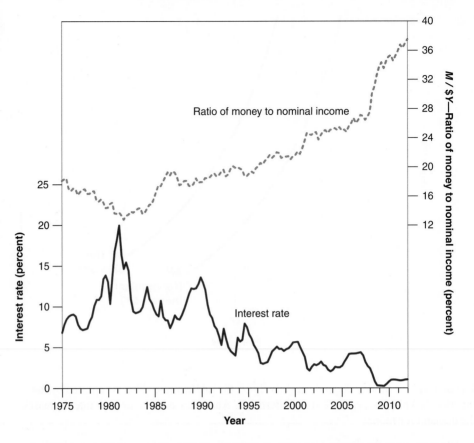

The ratio of money to nominal income is constructed as follows: Money, *M*, is the sum of currency outside banks plus personal and nonpersonal chequable deposits held at chartered banks plus all chequable deposits at trust and mortgage loan companies, credit unions, and caisses populaires as described in the notes to Table E1 (*Bank of Canada Banking and Financial Statistics*). This measure of money is called *M1+* (said *M*1 plus). Nominal income is measured by nominal GDP, *$Y*. The interest rate, *i*, is the average interest rate paid by government bonds during each year.

Figure 4–2 has two characteristics:

(1) The first is the decline in the ratio of money to nominal income exactly when nominal interest rates peak in the entire period from 1980 to 1990. Households and firms reduced their holdings of money when higher interest returns were available on assets, such as money market funds.

Economists sometimes refer to the inverse of the ratio of money to nominal income—that is, to the ratio of nominal income to money—as the **velocity** of money. The word "velocity" comes from the intuitive idea that when the ratio of nominal income to money is higher, the number of transactions for a given quantity of money is higher, and it must be the case that money is changing hands faster; in other words, the *velocity* of money is higher. Therefore, another equivalent way of stating the first characteristic of Figure 4–2 is that the velocity of money is highest when nominal interest rates are highest.

(2) The second is the negative relation between year-to-year movements in the ratio of money to nominal income and the interest rate. A better way to look at year-to-year movements is with a scatter diagram. Figure 4–3 plots the *change in the ratio of money to nominal income* versus the *change in the interest rate* from year to year. Changes in

More precisely, the interest rate is the average over the year of the three-month Treasury bill rate. A precise definition of Treasury bills is given in section 4-2.

$$\frac{1}{(M/\$Y)} = \frac{\$Y}{M}$$
$$= velocity$$

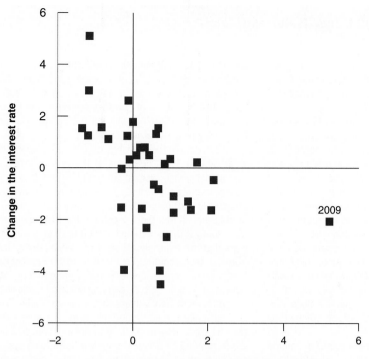

FIGURE 4-3

**Changes in the Ratio of Money to Income and Changes in the Interest Rate, 1976–2012**

Increases in the interest rate are typically associated with a decrease in the ratio of money to nominal income; decreases in the interest rate are typically associated with an increase in that ratio.

*Source:* See Figure 4–2.

the interest rate are measured on the vertical axis. Changes in the ratio of money to nominal income are measured on the horizontal axis. Each point (shown as a square) in the figure corresponds to a given year. The figure shows a negative relation between year-to-year changes in the interest rate and changes in the ratio. The relation is not tight, but if we were to draw a line that best fits the cloud of points, it would clearly be downward sloping, as predicted by our money demand equation. There is a very large increase in money held in 2009, the year of the global financial crisis. This increase cannot be explained by the conventional demand for money relationship.

Note that most of the points lie either in the upper-left quadrant (increases in the interest rate, decreases in the ratio) or the lower-right quadrant (decreases in the interest rate, increases in the ratio).

# 4-2 | The Determination of the Interest Rate: I

We have looked at the demand for money. We now need to look at the supply of money. In reality, there are two suppliers of money: banks supply chequable deposits, and the central bank supplies currency. In this section, we will assume that all money is currency, supplied by the central bank. In the next section, we will reintroduce chequable deposits and look at the role of banks. Introducing banks makes the discussion more realistic. But it also makes the mechanics of money supply more complicated, and it is better to build the intuition in two steps.

Throughout this section, "money" stands for "central bank money" or "currency."

## Money Demand, Money Supply, and the Equilibrium Interest Rate

Suppose that the central bank decides to supply an amount of money equal to *M*. (Let us leave aside for the moment the issue of how the central bank chooses and changes the amount of money in the economy. We will return to it in a few paragraphs.)

FOCUS    How Much of Money Is Currency?

You might think that with debit cards, credit cards, prepaid cash cards for food and phones, and other more exotic forms of payment, very little money is actually held in the form of currency. And in a sense, you are correct.

The Bank of Canada presents information as of December 31 of each year concerning how much Canadian currency is outstanding, that is, all banknotes that have ever been printed and then not destroyed. Part of the Bank of Canada's job is to replace worn bills with new bills. The cost of the replacement operation is the most important reason Canada went to the loonie and the toonie, our one-dollar and two-dollar coins. One-dollar and two-dollar bills were used so frequently that they wore out more quickly than other bills and it was expensive to constantly replace them. Although the coins are more expensive to produce, they last much longer. As of December 31, 2011, there remained $153,988,000 in one-dollar bills and $213,049,000 in two-dollar bills issued at some point by the Bank of Canada and not yet destroyed. The one-dollar and two-dollar bills form only a tiny proportion of the outstanding currency.

The remaining currency issued by the Bank of Canada comprises notes with denominations of $5, $10, $20, $25, $50, $100, $500, and $1000. Yes, there is $46,000 in $25 bills, that is, 1840 such bills issued by the Bank of Canada in 1935 to celebrate the silver jubilee of King George V were never destroyed. There is an additional $20,000 in $500 bills

issued in 1911 and again in 1935. These rare bills are almost certainly in the hands of collectors. A 1911 Queen Mary $500 bill sold at auction in the fall of 2008 for US$322,000, a record price. The face value of currency issued by the Bank of Canada totals $61,028,761,000. All this money is somewhere. Some may be lost, burned, or buried.

According to the Statistics Canada population clock there were 34,671,306 Canadians at the end of 2011. Thus on average every man, woman, and child in Canada held $1760.21 dollars in currency. Some of that money is in the banks and other financial institutions so that when you put your debit card in a machine, there is cash in the machine. But most of that money is thought to be hoarded cash to carry out transactions that are either illegal or, if not illegal, are being hidden from the tax authorities. For this reason the Bank of Canada no longer issues notes in the $1000 denomination. When the largest bill issued is $100, carrying out large-scale illegal transactions is more inconvenient simply because a large volume of bills has to be carried around. However, it is noteworthy that of the $61 billion dollars in currency outstanding, $32 billion is in the form of $100 bills and very few individuals systematically carry around $100 bills. Many "legitimate" businesses will not accept $100 bills in a transaction. In fact, the proportion of large currency bills has been used by some economists as a way to compare the size of the illegal economy in different countries.

The name of the relation (*LM*) is more than 50 years old. *L* stands for liquidity: Economists use liquidity as a measure of how easily and how cheaply an asset can be exchanged for money. Money is fully liquid, other assets less so; we can think ▶ of the demand for money as a demand for liquidity. *M* stands for money. The demand for liquidity must equal the supply of money.

Equilibrium in financial markets requires that money supply be equal to money demand, that $M^s = M^d$. Using equation (4.1) for money demand, the equilibrium condition is:

$$\text{Money supply} = \text{Money demand}$$
$$M = \$Y\,L(i) \tag{4.3}$$

This equation tells us that the interest rate must be such that people are willing to hold an amount of money equal to the existing money supply. This equilibrium relation is called the ***LM* relation**.

This equilibrium condition is represented graphically in Figure 4–4. Just as in Figure 4–1, money is measured on the horizontal axis, and the interest rate is measured on the vertical axis. The demand for money, $M^d$, drawn for a given level of nominal income, is downward sloping: A higher interest rate implies a lower demand for money. The supply of money is drawn as the vertical line denoted $M^s$: The money supply equals $M$ and is independent of the interest rate. Equilibrium is at point $A$, with interest rate $i$.

With this characterization of the equilibrium, we can then look at the effects of changes in nominal income or in the money stock on the equilibrium interest rate.

Figure 4–5 shows the effects of an increase in nominal income on the interest rate. The figure replicates Figure 4–4, and the initial equilibrium is at point $A$. An increase in nominal income increases the level of transactions, which increases the demand for money at any interest rate. The demand curve shifts to the right, from $M^d$ to $M^{d\prime}$. The equilibrium moves along the fixed money supply, from $A$ to $A\prime$, and the equilibrium interest rate increases from $i$ to $i\prime$: *An increase in nominal income leads to an increase in the interest rate.* The reason: At the initial interest rate, the demand for money exceeds the unchanged supply. An increase in

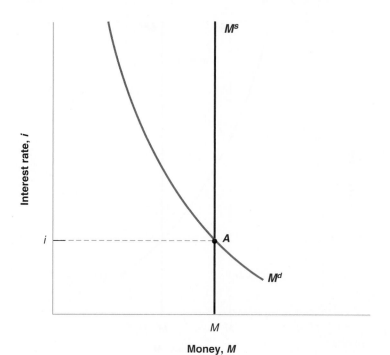

FIGURE 4–4

**The Determination of the Interest Rate**

The interest rate must be such that the supply of money is equal to the demand for money.

the interest rate is needed to decrease the amount of money people want to hold and re-establish equilibrium.

Figure 4–6 shows the effects of an increase in the money supply on the interest rate. The initial equilibrium is at point *A*, with interest rate *i*. An increase in the money supply, from *M* to *M′*, leads to a shift of the supply curve to the right, from $M^s$ to $M^{s'}$. The equilibrium moves from *A* to *A′*, and the interest rate decreases from *i* to *i′*. Thus, *an increase in the supply of money leads to a decrease in the interest rate.* The decrease in the interest rate increases the demand for money so that it equals the larger money supply.

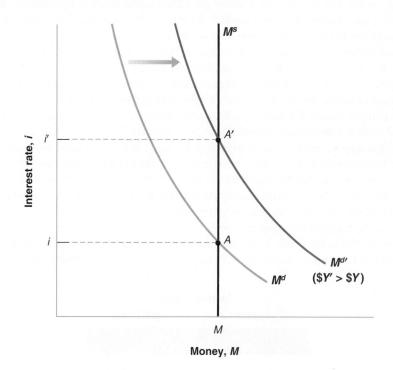

FIGURE 4–5

**The Effects of an Increase in Nominal Income on the Interest Rate**

An increase in nominal income leads to an increase in the interest rate.

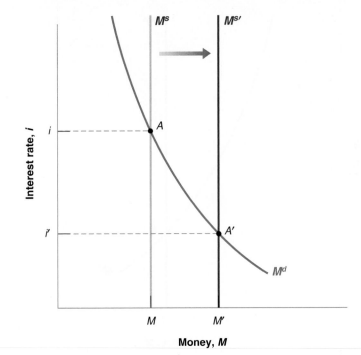

**FIGURE 4–6**

**The Effects of an Increase in the Money Supply on the Interest Rate**

An increase in the supply of money leads to a decrease in the interest rate.

## Monetary Policy and Open Market Operations

We can get a better intuition for the results in Figures 4–5 and 4–6 by looking more closely at how the central bank actually changes the money supply and what happens when it does so.

Assume that the central bank changes the amount of money in the economy by buying or selling bonds in the bond market. If it wants to increase the amount of money in the economy, it buys bonds and pays for them by printing money. If it wants to decrease the amount of money in the economy, it sells bonds and removes from circulation the money it receives in exchange for the bonds. Such operations are called **open market operations**, so called because they take place in the "open market" for bonds. They are one of the standard methods central banks use to change the money stock in modern economies.

The balance sheet of the central bank is given in Figure 4–7. The assets of the central bank are the bonds that it holds in its portfolio. Its liabilities are the stock of money in the economy. Open market operations lead to equal changes in assets and liabilities. If the central bank buys, say, $1 million worth of bonds, the amount of bonds it holds is higher by $1 million, and so is the amount of money in the economy. If it sells $1 million worth of bonds, both the amount of bonds held by the central bank and the amount of money in the economy are lower by $1 million.

The other step we need to take is to look at the relation between bond prices and interest rates. We have focused so far on the interest rate on bonds. In fact, what is determined in bond markets is not interest rates but bond *prices*; the interest rate on a bond can then be inferred from the price of the bond. Understanding the relation between the interest rate and the price of a bond will prove useful both here and later in the book.

Suppose the bonds in our economy are one-year bonds—bonds that promise a payment of a given number of dollars, say, $100, a year hence. In Canada, such bonds, when issued by government and promising payment in a year or less, are called **Treasury bills** or **T-bills**.

> The balance sheet of a bank (or firm or individual) is a list of its assets and liabilities. The assets are the sum of what the bank owns and what is owed to the bank; the liabilities are what the bank owes to others.

**FIGURE 4–7**

**The Balance Sheet of the Central Bank**

The assets of the central bank are the bonds it holds. The liabilities are the stock of money in the economy. An open market operation in which the central bank buys bonds and issues money increases both assets and liabilities by the same amount.

**Central Bank**

| Assets | Liabilities |
|--------|-------------|
| Bonds | Money (currency) |

You can think of the bonds in our economy as one-year T-bills. Let the price of a bond today be $\$P_B$, where $B$ stands for "bond." If you buy the bond today and hold it for a year, the rate of return on holding the bond for a year is equal to $(\$100 - \$P_B)/\$P_B$. Therefore, the interest rate on the bond is:

What you get for the bond a year from now ($100) minus what you pay for the bond today ($P_B$), divided by the price of the bond today, ($P_B$).

$$i = \frac{\$100 - \$P_B}{\$P_B}$$

If $\$P_B$ is $95, the interest rate equals $5/$95 = 0.053, or 5.3%. If $\$P_B$ is $90, the interest rate is 11.1%. *The higher the price of the bond, the lower is the interest rate.*

Equivalently, if we are given the interest rate, we can infer the price of the bond. Reorganizing the formula above, the price today of a one-year bond paying $100 a year from today is given by:

$$\$P_B = \frac{\$100}{1+i}$$

The price of the bond is equal to the final payment divided by 1 plus the interest rate. If the interest rate is positive, the price of the bond is less than the final payment. The higher the interest rate, the lower is the price today. When newspapers write that "bond markets went up today," they mean that *the prices of bonds went up* and therefore that *interest rates went down.*

We are now ready to return to the effects of an open market operation. Consider an **expansionary open market operation**—an operation in which the central bank increases the supply of money. In such a transaction, the central bank buys bonds in the bond market and pays for them by creating money. As the central bank buys bonds, the demand for bonds goes up, increasing the price of bonds. Equivalently, the interest rate on bonds goes down. When the central bank wants instead to decrease the supply of money—a **contractionary open market operation**—it sells bonds. This leads to a decrease in their price, an increase in the interest rate.

To summarize:

- The interest rate is determined by the equality of the supply of money and the demand for money.
- By changing the supply of money, the central bank can affect the interest rate.
- The central bank changes the supply of money through open market operations, which are purchases or sales of bonds for money.
- Open market operations in which the central bank increases money supply by buying bonds lead to an increase in the price of bonds—equivalently, a decrease in the interest rate.
- Open market operations in which the central bank decreases the money supply by selling bonds lead to a decrease in the price of bonds—equivalently, an increase in the interest rate.

Our economy with its two assets, money and bonds, is a much simplified version of actual economies with their many financial assets and many financial markets. But, as we will see later in the book, the basic lessons we have just seen apply very generally. The only change we will have to make is to replace "interest rate" in our conclusions by "short-term interest rate." We will see that the short-term interest rate is determined by the condition that money supply equals money demand; that the central bank can change the amount of money and the short-term interest rate.

The complication: The short-term interest rate—the rate directly affected by monetary policy—is not the only interest rate in the economy. The determination of other interest rates and asset prices (such as stock prices) is the topic of Chapter 19.

There is one dimension, however, in which our model must be extended. We have assumed that all money was currency, supplied by the central bank. In the real world, money includes not only currency but also chequable deposits. Chequable deposits are supplied not by the central bank, but by (private) banks. How the presence of banks, and of chequable deposits, changes our conclusions is the topic of the next section. The section is optional. For those of you who decide to skip it, let us state its basic conclusion. In an economy in which money includes both currency and chequable deposits, the central bank no longer controls the total amount of money directly. It does, however, control it indirectly. In particular, it can still use open market operations—purchases and sales of bonds—to increase or decrease the supply of money and affect the interest rate. The Bank of Canada can also use other methods as described in Chapter 24.

## *4-3 | The Determination of the Interest Rate: II

To understand what determines the interest rate in an economy with both currency and chequable deposits, we must first look at what banks do.

### What Banks Do

Modern economies are characterized by the existence of many types of **financial intermediaries**, institutions that receive funds from people and firms and use these funds to buy bonds or stocks or make loans to other people and firms. Their liabilities are the funds that they owe to the people and firms from whom they have received funds. Their assets are the stocks and bonds they own and the loans they have made.

Banks are one type of financial intermediary. What makes banks special—and the reason we focus on banks here rather than financial intermediaries in general—is that their liabilities are money: People can pay for transactions by writing cheques up to the amount of their account balance. Let us look more closely at what they do.

Banks receive funds from depositors. They keep some of these funds as reserves and use the rest to make loans and purchase bonds. Their balance sheet is shown in Figure 4–8(a). Their liabilities consist of chequable deposits, the funds deposited by people and firms. Their assets consist of reserves, loans, and bonds.

Banks receive funds from people and firms who either deposit funds or have funds sent to their chequing account (their paycheque, for example). At any point in time, people and firms can write cheques or withdraw up to the full amount of their account balance. Thus, the liabilities of the banks are equal to the total value of *chequable deposits.*[1]

Banks keep as **reserves** some of the funds they have received. These reserves are reserves of central bank money; they are held partly in cash and partly on an account the banks have at the central bank, on which they can draw when they need to.

Why do banks hold reserves? For three reasons:

- On any given day, some depositors withdraw cash from their chequing account, while others deposit cash into their account. There is no reason for the inflows and outflows of cash to be equal, so the bank must keep some cash on hand.
- In the same way, on any given day, people with accounts at a bank, bank A, write cheques to people with accounts at other banks, and people with accounts at other banks write cheques to people with accounts at bank A. What bank A, as a result of these transactions, owes to other banks may be greater or less than what other banks owe to bank A. For this reason also, a bank needs to keep reserves. If, at the end of a business day, a bank

[1]**DIGGING DEEPER.** This description simplifies reality in two ways. First, banks also offer other types of deposits, such as savings and time deposits. These cannot be used directly in transactions, and so they are not money. We will ignore this part of the banks' activity, which is not central for our purposes. Also, banks are the main but not the only financial intermediary to offer chequable deposits; other savings institutions and credit unions also offer such deposits. We also ignore this complication here and use "banks" to denote all suppliers of chequable deposits.

*This section is optional.

FIGURE 4-8

(a)

**Banks**

| Assets | Liabilities |
|--------|-------------|
| Reserves<br>Loans<br>Bonds | Chequable deposits |

(b)

**Central Bank**

| Assets | Liabilities |
|--------|-------------|
| Bonds | Central bank money<br>= reserves<br>+ currency |

The Balance Sheet of Banks (a) and the Balance Sheet of the Central Bank Revisited (b)

is short of reserves, it must borrow these reserves from other banks or from the Bank of Canada. Banks keep reserves to avoid these costly loans.

● The first two reasons imply that banks would want to keep some reserves even if they were not required to. But, in addition, in some countries (the United States, for example), banks are subject to legal reserve requirements, which require them to hold reserves in some proportion to chequable deposits. In these countries, reserve requirements are set by their central banks and vary by size of deposits as well as over time. The actual **reserve ratio**, the ratio of bank reserves to chequable deposits, is about 1% in Canada today.

Leaving aside reserves, banks use the remainder of their funds to make loans to firms and consumers or to buy bonds. Loans represent roughly 80% of banks' assets. Bonds account for the rest, thus 20%. The distinction between bonds and loans is unimportant for our purpose—understanding the determination of money supply. Both represent different kinds of lending. In what follows, we will assume for simplicity that banks do not make loans and thus hold only reserves and bonds as assets. However, the distinction between loans and bonds is important for other purposes, from the likelihood of bank runs to the role of federal deposit insurance. These topics are explored in the Focus box "Bank Runs and Bank Collapses."

Figure 4–8(b) gives the balance sheet of the central bank in an economy with banks. It is very similar to the balance sheet in Figure 4–7. The asset side is the same as before: The assets of the central bank are the bonds that it holds. The liabilities of the central bank are the money it has issued, **central bank money**. The new feature is that not all of central bank money is held as currency by the public. Some of it is held as reserves by banks.

## The Supply and Demand for Central Bank Money

The easiest way to think about the determination of the interest rate in this economy is by thinking in terms of the supply and the demand for central bank money. The demand for central bank money is equal to the demand for currency by people plus the demand for reserves by banks. The supply of central bank money is under the direct control of the central bank. The equilibrium interest rate is such that the demand and the supply for central bank money are equal.

Figure 4–9 shows the structure of demand and supply in more detail. Start from the left side. The demand for money is a demand for both chequable deposits and currency. Banks have to hold reserves against chequable deposits: The demand for chequable deposits leads to a demand for reserves by banks. The demand for central bank money is equal to the demand for reserves by banks plus the demand for currency by people. The supply of central bank money is determined by the central bank. The interest rate must be such that the demand and the supply are equal.

◄ Be careful in this section to distinguish among:

The demand for money (demand for currency and chequable deposits)

The demand for bank money (demand for chequable deposits)

The demand for central bank money (demand for currency by people and demand for reserves by banks)

Banks are actually even more complicated than has been outlined in the text. Figure 1 shows that banks make loans: These can be made to either firms or households. A bank may also lend money to the government by buying government bonds. Nongovernment bonds are issued by the private sector: other banks or nonbank firms. For convenience, the analysis in section 4-3 did not distinguish among these three types of loans that are all assets of a bank. In one sense, these loans are similar; they all are intended to pay interest to and then be repaid to the owners of the bank.

In another sense, making a loan to the government is very different from making a loan to a firm or a household. Government bonds are very liquid; the bank can always sell a government bond for cash since government bonds are backed by the tax revenue of the state. There are usually also markets for nongovernment bonds, where these bonds can also be sold for cash. However at the height of the financial crisis in 2008, the usual situation did not prevail.

On the liability side of the balance sheet, we can see that the bank borrows from its customer base in the form of chequable deposits. At any time depositors can withdraw their money. Banks also borrow in the form of very short-term deposits or commercial paper, where the bank promises to pay the depositor or the purchaser of the commercial paper principal and interest in 3, 6, or 12 months. If it is a 12-month unit of commercial paper worth $1 million at an interest rate of 10%, then the owner gets $1.1 million in 365 days.

The last item on the bank's liability side is labelled "equity," which is the shares of the bank that are owned by individuals and by pension funds. These shares have value (we will be more formal in Chapter 20, section 2) because they entitle the owner to a share of the profits of the bank. Where do these profits come from? If the interest rate the bank pays on its deposits and commercial paper is less than the interest rate earned on its loans and its holdings of bonds of both types, then the bank makes a profit.

This system works only if a bank has a healthy portfolio of loans, that is, loans that are paying it enough interest to be able to pay the interest on the deposits and the commercial paper, and to give the bank's shareholders a profit. If too many loans are in default and not paying interest, this is a problem.

What is really interesting is that the system works only if the bank's depositors and the owners of the bank's commercial paper believe that a specific bank's portfolio of loans is healthy. If a rumour starts that that specific bank has made poor decisions about its loans, then people holding deposits at that particular bank will want to "run" to the bank and get their cash. If enough people want to do this, the bank will run out of cash reserves even if it sells all its government bonds. It will be forced to close.

We have now learned that even a rumour that a bank has made poor loan choices, whether true or not, can lead to a bank run. This can happen even if the rumour is false. **Bank runs** are fairly common in history. They even occur in the movies. In *It's a Wonderful Life*, the bank manager played by Jimmy Stewart faces a bank run and successfully halts the run by convincing the depositors that the rumour is false. However this is a feel-good Hollywood ending. More practical policies help to avoid bank runs in Canada and other countries.

Bank runs are avoided in Canada through the combination of federal **deposit insurance** and regulation. In 1967, the **Canada Deposit Insurance Corporation** (CDIC) was created. The Canadian government through the CDIC insures each account up to a maximum of $100,000. There is no reason for most depositors to panic and try to get their money out as long as their deposit is less than that amount. But a bank can use the CDIC only if it submits to a regulatory procedure that is supposed to ensure it has chosen a healthy and well-diversified portfolio of loans. Through the crisis, it was clear that Canadian regulated banks had been well regulated and did hold a well-diversified portfolio of loans. In particular, Canadian banks did not hold excessively large quantities of non-government bonds that were backed by payments on mortgages in the United States.

But deposit insurance is not a perfect solution. Depositors, who do not have to worry about their deposits, no longer look at the activities of the banks in which they have their deposits and the banks may have the incentive to misbehave. In fact, bank managers have the incentive to make very risky higher return loans to generate higher profits for their shareholders and higher salaries for the banks' executives.

In the U.S. and the U.K. in 2008 housing prices fell sharply. Many of the loans held by banks in those countries were either mortgage loans or nongovernment bonds that were "backed by" mortgages called "mortgage-backed securities." These mortgage-backed securities stopped paying interest when the homeowners who had taken out these mortgages stopped paying the interest on them. These homeowners

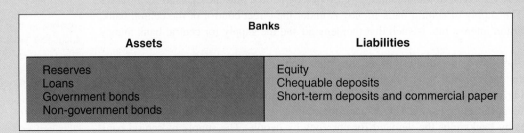

| Banks | |
|---|---|
| **Assets** | **Liabilities** |
| Reserves | Equity |
| Loans | Chequable deposits |
| Government bonds | Short-term deposits and commercial paper |
| Non-government bonds | |

**FIGURE 1    A slightly more complicated bank balance sheet**

stopped paying their interest because the prices of the houses were below the value of the mortgages. It made sense for the homeowners to let the mortgage holders, the banks, take over the houses.

Now the banks had financial assets, either mortgage loans or nongovernment bonds backed by mortgage loans, that were not paying interest. But the banks owed that interest to the depositors and to the persons who held the commercial paper issued by the banks. In some countries, Britain in particular, there were bank runs as depositors such as the ones in Northern Rock lined up to get their money. In other countries, buyers of bank commercial paper refused to buy any more commercial paper from any bank since they did not know which banks had a good portfolio of loans and bonds and which banks were concentrated in housing loans and bonds. Banks could not sell new shares since the expected market price on these shares would be too low. Without the ability to borrow in the short-term deposit market, banks could not make loans to any customers. The inability of even good cus-

tomers to get loans threatened a general slowdown in the entire world economy. We will explore that effect much more extensively in Chapter 11. It is clear that much of the world economic crisis was caused by poor regulation of banks in the United States and, to a lesser degree, in other countries.

As the world economic crisis comes to an end (we hope), it is clear that governments in the United States and the United Kingdom took unprecedented steps in various ways to prevent bank runs. They guaranteed the commercial paper of banks to ensure banks had a way to continue to make loans to good customers as well as to pay the interest due on deposits. Governments also bought shares, both preferred (the usual case) and common shares, in some banks in order to avoid bank runs and allow the banks to continue to function. The past four years have been occupied by discussions between government and the financial industry as they trying to write and implement new regulations that would avoid a repeat of the financial crisis. This has been a long and complicated task that is not yet complete.

---

Let us go through each of the steps in Figure 4–9 and ask the following: What determines the demand for chequable deposits and the demand for currency? What determines the demand for reserves by banks? How does the interest rate reconcile the demand and the supply of central bank money?

**The Demand for Money.** When people can hold both currency and chequable deposits, the demand for money involves two decisions. First, people must decide how much money to hold. Second, they must decide how much of this money to hold in currency and how much to hold in chequable deposits.

It is reasonable to assume that the overall demand for money is given by the same factors as before. The higher the level of transactions and the lower the interest rate on bonds, the more money people will hold. So, we assume that overall money demand is given by the same equation as before (equation [4.1]):

$$M^d = \$Y\, L(i) \tag{4.4}$$
$$(-)$$

That brings us to the second decision. How do people decide how much to hold in currency and how much in chequable deposits? Currency is more convenient for small transactions. Cheques are more convenient for large transactions. Holding money in your chequing account is safer than holding it in cash. We will simply assume here that people hold a fixed proportion of their money in currency—call this proportion $c$—and, by implication, a fixed proportion $(1 - c)$ in chequable deposits. In Canada, people hold 40% of their money in the form of currency; so, think of $c$ as equal to 0.4.

A Federal Reserve Board study suggests that more than half of U.S. currency is held abroad! It is a reasonable guess that part of these foreign holdings of U.S. currency is associated with illegal transactions and that U.S. currency is the currency of choice for illegal transactions around the world. It is unlikely that much Canadian currency is held by foreign residents to carry out illegal transactions in foreign countries. Some Canadian currency is held within Canada to carry out illegal transactions.

FIGURE 4–9

**Determinants of the Demand and the Supply of Central Bank Money**

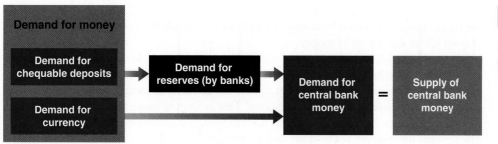

Call the demand for currency $CU^d$ ($CU$ for currency, and $d$ for demand). Call the demand for chequable deposits $D^d$ ($D$ for deposits, and $d$ for demand). The two demands are thus given by:

$$CU^d = cM^d \tag{4.5}$$

$$D^d = (1 - c)M^d \tag{4.6}$$

Equation (4.5) gives the first component of the demand for central bank money, the demand for currency by the public. Equation (4.6) gives the demand for chequable deposits. This demand for chequable deposits leads to a demand by banks for reserves, the second component of the demand for central bank money. To see how, let us turn to the behaviour of banks.

**The Demand for Reserves.** The larger the amount of chequable deposits, the larger is the amount of reserves the banks must hold to allow customers to retrieve cash or to clear cheques between banks. Let $\theta$ (the Greek lowercase letter theta) be the reserve ratio, the amount of reserves banks hold per dollar of chequable deposits. Let $R$ denote the dollar amount of reserves of banks. Let $D$ denote the dollar amount of chequable deposits. Then, by the definition of $\theta$, the following relation holds between $R$ and $D$:

$$R = \theta D \tag{4.7}$$

We saw earlier that in Canada today, the reserve ratio is roughly equal to 1%. Thus, $\theta$ is roughly equal to 0.01.

If people want to hold $D^d$ in deposits, then, from equation (4.7) banks must hold $\theta D^d$ in reserves. Combining equations (4.6) and (4.7), the second component of the demand for central bank money—the demand for reserves by banks—is given by:

$$R^d = \theta (1 - c)M^d \tag{4.8}$$

**The Determination of the Interest Rate.** We are now ready to characterize the equilibrium. Let $H$ be the supply of central bank money; $H$ is directly controlled by the central bank, which can change the amount of $H$ through open market operations. The demand for central bank money is equal to the sum of the demand for currency and the demand for reserves. The equilibrium condition is that the supply of central bank money be equal to the demand for central bank money:

More on open market operations coming next.

$$H = CU^d + R^d \tag{4.9}$$

Replace $CU^d$ and $R^d$ by their expressions from equations (4.5) and (4.8) to get:

$$H = cM^d + \theta(1 - c)M^d = [c + \theta(1 - c)]M^d$$

Finally, replace the overall demand for money, $M^d$, by its expression from equation (4.4) to get:

$$H = [c + \theta (1 - c)]\$Y L(i) \tag{4.10}$$

The supply of central bank money (the left side) is equal to the demand for central bank money (the right side), which is equal to the term in brackets times the overall demand for money.

Look at the term in brackets more closely. Assume that people hold only currency: $c = 1$. Then, the term in brackets is equal to 1, and the equation is exactly the same as equation (4.3) in section 4-2 (with the letter $H$ replacing the letter $M$ on the left side, but both $H$ and $M$ standing for the supply of central bank money). In this case, people hold only currency, and banks play no role in the supply of money.

Assume, instead, that people do not hold currency at all but hold only chequable deposits. In this case, $c = 0$, and the term in brackets is equal to $\theta$. Suppose for example that $\theta = 0.01$, and so the term in brackets equals 0.01. Then, the demand for central bank money is one-hundredth of the overall demand for money. This is easy to understand: People hold only chequable deposits. For every dollar they want to hold, banks need to have 1 cent in reserves. The demand for reserves is 1% of the overall demand for money.

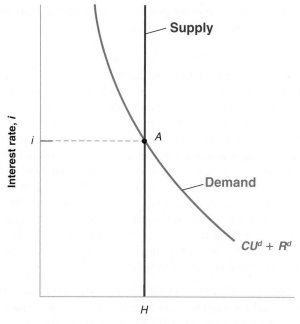

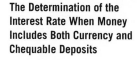

FIGURE 4-10

**The Determination of the Interest Rate When Money Includes Both Currency and Chequable Deposits**

The equilibrium interest rate is such that the supply of central bank money is equal to the demand for central bank money.

Leaving aside these two extreme cases, note that as long as people hold some chequable deposits (so that $c < 1$), the term in brackets is less than 1: The demand for central bank money is less than the overall demand for money. This comes from the fact that the demand for reserves by banks is only a fraction of the demand for chequable deposits.

The equilibrium condition in equation (4.10) is represented graphically in Figure 4–10. The figure looks the same as Figure 4–4 but with central bank money rather than money on the horizontal axis. The interest rate is measured on the vertical axis. The demand for central bank money, $CU^d + R^d$, is drawn for a given level of nominal income. A higher interest rate implies a lower demand for central bank money for two reasons. The demand for currency goes down; the demand for chequable deposits also goes down, leading to a decrease in the demand for reserves by banks. The supply of money is fixed and is represented by a vertical line at $H$. Equilibrium is at point $A$, with interest rate $i$.

The effects of either changes in nominal income or changes in the supply of central bank money are qualitatively the same as in the previous section. In particular, an increase in the supply of central bank money leads to a shift in the vertical supply line to the right. This leads to a lower interest rate. As before, an increase in central bank money leads to a decrease in the interest rate; symmetrically, a decrease in central bank money leads to an increase in the interest rate. The rest of this section is spent exploring this result further.

## Two Alternative Ways of Looking at the Equilibrium

We have looked at the equilibrium through the condition that the supply and the demand of central bank money be equal. There are two alternative ways of looking at the equilibrium. One is through the condition that the supply and demand of *reserves* be equal. The other is through the condition that the supply and the demand of *money* be equal. Going through each will strengthen your intuition.

**The Supply and Demand for Reserves.** Take the equilibrium condition (4.9) and move the demand for currency to the left side to get:

$$H - CU^d = R^d$$

The left side gives the *supply of reserves* as the amount of central bank money minus what people hold as currency. The right side gives the *demand for reserves*. The equilibrium condition now reads: The supply of reserves must be equal to the demand for reserves.

This way of looking at the equilibrium is attractive because in Canada, there is, indeed, a market for reserves, in which the interest rate that reconciles the demand and the supply of reserves is determined. The market is called the **market for overnight funds**. Banks that have excess reserves at the end of the day lend them to banks that have insufficient reserves. In equilibrium, the total demand for reserves by all banks, $R^d$, must be equal to the supply of reserves, $H - CU^d$—the equilibrium condition above. The interest rate determined in that market is called the **overnight interest rate** (sometimes shortened to the "overnight rate"). Because the Bank of Canada can change the supply of central bank money, $H$, it can, in effect, choose the overnight rate. The Bank of Canada, as of 2013 and for many years before, announces a 0.5% range for the overnight rate approximately every six weeks. The **Bank Rate** is the highest value that the Bank of Canada will allow the overnight rate to attain. The lowest allowed value is the Bank Rate minus 0.5%. Announcements of the Bank Rate are indicators of Bank of Canada policy, reflecting the overnight rate desired by the Bank. The Bank Rate appears on the Bank of Canada website.

**The Supply and Demand for Money.** Yet another, but still equivalent, way of looking at the equilibrium is as the condition that the overall demand for money is equal to the overall supply of money. To see this, take equation (4.10) and divide both sides by $[c + \theta (1 - c)]$ to get:

$$\frac{1}{[c + \theta (1 - c)]} H = \$Y \, L(i) \tag{4.11}$$

Supply of money = Demand for money

The right side of the equation gives the overall demand for money (currency plus chequable deposits). The left side gives the overall supply of money (currency plus chequable deposits). The equilibrium condition is that demand and supply be equal.

Note that the overall supply of money is equal to a constant term times central bank money. Note that because $c + \theta(1 - c)$ is less than 1, its inverse—the constant term on the left of the equation above—is greater than 1. This term is often called the **money multiplier**. Equation (4.11) then tells us that the overall supply of money is a multiple of the supply of central bank money, with the multiple given by the money multiplier. Suppose $c = 0.4$ and $\theta = 0.01$. Then $[c + \theta(1 - c)] = [0.4 + 0.01(0.6)] = 0.406$, and the multiplier equals $1/0.406$, or about 2.46. A multiplier of 2.46 implies that the overall money supply is equal to about 2.46 times the supply of central bank money. To reflect the fact that the overall money supply in the end depends on central bank money, central bank money is often called **high-powered money** (this is where the letter $H$ we used to denote central bank money comes from), or the **monetary base**.

> "High-powered" because increases in $H$ lead to more than one-for-one increases in the supply of money—the left side of equation (4.11): Increases in $H$ are high-powered.

The multiplier in equation (4.11) implies that a given change in central bank money has a larger effect on money supply—and, in turn, a larger effect on interest rates—in an economy with banks than in an economy without banks. In an economy without banks—the economy we studied in section 4-2—the effect of a change in central bank money on money supply is simply one for one, as central bank money and money are the same thing. Here, the effect is given by the multiplier: The effect on money supply is a multiple of the original change in central bank money. To give you more intuition for this result, the last subsection looks at the effects of an open market operation in an economy in which people hold chequable deposits.

## Open Market Operations Revisited

Consider the special case where people hold only chequable deposits; so, $c = 0$. In this case, the multiplier is $1/\theta$: An increase of one dollar of high-powered money leads to an increase of $1/\theta$ dollars in money supply. Assume further that $\theta = 0.01$ so that the multiplier equals $1/0.01 = 100$. The purpose of what follows is to get more intuition for where this multiplier comes from and, more generally, for how the initial increase in central bank money leads to a 10-fold increase in the overall money supply.

Suppose the Bank of Canada buys $100 worth of bonds in an open market operation. It pays the seller—call him seller 1—$100, creating $100 in central bank money. At this point, the increase in central bank money is $100. When we looked earlier at the effects of an open market operation in an economy in which there were no banks, this was the end of the story. Here, it is just the beginning:

- Seller 1 (who, we have assumed, does not want to hold any currency) deposits the $100 in a chequing account at his bank—call it bank A. This leads to an increase in chequable deposits of $100.
- Bank A keeps $100 × 0.01 = $1 in reserves and buys bonds with the rest, $100 × 0.99 = $99. It pays $99 to the seller of those bonds—call her seller 2.
- Seller 2 deposits $99 in a chequing account in her bank—call it bank B. This leads to an increase in chequable deposits of $99.
- Bank B keeps $99 × 0.01 = $0.99 in reserves and buys bonds with the rest, $99 × 0.99 = $98.01. It pays $98.01 to the seller of those bonds—call him seller 3.
- Seller 3 deposits $98.01 in a chequing account in his bank—call it bank C. And so on.

By now, the chain of events should be clear. What is the eventual increase in money supply? The increase in chequable deposits is $100 when seller 1 deposits the proceeds of his sale of bonds in bank A, plus $99 when seller 2 deposits the proceeds of her sale of bonds in bank B, plus $98.01 when seller 3 does the same, and so on. Let us write the sum as:

$$\$100 \, (1 + 0.99 + 0.99^2 + \cdots )$$

The series in parentheses is a geometric series, so its sum is equal to $1/(1 - 0.99) = 100$. Money supply increases by $10,000, 100 times the initial increase in central bank money.

This derivation gives us another way of thinking about the money multiplier: We can think of the ultimate increase in money supply as the result of *successive rounds of purchases of bonds*—the first by the Bank of Canada in its open market operation, the following ones by banks. Each successive round leads to an increase in money supply; eventually, the increase in money supply is equal to 100 times the initial increase in central bank money.

When we take into account the fact that money is composed of both currency and chequable deposits, the best way to think about the determination of the interest rate is as the condition that the demand for central bank money equals the supply of central bank money. Changes in the supply of central bank money, carried out by the central bank through open market operations, affect the equilibrium interest rate. Increases in central bank money decrease the interest rate; decreases in central bank money increase the interest rate.

◀ There is a parallel between our interpretation of the money multiplier as the result of successive purchases of bonds and the interpretation of the goods market multiplier (Chapter 3) as the result of successive rounds of spending. Multipliers can often be derived as the sum of a geometric series and be interpreted as the result of successive rounds of decisions. This interpretation often gives a better intuition for the process at work.

◀ See Appendix 2 at the end of the book for a refresher on geometric series.

◀ Work out the case where $c > 0$. In each round, take into account that not all money is deposited in a chequing account.

# 4-4 | Target Interest Rate Setting by the Central Bank

The Bank of Canada and many central banks do not directly announce changes in the money supply. Instead they announce the level of the interest rate that will prevail in financial markets between this announcement and the next announcement. We will look at the details of these announcements in Chapter 24. Here we use the analysis of financial markets in sections 4-2 and 4-3 to understand how an announcement of a target rate of interest is implemented.

## A Target Interest Rate Announcement and the Supply of Money

Figure 4–11 shows the money market using our first model of the determination of interest rates. The **target interest rate** is $i_A$ and is announced by the central bank. It is the interest rate that will prevail over the period between this announcement and the next announcement. We

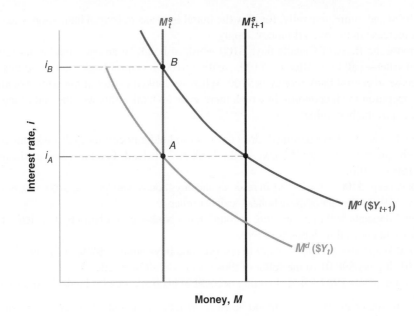

FIGURE 4-11

**The Equilibrium in the Money Market when the Central Bank Makes an Interest Rate Announcement**

The central bank has announced that the interest rate will remain at $i_A$ during both period $t$ and $t+1$. The figure shows that if the demand for money increases between period $t$ and period $t+1$, the central bank must increase the money supply to keep interest rates from rising to $i_B$.

now have to be more specific about time periods. Suppose there are two time periods, period $t$ and $t+1$, between now and the next announcement. You could think of these as months. The interest rate announcement is made by the central bank at the beginning of period $t$. There is a demand for money in period $t$ that depends on nominal income in period $t$. There is a demand for money in period $t+1$ that depends on nominal income in period $t+1$. In the example in Figure 4–11, there is an increase in nominal GDP between $t$ and $t+1$ and the demand for money shifts to the right. What are the implications for the central bank and financial markets?

Figure 4–11 makes the necessary actions of the central bank clear. Once the central bank has committed to a target interest rate $i_A$ for both periods $t$ and $t+1$, it is committing to changing the money supply as needed to keep the interest rate at $i_A$ over both months. Thus when money demand rises, the money supply must rise to $M_{t+1}^s$. If nominal income were to fall between period $t$ and period $t+1$, then in order to keep interest rates from falling, the central bank would have to reduce the money supply. The interest rate announcement is a promise to move the money supply as needed over the next two months in a way that keeps the interest rate constant.

We could also use Figure 4–11 to show that if a central bank announces a reduction in the target interest rate to prevail over the next two months, as long as nominal income is the same, the bank is announcing that there will be in increase in the money supply.

In Chapter 2 we saw that the Bank of Canada did keep interest rates constant for a very long period of time over 2012. Thus the Bank of Canada must have adjusted the money supply to equal money demand.

## A Target Interest Rate Announcement and Activity in the Market for Central Bank Money*

Figure 4–12 is used to show how a target interest rate announcement is implemented in the market equilibrium for central bank money. The analysis is very similar to that just done in Figure 4–11. The target interest rate announcement again promises to keep the interest rate at $i_A$ for the next two months, month $t$ and month $t+1$.

---

*This section should be skipped if you choose not to cover optional section 4-3.

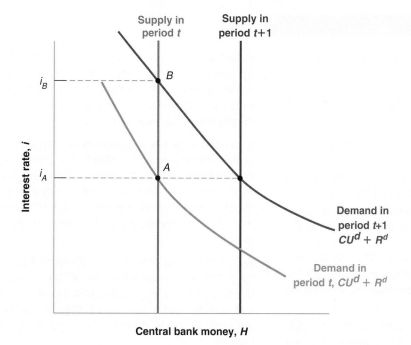

FIGURE 4-12

**The Equilibrium in the Market for Central Bank Money when the Central Bank Makes an Interest Rate Announcement**

The central bank has announced that the interest rate will remain at $i_A$ during both period $t$ and $t+1$. The figure shows that if the demand for central bank money increases between period $t$ and period $t+1$, the central bank must increase the supply of central bank money to keep interest rates from rising from $i_A$ to $i_B$.

In Figure 4–12, we again allow the level of nominal income to be higher in period $t+1$ than in period $t$. The increase in nominal income shifts the demand curve for central bank money to the right. As nominal income rises, there is a larger demand for currency at any level of the interest rate. As nominal income rises, there is a larger demand for reserves as banks have a higher level of deposits against which they hold the reserves. If the central bank did not increase the supply of central bank money, the interest rate would have to increase to $i_B$. The central bank would not achieve its target interest rate. But the commitment to keep the interest rate constant at $i_A$ requires that the central bank increase the supply of central bank money when nominal income rises.

To maintain the interest rate at the target $i_A$, the central bank must enter financial markets and supply reserves and currency. This means the central bank must conduct an expansionary monetary policy and buy government bonds in an open market operation.

The promise to keep the interest rate constant at a pre-announced target for a fixed period of time between announcements is a promise to adjust the supply of central bank money to meet the demand for central bank money at the announced interest rate.

## 4-5 | Summary

We have looked at three ways that a central bank can change the interest rate in financial markets. In Section 4-2, the central bank directly set the money supply. In Section 4-3, the central bank set the quantity of central bank money. In either case, the central bank, if it conducted an expansionary open market operation, would cause a reduction in interest rates and if it conducted a contractionary open market operation would cause an increase in interest rates.

In Section 4-4, we noted that many central banks simply announce the target interest rate to prevail for a specific period of time, the time between announcements. This means that the central bank must be willing to adjust the money supply or the supply of central bank money to achieve its target interest rate. In all three cases, the message is the same. Through its activities in financial markets the central bank can control the interest rate.

- The demand for money depends positively on the level of transactions in the economy and negatively on the interest rate.

- Given the supply of money, an increase in income leads to an increase in the demand for money and an increase in the interest rate. An increase in money supply leads to a decrease in the interest rate.

- The central bank affects the interest rate through open market operations. Open market operations in which the central bank increases money supply by buying bonds lead to an increase in the price of bonds—equivalently, a decrease in the interest rate.

    Open market operations in which the central bank decreases money supply by selling bonds lead to a decrease in the price of bonds—equivalently, an increase in the interest rate.

- When people hold currency and chequable deposits, the central bank does not directly control money supply. But it controls the supply of central bank money. The interest rate must be such that the supply of central bank money is equal to the demand for central bank money, which is itself the sum of the demand for currency by people and of reserves by banks.

- In an economy where people hold both currency and chequable deposits, the effect of a given change in central bank money on money supply is given by the money multiplier. The larger the money multiplier, the larger is the effect of a given change in central bank money on money supply and, in turn, on the interest rate.

- An announcement of a target interest rate by a central bank, that is, an interest rate that will prevail over a number of future periods, requires that the central bank adjust money supply so money supply equals money demand in each period when the announcement prevails.

## KEY TERMS

- Bank of Canada, 58
- Bank Rate, 74
- bank runs, 70
- bonds, 59
- Canada Deposit Insurance Corporation, 70
- central bank money, 69
- chequable deposits, 59
- contractionary open market operation, 67
- currency, 59
- deposit insurance, 70
- expansionary open market operation, 67
- financial intermediaries, 68
- financial investment, 59
- financial markets, 58
- financial wealth, 59
- flow, 59
- high-powered money, 74
- income, 59

- *LM* relation, 64
- *M*1+, 62
- market for overnight funds, 74
- monetary base, 74
- money, 59
- money market funds, 60
- money multiplier, 74
- open market operation, 66
- overnight interest rate, 74
- reserve ratio, 69
- reserves, 68
- savings, 59
- stock, 59
- target interest rate 75
- Treasury bills, or T-bills, 66
- velocity, 62
- wealth, 59

## QUESTIONS AND PROBLEMS

1. **TRUE/FALSE/UNCERTAIN**

a. Income and financial wealth are both examples of stock variables.

b. The demand for money does not depend on the interest rate because only bonds earn interest.

**c.** Given their financial wealth, if people are satisfied with the amount of money they hold, then they must also be satisfied with the amount of bonds they hold.

**d.** Financial innovations slowly change velocity.

**e.** In the past 25 years, the ratio of money to nominal income has moved in the same direction as the interest rate.

**f.** The central bank can increase the supply of money by selling bonds in the market for bonds.

**g.** By construction, bond prices and interest rates always move in opposite directions.

## 2. MONEY DEMAND

Suppose that a person's wealth is $50,000 and that her yearly income is $60,000. Also, suppose that her money demand function is given by:

$$M^d = \$Y(0.35 - i)$$

**a.** What is her demand for money and her demand for bonds when the interest rate is 5%? 10%? Remember that the sum of money and bonds demanded is total wealth.

**b.** Describe the effect of the interest rate on money demand and bond demand. Is it consistent with the theory in Chapter 4? Why?

**c.** Suppose that the interest rate is 10%. In percentage terms, what happens to her demand for money if her yearly income is reduced by 50%?

**d.** Suppose that the interest rate is 5%. In percentage terms, what happens to her demand for money if her yearly income is reduced by 50%?

**e.** Summarize the effect of income on money demand. How does it depend on the interest rate?

## 3. BONDS AND THE INTEREST RATE

A bond promises to pay $100 in one year.

**a.** What is the interest rate on the bond if its price today is $75? $85? $95?

**b.** What is the relation between the price of the bond and the interest rate?

**c.** If the interest rate is 8%, what is the price of the bond today?

## 4. FINANCIAL MARKETS EQUILIBRIUM

Suppose that money demand is given by:

$$M^d = \$Y(0.25 - i)$$

where $Y is $100. Also, suppose that the supply of money is $20. Assume equilibrium in financial markets.

**a.** What is the interest rate?

**b.** If the Bank of Canada wants to increase $i$ by 10% (from, say, 2% to 12%), at what level should it set the supply of money?

## 5. BOND DEMAND

Suppose that a person's wealth is $50,000 and that her yearly income is $60,000. Also, suppose that her money demand function is given by:

$$M^d = \$Y(0.35 - i)$$

**a.** Derive the demand for bonds. What is the effect of an increase in the interest rate of 10% (from, say, 2% to 12%) on the demand for bonds?

**b.** What are the effects of an increase in wealth on money demand and on bond demand? Explain in words.

**c.** What are the effects of an increase in income on money and on bond demand? Explain in words.

**d.** "When people earn more money, they obviously want to hold more bonds." What is wrong with this statement?

## 6. THE MONEY MULTIPLIER

Suppose the following assumptions hold:

1. The public holds no currency.
2. The ratio of reserves to deposits is 0.1.
3. The demand for money is given by:

$$M^d = \$Y(0.8 - 4i)$$

Initially, the monetary base is $100 billion, and nominal income is $5 trillion.

**a.** What is the demand for high-powered money?

**b.** Find the equilibrium interest rate by setting the demand for high-powered money equal to the supply of high-powered money.

**c.** What is the overall supply of money? Is it equal to the overall demand for money at the interest rate you found in (b)?

**d.** What is the impact on the interest rate if high-powered money is increased to $300 billion?

**e.** If the overall money supply increases to $3000 billion, what will be the impact on $i$? (*Hint:* Use what you learned in d.)

## 7. ATMS AND CREDIT CARDS

In this problem, we examine the effect of the introduction of ATMs and credit cards on money demand. For simplicity, let us examine a person's demand for money over a period of four days.

Suppose ATMs and credit cards do not exist and a person goes to the bank once at the beginning of each four-day period and withdraws from his savings account all the money he needs for the next four days. He spends $4 per day.

**a.** How much does he withdraw each time he goes to the bank?

Compute the person's money holdings for days 1 through 4 (in the morning, before he spends any of the money he withdraws).

**b.** What is the amount of money he holds on average?

After the advent of ATMs, he now withdraws money once every two days.

**c.** How much does he withdraw each time he goes to the ATM?

**d.** What is the amount of money he holds on average?

Finally, with the advent of credit cards, the person pays for all his purchases using his card. He withdraws no money from his savings account until the fourth day, when he withdraws the whole amount necessary to pay for his credit card purchases over the previous four days.

**e.** Compute the person's money holdings for days 1 through 4.

**f.** What is the amount of money he holds on average?

**g.** On the basis of your answers to (b), (d), and (f), what has been the effect of ATMs and credit cards on money demand?

### 8. THE VELOCITY OF MONEY

Let money demand be given by:

$$M^d = \$Y\, L(i)$$

**a.** Derive an expression for velocity as a function of $i$. How does it depend on $i$?

**b.** Look at Figure 4–2. What has happened to the velocity of money from 1975 to 2012?

### 9. TARGETING AN INTEREST RATE

Suppose that $M^d = \$Y\,(0.25 - i)$ where $i$ is expressed in decimal form, that is 10% = 0.10.

**a.** If nominal income is \$1000, and the interest rate target is 5%, what money supply must the Bank of Canada provide to achieve its target?

**b.** The interest rate target announced in March 2013 is 5%. If nominal income is \$1000 in March 2013, but rises to \$1010 in April 2013, how much does the Bank of Canada have to increase the money supply between March and April to achieve its target?

**c.** The central bank often announces the money supply. Suppose that when the targeted interest rate is 3% and the central bank is achieving the interest rate target, I observe that the nominal money supply is falling between this month and last month? What would I believe was happening to nominal income?

**d.** Visit the Bank of Canada website. What is the current target interest rate? When was the most recent announcement? When is the next announcement?

---

### FURTHER READING

The Bank of Canada maintains a useful website (www.bankofcanada.ca) that contains data on financial markets as well as information on what the Bank of Canada is doing and the current announcement of the Bank Rate.

It is very likely that your university has a course in money and banking. This course would explore many of the issues raised in this chapter in more detail.

# Goods and Financial Markets: The *IS-LM* Model

## The Core: The Short Run

We looked at the goods market in Chapter 3 and at financial markets in Chapter 4. We now look at goods and financial markets together. By the end of this chapter, you will have a framework to think about how output and the interest rate are determined in the short run.

In developing this framework, we follow a path first traced by two economists, John Hicks and Alvin Hansen, in the late 1930s and the early 1940s. When Keynes's *General Theory* was published in 1936, there was much agreement that the book was both fundamental and nearly impenetrable. (Look at it, and you will agree.) There were many debates about what Keynes really meant. In 1937, John Hicks summarized what he saw as one of Keynes's main contributions: the joint description of goods and financial markets. His analysis was later extended by Alvin Hansen. Hicks and Hansen called their formalization the *IS-LM* model.

Macroeconomics has made substantial progress since the early 1940s. This is why the *IS-LM* model is treated in Chapter 5 rather than in the last chapter of this book. (Think of it: If you had taken this course 40 years ago, you would be nearly done.) But to most economists, the *IS-LM* model still represents an essential building block—one that, despite its simplicity, captures much of what happens in the economy in the short run. This is why the *IS-LM* model is still taught and used today.

# 5-1 | The Goods Market and the *IS* Relation

Let us first summarize what we learned in Chapter 3:

The exact relation, from Chapter 3:

$$Y = Z \Leftrightarrow$$
$$I = S + (T - G)$$

- We characterized equilibrium in the goods market as the condition that production, $Y$, be equal to the demand for goods, $Z$.
- In section 3-4, we called the equality of demand and production the *IS* relation because it had been historically reinterpreted as the equality of $I$ (investment) and $S$(saving). The name has stuck and we use that name throughout this chapter.
- We defined demand as the sum of consumption, investment, and government spending. We assumed that consumption was a function of disposable income (income minus taxes) and took investment spending, government spending, and taxes as given. The equilibrium condition was given by:

$$Y = C(Y - T) + \bar{I} + G$$

- Using this equilibrium condition, we then looked at the factors that changed equilibrium output. We looked, in particular, at the effects of changes in government spending and of shifts in consumption demand.

We will do this in Chapter 21, where we will look at the effects of interest rates on both consumption and investment. We could denote G and T as G as G bar and T bar to show G and T are also exogenous. Since these two variables remain exogenous, we lighten notation and just use G and T throughout.

The two simplifications of this first model were that (1) the interest rate did not affect the demand for goods, and (2) exports, imports, and net exports were zero. Our task in this chapter is to remove the first simplification, to introduce the interest rate in our model of goods–market equilibrium. For the time being, we will focus only on the effect of the interest rate on investment and take up a discussion of its effects on the other components of demand later. The task in the next chapter is to include exports and imports in our model.

## Investment, Sales, and the Interest Rate

In our first model of output determination, investment was left unexplained—we assumed investment was constant, even when output changed. Investment—spending on new machines and plants by firms—is, in fact, far from constant, and it depends primarily on two factors:

- *The level of sales.* A firm facing an increase in sales needs to increase production. To do so, it may need to buy additional machines or build an additional plant. A firm facing low sales will feel no such need and will spend little, if anything, on investment.
- *The interest rate.* Consider a firm deciding whether to buy a new machine. To buy the new machine, the firm must borrow, either by taking a loan from a bank or by issuing bonds. The higher the interest rate, the less likely the firm is to borrow and buy the machine. At a high enough interest rate, the additional profits from the new machine will not cover interest payments, and the new machine will not be worth buying.

To capture these two effects, we write the investment relation as follows:

$$I = I(Y, \ i) \tag{5.1}$$
$$(+, -)$$

Equation (5.1) states that investment, $I$, depends on production, $Y$, and the interest rate, $i$. Although our discussion suggests that sales may be a more appropriate variable, we will assume that sales and production are equal—in other words, we will assume that inventory investment always equals zero—and use production instead. The positive sign under $Y$ indicates that an increase in production leads to an increase in investment. The negative sign under the interest rate $i$ indicates that an increase in the interest rate leads to a decrease in investment.

$$Y\uparrow \Rightarrow I\uparrow$$
$$i\uparrow \Rightarrow I\downarrow$$

## The *IS* Curve

Taking into account the investment relation (5.1), the equilibrium condition in the goods market becomes:

$$Y = C(Y - T) + I(Y,i) + G \tag{5.2}$$

The supply of goods (the left side) must be equal to the demand for goods (the right side). Equation (5.2) and the curve to be derived is our expanded *IS* relation. We can now look at what happens to demand and thus to output when the interest rate changes.

Start with Figure 5–1. Demand (the right side of equation [5.2]) is measured on the vertical axis. Output (equivalently, production or income) is measured on the horizontal axis. The curve *ZZ* plots demand as a function of output for a given value of the interest rate, *i*. As output, and thus income, increases, so does consumption; we studied this relation in Chapter 3. As output increases, investment also increases; this is the relation between investment and production that we have introduced in this chapter. Through its effects on both consumption and investment, an increase in output leads to an increase in demand: *ZZ* is upward sloping.

◀ Remember that (1) production is a synonym for output, and (2) production and income are always equal.

Note that we have drawn *ZZ* so that it is flatter than the 45-degree line. Put another way, we have assumed that an increase in output leads to a less than one-for-one increase in demand. In Chapter 3, where investment was constant, this restriction naturally followed from the restriction that consumers spend only part of their additional income on consumption. But now that we allow investment to respond to production, this restriction may no longer hold. When output increases, the sum of the increase in consumption and the increase in investment could exceed the initial increase in output. Although this is a theoretical possibility, the empirical evidence suggests that it is not the case in practice. That is why we will assume the response of demand to output is less than one-for-one and draw *ZZ* flatter than the 45-degree line.

◀ Since we have not assumed that the consumption and investment relations in equation (5.2) are linear, *ZZ* is, in general, a curve rather than a line. Thus, we draw it as a curve in Figure 5–1.

Equilibrium is reached at the point where demand equals production, at point *A*—the intersection of *ZZ* and the 45-degree line. The equilibrium level of output is given by *Y*.

We have drawn the demand relation, *ZZ*, for a given value of the interest rate. Suppose that the interest rate exogenously increases from its initial value *i* to a new higher value *i'*. At any level of output, investment decreases. The demand curve *ZZ* shifts down to *ZZ'*: At a given level of output, demand is lower. The new equilibrium is at the intersection of the lower demand curve *ZZ'* and the 45-degree line, at point *A'*. The equilibrium level of output is now *Y'*.

◀ Equilibrium in the goods market: $i\uparrow \Rightarrow Y\downarrow$

In words: An increase in the interest rate investment. The decrease in investment leads to a decrease in output, which further decreases consumption and investment. In other words, the initial decrease in investment leads to a larger decrease in output through the multiplier effect.

Using Figure 5–1, we can find the equilibrium value of output associated with *any* value of the interest rate. The relation between equilibrium output and the interest rate is derived in Figure 5–2. Figure 5–2(a) reproduces Figure 5–1. The interest rate *i* implies a level of output equal to *Y*. The higher interest rate *i'* implies a lower level of output, *Y'*. Figure 5–2(b) plots

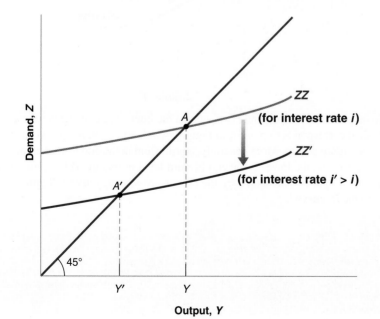

Output, *Y*

**FIGURE 5–1**

**The Effects of an Increase in the Interest Rate on Output**

An increase in the interest rate decreases the demand for goods at any level of output. Because we have not assumed that the consumption and investment relations in equation (5.2) are linear, *ZZ* is, in general, a curve rather than a line, as shown. But all the arguments that follow would apply if we assumed that the consumption and investment relations were linear and that *ZZ* was a line instead.

### FIGURE 5–2

**The Derivation of the IS Curve**

Equilibrium in the goods market implies that output is a decreasing function of the interest rate. The *IS* curve is downward sloping.

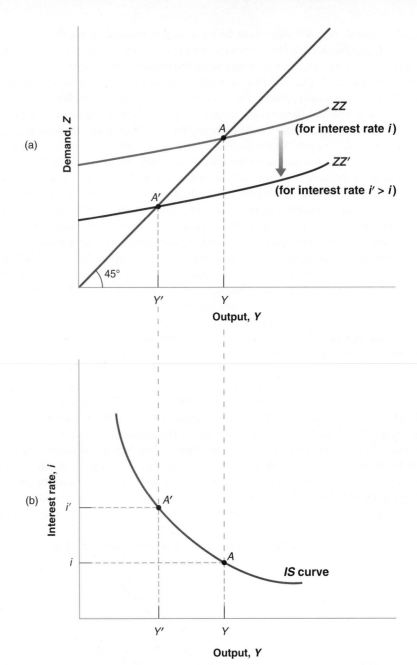

(a)

(b)

equilibrium output $Y$ on the horizontal axis against the interest rate on the vertical axis. Point $A$ in Figure 5–2(b) corresponds to point $A$ in Figure 5–2(a), and point $A'$ in Figure 5–2(b) corresponds to $A'$ in Figure 5–2(a). More generally, equilibrium in the goods market implies that the higher the interest rate, the lower is the equilibrium level of output. This relation between the interest rate and output is represented by the downward-sloping curve in Figure 5–2(b). This curve is called the **IS curve**.[1]

Equilibrium in the goods market implies that output is a decreasing function of the interest rate. This relation is represented by the downward-sloping *IS* curve.

[1]**DIGGING DEEPER.** Consider what happens to investment and saving as we move down the *IS* curve. As we move down, the interest rate decreases, and production increases; both factors increase investment. As we move down, income increases so that saving increases. Thus, as income increases and we move down the *IS* curve, both investment and saving increase; indeed, by the construction of the *IS* curve, they increase by the same amount so that investment remains equal to saving. Reminder: This relation between investment ($I$) and saving ($S$) along the *IS* curve is the source of the name of the curve.

FIGURE    5-3

**Shifts in the *IS* Curve**

An increase in taxes shifts the *IS* curve to the left.

## Shifts in the *IS* Curve

Note that we have derived the *IS* curve in Figure 5–2 for given values of taxes, *T*, and government spending, *G*. Changes in either *T* or *G* will shift the *IS* curve.

To see how, consider Figure 5–3. The *IS* curve gives the equilibrium level of output as a function of the interest rate. It is drawn for given values of taxes and spending. Now, consider an increase in taxes, from *T* to *T'*. At a given interest rate, say, *i*, consumption decreases, leading to a decrease in the demand for goods and, through the multiplier, to a decrease in equilibrium output. The equilibrium level of output decreases, say, from *Y* to *Y'*. Put another way, the *IS* curve shifts to the left: At any interest rate, the equilibrium level of output is lower than it was before the increase in taxes.

◀ For a given $i$, $T \uparrow \Rightarrow Y \downarrow$

More generally, any factor that, for a given interest rate, decreases the equilibrium level of output, leads the *IS* curve to shift to the left. We have looked at an increase in taxes, but the same would hold for a decrease in government spending or a decrease in consumer confidence (which decreases consumption given disposable income). In contrast, any factor that, for a given interest rate, increases the equilibrium level of output—a decrease in taxes, an increase in government spending, an increase in consumer confidence—leads the *IS* curve to shift to the right.

Let us summarize:

● Equilibrium in the goods market implies that output is a decreasing function of the interest rate.
● This relation is represented by the downward-sloping *IS* curve.
● Changes in factors that decrease or increase the demand for goods given the interest rate shift the *IS* curve to the left or to the right.

## 5-2 | Financial Markets and the *LM* Relation

Let us now turn to financial markets. We saw in Chapter 4 that the interest rate is determined ◀ by the equality of the supply of and the demand for money.

$$M = \$Y\, L(i)$$

The variable *M* on the left side is the nominal money supply. We will ignore here the details of the money-supply process and simply think of the central bank as controlling *M*

Left side: Money supply
$$M^s = M$$
Right side: Money demand
$$M^d = \$Y\, L(i)$$

directly. The right side gives the demand for money, which is a function of nominal income, $\$Y$, and of the nominal interest rate, $i$; an increase in nominal income increases the demand for money; an increase in the interest rate decreases the demand for money. Equilibrium requires that money supply (the left side of the equation) be equal to money demand (the right side of the equation).

## Real Money, Real Income, and the Interest Rate

The equation $M = \$Y\,L(i)$ gives a relation among money, nominal income, and the interest rate. In order to place the money market relation in a graph with real output on the axis, we rewrite it as a relation among real money (that is, money in terms of goods), real income (that is, income in terms of goods), and the interest rate.

From Chapter 2:
$$\frac{\$Y}{P} = Y$$

Recall that nominal income divided by the price level equals real income, $Y$. Dividing both sides of the equation by the price level $P$ (which we take as given here) gives:

$$\frac{M}{P} = Y\,L(i) \tag{5.3}$$

Hence, we can restate our equilibrium condition as the condition that *real money supply*—that is, the money supply in terms of goods, not dollars—be equal to *real money demand*, which depends on real income $Y$ and the interest rate $i$. The notion of a "real" demand for money may feel a bit abstract, so an example may help. Think not of your demand for money in general but just of your demand for coins. Suppose you like to have coins in your pocket to buy four cups of coffee during the day. If a cup costs 60 cents, you will want to keep about $2.40 in coins: This is your nominal demand for coins. Equivalently, you want to keep enough coins in your pocket to buy four cups of coffee. This is your demand for coins in terms of goods— here, in terms of cups of coffee.

From now on, we will refer to equation (5.3) as the *LM relation*. The advantage of writing things this way is that *real income*, $Y$, appears on the right side of the equation instead of *nominal income*, $\$Y$. And real income (equivalently real output) is the variable we focus on when looking at equilibrium in the goods market. To make the reading lighter, we will refer to the right and left sides of equation (5.3) simply as "money supply" and "money demand" rather than the more accurate but heavier "real money supply" and "real money demand." Similarly, we will refer to "income" rather than "real income."

## The *LM* Curve

To see the relation between output and the interest rate implied by equation (5.3), let us start with Figure 5–4. Let the interest rate be measured on the vertical axis and (real) money be measured on the horizontal axis. Money supply is given by the vertical line at $M/P$ and is denoted $M^s$. For a given level of income, $Y$, money demand is a decreasing function of the interest rate. It is drawn as the downward-sloping curve denoted $M^d$. Except for the fact that we measure real rather than nominal money on the horizontal axis, the figure is similar to Figure 4–4 in Chapter 4. The equilibrium is at point $A$, where money supply is equal to money demand, and the interest rate is equal to $i$.

Now, consider an increase in income from $Y$ to $Y'$, which leads people to increase their demand for money at any given interest rate. Money demand shifts to the right, to $M^{d'}$. The new equilibrium is at $A'$, with a higher interest rate, $i'$. Why does an increase in income lead to an increase in the interest rate? When income increases, money demand increases. But money supply is a given. Thus, the interest rate must go up until the two opposite effects on the demand for money—the increase in income that leads people to want to hold more money and the increase in the interest rate that leads people to want to hold less money—cancel each other. At that point, the demand for money is equal to the unchanged money supply, and financial markets are again in equilibrium.

Equilibrium in financial markets: For a given $M$,
$Y\!\uparrow \;\Rightarrow\; i\!\uparrow$

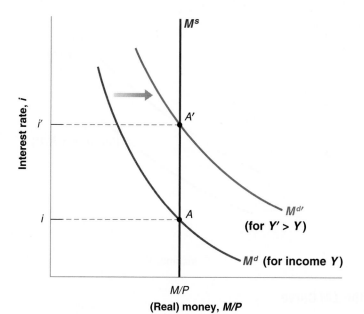

FIGURE 5–4

**The Effects of an Increase in Income on the Interest Rate**

An increase in income leads, at a given interest rate, to an increase in the demand for money. Given the money supply, this leads to an increase in the equilibrium interest rate.

Using Figure 5–4, we can find out the value of the interest rate associated with *any* value of income for a given money supply. The relation is derived in Figure 5–5. Figure 5–5(a) reproduces Figure 5–4. When income is equal to $Y$, money demand is given by $M^d$ and the equilibrium interest rate is equal to $i$. When income is equal to the higher value $Y'$, money demand is given by $M^{d'}$ and the equilibrium interest rate is equal to $i'$. Figure 5–5(b) plots the equilibrium interest rate $i$ on the vertical axis against income on the horizontal axis. Point $A$ in Figure 5–5(b) corresponds to point $A$ in Figure 5–5(a), and point $A'$ in Figure 5–5(b) corresponds to point $A'$ in Figure 5–5(a). More generally, equilibrium in financial markets implies that the higher the level of output, the higher is the demand for money and therefore the higher is the equilibrium interest rate. This relation between output and the interest rate is represented by the upward-sloping curve in Figure 5–5(b). This curve is called the ***LM* curve**. Economists sometimes characterize this relation by saying that "higher economic activity puts pressure on interest rates." Make sure you understand the steps behind this statement.

Equilibrium in financial markets implies that for a given money supply, the interest rate is an increasing function of the level of income. This relation is represented by the upward-sloping *LM* curve.

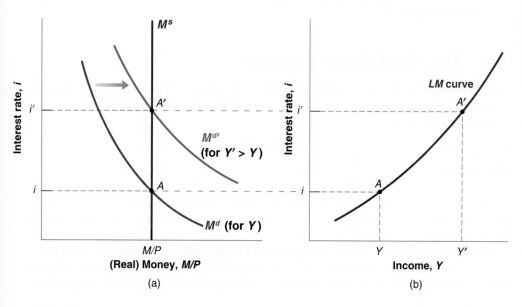

FIGURE 5–5

**The Derivation of the *LM* Curve**

Equilibrium in financial markets implies that the interest rate is an increasing function of the level of income. The *LM* curve is upward sloping.

FIGURE 5-6

**Shifts in the *LM* Curve**

An increase in the money supply leads the *LM* curve to shift down.

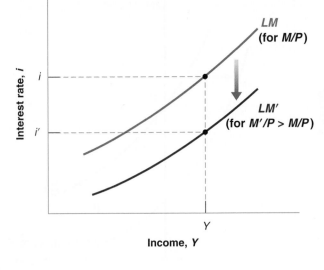

**Shifts in the *LM* Curve**

We have derived the *LM* curve in Figure 5–5 taking both the nominal money supply, *M*, and the price level, *P*—and, by implication, their ratio, the real money supply, *M/P*—as given. Changes in *M/P*, whether they come from changes in the nominal money supply, *M*, or from changes in the price level, *P*, will shift the *LM* curve.

> We look at how price changes shift the LM curve in much more detail in Chapters 10 and 13.

To see how, consider Figure 5–6. The *LM* curve gives the interest rate as a function of the level of income. It is drawn for a given value of *M/P*. Now, consider an increase in nominal money supply, from *M* to *M′*, so that at an unchanged price level, real money supply increases from *M/P* to *M′/P*. At a given level of income, *Y*, this increase in the money supply leads to a decrease in the equilibrium interest rate from *i* to *i′*. Put another way, the *LM* curve shifts down; at any level of income, an increase in the money supply leads to a decrease in the equilibrium

> For a given *Y*, *M/P*↑ ⇒ *i*↓ An increase in money shifts the *LM* curve down.

interest rate. By the same reasoning, at any level of income, a decrease in the money supply leads to an increase in the interest rate. A decrease in the money supply leads the *LM* curve to shift up.

Let us summarize:

> Why do we talk about shifts of the *IS* curve to the left and to the right but about shifts of the *LM* curve up or down?
>
> We think of the goods market as determining *Y*, given *i*; so, we want to know what happens to *Y* when some exogenous variable changes. *Y* is measured on the horizontal axis and moves right or left.
>
> We think of financial markets as determining *i*, given *Y*; so, we want to know what happens to *i* when some exogenous variable changes. *i* is measured on the vertical axis and moves up or down.

- Equilibrium in financial markets implies that the interest rate is an increasing function of the level of income. This relation is represented by the upward-sloping *LM* curve.
- Increases in the money supply shift the *LM* curve down; decreases in the money supply shift the *LM* curve up.

## 5-3 | The *IS-LM* Model: Exercises

We can now put the *IS* and *LM* relations together. At any point in time, the supply of goods must be equal to the demand for goods. And the supply of money must be equal to the demand for money. Both the *IS* and *LM* relations must hold:

*IS* relation $\qquad\qquad Y = C(Y - T) + I(Y,i) + G$

*LM* relation $\qquad\qquad \dfrac{M}{P} = Y\,L(i)$

Figure 5–7 plots both the *IS* curve and the *LM* curve on one graph. Output—equivalently production or income—is measured on the horizontal axis. The interest rate is measured on the vertical axis.

Any point on the downward-sloping *IS* curve corresponds to equilibrium in the goods market. Any point on the upward-sloping *LM* curve corresponds to equilibrium in financial markets. Only at point *A* are both equilibrium conditions satisfied. That means point *A*, with

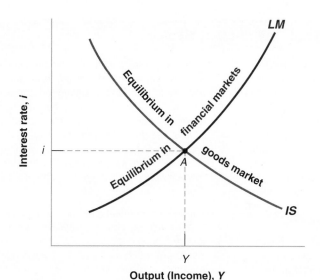

FIGURE 5-7

**The *IS-LM* Model**

Equilibrium in the goods market implies that output is a decreasing function of the interest rate. Equilibrium in financial markets implies that the interest rate is an increasing function of output. Only at point *A* are both goods and financial markets in equilibrium.

associated level of output *Y* and interest rate *i*, is the overall equilibrium, the point at which there is equilibrium in both the goods market and the financial markets.

The *IS* and *LM* relations that underlie Figure 5-7 contain a lot of information about consumption, investment, money demand, and equilibrium conditions. But you may ask, so what if the equilibrium is at point *A*? How does this fact translate into anything directly useful about the world? Do not despair: Figure 5-7 does, in fact, hold the answer to many questions in macroeconomics. Used properly, it allows us to study what happens to output and the interest rate when the central bank decides to increase the money supply, or when government decides to increase taxes, or when consumers become more pessimistic about the future, and so on.

Let us now see what the *IS-LM* model can do.

## Fiscal Policy, Activity, and the Interest Rate

Suppose government decides to reduce the budget deficit and does so by increasing taxes while keeping government spending unchanged. Such a policy, aimed at reducing the budget deficit, is often called a **fiscal contraction** or a **fiscal consolidation**. (An *increase* in the deficit, either due to an increase in spending or to a decrease in taxes, is called a **fiscal expansion**.) What are the effects of such a fiscal contraction on output, on its components, and on the interest rate?

In answering this or any question about the effects of changes in policy, always follow these three steps:

**Step 1.** Ask how this change affects goods and financial markets equilibrium relations, that is, how it shifts the *IS* or/and the *LM* curve.

**Step 2.** Characterize the effects of these shifts on the equilibrium.

**Step 3.** Describe the effects in words.

With time and experience, you will often be able to go directly to step 3; by then you will be ready to give an instant commentary on the economic events of the day. But until you achieve that level of expertise, go step by step.

Going through step 1, the first question is how the increase in taxes affects equilibrium in the goods market—that is, how it affects the *IS* curve.

Let us draw, in Figure 5-8(a) on page 91, the *IS* curve corresponding to equilibrium in the goods market before the increase in taxes. Take an arbitrary point, *B*, on this *IS* curve. By construction of the *IS* curve, output $Y_B$ and the corresponding interest rate $i_B$ are such that the supply of goods is equal to the demand for goods.

Decrease in $G - T \Leftrightarrow$ Fiscal contraction $\Leftrightarrow$ Fiscal consolidation

Increase in $G - T \Leftrightarrow$ Fiscal expansion

From the 1950s to the 1970s, the *IS-LM* model was the domi-nant model in macroeconomics. Nearly every question was recast in terms of whether the *IS* curve or the *LM* curve shifted and how this shift led to a change in output.

The dominance of the *IS-LM* model led Axel Leijonhufvud, an economist at the University of California, Los Angeles, to write a satire of macroeconomics. In "Life among the Econ," he pretended to be an "econologist"—an anthropologist study-ing a tribe called the Econ. He described the tribe as divided into castes, the "Micros" and the "Macros," each with "elders" and "grads," each making "models," and each with its own totems. Here is how he describes macro and the *IS-LM*:

> Consider the totems of the Micro and the Macro. Both could be roughly described as formed by two carved sticks joined together in the middle somewhat in the form of a pair of scissors. [See Figure 1.]

> Certain ceremonies connected with these totems are of great interest to us. . . . The following account of the "prospecting" ceremony among the Macro brings out several riddles that currently perplex econologists working in the area:

> The elder grasps the LM *with his left hand and the* IS *with his right hand and, holding the totem out in front of himself, with elbows slightly bent, proceeds in a straight line—gazing neither left nor right, in the words of their ritual—out over the chosen terrain. . . . At long last, the totem vibrates, then oscillates more and more; finally, it points, quivering, straight down. The elder waits for the grads to gather around and then pronounces, with great solemnity: "Behold, the Truth and the Power of Macro."* . . .

> The Macro maintain that they strike gold this way. Some travellers and investigators support the con-tention, others dismiss it as mere folklore. The issues are much the same as those connected with attempts to appraise the divining-rod method of finding water. Numerous people argue that it works—but no scientific explanation of why it would has ever been advanced.

*Source:* Demand/Supply and *IS-LM*, from Axel Leijonhufvud, "Life among the Econ," *Western Economic Journal,* 11 (3), 1973: pp. 327–337. © 1973 Western Economic Association. Reprinted with permission.

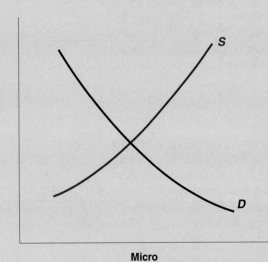

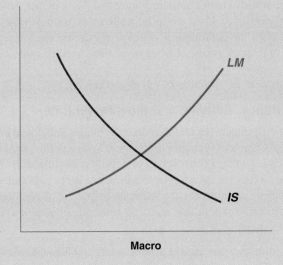

**Figure 1    Totems of the Micro and the Macro.**

Now, at the interest rate $i_B$, ask what happens to output if taxes increase from $T$ to $T'$. We saw the answer in section 5-1. Because people have less disposable income, the increase in taxes decreases consumption and, through the multiplier, decreases output. At interest rate $i_B$, output decreases from $Y_B$ to $Y_C$. More generally, at *any* interest rate, higher taxes lead to lower output: The *IS* curve shifts to the left from *IS* to *IS'*.

> Taxes appear in the *IS* relation ⟺ Taxes shift the *IS* curve.

Next, let us see if anything happens to the *LM* curve. Figure 5–8(b) on page 91 draws the *LM* curve corresponding to financial-markets equilibrium before the increase in taxes. Take an arbitrary point, $F$, on this *LM* curve. By construction of the *LM* curve, the interest rate $i_F$ and income $Y_F$ are such that the supply of money is equal to the demand for money.

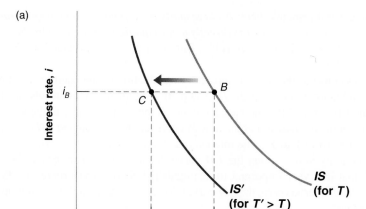

(a)

FIGURE 5-8

**The Effects of an Increase in Taxes**

An increase in taxes shifts the *IS* curve to the left, and leads to a decrease in equilibrium output and the equilibrium interest rate.

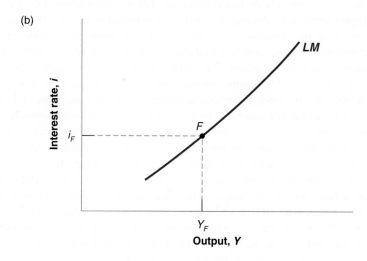

(b)

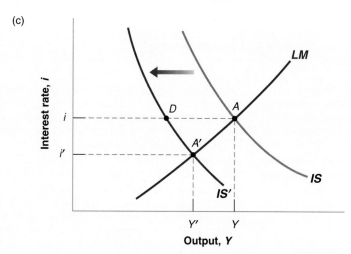

(c)

What happens to the *LM* curve when taxes are increased? The answer: nothing. At the given level of income $Y_F$, the interest rate at which the supply of money is equal to the demand for money is the same as before, namely, $i_F$. In other words, because taxes do not appear in the *LM* relation, they do not affect the equilibrium condition. They do not affect the *LM* curve.

Taxes do not appear in the *LM* relation ⇔ Taxes do not shift the *LM* curve.

A reminder: Exogenous variables are variables we take as given, unexplained within the model. ▶

Note the general principle here: *A curve shifts in response to a change in an exogenous variable only if this variable appears directly in the equation represented by that curve.* Taxes enter equation (5.2), so the *IS* curve shifts. But taxes do not enter equation (5.3), so the *LM* curve does not shift.

Now let us consider the second step, the determination of the equilibrium. Let the initial equilibrium in Figure 5–8(c) on page 91 be at point *A*, at the intersection between the initial *IS* curve and the *LM* curve. After the increase in taxes, the *IS* curve shifts to the left, and the new equilibrium is at the intersection of the new *IS* curve and the unchanged *LM* curve, at point *A'*. Output decreases from *Y* to *Y'*. The interest rate decreases from *i* to *i'*. Thus, as the *IS* curve *shifts*, the economy *moves along* the *LM* curve, from *A* to *A'*. The reason these words are italicized is that it is very important to distinguish *shifts in* curves (here, the *IS* curve) and *movements along* a curve (here, the *LM* curve). Many mistakes result from not distinguishing between the two.

$T \uparrow \Rightarrow$ The *IS* curve shifts. The *LM* curve does not shift. The economy moves along the *LM* curve. ▶

The third and final step is to tell the story in words: The increase in taxes leads to lower disposable income, which causes people to consume less. This leads, through the multiplier effect, to a decrease in output and income. The decrease in income reduces the demand for money, leading to a decrease in the interest rate. The decline in the interest rate reduces but does not completely offset the effect of higher taxes on the demand for goods, that is, output at *A'* is less than output at *A*.

If the interest rate did not decline, the economy would go from point *A* to point *D* in Figure 5–8(c), and output would be directly below point *D*. Because of the decline in the interest rate—which stimulates investment—the decline in activity is only to point *A'*. ▶

What happens to the components of demand? By assumption, government spending remains unchanged: We have assumed that the reduction in the budget deficit takes place through an increase in taxes. Consumption surely goes down, both because taxes go up and because income goes down: Disposable income goes down on both counts. But what happens to investment? On the one hand, lower output means lower sales and lower investment. On the other hand, a lower interest rate leads to higher investment. Without knowing more about the exact form of the investment relation, equation (5.1), we cannot tell which effect dominates. If investment depends only on the interest rate, then investment surely increases; if investment depends only on sales, then investment surely decreases. In general, investment depends on both the interest rate and sales, so we cannot tell. Contrary to what is often stated by politicians, a reduction in the budget deficit does not necessarily lead to an increase in investment. (The Focus box "Deficit Reduction: Good or Bad for Investment?" discusses this at more length.) We will return to the relation between fiscal policy and investment many times in this book, and we will qualify this first answer in many ways. But the result that *in the short run*, *deficit reduction may decrease investment* will remain.

## FOCUS — Deficit Reduction: Good or Bad for Investment?

You may have heard the argument before: "Private saving goes toward either financing the budget deficit or financing investment. It does not take a genius to conclude that reducing the budget deficit leaves more saving available for investment, which increases investment."

This argument sounds simple and convincing. How do we reconcile it with what we just saw in the text, that deficit reduction may decrease rather than increase investment?

Remember from Chapter 3 that we can also think of the goods-market equilibrium condition as:

$$I \qquad = \qquad S \qquad + \qquad (T - G)$$
$$\text{Investment} \qquad \text{Private saving + Public saving}$$

In equilibrium, investment is equal to private saving plus public saving. If public saving is positive, government is said to run a budget surplus; if public saving is negative, government runs a budget deficit. So, it is true that given private saving, if government reduces its deficit—either by increasing taxes or reducing government spending so that $T - G$ goes up—investment must go up. Given $S$, $T - G$ going up implies that $I$ goes up.

The crucial part of this statement, however, is "given private saving." And a fiscal contraction affects private saving as well: A fiscal contraction leads to lower output, that is, lower income; as consumption goes down by less than income, private saving also goes down. And it may go down by more than the reduction in the budget deficit, leading to a decrease rather than an increase in investment. In terms of the equation above: If $S$ decreases more than $T - G$ increases, then $I$ will decrease, not increase. To sum up, a fiscal contraction may decrease investment. Or, looking at the reverse case, a fiscal expansion—a decrease in taxes or an increase in spending—may actually increase investment.

## Monetary Policy, Activity, and the Interest Rate

An increase in the money supply is called a **monetary expansion**. A decrease in the money supply is called a **monetary contraction** or **monetary tightening**.

Let us take the case of a monetary expansion. Suppose that the central bank increases nominal money, $M$, through an open market operation. Given our assumption that the price level is fixed, this increase in nominal money leads to a one-for-one increase in real money, $M/P$. Let us denote the initial real money supply by $M/P$ and the new higher one by $M'/P$, and trace the effects of money supply increase on output and the interest rate.

The first step is again to see whether and how the *IS* and the *LM* curves shift. Let us look at the *IS* curve first. Money supply does not affect directly either the supply of or the demand for goods. In other words, $M$ does not appear in the *IS* relation. Thus, a change in $M$ does not shift the *IS* curve.

Money enters the *LM* relation, however, so that the *LM* curve shifts when money supply changes. As we saw in section 5-2, an increase in money shifts the *LM* down: At a given level of income, an increase in money leads to a decrease in the interest rate.

Putting things together, a monetary expansion shifts the *LM* curve and does not affect the *IS* curve. Thus, in Figure 5–9, the economy moves along the *IS* curve, and the equilibrium moves from point $A$ to point $A'$. Output increases from $Y$ to $Y'$, and the interest rate decreases from $i$ to $i'$. In words: The increase in money leads to a lower interest rate. The lower interest rate leads to an increase in investment and, through the multiplier, to an increase in demand and output.

In contrast to the case of a fiscal contraction, we can tell exactly what happens to the different components of demand after a monetary expansion. With higher income and unchanged taxes, consumption goes up. With both higher sales and a lower interest rate, investment also unambiguously goes up. A monetary expansion is more investment friendly than a fiscal expansion.

To summarize:

- You should remember the method we have developed in this section to look at the effects of changes in policy on output and the interest rate. We will use it throughout the book.
- We have used this method to look at the effects of fiscal and monetary policies on output and the interest rate. Table 5–1 summarizes what we have learned. But you can use the same method to look at other changes as well. For example, you may want to trace the effects of a decrease in consumer confidence through its effect on consumption demand or of the introduction of new, more convenient credit cards through their effect on the demand for money.

Increase in $M \Leftrightarrow$ Monetary expansion.

Decrease in $M \Leftrightarrow$ Monetary contraction $\Leftrightarrow$ Monetary tightening.

$P$ fixed, $M$ increases by 10% $\Rightarrow$ $M/P$ increases by 10%.

Money does not appear in the *IS* relation $\Leftrightarrow$ Money does not shift the *IS* curve.

Money appears in the *LM* relation $\Leftrightarrow$ Money shifts the *LM* curve.

$M\uparrow \Rightarrow$ The *IS* curve does not shift. The *LM* curve shifts down. The economy moves along the *IS* curve.

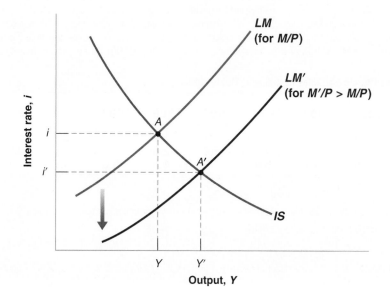

**FIGURE  5-9**

**The Effects of a Monetary Expansion**

A monetary expansion leads to higher output and a lower interest rate.

## TABLE 5-1 The Effects of Fiscal and Monetary Policies

| | Shift in *IS* | Shift in *LM* | Movement in Output | Movement in Interest Rate |
|---|---|---|---|---|
| Increase in taxes | left | none | down | down |
| Decrease in taxes | right | none | up | up |
| Increase in spending | right | none | up | up |
| Decrease in spending | left | none | down | down |
| Increase in money | none | down | up | down |
| Decrease in money | none | up | down | up |

## FOCUS    The Martin–Thiessen Policy Mix: A Successful Fiscal Consolidation

When Jean Chretien's first term of office as prime minister began in 1993, Canada had come through some difficult macroeconomic times. As Table 1 shows, there had been a severe recession in 1991 and slow growth in 1992, and even in 1993 growth in real GDP was far below its normal level. Unemployment had been high for the past three years. Anger at the economic outcomes associated with the previous Conservative government was one important reason for the Liberal election victory in 1993. How could this government do better than its predecessor?

The second line of Table 1 shows the other macroeconomic problem faced by the new Liberal government. The federal government had an enormous budget deficit. Tax revenues were far short of federal government outlays. Finance Minister Paul Martin was clear that this deficit must be reduced. From the Budget Speech (February 27, 1995):

*Canadians want more than temporary fiscal remission. They want full fiscal health. It is absolutely essential that once we meet our interim target we do not stall. We will continue to set firm, short-term deficit goals—rolling two-year targets, until the deficit is erased[†].*

Two years later, the federal budget deficit was erased. This deficit was erased using some tax rate increases, some spending decreases, and the happy coincidence for Mr. Martin of a booming U.S. economy. The increase in American income led to increases in Canadian exports and higher GDP growth in Canada. Some of his success at deficit reduction was good luck. Some of his success was a good choice of policies by the Bank of Canada and the federal government. We can use the *IS-LM* framework to understand these choices.

Tax increases and expenditure reductions should, by themselves, shift the *IS* curve down. This is shown in Figure 1 as the movement from *IS* to *IS'*. Without further changes, the economy should experience a recession at *B*. But the Bank of Canada, as shown in the third row of Table 1, reduced interest rates in most years from 1991 to 1997 (with a one-year rise in rates in 1995). The reduction in interest rates is associated with a downward shift in the *LM* curve in Figure 1 from the curve labelled *LM* to the curve labelled *LM'*. The final outcome is represented as *A'*, a lower interest rate without adverse effects on output.

The combined effect of the policy actions by the federal Department of Finance to reduce the deficit and the Bank of Canada to lower interest rates allowed output to grow rapidly in 1994, 1995, 1997, 1998, and 1999. The rapid output growth, in turn, increased tax revenues to the federal government and helped turn the large deficit into a large surplus.

The time period we have just studied may seem like ancient history. In fact, as Table 2 shows, the deficit situation faced by Canada in 1991–1993, an average deficit of 5% of

## TABLE 1 Selected Macro Variables for Canada, 1991–1999

| Year | 1991 | 1992 | 1993 | 1994 | 1995 | 1996 | 1997 | 1998 | 1999 |
|---|---|---|---|---|---|---|---|---|---|
| (1) | −2.0 | 0.9 | 2.4 | 4.7 | 2.7 | 1.5 | 4.4 | 3.9 | 5.0 |
| (2) | −5.4 | −5.1 | −5.4 | −4.5 | −3.9 | −2.0 | 0.7 | 1.0 | 0.9 |
| (3) | 8.8 | 6.5 | 4.9 | 5.4 | 7.0 | 4.3 | 3.2 | 4.7 | 4.7 |

(1) Real GDP growth (percent) (*Source:* Using CANSIM II variable V1992259.)

(2) Budget surplus (percent of GDP) (*Source:* Table 46: *Fiscal Reference Tables 2001*, Department of Finance, Canada.)

(3) Interest rate (percent) (*Source:* Using CANSIM II variable V122484.)

---

[†]The Budget Speech, The Honourable Paul Martin, P.C., M.P. Minister of Finance, February 22, 1994, Department of Finance Canada

| TABLE | 2 | General Government Deficits in the G7 Countries in 2011, Percentage of GDP | | | | | |
|---|---|---|---|---|---|---|---|
| Country | Canada | France | Germany | Italy | Japan | United Kingdom | United States |
| Deficit | 4.3 | 5.2 | 0.8 | 3.8 | 9.7 | 8.5 | 10.0 |

*Source:* Data from International Monetary Fund, World Economic Outlook, October 2012. The term "General Government" means that all levels of government are treated as one. This makes the deficits comparable across these countries.

GDP, is very similar to the deficit situation faced by a number of countries following the world economic crisis of 2009. Table 2 shows the size of the 2011 deficit in each G7 countries. Germany has by far the smallest deficit. The other 6 countries have much larger deficits. The process to reducing such large deficits is called fiscal consolidation. How to manage each country's fiscal consolidation without generating a recession is the enormous policy challenge facing the world. The larger the deficit, the bigger the challenge! The Canadian success of the 1990s is an example of a successful fiscal consolidation.

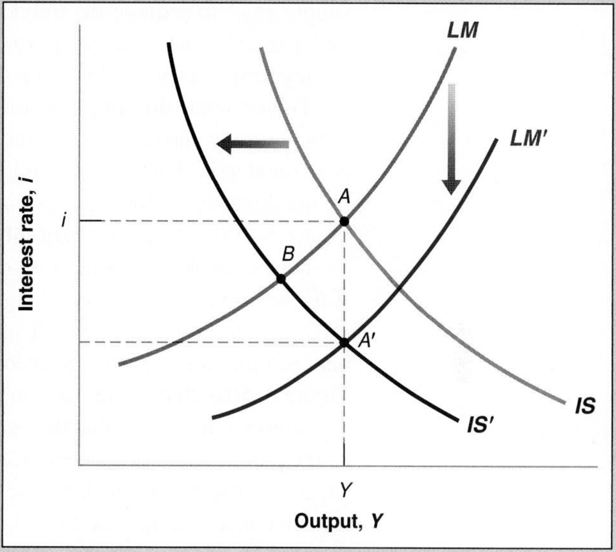

**FIGURE 1  Deficit Reduction and Monetary Expansion**
The right combination of deficit reduction and monetary expansion can achieve a reduction in the deficit without adverse effects on output.

# 5-4 | Using a Policy Mix

We have looked so far at fiscal and monetary policies in isolation. Our purpose was to show how each worked. In practice, the two are often used together. The combination of monetary and fiscal policies is known as the **monetary–fiscal policy mix**, or simply the **policy mix**.

Sometimes, monetary and fiscal policies are used for a common goal. For example, expansionary monetary policy is used to offset the adverse effect on the demand for goods of a fiscal contraction. This was the case in Canada, where, used in combination, fiscal and monetary policies have delivered both sustained deficit reduction and output growth. How it was done and how much of the credit should go to Finance Minister Paul Martin and Bank of Canada Governor Gordon Theissen is described in the Focus box "The Martin–Thiessen Policy Mix" on page 94.

Sometimes, the monetary–fiscal policy mix emerges from tensions or even disagreements between government (which is in charge of fiscal policy) and the central bank (which is in charge of monetary policy). A typical scenario is one in which the central bank, disagreeing with what it considers a dangerous fiscal expansion, embarks on a course of monetary contraction to offset some of the effects of the fiscal expansion on activity. An example of such a tension is what happened in Germany after unification in the early 1990s, described in the Focus box "German Unification, Interest Rates, and the EMS."

Fiscal contraction ⇔ Reduction in budget deficit.

See the boxes "German Unification, Interest Rates, and the EMS" in Chapter 8, and "Anatomy of a Crisis: The September 1992 EMS crisis" in Chapter 14.

## 5-5 | The *LM* Relation When the Central Bank Directly Targets the Interest Rate

Up to this point in the chapter, we derived the *LM* relation under the assumption that *the real money supply remained constant*. This gave us the positive relation between the interest rate and income shown, for example, in Figure 5–5(b).

As we discussed in Chapter 4, section 4-4, however, the assumption that the central bank keeps the real money supply constant and lets the interest rate adjust is not always the way central banks operate monetary policy. Many central banks, including the Bank of Canada, think instead in terms of setting the interest rate for a period of time, and adjusting the money supply so as to achieve the interest rate they want. In this section, we derive the *LM* relation under the alternative assumption that the central bank sets the interest rate and adjusts the money supply as needed to achieve that goal.

To see what this implies, turn to Figure 5–10(a). Like Figure 5–5(a), the panel plots money supply and money demand, with the interest rate on the vertical axis and money on the horizontal axis. The money supply is given by the vertical line. Real money demand is given by the downward-sloping curve associated with a specific level of real income, denoted $Y$ in Figure 5–10(b). The initial equilibrium in the money market is at point $A$ with interest rate $i_A$.

Now consider an increase in real income to $Y'$ that shifts money demand from $M^d$ to $M^{d'}$. If the central bank does not change the money supply, then the equilibrium will move from $A$ to $B$ and the interest rate will increase from $i_A$ to $i_B$. The implied *LM* curve, the relation between the interest rate and income, is drawn in Figure 5–10(b). It is exactly the same as in Figure 5–5(b), that is, the *LM* curve that we have used elsewhere in this chapter.

Suppose, however, that the central bank wants to keep the interest rate constant in the face of the increase in real income. Can it do it? Yes. How can it do it? By increasing the money supply in response to the increase in income, from $M^s$ to $M^{s'}$. If it does so, the interest rate will remain constant at $i_A$. The *IS-LM* equilibrium will move from $A$ to $C$. The resulting *LM* curve, denoted by $LM'$ in Figure 5–10(b), will be horizontal: In response to the increase in income, the central bank will adjust the money supply so as to keep the interest rate constant over the period of the interest rate target.

### Monetary Policy with an Interest Rate Target

It is straightforward to characterize monetary policy in the *IS-LM* framework when the central bank has an interest rate target. This is shown in Figure 5–11. When the interest rate target is $i_A$, the equilibrium level of income is $Y$.

A contractionary monetary policy is an increase in the **target interest rate**. The central bank announces a new higher interest rate target, $i_B$. To implement that target, as demand and

**FIGURE  5–10**

The *LM* Relation When There Is an Interest Rate Target

(a) The real money supply must be altered to keep the interest rate constant at the target as income changes.
(b) If the central bank sets an interest rate target, $i_A$, then, during the target period, the *LM* relation that describes equilibrium in financial markets is horizontal at the target interest rate.

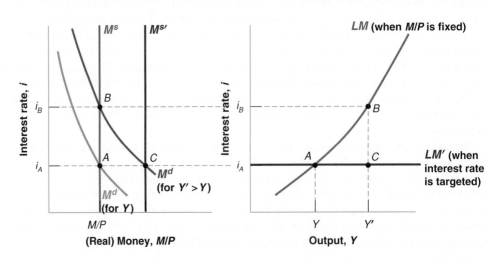

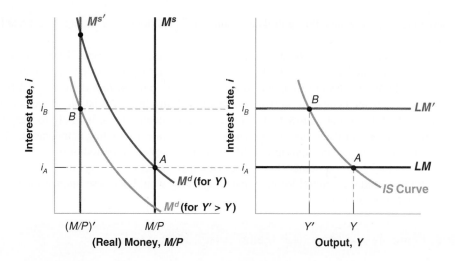

FIGURE 5-11

**The Effects of an Increase in the Interest Rate Target**

(a) As income falls with demand, the central bank reduces the money supply.
(b) If the central bank increases the target interest rate from $i_A$ to $i_B$, then demand and output fall as interest rates rise.

output fall, the central bank must reduce the money supply from $M^s$ to $M^{s'}$. You can use Figure 5–11(a) to show the necessary reduction in the money supply. The $LM$ curve is now horizontal at the new higher target rate of interest. That curve is labeled $LM'$.

## Fiscal Policy with an Interest Rate Target

It is also possible to consider an expansionary fiscal policy when the central bank has an interest rate target. This is shown in Figure 5–12. The interest rate target is set at $i_A$ and is assumed to remain in place for the entire fiscal expansion. The $LM$ curve is horizontal at $i_A$.

The increase in government spending shifts the $IS$ curve to the right, the curve labelled $IS'$ in Figure 5–12(b). As real income rises and real money demand rises, in order to prevent an increase in interest rates to $i_B$, the central bank must increase the real money supply to $M^{s'}$. This increase is shown in Figure 5–12(a).

It should be clear that an expansionary fiscal policy with a strict interest rate target will be much more effective at increasing the level of output than the same increase in government spending where the central bank keeps the real money supply constant. Figure 5–12 includes the $LM$ curve drawn with the real money supply held constant. You can see that the same expansion in government spending would increase output substantially less; however, it is not really a fair comparison. Maintaining the target interest rate requires that the central bank increase the money supply, that is, expand its balance sheet as government spending is increased.

To summarize: The $LM$ relation we derived in the text gave us the relation between the interest rate and income for a *given real money supply*. The $LM$ relation derived in this section

FIGURE 5-12

**The Effects of an Increase in Government Spending When There Is an Interest Rate Target**

(a) As income increases with the increase in government spending, real money demand increases. The central bank must increase the real money supply to $M^{s'}$ to prevent interest rates from rising.
(b) The increase in government spending shifts the $IS$ curve to the right and increases aggregate demand and output at the same interest rate, $i_A$. Output rises from $Y$ to $Y'$.

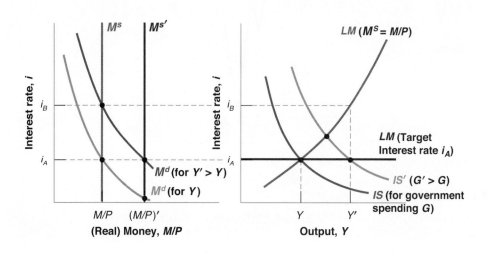

is a horizontal relation where the central bank commits to maintaining a target interest rate for a fixed period of time.

Which *LM* relation should you use? It depends on the question at hand. Take, for example, the case of an increase in government spending, shifting the *IS* curve to the right. You may want to know what would happen to output and the interest rate if the central bank money supply remained constant, in which case you will use the *LM* relation derived earlier in the chapter. But you may know that, for example, the central bank is likely to keep the interest rate constant for the entire period where the government spending is increased. Then the horizontal *LM* curve is the appropriate *LM* curve to use over the period of time where the interest rate is to remain constant. This is not just a theoretical possibility. In 2013 both the Bank of England and the Federal Reserve announced they would not raise interest rates for a considerable period of time into the future.

## FOCUS    The U.S. Economy and the *IS-LM* Model from 2000 to 2012

Following the ups and downs of the U.S. economy is important for Canadians because the United States is by far our biggest export market. The *IS-LM* model can be used to trace the short-run movements of the U.S. economy from 2000 to 2012. The United States experienced two recessions in this period: 2001 and 2008–09. The United States made extensive use of both monetary and fiscal policy over this decade.

The decade of the 1990s finished a long period of strong real growth in the U.S. economy. Quarterly growth rates of real GDP were around 1%, as Figure 1 shows. GDP growth was negative in two of the four quarters in 2001. The National Bureau of Economic Research (NBER), a nonprofit organization that traditionally dates U.S. recessions and expansions, concluded that there was a U.S. recession from March 2001 to December 2001. There was a much more obvious and dramatic recession in 2008 and 2009 during which GDP growth was negative throughout the last half of 2008 and the first half of 2009.

What triggered the 2001 recession was a sharp decline in investment demand. Nonresidential investment—the demand for plant and equipment by firms—decreased by 4.5% in 2001. The cause was the end of what Alan Greenspan has dubbed a period of "irrational exuberance." During the second part of the 1990s, firms had been extremely optimistic about the future and the rate of investment had been very high. The average yearly growth of investment from 1995 to 2000 exceeded 10%. By 2001 it became clear to firms that they had been overly optimistic and had invested too much. This led them to cut back on investment, leading to a decrease in demand and, through the multiplier, a decrease in GDP.

The trigger for the 2008–2009 recession was the collapse of house prices and the fall in investment in new housing. New house construction is also part of investment. In addition consumers, made poorer as their houses fell in value, cut back consumption. As consumption demand fell, firms would also reduce investment. In both recessions, as labelled in Figure 4,

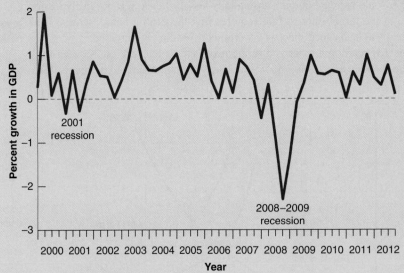

**FIGURE 1   The Growth Rate of U.S. Real GDP**

*Source:* Data from Federal Reserve Bank of St. Louis, FRED Database: Variable GDPC.

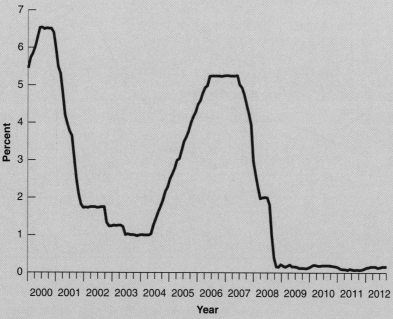

**FIGURE 2    The Federal Funds Rate, 2000–2012**

*Source:* Federal Reserve Bank of St. Louis, FRED Database: Variable FEDFUNDS.

there is a large leftward shift in the *IS* curve as "Drop in demand."

In both cases, it is reasonable to argue that the recessions could have been much worse. Both recessions were met by a strong macroeconomic policy response that certainly reduced the depth and length of each recession.

Take monetary policy first. Starting in early 2001, the Federal Reserve, the U.S. central bank, started increasing the money supply and aggressively decreasing the federal funds rate, the short-term interest rate on loans between U.S. banks. Figure 2 shows the fall in the federal funds rate from 6.5% in January 2001 to 2% in December 2001, at that time a very low level for the interest rate. The pattern of the monetary policy response is repeated in 2008. The Federal Reserve immediately cut interest rates from 5% to zero where they remained to 2012. This was indeed a very strong monetary policy response to a very deep recession.

Now consider the fiscal policy responses in the two recession. During the presidential election campaign in 2000, candidate George W. Bush had run on a platform of lower taxes. Bush made the argument that the United States had a large surplus of federal revenue over federal spending, as shown in Figure 3, and that there was room to cut tax rates and leave the federal budget in balance. When Bush took office in January 2001, it was then also clear that the rate of economic growth was slowing and a tax cut would increase aggregate demand. Both the 2001 and 2002 federal budgets included substantial tax cuts. After the events of September 11, 2001, there was also a substantial federal spending increase on defence and homeland security. These tax cuts and spending increases can be seen in Figure 3. The combination of these

tax cuts and spending increases would shift the *IS* curve to the right as shown in Figure 4.

It was very clear partway through 2008 that a major recession was going to occur. As we noted above, the Fed took immediate action to reduce interest rates. Federal fiscal policy became very expansionary. There were large and very swift tax cuts. In February 2008, Congress passed legislation that saw individual American taxpayers receive $600 each and families with children receive an additional $300 per child. Rebates were slightly smaller for higher-income Americans. The rebate cheques were sent in April 2008. This was an extremely rapid fiscal policy response—almost unprecedented. Federal spending also increased as a response to the recession. There was a combination of spending on infrastructure as well as significant transfers to individuals through extended unemployment benefits. There were large transfers to state governments to allow spending at that level of government to continue.

Figure 4 can now be reviewed to understand the events around both the 2001 and 2008–2009 recessions in the United States. The large left shift in the *IS* curve from *IS* to *IS″* represents the decline in investment spending, whether by corporations or by household spending on new houses. Without any policy response, output would fall to *Y″* at point *A″*. The right shift in the *LM* curve from *LM* to *LM′* represents the Federal Reserve decision to cut interest rates and increase the money supply in both recessions. The shift in the *IS* curve from *IS* to *IS′* represents the increase in federal spending and cuts in taxes in both recessions. The recession that would have found the economy at *A″* without the changes in fiscal and monetary policy outlined above, would now be smaller. The reduction in output, which would have been from *Y* to *Y″* without the policy

*(continued)*

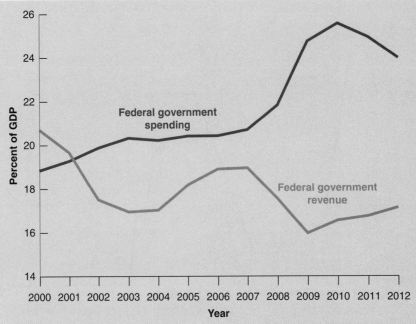

FIGURE 3 U.S. Federal Government Revenues and Spending (percent of GDP), 1998: 1–2008:2

*Source:* Federal Reserve Bank of St. Louis, FRED Database: Spending Is Variable FGEXPND; Revenue Is Variable FGRECPT: Nominal GDP Is Variable GDP.

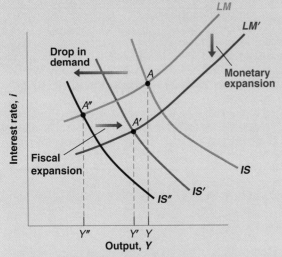

FIGURE 4 Policies to Fight Recessions in the United States in 2001 and 2008–2009

changes is now from *Y* to *Y'* with the policy changes. The policies followed made the recession less severe. Several questions should occur to you as you think about this diagram.

First question: Why was (is) it not possible to avoid all recessions by cutting interest rates and taxes or increasing spending at just the right time? There are two reasons. First, policy makers, the people who have to decide whether to cut interest rates and make fiscal policy decisions, like you and I, operate with less than complete information at the time decisions have to be made. Second, even when a decision is made, the effects of cuts in interest rates, cuts in taxes, and increases in spending on aggregate demand and output occur only with a lag. Thus, as it became clear there was a recession and policies were changed, it took time to see the effects of those changes. Neither recession was completely avoided. This is a general lesson in policy making and is just as valid for Canada as for the United States. We will address this issue further in Chapters 23 and 25.

Second question: Was the monetary and fiscal policy mix used to fight the 2001 recession in the United States a "textbook" example of excellent policy—policy as it should be? The 2001 recession was very mild. On this economists differ. Most agree that it was good that the Federal Reserve sharply cut interest rates as the economy slowed in 2000. The very large tax cuts were permanent, not temporary tax cuts. It may have been better if the tax cuts were temporary, that is, lasted only the two years needed to increase demand during the period of low investment demand. The permanent tax cuts, combined with permanent increases in federal spending on both military and nonmilitary items through the eight George W. Bush years, led to a very large U.S. federal budget deficit. This large deficit may have other consequences that we will discuss in Chapter 25.

Third question: If policy was so successful in reducing the severity of the 2001 recession, why was policy not equally effective in fighting the 2008–2009 recession? The short answer: the shift left in the *IS* curve was much larger in 2008 than in 2001. Most economists would argue the 2008–2009 recession would have been much larger without the monetary and fiscal stimulus.

Fourth question: Figure 2 shows interest rates of zero in and after the 2008–2009 recession. In Figure 4, interest rates do not fall to zero. How did zero interest rates come about? We answer that question in Chapter 11.

## 5-6 | Does the *IS-LM* Model Actually Capture What Happens in the Economy?

The *IS-LM* model gives us a way of thinking about the determination of output and the interest rate. But it is a theory based on many assumptions and many simplifications. How do we know that we have made the right simplifications? How much should we believe the answers given by the *IS-LM* model?

These are the questions facing any theory, whether in macroeconomics or anywhere else. A theory must pass two tests.

- First, the assumptions and the simplifications must be reasonable. What "reasonable" means is not entirely clear. Surely assuming—as we have done—that there is only one type of good in the economy is factually wrong. But it may still be a reasonable simplification of reality if allowing for more than one type of good leads to a more complicated model, but roughly the same results for aggregate activity, the interest rate, and so on. One assumption we have made in Chapters 3, 4, and 5 is factually wrong. We assumed net exports were zero and that exports and imports did not vary. In the next chapter, we will change that aspect of the model.

- Second, the major implications of the theory must be consistent with what we actually see in the world. This is easier to check. Using econometrics, we can trace the effects of changes in monetary policy and fiscal policy and see how close the effects correspond to the predictions of the *IS-LM* model. And it turns out that the *IS-LM* model does quite well.

Figure 5–13 considers the evidence on the usefulness of the *IS-LM* model in the Canadian economy. The Bank of Canada undertook a major comparison of 12 different models of the Canadian economy and published the results in 2003. The Figure shows how two different events in the 12 models affect Canadian GDP. The sets of initials associated with each line denote different models. The time periods on the $x$-axis of these figures are quarters. The measure on the $y$-axis is a percentage point of GDP.

In panel (a) the models are exposed to a temporary increase in domestic demand. This is an increase in the level of consumption and investment (a right shift in the *IS* curve) of 1% in the first quarter, 0.75% in the second quarter, 0.5% in the third quarter, and 0.25% in the fourth quarter. The right shift in the *IS* curve is over in the fifth and subsequent quarters in the experiment. Panel (a) does show an increase in GDP that follows the right shift in the *IS* curve. However the different models show a wide variety of sizes of this increase and also show variety in the length of time the increase persists. Two of the models show a very long-lasting effect of the temporary increase in domestic demand. Thus, the forecast of the exact size and duration of the increase in GDP that follows the increase in domestic demand will differ, depending on which model you use. The evidence suggests that the response of output to a change in demand is not instantaneous. There is a lag between the change in demand and the change in output.

In panel (b) of Figure 5–13, the experiment increases short-term interest rates by 1% in the first quarter, 0.75% in the second quarter, 0.5% in the third quarter, and 0.25% in the fourth quarter. This corresponds to a sharp shift to the left in the *LM* curve followed by a return to its original position. Here the different models all show that the effect of a temporary increase in interest rates is temporary. This makes sense. All the models show a decline in GDP following interest rate increases. The size of the decline in GDP varies from as much as 0.75% of GDP to as little as 0.25% of GDP. This is quite a wide range. The length of time it takes for the increase in interest rates to affect real GDP also varies: in several models it is virtually immediate and in most models the largest effect seems to be about a year later.

We make the same observation about lags and the effect of a change in interest rates. Although the interest rate change is immediate, the effect on output takes place over the next

FIGURE 5–13

**(a)** The effects of a temporary increase in domestic demand on GDP

**The Empirical Representation of the *IS-LM* Model in the Canadian Economy**

*Source:* Data from Denise Côté, John Kuszczak, Jean-Paul Lam, Ying Liu, and Pierre St-Amant, *A Comparison of Twelve Macroeconomic Models of the Canadian Economy* (Ottawa: Bank of Canada, 2003).

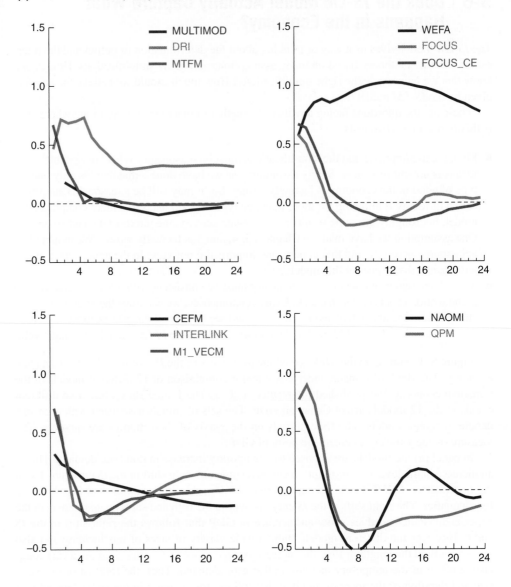

one to two years, depending on the model used. The models agree that an increase in the interest rate will reduce output; they do not agree on exactly when the reduction in output will occur.

Figure 5–13 is comforting. It shows that the implications of the *IS-LM* model are consistent with what we observe in the economy. This does not *prove* that the *IS-LM* model is right. It may be that what we observe in the economy is the result of a completely different mechanism and that the fact that the *IS-LM* model fits well is a coincidence. But this seems unlikely. The *IS-LM* model looks like a solid basis on which to build to look at movements in activity in the short run. In the next three chapters, we look at the implications of openness in both goods and financial markets in the short run. Then, we return to what determines output in the medium run and then the long run.

**(b)** The effects of a temporary increase in short-term interest rates on GDP

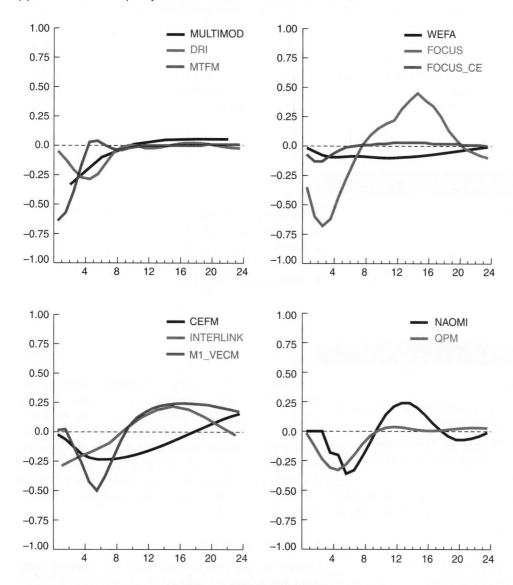

**S U M M A R Y**

- The *IS-LM* model characterizes the implications of equilibrium in both the goods and the financial markets.

- The *IS* relation and the *IS* curve show the combinations of the interest rate and the level of output that are consistent with equilibrium in the goods market. An increase in the interest rate leads to a decline in output.

- The *LM* relation and the *LM* curve show the combinations of the interest rate and the level of output consistent with equilibrium in financial markets. Given the real money supply, an increase in output leads to an increase in the interest rate.

- A fiscal expansion shifts the *IS* curve to the right, leading to an increase in output and an increase in the interest rate. A monetary expansion shifts the *LM* curve down, leading to an increase in output and a decrease in the interest rate.

- The combination of monetary and fiscal policies is known as the monetary–fiscal policy mix, or simply the policy mix. Sometimes monetary and fiscal policies are used for a common goal. Sometimes, the monetary–fiscal mix emerges from tensions or even disagreements between government (which is in charge of fiscal policy) and the central bank (which is in charge of monetary policy).

- The *IS-LM* framework can be extended to the case where the central bank has a target interest rate. The *LM* curve becomes horizontal at the target interest rate. The horizontal *LM* curve moves up or down when the central bank changes the target interest rate. The central bank must adjust the money supply to maintain the target interest rate when income changes.

- The *IS-LM* model appears to describe the behaviour of the economy well in the short run. The effects of monetary policy appear to be similar to those implied by the *IS-LM* model once dynamics are introduced in the model. An increase in the interest rate due to a monetary contraction leads to a steady decrease in output. An increase in investments or consumption leads to an increase in output.

## KEY TERMS

- fiscal consolidation, 89
- fiscal contraction, 89
- fiscal expansion, 89
- *IS* curve, 84
- *LM* curve, 87

- monetary contraction, 93
- monetary expansion, 93
- monetary tightening, 93
- monetary–fiscal policy mix, policy mix, 95
- target interest rate, 96

## QUESTIONS AND PROBLEMS

### 1. TRUE/FALSE/UNCERTAIN

**a.** The main determinants of investment are the level of sales and the interest rate.

**b.** If all the exogenous variables in the *IS* relation are constant, then a higher level of output can be achieved only at a lower interest rate.

**c.** The *IS* curve is downward sloping because goods–market equilibrium implies that an increase in taxes leads to a lower level of output.

**d.** If both government spending and taxes increase by the same amount, the *IS* curve does not shift.

**e.** The *LM* curve is upward sloping because a higher level of money supply is needed to increase output.

**f.** An increase in government spending decreases investment.

**g.** An increase in output at a constant interest rate can be achieved only by using a monetary–fiscal policy mix.

**h.** Fiscal policy will have a larger effect on output when the central bank follows an interest rate target

**i.** Changes in consumer and business confidence will have a smaller effect on output when the central bank maintains an interest rate target.

### 2. INVESTMENT AND THE INTEREST RATE

The chapter argues that the reason investment depends negatively on the interest rate is the following: When the interest rate increases, the cost of borrowing funds also increases, and this discourages investment. However, firms often finance their investment projects using their own funds. Because no borrowing actually occurs, will higher interest rates discourage investment in this case? Explain. (*Hint:* Think of yourself as an owner of a firm who is considering financing new investment projects in your firm using the profits your firm just earned, or buying bonds. Will your decision to invest in new projects in your firm be affected by the interest rate?)

### 3. THE MULTIPLIER REVISITED

Consider first the goods market model with constant investment that we saw in Chapter 3:

$$C = c_0 + c_1(Y - T), \text{ and } I, G, \text{ and } T \text{ are given.}$$

**a.** Solve for equilibrium output. What is the value of the multiplier?
Now, let investment depend on both sales and the interest rate:

$$I = b_0 + b_1 Y - b_2 i$$

**b.** Solve for equilibrium output. At a given interest rate, is the effect of change in autonomous spending bigger than what it was in (a)? Why? (Assume $c_1 + b_1 < 1$).

Next, let us introduce the financial market equilibrium condition with real money demand equal to real money supply.

$$M/P = d_1 Y - d_2 i$$

**c.** Solve for equilibrium output. (*Hint:* Eliminate the interest rate in the *IS* equation using the expression from the *LM* equation.) Derive the multiplier (the effect of a one-unit change in $b_0$ on output).

**d.** Is the multiplier you obtained smaller or larger than the multiplier you derived in your answer to (a)? Explain how your answer depends on the behavioural equations for consumption, investment, and money demand.

## 4. THE RESPONSE OF INVESTMENT TO FISCAL POLICY

**a.** Using the *IS-LM* graph, determine the effects on output and the interest rate of a decrease in government spending. Why is the effect on investment ambiguous?

With more information on the parameters of the *IS* and *LM* relation, we may be able to determine, for example, whether deficit reduction is good or bad for *I* in the short run. Consider the following equations for consumption, investment, and money demand:

$$C = c_0 + c_1(Y - T)$$
$$I = b_0 + b_1 Y - b_2 i$$
$$M/P = d_1 Y - d_2 i$$

**b.** Solve for equilibrium output. (*Hint:* You may want to work through question 3 if you are having trouble with this step.)

**c.** Solve for the equilibrium interest rate. (*Hint:* Use the *LM* relation.)

**d.** Solve for investment.

**e.** Under what condition on the parameters of the model (for example, $c_0$, $c_1$, and so on) will investment increase when *G* decreases?

**f.** Explain the condition you derived in (e).

## 5. MONETARY AND FISCAL POLICIES: AN EXAMPLE

Consider the following *IS-LM* model:

$$C = 200 + 0.25Y_D$$
$$I = 150 + 0.25Y - 1000i$$
$$G = 250$$
$$T = 200$$
$$(M/P)^d = 2Y - 8000i$$
$$M/P = 1600$$

**a.** Derive the equation for the *IS* curve. (*Hint:* You want an equation with *Y* on the left-hand side and all else on the right.)

**b.** Derive the equation for the *LM* curve. (*Hint:* It will be convenient for later use to write this equation with *i* on the left side and all else on the right.)

**c.** Solve for equilibrium real output. (*Hint:* Substitute the expression for the interest rate given by the *LM* equation into the *IS* equation, and solve for output.)

**d.** Solve for the equilibrium interest rate. (*Hint:* Substitute the value you obtained for *Y* in (c) into either the *IS* or the *LM* equation, and solve for *i*. If your algebra is correct, you should get the same answer from both equations.)

**e.** Solve for the equilibrium values of *C* and *I*, and verify the value you obtained for *Y* by adding up *C*, *I*, and *G*.

**f.** Now, suppose that money supply increases to $M/P =$ 1840. Solve for *Y*, *i*, *C*, and *I*, and explain in words the effects of expansionary monetary policy.

**g.** Set $M/P$ equal to its initial value of 1600. Now, suppose government spending increases to $G = 400$. Summarize the effects of expansionary fiscal policy on *Y*, *i*, and *C*.

**h.** (Try this question only if you have already answered question 4.) Without solving for *Y* and *i*, can you tell whether contractionary fiscal policy will increase or decrease *I*? To verify your answer, set all exogenous variables back to their initial values, and solve for investment when government spending decreases to $G = 100$.

## 6. MONETARY AND FISCAL POLICY WITH AN INTEREST RATE TARGET

**a.** What is the slope of the *LM* curve when there is an interest rate target?

**b.** What is the intercept of the *LM* curve when there is an interest rate target?

**c.** If the level of investment responds strongly to the rate of interest, and the central bank is following an interest rate target, draw the consequences for output when the interest rate target is increased.

**d.** When is fiscal policy more effective at changing the level of output: when the central bank maintains a fixed real money supply or when the central bank sets an interest rate target?

## 7. POLICY RECOMMENDATIONS

Suggest a policy or a policy mix to achieve the following objectives:

**a.** Increase *Y* while keeping *i* constant.

**b.** Decrease the deficit while keeping *Y* constant. What happens to *i*? To investment?

The Bank of Canada issues, on a regular basis, a policy announcement of the current target for the interest rate. There is a discussion about why that choice was made and how long that target is likely to be maintained. The stance of fiscal policy at the federal level is usually outlined twice a year, in a spring Budget and in a Fall Economic Statement. However, the fiscal documents are very much political statements designed to shape public opinion. Read them with some care.

# Openness in Goods and Financial Markets

## The Core: The Short Run

We have assumed so far that the economy was *closed*—that it did not interact with the rest of the world. We started this way to keep things simple and build up your intuition for the basic macroeconomic mechanisms. We are now ready to open the economy. Understanding the macroeconomic implications of openness will occupy us in this and the next two chapters.

"Openness" has three distinct dimensions:

1. **Openness in goods markets**: the opportunity for consumers and firms to choose between domestic and foreign goods. This choice is not completely free of restrictions. Even the countries most committed to free trade have tariffs and quotas on at least some foreign goods. (**Tariffs** are taxes on imported goods; **quotas** are restrictions on the quantities of goods that can be imported.) At the same time, in most countries, average tariffs are low and getting lower.
2. **Openness in financial markets**: the opportunity for financial investors to choose between domestic and foreign financial assets. Until recently, even some of the richest countries, such as France and Italy, had **capital controls**, tight restrictions on the foreign assets their domestic residents could hold as well as on the domestic assets foreigners could hold. These restrictions are rapidly disappearing. As a result, world financial markets are becoming more and more closely integrated.
3. **Openness in factor markets**: the opportunity for firms to choose where to locate production and for workers to choose where to work and whether or not to migrate. Here also, trends are clear. More and more companies move their operations around the world to take advantage of low costs. Much of the debate about the **North American Free Trade Agreement (NAFTA)**, signed in 1993 by the United States, Canada, and Mexico, centred on its implications for the relocation of U.S. firms to Mexico. Immigration from low-wage countries to high-wage countries is a hot political issue in countries ranging from Germany to the United States. At the time of writing, Canada was actively pursuing agreements similar to NAFTA with both the European Community and a large group of nations around the Pacific Ocean, called the Trans-Pacific Partnership. Neither agreement had been signed as of February 2013.

In the short run—the focus of this and the next two chapters—openness in factor markets plays much less of a role than openness in either goods or financial markets. Thus, we will ignore openness in factor markets and focus only on the first two dimensions of openness here. We consider openness in factor markets in Chapter 18 as part of the analysis of growth in the open economy. In this chapter, section 6-1 looks at the implications of openness in the goods market. Section 6-2 looks at the implications of openness in financial markets.

# 6-1 | Openness in Goods Markets

Figure 6–1 plots the evolution of Canadian exports and imports, as ratios to GDP, since 1961. ("Canadian exports" means exports *from* Canada; "Canadian imports" means imports *to* Canada.) What is striking is how these ratios have increased over time. Exports and imports, which were equal to around 15% of GDP as recently as the 1960s, now stand around 30% of GDP. Canada trades substantially more with the rest of the world than it did just 50 years ago.

A closer look at Figure 6–1 reveals two interesting patterns:

Recall from Chapter 3 that the trade balance is equal to the difference between exports and imports. If exports are larger than imports, then there is a trade surplus (equivalently, a positive trade balance). If exports are smaller than imports, then there is a trade deficit (equivalently, a negative trade balance).

- For most of the last 50 years, Canada ran a trade surplus, that is, exports of goods and services were larger than imports of goods and services. This feature of the data receives further consideration in Chapter 18, Economic Growth in the Open Economy.
- Although Canada usually has a trade surplus, the size of that trade surplus has varied over time. There were very large trade surpluses between 1997 and 2007, with the peak trade surplus at 5% of GDP. There were also large trade surpluses in 1970 and 1971 and between 1982 and 1985. Intervening years had much smaller trade surpluses and some small trade deficits. There has been a substantial trade deficit since 2009.

Given the constant media talk about *globalization*, the data in Figure 6–1 are one aspect of the reality of globalization. Canada produces many goods and services consumed by people living in other countries. Canadians consume many goods and services produced in other countries. With exports around 30% of GDP, Canada has one of the largest ratios of exports to GDP among the rich countries of the world. Table 6–1 gives ratios for eight other OECD countries.

For more on the OECD and for the list of member countries, see Chapter 1.

The United States and Japan are at the low end of the range of export ratios. The large European countries, such as Germany and the United Kingdom, have ratios that are two to three times larger. Germany is similar to Canada, and the smaller European countries have even larger ratios than does Canada.

Do these numbers indicate that the United States or Japan has more trade barriers than, say, Belgium or Canada? No. The main factors behind these differences are geography and size. Distance from other markets explains a good part of the low Japanese ratio. Size also matters: The smaller the country, the more it must specialize in only a few products, produce and export them, and rely on imports for the others. Austria can hardly afford to produce the range of goods produced by the United States, a country with a GDP more than 300 times

Iceland is both isolated and small. What would you expect its export ratio to be?

---

**FIGURE 6–1**

**Canadian Exports and Imports as a Ratio of GDP, 1961–2012**

Exports and imports, which in the 1960s were less than 20% of GDP, peaked in 2000 at over 40% of GDP. Since then, both exports and imports have dropped as a percent of GDP. Exports have fallen faster than imports. A trade deficit emerged after 2009.

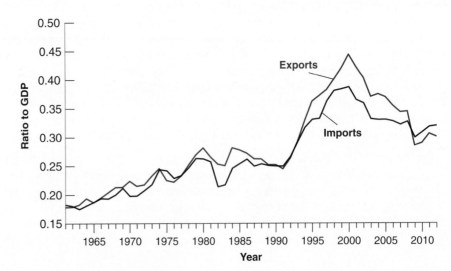

*Source:* Data from CANSIM II Variables: from 1961 to 1980; Export share (V498103/V498086), Import share (V498106/ V498086); from 1981 to 2012; Export share (V62305776/V62305783), Import share (V62305779/V62305783).

TABLE 6-1 Ratios of Exports to GDP for Selected OECD Countries, 2010

| Country | Export Ratio (%) | Country | Export Ratio (%) |
|---|---|---|---|
| United States | 13 | Switzerland | 54 |
| Japan | 15 | Austria | 55 |
| United Kingdom | 30 | Netherlands | 78 |
| Germany | 46 | Belgium | 81 |

*Source:* Data from OECD National Accounts.

larger. Part of the reason Canada's exports-to-GDP ratio is so large is the full integration of automobile production across Canada and the United States.

## The Choice between Domestic and Foreign Goods

How does openness in goods markets force us to rethink the way we look at equilibrium in the *goods* market? When thinking about consumers' decisions in the goods market, we have focused so far on their decision to save or to consume. But when goods markets are open, domestic consumers face another decision: whether to buy domestic goods or foreign goods. Other domestic buyers (firms, government) and foreign buyers also face this decision. If they decide to buy more domestic goods, the demand for domestic goods increases, and so does domestic output. If they decide to buy more foreign goods, then foreign output increases instead.

Central to consumers' and firms' decisions to buy foreign or domestic goods is the price of foreign goods in terms of domestic goods. We call this relative price the **real exchange rate**. The real exchange rate is not directly observable, and you will not find it in the newspapers. What you will find there are *nominal exchange rates*, the relative prices of currencies. Let us start by looking at nominal exchange rates, then see how we can use them to construct real exchange rates.

> In a closed economy, consumers have to make one decision: save or buy (consume). In an open economy, consumers have to make two decisions: (1) save, or (2) buy domestic or foreign.

## Nominal Exchange Rates

Nominal exchange rates between two currencies are quoted in two ways: (1) the price of the domestic currency in terms of the foreign currency, or (2) the price of the foreign currency in terms of the domestic currency. In 2011, for example, the nominal exchange rate between the Canadian dollar and the American dollar could be quoted as either the price of a Canadian dollar in terms of American dollars (C\$1 = US\$1.0108) or as the price of an American dollar in terms of Canadian dollars (US\$1 = 1/1.0108 = C\$0.9892). It is annoying that both Canada and the United States call

---

## FOCUS   Can Exports Exceed GDP?

Can a country have exports larger than its GDP—an export ratio greater than 1?

At first, it would seem that countries cannot export more than they produce so that the export ratio must be less than 1. Not so. The trick is to realize that exports and imports may include exports and imports of intermediate goods.

For example, take a country that imports intermediate goods for \$1 billion. Suppose it transforms them into final goods using only labour. Say that total wages equal \$200 million and there are no profits. The value of final goods is thus equal to \$1200 million. Assume that \$1 billion worth of final goods is exported and the rest is consumed domestically.

Exports and imports therefore both equal \$1 billion. What is GDP in this economy? Remember that GDP is value added *in* the economy (see Chapter 2). So, in this example, GDP equals \$200 million, and the ratio of exports to GDP equals \$1000/\$200 = 5.

Hence exports can exceed GDP. This is actually the case for a number of small countries where economic activity is organized around a harbour and import–export activities. In Singapore in 2010 the ratio of exports to GDP was 211%.

their unit of currency a dollar. In newspapers, exchange rates really are quoted to four decimal places. The extra places matter if the transaction involves billions of dollars, of either country!

To compound the confusion, in 2012, the average Canadian dollar value of the U.S dollar was $0.9993. The inverse of this value, the number of U.S. dollars per Canadian dollar is $1.0006. On average, the Canadian dollar and U.S dollar traded one-for-one over this particular calendar year. Using either definition, the value of the exchange rate was 1. Very confusing! Although confusion about which definition of an exchange rate is usual, it is not the usual situation that the nominal exchange rate between two currencies is 1 and thus both definitions of the nominal exchange rate generate the same numerical value.

In this book, we will define the **nominal exchange rate** as *the price of foreign currency in terms of domestic currency* and denote it by $E$. When, for example, looking at the exchange rate between Canada and the United States (from the viewpoint of Canada, the Canadian dollar is the domestic currency), $E$ will denote the price of a U.S. dollar in terms of Canadian dollars—so, as of December 2012, this is $0.9895.

Exchange rates between foreign currencies and the dollar change every day, every minute of the day. These changes are called *nominal appreciations* or *nominal depreciations*—appreciations or depreciations for short. An **appreciation** of the domestic currency is an increase in the price of the domestic currency in terms of a foreign currency. Given our definition of the exchange rate as the price of the foreign currency in terms of domestic currency, an appreciation of the domestic currency corresponds to a *decrease* in the exchange rate, $E$.

This is more intuitive than it seems: Consider the Canadian dollar and the American dollar (from the viewpoint of Canada). An *appreciation* of the Canadian dollar means that the price of the Canadian dollar in terms of the U.S. dollar goes up. Equivalently, the price of the American dollar in terms of Canadian dollars goes down, which is the same as saying that the exchange rate has decreased. A **depreciation** of the Canadian dollar means the price of the Canadian dollar in terms of American dollars goes down. Equivalently, the price of the American dollar in terms of Canadian dollars goes up, the same as saying that the exchange rate has increased.

That an appreciation corresponds to a decrease in the exchange rate and a depreciation to an increase in the exchange rate will almost surely be confusing to you at first—indeed, it confuses many professional economists—but it will eventually become familiar as your understanding of open-economy macroeconomics deepens. Until then, consult Figure 6–2,

A definition to remember: $E$ is the nominal exchange rate or the price of foreign currency in terms of domestic currency. (For example, from the point of view of Canada, it is the price of U.S. dollars in terms of Canadian dollars.)

*Warning:* Defining exchange rates as the price of foreign currency in terms of domestic currency is the convention in economic articles and books on the North American side of the Atlantic. On the other side of the Atlantic, however, economists more often use the alternative definition, defining exchange rates as the price of domestic currency in terms of foreign currency.

**FIGURE 6–2**

The Nominal Exchange Rate, Appreciation, and Depreciation: Canada and the United States (from the viewpoint of Canada)

**From the viewpoint of Canada looking at the United States**

**Nominal exchange rate $E$**
Price of the American dollar in terms of Canadian dollars

**Appreciation of the Canadian dollar**

Price of Canadian dollars in U.S. dollars increases equivalently:
Price of U.S. dollars in Canadian dollars decreases equivalently:
Exchange rate decreases: $E\downarrow$

**Depreciation of the Canadian dollar**

Price of Canadian dollars in U.S. dollars decreases equivalently:
Price of U.S. dollars in Canadian dollars increases equivalently:
Exchange rate increases: $E\uparrow$

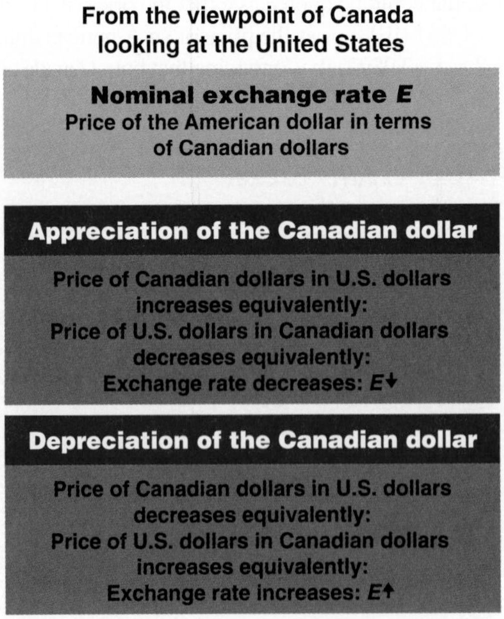

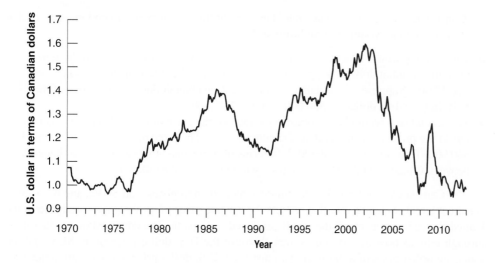

**FIGURE 6-3**

**The Nominal Exchange Rate between the American Dollar and the Canadian Dollar, 1970–2012**

There was a long depreciation of the Canadian dollar from 1977 to 1988. There was a sharp appreciation from 1988 to 1991. This was followed by a long depreciation from 1991 to 2001. Since 2001, the Canadian dollar has experienced a substantial appreciation. There have been several periods since 2001 where the Canadian dollar has been more valuable that the American dollar. There is a rapid depreciation in 2008 followed by an equally rapid appreciation in 2009.

*Source:* Data from CANSIM II variable V37426.

which summarizes the terminology. (You may have encountered two other words for movements in exchange rates: "revaluations" and "devaluations." These two terms are used when countries operate under **fixed exchange rates**—a system in which two or more countries maintain an unchanging exchange rate between their currencies. Under such a system, decreases in the exchange rate—infrequent, by definition—are called **revaluations** (rather than appreciations). Increases in the exchange rate are called **devaluations** (rather than depreciations). We discuss fixed exchange rates in Chapter 8.)

Keep in mind these definitions as we move on to Figure 6–3, which plots the nominal exchange rate between the American dollar and the Canadian dollar since 1970. The figure has four important features:

1. *The trend increase in the exchange rate.* In 2007, it cost about C$1.07 to buy US$1. From 1970 to 1975, US$1 cost a Canadian roughly C$1. Over the last 30 years or so, there has been a sustained depreciation of the Canadian dollar.
2. There was a significant period from 1988 to 1991 when the Canadian dollar appreciated. At the end of 1987, US$1 cost C$1.31. At its most valuable point between 1998 and 1991, in October 1991, US$1 cost only C$1.13.
3. A significant appreciation from 2002, where US$1 cost C$1.57 to 2012, where US$1 cost C$1.00.
4. The nominal exchange rate exhibits a lot of movement or, to use another word, is very volatile. Figure 6–3 is drawn using a monthly average of daily observations. It would look more volatile if we had plotted the daily data. One particular episode of volatility stands out. There is a sharp depreciation in 2008 and an equally rapid appreciation in 2009.

◀ Remember,
Increase in the exchange rate ⇔ Depreciation
Decrease in the exchange rate ⇔ Appreciation

Figure 6–3 tells us only about movements in the relative price of the two currencies. To Canadian tourists thinking of visiting the United States, the question is not, however, how much one American dollar costs in terms of Canadian dollars but also how many goods their Canadian dollar will buy. It does them little good to get more American dollars per Canadian dollar if the American dollar prices of goods have increased in roughly the same proportion. This takes us closer to where we want to go—to the construction of real exchange rates.

## Real Exchange Rates

How do we construct the real exchange rate between Canada and the United States—the price of American goods in terms of Canadian goods?

Suppose the United States produced only one good, an SUV (sport utility vehicle) (this is one of those completely counterfactual "suppose" statements, but we will become more realistic shortly) and Canada also produced only one good, say, a minivan.

Constructing the real exchange rate, the price of this one American good in terms of that one Canadian good would be straightforward.

Computing the relative price of SUVs in terms of minivans:

SUV:
US$30,000 × 1.5
         = C$45,000
Minivan:   = C$40,000

Relative price of SUVs in terms of minivans:

$$\frac{\$45,000}{\$40,000} = 1.125$$

- The first step would be to take the price of the SUV in U.S. dollars and convert it to a price in Canadian dollars. Suppose the price of the SUV in the United States is US$30,000. Suppose a U.S. dollar is worth 1.5 Canadian dollars. So, the price of the SUV in Canadian dollars is $30,000 × 1.5 = $45,000.
- The second step would be to compute the ratio of the price of the SUV in Canadian dollars to the price of the minivan in Canadian dollars. The price of a minivan in Canada is $40,000. Thus, the price of the SUV in terms of minivans—that is, the real exchange rate between Canada and the United States—would be $45,000/$40,000 = 1.125.

But Canada and the United States produce more than minivans and SUVs, and we want to construct a real exchange rate that reflects the relative price of *all* the goods produced in the United States in terms of *all* the goods produced in Canada. The computation we just went through tells us how to proceed. Rather than use the U.S. dollar price of an SUV and the Canadian dollar price of a minivan, we must use a U.S. dollar price index for all goods produced in the United States and a Canadian dollar price index for all goods produced in Canada. This is exactly what the GDP deflators we introduced in Chapter 2 do: They are, by definition, price indexes for the set of final goods and services produced in the economy.

So, let $P$ be the GDP deflator for Canada, $P^*$ be the GDP deflator for the United States (as a rule, we will denote foreign variables by an asterisk), and $E$ be the U.S. dollar–Canadian dollar nominal exchange rate. Figure 6–4 shows the steps needed to construct the real exchange rate.

Another definition to remember: $\epsilon$ is the real exchange rate or the price of foreign goods in terms of domestic goods. (For example, from the point of view of Canada, it is the price of U.S. goods in terms of Canadian goods.)

- The price of U.S. goods in U.S. dollars is $P^*$. Multiplying it by the exchange rate, $E$ (the price of U.S. dollars in terms of Canadian dollars), gives us the price of U.S. goods in Canadian dollars, $EP^*$.
- The price of Canadian goods in Canadian dollars is $P$. The real exchange rate, the price of U.S. goods in terms of Canadian goods, which we shall call $\epsilon$ (the Greek lowercase epsilon), is thus given by

$$\epsilon = \frac{EP^*}{P} \tag{6.1}$$

Note that, unlike the price of an SUV in terms of a minivan, the real exchange rate is an index number: That is, its level is arbitrary and thus uninformative. This is because the GDP deflators used in the construction of the real exchange rate are themselves index numbers; as we saw in Chapter 2, they are equal to 1 (or 100) in whatever year is chosen as the base year. But while its level is uninformative, relative changes in the real exchange rate are informative: If, for example, the real exchange rate between the United States and Canada increases by 10%, this tells us Canadian goods are now 10% cheaper relative to U.S. goods than they were before.

An increase in the relative price of domestic goods in terms of foreign goods is called a **real appreciation**; a decrease is called a **real depreciation**. *Real* indicates that we are referring to changes in the relative price of *goods*, not the relative price of currencies. Given our definition of the real exchange rate as the price of foreign goods in terms of domestic goods,

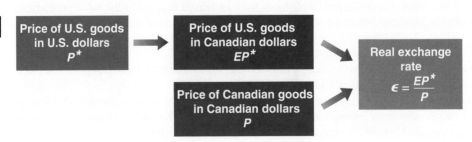

**FIGURE  6–4**

**The Construction of the Real Exchange Rate**

a real appreciation corresponds to a *decrease* in the real exchange rate, $\epsilon$. Similarly, a real depreciation corresponds to an *increase* in $\epsilon$. These definitions are summarized in Figure 6–5, which does for the real exchange rate what Figure 6–2 did for the nominal exchange rate.

Figure 6–6 plots the evolution of the real exchange rate between the United States and Canada from 1970 to 2012. For convenience, it also reproduces the evolution of the nominal exchange rate from Figure 6–3. Real and nominal exchange rates were both about 1 in 1976. But remember the units of the real exchange rate are arbitrary.

Figure 6–6 has three distinct sections:

- From 1970 to 1984, the nominal exchange rate depreciated: the Canadian dollar price of an American dollar increased from about C$1 per US$1 to C$1.25 per US$1. In spite of this nominal depreciation, the value of the real exchange rate in 1984 was roughly the same as in 1970.

  How can this be? Given the increase in the nominal exchange rate over the period, why did the real exchange rate remain roughly the same? The answer: Although the Canadian dollar depreciated from 1970 to 1984 by 25%, the price level in Canada increased more than the price level in the United States. To see this more clearly, return to the definition of the real exchange rate:

  $$\epsilon = \frac{EP^*}{P}$$

  Two things happened between 1970 and 1984. First, $E$ went up: The U.S. dollar cost more in terms of Canadian dollars—this is the nominal depreciation we saw earlier. Second, inflation was higher in Canada than in the United States, leading to a larger increase in the Canadian price level, $P$, than in the American price level, $P^*$. This has led to a decrease in $P^*/P$. The increase in $E$ and the decrease in $P^*/P$ roughly cancelled out between 1970 and 1984, leading to an unchanged real exchange rate.

  To make this more concrete, return to our American tourists thinking of visiting Canada. They could buy 25% more Canadian dollars per American dollar in 1984 than in 1970. Does this imply their trip would be 25% cheaper? No. When they arrived in Canada, they would have discovered that the prices of goods in Canada had increased by 25% more than the prices of goods in the United States, roughly cancelling the increase in the value of the American dollar in terms of Canadian dollars. Their trip would have been no cheaper in 1984 than it would have been in 1970.

**From the viewpoint of Canada looking at the United States**

**Real exchange rate $\epsilon$**
Price of American goods in terms of Canadian goods

**Real appreciation**

Price of Canadian goods in terms of American goods increases equivalently.
Price of American goods in terms of Canadian goods decreases equivalently.
Real exchange rate decreases: $\epsilon\downarrow$

**Real depreciation**

Price of Canadian goods in terms of American goods decreases equivalently.
Price of American goods in terms of Canadian goods increases equivalently.
Real exchange rate increases: $\epsilon\uparrow$

**FIGURE 6–5**

The Real Exchange Rate, Real Appreciation, and Real Depreciation: The United States and Canada (from the viewpoint of Canada)

FIGURE 6-6

**Real and Nominal Exchange Rates between Canada and the United States, 1970–2012**

The nominal and real exchange rates move together for most of this period. The real exchange rate is an index value, so its absolute value means little. A decline in the index means Canadian goods and services are becoming more expensive for Americans to purchase and American goods are becoming cheaper for Canadians to purchase.

*Source:* Data from Nominal exchange rate CANSIM II Variable V37426. Real exchange rate is the nominal exchange rate multiplied by the U.S. GDP deflator divided by the Canadian GDP deflator. The U.S. GDP deflator is nominal GDP (variable GDP, Federal Reserve Bank of St. Louis FRED database) divided by real GDP (variable GDPC1, Federal Reserve Bank of St. Louis FRED database); rebased so 2007=100. The Canadian GDP deflator from 1981 through 2012 is nominal GDP (V62305783) divided by real GDP (V62305752). From 1970 to 1980 the Canadian GDP deflator is nominal GDP (V498086) divided by real GDP (V1992067).

> Can there be a real appreciation with no nominal appreciation? Can there be a nominal appreciation with no real appreciation?

> Between 1970 and 2001, the difference between the American inflation rate and the Canadian inflation rate was usually less than 1% in a given year. In other words, the change in $P*/P$ from one year to the next was usually 1% or less. In contrast, there have been several years when the nominal exchange rate has changed by much more than 5% within the year.

There is a general lesson here. Over long periods of time, depending on differences in inflation rates across countries, nominal and real exchange rates can move quite differently. We will return to this issue in Chapter 14.

● From 1992 to 2002, both the nominal and real exchange rates depreciated. The American dollar, which cost a Canadian about C$1.25 in 1984, cost C$1.57 in 2002. This is the "dead duck" description of the loonie over the decade of the 1990s. Throughout most of the decade, the Canadian dollar fell in value or the U.S. dollar became more expensive for Canadians.

In the 1990s, Canada had a lower average inflation rate than did the United States. The ratio $P*/P$ actually increased. This can be seen in Figure 6–6, where the increase in the real exchange rate from 1997 to 2001 is slightly larger than the increase in the nominal exchange rate.

● The third and fourth observations to make concerning Figure 6–6 is to look at the periods of real exchange rate appreciation. The first period is from 1987 to 1991. In this period, as the Canadian dollar appreciated from C$1.30 per US$1 to C$1.15 per US$1, American goods became 15% cheaper to Canadians, or Canadian goods became 15% more expensive for Americans (these are the same statements). Cross-border shopping became a major recreational activity for Canadians as they flocked across the American border in search of cheaper American goods. And Americans stopped shopping in Canada! We need to understand the source of this massive real and nominal appreciation of the Canadian dollar from 1987 to 1991. The second period is from 2002 to 2012 with the strange break in 2008 and 2009. In 2008 there was a large and rapid depreciation of the Canadian dollar. In 2009 there was an equally rapid appreciation of the Canadian dollar. We return to this period in our discussion of long-run equilibrium real exchange rate in section 20-5 as well as in the general discussion of recent Canadian monetary policy in Chapter 24.

We have one last step to take. Canada trades mostly with the United States, as noted in Table 6–2. The numbers refer to **merchandise trade**—exports and imports of goods; they do not include exports and imports of services, such as travel services and tourism.

> *Bi-* means two. *Multi-* means many.

The United States accounts for 72% of Canada's merchandise exports and, a slightly smaller percentage, only 62% of Canada's merchandise imports. The only exchange rate of

| Countries | Exports to | | Imports from | |
|---|---|---|---|---|
| | $ Billions | Percent | $ Billions | Percent |
| United States | 331 | 72.3 | 281 | 61.7 |
| Japan | 11 | 2.5 | 9 | 2.0 |
| United Kingdom | 19 | 4.2 | 11 | 2.3 |
| Other European Community Countries | 23 | 5.0 | 35 | 7.8 |
| Other OECD Countries | 21 | 4.5 | 33 | 7.2 |
| Other Countries | 53 | 11.5 | 87 | 19.0 |
| **Total** | **458** | **100.0** | **456** | **100.0** |

Source: Data from CANSIM II Table 228-0003.

vital interest to Canadians is the exchange rate with respect to the United States. Sometimes, this is called our **bilateral real exchange rate**; implicitly for Canada, we mean the exchange rate with the United States.

Canada, as Table 6–2 shows, also trades with Japan, the United Kingdom, the rest of Europe, and, indeed, the rest of the world. We could calculate a bilateral real exchange rate with Japan, the United Kingdom, and every other country. The **multilateral real exchange rate** is a weighted average of bilateral real exchange rates. The weights could be either export shares or import shares (or an average of these two shares). Canadians, because the United States accounts for 72% of exports and 62% of imports, rarely bother to calculate a multilateral real exchange rate. If you planned a graduation trip to the United Kingdom, the rest of Europe, or more exotic destinations, you would have to make a multilateral real exchange rate calculation to calculate the cost of your trip around the world.

> A multilateral real exchange rate is also called the **trade-weighted real exchange rate**, or an **effective real exchange rate**. The Bank of Canada posts a multilateral real exchange rate for Canada on its website.

# 6-2 | Openness in Financial Markets

Openness in financial markets allows financial investors to hold both domestic and foreign assets, to diversify their portfolios, to speculate on movements in foreign versus domestic interest rates, exchange rates, and so on. And diversify and speculate they do. Given that buying or selling foreign assets implies, as part of the operation, buying or selling foreign currency (sometimes called **foreign exchange**), the size of transactions in foreign-exchange markets gives a sense of the importance of international financial transactions.

International financial markets are dominated by trades in assets. Here is an example. In 2010, the recorded *daily* volume of foreign-exchange transactions in the world was $4 trillion, of which 85%—about $3.4 trillion—involved U.S. dollars on one side of the transaction. To get a sense of the magnitude of these numbers, the sum of U.S. exports and imports in 2010 totalled $4.1 trillion *for the year,* or about $11 billion a day. If the only dollar transactions in foreign-exchange markets had been on one side by U.S. exporters selling their foreign currency earnings and on the other side by U.S. importers buying the foreign currency they needed to buy foreign goods, the volume of transactions would have been $11 billion a day, or about 0.3% of the actual daily volume of dollar transactions ($3.4 trillion) involving dollars in foreign-exchange markets. This computation yields a simple conclusion: Most of the transactions are associated not with trade but with purchases and sales of financial assets. The volume of transactions in foreign-exchange markets is not only high but also increasing rapidly. The volume of foreign exchange transactions more than quadrupled between 2001 and 2010. Again, this activity reflects an increase in financial transactions rather than an increase in trade.

> Daily volume of foreign exchange transactions with U.S. dollars on one side of the transaction: $3.4 trillion.
> Daily volume of trade of the United States with the rest of the world: $11 billion (0.3% of the volume of foreign exchange transactions).

For a country as a whole, openness in financial markets has an important implication. It allows the country to run trade surpluses and trade deficits. A country running a trade deficit is buying more from the rest of the world than it is selling to the rest of the world and must borrow the difference. It borrows by making it attractive for foreign financial investors to increase their holdings of domestic assets—in effect, to lend to the country. This lending from one country to another plays a key role in economic growth. We explore this feature of economic growth in Chapter 18. In the meantime, international forces also play an important role in the short-run macroeconomic outcome in Canada and in other countries. These forces are measured using a set of accounts called the balance of payments.

## The Balance of Payments

A country's transactions with the rest of the world are summarized by a set of accounts called the **balance of payments**. Table 6–3 presents the Canadian balance of payments for 2012.

In this presentation, the table has two parts, separated by a line. Transactions are referred to as either **above the line** or **below the line**.

**The Current Account.** The transactions above the line all record payments to and from the rest of the world. These are called **current account** transactions.

The first two lines of Table 6–3 record exports and imports of goods and services. Exports lead to payments from the rest of the world and imports lead to payments to the rest of the world. In 2012, imports exceeded exports, leading to a Canadian trade deficit of $36.5 billion. Note that in Table 6–2, Canada exported slightly more goods than it imported in 2011. However the numbers in Table 6–3 refer to exports and imports of both goods and services. Table 6–2 refers only to trade in goods. Canada imports a lot more services than it exports.

Exports and imports of goods and services are not the only sources of payments to and from the rest of the world. The Current Account records, under the categories **primary income received** and **primary income paid**, two types of payments made and received. One type is small, the other very large. The small type is compensation of employees. A foreign resident may be paying a Canadian resident as an employee. That is a payment by a foreigner to a Canadian. A Canadian resident may pay a foreigner as an employee. That is a payment to a foreigner.

| TABLE 6–3 | The Canadian Balance of Payments, 2012, in Billions of Canadian Dollars* | |
|---|---|---|
| **Current Account** | | |
| Exports of Goods and Services | 554.8 | |
| Imports of Goods and Services | −582.3 | |
| Trade balance: Item (1) | | −36.5 |
| Primary income received | 69.5 | |
| Primary income paid | −96.3 | |
| Primary income balance: Item (2) | | −26.8 |
| Secondary income balance: Item (3) | | −3.7 |
| Current Account Balance: (1) + (2) + (3) | | −67.0 |
| **Financial Account** | | |
| Increase in foreign holdings of Canadian assets | 182.7 | |
| Increase in Canadian holdings of foreign assets | −119.0 | |
| Net lending (−)/borrowing (+) on financial account | | 63.7 |
| Statistical Discrepancy (Net Errors and Omissions) | | 3.3 |

*A surplus on a balance item is indicated as positive.

Source: Data from Tables 1 and 2: Canada's Balance of International Payments, Fourth Quarter, 2012, as released in The Daily, February 28, 2012.

These are very small payments in total. The very large type of payment in the primary income category, both received and paid, more than 95% of the total, is **investment income**.

Canadians receive investment income, interest and dividends, on their holdings of foreign assets. Canadians pay interest on loans made in the past by foreigners to Canadians. Canadians pay dividends to foreigners for their holdings of equity in firms that operate in Canada. The **primary income balance** is −$26.8 billion. This indicates that Canada pays a lot more in interest and dividends to foreigners than it receives in interest and dividends from foreigners.

The last item in the Current Account is the **secondary income balance** of −$3.7 billion. This relatively small item used to be called **net transfers paid**. That name evokes the idea that Canadians give money to foreigners to help them. Some of the money is given privately through organizations like UNICEF and Mennonite Central Committee. Some of the money is given by the government through agencies like CIDA, the Canadian International Development Agency. However foreigners also "give" money to Canadians—in two ways. First foreigners do pay some taxes to various Canadian governments. Second, when a person emigrates from another part of the world to Canada and becomes a Canadian resident, any money that immigrant brings with him or her is treated as a transfer from a foreign resident (that person) to a Canadian resident (that same person) at the instant the immigrant arrives to stay in Canada.

Keeping track of the details of the balance of payments can be an overwhelming task. Table 6–3 is a much-simplified version of all the data available. The crucial figure in Table 6–3 is the sum of Items (1), (2), and (3), which add up to −$67.0 billion. This sum is called the **current account balance**.

**The Financial Account**. The fact that Canada had current account deficit of $67.0 billion in 2012 implies it had to, on net, borrow that amount of money from the rest of the world. The **financial account**, the items below the line in Table 6–3, explains how this borrowing occurred.

The measured increase in Canadian assets held abroad in 2012 was $119 billion. Canadians made loans to foreigners or bought foreign equity in 2012 in that amount. But at the same time, there was an increase in foreign assets held in Canada of $182.7 billion. Foreigners make loans to Canadians or buy Canadian equity.

The **net capital flow** into Canada was $182.7 − $119.0 = $63.7 billion. This is a positive value since foreigners are investing more in Canada than Canadians are investing abroad. When Canada has a current account surplus, the net capital flow into Canada is negative or, equivalently, Canada experiences a net capital outflow.

Shouldn't the net capital flow ($63.7 billion) be exactly equal to the current account deficit ($67.0 billion)? Yes. But the numbers for the current account and the financial account are constructed from different sources; although they should give the same answers, they typically do not. In 2012, the difference between the two, the **statistical discrepancy**, was $3.3 billion.

The increase in foreign holdings of Canadian assets in Table 6–3 is positive, and we imagine Canadians receive foreign currency as foreigners buy factories in Canada. The increase in Canadian holdings of foreign assets has a negative sign as Canadians pay foreign currency to buy foreign assets. Above the line, Canadians needed $67.0 billion in foreign currency. Below the line, these $67.0 billion are found. Using the first two lines of the financial account finds only $63.7 of the required $67.0 billion dollars. Thus the statistical discrepancy represents an additional $3.3 billion in loans made by foreigners to Canadians that were not recorded.

It is unusual that the statistical discrepancy is positive. If the discrepancy is negative, then there are some purchases of foreign assets by Canadians that are not reported to the Canadian ◄ government. For example, a Canadian could purchase a condominium in Florida to rent to others and, in not wishing to report the rental income, would also not wish to report the purchase. As indicated in the margin note, when the discrepancies are added for all countries in the world, the result is a large negative number.

Now that we have looked at the current account, we can return to an issue we touched on in Chapter 2, the difference between GDP, the measure of output we have used so far, and

Here is a variant on the same statistical problem: The sum of the current account deficits of all countries should be equal to zero: One country's deficit should show up as a surplus for the other countries taken as a whole. This is not, however, the case in the data: If we added the published current account deficits of all the countries in the world, it would appear that the world is running a large current account deficit. Some economists speculate that the explanation is unrecorded trade with the Martians. Most others believe that mismeasurement is the explanation.

GNP, another measure of aggregate output. This is done in the Focus box "GDP versus GNP: The Example of Kuwait."

## The Choice between Domestic and Foreign Assets

Why were Canadian investors willing, in 2012, to increase their holdings of foreign assets by $119 billion? To answer this question, we must look at the choice investors face in holding domestic versus foreign assets.

It might appear that we have to think about at least two new decisions: the choice of holding domestic versus foreign *money* and the choice of holding domestic versus foreign *interest-paying assets*. But remember why people hold money: to engage in transactions. For somebody who lives in Canada whose transactions are thus mostly in Canadian dollars, there is little point in holding foreign currency: It cannot be used for transactions, and if the goal is to hold foreign assets, holding foreign currency is clearly less desirable than holding foreign bonds, which, at least, pay interest. Thus, the only new choice we have to think about is the choice between domestic and foreign interest-paying assets.

Let us think of them for now as domestic and foreign one-year bonds and consider the choice between Canadian and American one-year bonds.

There are three qualifications to this statement: Canadians involved in illegal activities often hold American dollars in cash. Some Canadians hold U.S. dollar bank accounts for convenience, even in Canadian banks. Also, in times of very high inflation, people sometimes switch to the use of a foreign currency, often the American dollar, even for some domestic transactions. This is known as the dollarization of an economy. Inflation in Canada is not high enough to create dollarization.

- Suppose you decide to hold Canadian bonds. Let $i_t$ be the one-year Canadian nominal interest rate. Then, as Figure 6–7 shows, for every Canadian dollar you put in Canadian bonds, you will get $(1 + i_t)$ Canadian dollars next year.
- Suppose you decide instead to hold American bonds. To buy American bonds, you must first buy American dollars. Let $E_t$ be the nominal exchange rate between the Canadian dollar and the American dollar. For every Canadian dollar, you get $(1/E_t)$ American dollars.

Let $i_t^*$ denote the one-year nominal interest rate on American dollar bonds. When the next year comes, you will have US$$(1/E_t)(1 + i_t^*)$. You will then have to convert your American dollars back into Canadian dollars. If you expect the nominal exchange rate next year to be $E_{t+1}^e$, you can expect to have $(1/E_t)(1+i_t^*)E_{t+1}^e$ Canadian dollars next year for every Canadian dollar you invested. The Canadian investor cares about the number of Canadian dollars available for next year's spending. This set of steps is represented in the lower part of Figure 6–7. We will look at the expression we just derived in more detail soon. But note already its basic implication: In assessing the attractiveness of American dollar bonds, you cannot look just at the American and Canadian interest rates; you must also assess what you think will happen to the exchange rate between this year and the next.

This is the simplest assumption. You and other investors in the financial markets also consider the riskiness of assets as well as the length of time you expect to hold the assets. Nonetheless, the expected rate of return is a major factor in your asset choices.

Let us now make the simplest assumption concerning the choices made in financial markets. We will assume that you and other financial investors want only to hold the asset with the highest expected rate of return when held for the same length of time. The one-year interest rates we have been discussing are just that, assets held for one year. In that case, if both American dollar and Canadian dollar one-year bonds are to be held, they must have the same expected rate of return, so the following *arbitrage relation* must hold.

$$1 + i_t = \left(\frac{1}{E_t}\right)(1 + i_t^*)(E_{t+1}^e)$$

FIGURE  6–7

Expected Returns from Holding One-Year Canadian Dollar or American Dollar Bonds

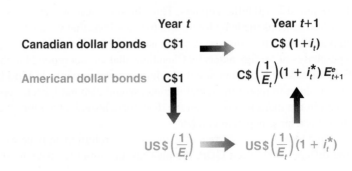

Should value added in an open economy be defined as

● The value added domestically (that is, within the country)?
● The value added by domestically owned factors of production?

The two definitions are not the same. Some domestic output is produced with capital owned by foreigners, while some foreign output is produced with capital owned by domestic residents.

The answer is that either definition is fine, and economists use both. **Gross domestic product (GDP)**, the measure we have used so far, corresponds to value added domestically. **Gross national product (GNP)** corresponds to the value added by domestically owned factors of production. To go from GDP to GNP, one must start from GDP, add factor payments received from the rest of the world, and subtract factor payments paid to the rest of the world. Put another way, GNP is equal to GDP plus net factor payments from the rest of the world. While GDP is now the measure most commonly mentioned, GNP was widely used until the early 1990s, and you will still encounter it in newspapers and academic publications.

For most countries, the difference between GNP and GDP is typically small because factor payments to and from the rest of the world roughly cancel one another. For Canada, the difference between GDP and GNP in 2012 is approximately the primary income balance in Table 6–3, –$26.8 billion. The primary income balance was 1.4% of 2012 GDP, of $1833 billion a relatively small number. This is the case for most countries.

There are a few exceptions. Among them is Kuwait. When oil was discovered in Kuwait, Kuwait's government decided that a portion of oil revenues would be saved and invested abroad, rather than spent, so as to provide future Kuwaiti generations with investment income when oil revenues came to an end.

Kuwait ran a large current account surplus, steadily accumulating large foreign assets. As a result, it now has large holdings of foreign assets and receives substantial investment income from the rest of the world. Table 1 gives GDP, GNP, and net factor payments for Kuwait, from 1989 to 1994.

Note how much larger GNP is compared with GDP throughout the period. Note also how net factor payments decreased after 1989. This is because Kuwait had to pay its allies for part of the cost of the 1990–1991 Gulf War and to pay for reconstruction after the war. It did so by running a current account deficit—that is, by decreasing its net holdings of foreign assets. This, in turn, led to a decrease in the income it earned from foreign assets and, by implication, a decrease in its net factor payments.

Since the Gulf War, Kuwait has rebuilt a sizeable net foreign asset position. Net income from abroad, the primary balance in Kuwait was 37% of GDP in 2010.

| TABLE | 1 | GDP, GNP, and Net Factor Payments in Kuwait, 1989–1994 |
|---|---|---|

| Year | GDP | GNP | Net Factor Payments |
|---|---|---|---|
| 1989 | 7143 | 9616 | 2473 |
| 1990 | 5328 | 7560 | 2232 |
| 1991 | 3131 | 4669 | 1538 |
| 1992 | 5826 | 7364 | 1538 |
| 1993 | 7231 | 8386 | 1151 |
| 1994 | 7380 | 8321 | 941 |

*Source*: Excerpts & graph from *International Financial Statistics*, IMF. Used by permission of IMF. All numbers are in millions of Kuwaiti dinars, with 1 dinar = US$3.3 (2003).

Or, reorganizing slightly,

$$1 + i_t = (1 + i_t^*)\left(\frac{E_{t+1}^e}{E_t}\right) \tag{6.2}$$

Equation (6.2) is called the **uncovered interest parity relation**, or simply the **interest parity condition**.[1]

[1]**DIGGING DEEPER**. The word "uncovered" is used to distinguish this relation from another relation called the *covered interest parity* condition. That condition is derived by looking at the following choice: Buy and hold Canadian dollar bonds for one year. Or buy an American dollar bond today, buy one-year American dollar bonds with the proceeds, and agree to sell the American dollars for Canadian dollars a year ahead at a predetermined price, called the *forward exchange rate*. The rate of return to these two alternatives, which can both be realized at *no risk today*, must be the same. The covered interest parity condition is a *riskless arbitrage condition*.

The assumption that financial investors will hold only the bonds with the highest expected rate of return is obviously too strong, for two reasons:

- It ignores transaction costs: Going in and out of American dollar bonds requires three separate transactions, each with a transaction cost.
- It ignores risk: The exchange rate a year from now is uncertain; that means that holding American dollar bonds is more risky, in terms of Canadian dollars, than holding Canadian dollar bonds.[2]

But as a characterization of capital movements among the major world financial markets (New York, Frankfurt, London, Tokyo, and perhaps Toronto), it is not far off. Small changes in interest rates and rumours of impending appreciation or depreciation can lead to movements of tens of billions of dollars within minutes. For the rich countries of the world, the arbitrage assumption in equation (6.2) is a good approximation of reality. Other countries, those whose capital markets are smaller and less developed or those that have various forms of capital control, have more leeway in choosing their domestic interest rate than is implied by equation (6.2). We will return to this issue at the end of Chapter 14.

To get a better sense of what arbitrage implies, rewrite equation (6.2) as:

$$1 + i_t = (1 + i_t^*)\left(1 + \frac{E_{t+1}^e - E_t}{E_t}\right) \qquad (6.3)$$

This gives a relation among the domestic nominal interest rate, the foreign nominal interest rate, and the expected rate of depreciation. Remember that an increase in $E$ is a depreciation, so $(E_{t+1}^e - E_t)/E_t$ is the expected rate of depreciation of the domestic currency. (If the domestic currency is expected to appreciate, then this term is negative.) As long as interest rates or the expected rate of depreciation are not too large (say, below 20% a year) a good approximation to this equation is given by:

> This follows from proposition 3 in Appendix 2.

$$i_t \approx i_t^* + \frac{E_{t+1}^e - E_t}{E_t} \qquad (6.4)$$

> An important relation to remember: Under the uncovered interest parity condition, the domestic interest rate must approximately equal the foreign interest rate plus the expected depreciation of the domestic currency.

This is the relation you must remember: Arbitrage implies that *the domestic interest rate must be (approximately) equal to the foreign interest rate plus the expected depreciation rate of the domestic currency.*

Let us apply this equation to American dollar versus Canadian dollar bonds. Suppose the one-year nominal interest rate is 4% in Canada and 2.5% in the United States. Should you hold American dollar or Canadian dollar bonds? It depends on whether you expect the Canadian dollar to depreciate vis-à-vis the U.S. dollar by more or less than 4% − 2.5% = 1.5% over the coming year. If you expect the Canadian dollar to depreciate by more than 1.5%, then, despite the fact that the interest rate is lower in the United States than in Canada, investing in American bonds is more attractive than investing in Canadian bonds. By holding American bonds, you will get fewer American dollars a year from now, but the U.S. dollars will also be worth more in terms of Canadian dollars a year from now, making investing in American dollar bonds more attractive than investing in Canadian dollar bonds. However, if you expect the Canadian dollar to depreciate by less than 1.5% or even to appreciate, then the reverse holds, and Canadian dollar bonds are more attractive than American dollar bonds.

In other words, the uncovered interest parity condition tells us that financial investors must be expecting, on average, a depreciation of the Canadian dollar with respect to the

---

[2]**DIGGING DEEPER**. Whether holding American dollar or Canadian dollar bonds is more risky depends on which investors we are looking at. Holding American dollar bonds is more risky from the point of view of Canadian investors. Holding Canadian dollar bonds is more risky from the point of view of American investors. (Why?)

**FOCUS**     **Buying Brazilian Bonds**

Put yourself back in September 1993 (the very high interest rate in Brazil at the time helps make the point we want to get across here). Brazilian bonds are paying a *monthly* interest rate of 36.9%. This seems very attractive compared with the *annual* rate of 3% on U.S. bonds—corresponding to a *monthly* interest rate of about 0.2%. Shouldn't you buy Brazilian bonds?

The discussion in this chapter tells you that to decide, you need one more crucial element, the expected rate of appreciation of the dollar vis-à-vis the cruzeiro (the name of the Brazilian currency at the time; the currency is now called the real). You need this information because (as Figure 6–7 makes clear) the return in dollars from investing in Brazilian bonds for a month is:

$$(1 + i_t^*) \frac{E_{t+1}^e}{E_t} = (1.369) \frac{E_{t+1}^e}{E_t}$$

What rate of cruzeiro depreciation should you expect over the coming month? Assume that the rate of depreciation next month will be equal to the rate of depreciation last month. You know that 100,000 cruzeiros, worth $1.01 at the end of July 1993, were worth only $0.75 at the end of August 1993. If depreciation continues at the same rate, the return from investing in Brazilian bonds for a month is:

$$(1 + i_t^*) \frac{E_{t+1}^e}{E_t} = (1.369) \left( \frac{0.75}{1.01} \right) = 1.016$$

The expected rate of return in dollars from holding Brazilian bonds is only $(1.016 - 1) = 1.6\%$ per month, not the 36.9% per month that looked so attractive. Note that 1.6% per month is still much higher than the monthly interest rate on U.S. bonds (about 0.2%). But think of the risk and the transaction costs—all the elements we ignored when we wrote the arbitrage condition. When these are taken into account, you may well decide to keep your funds out of Brazil.

---

American dollar of about 1.5% over the coming year, and this is why they are willing to hold American dollar bonds despite their lower interest rate. (Another example is provided in the Focus box "Buying Brazilian Bonds.")

The arbitrage relation between interest rates and exchange rates in equation (6.4) will play a central role in the following chapters. It suggests that unless financial markets expect large depreciations or appreciations, domestic and foreign interest rates are likely to move very much together. Take the extreme case of two countries that commit to maintaining their bilateral exchange rates at a fixed value. If markets have faith in this commitment, they will expect the exchange rate to remain constant, and the expected depreciation will be zero. In that case, the arbitrage condition implies that interest rates in the two countries will have to move together exactly. Most of the time, as we will see, governments do not make such absolute commitments, but they often do try to avoid large movements in the exchange rate. This puts sharp limits on how much they can allow their interest rate to deviate from interest rates elsewhere in the world.

How much do nominal interest rates actually move together between major countries? Figure 6–8 plots nominal interest rates in Canada and the United States since 1970. The impression is, indeed, one of closely related but not identical movements. Interest rates were high (by historical standards) in both countries around 1980, lower in the late 1970s, and lower in the 1990s. At the same time, differences between the two are sometimes large. In 1989–1990, the Canadian interest rate was nearly 5% above the U.S. interest rate. More recently, by contrast, the Canadian interest rate has been both slightly below and slightly above the U.S. interest rate. In the coming chapters, we will return to why these differences emerged and what their implications were.

Meanwhile, do the following: Look at the back pages of a recent issue of *The Economist* for short-term interest rates in different countries relative to the United States. Which are the currencies against which the dollar is expected to depreciate?

## 6-3 | Conclusions and a Look Ahead

We have now set the stage for the study of the open economy. Openness in goods markets allows a choice between domestic and foreign goods. This choice depends primarily on the *real exchange rate*—the relative price of foreign goods in terms of domestic goods.

FIGURE 6-8

**Canadian and American Treasury Bill Rates, 1970–2012**

Canadian and American nominal interest rates, in this figure interest rates on six-month Treasury bills, have moved closely together over the years. But the interest rates are not identical. The lowest line is the Canadian rate minus the American rate. There are periods where the gap between the two rates is quite large, both positive and negative.

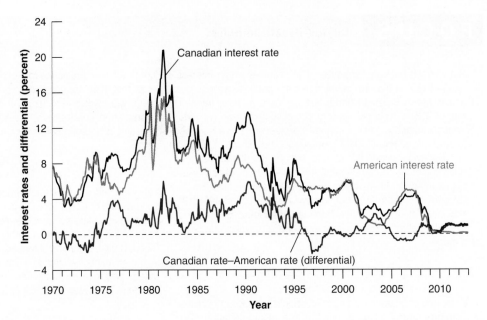

*Source:* Data from Canadian interest rate is CANSIM II V122552. American interest rate is variable DTB6 FRED, Federal Reserve Bank of St. Louis database.

Openness in financial markets allows a choice between domestic and foreign assets. This choice depends primarily on their relative rates of return, which depend, in turn, on domestic and foreign interest rates and on the expected rate of depreciation of the domestic currency.

In the next chapter, Chapter 7, we look at the implications of openness in goods markets. Chapter 8 brings in openness in financial markets. Later, in Chapter 14, we look at the medium run in an open economy, and we discuss the pros and cons of different exchange rate regimes.

## SUMMARY

- Openness in goods markets allows people and firms to choose between domestic and foreign goods. Openness in financial markets allows financial investors to choose between domestic or foreign financial assets.

- The nominal exchange rate is the price of foreign currency in terms of domestic currency. From the viewpoint of Canada, the nominal exchange rate between Canada and the United States is the price of the American dollar in terms of Canadian dollars.

- A nominal appreciation (an appreciation, for short) is an increase in the price of the domestic currency in terms of foreign currency; given the definition of the exchange rate, it corresponds to a decrease in the exchange rate. A nominal depreciation (a depreciation, for short) is a decrease in the price of the domestic currency in terms of foreign currency; it corresponds to an increase in the exchange rate.

- The real exchange rate is the relative price of foreign goods in terms of domestic goods. It is equal to the

nominal exchange rate times the foreign price level divided by the domestic price level.

- A real appreciation is an increase in the relative price of domestic goods in terms of foreign goods; it corresponds to a decrease in the real exchange rate. A real depreciation is a decrease in the relative price of domestic goods; it corresponds to an increase in the real exchange rate.

- The multilateral real exchange rate, or real exchange rate, for short, is a weighted average of bilateral real exchange rates, with weights equal to trade shares.

- The balance of payments records a country's transactions with the rest of the world. The current account balance is equal to the sum of the trade balance, the primary income balance and the secondary income balance. The capital account balance is equal to capital flows from the rest of the world minus capital flows to the rest of the world.

- The current account and the capital account are mirror images of each other. A current account deficit is financed by net capital flows from the rest of the world, thus by a capital account surplus. Similarly, a current account surplus corresponds to a capital account deficit.

- Uncovered interest parity, or interest parity, for short, is an arbitrage condition stating that the expected rates of return in terms of domestic currency on domestic and foreign bonds must be equal. Interest parity implies that the domestic interest rate approximately equals the foreign interest rate plus the expected depreciation rate of the domestic currency.

## KEY TERMS

- above the line, below the line, 116
- appreciation, 110
- balance of payments, 116
- bilateral real exchange rate, 115
- capital controls, 107
- current account, 116
- current account balance, 117
- depreciation, 110
- devaluation, 111
- effective real exchange rate, 115
- financial account, 117
- fixed exchange rates, 111
- foreign exchange, 115
- Gross Domestic Product (GDP), 119
- Gross National Product (GNP), 119
- investment income, 117
- merchandise trade, 114
- multilateral real exchange rate, 115
- net capital flow, 117
- net transfers paid, 117

- nominal exchange rate, 110
- North American Free Trade Agreement (NAFTA), 107
- openness in factor markets, 107
- openness in financial markets, 107
- openness in goods markets, 107
- primary income balance, 117
- primary income paid, 116
- primary income received, 116
- quotas, 107
- real appreciation, 112
- real depreciation, 112
- real exchange rate, 109
- revaluation, 111
- secondary income balance, 117
- statistical discrepancy, 117
- tariffs, 107
- trade-weighted real exchange rate, 115
- uncovered interest parity relation, or interest parity condition, 119

## QUESTIONS AND PROBLEMS

### 1. TRUE/FALSE/UNCERTAIN

**a.** Countries with net capital inflows must be running current account deficits.

**b.** Although the export ratio can be larger than one (as it is in Belgium and Luxembourg), the same cannot be true of the ratio of imports to GDP.

**c.** That a rich country such as Japan has such a small ratio of imports to GDP is clear evidence of an unfair playing field for exporters in other countries.

**d.** Uncovered interest parity implies that real interest rates must be the same across countries.

**e.** If the nominal exchange rate between the American dollar and the Canadian dollar is 0.70, it means that one American dollar is worth 70 Canadian cents.

**f.** If the real exchange rate between the United States and Canada is 2, this means that goods are twice as expensive in the United States as in Canada.

### 2. BALANCE OF PAYMENTS

Consider two fictional economies, one the "domestic country" and the other the "foreign country." Construct a balance of payments for each country given the following list of transactions:

The domestic country purchased $100 in oil from the foreign country.

Foreign tourists spent $25 on domestic ski slopes.

Domestic residents purchased $45 in life insurance in the foreign country.

Domestic residents purchased $5 in illegal substances from foreigners.

Foreign investors were paid $20 in dividends from their holdings of domestic equities.

Foreign residents paid Canadian residents $5 as employment income

Domestic residents sent $25 to foreign charities.

Foreign businessmen spent $35 in bribes to domestic government officials.

Domestic businesses borrowed $65 from foreign banks.

Foreign investors purchased $15 in domestic junk bonds.

Domestic investors sold off $50 in holdings of foreign government bonds.

## 3. UNCOVERED INTEREST PARITY

Consider the following prices for government bonds and foreign exchange in Canada and the United States. Assume that both government securities are one-year bonds, paying the face value of the bond one year from now. The exchange rate $E$ stands at US$1 = C$0.95.

The face values and prices on the two bonds are given by:

|  |  | Face Value | Price |
|---|---|---|---|
| Canada | 1-year bond | C$10,000 | C$9,615.38 |
| United States | 1-year bond | US$13,333 | US$12,698.10 |

**a.** Compute the nominal interest rate on each of the bonds.

**b.** Compute the expected exchange rate next year consistent with uncovered interest parity.

**c.** If you expect the Canadian dollar to depreciate relative to the American dollar, which bond should you buy?

**d.** Assume you are a Canadian investor. You exchange your dollars for U.S. dollars and purchase the American bond. One year from now, it turns out $E$ is actually 0.90 (US$1 = C$0.90). What is your realized return in Canadian dollars compared with the realized return you would have made had you held the Canadian dollar bond?

**e.** Are the differences in returns in (d) consistent with the uncovered interest parity condition? Why, or why not?

## 4. REAL EXCHANGE RATES

$E$ units of domestic currency per unit of foreign currency; $P$, $P^*$ are the domestic and foreign price index respectively.

| Year | $E$ | $P$ | $P^*$ | $EP^*/P$ |
|---|---|---|---|---|
| 1 | 1.0 | 100 | 100 | 1.0 |
| 2 | 1.1 | 110 | — | 1.0 |
| 3 | 1.1 | — | 110 | 1.1 |
| 4 | 1.1 | 110 | 121 | — |
| 5 | — | 110 | 121 | 1.155 |

Fill in the missing elements of the table above and answer the following questions:

**a.** Between which years did the domestic nominal exchange rate change?

**b.** Between which years did the domestic real exchange rate change?

**c.** Did the domestic nominal exchange rate depreciate or appreciate between Year 1 and Year 5?

**d.** Did the domestic real exchange rate depreciate or appreciate between Year 1 and Year 5?

## FURTHER READING

If you want to learn more about international trade and international economics, read the textbook by Paul Krugman, Maurice Obstfeld, and Marc Melitz, *International Economics, Theory and Policy*, 9th ed. (New York: Pearson, 2013).

If you want to know current exchange rates between the Canadian dollar and any currency in the world, look at the "currency converter" at the Bank of Canada homepage (www.bankofcanada.ca).

# The Goods Market in an Open Economy

## The Core: The Short Run

When Canada experiences stronger economic growth, politicians often take the credit and make sure through extensive advertising campaigns that the public understands how their policies are responsible for Canada's economic success. Witness the endless advertising related to "Canada's Economic Action Plan" vintage 2009, 2010, 2011, 2012, and 2013. However, when there are difficulties in the Canadian economy, the same politicians will carefully explain that Canada is part of a broader world economy and is frequently buffeted by events completely beyond their control. Which view of the Canadian economy is closer to the truth?

As usual, the answer to this kind of question is not simple. Good economic policy matters, which is why you are studying macroeconomics. And there is truth to the statements that the world economy has a very large impact on Canada. The slowdown in growth in Canada in 2001 and the substantial recession in 2009 were clearly related to a decline in economic activity in the United States and, in the more recent period, in the whole world.

Do foreign events dominate Canada's economy? If so, how much? To answer this question, we need to expand the treatment of the goods market from Chapter 3 to take into account openness. That is what we do in this chapter.

# 7-1 | The *IS* Relation in the Open Economy

The terms "the domestic demand for goods" and "the demand for domestic goods" may sound close. But, in an open economy, they need not be equal.

When we were assuming that the economy was closed to trade, there was no need to distinguish between the domestic demand for goods and the demand for domestic goods: They were clearly the same. Now, we must distinguish between the two: Some domestic demand falls on foreign goods, and some of the demand for domestic goods comes from foreigners. Let us look at this distinction more closely.

## The Demand for Domestic Goods

In an open economy, the **demand for domestic goods** is given by:

$$Z \equiv C + I + G - \epsilon Q + X \qquad (7.1)$$

The first three terms—consumption ($C$), investment ($I$), and government spending ($G$)—constitute the **domestic demand for goods**. If the economy were closed, $C + I + G$ would also be the demand for domestic goods. This is why, until now, we looked only at $C + I + G$. But now we have to make two adjustments.

In Chapter 3, we ignored this and subtracted Q. This was wrong, but we did not want to have to talk about the real exchange rate and complicate matters so early in the book.

- First, we must subtract imports, that part of domestic demand that falls on foreign goods. We must be careful here. Foreign goods are different from domestic goods, so we cannot just subtract the quantity of imports, $Q$; if we were to do so, we would be subtracting apples (foreign goods) from oranges (domestic goods). We must first express the value of imports in terms of domestic goods. This is what $\epsilon Q$ in equation (7.1) stands for: As we saw in Chapter 6, $\epsilon$ is the real exchange rate, the price of foreign goods in terms of domestic goods. Thus, $\epsilon Q$ (the price times the quantity of imports) is the value of imports in terms of domestic goods.

- Second, we must add exports, the demand for domestic goods that comes from abroad. This is captured by the term $X$ in equation (7.1).

## The Determinants of the Demand for Domestic Goods

Domestic demand for goods ($C + I + G$)
− Domestic demand for foreign goods (imports, $\epsilon Q$)
+ Foreign demand for domestic goods (exports, $X$)
= Demand for domestic goods ($C + I + G - \epsilon Q + X$)

Having listed the five components of demand, our next task is to specify their determinants. Let us start with the first three: $C$, $I$, and $G$.

**The Determinants of *C*, *I*, and *G*.** Now that we are assuming that the economy is open, how should we modify our earlier descriptions of consumption, investment, and government spending? The answer is not very much, if at all. How much consumers decide to spend still depends on their income and their wealth. Although the real exchange rate surely affects the *composition* of consumption spending between domestic and foreign goods, there is no obvious reason why it should affect the overall *level* of consumption. The same is true of investment: The real exchange rate may affect whether firms buy domestic or foreign machines, but it should not affect total investment.

This is good news because it implies that we can use the descriptions of consumption, investment, and government spending that we developed earlier. Therefore,

$$\text{Domestic demand:} \quad C + I + G = C(Y - T) + I(Y, i) + G$$
$$( \quad + \quad ) \quad (+, -)$$

Domestic demand ($C + I + G$) depends on income ($Y$), the interest rate ($i$), taxes ($T$), and the level of government spending ($G$).

We assume that consumption depends positively on disposable income ($Y - T$) and that investment depends positively on production ($Y$) and negatively on the interest rate ($i$). We continue to take government spending ($G$) as a given.

**The Determinants of Imports.** What does the quantity of imports, $Q$, depend on? Primarily on the overall level of domestic demand: the higher the level of domestic demand, the higher the demand for all goods, both domestic and foreign. But $Q$ also clearly depends on the real exchange rate: the higher the price of foreign goods relative to domestic goods, the lower the relative domestic demand for foreign goods and the lower the quantity of imports.

Thus, we write imports as:

$$Q = Q(Y, \epsilon) \qquad (7.2)$$
$$(+, -)$$

Imports depend on income (or, equivalently, output—the two are still the same in an open economy), $Y$: Higher income leads to higher imports.[1] Imports also depend on the real exchange rate. Recall that the real exchange rate, $\epsilon$, is defined as the price of foreign goods in terms of domestic goods. A higher real exchange rate means that foreign goods are relatively more expensive, leading to a decrease in the quantity of imports, $Q$. This negative effect of the real exchange rate on imports is captured by the negative sign under $\epsilon$ in the import equation.

**The Determinants of Exports.** The export of one country is, by definition, the import of another. In thinking about what determines Canadian exports, we can ask, equivalently, what determines foreign imports. From our discussion of the determinants of imports in the preceding paragraph, we know that foreign imports are likely to depend on foreign activity and on the relative price of foreign goods. Thus, we can write exports as:

$$X = X(Y^*, \epsilon) \qquad (7.3)$$
$$(+, +)$$

$Y^*$ is income in the rest of the world, or simply *foreign* income (equivalently foreign output). An increase in foreign income leads to an increase in the foreign demand for all goods, some of which falls on Canadian goods, leading to higher Canadian exports. An increase in $\epsilon$ —an increase in the relative price of foreign goods in terms of Canadian goods—makes Canadian goods relatively more attractive, leading to an increase in exports.

For Canada, $Y^*$ is usually real income in the United States and $\epsilon$ is usually the real exchange rate between Canada and the United States. Although we trade with other countries, as we saw in the previous chapter, the United States is our dominant trading partner.

We can represent what we have learned so far in Figure 7–1, which plots the various components of demand against output, keeping constant all other variables that affect demand (the interest rate, taxes, government spending, foreign output, and the real exchange rate).

In Figure 7–1(a), the line $DD$ plots *domestic demand*, $C + I + G$, as a function of output, $Y$. This relation between demand and output is familiar from Chapter 3. Under our standard assumptions, the slope of the relation between demand and output is positive but less than 1: An increase in output (equivalently, in income) increases demand but less than one for one. (In the absence of good reasons to the contrary, we draw the relation between demand and output, as well as the other relations in this chapter, as lines rather than curves. This is purely for convenience, and none of the discussions that follow depend on that assumption.)

To arrive at the *demand for domestic goods*, we must first subtract imports. This is done in Figure 7–1(b) and gives us the line $AA$: The distance between $DD$ and $AA$ equals the value of imports, $\epsilon Q$. Because the quantity of imports increases with income, the distance between the two lines increases with income. We can establish two facts about line $AA$, which will be useful later in the chapter:

As $\epsilon$ goes up while $Q$ goes down, what happens to $\epsilon Q$, the value of imports in terms of domestic goods, is ambiguous. We return to this point later.

The volume of imports ($Q$) depends on the level of output ($Y$), and the real exchange rate ($\epsilon$).

Recall that asterisks refer to foreign variables.

Exports depend on the level of foreign income ($Y^*$) and the real exchange rate ($\epsilon$).

For a given real exchange rate $\epsilon$, $\epsilon Q$ (the value of imports in terms of domestic goods) moves exactly with $Q$ (the volume of imports).

[1]**DIGGING DEEPER**. We cheat a bit here. Our discussion suggests that we should be using domestic demand, $C + I + G$, instead of income, $Y$. You might also dispute the assumption that imports depend on the sum of domestic demand and not on its composition: It may well be that the proportion of imports in investment differs from that of imports in consumption. For example, many poor countries import most of their capital equipment but consume mostly domestic goods. In that case, the composition of demand would matter for imports. We leave these complications aside.

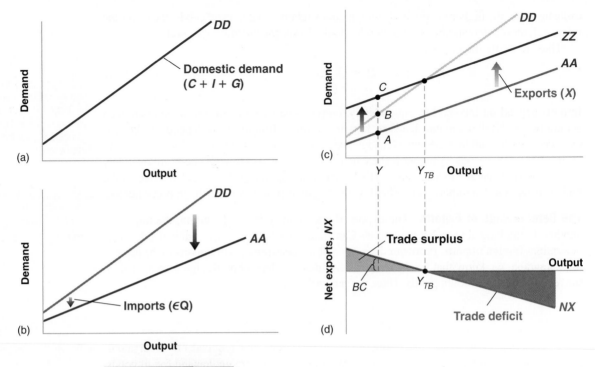

## FIGURE 7–1

**The Demand for Domestic Goods and Net Exports**

The domestic demand for goods is an increasing function of income. The demand for domestic goods is obtained by subtracting the value of imports from domestic demand and then adding exports. The trade balance is a decreasing function of output.

1. *AA* is flatter than *DD*: As income increases, some of the additional domestic demand falls on foreign goods rather than on domestic goods. As income increases, the domestic demand for domestic goods increases less than does total domestic demand.

2. As long as some of the additional demand falls on domestic goods, *AA* has a positive slope: An increase in income leads to some increase in the demand for domestic goods.

Finally, we must add exports. This is done in Figure 7–1(c) and gives us the line *ZZ*, which is above *AA*. The distance between *ZZ* and *AA* equals exports. Because exports do not depend on domestic output, the distance between *ZZ* and *AA* is constant, so the two lines are parallel. Because *AA* is flatter than *DD*, *ZZ* is flatter than *DD* as well.

From the information in Figure 7–1(c) we can characterize the behaviour of net exports—the difference between exports and imports $(X - \epsilon Q)$—as a function of output. At output level $Y$ for example, exports are given by the distance $AC$ and imports by the distance $AB$, so net exports are given by the distance $BC$.

> Recall that *net exports* is synonymous with trade balance. Positive net exports correspond to a trade surplus, negative net exports to a trade deficit.

This relation between net exports and output is represented as the line denoted *NX* (for net exports) in Figure 7–1(d). Net exports are a decreasing function of output: As output increases, imports increase and exports are unaffected, leading to lower net exports. Call $Y_{TB}$ (*TB* for trade balance) the level of output at which the value of imports is just equal to exports so that net exports are equal to zero. Levels of output above $Y_{TB}$ lead to higher imports, leading to a trade deficit. Levels of output below $Y_{TB}$ lead to lower imports and to a trade surplus.

## 7-2 | Equilibrium Output and the Trade Balance

The goods market is in equilibrium when domestic output equals the demand for domestic goods:

$$Y = Z$$

Collecting the relations we derived for the components of the demand for domestic goods, $Z$:

$$Y = C(Y - T) + I(Y, i) + G - \epsilon Q(Y, \epsilon) + X(Y^*, \epsilon) \quad (7.4)$$

This equilibrium condition determines output as a function of all the variables we take as givens, from taxes to the real exchange rate to foreign output. This is not a simple relation; Figure 7–2 represents it in a more user-friendly way. In Figure 7–2(a), demand is measured on the vertical axis, output (equivalently, income) on the horizontal axis. The line $ZZ$ plots demand as a function of output; this line just replicates the line $ZZ$ in Figure 7–1; $ZZ$ is upward sloping, but with slope less than 1.

Equilibrium output is at the point where demand equals output, at the intersection of the line $ZZ$ and the 45-degree line, so at point $A$ in the figure, with associated output level $Y$.

Figure 7–2(b) replicates Figure 7–1(d), drawing net exports as a decreasing function of output. There is, in general, no reason why the equilibrium level of output, $Y$, should be the same as the level of output at which trade is balanced, $Y_{TB}$. As we have drawn the figure, equilibrium output is associated with a trade surplus, equal to the distance $BC$.

We now have the tools needed to answer the questions we asked at the beginning of this chapter.

> Equilibrium in the goods market requires that domestic output be equal to the demand for domestic goods.

> The equilibrium level of output is given by the condition $Y = Z$. The level of output at which there is trade balance is given by the condition $\epsilon Q = X$. These are two different conditions.

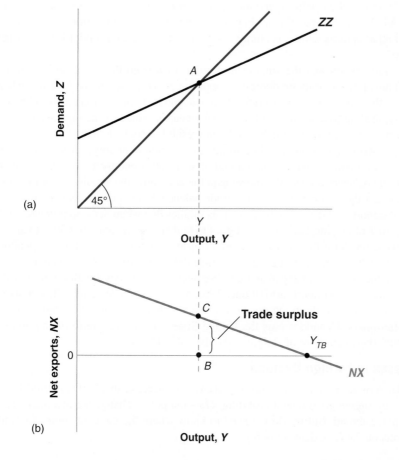

**FIGURE 7–2**

**Equilibrium Output and Net Exports**

The goods market is in equilibrium when production is equal to the demand for domestic goods. At the equilibrium level of output, the trade balance may show a deficit or a surplus.

## 7-3 | Increases in Demand, Domestic or Foreign

How do changes in demand affect output in an open economy? Let us start with a variation of what is by now an old favourite, an increase in government spending, and then turn to a new exercise, the effects of an increase in foreign activity.

### Increases in Domestic Demand

As in Chapter 3 we start by ignoring all markets other than the goods market; the conclusions we derive here will still apply when we introduce financial and labour markets later on.

Suppose the economy is in recession and government decides to increase government spending to increase domestic demand and output. What will be the effects on output and on the trade balance?

The answer is given in Figure 7–3. Before the increase in government spending, demand is given by ZZ in Figure 7–3(a), and the equilibrium is at point A, where output equals Y. Let us assume (though, as we have seen, there is no reason why this should be true in general) that trade is initially balanced, so, in Figure 7–3(b), $Y = Y_{TB}$.

What happens if government increases spending by $\Delta G$? At any level of output, demand is higher by $\Delta G$, shifting the demand relation up by $\Delta G$ from ZZ to ZZ'. The equilibrium point moves from A to A', and output increases from Y to Y'. The increase in output is larger than the increase in government spending: There is a multiplier effect.

So far, the story sounds like what happened in the closed economy earlier (see Chapter 3). However, let us look more closely: There is now an effect on the trade balance. Because government spending enters neither the exports relation nor the imports relation directly, the relation between net exports and output in Figure 7–3(b) does not shift. Thus, the increase in output from Y to Y' leads to a trade deficit equal to BC.

Starting from trade balance, an increase in government spending leads to a trade deficit.

Not only does government spending now generate a trade deficit, but its effect on output is smaller than in the closed economy. Recall from Chapter 3 that the smaller the slope of the demand relation, the smaller is the multiplier (for example, if ZZ were horizontal, the multiplier would be 1). And recall from Figure 7–1 that the demand relation, ZZ, is flatter than the demand relation in the closed economy, DD. That means the multiplier is smaller in the open economy.

The smaller multiplier and the trade deficit have the same underlying cause: Some domestic demand falls on foreign goods, not on domestic goods.

The trade deficit and the smaller multiplier arise from the same cause: An increase in demand now falls not only on domestic goods but also on foreign goods. Thus, when income increases, the effect on the demand for domestic goods is smaller than it would be in a closed economy, leading to a smaller multiplier. And because some of the increase in demand falls on imports—and exports are unchanged—the result is a trade deficit.

These two implications are important. In an open economy, an increase in domestic demand has a smaller effect on output than in a closed economy as well as an adverse effect on the trade balance. Indeed, the more open the economy, the smaller is the effect on output and the larger the adverse effect on the trade balance. For example, take Belgium, which has a ratio of imports to GDP close to 70%. This implies that when demand increases in Belgium, roughly 70% of this increased demand goes to higher imports and only 30% to an increase in the demand for domestic goods. The effect of an increase in government spending is thus likely to be a large increase in Belgium's trade deficit and only a small increase in its output, making domestic demand expansion a rather unattractive policy for Belgium. For the United States, which has an import ratio of only 13%, an increase in demand will be associated with some deterioration in the trade position. (This conclusion is discussed further in the Focus box "Multipliers: Canada versus the United States.") Canada's ratio of imports to GDP is about 30% (between those of Belgium and the United States).

### Increases in Foreign Demand

Consider now an increase in foreign activity, an increase in $Y^*$. This could be due to an increase in foreign government spending, $G^*$—the policy change we just analyzed, but now taking place abroad. But we do not need to know where the increase comes from to analyze the effects on the Canadian economy.

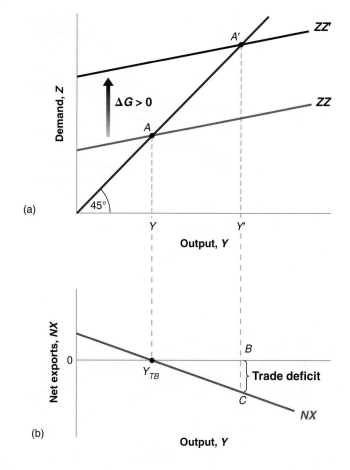

FIGURE    7-3

**The Effects of Higher
Government Spending**

An increase in government
spending leads to an
increase in output and a
trade deficit.

Figure 7–4 shows the effects of an increase in foreign activity on domestic output and the trade balance. The initial demand for domestic goods is given by $ZZ$ in Figure 7–4(a). The equilibrium is at point $A$, with output level $Y$. Let us assume trade is balanced so that in Figure 7–4(b) the net exports associated with $Y$ equal zero.

It will be useful to refer to the line that gives the domestic demand for goods $C + I + G$ as a function of income. This line is drawn as $DD$. Recall from Figure 7–1 that $DD$ is steeper than $ZZ$. The difference between $ZZ$ and $DD$ equals net exports so that if trade is balanced at point $A$, then $ZZ$ and $DD$ intersect at point $A$.

Now, consider the effects of an increase in foreign output, $\Delta Y^*$. Higher foreign output means higher foreign demand, including higher foreign demand for Canadian goods. So, the direct effect of the increase in foreign output is to increase Canadian exports by some amount, call it $\Delta X$. For a given level of output, this increase in exports leads to an increase in the demand for Canadian goods by $\Delta X$, so the line giving the demand for domestic goods as a function of output shifts up by $\Delta X$, from $ZZ$ to $ZZ'$. As exports increase by $\Delta X$ at a given level of output, the line giving net exports as a function of output in Figure 7–4(b) also shifts up by $\Delta X$, from $NX$ to $NX'$.

The new equilibrium is at point $A'$, with output level $Y'$. The increase in foreign output leads to an increase in domestic output. The reason is clear: Higher foreign output leads to higher exports of domestic goods, which increases domestic output and the domestic demand for goods through the multiplier.

What happens to the trade balance? We know that exports go up. But could it be that the increase in domestic output leads to such a large increase in imports that the trade balance actually deteriorates? The answer is no: The trade balance must improve. To see why, note

*DD* is the domestic demand for goods. *ZZ* is the demand for domestic goods.

$Y^* \uparrow \Rightarrow X = X(Y^*, \epsilon) \uparrow$

FIGURE 7-4

**The Effects of Higher Foreign Demand**

An increase in foreign demand leads to an increase in output and to a trade surplus.

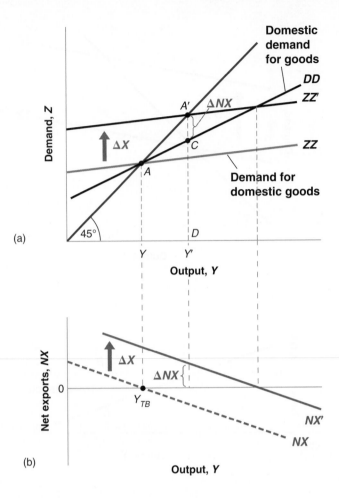

(a)

(b)

$Y^*$ directly affects exports and so enters the relation between the demand for domestic goods and output. An increase in $Y^*$ leads to a shift in $ZZ$.

$Y^*$ does not affect consumption, investment, or government spending directly and so does not enter the relation between the domestic demand for goods and output. An increase in $Y^*$ does not lead to a shift in $DD$.

An increase in foreign output increases output and improves the trade balance.

that when foreign demand increases, the demand for domestic goods shifts up from $ZZ$ to $ZZ'$; but the line $DD$, which gives domestic demand for goods as a function of output, does not shift. At the new equilibrium level of output $Y'$, domestic demand is given by the distance $DC$, and the demand for domestic goods is given by $DA'$. Net exports are thus given by the distance $CA'$—which, because $DD$ is necessarily below $ZZ'$, is necessarily positive. Thus, although imports increase, the increase does not offset the increase in exports, and the trade balance improves.

## Games that Countries Play

We have derived two basic results so far:

- An increase in domestic demand leads to an increase in output but also to an increase in the trade deficit or a reduction in the trade surplus. (We looked at an increase in government spending, but the results would have been the same for a decrease in taxes, an increase in consumer spending, and so on.)
- An increase in foreign demand (which could come from the same types of changes taking place abroad) leads to an increase in domestic output and a trade surplus.

Governments do not like trade deficits, and for good reasons. The main reason is that a country that runs a trade deficit accumulates debt vis-à-vis the rest of the world and therefore has to pay higher interest payments to the rest of the world. Thus, it is no wonder that countries prefer increases in foreign demand (which lead to an improvement in the trade balance) to increases in domestic demand (which lead to a deterioration in the trade balance).

If we assume that the various relations in equation (7.4) are linear, we can compute the effects of government spending, foreign output, and so forth, on both output and the trade balance. Here, we will focus on the differences between the effects of government spending in a large country, such as the United States, and in a small country, such as Canada.

Assume that consumption increases with disposable income and that investment increases with output:

$$C = c_0 + c_1(Y - T)$$
$$I = d_0 + d_1 Y$$

For simplicity, ignore movements in the real exchange rate, and assume that the real exchange rate is equal to 1. Also, assume that imports are proportional to domestic output and exports are proportional to foreign output:

$$Q = q_1 Y$$
$$X = x_1 Y^*$$

In the same way we referred to $c_1$ as the marginal propensity to consume, $q_1$ is the **marginal propensity to import**.

The equilibrium condition is that output be equal to the demand for domestic goods:

$$Y = C + I + G - Q + X$$

(Recall that we are assuming that $\epsilon$ is equal to 1.) Replacing the components by the expressions from above gives:

$$Y = [c_0 + c_1(Y - T)] + (d_0 + d_1 Y) + G - q_1 Y + x_1 Y^*$$

Regrouping terms gives:

$$Y = (c_1 + d_1 - q_1)Y + (c_0 + d_0 - c_1 T + G + x_1 Y^*)$$

Bringing the terms in output together, and solving, gives:

$$Y = \frac{1}{1 - (c_1 + d_1 - q_1)}$$
$$\times (c_0 + d_0 - c_1 T + G + x_1 Y^*)$$

Output is equal to the multiplier times the term in parentheses, which captures the effect of all the variables we take as givens in explaining output.

Consider the multiplier. More specifically, consider the term $(c_1 + d_1 - q_1)$ in the denominator. As in the closed economy, $(c_1 + d_1)$ gives the effects of an increase in output on consumption and investment demand; $(-q_1)$ captures the fact that some of the increased demand falls not on domestic goods but on foreign goods. In the extreme case where all the additional demand falls on foreign goods—that is, when $q_1 = c_1 + d_1$—an increase in output has no effect back on the demand for domestic goods; in that case, the multiplier is equal to 1. In general, $q_1$ is less than $(c_1 + d_1)$ so that the multiplier is larger than 1. But it is smaller than it would be in a closed economy.

Using this equation, we can easily characterize the effects of an increase in government spending of $\Delta G$. The increase in output is equal to the multiplier times the change in government spending, thus:

$$\Delta Y = \frac{1}{1 - (c_1 + d_1 - q_1)} \Delta G$$

The increase in imports that follows from the increase in output implies a change in net exports of:

$$\Delta NX = -q_1 \Delta Y$$
$$= -\frac{q_1}{1 - (c_1 + d_1 - q_1)} \Delta G$$

Let us see what these formulas imply by choosing numerical values for the parameters. Take $c_1 + d_1$ equal to 0.6. What value should we choose for $q_1$? We saw in Chapter 6 that in general, the larger the country, the more self-sufficient it is and the less it imports from abroad. So, let us choose two values of $q_1$—a small value, say, 0.1, for a large country, such as the United States, and a larger one, say, 0.3, for a small country, such as Canada. Note that we can think of $q_1/(c_1 + d_1)$ as the proportion of an increase in demand that falls on imports so that an equivalent way of stating our choices of $q_1$ is that in the large country, one-sixth of demand falls on imports, versus half in the small country.

For the large country, the effects on output and the trade balance are given by:

$$\Delta Y = \frac{1}{1 - (0.6 - 0.1)} \Delta G = 2.0\, \Delta G$$

and

$$\Delta NX = -0.1\, \Delta Y = \frac{-0.1}{1 - (0.6 - 0.1)} \Delta G = -0.2\, \Delta G$$

For the small country, the effects are given by:

$$\Delta Y = \frac{1}{1 - (0.6 - 0.3)} \Delta G = 1.43\, \Delta G$$

and

$$\Delta NX = -0.3\, \Delta Y = \frac{-0.3}{1 - (0.6 - 0.3)} \Delta G = -0.43\, \Delta G$$

These computations show how different the trade-offs faced by both countries are. In the large country, the effect of an increase in $G$ on output is large and the effect on the trade balance is small. In the small country, the effect on output is small, and the deterioration of the trade balance is over 40% of the increase in government spending.

This example makes clear how drastically openness binds the hands of policy makers in small countries. We will see more examples of this proposition as we go along.

These preferences may have disastrous implications. Consider a group of countries, all trading a lot with one another so that an increase in demand in any one country falls largely on the goods produced in the other countries. Suppose all these countries are in recession and each has roughly balanced trade to start. Each country may be very reluctant to increase domestic demand: The result would be a small increase in output but also a large trade deficit. Each country may just wait for others to increase their own demand. But if they all wait, nothing happens, and the recession may endure.

Is there a way out of this situation? Yes, at least in theory. If all countries coordinate their macroeconomic policies to increase domestic demand simultaneously, each can expand without increasing its trade deficit (vis-à-vis the others; their combined trade deficit with respect to the rest of the world will still increase). The reason is clear: The coordinated increase in demand leads to increases in both exports and imports in each country. It is still true that domestic demand expansion leads to larger imports; but this increase in imports is offset by the increase in exports, which comes from the foreign demand expansions.

**Coordination** is a word that governments often invoke. The eight major countries of the world—the so-called **G-8** (the United States, Japan, France, Germany, the United Kingdom, Italy, Russia, and Canada)—meet regularly to discuss their economic situations; the communiqué at the end of the meeting rarely fails to mention coordination. But the evidence is that there is, in fact, very limited macrocoordination among countries. Here are some reasons why.

Coordination may imply that some countries have to do more than others. They may not want to do so:

- Suppose that only some countries are in recession. Countries that are not in a recession will be reluctant to increase their own demand; but if they do not, the countries that expand will run a trade deficit vis-à-vis the countries that do not.
- Suppose instead that some countries are already running a large budget deficit. These countries will not want to cut taxes or increase spending further and will ask other countries to take on more of the adjustment. Those other countries may be reluctant to do so.

Another reason is that countries have a strong incentive to promise to coordinate and then not deliver on that promise. Once all countries have agreed, say, to an increase in spending, each country has an incentive not to deliver in order to benefit from the increase in demand elsewhere and thereby improve its trade position. But if each country cheats, or does not do everything it promised, there will be insufficient demand expansion to get out of the recession.

Although most attempts at coordinated fiscal expansion have failed, there is always the exception that proves the rule. When things get really bad, coordination does appear to take hold. This was the case for the world economy in 2009 and it is explored in the Focus box "The G20 and the 2009 Fiscal Stimulus."

## FOCUS | The G20 and the 2009 Fiscal Stimulus

On November 14–15, 2008, the leaders of the G20 met in an emergency meeting in Washington. The G20, a group of ministers of finance and central bank governors from 20 countries, including both the major advanced and the major emerging countries in the world, had been created in 1999 but had not played a major role until the crisis. With mounting evidence that the world economic downturn was going to be both deep and widespread, the group met to coordinate their responses in terms of both macroeconomic and financial policies.

On the macroeconomic front, it had become clear that interest rates had already been reduced substantially and

monetary policy would not be enough. The focus of the group turned to fiscal policy. The decrease in output was going to lead to a decrease in revenues, and thus to an increase in budget deficits. Dominique Strauss-Kahn, then the managing director of the International Monetary Fund, argued that further fiscal actions were needed and suggested taking additional discretionary measures—either decreases in taxes or increases in spending—adding up to roughly 2% of GDP on average for each country. Here is what he said:

"The fiscal stimulus is now essential to restore global growth. Each country's fiscal stimulus can be twice as effective in raising domestic output growth if its major trading partners also have a stimulus package."[†]

Strauss-Kahn noted that some countries had more room to manoeuvre than others. "We believe that those countries—advanced and emerging economies—with the strongest fiscal policy frameworks, the best ability to finance fiscal expansion, and the most clearly sustainable debt should take the lead."

Over the next few months, most countries indeed adopted discretionary measures, aimed at either increasing private or public spending. For the G20 as a whole, discretionary measures added up to about 2.3% of GDP in 2009. Some countries, with less fiscal room, such as Italy, did less. Some countries, such as the United States or France, did more.

Canada was in a very odd situation relative to most G20 countries. In fiscal year 2007–08, the federal government was in surplus; in fiscal year 2008–09, there was a small deficit. Canada was a country with a lot of room to manoeuvre, in Strauss-Kahn's language. However, on November 27, 2008, in his November Economic Update after the G20 meeting in which Canada participated, Finance Minister Flaherty indicated the government would take action to "restrain spending" and "return quickly to balanced budgets." This ignored the advice of the G20 meeting held two weeks earlier. At that time, the Conservative government held a minority of seats in Parliament.

The Economic Update faced certain defeat in the House of Commons, which would have resulted in an election. Prime Minister Harper prorogued Parliament, effectively putting off the vote of confidence on the Update. On January 27, 2009, just two months after announcing spending restraints and a rapid return to balanced budgets, the same finance minister joined in with the G20 plan and announced the first Economic Action Plan in the Budget. That Budget presented a substantial increase in spending and a substantial reduction in taxes with the consequent deficit.

> "We are not acting alone," said Minister Flaherty. "These actions fulfill Canada's commitments to its global partners at the G20 leaders' summit to provide timely stimulus to domestic demand, while maintaining long-run fiscal sustainability.[†]

The January 2009 Budget with its fiscal stimulus passed through the minority Parliament.

Were the Canadian and world fiscal stimulus packages successful? Some have argued that they were not: After all, the world economy had large negative growth in 2009. The issue here is one of counterfactuals. What would have happened in the absence of the stimulus? Many believe that, absent the fiscal stimuli, growth would have been even more negative, perhaps catastrophically so. Counterfactuals are hard to prove or disprove, and thus the controversy is likely to go on. (On the issue of counterfactuals and the difference between economists and politicians, here is a very nice quote from U.S. congressman Barney Frank: "Not for the first time, as an elected official, I envy economists. Economists have available to them, in an analytical approach, the counterfactual. Economists can explain that a given decision was the best one that could be made, because they can show what would have happened in the counterfactual situation. They can contrast what happened to what would have happened. No one has ever gotten re-elected where the bumper sticker said, 'It would have been worse without me.' You probably can get tenure with that. But you can't win office.")[†]

Were these fiscal stimuli dangerous? Some have argued that they have led to a large increase in debt, which is now forcing governments to adjust, leading to a fiscal contraction and making recovery more difficult. This argument is largely misplaced. Most of the increase in debt does not come from the discretionary measures that were taken, but from the decrease in revenues that came from the decrease in output during the crisis. And a number of countries, although not Canada, were running large deficits before the crisis. It remains true, however, that this large increase in debt is now making it more difficult to use fiscal policy to help the recovery.

For more discussion at the time, see "Financial Crisis Response: IMF Spells Out Need for Global Fiscal Stimulus," *IMF Survey Magazine Online*, December 29, 2008. (http://www.imf.org/external/pubs/ft/survey/so/2008/int122908a.htm)

---

[†]IMF Managing Director Dominique Strauss-Kahn Calls G-20 Action Plan Significant Step toward Stronger International Cooperation," Press Release No. 08/286, November 15, 2008, International Monetary Fund
[†]Budget 2009: Canada's Economic Action Plan," Ottawa, January 27, 2009, 2009–011, Department of Finance Canada
[†]U.S. Congressman Barney Frank

# 7-4 | Depreciation, the Trade Balance, and Output

Suppose the Canadian government takes policy measures that lead to a depreciation of the dollar. Up to this point in the chapter, we have held the real exchange rate constant. (We shall see in Chapter 8 how it can do so using monetary policy; for the moment, we assume that government can simply choose the exchange rate.)

Recall that the real exchange rate is given by:

$$\epsilon \equiv \frac{EP^*}{P}$$

The real exchange rate, $\epsilon$ (the price of foreign goods in terms of domestic goods), equals the nominal exchange rate, $E$ (the price of foreign currency in terms of domestic currency), times the foreign price level, $P^*$, divided by the domestic price level, $P$. Under our maintained assumption that the price levels are given, a nominal depreciation is thus reflected one for one in a real depreciation. More concretely, if the Canadian dollar depreciates vis-à-vis the American dollar by 5% (a 5% nominal depreciation), and if the price levels in Canada and the United States do not change, Canadian goods will be 5% cheaper compared with American goods (a 5% real depreciation).

Let us now ask what the effects of this real depreciation will be on the Canadian trade balance and on Canadian output.

A look ahead: In Chapter 14, after we understand the adjustment of the price level, we will have a second look at the effects of a nominal depreciation. We will see that a nominal depreciation leads to a real depreciation in the short run but not in the medium run.

## Depreciation and the Trade Balance: The Marshall–Lerner Condition

Return to the definition of net exports:

$$NX \equiv X - \epsilon Q$$

Replace $X$ and $Q$ by their expressions from equations (7.2) and (7.3):

$$NX = X(Y^*, \epsilon) - \epsilon Q(Y, \epsilon)$$

As the real exchange rate $\epsilon$ enters in three places, this equation makes clear that the real depreciation—an increase in $\epsilon$—affects the trade balance through three channels.

If the Canadian dollar depreciates vis-à-vis the American dollar by 5%, Canadian goods will be cheaper in the United States, leading to a larger volume of Canadian exports to the United States.

▶ 1. *X increases.* The real depreciation makes Canadian goods relatively cheaper abroad, leading to an increase in foreign demand for Canadian goods—an increase in Canadian exports.

American goods will be more expensive in Canada, leading to a smaller volume of imports of American goods to Canada.

▶ 2. *Q decreases.* The real depreciation makes foreign goods relatively more expensive in Canada, leading to a shift in domestic demand toward domestic goods, to a decrease in the quantity of imports.

American goods will be more expensive, leading to a higher import bill for a given volume of imports of American goods to Canada.

▶ 3. *The relative price of foreign goods, $\epsilon$, increases.* This tends to increase the import bill, $\epsilon Q$. The same quantity of imports now costs more to buy (in terms of domestic goods).

For the trade balance to improve following a depreciation, exports must increase enough and imports must decrease enough to compensate for the increase in the price of imports. The condition under which a real depreciation leads to an increase in net exports is known as the **Marshall–Lerner condition**. (The condition is named for the two economists, Alfred Marshall and Abba Lerner, who stated it first.) It is derived formally in this chapter's appendix. It turns out—with a caveat, which we will state when we introduce dynamics later in this chapter—that this condition is satisfied in reality. So, for the rest of this book, we will assume that an increase in $\epsilon$, a real depreciation, leads to an increase in net exports.

## The Effects of a Depreciation

We have looked so far only at the *direct* effects of a depreciation on the trade balance, that is, the effects *given Canadian and foreign outputs*. But the effects do not end there. The change in net exports changes domestic output, which affects net exports further.

Because the effects of a real depreciation are very much like those of an increase in foreign output, we can use Figure 7–4, the same figure that we used to show the effects of an increase in foreign output earlier.

Just like an increase in foreign output, a depreciation leads to an increase in net exports (assuming, as we do, that the Marshall–Lerner condition holds), at any level of output. Both the demand relation (ZZ in Figure 7–4a) and the net exports relation (NX in Figure 7–4b) shift up. The equilibrium moves from A to A'; output increases from Y to Y'. By the same argument we used earlier, the trade balance improves: The increase in imports induced by the increase in output is smaller than the direct improvement in the trade balance induced by the depreciation.

To summarize: The depreciation leads to a shift in demand, both foreign and domestic, toward domestic goods. This leads, in turn, both to an increase in domestic output and to an improvement in the trade position.

Although a depreciation and an increase in foreign output each have the same effect on domestic output and the trade balance, there is a subtle but important difference between the two. A depreciation works by making foreign goods relatively more expensive. But this means that given their income, people—who now have to pay more to buy foreign goods because of the depreciation—are worse off. This mechanism is strongly felt in countries that undergo a major depreciation. Governments that try to achieve a major depreciation often find themselves with strikes and riots, as people react to the much higher prices of imported goods. This was the case in Mexico, where the large depreciation of the peso in 1994–1995 (from 3.44 pesos per U.S. dollar in November 1994 to 5.88 pesos per dollar in May 1995) led to a large decline in workers' living standards and to strong social tensions. A more recent example is that of Indonesia in 1998.[2] A depreciation of the Canadian dollar makes purchases of American goods and services more expensive. Winter trips to Florida and Hawaii are important parts of Canadian purchases of U.S. goods and services.

## Combining Exchange-Rate and Fiscal Policies

Suppose a government wants to reduce the trade deficit without changing the level of output. A depreciation alone will not do: It will reduce the trade deficit, but it also will increase output. Nor will a fiscal contraction do: It will reduce the trade deficit, but it will decrease output. What should that government do? The answer is to use the right combination of depreciation and fiscal contraction. Figure 7–5 shows what this combination should be.

The initial equilibrium in Figure 7–5(a) is at $A$, associated with output $Y$. The trade deficit is given by the distance $BC$ in Figure 7–5(b). If government wants to eliminate the trade deficit without changing output, it must do two things:

- First, it must achieve a depreciation sufficient to eliminate the trade deficit at the initial level of output. So, the depreciation must shift the net exports relation from $NX$ to $NX'$ in Figure 7–5(b). But this depreciation, and the associated increase in net exports, also shifts the demand relation in Figure 7–5(a) from $ZZ$ to $ZZ'$. In the absence of other measures, the equilibrium would move from $A$ to $A'$, and output would increase from $Y$ to $Y'$.
- Second, to avoid the increase in output, government must reduce government spending so as to shift $ZZ'$ back to $ZZ$. This combination of a depreciation and a fiscal contraction leads to the same level of output and an improved trade balance.

There is a general point behind this example. To the extent that governments care about *both* the level of output and the trade balance, they have to use *both* fiscal and exchange-rate policies. We just saw one such combination. Table 7–1 shows others, depending on the initial output and trade situation. Take, for example, the case represented in the top-right corner of the table. Initial output is too low (put another way, the unemployment rate is too high), and the economy has a trade deficit. A depreciation will help on both the trade and the output fronts: It reduces the trade deficit and increases output. But there is no reason for the depreciation to achieve both the right increase in output and the elimination of the trade deficit. Depending on the initial situation and the relative effects of the depreciation on output and the trade balance, government may need to complement the depreciation with either an increase or a decrease in government spending. This ambiguity is captured by the question mark in the box. Make sure that you understand the logic behind each of the other three cases.

[2] **DIGGING DEEPER**. There is an alternative to strikes and riots: asking for and obtaining an increase in wages. But if wages increase, presumably the prices of domestic goods will increase as well, leading to a smaller real depreciation. To discuss this mechanism, we need to look at the supply side in more detail than we have done so far. We return to the dynamics of depreciation, wage movements, and price movements in Chapter 14.

FIGURE  7–5

**Reducing the Trade Deficit without Changing Output**

To reduce the trade deficit without changing output, government must achieve a depreciation and decrease government spending.

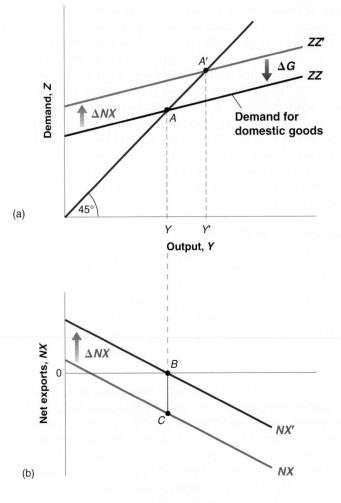

(a)

(b)

| TABLE | 7–1 | Exchange Rate and Fiscal Policy Combinations | |
|---|---|---|---|
| **Initial Conditions** | | **Trade Surplus** | **Trade Deficit** |
| Low output | | $\epsilon$ ? $G\uparrow$ | $\epsilon\uparrow$ $G$? |
| High output | | $\epsilon\downarrow$ $G$? | $\epsilon$ ? $G\downarrow$ |

## 7-5 | Looking at Dynamics: The J-Curve

We have ignored dynamics so far in this chapter. It is time to reintroduce them. The dynamics of consumption, investment, sales, and production we discussed in Chapter 3 are as relevant to the open economy as they were to the closed economy. But there are additional dynamic effects as well, which come from the dynamics of exports and imports. We focus on these effects here.

Return to the effects of the exchange rate on the trade balance. We argued earlier that a depreciation leads to an increase in exports and to a decrease in imports. But these effects do not happen overnight. Think of the dynamic effects of, say, a 5% depreciation of the Canadian dollar. In the first few months following the depreciation, the effect of the deprecia-tion is likely to be reflected much more in prices than in quantities. The price of imports to

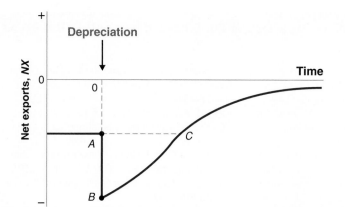

FIGURE    7–6

**The J-Curve**

A real depreciation leads initially to a deterioration and then to an improvement of the trade balance.

Canada goes up, the price of Canadian exports abroad goes down.[3] But the quantities of imports and exports are likely to adjust slowly: It takes a while for consumers to realize that relative prices have changed, it takes a while for firms to shift to cheaper suppliers, and so on. Thus, a depreciation may well lead to an initial deterioration of the trade balance; $\epsilon$ increases, but neither $X$ nor $Q$ adjusts very much initially, leading to a decline in net exports $(X - \epsilon Q)$.

As time passes, the effects of the change in the relative prices of both exports and imports become stronger. Exports increase, and imports decrease. If the Marshall–Lerner condition eventually holds—and we have argued that it does—the response of exports and imports eventually becomes stronger than the adverse price effect, and the eventual effect of the depreciation is to improve the trade balance.

> The response of the trade balance to the real exchange rate:
> Initially:
> $(X,Q)$ unchanged, $\epsilon \uparrow \Rightarrow$
> $(X - \epsilon Q) \downarrow$
> Eventually:
> $(X \uparrow, Q \downarrow, \epsilon \uparrow) \Rightarrow$
> $(X - \epsilon Q) \uparrow$

Figure 7–6 captures this adjustment by plotting the evolution of the trade balance against time in response to a real depreciation. The trade deficit before the depreciation is $OA$. The depreciation initially *increases* the trade deficit to $OB$: $\epsilon$ goes up, but neither $Q$ nor $X$ changes right away. Over time, exports increase and imports decrease, reducing the trade deficit. Eventually, the trade balance improves beyond its initial level; this is what happens from point $C$ on in the figure. Economists refer to this adjustment process as the **J-curve** because—admittedly, with a bit of imagination—the curve in the figure resembles a "J": first down, then up.

The importance of the effects of the real exchange rate on the trade balance can be seen from the evidence: Figure 7–7 plots the Canadian trade balance against the real exchange rate from 1970 to 2012. As we saw in the last chapter, the period from 1987 to 1991 was one of sharp real appreciation and the period from 1992 to 2002 one of sharp real depreciation, followed by a dramatic trend real appreciation since 2002. There is a strange and very hard to explain nearly 10% real depreciation from 2008 to 2009 and an even larger real appreciation from 2009 to 2010 as part of the trend real appreciation from 2002 to 2012. Figure 7–7 shows that there is a strong relationship between the real exchange rate and net exports. When the Canadian dollar experiences a real depreciation, net exports rise. When the Canadian dollar experiences a real appreciation, net exports fall. In the case of Canada, the J-curve related lags seem quite short and it is very clear that the real exchange rate is an important macroeconomic variable. The Focus Box "Was the Canadian Recession in 2009 Caused by a Fall in

---

[3]**DIGGING DEEPER**. The price of imported goods may not go up by 5%, however. The price would go up 5% if importers adjusted their dollar price fully for the dollar depreciation. To keep their market share, or because they are committed under previous contracts to deliver at a given dollar price, importers may decide instead to pass along only part of the dollar depreciation and take a reduction in their profit margins. This is what we observe in practice: Whereas import prices respond to a depreciation, they respond less than one for one. The same logic applies to the prices of exports. We stay away from these complications here.

The chapter opened asking if recessions in Canada were usually caused by recessions in the rest of the world. In this box, we look at the evidence specific to the 2009 recession. Look at the first column of Table 1. That column shows GDP growth in Canada in each year from 2007 to 2010. The recession is obvious. GDP growth in Canada is negative in 2009.

Even before the 2009 recession, Canadian real GDP growth drops by 1 percentage point between 2007 and 2008. The table shows that some of this decline in growth is due to the decline in net exports. Net exports decline from 2.1 percent of GDP to 1.7 percent of GDP. The reduction in net exports occurs in spite of a large depreciation of the real exchange rate. Thus in 2008 there are two opposite effects on net exports: the depreciation of the Canadian dollar and a decline in U.S. real GDP. The United States is by far the largest customer for Canadian exports and it is certain that the decline in U.S. real GDP would reduce the demand for Canadian exports. The J-curve makes it more complicated to be certain that a depreciation of the Canadian dollar would have an immediate impact on the trade balance. However as pointed out in the text, the lags in the effect of a real depreciation on Canada may well be shorter than for other rich countries.

After falling by 0.3 percentage points in 2008, U.S. real GDP then falls by a further 3.1 percentage points in 2009. This is the world economic crisis. Remember that, for Canada, the United States is a large portion of the world. It is not surprising that Canadian net exports swing from PLUS 1.7 percent of GDP in 2008 to NEGATIVE 1.5 percent of GDP in 2009. Part of that swing would clearly be attributed to the large decline in American real GDP. A further portion of the swing could easily be attributed to both the continued trend appreciation of the real exchange rate from 2007 through to 2010 as well as a very large and sudden real appreciation of the Canadian dollar from 2008 to 2009.

Separating these two effects in a precise way is difficult. Note that in 2010, net exports from Canada to the United States continue to decline even as American GDP growth turns positive. The Canadian dollar experienced a further real appreciation from 2009 to 2010.

The conclusion: There is lots of evidence that the primary cause of the 2009 recession in Canada was the recession in the United States. Many economists would also suggest that a real appreciation of the Canadian dollar of almost 10 percentage points from 2007 to 2010 also played a role in reducing net exports over that period.

**TABLE   1**

| Year | GDP Growth in Canada (percent) | GDP Growth in the United States (percent) | Net exports from Canada (percent of GDP) | Real exchange rate (index) |
|------|-------------------------------|-------------------------------------------|------------------------------------------|----------------------------|
| 2007 | 2.1 | 1.9 | 2.1 | 1.07 |
| 2008 | 1.1 | −0.3 | 1.7 | 1.15 |
| 2009 | −2.8 | −3.1 | −1.5 | 1.03 |
| 2010 | 3.2 | 2.4 | −1.9 | 0.97 |

Source: Data from Canadian Real GDP: CANSIM Variable V62305752; United States Real GDP: Variable GDPC1, Federal Reserve Bank of St. Louis FRED database; Net exports and real exchange rate see Figure 7–7.

This effect is sometimes an issue in the developing countries. International organizations, such as the International Monetary Fund or the World Bank, recommend a devaluation to improve economic conditions. When the improvement is slow due to the J-curve, this can lead to considerable political unrest and a tendency to blame the international organizations involved. ▶

Net Exports?" further explores the relationships between the real exchange rate and net exports as they pertain to the cause of the 2009 recession in Canada. However, for other countries, particularly the United States, the slow effect of a real exchange rate change on trade is an important policy constraint.

In general, the statistical evidence on the dynamic relation among exports, imports, and the real exchange rate suggests that in rich countries, a real depreciation eventually leads to a trade balance improvement. But it also suggests that this process may take some time, typically between six months and a year. These lags have implications not only for the effects of a depreciation on the trade balance but also for the effects of a depreciation on output. If a depreciation initially decreases net exports, it also initially exerts a contractionary effect on output. Thus, if a government relies on a depreciation to both improve the trade balance and expand domestic output, the effects will go the "wrong" way for a while.

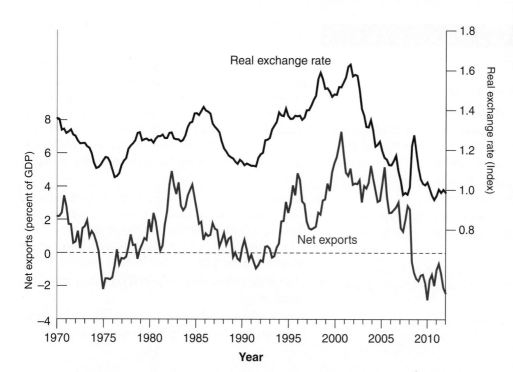

FIGURE 7-7

**The Real Exchange Rate and the Ratio of Net Exports to GDP in Canada, 1970–2012**

The level of the real exchange rate has a powerful influence on net exports. A real depreciation increases net exports, and a real appreciation reduces net exports. Net exports are measured as a percent of GDP. The appreciation after 2002 did reduce net exports.

Source: Real exchange rate index see Figure 6–6. Net exports as a percent of GDP: from 1970 to 1980, CANSIM variables (V498103–V498106)/V498086; from 1981 to 2012, (V62305776–V62305779)/V62305783.

## SUMMARY

- In an open economy, the demand for domestic goods is equal to the domestic demand for goods (consumption plus investment plus government spending) minus imports plus exports.

- An increase in domestic demand leads to a smaller increase in output in an open economy than in a closed economy because some of the additional demand falls on imports. It also leads to a deterioration of the trade balance.

- An increase in foreign demand leads, as a result of increased exports, to an increase in domestic output and an improvement in the trade balance.

- Because increases in foreign demand improve the trade balance and increases in domestic demand worsen it, countries may be tempted to wait for increases in foreign demand to move them out of a recession. When a group of countries is in recession, coordination can help them get out of it.

- If the Marshall–Lerner condition is satisfied—and econometric evidence suggests that it is—a real depreciation leads to an improvement in net exports.

- The typical response of the trade balance to a real depreciation is first a deterioration and then an improvement. This adjustment process is known as the J-curve.

## KEY TERMS

- coordination, 134
- demand for domestic goods, 126
- domestic demand for goods, 126
- G-8, 134
- J-curve, 139
- marginal propensity to import, 133
- Marshall–Lerner condition, 136

## 1. TRUE/FALSE/UNCERTAIN

**a.** Trade deficits generally reflect high investment.

**b.** Budget deficits cause trade deficits.

**c.** It is much easier for the government of a small open economy to maintain output at a given level than for the government of a large closed economy.

**d.** The only way a country can eliminate a trade surplus is through an appreciation of its currency.

**e.** A small open economy can reduce its trade deficit through fiscal contraction at a smaller cost in output than can a large economy.

**f.** If the trade deficit is equal to zero, the domestic demand for goods and the demand for domestic goods are the same.

**g.** The Canadian dollar experienced a real depreciation from 2002 to 2012.

## 2. REAL EXCHANGE RATES AND THE BALANCE OF TRADE

**a.** Using the definition of the real exchange rate, verify that the following is true (you may want to use propositions 7 and 8 of Appendix 2 at the end of the book):

$$\frac{\Delta \epsilon}{\epsilon} = \frac{\Delta E}{E} + \frac{\Delta P^*}{P^*} - \frac{\Delta P}{P}$$

**b.** If domestic inflation is higher than foreign inflation but the domestic country has a fixed exchange rate, what happens to net exports over time? Assume that the Marshall–Lerner condition holds. If needed, read the appendix. Explain in words.

## 3. COORDINATION AND FISCAL POLICY

Consider the following open economy. The real exchange rate is fixed and equal to one. Consumption, investment, government spending, and taxes are given by:

$$C = 10 + 0.8(Y - T) \quad I = 10 \quad G = 10 \quad T = 10$$

Imports and exports are given by:

$$Q = 0.3Y \quad X = 0.3Y^*$$

where an asterisk denotes a foreign variable.

**a.** Solve for equilibrium income in the domestic economy, given $Y^*$. What is the multiplier in this economy? If we were to close the economy (so that exports and imports were equal to zero), what would the multiplier be? Why are the two multipliers different?

**b.** Assume the foreign economy has the same equations as the domestic economy (remove the asterisk from all the variables with an asterisk, and add an asterisk to all the variables without an asterisk). Use the two sets of equations to solve for the equilibrium income of each country. What is the multiplier for each country now? Why is it different from the open economy multiplier above?

**c.** Assume both countries have a target level of output of 125. What is the increase in $G$ necessary in either of these countries, assuming that the other country does not change $G$, to achieve target output? Solve for net exports and the budget deficit in each country.

**d.** What is the common increase in $G$ necessary to achieve target output?

**e.** Why is fiscal coordination (such as the common increase in $G$ in (d) difficult to achieve in practice?

## 4. A U.S. RECESSION AND THE CANADIAN ECONOMY

**a.** The share of American spending on Canadian goods is about 80% of Canadian exports, which are themselves equal to about 40% of GDP. What is the share of American spending on Canadian goods relative to Canadian GDP?

**b.** Assume the multiplier in Canada is 2 and that a recession in the U.S. has reduced output by 5% (relative to its natural level). U.S. imports are about 10% of U.S. GDP. What is the impact of the U.S. slowdown on Canadian GDP?

**c.** If the U.S. recession also leads to a slowdown of the other economies that import goods from Canada, the effect could be larger. Assume exports to all countries fall by 5% (of themselves). What is the impact on the Canadian GDP?

**d.** Comment on the following statement from an economist on television: "Unless the U.S. recovers from recession quickly, growth will grind to a halt in Canada."

## 5. DYNAMICS OF A DEPRECIATION

Consider an economy with a fixed exchange rate. Assume that the price level is fixed.

**a.** What is the effect of a depreciation on equilibrium income and trade balance in the first six months after the depreciation?

**b.** What is the effect of the depreciation on equilibrium income and trade balance after the first six months?

## 6. EXPORT RATIOS

Look at a recent issue of the *International Financial Statistics,* published monthly by the IMF. Find the list of countries in the table of contents. Make a list of five countries you would expect to have high ratios of exports to GDP. Then, go to the page corresponding to each country, and find the numbers for exports and for GDP for the most recent year available. (Make sure that you are comparing exports and GDP measured in the same units—either domestic currency or dollars. If one variable is in domestic currency and the other variable is in dollars, use the exchange rate to convert the two to the same currency.) Compute the export ratios. How good were your guesses?

---

## APPENDIX

# DERIVATION OF THE MARSHALL–LERNER CONDITION

Start from the definition of net exports, $NX \equiv X - \epsilon Q$, and assume trade to be initially balanced so that $X = \epsilon Q$. The Marshall–Lerner condition is the condition under which a real depreciation, an increase in $\epsilon$, leads to an increase in net exports.

To derive this condition, consider an increase in the real exchange rate of $\Delta \epsilon$. The change in the trade balance thus is given by:

$$\Delta NX = \Delta X - \epsilon \Delta Q - Q \Delta \epsilon$$

The first term on the right ($\Delta X$) gives the change in exports, the second ($\epsilon \Delta Q$) the real exchange rate times the change in the quantity of imports, and the third ($Q \Delta \epsilon$) the quantity of imports times the change in the real exchange rate.

Divide both sides of the equation by $X$ to get:

$$\frac{\Delta NX}{X} = \frac{\Delta X}{X} - \frac{\epsilon \Delta Q}{X} - \frac{Q \Delta \epsilon}{X}$$

Use the fact that $\epsilon Q = X$ to replace $\epsilon / X$ by $1/Q$ in the second term on the right and to replace $Q/X$ by $1/\epsilon$ in the third term on the right. This substitution gives:

$$\frac{\Delta NX}{X} = \frac{\Delta X}{X} - \frac{\Delta Q}{Q} - \frac{\Delta \epsilon}{\epsilon}$$

This equation says that the change in the trade balance in response to a real depreciation, normalized by exports, is equal to the sum of three terms. The first is the proportional change in exports, $\Delta X/X$, induced by the real depreciation. The second term is equal to minus the proportional change in imports, $-\Delta Q/Q$, induced by the real depreciation. The third term is equal to minus the proportional change in the real exchange rate, $-\Delta \epsilon/\epsilon$, or equivalently, minus the rate of real depreciation.

The Marshall–Lerner condition is the condition that the sum of these three terms be positive. If it is satisfied, a real depreciation leads to an improvement in the trade balance.

A numerical example will help here. Suppose that a 1% depreciation leads to a relative increase in exports of 0.9% and to a relative decrease in imports of 0.8%. (Econometric evidence on the relation of exports and imports to the real exchange rates suggests that these are, indeed, reasonable numbers.) In that case, the right-hand side of the equation is equal to 0.9% − (−0.8%) − 1% = 0.7%. Thus, the trade balance improves: The Marshall–Lerner condition is satisfied.

# Output, the Interest Rate, and the Exchange Rate

## The Core: The Short Run

In Chapter 7, we treated the exchange rate as one of the policy instruments available to government. But the exchange rate is not a policy instrument. Rather, it is determined in the foreign-exchange market—a market where, as we saw in Chapter 6, there is an enormous amount of trading. This fact raises two obvious questions: What determines the exchange rate? How can government affect it?

These are the questions that motivate this chapter. More generally, we examine the implications of equilibrium in both the goods and financial markets, including the foreign-exchange market. This allows us to characterize the joint movements of output, the interest rate, and the exchange rate in an open economy. The model we develop is an extension of the open economy of the *IS-LM* model we saw in Chapter 5 and is known as the **Mundell–Fleming model**, after the two economists Robert Mundell and Marcus Fleming, who first put it together in the 1960s. (The model presented here keeps the spirit but differs in its details from the original Mundell–Fleming model.)

Sections 8-1 and 8-2 look at equilibrium in the goods and financial markets, respectively. Section 8-3 puts the two equilibrium conditions together and looks at the determination of output, the interest rate, and the exchange rate. Section 8-4 looks at the role of policy under flexible exchange rates, and section 8-5 does the same under fixed exchange rates.

# 8-1 | Equilibrium in the Goods Market

Equilibrium in the goods market was the focus of Chapter 7, where we derived the following equilibrium condition:

$$Y = C(Y - T) + I(Y, i) + G - \epsilon Q(Y, \epsilon) + X(Y^*, \epsilon)$$

$$( + ) \quad (+,-) \qquad (+,-) \qquad (+,+)$$

For the goods market to be in equilibrium, output (the left side of the equation) must be equal to the demand for domestic goods (the right side of the equation).

Demand, in turn, is equal to consumption plus investment plus government spending minus imports plus exports. Consumption depends positively on disposable income. Investment depends positively on output and negatively on the interest rate. Government spending is taken as a given. The volume of imports depends positively on output and negatively on the real exchange rate. Exports depend positively on foreign output and positively on the real exchange rate.

It will be convenient in what follows to regroup the last two terms under "net exports," defined as exports minus imports, $X - \epsilon Q$:

$$NX(Y, Y^*, \epsilon) \equiv X(Y^*, \epsilon) - \epsilon Q(Y, \epsilon)$$

It follows from our assumptions about imports and exports that net exports depend on domestic output, foreign output, and the real exchange rate. An increase in domestic output increases imports and thus decreases net exports. An increase in foreign output increases exports, thus increasing net exports. An increase in $\epsilon$—a real depreciation—leads (under the Marshall–Lerner condition, which we will assume to hold throughout this chapter) to an increase in net exports.

Using this definition of net exports, we can rewrite the equilibrium condition as:

$$Y = C(Y - T) + I(Y, i) + G + NX(Y, Y^*, \epsilon) \tag{8.1}$$

$$( + ) \quad (+, -) \qquad (-, +, +)$$

For our purposes, the essential implication of equation (8.1) is the dependence of demand, and so of equilibrium output, on both the interest rate and the real exchange rate:

- An increase in the interest rate leads to a decrease in investment spending, and so to a decrease in the demand for domestic goods. This leads, through the multiplier, to a decrease in output.
- An increase in the exchange rate—a real depreciation—leads to a shift in demand toward domestic goods, and thus an increase in net exports. The increase in net exports increases demand and output.

In writing (8.1), we have assumed that the domestic price level, $P$, is fixed in the short run. We make a similar assumption about the foreign price level in the short run so that $P^*$ is fixed. Extending this assumption to the foreign price level means the real exchange rate ($\epsilon = EP^*/P$) and the nominal exchange rate ($E$) move together. A nominal depreciation leads, one for one, to a real depreciation. If for notational convenience, we choose $P$ and $P^*$ so that $P = P^* = 1$ (and we can do so because they are index numbers), then $\epsilon = E$ and we can replace $\epsilon$ by $E$ in equation (8.1).

With these simplifications, equation (8.1) becomes:

$$Y = C(Y - T) + I(Y, i) + G + NX(Y, Y^*, E) \tag{8.2}$$

Equilibrium output in the goods market depends on both the nominal interest rate and the nominal exchange rate in the short run.

> Goods-market equilibrium condition (*IS*): Output = Demand for domestic goods.

> A reminder: A real depreciation is represented by an increase in the real exchange rate—an increase in the price of foreign goods in terms of domestic goods.

> Simplification:
> $P = P^* = 1$, so $\epsilon = E$

## 8-2 | Equilibrium in Financial Markets

When we looked at financial markets in the *IS-LM* model, we assumed that people chose between only two financial assets: money and bonds. Now that we look at a financially open economy, we must allow for a second choice—the choice between domestic bonds and foreign bonds. Let us consider each choice in turn.

### Money versus Bonds

When looking at the determination of the interest rate in the *IS-LM* model, we wrote the condition that the supply of money be equal to the demand for money as:

$$\frac{M}{P} = Y\, L(i) \tag{8.3}$$

We took the real supply of money (the left side of equation [8.3]) as a given. We assumed that the real demand for money (the right side of equation [8.3]) depended on the level of transactions in the economy, measured by real output (*Y*), and on the opportunity cost of holding money rather than bonds, the nominal interest rate on bonds (*i*).

How should we change this characterization now that the economy is open? The answer is not very much, if at all.

In an open economy, the demand for domestic money is still mostly a demand by domestic residents. There is not much reason for, say, Canadians to hold American currency or American dollar–denominated demand deposits. They cannot use them for transactions in Canada, which require payment in Canadian money. If they want to hold American dollar-denominated assets, they are better off holding U.S. bonds, which at least pay a positive interest rate. And the demand for money by domestic residents still depends on the same factors as before: their level of transactions, that we proxy by domestic real output, and the opportunity cost of holding money, the nominal interest rate on bonds.[1]

Therefore, we can still use equation (8.3) to think about the determination of the nominal interest rate in an open economy. The interest rate must be such that the supply and the demand for money are equal. An increase in money supply leads to a decrease in the interest rate. An increase in money demand, say, as a result of an increase in output, leads to an increase in the interest rate.

### Domestic Bonds versus Foreign Bonds

In looking at the choice between domestic bonds and foreign bonds, we will rely on the assumption we introduced in Chapter 6: Financial investors, domestic or foreign, go for the highest expected rate of return. This implies that in equilibrium, both domestic bonds and foreign bonds must have the same expected rate of return; otherwise, investors would be willing to hold only one or the other, but not both, and this could not be an equilibrium.

Like most economic relations, the interest rate parity relation is only an approximation to reality and does not always hold exactly. There is further discussion of extreme situations where interest rate parity breaks down in the Focus box "Sudden Stops, Safe Havens, and the Limits to the Interest Rate Parity Condition." However, the rest of this chapter makes use of the interest rate parity condition written as:

Recall from Chapter 6 that this is only an approximation (but a good one). For notational convenience, we replace the earlier approximation symbol ($\approx$) with an equal sign (=).

$$i_t = i_t^* + \frac{E_{t+1}^e - E_t}{E_t}$$

[1] **DIGGING DEEPER.** Given that domestic residents can now hold both domestic and foreign bonds, the demand for money should depend on the expected rates of return on both domestic and foreign bonds. But our next assumption—interest parity—implies that these two expected rates of return are equal so that we can write the demand for money directly as we did in equation (8.3).

The domestic interest rate $i_t$ must be equal to the foreign interest rate $i_t^*$ plus the expected rate of depreciation of the domestic currency $(E_{t+1}^e - E_t)/E_t$.

For now, we will take the expected future exchange rate as given and denote it as $\overline{E}^e$ (we will relax this assumption in Chapters 14 and 20). Under this assumption, and dropping time indexes, the interest rate parity condition becomes:

$$i = i^* + \frac{\overline{E}^e - E}{E} \tag{8.4}$$

Multiplying both sides by $E$, bringing the terms in $E$ to the left side, and dividing both sides by $(1 + i - i^*)$ give the current exchange rate as a function of the expected future exchange rate and the domestic and foreign interest rates:

$$E = \frac{\overline{E}^e}{1 + i - i^*} \tag{8.5}$$

Equation (8.5) implies a negative relation between the domestic interest rate and the exchange rate. Given the expected future exchange rate and the foreign interest rate, *an increase in the domestic interest rate leads to a decrease in the exchange rate—equivalently, to an appreciation of the domestic currency. A decrease in the domestic interest rate leads to an increase in the exchange rate—to a depreciation.*

◀ An increase in the domestic interest rate leads to an appreciation of the domestic currency. An increase in the foreign interest rate leads to a depreciation of the domestic currency.

---

## FOCUS    Sudden Stops, Safe Havens, and the Limits to Interest Rate Parity Condition

The interest rate parity condition assumes that financial investors care only about expected returns. We all know that investors care not only about expected returns, but also about risk and about liquidity—how easy it is to buy or sell the asset. Much of the time, we can ignore these other factors. Sometimes, however, these factors play a big role in investors' decisions and in determining exchange rate movements.

This is an issue that many emerging countries know well. Perceptions of risk play an important role in the decision of large foreign investors, such as pension funds, to invest or not invest in a country. Sometimes, the perception that risk has decreased leads many foreign investors to simultaneously buy assets in the country. Sometimes, the perception that risk has increased leads the same investors to want to sell all the assets they have in the country, no matter what the interest rate. These selling episodes, which have affected many Latin American and Asian emerging economies, are known as **sudden stops**. During these episodes, the interest parity condition fails, and the exchange rate may decrease a lot, without much change in domestic or foreign interest rates.

Indeed, the start of the crisis in 2008 and 2009 was associated with large capital movements which had little to do with expected returns. Worried about uncertainty, many investors from advanced countries decided to take their funds home, where they felt safer. The result was large capital outflows from a number of emerging countries, leading to strong downward pressure on their exchange rates and serious financial problems: This is best shown in Figure 1, which plots the net flows from funds that invest in emerging market bonds (figure on top) and in emerging market stocks (figure on bottom) from January 2010 to August 2011. What you should take from Figure 1 is the volatility of these net flows: This volatility is not primarily due to movements in interest rates, either in advanced or in emerging countries, but to fluctuations in perceived uncertainty.

A symmetrical phenomenon is at play in some advanced countries. Because of their characteristics, some countries are seen as particularly attractive by investors. This is the case for the United States and, to a lesser degree, Canada.

Even in normal times, there is a large foreign demand for U.S. T-bills by world investors. The reason is the size and the liquidity of the U.S. T-bill market: One can sell or buy large quantities of T-bills quickly and without moving the price very much.

In crisis times, the preference for U.S. T-bills becomes even stronger. The United States is widely seen by investors as being a **safe haven**, a country in which it is safe to move funds. The result is that times of higher uncertainty are often associated with a stronger demand for U.S. assets and thus upward pressure on the dollar. At the beginning of the crisis, the U.S. dollar experienced a large appreciation. There is some irony here, given that the crisis originated in the United States. A large real appreciation would further reduce the demand for American exports.

Indeed, some economists wonder how long, given the large budget deficits that it is running, the United States will continue to be perceived as a safe haven. If this were to change, the dollar would depreciate and be expected to depreciate. Using interest rate parity, this would lead U.S. interest rates to be higher than interest rates in the rest of the world.

Interest rate parity is a tool to understand monetary policy in "normal" times. This box reminds us that risk and perceptions of risk can play an important role in the determination of interest rates and exchange rate in "abnormal" times.

*(continued)*

**FURTHER READING**

Among the countries affected by large capital outflows in 2008 and 2009 were also a number of small advanced countries, notably Ireland and Iceland. These two countries had experienced the changes in the banking system that we will discuss in Chapter 11. Thus the world economic crisis hit these countries as hard as it hit the United States. A very good and easy-to-read discussion can be found in Michael Lewis's chapters on Ireland and Iceland in *Boomerang: Travels in a New Third World*, (Norton 2011).

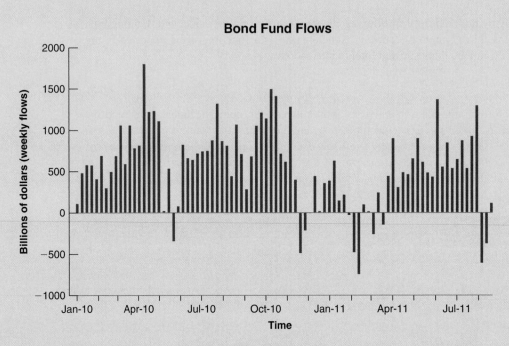

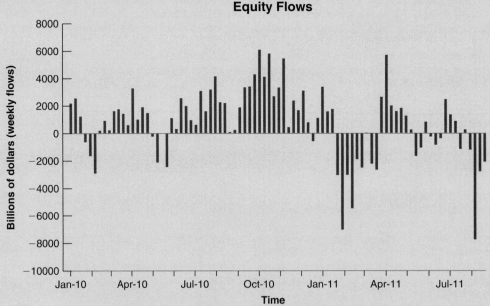

**FIGURE 1    The Volatility of Capital Flows to Emerging Countries since January 2010**

Capital flows have been very volatile during the crisis, reflecting mostly changes in perceived uncertainty.

*Source:* Data from International Monetary Fund

This relation between the exchange rate and the domestic interest rate plays a central role in the real world and will play a central role in the rest of this chapter. To understand it further, think about the sequence of events that takes place in financial and foreign exchange markets after an increase in the Canadian interest rate above the American interest rate:

- Suppose that, to start with, the Canadian and American interest rates are equal so that $i = i^*$. This implies, from equation (8.5), that the current exchange rate equals the expected future exchange rate: $E = E^e$.
- Suppose, as a result of a Canadian monetary contraction, the Canadian interest rate increases. At an unchanged exchange rate, Canadian bonds become more attractive, so financial investors want to shift out of American bonds and into Canadian bonds. To do so, they must sell American bonds for American dollars, then sell American dollars for Canadian dollars, and then use the Canadian dollars to buy Canadian bonds. As investors sell American dollars and buy Canadian dollars, the Canadian dollar appreciates.
- That an increase in the Canadian interest rate leads to an appreciation of the Canadian dollar is intuitively straightforward: An increase in the demand for Canadian dollars leads to an increase in the price of Canadian dollars. What is less intuitive is *by how much* the Canadian dollar must appreciate. The important point here is that if financial investors do not change their expectation of the future exchange rate, then *the more the Canadian dollar appreciates today*, the more investors expect it to *depreciate in the future* (as they expect it to return to the same value in the future). Other things being equal, this expectation makes American dollar bonds more attractive: When the Canadian dollar is expected to depreciate, a given rate of return in American dollars means a higher rate of return in Canadian dollars.
- This gives us the answer: The initial Canadian dollar appreciation must be such that the expected future depreciation compensates for the increase in the Canadian interest rate. When this is the case, investors are again indifferent, and equilibrium prevails.

A numerical example will help. Assume one-year Canadian and American interest rates are both equal to 4%. Suppose the Canadian interest rate now increases to 10%. The Canadian dollar will appreciate by 6% today. Why? Because if the Canadian dollar appreciates by 6% today and investors do not change their expectation of the exchange rate one year ahead, the Canadian dollar is now expected to depreciate by 6% over the coming year. Put the other way, the American dollar is expected to appreciate by 6% relative to the Canadian dollar over the coming year so that holding American bonds yields an expected rate of return of 10%—the 4% rate of return in U.S. dollars plus the expected 6% appreciation of the U.S. dollar. Holding Canadian bonds or holding American bonds both yield an expected rate of return of 10% in Canadian dollars. Financial investors are willing to hold either one, so there is equilibrium in the foreign exchange market. In terms of equation (8.4):

$$i = i^* + \frac{\bar{E}^e - E}{E}$$
$$10\% = 4\% + 6\%$$

Make sure you understand the three steps in the argument: (1) The one-year interest rate on Canadian bonds increases by 6%. Investors then buy Canadian bonds and Canadian dollars. (2) The Canadian dollar appreciates until it is expected to depreciate by 6% during the coming year. (3) This happens when the Canadian dollar has appreciated today by 6%.

The rate of return from holding Canadian dollar bonds (the left side) is equal to 10%. The expected rate of return from holding American dollar bonds, expressed in Canadian dollars, (the right side) is equal to the U.S. interest rate, 4%, plus the expected depreciation of the Canadian dollar, 6%.

Figure 8–1 plots the relation between the (domestic) interest rate and the exchange rate implied by equation (8.5)—the interest parity relation. It is drawn for a given expected future exchange rate, $\bar{E}^e$, and a given foreign interest rate, $i^*$. The lower the interest rate, the higher the exchange rate: The relation is thus drawn as a downward-sloping curve. Equation (8.5)

FIGURE    8–1

**The Relation between the Interest Rate and the Exchange Rate Implied by Interest Parity**

A lower domestic interest rate leads to a higher exchange rate—to a depreciation of the domestic currency. A higher domestic interest rate leads to a lower exchange rate—to an appreciation of the domestic currency.

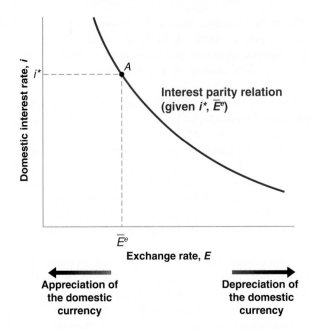

*Domestic interest rate, i*

$i^*$ — — — — $A$

**Interest parity relation (given $i^*$, $\bar{E}^e$)**

$\bar{E}^e$

**Exchange rate, E**

← **Appreciation of the domestic currency**

→ **Depreciation of the domestic currency**

What happens to the curve if ▶ $i^*$ increases? If $\bar{E}^e$ increases?

also implies that when the domestic interest rate is equal to the foreign interest rate, the exchange rate is equal to the expected future exchange rate: When $i = i^*$, then $E = \bar{E}^e$. This point is denoted $A$ in the figure.[2]

## 8-3 | Putting Goods and Financial Markets Together

We now have all the elements we need to understand the movements of output, the interest rate, and the exchange rate.

Goods–market equilibrium implies that output depends on, among other factors, the interest rate and the exchange rate:

$$Y = C(Y - T) + I(Y, i) + G + NX(Y, Y^*, E)$$

The interest rate is determined by the equality of money supply and money demand:

$$\frac{M}{P} = Y L(i)$$

And the interest parity condition implies a negative relation between the domestic interest rate and the exchange rate:

$$E = \frac{\bar{E}^e}{1 + i - i^*}$$

[2]**DIGGING DEEPER.** The argument in this text relies heavily on the assumption that when the interest rate changes, the expected exchange rate remains unchanged. This implies that an appreciation today (a decrease in the current exchange rate) leads to an expected depreciation in the future (as the exchange rate is expected to return to the same, unchanged value). We will relax the assumption that the future exchange rate is fixed in Chapter 20. But the two basic conclusions will remain: (1) An increase in the domestic interest rate leads to an appreciation. (2) An increase in the foreign interest rate leads to a depreciation.

Together, these three relations determine output, the interest rate, and the exchange rate. Working with three relations is not very easy. But we can easily reduce them to two by using the interest parity condition to eliminate the exchange rate in the goods-market equilibrium relation. Doing this gives us the following two equations, the open-economy versions of our old *IS* and *LM* relations:

*IS*:
$$Y = C(Y - T) + I(Y, i) + G + NX\left(Y, Y^*, \frac{\bar{E}^e}{1 + i - i^*}\right)$$

*LM*:
$$\frac{M}{P} = Y L(i)$$

Take the *IS* relation first, and consider the effects of an increase in the interest rate on output. An increase in the interest rate now has two effects:

- The first, which was already present in a closed economy, is the direct effect on investment. A higher interest rate leads to a decrease in investment, and so to a decrease in the demand for domestic goods and a decrease in output.
- The second, which is present only in the open economy, is the effect through the exchange rate. An increase in the domestic interest rate leads to an appreciation of the domestic currency. The appreciation, which makes domestic goods more expensive relative to foreign goods, leads to a decrease in net exports, and thus to a decrease in the demand for domestic goods and a decrease in output.

Both effects work in the same direction: An increase in the interest rate decreases demand directly, and also indirectly through the adverse effect of the appreciation. Note that the multiplier is smaller than in the closed economy. This is because part of demand falls on foreign goods rather than all on domestic goods.

The *IS* relation between the interest rate and output is drawn in Figure 8–2(a) for given values of all the other variables in the relation—namely, *T*, *G*, $Y^*$, $i^*$, and $\bar{E}^e$. The *IS* curve is downward sloping: An increase in the interest rate leads to a decrease in output. It looks very much the same as in the closed economy, but it hides a more complex relation than before: The interest rate affects output not only directly but also indirectly through the exchange rate.

An increase in the interest rate leads, both directly and indirectly (through the exchange rate), to a decrease in output.

The *LM* relation is exactly the same as in the closed economy. The *LM* curve is upward sloping. For a given value of the real money stock, (*M/P*), an increase in output leads to an increase in the demand for money and to an increase in the equilibrium interest rate.

Equilibrium in the goods and financial markets is attained at point *A* in Figure 8–2(a), with output level *Y* and interest rate *i*. The equilibrium value of the exchange rate cannot be read directly from the graph. But it is easily obtained from Figure 8–2(b), which replicates Figure 8–1 and gives the exchange rate associated with a given interest rate. The exchange rate associated with the equilibrium interest rate *i* is equal to *E*.

To summarize: We have derived the *IS* and the *LM* relations for an open economy. The *IS* curve is downward sloping: An increase in the interest rate leads directly, and indirectly through the exchange rate, to a decrease in demand and a decrease in output. The *LM* curve is upward sloping: An increase in income increases the demand for money, requiring an increase in the equilibrium interest rate. Equilibrium output and the equilibrium interest rate are given by the intersection of the *IS* and the *LM* curves. Given the foreign interest rate and the expected future exchange rate, the equilibrium interest rate determines the equilibrium exchange rate.

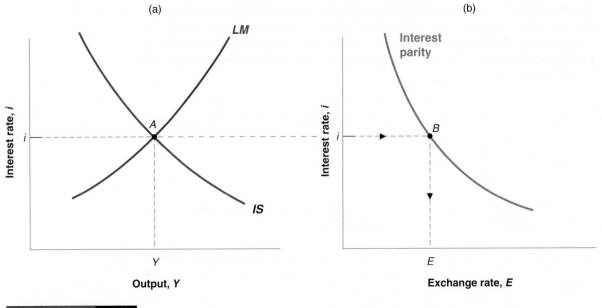

(a)                                    (b)

**FIGURE 8-2**

**The *IS-LM* Model in the Open Economy**

An increase in the interest rate reduces output both directly and indirectly (through the exchange rate): The *IS* curve is downward sloping. Given the real money stock, an increase in income increases the interest rate: The *LM* curve is upward sloping.

## 8-4 | The Effects of Policy in an Open Economy

Having derived the *IS-LM* model for the open economy, we can now put it to use and look at the effects of policy.

### The Effects of Fiscal Policy in an Open Economy

Let us look again at a change in government spending. Suppose that starting from budget balance, government decides to increase infrastructure spending and thus to run a budget deficit. What happens to the level of output and to its composition? To the interest rate? To the exchange rate?

The answers are given in Figure 8–3(a): The economy is initially at point *A*. An increase in government spending from *G* to *G'* increases output at a given interest rate, shifting the *IS* curve to the right, from *IS* to *IS'*. Because government spending does not enter the *LM* relation, the *LM* curve does not shift. The new equilibrium is at point *A'*, with a higher level of output and a higher interest rate. As shown in Figure 8–3(b), the higher interest rate leads to a decrease in the exchange rate—an appreciation of the domestic currency. Thus, *an increase in government spending leads to an increase in output, an increase in the interest rate, and an appreciation.*

In words: An increase in government spending leads to an increase in demand, leading to an increase in output. As output increases, so does the demand for money, leading to upward pressure on the interest rate. The increase in the interest rate, which makes domestic bonds more attractive, also leads to an appreciation of the domestic currency. Both the higher interest rate and the appreciation decrease the domestic demand for goods, offsetting some of the effect of government spending on demand and output.

> An increase in government spending shifts the *IS* curve to the right. It shifts neither the *LM* curve nor the interest parity curve.

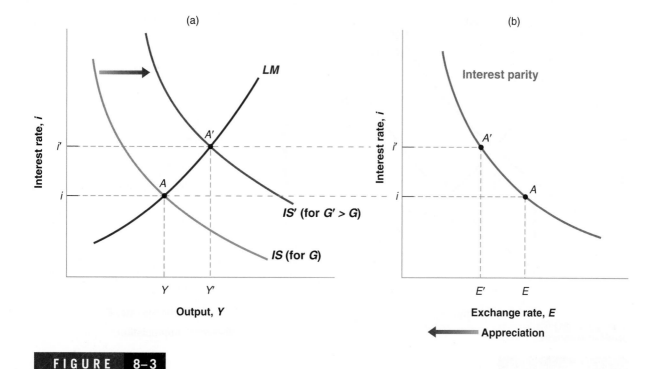

(a)                                                      (b)

FIGURE    8-3

**The Effects of an Increase in Government Spending**

An increase in government spending leads to an increase in output, an increase in the interest rate, and an appreciation.

Can we tell what happens to the various components of demand?

- Clearly, both consumption and government spending go up—consumption goes up because of the increase in income, and government spending goes up by assumption.
- What happens to investment is ambiguous. Recall that investment depends on both output and the interest rate: $I = I(Y, i)$. On the one hand, output goes up, leading to an increase in investment. But on the other, the interest rate also goes up, leading to a decrease in investment. Depending on which of these two effects dominates, investment can go up or down.
- Recall that net exports depend on domestic output, foreign output, and the exchange rate: $NX = NX(Y, Y^*, E)$. Thus, both the appreciation and the increase in output combine to decrease net exports: The appreciation decreases exports and increases imports, and the increase in output increases imports further. The budget deficit leads to a deterioration of the trade balance. If trade is balanced to start with, then the budget deficit due to the increase in G leads to a trade deficit.

> The effect of a change in government spending on investment was ambiguous in the closed economy; it remains ambiguous in the open economy.

> *Note:* Although an increase in the budget deficit increases the trade deficit, the effect is far from mechanical. It works through the effect of the budget deficit on output and on the exchange rate.

## The Effects of Monetary Policy in an Open Economy

The effects of our other favourite policy experiment, a monetary contraction, are shown in Figure 8–4. At a given level of output, a decrease in the money stock, from $M/P$ to $M'/P$, leads to an increase in the interest rate: The *LM* curve in Figure 8–4(a) therefore shifts up, from *LM* to *LM'*. Because money does not directly enter the *IS* relation, the *IS* curve does not shift. The equilibrium moves from point *A* to point *A'*. The increase in the interest rate leads to an appreciation of the domestic currency (Figure 8–4b).

Thus, *a monetary contraction leads to a decrease in output, an increase in the interest rate, and an appreciation*. The story is easy to tell. A monetary contraction leads to an increase

> A monetary contraction shifts the *LM* curve up. It shifts neither the *IS* curve nor the interest parity curve.

> Can you tell what happens to consumption, investment, and net exports?

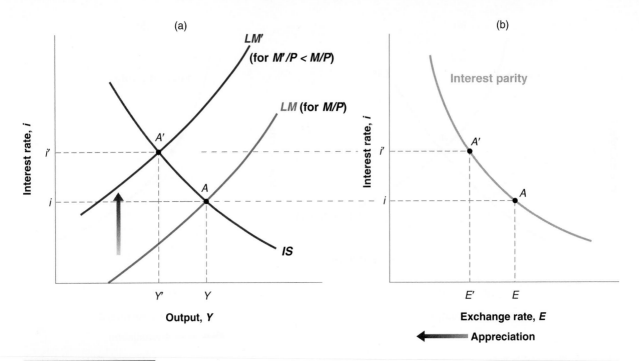

(a)

LM′
(for M′/P < M/P)

LM (for M/P)

Interest rate, i

i′ — — — — A′

i — — — — A

IS

Y′  Y

Output, Y

(b)

Interest parity

Interest rate, i

i′ — — — — A′

i — — — — A

E′  E

Exchange rate, E

◀ Appreciation

## FIGURE 8–4

**The Effects of a Monetary Contraction**

A monetary contraction leads to a decrease in output, an increase in the interest rate, and an appreciation.

That these experiments were instructive for economists does not imply they were good for the Canadian economy. How costly the large budget deficits have turned out to be is taken up ▶ in Chapter 25.

in the interest rate, making domestic bonds more attractive and triggering an appreciation. The higher interest rate and the appreciation both decrease demand and output. As output decreases, money demand decreases, leading to a decrease in the interest rate, offsetting some of the initial increase in the interest rate and some of the initial appreciation.

How well do the implications of this model fit the facts? To answer, one could hardly design a better experiment than the sharp monetary contraction in Canada from 1988 to 1991. This is described in the Focus box "Monetary Contraction in Canada, 1989–1992." The Mundell–Fleming model and its predictions pass with flying colours.

## FOCUS  Monetary Contraction in Canada, 1989–1992

From 1988, the Bank of Canada decided to engage in a sharp monetary contraction. Its goal was to reduce inflation. We will consider that issue in detail in Chapters 9 through 13 when we adapt the *IS-LM* model to allow prices to adjust slowly. However, the monetary contraction is a "textbook example" of the effects of tight monetary policy in an open economy. Table 1 walks us through these effects.

First, the Bank of Canada policy was effective. Growth in real GDP declined sharply in 1989 and again in 1990. Growth in real GDP was negative 2% in 1991, the most severe recession in Canada since the Great Depression of the 1930s. With a lag of one year, the unemployment rate in Canada increased sharply. In both 1991 and 1992, more than 1 in 10 Canadians in the labour force were unemployed. What caused demand for Canadian-produced goods and services to fall?

The Bank of Canada raised interest rates from 9.4% in 1988 to over 12% in both 1989 and 1990. This reduced investment. It also generated a very large real appreciation of the Canadian dollar. The increase in Canadian interest rates was much larger than the increase in American interest rates. The gap between Canadian and American interest rates was 5.3% in 1990.

The real exchange rate appreciation greatly reduced Canada's net exports. Net exports of goods and services were 1.2% of GDP, a large surplus in 1987. Canada usually has a trade surplus. But in 1991 and 1992 (you can see a small J-curve effect in these data), Canada's trade balance was negative.

Monetary policy is a powerful tool to affect aggregate demand and output in an open economy. Canada, from 1990 to 1992, provides an excellent example of this fact.

| TABLE 1 | Some Major Canadian Macroeconomic Variables, 1987–1992 | | | | | |
|---|---|---|---|---|---|---|
| | **1987** | **1988** | **1989** | **1990** | **1991** | **1992** |
| GDP growth (%) | 4.0 | 4.8 | 2.5 | 0.3 | −2.0 | 1.0 |
| Unemployment rate (%) | 8.8 | 7.8 | 7.5 | 8.1 | 10.3 | 11.2 |
| Canadian interest rate (%) | 8.2 | 9.4 | 12.0 | 12.8 | 8.8 | 6.5 |
| American interest rate (%) | 5.8 | 6.7 | 8.1 | 7.5 | 5.4 | 3.4 |
| Interest rate differential (%) | 2.4 | 2.7 | 3.9 | 5.3 | 3.4 | 3.1 |
| Real exchange rate | 1.33 | 1.21 | 1.16 | 1.15 | 1.14 | 1.21 |
| Trade surplus (Trade deficit if negative) as a % of GDP | 1.2 | 0.8 | 0.0 | 0.1 | −0.6 | −0.4 |

*Sources:* Data from Real GDP growth using CANSIM II variable V3862685; unemployment rate using CANSIM II variable V159752; Canadian one-year Treasury bill rate using CANSIM II; *U.S. one-year Treasury bill rate* using Federal Reserve Board variable RIFSGFSM03_N.M.; *real exchange rate:* Nominal exchange rate using CANSIM II variable V37426; United States GDP deflator using CANSIM II variable V122054/V149258; Canada GDP deflator using CANSIM II variable V498918/V1992259; *trade surplus* using CANSIM II variables (V646954–V646957)/V646937.

# 8-5 | Fixed Exchange Rates

We have assumed so far that the central bank chose money supply and let the exchange rate adjust in whatever manner was implied by equilibrium in the foreign-exchange market. In many or even most countries, this assumption does not reflect reality: Central banks act under implicit or explicit exchange-rate targets and use monetary policy to achieve those targets. The targets are sometimes implicit, sometimes explicit; they are sometimes specific values, sometimes bands or ranges. These exchange-rate arrangements come under many names. Let us first see what these various names mean.

## Pegs, Crawling Pegs, Bands, the EMS, and the Euro

At one end of the spectrum, there are geographic units, usually countries, with flexible exchange rates. These units, usually countries, have no explicit exchange-rate targets. The largest economic units in the world operate under this arrangement, including the United States, Canada, Japan, the United Kingdom, and the euro area, the collective of countries that jointly use the euro as their currency and unit of account. Although their central banks surely do not ignore movements in the exchange rate, they have shown themselves quite willing to let their exchange rates fluctuate considerably.

The euro is, of course, the reason we have to allow for geographic units sharing currencies that are not countries.

At the other end, there are countries that operate under fixed exchange rates. These countries maintain a fixed exchange rate in terms of some foreign currency. Some **peg** their currency to the U.S. dollar: The list ranges from the Bahamas to Oman. Canada pegged its currency to the U.S. from 1962 to 1970. Swaziland and Lesotho, two small countries adjacent to South Africa, peg their currencies to the South African rand. Others peg to a basket of currencies, with the weights reflecting the composition of their trade. The label "fixed" is a bit misleading: It is not the case that the exchange rates in countries with fixed exchange rates actually never change. But changes are rare. An extreme case is that of the African countries pegged to the French franc. When their exchange rates were readjusted in January 1994, this was the first adjustment in 45 years. Because these changes are rare, economists use specific words to distinguish them from the daily changes that occur under flexible exchange rates. They refer to an increase in the exchange rate under a fixed exchange rate regime as a *devaluation* rather than a depreciation and to a decrease in the exchange rate under a fixed exchange rate regime as a *revaluation* rather than an appreciation.

Recall the definition of the real exchange rate $\epsilon = EP^*/P$. If domestic inflation is higher than foreign inflation: $P$ increases faster than $P^*$. Equivalently, $P^*/P$ decreases. If the nominal exchange rate $E$ is fixed, $EP^*/P$ decreases; there is a steady real appreciation, and domestic goods become steadily more expensive relative to foreign goods.

Between these extremes are the countries with various degrees of commitment to an exchange rate target. For example, some countries operate under a **crawling peg**. The name describes it well: These countries often have inflation rates that exceed the inflation rate in the United States. Since most of these countries peg their nominal exchange rate to the U.S. dollar, the more rapid increase in their domestic price level over the U.S. price level would lead to a steady real appreciation and rapidly make their goods noncompetitive. To avoid this effect, these countries choose a predetermined rate of depreciation against the U.S. dollar. They choose to "crawl" (move slowly) vis-à-vis the U.S. dollar.

We look at the 1992 crisis in Chapter 14.

You can think of countries adopting a common currency as adopting an extreme form of fixed exchange rates: Their "exchange rate" is fixed at one to one between any pair of countries.

Yet another arrangement is for a group of countries to maintain their bilateral exchange rates (the exchange rate between each pair of countries) within some bands. The most prominent example is the **European Monetary System (EMS)**—which determined the movements of exchange rates within the European Union from 1978 to 1998. Under the rules of this **exchange rate mechanism**, or **ERM**, member countries agreed to maintain their exchange rate vis-à-vis the other currencies in the system within narrow limits or **bands** around a **central parity**. Changes in the central parity and devaluations or revaluations of specific currencies could occur, but only by common agreement among member countries. After a major crisis in 1992, which forced several countries to drop out of the EMS altogether, exchange rate adjustments became more and more infrequent, leading several countries to move one step further and adopt a common currency, the *euro*. Conversion from domestic currencies to the euro started in earnest on January 1, 1999. Full conversion was achieved in 2002. We will return to the implications of the move to the euro in Chapter 14.

We will discuss the pros and cons of different exchange regimes in Chapter 14 as well. But first, we must understand how pegging the exchange rate affects the scope for and the effects of monetary and fiscal policies. This is what we do in the rest of this chapter.

## Pegging the Exchange Rate and Monetary Control

Until now, we looked at macroeconomic policy under flexible exchange rates. We now look at policy under fixed exchange rates.

Suppose a country decides to peg its exchange rate at some chosen value, call it $\overline{E}$. How does it actually achieve this? It cannot just announce the value of the exchange rate and do nothing further. Rather, it must take measures so that the chosen exchange rate will prevail in the foreign-exchange market. Let us look at the implications and mechanics of pegging.

**Perfect capital mobility** means that there are no regulatory controls or barriers placed on the purchase of assets across borders.

Pegging or not pegging, under the assumption of perfect capital mobility, the exchange rate and the nominal interest rate, must satisfy the interest parity condition:

$$i_t = i_t^* + \frac{E_{t+1}^e - E_t}{E_t}$$

Now, suppose the country pegs the exchange rate at $\overline{E}$, so the current exchange rate $E_t = \overline{E}$. If financial and foreign exchange markets believe that the exchange rate will remain pegged at this value in the future, their expectation of the future exchange rate, $E_{t+1}^e$, is also equal to $\overline{E}$, and the interest parity relation becomes

$$i_t = i_t^* + \frac{\overline{E} - \overline{E}}{\overline{E}} = i_t^*$$

Fixing the exchange rate means giving up the freedom to choose the interest rate (which must equal the foreign interest rate).

In words: If financial investors expect the exchange rate to remain fixed, they will require the same nominal interest rate in both countries. *Under a fixed exchange rate and perfect capital mobility, the domestic interest rate must be equal to the foreign interest rate.*

This condition has one further important implication. Return to the equilibrium condition that the supply of money and demand for money be equal. Now that $i = i^*$, this condition becomes:

$$\frac{M}{P} = Y L(i^*) \tag{8.6}$$

Suppose an increase in domestic output increases the demand for money. In a closed economy, the central bank could leave the money stock unchanged, leading to an increase in the equilibrium interest rate. In an open economy, and under flexible exchange rates, the central bank can still do the same: The result will be both an increase in the interest rate and an appreciation of the domestic currency. But under a fixed exchange rate, the central bank cannot keep the money stock unchanged. If it did, the domestic interest rate would increase above the foreign interest rate, leading to an appreciation of the domestic currency. To maintain the exchange rate, it must increase the supply of money in line with the increase in the demand for money so the equilibrium interest rate does not change. Given the price level, $P$, nominal money $M$ must adjust so that equation (8.6) holds.

To summarize: *Under fixed exchange rates, the central bank gives up monetary policy as a policy instrument.* A fixed exchange rate implies a domestic interest rate equal to the foreign rate. And the money supply must adjust to maintain that interest rate.

These results depend very much on the assumption of perfect capital mobility. The case of fixed exchange rates with imperfect capital mobility, which is more relevant for middle-income countries such as those in Latin America or Asia, is treated in the appendix to this chapter.

## Fiscal Policy under Fixed Exchange Rates

If monetary policy can no longer be used under fixed exchange rates, what about fiscal policy? To answer, we use Figure 8–5.

Figure 8–5 starts by replicating Figure 8–3(a), which we used earlier to analyze the effects of fiscal policy under flexible exchange rates. In that case, we saw that a fiscal expansion shifted the *IS* curve to the right from *IS* to *IS'*. Under flexible exchange rates, the money stock remained unchanged, leading to a movement in the equilibrium from *A* to *B*, with an increase in output from $Y_A$ to $Y_B$, an increase in the interest rate, and a decrease in the exchange rate—an appreciation of the domestic currency.

However, under fixed exchange rates, the central bank cannot allow the currency to appreciate. As the increase in output leads to an increase in the demand for money, the central bank must accommodate this increased demand for money by increasing money supply. In terms of Figure 8–5, the central bank must shift the *LM* curve down as the *IS* curve shifts to the right so that the interest rate and, by implication, the exchange rate do not change. Therefore, the equilibrium moves from *A* to *C*, with higher output $Y_C$ and unchanged interest and exchange rates. Thus, under fixed exchange rates, fiscal policy is more powerful than it is under flexible exchange rates. This is because fiscal policy triggers monetary accommodation.

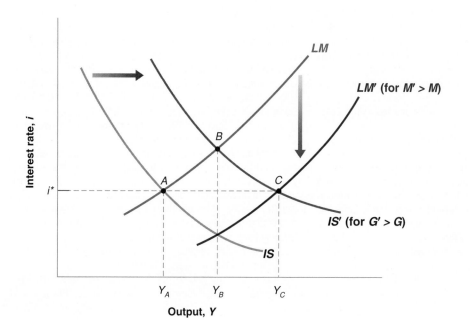

FIGURE    8–5

**The Effects of a Fiscal Expansion under Fixed Exchange Rates**

Under flexible exchange rates, a fiscal expansion increases output from $Y_A$ to $Y_B$. Under fixed exchange rates, output increases from $Y_A$ to $Y_C$.

Is the effect of fiscal policy stronger in a closed economy or in an open economy with fixed exchange rates? (*Hint:* The answer is ambiguous.) ▶

As this chapter comes to an end, a question should have started to form in your mind. Why would a country choose to fix its exchange rate? We have seen several reasons why this appears to be a bad idea:

1. By fixing the exchange rate, a country gives up a powerful tool for correcting trade imbalances or changing the level of economic activity.

2. By committing to a particular exchange rate, a country also gives up control of its interest rate. It must match movements in the foreign interest rate, at the risk of unwanted effects on its own activity. This is what happened in the early 1990s in Europe. Because of the increase in demand due to reunification, Germany felt it had to increase its interest rate. To maintain their parity with the deutschmark (DM), other countries in the European Monetary System (EMS) also were forced to increase their interest rate, something that they would rather have avoided. (This is the topic of the Focus box "German Unification, Interest Rates, and the EMS.") This tension was the cause of a major exchange rate crisis within the EMS in 1992, which we study in Chapter 14.

3. While the country retains control of fiscal policy, one policy instrument is not enough. As we saw in Chapter 7, for example, a fiscal expansion can help the economy get out of a recession, but only at the cost of a larger trade deficit. And a country that wants to decrease its budget deficit cannot, under fixed exchange rates, use monetary policy to offset the contractionary effect of its fiscal policy on output.

So, why do some countries fix their exchange rates? Why have 17 European countries adopted a common currency? To answer these questions, we must do some more work. We must look at what happens not only in the short run—which is what we did in this chapter—but also in the medium run, when the price level can adjust. Chapters 9, 10, 11, 12, and 13 allow the price level to adjust in a closed economy. Once we have done this, we will then be able to give an assessment of the pros and cons of exchange rate regimes. These are the open economy topics we return to in Chapter 14.

# FOCUS     German Unification, Interest Rates, and the EMS

Under a system of fixed exchange rates, such as the EMS (let us ignore here the degree of flexibility afforded by the bands), no individual country can change its interest rate if the others do not change theirs as well. So how do interest rates actually change? Two arrangements are possible. One is for the member countries to coordinate all changes in their interest rates. Another is for one of the countries to take the lead and for the other countries to follow—this is what happened in the EMS, with Germany as the leader.

During the 1980s, most European central banks shared similar goals and were happy to let the Bundesbank (the German central bank) take the lead. But in 1990, German unification led to a sharp divergence in goals between the Bundesbank and the other EMS nations' central banks. Both the need for large transfers to eastern Germany and an investment boom led to a large increase in demand in Germany. The Bundesbank's fear that this shift would generate too strong an increase in activity led it to adopt a restrictive monetary policy. The result was, as we saw, strong growth in Germany together with a large increase in interest rates.

This may have been the right policy mix for Germany. But for other countries, the effects of German unification were less appealing. The other countries had not experienced the same increase in demand, but to stay in the EMS, they had to match German interest rates. The net result was a sharp decrease in demand and in output in the other countries. These results are presented in Table 1, which gives nominal and real interest rates, inflation rates, and GDP growth from 1990 to 1992 for Germany and for two of its EMS partners, France and Belgium.

Note first how the high German nominal interest rates were matched by both France and Belgium. Nominal interest rates were actually higher in France than in Germany in all three years! This is because France needed higher interest rates than did Germany to maintain the DM/franc parity; the reason for this is that financial markets were not sure that France would actually keep the parity of the franc vis-à-vis the DM. Worried about a possible devaluation of the franc, they asked for a higher interest rate on French bonds than on German bonds.

Although they had to match—or, as we have just seen, more than match—German nominal rates, France and

| TABLE | 1 | German Unification, Interest Rates, and Output Growth: Germany, France, and Belgium, 1990–1992 | | | | | |
|---|---|---|---|---|---|---|---|
| | **Nominal Interest Rates** | | | **Inflation** | | | |
| | **1990** | **1991** | **1992** | **1990** | **1991** | **1992** | |
| Germany | 8.5 | 9.2 | 9.5 | 2.7 | 3.7 | 4.7 | |
| France | 10.3 | 9.6 | 10.3 | 2.9 | 3.0 | 2.4 | |
| Belgium | 9.6 | 9.4 | 9.4 | 2.9 | 2.7 | 2.4 | |
| | **Real Interest Rates** | | | **Real GDP Growth** | | | |
| | **1990** | **1991** | **1992** | **1990** | **1991** | **1992** | |
| Germany | 5.7 | 5.5 | 4.8 | 5.7 | 4.5 | 2.1 | |
| France | 7.4 | 6.6 | 7.9 | 2.5 | 0.7 | 1.4 | |
| Belgium | 6.7 | 6.7 | 7.0 | 3.3 | 2.1 | 0.8 | |

The *nominal interest rate* is the short-term nominal interest rate. The *real interest rate* is the realized real interest rate over the year—that is, the nominal interest rate minus actual inflation over the year. All rates are annual.

*Source:* Data from *OECD Economic Outlook.*

Belgium had lower inflation than Germany. The result was very high real interest rates, higher than in Germany. In both France and Belgium, average real interest rates from 1990 to 1992 were close to 7%. And in both countries, the period 1990 to 1992 was characterized by slow growth and rising unemployment. Unemployment in France in 1992 was 10.4%, up from 8.9% in 1990. Unemployment in Belgium in 1992 was 12.1%, up from 8.7%.

Although we have looked at only two of Germany's EMS partners, a similar story was unfolding for the others. Average unemployment in the European Union, which stood at 8.7% in 1990, had increased to 10.3% in 1992. The effects of high real interest rates on spending were not the only cause of this slowdown, but they were the main one.

By 1992, an increasing number of countries were wondering whether to keep defending their EMS parity or to give it up and lower their interest rates. Worried about the risk of devaluations, financial markets started to ask for higher interest rates in those countries where they thought devaluation was more likely. The result was two major exchange rate crises, one in the fall of 1992 and the other in the summer of 1993. By the end of these two crises, two countries, Italy and the United Kingdom, had left the EMS. We look at these crises, their origins and their implications, in Chapter 14.

## SUMMARY

- In an open economy, the demand for goods depends on both the interest rate and the exchange rate. A decrease in the interest rate increases the demand for goods. An increase in the exchange rate—a depreciation—also increases the demand for goods.

- The interest rate is determined by the equality of money demand and money supply. The exchange rate is determined by the interest parity condition, which states that the domestic interest rate must equal the foreign interest rate plus the expected rate of depreciation.

- Given the expected future exchange rate and the foreign interest rate, increases in the domestic interest rate lead to a decrease in the exchange rate (an appreciation), and decreases in the domestic interest rate lead to an increase in the exchange rate (a depreciation).

- Under flexible exchange rates, an expansionary fiscal policy leads to an increase in output, an increase in the interest rate, and an appreciation. A contractionary monetary policy leads to a decrease in output, an increase in the interest rate, and an appreciation.

- There are many types of exchange-rate arrangements. They range from fully flexible exchange rates to crawling pegs, to pegs, to fixed exchange rates, to the adoption of a common currency. Under fixed exchange rates, a country maintains a fixed exchange rate in terms of a foreign currency or a basket of currencies.

- Under fixed exchange rates and perfect capital mobility, a country must maintain an interest rate equal to the foreign interest rate. Thus, the central bank loses the use of monetary policy as a policy instrument. Fiscal policy becomes more powerful, however, because fiscal policy triggers monetary accommodation and thus does not lead to offsetting changes in the domestic interest rate and exchange rate.

## KEY TERMS

- bands, 156
- central parity, 156
- crawling peg, 156
- European Monetary System (EMS), 156
- exchange rate mechanism (ERM), 156
- foreign-exchange reserves, 161

- Mundell–Fleming model, 144
- peg, 155
- perfect capital mobility, 156
- safe haven, 147
- sudden stops, 147

## QUESTIONS AND PROBLEMS

**1. TRUE/FALSE/UNCERTAIN**

**a.** Because the multiplier is smaller in an open economy than in a closed economy, fiscal policy is more effective in an open economy than in a closed economy.

**b.** Monetary policy is more effective in a closed economy than in an open economy with flexible exchange rates.

**c.** If financial investors expect the exchange rate to be higher next year, interest parity implies that it will be higher today.

**d.** If financial investors expect the American dollar to depreciate vis-à-vis the yen over the coming year, one-year interest rates will be higher in the United States than in Japan.

**e.** If the Japanese interest rate is equal to zero, foreigners will not want to hold Japanese bonds.

**f.** Under fixed exchange rates, the money stock must be constant.

**2. A CURRENCY CRISIS**

**a.** Consider an economy with fixed exchange rates. Suppose that government devalues unexpectedly and that investors believe that there will be no further devaluation. What will be the effects of the devaluation on output and on the interest rate?

**b.** Suppose instead that after the devaluation investors believe that another devaluation is likely to come soon. What will be the effects of the initial devaluation on output and on the interest rate?

**3. FIXED EXCHANGE RATES AND MONETARY POLICY**

Consider a group of open economies with perfect capital mobility among them.

**a.** Assume that there is a Leader country. All other countries (referred to as the Follower countries) fix their exchange rates to the Leader country. Discuss the effectiveness of monetary policy in the Follower countries.

**b.** If all the Follower countries fix their exchange rate vis-à-vis the Leader country, is the Leader country's exchange rate not also fixed? What does this imply for the effectiveness of the Leader country's monetary policy?

**c.** If the Leader country reduces its money supply to fight inflation, what must the Follower countries do to enforce their fixed exchange rates? What is the effect on their economies? What would happen if the Follower countries did nothing?

**4. THE EFFECTS OF CHANGES IN FOREIGN VARIABLES**

Consider the *IS* and *LM* equations in section 8-3.

**a.** Show the effect of a decrease in foreign output $Y^*$ on domestic output $Y$. Explain in words.

**b.** Show the effect of an increase in the foreign interest rate $i^*$ on domestic output $Y$. Explain in words.

**c.** "A monetary contraction abroad is likely to lead to a recession at home." Discuss this statement.

**5. ELIMINATING A TRADE DEFICIT UNDER FIXED EXCHANGE RATES**

Consider a small, open *IS-LM* economy with a fixed exchange rate, where output is at its natural level but there is a trade deficit. What is the appropriate fiscal–monetary policy mix?

**6. MONETARY POLICY AND THE COMPONENTS OF GDP**

Consider a monetary expansion in an economy operating under flexible exchange rates. Discuss the effects on consumption, investment, and net exports.

---

**APPENDIX**

# FIXED EXCHANGE RATES, INTEREST RATES, AND CAPITAL MOBILITY

The assumption of perfect capital mobility is a good approximation of what happens in countries with highly developed financial markets and few capital controls, such as the United States, the United Kingdom, Japan, and Canada. But the assumption is more questionable in countries that have less developed financial markets or have a battery of capital controls in place. There, domestic financial investors may have neither the savvy nor the legal right to move easily into foreign bonds when domestic interest rates are low. The central bank may then be able both to decrease interest rates and to maintain a given exchange rate.

To look at these issues, let us start with the balance sheet of the central bank. In Chapter 4, we assumed the only asset held by the central bank was domestic bonds. In an open economy, the central bank actually holds two types of assets: (1) domestic bonds, and (2) **foreign-exchange reserves**, which we shall think of as foreign currency, although they also take the form of foreign bonds or foreign interest-paying assets. The balance sheet of the central bank is represented in Figure 8A–1. On the asset side are bonds and foreign currency reserves, and on the liability side is the monetary base. There are now two ways in which the central bank can change the monetary base: either by purchases or sales of bonds in the bond market or by purchases or sales of foreign currency in the foreign-exchange market.[†]

## Perfect Capital Mobility and Fixed Exchange Rates

Consider first the effects of an open market operation under the assumptions of perfect capital mobility and fixed exchange rates (the assumptions we made in the last section of this chapter).

- Assume that the domestic and foreign nominal interest rates are initially equal so that $i = i^*$. Suppose the central bank embarks on an expansionary open-market operation, buying bonds in the bond market in amount $\Delta B$ and creating money—increasing the monetary base—in exchange. This purchase of bonds leads to a decrease in the domestic interest rate, $i$. This is, however, only the beginning of the story.

- Now that the domestic interest rate is lower than the foreign interest rate, financial investors prefer to hold foreign bonds. To buy foreign bonds, they must first buy foreign currency. They go to the foreign exchange market and sell domestic currency for foreign currency.

- If the central bank did nothing, the price of domestic currency would fall, and the result would be a depreciation. Under its commitment to a fixed exchange rate, the central bank cannot allow the currency to depreciate. Thus, it must intervene in the foreign-exchange market and sell foreign currency for domestic currency. As it buys domestic money, the monetary base decreases.

- How much foreign currency must the central bank sell? It must keep selling until the monetary base is back to its pre–open-market operation level, so the domestic interest rate is again equal to the foreign interest rate. Only then are financial investors willing to hold domestic bonds.

How long do all these steps take? Under perfect capital mobility, all this may happen within minutes or so of the original open-market operation. After these steps, the balance sheet of the central bank looks as in Figure 8A–2. Bond holdings are up by $\Delta B$, reserves of foreign currency are down by $\Delta B$, and the monetary base is unchanged,

| Assets | Liabilities |
|---|---|
| Bonds<br>Foreign exchange<br>reserves | Monetary base |

**FIGURE 8A–1**

**Balance Sheet of the Central Bank**

---

[†]**DIGGING DEEPER**. If you have not read section 4-3 in Chapter 4, substitute "monetary base" with "money supply," and you will get the sense of the argument. If you have read that section, recall that money supply is equal to the monetary base times the money multiplier. Take the money multiplier as a given, and our conclusions about the monetary base extend straightforwardly to money supply.

| Assets | | Liabilities |
|---|---|---|
| Bonds: | $\Delta B$ | Monetary base: $\Delta B - \Delta B$ |
| Reserves: | $-\Delta B$ | = 0 |

### FIGURE 8A–2

**Balance Sheet of the Central Bank after an Open Market Operation and the Induced Intervention in the Foreign-Exchange Market**

having gone up by $\Delta B$ in the open-market operation and down by $\Delta B$ as a result of the sale of foreign currency in the foreign-exchange market.

To summarize: Under fixed exchange rates and perfect capital mobility, the only effect of the initial open-market operation is to change the *composition* of the central bank's balance sheet but not the monetary base.

### Imperfect Capital Mobility and Fixed Exchange Rates

Let us now move away from the assumption of perfect capital mobility. Suppose it takes some time for financial investors to shift between domestic and foreign bonds.

An expansionary open market operation can now initially bring the domestic interest rate below the foreign interest rate. But over time, investors shift to foreign bonds, leading to an increase in the demand for foreign currency in the foreign-exchange market. To avoid a depreciation of the domestic currency, the bank must again stand ready to sell foreign currency and buy domestic currency. Eventually, the central bank buys enough domestic currency to offset the effects of the initial open-market operation. The monetary base is back to its pre–open-market operation level, and so is the interest rate. The central bank holds more bonds and smaller reserves of foreign currency.

The difference between this case and the preceding one is that by accepting a loss in foreign-exchange reserves, the central bank is now able to decrease interest rates *for some time*. If it takes just a few days for financial investors to

adjust, the trade-off is rather unattractive—as many countries have discovered. But, if the central bank can affect the domestic interest rate for a few weeks or months, it may, in some circumstances, be willing to do so.

Now, let us move further from perfect capital mobility. Suppose, in response to a decrease in the domestic interest rate, financial investors are either unwilling or unable to move much of their portfolio into foreign bonds. This is the relevant case for many middle-income countries, from Latin America to Eastern Europe to Asia. After an expansionary open-market operation, the domestic interest rate decreases, making domestic bonds less attractive. Some domestic investors move into foreign bonds, selling domestic currency for foreign currency. To maintain the exchange rate, the central bank must buy domestic currency and supply foreign currency. However, the foreign-exchange intervention may now be small compared with the initial open-market operation. And if capital controls truly prevent investors from moving into foreign bonds at all, there may be no need at all for such an intervention.

Even leaving this extreme case aside, the net effect is likely to be an increase in the monetary base, a decrease in the domestic interest rate, an increase in the central bank's bond holdings, and some (but smaller) loss in reserves of foreign currency. With imperfect capital mobility, a country has some freedom to move the domestic interest rate while maintaining its exchange rate. Its freedom to do so depends primarily on three factors:

- The degree of development of its financial markets, and how willing domestic and foreign investors are to shift between domestic and foreign assets.
- The degree of capital controls it is able to impose on both domestic and foreign investors.
- The amount of foreign-exchange reserves it holds: The higher the amount, the more it can afford the loss in reserves it is likely to sustain if it decreases the interest rate at a given exchange rate.

# The Core: The Medium Run

The next six chapters focus on the medium run.

## Chapter 9

Chapter 9 looks at equilibrium in the labour market. It derives the natural rate of unemployment as the unemployment rate to which the economy tends to return in the medium run. Associated with the natural rate of unemployment is a natural level of output.

## Chapter 10

Chapter 10 looks at equilibrium in all three markets—goods, financial, and labour—together. It shows how, in the short run, output can deviate from its natural level and how it tends to return to this natural level in the medium run. The model developed in Chapter 10 is called the *AS-AD* model and is, like the *IS-LM* model, one of the workhorses of macroeconomics.

## Chapter 11

This chapter continues the *AS-AD* model and extends it to analyze macroeconomic outcomes and policy in 'abnormal' times. These policy issues arise from two infrequent shocks. It is good these shocks are infrequent. One shock is a large change in world oil prices. The second shock is the collapse of a financial system, either within a specific country or, as occurred in the world economic crisis of 2009, across several countries at the same time. Both types of shock make for difficult macroeconomic times and difficult policy choices.

## Chapter 12

Chapter 12 looks more closely at the relation between inflation and unemployment, a relation known as the Phillips curve. It shows that in Canada today, low unemployment leads to an increase in inflation and high unemployment to a decrease in inflation.

## Chapter 13

This chapter looks in detail at the time path of a disinflation, a policy to reduce the rate of inflation. It shows that once inflation is established, it is costly to reduce inflation. This cost of reducing inflation partly explains the strong aversion to inflation shown by central banks.

## Chapter 14

Chapter 14 focuses on the implications of fixed and flexible exchange rates in the medium run. When prices can change, the real exchange rate can change even under a fixed exchange rate regime. This may trigger a foreign exchange rate crisis. The chapter ends by discussing the pros and cons of various exchange rate regimes, including the adoption of a common currency.

# The Labour Market

## The Core: The Medium Run

Think about what happens when firms respond to an increase in demand by stepping up production:

- Higher production requires an increase in employment.
- Higher employment leads to lower unemployment.
- Lower unemployment puts pressure on wages.
- Higher wages increase production costs, forcing firms, in turn, to increase prices.
- Higher prices lead workers to ask for higher wages, and so on.

In the previous six chapters, for both closed and open economies, we ignored this sequence of events: We assumed that firms were able and willing to supply any level of output at a given price level. So long as our focus was on the *short run*, this was an acceptable simplification. As our attention turns to what happens in the *medium run*, we must now relax this assumption, explore how prices and wages adjust over time, and how this, in turn, affects the response of output. This will be our task in this and the next four chapters.

At the centre of the process described above is the *labour market*, the market in which wages and employment are determined. This chapter starts with an overview of the labour market and takes a first pass at deriving equilibrium in the labour market. In particular, it derives the central notion of the *natural rate of unemployment*. We then combine our earlier treatment of goods and financial markets with our newly acquired knowledge of the labour market. The last chapter in this section looks at an open economy in the medium run. When we are done, you will know how to think about movements in output and the price level, both in the short run and in the medium run.

# 9-1 | A Tour of the Labour Market

The total Canadian population in 2012 was 34.8 million. The relevant population available for civilian employment is the able-bodied population of working age (15 years of age or older). Specifically excluded are full-time members of the Canadian Armed Forces and inmates of institutions (penal institutions or long-term care facilities). Also excluded, for the most part because they are difficult to sample, are residents of the three territories and persons living on native reserves. Together, these excluded groups represent approximately 2% of the working-age population. In 2012, the over-15 population in Canada was 28.3 million (Table 9–1).

The **labour force**—the sum of those either working or looking for work—was, however, only 18.9 million. The other 9.4 million people were not in the labour force, neither working in the marketplace nor looking for work. (Work in the home, such as cooking or raising children, is not classified as work in official statistics. The reason is simply the difficulty of measuring these activities, not a value judgment as to what is work or not work.) The participation rate, defined as the ratio of the labour force to the noninstitutionalized population, was thus equal to 18.9/28.3 or 66.7%. The participation rate has, until recently, steadily increased over time; it stood at only 61.5% in 1976. This increase reflects the steadily increasing participation rate of women. The participation rate in 2012 is about 1 percentage point below its 2008 peak.

Of those in the labour force, 17.5 million were employed, and 1.4 million were unemployed. The unemployment rate, defined as the ratio of the unemployed to the labour force in percentage terms, was thus equal to 1.4/18.9 or 7.4%. A convenient approximation to keep in mind is that a 1% increase in the Canadian unemployment rate corresponds roughly to 180,000 more people unemployed.

These numbers tell us where people were (whether they were employed, unemployed, or not in the labour force) at one point in time—in this case, 2012. But they do not tell us what typically happens to them over time. Do those out of the labour force stay out all the time, or do they go back and forth between participation and nonparticipation? How long do the unemployed remain unemployed? How long do the employed remain employed? To answer these questions, we must turn to the evidence on flows rather than stocks.

## The Large Flows of Workers

To think further about unemployment, the following analogy will be helpful: Take an airport full of passengers. This may be because it is a busy airport with many planes taking off and landing. Many passengers are quickly moving in and out of the airport. Or it may be because bad weather is delaying flights and passengers are stuck, waiting for the weather to improve. The number of passengers in the airport may be the same in both cases, but their plight is quite different. In the same way, a given unemployment rate may reflect two very different realities. It may reflect an active labour market, with many **separations** (workers leaving or losing their jobs), many **hires**, and lots of workers entering and exiting unemployment; or it may reflect a inactive labour market, with few separations, few hires, and a stagnant unemployment pool.

| TABLE 9–1 | Population, Labour Force, Employment, and Unemployment (Millions) in Canada, 2012 |
|---|---|
| Total population | 34.8 |
| Age 15 and over | 28.3 |
| Labour force | 18.9 |
| Employed | 17.5 |
| Unemployed | 1.6 |

*Source:* Data from Statistics Canada, CANSIM II Tables 282-0002, 282-0022.

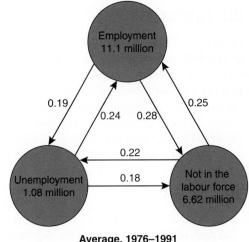

**FIGURE    9–1**

**Average Monthly Flows among Employment, Unemployment, and Nonparticipation in Canada, February 1976 to October 1991**

(1) The flows of workers into and out of employment are large. (2) The flows into and out of unemployment are large in relation to the number of unemployed. (3) There are also large flows into and out of the labour force, much of it directly to and from employment.

*Source:* See footnote 1.

**Average, 1976–1991**
**All numbers in millions.**

Finding out what reality hides behind the aggregate unemployment rate requires data on the movements of workers. Such data are available in Canada from the Labour Force Survey (LFS). Average monthly flows, computed from the LFS for Canada from 1976 to 1991, are reported in Figure 9–1.[1] (For more on the ins and outs of the LFS, see the Focus box "The Labour Force Survey.")

Figure 9–1 has three striking features:

1.  *The size of the flows into and out of employment:* The average monthly flow into employment is almost half a million: 0.24 million from unemployment plus 0.25 million from nonparticipation in the labour force. The average monthly flow out of employment is 0.47 million: 0.19 million to unemployment plus 0.28 million to nonparticipation in the labour force. Put another way, over this sample period, hires by firms and separations from firms equalled, respectively, 4.4% and 3.3% of employment *each month.*[2]

    Why are these flows so large? About half of separations (the flows from employment) are **quits**, workers leaving their jobs in search of better alternatives. The other half are **layoffs**. These come mostly from changes in employment levels across firms: The slowly changing aggregate employment numbers hide a reality of continual job destruction and job creation across firms. At any time, some firms are experiencing decreases in demand and decreasing their employment; others are experiencing increases in demand and increasing employment.

Think of it this way: Suppose the number of unemployed is constant. If each unemployed person remains unemployed for $n$ months, then it must be that a proportion $1/n$ is leaving unemployment each month (and, as the number of unemployed is constant, an equal number enters unemployment). More formally, the proportion of people leaving unemployment is the inverse of unemployment duration. Conversely, unemployment duration is the inverse of the proportion of people leaving unemployment.

2.  *The size of the flows into and out of unemployment in relation to the total number of unemployed.* The average monthly flow out of unemployment each month is 0.42 million: 0.24 million to employment plus 0.18 million to nonparticipation in the labour force. Put another way, the proportion of unemployed leaving unemployment is equal to 0.42/1.08, or 39% each month. Put yet another way, the average **duration of unemployment** is about three months.[3]

---

[1]**DIGGING DEEPER.** The data used in Figure 9–1 are taken from Stephen R.G. Jones, "Cyclical and Seasonal Properties of Canadian Gross Flows of Labour," *Canadian Public Policy,* XIX:1 (1993). This study has not been updated. Used by permission of Canadian Public Policy.

[2]**DIGGING DEEPER.** This is actually an underestimate because it excludes movements of workers directly from one job to another.

[3]**DIGGING DEEPER.** For those who know statistics: If $p$ is the probability of finding a job each month, the expected duration of unemployment is equal to $1/p$. Here, $p$ is equal to 39%, so the expected time—equivalently, the duration of unemployment—is 1/0.39, or 2.6 months.

Since its inception in 1945, the Labour Force Survey (LFS) is the main source of statistics on the labour force, employment, and participation in Canada.

The LFS has been a monthly survey since 1952. Its coverage has expanded over the years, and there were major redesigns of the survey content in 1976 and again in 1997. The most recent changes provide a number of improvements, including data on wages and union status and more detailed information on job status and hours worked. Since July 1995, a total of 54,000 households across Canada are surveyed each month; this amounts to over 100,000 respondents. The sample is not random, but it is chosen to obtain reasonably accurate estimates for different demographic groups (determined by age and gender) and at various geographic levels: national, provincial, census metropolitan areas (large cities), and employment insurance regions. The LFS follows a rotating panel design; each household stays in the survey for six months before it is replaced. From month to month, one-sixth of the survey is replaced. The initial interview is done through a personal visit, and a large amount of socio-demographic information for each person in the household is collected. Subsequent interviews are conducted by telephone. Since 1994, the data have been entered directly into a laptop computer to reduce processing time and transcription errors. A curiosity: participation in the Labour Force Survey is mandatory. Readers may recall that part of the Canadian Census was controversially changed from mandatory to voluntary in 2011.

Although the survey is conducted monthly, labour force status is determined by looking at what happened during a single week, called the **reference week**, for that month. Persons are classified as employed if they do any work at all at a job or business during the reference week (including unpaid work for a family business) or if they had a job but were away because of illness, vacation, labour dispute, or similar reasons. The concept of being unemployed is a bit fuzzier. Anyone available for work is called unemployed when he or she is (a) on a temporary layoff, (b) without work and has been actively looking for work in the past four weeks, or (c) waiting to start a job at a future date. Full-time students looking for full-time work are not included in this list. Anyone not considered employed or unemployed is deemed to be not in the labour force. The notion of "actively looking for work" is a bit loose. In the United States, the criteria require the individual to actually contact potential employers; in Canada, it is enough to check the newspaper.

This fact has an important implication. You should not think of unemployment in Canada as a stagnant pool of workers waiting indefinitely for jobs. For most of the unemployed, being unemployed is more a way-station between jobs: For the period 1976–1991, the proportion of unemployed getting a job was just over 20% (0.24/1.08) each month.

3.  *The size of the flows into and out of the labour force.* One might have expected these flows to be small, composed on one side of those finishing school and entering the labour force for the first time and on the other side of workers going into retirement. But these groups actually represent a small fraction of the total flows. The fact is that many of those classified as not in the labour force are, in fact, willing to work and move back and forth between participation and nonparticipation. The flow from nonparticipation in the labour force to employment is larger than the flow from unemployment to employment.

This fact also has an important implication. The sharp focus on the unemployment rate by economists, policy makers, and newspapers is partly misdirected. Some of those classified as not in the labour force are, in fact, very much like the unemployed; they are in effect discouraged workers, and although they are not actively looking for a job, they will take it if they find it. This is why economists sometimes focus on the **employment rate**, the ratio of employment to population, rather than the unemployment rate. We will follow tradition and focus on the unemployment rate, but keep in mind that the unemployment rate typically underestimates the number of people available for work.

## Differences across Workers

The aggregate picture is one of large flows among employment, unemployment, and nonparticipation. However, this picture conceals important differences across groups of workers. Table 9–2, based on evidence from the LFS, shows some of the differences in separation rates by age and gender, again for the period 1976–1991.

| TABLE 9–2 | Monthly Separation Rates for Different Groups, 1976–1991 |
|---|---|
| **Category** | **Monthly Separation Rate (%) (Quits and Layoffs)** |
| Young (15–24 years old) | 8.7 |
| Older (25+) | 2.9 |
| Male | 3.7 |
| Female | 4.9 |

The separation rate is defined as the monthly flow out of employment divided by the initial level of employment. The number is the average separation rate for the period 1976–1991.

*Source:* See footnote 1.

On average, 8.7% of workers aged 15 to 24 leave their jobs each month. By contrast, the rate is only 2.9% among workers aged 25 and over. Slightly more women than men leave their jobs every month, 4.9% versus 3.7%; the difference is largely due to a higher rate of going from employment to nonparticipation in the labour force. These different separation rates are reflected in different unemployment rates for the different groups. In 2012, although the average unemployment rate was 7.2%, the average unemployment rate for those aged 15–24 was 14.3%.

Where do these differences come from? Young people often hold low-paying jobs, such as the starter job at McDonalds, which are often only marginally more attractive than unemployment. Young workers have little seniority and are often the first to be laid off when a firm needs to downsize its workforce. Thus, young workers frequently move among jobs, unemployment, and nonparticipation. Middle-aged males, in contrast, tend to keep the jobs they have. This is because the jobs are typically better and because family responsibilities make it much more difficult to give up the jobs they have for a chance at a better one.

The variations in labour-market experiences reflect, in part, life-cycle considerations, with the young going from one job to the next until they eventually find one they like and settle down. But they also reflect permanent differences among workers, including education level, skill, and race. Unskilled workers, whatever their age, typically have higher unemployment rates.

These differences across jobs and workers have sometimes led macroeconomists and labour economists to model the labour market as a **dual labour market** that includes a **primary labour market**, where jobs are good, wages are high, and turnover is low, and a **secondary labour market**, where jobs are poor, wages are low, and turnover is high. This is not a distinction that we will pursue in this book.

## 9-2 | Movements in Unemployment

Let us now turn to movements in the unemployment rate over time. Figure 9–2 shows the average annual value of the unemployment rate for the years 1926 to 2012. Three different sources are cited because the methods used to count the unemployed vary slightly over time. However, the data are consistent since 1976 and reasonably consistent since 1953.

The most prominent feature of Figure 9–2 is the very high, over 20%, rate of unemployment in the 1930s, during the Great Depression. In this period, one in five Canadians was unemployed. This macroeconomic disaster led to the study of macroeconomics (see Chapter 26 for a brief discussion of Keynes). World War II ended unemployment as men and women entered the armed forces. Most economists believe that a combination of bad trade policy, bad monetary policy, and bad fiscal policy in both Europe and North America had led to the Great Depression. During the stock market turmoil of October 2008, there were frequent references to the Great Depression. We will look at the Great Depression in more detail in Chapter 11.

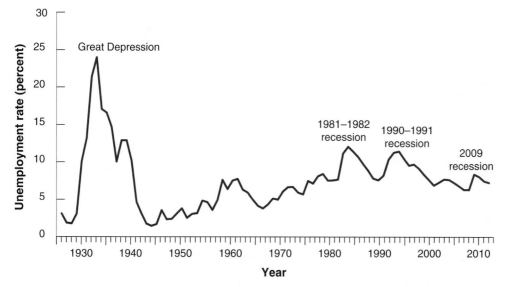

FIGURE 9-2

**Movements in the Canadian Unemployment Rate, 1926–2012**

The enormously high unemployment rate during the Great Depression of the 1930s is the most noticeable feature here. The three most recent recessions are labelled: 1981–1982; 1990–1991; and 2009. The most recent recession was less severe than the previous two recessions; unemployment did not reach double digits. Finally, there appears to be an overall upward trend in the unemployment rate since 1950.

*Source:* Data from 1926–1952 using *Historical Statistics of Canada*; 1953–1975 using CANSIM I variable D767611; 1976–2012 using CANSIM II variable V159752.

The second feature of the data in Figure 9–2 is a trend increase in the unemployment rate in Canada. On average, unemployment has been higher from 1980 to 2012 than it was from 1950 to 1960. The 1970s was a period of steadily rising unemployment. This suggests that the average rate of unemployment can change over time.

The third prominent feature of Figure 9–2 is two long periods of high unemployment associated with the 1981–1982 recession and the 1990–1991 recession. In both cases, Canadians experienced four consecutive years with unemployment rates exceeding 10%. The recession in 2009 is also labelled. Here the rise in the unemployment rate is much smaller than in the previous two recessions and, at least in Canada although not in the rest of world, shorter-lived.

How do fluctuations in the *aggregate unemployment rate* affect *individual workers*? This is an important question for two reasons. The answer determines both the effect of movements in unemployment on the welfare of workers and the effect of unemployment on wages.

Think about how firms can decrease their employment in response to a decrease in demand. They can hire fewer new workers, or they can lay off the workers they currently employ. Typically, firms prefer first to slow or stop the hiring of new workers, relying on quits and retirements to achieve a decrease in employment. But if the decrease in demand is large, this may not be enough, and firms may then have to lay off workers.

Now, think about the implications for workers, employed or unemployed. If the adjustment takes place through a decrease in hires, the effect is to decrease the chance that an unemployed worker will find a job. Fewer hires means fewer job openings; higher unemployment means more job applicants. Fewer openings and more applicants combine to make it harder for the unemployed to find jobs. If the adjustment takes place instead through higher layoffs, then the employed workers are at a higher risk of losing their jobs. In general, when firms use both margins of adjustment, the result is likely to be both a higher chance of losing a job if employed and a lower chance of finding a job if unemployed.

The first effect is clear in Figure 9–3. In recessions, a larger percentage of the unemployed fall into the category of job losers—those on permanent or temporary layoff. Figure 9–3 also shows that a recession reduces the percentage of the unemployed who voluntarily left their job—the job leavers. When times are bad, workers are less likely to leave an existing job and become unemployed.

Figure 9–3 also shows that a large percentage of the unemployed, between 30 and 50%, are persons who are either entering the labour force for the first time or re-entering the labour force. This percentage of the unemployed has risen over time. This reason for unemployment

FIGURE 9-3

**A Decomposition of Unemployment, 1976–2012**

The upper line with scaling on the right-hand axis is the unemployment rate. The three recessions each show large increases in the unemployment rate. Each of the three lower lines with the scale on the left-hand axis is the percentage of the total number of unemployed persons who became unemployed in one of three ways: through losing their job—the Job Losers; through leaving their job, the Job Leavers; or through entering or re-entering the labour force, New or Re-entrants. Recessions increase the percentage of Job Losers and reduce the percentage of Job Leavers. There is clearly an increase since the 1990s in the percentage of the unemployed who are new entrants or re-entrants to the labour force.

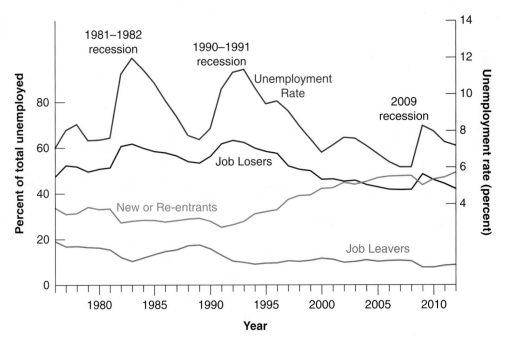

*Source:* Data from Unemployment rate—see Figure 9–2. Percentage of unemployed previous labour market status: authors' calculations from CANSIM II Table 282-0215.

also shows an effect of recessions—when the national unemployment rate is high, people will stay in school longer.

The factors discussed in Figure 9–3 combine to show the very important effect in Figure 9–4. There is a nearly exact relationship between the average level of the unemployment rate and the average length of time (called duration) a person remains unemployed. The higher the unemployment rate, the higher the average duration of unemployment.

To summarize, when the unemployment rate is high, workers are worse off in a variety of ways. If they have a job, the probability that they will lose their job is higher. Leaving a job

FIGURE 9-4

**The Unemployment Rate and the Average Duration of Unemployment, 1976–2012**

When unemployment is high, it takes a longer time for the unemployed to find a new job.

*Source:* Data from Unemployment rate, CANSIM II V2062815; Duration of Unemployment, CANSIM II V2349178

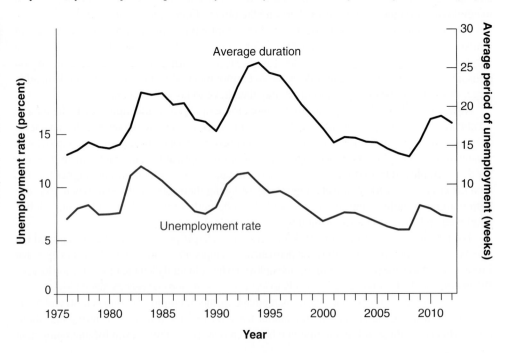

voluntarily to look for a better job is a high-risk strategy when the unemployment rate is high. Thus voluntary quits in the expectation of finding a better job fall. And the time an unemployed worker remains unemployed, whether that worker has left a job or is a new entrant to the labour force, is much longer. All of these factors combine to reduce the bargaining power of workers in the labour market.

# 9-3 | Wage Determination

Having looked at the nature of unemployment, let us turn to wage determination and to the relation between wages and unemployment.

Wages are set in many ways. Sometimes, they are set by **collective bargaining**, that is, bargaining between firms and unions. In Canada, however, collective bargaining plays a limited role, especially outside the manufacturing and public sectors. Today, between 25 and 35% of workers are covered by collective bargaining agreements. For the rest, wages are set either by employers or by individual bargaining between the employer and the employee. The higher the skills needed to do the job, the more typical is individual bargaining. Wages offered for entry-level jobs at McDonald's are on a take-it-or-leave-it basis. New college graduates can typically negotiate a few aspects of their contract. CEOs and sports stars can negotiate a lot more.

There are also large differences across countries. In the United States, less than 15% of the labour force is involved in collective bargaining. In European countries, such as Germany and France, over 90% of the paid workers have wages determined by collective bargaining, although a smaller proportion of workers are actually members of unions. Negotiations may take place at the level of the firm, at the level of industry, or at the national level. Contract agreements sometimes apply only to those firms that have signed the agreement; sometimes, they are automatically extended to all firms and all workers in the sector or the economy.

Given these differences across workers and across countries, can we hope for anything like a general theory of wage determination? Yes. Although institutional differences play a role, there are common forces at work in all countries. Two sets of facts stand out:

1. Workers are typically paid a wage that exceeds their **reservation wage**, the wage that would make them indifferent to working or becoming unemployed. In other words, most workers are paid a high enough wage that they prefer to be employed rather than unemployed.
2. Wages and wage increases typically depend on labour-market conditions: The lower the unemployment rate, the higher are the wages.

To think about these facts, economists have focused on two broad lines of explanation. The first is that even in the absence of collective bargaining, workers have some bargaining power, which they can and do use to obtain wages above their reservation wage. The second is that firms themselves may, for a number of reasons, want to pay wages higher than the reservation wage. Let us look at each explanation.

## Bargaining

How much **bargaining power** a worker has depends on two factors. The first is how easy it would be for the firm to replace him, were he to leave the firm. The second is how easy it would be for him to find another job, were he to leave the firm. The harder it is for the firm to replace him, or the easier it is for him to find another job, the stronger he will be in bargaining.

This has two implications. First, how much bargaining power a worker has depends on the nature of his job. Replacing a worker at McDonald's is not very costly; the required skills can be taught quickly, and typically a large number of willing applicants have already filled out job application forms. In this situation, the worker is unlikely to have much bargaining power. If he asks for a higher wage, the firm can lay him off and find a replacement at minimum cost. In contrast, a highly skilled worker who has proven unusually good at his job may be very difficult to replace. This gives him more bargaining power. If he asks for a higher wage, the firm may decide that it is best to give it to him.

Second, how much bargaining power workers have depends on labour market conditions. When the unemployment rate is low, it is more difficult for firms to find acceptable replacements, and it is easier for workers to find other jobs. Under such conditions, workers are in a stronger bargaining position and may be able to obtain a higher wage. Conversely, when the unemployment rate is high, finding good replacements is easier for firms, whereas finding another job is harder for workers. Being in a weaker bargaining position, workers may have no choice but to accept a lower wage.

## Efficiency Wages

Leaving aside workers' bargaining power, firms themselves may want to pay more than the reservation wage. Firms want their workers to be productive, and the wage can help them achieve that goal.

If, for example, it takes a while for workers to learn how to do a job correctly, firms will want their workers to stay. But if workers are paid just their reservation wage, they will be indifferent between staying or leaving. Many of them may quit, and turnover may be high. In such a situation, paying a wage above the reservation wage will make it financially attractive for workers to stay. It will decrease turnover and increase productivity.

Behind this example lies a more general proposition: Most firms want their workers to feel good about their jobs. Feeling good promotes good work, which leads to higher productivity. Paying a high wage is one instrument the firm can use to achieve these goals. (See the Focus box "Henry Ford and Efficiency Wages.") Economists call the theories that

## FOCUS    Henry Ford and Efficiency Wages

In 1914, Henry Ford—the builder of the most popular car in the world at the time, the Model T—made a stunning announcement. His company would pay all qualified employees a minimum of $5 a day for an eight-hour day. This was a very large salary increase for most employees, previously earning on average $2.34 for nine-hour days. Although company profits were substantial, this increase in pay was far from negligible—it represented about half of the company's profits at the time.

What Ford's motivations were is not entirely clear. Ford himself gave too many reasons for us to know which ones he actually believed. The reason was not that the company had a hard time finding workers at the previous wage. But the company clearly had a hard time retaining workers. There was a very high turnover rate as well as high dissatisfaction among workers.

Whatever the reasons behind Ford's decision, the results of the wage increase were astounding, as Table 1 shows.

The annual turnover rate (the ratio of separations to employment) plunged from a high of 370% in 1913 to a low of 16% in 1915. (An annual turnover rate of 370% means that on average 31% of the company's workers left each month, so that over the year the ratio of separations to employment was 31% × 12 ≈ 370%.) The layoff rate collapsed from 62% to nearly 0%. Other measures point in the same direction. The average rate

of absenteeism (not shown in the table), which ran at 10% in 1913, was down to 2.5% a year later. There is little question that higher wages were the main source of these changes.

Did productivity at the Ford plant increase enough to offset the cost of increased wages? The answer to this question is less clear. Productivity was much higher in 1914 than in 1913; estimates of productivity increases range from 30 to 50%. Despite higher wages, profits were also higher in 1914 than in 1913. But how much of this increase in profits was due to changes in workers' behaviour and how much was due to the increasing success of Model-T cars is harder to establish.

Although the effects support efficiency-wage theories, it may be that the increase in wages to $5 a day was excessive, at least from the point of view of profit maximization. But Henry Ford probably had other objectives as well, from keeping the unions out—which he did—to generating publicity for himself and the company—which he surely did as well.

*Source:* Dan Raff and Lawrence Summers, "Did Henry Ford Pay Efficiency Wages?" Journal of Labor Economics 1987 5 (No. 4 Part 2): pp. S57–S87. p. 119: "Did Henry Ford Pay Efficiency Wages?" by Dan Raff and Lawrence Summers from *The Journal Of Labor Economics,* 5: 4, October 1987. Copyright © 1987 University of Chicago Press.

### TABLE    1    Annual Turnover and Layoff Rates (%) at Ford, 1913–1915

|  | 1913 | 1914 | 1915 |
| --- | --- | --- | --- |
| Turnover rate | 370 | 54 | 16 |
| Layoff rate | 62 | 7 | 0.1 |

link the *productivity* or the *efficiency* of workers to the wage they are paid **efficiency wage theories**.

Like theories based on bargaining, efficiency wage theories suggest that wages depend both on the nature of the job and on labour-market conditions.

The evidence is that workers who operate more expensive machinery are typically paid more. Can efficiency wage theories explain this fact?

- Firms—such as high-tech firms—that see employees' morale and commitment as essential to the quality of their work will pay more than firms in sectors where workers' activity is more routine.
- Labour-market conditions will affect the wage. Lower unemployment makes it more attractive for employed workers to quit: Lower unemployment makes it easier to find another job. A firm that wants to avoid an increase in quits will have to counteract the effects of lower unemployment by increasing the wage it pays its workers. In short, lower unemployment will lead to higher wages.

## Wages and Unemployment

The following equation captures the main conclusions of our discussion of wage determination:

$$W = P^e F(u, z) \qquad (9.1)$$
$$(-,+)$$

where $W$, the nominal wage, depends on three factors:

- The expected price level, $P^e$.
- The unemployment rate, $u$.
- A catchall variable, $z$, that stands for all other variables that affect the outcome of wage setting.

Let us look at each factor in turn.

**The Expected Price Level.** Leave aside first the difference between the expected and the actual price level, and ask: Why does the price level affect wages? Quite simply because workers and firms care about *real wages*, not nominal wages.

- Workers care not about how many dollars they receive but about how many goods they can buy with their wages. In other words, they care about their wage in terms of goods, about $W/P$.
- In the same way, firms care not about the nominal wages they pay workers but about the nominal wages they pay in terms of the price of the output they sell. So, firms also care about $W/P$.

If both workers and firms knew that the price level was going to double, they would agree to doubling the nominal wage. This relation between the wage and the expected price level is captured in equation (9.1). A doubling in the expected price level leads to a doubling of the nominal wage chosen in wage setting.

$P^e \uparrow \Rightarrow W \uparrow$

Returning to the distinction we put aside at the start of the preceding paragraph: Why do wages depend on the *expected price level, $P^e$*, rather than the *actual price level, $P$*? Because wages are set in nominal (dollar) terms, when they are set, what the relevant price level will be is not yet known. For example, in many union contracts, nominal wages are set in advance for three years. Unions and firms have to decide what nominal wages will be over the following three years based on what they expect the price level to be over those three years. Even when wages are set by firms, or by bargaining between the firm and each worker, nominal wages are typically set for a year. If the price level goes up unexpectedly during the year, nominal wages are typically not re-adjusted. (How workers and firms form expectations of the price level will occupy us for much of the next three chapters; we leave this issue aside for the moment.)

**The Unemployment Rate.** Also affecting the aggregate wage in equation (9.1) is the unemployment rate. The minus sign under $u$ indicates that an increase in the unemployment rate *decreases* wages.

This is one of the main implications of our earlier discussion of wage determination. If we think of wages as being determined by bargaining, higher unemployment weakens workers' bargaining power, forcing them to accept lower wages. If we think of wages as being determined by efficiency wage considerations, higher unemployment allows firms to pay lower wages and still keep workers willing to work.

$u\uparrow \Rightarrow W\downarrow$

**The Other Factors.** The third variable in equation (9.1), $z$, is a catch-all variable that stands for all the factors that affect wages given the expected price level and the unemployment rate. By convention, $z$ is defined in such a way that an increase in $z$ leads to an increase in the wage—hence the plus sign under $z$. Our earlier discussion suggests a long list of such factors. For instance:

$z\uparrow \Rightarrow W\uparrow$

In most countries what Canadians call employment insurance is called unemployment insurance, that is, a system where a payment is received when you become unemployed.

- Employment insurance offers workers protection from a complete loss of income if they become unemployed. There are good reasons why society should provide at least partial insurance to workers who lose their jobs and find it difficult to find another. But there is little question that by making the prospects of unemployment less distressing, more generous benefits while you are unemployed do increase wages. To take an extreme example, suppose employment insurance did not exist. Workers would then be willing to accept very low wages to avoid being unemployed. But employment insurance does exist, and it allows unemployed workers to hold out for higher wages. In this case, we can think of $z$ as standing for the level of benefits: Higher unemployment benefits increase wages.
- Suppose the economy undergoes a period of structural change, so more jobs are created and more jobs are destroyed, leading to larger flows into and out of unemployment. This implies that at a given level of unemployment, there are more job openings and thus a better chance of finding a job while unemployed. If it is easier to get a job while unemployed, then unemployment is less of a threat to workers. At a given level of unemployment, workers are in a stronger bargaining position, and wages increase. In this case, we can think of $z$ as standing for an increase in the rate of structural change in the economy.

It is easy to think of other examples, from changes in minimum-wage legislation to changes in restrictions on firing and hiring, and so on. We will explore the implications of some of these as we go along.

## 9-4 | Price Determination

Having looked at the determination of wages given expected prices, let us now look at the determination of prices given wages.

Prices depend on costs. Costs depend on the nature of the **production function**—the relation between the inputs used in production and the quantity of output produced. We will assume that firms produce goods using labour as the only factor of production, and according to the production function:

$$Y = AN$$

where $Y$ is output, $N$ is employment, and $A$ is labour productivity. This implies that **labour productivity**—the ratio of output per worker—is constant and equal to $A$.

Using a term from microeconomics, this assumption implies *constant returns to labour in production*. If firms double the amount of labour they use, they can double the amount of output they produce.

It should be clear that this assumption is a drastic simplification of reality. Firms use other factors of production than labour. They use capital—machines and plants. They use raw materials—oil, for example. We know that there is technological progress so that labour productivity ($A$) is not constant but instead steadily increases over time. We will face these realities later. We will introduce raw materials in section 11-4 when we discuss the oil crises of the 1970s. We will focus on the role of capital and technological progress when we turn to the determination of output in the *long run* in Chapters 15 to 18. For the moment, the simple relation between output and employment will make our lives easier and still serve our purposes.

Given the assumption that labour productivity, $A$, is constant, we can make one further simplification. We can choose the units for output so that one worker produces one unit of output—so that $A = 1$. (This way we do not have to carry the letter $A$ around, and this will simplify notation.) With that choice, the production function becomes:

$$Y = N \qquad (9.2)$$

The production function $Y = N$ implies that the cost of producing one more unit of output is the cost of employing one more worker, at wage $W$. Using the terminology introduced in your microeconomics course, the marginal cost of production is equal to $W$. Marginal cost is the extra cost to a firm of producing one more unit of output. If one more unit of output is produced using one more unit of labour, and a unit of labour is paid wage $W$, then one more unit of output costs $W$. If there were perfect competition in the goods market, the price of a unit of output would be equal to marginal cost: $P$ would be equal to $W$. But many goods markets are not competitive, and firms charge a price higher than their marginal cost. A simple way of capturing this fact is to assume that firms set their price according to:

$$P = (1 + m)W \qquad (9.3)$$

where $m$ is the markup of price over cost. If goods markets were perfectly competitive, the price would simply equal the cost and $m$ would equal zero. To the extent that they are not competitive and that firms have market power, the price will be higher than the cost, and $m$ will be positive.

> If we had not put $A$ equal to 1, then to produce one unit of goods, the firm would need $1/A$ units of labour, at cost $W/A$ (the wage times the number of units of labour). Thus, $P$ would equal $(1 + m)W/A$.

## 9-5 | The Natural Rate of Unemployment

Let us now look at the implications of wage and price determination for unemployment. Let us do so under the assumption that in wage determination, nominal wages depend on the actual price level, $P$, rather than on the expected price level, $P^e$ (why we assume this will become clear soon). Under this assumption, wage setting and price setting determine the equilibrium rate of unemployment. Let us see how.

> An important assumption for the rest of the chapter: $P^e = P$.

### The Wage-Setting Relation

Given the assumption that nominal wages depend on the actual price level ($P$) rather than on the expected price level ($P^e$), equation (9.1), which characterizes wage determination, becomes

$$W = P \, F(u, z)$$

Or, dividing both sides by the price level,

$$\frac{W}{P} = F(u, z) \qquad (9.4)$$
$$(-,+)$$

Wage determination implies a negative relation between the real wage, $W/P$, and the unemployment rate, $u$: *The higher the unemployment rate, the lower is the real wage chosen by wage setters*. The intuition is straightforward: The higher the unemployment rate, the weaker the workers are in bargaining, and so the lower the real wage.

This relation between the real wage and the rate of unemployment—let us call it the **wage-setting relation**—is drawn in Figure 9–5. The real wage is measured on the vertical axis. The unemployment rate is measured on the horizontal axis. The wage-setting relation is drawn as the downward-sloping curve WS (for wage setting): The higher the unemployment rate, the lower is the real wage.

> "Wage setters" means unions and firms if wages are set by collective bargaining; it means individual workers and firms if wages are set in bilateral bargaining; it means firms if wages are set on a take-it-or-leave-it basis.

### The Price-Setting Relation

Turn now to the implications of price determination. If we divide both sides of the price-determination equation (9.3), by the nominal wage, we get:

$$\frac{P}{W} = 1 + m \qquad (9.5)$$

FIGURE    9–5

**The Wage-Setting Relation, the Price-Setting Relation, and the Natural Rate of Unemployment**

The real wage chosen in wage setting is a decreasing function of the unemployment rate. The real wage implied by price setting is constant—independent of the unemployment rate. The natural rate of unemployment is the unemployment rate such that the real wage chosen in wage setting is equal to the real wage implied by price setting.

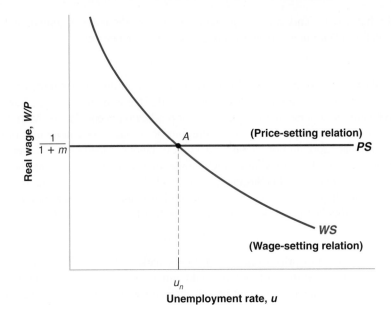

More help with the intuition: If the firm in which I work increases its markup and so increases the price of its products, my real wage does not change very much, if at all. I am still paid the same wage, and, even if one of the goods I buy is the good produced by the firm, it is at most a very small part of my consumption basket. But, if not only the firm I work for but all firms increase their markup and the price of their products, then the prices of all the goods I buy go up. My real ▶ wage goes down.

The ratio of the price level to the wage implied by the price-setting behaviour of firms equals 1 plus the markup. Now, invert both sides of this equation to get the implied real wage:

$$\frac{W}{P} = \frac{1}{1 + m} \qquad (9.6)$$

*Price-setting decisions determine the real wage paid by firms.* An increase in the markup leads firms to increase prices, given wages; equivalently, it leads to a decrease in the real wage.

The step from equation (9.5) to equation (9.6) is algebraically straightforward. But how price setting actually determines the real wage paid by firms may not be intuitively obvious. A numerical example will help. Suppose it takes one hour of work to produce one unit of output, firms pay a wage of \$10 per hour, and the firms' markup is 20%, so they sell each unit of output for \$10 × 1.2 = \$12. The real wage—how many units of the good workers can buy if they work for an hour—is 10/12 = 0.83 units of the good. If firms increase their markup to 30%, the real wage falls to 10/13 = 0.76 units. The markup determines the real wage. This is what is captured in equation (9.6).

The **price-setting relation** in equation (9.6) is drawn as the horizontal line *PS* (for price setting) in Figure 9–5. The real wage implied by price setting is constant, equal to $1/(1 + m)$, and therefore independent of the unemployment rate.

### Equilibrium Real Wages and Unemployment

Equilibrium in the labour market requires that the real wage chosen in wage setting be equal to the real wage implied by price setting. (This way of stating equilibrium may sound strange if you learned to think in terms of labour supply and labour demand in your microeconomics course. The relation between wage setting and price setting on the one hand and labour supply and labour demand on the other is closer than it looks at first and is explored further in the appendix at the end of this chapter.) In Figure 9–5, equilibrium is therefore given by point $A$, and the equilibrium unemployment rate is given by $u_n$.

We can also characterize the equilibrium unemployment rate algebraically; eliminating $W/P$ between equations (9.4) and (9.6) gives:

$$F(u_n, z) = \frac{1}{1 + m} \qquad (9.7)$$

The equilibrium unemployment rate, $u_n$, is such that the real wage chosen in wage setting—the left side of equation (9.7)—is equal to the real wage implied by price setting—the right side of equation (9.7).

The equilibrium unemployment rate ($u_n$) is called the **natural rate of unemployment** (which is why we used the subscript $n$ to denote it). The terminology has become standard, so we will adopt it, but this is actually a bad choice of words. The word "natural" suggests a constant of nature, one that is unaffected by institutions and policy. As its derivation makes clear, however, the "natural" rate of unemployment is anything but natural. The positions of the wage-setting and price-setting curves, and thus the equilibrium unemployment rate, depend on both $z$ and $u$. Consider two examples:

◀ "Natural," in *Webster's Dictionary,* means "in a state provided by nature, without man-made changes."

- *An increase in unemployment benefits.* An increase in unemployment benefits can be represented by an increase in $z$. Because an increase in benefits makes the prospect of unemployment less painful, it increases the wage set by wage setters at a given unemployment rate. So, it shifts the wage-setting relation up, from $WS$ to $WS'$ in Figure 9–6. The economy moves along the $PS$ line, from $A$ to $A'$. The natural rate of unemployment increases from $u_n$ to $u_n'$.

  In words: At a given unemployment rate, higher unemployment benefits lead to a higher real wage. A higher unemployment rate is needed to bring the real wage back to what firms are willing to pay.

- *A less stringent enforcement of existing antitrust legislation.* To the extent that this allows firms to collude more easily and increase their market power, it leads to an increase in their markup—an increase in $m$. The increase in $m$ implies a decrease in the real wage paid by firms, so it shifts the price-setting relation down, from $PS$ to $PS'$ in Figure 9–7. The economy moves along $WS$. The equilibrium moves from $A$ to $A'$, and the natural rate of unemployment increases from $u_n$ to $u_n'$.

  In words: By letting firms increase their prices, given the wage, less stringent enforcement of antitrust legislation leads to a decrease in the real wage. Higher unemployment is required to make workers accept this lower real wage, leading to an increase in the natural rate of unemployment.

An increase in unemployment benefits shifts the wage-setting curve up. The economy moves along the price-setting curve. Equilibrium unemployment increases. ◀

◀ This has led some economists to call unemployment a "discipline device." Higher unemployment is the device that returns wages to the level firms are willing to pay.

An increase in the markup shifts the price-setting curve (line in this case). The economy moves along the wage-setting curve. Equilibrium unemployment increases. ◀

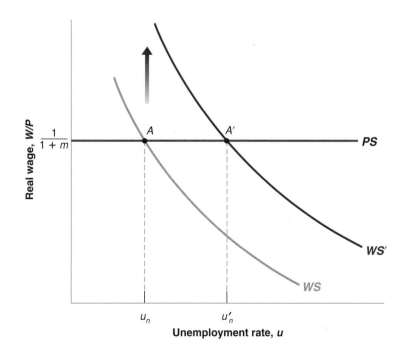

**FIGURE  9–6**

**Unemployment Benefits and the Natural Rate of Unemployment**

An increase in unemployment benefits leads to an increase in the natural rate of unemployment.

FIGURE  9-7

**Markups and the Natural Rate of Unemployment**

An increase in markups decreases the real wage and leads to an increase in the natural rate of unemployment.

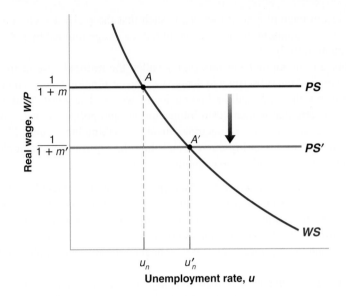

Such factors as the generosity of unemployment benefits or antitrust legislation can hardly be thought of as the result of nature. Rather, they reflect various characteristics of the structure of the economy. For that reason, a better name for the equilibrium rate of unemployment would be the **structural rate of unemployment**, but so far, the name has not caught on.

> This name has been suggested by Edmund Phelps, from Columbia University.

## From Unemployment to Employment

Associated with the natural rate of unemployment is a **natural level of employment**, the level of employment that prevails when unemployment is equal to its natural rate.

Let us review the relation among unemployment, employment, and the labour force. Let $U$ denote unemployment, $N$ denote employment, and $L$ the labour force. Then,

$$u \equiv \frac{U}{L} = \frac{L - N}{L} = 1 - \frac{N}{L}$$

The first step follows from the definition of the unemployment rate ($u$). The second follows from the fact that, from the definition of the labour force, the level of unemployment ($U$), equals the labour force ($L$), minus employment ($N$). The third step follows from simplifying the fraction. Putting all three steps together, the unemployment rate, $u$, equals one minus the ratio of employment, $N$, to the labour force, $L$.

> $L = N + U \Rightarrow U = L - N$

Rearranging to get employment in terms of the labour force and the unemployment rate gives:

$$N = L(1 - u)$$

Employment, $N$, is equal to the labour force, $L$, times one minus the unemployment rate, $u$.

So, if the natural rate of unemployment is $u_n$, and the labour force is equal to $L$, the natural level of employment, $N_n$, is given by:

$$N_n = L(1 - u_n)$$

For example, if the labour force is 30 million and the natural rate of unemployment is 5%, then the natural level of employment is 28.5 million.

## From Employment to Output

Finally, associated with the natural level of employment is the **natural level of output**, the level of production when employment is equal to the natural level of employment.

Given the production function we used in this chapter ($Y = N$), the natural level of output, $Y_n$, is easy to derive. It is given by:

$$Y_n = N_n = L(1 - u_n)$$

Using equation (9.7) and the relations among the unemployment rate, employment, and the output we just derived, the natural level of output satisfies the following equation:

$$F\left(1 - \frac{Y_n}{L}, z\right) = \frac{1}{1 + m} \tag{9.8}$$

The natural level of output ($Y_n$) is such that at the associated rate of unemployment ($u_n = 1 - Y_n/L$), the real wage chosen in wage setting—the left side of equation (9.8)—is equal to the real wage implied by price setting—the right side of equation (9.8). Equation (9.8) will turn out to be very useful in the next chapter.

We have gone through many steps in this section. Let us summarize.

Assume that the expected price level is equal to the actual price level ($P^e = P$). Then,

- The real wage chosen in wage setting is a decreasing function of the unemployment rate.
- The real wage implied by price setting is constant.
- Equilibrium in the labour market requires that the real wage chosen in wage setting be equal to the real wage implied by price setting. This determines the unemployment rate.
- This equilibrium unemployment rate is known as the natural rate of unemployment.
- Associated with the natural rate of unemployment is a natural level of employment and a natural level of output.


# 9-6 | Where Do We Go from Here?

We have just seen how the equilibrium in the labour market determines the natural rate of unemployment, which then determines the natural level of output. So, what have we been doing in the previous three chapters? If our primary goal was to understand the determination of output, why did we spend so much time looking at the goods and financial markets? What about our earlier conclusions that the level of output was determined by such factors as monetary policy, fiscal policy, consumer confidence, and so on—all factors that do not enter equation (9.7) and thus do not affect the natural level of output?

The key to the answers is simple, yet important.

- We have derived the natural rate of unemployment and the associated levels of unemployment and output under two assumptions. We have assumed equilibrium in the labour market. We have assumed that the price level was equal to the expected price level.
- There is no reason for the second assumption to be true in the *short run*. The price level may turn out to be different from what was expected by wage setters when nominal wages were set. Hence, in the short run, there is no reason for unemployment to be equal to the natural rate or for output to be equal to its natural level. As we will see in the next chapter, the factors that determine movements in output *in the short run* are the factors we focused on in the preceding six chapters: monetary policy, fiscal policy, and so on. Your time (or ours) was not wasted.
- But expectations of the price level are unlikely to be systematically wrong forever (say, always too high or always too low). That is why, in the medium run, unemployment tends to return to the natural rate, and output tends to return to the natural level. *In the medium*

> In the short run, the factors that determine movements in output are the factors we focused on in the preceding six chapters: monetary policy, fiscal policy, and so on.
>
> In the medium run, output tends to return to the natural level, and the factors that determine output are the factors we have focused on in this chapter.

*run*, the factors that determine unemployment and output are the factors that appear in equations (9.7) and (9.8).

These, in short, are the answers to the questions asked in the first paragraph. Developing these answers in detail will be our task in our remaining analysis of the medium run.

## SUMMARY

- The labour force is composed of those who are working (employed) or looking for work (unemployed). The unemployment rate is equal to the ratio of the number of unemployed to the labour force. The participation rate is equal to the ratio of the labour force to the population of working age.

- The labour market is characterized by large flows between employment and unemployment and out of the labour force. Each month, on average, more than one-third of the unemployed move out of unemployment, either to take a job or to drop out of the labour force.

- Many people who are not actively searching for jobs and are therefore not counted as unemployed are, in fact, willing to work if they find a job. This is one reason why the unemployment rate is an imperfect measure of the number of people not working but willing to work.

- There are important differences across groups of workers in terms of their average unemployment rate and in terms of their average duration of unemployment. Unemployment rates are typically higher among the young, the low-skilled, and minorities.

- Unemployment is high in recessions and low in expansions. During periods of high unemployment, the probability of losing a job increases and the probability of finding a job if unemployed decreases.

- Wages depend negatively on the unemployment rate. Wages depend positively on expected prices. The reason wages depend on expected rather than actual prices is that wages are typically set in nominal terms for some period of time. During that time, even if prices turn out to be different from what was expected, wages are typically not re-adjusted.

- Prices set by firms depend on wages and on the markup of prices over wages. The higher the markup chosen by firms, the lower is the real wage implied by price-setting decisions.

- Equilibrium in the labour market requires that the real wage chosen in wage setting be equal to the real wage implied by price setting. Under the additional assumption that the actual price level is equal to the expected price level, equilibrium in the labour market determines the unemployment rate. This unemployment rate is known as the *natural rate of unemployment*.

- In general, the actual price level may turn out to be different from what was expected by wage setters, and therefore the unemployment rate need not be equal to the natural rate. The coming chapters will show that in the short run, unemployment and output are determined by the factors we focused on in the preceding six chapters but that in the medium run, unemployment tends to return to the natural rate and output tends to return to its natural level.

## KEY TERMS

- bargaining power, 171
- collective bargaining, 171
- dual labour market, 168
- duration of unemployment, 166
- efficiency wage theories, 173
- employment rate, 167
- hires, 165
- labour force, 165
- labour productivity, 174
- layoffs, 166
- natural level of employment, 178
- natural level of output, 179

- natural rate of unemployment, 177
- price-setting relation, 176
- primary labour market, 168
- production function, 174
- quits, 166
- reference week, 167
- reservation wage, 171
- secondary labour market, 168
- separations, 165
- structural rate of unemployment, 178
- wage-setting relation, 175

## QUESTIONS AND PROBLEMS

### 1. TRUE/FALSE/UNCERTAIN

**a.** Since 1950, the participation rate in Canada has remained roughly constant at 60%.

**b.** Each month, the flows in and out of employment are very small compared with the size of the labour force.

**c.** One-third of all unemployed workers exit the unemployment pool each year.

**d.** The unemployment rate tends to be high in recessions and low in expansions.

**e.** Most workers are typically paid their reservation wage.

**f.** Workers who do not belong to unions have very little bargaining power.

**g.** It may be in the best interests of employers to pay wages higher than their workers' reservation wage.

**h.** The natural rate of unemployment is unaffected by policy changes.

**i.** The natural rate of unemployment could equally be called the structural rate of unemployment.

### 2. LABOUR-MARKET NUMBERS

Answer the following questions using the information about Canada in Figure 9–1.

**a.** As a percentage of the employed workers, what is the size of the flows in and out of employment (that is, hires and separations) each month?

**b.** As a percentage of the unemployed workers, what is the size of the flows from unemployment into employment each month?

**c.** As a percentage of the unemployed, what is the size of the total flows out of unemployment each month? What is the average duration of unemployment?

**d.** As a percentage of the labour force, what is the size of the total flows in and out of the labour force each month?

**e.** New workers enter the labour force through gaining employment. Retirees (and others) leave the labour force without experiencing unemployment. Calculate this total flow as a percent of employment.

### 3. THE LABOUR MARKET AT A GLANCE

Go to the Web site maintained by Statistics Canada, www. statcan.gc.ca. Look for the latest release of the *Labour Force Survey*. This might be found on the opening page of the website or may be found by a search of *The Daily*.

**a.** What are the latest monthly data on the size of the Canadian labour force, the number of unemployed people, and the unemployment rate?

**b.** How many people are employed?

**c.** Compute the change in the number of unemployed from the first available number to the most recent month in the table. Do the same for the number of employed workers. Is the decline in unemployment equal to the increase in employment? Explain in words.

### 4. UNEMPLOYMENT SPELLS AND LONG-TERM UNEMPLOYMENT

According to the data presented in this chapter, about one of every three unemployed workers leaves unemployment each month, that is, the probability of finding a job when unemployed in a given month is 0.39.

**a.** What is the probability a worker will still be unemployed after one month? Three months? Six months?

**b.** What proportion of the unemployed has been unemployed for six months or more?

### 5. RESERVATION WAGES

In the mid-1980s, a famous supermodel once said that she would not get out of bed for less than $10,000 (presumably per day).

**a.** What is your own reservation wage?

**b.** Did your first job pay more than your reservation wage at the time?

**c.** Relative to your reservation wage at the time you accept each job, which job pays more: your first one or the one you expect to have in 10 years?

**d.** Explain your answers in terms of the efficiency wage theory.

### 6. BARGAINING POWER AND WAGE DETERMINATION

Even in the absence of collective bargaining, workers do have some bargaining power that allows them to receive a wage higher than their reservation wage. Each worker's bargaining power depends both on the nature of the job and on the economy-wide labour-market conditions. Let us consider each factor in turn.

**a.** Compare the job of a delivery person and the job of a computer network administrator. In which of these jobs does a worker have more bargaining power? Why?

**b.** For any given job, how do labour-market conditions affect the workers' bargaining power? Which labour-market variable would you look at to assess labour-market conditions?

## 7. THE NATURAL RATE OF UNEMPLOYMENT AND THE NATURAL LEVEL OF OUTPUT

Suppose that the firms' mark-up over costs is 5% and the wage-setting equation is $W = P(1 - u)$ where $u$ is the unemployment rate.

**a.** What is the real wage as determined by the price-setting relationship?

**b.** Solve for the natural rate of unemployment, that is, the rate of unemployment at the real wage determined by the price-setting relationship. You will need to use further information scattered through the chapter.

**c.** Using the production function in expression (9.2), and the notation that the total labour force is equal to $L$ when employment equals $N$, solve for the natural level of output. $Y_n = N$ where employment is at the natural rate $= (1 - u_n) * L$

**d.** Suppose the mark-up of prices over costs increases to 10%. What happens to the natural rate of unemployment? Explain the logic behind the answer and the sense in which there is nothing "natural" about the natural rate of unemployment.

### FURTHER READING

An in-depth discussion of unemployment along the lines of this chapter is given by Richard Layard, Stephen Nickell, and Richard Jackman in *The Unemployment Crisis* (Oxford University Press, 1994).

## APPENDIX

# WAGE- AND PRICE-SETTING RELATIONS VERSUS LABOUR SUPPLY AND LABOUR DEMAND

In your microeconomics course, you probably saw a representation of labour market equilibrium in terms of labour supply and labour demand. You may therefore be asking yourself: How does the representation in terms of wage setting and price setting relate to the representation of the labour market I saw in my microeconomics course?

In an important sense, the two representations are similar.

To see why, let us redraw Figure 9–6 in terms of the real wage and the level of *employment* (rather than the unemployment rate). We do this in Figure 9A–1.

Employment, $N$, is measured on the horizontal axis. The level of employment must be somewhere between zero and $L$, the labour force. Employment cannot exceed the number of people available for work, the labour force. For any employment level, $N$, unemployment is given by $U = L - N$.

**FIGURE  9A–1**

**Wage and Price Setting and the Natural Level of Employment**

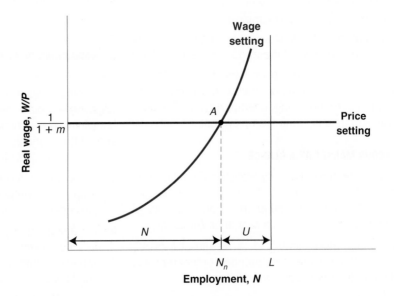

Knowing that, we can measure unemployment by starting from $L$ and *moving to the left* on the horizontal axis. Unemployment is given by the distance between $L$ and $N$. The lower employment, $N$, is, the higher unemployment is and, by implication, the higher the unemployment rate, $u$.

Let us now draw the wage-setting and price-setting relations and characterize the equilibrium:

- An increase in employment (a movement to the right along the horizontal axis) implies a decrease in unemployment, and therefore an increase in the real wage chosen in wage setting. Thus, the wage-setting relation is now *upward sloping*. Higher employment implies a higher real wage.
- The price-setting relation is still a horizontal line at $W/P = 1/(1 + m)$.
- The equilibrium is given by point $A$, with "natural" employment level $N_n$ (and an implied natural unemployment rate equal to $u_n = [L - N_n]/L$).

In this figure, the wage-setting relation looks like a labour-supply relation. As the level of employment increases, the real wage paid to workers increases as well. For that reason, the wage-setting relation is sometimes called the "labour supply" relation (in quotes).

What we have called the price-setting relation looks like a flat labour-demand relation. The reason it is flat rather than downward sloping has to do with our simplifying assumption of constant returns to labour in production. Had we assumed, more conventionally, that there were decreasing returns to labour in production, our price-setting curve would, like the standard labour-demand curve, be downward sloping. As employment increased, the marginal cost of production would increase, forcing firms to increase their prices, given the wages they pay. In other words, the real wage implied by price setting would decrease as employment increased.

But, in a number of ways, the two approaches are different:

- The standard labour-supply relation gives the wage at which a given number of workers are willing to work.

The higher the wage is, the larger the number of workers who are willing to work.

In contrast, the wage corresponding to a given level of employment in the wage-setting relation is the result of a process of bargaining between workers and firms or unilateral wage setting by firms. Such factors as the structure of collective bargaining or the use of wages to deter quits affect the wage-setting relation. In the real world, they seem to play an important role. Yet they play no role in the standard labour-supply relation.

- The standard labour-demand relation gives the level of employment chosen by firms at a given real wage. It is derived under the assumption that firms operate in competitive goods and labour markets and therefore take wages and prices—and by implication, the real wage—as givens.

In contrast, the price-setting relation takes into account the fact that in most markets, firms actually set prices. Such factors as the degree of competition in the goods market affect the price-setting relation by affecting the markup. But these factors are not considered in the standard labour-demand relation.

- In the labour-supply–labour-demand framework, those unemployed are *willingly unemployed*. At the equilibrium real wage, they prefer to be unemployed rather than to work.

In contrast, in the wage-setting–price-setting framework, unemployment is likely to be involuntary. For example, if firms pay an efficiency wage—a wage above the reservation wage—workers would rather be employed than unemployed. Yet, in equilibrium, there is still involuntary unemployment. This also seems to capture reality better than does the labour-supply–labour-demand framework.

These are the three reasons why we have relied on the wage-setting and the price-setting relations rather than on the labour-supply–labour-demand approach to characterize equilibrium in this chapter.

# All Markets Together: The *AS-AD* Model—The Basics

## The Core: The Medium Run

We are now ready to think about the determination of output in both the short run and in the medium run. This requires taking into account equilibrium in *all* markets (goods, financial, and labour). We do so by deriving two relations:

- The aggregate supply relation captures the implications of equilibrium in the labour market; it builds on what we learned in Chapter 9.

- The aggregate demand relation captures the implications of equilibrium in both the goods and financial markets; it builds on what we learned in Chapter 5.

Using both relations, we can characterize the equilibrium level of output and prices over time. This is what we do in this and the next four chapters. This chapter develops a basic version of the model, called the *AS-AD* (for aggregate supply–aggregate demand) model. When confronted with macroeconomic questions, it is the model that we typically use to organize our thoughts. For some questions, however, it must be refined and extended. In Chapter 11 the model is extended to consider both periods where the interest rate is zero as well as a case where there are supply shocks. In Chapters 12 and 13, the model is extended to study inflation, periods where there is a continuous increase in prices. In Chapter 14, we will extend this model to the open economy in the medium run.

# 10-1 | Aggregate Supply

The **aggregate supply relation** captures the effects of output on the price level. It is derived from equilibrium in the labour market.

## The Derivation of the Aggregate Supply Relation

Recall our characterization of wage and price determination in Chapter 9:

$$W = P^e F(u, z)$$
$$P = (1 + m)W$$

- The nominal wage ($W$), set by wage setters, depends on the expected price level ($P^e$), the unemployment rate ($u$), and the catchall variable ($z$) that stands for all the other factors that affect wage determination, from unemployment benefits to the form of collective bargaining.
- The price level ($P$) set by price setters is equal to the nominal wage ($W$), times 1 plus the markup ($m$).

Combining these two equations by replacing the wage in the second equation by its expression from the first gives:

$$P = P^e(1 + m) F(u, z)$$

The price level is a function of the expected price level and the unemployment rate. It will be more convenient in this chapter to express the price level as a function of the level of output rather than as a function of the unemployment rate. To do this, recall from Chapter 9 the relation between the unemployment rate, employment, and output:

$$u \equiv \frac{U}{L} = 1 - \frac{N}{L} = 1 - \frac{Y}{L}$$

The first step follows from the definition of the unemployment rate, the second from the definition of unemployment ($U \equiv L - N$). The last follows from our specification of the production function, which says that one unit of output requires one worker so that $Y = N$.

Replacing $u$ in the previous equation gives the aggregate supply relation among the price level, the expected price level, and output:

$$P = P^e(1 + m) F\left(1 - \frac{Y}{L}, z\right) \qquad (10.1)$$

> A better name would be "the labour market equilibrium relation." But because the relation looks graphically like a supply curve (that is, a positive relation between output and the price), it has become traditional to call it "the aggregate supply relation." We will follow tradition.

Note two things about equation (10.1):

1. *A higher expected price level leads, one for one, to a higher actual price level.* For example, if the expected price level doubles, then the price level will also double. This effect works through wages: If wage setters expect higher prices, they set higher nominal wages. This, in turn, leads firms to set higher prices.

2. *An increase in output leads to an increase in the price level.* This is the result of four underlying steps:

   - An increase in output leads to an increase in employment.
   - The increase in employment leads to a decrease in unemployment, and therefore a decrease in the unemployment rate.
   - The lower unemployment rate leads to an increase in nominal wages.
   - The increase in nominal wages leads to an increase in costs, which leads firms to increase prices.

> $P^e\uparrow \Rightarrow P\uparrow$
>
> $P^e\uparrow \Rightarrow W\uparrow$
> $W\uparrow \Rightarrow P\uparrow$

> $Y\uparrow \Rightarrow P\uparrow$
>
> $Y\uparrow \Rightarrow N\uparrow$
> $N\uparrow \Rightarrow u\downarrow$
>
> $u\downarrow \Rightarrow W\uparrow$
> $W\uparrow \Rightarrow P\uparrow$

**FIGURE 10-1**

**The Aggregate Supply Curve**

(a) Given the expected price level, an increase in output leads to an increase in the price level. (b) An increase in the expected price level shifts the aggregate supply curve up.

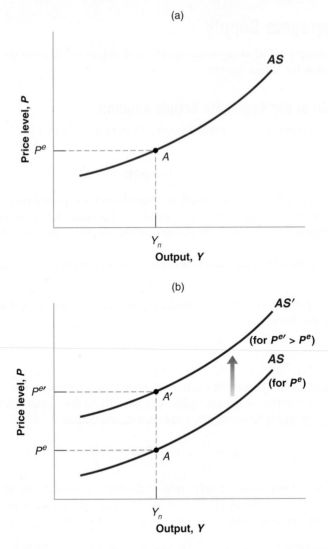

(a)

(b)

The aggregate supply relation between output and the price level is represented by the *aggregate supply curve AS* in Figure 10–1(a). This aggregate supply curve has two characteristics:

> Here is an informal way of saying the same thing: High activity puts pressure on prices.

- It is upward sloping: For a given value of the expected price level, $P^e$, an increase in output leads to an increase in the price level.
- It goes through point A, where $Y = Y_n$ and $P = P^e$. That is, if output is equal to its natural level $Y_n$, then the price level is equal to the expected price level: $P = P^e$. We know this from the definition of the natural level of output in Chapter 9: We derived the natural rate of unemployment (and, by implication, the natural level of output) as the unemployment rate (and, by implication, the level of output) that prevails if the price level and the expected price level are equal.

These characteristics have, in turn, two implications; both will be useful when we trace movements in equilibrium output later in this chapter:

- When output is above its natural level, the price level is higher than expected: $P > P^e$. Conversely: When output is below its natural level, the price level is lower than expected: $P < P^e$. This is shown in Figure 10–1(a). To the left of A, the price level is lower than was expected. To the right of A, the price level is higher than was expected.
- An increase in the expected price level shifts the aggregate supply curve up. Conversely, a decrease in the expected price level shifts the aggregate supply curve down.

This second implication is shown in Figure 10–1(b). If the expected price level increases from $P^e$ to $P^{e'}$, the aggregate supply curve shifts up: Instead of going through point $A$ (where $Y = Y_n$ and $P = P^e$), it now goes through point $A'$ (where $Y = Y_n$, $P = P^{e'}$).

To summarize: We have derived the *aggregate supply relation*, the first of the two relations we need to characterize the equilibrium. This relation is derived from equilibrium in the labour market. It says that the price level is an increasing function of the level of output and of the expected price level. It is represented by an upward sloping curve. Changes in the expected price level shift the curve up or down.

## 10-2 | Aggregate Demand

The **aggregate demand relation** captures the effect of the price level on output. It is derived from equilibrium in the goods and financial markets.

Borrowing from Chapter 5, the two equations that characterize equilibrium in goods and financial markets were:

(Goods market) $\quad$ $IS$: $\quad Y = C(Y - T) + I(Y, i) + G$

(Financial markets) $\quad$ $LM$: $\quad \dfrac{M}{P} = YL(i)$

Equilibrium in the goods market requires that the supply of goods equal the demand for goods—the sum of consumption, investment, and government spending. This is the $IS$ relation.

Equilibrium in financial markets requires that the supply of money equal the demand for money; this is the $LM$ relation. Note that what appears on the left side of the $LM$ equation is the real money stock, $M/P$. We have focused so far on changes in the real money stock that came from changes in nominal money, $M$—monetary contractions or expansions implemented by the central bank. But changes in $M/P$ also can come from changes in the price level. A 10% increase in the price level has the same effect on $M/P$ as does a 10% decrease in the stock of nominal money: Both lead to a 10% decrease in the real money stock.

Figure 10–2 derives the relation between the price level and output implied by equilibrium in the goods and the financial markets. Figure 10–2(a) draws the $IS$ and $LM$ curves. The $IS$ curve is downward sloping: An increase in the interest rate leads to a decrease in demand and in output. The $LM$ curve is upward sloping: An increase in output increases the demand for money, and the interest rate must increase so as to maintain equality of money demand and the (unchanged) money supply. The initial equilibrium is at point $A$.

While still looking at Figure 10–2(a), consider an increase in the price level from $P$ to $P'$. Given the stock of nominal money, $M$, the increase in the price level decreases the real money stock, $M/P$, and the $LM$ curve shifts up: At a given level of output, the lower real money stock leads to an increase in the interest rate. The equilibrium moves from $A$ to $A'$; the interest rate increases from $i$ to $i'$, and output decreases from $Y$ to $Y'$. The increase in the price level leads to a decrease in output.

In words: As the price level increases, the demand for *nominal* money increases. Because the supply of nominal money is fixed, the interest rate must increase to induce people to decrease their demand for money, and re-establish equilibrium. The increase in the interest rate leads, in turn, to a decrease in the demand for goods and a decrease in output.[1]

The implied negative relation between output and the price level is drawn as the downward-sloping curve $AD$ in Figure 10–2(b). Points $A$ and $A'$ in Figure 10–2(b) correspond to points $A$ ◄

A better name would be "the goods and financial markets equilibrium relation." But because this is a long name and because the relation looks graphically like a demand curve (that is, a negative relation between output and the price), it has become traditional to call it the "aggregate demand relation." Be aware, however, that the aggregate supply and aggregate demand relations are very different from regular supply and demand curves.

---

[1]**DIGGING DEEPER.** When we extend the model to the open economy, the increase in $i$ causes an exchange rate appreciation. This is, given fixed prices, a real exchange rate appreciation. The price rise in Canada ($P$ rising) adds to the real exchange rate appreciation and further reduces the demand for Canadian goods. Thus, the $AD$ curve is also negatively sloped in the open economy. To keep things simple in this and the next two chapters, we will work in the closed economy. The open economy effects are not difficult to incorporate.

and $A'$ in Figure 10–2(a). An increase in the price level from $P$ to $P'$ leads to a decrease in output from $Y$ to $Y'$. We will call this curve the aggregate demand curve and call the underlying negative relation between output and the price level the aggregate demand relation.

Any variable other than the price level that shifts either the $IS$ curve or the $LM$ curve in Figure 10–2(a) also shifts the aggregate demand curve in Figure 10–2(b). Take, for example, an increase in consumer confidence, which shifts the $IS$ curve to the right and so leads to higher output. At the same price level, output is higher: The aggregate demand curve shifts to the right. Or take a contractionary open-market operation, which shifts the $LM$ curve up and decreases output. At the same price level, output is lower: The aggregate demand curve shifts to the left.

Recall that a contractionary open market operation is a decrease in nominal money, $M$, implemented through the sale of bonds by the central bank.

We represent the aggregate demand relation by:

$$Y = Y\left(\frac{M}{P}, G, T\right)$$ (10.2)

$$(+,+,-)$$

Output is an increasing function of the real money stock, an increasing function of government spending, and a decreasing function of taxes. Other factors, such as consumer confidence, could be introduced in this equation but are omitted for simplicity. Given monetary and fiscal policies—that is, given $M$, $G$, and $T$—an increase in the price level, $P$, leads to a decrease in the real money stock, $M/P$, which leads to a decrease in output. This is the relation captured by the $AD$ curve in Figure 10–2(b).

To summarize: We have derived the *aggregate demand relation*, the second of the two relations we need to characterize the equilibrium. This relation is derived from equilibrium in

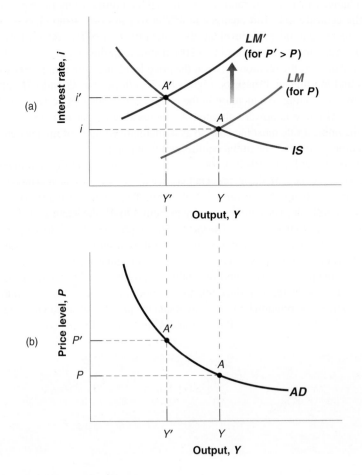

**FIGURE 10–2**

**The Derivation of the Aggregate Demand Curve**

An increase in the price level leads to a decrease in output. Any variable other than the price level that shifts either the $IS$ curve or the $LM$ curve in (a) also shifts the aggregate demand relation in (b).

the goods and financial markets. It says that the level of output is a decreasing function of the price level and is represented by a downward-sloping curve. Changes in monetary or fiscal policy—or more generally, in any factor that shifts the $IS$ or the $LM$ curves—shift the aggregate demand curve to the right or to the left.

## 10-3 | Equilibrium Output in the Short Run and the Medium Run

We now put the $AS$ and the $AD$ relations together. From sections 10-1 and 10-2, the two relations are given by:

$$AS \text{ relation} \qquad P = P^e(1 + m) F\left(1 - \frac{Y}{L}, z\right)$$

$$AD \text{ relation} \qquad Y = Y\left(\frac{M}{P}, G, T\right)$$

Figure 10–3 plots the two corresponding curves. The aggregate supply curve, $AS$, drawn for a given value of $P^e$, is upward sloping. Recall from the derivation of the aggregate supply curve in section 10-1 that when output is equal to its natural level, the price level is equal to the expected price level. This implies that the aggregate supply curve goes through point $B$—if output is equal to $Y_n$, the price level is equal to the expected price level, $P^e$. The aggregate demand curve $AD$ is downward sloping. Its position depends on the values of $M$, $G$, and $T$.

The equilibrium is given by the intersection of the two curves at point $A$. By construction, at point $A$, the goods, financial, and labour markets are *all* in equilibrium. The fact that the labour market is in equilibrium comes from the fact that point $A$ is on the aggregate supply curve. The fact that the goods and financial markets are in equilibrium comes from the fact that point $A$ is also on the aggregate demand curve. The equilibrium level of output and price level are given by $Y$ and $P$.

Note that there is no reason why, in a particular year, equilibrium output $Y$ should be equal to the natural level of output $Y_n$. Equilibrium output depends on both the position of the aggregate supply curve—thus on the value of $P^e$—and the position of the aggregate demand curve—thus on the values of $M$, $G$, and $T$. As we have drawn the two curves, the equilibrium is such that $Y$ is larger than $Y_n$: The economy is operating above its natural level of output. But we could clearly have drawn the $AS$ and the $AD$ curves so that equilibrium output was smaller than its natural level. It all depends on the specific values of the expected price level and the values of the variables affecting the position of aggregate demand.

> Equivalently, the unemployment rate is below the natural rate.

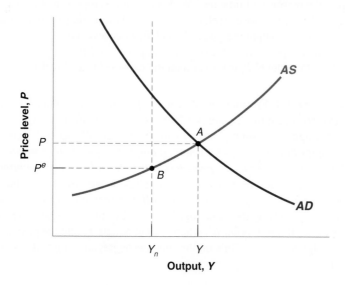

FIGURE 10-3

**Equilibrium Output and Price Level**

The equilibrium is given by the intersection of the aggregate supply and the aggregate demand curves. At point $A$, the labour, goods, and financial markets are all in equilibrium.

This gives us our first result: In the short run, there is no reason why output should equal its natural level. We can, however, go further and ask: What happens over time? More specifically, suppose that (as in Figure 10–3) output is above its natural level. Now, suppose that the economy is left to itself; that is, policy and other exogenous variables remain constant. What will happen to output over time? Will it return to its natural level? If so, how? These are the questions we take up in the rest of this section.

## The Dynamics of Output and the Price Level

To study the movement of output over time, we must first specify how wage setters form expectations. In drawing Figure 10–3, we took the expected price level, $P^e$, as a given. But $P^e$ is likely to change over time: If the price level last year turned out to be different from what they expected, wage setters are likely to take this into account when forming expectations of what the price level will be this year. We will assume in this chapter that wage setters always expect the price level this year to be equal to the price level last year. This assumption is too simple, and we will improve on it in the next two chapters. But starting with it will make it easier to understand the basic mechanisms at work.

As we now look at the evolution of output and other variables over time, the other thing we need to do is to introduce time indexes. So, $P_t$ will refer to the price level in year $t$, $P_{t-1}$ to the price level in year $t - 1$, $P_{t+1}$ to the price level in year $t + 1$, and so on.

Using this notation, the assumption that the expected price level equals the price level last year is written as:

$$P_t^e = P_{t-1}$$

And the aggregate supply and demand relations must now be written as:

AS relation $\qquad P_t = P_{t-1}(1 + m) F\left(1 - \frac{Y_t}{L}, z\right)$ (10.3)

AD relation $\qquad Y_t = Y\left(\frac{M}{P_t}, G, T\right)$ (10.4)

Note that the parameters $(m, z)$ and the exogenous variables ($L$ in the aggregate supply relation, $M$, $G$, and $T$ in the aggregate demand relation) do not have a time subscript. This is because we will assume they remain constant, so there is no need for a time subscript.

With the help of Figure 10–4, we can now look at the evolution of output over time.

1.  Assume that in year $t$, the equilibrium is the same as the equilibrium characterized in Figure 10–3. So, Figure 10–4(a), which gives the equilibrium for year $t$, replicates Figure 10–3; the only change is the presence of time indexes. Under our assumption that the expected price level is equal to last year's price level, $P_t^e = P_{t-1}$, and the aggregate supply curve goes through point $B$, where output is equal to $Y_n$ and the price level equals $P_{t-1}$.

    Equilibrium is at point $A$, with output $Y_t$ and price level $P_t$. Output $Y_t$ is above its natural level $Y_n$. Price level $P_t$ is higher than the expected price level $P_t^e$, hence higher than $P_{t-1}$.

2.  Now, turn to year $t + 1$. Equilibrium in year $t + 1$ is shown in Figure 10–4(b). The curves AS and AD repeat the AS and AD for year $t$ from Figure 10–4(a).

    To draw the aggregate supply curve for year $t + 1$, recall that *the aggregate supply curve always goes through the point where, if output is equal to its natural level, the price level is equal to the expected price level—which, under our assumptions, is itself equal to the price level the year before.* This implies, as we saw earlier, that the aggregate supply curve for year $t$ goes through point $B$, where output equals $Y_n$ and the price level is equal to $P_{t-1}$. Using the same logic, this implies that the aggregate supply curve for year $t + 1$ goes through point $B'$, where output equals $Y_n$ and the price level is equal to $P_t$. As $P_t$ is higher than $P_{t-1}$, this implies that the aggregate supply shifts up from year $t$ to year $t + 1$.

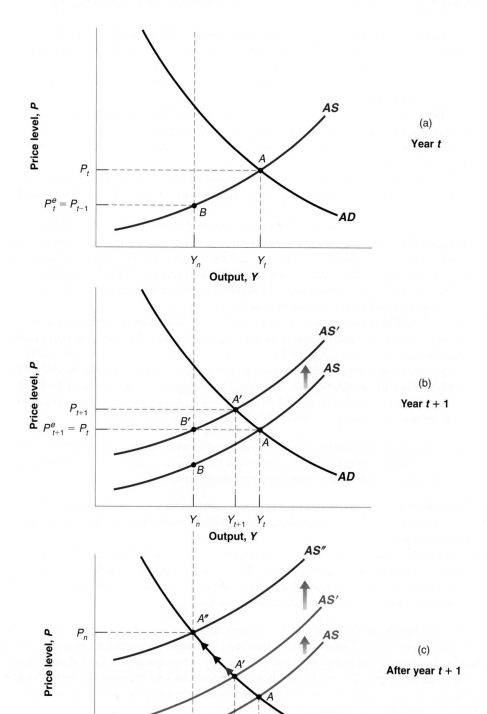

FIGURE 10-4

**The Dynamics of Adjustment to the Natural Level of Output**

(a) Output is above its natural level. The price level is higher than expected. (b) As wage setters revise their price expectations up, the aggregate supply curve shifts up. Output declines. The price level increases. (c) The aggregate supply curve keeps shifting up, until, in the medium run, output is equal to its natural level.

Make sure you understand the steps in the previous paragraph. But do not lose track of the basic intuition for why the aggregate supply curve shifts up. In year $t$, output is higher than its natural level, so prices turn out to be higher than expected. This leads wage setters in year $t + 1$ to increase their price expectations, leading the aggregate supply curve to shift up.

Turn to the aggregate demand curve. Note that it does not shift: The aggregate demand curve gives the relation between output and the price level from goods and financial markets equilibrium, for given values of $M$, $G$, and $T$. And by assumption, $M$, $G$, and $T$ remain constant.

The shift in the aggregate supply curve implies that the economy moves from $A$ in year $t$ to $A'$ in year $t + 1$. Price level $P_{t+1}$ is higher than $P_t$. Output $Y_{t+1}$ is lower than $Y_t$, thus closer to the natural level of output $Y_n$.

In words: Because output is above its natural level in year $t$, the price level in year $t$ is higher than expected. This leads wage setters to increase their expectations of the price level in year $t + 1$, leading to a higher price level in year $t + 1$. Given nominal money, a higher price level leads to a lower real money stock in year $t + 1$. The lower real money stock leads to a higher interest rate. The higher interest rate leads to a lower demand for goods, and a lower level of output in year $t + 1$.

3. We have looked at what happens in years $t$ and $t + 1$. What happens in the following years is now easy to describe and is shown in Figure 10–4(c). As long as output is higher than its natural level, the price level keeps increasing, and the aggregate supply curve keeps shifting up. Output keeps decreasing. The economy moves up along the $AD$ curve, until it eventually reaches point $A''$. At point $A''$, the aggregate supply curve is given by $AS''$ and output is equal to its natural level. There is no longer any pressure on prices to increase, and the economy settles at $Y_n$, with associated price level $P_n$.[2]

This is the basic mechanism through which the economy returns to its natural level. We will use it in the next three sections to understand the dynamic effects of various shocks and changes in policy. But we can already draw two important lessons:

- In the *short run*, output can be above or below its natural level. Changes in any of the variables that enter the aggregate supply or aggregate demand relation lead to changes in output and prices.
- In the *medium run/long run*, however, output eventually returns to its natural level. The adjustment process works through prices. When output is above its natural level, prices increase. Higher prices decrease demand and output. When output is below its natural level, prices decrease, increasing demand and output.

We now use the model to look at the dynamic effects of two changes in policy or in the economic environment. These are old favourites by now: an open-market operation, which changes the stock of nominal money, and a decrease in the budget deficit. Each shock is interesting in its own right. The model will help us understand why reducing the budget deficit could lead to a reduction in output. First, we turn to understanding the short- and medium-run effects of a monetary expansion.

*Warning:* There are many steps here: A higher expected price level leads to a higher price level. A higher price level leads to a lower real money stock. A lower real money stock leads to a higher interest rate. A higher interest rate leads to lower output. Make sure you understand each, but do not worry: You will get more training in the next three sections.

Short run: $Y \neq Y_n$

Medium run: $Y \rightarrow Y_n$

[2]**DIGGING DEEPER.** What if the aggregate supply curve shifts up so much from one period to the next that equilibrium output ends up below its natural level? That may happen. If so, with output below the natural level, the price level is lower than the expected price level, and the aggregate supply curve starts shifting down. In short, the return to the natural level may involve oscillations of output rather than a smooth adjustment of output to $Y_n$. These oscillations are not important for our purposes, and we will not consider them further.

# 10-4 | The Effects of a Monetary Expansion

What are the short- and medium-run effects of an expansionary monetary policy, say, an increase in the level of nominal money from $M$ to $M'$?

## The Dynamics of Adjustment

Assume that before the change in nominal money, output is at its natural level. In Figure 10–5, aggregate demand and aggregate supply cross at point $A$, and the level of output at $A$ equals $Y_n$.

Now consider an increase in nominal money. Recall the specification of aggregate demand from equation (10.4):

$$Y_t = Y\left(\frac{M}{P_t}, G, T\right)$$

For a given price level $P_t$, the increase in money leads to an increase in $M/P_t$, leading to an increase in output. The aggregate demand curve shifts to the right, from $AD$ to $AD'$. The equilibrium moves from point $A$ to $A'$. Output is higher, and so is the price level.

Over time, the adjustment of price expectations comes into play. Seeing higher prices, wage setters ask for higher nominal wages, which lead to higher prices. Prices keep rising. Equivalently, as long as output exceeds its natural level, the aggregate supply curve shifts up. The economy moves up along the aggregate demand curve $AD'$. The adjustment process stops when output has returned to its natural level. In the medium run, the aggregate supply curve is given by $AS''$, and the economy is at point $A''$: Output is back to its natural level, and the price level is higher.

We can pin down exactly the size of the eventual increase in the price level. If output is back to its natural level, the real money stock must also be back to its initial value. In other words, the proportional increase in prices must be equal to the proportional increase in the nominal money stock: If the initial increase in nominal money is equal to 10%, then the price level ends up 10% higher.

## Looking Behind the Scene

It is useful to look behind the scene at what happens in terms of the underlying *IS-LM* model. This is done in Figure 10–6. Figure 10–6(a) reproduces Figure 10–5, showing the adjustment of output and the price level. Figure 10–6(b) shows the adjustment of output and the interest rate, by looking at the adjustment in terms of the *IS-LM* model.

We leave the more difficult question of the effects of a change in the rate of growth of money—rather than a change in the level of money—to Chapters 12 and 13.

We think of shifts in the aggregate demand curve as shifts to the right and the left. It is because we think of the aggregate demand relation as giving output, given the price level. We then ask: At a given price level, does output increase (a shift to the right) or decrease (a shift to the left)? We think of shifts in the aggregate supply curve as shifts up or down. It is because we think of the aggregate supply relation as giving the price level, given output. We then ask: At a given output level, does the price level increase (a shift up) or decrease (a shift down)?

If $M/P$ is unchanged, it must be that $M$ and $P$ increase in the same proportion.

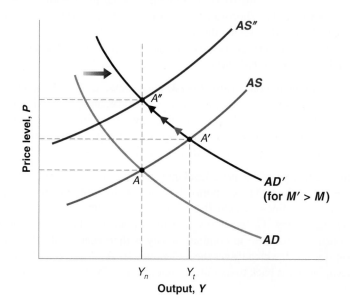

**FIGURE 10–5**

**The Dynamic Effects of a Monetary Expansion**

A monetary expansion leads to an increase in output in the short run but has no effect on output in the medium run.

FIGURE 10-6

**The Dynamic Effects of a Monetary Expansion on Output and the Interest Rate**

The increase in nominal money initially shifts the *LM* curve down, decreasing the interest rate and increasing output. Over time, the price level increases, shifting the *LM* curve back up until output is back at its natural level. Look back at Figure 10–5. There is a movement along AD′ and a series of shifts in the *AS* curve from *AS* to *AS′*.

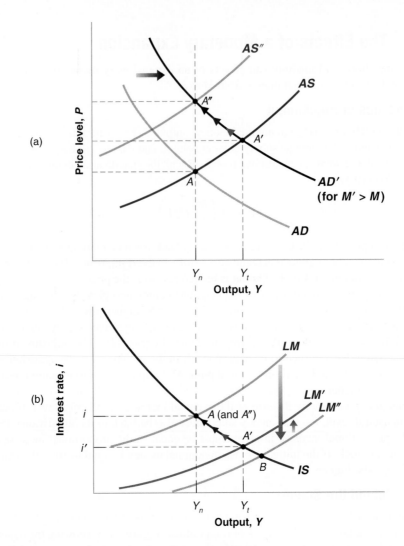

Look at Figure 10–6(b). Before the change in money, the economy is at point *A* (which corresponds to point *A* in Figure 10–6(a)). Output is equal to its natural level, $Y_n$, and the interest rate is given by *i*. The short-run effect of the monetary expansion is to shift the *LM* curve down from *LM* to *LM′*, moving the equilibrium from *A* to *A′* (which corresponds to *A′* in Figure 10–6(a)). The interest rate is lower; output is higher. Note that there are two effects at work behind the shift in the *LM* curve:

Why only partially? Suppose the increase in the price level fully cancelled the increase in nominal money, leaving the real money stock unchanged. If the real money stock were unchanged, output would remain unchanged as well. But if output were unchanged, the price level would not ▶ increase, in contradiction with our premise.

- The increase in nominal money shifts the *LM* curve down to *LM″*. If the price level did not change—as was our assumption in Chapter 5—the economy would move to point *B*.
- But even in the short run, the price level increases with output as the economy shifts along the aggregate supply curve. So, this increase in the price level shifts the *LM* curve upward from *LM″* to *LM′*, partially offsetting the effect of the increase in nominal money.

Over time (after the first year), the price level increases further, reducing the real money stock and shifting the *LM* back up. The economy thus moves along the *IS* curve: The interest rate increases and output declines. Eventually, the *LM* curve returns to where it was before the increase in nominal money. The economy ends up at point *A*, which corresponds to point *A″* in Figure 10–6(a). The increase in nominal money is then exactly offset by a proportional increase in the price level, which leaves the real money stock unchanged. With the real money stock unchanged, output is back to its initial value, $Y_n$, and the interest rate also returns to its initial value, *i*.

## The Neutrality of Money

Let us summarize what we have learned about the effects of monetary policy in this section:

- In the short run, a monetary expansion leads to an increase in output, a decrease in the interest rate, and an increase in the price level. How much of the initial effect falls on output and how much falls on prices depends on the slope of the aggregate supply curve. In Chapter 5, we assumed that the aggregate supply curve was flat so that the price level did not increase at all in response to an increase in output. This was a simplification, but empirical evidence shows that the initial effect of changes in output on prices is quite small.

- Over time, prices increase, and the effects of the monetary expansion on output and the interest rate disappear. In the medium run, the increase in nominal money is reflected entirely in a proportional increase in the price level; it has no effect on output or the interest rate. (How long it takes for the effects of money on output to disappear is the topic of the Focus box "How Long Lasting Are the Real Effects of Money?") Economists refer to the absence of medium-run effects of money on output and the interest rate by saying that money is *neutral in the medium run.*

> Actually, the way the proposition is typically stated is that money is neutral in the *long run.* This is because many economists use "long run" to refer to what we call in this book the "medium run."

  The **neutrality of money** does not imply that monetary policy cannot or should not be used: An expansionary monetary policy can, for example, help the economy move out of a recession and return faster to its natural level. But it is a warning that monetary policy cannot sustain higher output forever.

---

## FOCUS    How Long Lasting Are the Real Effects of Money?

How long lasting are the effects of an increase in money on output?

One way to answer is to turn to macroeconometric models. These models, which are used both to forecast activity and to look at the effects of alternative macroeconomic policies, are large-scale versions of the aggregate supply and aggregate demand model presented in the text. Figure 1 shows the effects in such a model—a model built by John Taylor of Stanford University—of a 3% permanent increase in nominal money. The increase in nominal money is assumed to take place over the four quarters of year 1: 0.1% in the first quarter, another

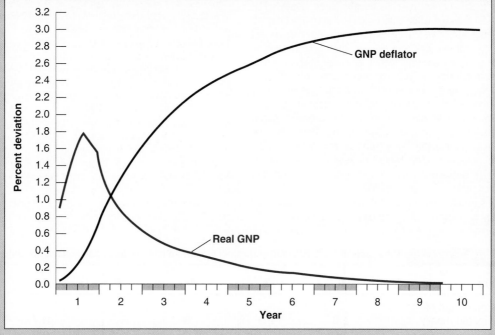

**FIGURE 1   The Effects of an Expansion in Nominal Money in the Taylor Model**

*Source:* John Taylor, Macroeconomic Policy in a World Economy (New York: W.W. Norton, 1993), Figure 5–1A, p. 138. Used by permission of the author.

*(continued)*

0.6% in the second, another 1.2% in the third, and another 1.1% in the fourth. After these four-step increases, nominal money remains at its new higher level forever.

The effects of money on output reach a maximum after three quarters. By then, output is 1.8% higher than it would have been without the increase in nominal money. Over time, however, prices increase, and output returns to its natural level. In year 4, the price level is up by 2.5%, whereas output is up by only 0.3%. Therefore, the Taylor model suggests that it takes roughly four years for money to be neutral.

Some economists are skeptical of the results of simulations from such large models. Building such a model requires making decisions about which equations to include, which variables to include in each equation, and which ones to leave out. Some decisions are bound to be wrong. Because the models are so large, it is difficult to know how each of these decisions affects the outcome of a particular simulation. So, they argue, whenever possible, one should use simpler methods.

One such method is simply to trace out, using econometrics, the effects of a change in money on output. This method is not without its problems: A strong relation between money and output may not come from an effect of money on output but rather from an effect of output on the conduct of monetary policy and thus on nominal money (the econometric problems raised by such two-way causation are discussed further in Appendix 3 at the end of the book). But the method can provide a useful first pass. The results of such a study by Frederic Mishkin, building on earlier work by Robert Barro, are summarized in Table 1.

Following Barro, Mishkin first separates movements in nominal money into those movements that could have been predicted on the basis of the information available up to that time (a component he calls **anticipated money**) and those that could not (a component he calls **unanticipated money**). The motivation for this distinction should be clear from this chapter: If wage setters anticipate increases in money, they may expect the price level to be higher and ask for higher wages. Thus, to the extent that they are anticipated, changes in money may have a larger effect on prices and a smaller effect on output.

The results in Table 1 confirm that changes in money have stronger effects when they are unanticipated. Whether anticipated or unanticipated, the effects of changes in money on output peak after about two quarters. The effects are substantially larger than in the Taylor model (which looked at a 3% increase in nominal money; Table 1 looks at the effects of 1% increase). As in the Taylor model, the effects disappear after three to four years (12 to 16 quarters).

Zisimos Koustas has tested the validity of the proposition that money is neutral in the long run in Canada. He uses a third approach to the problem. He does not distinguish between anticipated and unanticipated money. He does allow lags of real output growth to cause money growth—remember from Chapter 4 that money is primarily bank deposits. If real output grows, then people with more income may take out more loans. In our language, money becomes endogenous. Thus, output may be changed in the short term by changes in the money stock, and over time, the money stock may be changed by real output in the short term. But our model predicts that in the long term, all the effect of money on real output goes away, and the entire increase in the level of the money supply is taken up with higher prices. Real money $M/P$ remains the same. Koustas does not test whether $M/P$ remains the same. He does find that the increase in money has no long-run impact on the level of real output and infers that the impact of money is felt entirely on prices.

Paul DeGrauve and Claudia Costa Storti analyze the effect of monetary policy on prices and output using a "meta-analysis." They consider 43 published studies from more than 19 different countries. The key result—a monetary contraction reduces output in the short run. The effect on output goes away in the longer run.

Finally, George McCandless and Warren Weber have presented data on money growth (three different definitions of money) and inflation across 110 countries over 30 years. They find that money is neutral. Growth rates of money and growth rates of prices are highly correlated in the long run.

Although the results using the five approaches are not identical, they share a number of features. Money has a strong effect on output in the short run. But the effect is largely gone after four years. By then, the effect of higher nominal money is largely reflected in higher prices, not higher output.

*Sources:*

Figure 1 is reproduced from John Taylor, *Macroeconomic Policy in a World Economy* (New York: W.W. Norton, 1993), Figure 5–1A, p. 138. Used by permission of the author.

Table 1 is taken from Frederic Mishkin, *A Rational Expectations Approach to Macroeconometrics*, Table 6.5, p. 122. © 1983 University of Chicago Press. Used by permission of the publisher.

The study by Mishkin builds, in turn, on Robert Barro, "Unanticipated Money Growth in the United States," *American Economic Review* 67, March 1977: pp. 101–115.

Koustas's work, which is quite technical, is found in "Canadian Evidence on Long-Run Neutrality Propositions," *Journal of Macroeconomics* 20 (2), 1998: pp. 397–411.

Paul DeGrauve and Claudia Costa Storti, *The Effects of Monetary Policy: A Meta Analysis.* CESifo Working Paper No. 1224, February 2004.

The study by George McCandless and Warren Weber "Some Monetary Facts" is found in *The Federal Reserve Bank of Minneapolis Quarterly Review* 19 (3), 1995: pp. 2–11.

| TABLE 1 | The Effects of a 1% Increase in Nominal Money, Anticipated and Unanticipated, on Output (Percent) | | | | | |
|---|---|---|---|---|---|---|
| Quarters | 0 | 2 | 4 | 6 | 12 | 16 |
| Effects on output of: | | | | | | |
| Anticipated money | 1.3 | 1.9 | 1.8 | 1.3 | 0.7 | −0.6 |
| Unanticipated money | 2.0 | 2.3 | 2.2 | 2.0 | 0.5 | −0.4 |

*Source: Frederic Mishkin, A Rational Expectations Approach to Macroeconometrics, Table 6.5, p. 122. © 1983 University of Chicago Press. Used by permission of the publisher.*

# 10-5 | A Decrease in the Budget Deficit

The policy we just looked at—a monetary expansion—led to a shift in aggregate demand coming from a shift in the *LM* curve. Let us now look at the effects of a shift in the *IS* curve.

Suppose that government was running a budget deficit and decides to eliminate it. As of 2013, almost all developed countries have significant budget deficits, and most intend to reduce these budget deficits over time. It could accomplish this task by decreasing government spending (*G*) while leaving taxes unchanged. How will this affect the economy in the short run and the medium run?

Assume that output is initially at its natural level so that the economy is at point *A* in Figure 10–7: Output equals $Y_n$. The decrease in government spending shifts the aggregate demand curve to the left, from *AD* to *AD'*: At a given price level, the demand for output is lower. The economy therefore moves from *A* to *A'*, leading to lower output and lower prices. The initial effect of deficit reduction is thus to trigger a recession. We first derived this result in Chapter 3 and confirmed it in Chapter 5, and it holds here as well.

What happens over time? As long as output is below its natural level, the aggregate supply curve keeps shifting down. The economy moves down along the aggregate demand curve *AD'* until the aggregate supply curve is given by *AS"* and the economy reaches point *A"*. By then, the initial recession is over, and output is back at $Y_n$.

So, just like an increase in nominal money, a reduction in the budget deficit does not affect output forever. Eventually, output returns to its natural level; unemployment returns to the natural rate. But there is an important difference between the effects of a change in money and the effects of a change in the deficit: At point *A"*, not everything is the same as before. Output is back to its natural level, but the price level and the interest rate are now lower than before the shift. The best way to see why is to look at the adjustment in terms of the underlying *IS-LM* model.

## The Budget Deficit, Output, and the Interest Rate

Figure 10–8 shows the adjustment in terms of output and the interest rate. Figure 10–8(a) reproduces Figure 10–7. Figure 10–8(b) shows the adjustment in terms of the *IS-LM* model.

Look at Figure 10–8(b). The economy is initially at point *A* (which corresponds to *A* in Figure 10–8[a]). Output is equal to its natural level, $Y_n$, and the interest rate is equal to *i*. As the government reduces the budget deficit, the *IS* curve shifts to the left, to *IS'*. If the price level did not change, the economy would move from point *A* to point *B*. But because prices decline in response to the decrease in output, the real money stock increases, leading to a partly offsetting shift of the *LM* curve downward, to *LM'*. The initial effect of deficit reduction is thus to move

> That the price level decreases as the economy goes first from *A* to *A'* and then from *A'* to *A"* over time feels strange: We rarely observe deflation. This result comes, however, from our assumption that there is no money growth so that there is zero inflation in the medium run. In the real world, money growth is typically positive, and inflation is positive. Recessions generate a temporary decrease in inflation, not a decrease in the price level. We will explore the implications of positive money growth in Chapters 12 and 13.

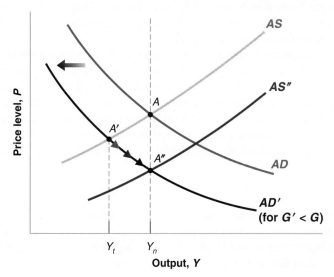

**FIGURE 10–7**

**The Dynamic Effects of a Decrease in the Budget Deficit**

A decrease in the budget deficit leads initially to a decrease in output. Over time, output returns to its natural level.

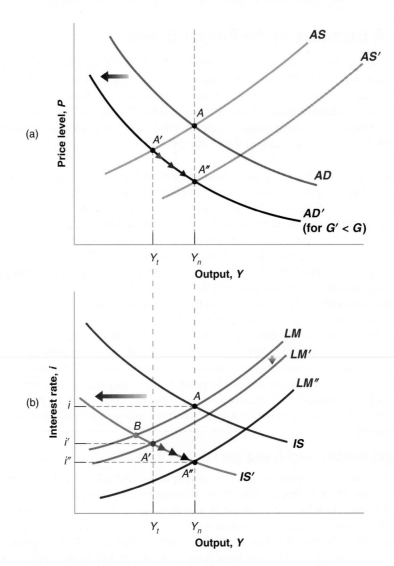

FIGURE 10-8

**The Dynamic Effects of a Decrease in the Budget Deficit on Output and the Interest Rate**

Deficit reduction leads in the short run to a decrease in output and in the interest rate. In the medium run, output returns to its natural level, whereas the interest rate declines further.

Effects of a deficit reduction:

Short run: $Y\downarrow$ and $i\uparrow\downarrow$?

Medium run:
    $Y$ unchanged and $i\uparrow$

We saw in Chapter 5 that Canada reduced deficits in the 1990s without a reduction in output. What happened and what was needed was that a reduction in interest rates led to more aggregate demand at the same time that the deficit was reduced.

the economy from $A$ to $A'$; point $A'$ corresponds to point $A'$ in Figure 10–8(a). Both output and the interest rate are lower than before the fiscal contraction. Note, for later use, that whether investment increases or decreases in the short run is ambiguous: Lower output decreases investment, but the lower interest rate increases it.

Over time, output below the natural level—equivalently, unemployment above the natural rate—leads to a further decrease in prices. As long as output is below its natural level, prices decrease, and the $LM$ curve shifts down. The economy moves down from point $A'$ along $IS'$ and eventually reaches $A''$ (which corresponds to $A''$ in Figure 10–8(a)). At $A''$, the $LM$ curve is given by $LM''$. Output is back at its natural level. But the interest rate is now equal to $i''$, lower than it was before deficit reduction. The composition of output is now different. To see how and why, let us rewrite the $IS$ relation, taking into account that at $A''$, output is back at its natural level so that $Y = Y_n$:

$$Y_n = C(Y_n - T) + I(Y_n, i) + G$$

Because neither income nor taxes have changed, consumption is the same as before deficit reduction. By assumption, government spending, $G$, is lower than before; therefore, investment, $I$, must be higher than before deficit reduction—higher by an amount exactly equal to the decrease in the budget deficit. Put another way, in the medium run, a reduction in the budget deficit unambiguously leads to a decrease in the interest rate and an increase in investment. In the short run, the reduction in the budget deficit as a stand-alone policy leads to a reduction in output.

# 10-6 | Conclusions

This has been an important chapter. Let us repeat and develop some of the conclusions.

## The Short Run versus the Medium Run

One message of this chapter is that changes in aggregate demand typically have different short-run and medium-run effects. We looked at the effects of a monetary expansion and of a deficit reduction.

## Shocks and Propagation Mechanisms

This chapter also gives us a first way of thinking about **output fluctuations** (sometimes called **business cycles**)—movements in output around its trend (a trend that we have ignored so far but will focus on in Chapters 15 to 18.)

In this first way to understand the business cycle, the economy is constantly buffeted by **shocks** to aggregate demand. These shocks may be shifts in consumption coming from changes in consumer confidence, or shifts in investment with changes in business confidence. Or they may come from changes in policy—from the introduction of a new tax law, to a new ◄ program of infrastructure investment, to the decision by the central bank to fight inflation through tight money. In Canada's case, many demand shocks will come from abroad. If GDP in the United States falls, Canada's exports fall and, as in the case of the reduction in the budget deficit, the *IS* and *AD* curves shift to the left.

Each shock has dynamic effects on output and its components. These dynamic effects are called the **propagation mechanism** of the shock. Propagation mechanisms are different for different shocks. The effects on activity may be largest at the beginning and then may decrease over time. Or the effects may build up for a while and then decrease and eventually disappear. We saw, for example, that the effects of an increase in money on output peak after six to nine months and then slowly decline afterward, as prices eventually increase in proportion to the increase in money. In both shocks, output eventually returns to its original level.

The implication of a shock having a propagation mechanism is that the negative effects of a shock may last for a considerable period of time. If the period of high unemployment is long, should policy be used to try to shorten that period of unemployment or make it less severe.

> Defining *shocks* is harder than it appears. Suppose a failed economic program in a foreign country leads to the fall of democracy in that country, which leads to an increase in the risk of nuclear war, which leads to a fall in domestic consumer confidence in our country, which leads to a drop in consumption. What is the "shock"? The failed program? The fall of democracy? The increased risk of nuclear war? Or the decrease in consumer confidence? In practice, we have to cut the chain of causation somewhere. Thus, we may refer to the drop in consumer confidence as "the shock," ignoring its underlying causes.

## First Observations on Policy and the Business Cycle in the *AS-AD* Model

We have much more to say about the role of macroeconomic policy as we continue through the rest of the book, particularly in Chapters 23, 24, and 25. Even at this point we use the *AS-AD* model in this chapter to frame two important questions. These questions are themes we have considered before and will consider again.

Where do fluctuations in output come from? In our two examples in the chapter, the fluctuations in output come directly from monetary and fiscal policy actions. The one-time increase in the money supply we studied led to a temporary increase in output followed by a return to the same level of output and employment and investment at a higher price level. In this example, there is no sensible role for changes in the money supply. The best policy is to keep the money supply constant and the economy will be perfectly stable. Monetary policy does not seem to be needed, and if it is used, leads to larger fluctuations in output.

However we know fluctuations in aggregate demand can come from sources other than policy. In Chapter 3 we looked at changes in consumer confidence and business confidence that changed aggregate demand and output. Thus when consumer confidence or business confidence falls, an increase in the money supply at the same time could reduce interest rates and increase aggregate demand. This would reduce the decrease in output and stabilize the economy. In Chapter 7 we looked at a decline in aggregate demand due to a decline in exports when foreign income fell. If the money supply is not changed, then this leads to a fall in GDP and a recession. A well-timed increase in the money supply could reduce interest rates, depreciate the Canadian dollar, and offset part of the decrease in aggregate demand. The argument for monetary policy in these cases depends crucially on your assessment concerning the length of time the economy takes to return to full employment without any change in policy. If that time is short, then policy is not needed.

We also studied a decrease in the budget deficit and learned that a decrease in the budget deficit would usually reduce output. Output returns to the natural level after some time. However the interest rate is lower and investment is higher. As pointed out in the chapter, higher investment could lead to more output in the future. Here the short run negative effects on output that accompany the reduction in the budget deficit could be offset by future benefits. There is a clear reason to reduce the budget deficit.

We can also make the same arguments about using fiscal policy to stabilize output in the face of the other shocks to aggregate demand—changes in consumer and business confidence as well as changes in exports. If the time for the economy to return to the natural level of output is long, we may use fiscal and monetary policy to speed the return to the natural level of output.

Your views on macroeconomic policy depend to a large degree on your view on the length of time for the economy to return to the natural level of output without any policy change. If this time is short, you will be much less inclined to change monetary and fiscal policy when shocks occur.

Aggregate demand shocks seem relatively simple to analyze. Policy in response to aggregate demand shocks seems simple—if you are faced with a negative shock to aggregate demand, the appropriate response is to increase the money supply or increase the budget deficit and output will not fall as much as it would have. Although there are many complications to be considered, including those explored in the next chapter as well as in the rest of the book, that statement is partly true. The Focus box "Canada's Macroeconomic Policy Response to the World Economic Crisis" is a brief look at monetary and fiscal policy in Canada in 2008 and 2009 as output in the rest of the world fell.

There is an important question yet to be asked in the *AS-AD* framework: Are there shocks where output does not return to the same natural level of output? We answer this question in Chapter 11.

## FOCUS    Canada's Macroeconomic Policy Response to the World Economic Crisis

In 2009, the level of world output fell. Exports from Canada to the rest of the world fell. This reduced business confidence in Canada. Canadian firms who export knew that their sales were falling and less capital would be needed. For these reasons, there was a large reduction in aggregate demand in Canada in 2008 and especially in 2009.

There was an immediate monetary policy response in Canada. On October 21, 2008 the Bank of Canada lowered its interest rate from 2.5% to 2.25%. This was followed by a much more dramatic reduction of the interest rate on December 9, 2008 from 2.25% to 1.5%, a very large reduction. These were followed through 2009 by interest rate reductions on January 20 (to 1%); March 3 (to ½%) and April 21 (to ¼%). The nominal money supply was increased by more than 10% from 2008 to 2009, a percentage far in excess of inflation of less than 2%. Monetary policy responded to the decrease in

© Francis Vachon/Alamy

the demand for exports by reducing interest rates and increasing the money supply.

Fiscal policy was also (eventually) expansionary. The Economic Statement delivered November 27, 2008 made no accommodation for weakening aggregate demand in the rest of the world. That Statement proposed a balanced budget in every fiscal year from 2008–2009 through to 2012–2013. Fiscal years begin on April 1 and end on March 31 the following year. Federal government spending, revenue, and deficits are often reported by fiscal year.

However, with the threat of a defeat in the House of Commons over the contents of the November Economic Statement, the government shut down the House and returned to table a completely different fiscal plan on January 27, 2009. That plan forecast a substantial increase in federal government spending and a substantial decrease in taxes. The forecast budget deficit was 2.2% of GDP in 2009–2010 and 1.8% of GDP in 2010–2011. The Conservative government dubbed this Canada's Economic Action Plan—a moniker that has been repeated for every Conservative economic policy statement since that time. Whether by accident of politics or by design of policy, Canada did engage in an expansionary fiscal policy just as output fell most severely in the rest of the world. Most economists would argue that the recession in Canada was less severe than it would have been without this expansionary fiscal policy, particularly when combined with an extremely expansionary monetary policy.

## SUMMARY

- The aggregate supply–aggregate demand model describes the movements in output and prices when account is taken of equilibrium in the goods, financial, and labour markets.

- The aggregate supply relation captures the effects of output on the price level. It is derived from equilibrium in the labour market. It is a relation among the price level, the expected price level, and the level of output. An increase in output decreases unemployment, increases wages, and, in turn, increases the price level. A higher expected price level leads, one for one, to a higher increase in the actual price level.

- The aggregate demand relation captures the effects of the price level on output. It is derived from equilibrium in the goods and financial markets. An increase in the price level decreases the real money stock, increases interest rates, and decreases output.

- In the short run, movements in output can come from changes in aggregate demand. In the medium run, after a fluctuation in output caused by a change in aggregate demand, output returns to the unchanged natural level of output determined in the labour market.

- An expansionary monetary policy leads, in the short run, to an increase in the real money stock, a decrease in the interest rate, and an increase in output. Over time, the price level increases, leading to a decrease in the real money stock until output has returned to its natural level. In the medium run, money is neutral: It does not affect output, and changes in money are reflected in proportional increases in the price level.

- A decrease in the budget deficit leads, in the short run, to a decrease in the demand for goods and thus a decrease in output. Over time, the price level decreases, leading to an increase in the real money stock and a decrease in the interest rate. In the medium run, output is back to its natural level, but the interest rate is lower and investment is higher.

- The difference between short- and medium-run effects of policies is one of the main reasons economists disagree in their policy recommendations. Some economists believe that the economy adjusts quickly to its medium-run equilibrium and thus emphasize medium-run implications of policy. Others believe that the adjustment mechanism through which output returns to its natural level is a slow one at best and put more emphasis on short-run effects.

- Economic fluctuations are partly the result of a constant stream of shocks to aggregate demand and of the dynamic effects of each of these shocks on output. Sometimes, the shocks are sufficiently adverse, alone or in combination, that they lead to a recession.

## KEY TERMS

## 1. TRUE/FALSE/UNCERTAIN

**a.** The aggregate supply relation implies that an increase in output leads to an increase in the price level.

**b.** The natural level of output can be determined by looking only at the aggregate supply relation.

**c.** The aggregate demand relation implies that an increase in the price level leads to an increase in output.

**d.** In the absence of changes in fiscal and/or monetary policy, the economy will always remain at the natural level of output.

**e.** Expansionary monetary policy has no effect on the level of output in the medium run.

**f.** Fiscal policy cannot affect investment in the medium run because output always returns to its natural level.

**g.** In the medium run, prices and output always return to the same value after a demand shock.

**h.** After a fall in consumer confidence, the money supply could be decreased to help output return to its natural level.

## 2. SPENDING SHOCKS AND THE MEDIUM RUN

Using the *AS-AD* model developed in this chapter, show the effects of each of the following shocks on the position of the *IS*, *LM*, *AD*, and *AS* curves in the medium run. Then, show the effect on output, the interest rate, and the price level, also in the medium run. Assume that before the changes, the economy was at the natural level of output.

**a.** An increase in consumer confidence

**b.** An increase in taxes

## 3. THE NEUTRALITY OF MONEY

**a.** In what sense is money neutral? Why is monetary policy useful, even though money is neutral?

**b.** Fiscal policy, just like monetary policy, cannot change the natural level of output. Why then is monetary policy considered neutral but fiscal policy is not?

**c.** Discuss this statement: "Because neither fiscal nor monetary policy can affect the natural level of output, it follows that in the medium run, the natural level of output is independent of all government policies."

## 4. WHAT IF THE INTEREST RATE HAD NO EFFECT ON INVESTMENT?

Suppose that investment is not responsive to the interest rate.

**a.** Can you think of a situation where that may happen?

**b.** What does this imply for the *IS* curve?

**c.** What does this imply for the *LM* curve?

**d.** What does this imply for the *AD* curve?

## 5. INVESTMENT AND MONETARY POLICY

Consider the following model of the economy (we ignore the role of *G* and *T* on demand; also, to simplify the algebra, we assume that output depends on the difference between *M* and *P* rather than on their ratio):

$$AD: \quad Y = c(M - P)$$
$$AS: \quad P = P^e + d(Y - Y_n)$$

where *c* and *d* are parameters.

**a.** What is the natural level of output? If nominal money is equal to $M_0$, what is the initial price level? Call this initial price level $P_0$. Assume the expected price level is the initial price level.

Suppose that in an effort to increase investment, the Bank of Canada decides to pursue an expansionary monetary policy and doubles the nominal money stock: $M_1 = 2M_0$.

**b.** Solve for the equilibrium value of output in the short run.

**c.** What happens to investment behind the scene? Explain in words.

**d.** Solve for the equilibrium value of output in the medium run.

**e.** What happens to investment in the medium run? Explain in words.

## 6. SPENDING SHOCKS, POLICY IN THE SHORT AND MEDIUM RUNS

**a.** Supposed there is an increase in consumer confidence. Show the short-run effects on these curves: *IS, LM, AD, AS*. Will output rise or fall in the short run in the absence of policy action? Assume that before the change in consumer confidence, the economy was at its natural level of output.

What monetary policy action will prevent a change in output when there in an increase in consumer confidence? What curves shift?

How does the composition of output change in the medium run? What justifies this policy?

b.  Suppose there is a decrease in business confidence. Show the short-run effects on these curves: *IS, LM, AD, AS*. Will output rise or fall in the short run in the absence of policy action? Assume that before the change in consumer confidence, the economy was at its natural level of output.

What change in government spending will prevent a change in output when there in a decrease in business consumer confidence? What curves shift?

How does the composition of output change in the medium run? What justifies this policy?

# All Markets Together: The *AS-AD* Model—Liquidity Traps and Supply Shocks

## The Core: The Medium Run

We looked at the basics of the *AS-AD* model in the previous chapter. We found equilibrium in all three markets: goods markets, financial markets, and labour markets. This chapter looks at two important complications.

- When we had small shocks to aggregate demand in Chapter 10, output would, in time, return to its natural level. Monetary policy could also be used to speed the return of output to the natural level. We show in this chapter that a very large negative shock to aggregate demand will place the economy in a **liquidity trap**. In this case output will not return to its natural level regardless of how long we wait. An expansion of the money supply cannot return the economy to full employment.

- We introduce the possibility of a **supply shock**, a macroeconomic event that reduces the level of natural output.

Are these complications to the basic *AS-AD* framework necessary? Three important economies experienced a liquidity trap in the last 100 years: North America in the **Great Depression** of the 1930s, the prolonged Japanese slump of the 1990s, and the United States in 2009 as part of the world economic crisis of 2009. Although these events are rare, the reduction in output in a liquidity trap is large and long. Studying why these events occur, how to avoid them, and what to do when they occur is important.

A large shock to aggregate supply occurred when the real price of oil increased sharply in the 1970s. The shock led to both inflation and unemployment, a very unpleasant combination. Understanding how such an outcome could occur is worthwhile.

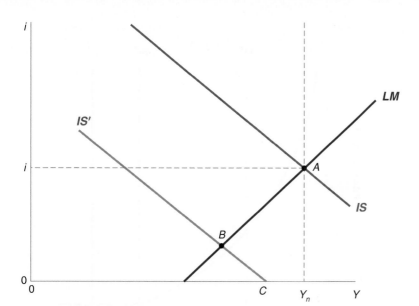

FIGURE 11-1

**The Shift in Aggregate Demand Needed to Create a Liquidity Trap in the *IS-LM* Model**

This diagram shows a negative shock to aggregate demand that is large enough to create a liquidity trap. The intersection of the *IS* curve and the horizontal axis at point *C* is considerably to left of the natural rate of output. Even at a zero rate of interest, aggregate demand is much less than $Y_n$. The economy is in a liquidity trap. Point *C* is the level of output when the economy is in the liquidity trap.

## 11-1 | The Liquidity Trap and the Risk of Deflation

The first step in understanding the liquidity trap returns us to the *IS-LM* model in Figure 11–1. The figure depicts an *IS* curve and an *LM* curve starting at the natural level of output and interest rate *i*, the point labeled *A*. There is a large negative shock to demand that shifts the *IS* curve to *IS'*. In section 11–2 and the Focus boxes in this chapter, we analyze the source of such a large shock. Suffice it to say that a very large decline in consumer confidence, a very large decline in business confidence, or the combination of the two are sufficient to generate such a large shift. For now, we just accept that there is such a large shock and consider its consequences.

With such a large shock, even if the interest rate falls to zero, Figure 11–1 shows that the *IS* curve intersects the horizontal axis at point C, at a level of output much lower than the natural rate of output, $Y_n$. The economy is in the liquidity trap. Why does it have this name?

> In short, the liquidity trap occurs when the *IS* curve crosses the horizontal axis at an interest rate of zero to the left of the natural level of output.

### The Limits of Monetary Policy: The Liquidity Trap

To answer this question, we must first go back first to our characterization of the demand and the supply of money in Chapter 4. There we drew the demand for money, for a given level of income, as a decreasing function of the interest rate. The lower the interest rate, the larger the demand for money—equivalently, the smaller the demand for bonds. What we did not ask in Chapter 4 is what happens to the demand for money when the interest rate becomes equal to zero. The answer: Once people hold enough money for transaction purposes, they are then indifferent between holding the rest of their financial wealth in the form of money or in the form of bonds. The reason they are indifferent is that both money and bonds pay the same interest rate, namely zero. Thus, the demand for money is as shown in Figure 11–2.

> If you look at Figure 4–1, you will see that we avoided the issue by not drawing the demand for money for interest rates close to zero.

- As the interest rate decreases, people want to hold more money (and thus less bonds): The demand for money increases.
- As the interest rate becomes equal to zero, people want to hold an amount of money at least equal to the distance *OB*: this is what they need for transaction purposes. But they are willing to hold even more money (and therefore hold less bonds) because they are indifferent between money and bonds. Therefore, the demand for money becomes horizontal beyond point *B*.

**FIGURE** 11–2

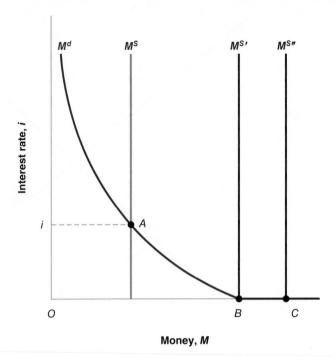

**Money Demand, Money Supply, and the Liquidity Trap**

When the interest rate is equal to zero, and once people have enough money for transaction purposes, they become indifferent between holding money and holding bonds. The demand for money becomes horizontal. This implies that, when the interest rate is equal to zero, further increases in the money supply have no effect on the interest rate.

Now consider the effects of an increase in the money supply.

- Consider the case where the money supply is $M^s$, so the interest rate consistent with financial market equilibrium is positive and equal to $i$. (This is the case we considered in Chapter 4.) Starting from that equilibrium, an increase in the money supply—a shift of the $M^s$ line to the right—leads to a decrease in the interest rate.
- Now consider the case where the money supply is $M^{s'}$, so the equilibrium is at point B; or the case where the money supply is $M^{s''}$, so the equilibrium is given at point C. In either case, the initial interest rate is zero. An increase in the money supply from B to C has no effect on the interest rate. Think of it this way:

> From Chapter 4: The central bank changes the money stock through open market operations, in which it buys or sells bonds in exchange for money.

Suppose the central bank increases the money supply. It does so through an open market operation in which it buys bonds and pays for them by creating money. As the interest rate is zero, people are indifferent to how much money or bonds they hold, so they are willing to hold less bonds and more money at the same interest rate, namely zero. The money supply increases, but with no effect on the interest rate—which remains equal to zero.

In short: Once the interest rate is equal to zero, expansionary monetary policy becomes powerless. Or to use the words of Keynes, who was the first to point out the problem, the increase in money falls into a liquidity trap: People are willing to hold more money (*more liquidity*) at the same interest rate.

The derivation of the *LM* curve when one takes into account the possibility of a liquidity trap is shown in the two panels of Figure 11–3. Recall that the *LM* curve gives, for a given real money stock, the relation between the interest rate and the level of income implied by equilibrium in financial markets. To derive the *LM* curve, Figure 11–3(a) looks at equilibrium in the financial markets for a given value of the real money stock and draws three money demand curves, each corresponding to a different level of income:

- $M^d$ shows the demand for money for a given level of income $Y$. The equilibrium is given by point A, with interest rate equal to $i$. This combination of income $Y$ and interest rate $i$ gives us the first point on the *LM* curve, point A in Figure 11–3(b).
- $M^{d'}$ shows the demand for money for a lower level of income, $Y' < Y$. Lower income means fewer transactions and, therefore, a lower demand for money at any interest rate.

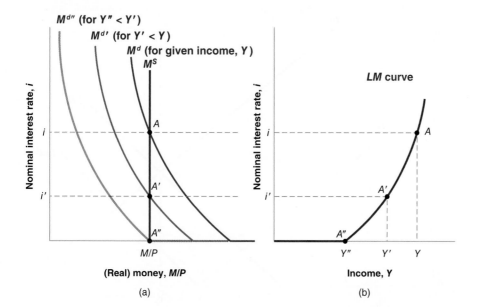

FIGURE 11-3

**The Derivation of the *LM* Curve in the Presence of a Liquidity Trap**

For low levels of output, the *LM* curve is a flat segment, with an interest rate equal to zero. For higher levels of output, it is upward sloping: An increase in income leads to an increase in the interest rate.

In this case, the equilibrium is given by point $A'$, with interest rate equal to $i'$. This combination of income $Y'$ and interest rate $i'$ gives us the second point on the *LM* curve, point $A'$ in Figure 11–3(b).

- $M^{d''}$ gives the demand for money for a still lower level of income $Y'' < Y'$. In this case, the equilibrium is given by point $A''$ in Figure 11–3(a), with interest rate equal to zero. point $A''$ in Figure 11–3(b) corresponds to $A''$ in Figure 11–3(a).
- What happens if income decreases below $Y''$, shifting the demand for money further to the left in Figure 11–3(a)? The intersection between the money supply curve and the money demand curve takes place on the horizontal portion of the money demand curve. The interest rate remains equal to zero.

So far, the derivation of the *LM* curve is exactly the same as in Chapter 5. It is only when income is lower than $Y''$, that things become different.

Let's summarize: In the presence of a liquidity trap, the *LM* curve is given by Figure 11–3(b). For values of income greater than $Y''$, the *LM* curve is upward sloping—just as it was in Chapter 5 when we first characterized the *LM* curve. For values of income less than $Y''$, it is flat at $i = 0$. Intuitively: The interest rate cannot go below zero.

Having derived the *LM* curve in the presence of a liquidity trap, we can look at the properties of the *IS–LM* model modified in this way. Figure 11–4 contains the same large shift in the *IS* curve to the left from *IS* to *IS'* that we introduced in Figure 11–1. If there is no response from the central bank and the real money supply remains the same, the *LM* curve does not shift. Goods markets and financial markets would be in equilibrium at point $B$. There is a very low level of income $Y'$ and low rate of interest $i'$.

The question is: Can monetary policy help the economy return to the natural level of output, $Y_n$? Suppose the central bank increases the money supply, shifting the *LM* curve from *LM* to *LM'*. The equilibrium does move from point $B$ to point $C$ and output does increase from $Y'$ to $Y''$. However, as we discussed in Figures 11–2 and 11–3, a further increase in the money supply will not increase output. Once the interest rate is zero, it remains at zero and output remains at $Y''$ at point $C$.

In words: When the interest rate is equal to zero, the economy falls into a *liquidity trap*: The central bank can increase *liquidity*—that is, increase the money supply. But this *liquidity* falls into a *trap*: The additional money is willingly held by people at an unchanged interest rate, namely zero. Since the interest rate remains at zero, the demand for goods does not change. There is nothing further an expansion of the money supply can do to increase output.

The lesson is that with a very large decrease in aggregate demand—that is, a very large shift in the *IS* curve to the left—the decline in output can be so large that the economy falls

**FIGURE   11-4**

**The *IS–LM* Model and the Liquidity Trap**

In the presence of a liquidity trap, an expansion of the money supply cannot return output to the natural level of output. Even after the money supply is increased and the interest rate hits zero, the economy is trapped well below the natural level of output at point *C*.

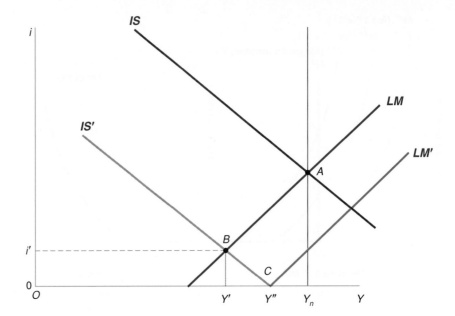

into a liquidity trap. Unfortunately, if we extend the analysis to the *AS-AD* model, the situation can become even worse.

## The Risk of Deflation

In the presence of a liquidity trap, the process of adjustment in the *AS-AD* model fails to return the economy to the natural level of output. Recall from Chapter 10 how the mechanism typically works:

- A decrease in output below its natural level leads to a decrease in the price level.
- This leads to an increase in the real money stock, which in turn leads to a decrease in the interest rate.
- The decrease in the interest rate leads then to an increase in spending, which in turn leads to an increase in output.

The process goes on until output has returned to its natural level. The process can be made faster by using either monetary policy (that is, by increasing the money stock, which leads to a larger decrease in the interest rate) or fiscal policy, which increases demand directly. At the core of the adjustment is the aggregate demand relation (equation (10.2) in Chapter 10):

$$Y = Y\left(\frac{M}{P}, G, T\right)$$

Now think about what happens when the economy is in the liquidity trap, with the interest rate equal to zero. In this case, an increase in the real money stock, $M/P$, whether it comes from an increase in $M$ or from a decrease in $P$, has no effect on the interest rate, which remains equal to zero. So not only does monetary policy not affect spending, but the adjustment mechanism that returns output to its natural level in the *AS–AD* model also does not work: The decrease in the price level leads to a higher real money stock but does not lead to a lower interest rate and does not lead to higher spending.

Let's formally introduce this in our *AS–AD* model. If the economy is in the liquidity trap, the aggregate demand relation takes the following form:

$$Y = Y(G, T) \tag{11.1}$$

As before, increases in government spending or decreases in taxes increase demand. But in the liquidity trap, aggregate demand no longer depends on the real money stock.

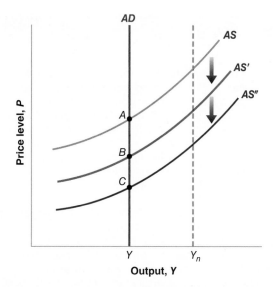

FIGURE 11-5

**The Liquidity Trap and Adjustment Failure**

If the economy is in the liquidity trap and output is below its natural level, the price level may decrease over time, but output does not increase.

What may then happen to the economy is represented in Figure 11–5, using the *AS–AD* model. Aggregate supply is still represented by an upward sloping curve in the figure: The higher the level of output, the higher the price level, given the expected price level. Conversely, and more relevantly for our case, the lower the output, the lower the price level.

The aggregate demand relation is now vertical over the range of prices through A, B and C. The curve is drawn for the liquidity trap case. For given values of $G$, $T$, aggregate demand does not depend on the real money stock and thus does not depend on the price level. Suppose that the initial aggregate supply and demand curves are given by *AS* and *AD* respectively, so the initial equilibrium is at point *A*, with output $Y$ below the natural level $Y_n$. In other words, output is low, and the economy is in the liquidity trap. As output is below its natural level, the aggregate supply curve shifts down over time. (Recall the mechanism: Low output implies high unemployment, which puts downward pressure on wages, and in turn on prices.) The equilibrium moves over time from *A* to *B* to *C*: The price level keeps decreasing, but this does not lead to an increase in output.

A constant decrease in the price level is called **deflation**. You can think of deflation as a series of years of negative inflation as prices fall when the economy moves from point *A* to point *B* to point *C* in Figure 11–5. Although it is not included in the modified aggregate demand relation (11.1), there are reasons to believe the expected deflation would further reduce aggregate demand, that is, shift the aggregate demand curve in Figure 11–5 further to the left and shift the *IS* curves in Figures 11–1 and 11–4 further to the left. Why might this happen? Imagine you are a consumer waiting to buy a new car or appliance. If you thought the price level was going to fall by 10% between now and next year, you might decide to wait to buy the new car at a lower price.

The last sustained deflation in North America took place during the Great Depression in the 1930s. See the Focus box "The Great Depression in North America"

# 11-2 | The Most Recent Liquidity Trap: The United States in 2009

For an economy to enter a liquidity trap, an exceptionally large decrease in aggregate demand must occur. The most prominent examples of liquidity traps and the major declines in economic output are labelled **depressions**, prolonged periods of low economic activity. The Focus box "The Great Depression in North America" explores the depression of the 1930s, a liquidity trap. The distinction between a recession and a depression is subjective; the latter is longer and more severe than the former in terms of lower output and higher unemployment. In this section, we join theory and empirical evidence to explore how the major decline in

We hope Table 1 is the most depressing economic data you will ever see! It presents, for Canada and the United States, the unemployment rate, the output growth rate, the price level, and the nominal money supply for the years from 1929 to 1942. There was a dramatic fall in aggregate demand in 1929 in the United States and, with the United States as Canada's biggest export market, demand and output fell in Canada as well. The Great Depression in Canada was, as is usually the case for Canadian slumps, primarily a slump in the foreign countries that are our export markets. But the size of the fall in output in the Great Depression was unprecedented.

Output in the United States fell every year between 1929 and 1932: four consecutive years! The total fall in output was about 30 percentage points of the level of output in 1928. In Canada, output fell from 1930 to 1933. The unemployment rate peaked in the United States at 24.9% and at 19.5% in Canada in 1933. The Great Depression was an economic disaster.

Were the 1930s a liquidity trap? Interest rates In America throughout the 1930s were near zero. If you use the nominal money supply and the price levels in Table 1 to calculate the real money supply in each year, you would find that in America the real money supply increased from 1929 to 1932 while output continued to fall over these years. In Canada, where output fell by 30% between 1929 and 1933, the real money supply fell by only 5%. The real money supply in both countries increased steadily from 1933 onwards with only a very slow decline in unemployment. The ineffectiveness of monetary policy at raising the level of output and returning the economy to full employment appears to be amply demonstrated by the Great Depression.

The tough times in North America went on for a long time. Output did not recover its 1929 level in the United States until 1936, falling in 1937 and finally regaining its 1928 level in 1938. Canadian output followed a similar pattern. The unemployment rate remained high in both countries until 1942. Canada entered the Second World War in September 1939; the United States entered the Second World War in late 1941. Wartime demand for men and material led to the decline in the unemployment rate and the very large increases in output in both countries. The end of the Great Depression certainly coincided with the onset of World War II or, in our *IS-LM* language, a very expansionary fiscal policy.

| TABLE | 1 | North America in the Great Depression |

| Year | Unemployment Rate (%) | | Output Growth Rate (%) | | Price Level | | Nominal Money Supply | |
|------|---------|------|--------|------|--------|------|----------------------|----------------------|
| | Canada | U.S. | Canada | U.S. | Canada | U.S. | Canada C$ millions | U.S. US$ billions |
| 1929 | 2.9 | 3.2 | 0.9 | −9.8 | 100.0 | 100.0 | 787.8 | 26.4 |
| 1930 | 9.1 | 8.7 | −3.3 | −7.6 | 96.7 | 97.4 | 722.0 | 25.4 |
| 1931 | 11.6 | 15.9 | −11.2 | −14.7 | 90.1 | 88.8 | 683.6 | 23.6 |
| 1932 | 17.6 | 23.6 | −9.3 | −1.8 | 81.8 | 79.7 | 605.8 | 19.4 |
| 1933 | 19.3 | 24.9 | −7.2 | 9.1 | 80.2 | 75.6 | 603.6 | 21.5 |
| 1934 | 14.5 | 21.7 | 10.4 | 9.9 | 81.8 | 78.1 | 633.3 | 25.5 |
| 1935 | 14.2 | 20.1 | 7.2 | 13.9 | 82.6 | 80.1 | 704.2 | 29.2 |
| 1936 | 12.8 | 16.9 | 4.6 | 5.3 | 85.1 | 80.9 | 757.3 | 30.3 |
| 1937 | 9.1 | 14.3 | 8.8 | −5.0 | 87.6 | 83.8 | 851.1 | 30.0 |
| 1938 | 11.4 | 19.0 | 1.4 | 8.6 | 86.8 | 82.2 | 857.0 | 30.0 |
| 1939 | 11.4 | 17.2 | 7.5 | 8.5 | 86.8 | 81.0 | 929.6 | 33.6 |
| 1940 | 9.2 | 14.6 | 13.3 | 16.1 | 90.9 | 81.8 | 1146.6 | 39.6 |
| 1941 | 4.4 | 9.9 | 13.3 | 12.9 | 97.5 | 85.9 | 1453.6 | 46.5 |
| 1942 | 3.0 | 4.7 | 17.6 | 13.2 | 102.5 | 95.1 | 1844.9 | 55.3 |

*Source*: *For Canada*: *Unemployment rate* using Statistics Canada, CANSIM Series D31253 and D31254; *output growth, GDP growth*, using CANSIM Series D14442; *price level, GDP deflator* (1929 = 100) using CANSIM Series D14476; *money supply*, M1 from C. Metcalf, A. Redish, R. Shearer, "New Estimates of the Canadian Money Stock, 1871–1967," *Canadian Journal of Economics*, 1998: pp. 104–124.

*For the U.S.: Unemployment rate: Historical Statistics of the United States* using U.S. Department of Commerce, Series D85-86; *output growth, GNP growth* using Series F31; *price level*, CPI (1929 = 100) using Series E135; *money stock*, M1 using Series X414; *Historical Statistics of the United States*, U.S. Department of Commerce.

**FURTHER READING**

For more on the Great Depression in Canada, see Kenneth, Norrie, and Douglas, *A History of the Canadian Economy* (Toronto: Harcourt Brace, 1996), Chapter 17, which gives the basic facts.

Ed Safarian's book, *The Canadian Economy in the Great Depression* (Toronto: University of Toronto Press, 1959) is the classic reference.

A description of the Great Depression through the eyes of those who suffered through it is given by Barry Broadfoot's *Ten Lost Years 1929–1939* (Toronto: McClelland and Stewart, 1997). This book, which has been turned into both a play and a video, is a moving account of the Great Depression in Canada.

There is a series of made-for-television movies that follow the adventures of a young girl named Booky who lives in Toronto in the Great Depression.

For more on the Great Depression in the United States, see Lester Chandler's *America's Greatest Depression* (New York: Harper and Row, 1970), which gives the basic facts. So does the book by John A. Garraty, *The Great Depression* (New York: Harcourt Brace Jovanovich, 1986).

Peter Temin's *Did Monetary Forces Cause the Great Depression?* (New York: W.W. Norton, 1976) looks more specifically at the macroeconomic issues. So do the articles presented in a symposium on the Great Depression in the *Journal of Economic Perspectives*, Spring 1993.

house prices in America interacted with a fragile financial system to generate the large decline in aggregate demand that led the American (and world) economy into the major recession and the liquidity trap in 2009.

> ◀ The period of time from 2008 to 2009 is often called the World Economic Crisis.

## Housing Prices and Subprime Mortgages

From 2000 to 2006, house prices in the United States roughly doubled. In 2006, as housing prices started to decline in the United States, most economists forecast this decline would lead to a decrease in aggregate demand and a slowdown in growth. Only a few economists anticipated that it would lead to a major macroeconomic crisis and a liquidity trap. These economists had not anticipated the effect of the decline of housing prices on the financial system, the focus of this section.

Figure 11–6 shows the evolution of an index of U.S. housing prices from 2000 on. The index is known as the Case-Shiller index, named for the two economists who have constructed it. The index is normalized to equal 100 in January 2000. You can see the large increase in prices in the early 2000s, followed by a large and rapid decrease from 2006 to 2008. From 2010 to 2012, the average value of the index was around 130.

> ◀ Type "Case-Shiller" on the Internet if you want to find the index and see its recent evolution. Canada has a similar house price index found at www.housepriceindex.ca/

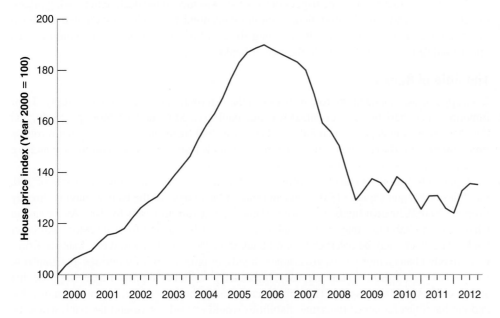

**FIGURE 11–6**

**House Prices in the United States, 2000–2012**

Prior to the World Economic Crisis, house prices in the United States rose from 2000 to 2006 and then declined sharply.

*Source:* House Prices: Case-Shiller Home Price Indices, http://www.standardandpoors.com/indices/main/en/us.

Was the sharp increase in house prices from 2000 to 2006 justified? In retrospect, and given the ensuing collapse, surely not. But, at the time, when prices were increasing, economists were not so sure. *Some* increase in prices was clearly justified:

Even if people did not finance the purchase of a house by taking a mortgage, low interest rates would lead to an increase in the price of houses. You will learn more about this when we discuss present discounted values in Chapter 19.

- The 2000s were a period of unusually low interest rates. As a result, mortgage rates were also low, increasing the demand for housing and thus pushing up the price.
- Other factors were also at work. **Mortgage lenders** became increasingly willing to make loans to more risky borrowers. These mortgages, known as **subprime mortgages**, or **subprimes** for short, had existed since the mid-1990s but became more prevalent in the 2000s. By 2006, about 20% of all U.S. mortgages were subprimes. Was it necessarily bad? Again, at the time, this was seen by most economists as a positive development: It allowed more people to buy homes, and, under the assumption that housing prices would continue to increase so the value of the mortgage would decrease over time relative to the price of the house, it looked safe both for lenders and for borrowers. Judging from the past, the assumption that housing prices would not decrease also seemed reasonable: As you can see from Figure 11–6, house prices had not decreased during the 2000–2001 recession in the United States.

Some economists were worried even as prices were going up. Robert Shiller, one of the two economists behind the Case-Shiller index, was among them, warning that the price increase was a bubble that would most likely burst.

In retrospect, again, these developments were much less benign than most economists thought. First, housing prices could go down, as became evident from 2006 on. When this happened, many borrowers found themselves in a situation where the mortgage they owed now exceeded the value of their house (when the value of the mortgage exceeds the value of the house, the mortgage is said to be **underwater**). Second, it became clear that, in many cases, the mortgages were in fact much riskier than either the lender pretended or the borrower understood. In many cases, borrowers had taken mortgages with low initial interest rates and thus low initial interest payments, probably not fully realizing that payments would increase sharply over time. Even if house prices had not declined, many of these borrowers would have been unable to meet their mortgage payments.

Some of these loans became known as NINJA loans (for no income, no job, no assets).

Thus, as house prices fell so quickly and many borrowers defaulted, many banks found themselves faced with large losses. In mid-2008, losses on mortgages were estimated to be around $300 billion. This is obviously a large number, but relative to the size of the U.S. economy, it is not a very large number: $300 billion is only about 2% of U.S. GDP. One might have thought that the U.S. financial system could absorb the shock and that the adverse effect on output would be limited.

This was not to be. While the trigger of the crisis was indeed the decline in housing prices, its effects were enormously amplified. Even those economists who had anticipated the housing price decline did not realize how strong the amplification mechanisms would be. To understand them, we must return to the role of banks.

## The Role of Banks

In Chapter 4, we looked at the role of banks in the determination of the money supply. Their important characteristic in that context was that banks issued money, or, more precisely, that they had chequable deposits as liabilities. Here, we shall focus on their more general role as **financial intermediaries**, institutions that receive funds from those who wish to save and use those funds to make loans to those who wish to borrow.

See section 4-3.

Figure 11–7 shows a (much simplified) bank balance sheet. The bank has assets of 100, liabilities of 80, and capital of 20. You can think of the owners of the bank as having directly invested 20 of their own funds, borrowed 80 and bought various assets for 100. As we saw in Chapter 4, the liabilities may be chequable deposits, or borrowing from investors and other banks. The assets may be reserves (central bank money), loans to consumers, loans to firms, loans to other banks, mortgages, government bonds, or other forms of securities. In Chapter 4, we ignored capital. But, for our purposes, introducing capital is important here. Suppose that a bank did not hold any capital. Then, if, for any reason, the assets it held went down in value and the liabilities remained the same, liabilities would exceed assets, and the bank would be

One wishes that the balance sheets of banks were this simple and transparent. Had it been the case, the crisis would have been much more limited.

bankrupt—that is, unable to pay off its depositors. It is thus essential for the bank to hold enough capital to limit the risk of bankruptcy.

How can things go wrong even if the bank holds some capital, as in our example? First, the assets may decline in value by so much that the capital the bank holds is not enough to cover its losses. In our example, this will happen if the value of the assets decreases below 80. The bank will become insolvent. This is not, however, the only way the bank can get in trouble. Suppose that some of the investors who have loaned to the bank (made a deposit in the bank) want their funds back right away. If the bank can sell some of its assets, it can get the funds and pay the depositors. But it may be difficult for the bank to sell the assets quickly: Calling back loans is difficult; some securities may be hard to sell. The problem of the bank in this case is not **solvency**, but **illiquidity**. The bank is still solvent, but it is illiquid. The more liquid its liabilities, or the less liquid its assets, the more likely the bank is to find itself in trouble.

What happened in this crisis when American house prices fell was a combination of all these factors. Banks had too little capital. Liabilities, both deposits and other securities issued by banks, were very liquid. Assets were often very illiquid. The outcome was a combination of both solvency and liquidity problems, which quickly paralyzed the financial system. We now look at three specific aspects of the crisis that affected banks (and other financial intermediaries) in more detail.

## Leverage

Consider two banks. As in Figure 11–7, bank A has assets of 100, liabilities of 80, and capital of 20. Its **capital ratio** is defined as the ratio of capital to assets and is thus equal to 20%. Its **leverage ratio** is defined as the ratio of assets to capital (the inverse of the capital ratio) and is thus equal to 5. Bank B has assets of 100, liabilities of 95, and capital of 5. Thus, its capital ratio is equal to 5%, and its leverage ratio to 20.

Now suppose that some of the assets in each of the two banks go bad. For example, some borrowers cannot repay their loans. Suppose, as a result, that for both banks, the value of the assets decreases from 100 to 90. Bank A now has assets of 90, liabilities of 80, and capital of $90 - 80 = 10$. Bank B has assets of 90, liabilities of 95, and thus *negative* capital of $90 - 95 = -5$. Its liabilities exceed its assets: In other words, it is bankrupt. This is indeed what happened in 2008 and 2009, both in the United States and in other countries. Many banks had such a high leverage ratio that even limited losses on assets related to mortgages greatly increased the risk of bankruptcy.

Why was leverage so high? The example suggests a simple answer: Higher leverage means higher expected profit, or, more precisely, a higher rate of return on capital invested. Suppose, for example, that assets pay an expected rate of return of 5%, and liabilities pay an expected rate of return of 4%. Then the owners of bank A have an expected rate of return on their capital of $(100 \times 5\% - 80 \times 4\%)/20 = 9\%$, and the owners of bank B have an expected rate of return of $(100 \times 5\% - 95 \times 4\%)/5 = 24\%$, more than twice as high. But, as the example we just saw also makes clear, leverage also increases risk: The higher the leverage, the more likely the bank is to go bankrupt. What happened throughout the 2000s is that banks all over the world, but particularly in the United States, decided to get a higher return and thus to take on more risk as well through increases in leverage.

Why did banks opt to take on more risk? This is the subject of much discussion. There appears to be a number of reasons: First, banks probably underestimated the risk they were taking: Times were good, and, in good times, banks, just like people, tend to underestimate

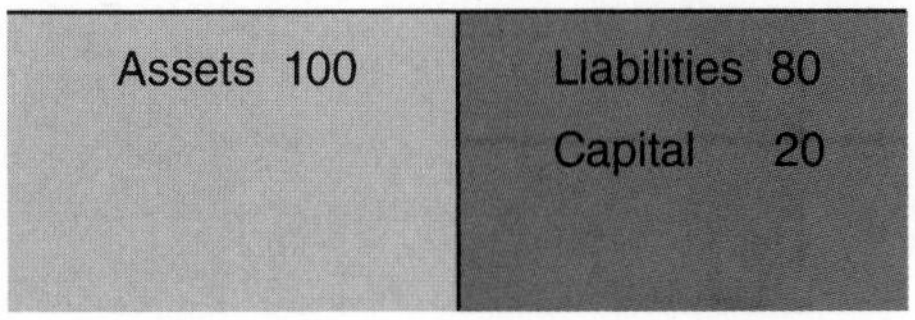

No matter how careful a bank is, just with bad luck, some of the bank's loans will always default. The bank's capital is sufficient for loan failure at the usual rate.

See the Focus box "Bank Runs and Bank Collapses" in Chapter 4.

Northern Rock was the most well-known bank failure in the United Kingdom.

Some liabilities may actually pay a zero rate of return. Recall from Chapter 4 that a large part of these liabilities is chequing deposits, which typically pay at most a low interest rate.

| Assets  100 | Liabilities  80 |
|             | Capital     20  |

**FIGURE   11–7**

**Bank Assets, Capital, and Liabilities**

the risk of bad times. Second, the compensation and bonus system gave incentives to managers to pursue high expected returns without fully taking the risk of bankruptcy into account. Third, while financial regulation required banks to keep their capital ratio above some minimum, many banks found new ways of avoiding the regulation, by creating new financial structures such as *SIVs*. What these are and how banks used them is explained in the Focus box "Increasing Bank Leverage in the United States—the SIV."

## Complexity

One crucial difference between Canada and the United States has always been that banks in Canada are national with assets in all provinces. The failure of the two Alberta banks, Northland and Canadian Commercial, in the 1980s, are the exceptions that prove the rule. These banks held assets heavily concentrated in Alberta.

Another important development of the 1990s and the 2000s was the growth of **securitization**. Traditionally, the financial intermediaries that made loans or issued mortgages kept them on their own balance sheet. This had obvious drawbacks. A local bank, with local loans and mortgages on its books, was very much exposed to the local economic situation. When, for example, oil prices had come down sharply in the mid-1980s and both Texas and Alberta fell into a serious recession, local banks went bankrupt. Had banks in Texas or Alberta had a more diversified portfolio of mortgages, say mortgages from many parts of the country, these banks might have avoided bankruptcy.

This is the idea behind securitization. Securitization is the creation of securities based on a bundle of assets (for example, a bundle of loans, or a bundle of mortgages). For instance, a **mortgage-backed security**, or **MBS**, is a title to the returns from a bundle of mortgages, with the number of underlying mortgages often in the tens of thousands. The advantage is that many investors who would not want to hold individual mortgages will be willing to buy and hold these securities. This increase in the supply of funds from investors is, in turn, likely to decrease the cost of borrowing.

One can think of further forms of securitization. For example, instead of issuing identical claims to the returns on the underlying bundle of assets, one can issue different types of securities. For example, one can issue two types of securities: **senior securities**, which have first claims on the returns from the bundle, and **junior securities**, which come after and pay only if something is left after the senior securities have been paid. Senior securities will appeal to investors who want little risk; junior securities will appeal to investors who are willing to take

| FOCUS | Increasing Bank Leverage in the United States—the SIV |
|---|---|

SIV stands for **structured investment vehicle**. Think of it as a virtual bank created by an actual bank. On the liability side, it borrows from investors, typically in the form of short-term debt. On the asset side, it holds various forms of securities. To reassure the investors that they will get repaid, the SIV typically has a guarantee from the actual bank that, if needed, the bank will provide funds to the SIV.

While the first SIV was set up by Citigroup in 1988, SIVs rapidly grew in size in the 2000s. You may ask why banks did not simply do all these things on their own balance sheet rather than create a separate vehicle. The main reason was to be able to increase leverage. If the banks had done these operations themselves, the operations would have appeared on their balance sheet and been subject to regulatory capital requirements, forcing them to hold enough capital to limit the risk of bankruptcy. But doing these operations through an SIV did not require banks to put capital down. For that reason, through setting up an SIV, banks could increase leverage and increase expected profits, and they did.

When housing prices started declining, and many mortgages turned bad, the securities held by the SIVs decreased in value. Investors became reluctant to lend to the SIVs out of fear that they might be insolvent. The banks that had created the SIVs had to honour their obligations by paying investors, but had limited capital to do so. It became clear that banks had in effect created a **shadow banking system**, and that leverage of the banking system as a whole (i.e, including the shadow banking part) was much higher than had been perceived. Small losses could lead to bankruptcies. As of October 2008, no SIVs were left; they had either closed, or all their assets and liabilities had been transferred to the banks that had created them.

For a variety of reasons, including tighter bank regulation in Canada and the refusal of the federal government to allow two large bank mergers (BMO with RBC, TD with CIBC) in 1998, the large Canadian banks did not set up SIVs or participate as widely in the banking changes of the 2000s. Canadian banks did not hold a large number of assets backed by subprime U.S. mortgages. These decisions have given Canada a partly deserved and a partly accidental reputation in the rest of the world for sound banking.

more risk. Such securities, known as **collateralized debt obligations**, or **CDOs**, were first issued in the late 1980s but, again, grew in importance in the 1990s and 2000s.

Securitization would seem like a good idea: a way of diversifying risk and getting a larger group of investors involved in lending to households or firms. And, indeed, it is. But it also came with a large cost, which became clear only during the crisis. It was a risk that **rating agencies**, those firms that assess the risk of various securities, had largely missed: When underlying mortgages went bad, assessing the value of the underlying bundles in the MBSs, or, even more so, of the underlying MBSs in the CDOs, was extremely hard to do. These assets came to be known as **toxic assets**. It led investors to assume the worst and be very reluctant either to hold them or to continue lending to those institutions that did hold them.

## Liquidity

Yet another development of the 1990s and 2000s was the development of other sources of finance than chequable deposits by banks (the 80 dollars they borrowed in our example above). Increasingly, they relied on borrowing from other banks or other investors, in the form of short-term debt, to finance the purchase of their assets, a process known as **wholesale funding**. SIVs, the financial entities set up by banks that we saw earlier, were entirely funded through such wholesale funding.

Wholesale funding again would seem like a good idea, giving banks more flexibility in the amount of funds they can use to make loans or buy assets. But it has a cost, which again became clear during the crisis. If investors or other banks, worried about the value of the assets held by the bank, decide to stop lending to the bank, the bank may find itself short of funds and be forced to sell some of its assets. If these assets are complex and hard to sell, it may have to sell them at very low prices, often referred to as **fire sale prices**.

This is the modern equivalent of bank runs, when people ran to the bank to take their money out. Deposit insurance has largely eliminated that risk. There is relatively little concern that small depositors will perceive their deposits to be threatened. Again see the Focus box "Bank Runs and Bank Collapses" in Chapter 4. However, the bank's liabilities that are short-term deposits in amounts much larger than any covered by deposit insurance can still be withdrawn if the owners of the large deposits perceive the bank's solvency is threatened. This is the present-day analogue to an old-fashioned bank run.

We now have all the elements in place we need to explain what happened when housing prices declined, why this led to a major financial crisis, and why it ultimately led to the liquidity trap in the United States in 2009.

## Amplification Mechanisms

As the crisis worsened, solvency and liquidity concerns increased sharply, each reinforcing the other.

- When housing prices declined, and some mortgages went bad, high leverage implied a sharp decline in the capital of banks. This in turn forced them to sell some of their assets. Because these assets were often hard to value, they had to be sold at fire sale prices. This, in turn, decreased the value of similar assets remaining on the bank's balance sheet, or on the balance sheet of other banks, leading to a further decline in capital ratio and forcing further sales of assets and further declines in prices.
- The complexity of the securities (MBS, CDOs) and of the true balance sheets of banks (banks and their SIVs) made it very difficult to assess the solvency of banks and their risk of bankruptcy. Thus, investors became very reluctant to continue to lend to them, and wholesale funding came to a stop, forcing further asset sales and price declines. Banks even became very reluctant to lend to each other. This is shown in Figure 11–8, which shows the difference between the riskless rate (measured by the rate of three-month government bonds), which you can think of as the rate determined by monetary policy, and the rate at which banks are willing to lend to each other (known as the **Libor rate**). This difference is known as the **TED spread**.

FIGURE 11-8

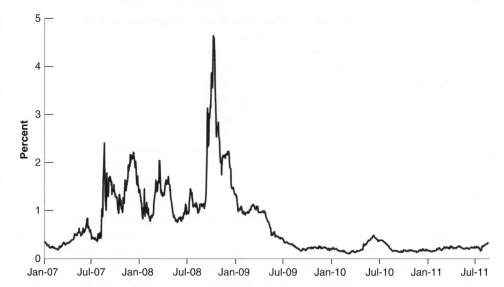

**The TED Spread in the U.S. Financial Crisis**

The rate spread, which reflects the risk banks perceive in lending to each other, went sharply up in September 2008.

*Source:* Data from Bloomberg L.P.

If banks perceived no risk in lending to each other, the TED spread would be equal to zero. And, indeed, until mid-2007, it was very close to zero. Note, however, how it became larger in the second half of 2007 and then increased sharply in September 2008. Why was there a sharp increase in September 2008? Because, on September 15, 2008, Lehman Brothers, a major bank with more than $600 billion in assets, declared bankruptcy, leading financial participants to conclude that many, if not most, other banks and financial institutions in the United States and indeed in other countries (non-U.S. banks owned some of the mortgage-backed securities) were indeed at risk.

By mid-September 2008, both mechanisms were in full force. The financial system had become paralyzed: Banks had essentially stopped lending to each other or to anyone else. A financial crisis turned into a macroeconomic crisis, a collapse in aggregate demand.

In section 11-1 we made the argument that to move to a liquidity trap required a very large decline in aggregate demand, a shift to the left in the *IS* curve that was so dramatic that, even at a zero rate of interest, aggregate demand and output would be far below the natural level of output. GDP in the United States fell by 0.3% in 2008 and a further 3.1% in 2009. The unemployment rate jumped from 5.8% in 2008 to 9.3% in 2009 and it continued to rise into 2010. Interest rates in the United States were reduced to zero by the end of 2008 as shown in Figure 11–9. In spite of

FIGURE 11-9

**Interest rates in the United States, 2006 to 2011**

As demand declined sharply in the United States, the Federal Reserve reduced interest rates from 5% in 2007 to zero as of December 2008.

*Source:* FRED, Federal Reserve Economic Data, Federal Reserve Bank of St. Louis: 3-Month Treasury Bill: Secondary Market Rate [TB3MS]; Board of Governors of the Federal Reserve System; http://research.stlouisfed.org/fred2/series/TB3MS

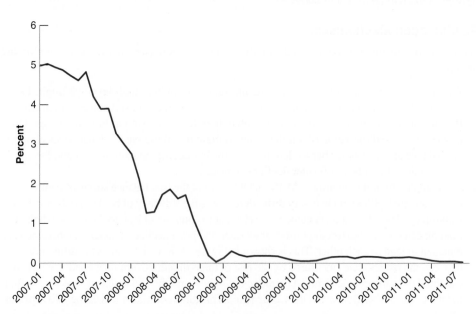

the reduction in interest rates to zero, sales of houses and cars collapsed. Other investment also fell dramatically, partly as aggregate demand fell and partly as business confidence fell. The United States was caught in the liquidity trap.

# 11-3 | Policy Choices in a Liquidity Trap and a Banking Collapse

The making of policy in a liquidity trap and banking crisis is difficult. First we look at the role of fiscal policy, the conventional method of increasing aggregate demand and escaping from a liquidity trap. Second, we look at the set of policies used to deal with a banking system that is threatened with collapse.

## Fiscal Policy as the Way Out of the Liquidity Trap

An expansion of the real or nominal money supply does not increase aggregate demand when the economy is in the liquidity trap. A reasonable question: Could fiscal policy work? Look at Figure 11–10. The liquidity trap equilibrium is at point $A$, well below the natural level of output. The interest rate is at zero and the $LM$ curve through point $A$ is associated with a real money supply ($M/P$). Remember it would not matter if the money supply were increased from point $A$ since the interest rate is already zero.

An expansionary fiscal policy shifts the $IS$ curve to $IS'$. If the money supply remained at ($M/P$), the level associated with $LM$, then interest rates would rise to $i_B$. The fiscal expansion would increase output and be partly successful. The fiscal multiplier is positive. The fiscal expansion would be much more successful if, while the government deficit increased, the central bank acted to maintain the interest rate at zero. In Figure 11–10 this is shown by shifting the $LM$ curve to $LM'$, associated with a larger real money supply, ($M/P'$). Such an expansion of the money supply is called **accommodative**; it accommodates the fiscal expansion so the fiscal expansion has the largest possible effect. In fact, if monetary policy is fully accommodative, and the interest rate remains at zero, then the fiscal policy multipliers are the multipliers calculated in Chapter 3.

◀ See section 3-3.

## Examples of Fiscal Policy in the Liquidity Trap

We have already seen that in 2009, when the world economic crisis occurred, Canada practised a combination of an expansionary fiscal policy and accommodative monetary policy. This is exactly as drawn in Figure 11–10. In January 2009, the plan was to increase the Canadian federal deficit from 0% of GDP to about 2% of GDP. Interest rates were kept at or near zero in order to allow the fiscal expansion to have the largest possible effect. What about our neighbours to the south?

See the Focus box "Canada's Macroeconomic Policy Response to the World ◀ Economic Crisis" in Chapter 10. In fact, the federal deficit increased to more than 3% of GDP.

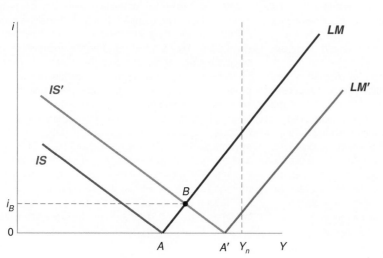

**FIGURE 11–10**

**Fiscal Policy in a Liquidity Trap**

If the economy is in the liquidity trap and output at the zero rate of interest is well below the natural level of output, expansionary fiscal policy could be used to increase the level of output.

President Obama was first elected in November 2008. The American Congress passed the **American Recovery and Reinvestment Act** in February 2009. This act contained substantial spending increases and tax cuts over 2009 and 2010, a total of $780 billion. As usual, it is better to measure fiscal stimulus as a percentage of GDP. By that measure, the American federal deficit increased from 3.2% of GDP in 2008 to 10.1% of GDP in 2009 and 9.0% of GDP in 2010. Some of the increase in the deficit was the result of large declines in tax revenues as GDP fell in the crisis. But part of the increases in the deficits in 2009 and 2010 were due to stimulative fiscal policy. The policy of the Federal Reserve was, as we saw in Figure 11–9, to fully accommodate the expansionary fiscal policy and keep interest rates at zero. Although no one claims the expansionary fiscal policies successfully prevented the large decline in output from 2008 to 2009, most economists argue that the 2009 recession would have been worse without these policies, policies in fact carried out around the world.

See the Focus box "The G20 and the 2009 Fiscal ▶ Stimulus" in Chapter 7.

## The Limits of Fiscal Policy: High Debt

Does fiscal policy have limits? In Figure 11–10, the government is running a deficit. If people or firms do not eventually become more optimistic and increase spending, or if exports do not eventually recover, the government must continue to run deficits to sustain higher demand and output. Continuing large deficits lead, however, to steadily higher public debt. In advanced countries, the ratio of government debt to GDP has increased from 46% in 2006 to 70% in 2011. High debt implies that, sooner or later, either taxes will have to increase, or spending will have to decrease, or the government will be unable to repay the debt. And when investors become worried about repayment of the debt, they start asking for higher interest rates on government bonds, making it even harder for the government to repay the debt. These worries are already leading to higher interest rates on government bonds in a number of European countries. They have not yet led to higher interest rates on government bonds in the United States. But the risk that interest rates might rise in the future is forcing the U.S. government to look for ways to begin to reduce its budget deficit now. This may eventually limit the contribution of fiscal policy to demand and to a recovery from a liquidity trap. The experience of Japan in a liquidity trap, outlined in the Focus box "Japan, the Liquidity Trap, and Fiscal Policy," has been studied quite extensively. Japan's experience is discouraging. Very expansionary fiscal policy in Japan over a number of years has not restored vigorous economic activity.

The increase over the course of the recession in Canada's federal public debt was relatively small. The increase in Canada's overall public ▶ debt, including provincial debt, is relatively large. We look at these issues in Chapter 25 in more detail.

---

## FOCUS  Japan, the Liquidity Trap, and Fiscal Policy

Japan, through the 1990s and into the first decade of the 21st century, appears to be another example of an economy in a liquidity trap. The similarities between Japan, the 2009 American crisis, and the Great Depression are striking and, if we are honest, disturbing.

The Japanese stock market, which had boomed earlier, suddenly crashed. The **Nikkei index**, a broad index of Japanese stock prices, had gone up from 7000 in 1980 to 35,000 at the beginning of 1990. Then, within two years, it went down to 16,000 and continued to decline after that, reaching a trough of 7000 in 2003. (In July 2013, the Nikkei index is around 14,000.) This decline in stock prices was followed by a decline in spending, and, in response to the decline in spending, the Japanese central bank cut the interest rate. As you can see from Figure 1, by the mid-1990s, the interest rate was down to less than 1%, and it has remained below 1% since.

With little room left for using monetary policy, fiscal policy was used to sustain demand. Figure 2 shows the evolution of government spending and revenues as a percentage of GDP since 1990. You can see the dramatic increase in spending since the early 1990s. Much of the increased spending has taken the form of public works projects, and a joke circulating in Japan is that, by the time the Japanese economy has recovered, the entire shoreline of the Japanese archipelago will be covered in concrete. The result of this strong fiscal expansion, however, has been a sharp increase in debt. The ratio of government debt to GDP, which stood at 13% of GDP in 1991, is now above 120%. Meanwhile, the Japanese economy is still in a slump: GDP growth, which averaged 4.4% in the 1980s, was down to 1.4% in the 1990s, and 0.9% in the 2000s.

Several lessons appear from the Japanese experience. What has happened in Japan since 1990 is a tough warning to

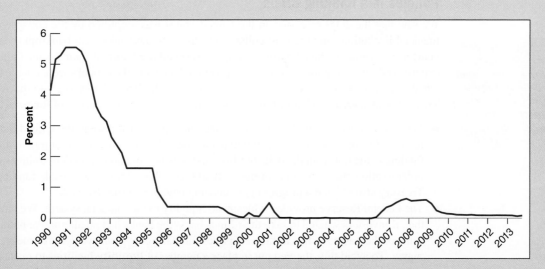

**FIGURE 1    The Interest Rate in Japan since 1990**

Japan has been in a liquidity trap since the mid-1990s.

*Source:* Data from One-year government bond rate, DLX, International Monetary Fund database.

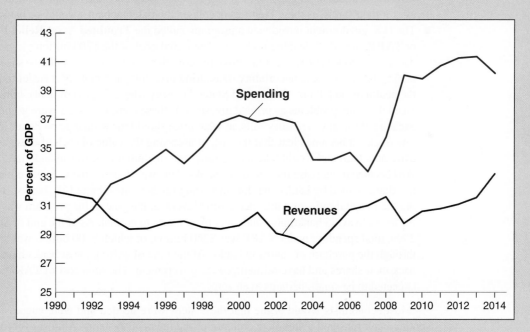

**FIGURE 2    Government Spending and Revenues (as a percentage of GDP), Japan, since 1990**

Increasing government spending and decreasing revenues have led to steadily larger deficits.

*Source:* Data from IMF World Economic Outlook databases

other advanced countries that it may take a long time to recover from a slump associated with a collapse in asset prices. It is also noteworthy that Japan was able to run large government deficits for many years. The fiscal reckoning associated with the increase in deficits and debt may take many, many years to come about.

## Policies in a Banking Crisis

We saw that the 2009 recession in the United States was amplified by the collapse of some financial institutions and the near collapse of others. Some banks went bankrupt (were insolvent) as the value of their liabilities simply exceeded the value of their assets. Other banks experienced severe liquidity problems as potential lenders to those banks were unable to assess whether that bank was insolvent or merely illiquid. The Federal Reserve and the American Treasury took a variety of short-term steps to prevent a complete collapse of financial markets.

The United Kingdom took similar short-term steps. These steps were not needed in Canada. Longer-term international policy changes applied to the banking industry are presented in Chapter 24.

- In order to prevent a run by depositors, federal deposit insurance in the United States was increased from $100,000 to $250,000 per account. Recall, however, that much of banks' funding came not from deposits but from the issuance of short-term debt to investors. In order to allow the banks to continue to fund themselves through wholesale funding, the Treasury also offered a program guaranteeing new debt issues by banks.

- The Federal Reserve provided widespread liquidity to the financial system. We have seen that, if investors wanted to take their funds back, the banks had no alternative but to sell some of their assets, often at fire sale prices. In many cases, this would have meant bankruptcy. To avoid this, the Fed put in place a number of **liquidity facilities** to make it easier to borrow from the Fed. It allowed not only banks, but also other financial institutions, to borrow from the Fed. Finally, it increased the set of assets that financial institutions could use as **collateral** when borrowing from the Fed (*collateral* refers to the asset a borrower pledges when borrowing from a lender. If the borrower defaults, the asset then goes to the lender). Together, these facilities allowed banks and financial institutions to pay back investors without having to sell their assets. It also decreased the incentives of investors to ask for their funds, as these facilities decreased the risk that banks would go bankrupt.

- The U.S. government introduced a program, called the **Troubled Asset Relief Program**, or **TARP**, aimed at cleaning up banks. The initial goal of the $700 billion program, introduced in October 2008, was to remove the complex assets from the balance sheet of banks, thus decreasing uncertainty, reassuring investors, and making it easier to assess the health of each bank. The United States Treasury (the U.S. government), however, faced the same problems as private investors. If these complex assets were going to be exchanged for, say, Treasury bills, at what price should the exchange be done? Within a few weeks, it became clear that the task of assessing the value of each of these assets was extremely hard and would take a long time, and the initial goal was abandoned. The new goal became to increase the capital of banks. This was done by the U.S. government buying shares issued by banks and thus providing funds to most large U.S. banks. By increasing their capital ratio, and thus decreasing leverage, the goal of the program was to allow the banks to avoid bankruptcy and, over time, return to normal. As of the end of September 2009, total spending under TARP was $360 billion, of which $200 billion was spent through the purchase of shares in banks. At the time of writing, most banks have bought back their shares and have reimbursed the government. The final cost of TARP is expected to be small, perhaps even zero.

Most economists would argue that these steps were needed and were successful at preventing bank runs and a complete collapse of the financial systems. Almost everyone agrees that the 2009 crisis, bad as it was, would have been much worse without the active fiscal policy to increase aggregate demand and the various policies used to prevent banking sector collapse. The Great Depression did not re-occur.

See again, the Focus box "The Great Depression in North America."

## 11-4 | Supply Shocks: An Increase in the Price of Oil

We close our study of the *AS-AD* model in this chapter by looking at shocks that shift the aggregate supply curve. For both analytical and historical reasons, a very large movement in the real price of oil is the obvious candidate to shift the aggregate supply curve.

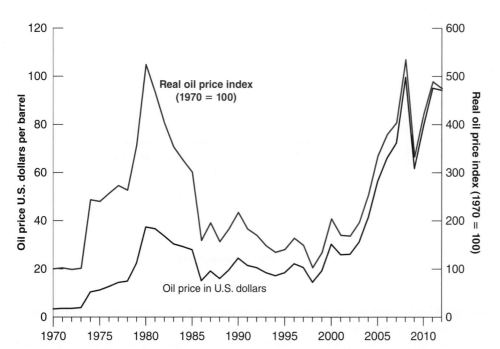

**FIGURE 11–11**

**The Nominal and the Real Prices of Oil, 1970–2012**

Over the last 40 years, world oil prices have fluctuated a great deal. The value of the index on the right-hand axis, the **real oil price**, doubled from 1973 to 1974. It then doubled again between 1978 and 1980. There was a much more gradual run-up in real oil prices from 2001 to 2008, a sharp drop in 2009, and a recovery in 2010.

*Source:* Series OILPRICE, CPIAUSCL Federal Reserve Economic Data (FRED), http://research.stlouisfed.org/fred2/

Figure 11–11 plots two series. One is the dollar price of oil—that is, the price of a barrel of oil in dollars—since 1970. It is measured on the vertical axis on the left. This is the series you observe more or less every day as part of world financial reporting. Oil prices are quoted in U.S. dollars because oil is a world commodity. What matters, however, for economic decisions is not the dollar price, but the real price of oil—that is, the dollar price of oil divided by the price level. The second series in the figure shows the real price of oil, constructed as the dollar price of oil divided by the U.S. Consumer Price Index. Note that the real price is an index; it is normalized to equal 100 in 1970. It is measured on the vertical axis on the right.

> Since the nominal price of oil is measured in U.S. dollars, it makes sense to deflate by the U.S. Consumer Price Index.

One striking feature of Figure 11–11 is the large increase in the real price of oil in the 2000s: In 10 years, from 1998 to 2008, the index for the real price went from about 100 to more than 500, a more than five-fold increase. But as the figure also shows, there were similar but more abrupt increases in the price of oil in the 1970s, Oil prices doubled in two years from from 1973 to 1975. Oil prices doubled again from 1977 to 1980.

What was behind these large increases in oil prices? In the 1970s, the main factors were the formation of **OPEC** (Organization of the Petroleum Exporting Countries), a cartel of oil producers that was able to act as a monopoly and increase prices, and disruptions due to wars and revolutions in the Middle East. In the 2000s, the main factor was quite different, namely the fast growth of emerging economies, in particular China, which led to a rapid increase in the world demand for oil and, by implication, a steady increase in real oil prices. Whether coming from changes in supply in the 1970s or from changes in the demand from emerging countries in the 2000s, the implication for the world economy was the same: more expensive oil, more expensive energy.

> At the time of writing, removing natural gas and oil from shale is the new energy technology. It is possible energy prices could fall and we would have a positive supply shock. Simply reverse the analysis below.

In thinking about the macroeconomic effects of such large oil price increases, it is clear that we face a serious problem in using the model we have developed so far: The price of oil appears neither in our aggregate supply relation nor in our aggregate demand relation! The reason is that, until now, we have assumed that output was produced using only labour. One way to extend our model would be to recognize explicitly that output is produced using labour *and* other inputs (including energy), and then figure out what effect an increase in the price of oil has on the price set by firms and on the relation between output and employment. An easier way, and the way we shall go here, is simply to capture the increase in the price of oil by an increase in $m$—the markup of the price over the nominal wage. The justification is

FIGURE 11-12

**The Effects of an Increase in the Real Price of Oil on the Natural Rate of Unemployment**

An increase in the price of oil leads to a lower real wage and a higher natural rate of unemployment.

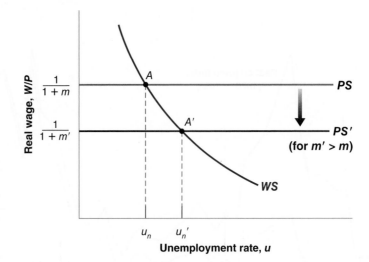

straightforward: Given wages, an increase in the price of oil increases the cost of production, forcing firms to increase prices.

Having made this assumption, we can then track the dynamic effects of an *increase in the markup* on output and the price level. It will be easiest here to work backward in time, first asking what happens in the medium run, and then working out the dynamics of adjustment from the short run to the medium run.

## Effects on the Natural Rate of Unemployment

Let's start by asking what happens to the natural rate of unemployment when the real price of oil increases (for simplicity, we shall drop "real" in what follows). Figure 11–12 reproduces the characterization of labour-market equilibrium from Figure 9–4 in Chapter 9.

The wage-setting curve is downward sloping. The price-setting relation is represented by the horizontal line at $W/P = 1/(1 + m)$. The initial equilibrium is at point $A$, and the initial natural unemployment rate is $u_n$. An increase in the markup leads to a downward shift of the price-setting line, from $PS$ to $PS'$: The higher the markup, the lower the real wage implied by price setting. The equilibrium moves from $A$ to $A'$. The real wage is lower. The natural unemployment rate is higher: Getting workers to accept the lower real wage requires an increase in unemployment.

The increase in the natural rate of unemployment leads in turn to a decrease in the natural level of employment. If we assume that the relation between employment and output is unchanged—that is, that each unit of output still requires one worker in addition to the energy input—then the decrease in the natural level of employment leads to a decrease in the natural level of output. Putting things together: An increase in the price of oil leads to a decrease in the natural level of output.

> This assumes that the increase in the price of oil is permanent. If, in the medium run, the price of oil goes back to its initial value, then the natural rate is unaffected. ▶

## The Dynamics of Adjustment

Let's now turn to dynamics. Suppose that before the increase in the price of oil, the aggregate demand curve and the aggregate supply curve are given by $AD$ and $AS$, respectively, so the economy is at point $A$ in Figure 11–13, with output at the natural level of output, $Y_n$, and by implication $P = P^e$.

We have just established that the increase in the price of oil decreases the natural level of output. Call this lower level $Y'_n$. We now want to know what happens in the short run and how the economy moves from $Y_n$ to $Y'_n$.

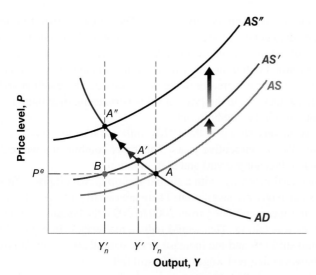

FIGURE 11-13

**The Dynamic Effects of an Increase in the Prices of Oil**

An increase in the price of oil leads, in the short run, to a decrease in output and an increase in the price level. Over time, output decreases further and the price level increases further.

To think about the short run, recall that the aggregate supply relation is given by

$$P = P^e(1 + m)F\left(1 - \frac{Y}{L}, z\right)$$

Recall that we capture the effect of an increase in the price of oil by an increase in the markup $m$. So, in the short run (given $P^e$), the increase in the price of oil shows up as an increase in the markup $m$. This increase in the markup leads firms to increase their prices, leading to an increase in the price level $P$ at any level of output $Y$. The aggregate supply curve shifts up.

We can be more specific about the size of the shift, and knowing the size of this shift will be useful in what follows. We know from section 10-1 that the aggregate supply curve always goes through the point such that output equals the natural level of output and the price level equals the expected price level. Before the increase in the price of oil, the aggregate supply curve in Figure 11–13 goes through point $A$, where output equals $Y_n$ and the price level is equal to $P^e$. After the increase in the price of oil, the new aggregate supply curve goes through point $B$, where output equals the new lower natural level of output $Y'_n$ and the price level equals the expected price level, $P^e$. The aggregate supply curve shifts left from $AS$ to $AS'$.

Does the aggregate demand curve shift as a result of the increase in the price of oil? The answer is: maybe. There are many channels through which demand might be affected at a given price level: The higher price of oil may lead firms to change their investment plans, cancelling some investment projects and/or shifting to less energy-intensive equipment. The high price of oil may increase business investment in the capital needed to produce more oil. The increase in the price of oil also redistributes income from oil buyers to oil producers. Oil producers may spend less than oil buyers, leading to a decrease in consumption demand. Let's take the easy way out: Because some of the effects shift the aggregate demand curve to the right and others shift the aggregate demand curve to the left, let's simply assume that the effects cancel each other out and that aggregate demand does not shift.

◄ It is clear that the increase in oil prices in the 2000s did lead to a boom in the oilsands in Alberta. An oil price increase may slightly increase aggregate demand in Canada since Canada is a net energy exporter. To keep things simpler, we will set aside this effect in this chapter.

Under this assumption, in the short run, only the $AS$ shifts. The economy therefore moves along the $AD$ curve, from $A$ to $A'$. Output decreases from $Y_n$ to $Y'$. The increase in the price of oil leads firms to increase their prices. This increase in the price level then decreases demand and output.

What happens over time? Although output has fallen, the natural level of output has fallen even more: At point $A'$, output $Y'$ is still above the new natural level of output $Y'_n$, so the aggregate supply curve continues to shift up. The economy therefore moves over time along the aggregate demand curve, from $A'$ to $A''$. At point $A''$, output $Y'$ is equal to the new lower natural level of output $Y'_n$, and the price level is higher than before the oil shock: Shifts in aggregate supply affect output not only in the short run but in the medium run as well.

To summarize: Permanent increases in the price of oil decrease output and increase prices in the short run. If the increase in the price of oil is permanent, then output is lower not only in the short run, but also in the medium run.

These effects were very strong in the 1970s. Inflation rose to over 10%. The unemployment rate was over 8% in consecutive years. This nasty combination was called **stagflation**, high unemployment (stagnant growth) and high inflation.

An interesting question is why, with a similar run-up in real oil prices from the year 2000 to 2008, we did not also observe stagflation. There are two hypotheses. One hypothesis is that at the same time oil prices were rising from 2000 to 2008, the bargaining power of workers in developed countries was falling. This would reduce real wages. In Figure 11–12, the wage-setting curve would shift left and the increase in the natural rate of unemployment would be mitigated. Note however that real wages would still fall.

The second hypothesis is that monetary policy in the period from 2000 to 2008 was better managed. In the 1970s, as prices rose, people began to expect higher prices and, as shown in Figure 11–13, the $AS$ curve shifted left as $P^e$ increased. If central banks around the world had convinced the public that prices would not rise, then $P^e$ would not increase and the $AS$ curve might shift less. In the extreme case—refer back to Figure 11–13—suppose that $P^e$ does not change. There would be a single shift in the $AS$ curve from $AS$ to $AS'$. Monetary policy would have to reduce the money supply and shift $AD$ to the right to pass through B (not shown on the diagram). The oil price increase would still cause a decline in output but without the increase in inflation—you would only have the stagnation part of *stagflation*.

Did output decline in the oil-consuming countries of the world as oil prices rose through the 2000s? There was no recession. Table 11–1 shows there was a substantial reduction in the rate of economic growth in the developed world as oil prices rose. Economic growth fell by one percentage point per year in the five years of rising oil prices compared to the five years of stable oil prices. The rise in oil prices would be the one shock that would have affected all of the advanced economies at the same time. This table does not prove that rising oil prices slowed economic growth. It certainly suggests this hypothesis is not to be immediately rejected.

> We do not want the crisis years in the comparison group so the comparison ends in 2005.

## 11-5 | Conclusions

We are partway through our analysis of the medium run. Although we have introduced the price level into our analysis, most discussion of the price level, as we saw in Chapter 2, focuses on inflation. Inflation is the annual percentage change in the price level. In the next two chapters, we take up the analysis of variation in inflation. We use the same structure. Chapter 12 looks at the basic model and the straightforward issues. Chapter 13 addresses two important extensions. Chapter 14 takes us into the open economy to close our analysis of the medium run.

| TABLE 11–1 | Average Economic Growth, 1995–2005* | |
|---|---|---|
| Country Group | 1995–2000 | 2001–2005 |
| Advanced Economies | 3.2 | 2.1 |

*Averages of annual growth rate of real GDP over the years listed.

*Source:* World Economic Outlook Database, International Monetary Fund.

- A large fall in aggregate demand can create a situation where, even at a zero rate of interest, the level of aggregate demand and output is much lower than the natural level of output. This situation is called a liquidity trap.

- A liquidity trap means that increases in the real money supply will not increase lower interest rates nor increase aggregate demand.

- If output is far below the natural level and prices begin to fall, expectations of deflation may occur. Expected deflation may further reduce aggregate demand and output.

- The Great Depression of the 1930s was a decade of output lower than the natural level, zero interest rates, and both actual and expected deflation. The Great Depression was an economy in a liquidity trap.

- The U.S. and world economic crisis of 2009 exhibits many of the characteristics of a liquidity trap.

- There was a large reduction in aggregate demand triggered by a decrease in U.S. house prices.

- The effect of lower house prices was considerably amplified by the effects on the banking system. Banks became bankrupt as well as illiquid. Banks stopped making loans.

- Although monetary policy was immediately employed to reduce interest rates to zero, output remained far below the natural level.

- Expansionary fiscal policy was used to increase aggregate demand. All countries, including the United States and Canada, increased their budget deficits.

- A suite of policies was used by governments and central banks around the world to prevent complete collapse of the banking system in the world economic crisis of 2009. These included direct purchases of bank shares, lending to banks and government guarantees on bond issues by banks as well as on bank deposits. Problems in appropriate regulation of banks, particularly off-balance sheet activities of banks, played a significant role in the financial system collapse.

- Japan experienced slow growth and a liquidity trap through the 1990s and into the 2000s. Very expansionary fiscal policy was not completely successful in restoring economic growth.

- An increase in the price of oil leads, in both the short run and in the medium run, to a decrease in output. In the short run, it leads to an increase in the price level, which decreases the real money stock and leads to a contraction of demand and output. In the medium run, an increase in the price of oil decreases the real wage paid by firms, increases the natural rate of unemployment, and therefore decreases the natural level of output. These effects were observed in the 1970s. Although oil prices rose steeply in the 2000s, there appeared to be little effect on prices or inflation and a much smaller effect on output than the effect observed in the 1970s.

- accommodative, 217
- American Recovery and Reinvestment Act, 218
- capital ratio, 213
- collateral, 220
- collateralized debt obligation (CDO), 215
- deflation, 209
- depression, 209
- financial intermediaries, 212
- fire sale prices, 215
- Great Depression, 204
- illiquidity, 213
- junior securities, 214
- leverage ratio, 213
- Libor rate, 215
- liquidity facilities, 220
- liquidity trap, 204
- mortgage lenders, 212
- mortgage-backed security (MBS), 214

- Nikkei index, 218
- OPEC (Organization of Petroleum Exporting Countries) 221
- rating agencies, 215
- real oil price, 221
- securitization, 214
- senior securities, 214
- shadow banking system, 214
- solvency, 213
- supply shock, 204
- stagflation, 224
- structured investment vehicle (SIV), 214
- subprime mortgages (subprimes), 212
- TED spread, 215
- toxic assets, 215
- Troubled Asset Relief Program (TARP), 220
- underwater mortgage, 212
- wholesale funding, 215

## 1. TRUE/FALSE/UNCERTAIN

Using information in this chapter, label each of the following statements true, false, or uncertain. Explain briefly.

**a.** The interest rate is zero in a liquidity trap.

**b.** Liquidity traps occur whenever aggregate demand falls.

**c.** An increase in a bank's leverage ratio tends to increase both the expected rate of return on the bank's capital and the risk of the bank going bankrupt.

**d.** Since the financial crisis ultimately led to a global recession, the policy measures (adopted in many countries) that provided substantial liquidity to financial institutions and that recapitalized banks (through the purchase of shares by governments) failed.

**e.** The fiscal stimulus programs adopted by many countries in response to the financial crisis of 2009 helped offset the decline in aggregate demand and reduce the size of the recession.

**f.** The fiscal stimulus program adopted by many countries in response to the financial crisis did not lead to a large increase in the debt-to-GDP ratio.

**g.** Fiscal and monetary policy successfully saved Japan from a decade of slow growth following its financial crisis in the early 1990s.

**h.** A supply shock will cause a temporary but not a permanent reduction in output.

## 2. TRADITIONAL MONETARY AND FISCAL POLICY IN A LIQUIDITY TRAP — THE *IS-LM* VIEW

Consider an economy described by Figure 11–4, with output lower than the natural level of output and the nominal interest rate at zero.

**a.** Redraw Figure 11–4. Is output at point B less than the natural rate of output? What does this imply for the unemployment rate?

**b.** If the central bank increases the money supply, what will happen to the *IS-LM* diagram you drew in part (a)? Will equilibrium output move to the natural level?

**c.** Given your answer to part (b), what fiscal policy options are available to the government to try to increase output? How does your answer relate to the policy decisions of the Obama administration and the U.S. Congress in February 2009? How does your answer relate to the policy decisions of the Canadian federal government in January 2009 (see Chapter 10)?

## 3. TRADITIONAL MONETARY AND FISCAL POLICY IN A LIQUIDITY TRAP—THE *AS-AD* VIEW

Consider an economy described by Figure 11–5, with output lower than the natural level of output and the nominal interest rate at zero.

**a.** Draw Figure 11–5 and explain why the *AD* curve is vertical.

**b.** If the central bank increases the money supply, what will happen to the *AS-AD* diagram you drew in part (a)? Will equilibrium output move closer to the natural level?

**c.** Given your answers to part (b), what fiscal policy options are available to the government to try to increase output? How does your answer relate to the policy decisions of the Obama administration and the U.S. Congress in February 2009? How does your answer relate to the policy decisions of the Canadian federal government in January 2009 (see Chapter 10)?

## 4. MODERN BANK RUNS

Consider a simple bank that has assets of 100, capital of 20, and chequing deposits of 80. Recall from Chapter 4 that chequing deposits are liabilities of a bank.

**a.** Set up the bank's balance sheet.

**b.** Now suppose that the perceived value of the bank's assets falls by 10. What is the new value of the bank's capital?

**c.** Suppose the deposits are insured by the government. Despite the decline in the value of bank capital, is there any immediate reason for depositors to withdraw their funds from the bank? Would your answer change if the perceived value of the bank's assets fell by 15? 20? 25? Explain.

Now consider a different sort of bank, still with assets of 100 and capital of 20, but now with their liabilities as short-term credits (think of one-month term deposits) of 80 instead of chequable deposits. Short-term credit must be repaid or rolled over (borrowed again) when it comes due.

**d.** Set up this bank's balance sheet.

**e.** Again suppose the perceived value of the bank's assets falls. If lenders are nervous about the solvency of the bank, will they be willing to continue to provide short-term credit to the bank at low interest rates?

**f.** Assuming that the bank cannot raise additional capital, how can it raise the funds necessary to repay its debt coming due? If many banks are in this position at the same time (and if banks hold similar kinds of assets), what will likely happen to the value of the assets of these banks? How will this affect the willingness of lenders to provide short-term credit?

## 5. THE TROUBLED ASSET RELIEF PROGRAM (TARP) IN THE UNITED STATES

Consider a bank that has assets of 100, capital of 20, and short-term credit of 80. Part of the bank's assets are securitized assets whose value depends on the price of houses. These assets have a value of 50. The remaining assets are loans.

**a.** Set up the bank's balance sheet.

Suppose that as a result of a housing price decline, the value of the bank's securitized assets falls by an uncertain amount, so that these assets are now worth somewhere between 25 and 45. Call the securitized assets "troubled assets." The value of the other assets remains at 50. As a result of the uncertainty about the value of the bank's assets, lenders are reluctant to provide any short-term credit to the bank.

**b.** Given the uncertainty about the value of the bank's assets, what is the range in the value of the bank's capital?

As a response to this problem, the government considers purchasing the troubled assets, with the intention of reselling them again when the markets stabilize. (This is the original version of TARP.)

**c.** If the government pays 25 for the troubled assets, what will be the value of the bank's capital? How much would the government have to pay for the troubled assets to ensure that the bank's capital does not have a negative value? If the government pays 45 for the troubled assets, but the true value turns out to be much lower, who bears the cost of this mistaken valuation? Explain.

Suppose, instead of buying the troubled assets, the government provides capital to the bank by buying ownership shares, with the intention of reselling the shares again when the markets stabilize. (This is what TARP ultimately became.) The government exchanges treasury bonds (which become assets for the bank) for ownership shares.

**d.** Suppose the government exchanges 25 of government bonds for ownership shares. Assuming the worst-case scenario (so that the troubled assets are worth only 25), set up the new balance sheet of the bank. (Remember that the firm now has three assets: 50 of untroubled assets, 25 of troubled assets, and 25 of government

bonds.) What is the total value of the bank's capital? Will the bank be insolvent?

**e.** Given your answers and the material in the text, why might recapitalization be a better policy than buying the troubled assets?

## 6. THE TED SPREAD

The text described the fluctuations in the TED spread that occurred during the financial crisis. Do an Internet search and find the recent history of the TED spread. You can find this information easily from various sources.

**a.** Consult Figure 11–8 to compare the current value of the TED spread to its value before and during the financial crisis. How does the current value of the TED spread compare to its highest values during the crisis? How does the current value of the TED spread compare to its value at the beginning of 2007? (Note that the TED spread is often quoted in basis points. One hundred basis points equals one percentage point.)

**b.** Has the TED spread been relatively stable in recent months? In what range of values has the spread fluctuated?

**c.** What do you conclude about the willingness of banks to lend to one another now as compared to the beginning of 2007 or the fall of 2008?

## 7. SUPPLY SHOCKS AND DEMAND MANAGEMENT

Assume that the economy starts at the natural level of output. Now suppose there is an increase in the price of oil.

**a.** In an AS-AD diagram, show what happens to output and the price level in the short run and the medium run.

**b.** What happens to the unemployment rate in the short run? in the medium run?

Suppose that the central bank decides to respond immediately to the increase in the price of oil. In particular, suppose that the central bank wants to prevent the unemployment rate from changing in the short run after the increase in the price of oil. Assume that the central bank changes the money supply once—immediately after the increase in the price of oil—and then does not change the money supply again.

**c.** What should the central bank do to prevent the unemployment rate from changing in the short run? Show how the central bank's action affects the AS-AD diagram in the short run and the medium run.

**d.** How do output and the price level in the short run and the medium run compare to your answers from part (a)?

**e.** How do the short-run and medium-run unemployment rates compare to your answers from part (b)?

## FURTHER READING

- There are many good books on the crisis: among them Michael Lewis's *The Big Short* (W.W. Norton, 2010) and Gillian Tett's *Fool's Gold* (Free Press, 2009). Both books show how the financial system became increasingly risky until it finally collapsed. Both read like detective novels, with a lot of action and fascinating characters.

- *In Fed We Trust* (Crown Business, 2009), written in 2009 by David Wessel, the economics editor of *The Wall Street Journal*, describes how the Fed reacted to the crisis. It also makes for fascinating reading.

# The Phillips Curve, the Natural Rate of Unemployment, and Inflation

## The Core: The Medium Run

In 1958, A.W. Phillips drew a diagram plotting the rate of inflation against the rate of unemployment in the United Kingdom for each year from 1861 to 1957. He found clear evidence of a negative relation between inflation and unemployment: When unemployment was low, inflation was high, and when unemployment was high, inflation was low, often even negative. As is common in the social sciences, the same experiment was repeated using the data from other countries.

Figure 12–1 shows the evidence that Phillips would have had for Canada. It plots the inflation rate, measured as the percent change in the Consumer Price Index, against the unemployment rate. There appears to be a negative relationship between inflation and unemployment in Canada also. In the three years in the heart of the Great Depression, unemployment is very high and the rate of inflation is negative.

This relation, which became known as the Phillips curve, rapidly became central to macroeconomic thinking and policy. It appeared to imply that countries could choose among different combinations of unemployment and inflation. They could achieve low unemployment if they were willing to tolerate higher inflation, or they could achieve price level stability—zero inflation—if they were willing to tolerate higher unemployment. Much of the discussion about macroeconomic policy became a discussion about which point to choose on the Phillips curve.

In the 1970s, however, the relation broke down. In Canada, the United States, and most OECD countries, there was both high inflation *and* high unemployment, clearly contradicting the original Phillips curve. A relation reappeared, but it was now a relation between the unemployment rate and the *change* in the inflation rate. Today, in both Canada and the United States, high unemployment leads not to low inflation but instead to a decrease in inflation. This is the central relationship in the control of inflation and in the achievement of Canada's inflation target.

The purpose of this chapter is to explore the mutations of the Phillips curve and, more generally, to understand the relation between inflation and unemployment. We will see that what Phillips discovered was the aggregate supply relation and that the mutations of the Phillips curve came from changes in the way people and firms formed expectations. A critical unemployment rate emerges from this analysis: the *natural rate of unemployment*. We close with the mathematics of inflation and money growth to understand that these two growth rates—money and prices—go hand in hand.

FIGURE 12–1

**Inflation and Unemployment in Canada, 1927–1959**

During the period 1927–1959 in Canada, low unemployment was typically associated with high inflation, and high unemployment was typically associated with low or negative inflation. The years 1931, 1932, and 1933 are notable for very high unemployment rates and large negative inflation rates. These years are the beginning of the Great Depression.

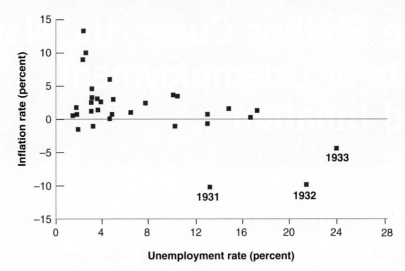

*Source:* Data from Inflation rate using CANSIM II variable V35319; unemployment rate 1927–1952 using *Historical Statistics of Canada*, and 1953–1975 using CANSIM I variable D7676.

We will from now on refer to the inflation rate as "inflation," and to the unemployment rate as "unemployment." ▶

After deriving this relation ▶ in Chapter 10, we replaced the unemployment rate by its expression in terms of output to obtain a relation among the price level, the expected price level, and output. It will be more convenient in this chapter to stay with the relation in terms of unemployment rather than output.

# 12-1 | Inflation, Expected Inflation, and Unemployment

Our first step will be to show that the aggregate supply relation we derived in Chapter 10 can be rewritten as a relation between *inflation* and *unemployment*, given *expected inflation*.

To do this, go back to the relation among the *price level*, the *expected price level*, and the *unemployment rate* we derived in Chapter 10:

$$P_t = P_t^e(1 + m) F(u_t, z)$$

Recall that the function $F$ captures the effects on the wage of the unemployment rate, $u_t$, and of the other factors that affect wage setting, represented by the catch-all variable, $z$. It will be convenient here to assume a specific form for the function $F$:

$$F(u_t, z) = 1 - \alpha u_t + z$$

This captures the notion that the higher the unemployment rate, the lower is the wage, and the higher $z$, the higher is the wage. The parameter $\alpha$ (the Greek lowercase letter alpha) captures the strength of the effect of unemployment on wages: The larger the $\alpha$, the stronger is the (negative) effect of unemployment on wages.

$P^e\uparrow \Rightarrow P\uparrow; \ u\uparrow \Rightarrow P\downarrow$ ▶

Replacing in the earlier equation gives:

$$P_t = P_t^e(1 + m)(1 - \alpha u_t + z)$$

With a few manipulations, this relation can be rewritten as a relation among the *inflation rate*, the *expected inflation rate*, and the *unemployment rate*:

$\pi^e\uparrow \Rightarrow \pi\uparrow; \ u\uparrow \Rightarrow \pi\downarrow$ ▶

$$\pi_t = \pi_t^e + (m + z) - \alpha u_t \qquad (12.1)$$

where $\pi_t$ denotes the inflation rate, defined as the rate of change of prices from last year to this year, and $\pi_t^e$ denotes the corresponding expected inflation rate—the rate of change of prices from last year to this year, expected by wage setters as of last year.

In short, equation (12.1) tells us that *inflation depends positively on expected inflation and negatively on unemployment.*

- *Higher expected inflation leads to higher inflation.* We saw in Chapter 10 how higher expected prices lead to higher nominal wages, which lead to higher prices. But note that given last year's prices, higher prices this year imply higher inflation this year; similarly, higher expected prices imply higher expected inflation. So, higher expected inflation leads to higher actual inflation.
- *Given expected inflation, the higher the markup chosen by firms,* m, *or the higher the factors that affect wage determination,* z, *the higher is inflation.* We saw in Chapter 10 and 11 how a higher markup leads to higher prices, given expected prices. We can restate this proposition as follows: A higher markup leads to higher inflation, given expected inflation. The same argument applies to increases in any of the factors that affect wage determination.
- *Given expected inflation, the higher the unemployment, the lower is inflation.* We saw in Chapter 10 that given expected prices, a higher unemployment rate leads to lower prices. We can restate this proposition as follows: Given expected inflation, a higher unemployment rate leads to lower actual inflation.

With this reformulation of the aggregate supply relation, we can now return to the tribulations of the Phillips curve.

> Going from the relation between the expected price level and the price level to a relation between inflation and expected inflation.
> Start with:
> $$P_t^e \uparrow \Rightarrow P_t \uparrow$$
> Subtract $P_{t-1}$ from both sides, and divide both sides by $P_{t-1}$:
> $$(P_t^e - P_{t-1})/P_{t-1} \Rightarrow$$
> $$(P_t - P_{t-1})/P_{t-1}$$
> Recall the definitions of expected inflation
> $$(\pi_t^e = (P_t^e - P_{t-1})/P_{t-1})$$
> and actual inflation
> $$(\pi_t = (P_t - P_{t-1})/P_{t-1}),$$
> and replace:
> $$\pi_t^e \uparrow \Rightarrow \pi_t \uparrow$$

# 12-2 | The Phillips Curve

Let us start with the relation between unemployment and inflation as it was first discovered by Phillips, circa 1960.

## The Early Incarnation

Think of an economy where inflation is positive in some years, negative in others, and on average equals zero. This is clearly not the way things are in Canada today: The last year during which inflation was negative—the last year during which there was **deflation**—was 1953, when inflation was −1%. But as we will see later in this chapter, average inflation *was* close to zero during much of the period that Phillips were examining.

Think of wage setters choosing nominal wages for the coming year and thus having to forecast what inflation will be over the year. With the average inflation rate equal to zero in the past, it is reasonable for them to expect that inflation will be equal to zero over the next year as well. Assuming that $\pi_t^e = 0$ in equation (12.1) gives the following relation between unemployment and inflation:

$$\pi_t = (m + z) - \alpha u_t \tag{12.2}$$

This is precisely the negative relation between unemployment and inflation that Phillips found for the United Kingdom and that seems to be in the Canadian data in Figure 12–1. The story behind it is simple: Given expected prices, which workers simply take to be last year's prices, lower unemployment leads to higher nominal wages. Higher nominal wages lead to higher prices. Putting the steps together, lower unemployment leads to higher prices this year compared with last year's prices—that is, to higher inflation.

This mechanism has sometimes been called the **wage-price spiral**, and this phrase captures well the basic mechanism at work:

- Low unemployment leads to higher nominal wages.
- In response to higher wages, firms increase their prices.
- In response to higher prices, workers ask for higher nominal wages.
- Firms further increase prices, so workers ask for further increases in wages.
- And so on, with the result being steady wage and price inflation.

## Mutations

The combination of an apparently reliable empirical relation, together with a plausible story to explain it, led to the adoption of the Phillips curve by macroeconomists and policy makers alike. Macroeconomic policy in the 1960s was aimed at maintaining unemployment in the range that appeared consistent with moderate inflation. And, throughout the 1960s, the negative relation between unemployment and inflation provided a reliable guide to the joint movements in unemployment and inflation. Figure 12–2 plots the combinations of inflation and unemployment in Canada for each year from 1960 to 1969. Note how well the relation held during the 1960s.

From 1970 on, however, the relation broke down. Figure 12–3 gives the combination of inflation and unemployment in Canada for each year from 1970 to 2012. The points are scattered in a roughly symmetric cloud: There is no relation between the unemployment rate and the inflation rate.

Why did the original Phillips curve vanish? There are two main reasons:

- As we saw in Chapter 11, in the 1970s, there were two periods where the price of oil increased rapidly. The effect of this increase in nonlabour costs was to force firms to increase their prices given wages, to increase $m$. As shown in equation (12.1), an increase in $m$ leads to an increase in inflation, even at a given rate of unemployment, and this indeed happened in the 1970s. But the main reason for the breakdown of the Phillips curve relation was elsewhere.
- The main reason was that wage setters changed the way they formed expectations. This change came from a change in the process of inflation itself. Look at Figure 12–4, which plots the Canadian inflation rate for each year from 1927 to 2012. Starting around 1960, there was a clear change in the way the rate of inflation moved over time. First, rather than being sometimes positive and sometimes negative, as it had for the first part of the century, the rate of inflation became consistently positive. Second, inflation became more persistent. High inflation in one year became more likely to be followed by high inflation the next year.

The persistence of inflation led workers and firms to revise the way they formed their expectations. When inflation is consistently positive, expecting that prices this year will be the same as last year becomes systematically incorrect; indeed, it becomes foolish. People do not like to make the same mistake repeatedly. So, as inflation became consistently positive and more persistent, expectations started to take into account the presence of inflation. This change in expectation formation changed the nature of the relation between unemployment and inflation.

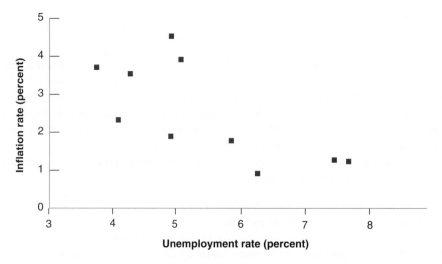

**FIGURE 12–2**

**Inflation and Unemployment in Canada, 1960–1969**

In the nine years following the discovery of the Phillips curve, the Canadian economy behaved as predicted. If unemployment was lower, inflation was higher.

*Source:* Data from Inflation rate using CANSIM II variable V35319; unemployment rate 1927–1952 using Historical Statistics of Canada, and 1953–1975 using CANSIM I variable D7676.

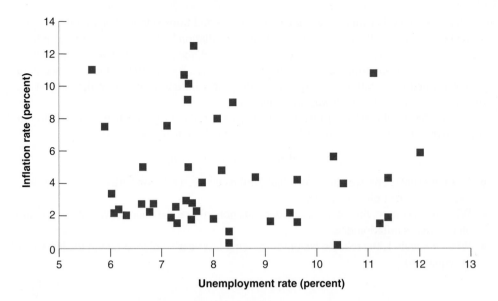

**FIGURE 12-3**

**Inflation and Unemployment in Canada, 1970–2012**

Beginning in 1970, the relation between the unemployment rate and the inflation rate disappeared in Canada.

*Source:* Data from Inflation rate using, CANSIM II variable V41690973; unemployment rate using CANSIM II variable V2062815.

To understand what happened, suppose expectations are formed according to:

$$\pi_t^e = \theta \pi_{t-1} \tag{12.3}$$

The value of the parameter $\theta$ (the Greek lowercase letter theta) captures the effect of last year's inflation rate on this year's expected inflation rate. The higher the value of $\theta$, the more last year's inflation leads workers and firms to revise their expectations of what inflation will be this year and so the higher expected inflation is.

We can then think of what happened from 1970 on as an increase in the value of $\theta$ over time. As long as inflation was low and not very persistent, it was reasonable for workers and firms to ignore past inflation and to assume that this year's price level would be roughly the same as last year's. For the period that Phillips had looked at, $\theta$ was close to zero, expectations were roughly given by $\pi_t^e = 0$, and the relation between the inflation and unemployment rates was given by equation (12.2).

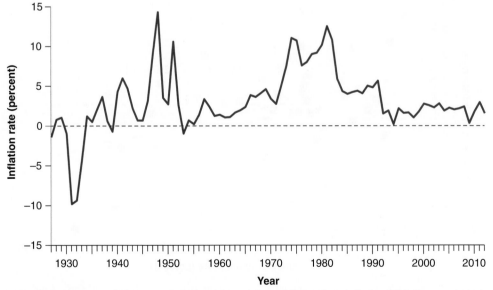

**FIGURE 12-4**

**Canadian Inflation, 1927–2012**

Since the 1960s, Canadian inflation has been consistently positive. Inflation has also become more persistent: High inflation in the current year is more likely to be followed by high inflation the following year. In the last decade, inflation has been very close to 2%, which is its target. We would anticipate that expected inflation has been near 2% as well.

*Source:* Data from Annual inflation calculated using the Consumer Price Index. All items, CANSIM II variable V41690973.

But as inflation became more persistent, workers and firms started changing the way they formed expectations. They started assuming that if inflation had been high last year, inflation was likely to be high this year as well. The parameter $\theta$, the effect of last year's inflation rate on this year's expected inflation rate, steadily increased. By the 1970s, the evidence is that people formed expectations by expecting this year's inflation rate to be the same as last year's—in other words, that $\theta$ was now equal to 1.

To see the implications of different values of $\theta$ for the relation between inflation and unemployment, replace equation (12.3) in equation (12.1). Doing so gives:

$$\pi_t = \theta \pi_{t-1} + (m + z) - \alpha u_t$$

- When $\theta$ equals zero, we get the original Phillips curve, a relation between the inflation rate and the unemployment rate.
- When $\theta$ is positive, the inflation rate depends not only on the unemployment rate but also on last year's inflation rate.
- When $\theta$ equals 1, the relation becomes (moving last year's inflation rate to the left side of the equation):

$$\pi_t - \pi_{t-1} = (m + z) - \alpha u_t \qquad (12.4)$$

So when $\theta = 1$, the unemployment rate affects not the inflation rate, but rather the *change* in the inflation rate: High unemployment leads to decreasing inflation; low unemployment leads to increasing inflation.

To distinguish equation (12.4) from the original Phillips curve (equation (12.2)), it is often called the **modified Phillips curve**, or the **expectations-augmented Phillips curve** (to indicate that the term $\pi_{t-1}$ stands for expected inflation), or the **accelerationist Phillips curve** (to indicate that a low unemployment rate leads to an increase in the inflation rate and thus an *acceleration* of the price level). We will simply call equation (12.4) the Phillips curve and refer to the earlier incarnation, equation (12.2), as the *original* Phillips curve.

This discussion gives the key to what happened from 1970 on. As $\theta$ increased from 0 to 1, the simple relation between unemployment and inflation disappeared. This is what we saw in Figure 12–3. But equation (12.4) tells us what to look for: a relation between unemployment and the *change* in inflation. This relation is shown in Figure 12–5, which plots the change in

Original Phillips curve:

$$u_t \uparrow \Rightarrow \pi_t \downarrow$$

Modified Phillips curve:

$$u_t \uparrow \Rightarrow (\pi_t - \pi_{t-1}) \downarrow$$

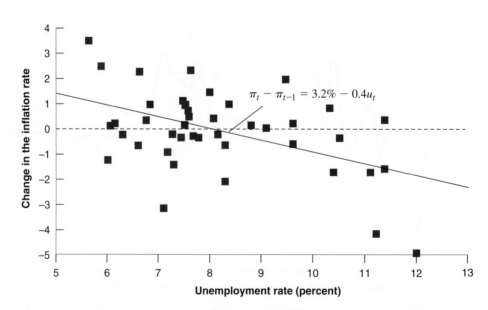

**FIGURE 12–5**

**Change in Inflation versus Unemployment in Canada, 1970–2012**

Since 1970, there has been a negative relation between the unemployment rate and the change in the inflation rate in Canada.

$$\pi_t - \pi_{t-1} = 3.2\% - 0.4u_t$$

*Source:* Data from Inflation rate using CANSIM II variable V735319; unemployment rate 1927–1952 using *Historical Statistics of Canada*, 1953–1975 using CANSIM I variable D767611, and 1976–2007 using CANSIM II variable V2062815.

the inflation rate versus the unemployment rate for each year between 1970 and 2012. It shows a negative relation between unemployment and the change in inflation. A line that roughly fits the scatter of points for the period 1970–2012 is:

$$\pi_t - \pi_{t-1} = 3.2\% - 0.4u_t \qquad (12.5)$$

The corresponding line is drawn in Figure 12–5. For low unemployment, the change in inflation is positive. For unemployment larger than 8.0% (2.5 times 3.2%), the change in inflation is negative.

This line is obtained using econometrics. (See Appendix 3 at the end of the book.) Note that the line does not fit the cloud of points very tightly. There are years when the change in inflation is much larger than implied by the line, and years when the change in inflation is much less than implied by the line. We return to this point below.

## Back to the Natural Rate of Unemployment

The history of the Phillips curve is closely related to the discovery of the concept of the natural unemployment rate that we developed in Chapter 9.

The original Phillips curve implied that there was no such thing as a natural unemployment rate: If policy makers were willing to tolerate a higher inflation rate, they could maintain a lower unemployment rate forever.

In the late 1960s, and even while the original Phillips curve still gave a good description of the data, two economists, Milton Friedman and Edmund Phelps, questioned the existence of such a trade-off between unemployment and inflation. They questioned it on logical grounds. They argued that such a trade-off could exist only if wage setters systematically underpredicted inflation and that they were unlikely to do so forever. They also argued that if government attempted to sustain lower unemployment by accepting higher inflation, the trade-off would ultimately disappear; the unemployment rate could not be sustained below a certain level, a level they called the "natural rate of unemployment." Events proved them right, and the trade-off between the unemployment rate and the inflation rate indeed disappeared. (See the Focus box "Theory ahead of the Facts: Milton Friedman and Edmund Phelps.") Today, most economists accept the notion of a *natural rate of unemployment*—subject to the many caveats we state in the next section.

Let us make explicit the connection between the Phillips curve and the natural rate of unemployment. By definition, the natural rate of unemployment is that unemployment rate at which the actual price level turns out equal to the expected price level. Equivalently, and more conveniently here, the natural rate of unemployment is the unemployment rate at which the actual inflation rate is equal to the expected inflation rate. Denote the natural unemployment rate by $u_n$. Then, imposing the condition that actual inflation and expected inflation be the same ($\pi_t = \pi_t^e$) in equation (12.1) gives:

In Chapter 9, we derived the natural rate of unemployment as the rate of unemployment in which the expected and actual price level are the same. In Chapter 10, when drawing the aggregate supply curve, we emphasized that when output is equal to its natural level (hence unemployment is at the natural rate), the price level is equal to the expected price level.

$$0 = (m + z) - \alpha u_n$$

Solving for the natural rate $u_n$,

$$u_n = \frac{m + z}{\alpha} \qquad (12.6)$$

If $P_t^e = P_t$, then
$$\pi_t^e \equiv (P_t^e - P_{t-1})/P_{t-1}$$
$$= (P_t - P_{t-1})/P_{t-1} = \pi_t$$

Thus, the higher the markup, $m$, or the higher the factors that affect wage setting, $z$, the higher the natural rate is.

From equation (12.6), $\alpha u_n = m + z$. Replacing $(m + z)$ by $\alpha u_n$ in equation (12.1) and rearranging gives:

$$\pi_t - \pi_t^e = -\alpha(u_t - u_n) \qquad (12.7)$$

If the expected rate of inflation ($\pi_t^e$) is well approximated by last year's inflation rate ($\pi_{t-1}$), the relation finally becomes:

$$\pi_t - \pi_{t-1} = -\alpha(u_t - u_n) \qquad (12.8)$$

Economists are usually not very good at predicting major changes before they happen, and most of their insights are derived after the fact. Here is an exception.

In the late 1960s—precisely as the original Phillips curve relation was working like a charm—two economists, Milton Friedman and Edmund Phelps, argued that the appearance of a trade-off between inflation and unemployment was an illusion.

Here are a few quotations from Milton Friedman. Talking about the Phillips curve, he said,

*Implicitly, Phillips wrote his article for a world in which everyone anticipated that nominal prices would be stable and in which this anticipation remained unshaken and immutable whatever happened to actual prices and wages. Suppose, by contrast, that everyone anticipates that prices will rise at a rate of more than 75% a year—as, for example, Brazilians did a few years ago. Then, wages must rise at that rate simply to keep real wages unchanged. An excess supply of labor will be reflected in a less rapid rise in nominal wages than in anticipated prices, not in an absolute decline in wages.*

He went on to say,

*To state [my] conclusion differently, there is always a temporary trade-off between inflation and unemployment;*

*there is no permanent trade-off. The temporary trade-off comes not from inflation per se, but from a rising rate of inflation.*

He then tried to guess how much longer the apparent trade-off between inflation and unemployment would last in the United States:

*But how long, you will say, is "temporary"? . . . I can at most venture a personal judgment, based on some examination of the historical evidence, that the initial effect of a higher and unanticipated rate of inflation lasts for something like two to five years; that this initial effect then begins to be reversed; and that a full adjustment to the new rate of inflation takes as long for employment as for interest rates, say, a couple of decades.*

Friedman could not have been more right. A few years later, the original Phillips curve started to disappear, in exactly the way Friedman had predicted.

*Source:* Excerpts from "The Role of Monetary Policy" by Milton Friedman. *American Economic Review,* Vol.58, No.1, pp.1–17 March, 1968. Used by permission of American Economic Association.

---

Equation (12.8) gives us another way of thinking about the Phillips curve, as a relation among the actual unemployment rate, the natural unemployment rate, and the change in the inflation rate: *The change in inflation depends on the difference between the actual and the natural unemployment rates. When the actual unemployment rate is higher than the natural unemployment rate, inflation decreases; when the actual unemployment rate is lower than the natural unemployment rate, inflation increases.*

> Calling the natural rate "the nonaccelerating inflation rate of unemployment" is actually wrong. It should be called "the nonincreasing inflation rate of unemployment," or NIIRU. But NAIRU has now become so standard that it is too late to change it.

Equation (12.8) also gives us another way of thinking about the natural rate of unemployment: It is the rate of unemployment required to keep inflation constant. This is why the natural rate is also called the **nonaccelerating inflation rate of unemployment**, or **NAIRU**.

What has been the natural rate of unemployment in Canada since 1970? In other words, what is the unemployment rate such that, on average, inflation has been constant? We can find the answer by returning to equation (12.5). Putting the change in inflation equal to zero in equation (12.5) implies a value for the natural unemployment rate of 3.2%/0.4 = 8.0%. In other words, the evidence suggests that since 1970, in Canada, the rate of unemployment required to keep inflation constant has been, on average, around 8.0%.

## 12-3 | The Natural Rate of Unemployment, Money Growth, and Inflation

In Chapter 10, we looked at an important proposition in the *AS-AD* model: that money was neutral in the medium run. More specifically, we showed that if there was a one-time increase in the level of the nominal money supply in that model, a proportional one-time increase in the price level would return output to its natural level. The real money stock and indeed all the

> See section 10-4.

real variables in this economy were left unchanged. These results need to be extended so we can better understand inflation, the situation where the price level rises every year.

We return to equation (12.8)

$$\pi_t - \pi_{t-1} = -\alpha(u_t - u_n)$$

Unemployment above the natural rate leads to a decline in inflation, unemployment below the natural rate leads to an increase in inflation. The purpose of re-writing the equation is to emphasize that when inflation does not change, unemployment is equal to the natural rate of unemployment. This can only be the case if output is at the natural level, $Y_n$.

To understand the level of inflation, we must return to the aggregate demand relation, equation (10.2):

As we have done until this point, we ignore output growth and thus assume output is constant in the medium run. We allow for output growth in Chapter 13 and explain output growth in Chapters 15–18.

$$Y = Y\left(\frac{M}{P}, G, T\right)$$

When inflation is not changing and unemployment is at the natural rate of unemployment, we use equation (10.2) and set the unchanging natural level of output equal to the unchanging level of aggregate demand:

$$Y_n = Y\left(\frac{M}{P}, G, T\right) \tag{12.9}$$

If $Y_n$ is constant, for this equality to hold (that is, for aggregate demand to be equal to the natural level of output), the right-hand side of the equation (12.9) must be constant. If we assume unchanged fiscal policy (that is, constant $G$ and constant $T$), this implies that the real money stock must also be constant. This implies in turn that the rate of inflation must be equal to the **money growth rate**.

See Proposition 8 in Appendix 2. $g_M$ is the notation for the rate of growth of the nominal money stock.

$$\pi = g_M$$

This is an important result: In the medium run, the rate of inflation is determined by the rate of money growth. Milton Friedman put it this way: *Inflation is always and everywhere a monetary phenomenon*. The implication here is that when a central bank or a government chooses a rate of money growth, they are choosing a rate of inflation. Or, to say the same thing in different words, choosing a rate of inflation is also choosing a rate of growth of money. As we have seen, factors such as the monopoly power of firms, strong unions, strikes, fiscal deficits, and increases in the price of oil do affect the price level and, by implication, do affect inflation in the short run. But, unless they affect the rate of money growth, they have no effect on inflation in the medium run.

In Chapter 24, the choice of the best level of the inflation rate, 0%, 2%, 4%, or higher, is discussed at length.

The "unless" is important here. It could be, for example, that some of these shocks lead to a change in the rate of money growth. For example, a wage explosion or a large budget deficit may lead to higher money creation (more on deficits and inflation in Chapter 25). If this is the case, these shocks will, indirectly, affect inflation even in the medium run.

# 12-4 | A Summary and Many Warnings

To summarize: The aggregate supply relation is well captured in Canada today by the Phillips curve, which is a relation between the change in the inflation rate and the deviation of unemployment from its natural rate (equation (12.8)). When unemployment exceeds the natural rate, inflation decreases. When unemployment is below the natural rate, inflation increases.

This relation has held quite well since 1970. But its earlier history points to the need for several warnings. All of them point to one main fact: The relation can change, and it often has.

## The Inflation Process and the Phillips Curve

Recall how the Canadian Phillips curve changed as inflation became more persistent and the way wage setters formed inflation expectations changed as a result. The lesson is a general one: The relation between unemployment and inflation is likely to change with the inflation

More concretely, when inflation runs on average at 5% a year, wage setters can be confident the rate will be, say, between 3 and 7%. When inflation runs on average at 30% a year, wage setters can be confident the rate will be, say, between 20 and 40%. If they set a nominal wage, their real wage may vary in the first case by 2% up or down relative to what they expected; in the second case, it may vary by as much as 10% relative to what they expected. There is much more uncertainty in the second case.

This assumption is actually too strong. Indexation clauses typically adjust wages not for current inflation (which is known only with a lag) but for inflation in the recent past, so there remains a short lag between inflation and wage adjustments. We ignore this lag here.

process. Evidence from countries with high inflation confirms this lesson. Not only does the way in which workers and firms form expectations change, but institutional arrangements change as well.

When the inflation rate becomes high, inflation also tends to become more variable. Workers and firms become more reluctant to enter into labour contracts that predetermine nominal wages for a long period of time: If inflation turns out to be higher than expected, real wages may plunge and workers may suffer a large cut in their standard of living. If inflation turns out to be lower than expected, real wages may explode, and firms may go bankrupt.

For this reason, the form of wage agreements changes with the level of inflation. Nominal wages are set for shorter periods of time, down from a year to a month or even less. **Wage indexation**, a rule that increases wages automatically in line with inflation, becomes more prevalent.

These changes lead to a stronger response of inflation to unemployment. To see this, an example based on wage indexation will help. Think of an economy that has two types of labour contracts. A proportion $\lambda$ (the Greek lowercase letter lambda) of labour contracts is indexed: Nominal wages in those contracts move one for one with variations in the actual price level. A proportion $1 - \lambda$ of labour contracts is not indexed: Nominal wages are set on the basis of expected inflation. Finally, assume expected inflation is equal to last year's inflation.

Under this assumption, equation (12.7) becomes:

$$\pi_t = [\lambda \pi_t + (1 - \lambda)\pi_{t-1}] - \alpha(u_t - u_n)$$

The term in square brackets on the right reflects the fact that a proportion $\lambda$ of contracts responds to actual inflation ($\pi_t$), and a proportion $(1 - \lambda)$ responds to expected inflation, which we have assumed is equal to last year's inflation ($\pi_{t-1}$).

When $\lambda = 0$, all wages are set on the basis of expected inflation—which is equal to last year's inflation, $\pi_{t-1}$—and the equation reduces to equation (12.8). When $\lambda$ is positive, however, a proportion $\lambda$ of wages is set on the basis of actual rather than expected inflation.

Reorganizing the equation gives

$$\pi_t - \pi_{t-1} = -\frac{\alpha}{(1 - \lambda)}(u_t - u_n)$$

Indexation increases the effect of unemployment on inflation: The higher the proportion of indexed contracts—the higher the $\lambda$—the larger the effect of the unemployment rate on the change in inflation, and the higher the coefficient $\alpha/(1 - \lambda)$.

The intuition is as follows: Without indexation, lower unemployment increases wages, which, in turn, increases prices. But because wages do not respond to prices right away, there is no further effect within the year. With wage indexation, however, an increase in prices leads to a further increase in wages within the year, which, in turn, leads to a further increase in prices, and so on, so the effect of unemployment on inflation within the year is higher.

If and when $\lambda$ gets close to 1—when most labour contracts allow for wage indexation—small changes in unemployment can lead to very large changes in inflation. Put another way, there can be large changes in inflation with nearly no change in unemployment. This is, indeed, what happens in countries where inflation is very high: The relation between inflation and unemployment becomes more and more tenuous and eventually disappears altogether.

### Deflation and the Phillips Curve Relation

We have just looked at what happens to the Phillips curve when inflation is very high. Another issue is what happens when inflation is low, and possibly negative—when there is deflation.

The motivation for asking this question is given by an aspect of Figure 12–1 that we mentioned at the start of the chapter but then left aside. In that figure, note how the points corresponding to 1931, 1932, and 1933 lie to the right of the others. Not only is unemployment unusually high—this is no surprise because we are looking at the years corresponding to the Great Depression—but given the high unemployment rate, the inflation rate may be surprisingly high in 1932 and 1933. In other words, given the very high unemployment rate, we would have expected not merely deflation, but a large rate of deflation. In fact, deflation was limited.

How do we interpret that fact? There are two potential explanations.

One is that the Great Depression was associated with an increase not only in the actual unemployment rate but also in the natural unemployment rate. This seems unlikely. Most economic historians see the Great Depression primarily as the result of a large adverse shift in aggregate demand leading to an increase in the actual unemployment rate over the natural rate of unemployment rather than an increase in the natural rate of unemployment itself.

For more on the Great Depression, see Chapter 11.

The other explanation is it may be that when the economy starts experiencing deflation, the Phillips curve relation breaks down. One possible reason is the reluctance of workers to accept decreases in their nominal wages. Workers will unwittingly accept a cut in their real wages that occurs when their nominal wages increase more slowly than inflation does. However, they are likely to fight the same cut in their real wages if it results from an overt cut in their nominal wages. If this argument is correct, this implies that the Phillips curve relation between the change in inflation and unemployment may disappear or at least become weaker when the economy is close to zero inflation.

Consider two scenarios. In one, inflation is 4%, and your nominal wage goes up by 2%. In the other, inflation is 0%, and your nominal wage is cut by 2%. Which do you dislike most? You should be indifferent between the two. In both cases, your real wage goes down by 2%. There is some evidence, however, that most people find the first scenario less painful.

This issue is a crucial one at this stage because in many countries, inflation is now very low, and in some countries, negative. What happens to the Phillips curve relation in this environment of low inflation or even deflation is one of the developments closely watched by macroeconomists today. Chapter 11 had some discussion of deflation in a liquidity trap. Chapter 24 will have further discussion of the best choice of an inflation rate, including the possibility that a very low rate of inflation leads to policy challenges.

## Differences in the Natural Rate between Canada and the United States

Recall from equation (12.6) that the natural rate of unemployment depends on all the factors that affect wage setting, represented by the catch-all variable, $z$; on the markup set by firms, $m$; and on the response of inflation to unemployment, represented by $\alpha$. To the extent that these factors differ across countries, there is no reason to expect different countries to have the same natural rate of unemployment. And, indeed, natural rates differ across countries. Consider the unemployment rates in Canada and the United States shown from 1950 to 2012 in Figure 12–6. Until the middle of the 1960s, the two rates were very similar. Remember that recessions in the United States nearly always cause recessions in Canada. From 1950 to 1969, average unemployment in Canada was 4.9%; in the United States, average unemployment was 4.6%. The situation changed dramatically after 1970. From 1970 to 2001, unemployment in Canada averaged 8.5%, while unemployment averaged 6.3% in the United States. In the years from 2009 to 2012, Canada's unemployment rate was lower than the unemployment rate in the United States.

What might account for these differences? The Focus box "Small Differences That Matter" explores this issue further.

## Variations in the Natural Rate over Time

In estimating equation (12.6), we treated $m + z$ as a constant. But there is no reason to believe that $m$ and $z$ are constant over time. The composition of the labour force, the structure of wage bargaining, the system of unemployment benefits, and so on are likely to change over time, leading to changes in the natural rate of unemployment.

Changes in the natural unemployment rate over time are hard to measure. Again, the reason is that we do not observe the natural rate, only the actual rate. But broad evolutions can be established by comparing average unemployment rates across decades. We see in Figure 12–6 that the natural rate of unemployment almost certainly increased in Canada after 1970. Many economists observe the sharp increase just after 1970. In 1971, the Canadian employment insurance system (now called Employment Insurance, or EI) was changed. A larger proportion of

In a 1993 book with the wonderful title *Small Differences That Matter*, a group of economists looked at various aspects of the labour market in Canada and the United States. From the title, you can guess the theme of the book. Small differences in the institutions related to labour markets were found to have substantial impacts on the lives of working Canadians and Americans.

The topics addressed included how wage inequality varies across the two countries, how the social safety net varies, and how immigration policies have differed. There are also the differences in the roles and sizes of unions. For this chapter, we want to learn why the natural rate of unemployment seems to be so much higher after 1970 in Canada than in the United States. Like in any good detective story, there are a number of suspects.

The usual suspect was already mentioned in the text: the more generous Canadian employment insurance system. This is quite clearly the case. Canada's employment insurance system covers more workers, pays higher benefits, includes maternity benefits, and generally encourages labour force participation.

There are more unusual suspects as well. These measurement differences account for about 0.7% of the gap from 1993 to the present day. In Canada, by definition, a full-time student cannot be considered unemployed. In the U.S. survey, a full-time student can state he or she is looking for a job and be considered unemployed. In the United States, a person is counted as unemployed only if he or she "actively searches," that is, takes action to find a job. In Canada, "passive search," even just looking at an ad, is sufficient to count as unemployed. There are differences in the treatment of those who are

waiting for a known job to start. In Canada, these persons are unemployed; in the United States, they are not. There is the higher rate of incarceration in the United States. The prison population in the United States almost doubled between the mid-1980s and the mid-1990s. This removes from the labour force a large number of persons who would be likely to be counted as unemployed. There are also some differences in the way Aboriginal people are treated in the measurement of the unemployed. In both countries, Aboriginal people are more likely to be unemployed.

Figure 1 replicates Figure 12–5 but with American data from 1970 to 2012. The estimated regression line in the graph is $\pi_t - \pi_{t-1} = 3.2\% - 0.5u_t$. Using the methodology developed earlier, this line says that the natural rate of unemployment in the United States is $3.2/0.5 = 6.4\%$. This is, indeed, lower than the estimate for Canada using the data in Figure 12–5. As shown in Figure 12-6, from 2009 to 2012 Canadian unemployment rates have been about one percentage point lower than American unemployment rates. It remains to be seen if this is a temporary or permanent situation.

*Sources:*
David Card and Richard B. Freeman, eds., *Small Differences That Matter: Labor Markets and Income Maintenance in Canada and the United States* (Chicago: University of Chicago Press, 1993).

Craig W. Riddell, "Why Is Canada's Unemployment Rate Persistently Higher than in the United States?" *Canadian Public Policy* 31 (March 2005): pp. 93–100.

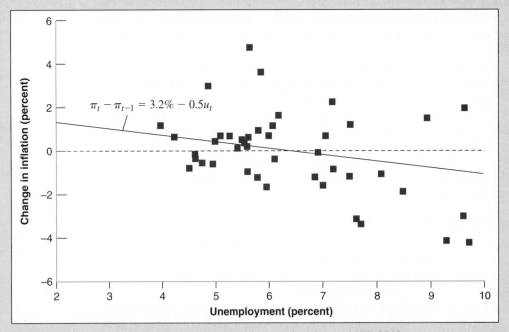

**FIGURE 1**    **Change in inflation versus unemployment in the United States, 1970–2012**

*Source:* Data from U.S. Consumer Price Index Variable CPIAUSI, Federal Reserve Bank of St. Louis FRED data base; U.S. unemployment rate Variable UNRATE, Federal Reserve Bank of St. Louis FRED data base.

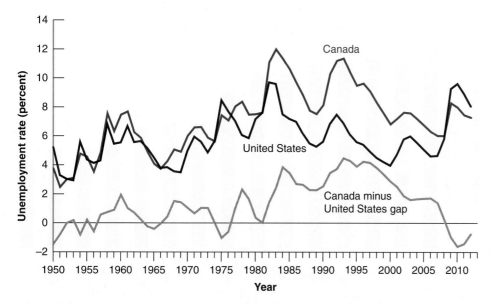

FIGURE 12-6

**Unemployment Rates in Canada and the United States, 1950–2012**

The impact of U.S. recessions on Canadians seems clear. Until 1980, the levels of the unemployment rate in Canada and the United States were very similar. From 1980 until 2007 the unemployment rate in Canada averaged 2.6 percentage points higher than the unemployment rate in the United States. There was a large gap for many years. The world economic crisis after 2007 hit the United States much harder than Canada and from 2008 to 2012, the Canadian unemployment rate fell below the U.S. unemployment rate. It remains to be seen if the gap will return.

*Source:* Data from Canadian unemployment rate 1950–1952 using *Historical Statistics of Canada*; 1953–1975 using CANSIM I variable D767611; and 1976–2007 using CANSIM II variable V12062815; United States unemployment rate using CANSIM II variable V122076.

workers were included in coverage. The benefits were increased and the number of weeks of work required to qualify was reduced. Some of these changes were partially reversed in 1996. In the Budget of 2012, further changes were made to EI that made it less accessible to seasonal workers. It seems likely these changes would decrease the natural rate of unemployment over time.

## The Limits of Our Understanding

The theory of the natural rate gives macroeconomists directions in which to look for differences in natural rates across countries or for variations in the natural rate over time in a given country. But the truth is that macroeconomists' understanding of exactly which factors determine the natural rate of unemployment is still very limited. In particular, there is considerable uncertainty about the exact list of factors behind $z$ and about the dynamic effects of each factor on the natural unemployment rate.

One way to see the limits of our understanding is to look at countries beyond Canada and the United States for evidence on the natural rate of unemployment. Olivier Blanchard has done much of this work and gives us Figure 12–7, which shows the unemployment rate in 15 European countries in 2006. In these countries, inflation did not change very much between 2005 and 2006 and it is reasonable to look at this variation in the unemployment rate as variation in the natural rate of unemployment. The lowest rate, in Denmark, is around 4%; the highest rate, in France, is 9%. This is indeed a very wide range.

Blanchard concludes from this range that the devil is in the details when it comes to the determination of the natural rate of unemployment. While European countries are broadly similar in having relatively generous unemployment insurance systems compared to those in North America and having a higher degree of employment protection than exists in North America, there is still enough variation within Europe to generate Figure 12–7. Details that matter include the incentives to return to work within the unemployment insurance system and the exact structure and type of severance payments on layoff. If there is a large cost to firms laying off workers in a recession, then firms may hesitate to take on workers in booms. This may lead to a higher "natural" rate of unemployment. Work on understanding international differences between labour market institutions is an important part of the macroeconomic research agenda.

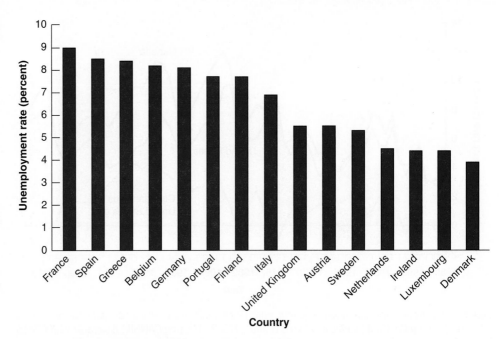

**FIGURE 12-7**

**Unemployment Rates in 15 European Countries, 2006**

In 2006, the change in inflation in most of Western Europe was zero. This implies countries were at or near the natural rate of unemployment. Even though the countries in Western Europe share broadly similar characteristics relative to North America in terms of their attitudes toward social protection—relatively high unemployment and more generous social welfare benefits—the natural rate of unemployment varies widely across these countries.

*Source:* For more, read Olivier Blanchard, "European Unemployment: The Evolution of Facts and Ideas," *Economic Policy*, Volume I (2006): 1–54.

## SUMMARY

- The aggregate supply relation can be expressed as a relation among inflation, expected inflation, and unemployment rate: The higher the expected inflation, the higher the actual inflation; the higher the unemployment rate, the lower the inflation.

- When inflation is not very persistent, expected inflation does not depend very much on past inflation. Thus, the aggregate supply relation becomes a relation between inflation and unemployment. This is what Phillips in the United Kingdom discovered when he looked in the late 1950s at the joint behaviour of unemployment and inflation.

- As inflation became more persistent in the 1970s and 1980s, expected inflation became increasingly dependent on past inflation. In Canada today, the aggregate supply relation takes the form of a relation between unemployment and the change in inflation. High unemployment leads to decreasing inflation; low unemployment leads to increasing inflation.

- The natural unemployment rate is the unemployment rate at which inflation remains constant. When the actual unemployment rate exceeds the natural rate, inflation decreases; when the actual unemployment rate is less than the natural rate, inflation increases.

- In the medium run when output is not growing, the inflation rate is equal to the growth rate of money.

- Changes in the way the inflation rate varies over time affect the way wage setters form expectations and how much they use wage indexation. When wage indexation is widespread, small changes in unemployment can lead to very large changes in inflation. At very high rates of inflation, the relation between inflation and unemployment disappears altogether.

- The natural rate of unemployment depends on many factors that differ across countries and can change over time. It seems clear that from 1970 to at least 2000, the natural rate of unemployment in Canada was higher than the natural rate of unemployment in the United States. It is clear that the natural rate of unemployment varies across countries within Europe.

## KEY TERMS

- accelerationist Phillips curve, 234
- deflation, 231
- expectations-augmented Phillips curve, 234
- modified Phillips curve, 234
- money growth rate, 237

- nonaccelerating inflation rate of unemployment (NAIRU), 236
- wage indexation, 238
- wage-price spiral, 231

## 1. TRUE/FALSE/UNCERTAIN

**a.** The original Phillips curve is the negative relation between unemployment and inflation first observed by Phillips for the United Kingdom.

**b.** The original Phillips curve relation has proven to be very stable across both countries and time.

**c.** The aggregate supply relation is consistent with the Phillips curve as observed before the 1970s, but not since.

**d.** Policy makers can only temporarily exploit the inflation–unemployment trade-off.

**e.** Before the 1970s, there was no natural rate of unemployment, and policy makers could achieve as low a rate of unemployment as they wanted.

**f.** The expectations-augmented Phillips curve is consistent with workers and firms adapting their expectations following the macroeconomic experience of the 1960s.

**g.** Inflation is always equal to money growth.

## 2. THE PHILLIPS CURVE

Discuss the following statements:

**a.** The Phillips curve implies that when unemployment is high, inflation is low, and vice versa. Therefore, we may experience either high inflation or high unemployment, but we will never experience both together.

**b.** As long as we do not mind having high inflation, we can achieve as low a level of unemployment as we want. All we have to do is increase the demand for goods and services by using, for example, expansionary fiscal policy.

## 3. MAINTAINING LOW UNEMPLOYMENT

Suppose that the Phillips curve is given by:

$$\pi_t = \pi_t^e + 0.1 - 2u_t$$

where

$$\pi_t^e = \theta \pi_{t-1}$$

Also, suppose that $\theta$ is initially equal to zero.

**a.** What is the natural rate of unemployment?

Suppose that the rate of unemployment is initially equal to the natural rate. In year $t$, the authorities decide to bring the unemployment rate down to 3% and hold it there forever.

**b.** Determine the rate of inflation in years $t$, $t+1$, $t+2$, $t+10$, $t+15$.

**c.** Do you believe the answer you gave in (b)? Why, or why not? (*Hint:* Think about how inflation expectations are formed.)

Now, suppose that in year $t+5$, $\theta$ increases from 0 to 1.

**d.** Why might $\theta$ increase like this? What is the effect on $u_n$?

Suppose that government is still determined to keep $u$ at 3% forever.

**e.** What will the inflation rate be in years $t+5$, $t+10$, and $t+15$?

**f.** Do you believe the answer given in (e)? Why, or why not?

## 4. INDEXATION OF WAGES

Suppose that the Phillips curve is given by:

$$\pi_t - \pi_t^e = 0.1 - 2u_t$$

where

$$\pi_t^e = \pi_{t-1}$$

Suppose that inflation in year $t-1$ is zero. In year $t$, the authorities decide to keep the unemployment rate at 4% forever.

**a.** Compute the rate of inflation for years $t$, $t+1$, $t+2$, and $t+3$.

Now, suppose that half the workers have indexed labour contracts.

**b.** What is the new equation for the Phillips curve?

**c.** Repeat the exercise in (a).

**d.** What is the effect of indexation on the relation between $\pi$ and $u$?

## 5. OIL SHOCKS, INFLATION, AND UNEMPLOYMENT

Suppose that the Phillips curve is given by:

$$\pi_t - \pi_t^e = 0.08 + 0.1m - 2u_t$$

where $m$ is the markup of prices over wages.

Suppose that $m$ is initially equal to 20% but that as a result of a sharp increase in oil prices, $m$ increases to 40% in year $t$ and after.

**a.** Why would an increase in oil prices result in an increase in $m$?

**b.** What is the long-run effect of the increase in $m$ on the natural rate of unemployment?

### 6. FAVOURABLE OIL SHOCKS, UNEMPLOYMENT, AND INFLATION

In sharp contrast to the oil shocks of the 1970s, the price of oil substantially declined in the early part of the 1990s.

**a.** Can this explain the good performance of both inflation and unemployment in the 1990s?

**b.** What has been the probable effect on the natural rate of unemployment?

### 7. USING THE NATURAL RATE OF UNEMPLOYMENT MODEL [WEB]

In the chapter, using data from 1970 to 2012, the equation $\pi_t - \pi_{t-1} = 3.2\% - 0.4u_t$ was found to best predict changes in inflation in Canada. You can check to see if the equation continues to describe changes in inflation after this book was written.

At the Statistics Canada website (www.statcan.gc.ca), follow the links through Canadian Statistics, Economic Conditions, and then to Prices (here, you will find annual inflation rates for the last five calendar years under Consumer Prices). You will have to "go back" to Economic Conditions, and under the Labour Force and Unemployment Rates, you will find unemployment rates for the last five calendar years.

**a.** Calculate the change in inflation predicted by the equation $\pi_t - \pi_{t-1} = 3.2\% - 0.4u_t$ using the data from the five years listed. There will be four observations of $\pi_t - \pi_{t-1}$ and four matching observations of the corresponding value of $u_t$.

**b.** Graph your four observations. You could try to place these points on Figure 12–5 or draw your own graph.

**c.** Does it seem like the natural rate of unemployment is still 8.0%? Why, or why not?

---

**APPENDIX**

# FROM THE AGGREGATE SUPPLY RELATION TO THE PHILLIPS CURVE

The purpose of this appendix is to derive equation (12.1), expressing the relation among inflation, expected inflation, and unemployment.

The starting point is the aggregate supply relation among the price level, the expected price level, and the unemployment rate derived in Chapter 10:

$$P_t = P_t^e(1 + m)(1 - \alpha u_t + z)$$

Divide both sides by last year's price level, $P_{t-1}$:

$$\frac{P_t}{P_{t-1}} = \frac{P_t^e}{P_{t-1}}(1 + m)(1 - \alpha u_t + z) \qquad (12A.1)$$

Rewrite the fraction $P_t/P_{t-1}$ on the left side as:

$$\frac{P_t}{P_{t-1}} = 1 + \frac{P_t - P_{t-1}}{P_{t-1}} = 1 + \pi_t$$

where the first equality follows from adding and subtracting one, and the second from the definition of the inflation rate: $\pi_t \equiv (P_t - P_{t-1})/P_{t-1}$.

Do the same for the fraction $P_t^e/P_{t-1}$ on the right side, using the definition of the expected inflation rate: $\pi_t^e \equiv (P_t^e - P_{t-1})/P_{t-1}$.

$$\frac{P_t^e}{P_{t-1}} = 1 + \frac{P_t^e - P_{t-1}}{P_{t-1}} = 1 + \pi_t^e$$

Replacing $P_t/P_{t-1}$ and $P_t^e/P_{t-1}$ in equation (12A.1) by the expressions we have just derived,

$$(1 + \pi_t) = (1 + \pi_t^e)(1 + m)(1 - \alpha u_t + z)$$

This gives us a relation among inflation ($\pi_t$), expected inflation ($\pi_t^e$), and the unemployment rate ($u_t$). The remaining steps make the relation look more friendly:

Divide both sides by $(1 + \pi_t^e)(1 + m)$:

$$\frac{(1 + \pi_t)}{(1 + \pi_t^e)(1 + m)} = 1 - \alpha u_t + z$$

As long as inflation, expected inflation, and the markup are not too large, a good approximation to this equation is given by (see propositions 3 and 6 in Appendix 2 at the end of the book):

$$1 + \pi_t - \pi_t^e - m = 1 - \alpha u_t + z$$

Rearranging gives:

$$\pi_t = \pi_t^e + (m + z) - \alpha u_t$$

This is equation (12.1) in the text. The inflation rate depends on the expected inflation rate and the unemployment rate, $u_t$. The relation depends on the markup, $m$, on the factors that affect wage setting, $z$, and on the effect of the unemployment rate on wages, $\alpha$.

# Inflation, Economic Growth, and Money Growth

## The Core: The Medium Run

On January 8, 1988, Governor John Crow, head of the Bank of Canada at the time, used the Hanson lecture at the University of Alberta to lay out the agenda for monetary policy in Canada during his seven-year term. In 1987, inflation was 4.2% measured using the Consumer Price Index (CPI) and 4.6% measured using the GDP deflator. The speech surprised Canadian economists because Governor Crow stated unequivocally, "Monetary policy should be conducted so as to achieve a pace of monetary expansion that promotes stability in the value of money. This means pursuing a policy aimed at achieving and maintaining stable prices." By 1992, both measures of inflation were less than 2%. Since then, inflation has remained less than 3%. The Bank of Canada achieved its goal of reducing inflation; however, the 1990–1991 recession was a long, severe recession. The Focus box "Recessions in Canada since 1981" in Chapter 3 compares this recession to the most recent and relatively mild recession in 2009. Was this very severe recession needed to reduce inflation?

Why did Governor Crow decide to reduce inflation? How was it done? Why was there a recession? More generally, what are the effects of money growth on inflation and on economic activity? Our treatment of expectations in Chapter 10 was too simple to allow us to tackle these issues. Our treatment of output growth (there was no output growth) in Chapter 12 was too simple as well. But with our discussion of expectations and the introduction of the Phillips curve relation in Chapter 12, we now have what we need. In this chapter, we ask how inflation was reduced and model the recession that followed. In Chapter 24, we consider the choice of the optimal (best) rate of inflation.

The first section of this chapter looks at the links among output, unemployment, and inflation. The next several sections put these links together and discuss both the short-run and the medium-run effects of money growth on inflation and activity. The last section returns to the Canadian disinflation following the 1988 Hanson lecture. The central lesson of the chapter is clear. There is a lot of evidence that a permanent reduction in the rate of inflation from a higher rate of inflation to a lower rate of inflation is associated with a prolonged recession. This lesson helps us understand why central banks are so averse to risking higher inflation; they are averse to the recession that seems to be needed to lower inflation.

# 13-1 | Output, Unemployment, and Inflation

In thinking about the interactions among output, unemployment, and inflation, you must keep in mind three relations:

1. Okun's law, first introduced in Chapter 1, which relates the change in unemployment to the deviation of output growth from normal.
2. The Phillips curve, introduced in Chapter 12, which relates the change in inflation to the deviation of unemployment from the natural rate.
3. The aggregate demand relation, from Chapter 12, which relates output growth to the rate of growth of nominal money minus the rate of inflation.

This section looks at each relation on its own. The rest of the chapter looks at their joint implications.

## Okun's Law: Output Growth and Changes in Unemployment

When we wrote the relation between output and unemployment in Chapter 9, we did so under two convenient but restrictive assumptions. We assumed that output and employment moved together, so changes in output led to equal changes in employment. And we assumed that the labour force was constant, so changes in employment were reflected one for one in opposite changes in unemployment.

We must now move beyond these assumptions. To see why, think about what they imply for the relation between the rate of output growth and the unemployment rate. As output and employment move together, a 1% increase in output leads to a 1% increase in employment. And because movements in employment are reflected in opposite movements in unemployment, a 1% increase in employment leads to a decrease of 1% in the unemployment rate.[1] Let $g_{yt}$ denote the growth rate of output. Then, under these two assumptions, the following relation should hold:

$$u_t - u_{t-1} = -g_{yt} \tag{13.1}$$

The change in the unemployment rate should be equal to the negative of the growth rate of output. If output growth is, say, 4%, then the unemployment rate should decline by 4%.

Contrast this with the actual relation between output growth and the change in the unemployment rate, the relation known as Okun's law. Figure 13–1 plots the change in the unemployment rate against the rate of output growth for each year between 1982 and 2012. It also plots the regression line that best fits the scatter of points. The relation corresponding to the line is given by:

$$u_t - u_{t-1} = -0.4(g_{yt} - 2.5\%) \tag{13.2}$$

Equation (13.2) differs in two ways from equation (13.1):

If $g_{yt} = 2.5\%$, then

$u_t - u_{t-1}$
$= -0.4(2.5\% - 2.5\%)$
$= 0$

▶ • Annual output growth has to be at least 2.5% to prevent the unemployment rate from rising. See the Focus box "The Release of GDP Growth Measures in Canada and the

[1]**DIGGING DEEPER.** This last step is only approximately correct. Remember the definition of the unemployment rate:

$$u \equiv U/L = 1 - N/L$$

If the labour force, $L$, is fixed,

$$\Delta u = \Delta U/L = -\Delta N/L = -(\Delta N/N)(N/L)$$

where the last equality follows from multiplying and dividing by $N$. If $N/L$ is equal to, say, 0.95, then a 1% increase in employment leads to a decrease of 0.95% in the unemployment rate. The result in the text is based on approximating $N/L$ by 1, so a 1% increase in employment leads to a decrease of 1% in the unemployment rate.

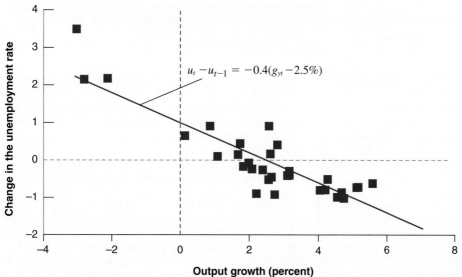

FIGURE    13-1

**Changes in the Unemployment Rate versus Output Growth in Canada, 1982–2012**

High output growth is associated with a reduction in the unemployment rate; low output growth is associated with an increase in the unemployment rate.

$$u_t - u_{t-1} = -0.4(g_{yt} - 2.5\%)$$

*Source:* Real GDP CANSIM II Variable V62305752; Unemployment rate, CANSIM II Variable V2062815.

United States: Numbers to Watch." GDP growth releases are, because of their relation through Okun's Law, among the most closely watched economic data. This is because of two factors we have neglected so far—both the labour force and the productivity of labour are growing over time.

Suppose the labour force grows at 1.5% a year. To maintain a constant unemployment rate, employment must grow at the same rate as the labour force, at 1.5% a year.

Suppose also that labour productivity—output per worker—is growing at 1.0% a year. If employment grows at 1.5% and labour productivity grows at 1.0%, output will grow at $1.0\% + 1.5\% = 2.5\%$. In other words, to maintain a constant unemployment rate, output growth must be equal to 2.5%. In Canada, the sum of the rate of labour-force growth and of labour-productivity growth has been equal to 2.5% on average since 1982, and this is why the number 2.5% appears on the right side of equation (13.2). We will call the rate of output growth needed to maintain a constant unemployment rate the **normal growth rate** in what follows.

More details on the normal rate of growth follow in our discussion of the long run in Chapters 15 to 18.

● The coefficient on the deviation of output growth from the normal growth rate is $-0.4$ in equation (13.2), not $-1$ as in equation (13.1). Put another way, output growth of 1% in excess of the normal growth rate leads to only a 0.4% reduction in the unemployment rate rather than a 1% reduction. There are two reasons why:

1. Firms adjust employment less than one for one in response to deviations of output growth from the normal growth rate. More specifically, output growth that is 1% above normal for one year leads to only a 0.6% increase in the employment rate.

   One reason is that some workers are needed no matter what the level of output is. The accounting department of a firm, for example, needs roughly the same number of employees whether the firm is selling more or less than normal.

   Another reason is that training new employees is costly. That is why many firms prefer to keep current workers rather than lay them off when output is lower than normal, and to ask them to work overtime rather than hire new employees when output is higher than normal. In bad times, firms, in effect, hoard labour; this behaviour is called **labour hoarding**.

GDP growth figures usually make the headlines—at least in the business news. The main reason is Okun's Law. The unemployment rate is what matters the most to people. Can they get a job? Can their son or daughter get a job? Through Okun's Law, GDP growth determines the changes in the unemployment rate. It takes sustained growth in real GDP over a long period of time to gradually reduce the unemployment rate.

Statistics Canada makes two announcements of GDP growth. Every month, there is an announcement of GDP growth. This announcement is organized by industry. The release describes growth prior to the announcement month. It takes time to collect and analyze the data. The January release, for example, presents growth in GDP from October to November of the previous year. Growth is expressed at an annual rate. The growth is seasonally adjusted so that known influences of the seasons are removed from the data. There are weather-related seasons—harvesting and construction. There are seasons related to calendar effects. The latter could involve more production than usual—think of Christmas retail sales. Seasons can also involve less production than usual—think of the propensity of people to take more holidays in the summer. Seasonal effects may be quite strong on a monthly level. We depend on statistical agencies to remove these effects. One item to note—Statistics Canada often makes it easier to think in annual terms, as in Okun's Law, by comparing the rate of growth of the most recent month reported with the same month in the previous year.

Statistics Canada makes a second and much more important announcement of quarterly GDP growth. There is again a lag—the announcement made in March presents the estimate of GDP growth from quarter 3 to quarter 4 in the previous year. Quarter 3 is July, August, and September. Quarter 4 is October, November, and December. Again the data are seasonally adjusted and growth rates are presented at annual rates. This release is organized by category of expenditure, consumption, investment, and net exports. The release often emphasizes the real growth in GDP from the most recent quarter of data from the same quarter in the previous year as the simplest way to remove seasonal effects.

The United States follows a similar but more complex pattern of real GDP growth releases. Their statistical agency is called the Bureau of Economic Analysis (BEA). Estimates of the quarterly rate of growth of real GDP are released three times. The third estimate corresponds to the Statistics Canada timing—in late March, the third estimate of GDP growth from third quarter to fourth quarter of the previous year is released. There are often substantial revisions between the first estimate, called the advance estimate, and the third estimate. U.S. GDP data are very closely watched by Canadian business and government economists.

As a general principle, the longer the time period of the estimate, the more useful is the data on GDP growth. A reduction in the month-to-month growth rate is not as serious as a reduction in the quarterly growth rate of real GDP.

Okun's Law helps us to understand whether a GDP release is "good" or "bad." Very roughly, if the unemployment rate is high, then a reduction in the unemployment rate over the medium term requires a number of quarters of substantial real GDP growth. An announcement of annual GDP growth of 1 percentage point is actually bad news—this level of GDP growth, using Okun's law, would indicate the unemployment rate is increasing.

*Note:* If you open the home page of Statistics Canada, www. statcan.gc.ca, the latest GDP release is usually immediately available. This is the monthly release. You can search The Daily to find the most recent quarterly release.

---

Putting the two steps together:

1% increase in output above normal ⇒
0.6% increase in employment ⇒ ▶
0.4% decrease in the unemployment rate.

Okun's law:

$$g_{yt} > \overline{g}_y \Rightarrow u_t < u_{t-1}$$ ▶

2. An increase in the employment rate does not lead to a one-for-one decrease in the unemployment rate. More specifically, a 0.6% increase in the employment rate leads to only a 0.4% decrease in the unemployment rate.

   The reason is that labour participation increases. When employment increases, not all the new jobs are filled by the unemployed. Some of the jobs go to people who were classified as *out of the labour force*, meaning they were not actively looking for a job. And as labour-market prospects improve for the unemployed, some discouraged workers—who were previously classified as out of the labour force—decide to start actively looking for a job and become classified as unemployed. For both reasons, the decrease in unemployment is smaller than the increase in employment.

Using letters rather than numbers, let us write the relation between output growth and the change in the unemployment rate as:

$$u_t - u_{t-1} = -\beta(g_{yt} - \overline{g}_y) \tag{13.3}$$

where $\bar{g}_y$ is the normal growth rate of the economy (about 2.5% for Canada between 1982 and 2012), and $\beta$ (the Greek lowercase letter beta) tells us how growth in excess of normal growth translates into decreases in the unemployment rate. In Canada, $\beta$ equals 0.4.

## The Phillips Curve: Unemployment and the Change in Inflation

We derived in Chapter 12 the following relation among inflation, expected inflation, and unemployment (equation (12.7)):

$$\pi_t = \pi_t^e - \alpha(u_t - u_n) \tag{13.4}$$

Inflation depends on expected inflation and on the deviation of unemployment from the natural rate.

We then argued that expected inflation appears to be well approximated by last year's inflation so that we can replace $\pi_t^e$ by $\pi_{t-1}$. With this assumption, the relation between inflation and unemployment takes the form:

$$\pi_t - \pi_{t-1} = -\alpha(u_t - u_n) \tag{13.5}$$

Unemployment above the natural rate leads to a decrease in inflation; unemployment below the natural rate leads to an increase in inflation. The parameter $\alpha$ gives the effect of unemployment on the change in inflation. We saw in Chapter 12 that since 1970, in Canada, the natural unemployment rate has been on average equal to 8.0% and $\alpha$ roughly equal to 0.4. This value of $\alpha$ means that an unemployment rate of 1% above the natural rate for one year leads to a decrease in the inflation rate of about 0.4%. We will refer to equation (13.5) as the Phillips curve.

> Phillips curve:
> $u_t < u_n \Rightarrow \pi_t > \pi_{t-1}$

> We should call equation (13.5) the "Phillips relation" and reserve the expression "Phillips curve" for the curve that represents the relation. But the tradition is to use "Phillips curve" to denote equation (13.5). Tradition is respected here.

## The Aggregate Demand Relation: Money Growth, Inflation, and Output Growth

In Chapter 10 and Chapter 12, we wrote the aggregate demand relation as a relation between output and the real money stock, government spending, and taxes. To focus on the relation between the real money stock and output, we will ignore changes in factors other than real money here and write the aggregate demand relation simply as:

$$Y_t = \gamma \frac{M_t}{P_t} \tag{13.6}$$

where $\gamma$ (the Greek lowercase gamma) is a positive parameter. This equation states that the demand for goods, and thus output, is simply proportional to the real money stock. This simplification will make our life easier. You should keep in mind, however, that behind this relation hides the set of steps we saw in the *IS-LM* model:

- An increase in the real money stock leads to a decrease in the interest rate.
- The decrease in the interest rate leads to an increase in the demand for goods and to an increase in output.

> $M/P\uparrow \Rightarrow i\downarrow$
> $i\downarrow \Rightarrow Y\uparrow$
> Putting the two steps together: $(M/P)\uparrow \Rightarrow Y\uparrow$

For our purposes, we need to move from the relation between levels (the output level, the level of nominal money, and the price level) in equation (13.6) to a relation between growth rates (of output, nominal money, and prices). Let $g_{yt}$ be the growth rate of output. Let $g_{Mt}$ be the growth rate of nominal money, and let $\pi_t$ be the growth rate of prices—the rate of inflation. Then, from equation (13.6), it follows that:

$$g_{yt} = g_{Mt} - \pi_t \tag{13.7}$$

> If a variable is the ratio of two variables, its growth rate is the difference between the growth rates of these two variables (proposition 8 in Appendix 2 at the end of the book). So, if $Y = \gamma M/P$, and $\gamma$ is constant, $g_y = g_M - \pi$.

The growth rate of output is equal to the growth rate of nominal money minus the rate of inflation. Given money growth, high inflation leads to a decrease in the real money stock and a decrease in output; low inflation leads to an increase in the real money stock and an increase in output.

> Aggregate demand relation:
> $g_{Mt} > \pi_t \Rightarrow g_{yt} > 0$

## 13-2 | The Medium Run

Let's collect the three relations among inflation, unemployment, and output growth we derived in section 13-1. Okun's law relates the change in the unemployment rate to the deviation of output growth from normal (equation (13.3)):

$$\begin{matrix} \text{Change in the} \\ \text{unemployment rate} \end{matrix} = \begin{matrix} \text{Deviation of output} \\ \text{growth from normal} \end{matrix}$$

$$u_t - u_{t-1} = -\beta(g_{yt} - \bar{g}_y)$$

The Phillips curve relates the change in inflation to the deviation of the unemployment rate from its natural rate (equation (13.5)):

$$\begin{matrix} \text{Change in the} \\ \text{inflation rate} \end{matrix} = \begin{matrix} \text{Deviation of unemployment} \\ \text{from the natural rate} \end{matrix}$$

$$\pi_t - \pi_{t-1} = -\alpha(u_t - u_n)$$

The aggregate demand relation relates output growth to the difference between nominal money growth and inflation (equation (13.7)):

$$\begin{matrix} \text{Rate of growth} \\ \text{of output} \end{matrix} = \begin{matrix} \text{Rate of growth of nominal} \\ \text{money minus rate of inflation} \end{matrix}$$

$$g_{yt} = g_{Mt} - \pi_t$$

$g_M\downarrow \Rightarrow (g_m - \pi)\downarrow \Rightarrow g_y\downarrow$
$g_y\downarrow \Rightarrow u\uparrow$
$u\uparrow \Rightarrow \pi\downarrow$

Our task is now to see what these three relations imply for the effects of money growth on output, unemployment, and inflation. We can go some way already. Take, for example, a decrease in money growth:

- From the aggregate demand relation, given inflation, lower money growth implies a decrease in output growth.
- From Okun's law, this decrease in growth leads to an increase in unemployment.
- From the Phillips curve, higher unemployment implies a decrease in inflation.

We can already see that the initial effects of lower money growth are to slow output growth, increase unemployment, and decrease inflation. But what happens after this initial response is harder to tell: Does unemployment keep going up? What happens to inflation? The easiest way to answer these questions is to work backward in time, to start by looking at the medium run—that is, where the economy ends when all the dynamics have worked themselves out—and then to return to the dynamics. This section looks at the *medium run*. The following sections return to dynamics.

Assume that the central bank maintains a constant growth rate of nominal money, call it $\bar{g}_M$. What will be the values of output growth, unemployment, and inflation in the medium run?

Medium run: $g_y = \bar{g}_y$

- In the medium run, unemployment must be constant; unemployment cannot be increasing or decreasing forever. Putting $u_t = u_{t-1}$ in Okun's law implies that $g_{yt} = \bar{g}_y$. *In the medium run, output grows at its normal rate of growth,* $\bar{g}_y$.
- With money growth equal to $\bar{g}_M$ and output growth equal to $\bar{g}_y$, the aggregate demand relation implies that inflation is constant and satisfies:

$$\bar{g}_y = \bar{g}_M - \pi$$

Moving $\pi$ to the left, and $\bar{g}_y$ to the right, gives

$$\text{Inflation rate} = \begin{matrix} \text{Rate of growth} \\ \text{of nominal money} \end{matrix} - \begin{matrix} \text{Normal growth} \\ \text{rate of output} \end{matrix}$$

$$\pi = \bar{g}_M \qquad\qquad\qquad - \bar{g}_y \qquad\qquad (13.8)$$

Medium run: $\pi = \bar{g}_M - \bar{g}_y$

In the medium run, inflation is equal to nominal money growth minus normal output growth. It will be convenient to call nominal money growth minus normal output growth

**adjusted nominal money growth** so that this result can be stated as: *In the medium run, inflation equals adjusted nominal money growth.*

One way to think about this result is as follows: A growing level of output implies a growing level of transactions and thus a growing demand for real money. If output is growing at 2.5%, the real money stock must also grow at 2.5% per year. If the nominal money stock grows at a rate different from 2.5%, the difference must show up in inflation (or deflation). For example, if nominal money growth is 6%, then inflation must be equal to 4.5%.

- If inflation is constant, then $\pi_t = \pi_{t-1}$. Putting $\pi_t = \pi_{t-1}$ in the Phillips curve implies that $u_t = u_n$. *In the medium run, the unemployment rate must be equal to the natural rate.*

◄ Medium run: $u = u_n$

These results are the natural extension of the results we derived in Chapter 10 and Chapter 12. There, we saw that *changes in the level of money* were neutral in the medium run: They had no effect on either output or unemployment but were reflected one for one in changes in the price level. We see here that a similar neutrality result applies to *changes in the rate of growth of money*. Changes in nominal money growth have no effect on output or unemployment in the medium run but are reflected one for one in changes in the rate of inflation.

Another way to state this last result is that the only determinant of inflation in the medium run is adjusted money growth. Milton Friedman put it this way: *Inflation is always and everywhere a monetary phenomenon.* Unless they lead to higher nominal money growth, such factors as the monopoly power of firms, strong unions, strikes, fiscal deficits, the price of oil, and so on have no effect on inflation *in the medium run.*

We can summarize the results of this section with the help of Figure 13–2, which plots the unemployment rate on the horizontal axis and the inflation rate on the vertical axis.

In the medium run, the unemployment rate is equal to the natural rate. The economy must thus be somewhere on the vertical line at $u = u_n$.

In the medium run, inflation must be equal to adjusted money growth—the rate of nominal money growth minus the normal rate of growth of output. This is represented by the horizontal line at $\pi = \bar{g}_M - \bar{g}_y$.

A decrease in nominal money growth from $\bar{g}_M$ to $\bar{g}'_M$ shifts the horizontal line downward, moving the equilibrium from point $A$ to point $B$. The inflation rate decreases by the same amount as the decrease in nominal money growth. There is no change in the unemployment rate, which is still equal to $u_n$.

Having looked at what happens in the medium run, we can now return to the dynamics of adjustment. This is the focus of the next three sections.

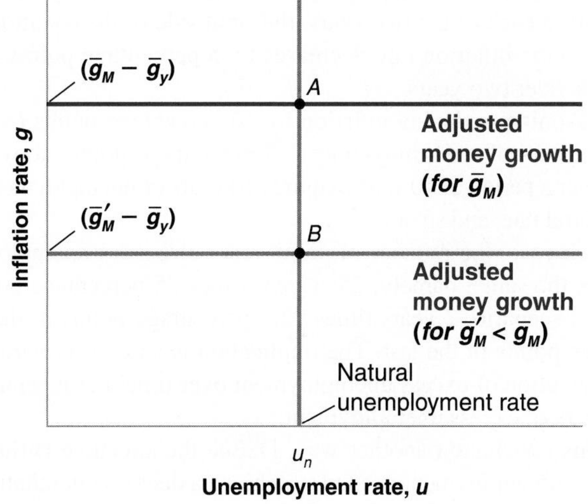

In the medium run, changes in money growth have no effect on output growth or on unemployment. They are reflected one for one in changes in the rate of inflation.

You may recall seeing the same quote in Chapter 12. Here we add the important adjustment of the normal rate of growth in output.

The "unless" qualification is important. When we study episodes of very high inflation in Chapter 25, we will see that fiscal deficits often lead to money creation and to higher nominal money growth.

**FIGURE  13–2**

**Inflation and Unemployment in the Medium Run**

In the medium run, unemployment is equal to the natural rate, and inflation is equal to adjusted money growth.

# 13-3 | Disinflation: A First Pass

What is so bad about high inflation if growth is proceeding at a normal rate and unemployment is at its natural rate? To answer, we need to discuss the costs of inflation and why policy makers take steps to decrease inflation. We will do this in Chapters 24 and 25. ▶

Suppose the economy is in medium-run equilibrium: Unemployment is at its natural rate, and the rate of growth of output is equal to the normal growth rate. But the inflation rate is high, and there is a general consensus that it must be reduced.

We know from the previous section that achieving lower inflation requires lowering money growth and thus lowering aggregate demand. But we also know that a decrease in money growth will slow output growth and increase unemployment, at least initially. Knowing this, how should the central bank achieve **disinflation**—that is, the decrease in inflation? Should it decrease money growth quickly or slowly? Let us see what our equations imply.

## How Much Unemployment? And for How Long?

Start with the Phillips curve relation (equation (13.5)):

$$\pi_t - \pi_{t-1} = -\alpha(u_t - u_n)$$

We came to the same conclusion at the end of Chapter 12. ▶

This relation makes it clear that disinflation can be obtained only at the cost of higher unemployment. For the left side of the equation to be negative—that is, for inflation to decrease—the term $(u_t - u_n)$ must be positive: The unemployment rate must exceed the natural rate.

The equation actually has a stronger and quite startling implication: The total amount of unemployment required for a given decrease in inflation does not depend on the speed at which disinflation is achieved. In other words, disinflation can be achieved quickly, at the cost of very high unemployment for a few years; or it can be achieved more slowly, with a smaller increase in unemployment spread over more years. In both cases, the total amount of unemployment, summing over the years, will be the same.

When should we use "percentage point" rather than "percent"? Suppose you are told that the unemployment rate, which was equal to 10%, has increased by 5%. Is it 5% of itself, in which case the unemployment rate is equal to $(1.05) \times 10\% = 10.5\%$? Or is it 5 percentage points, in which case it is equal to $10\% + 5\% = 15\%$? The use of "percentage point" rather than "percent" helps avoid the ambiguity. If you are told the unemployment rate has increased by 5 percentage points, this means that the unemployment rate is $10\% + 5\% = 15\%$.

Let us now see why this is. Define first a **point-year of excess unemployment** as a difference between the actual and the natural unemployment rate of 1 percentage point for one year. For example, if the natural rate is 8.0%, an actual unemployment rate of 11.0% four years in a row corresponds to $4 \times (11.0 - 8.0) = 12.0$ point-years of excess unemployment.

Now, suppose a central bank wants to reduce inflation by $x$ percentage points. To make things simpler, let us use specific numbers: Assume that the central bank wants to reduce inflation from 14% to 4% so that $x$ is equal to 10 percentage points. Let us also assume that $\alpha$ equals 0.4.

Suppose it wants to achieve the reduction in inflation in just one year. Equation (13.5) tells us that what is required is one year of unemployment at 25 percentage points above the natural rate. In this case, the right side of the equation is equal to $-10$ percentage points, and the inflation rate decreases by 10 percentage points within a year.

Suppose it wants to achieve the reduction in inflation over a period of two years. Equation (13.5) tells us that two years of unemployment are required at 12.5 percentage points above the natural rate. During each of the two years, the right side of the equation is equal to $-12.5$ percentage points, so the inflation rate decreases by 5 percentage points each year, thus by 10 percentage points over two years.

By the same reasoning, reducing inflation by 10 percentage points over a period of five years requires five years of unemployment at 5 percentage points above the natural rate; reducing inflation over a period of 10 years requires 10 years of unemployment at 2.5 percentage points above the natural rate, and so on.

Note that in each case, the number of point-years of excess unemployment required to decrease inflation is the same, namely, 25: 1 year times 25 percentage points excess unemployment in the first scenario, 2 years times 12.5 percentage points in the second, 10 years times 2.5 percentage points in the last. The implication is straightforward: The central bank can choose the distribution of excess unemployment over time, but it cannot change the total number of point-years of excess unemployment.

Sacrifice ratio

$$= \frac{\text{Excess point-years of unemployment}}{\text{Decrease in inflation}}$$

◀ We can state this conclusion another way. Define the **sacrifice ratio** as the number of point-years of excess unemployment needed to achieve a decrease in inflation of 1 percentage point. Then, equation (13.5) implies that this ratio is independent of policy and simply equal to $(1/\alpha)$. If $\alpha$ roughly equals 0.4, as the estimated Phillips curve suggests, then the sacrifice ratio is roughly equal to 2.5.

If the sacrifice ratio is constant, does this imply that the speed of disinflation is irrelevant? No. Suppose that the central bank tried to achieve the 10 percentage points decrease in inflation in one year. As we have just seen, this would require an unemployment rate of 25 percentage points above the natural rate for one year. With a natural unemployment rate of 8.0%, this would require increasing the actual unemployment rate to 33.0% for one year. From Okun's law, using a value of 0.4 for $\beta$ and a normal output growth rate of 2.5%, output growth would have to satisfy:

$$u_t - u_{t-1} = -\beta(g_{yt} - \bar{g}_y)$$
$$33.0\% - 8.0\% = -0.4(g_{yt} - 2.5\%)$$

This implies a value for $g_{yt} = -(25\%)/0.4 + 2.5\% = -60.0\%$. In words, output growth would have to equal $-60.0\%$ for a year! For comparison, the largest negative growth rate in Canada this century was $-12\%$ in 1931, during the Great Depression. It is fair to say that macroeconomists do not know with great confidence what would happen if monetary policy were aimed at inducing such a large negative growth rate. But most would surely be unwilling to try. The increase in the overall unemployment rate would lead to extremely high unemployment rates for some groups—specifically the young and the unskilled. Not only would the welfare costs for these groups be large, but such high unemployment might leave permanent scars. The sharp drop in output would most likely also lead to a large number of bankruptcies, with long-lasting effects on economic activity. In short, the disruptions from such a fast disinflation would be very large indeed.

## Working Out the Required Path of Money Growth

Let us assume that based on the computations we just went through, the central bank decides to decrease the inflation rate from 6% to 2% in four years. This is a more plausible disinflation. Clearly, the central bank does not control either inflation or unemployment directly. What it controls is money growth. Using our equations, we can solve for the path of money growth that will achieve the disinflation.

As we saw in Chapter 4, what the central bank actually controls is central bank money, not the money stock itself. We will ignore this complication here.

Let us make the same numerical assumptions as before. Normal output growth is 2.5%. The natural rate of unemployment is 8.0%. The parameter $\alpha$ in the Phillips curve is equal to 0.4; $\beta$ in Okun's law is equal to 0.4. These are the values estimated from Canadian data over the past two chapters. It is a coincidence that both values are 0.4. Table 13–1 shows how to derive the path of money growth needed to achieve 4% disinflation over four years.

In year 0, before the disinflation, output growth is proceeding at its normal rate of 2.5%. Unemployment is at the natural rate, 8.0%; inflation is running at 6%; nominal money growth is equal to 8.5%. Real money growth equals $8.5\% - 6\% = 2.5\%$, the same as output growth.

The decision is then made to reduce inflation from 6 to 2% over five years, starting in year 1.

The easiest way to solve for the path of money growth is to start from the desired path of inflation, find the required path of unemployment and the required path of output growth, and, finally, derive the required path of money growth.

The way to read the rest of this section is first to follow the logic of the step-by-step computations; do not worry about understanding the broader picture. When you have done this, step back and look at the way the economy adjusts over time. Make sure you can tell the story in words.

- The first line of Table 13–1 gives the *target path of inflation*. Inflation starts at 6% before the change in monetary policy, decreases by 1 percentage point a year from year 1 to year 4, and then remains at its lower level of 2% thereafter.

From the inflation path.

- The second line gives the required *path of unemployment* implied by the Phillips curve. If inflation is to decrease by 1 percentage a year and $\alpha = 0.4$, the economy must accept four years of unemployment at 2.5 percentage point above the natural rate. Each year of unemployment 2.5 percentage points in excess of the natural rate of unemployment reduces inflation by 1 percentage point. Thus, from year 1 to year 4, the unemployment rate must equal $8.0\% + 2.5\% = 10.5\%$.

To the path of unemployment.

| TABLE 13–1 | Engineering Disinflation | | | | | | | | |
|---|---|---|---|---|---|---|---|---|---|
| | **Before** | **Year** **Disinflation** | | | | | **After** | | |
| | 0 | 1 | 2 | 3 | 4 | 5 | 6 | 7 | |
| Inflation (%) | 6 | 5 | 4 | 3 | 2 | 2 | 2 | 2 | |
| Unemployment rate (%) | 8 | 10.5 | 10.5 | 10.5 | 10.5 | 8.0 | 8.0 | 8.0 | |
| Output growth (%) | 2.5 | –3.75 | 2.5 | 2.5 | 2.5 | 8.75 | 2.5 | 2.5 | |
| Nominal money growth (%) | 8.5 | 1.25 | 6.5 | 5.5 | 4.5 | 10.25 | 4.5 | 4.5 | |

**To the path of output growth.** ▶ ● The third line gives the required *path of output growth*. From Okun's law, we know that the initial increase in unemployment requires lower output growth. With $\beta$ equal to 0.4, an initial increase in unemployment of 2.5 percentage points requires the rate of output growth to be lower than normal by $2.5\% \div 0.4 = 6.25$ percentage points. Given a normal growth rate of 2.5%, the economy must therefore have a growth rate of $2.5\% - 6.25\% = -3.75\%$ in year 1. There must be a significant recession in year 1.

From years 2 to 4, growth must proceed at a rate sufficient to maintain the unemployment rate constant at 10.5%. Thus, output must grow at its normal rate, 2.5%. In other words, from years 2 to 4, the economy grows at a normal rate but has an unemployment rate that exceeds the natural rate by 2.5 percentage points. In this situation, inflation falls by 1 percentage point in each year.

Once disinflation is achieved, a burst of output growth in year 5 is needed to return unemployment to normal: To decrease the unemployment rate by 2.5 percentage points in a year, the rate of output growth must exceed normal growth by $2.5\% \div 0.4$, thus by 6.25%. The economy must therefore grow at $2.5\% + 6.25\% = 8.75\%$ for one year.

**To the path of nominal money growth.** ▶ ● The fourth line gives the implied path of *nominal money growth*. From the aggregate demand relation, (equation (13.7)), we know that output growth equals nominal money growth minus inflation or, equivalently, that nominal money growth equals output growth plus inflation. Adding the numbers for inflation in the first line and for output growth in the third gives us the required path for the rate of nominal money growth.

The path looks surprising at first: Money growth goes down sharply in year 1, then up again, then slowly down for two years, then up again in the year following disinflation, to finally reach its permanent lower level of 4.5%. But this is easy to explain: To start disinflation, the central bank must induce an increase in unemployment. This requires a sharp contraction in money growth in year 1. The decrease in nominal money growth—from 8.5 to 1.25%—is much sharper than the decrease in inflation—from 6 to 5%. The result is thus a sharp decrease in real money growth, decreasing demand and output, which increases the unemployment rate.

For the next three years, monetary policy is aimed at maintaining unemployment at 10.5%, not at increasing unemployment further. Nominal money growth is aimed at allowing demand and therefore output to grow at the normal growth rate. Put another way, nominal money growth is set equal to inflation plus the normal growth rate of 2.5%. And as inflation decreases—because of high unemployment—so does nominal money growth.

At the end of the disinflation, the central bank must allow unemployment to return to its natural rate (otherwise, inflation would continue to decrease). This implies that it provides in year 5 a one-time increase in money growth before returning, from year 6 on, to the new lower rate of money growth.

Figure 13–3 shows the path of unemployment and inflation implied by this disinflation path. In year 0, the economy is at point *A*: The unemployment rate is 8.0%, and the inflation

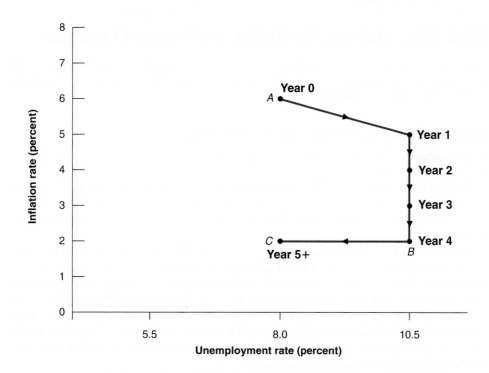

**FIGURE** **13–3**

**A Disinflation Path**

Four years of unemployment above the natural rate lead to a permanent decrease in inflation.

rate is 6%. Years 1 to 4 are years of disinflation, during which the economy moves from *A* to *B*. Unemployment is higher than the natural rate, leading to a steady decline in inflation. Inflation decreases until it reaches 2%. From year 5 on, the economy remains at point *C*, with unemployment back down to its natural rate and an inflation rate of 2%. *In the medium run, money growth and inflation are lower, and the unemployment rate and output growth are back to normal;* this is the neutrality result we obtained in section 13-2. *But the transition to lower money growth and lower inflation is associated with a period of higher unemployment.*

The disinflation path drawn in Figure 13–3 is one of many possible paths. We could have looked instead at a path that front-loaded the increase in the unemployment rate and allowed it to return slowly to the natural rate, avoiding the awkward increase in money growth that takes place at the end of our scenario (year 5 in Table 13–1). Or we could have looked at a path where the central bank decreased the rate of money growth from 8.5% to 4.5% at once, letting inflation and unemployment adjust over time.[2] But all the paths we would draw would share one characteristic: The total unemployment cost—that is, the number of point-years of excess unemployment—would be the same. Put another way, *unemployment has to remain above the natural rate by a large enough amount, and/or long enough, to achieve disinflation.*

The analysis we have just developed is very much the type of analysis economists at central banks were conducting in the late 1970s. The econometric model they used, as well as most econometric models in use at the time, shared our simple model's property that policy could change the timing, but not the number of point-years of excess unemployment. We will call this the *traditional approach* in what follows. This traditional approach was challenged by two groups of academic economists. The next section presents their arguments and the discussion that followed.

---

[2]**DIGGING DEEPER**. It would seem natural to look at a policy where the central bank permanently decreases the rate of money growth, say, from 8.5 to 4.5%. If you trace the effects of such a policy on output, unemployment, and inflation (solve for output, unemployment, and inflation for time *t*, then for *t* + 1, and so on), you will find that it leads to a complicated path of inflation and unemployment, with inflation actually being lower than its new medium-run value for some time.

## 13-4 | Expectations, Credibility, and Nominal Contracts

The focus of both groups of economists was the role of expectations and how changes in expectation formation might affect the unemployment cost of disinflation. But despite this common focus, they reached quite different conclusions.

### Expectations and Credibility: The Lucas Critique

The conclusions of the first group were based on the work of Robert Lucas and Thomas Sargent of the University of Chicago.

In what has become known as the **Lucas critique**, Lucas pointed out that when trying to predict the effects of a major change in policy—such as the change considered by the Bank of Canada in 1988—it could be very misleading to take as given the relations estimated from past data.

In the case of the Phillips curve, taking equation (13.5) as a given was equivalent to assuming that wage setters would keep expecting inflation in the future to be the same as in the past, that the way wage setters formed expectations would not change in response to the change in policy. This was an unwarranted assumption, Lucas argued. Why shouldn't wage setters take policy changes into account? If they believed that the Bank of Canada was committed to lower inflation, they might well expect inflation to be lower in the future than in the past. If they lowered their expectations of inflation, then actual inflation would decline without the need for a protracted recession.

The logic of Lucas's argument can be seen by returning to equation (13.4):

$$\pi_t = \pi_t^e - \alpha(u_t - u_n)$$

If $\pi_t^e = \pi_{t-1}$, the Phillips curve is given by

$$\pi_t - \pi_{t-1} = -\alpha(u_t - u_n)$$

To achieve $\pi_t < \pi_{t-1}$, one must have $u_t > u_n$.

If wage setters kept forming expectations of inflation by looking at last year's inflation (if $\pi_t^e = \pi_{t-1}$), then the only way to decrease inflation would, indeed, be to accept higher unemployment for some time; we explored the implications of this assumption in the preceding section.

But if wage setters could be convinced that inflation was, indeed, going to be lower than in the past, they would decrease their expectations of inflation. This would, in turn, reduce actual inflation, without necessarily any change in the unemployment rate. For example, if wage setters were convinced that inflation, which had been running at 6% in the past, would be only 2% in the future, and if they formed expectations accordingly, then inflation would decrease to 2%, *even if unemployment remained at the natural rate*:

$$\pi_t = \pi_t^e - \alpha(u_t - u_n)$$
$$2\% = 2\% - \alpha(0\%)$$

Money growth, inflation, and expected inflation could all be reduced without the need for a recession. Put another way, decreases in money growth could be neutral not only in the medium run but also in the short run.

Lucas and Sargent did not believe that disinflation could really take place without some increase in unemployment. But Sargent, looking at the historical evidence on the end of several very high inflations, concluded that the increase in unemployment could be small. The sacrifice ratio—the amount of excess unemployment needed to achieve disinflation— might be much lower than suggested by the traditional approach. The essential ingredient of successful disinflation, he argued, was **credibility** of monetary policy—the belief by wage setters that the central bank was truly committed to reducing inflation. Only credibility would lead wage setters to change the way they formed expectations. Furthermore, he argued, a clear and quick disinflation program was much more likely to be credible than a protracted one that offered plenty of opportunities for reversal and political infighting along the way.

The credibility view: Fast disinflation is likely to be more credible than slow disinflation. Credibility decreases the unemployment cost of disinflation. Thus, the central bank should implement a fast disinflation.

## Nominal Rigidities and Contracts

A contrary view was taken by Stanley Fischer of the Massachusetts Institute of Technology (MIT), and John Taylor, then at Columbia University. Both emphasized the presence of **nominal rigidities**, meaning that in modern economies, many wages and prices are set in nominal terms for some time and are typically not readjusted when there is a change in policy.

Fischer argued that even with credibility, too rapid a decrease in money growth would lead to higher unemployment. Even if the Bank of Canada fully convinced workers and firms that money growth was going to be lower, the wages set before the change in policy would reflect expectations of inflation prior to the change in policy. In effect, inflation would already be built into existing wage agreements and could not be reduced costlessly and instantaneously. At the very least, Fischer said, a policy of disinflation should be announced sufficiently in advance of its actual implementation to allow wage setters to take it into account when setting wages.

Taylor's argument went one step further. An important characteristic of wage contracts, he argued, is that they are not all signed at the same time. Instead, they are staggered over time. He showed that this **staggering of wage decisions** imposed strong limits on how fast disinflation could proceed without triggering higher unemployment, even if the Bank of Canada's commit- ◄ ment to inflation was fully credible. Why the limits? If workers cared about relative wages—that is, cared about their wages relative to the wages of other workers—each wage contract would choose a wage not very different from wages in the other contracts in force at the time. Too rapid a decrease in nominal money growth would not lead to a proportional decrease in inflation. So, the real money stock would decrease, triggering a recession and an increase in the unemployment rate.

> The nominal rigidities view: Many wages are set in nominal terms, sometimes for many years. The way to decrease the unemployment cost of disinflation is to give wage setters time to take the change in policy into account. Thus, the central bank should implement a slow disinflation.

Taking into account the time pattern of wage contracts in the United States, which is similar to the time pattern of contracts in Canada, Taylor then showed that under full credibility of monetary policy, there *was* a path of disinflation consistent with no increase in unemployment. This path is shown in Figure 13–4.

Disinflation starts in quarter 1 and lasts for 16 quarters. Once it is achieved, the inflation rate, which started at 10%, is 3%. The striking feature is how slowly disinflation proceeds at the beginning. One year (four quarters) after the announcement of the change in policy, inflation is still 9.9%. But then disinflation occurs faster. By the end of the third year, inflation is down to 4%, and by the end of the fourth year, the desired disinflation is achieved.

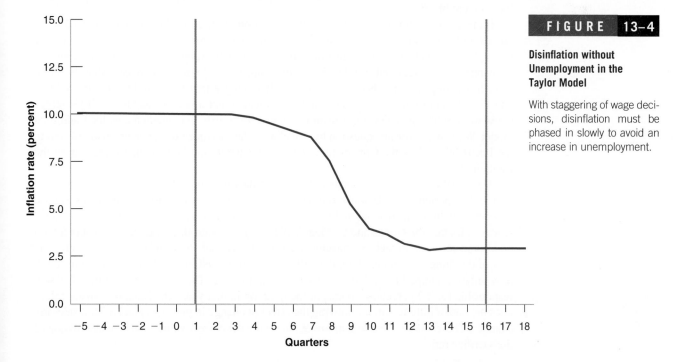

### FIGURE 13–4

**Disinflation without Unemployment in the Taylor Model**

With staggering of wage decisions, disinflation must be phased in slowly to avoid an increase in unemployment.

The reason for the slow decrease in inflation at the beginning—and, behind the scene, for the slow decrease in nominal money growth—is straightforward. Wages in force at the time of the policy change are the result of decisions made before the policy change so that the path of inflation in the near future is largely predetermined. If nominal money growth were to decrease sharply, inflation could not decrease very much right away, and the result would be a decrease in real money and a recession. Thus, the best policy is for the Bank of Canada to proceed slowly at the beginning, while announcing it will proceed faster in the future. This announcement leads new wage settlements to take the new policy into account. When most wage decisions in the economy come from decisions made after the change in policy, disinflation can proceed much faster. This is what happens in the third year following the policy change.

Like Lucas and Sargent, Taylor did not believe that disinflation really could be implemented without increasing unemployment. For one thing, he realized that the path of disinflation drawn in Figure 13–4 might not be credible. The announcement this year that money growth will be decreased two years from now is likely to run into a serious credibility problem. Wage setters are likely to ask themselves: If the decision has been made to disinflate, why should the central bank wait two years? Without credibility, inflation expectations might not change, defeating the hope of disinflation without an increase in the unemployment rate. But Taylor's analysis had two clear messages. First, like Lucas and Sargent's analysis, it emphasized the role of expectations. Second, it suggested that a slow but credible disinflation might have a cost lower than that implied by the traditional approach.

With this discussion in mind, let us end the chapter with a look at what happened in Canada from 1988 to 1993.

## 13-5 | The Canadian Disinflation, 1988 to 1993

In 1988, as shown in row 8 of Table 13–2, Consumer Price Index inflation in Canada was 4%. The unemployment rate was 7.8%, slightly (but not significantly) below our estimate of the natural rate of 8.0%. Other factors also influence inflation. The Bank of Canada's Governor Crow decided to publicly announce that the Bank of Canada had a new policy goal: price stability. The quote from the Hanson lecture that opened this chapter made this goal clear to Canadians. Did they believe Governor Crow or, in the language of section 13-4, was the disinflation credible?

If the disinflation was credible, then the reduction in inflation should have occurred without a significant increase in unemployment. Figure 13–5 reminds us that as monetary policy was tightened and Canadian interest rates rose higher than American rates, the Canadian real exchange rate appreciated. Table 13–2 shows that unemployment increased sharply, GDP growth was negative in 1991, and there is little evidence that the disinflation was credible. Our discussion of credibility in section 13-4 indicated that a second way to ask if Governor Crow was credible is to ask if this disinflation was less costly than predicted by the traditional model. We can answer this question by calculating the sacrifice ratio. You are also referred to the Focus box, "Was the Cost of the 1988–1993 Disinflation Higher than Expected by the Bank of Canada?"

The sacrifice ratio can be calculated using the data in Table 13–2. There is one complication. In this period, Canada was switching to make more extensive use of sales taxes to raise revenue at both the provincial and federal levels. In particular, on January 1, 1991, a "new" federal sales tax, the Goods and Services Tax (GST), was introduced. Because this tax fell on goods and services bought by consumers and the Consumer Price Index (CPI) measures the cost of the things consumers buy, the CPI jumped from 1990 to 1991. You can see in row 8 how inflation jumped from 4.7% in 1990 to 5.5% in 1991. The introduction of the GST was responsible for 2.2 percentage points of the inflation in that year. The Bank of Canada calculates the rate of inflation after removing the effect of change in provincial and federal sales tax changes. These values are found in row 9. These are the correct values to use in calculation of the sacrifice ratio.

TABLE 13-2 Inflation and Unemployment in Canada, 1988–1993

| Variable | 1988 | 1989 | 1990 | 1991 | 1992 | 1993 |
|---|---|---|---|---|---|---|
| 1. GDP growth (%) | 4.8 | 2.5 | 0.3 | −2.0 | 1.0 | 2.4 |
| 2. Unemployment rate (%) | 7.8 | 7.5 | 8.1 | 10.3 | 11.2 | 11.4 |
| 3. Canadian interest rate (%) | 9.4 | 12.0 | 12.8 | 8.8 | 6.5 | 4.9 |
| 4. U.S. interest rate (%) | 6.7 | 8.1 | 7.5 | 5.4 | 3.4 | 3.0 |
| 5. Interest rate differential (%) | 2.7 | 3.9 | 5.3 | 3.4 | 3.1 | 1.9 |
| 6. Real exchange rate | 1.21 | 1.16 | 1.15 | 1.14 | 1.21 | 1.3 |
| 7. Trade surplus (% of GDP) | 0.8 | 0.0 | 0.1 | −0.6 | −0.4 | 0.0 |
| 8. CPI inflation | 4.0 | 4.9 | 4.7 | 5.5 | 1.5 | 1.8 |
| 9. CPI inflation without indirect tax changes | 3.2 | 4.2 | 4.2 | 3.3 | 1.0 | 1.6 |
| 10. Cumulative unemployment | — | — | — | 2.3 | 5.5 | 8.9 |
| 11. Cumulative disinflation | — | — | — | 0.9 | 3.2 | 2.6 |
| 12. Sacrifice ratio | — | — | — | 2.5 | 1.7 | 3.4 |

The only new variable in Table 13–2 is found in row 9, CPI inflation without indirect tax changes. This variable is created by the Bank of Canada. Indirect taxes is a term used for sales taxes. Since consumers pay sales taxes, the CPI in row 8 includes the effects of sales-tax increases. The year 1991 saw the introduction of the federal consumer sales tax, the Goods and Services Tax (GST). In 1991, CPI inflation in row 8 is much larger than CPI inflation without indirect tax changes in row 9. The row-9 variable is the correct inflation rate to use to calculate the sacrifice ratio.

Cumulative unemployment is the sum of point-years of excess unemployment from 1991 on, assuming a natural rate of unemployment of 8.0%

Cumulative disinflation is the difference between CPI inflation without indirect tax changes in a given year and CPI inflation without indirect tax changes in 1990. The sacrifice ratio is the ratio of cumulative unemployment to cumulative disinflation.

To calculate the sacrifice ratio in Table 13–2, we first need the cumulative number of point-years of excess unemployment (assuming a natural rate of 8.0%). This is calculated in row 10, starting in 1991, the first year where unemployment substantially exceeds the natural

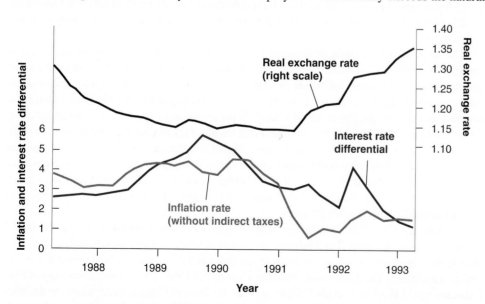

FIGURE 13-5

**Monetary Policy and Inflation, 1988–1993**

Here, we add the inflation rate (measured without indirect taxes) and the real exchange rate to the Canadian and American interest rate differential from Figure 6–8. The Bank of Canada raised interest rates in Canada relative to interest rates in the United States. The resulting real appreciation raised unemployment and lowered inflation.

*Source:* Real exchange rate using CANSIM II variables V37426, V122054, V149258, V498918, V1992259; interest rate differential using CANSIM II variable V122484, Federal Reserve Board RIFSGFSM03_N.M.

The model assessment in section 13-5 was not quite a fair test of our understanding of disinflation. In physical sciences, such as biology, we test a hypothesis with a controlled experiment. We hypothesize that there is a best amount of water. We take 10 seeds, put them in 10 flowerpots on the same windowsill, and give each pot a different amount of water at the same time each day. Both the plants that get too little water and those that get too much water die. We may even graph millilitres of water against biomass produced. We may even repeat the experiment 100 times. In the 101st repetition, we may even make a prediction on the best amount of water per day. This kind of experiment is difficult to conduct in macroeconomics. To measure the sacrifice ratio, we would like to repeat the same experiment of reducing inflation many times. We cannot do this. In section 13-5, the comparison of the calculated sacrifice ratio using Table 13–2 with the estimated sacrifice ratio in section 13-2 is not quite right. We used the data from the 1988 to 1993 disinflation to estimate $\alpha$, then checked our estimate of $\alpha$ with the data. Our reasoning, unlike the experiment with the plants, was quite circular.

One way out of this circularity is to estimate the sacrifice ratio with data up to 1988 and then use the model estimated with the pre-1988 data to predict the post-1988 behaviour of the economy. This predictive test is a much stronger test. Johnson and Gerlich (2002) did just such a predictive test for Canada. Fortunately for us, the Bank of Canada was very interested in the sacrifice ratio even before the 1988–1993 disinflation. Two Bank of Canada economists, Barry Cozier and

Gordon Wilkinson, published estimates of the sacrifice ratio estimated from the Canadian economy using data from 1964 to 1988. Using slightly different methodology from our methodology, they came up with three estimates of the sacrifice ratio—their estimates were scaled as the percent of GDP lost per unit decline in inflation. They estimated that a unit decline in inflation would require a 1 to 2% decline in output for one year. Using Okun's law, a 1 to 2% decline in output is 2.5 to 5 point-years of excess unemployment. These values are very close to the values Johnson and Gerlich (2002) estimated including all of the data from 1962 to 2001.[1]

It looks very much as though the traditional model of disinflation estimated with data before 1988 correctly predicts the cost of the disinflation after 1988. The Bank of Canada should not have been surprised that a reduction in Canada's inflation rate from 4 to 2% would involve a significant recession.

[1]Johnson and Gerlich (2002) also formally test the statistical hypothesis that the Cozier–Wilkinson model of inflation estimated with data from 1964 to 1988 continues to predict Canadian inflation from 1989 to 2001. This null hypothesis cannot be rejected.

*Sources:* David Johnson and Sebastian Gerlich, "How Has Inflation Changed in Canada? A Comparison of 1989–2001 to 1964–1988," *Canadian Public Policy* 28, 2002, pp. 563–579.

Barry Cozier and Gordon Wilkinson, "Some Evidence on Hysteresis and the Costs of Disinflation in Canada," *Bank of Canada Technical Report No. 55*, 1991.

rate and inflation begins to fall. Row 10 indicates that by 1993, Canada had experienced 8.9 point-years of excess unemployment. The cumulative fall in inflation from 1991 to 1993 was 2.6 percentage points. The sacrifice ratio calculated over that period was 3.4. Our simple model predicted a sacrifice ratio of about 2.5. The disinflation was even more costly than predicted by our estimate of $\alpha$.

The large actual sacrifice ratio suggests that Canada's 1988–1993 disinflation was not credible. A whole host of other evidence also points to this conclusion. According to Laidler and Robson (1993), direct measures of expected inflation are slow to adjust. According to Johnson (1997), there is evidence that expected inflation began to fall only after actual inflation fell and not during the Bank of Canada's presentation of the case for lower inflation. Finally, Johnson (1990) made the argument that fiscal policy in Canada depended on an inflation rate in excess of 3%, and monetary policy aimed at inflation less than 2%. This issue was not resolved until 1991. We will return to these issues in Chapters 24 and 25. There are three additional readings listed at the end of this chapter that are specific to the Canadian experience. The Canadian experience of disinflation was very similar to the disinflation experienced in other countries over the last 30 years.

In short, the Canadian disinflation from 1988 to 1993 was associated with a substantial increase in unemployment. The Phillips curve relation between the change in inflation and the deviation of the unemployment rate from the natural rate proved more robust than many economists anticipated. The Focus box "Was the Cost of the 1988–1993 Disinflation Higher than Expected by the Bank of Canada?" looks at what the Bank of Canada knew when the disinflation was started. Was this outcome due to a lack of credibility of the change in monetary policy or to the fact that credibility is not enough to reduce substantially the cost of disinflation?

Laurence Ball, of Johns Hopkins University, estimated sacrifice ratios for 65 disinflation episodes in 19 OECD countries over the last 30+ years. The study shows that the Canadian experience of disinflation was very typical. Ball reaches three main conclusions:

- Disinflations typically lead to higher unemployment for some time. Put another way, even if it is neutral in the medium run, a decrease in money growth leads to an increase in unemployment for some time.
- Faster disinflations are associated with smaller sacrifice ratios. This conclusion provides some evidence to support the expectation and credibility effects emphasized by Lucas and Sargent.
- Sacrifice ratios are smaller in countries that have shorter wage contracts. This provides some evidence to support Fischer and Taylor's emphasis on the importance of the structure of wage settlements.

## SUMMARY

- There are three relations linking inflation, output, and unemployment:

    The first is Okun's law, which relates the change in the unemployment rate to the deviation of the rate of growth of output from the normal growth rate. In Canada today, output growth of 1% above normal for a year leads to a decrease in the unemployment rate of about 0.4%.

    The second is the Phillips curve, which relates the change in the inflation rate to the deviation of the actual unemployment rate from the natural rate. In Canada today, an unemployment rate 1% below the natural rate for a year leads to an increase in inflation of about 0.4%.

    The third is the aggregate demand relation, which relates the rate of growth of output to the rate of growth of the real money stock. The growth rate of output is equal to the growth rate of nominal money minus the rate of inflation. Given nominal money growth, higher inflation leads to a decrease in output growth.

- In the medium run, the unemployment rate is equal to the natural rate, and output grows at its normal growth rate. Money growth determines the inflation rate: A 1% increase in money growth leads to a 1% increase in the inflation rate.

- In the short run, a decrease in money growth leads to a slowdown in growth and an increase in unemployment for some time. Thus, disinflation (a decrease in the inflation rate) can be achieved only at the cost of more unemployment. How much unemployment is required is a controversial issue.

- The traditional approach assumes that people do not change the way they form expectations when monetary policy changes so that the relation between inflation and unemployment is unaffected by the change in policy. This approach implies that disinflation can be achieved by a short but large increase in unemployment or by a longer and smaller increase in unemployment. But policy cannot affect the total number of point-years of excess unemployment.

- An alternative view is that if the change in monetary policy is credible, expectation formation may change, leading to a smaller increase in unemployment than predicted by the traditional approach. In its extreme form, this alternative view implies that if policy is fully credible, it can achieve disinflation at no cost in unemployment. A less extreme form recognizes that although expectation formation may change, the presence of nominal rigidities is likely to imply some increase in unemployment, although less than implied by the traditional answer.

- The Canadian disinflation from 1988 to 1993, during which inflation decreased by approximately 2%, was associated with a large recession. The unemployment cost was close to the predictions of the traditional approach.

## KEY TERMS

- adjusted nominal money growth, 251
- credibility, 256
- disinflation, 252
- labour hoarding, 247
- Lucas critique, 256

- nominal rigidities, 257
- normal growth rate, 247
- point-year of excess unemployment, 252
- sacrifice ratio, 252
- staggering of wage decisions, 257

### 1. TRUE/FALSE/UNCERTAIN

a. The Canadian unemployment rate will remain constant as long as output growth is positive.

b. Many firms prefer to keep workers around when demand is low (rather than lay them off), even if the workers are underutilized.

c. There are several different announcements of GDP growth that describe GDP growth over the same period of time in both the United States and Canada.

d. There is a reliable negative relation between the rate of inflation and the growth rate of output.

e. In the medium run, the rate of inflation is equal to the rate of nominal money growth.

f. According to the Phillips curve relation, the sacrifice ratio is independent on the speed of disinflation.

g. Contrary to the traditional Phillips curve analysis, Taylor's analysis of staggered wage contracts made a case for a slow approach to disinflation.

h. Johnson and Gerlich's analysis showed that the recession associated with the 1988–1993 disinflation could have been predicted by the Bank of Canada before 1988.

### 2. OKUN'S LAW

As shown by equation (13.2), the estimated Okun's law for Canada is given by

$$u_t - u_{t-1} = -0.4(g_{yt} - 2.5\%)$$

a. What growth rate of output leads to an increase in the unemployment rate of 1% per year? How can the unemployment rate increase even though the growth rate of output is positive?

b. What rate of growth output do we need to decrease unemployment by 1 percentage point over the next four years?

c. Suppose that we experience a second baby boom. How do you expect Okun's law to change if the rate of growth of the labour force increases by 2 percentage points?

### 3. REDUCING THE INFLATION RATE IN THE UNITED STATES

Blanchard, in an American edition of this text, finds that the U.S. economy can be described by the following three equations:

$$u_t - u_{t-1} = -0.4(g_{yt} - 3\%) \qquad \text{Okun's law}$$

$$\pi_t - \pi_{t-1} = -(u_t - 5\%) \qquad \text{Phillips curve}$$

$$g_{yt} = g_{Mt} - \pi_t \qquad \text{aggregate demand}$$

a. What is the natural rate of unemployment for this economy? How is it different from that of Canada?

b. Suppose that the unemployment rate is equal to the natural rate and that the inflation rate is 8%. What is the growth rate of output? What is the growth rate of the money supply?

c. Suppose that conditions are as in (b), when the authorities use monetary policy to reduce the inflation rate to 4% in year $t$ and keep it there. What must happen to the unemployment rate and output growth in years $t$, $t+1$, and $t+2$? What money growth rate in years $t$, $t+1$, and $t+2$ will accomplish this goal?

### 4. THE EFFECTS OF A PERMANENT DECREASE IN MONEY GROWTH

Suppose that the economy can be described by the following three equations:

$$u_t - u_{t-1} = -0.4(g_{yt} - 3\%) \qquad \text{Okun's law}$$

$$\pi_t - \pi_{t-1} = -(u_t - 5\%) \qquad \text{Phillips curve}$$

$$g_{yt} = g_{Mt} - \pi_t \qquad \text{aggregate demand}$$

a. Reduce the three equations to two by substituting $g_{yt}$ from the aggregate demand equation into Okun's law.

Assume initially that $u_t = u_{t-1} = 5\%$, $g_{Mt} = 13\%$, and $\pi_t = 10\%$. Now, suppose that this year's money growth is permanently reduced from 13% in period $t-1$ to 0% in period $t$ and all subsequent periods.

b. Compute the impact on unemployment and inflation this year and next year.

c. Compute the values of unemployment and inflation in the medium run.

### 5. POLICY RECOMMENDATIONS

Suppose that you are advising a government that wants to reduce its inflation rate. It is considering two options: a gradual reduction over several years and an immediate reduction.

a. Lay out the arguments for and against each option.

b. If the only criterion you were to consider was the sacrifice ratio, which option would you take? Why might you want to consider other criteria?

c. What particular features of the economy might you want to look at before giving your advice?

## FURTHER READING

The Lucas critique was first presented by Robert Lucas in "Econometric Policy Evaluation: A Critique," in *The Phillips Curve and Labor Markets*, Carnegie Rochester Conference, Vol. 1, 1976, pp. 19–46.

The article by Stanley Fischer arguing that credibility would not be enough to achieve costless disinflation is "Long-Term Contracts, Rational Expectations, and the Optimal Money Supply Rule," *Journal of Political Economy*, 85, 1977, pp. 163–190.

The article that derived the path of disinflation reproduced in Figure 13–4 is by John Taylor, "Union Wage Settlements," *American Economic Review* 73 (5), December 1983: pp. 981–993.

A celebration of Okun's law is found in Laurence Ball, Daniel Leigh, and Prakash Loungani (2013), "Okun's Law: Fit at 50?," NBER Working Paper 18668. The Okun coefficient is compared across a number of countries.

(All four preceding articles are relatively technical.)

A description of Canadian monetary policy in the 1988 to 1993 period is found in *The Great Canadian Disinflation: The Economics and Politics of Monetary Policy in Canada, 1988–93*, by David E.W. Laidler and William B.P. Robson. (Toronto: C.D. Howe Institute, 1993). The story told in this book extends into the material we discuss in Chapters 24 and 25.

Even more details on monetary policy in Canada in this period can be found in "An Evaluation of the Bank of Canada Zero Inflation Target: Do Michael Wilson and John Crow Agree?" *Canadian Public Policy* 16 (3), September 1990: pp. 308–325; "Expected Inflation in Canada 1988–1995: An Evaluation of Bank of Canada Credibility and the Effect of Inflation Targets," *Canadian Public Policy* 23 (3), September 1997: pp. 223–258; and "How Has Inflation Changed in Canada? A Comparison of 1989–2001 to 1964–1988," *Canadian Public Policy* 28, 2002: pp. 563–579. All three articles were written by David Johnson, one of the authors of this book. The last article was written jointly with Sebastian Cerlich.

# Exchange Rates in the Medium Run: Adjustments, Crises, and Regimes

## The Core: The Medium Run

In Chapters 6, 7, and 8, we introduced open economy considerations into the short-run macroeconomic model. We saw that the real exchange rate, the price of foreign goods in terms of domestic goods, is very important in an open economy. We saw that interest rate parity, the equalization of expected nominal returns, is a useful way to think about the links between financial markets across countries. These two concepts are used extensively in this chapter; you may need to review them as the analysis unfolds. We consider two choices available to policy makers in the open economy in the medium run. One choice: Should the nominal exchange rate be flexible, or should the nominal exchange rate be fixed in terms of the currency of your principal trading partner? In only one of the last five decades did Canada fix the value of the Canadian dollar in terms of U.S. dollars, from 1962 to 1970. For the remainder of the last half-century, the value of the Canadian dollar has been determined in the foreign exchange market. There have been serious suggestions, particularly in the years from 1995 to the present, that Canada should return to a fixed exchange rate. Which exchange rate system is better for Canada?

The same question has been faced by the international financial system over the years. The Bretton Woods agreement (Bretton Woods is a resort in New Hampshire, where a meeting was held in 1944 to consider whether exchange rates should be fixed or flexible when World War II was over) decided nominal exchange rates should be fixed. This agreement was implemented between the major trading countries in the world in the period 1950–1970. However, in 1973, the agreement fell apart, and since then, the major currencies in the world—the American dollar, the Japanese yen, and the major European currencies—have traded freely in financial markets. Their relative values, the various bilateral exchange rates, have been determined in those markets. Which exchange rate system is better for the world economy? You may have noticed that we said only the exchange rates between major countries have been freely determined in financial markets. For many smaller countries, nominal exchange rates were and still are fixed in value relative to the currency of their major trading partner. Thus, small European countries tended to fix their currency's value to the German Deutschmark (DM) or euro, and Latin American and Asian countries tended to fix the price of their currencies in terms of the U.S. dollar.

The second choice we consider is: If you do fix your nominal exchange rate in terms of the currency of your principal trading partner (and many countries do just that), are there circumstances in which you need to change the value of your currency? If there is never a reason to change the value of your nominal exchange rate, then logic suggests you should simply use the currency of another country or share currencies across nations. A few countries do use the currency of another country as their money. Examples include very small countries in Europe—Monaco used the French franc and San Marino the Italian lira, both before the creation of the euro. Many of you will know that as of January 1, 1999, most of the countries in Western Europe decided to replace their national currencies with a new shared currency, the euro. The creation of a new joint currency and a new joint central bank for this large an area and this many countries is an unprecedented experiment. We will discuss this experiment briefly at the end of the chapter. Both over time and across countries, there have been a variety of policy choices made to establish a value for the nominal exchange rate.

In section 14-1, we extend our medium run *AS-AD* model into a situation in which the nominal exchange rate is freely determined in financial markets. The main lesson: If a country chooses a flexible nominal exchange rate and chooses a higher inflation rate than the inflation rate in its principal trading partner, then the nominal exchange rate will continuously depreciate. The choice to have a flexible exchange rate is intimately linked to the choice to have an inflation rate different from that of your trading partner. This same point is explored in a different way in section 14-2. Here, we analyze the medium run in an open economy under fixed exchange rates. Remember, a fixed exchange rate is a fixed nominal exchange rate. In the short run, both domestic and foreign price levels are fixed, so the fixed nominal exchange rate implies a fixed real exchange rate as well. But in the medium run, price levels adjust, and even if the nominal exchange rate is fixed, the real exchange rate may change. We see this is indeed the case. However, we now have to provide an adjustment path to the "right" real exchange rate. This adjustment path, particularly the path of real output, can be quite different depending on whether it is the nominal exchange rate that is adjusted or the price level that is adjusted. In section 14-3, we look at exchange rate crises. Countries that fix their exchange rate often face serious crises. This was the case in 1973 for the countries that had operated under the Bretton Woods system when that system collapsed. It was the case in Europe in 1992 for countries operating within the European fixed exchange rate system. It was the case for many Asian countries in 1997 and 1998. Exchange rate crises typically start when participants in financial markets conclude the current nominal exchange rate is not sustainable and that the country will soon devalue its currency. To compensate investors for the perceived risk of devaluation, the central bank must increase the domestic interest rate, often to very high levels. The country is faced with a tough choice: maintain the interest rate at a very high level, which decreases the demand for goods and may trigger a recession, or give up the parity value of the nominal exchange rate and devalue the currency. Understanding such crises helps us assess one of the major problems associated with a fixed exchange rate.

Building on what we have done in sections 14-1, 14-2, and 14-3, the chapter closes in section 14-4 with a discussion of the pros and cons of flexible and fixed exchange rate regimes.

# 14-1 | Flexible Exchange Rates and the Adjustment of the Nominal Exchange Rate in the Medium Run

In this section, we present a country that operates with a flexible exchange rate and a positive rate of inflation. That rate of inflation will be constant at 5% throughout the following extensive example. The foreign country that is this country's major trading partner will have a zero rate of inflation. It is crucial that the two countries have a *different* rate of inflation but not crucial that one rate of inflation happens to be zero. Zero inflation in the foreign country simplifies the example just a little bit.

Our analysis in the last two chapters has shown us that an economy can operate with a sustained positive rate of inflation. We wrote that:

$$\pi_t = \pi_t^e - \alpha(u_t - u_n) \tag{14.1}$$

where inflation equalled expected inflation if the rate of unemployment were at the natural rate of unemployment. The evidence supporting this model is presented in Chapters 12 and 13. If expected inflation is equal to actual inflation, it follows that the expected price level equals the actual price level in each period. We use this fact below.

## Aggregate Supply

The aggregate supply relation is the relation between the price level and the output level implied by equilibrium in the labour market. In Chapter 10 (equation 10.1), we wrote:

$$P_t = P_t^e(1 + m) F\left(1 - \frac{Y_t}{L}, z\right) \qquad (14.2)$$

The price level depends on the expected price level for this year and the level of output. Recall the mechanisms at work:

- The price level expected to prevail in year $t$, $P_t^e$, affects the nominal wage in year $t$, which affects the actual price level in year $t$, $P_t$.
- Higher real output this year ($Y_t$) leads to lower unemployment, which leads to higher wages, which leads to a higher price level in this year.

We are now dealing in a world where expected inflation is positive. If $\pi_t^e$ is the expected rate of inflation (written as a decimal so that 10% equals 0.10), then we can rewrite our aggregate supply relationship as:

$$P_t = (1 + \pi_t^e)P_{t-1}(1 + m) F\left(1 - \frac{Y_t}{L}, z\right) \qquad (14.3)$$

This aggregate supply curve is placed in Figure 14–1 so that when output is at $Y_n$, the price level $P_t$ is at its expected level $P_t^e$. $Y_n$ is the full employment or natural level of output. This is point $A$ in Figure 14–1.

With aggregate supply in place, we need to review the elements of aggregate demand in the open economy.

FIGURE 14–1

**Aggregate Supply and Expected Inflation**

$P_{t-1}(1 + \pi_t^e) = P_t^e$ defines the expected price level prevailing in period $t$. $P_t^e$ is written as a decimal, and so 10% = 0.1. If prices are higher than expected, then output exceeds the natural level of output $Y_n$.

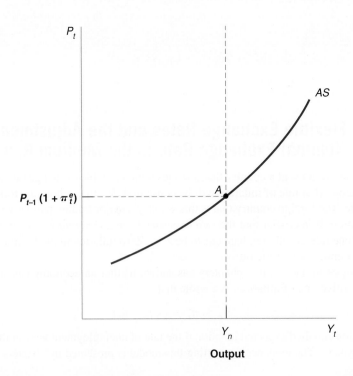

## Aggregate Demand

The aggregate demand relationship defines an equilibrium in the goods market between the goods people are willing to buy and those that are produced. From section 8-3 in Chapter 8, we write:

$$Y_t = C(Y_t - T) + I(Y_t, i_t) + G + NX\left(Y_t, Y^*, \frac{E_t P^*}{P_t}\right) \qquad (14.4)$$

$$\phantom{Y_t = C(Y_t} + \phantom{- T) + } - \phantom{I(Y_t,} + \ - \phantom{) + } + \phantom{G + NX(Y_t,} - \ + \ +$$

Because the price level varies in the medium run, the real exchange rate replaces the nominal exchange rate in the aggregate demand relation. For the goods-market equilibrium, the output produced, the left side of equation (14.4), must equal the output demanded, the right side of equation (14.4).

The signs below the variables, positive or negative, indicate how the variables in equation (14.4) affect demand. Let us review the influence of these variables:

- $G$ (+) represents the increase in the demand for domestic goods with higher government spending.
- $T$ (−) represents the decrease in demand for domestic goods with higher taxes.
- $Y_t$ (+) is the indirect influence of more domestic output on both consumption ($C$) and investment ($I$).
- The domestic nominal interest rate, $i_t$ (−), has a negative influence on aggregate demand. This effect was stressed in Chapter 5. Strictly speaking, now that expected inflation is positive, this variable should be the real interest rate. The discussion of the interaction among expected inflation, the nominal interest rate, and the real interest rate is deferred to Chapters 19 through 22. In this chapter, we want to focus only on the open economy interactions of prices and exchange rate. This is quite enough to do!
- $Y^*$ (+) represents the influence of foreign output on the demand for domestic goods. Higher foreign output means more net exports ($NX$) from Canada. $Y_t$ (−) in the $NX$ expression is the effect of more domestic output on imports (not exports).
- $\epsilon_t$, the real exchange rate, has a negative effect on imports and a positive effect on exports. A real exchange rate depreciation, an increase in $\epsilon_t$, means that imports fall and exports rise. This increases net exports ($NX$) hence a (+) sign under the real exchange rate. The Marshall–Lerner conditions discussed in Chapter 7 are assumed to hold.

In a world where the price level moves, we recognize that the value of the real exchange rate $\epsilon_t = E_t P^*/P_t$ changes. Such changes may occur because of any combination of movements in $E_t$, the nominal exchange rate; $P^*$, the foreign price level; and $P_t$ the domestic price level. It is these movements that we must understand and follow through the analytical exercise below.

There are two further equilibrium conditions in the financial market of the open economy. The first:

$$\frac{M_t}{P_t} = Y_t L(i_t) \qquad (14.5)$$

is the financial market equilibrium condition that characterized the $LM$ curve. Here, real money demand equals real money supply at the domestic interest rate, $i_t$.

The second condition is uncovered interest parity, where:

$$i_t = i^* + \left(\frac{E_{t+1}^e - E_t}{E_t}\right) \qquad (14.6)$$

means that expected returns on one-year bonds denominated in either currency are equal. The expected rate of depreciation of the domestic currency:

$$\frac{E_{t+1}^e - E_t}{E_t}$$

equals the interest rate difference between the domestic country and the foreign country. If bonds denominated in either currency earn equal expected returns, they will be held by the participants in either financial market.

You may have noticed time subscripts on some variables in equations (14.4), (14.5), and (14.6). We are going to allow these variables the possibility that they vary over time (but not all these variables will vary over time). Time will begin in period $t$, then move to period $t+1$, period $t+2$, period $t+3$, and so on. Some variables will never vary over time, specifically the foreign interest rate and foreign income, as well as domestic government spending and taxes. There are no subscripts on these variables. In addition to the four variables above, we are going to work in the situation where the foreign price level $P^*$ is held constant. This means the foreign inflation rate is zero. However, the analysis does generalize to the situation where the foreign country simply has a different inflation rate from the domestic country.

### A Full Employment Open Economy with Positive Inflation in the Medium Run

Figure 14–2 and Table 14–1 are used to illustrate a sequence of $AS$-$AD$ points that this economy could experience in a medium-run equilibrium. At each point in this example, actual inflation equals expected inflation.[1] Table 14–1 opens with four rows of foreign variables that are constant over time—that is, they take the same value in each period. The next four rows are the values of the domestic variables, which are predetermined for us in this analysis. Domestic inflation is 5% each year (row (6)). The actual price level (row (5)) and the expected domestic price level (row (7)) simply reflect the expected and actual inflation of 5% in each year. Because actual prices always equal expected prices, output is always at full employment, $Y_n$ (row (8)). Whatever happens on the demand side of this economy, in each period, the level of domestic prices rises by 5%, the $AS$ curve shifts up by 5%, and output remains at full employment. These shifts are illustrated in Figure 14–2 for periods $t$, $t+1$, and $t+2$. More periods could be added, but the diagram would simply get more cluttered. Figure 14–2 shows aggregate demand curves that also shift up each period so that the intersection of $AS$ and $AD$ remains at $Y_n$. How do we ensure this result?

FIGURE 14–2

Aggregate Demand and Aggregate Supply in an Open Economy with Expected Inflation

As the price level increases, the nominal exchange rate depreciates. At the same real exchange rate (points A, B, and C), demand for domestic output remains the same.

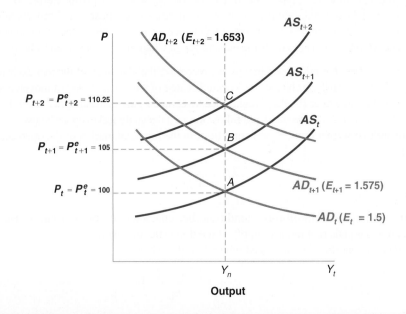

[1]**DIGGING DEEPER.** Implicitly, we have already considered various aspects of the situation in which actual inflation need not equal expected inflation in Chapters 6, 7, and 8, as well as in Chapters 10, 11, 12, and 13.

| Row | Symbol | Variable | $t$ | $t+1$ | $t+2$ | $t+3$ | $t+4$ |
|-----|--------|----------|-----|-------|-------|-------|-------|
| | | **TABLE 14–1 An Open Economy under Flexible Exchange Rates: An Example** | | | | | |
| (1) | $P^*$ | Foreign prices (index) | 100 | 100 | 100 | 100 | 100 |
| (2) | $\pi^*$ | Foreign inflation (%) | 0 | 0 | 0 | 0 | 0 |
| (3) | $i^*$ | Foreign interest rate (%) | 5 | 5 | 5 | 5 | 5 |
| (4) | $Y^*$ | Foreign output (index) | 100 | 100 | 100 | 100 | 100 |
| (5) | $P_t$ | Domestic prices (index) | 100 | 105 | 110.25 | 115.76 | 121.55 |
| (6) | $\pi_t$ | Domestic inflation | 5 | 5 | 5 | 5 | 5 |
| (7) | $P_t^e$ | Expected domestic price level | 100 | 105 | 110.25 | 115.76 | 121.55 |
| (8) | $Y_t$ | Output | $Y_n$ | $Y_n$ | $Y_n$ | $Y_n$ | $Y_n$ |
| (9) | $E_t$ | Nominal exchange rate (domestic currency per foreign currency) | 1.5 | 1.575 | 1.653 | 1.736 | 1.823 |
| (10) | $\epsilon_t$ | Real exchange rate (index) | 1.5 | 1.5 | 1.5 | 1.5 | 1.5 |
| (11) | $\dfrac{(E_{t+1}^e - E_t)}{E_t}$ | Expected rate of depreciation (%) | 5 | 5 | 5 | 5 | 5 |
| (12) | $i_t$ | Domestic interest rate (%) | 10 | 10 | 10 | 10 | 10 |
| (13) | $M_t$ | Money supply (dollars) | 1000 | 1050 | 1102.5 | 1115.76 | 1215.5 |
| (14) | $M_t/P_t$ | Real money supply (period $t$ dollars) | 1000 | 1000 | 1000 | 1000 | 1000 |

The data in this box are used in section 14-1 as an example of how an open economy can function when the domestic country chooses a different inflation rate from the inflation rate in its principal trading partner.

If output is to remain at $Y_n$, then total aggregate demand in equation (14.4) cannot change between period $t$ and period $t+1$. We have kept some of these elements in equation (14.4) constant in this problem—that is, $G$, $T$, and $Y^*$ are all constant. We need to calculate what will happen to $i_t$, the domestic interest rate, and $\epsilon_t$, the real exchange rate. Here is the methodology: We are going to propose a solution, a sequence of choices for $i_t$, and $\epsilon_t$ and then ask if our proposed choices make sense.

Rows (9), (10), and (11) of Table 14–1 are the first step. In these rows, a nominal depreciation of 5% between each period exactly offsets 5% domestic inflation (when foreign prices are fixed) so that the real exchange rate $\epsilon_t$ never changes. The domestic price level in period $t$ is 100. The nominal exchange rate in period $t$ is 1.5. The foreign price level in period $t$ is 100. (Remember these are index numbers where the initial values are arbitrary.) The real exchange rate in period $t$ is 1.5. If, in period $t+1$, the domestic price level moves to 105, a depreciation of the nominal exchange rate to 1.575 will leave the real exchange rate $\epsilon_t$ equal to the real exchange rate $\epsilon_{t+1}$ where both are equal to the period $t$ value of 1.5. The same logic repeats from period $t+2$ to $t+3$ and so on. The proposed solution has no variation in the real exchange rate and thus no variation in the demand for domestic goods from this source. Exports and imports remain unchanged in equation (14.4). This seems a promising first step to keeping the level of aggregate demand constant, that we should keep the real exchange rate constant. The next step is to deal with the domestic interest rate.

The variables needed for the analysis of interest rate parity (14.6) appear in rows (11) and (12), as well as in row (3). In the proposed solution, the uncovered interest parity condition, equation (14.6), holds between each period. Note the exchange rate in period $t+1$ (1.575 domestic currency units per unit of foreign currency), is the exchange rate expected in period $t+1$ as of period $t$. The same relationship holds in Table 14–1 between each set of periods. In each period, a 5% depreciation of the domestic currency is expected and occurs. In each period, the domestic nominal interest rate is 5% higher than the foreign interest rate. In Table 14–1, the domestic interest rate is constant and equal to 10%. There is no variation in aggregate

This box looks at the change in nominal exchange rates over a large number of years. In the analysis in section 14-1, we suggested that if a country had a higher rate of inflation than its trading partner, then it would need to depreciate its currency so that the real exchange rate stayed constant. Here, we look at the evidence from 22 countries over the most recent period of flexible exchange rates, 1973–1998. The end date, 1998, is chosen because many of these countries adopted the euro on January 1, 1999. Because the euro countries share one currency, we no longer have separate observations on their nominal exchange rates to the U.S. dollar. The countries used are Australia, Austria, Belgium, Canada, Denmark, Finland, France, Germany, Greece, Iceland, Ireland, Italy, Japan, Korea, the Netherlands, New Zealand, Norway, Portugal, Spain, Sweden, Switzerland, and the United Kingdom.

In each case, the average annual rate of inflation in the Consumer Price Index (CPI) was calculated from the data for the years 1973–1998. There is wide variation in the inflation outcome across countries. The highest inflation country was Iceland at 22% per year; the lowest inflation country was a tie—both Switzerland and Germany with average inflation of 3.1% per year. The United States was then treated as the principal trading partner of all these countries—that is, the average annual rate of depreciation in the bilateral exchange rates between each country and the United States dollar was calculated. Average inflation in the United States was 5.2% over the sample. Using our analysis in section 14-1, we would predict that countries with inflation less than 5.2% would experience an appreciation against the U.S. dollar, and countries with an inflation rate higher than 5.2% should experience a depreciation against the U.S. dollar.

Figure 1 and Table 1 show the results of these calculations. The horizontal axis in Figure 1 is the inflation in that country minus the inflation in the United States. The vertical axis is the average annual percent depreciation (a negative value is an appreciation) against the U.S. dollar. If the analysis in section 14-1 were exactly correct, then all these points in the scatter would lie on a 45-degree line through the centre of Figure 1. They are not exactly on such a line, but the fit is remarkably close. Differences in inflation rates account for most of the nominal exchange rate change between the United States and these 22 countries from 1973 to 1998. For example, in every country in which the inflation rate was lower than the American inflation rate, there is a nominal appreciation of that country's currency against the U.S. dollar. The opposite holds true for the countries with higher inflation than in the United States.

What of Canada? The Canadian average annual inflation rate from 1973 to 1988 was 0.22% higher than the inflation rate in the United States. All of this difference was early in this sample. Since 1991, Canada has had a lower inflation rate than has the United States. The Canadian dollar depreciated from 1973 to 1998 by an average of 1.59%. The Canadian dollar depreciated "too much," that is, we experienced a real depreciation. Canada is actually one of the countries that does not fit the model very well. Canada is labelled in Figure 1. You can use the data in the table to locate the points in the figure for the other countries.

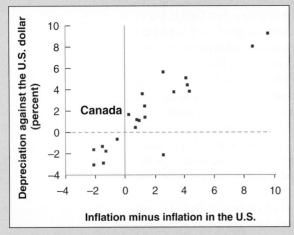

**FIGURE 1   Inflation Differences and Nominal Exchange Rate Change**

Countries with high inflation rates—in this case, higher inflation rates than the United States—see their currencies fall in value against the U.S. dollar.

| TABLE | 1 | | |
|---|---|---|---|
| Country | Inflation rate (%) | Inflation rate – U.S. inflation rate | Average depreciation (%) against the U.S. dollar |
| Australia | 6.3 | 1.1 | 3.5 |
| Austria | 3.9 | −1.3 | −1.8 |
| Belgium | 4.6 | −0.6 | −0.7 |
| Canada | 5.4 | 0.2 | 1.59 |
| Denmark | 5.8 | 0.6 | 0.40 |
| Finland | 6.5 | 1.3 | 1.3 |
| France | 6.0 | 0.8 | 1.1 |
| Germany | 3.1 | −2.1 | −1.7 |
| Greece | 14.7 | 9.5 | 9.2 |
| Iceland | 22.5 | 17.3 | 17.5 |
| Ireland | 7.7 | 2.5 | −2.2 |
| Italy | 9.3 | 4.1 | 4.3 |
| Japan | 3.7 | −1.5 | −2.9 |
| Korea | 9.2 | 4.0 | 5.0 |
| Netherlands | 3.7 | −1.5 | −1.4 |
| New Zealand | 8.4 | 3.2 | 3.7 |
| Norway | 6.0 | 0.8 | 1.1 |
| Portugal | 13.7 | 8.5 | 8.0 |
| Spain | 9.4 | 4.2 | 3.8 |
| Sweden | 6.5 | 1.3 | 2.4 |
| Switzerland | 3.1 | −2.1 | −3.1 |
| United Kingdom | 7.7 | 2.5 | 5.6 |
| United States | 5.2 | — | — |

*Source for data: International Financial Statistics Yearbook.* International Monetary Fund, 2001. Printed with permission.

demand from variation in the domestic interest rate. Thus, all the variables that determine aggregate demand are constant over time, and the solution we propose seems to be a viable solution. In each period, the aggregate demand curve shifts up to intersect the aggregate supply curve at $Y_n$. This shift is represented in Figure 14–2 by denoting that each aggregate demand curve is drawn for a different value of the nominal exchange rate.

The last step in this quite complicated analysis is to be certain that our solution allows the domestic financial market to be in equilibrium. Look again at equation (14.5). The right side of equation (14.5), the demand for real money, is constant in Table 14–1. $Y_n$ is the constant level of output (row (8)) and $i_t$ is the constant domestic interest rate equal to 10% (row (12)). If the right side of equation (14.5) is constant, the left side of equation (14.5) must be constant as well. Rows (13) and (14) that finish Table 14–1 show that as the domestic price level rises by 5% and the domestic nominal money supply also rises by 5%, then the real money supply, the very last row of Table 14–1, remains constant. This entire analysis is the open economy analogue of the analysis in Chapters 10 and 13. In Chapter 10, as long as prices rose in proportion to an increase in the money stock, money was neutral. In this analysis, the money stock continues to rise in proportion to prices, but in the open economy, the nominal exchange rate must also depreciate in proportion to the increase in domestic prices. When these conditions hold, as they do in the numerical example of Table 14–1, then the increase in the money stock is neutral in the open economy as well as in the closed economy.

## Conclusions

This exercise teaches us an important lesson. If the domestic country as a policy decides to have a higher inflation rate in the medium run than its principal foreign trading partner, then it must also undergo a nominal depreciation of its currency relative to its trading partner. To put this another way, higher inflation countries will experience a constantly declining value of their currency. The Focus box "What Makes the Canadian Dollar (and Other Currencies) Fall in Value?" tests this proposition using the data from 1973 to 1998, the long period in which major currencies floated against the United States dollar. Countries that chose to have a higher inflation rate than the United States also chose to have a currency that constantly depreciated against the United States dollar. We will see in section 14-2 that if a country chooses to have a fixed exchange rate, it must eventually adopt the inflation rate chosen by its principal trading partner. If it does not do so, then the conditions for an exchange rate crisis are set up, conditions discussed in section 14-3.

# 14-2 | Fixed Exchange Rates and the Adjustment of the Real Exchange Rate

Take a country operating under a fixed exchange rate regime. Suppose its currency is *overvalued*: At the real exchange rate implied by the fixed nominal exchange rate and the current domestic and foreign price levels, domestic goods are very expensive relative to foreign goods. As a result, the demand for domestic goods is low, and so is output: The country is in a recession.

To get out of the recession, the country has several options. Among them:

- *Devalue:* By making domestic goods cheaper relative to foreign goods, a devaluation leads to an increase in the demand for domestic goods, and thus to an increase in output and an improvement in the trade balance.
- *Do nothing:* Keep the nominal exchange rate fixed, and rely instead on the adjustment of the price level over time.

◀ Remember that under fixed exchange rates, a change in the exchange rate is called a devaluation (not a depreciation) or a revaluation (not an appreciation).

In this section, we compare the macro implications of these two options, both in the short run and in the medium run. To begin, we focus again on the aggregate demand and aggregate supply relations for an open economy under fixed exchange rates.

## Aggregate Demand under Fixed Exchange Rates

*Warning:* The understanding of the next paragraphs depends on what you learned in earlier chapters. Make sure you remember the definitions, the real exchange rate (Chapter 6), and the interest rate parity condition (Chapter 6).

Go back to the condition for goods-market equilibrium, equation (14.7), rewritten below:

$$Y = C(Y - T) + I(Y, i) + G + NX(Y, Y^*, \epsilon) \qquad (14.7)$$

For the goods market to be in equilibrium, output must be equal to the demand for domestic goods—the sum of consumption, investment, government spending, and net exports.

Recall that under fixed exchange rates, the nominal exchange rate is fixed. Denote by $\overline{E}$ the value at which it is fixed so that:

$$E = \overline{E}$$

Recall, finally, that under fixed exchange rates and perfect capital mobility, the domestic interest rate must be equal to the foreign interest rate:

$$i = i^*$$

Use these two relations to rewrite equation (14.4) when the exchange rate is fixed:

$$Y = C(Y - T) + I(Y, i^*) + G + NX\left(Y, Y^*, \frac{\overline{E}P^*}{P}\right)$$

This is a rich—if complicated—equilibrium condition. It tells us that in an open economy with fixed exchange rates equilibrium output (or, more precisely, the level of output implied by equilibrium in the goods, financial, and foreign exchange markets) depends on the variables we saw in section 14-1:

- *Government spending (G) and taxes (T).* An increase in government spending increases output, as does a decrease in taxes.
- *The domestic interest rate, which is equal to the foreign nominal interest rate (i\*).* An increase in the interest rate decreases output for the usual reasons.
- *Foreign output (Y\*).* An increase in foreign output increases exports and increases domestic output.
- *The real exchange rate, equal to the fixed nominal exchange rate* $(\overline{E})$ *times the foreign price level (P\*) divided by the domestic price level (P).* An increase in the real exchange rate, equivalently a real depreciation, leads to an increase in net exports, increasing output.

We will focus here on the effects of only three of these variables: the real exchange rate, government spending, and taxes. It will be convenient to write the relation between these three variables and output simply as:

$$Y = Y\left(\frac{\overline{E}P^*}{P}, G, T\right) \qquad (14.8)$$

$$= \quad (+, \quad +, -)$$

An increase in the real exchange rate—a real depreciation—increases output. So does an increase in government spending or a decrease in taxes. All the other variables that affect output in equation (14.7) are taken as givens and, to simplify notation, we simply omit them from equation (14.8).

Equation (14.8) gives us our *aggregate demand relation*, the relation between output and the price level implied by equilibrium in the goods market and in financial markets. This aggregate demand relation implies a negative relation between the price level and output: Given the fixed nominal exchange rate $(\overline{E})$ and the foreign price level ($P^*$), an increase in the domestic price level ($P$) leads to a decrease in the real exchange rate $\overline{E}P^*/P$—equivalently, a real appreciation. This real appreciation leads to a decrease in net exports and a decrease in $Y$.

In words, an increase in the price level makes domestic goods more expensive, decreasing the demand for domestic goods and, in turn, decreasing output.

Although the sign of the effect of the price level on output is the same as in the closed economy, the channel is quite different. In a closed economy, the price level affects output through its effect on the real money stock and, in turn, on the interest rate. In an open economy under fixed exchange rates, the interest rate is fixed—pinned down by the foreign interest rate. The way the price level affects output is, instead, through its effect on the real exchange rate.

In a closed economy:
$P\uparrow \Rightarrow (M/P)\downarrow \Rightarrow i\uparrow \Rightarrow Y\downarrow$

◄ In an open economy with fixed exchange rates:
$P\uparrow \Rightarrow (EP^*/P)\downarrow$
$\Rightarrow NX\downarrow \Rightarrow Y\downarrow$

## Aggregate Demand and Aggregate Supply

Rewrite the aggregate demand relation, equation (14.8), with time indexes—which will be needed as we look at dynamics later:

$$Y_t = Y\left(\frac{\overline{E}P^*}{P_t}, G, T\right) \qquad (14.9)$$

Note that we have put time indexes only on output and the price level. Given our assumption that the country operates under fixed exchange rates, the nominal exchange rate is fixed and does not need a time index. And, for convenience, we assume that the foreign price level and government spending and taxes are constant as well.

The aggregate demand curve implied by equation (14.9) is drawn as the $AD$ curve in Figure 14–3. The aggregate demand curve is downward sloping: An increase in the price level decreases output. As always, the relation is drawn for given values of all other variables, in particular for a given value of the nominal exchange rate.

Turn now to aggregate supply and the determination of the price level. Recall from Chapter 10 that the aggregate supply relation is the relation between the price level and output implied by equilibrium in the labour market. We will rely here on the simple version of the *aggregate supply relation* we derived in Chapter 10, equation (10.1):

$$P_t = P_{t-1}(1 + m)\,F\left(1 - \frac{Y_t}{L}, z\right) \qquad (14.10)$$

This equation was derived in Chapter 10 assuming that expected prices are equal to last year's prices. While we refined the assumption in later chapters, this assumption will do here as we focus on the dynamics ◄ around a misaligned fixed exchange rate.

The price level depends on the price level last year and on the level of output (this year). Recall the mechanisms at work:

● Last year's price level matters because it affects expectations of the price level this year, which affect nominal wages this year, which affect the price level this year.

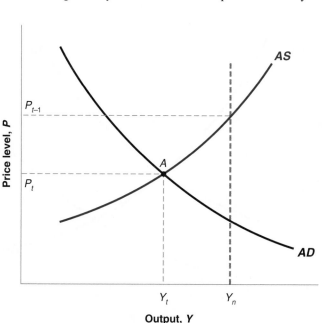

FIGURE  14–3

**Aggregate Demand and Aggregate Supply in an Open Economy under Fixed Exchange Rates**

An increase in the price level leads to a real appreciation and a decrease in output: The aggregate demand curve is downward sloping. An increase in output leads to an increase in the price level: The aggregate supply curve is upward sloping.

- Higher output matters because it leads to higher employment, which leads to lower unemployment, which leads to higher wages, which lead to a higher price level.

The aggregate supply curve is drawn as the *AS* curve in Figure 14–3, for a given value of last year's price level. It is upward sloping: Higher output leads to a higher price level.

The short-run equilibrium we want to consider is given by the intersection of the aggregate demand curve and the aggregate supply curve, point *A* in Figure 14–3. This equilibrium is at *A*, where output is below the natural level of output $Y_n$. The economy is in a recession. The rationale for looking at such a situation was given at the beginning of the section. We want to understand what will happen over time if government decides to either maintain the exchange rate or devalue.

Thinking about aggregate supply and aggregate demand can explain how this economy may have arrived at such a situation. $P_{t-1}$ is marked on Figure 14–3. It is where the *AS* curve (equation (14.9)) crosses $Y_n$. Something must have happened to reduce aggregate demand. In the *AD* curve (equation (14.9)), an increase in taxes or a decrease in government spending would cause *AD* to shift left. Taking advantage of other terms in equation (14.4), *AD* could shift to the left if $Y^*$ were lower—that is, if there were a recession in your trading partner. Whatever the source of the reduction in output, $Y_t$ is now less than $Y_n$, and government must decide how to act.

**Adjustment without a Devaluation.** Suppose, first, government does not devalue. What will happen over time is shown in Figure 14–4.

Need a refresher? Reread ▶ Chapter 10, section 10-3.

Recall that as long as output is below its natural level, the aggregate supply curve keeps shifting down. That is, at a given level of output, the price level in a given year will be below the price level the year before. In the absence of a change in the nominal exchange rate, the aggregate demand curve does not shift. Thus, starting from *A*, the economy will move over time along the aggregate demand curve, until it reaches *B*. At *B*, output is equal to its natural level. The price level is lower; by implication the real exchange rate is higher.

In words, the steady decrease in the price level over time will lead to a steady real depreciation. This real depreciation will lead to an increase in output until output has returned to its natural level.

This is an important conclusion. In the medium run, despite the fact that the nominal exchange rate is fixed, the economy achieves the real depreciation needed to return output to

FIGURE 14–4

**Adjustment without a Devaluation**

The aggregate supply shifts down, leading to a decrease in the price level, a real depreciation, and an increase in output over time. The process ends when output has returned to its natural level.

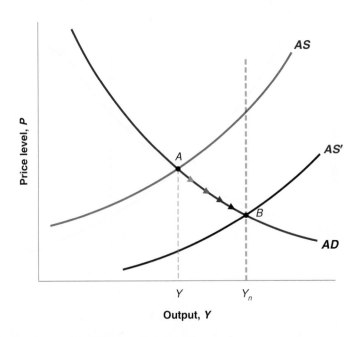

its natural level. This is an important qualification to the conclusions we reached in the previous chapter, where we were focusing only on the short run:

- In the short run, a fixed nominal exchange rate implies a fixed real exchange rate.
- In the medium run, a fixed nominal exchange rate is consistent with an adjustment of the real exchange rate. The adjustment is achieved through movements in the price level.[2]

**Adjustment with a Devaluation.** Now, suppose that instead of letting the economy adjust over time along the path AB, government decides to give up the existing parity and devalue.

For a given price level, a devaluation (an increase in the nominal exchange rate) leads to a real depreciation (an increase in the real exchange rate), and thus to an increase in output. In other words, a devaluation shifts the aggregate demand curve to the right: The demand for domestic output is higher at a given price level. We saw this in Figure 14–2: As the flexible currency depreciated in value, the AD curve shifted to the right.

This has a straightforward implication. A devaluation of the right size can take the economy directly back to the natural level of output. In terms of Figure 14–5, the right size revaluation can take the economy from point A to point C. The economy is initially at A, the same point A as in Figure 14–3. The right size devaluation shifts the aggregate demand curve from AD to AD', moving the equilibrium from A to C. At C, output is equal to its natural level $Y_n$. The real exchange rate is the same as at B. (We know this because output is the same at points B and C. From equation (14.9), and without changes in G or T, this implies that the real exchange rate must also be the same.)

That the "right size" devaluation can return output to its natural level right away—rather than over time, as was the case without the devaluation—sounds too good to be true, and in

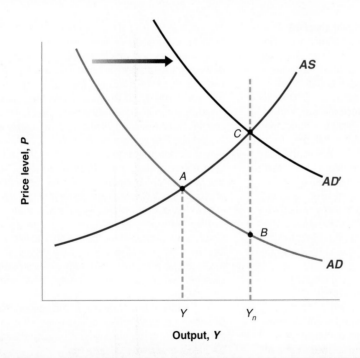

**FIGURE  14–5**

**Adjustment with a Devaluation**

The right size devaluation can shift aggregate demand to the right, moving the economy from point A to point C. At point C, output is back at its natural level.

[2]**DIGGING DEEPER**. Note that along the path of adjustment, the price level *decreases*. This would seem implausible, as we rarely observe countries going through deflation. (Japan in the late 1990s is a recent exception.) But this is the result of our assumption that the foreign price level is constant so that for domestic goods to become relatively cheaper, the domestic price level must *decrease*. If, instead, we had assumed that the foreign price level was increasing through time, the domestic price level would have to increase by less than the foreign price level or, put another way, domestic inflation would have to be lower than foreign inflation for some time.

practice, it is. Achieving the "right size" devaluation—the devaluation that takes output to $Y_n$ right away—is easier to achieve in a graph than in the real world:

See section 7-5 on the ▶ J-curve.

- In contrast to our simple aggregate demand relation (equation (14.9)), the effects of a real depreciation on output do not happen right away: Indeed, as we saw in Chapter 7, the initial effects of a depreciation on output may be contractionary, as people pay more for imports, and the quantities of imports and exports have not yet adjusted.

- Also, in contrast to our simple aggregate supply relation (14.10), there is likely to be a direct effect of the devaluation on the price level: As the price of imported goods increases, the price of a consumption basket increases. This is likely to lead workers to ask for higher nominal wages, forcing firms to increase their prices as well.

But these complications do not affect the basic conclusion: Allowing the nominal exchange rate to adjust can help output return to its natural level, if not right away, at least much faster than without a devaluation.

To summarize: We have learned that we must qualify some of the conclusions we reached in Chapter 8. Even under fixed *nominal* exchange rates, countries can adjust their *real* exchange rate in the medium run. They can do so by relying on adjustments in the price level. Nevertheless, the adjustment may be long and painful.

---

## FOCUS    The Return of Britain to the Gold Standard: Keynes versus Churchill

In 1925, Britain decided to return to the **gold standard**. The gold standard was a system in which each country fixed the price of its currency in terms of gold and stood ready to exchange gold for currency at the stated parity. This system implied fixed nominal exchange rates between countries.

The gold standard had been in place from 1870 until World War I. Because of the need to finance the war, and to do so, in part, by money creation, Britain had suspended the gold standard in 1914. In 1925, Winston Churchill, then Britain's Chancellor of the Exchequer (the British equivalent of the Minister of Finance in Canada), decided to return to the gold standard, and to do so at the prewar parity—that is, at the prewar value of the pound in terms of gold. But because prices had increased faster in Britain than in many of its trading partners, returning to the prewar parity implied a large real appreciation: At the same nominal exchange rate as before the war, British goods were now more expensive relative to foreign goods.

Keynes severely criticized the decision to return to the prewar parity. In *The Economic Consequences of Mr. Churchill*, a book he published in 1925, Keynes argued as follows: If Britain was going to return to the gold standard, it should have done so at a higher price of gold in terms of currency, at a nominal exchange rate higher than the prewar nominal exchange rate. In a newspaper article, he articulated his views as follows:

*There remains, however, the objection to which I have never ceased to attach importance, against the return to gold in actual present conditions, in view of the possible consequences on the state of trade and employment. I believe that our price level is too high, if it is converted to gold at the par of exchange, in relation to gold prices elsewhere; and if we consider the prices of those articles only which are not the subject of international trade, and of services, i.e., wages, we shall find that these are materially too high—not less than 5%, and probably 10%. Thus, unless the situation is saved by a rise of prices elsewhere, the Chancellor is committing us to a policy of forcing down money wages by perhaps 2 shillings in the Pound.*

*I do not believe that this can be achieved without the gravest danger to industrial profits and industrial peace. I would much rather leave the gold value of our currency where it was some months ago than embark on a struggle with every trade union in the country to reduce money wages. It seems wiser and simpler and saner to leave the currency to find its own level for some time longer rather than force a situation where employers are faced with the alternative of closing down or of lowering wages, cost what the struggle may.*

*For this reason, I remain of the opinion that the Chancellor of the Exchequer has done an ill-judged thing—ill judged because we are running the risk for no adequate reward if all goes well.*

Keynes's prediction turned out to be right. While other countries were growing, Britain was in a recession for the rest of the decade. Most economic historians attribute a good part of the blame to the initial overvaluation.

*Source:* Excerpts from *The Nation and Athenaeum*, May 2, 1925. © The New Statesman. Printed by permission.

---

Thus, whenever an exchange rate appears overvalued—be it because output is too low or the trade deficit too large—there is sure to be a debate about whether the country should devalue or, instead, stick to the existing parity.

● Those who want faster adjustment argue for devaluation. Perhaps the most forceful presentation of this view was made more than 70 years ago by Keynes, who argued against Winston Churchill's 1925 decision to return the English pound to its pre–World War I parity. His arguments are presented in the Global Macro box "The Return of Britain to the Gold Standard: Keynes versus Churchill." Most economic historians believe that history proved Keynes right and that overvaluation of the pound was one of the main reasons for Britain's poor economic performance after World War I.

● Those who oppose a devaluation argue that there are good reasons to choose fixed exchange rates and that too much willingness to devalue defeats the purpose of adopting a fixed exchange rate regime in the first place. They also argue that too much willingness on the part of governments to consider a devaluation may lead to an increased likelihood of exchange rate crises. To understand their arguments, we now turn to a discussion of these crises: what triggers them and what their implications might be.

## 14-3 | Exchange Rate Crises

Take a country operating under fixed exchange rates. Suppose that participants in financial markets start believing there may soon be an exchange rate adjustment—either a devaluation or a shift to a flexible exchange rate regime accompanied by a depreciation. Why might this be the case?

● The domestic currency may be overvalued. A real depreciation is called for. While this can be achieved without a devaluation, financial investors may conclude that government will take the quickest way out and devalue. Such an overvaluation often happens in countries that fix the nominal exchange rate while having an inflation rate higher than the inflation rate in the country they are pegging to. Higher relative inflation implies a steadily increasing price of domestic goods relative to foreign goods, a steady real appreciation, and so a steady worsening of the trade position. As time passes, the need for an adjustment of the real exchange rate steadily increases, and financial investors become more and more nervous.

● Internal conditions may call for a decrease in the domestic interest rate. A decrease in the domestic interest rate cannot be achieved under fixed exchange rates. But it can be achieved if the country is willing to shift to a flexible exchange rate regime. If a country lets the exchange rate float and then decreases its domestic interest rate, we know from Chapter 8 that this will trigger an increase in the nominal exchange rate—a nominal depreciation.

Whatever the reason, suppose financial markets believe a devaluation may be imminent. For the central bank to maintain the exchange rate requires an increase, often a large one, in the domestic interest rate. To see this, return to the interest parity condition we derived in Chapter 6 and used earlier in this chapter:

$$i_t = i_t^* + \frac{(E_{t+1}^e - E_t)}{E_t} \tag{14.11}$$

In Chapter 6, we interpreted this equation as a relation between the *one-year* domestic and foreign nominal interest rates, the current exchange rate and the expected exchange rate a year hence. But the choice of one year as the period was arbitrary. The relation holds over a day, a week, a month. If financial markets expect the exchange rate to be 2% higher a month from now, they will hold domestic bonds only if the one-month domestic interest rate exceeds the one-month foreign interest rate by 2% (or, if we express interest rates at an annual rate, if the domestic interest rate exceeds the foreign interest rate by approximately $2\% \times 12 = 24\%$).

Under fixed exchange rates, the current exchange rate $E_t$ is fixed at some level, say, $\overline{E}$. If markets expect the parity will be maintained over the period, then $E_{t+1}^e = \overline{E}$, and the interest parity condition simply states that the domestic and the foreign interest rates must be equal.

More precisely, the necessary interest rate differential is $(1.02)^{24} - 1 = 26.8\%$.

Suppose, however, that participants in financial markets start anticipating a devaluation—an increase in the exchange rate. Suppose that they believe that over the coming month, there is a 50% chance the parity will be maintained and a 50% chance there will be a 10% devaluation. Thus, the term $(E_{t+1}^e - E_t)/E_t$ in the interest parity equation (14.11), which we assumed equal to zero earlier, now equals $0.5 \times 0\% + 0.5 \times 10\%$ (a 50% chance of no change plus a 50% chance of a devaluation of 10%), thus equals 5%.

This implies that if the central bank wants to maintain the existing parity, it must now offer a monthly interest rate 5% higher—that is, $12 \times 5\% = 60\%$ higher at an annual rate! Sixty percent is the "annual" interest differential needed to convince investors to hold domestic bonds in view of the risk of a devaluation!

What, then, are the choices confronting government and the central bank?

In most countries, government is formally in charge of choosing the parity and the central bank formally in charge of defending it. In practice, choosing and defending the parity are joint responsibilities of government and the central bank.

In the summer of 1998, Boris Yeltsin announced that the Russian government had no intention of devaluing the ruble. Two weeks later, the ruble collapsed.

- First, government and the central bank can try to convince markets they have no intention of devaluing. This is always the first line of defence: Communiqués are issued, and prime ministers appear on TV to reiterate their absolute commitment to the existing parity. But words are cheap, and they rarely convince financial markets.
- Second, the central bank can increase the interest rate, but by less than needed to satisfy equation (14.11)—in our example, by less than 60%. Although domestic interest rates are high, they are not high enough to fully compensate for the perceived risk of devaluation. This action typically leads to a large capital outflow, as financial investors still see foreign bonds are more attractive. To maintain the parity, the central bank must buy domestic currency and sell foreign currency in the foreign exchange market. In doing so, it often loses most of its reserves of foreign currency. (The mechanics of central bank intervention were described in the appendix to Chapter 8.)
- Eventually—after a few hours or a few months—the choice for the central bank becomes either to increase the interest rate enough to satisfy equation (14.11) or to validate the market's expectations and devalue. Setting a very high short-term domestic interest rate can have a devastating effect on demand and on output. This course of action makes sense only if (1) the perceived probability of a devaluation is small, so the interest rate does not have to be too high, and (2) government believes markets will soon become convinced that no devaluation is coming, allowing domestic interest rates to decrease. Otherwise, the only option is to devalue.

To summarize: Expectations that a devaluation may be on the way can trigger an exchange rate crisis. Faced with such expectations, government has two options: (1) give in and devalue, or (2) fight and maintain the parity, at the cost of very high interest rates and a potential recession. Fighting may not work anyway: The recession may force government to change policy later on or force government out of office.

An interesting twist here is that a devaluation may occur even if the belief that a devaluation was imminent was initially groundless. Even if government initially had no intention of devaluing, it may be forced to devalue if financial markets believe that it will devalue: The cost of maintaining the parity would be a long period of high interest rates and a recession, so government prefers to devalue instead. Some economists believe that the exchange rate crises that hit many Asian countries in 1997 had such a self-fulfilling element. In the rest of the section, we focus on the exchange rate crisis that shook the European Monetary System in the early 1990s.

## Crises in the European Monetary System

At the start of the 1990s, the European Monetary System (EMS) appeared to work well. Started in 1979, it was an exchange rate system based on fixed parities with bands: Each member country (among them, France, Germany, Italy, and [starting in 1990] the United Kingdom) had to maintain its exchange rate vis-à-vis all other member countries within narrow bands. The first few years had been rocky, with many **realignments**—adjustment of parities—among member countries, but from 1987 to 1992, there were only two realignments.

There was increasing talk about narrowing the bands further and even moving to the next stage—to a common currency.

In 1992, however, financial markets became increasingly convinced that more realignments were soon to come. The reason was one we have seen already, namely, the implications of German reunification. Because of the pressure on demand coming from reunification, the Bundesbank was maintaining high interest rates to try to avoid too large an increase in output and an increase in inflation in Germany. Although Germany's trading partners needed lower interest rates to reduce a growing unemployment problem, they had to match the German interest rates to maintain their EMS parities. To financial markets, the position of Germany's partners looked increasingly untenable. Lower interest rates outside Germany, and thus devaluations of many currencies vis-à-vis the Deutchmark (DM), appeared increasingly likely. ◄

See the Global Macro box in Chapter 8 "German Unification, Interest Rates, and the EMS."

Throughout 1992, the perceived probability of a devaluation forced several of Germany's trading partners to maintain higher nominal interest rates than Germany. But the first major crisis did not come until September 1992. The day-by-day story is told in the Focus box "Anatomy of a Crisis: The September 1992 EMS Crisis." The belief, in early September, that a number of countries were soon going to devalue led to speculative attacks on several currencies,

## FOCUS   Anatomy of a Crisis: The September 1992 EMS Crisis

- **September 5–6.** The Ministers of Finance of the European Union meet in Bath, England. The official communiqué at the end of the meeting reaffirms their commitment to maintaining existing parities within the exchange rate mechanism (ERM) of the European Monetary System (EMS). The ERM was the agreement by some European countries within the EMS to intervene and maintain approximately fixed exchange rates.

- **September 8: The first attack.** The attack comes not against one of the currencies in the EMS but rather against the currencies of Scandinavian countries, which are also pegged to the DM. The Finnish authorities give in and decide to let their currency, the markka, **float**— that is, be determined in the foreign exchange market without central bank intervention. The markka depreciates by 13% vis-à-vis the DM. Sweden decides to maintain its parity and increases its overnight interest rate to 24% (at an annual rate). Two days later, it increases it further to 75%.

- **September 10–11: The second attack.** The Bank of Italy intervenes heavily to maintain the parity of the lira, leading the bank to sustain large losses of foreign exchange reserves. But on September 13, the lira is devalued by 7% vis-à-vis the DM.

- **September 16–17: The third and major attack.** Speculation starts against the British pound, leading to large losses in reserves by the Bank of England. The Bank of England increases its overnight rate from 10% to 15%. However, speculation continues against both the pound and (despite the previous devaluation) the lira. Both the United Kingdom and Italy announce they

are temporarily suspending their participation in the ERM and will no longer keep their exchange rates fixed. Over the following weeks, both currencies depreciate by roughly 15% vis-à-vis the DM.

- **September 16–17.** With the pound and the lira out of the ERM, the attack turns against the other currencies. To maintain its parity, Sweden increases its overnight rate to 500%! Ireland increases its overnight rate to 300%. Spain decides to stay in the ERM but to devalue by 5%.

- **September 20.** French voters narrowly approve the Maastricht treaty (the treaty that sets the timing for the transition to a common currency) in a referendum. A negative vote would surely have amplified the crisis. The narrow, but positive, vote is seen as the sign that the worst may be over and that the treaty will eventually be accepted by all EU members.

- **September 23–28.** Speculation against the franc forces the Banque de France to increase its short-term interest rate by 2.5 percentage points. To defend their parity without having to resort to very high short-term interest rates, both Ireland and Spain reintroduce capital controls.

- **End of September.** The crisis ends. Two countries, the United Kingdom and Italy, have moved to flexible exchange rates and thus left the EMS. Spain remains within the EMS, but only after a devaluation. The other countries have maintained their parity, but, for some of them, at the cost of large reserve losses.

*Source: World Economic Outlook*, October 1993. The September 1992 EMS Crisis. International Monetary Fund. Used by permission of IMF.

with financial investors selling in anticipation of an oncoming devaluation. All the lines of defence described earlier were used. First, solemn communiqués were issued, but with no discernible effect. Then, interest rates were increased, up to 500% for the overnight interest rate (the rate for lending and borrowing overnight) in Sweden (expressed at an annual rate). But they were not increased enough to prevent capital outflows and large losses of foreign exchange reserves by the central banks under pressure. Next, different courses of action were followed in different countries: Spain devalued its exchange rate, Italy and the United Kingdom suspended their participation in the EMS, and France decided to tough it out through higher interest rates until the storm was over.

By the end of September, financial markets believed no further devaluations were imminent. Some countries were no longer in the EMS, others had devalued but remained in the EMS, and those that had maintained their parity had shown their determination to stay in the EMS, even if this meant very high interest rates. But the underlying problem— the high German interest rates—was still there, and it was only a matter of time until the next crisis. In November 1992, further speculation forced a devaluation of the Spanish peseta, the Portuguese escudo, and the Swedish krona. The peseta and the escudo were further devalued in May 1993. In July 1993, after yet another large speculative attack, the EMS countries decided to adopt large bands of fluctuations (plus or minus 15%) around central parities, in effect moving to a system that allowed for very large exchange rate fluctuations. This system with wider bands was kept until the introduction of the euro in January 1999.

## 14-4 | Choosing between Exchange Rate Regimes

Let us return to one of the questions that started the chapter: Should countries choose flexible or fixed exchange rates? Are there circumstances when flexible rates dominate and others when fixed rates dominate?

On macroeconomic grounds, everything we have seen so far would seem to favour flexible exchange rates. The analysis in section 14-1 in this chapter showed that in the medium run, a flexible exchange rate allows a country to choose its own interest rate and inflation rate. This seems to give countries more choices and favour flexible exchange rates. But governments also care about what happens in the short run, and in the short run, flexible exchange rates also clearly dominate: Under fixed exchange rates, a country gives up control not only of its exchange rate but also—at least under perfect capital mobility—of its interest rate. The open economy macroeconomic model developed in Chapters 6, 7, and 8 assumed exchange rates were flexible. In the open economy, monetary policy works through both the interest rate and the real and nominal exchange rate. The Bank of Canada is firmly in favour of a flexible exchange rate for Canada. Canada has had a flexible exchange rate since 1970, about three years before flexible exchange rates became common in the rest of the world. Canada also had a flexible exchange rate throughout the 1950s when very few countries had flexible exchange rates. Between 1962 and 1970, the Canadian dollar was fixed at $1.08 Canadian per U.S. dollar. The Bank of Canada remains firmly against fixing the Canadian dollar to the U.S. dollar. In his testimony to a Parliamentary Committee on December 5, 2007, the incoming Bank of Canada governor said that "it would be a mistake" to fix the loonie to the U.S. dollar. He went on to say that "It would mean, de facto, Canada would adopt U.S. monetary policy, despite the reality that the structures of the economies are very different."

This continues to be the position of the Bank of Canada. ▶

How can it ever be a good idea to give up monetary policy in the short run? How can some economists still favour fixed exchange rates? There are three reasons:

- Flexible exchange rates are not without their own problems.
- In some cases, the costs of fixed exchange rates may not be that high.
- In some cases, the benefits of fixed exchange rates may be large.

Let us look at each of these arguments.

## The Problems of Flexible Exchange Rates

In the model we developed in Chapter 8, there was a simple relation between the interest rate and the exchange rate: The lower the interest rate, the higher is the exchange rate. This implied that a country that wanted to maintain a stable exchange rate simply had to maintain its interest rate close to the foreign interest rate. A country that wanted to achieve a given depreciation simply had to decrease its interest rate by the right amount.

◀ See Figure 8–1.

In the real world, the relation between the interest rate and the exchange rate is not so simple. Exchange rates often move even in the absence of movements in interest rates. The size of the effect of a given decrease in the interest rate on the exchange rate is often hard to predict, making it much harder for monetary policy to achieve its desired outcome. To see why, let us go back to the interest parity condition:

$$1 + i_t = \left(\frac{1}{E_t}\right)(1 + i_t^*)(E_{t+1}^e)$$

Rewrite it as:

$$E_t = \frac{1 + i_i^*}{1 + i_t} E_{t+1}^e \qquad (14.12)$$

Think of the time period as one year. The exchange rate this year depends on the domestic interest rate, the foreign interest rate, and the exchange rate expected for next year. We assumed in Chapter 8 that the expected exchange rate next year ($E_{t+1}^e$) was constant. But this was a simplification. The exchange rate expected one year hence is not constant. Using equation (14.12), but now for the next year, it is clear that the exchange rate one year hence will depend on the domestic and foreign interest rates expected for next year, on the expected exchange rate two years from now, and so on. Thus, any change in expectations of *current and future* domestic and foreign interest rates, as well as changes in the expected exchange rate in the far future, will affect the exchange rate today. This argument is further explored in Chapter 20, which looks at expectations in financial markets and focuses on exchange rate movements under flexible exchange rates. But, if the details are better left to later study, the two basic conclusions are simple:

Note the similarity with stock prices: The stock price depends on the current dividend and interest rate and on the expected stock price next year. The expected price next year depends on next year's expected dividend and interest rate, as well as on the expected stock price two years from now. And so on. This similarity is no coincidence: Exchange rates, like stock prices, depend on current and expected future conditions. Stock prices and interest rates are further explored in Chapter 20.

- The exchange rate can move for many other reasons than changes in the current domestic interest rate.
- The effect of a change in the current domestic interest rate on the exchange rate depends very much on how this change in the interest rate affects expectations of future interest rates.

In short, under flexible exchange rates, the exchange rate may move for many reasons, creating large changes in the real exchange rate and large fluctuations in output. Stabilizing the exchange rate may require large movements in the interest rate; these large interest movements may themselves lead to large fluctuations in output. Thus, controlling the economy under flexible exchange rates is much harder than we made it look in Chapter 8. Put another way, the benefits of a flexible exchange rate regime may be smaller than our previous arguments suggested.

## The Limited Costs of Fixed Exchange Rates

The costs of a fixed exchange rate regime may also be smaller than our previous arguments suggested. True, countries that operate under a fixed exchange rate regime are constrained to have the same interest rate. But how costly is that constraint? If they face roughly the same macroeconomic problems and the same shocks, they would have chosen similar policies in the first place. Forcing them to have the same monetary policy may not be much of a constraint.

This argument was explored by Robert Mundell, who looked at the conditions under which a set of countries might want to operate under fixed exchange rates or even adopt a

This is the same Mundell who put together the Mundell–Fleming model we saw in Chapter 8.

common currency. For countries to constitute an **optimal currency area**, Mundell argued, they need to satisfy one of two conditions:

- They have to experience similar shocks. We just saw the rationale for this: If they have similar shocks, then they would have chosen roughly the same policy anyway.
- Or, if they experience different shocks, they must have high factor mobility. For example, if workers are willing to move from countries doing poorly to countries doing well, factor mobility rather than macroeconomic policy can allow countries to adjust to shocks. The exchange rate is not needed.

Each province could have its own currency that freely floated against other provincial currencies. But this is not the case: Canada is a common currency area, with one currency, the Canadian dollar. ▶

Following Mundell's analysis, many economists have asked if a country or a group of countries is an optimal currency area. The 10 provinces (and three territories) of Canada are a common currency area. The first condition above is clearly not satisfied; provinces ("regions" is a better choice) do not suffer from the same shock. British Columbia has a large forestry sector, Manitoba and Saskatchewan a large grain sector, Ontario and Quebec large manufacturing sectors. The Atlantic provinces depend more heavily than other regions on forestry and fishery. Alberta is much more affected by oil prices than are other provinces. But the second condition is partly satisfied. There is considerable labour mobility among English-speaking provinces; many people from the rest of Canada have moved to Alberta and British Columbia in the past 30 years. Quebec, with language variation, is a special case. The Further Reading section in this chapter includes various discussions of whether Canada and the United States together form an optimal currency area.

## The Benefits of Fixed Exchange Rates

Finally, fixed exchange rate systems have several potential benefits:

- First, operating under fixed exchange rates simplifies things for firms. They can think about where to locate plants and how to increase sales without having to worry about potentially large fluctuations in the exchange rate. These advantages are very clear when countries decide not only to fix their bilateral exchange rates, but also to go all the way and adopt a common currency. The benefits of having a common currency for all provinces within a country for firms and consumers are obvious; think of how complicated life would be if you had to change currency every time you crossed a provincial line.

  This is true also of the major new common currency area, the euro zone. (The Focus box "The Euro: A Short History" gives you a short history of the euro and a discussion of current issues in that zone.) A report by the European Commission estimated that the adoption of the euro, which would eliminate foreign exchange transactions within the euro zone, would save 0.5% of the combined GDP of these countries. The benefits of the euro in terms of improved efficiency seemed likely to be much larger than just lower transaction costs. When prices are quoted in the same currency, it becomes much easier for buyers to compare prices, and competition among firms increases, benefiting consumers. There is some evidence that this happened in Europe. When shopping for cars, for example, European consumers look for the lowest price anywhere in the euro zone. This has already led to a decline in the price of cars in several countries.

- Second, there may be cases where a country may actually want to limit its ability to use monetary policy. We will look at this argument in more detail in Chapter 23 and in Chapter 24—where we look at monetary policy in general—but the essence of the argument is simple:

  Take a country that has had very high inflation in the recent past. This may be, for example, because it was unable to finance its budget deficit by any other means than through money creation, resulting in high money growth and high inflation. Suppose the country decides to reduce money growth and inflation. One way of convincing financial markets that it is serious about reducing money growth is to fix its exchange rate: The need to use money supply to maintain the parity then constrains the monetary authority. To the

- As the European Union celebrated its 30th birthday in 1988, a number of governments decided the time had come to plan a move to a common currency. They asked Jacques Delors, the president of the European Union, to prepare a report, which he presented in June 1989.

  The Delors report suggested moving to a European Monetary Union (EMU) in three stages: Stage I was the abolition of capital controls. Stage II was the choice of fixed parities, to be maintained except for "exceptional circumstances." Stage III was the adoption of a single currency.

- Stage I was implemented in July 1990.
- Stage II began in 1994, after the exchange rate crises of 1992–1993 had subsided. A minor but symbolic decision involved choosing the name of the new common currency. The French liked "Ecu" (European currency unit), which is also the name of an old French currency. But its partners preferred **euro**, and the name was adopted in 1995.
- In parallel, EU countries held referendums on whether they should adopt the **Maastricht treaty**. The treaty, negotiated in 1991, set three main conditions for joining the EMU: low inflation, a budget deficit below 3%, and a public debt below 60%. The Maastricht treaty was not very popular and, in many countries, the outcome of the popular vote was close. In France, the treaty passed with only 51% of the votes. In Denmark, the treaty was rejected.

- In 1996–1997, it looked as if few European countries would satisfy the Maastricht conditions. But a number of countries took drastic measures to reduce their budget deficits. When the time came to decide, in May 1998, which countries would be members of the euro area, 11 countries made the cut: Austria, Belgium, Finland, France, Germany, Italy, Ireland, Luxembourg, The Netherlands, Portugal, and Spain. The United Kingdom, Denmark, and Sweden decided to stay out, at least at the beginning. Greece did not qualify initially, and didn't join until 2001. (In 2004, it was revealed that Greece had partly "cooked the books" and understated the size of its budget deficit in order to qualify.) Since then, five more small countries, Cyprus, Malta, Slovakia, Slovenia, and Estonia, have joined.
- Stage III began in January 1999. Parities between the 11 currencies and the euro were "irrevocably" fixed. The new **European Central Bank** (ECB) based in Frankfurt became responsible for monetary policy for the euro area.

From 1999 to 2002, the euro existed as a unit of account, but euro coins and bank notes did not exist. In effect, the euro area was still functioning as an area with fixed exchange rates. The next and final step was the introduction of euro coins and bank notes in January 2002. For the first few months of 2002, national currencies and the euro then circulated side by side. Later in the year, national currencies were taken out of circulation.

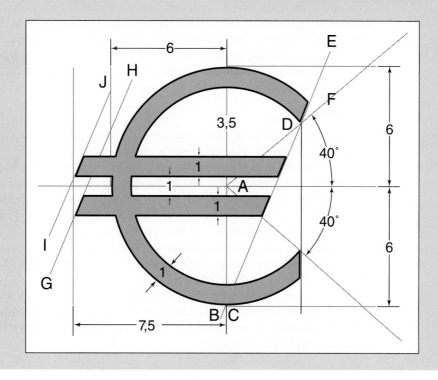

*(continued)*

The risk of adopting the euro is that one or more euro area members suffers from a large decline in demand and output but is unable to use either the interest rate or the exchange rate to increase its level of economic activity. The price level must drop to restore macroeconomic equilibrium. But, as we also saw in this chapter, this adjustment is likely to be long and painful. This is no longer a hypothetical worry.

Some euro countries, in particular Greece and Portugal, are suffering from low output and a large trade deficit. Without the option of a devaluation, achieving a real depreciation will require many years of high unemployment and downward pressure on wages and prices in Greece and Portugal relative to the rest of the euro area. And, at the time of writing, worries are extending beyond these two countries. While in better economic shape than Greece and Portugal, other countries, notably Spain and Italy, are also in a slump, suffering from low output and high unemployment. The slumps in these countries are associated with a need to raise taxes and cut government spending since they all face large budget deficits and large public debts. As members of the euro area, they also do not have the option of devaluation. In the case of Greece, there was considerabal discussion of a "Grexit"—an exit of Greece from the euro group. At the time of writing, this has not occurred and the possibility has been downplayed. The challenges faced by these countries in reducing budget deficits and maintaining aggregate demand within a currency union is the strongest challenge faced by euro area countries since the creation of the euro.

## FURTHER READING

For more on the euro, go to http://www.euro.ecb.int/. The Wikipedia page on the euro is also very good.

extent that financial markets expect the parity to be maintained, they will stop worrying about money growth being used to finance the budget deficit.

Note the qualifier *to the extent that financial markets expect the parity to be maintained*. Fixing the exchange rate is not a magic solution. The country needs to convince participants in financial markets that not only is the exchange rate fixed today, but it will also remain fixed in the future. This has two implications: (1) Fixing the exchange rate must be part of a more general macroeconomic package. (2) Fixing the exchange rate while continuing to run a large budget deficit will only convince financial markets that money growth will start again and that a devaluation is soon to come.

Making it symbolically or technically harder to change the parity may also be useful. With this aim, several countries have adopted an exchange rate regime known as a **currency board**. Under a currency board, a central bank stands ready to buy or sell foreign currency at the official exchange rate; furthermore, it cannot engage in open market operations—that is, buy or sell government bonds. Currency boards were quite popular in the 1990s. From 1991 to 2001, Argentina, for example, ran a currency board, with a highly symbolic parity of one U.S. dollar for one Argentinian peso. Giving up the currency board in 2001 and allowing the peso to float was a major defeat for government. The Argentine experience with a currency board is described in the Focus box "Argentina's Currency Board."

To summarize:

- For countries that are highly integrated, adopting fixed exchange rates can yield large benefits. If so, it makes sense for these countries to go all the way and adopt a common currency. Not only does it increase the benefits of fixed exchange rates, but it also eliminates the risk of exchange rate crises. Remember, however, if Mundell's conditions are not satisfied, the macroeconomic costs may be large. The situation in Europe, as discussed in the Focus box "The Euro: A Short History," is unclear and has become more unclear after a series of crises in Greece and Cyprus.
- For countries that have to establish or re-establish a reputation for responsible macroeconomic policy, a fixed exchange rate regime may also be useful. In this case, it may make sense to use a highly symbolic regime, such as the currency board.
- For other countries, it probably makes more sense to float. This does not imply ignoring the exchange rate altogether in the setting of monetary policy. But it means being willing to let the exchange rate move over time and to use the interest rate and the exchange rate to reduce output fluctuations.

When Carlos Menem became President of Argentina in 1989, he inherited an economic mess. Inflation was running at more than 30% a month. Output growth was negative.

Menem and his economic minister, Domingo Cavallo, quickly came to the conclusion that under these circumstances, the only way to bring money growth—and by implication, inflation—under control was to peg the peso (Argentina's currency) to the U.S. dollar, and to do this through a very hard peg. So, in 1991, Cavallo announced that Argentina would adopt a currency board. The central bank would stand ready to exchange pesos for dollars, on demand. Furthermore, it would do so at the highly symbolic rate of US$1 for 1 peso.

Both the creation of a currency board and the choice of a symbolic exchange rate had the same objective: to convince financial markets that government was serious about the peg and to make it more difficult for future governments to give up the parity and devalue. And so, by making the fixed exchange rate more credible in this way, they could decrease the risk of a foreign-exchange crisis.

For a while, the currency board appeared to work extremely well. Inflation, which had exceeded 2300% in 1990, was down to 4% by 1994! This was clearly the result of the tight constraints the currency board put on money growth. Even more impressive, this large decrease in inflation was accompanied by strong output growth. Output growth averaged 5% a year from 1991 to 1999.

Starting in 1999, however, growth turned negative, and Argentina went into a long and deep recession. Was the recession due to the currency board? Yes and no:

- Throughout the second half of the 1990s, the dollar steadily appreciated vis-à-vis other major world currencies. Because the peso was pegged to the dollar, the peso also appreciated. By the late 1990s, it was clear that the peso was overvalued, leading to a decrease in demand for goods from Argentina, a decline in output, and an increase in trade deficit.

- Was the currency board fully responsible for the recession? No—there were other causes. But the currency board made it much harder to fight it. Lower interest rates and a depreciation of the peso would have helped the economy recover; but under the currency board, this was not an option.

In 2001, the economic crisis turned into a financial and exchange rate crisis, along the lines we described in section 14-2:

- Because of the recession, the fiscal deficit had increased, leading to an increase in government debt. Worried that government might default on its debt, financial investors started asking for very high interest rates on government debt, making the fiscal deficit even larger and, by doing so, further increasing the risk of default.

- Worried that government would give up the currency board and devalue in order to fight the recession, financial investors started asking for very high interest rates in pesos, making it more costly for government to sustain the parity with the dollar, and so making it more likely that the currency board would be abandoned.

In December 2001, government defaulted on part of its debt. In early 2002, it gave up the currency board and let the peso float. The peso sharply depreciated, reaching 3.75 pesos for 1 U.S. dollar by June 2002! People and firms that, given their earlier confidence in the peg, had borrowed in dollars found themselves with a large increase in the value of their debts in pesos. Many went bankrupt. The banking system collapsed. Despite the sharp real depreciation, which should have helped exports, GDP fell by 11% in 2002, and unemployment increased to nearly 20%. In 2003, output growth turned positive and unemployment continued to decrease. It took until 2005 for GDP to reach its 1998 level again. More recently, Argentina has returned to pattern of high inflation. In fact, even knowing what the inflation rate in 2012 is in Argentina is a significant problem. Official inflation is around 10%, unofficial estimates of inflation are around 20%.

Does this mean that the currency board was a bad idea? Economists still disagree:

- Some argue that it was a good idea, but it did not go far enough. Argentina should have simply dollarized, that is, adopted the U.S. dollar as the currency, and eliminated the peso altogether. By eliminating the domestic currency, this solution would have eliminated the risk of a devaluation. The lesson, they argue, is that even a currency board does not provide a sufficiently hard peg for the exchange rate. Only dollarization will do.

- Others argue that the currency board may have been a good idea at the start but that it should not have been kept for so long. Once inflation was under control, Argentina should have moved from a currency board to a floating exchange rate regime. The problem was that Argentina kept the fixed parity with the dollar for too long, to the point where the peso was overvalued, and an exchange rate crisis was inevitable.

The debate about fixed versus flexible exchanges rates, currency boards, and common currencies continues.

(For a fascinating, fun, and strongly opinionated book about Argentina's crisis, read Paul Blustein, *And the Money Kept Rolling In (and Out): Wall Street, the IMF and the Bankrupting of Argentina* (New York: Public Affairs, 2005).

- If exchange rates are flexible, then in the medium run, a country with a higher inflation rate will experience a nominal deprecation of its currency. The real exchange rate will remain constant in the medium run to allow aggregate demand to be equal to the natural level of output.

- The higher inflation country, under flexible exchange rates, will have a higher nominal interest rate and uncovered interest parity will create an expected depreciation of the domestic currency. Expected returns on bonds denominated in the domestic currency will equal expected returns on bonds denominated in the foreign currency.

- Even under a fixed exchange rate regime, countries can adjust their *real* exchange rate in the medium run by relying on adjustments in the price level. Nevertheless, the adjustment may be long and painful. Nominal exchange rate adjustments can, in principle, allow the economy to adjust faster and reduce the pain.

- Exchange rate crises typically start when participants in financial markets believe a currency may soon be devalued. Defending the parity then requires very high interest rates, with potentially large adverse macroeconomic effects. These adverse effects may force the country to devalue, even if there were no plans for such a devaluation in the first place.

- In thinking about flexible versus fixed exchange rates, you must keep in mind four sets of arguments:

  1. Flexible exchange rates allow the central bank to use both the interest rate and the exchange rate for macroeconomic purposes. Fixed exchange rates and perfect capital mobility eliminate the scope for using either the exchange rate or the interest rate.

  2. Flexible exchange rates are often associated with large fluctuations in the exchange rate, making it difficult for the central bank to stabilize the economy.

  3. Fixed exchange rates may not be very costly if one of two conditions is satisfied: The countries that are pegging their exchange rate face largely the same shocks, or there is high labour mobility between them.

  4. Fixed exchange rates also have benefits. They reduce transaction costs and improve efficiency. These benefits are even larger if countries adopt not only fixed exchange rates, but also a common currency. Fixed exchange rates may also help governments establish or re-establish their reputation for responsible macroeconomic policy.

## KEY TERMS

- currency board, 284
- euro, 283
- European Central Bank (ECB), 283
- float, 279
- gold standard, 276
- Maastricht treaty, 283
- optimal currency area, 282
- realignments, 278

## QUESTIONS AND PROBLEMS

### 1. TRUE/FALSE/UNCERTAIN

a. Britain's return to the gold standard caused years of high unemployment.

b. If, in a country committed to a fixed exchange rate, investors suddenly fear a severe devaluation, they may well trigger an exchange rate crisis.

c. Because speculative behaviour by foreign investors can cause currency crises, small countries would be better off not allowing foreigners to hold domestic assets.

d. The countries of Southeast Asia would benefit if they formed a common currency area as they produce similar goods and are subject to largely similar shocks.

e. The large number of immigrants from Mexico to the United States every year indicates there is substantial labour mobility between the two countries, and thus they constitute an optimal currency area.

### 2. A CLOSER LOOK AT AGGREGATE DEMAND

Consider the specification of the aggregate demand relation in an open economy with fixed exchange rates given in the text:

$$Y = C(Y - T) + I(Y, i^*) + G$$
$$+ NX\left(Y, Y^*, \frac{\overline{E}P^*}{P}\right)$$

**a.** Discuss the effects on output, given the domestic price level, of an increase in the foreign price level.

**b.** Discuss the effects on output, given the domestic price level, of an increase in expected domestic inflation.

**c.** Discuss the effects on output of an increase in foreign interest rates. If the country wishes to keep its exchange rate fixed, how can it keep output constant?

## 3. EXCHANGE RATE CHANGES WITH DOMESTIC AND FOREIGN INFLATION

**a.** Use the data below in Table 1, Question 3 to calculate nominal exchange rates in period $t+1$, $t+2$, and $t+3$ that keep the real exchange rate constant.

**b.** If the foreign rate of interest is 8% each period and the expected exchange rate in period $t$ is the actual exchange rate in period $t+1$ (and similarly for periods $t+2$ and $t+3$), what is the domestic rate of interest when uncovered interest parity holds?

**c.** If you observed that during the 1970s Germany usually had a lower rate of interest than the United Kingdom, what would you expect of the exchange rate between the German mark and the British pound over this decade?

## 4. SHORT-RUN AND MEDIUM-RUN EFFECTS OF CHANGES IN GOVERNMENT SPENDING

Consider a country operating under fixed exchange rates, with aggregate demand and aggregate supply given by:

$$Y_t = Y\left(\frac{\bar{E}P^*}{P_t}, G, T\right)$$

and

$$P_t = P_{t-1}(1 + m)\, F\left(1 - \frac{Y_t}{L}, z\right)$$

Assume the economy is initially in medium-run equilibrium, with constant prices and output equal to its natural level.

**a.** Describe the short-run and the medium-run effects of an increase in government spending on output, the real exchange rate, and the interest rate.

**b.** Describe the short-run and medium-run effects of an increase in government spending on the components of spending: consumption, investment, and net exports.

**c.** Budget deficits lead to trade deficits. Discuss.

## 5. THE UNIFICATION OF GERMANY

When East Germany and West Germany were reunited in 1990, the exchange rate between the two countries was irrevocably fixed. In a symbolic gesture of equality between the two countries, it was decreed that one East German mark would be worth the same as one West German mark, even though the currency of the East was in reality worth much less.

**a.** Think of East Germany as the domestic economy. Suppose East Germany is initially in medium-run equilibrium before reunification (obviously a counterfactual assumption here, but one has to start somewhere . . .) and suppose that the exchange rate (vis-à-vis West Germany) is set much too low. Discuss the impact of that decision on equilibrium output and unemployment using *AS-AD* analysis.

**b.** What happens over time?

**c.** Suppose that prices in Western Germany are constant—there is no inflation. What has to happen to prices and wages in Eastern Germany?

### TABLE 1, QUESTION 3

| Symbol | Variable | $t$ | $t+1$ | $t+2$ | $t+3$ |
|---|---|---|---|---|---|
| $E$ | Nominal exchange rate (domestic currency per unit of foreign currency) | 1.5 | — | — | — |
| $\pi_t$ | Domestic inflation (%) | 3 | 3 | 3 | 3 |
| $\pi_t^*$ | Foreign inflation (%) | 5 | 5 | 5 | 5 |

## 6. THE PRESSURE ON CHINA TO REVALUE DURING 2005

Between 2004 and 2005, there was a tremendous pressure on China to revalue the yuan. The reasons are fairly clear. As the Chinese economy modernized and joined the world economy, it did so with a fixed exchange rate of 8.25 yuan per U.S. dollar. Over this period, China had a

very large trade surplus, particularly with the United States. The American policy response was to ask the Chinese to abandon a decade-long fixed exchange rate to the U.S. dollar.

**a.** If the yuan were to be revalued by 20%, calculate what its new value would be.

**b.** If both the price level in China and in the United States did not change when the yuan was revalued, what would be the percentage change in the real exchange rate?

**c.** Explain why, if the Chinese economy is booming and above full employment, the Chinese would favour a revaluation.

**d.** Explain how the proposed revaluation of the yuan would affect the U.S. economy already at full employment.

## FURTHER READING

The issue of whether or not Canada and the United States form an optimal currency area and thus should either share the same currency or at least have fixed exchange has been an active policy issue in Canada over the past 50 years. The debate is summarized in "The W. Irwin Gillespie Round Table on Public Policy: Canadian Exchange Rate Policy," *Canadian Public Policy* 25 (3), September 1999: pp. 307–324. A history of the early flexible exchange rate regime in Canada and of the movement to a fixed rate in 1962 is found in Paul Wonnacott's book *The Canadian Dollar, 1948–1962* (Toronto: University of Toronto Press, 1961).

# The Core: The Long Run

**The next four chapters focus on the long run. In the long run, what dominates is not fluctuations, but growth. The basic question now is, what determines growth?**

## Chapter 15

Chapter 15 looks at the facts of growth. Looking first at the OECD countries over the past 50 years, it documents the large increase in output, the convergence of output per capita across countries, and the slowdown in growth that has taken place since the mid-1970s. Taking a wider look, both across time and space, it shows that on the scale of human history, growth is a recent phenomenon and that convergence is not a worldwide phenomenon: Many countries are both poor and not growing.

## Chapter 16

Chapter 16 focuses on the role of capital accumulation in growth. It shows that capital accumulation cannot by itself sustain output growth but that it does affect the level of output. A higher saving rate typically leads to lower consumption initially but more consumption in the long run.

## Chapter 17

Chapter 17 turns to the role of technological progress. It shows how in the long run, the growth rate of an economy is determined by the rate of technological progress. It then returns to the facts of growth presented in Chapter 15 and shows how to interpret them in light of the theory we have developed.

## Chapter 18

Chapter 18 shows how growth in an open economy occurs. In an open economy, capital, labour, and technology are imported from or exported to the rest of the world.

# The Facts of Growth

## The Core: The Long Run

Our perceptions of how the economy is doing tend to be dominated by year-to-year fluctuations in activity. A recession leads to gloom, an expansion to optimism. But if we step back to get a look at activity over longer periods of time—say, over the course of many decades—we see a different picture. Fluctuations fade in importance. **Growth**—the steady increase in aggregate output over time—dominates the picture.

Figure 15–1 shows the evolution of Canadian GDP (in 2007 dollars) since 1926. The years after 1930 correspond to the large decrease in output during the Great Depression, and the years 1981–1982, 1990–1991, and 2008–2009 correspond to the three most recent recessions. Note how small these three episodes appear compared with the steady increase in output since 1926.

Our focus so far in the book has been on fluctuations. In this and the next three chapters, we focus instead on growth. Put another way, we turn from the study of the determination of output in the *short run* and *medium run*—where fluctuations dominate—to the determination of output in the *long run*—where growth dominates.

This chapter presents the facts of growth from Canada, within Canadian provinces, from the United States, and elsewhere, from the recent as well as the not so recent past, and introduces the framework economists use to think about growth. The framework is developed in the next two chapters. Chapter 16 focuses on the role of capital accumulation in growth. Chapter 17 focuses on the role of technological progress. Chapter 18 shows how we integrate the open economy into discussions of long-term growth.

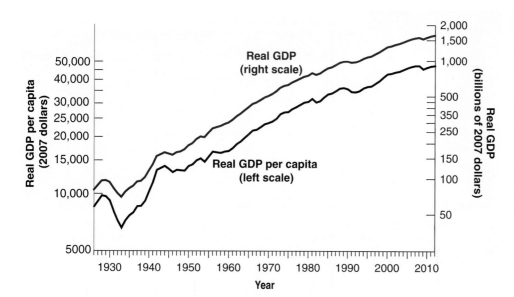

FIGURE  15–1

**Real GDP and Real GDP per Capita in Canada, 1926–2012**

Aggregate real output has increased by a factor of about 20 times in Canada since 1926. Per capita real output has increased by a factor of 5.6 times. The latter shows that the average Canadian was much better off in 2012 than in 1926.

*Source:* Real GDP using CANSIM I variable D14442 and CANSIM II variables V1992067; population using CANSIM II variable V1.

The scale used to measure GDP on the right-hand vertical axis in Figure 15–1 is called a **logarithmic scale**. It differs from the standard linear scale in the following way:

Take a variable that grows over time at a constant growth rate, say, 3% per year. Then, the larger the variable, the larger will be its increase from one year to the next. When GDP was $80 billion (in 2007 dollars) in 1926, a 3% increase meant an increase of $2.4 billion; in 2012, with GDP at $1658 billion (in 2007 dollars), a 3% increase meant an increase of $49.7 billion. If we were to plot GDP using a linear vertical scale, the increments for each year would become larger and larger over time. Using a logarithmic scale, the same proportional increase is represented by the same vertical distance on the scale. Put another way, the behaviour of a variable that grows at a constant rate is represented by a curve that becomes steeper and steeper when a linear scale is used but is represented by a straight line when a logarithmic scale is used. The slope of the line is equal to the rate of growth: If a variable grows at 3% per year, the slope of the line is 0.03.

Even when a variable has a growth rate that varies from year to year—as is the case for GDP—the slope at any point in time still gives the growth rate of the variable at that point in time. The slope of the line between two points at two different dates gives the average growth rate from the first to the second date. This is the reason for using a logarithmic scale to plot variables that grow over time: By looking at the slope, we can easily see what is happening to the growth rate.

Check that you have understood how to use a logarithmic scale. Look at Figure 15–1. In which 10-year period was output growth highest? Has average growth since 1970 been lower or higher than average growth from 1950 to 1970? What does the figure say about growth in per capita income since 2007?

# 15-1 | Growth in Rich Countries since 1950

Table 15–1 gives the evolution of **output per capita** (GDP divided by population) for Canada, France, Japan, the United Kingdom, and the United States since 1950. Output per capita is output per person. We have chosen these five countries not only because they are the world's major

| | 1950–1973 | 1974–1999 | 2000–2010 | 1950 | 2010 | Ratio of output per capita: 2010/1950 |
|---|---|---|---|---|---|---|
| Canada | 2.6 | 1.7 | 0.9 | 11141 | 37103 | 3.3 |
| France | 4.1 | 1.7 | 0.5 | 7084 | 31299 | 4.4 |
| Japan | 7.6 | 2.4 | 0.5 | 2787 | 31447 | 11.3 |
| United Kingdom | 2.4 | 2.5 | 1.2 | 8988 | 34268 | 3.8 |
| United States | 2.4 | 2.1 | 0.4 | 13069 | 41365 | 3.1 |
| Average | 3.8 | 2.1 | 0.7 | 8613 | 35096 | 5.2 |

*Source:* For these countries the data stops in 2010. Levels of per capita income are expressed in 2005 U.S. dollars at purchasing power parity exchange rates. Variable rgdpch: Alan Heston, Robert Summers and Bettina Aten, Penn World Table Version 7.1, Center for International Comparisons of Production, Income and Prices at the University of Pennsylvania, July 2012.

The Organisation for Economic Co-operation and Development (OECD) is an international organization that includes most of the world's rich economies. (See Chapter 1.)

Output: GDP
Output per capita: GDP divided by population

economic powers, but also because their experience is broadly representative of that of the advanced countries (the countries that are members of the OECD) over the last half century or so.

There are two reasons for looking here at the numbers for output *per capita* rather than the numbers for total output. The evolution of the standard of living is given by the evolution of output per capita, not total output. And, when comparing countries with different populations, output numbers must be adjusted to take into account these differences in population size. This is exactly what output per capita does.

Understanding the growth in incomes in Figure 15–1 gives practice in both thinking about growth and using the logarithmic scale. Where the slope of the line measuring total real GDP (the lower line) is steeper, its growth rate is faster. This makes perfect sense. In 1926, there were only 9.5 million Canadians; in 2012, there were 35 million Canadians. Total real output in Canada went up by a factor of about 20 times. Real output per capita went up by a factor of 5.6 times. It is important to adjust to per capita values.

Before discussing the table, we should discuss the way the output numbers are constructed. In constructing output numbers for other countries, you could use the straightforward method of taking that country's GDP expressed in that country's currency, then multiplying it by the current exchange rate to express it in terms of a common currency. But this simple computation will not do here, for two reasons.

First, exchange rates can vary a lot as we have already seen. The Canadian dollar depreciated from 1.35 Canadian dollars to 1.58 Canadian dollars per U.S. dollar, a depreciation of 17% between 1997 and 2001. It then appreciated to about one Canadian dollar per U.S. dollar in 2008, an appreciation of 36%. But the standard of living in Canada neither decreased by 17% nor increased by 36%. Most people lived in the same houses, wore similar clothes, and consumed similar food. Yet, if we compared GDP per capita using current exchange rates, we would conclude that Canadians had become 17% poorer or 36% richer in these 4-year periods. Neither is true.

The second reason goes well beyond fluctuations in exchange rates. In 2010, GDP per capita in India, using the current exchange rate, was $1300, compared with $47,300 in the United States. Surely nobody could live on $1300 a year in the United States. But people live on it—admittedly, not very well—in India, where the prices of basic goods, those goods needed for subsistence, are much lower than in the United States. The level of consumption of the average consumer in India, who consumes mostly basic goods, is not 36 times smaller than that of his or her U.S. counterpart. This pattern applies to other countries besides the United States and India: In general, the lower a country's income, the lower are the prices of food and basic services in that country.

Thus, when our focus is on comparing standards of living, either across time or across countries, we get more meaningful comparisons by correcting for the effects just discussed.

Let us consider two countries—say, the United States and Russia—but without attempting to fit the facts of these two countries very closely.

In the United States, annual consumption per capita equals $20,000. Individuals buy two goods. Every year, they buy a new car for $10,000, and spend the rest on food. The price of a yearly bundle of food is $10,000.

In Russia, annual consumption per capita equals 12,000 rubles. People keep their cars for 15 years. The price of a car is 60,000 rubles, so individuals spend, on average, 4000 rubles—60,000/15—a year on cars. They buy the same yearly bundle of food as their U.S. counterparts, at a price of 8000 rubles.

Russian and U.S. cars are of identical quality, and so are Russian and U.S. foods. (You may dispute the realism of these assumptions. Whether a car in country X is the same as a car in country Y is very much the type of problem confronting economists constructing PPP measures.) The exchange rate is such that one U.S. dollar is equal to six rubles. What is consumption per capita in Russia relative to consumption per capita in the United States?

One way to answer is by taking consumption per capita in Russia and converting it into dollars using the exchange rate. Using that method, Russian consumption per capita in dollars is US$2000 (12,000 rubles divided by the exchange rate, six rubles to the dollar), thus 10% of U.S. consumption.

Does this answer make sense? True, Russians are poorer, but food is relatively much cheaper in Russia. A U.S. consumer spending all of his $20,000 on food would buy ($20,000/$10,000) = 2 bundles of food. A Russian consumer spending all of the 12,000 rubles on food would buy (12,000 rubles/8000 rubles) = 1.5 bundles of food. In terms of food bundles, the difference between U.S. and Russian consumption per capita looks much smaller. And given that one-half of consumption in the United States and two-thirds of consumption in Russia go to spending on food, this seems like a relevant computation.

Can we improve on our initial answer? Yes. One way is to use the same set of prices for both countries and then measure the quantities of each good consumed in each country using this common set of prices. Suppose we use U.S. prices. In terms of U.S. prices, annual consumption per capita in the

United States is obviously still $20,000. What is it in Russia? Every year, the average Russian buys approximately 0.07 car (one car every 15 years) and one bundle of food. Using U.S. prices—specifically, $10,000 for a car and $10,000 for a bundle of food—gives Russian consumption per capita: [(0.07 × $10,000) + (1 × $10,000)] = ($700 + $10,000) = $10,700. This puts annual Russian consumption per capita at $10,700/$20,000 = 53.5% of annual U.S. consumption per capita, a better estimate of relative standards of living than we obtained using our first method (which gave only 10%).

This type of computation, namely, the construction of variables across countries using a common set of prices, underlies PPP estimates. Rather than using U.S. dollar prices as in our example (why use U.S. prices rather than Russian or, for that matter, French prices?), these estimates use average prices across countries; these prices are called international dollar prices. The estimates we use in Table 15–1 and elsewhere in this chapter are the result of an ambitious project known as the "Penn World Tables." Led by three economists—Irving Kravis, Robert Summers, and Alan Heston—over more than 15 years, this project has constructed PPP series not only for consumption (as we just did in our example), but also more generally for GDP and its components, going back to 1950, for most countries in the world.

In Canada, we are very concerned that an accurate comparison of GDP per capita between Canada and the United States is made. Each year, Statistics Canada cooperates with the OECD to construct a PPP estimate using the goods and services typical of North America, not those used in the Penn World Tables. These estimates are available from 1981 to the present. The International Monetary Fund and the OECD also construct PPP estimates to allow a better comparison of per capita income across countries.

**FURTHER READING**

For more on the construction of PPP numbers, read Robert Summers and Alan Heston, "The Penn World Table Mark 5: An Expanded Set of International Comparisons, 1950–1988," *Quarterly Journal of Economics*, 2, 1991: pp. 327–368.

---

This is what the numbers in Table 15–1 do. The details of construction are complicated, but the principle is simple: The numbers for GDP in Table 15–1 are constructed using a common set of prices for the goods and services produced in each economy. Such adjusted real GDP numbers, which you can think of as measures of **purchasing power** across time or across countries, are called **purchasing power parity (PPP)** numbers. Further discussion is given in the Focus box "The Construction of PPP Numbers."

The differences between PPP numbers and the numbers based on current exchange rates can be substantial. Make a comparison between India and the United States. Using PPP numbers, GDP per capita in the United States is roughly equal to 14 times GDP per capita in India. This is still a large difference, but less than the 36 times difference we derived using the current exchange rate. Or consider the ranking of rich countries by output per capita. In 2010, using current exchange rates, U.S. GDP per capita was 115% of Germany's output per capita;

◄ Bottom line: When comparing standards of living across countries, use PPP numbers.

using PPP numbers, it was 129%. Using PPP numbers, the United States and Canada still have the highest GDP per capita among the world's major countries.

We can now turn to the numbers in Table 15–1. You should draw three main conclusions from the table:

1. First and foremost is how strong growth has been in all five countries and how much the standard of living has improved since 1950. Growth from 1950 to 2010 has increased real output per capita by a factor of 3.3 in Canada, by a factor of 3.1 in the United States, by a factor of 4.4 in France, and by a factor of 11.3 in Japan.

These numbers show what is sometimes called the *force of compounding*. In a different context, you probably have heard how saving even a little while you are young will build to a large amount by the time you retire. For example, if the interest rate is 5.1% a year, an investment of $1, with the proceeds reinvested every year, leads to about $11 about 48 years later ($[\$1 + \$0.051]^{48} = \$10.9$). The same logic applies to the Japanese growth rate from 1950 to 2010. The average annual growth rate in Japan over the period was equal to 4.0%, leading to a 11-fold increase in real output per capita. Clearly, a better understanding of growth, if it leads to the design of policies that increase growth rates, can have a very large effect on the standard of living. A policy measure that increased the growth rate from, say, 2% to 3%, would lead, after 40 years, to a standard of living 100% higher than it would have been without the policy.

Needless to say, policy measures with such magic results have proven difficult ▶ to discover.

2. Growth rates have decreased since the mid-1970s and have declined even more since the turn of the century.

The first three columns of Table 15–1 show average growth rates, expressed as annual percent growth rates, for three sub-periods: 1950–1973; 1974–1999; and 2000–2010. The oil price shocks in the 1970s were widely thought to have decreased growth rates. It would appear that growth rates in all the countries except the United Kingdom fell quite substantially in the oil price shock period. In the last decade of data in Table 15–1, from 2000–2010, growth rates in all five countries dropped enormously.

The "rule of 70": If a variable ▶ grows at x% a year, then it will take approximately 70/x years for the variable to double. If x = 3.8, it will take about 18 years (70/3.8) for the variable to double. If x = 1.7, it will take about 37 years (70/1.9).

Reductions in growth rates have profound implications. At a growth rate of 3.8% per year, it takes only 18 years for the standard of living to double. At a growth rate of 2.1% per year, doubling income per capita takes 33 years. In the last decade, growth in per capita income has slowed even more dramatically. Incomes will, at the pace of growth in this decade, take much more than 70 years to double.

3. Levels of output per capita across the five countries have converged over time. Put another way, those countries that were behind have grown faster, reducing the gap between them and the United States.

In 1950, output per capita in Canada and the United States was around twice the level of output per capita in the United Kingdom and France, and more than six times that of Japan. Looking from Japan and Europe, North America was seen as the land of plenty, where everything was bigger and better. Today, these perceptions have faded, and the numbers explain why. Using PPP numbers, North American output per capita is still the highest, but in 2010, it was only about 20% above output per capita in the other four countries, a much smaller difference than in the 1950s.

This **convergence** of levels of output per capita across countries extends to the set of OECD countries. This is shown in Figure 15–2, which plots the average annual growth rate of output per capita from 1950 to 2009 against the initial level of output per capita in 1950 for the set of countries that are members of the OECD today. There is a clear negative relation between the initial level of output per capita and the growth rate since 1950: Countries that were behind in 1950 have typically grown faster. The relation is not perfect: Turkey, which had roughly the same low level of output per capita as Japan in 1950, has had a growth rate equal to only about half that of Japan. But the relation is clearly there.

The issue of convergence of output per capita has been a hot topic of macroeconomic research over the past decades. Some have pointed to a potential flaw in such graphs as

FIGURE    15–2

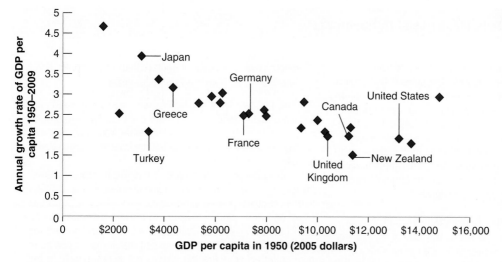

**Growth Rate of GDP per capita since 1950 versus GDP per capita in 1950; OECD Countries**

Countries with lower levels of output per capita in 1950 have typically grown faster.

*Source:* Data from Alan Heston, Robert Summers, and Bettina Aten, Penn World Table Version 7.0, Center for International Comparisons of Production, Income and Prices at the University of Pennsylvania, May 2011.

Figure 15–2. By looking at the set of countries that are members of the OECD today, what we have done, in effect, is to look at a club of economic winners: OECD membership is not officially based on economic success, but economic success is surely an important determinant of membership. But when you look at a club whose membership is based on economic success, you will find that those who came from behind had the fastest growth: This is precisely why they made it to the club. Thus, the finding of convergence could come, in part, from the way we selected the countries in the first place.

Thus, a better way of looking at convergence is to define the set of countries we look at not on the basis of where they are today—as we did in Figure 15–2 by looking at today's OECD members—but on the basis of where they were in, say, 1950. For example, we can look at all countries that had an output per capita of at least one-fourth of U.S. output per capita in 1950, then look for convergence within that group. It turns out that most of the countries in that group have, indeed, converged, and therefore convergence is not solely an OECD phenomenon. However, a few countries—Uruguay, Argentina, and Venezuela among them—have not converged. In 1950, these three countries had roughly the same output per capita as France. In 2009, they had fallen far behind; their level of output per capita stood only between one-fourth and one-half of the French level.

# 15-2 | A Broader Look across Time and Space

The three basic facts we will keep in mind and try to explain as we go along are:

- The large increase in the standard of living since 1950.
- The decrease in growth since the mid-1970s.
- The convergence of output per capita among rich countries.

Before we do so, however, it is useful to put these facts in a broader perspective. In this section, we look at the evidence on growth over a broader time span and over a larger set of countries. Then we look at how growth has varied among the provinces of Canada.

## Looking at Growth across Two Millennia

Has output per capita in the currently rich economies always grown at rates similar to the growth rates in Table 15–1? No. Estimates of growth are clearly harder to construct as we look further back in time. But there is agreement among economic historians about the main facts from the past 2000 years.

From the end of the Roman Empire to roughly 1500, there was essentially no growth of output per capita in Europe: Most workers were employed in agriculture, in which there was

Does money lead to happiness? Or, put more accurately, does higher income per capita lead to more happiness? The implicit assumption, when economists assess the performance of an economy by looking at its level of income per capita or at its growth rate, is that this is indeed the case. Early examinations of data on the relation between income and self-reported measures of happiness suggested that this assumption may not be right. They yielded what is now known as the **Easterlin paradox** (so named for Richard Easterlin, who was one of the first economists to look systematically at the evidence):

- Looking across countries, happiness in a country appeared to be higher, the higher the level of income per capita. The relation, however, appeared to hold only in relatively poor countries. Looking at rich countries, say the set of OECD countries (look at Chapter 1 for the list), there appeared to be little relation between income per capita and happiness.
- Looking over time, average happiness in rich countries did not seem to increase very much, if at all, with income. (There were no reliable data for poor countries.) In other words, in rich countries, growth did not appear to increase happiness.
- Looking across people within a given country, happiness appeared to be strongly correlated with income. Rich

people were consistently happier than poor people. This was true in both poor and rich countries.

The first two facts suggested that, once basic needs are satisfied, higher income per capita does not increase happiness. The third fact suggested that what was important was not the absolute level of income but the level of income relative to others.

If this interpretation is right, it has major implications for the way we think about the world and about economic policies. In rich countries, policies aimed at increasing income per capita might be misdirected because what matters is the distribution of income rather than its average level. Globalization and the diffusion of information, to the extent that it makes people in poor countries compare themselves not to rich people in the same country but to people in richer countries, may actually decrease rather than increase happiness. So, as you can guess, these findings have led to an intense debate and further research. As new data sets have become available better evidence has accumulated. The state of knowledge and the remaining controversies are analyzed in a recent article by Betsey Stevenson and Justin Wolfers. Their conclusions are well summarized in Figure 1 below.

The figure contains a lot of information. Let's go through it step by step.

The horizontal axis measures PPP GDP per capita for 131 countries. The scale is a logarithmic scale, so a given size

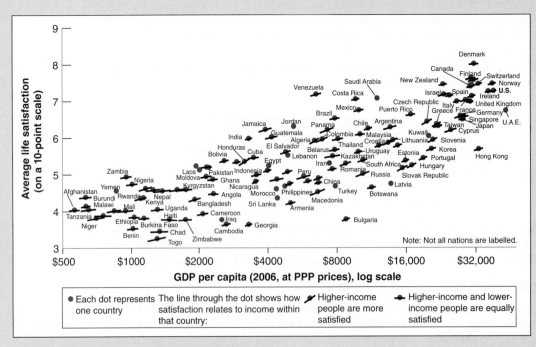

**FIGURE 1   Life Satisfaction and Income per Capita**

*Source:* Betsey Stevenson and Justin Wolfers, Wharton School at the University of Pennsylvania.

interval represents a given percentage increase in GDP. The vertical axis measures average life satisfaction in each country. The source for this variable is a 2006 Gallup World Poll survey, which asked about a thousand individuals in each country the following question:

*"Here is a ladder representing the "ladder of life." Let's suppose the top of the ladder represents the best possible life for you; and the bottom, the worst possible life for you. On which step of the ladder do you feel you personally stand at the present time?"*

The ladder went from 0 to 10. The variable measured on the vertical axis is the average of the individual answers in each country.

Focus first on the dots representing each country, ignoring for the moment the lines that cross each dot. The visual impression is clear: There is a strong relation across countries between average income and average happiness. The index is around 4 in the poorest countries, around 8 in the richest. And, more importantly in view of the early Easterlin paradox, this relation appears to hold both for poor and rich countries.

Focus now on the lines through each dot. The slope of each line reflects the estimated relation between life satisfaction and income across individuals within each country. Note first that all the lines slope upward: This confirms the third leg of the Easterlin paradox: In each country, rich people are happier than poor people. Note also that the slopes of most of these lines are roughly similar to the slope of the relation across countries. This goes against the Easterlin paradox: Individual happiness increases with income, whether this is because the country is getting richer or because the individual becomes relatively richer within the country.

Stevenson and Wolfers draw a strong conclusion from their findings: While individual happiness surely depends on much more than income, it definitely increases with income. Thus, it is not a crime for economists to focus first on levels and growth rates of GDP per capita. So, is the debate over? The answer is no. Even if we accept this interpretation of the evidence, clearly, many other aspects of the economy matter for welfare, income distribution surely being one of them. And not everybody is convinced by the evidence. In particular, the evidence on the relation between happiness and income per capita over time within a country is not as clear as the evidence across countries or across individuals presented in Figure 1. Given the importance of the question, the debate will continue for some time.

*Sources:* Betsey Stevenson and Justin Wolfers, "Economic Growth and Subjective Well–Being: Reassessing the Easterlin Paradox," Brookings Papers on Economic Activity, Vol. 2008 (Spring 2008): 1–79.
For a view closer to the Easterlin paradox and a fascinating discussion of policy implications, read Richard Layard, *Happiness: Lessons from a New Science* (London: Penguin Books, 2005).

little technological progress. Because agriculture's share of output was so large, inventions with applications outside agriculture could contribute little to overall production and output. Although there was some output growth, a roughly proportional increase in population led to roughly constant output per capita.

This period of stagnation of output per capita is often called the *Malthusian era*. Thomas Robert Malthus, an English economist, argued at the end of the eighteenth century that this proportional increase in output and population was not a coincidence. Any increase in output, he argued, would lead to a decrease in mortality, leading to an increase in population until output per capita was back to its initial level. Europe was in a Malthusian trap, unable to increase its output per capita.

Eventually, Europe was able to escape that trap. From about 1500 to 1700, growth of output per capita turned positive, but it was still small—only around 0.1% per year. It then increased to 0.2% per year from 1700 to 1820. Starting with the Industrial Revolution, growth rates increased, but from 1820 to 1950, the growth rate of output per capita in the United States was still only 1.5% per year. On the scale of human history, therefore, sustained growth of output per capita—especially the high growth rates we have seen since 1950—is definitely a recent phenomenon.

## Looking at Growth across Many Countries

We have seen how output per capita has converged among OECD countries. But what about other countries? Are the poorest countries also growing faster? Are they converging toward the United States, even if they are still far behind?

The answer is given in Figure 15–3, which plots, for 70 countries, the annual growth rate ◄ of output per capita since 1960 against output per capita in 1960.

The striking feature of Figure 15–3 is that there is no clear pattern: It is not the case that, in general, countries that were behind in 1960 have grown faster. Some have, but clearly many have not.

The numbers for 1950 are missing for too many countries to use 1950 as the initial year, as we did in Figure 15–2.

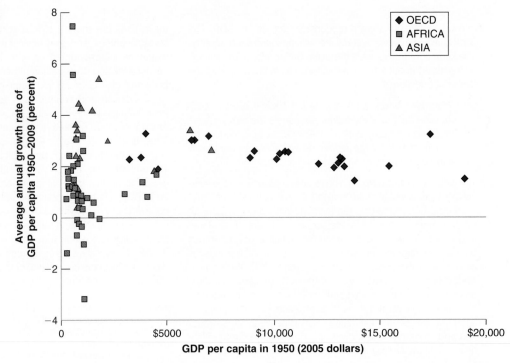

**FIGURE** 15–3

**Growth Rate of GDP per capita since 1960 versus GDP per capita in 1960 (2005 dollars); 76 Countries**

There is no clear relation between the growth rate of output per capita since 1960 and the level of output per capita in 1960.

*Source:* See Table 15–1.

The cloud of points in Figure 15–3 hides, however, a number of interesting patterns that appear when we put countries into different groups. Note that we have used different symbols in the figure: The diamonds represent OECD countries, the squares represent African countries, and the triangles represent Asian countries. Looking at patterns by groups yields three main conclusions:

1. The picture for the OECD countries (that is, for the rich countries) is much the same as in Figure 15–2, which looks at a slightly longer period of time (from 1950 onward rather than from 1960). Nearly all start at high levels of output per capita (say, at least one-third of the U.S. level in 1960), and there is clear evidence of convergence.

2. Convergence is also visible for most Asian countries: All the countries with growth rates above 4% over the period are in Asia. Japan was the first to grow and now has the highest level of output per capita in Asia. But a number of other Asian countries (represented by triangles) are trailing it closely. Starting in the 1960s, four countries—Singapore, Taiwan, Hong Kong, and South Korea, a group of countries sometimes called the **four tigers**—started catching up quickly. In 1960, their average output per capita was about 16% of the U.S. level; by 2004, it had increased to 65% of the U.S. level. More recently, the major story has been China—both because of its very high growth rates and because of its sheer size. Over the period, growth of output per capita in China has been 5.6%. But because it started very low, its output per capita is still only about one-sixth of the U.S. level. Economies with high growth rates but low output per capita are often called emerging economies.

Paradoxically, the two fastest growing countries in Figure 15–3 are Botswana and Equatorial Guinea, both in Africa. In both cases, however, high growth reflects primarily favourable natural resources—diamonds in Botswana, oil in Equatorial Guinea.

▶ 3. The picture is different, however, for African countries. Most African countries (represented by squares) were very poor in 1960, and most have not done well over the period. Many have suffered from either internal or external conflicts. Eight of them have had negative growth of output per capita—an absolute decline in their standard of living between 1960 and 2009. Growth averaged −1.0% in the Central African Republic and −0.7% in Niger. As a result, output per capita in the Central African Republic in 2009 is 60% of its level in 1960. Some hope, however, comes from more recent numbers: Growth of output per capita in sub-Saharan Africa, which averaged only 1.3% in the 1990s, was close to 5.0% in the 2000s.

Looking further back in time, a picture emerges. For much of the first millennium, and until the fifteenth century, China probably had the world's highest level of output per capita. For a couple centuries, leadership moved to the cities of northern Italy. But until the nineteenth century, differences across countries were typically much smaller than they are today. Starting in the nineteenth century, a number of countries, first in western Europe and then in North and South America, started growing faster than others. Since then, a number of other countries, most notably in Asia, have started growing fast and are converging. Many others, mainly in Africa, are not.

## Looking at Growth across Canadian Provinces

You can also ask if there is convergence across Canadian provinces (or American states). This is an important question, especially given the economic tensions within the Canadian federation between the have and have-not provinces and the complex structure of equalization payments and other federal transfers that both explicitly and implicitly create large flows of money between Canadian provinces.

Figure 15–4 shows the evidence on Canadian provinces between 1981 and 2010. Although the relationship is not perfect, there is a negative relationship. The provinces that were poorer in 1981 have grown more swiftly. The exception would appear to be Alberta, which was the richest province measured in per capita GDP in 1981. Alberta, of course, has more GDP derived from the exploitation of natural resources than do other Canadian provinces.

Our main focus in this chapter and the next is primarily on growth in rich and emerging countries. We do not take on some of the wider challenges raised by the facts we have just seen, such as why growth of output per capita started in earnest in the nineteenth century or why Africa has so far failed to achieve steady growth. Doing so would take us too far into economic history and *development economics*. But these facts put into perspective the two basic facts we discussed earlier when looking at the OECD: Neither growth nor convergence is a historical necessity.

Students who want to know more about convergence among Canadian provinces can read Serge Coulombe and Frank C. Lee, "Convergence across Canadian Provinces, 1961 to 1991," *Canadian Journal of Economics* 28 (4a), 1995: pp. 886–898.

The distinction between growth theory and development economics is fuzzy. A rough distinction: Growth theory takes many of the institutions of a country (for example, its legal system, its form of government) as given. Development economics asks what institutions are needed to sustain steady growth and how they can be put in place.

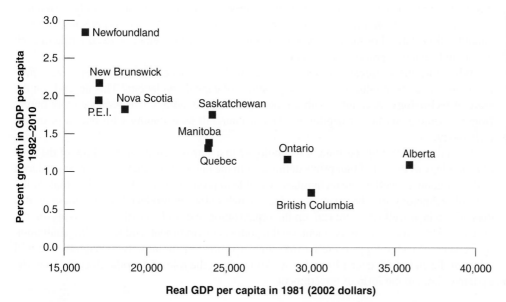

**Percent growth in GDP per capita 1982–2010**

**Real GDP per capita in 1981 (2002 dollars)**

*Source:* Real GDP in Canadian Provinces, CANSIM II Table 384002; Population in Canadian provinces, CANSIM II Table 051001.

### FIGURE 15–4

**Growth Rates of GDP per Capita 1982–2010 versus GDP per Capita in 1981 for 10 Provinces**

There is a reasonably clear relationship between the initial per capita GDP of provinces in Canada in 1981 and the growth rate of per capita real GDP between 1981 and 2010. The provinces that were richer in 1981 did grow more slowly.

# 15-3 | Thinking about Growth: A Primer

Solow's article, "A ▶
Contribution to the Theory
of Economic Growth,"
appeared in the *Quarterly
Journal of Economics*,
February 1956, pp. 65–94.
Solow received the Nobel
prize in 1987 for his work
on growth.

How do we explain the facts we saw in sections 15-1 and 15-2? What determines growth? What is the role of capital accumulation? What is the role of technological progress? To think about and answer these questions, economists use a framework developed originally by Robert Solow, from the Massachusetts Institute of Technology (MIT), and Trevor Swan from the Australian National University in the late 1950s. The framework has proven sturdy and useful, and we will use it here. This section provides an introduction. Chapters 16 and 17 provide a more detailed analysis, first of the role of capital accumulation and then of the role of technological progress in the process of growth. Chapter 18 extends the analysis to the open economy.

## The Aggregate Production Function

The starting point of any theory of growth is the **aggregate production function**, the relation between aggregate output and the inputs in production.

The aggregate production function we introduced in Chapter 9 to study the determination of output in the short and the medium run took a particularly simple form. Output was simply proportional to employment (equation (9.2)). This assumption was acceptable so long as our focus was on fluctuations in output and employment. But now that our focus shifts to growth, it will no longer do: It implies that output per worker is constant, ruling out growth (or at least growth of output per worker) altogether.

It is time to relax it. So, from now on, we will assume that aggregate output is produced using two inputs, capital and labour:

$$Y = F(K, N) \tag{15.1}$$

The aggregate production
function is:
$Y = F(K, N)$
Aggregate output (*Y*)
depends on the aggregate
capital stock (*K*) and ▶
aggregate employment (*N*).

As before, $Y$ is aggregate output; $K$ is capital—the sum of all the machines, plants, office buildings, and housing in the economy; $N$ is labour—the number of workers in the economy. The function $F$, which tells us how much output is produced for given quantities of capital and labour, is the aggregate production function. This way of thinking about aggregate production is clearly an improvement on our treatment in Chapter 9. It is still a drastic simplification of reality. Surely, machines and office buildings play very different roles in the production of aggregate output and should be treated as separate inputs. Surely, workers with Ph.D.s are different from high-school dropouts; yet, by constructing the labour input as simply the *number* of workers in the economy, we treat all workers as identical. We will relax some of these simplifications later. For the time being, equation (15.1), which emphasizes the role of both labour and capital in production, will do.

The function $F$ depends
on the state of technology.
The higher the state of
technology, the higher is
$F(K, N)$ for a given $K$ and a ▶
given $N$.

What does the aggregate production function $F$ itself depend on? In other words, how much output can be produced for given quantities of capital and labour? This depends on the **state of technology**. A country with a more advanced technology will produce more output from the same quantities of capital and labour than will an economy with only a primitive technology.

What do we mean by the state of technology? In a narrow sense, we can think of the state of technology as the list of blueprints defining both the range of products that can be produced in the economy as well as the techniques available to produce them. We can also think of the state of technology in a broader sense: How much output is produced in an economy also depends on how well firms are run, on the organization and sophistication of markets, on the system of laws and their enforcement, on the political environment, and so on. We shall think of the state of technology in the narrow sense for most of the next two chapters. We will return at the end of Chapter 17 to what we know about the role of the other factors, from the system of laws to the form of government.

Following up on growth
versus development eco-
nomics: Think of growth
theory as focusing on
the role of technology in
the narrow sense and
development economics
as focusing on the role of ▶
technology in the broader
sense.

**Returns to Scale and Returns to Factors.** Now that we have introduced the aggregate production function, what restrictions can we reasonably impose on this function?

Consider a thought experiment in which we doubled both the number of workers and the amount of capital in the economy. It is reasonable to guess that output would roughly double as well: In effect, we would have cloned the original economy, and the clone economy could produce output in the same way as the original economy. This property is called **constant returns to scale**: If the scale of operation is doubled—that is, if the quantities of capital and labour are doubled—then output will also double:

$$2Y = F(2K, 2N)$$

Or more generally, for any number $x$:

$$xY = F(xK, xN) \qquad (15.2)$$

"Constant returns to scale" refers to what happens to production when *both* capital and labour are increased. What should we assume when only *one* input—say, capital—is increased?

It is surely reasonable to assume that output will increase as well. It is also reasonable to assume that a given increase in capital will lead to smaller and smaller increases in output as the level of capital increases. Why? Think, for example, of a secretarial pool, composed of a given number of secretaries. Think of capital as computers. The introduction of just one computer will substantially increase the pool's production, as the computer assumes some of the more time-consuming tasks. As the number of computers increases and more secretaries in the pool get their own PCs, production will further increase, although by less per additional computer than was the case when the first one was introduced. Once each secretary has a PC, increasing the number of computers further is unlikely to increase production very much, if at all. Additional computers may simply remain unused and left in their shipping boxes and lead to no increase in output whatsoever.

Increases in capital lead to smaller and smaller increases in output as the level of capital increases. We will refer to this property as **decreasing returns to capital** (a property that will be familiar to those who have taken a course in microeconomics). A similar property holds for the other input, labour: Increases in labour, given capital, lead to smaller and smaller increases in output as the level of labour increases. (Return to our previous example, and think of what happens as you increase the number of secretaries for a given number of computers.) There are **decreasing returns to labour** as well.

**Output and Capital per Worker.** The aggregate production function we have written and the two properties we have just assumed imply a simple relation between output per worker and capital per worker.

To derive the relation between output per worker and capital per worker, we let $x = 1/N$ in equation (15.2) so that:

$$\frac{Y}{N} = F\left(\frac{K}{N}, 1\right) \qquad (15.3)$$

Note that $Y/N$ is output per worker, and $K/N$ is capital per worker. So, equation (15.3) says that the amount of output per worker depends on the amount of capital per worker. This relation between output per worker and capital per worker is drawn in Figure 15–5.

Output per worker ($Y/N$) is measured on the vertical axis and capital per worker ($K/N$) on the horizontal axis. The relation between the two is given by the upward-sloping curve. As capital per worker increases, so does output per worker. But because of decreasing returns to capital, increases in capital lead to smaller and smaller increases in output. At point $A$, where capital per worker is low, an increase in capital per worker equal to the distance $AB$ leads to an increase in output per worker of $A'B'$. At point $C$, where capital per worker is larger, the same increase in capital per worker, $CD$ (the distance $CD$ is equal to the distance $AB$), leads to a much smaller increase in output per worker, only $C'D'$. This is just as in our example of the secretarial pool, where additional computers led to less and less effect on total output.

You may question this assumption: Doubling the economy requires double the space. What about the fact that a country has a given size? This objection is correct in theory, but not very important in practice, except for economies where agriculture plays a central role. For example, Hong Kong, with very little land, has a thriving economy. For modern economies, constant returns to scale seems to be a good approximation to reality.

Even under constant returns to scale, there are decreasing returns to each factor, keeping the other factor constant:

- Given labour, there are decreasing returns to capital: Increases in capital lead to smaller and smaller increases in output as the level of capital increases.
- Given capital, there are decreasing returns to labour: Increases in labour lead to smaller and smaller increases in output as the level of labour increases.

Increases in capital per worker lead to smaller and smaller increases in output per worker as the level of capital per worker increases.

FIGURE 15-5

**Output and Capital per Worker**

Increases in capital per worker lead to smaller and smaller increases in output per worker.

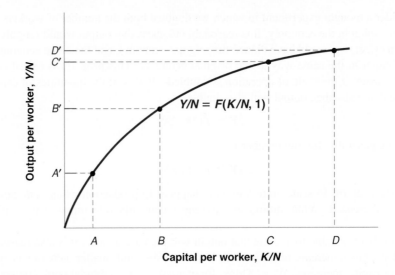

## The Sources of Growth

We are now ready to return to growth. Where does growth come from? Why does output per worker—or output per capita, if we assume the ratio of workers to the population as a whole remains roughly constant over time—go up over time? Equation (15.3) gives a simple answer:

> Increases in capital per worker: Movements along the production function. ▶

- Increases in output per worker ($Y/N$) can come from increases in capital per worker ($K/N$). This is the relation we just looked at in Figure 15–5. As ($K/N$) increases—as we move to the right on the horizontal axis—($Y/N$) increases.

> Improvements in the state of technology: Shifts of the production function. ▶

- Or they can come from improvements in the state of technology, which shift the production function, $F$, and lead to more output per worker *given* capital per worker. This is shown in Figure 15–6. An improvement in the state of technology shifts the production function from $F$ to $F'$. For a given level of capital per worker, the improvement in technology leads to an increase in output per worker. For example, for the level of capital per worker corresponding to point $A$, output per worker increases from $A'$ to $B'$.

Hence, we can think of growth as coming from **capital accumulation** and from **technological progress**—the improvement in the state of technology. We shall see, however, that these two factors play very different roles in the growth process:

- Capital accumulation by itself cannot sustain growth. A formal argument will have to wait until Chapter 16. But we can derive the basic intuition for this answer from Figure 15–6.

FIGURE 15-6

**The Effects of an Improvement in the State of Technology**

An improvement in the state of technology shifts the production function up, leading to an increase in output per worker for a given level of capital per worker.

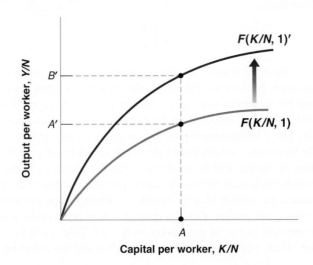

Because of decreasing returns to capital, sustaining a steady increase in output per worker would require larger and larger increases in the level of capital per worker. At some stage, society will not be willing to save and invest enough to further increase capital. At that stage, output per worker will stop growing.

Does this mean that an economy's **saving rate**—the proportion of income that is saved—is irrelevant? No. It is true that a higher saving rate cannot permanently increase the *growth rate* of output. But it can sustain a higher *level* of output. Let us state this in a slightly different way. Take two economies that differ only in their saving rate. The two economies will grow at the same rate; but at any point in time, the economy with the higher saving rate will have a higher level of output per capita than the other. How and how much the saving rate affects the level of output and whether such a country as Canada or the United States (both have a very low saving rate) should try to increase its saving rate will be one of the topics we take up in Chapter 16.

- Sustained growth requires sustained technological progress. This really follows from the first proposition: Given that the two factors that can lead to an increase in output per capita are capital accumulation and technological progress, if capital accumulation cannot sustain growth forever, then technological progress must be key—and it is. In Figure 15-6, as long as technological progress continues, output per worker grows at the same level of the capital stock per worker. We will see in Chapter 17 that the rate of growth of output per capita is eventually determined by the rate of technological progress.

This has a strong implication. In the long run, an economy that sustains a higher rate of technological progress will eventually overtake all other economies. This raises the question of what determines the rate of technological progress. What we know about the determinants of technological progress—from the role of spending on fundamental and applied research, to the role of patent laws, to the role of education and training—will be one of the topics taken up in Chapter 17.

## SUMMARY

- Over long periods of time, fluctuations in output are dwarfed by growth, the steady increase of aggregate output over time.

- Looking at growth in five rich countries (Canada, France, Japan, the United Kingdom, and the United States) since 1950, three main facts emerge:

  1. All five countries have experienced strong growth and a large increase in the standard of living. Growth from 1950 to 2010 increased real output per capita by factors of 3.3 in the United States and Canada, 4.4 in France, and 11.3 in Japan.

  2. Growth has decreased since the mid-1970s. The average growth rate of output per capita has gone from 2.6% per year in Canada from 1950 to 1973 to 1.7% from 1974 to 1999 to an even lower 0.9% from 2000 to 2010.

  3. The levels of output per capita across the five countries have converged over time. Put another way, those countries that were behind have grown faster, reducing the gap between them and the United States and Canada.

- Looking at the evidence across a broader set of countries and a longer period of time, the following facts emerge:

  1. On the scale of human history, sustained output growth is a recent phenomenon. From the end of the Roman Empire to roughly 1500 C.E., there was essentially no growth of output per capita in Europe. Even during the Industrial Revolution, growth rates were not high by current standards. The growth rate of output per capita from 1820 to 1950 in the United States was 1.5%.

  2. Convergence of levels of output per capita is not a worldwide phenomenon. Many Asian countries are rapidly catching up, but many African countries have both very low levels of output per capita and low growth rates.

- To think about growth, economists start from an aggregate production function relating aggregate output to two factors of production: capital and labour. How much output is produced given these inputs depends on the state of technology.

- Under the assumption of constant returns, the aggregate production function implies that increases in output per worker can come either from increases in capital per worker or from improvements in the state of technology.

- Capital accumulation by itself cannot permanently sustain growth of output per capita. Nevertheless, how much a country saves is very important because the saving rate determines the *level* of output per capita, if not its growth rate.

- Sustained growth of output per capita is ultimately due to technological progress. Perhaps the most important question in growth theory is what the determinants of technological progress are.

## KEY TERMS

- aggregate production function, 300
- capital accumulation, 302
- constant returns to scale, 301
- convergence, 294
- decreasing returns to capital, 301
- decreasing returns to labour, 301
- Easterlin paradox, 296
- four tigers, 298

- growth, 290
- logarithmic scale, 291
- output per capita, 291
- purchasing power, 293
- purchasing power parity (PPP), 293
- saving rate, 303
- state of technology, 300
- technological progress, 302

## QUESTIONS AND PROBLEMS

### 1. TRUE/FALSE/UNCERTAIN

**a.** Despite the Great Depression, Canadian output was higher in 1940 than in 1929.

**b.** On a log scale, a variable that increases at 5% a year will move along an upward-sloping line, with slope 0.05.

**c.** If Japan had continued to grow at the same rate during 1974 to 2010 as it had during 1950 to 1973, its output per capita in 2010 would have been more than twice U.S. output per capita.

**d.** The price of food is higher in poor countries than in rich countries.

**e.** Output per capita in most countries in the world is converging to the level of output per capita in the United States.

**f.** Capital accumulation does not affect the level of output in the long run. Only technological progress does.

**g.** The aggregate production function is a relation among output, labour, and capital.

**h.** Because eventually we will know everything, technological progress will end, and growth will eventually end as well.

### 2. THE DECREASE IN GROWTH SINCE 1973

Use Table 15–1 to answer the following questions:

**a.** Compute what output per capita would have been in 2010 for each of the five rich countries if the growth rate from 1973 to 2010 for each country had remained the same as during 1950 to 1973.

**b.** What would have been the ratio of output per capita in Japan relative to output per capita in the United States?

**c.** Did convergence continue during the growth slowdown from 1973 to 1999?

**d.** Make a graph with time on one axis and the natural logarithm of GDP per capita on the other (like the ln function on your calculator or in Excel). Plot the values of real output per capita in 1950 and 2010 from Table 15–1 for Japan and Canada. Calculate the slope of the line between 1950 and 2010 for both countries.

**e.** Compare the slope of the lines above to the growth rates of real output per capita in Canada and Japan listed in Table 15–1. What do you notice?

**f.** Use the "rule" of 70 to calculate how many times real output per capita doubled in Japan between 1950 and 1973.

### 3. PURCHASING POWER PARITY

Assume that typical consumers in Mexico and Canada buy the quantities and pay the prices indicated in the accompanying table:

| | Bread | | Car Services | |
|---|---|---|---|---|
| | Price | Quantity | Price | Quantity |
| Mexico | 1 peso | 400 | 7 pesos | 300 |
| Canada | $1 | 1000 | $2 | 2000 |

a. Compute Canadian consumption per capita in Canadian dollars.

b. Compute Mexican consumption per capita in pesos.

c. Suppose a peso is worth 20 cents ($0.20). Compute Mexican consumption per capita in dollars.

d. Using the purchasing power parity method and Canadian prices and quantities, compute Mexican consumption per capita in dollars.

e. Under each of the methods used in (c) and (d), how much lower is the standard of living in Mexico than in Canada? Does the choice of method make a difference?

### 4. THE PRODUCTION FUNCTION AND CONSTANT RETURNS TO SCALE

Consider the production function $Y = \sqrt{K}\sqrt{N}$

a. Compute output when $K = 49$ and $N = 81$.

b. If both capital and labour double, what happens to output?

c. Is this production function characterized by constant returns to scale? Explain.

d. Write this production function as a relationship between output per worker and capital per worker.

e. Let $K/N = 4$. What is $Y/N$? Now, double $K/N$ to 8. Does $Y/N$ more or less than double?

f. Does the relation between output per worker and capital per worker exhibit constant returns to scale?

g. Is your answer in (f) the same as your answer in (c)? Why, or why not?

h. Plot the relation between output per worker and capital per worker. Does it have the same general shape as the relation in Figure 15–5? Explain.

### 5. GROWTH AND TECHNOLOGICAL PROGRESS

Between 1950 and 1973, France and Japan experienced growth rates that were at least 2 percentage points higher than those in Canada or the United States. Yet, the most important technical advances of that period were made in North America. How can this be?

### 6. CONVERGENCE IN TWO SETS OF COUNTRIES

Go to the website containing the Penn World Table and collect data on real GDP per capita (chained series) from 1951 to the most recent year available for the United States, France, Belgium, Italy, Argentina, Venezuela, Chad, and Madagascar.

a. Define for each country the growth rate of real GDP per capita from 1951 to the latest available date.

b. Place all 6 countries on a graph similar to Figure 15-2. Does the graph support convergence for France, Belgium, Italy and the United States? Does the graph support convergence for Argentina, Venezuela, Chad, Madagascar and the United States?

### 7. GROWTH SUCCESSES AND FAILURES

Go to the website containing the Penn World Table and collect data on real GDP per capita (chained series) for 1970 for all available countries. Do the same for a recent year of data, say one year before the most recent year available in the Penn World Table. (If you choose the most recent year available, the Penn World Table may not have the data for some countries relevant to this question.)

a. Rank the countries according to GDP per capita in 1970. List the countries with the 10 highest levels of GDP per capita in 1970. Are there any surprises?

b. Carry out the analysis in part (a) for the most recent year for which you collected data. Has the composition of the 10 richest countries changed since 1970?

c. For each of the 10 countries for which you collected data, divide the recent level of GDP per capita by the level in 1970. Which of these countries has had the greatest proportional increase in GDP per capita since 1970?

d. Carry out the exercise in part (c) for all the countries for which you have data. Which country has had the highest proportional increase in GDP per capita since 1970? Which country had the smallest proportional increase? What fraction of countries has had negative growth since 1970?

e. Do a brief Internet search on either the country from part (c) with the greatest increase in GDP per capita or the country from part (d) with the smallest increase. Can you ascertain any reasons for the economic success, or lack of it, for this country?

Brad deLong at Berkeley maintains a very elaborate webpage http://delong.typepad.com/sdj/ (famous among economists). Some of the material relates to long-term economic growth and other material relates to current policy issues. A particularly useful introduction to economic history "Berkeley Faculty Lunch Talk: Main Themes of Twentieth Century Economic History" is found at http://econ161.berkeley.edu/TotW/berk_fac_lunch/lunch_Berkeley.html.

A broad presentation of facts about growth is given by Angus Maddison in *The World Economy. A Millenium Perspective* (Paris: OECD, 2001). The associated site www.theworldeconomy.org has a large number of facts and data on growth over the last two millenia.

Chapter 3 in *Productivity and American Leadership* by William Baumol, Sue Anne Batey Blackman, and Edward Wolff (Cambridge, MA: MIT Press, 1989) gives a vivid description of how life has been transformed by growth in the United States since the mid-1880s.

# Saving, Capital Accumulation, and Output

## The Core: The Long Run

Since 1970, the savings rate—the ratio of saving to GDP—has averaged about 20% in Canada and the United States. In China, the savings rate has averaged about 40% over the same period. In Japan, the savings rate has been 30%. Does a low savings rate in North America explain lower growth? Would increasing the savings rate in North America lead to sustained higher growth in the future?

We have already given the basic answer to these questions at the end of Chapter 15: The answer is no. Over the long run (an important qualification to which we will return), an economy's growth rate does not depend on its saving rate. Lower Canadian growth in the last 50 years is not due to the low saving rate. Nor should we expect that an increase in the saving rate would lead to sustained higher Canadian growth.

This conclusion does not imply, however, that we should not be concerned about the low Canadian saving rate. Even if the saving rate does not permanently affect the growth rate, it does affect the level of output and the standard of living. An increase in the saving rate would lead to higher growth for some time and eventually to a higher standard of living in Canada. In addition, as we will see in Chapter 18, a higher saving rate may pay off some foreign debts and allow higher future consumption.

The effects of the saving rate on capital and output are the topics of this chapter. The first two sections look at the interactions between output and capital accumulation and the effects of the saving rate. The third section plugs in numbers to give a better sense of the magnitudes involved. The fourth section extends the initial model to allow not only for physical capital, but also for human capital.

# 16-1 | Interactions between Output and Capital

To understand the determination of output in the long run, you must keep in mind two relations between output and capital.

- The amount of capital determines the amount of output being produced.
- The amount of output determines the amount of saving and investment, and thus the amount of capital being accumulated.

Together, these two relations, which are represented in Figure 16–1, determine the evolution of output and capital over time. We now look at each relation in turn.

## The Effects of Capital on Output

We started discussing the first of these two relations, the effect of capital on output, in section 15-3. There, we introduced the aggregate production function and saw that under the assumption of constant returns to scale, we can write the following relation between output and capital per worker:

$$\frac{Y}{N} = F\left(\frac{K}{N}, 1\right)$$

Output per worker ($Y/N$) is an increasing function of capital per worker ($K/N$). Under the assumption of decreasing returns to capital, the effects of an increase in capital per worker become smaller, the larger the initial ratio of capital per worker. When capital per worker is already very high, further increases have only a small effect on output.

To simplify notation, we rewrite this relation between output and capital per worker simply as:

$$\frac{Y}{N} = f\left(\frac{K}{N}\right)$$

where the function $f$ represents the same relation between output and capital per worker as the function $F$:

$$f(K/N) \equiv F(K/N, 1)$$

In this chapter, in order to focus on the role of capital accumulation, we will make two further assumptions:

- The first is that employment, $N$, is constant. Let us be more specific here. Start with the relations we saw in Chapter 2 (and again in Chapter 9) among population, the labour force, and employment. Employment is equal to the labour force times one minus the unemployment rate. The labour force, in turn, is equal to population times the participation rate. In this chapter, we will assume that population, the participation rate, and the unemployment rate are all constant. Constant population and a constant participation rate imply that the labour force is constant. A constant labour force and a constant unemployment rate imply that the level of employment, $N$, is constant. Note that under these assumptions, output per worker (output divided by employment), output per capita (output divided by population),

---

Suppose the function $F$ has the following "double square root" form:

$$F(K, N) = \sqrt{K}\sqrt{N}$$

Then,

$$Y/N = F(K/N, 1)$$
$$= \sqrt{K/N}\sqrt{N/N}$$
$$= \sqrt{K/N}$$

So, the function $f$ is simply the square root function:

$$f(K/N) = \sqrt{K/N}$$

---

Labour force ($L$) = Population × Participation rate

Employment ($N$) = Labour force ($L$) × [1 − Unemployment rate ($u$)]

If population, the participation rate, and the unemployment rate are constant, population, the labour force, and employment will be constant.

---

FIGURE 16–1

Capital, Output, and Saving/Investment

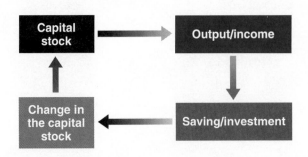

---

and output itself all move proportionately. Although we will usually refer to movements in output or capital *per worker*, to lighten the text we will sometimes just talk about movements in output or capital, leaving out the "per worker" or "per capita" qualification, where it is completely obvious.

The reason for assuming that $N$ is constant is to make it easier to focus on the role of capital accumulation in growth: If $N$ is constant, the only factor of production that changes over time is capital. The assumption is not very realistic, however, and we will relax it in the next two chapters. In Chapter 17, we will allow for steady population and employment growth. In Chapter 18, we will integrate the open economy into our analysis of the long run. But both steps are better left for later.

- The second assumption is that there is no technological progress, so the production function $f$ (or, equivalently, $F$) does not change through time. Again, the reason for making this—obviously counterfactual—assumption is to focus on the role of capital accumulation. In Chapter 17, we will introduce technological progress and see that the basic conclusions we derive here about the role of capital in growth also hold when there is technological progress. Again, this step is better left for the next chapter.

With these two assumptions, our first relation between output and capital per worker, from the production side, can be written as:

$$\frac{Y_t}{N} = f\left(\frac{K_t}{N}\right) \tag{16.1}$$

where we have introduced time indexes for output and capital (but not for labour, $N$, which we assume to be constant and so does not need a time index). In short, higher capital per worker leads to higher output per worker.

## The Effects of Output on Capital Accumulation

To derive the second relation, between output and capital accumulation, we proceed in two steps. First, we derive the relation between output and investment. Then, we derive the relation between investment and capital accumulation.

**Output and Investment.** To derive the relation between output and investment, we make three assumptions:

- We continue to assume that the economy is closed. As we saw in Chapter 3, this implies that investment is equal to saving, private and public:

$$I = S + (G - T)$$

- To focus on the behaviour of private saving, we ignore both taxes and government spending, so $G = T = 0$, and by implication public saving $(G - T) = 0$. (We will relax this assumption later when we focus on the implications of fiscal policy on growth.) Replacing in the equation above gives:

$$I = S$$

Investment is equal to private saving.
- We assume that private saving is proportional to income, so:

$$S = sY$$

The parameter $s$ is the saving rate, and has a value between 0 and 1. This assumption captures two basic facts about saving. The saving rate does not appear systematically to increase or decrease as a country becomes richer. And richer countries do not appear to have systematically higher or lower saving rates than poorer ones.

Combining the two relations above and introducing time indexes gives:

$$I_t = sY_t$$

Output per capita
$$= \frac{\text{Employment}}{\text{Population}}$$
$\times$ Output per worker

If the participation rate is 60% and the unemployment rate is 10%, then employment is 60% times $(1 - 0.10) = 54\%$ of the population. Output per capita is 54% of output per worker.

From the production side: The level of capital per worker determines the level of output per worker.

As we will see in Chapter 18, saving and investment need not be equal in an open economy. A country may save more than it invests and lend the difference to the rest of the world. In some decades Canada borrowed from the rest of the world while in other decades Canada lent to the rest of the world.

You have now seen two specifications of saving behaviour (equivalently consumption behaviour): one for the short run in Chapter 3 and one for the long run in this chapter. You may wonder how the two specifications relate to each other and whether they are consistent. The answer is yes. A full discussion is given in Chapter 21.

Recall that flows are
variables that have a time
dimension (that is, they are
defined per unit of time);
stocks are variables that
are defined at a point in
time. Output, saving, and
investment are flows.
Employment and the capital
stock are stocks.

Investment is proportional to output: the higher the level of output, the higher the level of investment.

**Investment and Capital Accumulation.** The second step relates investment, which is a flow (the new machines produced and new plants built during a given period), to capital, which is a stock (the existing machines and plants in the economy at a point in time).

Think of time as measured in years, so $t$ denotes year $t$, $t+1$ denotes year $t+1$, and so on. Think of capital as being measured at the beginning of each year, so $K_t$ refers to the capital stock at the beginning of year $t$, $K_{t+1}$ to the capital stock at the beginning of year $t+1$, and so on.

Assume that capital depreciates at rate $\delta$ (the lowercase Greek letter delta) per year: That is, from one year to the next, a proportion $\delta$ of the capital stock breaks down and becomes useless. The parameter $\delta$ is called the **depreciation rate**.

The evolution of the capital stock is then given by:

$$K_{t+1} = (1 - \delta)K_t + I_t$$

The capital stock at the beginning of year $t+1$, $K_{t+1}$, is equal to the capital stock at the beginning of year $t$, $K_t$, adjusted for depreciation—thus multiplied by $(1 - \delta)$—plus investment during year $t$, $I_t$.

We can now combine the relation between output and investment and the relation between investment and capital accumulation to obtain the second relation we need to think about growth, namely, the relation between output and capital accumulation.

Replacing investment by saving in the previous equation and dividing both sides by $N$ (the number of workers in the economy) gives:

$$\frac{K_{t+1}}{N} = (1 - \delta)\frac{K_t}{N} + s\frac{Y_t}{N}$$

In words: Capital per worker at the beginning of year $t+1$ is equal to capital per worker at the beginning of year $t$, adjusted for depreciation, plus investment per worker during year $t$. Investment per worker is, in turn, equal to the saving rate times output per worker during year $t$.

Moving $K_t/N$ to the left and reorganizing:

$$\frac{K_{t+1}}{N} - \frac{K_t}{N} = s\frac{Y_t}{N} - \delta\frac{K_t}{N} \tag{16.2}$$

In words: The change in the capital stock per worker—the term on the left—is equal to saving per worker (the first term on the right) minus depreciation per worker (the second term on the right.) This equation gives us the second relation between output and capital per worker.

# 16-2 | Implications of Alternative Saving Rates

From the saving side: The
level of output per worker
determines the change
in the level of capital per
worker over time.

We have derived two relations. From the production side, equation (16.1) shows how capital determines output. From the saving side, equation (16.2) shows how output, in turn, determines capital accumulation. Let us now put them together and see what they imply for the behaviour of output and capital over time.

## Dynamics of Capital and Output

Replacing output per worker ($Y_t/N$) in equation (16.2) by its expression in terms of capital per worker from equation (16.1) gives:

$$\frac{K_{t+1}}{N} - \frac{K_t}{N} = sf\left(\frac{K_t}{N}\right) - \delta\frac{K_t}{N} \tag{16.3}$$

$$\underset{\substack{\text{Change in capital} \\ \text{from year } t \text{ to year } t+1}}{} = \underset{\substack{\text{Investment} \\ \text{during year } t}}{} - \underset{\substack{\text{Depreciation} \\ \text{during year } t}}{}$$

This relation describes what happens to capital per worker. The change in capital per worker from this year to next year depends on the difference between two terms:

- Investment per worker, the first term on the right. The level of capital per worker this year determines output per worker this year. Given the saving rate, output per worker determines the amount of saving per worker, and thus of investment per worker this year.
- Depreciation per worker, the second term on the right. The capital stock per worker determines the amount of depreciation per worker this year.

$$K_t/N \Rightarrow Y_t/N = f(K_t/N)$$
$$f(K_t/N) \Rightarrow sf(K_t/N)$$

$$K_t/N \Rightarrow \delta K_t/N$$

If investment per worker exceeds depreciation per worker, the change in capital per worker is positive. Capital per worker increases. If investment per worker is less than depreciation per worker, the change in capital per worker is negative. Capital per worker decreases.

Given capital per worker, output per worker is then given by equation (16.1):

$$\frac{Y_t}{N} = f\left(\frac{K_t}{N}\right)$$

Equations (16.3) and (16.1) contain all the information we need to understand the dynamics of capital and output over time. The easiest way to interpret them is to use a graph. We do this in Figure 16–2, where output per worker is measured on the vertical axis, capital per worker on the horizontal axis.

In Figure 16–2, look first at the curve representing output per worker, $f(K_t/N)$, as a function of capital per worker. The relation is the same as in Figure 15–5. Output per worker increases with capital per worker, but the higher the level of capital per worker, the smaller is the effect.

Now, look at the two curves representing the two components on the right of equation (16.3).

The relation representing investment per worker, $sf(K_t/N)$, has the same shape as the production function, except that it is lower by a factor $s$. At the level of capital per worker $K_0/N$, for example, output per worker is given by the distance $AB$, and investment per worker is given by the distance $AC$, which is equal to $s$ times the distance $AB$. Thus, investment increases with capital, but by less and less as capital increases. When capital is already very high, the effect of a further increase in capital on output, and thus, in turn, on investment, is very small.

The relation representing depreciation per worker, $\delta K_t/N$ is represented by a line. Depreciation per worker increases in proportion to capital per worker, so the relation is represented

◀ To make the graph easier to read, we have assumed an unrealistically high saving rate. (Can you tell roughly what value we have assumed for $s$? What would be a plausible value for $s$?)

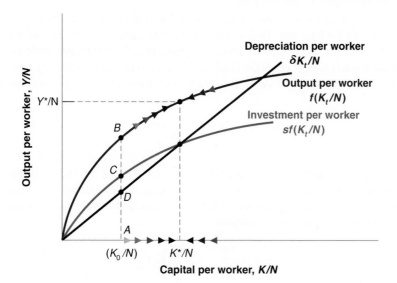

FIGURE   16–2

**Capital and Output Dynamics**

When capital and output are low, investment exceeds depreciation, and capital increases. When capital and output are high, investment is less than depreciation, and capital decreases.

by a straight line with slope equal to $\delta$. At the level of capital per worker given by $K_0/N$, depreciation is given by the distance $AD$.

The change in capital per worker is given by the difference between investment per worker and depreciation per worker. At $K_0/N$, the difference is positive and given by the distance $CD = AC - AD$. As we move to the right along the horizontal axis and look at higher and higher levels of capital per worker, investment increases by less and less, while depreciation keeps increasing in proportion to capital. For some level of capital per worker, $K^*/N$ in Figure 16–2, investment is just enough to cover depreciation, and capital per worker remains constant. To the left of $K^*/N$, investment exceeds depreciation, and capital per worker increases. This is indicated by the arrows pointing to the right along the curve representing the production function. To the right of $K^*/N$, depreciation exceeds investment, and capital per worker decreases. This is indicated by the arrows pointing to the left along the curve representing the production function.

Characterizing the evolution of capital per worker and output per worker over time is now easy. Consider an economy that starts with a low level of capital per worker—say, $K_0/N$ in Figure 16–2. Because investment exceeds depreciation, capital per worker increases. And because output moves with capital, output per worker increases as well. Capital per worker eventually reaches $K^*/N$, the level at which investment is equal to depreciation. Once the economy has reached the level of capital $K^*/N$, output and capital per worker remain constant at $Y^*/N$ and $K^*/N$, their long-run equilibrium levels.

For example, think of a country that loses part of its capital stock, perhaps as a result of a war. The mechanism we have just seen suggests that if it has suffered much larger capital losses than population losses, it will come out of the war with a low level of capital per worker, and so at a point to the left of $K^*/N$. It will then experience a large increase in both capital per worker and output per worker for some time. This appears to describe quite well what happened after World War II to countries that had proportionately larger destructions of capital than of human lives (see the Focus box "Capital Accumulation and Growth in France in the Aftermath of World War II").

If a country starts instead from a high level of capital per worker, from a point to the right of $K^*/N$, then capital per worker and output per worker will decrease: The initial level of capital per worker is too high to be sustained given the saving rate. This decrease in capital per worker will continue until the economy again reaches the point where investment is equal to depreciation, where capital per worker is equal to $K^*/N$. From then on, capital and output per worker will remain constant.

> When capital per worker is low, capital per worker and output per worker increase over time. When capital per worker is high, capital per worker and output per worker decrease over time.

> What does the model predict for postwar growth if a country suffers roughly proportional losses in population and in capital? Do you find this answer convincing? What elements may be missing from the model?

### Steady-State Capital and Output

Let us characterize the levels of output per worker and capital per worker to which the economy converges in the long run. This will be useful to us later. The state in which output per worker and capital per worker are no longer changing is called the **steady state** of the economy. Putting the left side of equation (16.3) equal to zero (in steady state, by definition, the change in capital per worker is zero), the steady-state value of capital per worker, $K^*/N$, is given by:

$$sf\left(\frac{K^*}{N}\right) = \delta\frac{K^*}{N} \tag{16.4}$$

The steady-state value of capital per worker is such that the amount of saving (the left side) is just sufficient to cover depreciation of the existing capital stock (the right side).

Given steady-state capital per worker ($K^*/N$), the steady-state value of output per worker ($Y^*/N$), is given by the production function:

$$\frac{Y^*}{N} = f\left(\frac{K^*}{N}\right) \tag{16.5}$$

When World War II ended in 1945, France had suffered some of the heaviest losses among all European countries. The losses in lives were large; more than 550,000 people had died, out of a population of 42 million. The losses in capital were much larger. Estimates are that the French capital stock in 1945 was about 30% below its prewar value. A more vivid picture of the destruction of capital is provided by the numbers in Table 1.

The model of growth we have just seen makes a clear prediction about what will happen to a country that loses a large part of its capital stock: The country will experience fast capital accumulation and output growth for some time. In terms of Figure 16–2, a country with capital per worker initially far below $K^*/N$ will grow rapidly as it converges to $K^*/N$ and output converges to $Y^*/N$.

This prediction fares well in the case of postwar France. There is plenty of anecdotal evidence that small increases in capital led to large increases in output. Minor repairs to a major bridge would lead to the reopening of a bridge. Reopening the bridge would lead, in turn, to large reductions in the travel time between two cities, leading to a large reduction in transport costs. A large reduction in transport costs would then allow a plant to receive much needed inputs and increase production and so on.

The more convincing evidence, however, comes directly from the numbers on growth of aggregate output itself. From 1946 to 1950, the annual growth rate of French real GDP was a very high 9.6% per year, leading to an increase in real GDP of about 60% over five years.

Was all the increase in French GDP due to capital accumulation? The answer is no. There were other forces in addition to the mechanism in our model. Much of the remaining capital stock in 1945 was old. Investment had been low in the 1930s (a decade dominated by the Great Depression) and nearly nonexistent during the war. Much of the postwar capital accumulation was associated with the introduction of more modern capital and the use of more modern production techniques. This was another reason for the high growth rates of the postwar period.

*Source:* Table & excerpts from Gilles Saint-Paul, "Economic Reconstruction in France, 1945–1958," in Rudiger Dornbusch, Willem Nolling, and Richard Layard, eds., *Postwar Economic Reconstruction and Lessons for the East Today* pp. 83–114. © 1993 MIT Press. Used by permission of MIT Press.

| TABLE | 1 | Proportion of the French Capital Stock Destroyed at the End of World War II | |
|---|---|---|---|
| Railways | | Rivers | |
| Tracks | 6% | Waterways | 86% |
| Stations | 38% | Canal locks | 11% |
| Engines | 21% | Barges | 80% |
| Hardware | 60% | Buildings | |
| Roads | | Dwellings | 1,229,000 |
| Cars | 31% | Industrial | 246,000 |
| Trucks | 40% | | |

*Source:* See source note for this box.

We now have the elements we need to discuss the effects of the saving rate on output per worker, both over time and in steady state.

## The Saving Rate and Output

We can now return to the question asked at the beginning of the chapter: What are the effects of the saving rate on the growth rate of output per worker? Our analysis leads to a three-part answer:

**1.** *The saving rate has no effect on the long-run growth rate of output per worker, which is equal to zero.*

This result is rather obvious: We have seen that eventually, the economy converges to a constant level of output per worker. In other words, in the long run, the growth rate of the economy is equal to zero, whatever the value of the saving rate.

There is, however, a way of thinking about this result that will be useful when we introduce technological progress in Chapter 17. Think of what would be needed to sustain a constant positive growth rate of output per worker in the long run. Capital per worker would

Some economists argue that the relatively high growth rate achieved by the Soviet Union from 1950 to 1990 was the result of such a steady increase in the saving rate over time and so could not be sustained forever. Paul Krugman has used the term "Stalinist growth" to denote this type of growth—growth resulting from a higher and higher saving rate over time.

have to increase. And because of decreasing returns to capital, it would have to increase faster than output per worker. This implies that each year the economy would have to save a larger and larger fraction of output and put it toward capital accumulation. At some point, the fraction of output that it would need to save would be greater than one: This is clearly not possible. This is why it is impossible to sustain a constant positive growth rate forever. In the long run, capital per worker must be constant and so must be output per worker.

2. Nonetheless, *the saving rate determines the level of output per worker in the long run.* Other things being equal, countries with a higher saving rate will achieve higher output per worker in the long run.

Figure 16–3 illustrates this point. Consider two countries with the same production function, the same level of employment, and the same depreciation rate, but different saving rates, say, $s_0$ and $s_1 > s_0$. Figure 16–3 draws their common production function, $f(K_t/N)$, and the functions giving saving/investment as a function of capital for each of the two countries, $s_0 f(K_t/N)$ and $s_1 f(K_t/N)$. In the long run, the country with saving rate $s_0$ will reach the level of capital per worker $K_0/N$ and output $Y_0/N$. The country with saving rate $s_1$ will reach the higher levels $K_1/N$ and $Y_1/N$.

3. *An increase in the saving rate will lead to higher growth of output per worker for some time, but not forever.*

This conclusion follows from the two propositions we just discussed. From the first, we know that an increase in the saving rate does not affect the long-run *growth rate of output per worker*, which remains equal to zero. From the second, we know that an increase in the saving rate leads to an increase in the long-run *level of output per worker*. It follows that as output per worker increases to its new higher level in response to the increase in the saving rate, the economy will go through a period of positive growth. This period of growth will come to an end when the economy reaches its new steady state.

We can use Figure 16–3 again to illustrate this point. Consider a country that has an initial saving rate of $s_0$. Assume that capital per worker is initially equal to $K_0/N$, with associated output per worker $Y_0/N$. Now, consider the effects of an increase in the saving rate from $s_0$ to $s_1$. (You can think of this increase as coming from tax changes that make it more attractive to save or from reductions in the budget deficit; the origin of the increase in the saving rate does not matter here.) The function giving saving/investment per worker as a function of capital per worker shifts upward from $s_0 f(K_t/N)$ to $s_1 f(K_t/N)$.

**FIGURE 16–3**

**The Effects of Different Saving Rates**

A country with a higher saving rate achieves a higher level of output in steady state.

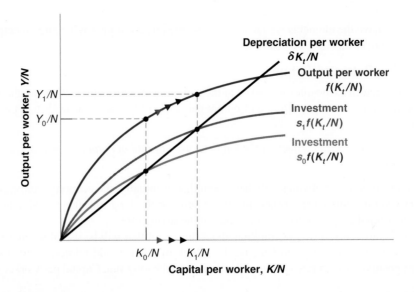

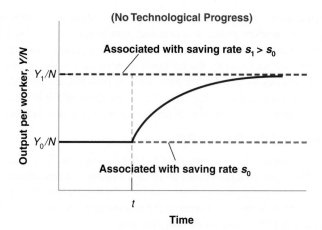

FIGURE  16–4

**The Effects of an Increase in the Saving Rate on Output per Worker**

An increase in the saving rate leads to a period of positive growth until output reaches its new higher steady-state level.

At the initial level of capital per worker, $K_0/N$, investment now exceeds depreciation, so capital per worker increases. As capital per worker increases, so does output per worker, and the economy goes through a period of positive growth. When capital eventually reaches $K_1/N$, investment is again equal to depreciation and growth ends. The economy remains from then on at $K_1/N$, with associated output per worker $Y_1/N$. The movement of output per worker is plotted against time in Figure 16–4. Output per worker is initially constant at level $Y_0/N$. After the increase in the saving rate at, say, time $t$, output per worker increases for some time until it reaches the higher level $Y_1/N$ and the growth rate returns to zero.

We have derived these three results under the assumption of no technological progress and thus no growth of output in the long run. But, as we will see in Chapter 17, the three results extend directly to an economy in which there is technological progress. Let us briefly indicate how.

An economy where there is technological progress has a positive growth rate of output per worker even in the long run. This growth rate is independent of the saving rate—the extension of the first result just discussed. The saving rate affects the level of output per worker, however— the extension of the second result. And an increase in the saving rate leads to growth greater than the steady-state growth rate for some time until the economy reaches its new higher path—the extension of our third result.

These three results are illustrated in Figure 16–5, which extends Figure 16–4 by plotting the effect of an increase in the saving rate in an economy with positive technological

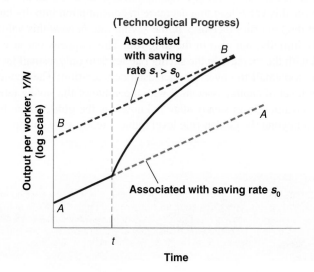

FIGURE  16–5

**The Effects of an Increase in the Saving Rate on Output per Worker in an Economy with Technological Progress**

An increase in the saving rate leads to a period of higher growth until output reaches a new, higher path.

See discussion of logarithmic scales below Figure 15–1 (p. 291).

progress. The figure uses a logarithmic scale to measure output per worker so that an economy where output per worker grows at a constant rate is represented by a line with slope equal to that growth rate. At the initial saving rate, $s_0$, the economy moves along $AA$. If, at time $t$, the saving rate increases to $s_1$, the economy experiences higher growth for some time until, eventually, it reaches its new higher path, $BB$. On path $BB$, the growth rate is again the same as before the increase in the saving rate (that is, the slope of $BB$ is the same as the slope of $AA$). But the level of output per worker is permanently higher than before.

## The Saving Rate and the Golden Rule

Governments can use various instruments to affect the saving rate. They can run budget deficits or surpluses. They can give tax breaks to saving, making it more attractive for people to save. What saving rate should governments aim for? To think about this question, we must shift our focus from the behaviour of *output* to the behaviour of *consumption*. What matters to people is not output per se but how much they consume.

It is clear that an increase in saving must come initially at the expense of lower consumption. (Except when we think it helpful, we will drop the "per worker" in this subsection and refer just to consumption rather than consumption per worker, capital rather than capital per worker, and so on.) A change in the saving rate this year has no effect on capital this year, and thus no effect on output and income *this year*. Therefore, an increase in saving comes initially with an equal decrease in consumption.[1]

Given the definition of $K_t$ as the capital stock at the beginning of year $t$, investment this year does not affect the capital stock this year: $I_t$ affects $K_{t+1}$, not $K_t$.

Does an increase in saving lead to an increase in consumption in the long run? Not necessarily. Consumption may decrease not only initially, but also in the long run. You may find this surprising. After all, we know from Figure 16–3 that an increase in the saving rate always leads to an increase in the level of *output* per worker. But output is not the same as consumption. To see why not, consider what happens for two extreme values of the saving rate:

- An economy in which the saving rate is (and has always been) zero is an economy in which capital is equal to zero. In this case, output is also equal to zero, and so is consumption. A saving rate equal to zero implies zero consumption in the long run.

- Now, consider the opposite extreme: an economy in which the saving rate is equal to 1. People save all their income. The level of capital, and thus output, will be very high. But because people save all their income, consumption is equal to zero. What happens is that the economy is carrying an excessive amount of capital: Simply maintaining that level requires that all output be devoted to replacing depreciation! A saving rate equal to 1 also implies zero consumption in the long run.

These two extreme cases suggest that there must be some value of the saving rate between 0 and 1 at which the steady-state level of consumption reaches a maximum value. Increases in the saving rate *below* this value lead to a decrease in consumption initially but to an increase in consumption in the long run. Increases in the saving rate *beyond* this value decrease consumption not only initially, but also in the long run. This happens because the increase in capital associated with the increase in the saving rate leads to only a small increase in output, an increase that is too small to cover the increased depreciation: The economy carries too much capital. The level of capital associated with the value of the saving rate that yields the highest level of consumption in steady state is known as the **golden-rule level of capital**. Increases in capital beyond the golden-rule level reduce steady-state consumption.

[1]**DIGGING DEEPER.** Because we assume that employment is constant, we are ignoring the short-run effect of an increase in the saving rate on output we focused on in Chapter 3. In the short run, not only does an increase in the saving rate reduce consumption given income, but it may also create a recession and decrease income further. We will return to a discussion of short- and long-run effects of changes in saving at various points in the book. See, for example, Chapter 25.

FIGURE  16-6

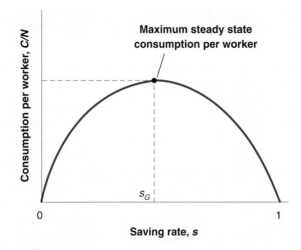

Maximum steady state
consumption per worker

**The Effects of the Saving
Rate on Consumption per
Worker in Steady State**

An increase in the saving
rate leads to an increase,
then to a decrease in consumption per worker in steady
state.

This argument is illustrated in Figure 16–6, which plots consumption per worker in steady state against alternative values of the saving rate. A saving rate equal to zero implies a capital stock per worker equal to zero, a level of output per worker equal to zero and, by implication, a level of consumption per worker equal to zero. For $s$ between 0 and $s_G$, ($G$ for golden rule) higher values of the saving rate imply higher values for capital per worker, output per worker, and consumption per worker. For $s$ larger than $s_G$, increases in the saving rate still lead to higher values of capital per worker and output per worker; but they lead to lower values of consumption per worker: This is because the increase in output is more than offset by the increase in depreciation due to the larger capital stock. For $s = 1$, consumption per worker is equal to zero. Capital per worker and output per worker are high, but all of output is used just to replace depreciation, leaving nothing for consumption.

If an economy already has so much capital that it is operating beyond the golden rule, then increasing saving further will decrease consumption not only now, but also later. Is this a relevant worry? Do some countries actually have too much capital? The empirical evidence indicates that most OECD countries are actually far below their golden-rule level of capital. If they were to increase the saving rate, it would lead to higher consumption in the future.

This conclusion implies that in practice, governments face a trade-off: An increase in the saving rate implies lower consumption initially but higher consumption later. What should governments do? How close to the golden rule should they try to get? That depends on how much weight they put on the welfare of current generations—who are more likely to lose from policies aimed at increasing the saving rate—versus the welfare of future generations—who are more likely to gain. However, future generations do not vote now. This implies that governments are unlikely to ask current generations for large sacrifices, which, in turn, means that capital is likely to stay far below its golden-rule level. These intergenerational issues are very much in evidence in the current debate on the age of retirement and receipt of age-related payments. This is explored in the Focus box "Old Age Pensions and Capital Accumulation in Canada."

# 16-3 | Getting a Sense of Magnitudes

How large is the effect of a change in the saving rate on output in the long run? For how long and by how much would an increase in the saving rate affect growth? What does the golden-rule level of capital look like? To get a better sense of the answers to these questions, let us now make more specific assumptions, plug in some numbers, and see what comes out.

Assume the production function is:

$$Y = \sqrt{K}\sqrt{N} \qquad (16.6)$$

There are three federal government programs that make significant payments to the elderly in Canada: **Old Age Security (OAS)**; the **Guaranteed Income Supplement (GIS)**; and the **Canada Pension Plan (CPP)**. OAS is a payment to all persons over a certain age, currently age 65. The GIS is a payment to very poor Canadians over 65 who, for whatever reason, have no other sources of retirement income. The Canada Pension Plan acts a bit like a regular pension plan—there are payments into the plan and the retiree collects benefits based on the payments. Residents of Quebec participate in the **Quebec Pension Plan (QPP)** which is similar to the CPP. In 2012, there were almost 5.3 million Canadians over 65 receiving such payments (15.1% of 34.8 million Canadians were over 65 in 2012). This number and percentage is forecast to increase rapidly over the next 30 years. Age-related payments are a very large proportion of the federal government's outlays.

Age-related government programming faces two critical decisions. What is the usual age when a person receives income from these programs? How are these programs funded?

In their Budget on March 29, 2012, the Harper government announced very substantial changes to the OAS and GIS system. The age of receipt of income from all these programs had been 65 since they started. As of April 2023, the age at which a person receives OAS or GIS will gradually rise from 65 to 67. The change will be fully implemented between 2023 and 2029. If you are born before March 31, 1958; you are not affected by these changes. All persons born after that date will receive benefits over a shorter period of their life. If you are born after February 1, 1962 (most of the readers of this book), then you will not receive your OAS until age 67. The Budget indicated that after discussions with the provinces, payment related to the Canada and Quebec Pension Plans would also start later in life, presumably at age 67, although as of writing, no specific details have been announced.

Changing the age of receipt of old-age payment is an important policy change. Canadians will receive taxpayer funded benefits for a shorter period of their life. How will this affect the savings rate? The answer (partly using analysis from Chapter 21) is: We simply do not know! Consider two extreme possibilities. Suppose Canadians continue to plan to retire at 65 but now have no OAS payments from age 65 to 67. To maintain the same level of retirement consumption when they are 66 and 67, they would have to save more when they are working. Savings rates must rise. This would generate a burst of growth starting now. It is also possible that Canadians will now decide to work until they turn 67. Then they have two fewer years of retirement consumption to save for and two additional years of work in which to save. The savings rate might fall and thus reduce growth. The age at which a Canadian receives OAS is a critical component of savings and retirement planning for Canadians. How the policy changes of 2012 will affect the national savings rate remains to be seen.

An equally important policy decision in a government-sponsored retirement system is the method of funding retirement income. Here the CPP/QPP and OAS/GIS models are completely different.

- The OAS/GIS systems taxes workers and distributes the tax contributions as benefits to retirees. Such a system is called a **pay-as-you-go** system: The system pays benefits out "as it goes," that is, as it collects them in contributions.
- The CPP/QPP systems tax workers, invest the contributions in financial assets, and pay back the principal plus the interest to workers when they retire. Such a system is called funded: At any time, the system has funds equal to the accumulated contributions of workers, and from which it will be able to pay out benefits when those workers retire. If the system if **fully funded**, then there are enough assets to pay all of the current and future benefits.

From the point of view of retirees, the two systems feel similar, but they are not identical. What the retirees receive in a pay-as-you-go system depends on demographics—the ratio of retirees to workers—and on the evolution of the tax rate set by the system; what they receive in a fully funded system depends on both the contribution rate and the rate of return on the financial assets held by the fund. But, in both cases, they pay contributions when they are employed and receive benefits later. In both cases, the contributions are mandatory.

From the point of view of the economy, the two systems are very different, however: In a pay-as-you-go system, the contributions are redistributed, not invested; in a fully funded system, they are invested, leading to a higher capital stock. So, a fully funded social security system leads to a higher capital stock.

The CPP and QPP were pay-as-you go plans when they started. For the first couple of decades of the CPP/QPP system, retirees received benefits without having contributed for very long. This gift to the initial retirees was widely perceived as fair: These were the generations that had suffered during the Great Depression and World War II. It also was not very costly: The number of eligible retirees was small at the beginning, so the contribution tax rate required to finance CPP pay-as-you-go benefits was low.

It is actually quite difficult to know if the CPP and its Quebec counterpart are now fully funded. That is certainly the objective of recent changes to these plans. The CPP and the QPP came into trouble in the 1990s because of demographic changes. Life expectancy and the average length of retirement have steadily increased. The large baby-boom generation is approaching retirement. As a result, the ratio of workers to retirees has steadily decreased and will continue to decrease over the next 50 years. By 2026, Statistics Canada projects that 21% of Canada's population will be over 65 years of age. If CPP (and QPP) contributions had not been increased, there would have been a growing imbalance between benefits and contributions. However, contribution rates were increased over the 1990s. Contributions are higher than benefits for the time being. In a change in policy, some of the excess of contributions over benefits is

*(continued)*

being invested in private sector financial instruments. This part is called the Canada Pension Plan Investment Board, and as of 2012, it held about $161 billion in various stocks, bonds, and real estate. The $161 billion in assets as well as the higher contribution rate is projected to maintain a balance between CPP benefits and CPP contributions for the next 75 years. The CPP is now fairly close to a fully-funded system. The OAS/GIS remains a completely pay-as-you-go system.

Is a fully-funded government system the best option for retirement savings? This is a controversial issue. One key fact is that all Canadians are required to participate in the Canada or Quebec Pension plans. This would raise savings rates assuming at least some of those Canadians would not choose to save in any other form. If the CPP and QPP make good investments, there is more capital and, in steady state, a higher level of output per person. But suppose that all of the Canadians would privately choose to save exactly what they are required to save in CPP and QPP and put those savings in private pension plans. If those private plans made the same investment decisions as the CPP and QPP, economic growth would be exactly the same. Most economists see some role for a mandatory public plan so that the Canadians who would not choose to save for their retirement do not end life in poverty. Another way to say this—most economists are willing to conclude a mandatory fully-funded public pension plan raises the national savings rate.

**FURTHER READINGS**

Two books that review recent pension policy in Canada are *The Future of Pension Policy: Individual Responsibility and State Support*, by William B.P. Robson, Publications of the British-North American Committee 41 (London: British North American Committee 1997) and *When We're 65: Reforming Canada's Retirement Income System*, by John P. Burbidge et al. (Toronto: C.D. Howe Institute, 1996). The website of the C.D. Howe Institute, www.cdhowe.org, contains a variety of research on the pension system in Canada.

Output equals the product of the square root of capital and the square root of labour. Note that this production function exhibits both constant returns to scale, and decreasing returns to either capital or labour.[2]

Dividing both sides by $N$ (because we are interested in output per worker) gives:

$$\frac{Y}{N} = \frac{\sqrt{K}\,\sqrt{N}}{N} = \frac{\sqrt{K}}{\sqrt{N}} = \sqrt{\frac{K}{N}}$$

The second equality follows from the following steps:
$$\sqrt{N}/N = \sqrt{N}/(\sqrt{N}\,\sqrt{N})$$
$$= 1/\sqrt{N}$$

Output per worker equals the square root of capital per worker. Put another way, the production function $f$ relating output per worker to capital per worker is given by:

$$f(K_t/N) = \sqrt{K_t/N}.$$

Now, using equation (16.3), which is repeated here for convenience:

$$\frac{K_{t+1}}{N} - \frac{K_t}{N} = sf\left(\frac{K_t}{N}\right) - \delta\frac{K_t}{N}$$

Replace $f(K_t/N)$ by $\sqrt{K_t/N}$:

$$\frac{K_{t+1}}{N} - \frac{K_t}{N} = s\sqrt{\frac{K_t}{N}} - \delta\frac{K_t}{N} \tag{16.7}$$

This equation describes the evolution of capital per worker over time. Let us now look at what it implies.

[2]**DIGGING DEEPER.** A more general specification for the production function would be:

$$Y = K^\alpha N^{1-\alpha}$$

where $\alpha$ is a number between 0 and 1.

The production function we use in the text assumes $\alpha = 0.5$, giving equal weights to capital and labour. (Taking the square root of a variable is the same as raising it to the power 0.5.) A more realistic production function would give more weight to labour and less to capital, for example $\alpha = 0.3$.

There are two reasons we use $\alpha = 0.5$: The first is that it makes the algebra much simpler. The second is based on a broader interpretation of capital than just physical capital. As we will see in section 16-4, we can think of the accumulation of skills, say, through education or on-the-job training, as a form of capital accumulation as well. Under this broader view of capital, a coefficient of 0.5 for capital is roughly appropriate.

## The Effects of the Saving Rate on Steady-State Output

How large is the effect of an increase in the saving rate on the steady-state level of output per worker?

Start with equation (16.7). In steady state, the amount of capital per worker is constant, so the left side of the equation equals zero.

This implies:

$$s\sqrt{\frac{K}{N}} = \delta\frac{K}{N}$$

(We have dropped time indexes, which are no longer needed because in steady state $K/N$ is constant.) Square both sides:

$$s^2\frac{K}{N} = \delta^2\left(\frac{K}{N}\right)^2$$

Divide both sides by $(K/N)$, and reorganize:

$$\frac{K}{N} = \left(\frac{s}{\delta}\right)^2 \tag{16.8}$$

This gives us an equation for steady-state capital per worker. From equations (16.6) and (16.8), steady-state output per worker is given by:

$$\frac{Y}{N} = \sqrt{\frac{K}{N}} = \sqrt{\left(\frac{s}{\delta}\right)^2} = \frac{s}{\delta} \tag{16.9}$$

Output per worker is equal to the ratio of the saving rate to the depreciation rate; capital per worker is equal to the square of that ratio. A higher saving rate and a lower depreciation rate both lead to higher capital per worker and output per worker in the long run.

Suppose the depreciation rate is 10% per year, and take the saving rate to be 10% as well. Then, using equations (16.8) and (16.9), we see that capital per worker and output per worker in steady state are both equal to 1. Now, suppose that the saving rate doubles, from 10% to 20%. It follows from equation (16.8) that in the new steady state, capital per worker increases from 1 to 4. And from equation (16.9), output per worker doubles, from 1 to 2. Thus, doubling the saving rate leads, in the long run, to doubling output: This is a large effect.

## The Dynamic Effects of an Increase in the Saving Rate

After an increase in the saving rate, how long does it take for the economy to reach the new higher level of output? Put another way, by how much and for how long does an increase in the saving rate affect the growth rate?

To answer these questions, we must use equation (16.7) and solve it for capital in year 0, year 1, and so on.

Suppose that the saving rate, which had always been equal to 0.1, increases in year 0 from 0.1 to 0.2 and remains at this higher value forever after. In year 0, nothing happens to the capital stock (recall that it takes one year for higher saving and higher investment to show up in higher capital). So, capital per worker remains equal to the steady-state value associated with a saving rate of 0.1. From equation (16.8), $K_0/N = (0.1/0.1)^2 = 1^2 = 1$.

In year 1, equation (16.7) gives:

$$\frac{K_1}{N} - \frac{K_0}{N} = s\sqrt{\frac{K_0}{N}} - \delta\frac{K_0}{N}$$

With a depreciation rate equal to 0.1 and a saving rate now equal to 0.2, this equation implies that $K_1/N - 1 = [(0.2)(\sqrt{1})] - [(0.1)1]$ so that $K_1/N = 1.1$.

In the same way, we can solve for $K_2/N$, and so on. Once we have the values of capital per worker in year 0, year 1, and so on, we can then use equation (16.6) to solve for output per

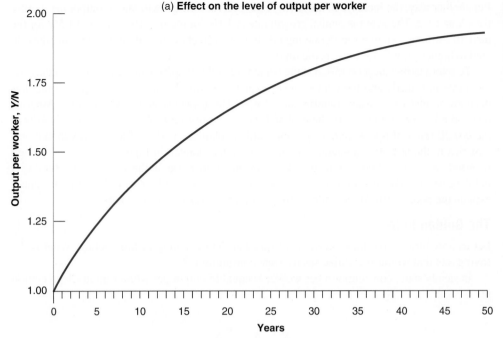

(a) **Effect on the level of output per worker**

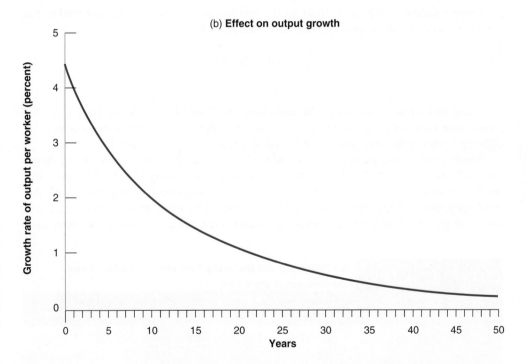

(b) **Effect on output growth**

**FIGURE 16–7**

**Dynamic Effects of an Increase in the Saving Rate from 10% to 20% on the Level and the Growth Rate of Output per Worker**

It takes a long time for output to adjust to its new higher level after an increase in the saving rate. Put another way, an increase in the saving rate leads to a long period of higher growth.

worker in year 0, year 1, and so on. The results of this computation are presented in Figure 16–7(a), which plots the *level* of output per worker against time. ($Y/N$) increases over time from its initial value of 1 in year 0 to its steady-state value of 2 in the long run. Figure 16–7(b) gives the same information in a different way, plotting instead the *growth rate* of output per worker against time. Growth of output per worker is highest at the beginning and then decreases over time. As the economy reaches its new steady state, growth of output per worker returns to zero.

Figure 16–7 clearly shows that the adjustment to the new, higher, long-run equilibrium takes a long time. It is only 40% complete after 10 years and is 63% complete after 20 years.

Put another way, the increase in the saving rate increases the growth rate of output per worker for a long time. The average annual growth rate is 3.1% for the first 10 years, and 1.5% for the next 10. Although changes in the saving rate have no effect on growth in the long run, they do lead to higher growth for quite some time.

To return to the question raised at the beginning of the chapter, can the lower saving/investment rate in Canada and the United States explain why the North American growth rate has been lower relative to Asian countries since 1970? The answer would be yes, if North America had had a higher saving rate in the past and *if this saving rate had decreased substantially in the last 50 years*. If this were the case, this could explain the period of lower growth in North America in the last 50 years along the lines of the mechanism in Figure 16–7 (with the sign reversed, as we would be looking at a decrease, not an increase, in the saving rate). But this is not the case: The North American saving rate has been low for a long time. Low saving cannot explain the poor North American growth performance over the last 40 years.

## The Golden Rule

Let us now turn to the third question we asked at the beginning of this section. What is the saving rate that would maximize steady-state consumption?

In steady state, consumption per worker is equal to output per worker minus depreciation per worker:

$$\frac{C}{N} = \frac{Y}{N} - \delta \frac{K}{N}$$

Using equations (16.8) and (16.9) for the steady-state values of output per worker and capital per worker, consumption per worker is thus given by:

$$\frac{C}{N} = s/\delta - \delta(s/\delta)^2$$
$$= s(1 - s)/\delta$$

Using this equation together with equations (16.8) and (16.9), Table 16–1 gives the steady-state values of capital per worker, output per worker, and consumption per worker for different values of the saving rate (and for a depreciation rate equal to 10%).

Steady-state consumption is largest when $s(1 - s)$ is largest; this occurs when $s$ equals one-half: The golden-rule level of capital is associated with a saving rate of 50%. Below that level, increases in the saving rate lead to an increase in long-run consumption. Above that level, they lead to a decrease. Few economies in the world today have saving rates above 40%, and (as we saw at the beginning of the chapter) the Canadian saving rate is about 20%.

Check your understanding of the issues: Using the equations in this section, argue the pros and cons of policy measures aimed at increasing the Canadian saving rate from its current value of about 20% to, say, 30%.

| TABLE 16–1 | The Saving Rate and the Steady-State Levels of Capital, Output, and Consumption per Worker | | |
|---|---|---|---|
| Saving Rate, *s* | Capital per Worker, *K/N* | Output per Worker, *Y/N* | Consumption per Worker, *C/N* |
| 0.0 | 0.0 | 0.0 | 0.0 |
| 0.1 | 1.0 | 1.0 | 0.9 |
| 0.2 | 4.0 | 2.0 | 1.6 |
| 0.3 | 9.0 | 3.0 | 2.1 |
| 0.4 | 16.0 | 4.0 | 2.4 |
| 0.5 | 25.0 | 5.0 | 2.5 |
| 0.6 | 36.0 | 6.0 | 2.4 |
| ... | ... | ... | ... |
| 1.0 | 100.0 | 10.0 | 0.0 |

As rough as it is, our computation suggests that in most economies, an increase in the saving rate would increase both output and consumption levels in the long run.

# 16-4 | Physical versus Human Capital

We have concentrated so far on physical capital—on machines, plants, office buildings, and so on. But economies have another type of capital: the set of skills of the workers in the economy, what economists call **human capital**. An economy with many highly skilled workers is likely to be much more productive than an economy in which most workers cannot read or write.

The increase in human capital has been as dramatic as the increase in physical capital over the last two centuries. At the beginning of the Industrial Revolution, only 30% of the population knew how to read. Today, the literacy rate in the OECD countries is above 95%. Schooling was not compulsory prior to the Industrial Revolution. Today it is, usually until the age of 16. Still, there are large differences across countries. Today, in the OECD countries, nearly 100% of children get a primary education, 90% get a secondary education, and 38% get a higher education. The corresponding numbers in poor countries, countries with GDP per capita below $400, are 95%, 32%, and 4%, respectively.

Even this comparison may be misleading. The quality of education may be quite different across countries.

How should we think about the effect of human capital on output? How does the introduction of human capital change our earlier conclusions? These are the questions we take up in this last section.

## Extending the Production Function

The most natural way of extending our analysis to allow for human capital is to modify the production function relation (16.1) to read:

$$\frac{Y}{N} = f\left(\frac{K}{N}, \frac{H}{N}\right)$$ (16.10)

$$(+, +)$$

The level of output per worker depends on both the level of physical capital per worker, $K/N$, and the level of human capital per worker, $H/N$. As before, an increase in capital per worker ($K/N$) leads to an increase in output per worker. And an increase in the average level of skill ($H/N$) also leads to more output per worker. More skilled workers can use more complex machines; they can deal more easily with unexpected complications; they can adapt faster to new tasks. All these lead to higher output per worker.

Note that we are using the same symbol, $H$, to denote the monetary base in Chapter 4, and human capital in this chapter. Both uses are traditional. Do not be confused.

We assumed earlier that increases in physical capital per worker increased output per worker but that the effect became smaller as the level of capital per worker increased. The same assumption is likely to apply to human capital per worker. Think of increases in $H/N$ as coming from increases in the number of years of education. The evidence is that the returns to increasing the proportion of children acquiring a primary education are very large. At the very least, the ability to read and write allows workers to use more sophisticated equipment. For rich countries, however, primary education—and, for that matter, secondary education—are no longer the relevant margins: Most children now get both. The relevant margin is higher education. The evidence here—and we are sure this will come as good news to most of you— is that higher education increases skills, at least as measured by the increase in wages for those who acquire it. But, to take an extreme example, it is not clear that forcing everybody to acquire a Ph.D. would increase aggregate output very much. Many people would end up overqualified and probably more frustrated rather than more productive.

How should we construct the measure for human capital, $H$? The answer is very much the same way we construct the measure for physical capital, $K$. In constructing $K$, we just add the values of the different pieces of capital so that a machine that costs $2000 gets twice the weight of a machine that costs $1000. Similarly, we construct the measure of $H$ such that workers who are paid twice as much get twice the weight.[3] Take, for example, an economy with 100 workers, half of them unskilled and half of them skilled. Suppose the relative wage of skilled workers is twice that of unskilled workers. We can then construct $H$ as $[(50 \times 1) + (50 \times 2)] = 150$. Human capital per worker, $H/N$, is equal to $150/100 = 1.5$.

## Human Capital, Physical Capital, and Output

How does the introduction of human capital change the analysis of the previous sections?

Our conclusions about *physical capital accumulation* remain valid: An increase in the saving rate increases steady-state physical capital per worker and therefore increases output per worker. But our conclusions now extend to *human capital accumulation* as well. An increase in how much society "saves" in the form of human capital—through education and on-the-job training—increases steady-state human capital per worker, which leads to an increase in output per worker.

Our extended model gives us a richer picture of the determination of output per worker. In the long run, it tells us, output per worker depends both on how much society saves and on how much it spends on education.

What is the relative importance of human and physical capital in the determination of output per worker? To answer this question, we can start by comparing how much is spent on formal education and how much is invested in physical capital. In Canada, spending on formal education is about 8% of GDP. This number includes both government and private expenditures. This number is between one-third and one-half of the gross investment rate for physical capital (which is around 20%). But this comparison is only a first pass. Consider the following complications:

- Education, especially higher education, is partly consumption—done for its own sake—and partly investment. We should include only the investment part for our purposes. However, the 8% number in the preceding paragraph includes both.

How large is your opportunity cost relative to your tuition? ▶

- At least for postsecondary education, the opportunity cost of a person's education is also forgone wages while one is acquiring the education. Spending on education should include not only the actual cost of education but also the opportunity cost. The 8% number does not include the opportunity cost.

- Formal education is only part of education. Much of what we learn comes from on-the-job training, formal or informal. Both the actual costs and the opportunity costs of on-the-job training should also be included. The 8% number does not include either cost.

- We should compare investment rates net of depreciation. Depreciation of physical capital, especially of machines, is likely to be higher than depreciation of human capital. Skills deteriorate but do so slowly. And, unlike physical capital, the more the skills are used, the more slowly they deteriorate.

For all these reasons, it is difficult to come up with reliable numbers for investment in human capital. The bulk of the evidence from recent research suggests that increases in physical capital and increases in human capital may have played roughly equal roles in the increase in output per worker over time. The implication is clear: Countries that save more and/or spend more on education can achieve substantially higher steady-state levels of output per worker.

[3]**DIGGING DEEPER.** The logic for using relative wages as weights is that they are supposed to capture the relative marginal products of different workers so that a worker who is paid three times as much as another has a marginal product that is three times higher.

This would be correct if labour markets were perfectly competitive: Recall from your microeconomics course that in a perfectly competitive labour market, each worker is paid a wage equal to his or her marginal product. But as we discussed in Chapter 9, labour markets are not perfectly competitive, and you may question whether relative wages accurately reflect relative marginal products. To take one, very controversial, example: In the same job, with the same seniority, women still often earn less than men. Does this fact reflect that their marginal product is lower? Should they be given a lower weight than men in the construction of human capital?

## Endogenous Growth

Note what the conclusion we just reached did and did not say. It did say that a country that saves more or spends more on education will achieve a *higher level* of output per worker in steady state. It did not say that by saving or spending more on education a country can sustain permanent *higher growth* of output per worker.

This conclusion, however, has been challenged in the past decade. Following the lead of Robert Lucas and Paul Romer, researchers have explored the possibility that the combination of physical and human capital accumulation may actually be enough to sustain growth. They have asked the following question: Given human capital, increases in physical capital will run into decreasing returns. And given physical capital, increases in human capital will also run into decreasing returns. But what if both physical and human capital increase in tandem? Can an economy grow forever just by having steadily more capital and more skilled workers?

We have mentioned Lucas once already, in connection with the Lucas critique in Chapter 13.

There are models where the answer to this question is yes—growth can continue forever. The simplest such model begins by assuming that population growth has stopped. To simplify the presentation, we set $N = 1$. Then, the more complicated production function (16.1) becomes:

$$Y_t = AK_t \tag{16.11}$$

where $A$ is a constant value over time. For obvious reasons, this is sometimes called the "$AK$" model. Equation (16.11) is rearranged so that:

$$K_t = \frac{Y_t}{A}$$

The accumulation of capital in this economy follows (16.3):

$$K_{t+1} - K_t = sY_t - \delta K_t$$

and when we substitute for $K_{t+1}$ and $K_t$, this yields:

$$\frac{Y_{t+1}}{A} - \frac{Y_t}{A} = sY_t - \delta\frac{Y_t}{A}$$

Now, factor out 1 over $A$ from the right-hand side, divide both sides by $Y_t$ and multiply both sides by $A$ to yield the basic growth equation in this economy:

$$\frac{Y_{t+1} - Y_t}{Y_t} = sA - \delta \tag{16.12}$$

In thinking about growth, even in this simplest model, this equation is very interesting. Why? Growth continues forever as long as $sA > \delta$. In stark contrast, go back and look at Figure 16–7. In the model presented earlier in the chapter, when the saving rate rises, after many years, the growth rate of output per person falls to zero.

The model is also called a **model of endogenous growth** because $s$, the saving rate, is a choice or is endogenous. The choice can be interpreted quite broadly. It can be a choice to accumulate more human capital as described in the previous section. A high value of $s$ could be a large amount of educational spending. A higher value of $s$ could be interpreted as a choice to spend more current income in creating technology, for example, by paying a lot of people to do basic research in physics or biology. Technology is explored in more detail in the next chapter. However, the contrast to the model presented in this chapter arises because capital does not encounter diminishing returns in equation (16.11). As long as $sA$ is larger than $s$, then growth is positive and can continue forever. The jury is still out, but the indications so far are that the conclusions we drew earlier need to be qualified but not abandoned. There is no evidence that countries can sustain higher growth just from capital accumulation and skill improvements.

To end this chapter, let us state our earlier conclusions, modified to take into account human capital: Output per worker depends on the level of both physical capital per worker and human capital per worker. Both forms of capital can be accumulated, one through physical investment, the other through education and training. Increasing either the saving rate or the fraction of output spent on education and training can lead to much higher levels of output per worker in the long run. However, for a given rate of technological progress, such measures are unlikely to lead to a permanently higher growth rate.

Note the qualifier in the last proposition: *for a given rate of technological progress*. But is technological progress unrelated to the level of human capital in the economy? Can't a better-educated labour force lead to a higher rate of technological progress? These questions take us to the topic of the next chapter, the sources and the effects of technological progress.

## SUMMARY

- In the long run, the evolution of output is determined by two relations. (To make the reading of this summary easier, we will omit "per worker" in what follows.) First, the level of output depends on the amount of existing capital. Second, capital accumulation depends, in turn, on the level of output, which determines saving and investment.

- These interactions between capital and output imply that starting from any level of capital (and ignoring technological progress, the topic of Chapter 17), an economy converges in the long run to a steady-state (constant) level of capital. Associated with this level of capital is a steady-state level of output.

- The steady-state level of capital and thus the steady-state level of output depend positively on the saving rate. A higher saving rate leads to a higher steady-state level of output; during the transition to the new steady state, a higher saving rate leads to positive output growth. But (again ignoring technological progress) in the long run, the growth rate of output is equal to zero and is thus independent of the saving rate.

- An increase in the saving rate requires an initial decrease in consumption. In the long run, the increase in the saving rate may lead to an increase or to a decrease in consumption, depending on whether the economy is below or above the golden-rule level of capital, the level of capital at which steady-state consumption is highest.

- Most countries appear to have a level of capital below the golden-rule level. Thus, an increase in the saving rate will lead to an initial decrease in consumption followed by an increase in the long run. In thinking about whether to take policy measures aimed at changing the saving rate, policy makers must decide how much weight to put on the welfare of current generations versus the welfare of future generations.

- Although most of the analysis of this chapter focuses on the effects of physical capital accumulation, output depends on the levels of both physical *and* human capital. Both forms of capital can be accumulated, one through investment and the other through education and training. Increasing the saving rate and/or the fraction of output spent on education and training can lead to large increases in output in the long run.

- In the model of endogenous growth, an increase in the saving rate can increase the growth rate.

## KEY TERMS

- Canada Pension Plan (CPP), 318
- Cobb–Douglas production function, 328
- depreciation rate, 310
- fully funded, 318
- golden-rule level of capital, 316
- Guaranteed Income Supplement (GIS), 318

- human capital, 323
- models of endogenous growth, 325
- Old Age Security (OAS), 318
- pay-as-you-go, 318
- Quebec Pension Plan (QPP), 318
- steady state, 312

### 1. TRUE/FALSE/UNCERTAIN

**a.** The saving rate is always equal to the investment rate.

**b.** A higher investment rate can sustain growth of output forever.

**c.** If capital never depreciated, growth could go on forever.

**d.** The higher the saving rate, the higher is consumption in steady state.

**e.** Output per capita in Canada is roughly equal to 60% of output per worker.

**f.** We should fully fund payments to the aged. This would increase consumption, now and in the future.

**g.** The Canadian capital stock is far below the golden-rule level. Government should give tax breaks for saving.

### 2. THE GROWTH RATE AND THE SAVING RATE

"The Chinese growth rate of output per worker will remain higher than that of Canada for as long as the Chinese saving rate exceeds that of Canada." Do you agree with this statement? Why, or why not?

### 3. THE PARADOX OF SAVING REVISITED

In Chapter 3, we saw that an increase in the saving rate can lead to a recession in the short run. You now can examine the effects beyond the short run. If the saving rate increases permanently, what will be the effect on the growth rate after 1 year, 10 years, 50 years? Explain in words.

### 4. THE DETERMINANTS OF OUTPUT PER WORKER IN STEADY STATE

Discuss the likely impact of the following changes on the level of output per worker in the long run:

**a.** The right to exclude saving from income when paying the income tax

**b.** A higher rate of female participation (but constant population)

### 5. GROWTH WITH A MORE GENERAL PRODUCTION FUNCTION, PART I

Suppose that the economy's production function is given by $Y = K^{\alpha}N^{1-\alpha}$. (This production function is called the **Cobb–Douglas production function**.) See the appendix for details. In section 16-3, we took $\alpha$ to be 1/2. Assume now that $\alpha = 1/3$.

**a.** Is this production function characterized by constant returns to scale? Explain.

**b.** Are there decreasing returns to capital?

**c.** Are there decreasing returns to labour?

**d.** Transform the production function into a relation between output per worker and capital per worker.

**e.** For a given saving rate ($s$) and a depreciation rate ($\delta$), give an expression for capital per worker in the steady state.

**f.** Give an expression for output per worker in the steady state.

**g.** Solve for the steady state level of output per worker when $\delta = 0.08$ and $s = 0.32$.

**h.** Suppose that the depreciation rate remains constant at $\delta = 0.08$, whereas the saving rate is reduced by half to $s = 0.16$. What happens to the steady state level of output per worker?

### 6. GROWTH WITH A MORE GENERAL PRODUCTION FUNCTION, PART II

Suppose that the economy's production function is $Y = K^{1/3}N^{2/3}$ and that both the saving rate ($s$) and the depreciation rate ($\delta$) are equal to 0.10.

**a.** What is the steady-state level of capital per worker?

**b.** What is the steady-state level of output per worker?

Suppose that the economy has reached its steady state in period $t$, and then, in period $t+1$, the depreciation rate doubles to 0.20.

**c.** Solve for the new steady-state levels of capital per worker and output per worker.

**d.** Compute the path of capital per worker and output per worker over the first three periods after the change in the depreciation rate.

### 7. SEARCHING FOR THE GOLDEN RULE

Suppose that the production function is given by $Y = 0.5\sqrt{K}\sqrt{N}$.

**a.** Derive the steady-state levels of $K/N$ and $Y/N$ in terms of the saving rate ($s$) and the depreciation rate ($\delta$).

**b.** Derive the equation for steady-state output per worker and steady-state consumption per worker in terms of $s$ and $\delta$.

**c.** Suppose that $\delta = 5\%$. With your favourite spreadsheet software, compute steady-state output per worker and steady-state consumption per worker for $s = 0, 0.1, 0.2, \ldots, 1.0$. Explain.

d. Use your software to graph the steady-state level of output per worker and consumption per worker as a function of the saving rate (that is, measure the saving rate on the horizontal axis of your graph and the corresponding values of output per worker and consumption per worker on the vertical axis).

e. Does the graph show that there is a value of $s$ that maximizes output per worker? Does the graph show that there is a value of $s$ that maximizes consumption per worker? If so, what is this value?

**8. USE THE MODEL OF ENDOGENOUS GROWTH IN EQUATIONS (16.11) AND (16.12)**

a. Graph $Y_t = AK_t$ as a function of $K_t$. Why is this production function *not* characterized by diminishing returns?

b. Is there a situation in which the rate of growth of output per person in this model is zero?

c. What is the effect of an increase in the savings rate on growth in the endogenous growth model?

d. Explain why the concept of the "golden rule" choice of a saving rate does not apply to the endogenous growth model.

### FURTHER READING

The classic treatment of the relation between the saving rate and output is provided by Robert Solow in *Growth Theory: An Exposition* (New York: Oxford University Press, 1970).

### APPENDIX

## APPENDIX: THE COBB–DOUGLAS PRODUCTION FUNCTION AND THE STEADY STATE

In 1928, Charles Cobb (a mathematician) and Paul Douglas (an economist who went on to become a U.S. senator) concluded that the following production function gave a very good description of the relation among output, physical capital, and labour in the United States from 1899 to 1922:

$$Y = K^{\alpha}N^{1-\alpha} \qquad (16.A1)$$

with $\alpha$ being a number between zero and one. Their findings proved surprisingly robust. Even today, the production function (16.A1), now known as the **Cobb–Douglas production function**, still gives a good description of the relation among output, capital, and labour in many countries, and it has become a standard tool in the economist's toolbox. (Verify for yourself that it satisfies the two properties we discussed in the text: constant returns to scale and decreasing returns to capital and to labour.)

The purpose of this appendix is to characterize the steady state of an economy when the production function is given by (16.A1). (All you need to follow the steps is a knowledge of the properties of exponents.)

Recall that in steady state, saving per worker must be equal to depreciation per worker. Let us see what this implies:

● To derive saving per worker, we must derive first the relation between output per worker and capital per worker implied by equation (16.A1). Divide both sides of equation (16.A1) by $N$:

$$Y/N = K^{\alpha}N^{1-\alpha}/N$$

Using the properties of exponents:

$$N^{1-\alpha}/N = N^{1-\alpha}N^{-1} = N^{-\alpha}$$

so, replacing in the preceding equation, we get:

$$Y/N = K^{\alpha}N^{-\alpha} = (K/N)^{\alpha}$$

Output per worker $Y/N$ is equal to the ratio of capital per worker $K/N$ raised to the power $\alpha$.

Saving per worker is equal to the saving rate times output per worker, so using the previous equation, it is equal to:

$$s(K^*/N)^{\alpha}$$

● Depreciation per worker is equal to the depreciation rate times capital per worker:

$$\delta(K^*/N)$$

● The steady-state level of capital, $K^*$, is determined by the condition that saving per worker be equal to depreciation per worker, so:

$$s(K^*/N)^{\alpha} = \delta(K^*/N)$$

To solve this expression for the steady-state level of capital per worker $K^*/N$, divide both sides by $(K^*/N)^\alpha$:

$$s = \delta(K^*/N)^{1-\alpha}$$

Divide both sides by $\delta$, and change the order of the equality:

$$(K^*/N)^{1-\alpha} = s/\delta$$

Finally, raise both sides to the power $1/(1-\alpha)$:

$$(K^*/N) = (s/\delta)^{1/(1-\alpha)}$$

This gives us the steady-state level of capital per worker.

From the production function, the steady-state level of output per worker is then equal to:

$$(Y^*/N) = (K/N)^\alpha = (s/\delta)^{\alpha/(1-\alpha)}$$

Let us see what this last equation implies:

- In the text, we actually worked with a special case of equation (16.A1), the case where $\alpha = 0.5$. (Taking a variable to the power 0.5 is the same as taking the square root of this variable). If $\alpha = 0.5$, the preceding equation means:

$$Y^*/N = s/\delta$$

Output per worker is equal to the ratio of the saving rate to the depreciation rate. This is the equation we discussed in the text. A doubling of the saving rate leads to a doubling in steady-state output per worker.

- The empirical evidence suggests, however, that if we think of $K$ as physical capital, $\alpha$ is closer to one-third than to one-half. Assuming $\alpha = 1/3$, then $\alpha(1 - \alpha) = (1/3)/(1 - (1/3)) = (1/3)/(2/3) = 1/2$, and the equation for output per worker yields:

$$Y^*/N = (s/\delta)^{1/2} = \sqrt{(s/\delta)}$$

This implies smaller effects of the saving rate on output per worker than was suggested by the computations in the text. A doubling of the saving rate, for example, means that output per worker increases by a factor of $\sqrt{2}$, or only about 1.4 (put another way, a 40% increase in output per worker).

- There is, however, an interpretation of our model in which the appropriate value of $\alpha$ is close to one-half, so the computations in the text are applicable. If, along the lines of section 16-4, we take human capital into account as well as physical capital, then a value of $\alpha$ around one-half for the contribution of this broader definition of capital to output is, indeed, roughly appropriate. Thus, one interpretation of the numerical results in section 16-3 is that they show the effects of a given saving rate, but that saving must be interpreted to include saving in both physical capital and in human capital (more machines and more education).

# Technological Progress and Growth

## The Core: The Long Run

Our conclusion in Chapter 16 that capital accumulation cannot, by itself, sustain growth has a straightforward implication: Sustained growth *requires* technological progress. This chapter looks at the relation between technological progress and growth.

Section 17-1 looks at the respective role of technological progress and capital accumulation in growth. It shows how, in steady state, the rate of growth of output per capita is simply equal to the rate of technological progress. This does not mean, however, that the saving rate is irrelevant: The saving rate affects the level of output per capita, if not its rate of growth. Section 17-2 turns to the determinants of technological progress, focusing in particular on the role of research and development (R&D). Section 17-3 returns to the facts of growth presented in Chapter 15 and interprets them in light of what we have learned in this and the preceding chapters. Section 17-4 looks at the role of institutions in growth.

# 17-1 | Technological Progress and the Rate of Growth

In an economy in which there is both capital accumulation and technological progress, at what rate will output grow? To answer this question, we need to extend the model developed in Chapter 16 to allow for technological progress. To do so, we must first revisit the aggregate production function.

In Chapter 16, we assumed that technology did not change, but only the amount ◄ of capital used in production. In this chapter, we take into account that technology itself changes over time.

## Technological Progress and the Production Function

Technological progress has many dimensions:

- It may mean larger quantities of output for given quantities of capital and labour. For example, think of a new type of lubricant that allows a machine to run at a higher speed.
- It may mean better products. For example, think of the steady improvement in car safety and comfort over time.
- It may mean new products. For example, think of the introduction of CD and then MP3 players and the stream of ever more sophisticated mobile wireless devices.
- It may mean a larger variety of products. For example, think of the steady increase in the types of breakfast cereals available at your local supermarket.

The average number of items carried by a supermarket increased from 2200 in 1950 to 38,700 in 2010. To get a sense of what this means, watch Robin Williams ◄ (who plays an immigrant from the Soviet Union) in the supermarket scene in the movie *Moscow on the Hudson*.

These dimensions are more similar than they may appear. If we think of consumers as caring not about the goods themselves but about the services these goods provide, then all these examples have something in common. In each case, consumers receive more services. A better car provides more safety, a new product such as the cell phone provides more communication services, and so on.

If we think of output as the set of underlying services provided by the goods produced in the economy, we can think of technological progress as leading to increases in output for given amounts of capital and labour. We can then think of the *state of technology* as a variable that tells us how much output can be produced from capital and labour at any time. Let us denote the state of technology by $A$ and rewrite the production function as:

$$Y = F(K, N, A)$$
$$(+,+,+)$$

This is our extended production function. Output depends on both capital and labour ($K$ and $N$) and on the state of technology ($A$): Given capital and labour, an improvement in the state of technology, $A$, leads to an increase in output.

For simplicity, we will ignore ◄ human capital here.

It will prove convenient to use a slightly more restrictive form of the preceding equation, namely:

$$Y = F(K, AN) \qquad (17.1)$$

This equation states that production depends on capital and on labour multiplied by the state of technology. This way of introducing the state of technology makes it easier to think about the effect of technological progress on the relation among output, capital, and labour.[1] Equation (17.1) implies that we can think of technological progress in two equivalent ways:

1. Given the existing capital stock, technological progress reduces the number of workers needed to achieve a given amount of output. A doubling of $A$ allows the economy to produce the same quantity of output with only half the original number of workers, $N$.

---

[1]**DIGGING DEEPER.** This way of writing the production function implies that technological progress is *labour augmenting*: It *augments* (that is, multiplies) labour in the production function. We could assume instead that technological progress is *capital augmenting* (that is, multiplies capital) or that it is both labour and capital augmenting. The justification for the assumption made here is convenience: It leads to a simpler characterization of growth in the long run.

*AN* is also sometimes called **labour in efficiency units**. The use of "efficiency" for "efficiency units" here and of "efficiency wages" in Chapter 9 is a coincidence: The two notions are unrelated.

**2.** Technological progress increases *AN*, the amount of **effective labour** in the economy. If the state of technology doubles, it is as if the economy had twice as many workers. In other words, we can can think of output being produced by two factors: capital (*K*) on the one hand and effective labour (*AN*) on the other.

What restrictions should we impose on the extended production function, equation (17.1)? We can build directly here on our discussion in Chapter 15.

It is again reasonable to assume constant returns to scale: *For a given state of technology (A), doubling both the amount of capital (K) and the amount of labour (N) is likely to lead to a doubling of output:*

$$2Y = F(2K, 2AN)$$

More generally, for any number *x*:

$$xY = F(xK, xAN)$$

It is also reasonable to assume decreasing returns to each of the two factors, capital and effective labour. Given effective labour, an increase in capital is likely to increase output, but at a decreasing rate. Symmetrically, given capital, an increase in effective labour is likely to increase output, but at a decreasing rate.

Per worker: divided by the number of workers (*N*).

Per effective worker: divided by the number of effective workers (*NA*)—the number of workers, *N*, times the state of technology, *A*.

It was convenient in Chapter 16 to think in terms of output and capital *per worker*. That was because the steady state of the economy was a state where output and capital *per worker* were constant. It is convenient here to look at output and capital *per effective worker*. The reason is the same: As we shall soon see, in steady state, output and capital *per effective worker* are constant.

To get a relation between output per effective worker and capital per effective worker, take $x = 1/AN$ in the preceding equation. This gives:

$$\frac{Y}{AN} = F\left(\frac{K}{AN}, 1\right)$$

Suppose that *F* has the "double square root" form:

$Y = F(K,AN) = \sqrt{K}\sqrt{AN}$

Then,

$Y/AN = \sqrt{K/AN}\sqrt{AN/AN}$
$= \sqrt{K/AN}$

So, the function *f* is simply the square root function:

$f(K/AN) = \sqrt{K/AN}$

Or, if we define the function *f* so that $f(K/AN) \equiv F(K/AN, 1)$:

$$\frac{Y}{AN} = f\left(\frac{K}{AN}\right) \qquad (17.2)$$

Output per effective worker $= f$ (Capital per effective worker)

Equation (17.2) gives us a relation between *output per effective worker* and *capital per effective worker*. Output per effective worker increases if and only if capital per effective worker increases. The relation between output per effective worker and capital per effective worker is drawn in Figure 17–1. It looks very much the same as the relation we drew in Figure 16–2 between output per worker and capital per worker in the absence of technological progress: Increases in *K/AN* lead to increases in *Y/AN*, but at a decreasing rate.

## FIGURE 17–1

**Output per Effective Worker versus Capital per Effective Worker**

Increases in capital per effective worker lead to smaller and smaller increases in output per effective worker.

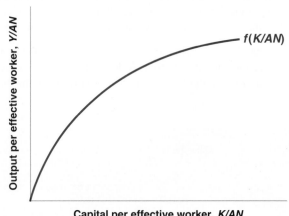

## Interactions between Output and Capital

We now have the elements we need to think about the determinants of growth. Our analysis will parallel the analysis of Chapter 16. There we looked at *output and capital per worker*. Here, we look at the dynamics of *output and capital per effective worker*.

In Chapter 16, we characterized the dynamics of output and capital per worker using Figure 16–2. In that figure, we drew three relations:

- The relation between output per worker and capital per worker
- The implied relation between investment per worker and capital per worker
- The relation between depreciation per worker—the investment per worker needed to maintain a constant level of capital per worker—and capital per worker

The dynamics of capital per worker and, by implication, of output per worker were determined by the relation between investment per worker and depreciation per worker. Depending on whether investment per worker was greater or smaller than depreciation per worker, capital per worker increased or decreased over time, and so did output per worker.

We follow exactly the same approach here in building Figure 17–2. The difference is that we focus on output, capital, and investment per effective worker, rather than per worker.

1. The relation between output per effective worker and capital per effective worker was derived in Figure 17–1. This relation is repeated in Figure 17–2. Output per effective worker increases with capital per effective worker, but at a decreasing rate.

2. Under the same assumptions as in Chapter 16—investment is equal to private saving, and the private saving rate is constant—investment is given by:

$$I = S = sY$$

Divide both sides by the number of effective workers, $AN$, to get:

$$\frac{I}{AN} = s\frac{Y}{AN}$$

Substituting output per effective worker $Y/AN$ by its expression from equation (17.2) gives:

$$\frac{I}{AN} = sf\left(\frac{K}{AN}\right)$$

The relation between investment per effective worker and capital per effective worker is drawn as the lower curve in Figure 17–2. It is equal to the upper curve—the relation between output per effective worker and capital per effective worker—multiplied by the saving rate, $s$ (which is less than one).

3. Finally, we need to derive the level of investment per effective worker needed to maintain a given level of capital per effective worker.

In Chapter 16, the answer was simple; for capital to be constant, investment had to be equal to the depreciation of the existing capital stock. Here, the answer is slightly more complicated. The reason is as follows: Now that we allow for technological progress, the number of effective workers ($AN$) is increasing over time. Thus, maintaining the same ratio of capital to effective workers ($K/AN$) requires an increase in the capital stock ($K$) proportional to the increase in the number of effective workers ($AN$). Let us look at this condition more closely.

Assume that population is growing at annual rate $g_N$. If we assume that the ratio of employment to the total population remains constant, the number of workers ($N$) also grows at annual rate $g_N$. Assume also that the rate of technological progress equals $g_A$. Together, these two assumptions imply that the growth rate of effective labour ($AN$) equals $g_A + g_N$. If

◀ Here is the key to understanding the results in this chapter: The results we derived for *output per worker* in Chapter 16 still hold in this chapter, but now for *output per effective worker*. For example, in Chapter 16, we saw that output per worker was constant in steady state. In this chapter, we will see that output per effective worker is constant in steady state.

In Chapter 16, we were assuming both $g_A$ and $g_N$ were equal to zero. Our main focus in this chapter is on the implications of technological progress, $g_A > 0$. But, once we allow for technological progress, introducing population growth $g_N > 0$ is ◀ straightforward. Thus, we allow for both.

The growth rate of the ▶
product of two variables is
the sum of the growth rates
of the two variables. See
proposition 7 in Appendix 2
at the end of the book.

the number of workers is growing at 1% per year and the rate of technological progress is 2% per year, then the growth rate of effective labour is equal to 3%.

Let $\delta$ be the depreciation rate of capital. Then the level of investment needed to maintain a given level of capital per effective worker is given by:

$$\delta K + (g_A + g_N)K$$

An amount $\delta K$ is needed just to keep the capital stock constant. If the depreciation rate is 10%, then investment must be equal to 10% of the capital stock just to maintain the same level of capital. An additional amount $(g_A + g_N)K$ is needed to ensure that the capital stock increases at the same rate as effective labour. If effective labour increases at 3% a year, then capital must increase by 3% a year to maintain the same level of capital per effective worker. Putting $\delta K$ and $(g_A + g_N)K$ together in this example, if the depreciation rate is 10% and the growth rate of effective labour is 3%, then investment must equal 13% of the capital stock to maintain a constant level of capital per effective worker.

Grouping the terms in $K$ in the preceding expression and dividing by the number of effective workers to get the amount of investment per effective worker needed to maintain a constant level of capital per effective worker gives:

$$(\delta + g_A + g_N)\frac{K}{AN}$$

The level of investment per effective worker needed to maintain a given level of capital per effective worker is represented by the upward-sloping line, "Required investment" in Figure 17–2. The slope of the line equals $\delta + g_A + g_N$.

### Dynamics of Capital and Output

We can now give a graphical description of the dynamics of capital per effective worker and output per effective worker. Consider in Figure 17–2 a given level of capital per effective worker, say, $(K/AN)_0$. At that level, output per effective worker equals the distance $AB$. Investment per effective worker is equal to $AC$. The amount of investment required to maintain that level of capital per effective worker is equal to $AD$. Because actual investment exceeds the investment level required to maintain the existing level of capital per effective worker, $K/AN$ increases.

Hence, starting from $(K/AN)_0$, the economy moves to the right, with the level of capital per effective worker increasing over time. This goes on until investment is just sufficient to

**FIGURE  17–2**

**Dynamics of Capital and Output per Effective Worker**

Capital and output per effective worker converge to constant values in the long run.

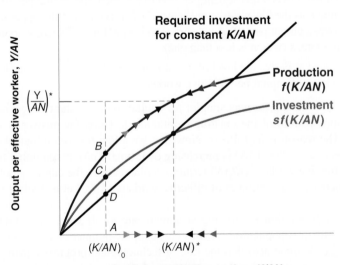

maintain the existing level of capital per effective worker, until capital per effective worker reaches $(K/AN)^*$. In the long run, capital per effective worker reaches a constant level, and so does output per effective worker. Put another way, the steady state of this economy is such that *capital per effective worker and output per effective worker are constant and equal to* $(K/AN)^*$ *and* $(Y/AN)^*$, *respectively.*

Note what this conclusion implies: *In steady state, in this economy, what is constant is not output but rather output per effective worker.* This implies that in steady state, output *(Y)* is growing at the same rate as effective labour *(AN)* (so that the ratio of the two is, indeed, constant). Because effective labour grows at rate $(g_A + g_N)$, output growth in steady state must also equal $(g_A + g_N)$. The same reasoning applies to capital. Because capital per effective worker is constant in steady state, capital is also growing at rate $(g_A + g_N)$.

These conclusions give us our first important result. *In steady state, the growth rate of output equals the rate of population growth $(g_N)$ plus the rate of technological progress $(g_A)$. By implication, the growth rate of output is independent of the saving rate.*

The best way to strengthen your intuition for this result is to go back to the argument we used in Chapter 16 to show that without technological progress and population growth, the economy could not sustain positive growth forever. The argument went as follows: Suppose the economy tried to achieve positive output growth. Because of decreasing returns to capital, capital would have to grow faster than output. The economy would have to devote a larger and larger proportion of output to capital accumulation. At some point, there would be no more output to devote to capital accumulation, and growth would come to an end.

Exactly the same logic is at work here. Effective labour grows at rate $(g_A + g_N)$. Suppose the economy tried to achieve output growth in excess of $(g_A + g_N)$. Because of decreasing returns to capital, capital would have to increase faster than output. The economy would have to devote a larger and larger proportion of output to capital accumulation. At some point, this would prove impossible. Thus, the economy cannot permanently grow faster than $(g_A + g_N)$.

We have focused on the behaviour of aggregate output. To get a sense of what happens, not to aggregate output but rather to the standard of living over time, we must look instead at the behaviour of output per worker (not output per *effective worker*). Because output grows at rate $(g_A + g_N)$ and the number of workers grows at rate $g_N$, output per worker grows at rate $g_A$. In other words, *in steady state, output per worker grows at the rate of technological progress.*

Because output, capital, and effective labour all grow at the same rate $(g_A + g_N)$ in steady state, the steady state of this economy is also called a state of **balanced growth**: In steady state, output and the two inputs, capital and effective labour, grow in balance (at the same rate). The characteristics of balanced growth will be helpful later in the chapter and are summarized in Table 17–1.

> If the number of effective workers is constant, then constant output per effective worker implies constant output. This was the case in Chapter 16, where we assumed there was neither population growth nor technological progress. But this is not the case here.

> If $Y/AN$ is constant, $Y$ must grow at the same rate as $AN$. So, it must grow at rate $g_A + g_N$.

> The standard of living is given by the level of output per worker (or, more accurately, the level of output per capita), not the level of output per effective worker.

> The growth rate of $Y/N$ is equal to the growth rate of $Y$ minus the growth rate of $N$ (see proposition 8 in Appendix 2 at the end of the book). So, the growth rate of $Y/N$ is given by $(g_Y - g_N) = (g_A + g_N) - g_N = g_A$.

| TABLE 17–1 The Characteristics of Balanced Growth | | Growth Rate |
| --- | --- | --- |
| 1. | Capital per effective worker | 0 |
| 2. | Output per effective worker | 0 |
| 3. | Capital per worker | $g_A$ |
| 4. | Output per worker | $g_A$ |
| 5. | Labour | $g_N$ |
| 6. | Capital | $g_A + g_N$ |
| 7. | Output | $g_A + g_N$ |

On the balanced growth path (equivalently, in steady state; equivalently, in the long run):

- Capital per effective worker and output per effective worker are constant; this is the result we derived in Figure 17–2.
- Equivalently, capital per worker and output per worker are growing at the rate of technological progress, $g_A$.
- Or, in terms of labour, capital, and output: Labour is growing at the rate of population growth, $g_N$; capital and output are growing at a rate equal to the sum of population growth and the rate of technological progress, $(g_A + g_N)$.

## The Effects of the Saving Rate

Note an important implication of our results so far: In steady state, the growth rate of output depends *only* on the rate of population growth and the rate of technological progress. Changes in the saving rate do not affect the steady-state growth rate. This does not mean, however, that the saving rate is irrelevant: Changes in the saving rate do affect the steady-state level of output per effective worker.

This result is best seen in Figure 17–3, which shows the effect of an increase in the saving rate from $s_0$ to $s_1$. The increase in the saving rate shifts the investment relation from $s_0 f(K/AN)$ to $s_1 f(K/AN)$. It follows that the steady-state level of capital per effective worker increases from $(K/AN)_0$ to $(K/AN)_1$, with a corresponding increase in the level of output per effective worker from $(Y/AN)_0$ to $(Y/AN)_1$.

Figure 17–4 is the same as Figure 16–5, which anticipated the derivation presented here.

For a description of logarithmic scales, see the discussion in Chapter 15.

When a logarithmic scale is used, a variable growing at a constant rate moves along a straight line. The slope of the line is equal to the rate of growth of the variable.

Following the increase in the saving rate, capital per effective worker and output per effective worker increase for some time as they converge to their new higher level. Figure 17–4 plots the evolution of output and capital against time. Both output and capital are measured on logarithmic scales. The economy is initially on the balanced growth path $AA$: Capital and output are growing at rate $(g_A + g_N)$—the slope of $AA$ is equal to $(g_A + g_N)$. After the increase in the saving rate at time $t$, output and capital grow faster for some time. Eventually, capital and output end up at higher levels than they would have been without the increase in saving. But their growth rate returns to $g_A + g_N$. In the new steady state, the economy grows at the same rate, but on a higher growth path, $BB$, which is parallel to $AA$, also has a slope equal to $(g_A + g_N)$.

To summarize: In an economy with technological progress and population growth, output grows over time. In steady state, output *per effective worker* and capital *per effective worker* are constant. Put another way, output *per worker* and capital *per worker* grow at the rate of technological progress. Put yet another way, output and capital grow at the same rate as effective labour, and thus at a rate equal to the growth rate of the number of workers plus

FIGURE **17–3**

**The Effects of an Increase in the Saving Rate: Part I**

An increase in the saving rate leads to an increase in the steady-state levels of output and capital per effective worker.

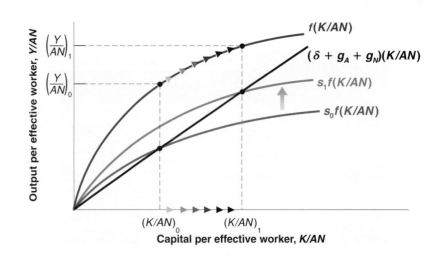

FIGURE 17–4

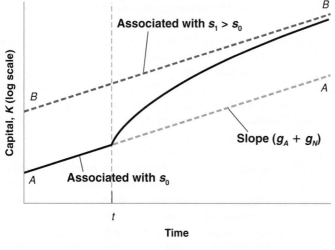

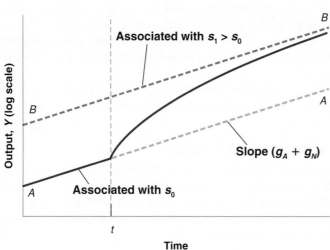

**The Effects of an Increase in the Saving Rate: Part II**

The increase in the saving rate leads to higher growth until the economy reaches its new, higher, balanced growth path.

the rate of technological progress. When the economy is in steady state, it is said to be on a balanced growth path.

The rate of output growth in steady state is independent of the saving rate. The saving rate affects the steady-state level of output per effective worker, however. And increases in the saving rate lead, for some time, to an increase in the growth rate above the steady-state growth rate.

## 17-2 | The Determinants of Technological Progress

We have just seen that the growth rate of output per worker is ultimately determined by the rate of technological progress. But what, in turn, determines the rate of technological progress? This is the question we take up in this section.

Technological progress brings to mind images of major discoveries: the invention of the microchip, the discovery of the structure of DNA, and so on. These discoveries suggest a process driven largely by scientific research and chance rather than by economic forces. But the truth is that most technological progress in modern economies is the result of a slower and more systematic process: the outcome of firms' **research and development (R&D)** activities. Industrial R&D expenditures account for between 2 and 3% of GDP in each of the five major rich countries we looked at in Chapter 15 (Canada, the United States, France, Japan, and the United Kingdom). About 75% of the roughly one million U.S. scientists and researchers working in R&D are employed by firms. U.S. firms' R&D spending equals more than 20% of their spending on gross investment and more than 60% of their spending on net investment. In Canada, about 1.7% of GDP was used each year for R&D purposes. There is slightly more public sector activity in Canada than in the United States: 30% of research funding passes through institutions of higher education, and 12% is done directly by government, leaving 58% of R&D spending in the hands of industry. Canadian industry does the smallest share of R&D spending among Canada, France, Germany, Japan, the United Kingdom, and the United States. This is a matter of some concern for policy, since many consider the most creative and most interesting jobs are associated with the R&D process.

Firms spend on R&D for the same reason they buy new machines or build new plants: to increase profits. By increasing spending on R&D, a firm increases the probability that it will discover and develop a new product. (We will use "product" as a generic term to denote new goods or new techniques of production.) If the new product is successful, the firm's profits will increase. There is, however, an important difference between purchasing a machine and spending more on R&D. The difference is that the outcome of R&D is fundamentally ideas. And, unlike a machine, an idea potentially can be used by many firms at the same time. A firm that has just acquired a new machine does not have to worry that another firm will use that particular machine. A firm that has discovered and developed a new product can make no such assumption.

This last point implies that the level of R&D spending depends not only on the *fertility* of the research process, but also on the *appropriability* of research results. Let us look at each aspect in turn.

## The Fertility of the Research Process

**Fertility of research** refers to how spending on R&D translates into new ideas and new products. If research is very fertile—if R&D spending leads to many new products—then, other things being equal, firms will have more incentives to do R&D; R&D and technological progress will be higher. The determinants of the fertility of research lie largely outside the realm of economics. Many factors interact here:

- The fertility of research depends on the successful interaction between basic research (the search for general principles and results) and applied research and development (the application of these results to specific uses and the development of new products). Basic research does not lead, by itself, to technological progress. But the success of applied R&D depends ultimately on basic research. Much of the computer industry's development can be traced to a few breakthroughs, from the invention of the transistor to the invention of the microchip.

In Chapter 16, we looked at the role of human capital as an input in production: More educated people can use more complex machines or handle more complex tasks. Here, we see a second role of human capital: better researchers and scientists and, by implication, a higher rate of technological progress. ▶

- Some countries appear more successful at basic research; others are more successful at applied R&D. Studies point to the relevance of the education system. For example, it is often argued that the French higher education system, with its strong emphasis on abstract thinking, produces researchers that are better at basic research than at applied R&D. Studies also point to the importance of a "culture of entrepreneurship," in which a big part of technological progress comes from the entrepreneurs' ability to organize the successful development and marketing of new products.

- It takes many years, and often many decades, for the full potential of major discoveries to be realized. The usual sequence is one in which a major discovery leads to the exploration of potential applications, then to the development of new products, then to the adoption of these new products. The Focus box "The Diffusion of New Technology: Hybrid Corn" shows the results of one of the first studies of this process of diffusion of ideas. Closer to us is the example of personal computers. Thirty years after the commercial introduction of the personal computer, it often feels as if we have just started discovering its potential.

An age-old worry is that most major discoveries have already been made and that technological progress will now slow down. This fear may come from thinking about mining, where

New technologies are not developed or adopted overnight. One of the first studies of the diffusion of new technologies was carried out in 1957 by Zvi Griliches, who looked at the diffusion of hybrid corn in different states in the United States.

Hybrid corn is, in the words of Griliches, "the invention of a method of inventing." Producing hybrid corn entails crossing different strains of corn to develop a type of corn adapted to local conditions. Introduction of hybrid corn can increase the corn yield by up to 20%.

Although the idea was first developed at the beginning of the twentieth century, the first commercial application of hybridization on a substantial scale did not take place until the 1930s in the United States. Figure 1 shows the rate at which hybrid corn was adopted in five U.S. states from 1932 to 1956.

Figure 1 shows two dynamic processes at work. One is the process through which appropriate hybrid corns were discovered for each state. Hybrid corn became available in the southern states (Texas, Alabama) many years after it had become available in the northern states (Iowa, Wisconsin, Kentucky). The other is the speed at which hybrid corn was adopted within each state. Within eight years of introduction, practically all corn in Iowa was hybrid corn. The process was much slower in the south. More than 10 years after its introduction, hybrid corn accounted for only 60% of total acreage in Alabama.

Why was the speed of adoption higher in Iowa than in the south? Griliches' article showed that the reason was an economic one: The speed of adoption in each state was a function of the profitability of introducing hybrid corn. And profitability was higher in Iowa than in the southern states.

*Source*: Table & excerpts from Zvi Griliches, "Hybrid Corn: An Exploration in the Economics of Technological Change," *Econometrica*, October 1957, Vol. 25, No 1. © The Econometric Society. Reprinted with permission from The Econometric Society.

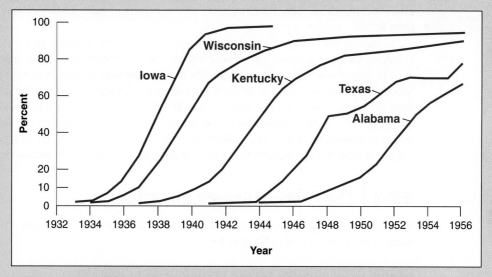

**FIGURE 1**   **Percentage of total corn acreage planted with hybrid seed, selected U.S. states, 1932–1956**

*Source*: See source note for this box.

high-grade mines were exploited first and where we have had to turn to lower-and-lower-grade mines as resources are depleted. But this is only an analogy, and so far there is no evidence that it applies.

## The Appropriability of Research Results

The second determinant of the level of R&D and of technological progress is the degree of **appropriability** of research results, the extent to which firms benefit from the results of their own R&D. If firms cannot appropriate the profits from the development of new products, they will not engage in R&D and technological progress will be slow. Many factors are also at work here:

● One is the nature of the research process itself. For example, if it is widely believed that the discovery of a new product will quickly lead to the discovery of an even better product, there may be little payoff to being first. Thus, a highly fertile field of research may not generate high levels of R&D. This example is extreme but revealing.

- Probably most important is the degree of protection given to new products by the law. Without legal protection, profits from developing a new product are likely to be small. Except in rare cases where the product is based on a trade secret (such as Coca-Cola), it generally will not take long for other firms to produce the same product, eliminating any advantage the innovating firm may have had initially. This is why countries have patent laws. **Patents** give a firm that has discovered a new product—usually a new technique or device—the right to exclude anyone else from the production or use of the new product for some time.

How should governments design patent laws? On the one hand, protection is needed to provide firms with the incentives to spend on R&D. On the other, once firms have discovered new products, it would be best for society if the knowledge embodied in those new products were made available to other firms and to people without restrictions. Take biogenetic research, for example. The prospect of large profits is what leads bioengineering firms to embark on expensive research projects. Once a firm has created a new product that can save many lives, it clearly would be best to make it available to all potential users at a price equal to the cost of production. But if such a policy were systematically followed, it would eliminate incentives for firms to do research in the first place. Patent law must strike a difficult balance: Too little protection will lead to little R&D. Too much protection will make it difficult for new R&D to build on the results of past R&D and may also lead to little R&D.

This type of dilemma is known as "time inconsistency." We will see other examples and discuss the issue at length in Chapter 23. ▶

Countries that are less technologically advanced often have poorer patent protection. For example, China is a country with poor enforcement of patent rights. Our discussion helps explain why. Poorer countries are typically users rather than producers of new technologies. Much of their improvement in productivity comes not from inventions within the country but from the adaptation of foreign technologies. In this case, the costs of weak patent protection are small because there would be few domestic inventions anyway. But the benefits of low patent protection are clear: They allow domestic firms to use and adapt foreign technology without having to pay royalties to the foreign firms that developed the technology.

# 17-3 | The Facts of Growth Revisited

We can now use the theory we have developed in this chapter and Chapter 16 to interpret some of the facts we saw in Chapter 15.

## Capital Accumulation versus Technological Progress in Rich Countries since 1950

Suppose we observe an economy with a high growth rate of output per worker over some period of time. Our theory implies that this fast growth may come from two sources:

- It may reflect a high rate of technological progress under balanced growth.
- It may reflect instead the adjustment of capital per effective worker, $K/AN$, to a higher level. As we saw in Figure 15–4, such an adjustment leads to a period of higher growth, even if the rate of technological progress has not increased.

Can we tell how much of the growth comes from one source and how much comes from the other? Yes. If high growth reflects high balanced growth, output per worker should be growing at a rate *equal* to the rate of technological progress (see Table 17–1, line 4). If high growth reflects instead the adjustment to a higher level of capital per effective worker, this adjustment should be reflected in a growth rate of output per worker that *exceeds* the rate of technological progress.

Let's apply this approach to interpret the facts about growth in four of the rich countries we saw in Table 15–1.

| TABLE 17–2 | Average Annual Rates of Growth of Output per Worker and Technological Progress in Four Rich Countries since 1985 | |
| --- | --- | --- |
| | Rate of Growth of Output per Worker (%) 1985–2009 | Rate of Technological Progress (%) 1985–2009 |
| France | 1.9 | 1.6 |
| Japan | 1.8 | 2.1 |
| United Kingdom | 2.1 | 1.6 |
| United States | 1.9 | 1.3 |
| Average | 1.9 | 1.7 |

*Source:* Calculations from the OECD Productivity Statistics

Table 17–2 gives, in column 1, the average rate of growth of output per worker ($g_Y - g_N$) and, in column 2, the average rate of technological progress $g_A$, between 1985 and 2009 (2008 for Japan, and 2007 for the United Kingdom), for four countries—France, Japan, the United Kingdom, and the United State. Note one difference between Tables 15–1 and 17–2: As suggested by the theory, Table 17–2 looks at the growth rate of output per worker. Table 15–1, which was focusing on the standard of living, looked at the growth rate of output per person. The differences are small. The rate of technological progress, $g_A$, is constructed using a method introduced by Robert Solow; the method and the details of construction are given in the appendix to this chapter.

Table 17–2 leads to two conclusions:

First, growth since 1985 has come from technological progress, not unusually high capital accumulation. This conclusion follows from the fact that, in all four countries, the growth rate of output per worker (column 1) has been roughly equal to the rate of technological progress (column 2). This is what we would expect when countries are growing along their balanced growth path.

Note what this conclusion does not say. It does not say that capital accumulation was irrelevant. Capital accumulation was such that it allowed these countries to maintain a roughly constant ratio of output to capital and achieve balanced growth. What it says is that, over the period, growth did not come from an unusual increase in capital accumulation (i.e., from an increase in the ratio of capital to output).

This is an important conclusion. One can think, in general, of two sources of convergence between countries. First: Poorer countries are poorer because they have less capital to begin with. Over time, they accumulate capital faster than the others, generating convergence. Second: Poorer countries are poorer because they are less technologically advanced than the others. Thus, over time, they become more sophisticated, either by importing technology from advanced countries or developing their own. As technological levels converge, so does output per worker. The conclusion we can draw from Table 17–2 is that, in the case of rich countries, the more important source of convergence in this case is clearly the second one (developing their own).

## Capital Accumulation versus Technological Progress in China since 1980

Going beyond growth in OECD countries, one of the striking facts in Chapter 15 was the high growth rates achieved by a number of Asian countries. This raises again the same questions we just discussed: Do these high growth rates reflect fast technological progress, or do they reflect unusually high capital accumulation?

In the United States, for example, the ratio of employment to population decreased slightly from 60.1% in 1985 to 59.3% in 2009. Thus output per person and output per worker grew at virtually the same rate over this period.

What would have happened to the growth rate of output per worker if these countries had had the same rate of technological progress, but no capital accumulation, during the period?

While the table only looks at four countries, a similar conclusion holds when we look at the set of all OECD countries. Countries that started behind in the 1950s after World War II converged mainly due to higher rates of technological progress since then.

Read more about Chinese growth in the Focus box "What Is behind Chinese Growth?"

Rapid growth in China could easily be considered the dominant economic event of the last two decades.

# FOCUS    What Is behind Chinese Growth?

From 1949—the year in which the People's Republic of China was established—to the late 1970s, China's economic system was based on central planning. Two major politico-economic reforms, the Great Leap Forward in 1958 and the Cultural Revolution in 1966, ended up as human and economic catastrophes. Output decreased by 20% from 1959 to 1962, and it is estimated that 25 million people died of famine during the same period. Output again decreased by more than 10% from 1966 to 1968.

After Chairman Mao's death in 1976, the new leaders decided to progressively introduce market mechanisms in the economy. In 1978, an agricultural reform was put in place, allowing farmers, after satisfying a quota due to the state, to sell their production in rural markets. Over time, farmers obtained increasing rights to the land, and today, state farms produce less than 1% of agricultural output. Outside of agriculture, and also starting in the late 1970s, state firms were given increasing autonomy over their production decisions, and market mechanisms and prices were introduced for an increasing number of goods. Private entrepreneurship was encouraged, often taking the form of Town and Village Enterprises, collective ventures guided by a profit motive. Tax advantages and special agreements were used to attract foreign investors.

The economic effects of these cumulative reforms have been dramatic: Average growth of output per worker has increased from 2.5% between 1952 and 1977 to more than 9% since then.

Is such high growth surprising? One could argue that it is not. Looking at the ten-fold difference in productivity between North and South Korea described in Focus box "The Importance of Institutions: North and South Korea" found later in this chapter, it is clear that central planning is a poor economic system. Thus, it would seem that, by moving from central planning to a market economy, countries could easily experience large increases in productivity. That answer is not so obvious, however, when one looks at the experience of the many countries that, since the late 1980s, have indeed moved away from central planning. In most Central European countries, this transition was typically associated initially with a 10 to 20% drop in GDP, and it took five years or more for output to exceed its pre-transition level. In Russia and in the new countries carved out of the Soviet Union, the drop was even larger and longer lasting. (Many transition countries now have strong growth, although their growth rates are far below that of China.)

In Central and Eastern Europe, the initial effect of transition was a collapse of the state sector, only partially compensated by slow growth of the new private sector. In China, the state sector has declined more slowly, and its decline has been more than compensated by strong private sector growth. This gives a proximate explanation for the difference between China and the other transition countries. But it still begs the question: How was China able to achieve this smoother transition?

Some observers offer a cultural explanation. They point to the Confucian tradition, based on the teachings of Confucius, which still dominates Chinese values and emphasizes hard work, respect for one's commitments, and trustworthiness among friends. All these traits, they argue, are the foundations of institutions that allow a market economy to perform well.

Some observers offer an historical explanation. They point to the fact that, in contrast to Russia, central planning in China lasted only for a few decades. Thus, when the shift back to a market economy took place, people still knew how such an economy functioned, and adapted easily to the new economic environment.

Most observers point to the strong rule of the communist party in the process. They point out that, in contrast to Central and Eastern Europe, the political system did not change, and the government was able to control the pace of transition. It was able to experiment along the way, to allow state firms to continue production while the private sector grew, and to guarantee property rights to foreign investors (in Figure 17–5, China has an index of property rights of 7.7, not far from its value in rich countries). With foreign investors has come the technology from rich countries, and, in time, the transfer of this knowledge to domestic firms. For political reasons, such a strategy was simply not open to governments in Central and Eastern Europe.

The limits of the Chinese strategy are clear. Property rights are still not well established. The banking system is still inefficient. So far, however, these problems have not stood in the way of growth.

## FURTHER READINGS

For more on China's economy, read Gregory Chow, *China's Economic Transformation* (Malden, MA: Blackwell Publishers, 2002).

For a comparison between transition in Eastern Europe and China, read Jan Svejnar, "China in Light of the Performance of Central and East European Economies," IZA Discussion Paper 2791, May 2007.

---

Warning: Chinese data for output, employment, and the capital stock (the latter is needed to construct $g_A$) are not as reliable as similar data for OECD countries. Thus, the numbers in the table should be seen as more tentative than the numbers in Table 17–2.

To answer the questions, we shall focus on China, because of its size and because of the astonishingly high output growth rate, nearly 10% since the late 1970s. Table 17–3 gives the average rate of growth, $g_Y$, the average rate of growth of output per worker, $g_Y - g_N$, and the average rate of technological progress, $g_A$, for two periods, 1978–1995 and 1995–2007.

Table 17–3 yields two conclusions: From the late 1970s to the mid-1990s, the rate of technological progress was close to the rate of growth of output per worker. China was roughly on a (very rapid) balanced growth path. Since 1995, however, while growth of output per worker has remained very high, the contribution of technological progress has decreased. Put another

| TABLE 17-3 | Average Annual Rate of Growth of Output per Worker and Technological Progress in China, 1978–2007 | | |
|---|---|---|---|
| Period | Rate of Growth of Output (%) | Rate of Growth of Output per Worker (%) | Rate of Technological Progress (%) |
| 1978–1995 | 10.2 | 8.6 | 7.8 |
| 1995–2007 | 9.9 | 9.4 | 6.0 |

Source: Barry Bosworth and Susan M. Collins, "Accounting for Growth: Comparing China and India," *Journal of Economic Perspectives*, 22(1) (2008): p. 49.

way, more recently, growth in China has come partly from unusually high capital accumulation—from an increase in the ratio of capital to output.

We can look at it another way. Recall, from Table 17–1, that under balanced growth, $g_K = g_Y = g_A + g_N$. To see what investment rate would be required if China had balanced growth, go back to equation (17.3) and divide both sides by output, $Y$, to get

$$\frac{I}{Y} = \left( \delta + g_A + g_N \right) \frac{K}{Y}$$

Let's plug in numbers for China for the period 1995–2007. The estimate of $\delta$, the depreciation rate of capital in China, is 5% a year. As we just saw, the average value of $g_A$ for the period was 6.0%. The average value of $g_N$, the rate of growth of employment, was 0.5%. The average value of the ratio of capital to output was 2.6. This implies a ratio of investment of output required to achieve balanced growth of (5.0% + 6.0% + 0.5%) × 2.6 = 30%. The actual average ratio of investment to output for 1995–2007 was a much higher 39%. Thus, both rapid technological progress and unusually high capital accumulation explain high Chinese growth. If the rate of technological progress were to remain the same, this suggests that, as the ratio of capital to output stabilizes, the Chinese growth rate will decrease somewhat, closer to 6% than to 9.4%.

Where does the technological progress in China come from? A closer look at the data suggests two main channels. First, China has transferred labour from the countryside, where productivity is very low, to industry and services in the cities, where productivity is much higher. Second, China has imported the technology of more technologically advanced countries. It has, for example, encouraged the development of joint ventures between Chinese firms and foreign firms. Foreign firms have come with better technologies, and, over time, Chinese firms have learned how to use them.

This leads to a more general point: The nature of technological progress is likely to be different between more advanced and less advanced economies. The more advanced economies, being by definition at the **technological frontier**, need to develop new ideas, new processes, and new products. They need to innovate. The countries that are behind can instead improve their level of technology by copying and adapting the new processes and products developed in the more advanced economies. They need to imitate. The farther behind a country is, the larger the role of imitation relative to innovation. As imitation is likely to be easier than innovation, this can explain why convergence, both within the OECD, and in the case of China and other countries, typically takes the form of **technological catch-up.** It raises, however, yet another question: If imitation is so easy, why is it that so many other countries do not seem to be able to do the same and grow? This points to the broader aspects of technology we discussed earlier in the chapter. Technology is more than just a set of blueprints. How efficiently these blueprints can be used and how productive an economy is depend on its institutions, on the quality of its government, and so on. We consider this issue in the next section.

Labour productivity growth is the increase in the level of output per worker. It is a key variable in the economy because, the higher the level of output per worker, the better off in a material sense is the average Canadian. In 2009, Statistics Canada made a detailed comparison of labour productivity growth in the business sector in Canada and the United States in sub-periods from 1961 to 2008. Table 1 updates this methodology to 2011.

The growth in output per hour worked is the best measure of the growth in $Y/N$ in our production function. If hours per worker are used in place of number of workers, then variations in part-time work, holidays taken, and differences in the average hours worked per week between the two countries are taken into account. There is a very large gap in the growth rate of output per hours worked in favour of Americans. That gap widens over time. The entries in the Table break down this gap into its components using our production function $Y = F(K,AN)$.

$K$, the national capital stock, increases. To be more precise, Statistics Canada has to estimate the contribution of the increase in the capital stock to the overall increase in output per hour worked. If there is more capital available to each worker, then each worker is more productive. In Chapter 16, we focused on growth associated with the increase in the capital stock per worker. Since 1980, in both countries, capital per hour worked rises by about the same amount, 1 percentage point per year.

The next component in the table is labelled "Contribution of labour composition." This is a measure of the education and experience level of the average worker and reflects our human capital discussion in Chapter 16. The average educational level of the workforce rises slowly. In Chapter 16 we downplayed the role of human capital. This decision is justified in part by the relatively small contribution of human capital to the growth rate of output per worker in Table 1, a value between 0.1 and 0.5 percentage points in both countries for all the sub-periods in Table 1. One note: the relatively small contribution of education to growth is a "rich country" phenomenon. In poorer countries, moving the labour force and particularly the female labour force from illiteracy to literacy through primary education is enormously important. This process is over in Canada and the United States.

The enormous and controversial difference between the two countries in Table 1 is found in the "Contribution of technological change" row of the table. It is this value that places Canada at such a huge disadvantage. In every sub-period, growth in labour productivity accounted for by technological change in the United States is much higher than in Canada. In the 1961 to 1980 period, the Canada–U.S. productivity gap is 0.9 percentage points per year. In the period from 1980 to 2000, the gap drops to 0.5 percentage points. Things seemed to be improving. The period from 2000 to 2011 was a disaster. Productivity growth in Canada was negative. What does this mean? It means that measured inputs of capital and labour actually grew more than output.

Productivity growth in the United States remained large and positive from 2000 to 2011. Canada had an enormous productivity gap. The negative productivity growth in Table 1 raised both eyebrows and concern!

There are very challenging issues around the measurement of productivity. The biggest issue is in the measurement of capital inputs. How quickly does capital wear out once installed? How do we add together the different types of capital—from a desk to a machine to a building? Diewert and Yu (2012) use a different methodology than Statistics Canada to construct a measure of the capital input. Their measure of the capital input is smaller and, as a consequence, the rate of

| TABLE 1 | Sources of Labour Productivity Growth in the Business Sector in Canada and the United States, 1961–2011 | | |
|---|---|---|---|
| | 1961–1980 | 1980–2000 | 2000–2011 |
| **Canada: % average annual growth** | | | |
| Output per hours worked | 2.9 | 1.6 | 0.9 |
| Contribution of capital deepening | 1.7 | 1.0 | 1.0 |
| Contribution of labour composition | 0.5 | 0.4 | 0.3 |
| Contribution of technological change | 0.7 | 0.2 | –0.4 |
| **United States: % average annual growth** | | | |
| Output per hours worked | 2.5 | 2.1 | 2.6 |
| Contribution of capital deepening | 0.9 | 0.9 | 1.0 |
| Contribution of labour composition | 0.1 | 0.3 | 0.3 |
| Contribution of technological change | 1.5 | 0.9 | 1.3 |

*Sources:* Calculations by author from CANSIM II Table 383-0021 and U.S. Bureau of Labor Statistics, Historical Multifactor Productivity Measures.

productivity growth is much larger. Much of the productivity gap between Canada and the United States is closed. This is not an abstract issue, since important policy arguments often rotate around raising Canada's productivity growth.

If there is a large productivity gap between Canada and the United States, closing that gap would make Canadians much better off. We would have more production with the same inputs of labour and capital. But everyone has a different perspective on the best policy to increase productivity. Some advocate cuts in corporate taxes. Others advocate moving from income taxes to broad-based sales taxes. Others advocate research and development spending, either direct spending by government, indirect spending of public research money at universities, or tax subsidies or other programs that pay for research and development at firms.

Some advocate freer trade with other countries as a way to increase Canadian productivity. Unfortunately there is little or no agreement on what policies would actually work to close the productivity growth gap between Canada and the United States.

*References:*

John Baldwin and Wulong Gu, "Productivity Performance in Canada, 1961 to 2008: An Update on Long-term Trends," *Canadian Productivity Review*, August 2009.

W. Erwin Diewert and Emily Yu, "New Estimates of Real Income and Multifactor Productivity Growth for the Canadian Business Sector, 1961–2011," *International Productivity Monitor* 24, 2012: 27–48.

# 17-4 | Institutions and Growth

It seems as though growth should be easy. If you are a poor country, technological progress is more a process of imitation rather than a process of innovation. As you save, you equip workers with more and more capital and their productivity and incomes rise. As we will see in the next chapter, if you are too poor to save, then you can borrow the necessary capital from the rest of the world. China and other Asian countries made growth look easy. So, why are so many other countries unable to do the same? As we indicated in Chapter 15, this question takes us from *macroeconomics* to *development economics*, and it would take a textbook in development economics to do it justice. But it is too important a question to leave aside entirely here. Here we look at a set of factors that economists call "institutions."

To get a sense of the issues, let us go beyond the set of rich countries we have focused on, and compare Kenya and the United States. In 2009, PPP GDP per capita in Kenya was about one-thirtieth of PPP GDP per capita in the United States. Part of the difference was due to a much lower level of capital per worker in Kenya. The other part of the difference was due to a much lower technological level in Kenya. It is estimated that $A$, the state of technology in Kenya, is about one-tenth of the U.S. level. Why is the state of technology in Kenya so low? After all, Kenya, like most poor countries, has access to most of the technological knowledge in the world. What prevents it from simply adopting much of the advanced countries' technologies, and quickly closing much of its technological gap with the United States?

> PPP stands for Purchasing Power Parity, PPP GDP per capita is measured using PPP exchanger rates—see the discussion in Chapter 15.

One can think of a number of potential answers, ranging from Kenya's geography and climate to its culture. Most economists believe, however, that the main source of the problem, for poor countries in general and for Kenya in particular, lies in their poor institutions.

What institutions do economists have in mind? At a broad level, the protection of property rights may well be the most important. Few individuals are going to create firms, introduce new technologies, and invest, if they expect that profits will be either appropriated by the state, extracted in bribes by corrupt bureaucrats, or stolen by other people in the economy. Figure 17–5 plots PPP GDP per capita in 1995 (using a logarithmic scale) for 90 countries, against an index measuring the degree of protection from expropriation, constructed for each of these countries by an international business organization. The positive correlation between the two is striking (the figure also plots the

FIGURE  17–5

**Protection from Expropriation and GDP per Capita**

There is a strong positive relation between the degree of protection from expropriation and the level of GDP per capita.

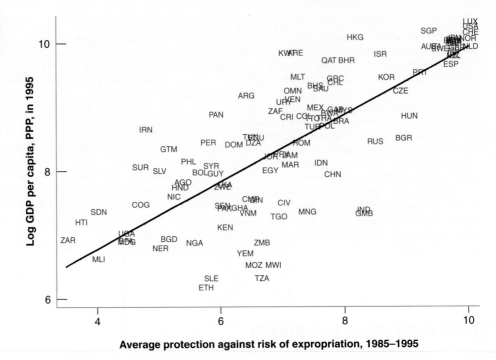

*Source:* Daron Acemoglu, "Understanding Institutions," Lionel Robbins Lectures, 2004.

The importance of property rights for growth was also painfully obvious during the transition of Eastern European countries from central planning to a market economy in the early 1990s. In many of these countries, poorly defined property rights, poorly enforced laws, and corrupt public officials severely constrained the growth of new firms and led to a decline in output.

This is where we move from the realm of growth theory to the fascinating realm of development economics.

regression line). Low property rights protection is associated with a low GDP per capita (at the extreme left of the figure are Zaire and Haiti); high protection is associated with a high GDP per capita (at the extreme right are the United States, Luxembourg, Norway, Switzerland, and the Netherlands).

What does "protection of property rights" mean in practice? It means a good political system, in which those in charge cannot expropriate or seize the property of the citizens. It means a good judicial system, where disagreements can be resolved efficiently and rapidly. Looking at an even finer degree of detail, it means laws against insider trading in the stock market so that people are willing to buy stocks and thus provide financing to firms; it means clearly written and well-enforced patent laws so that firms have incentive to do research and develop new products. It means good antitrust laws so that competive markets do not turn into monopolies with few incentives to introduce new methods of production and new products. And the list goes on. (A particularly clear example of the role of institutions is given in the Focus box "The Importance of Institutions: North and South Korea.")

This still leaves one essential question: Why don't poor countries adopt these good institutions? The answer is that it is hard! Good institutions are complex and difficult for poor countries to put in place. Surely, causality runs both ways in Figure 17–5. Low protection against expropriation leads to low GDP per capita. But it is also the case that low GDP per capita leads to worse protection against expropriation. Poor countries are often too poor to afford a good judicial system or to maintain a good police force, for example. Thus, improving institutions, and starting a virtuous cycle of higher GDP per capita and better institutions, is often very difficult. The fast-growing countries of Asia, although there are still some issues in China, appear to have succeeded in doing this. So far, much of Africa has been unable, however, to start such a virtuous cycle.

Following the surrender of Japan in 1945, Korea formally acquired its independence but became divided at the 38th parallel into two zones of occupation, with the Soviet armed forces occupying the North, and the U.S. armed forces occupying the South. Attempts by both sides to claim jurisdiction over all of Korea triggered the Korean War, which lasted from 1950 to 1953. At the armistice in 1953, Korea became formally divided into two countries, the "Democratic People's Republic of North Korea" and the "Republic of Korea" in the south.

An interesting feature of Korea before separation was its ethnic and linguistic homogeneity. The North and the South were inhabited by essentially the same people, with the same culture and the same religion. Economically, the two regions were also highly similar at the time of separation. PPP GDP per capita, in 1996 dollars, was roughly the same, about $700 in both the North and the South.

Yet, 50 years later, as shown in Figure 1, GDP per capita was 10 times higher in South Korea than in North Korea—$12,000 versus $1100! On the one hand, South Korea had joined the OECD, the club of rich countries. On the other, North Korea had seen its GDP per capita decrease by nearly two-thirds from its peak of $3000 in the mid-1970s and was facing famine on a large scale.

What happened? Institutions and the organization of the economy were dramatically different during that period in the South and in the North. South Korea relied on a capitalist organization of the economy, with strong state intervention, but also private ownership and legal protection of private producers. North Korea relied on central planning. Industries were quickly nationalized. Small firms and farms were forced to join large cooperatives so that they could be supervised by the state. There were no private property rights for individuals. The result was the decline of the industrial sector and the collapse of agriculture. The lesson is sad but transparent: Institutions matter very much for growth.

*Source:* Table and excerpts from *Why do Some Countries Produce So Much More Output per Worker than Others?* by Robert Hall and Charles Jones. NBER working paper, May 1998. © Hall and Jones.

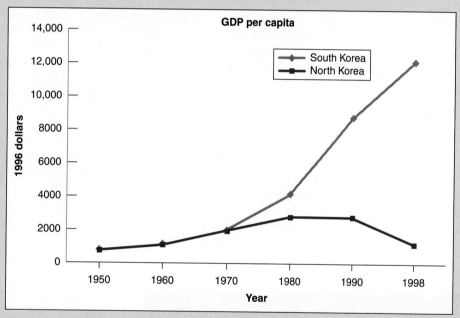

**FIGURE 1** PPP GDP per capita, North and South Korea, 1950–1998

# 17-5 | Epilogue: The Secrets of Growth

Why the rate of technological progress has declined since the mid-1970s is not the only unanswered question in the economics of growth. Many other questions remain.

We understand the basic mechanisms of growth in rich countries. But we are not very good at answering more specific questions: for example, what specific measures could be taken to increase growth? Are governments spending the right amount on basic research? Should patent laws be modified? Is there a case for an **industrial policy**, a policy aimed at helping specific sectors of the economy (for example, those sectors with the potential for high technological progress, and thus the potential for large spillovers for the rest of the economy)? What can we expect in terms of additional growth from increasing the average number of years of education by another year?

Turning from growth in rich countries since 1950 to growth over a longer time span or across a broader set of countries, our knowledge is also limited. For example, consider the fact that many countries in the world have a level of output per worker that is less than one-tenth the North American level of output per worker. The framework developed in this chapter and the previous one gives us a way of approaching this fact. If we think of output per worker as depending on physical capital per worker, human capital per worker, and the state of technology, we can ask: Are these countries poorer because they have less physical and human capital or because the state of their technology is lower?

The answer turns out that much of the difference comes from differences in the measured level of technology across countries. Compare, for example, the United States and China. GDP per worker ($Y/N$) is much higher in the United States than in China. If this ratio reflected only differences in the level of physical capital and human capital per worker between the two countries, then we would find that adjusting for differences in physical and human capital, the two economies had the same value of $A$: The level of technology would be the same in both countries. Existing estimates imply that $A$ is considerably higher in the United States than in China. In short, even if China suddenly acquired the same levels of physical capital and education per worker as the United States, output per worker would still be only a small fraction of what it is in the United States.

This answer is a useful first step, but it raises another question. Poor countries have access to most of the technological knowledge in the world. What prevents these countries from simply adapting much of the advanced countries' technologies, quickly closing a good part of their **technology gap**? It is clear that the answer to that question required us to take a broader interpretation of technology and to look at many of the factors we left aside in thinking about the determinants of the production function in Chapter 15. These include poorly established property rights, political instability, the lack of entrepreneurs, and poorly developed financial markets. In many countries, poorly defined property rights, poorly enforced laws, and corruption of public officials have severely constrained the growth of new firms. The list is easy to make. But the specific role of each of these factors is hard to pinpoint. And solving these problems is not easy: Many of them are as much the result of low income as they are the cause of low income.

The bottom line is clear: We have not yet fully unravelled the secrets of growth. In the next chapter, we explore growth in the open economy where capital and labour as well as technology flow between countries.

## SUMMARY

- When looking at the implications of technological progress for growth, it is useful to think of technological progress as increasing the amount of effective labour available in the economy (that is, labour multiplied by the state of technology). We can then think of output as being produced with capital and effective labour.

- In steady state, output *per effective worker* and capital *per effective worker* are constant. Put another way, output *per worker* and capital *per worker* grow at the rate of technological progress. Put yet another way, output and capital grow at the same rate as effective labour, thus at a rate equal to the growth rate of the number of workers plus the rate of technological progress. When the economy is in steady state, it is said to be on a balanced growth path.

- The rate of output growth in steady state is independent of the saving rate. However, the saving rate affects the steady-state level of output per effective worker. And increases in the saving rate lead, for some time, to an increase in the growth rate above the steady-state growth rate.

- Technological progress depends on both (1) the fertility of R&D, and (2) the appropriability of the results of R&D (that is, the extent to which firms benefit from the results of their R&D).

- In designing patent laws, governments must trade off protection for future discoveries with a desire to make existing discoveries available to potential users without restrictions.

- France, Japan, the United Kingdom, and the United States have had roughly balanced growth since 1985.
- There is no good explanation for the recent decline in the rate of technological progress in Canada in the last

decade. More generally, our understanding of the determinants of technological progress and its relation to such factors as the legal system or the political system remains limited.

## KEY TERMS

- appropriability, 339
- balanced growth, 335
- effective labour, or labour in efficiency units, 332
- fertility of research, 338
- industrial policy, 347
- patents, 340

- rate of growth of multifactor productivity, 351
- research and development (R&D), 337
- Solow residual, 351
- technological catch-up, 343
- technological frontier, 343
- technology gap, 348

## QUESTIONS AND PROBLEMS

### 1. TRUE/FALSE/UNCERTAIN

**a.** Writing the production function in terms of capital and effective labour implies that as the level of technology increases by a certain percentage, the number of workers required to achieve the same level of output decreases by the same percentage.

**b.** Because our production function exhibits constant returns to capital and effective labour, output per effective worker also exhibits constant returns to capital per effective worker.

**c.** If the rate of technological progress increases, investment must increase to keep capital per effective worker constant.

**d.** In steady state, output per effective worker grows at the rate of population growth.

**e.** In steady state, output per worker grows at the rate of technological progress.

**f.** A higher saving rate implies a higher level of capital per effective worker in the steady state, and thus a higher rate of growth of output per effective worker in steady state.

**g.** Even if the potential returns from R&D spending are identical to the potential returns from investing in a new machine, R&D spending is much riskier for firms than investing in new machines.

**h.** The fact that one cannot patent a theorem implies that private firms will not engage in basic research.

### 2. R&D SPENDING

Why is the amount of R&D spending important for growth? How do the appropriability and fertility of research affect the amount of R&D spending?

For each of the following policy proposals, determine how the appropriability and fertility of research are affected and what you expect the long-run effect to be on R&D and on output:

**a.** An international treaty that ensures that each country's patents are legally protected all over the world.

**b.** Tax credits for each dollar of R&D spending.

**c.** A decrease in funding of government-sponsored conferences between universities and corporations.

**d.** The elimination of patents on breakthrough drugs so that the drugs can be sold at low cost as soon as they are available.

### 3. PATENTS AND GROWTH

Where does technological progress come from for the economic leaders of the world? Where does it come from in the developing countries? Do you see any reasons why the developing countries may choose to have poor patent protection? Are there any dangers in such a policy (for the developing countries)?

### 4. DIFFUSION OF INVENTIONS

Use the medical and automobile industries to provide examples of technological advances that have not yet fully diffused in the economy. Can you think of some advances in those industries whose diffusion is relatively more important than that of others for society? Name a policy that would accelerate the diffusion process. Would such a policy also have disadvantages for society? Explain.

## 5. THE SLOWDOWN IN PRODUCTIVITY GROWTH

Consider the following two scenarios:

**i.** The rate of technological progress declines forever.

**ii.** The saving rate declines forever.

**a.** What is the impact of each of these scenarios on economic growth over the next five years?

**b.** Over the next five decades?

In both cases, make sure to consider the effects on both the growth rate and the level of output.

## 6. STEADY STATE OUTPUT AND TECHNOLOGICAL PROGRESS

Suppose that the economy's production function is:

$$Y = \sqrt{K}\sqrt{NA}$$

and that the saving rate ($s$) is equal to 16% and the rate of depreciation ($\delta$) is equal to 10%. Further, suppose that the number of workers grows at 2% per year and the rate of technological progress is 4% per year.

**a.** Find the steady state values of:
   The capital stock per effective worker.
   Output per effective worker.
   The growth rate of output per effective worker.
   The growth rate of output per worker.
   The growth rate of output.

**b.** Suppose that the rate of technological progress doubles to 8% per year. Recompute the answers to (a). Explain.

**c.** Now, suppose that the rate of technological progress is still equal to 4% per year but the number of workers now grows at 6% per year. Recompute the answers to (a). Are people better off in (a) or in (c)? Explain.

## 7. GROWTH ACCOUNTING

In the appendix to this chapter, it is shown how data on output, capital, and labour can be used to construct estimates of the rate of growth of technological progress.

Consider the following production function, which gives a good description of production in rich countries:

$$Y = K^{1/3}(NA)^{2/3}$$

Following the same steps as in the appendix, you can show that:

$$\text{Residual} = [g_Y - \tfrac{1}{3}g_K - \tfrac{2}{3}g_N]$$

or reorganizing:

$$\text{Residual} = [(g_Y - g_N) - \tfrac{1}{3}(g_K - g_N)]$$

The rate of technological progress is then obtained by dividing the residual by the share of labour, which, given the production function we have assumed, is equal to two-thirds:

$$g_A = \text{Residual}/(2/3) = (3/2)\,\text{Residual}$$

Download the series "Real GDP per worker" and "Nonresidential capital stock per worker" for both Japan and the United States for the period after 1965 from the *Penn World Tables*. (Unfortunately, the series on $K/N$ is not available for years prior to 1965.)

Input the series into your favourite spreadsheet program.

**a.** Compute the growth rate of $Y/N$, ($g_Y - g_N$), and $K/N$, ($g_K - g_N$), for each year and for each country.

**b.** For each country, calculate the average growth rate of $Y/N$ and $K/N$ for the sub-periods 1965–1973 and from 1974 on.

**c.** Using the equations above, compute the rate of technological progress for both sub-periods for both countries.

**d.** Do you find evidence of a slowdown? For which period?

**e.** The U.S. was the technological leader in both periods. So, why is it that Japan's growth rate of technological progress is so much higher than that of the U.S. in both periods? Why does the difference become smaller in the later sub-period?

**f.** Does the difference in $g_A$ explain all the difference in ($g_Y - g_N$)? If not, where does the rest come from?

---

### FURTHER READING

- For more on growth, both theory and evidence, read Charles Jones and Dietrich Vollrath, *Introduction to Economic Growth*, 3rd ed. (Norton, 2013).

- For more on patents, see *The Economist,* Special Report: Patents and Technology, October 20th, 2005.

- For more on growth in two large, fast growing countries, read Barry Bosworth and Susan M. Collins, "Accounting for Growth: Comparing China and India," *Journal of Economic Perspectives* 22 (1), 2008: pp. 45–66.

On two issues we have not explored in the text:

- Growth and global warming. Read the *Stern Review on the Economics of Climate Change*, 2006. You can find it at http://mudancasclimaticas.cptec.inpe.br/~rmclima/pdfs/destaques/sternreview_report_complete.pdf (The report is very long. Read just the executive summary.).

- Growth and the environment. Read The Economist Survey on *The Global Environment; The Great Race*, July 4, 2002, and the update entitled "The Anthropocene: A Man-made World," May 26, 2011.

## CONSTRUCTING A MEASURE OF TECHNOLOGICAL PROGRESS

In 1957, Robert Solow suggested a way of constructing an estimate of the rate of technological progress. The method, still used today, relies on one important assumption: Each factor of production is paid its marginal product.

Under this assumption, it is easy to compute the contribution of an increase in any factor of production to the increase in output. For example, if a worker is paid $30,000 a year, the assumption implies that her contribution to output is equal to $30,000. Now, suppose that this worker increases the amount of hours she works by 10%. The increase in output coming from the increase in her hours will therefore be equal to $30,000 × 10%, or $3000.

Let us write this more formally. Denote output by $Y$, labour by $N$, and the real wage by $W/P$. Then, as we just established, the change in output is equal to the real wage multiplied by the change in labour:

$$\Delta Y = \frac{W}{P} \Delta N$$

Divide both sides of the equation by $Y$, divide and multiply the right side by $N$, and reorganize:

$$\frac{\Delta Y}{Y} = \frac{WN}{PY} \frac{\Delta N}{N}$$

Note that the first term on the right ($WN/PY$) is equal to the share of labour in output—the total wage bill in dollars divided by the value of output in dollars. Denote this share by $\alpha$. Note that $\Delta Y/Y$ is the rate of growth of output, and denote it by $g_Y$. Note similarly that $\Delta N/N$ is the rate of change of the labour input, and denote it by $g_N$. Then, the previous relation can be written as:

$$g_Y = \alpha g_N$$

More generally, this reasoning implies that the part of output growth attributable to growth of the labour input is equal to $\alpha$ times $g_N$.

Similarly, we can compute the part of output growth attributable to growth of the capital stock. As there are only two factors of production—labour and capital—and as the share of labour is equal to $\alpha$, the share of capital in income must be equal to $(1 - \alpha)$. If the growth rate of capital is equal to $g_K$, then the increase in output attributable to growth of capital is equal to $(1 - \alpha)$ times $g_K$.

Putting the contributions of labour and capital together, the growth in output attributable to growth in both labour and capital is equal to $(\alpha g_N + (1 - \alpha)g_K)$.

We can then measure the effects of technological progress by computing what Solow called the residual, the excess of actual growth of output over the growth attributable to growth in labour and capital $(\alpha g_N + (1 - \alpha)g_K)$.

$$\text{Residual} \equiv \underset{\substack{\text{Actual} \\ \text{growth}}}{g_Y} - \underset{\substack{\text{Growth attributable to} \\ \text{growth of labour and capital}}}{[\alpha g_N + (1 - \alpha)g_K]}$$

This measure is called the **Solow residual**. All we need to know to compute it are the growth rates of output, labour, and capital, as well as the shares of labour and capital. The measurement of the capital input is actually quite difficult and researchers do not always agree on the correct estimate of the growth rate of technology.

The Solow residual is sometimes called the **rate of growth of multifactor productivity**. This is to distinguish it from the *rate of growth of labour productivity*, which is defined as $(g_Y - g_N)$, the rate of output growth minus the rate of labour growth.

| TABLE 1 | Estimates of Annual Multifactor Productivity Growth in Canada, 1962–2011 (percent) | | |
|---|---|---|---|
| | Business Sector | Business Sector: Goods Industries | Business Sector: Services Industries |
| 1962–1969 | 1.3 | 2.5 | 0.0 |
| 1970–1979 | 0.4 | 0.8 | 0.2 |
| 1980–1989 | −0.1 | 0.4 | −0.5 |
| 1990–1999 | 0.3 | 0.1 | −0.3 |
| 2000–2011 | −0.2 | −0.7 | 0.2 |

*Source:* Annual percent rates of change of indexes of multifactor productivity; CANSIM Table 383–220; Variables V417112881, V41712984, V4172895.

The Solow residual is related to the rate of technological progress in a simple way. The residual is equal to the share of labour times the rate of technological progress:

$$\text{Residual} = \alpha g_A$$

We will not derive this result here. But the intuition for this relation comes from the fact that what matters in the production function $Y = F(K, AN)$, equation (17.1), is the product of labour times the state of technology, $AN$. We saw that to get the contribution of labour growth to output growth, we must multiply the growth rate of labour by its share. Because $N$ and $A$ enter in the same way in the production function, it is clear that to get the contribution of technological progress to output growth, we must also multiply it by the share of labour.

If the Solow residual is equal to zero, so is technological progress. To construct an estimate of $g_A$, one must construct the Solow residual and then divide it by the share of labour. This is how the estimates of $g_A$ presented in the text are constructed.

As in the specific American-Canadian comparison in the Focus box "Labour productivity in Canada and the United States," there is no way to look at productivity growth in Canada, however measured, and think that there is not a problem.

*Sources:* Robert Solow, "Technical Change and the Aggregate Production Function," *Review of Economics and Statistics* 39 (3), 1957: pp. 312–320.

# Economic Growth in the Open Economy

## The Core: The Long Run

In the previous three chapters growth in output came from having more workers; each worker having more capital; or society increasing the level of technology, that is, producing more with the same number of workers and the same amount of capital. All of this discussion dealt only with a closed economy, an economy that does not trade with countries in the rest of the world. We need to modify this assumption. Other countries play a huge role in the growth of almost every national economy. We live in an interconnected world. In this chapter, we look at three different ways in which the international economy affects growth:

- The migration of people across international borders plays a large role in the growth of total output. In Canada's case, net immigration will provide the largest source of population growth in the next few decades. The level and structure of immigration are important policy choices.

- There is a great deal of lending and borrowing across international borders. A substantial portion of the capital stock in Canada is owned by foreigners. Residents of Canada sell their bonds to nonresidents. Residents of Canada take out loans from residents of other countries. Residents of other countries own shares in Canadian corporations. Canadians typically own some physical assets in foreign countries. Canadians frequently lend money to nonresidents and buy shares of corporations resident in other countries. We need to understand why international borrowing and lending in all these forms occurs; and we need to understand how to measure these flows of assets and incomes.

- It is clear that technology and knowledge flow across international borders. This means that technology is an international good. We touched on this issue in Chapter 17 but there is more to say. There are important policy issues around trade in technology.

In the appendix to this chapter, the issue of an optimal current account deficit is addressed. We show such an optimal deficit exists. If a country takes advantage of its interconnections with the rest of the world, growth takes place at a more rapid pace.

## 18-1 | Growth in the Labour Input to Production in Canada

The production function in the three previous chapters made use of a variable we called $N$. $N$ meant total employment. In the last chapter, $N$ grew at $g_N$ percent per year. $g_N$ was exogenous, with its value determined outside of any choices that are part of the economic or political policy process. $N$ has been measured as the number of workers. In this section, we want to be more precise about the measurement of $N$ and the sources of its growth over time. There is at least one important policy choice to be made by Canadians. There are three variables leading to the final value of $g_N$, one unique to the open economy and two variables common to both open and closed economies.

### The Ratio of Employment to Population and Average Hours of Work

Thus far, the variable $N$ has been total employment, representing the number of workers. If we wanted to be more precise about $N$ as a measure of the labour input to production, we should measure $N$ in terms of number of hours of work and not simply the number of workers. Statistics Canada reports that Canadians worked 585,290,830 hours in the year 2012, an incomprehensibly large number. We need to break this number down into its components.

First, realize that many people in the total population of Canada do not work. They are too young, too old, in school, or simply choose to remain out of paid employment for other reasons. Even if the total population of Canada remained constant, $N$, the number of persons working, could vary as more or fewer people are at work. Figure 18–1 shows the variation in the percentage of Canadians over 15 years of age who were employed. The data begin in 1976 and end in 2012. Values are presented for the total population, as well as males and females separately. These variables are called the **employment-to-population ratio**, the number of employed workers divided by the population 15 years of age and over.

The employment-to-population ratio for the combination of males and females in Canada has been increasing gradually since 1976. In 2012 about 62% of Canadians over the age of 15 had a job of some type. There are significant short-term fluctuations. In the large recessions of 1982, 1991, and 2009, a smaller proportion of Canadians were employed. We considered these fluctuations in the short-run and medium-run analyses in the preceding chapters. After the first two recessions, the employment-to-population ratio resumed its upward path, usually with a long delay. There has been little recovery in the employment-to-population ratio since its drop in 2009, at least to 2012.

| FIGURE | 18–1 |

**Employment-to-Population Ratio in Canada, 1976–2012**

Here, the percentage of the population aged 15 years and over that is employed is graphed from 1976 to 2012. The three recessions, 1982, 1991, and 2009, all create temporary declines in the employment-to-population ratio. From 1976 to 1989, a decline in the male employment-to-population ratio was offset by an increase in the female employment-to-population ratio.

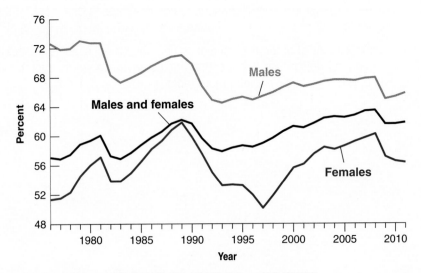

*Source:* Using CANSIM II variables V2461266, V2461476, and V2461687.

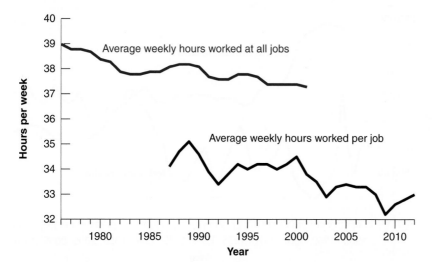

FIGURE 18-2

**Average Weekly Hours Worked by Canadians, 1976–2012**

Average weekly hours worked by Canadians at all jobs has declined slightly but steadily from 1976 to 2001. After 2001, Statistics Canada no longer measured this variable. Instead, Statistics Canada now calculates a measure of average hours per week per job. Average hours per week per job is now about 33 hours per week. It has also fallen slightly between 1987 and 2012. The figure makes it clear that some people have more than one job.

Source: *Average weekly hours worked at all jobs* 1976–2001 using CANSIM II variable V163865; *average weekly hours per job* from 1987–2004 using CANSIM II variable V2641490 divided by CANSIM II variable V2641481.

The employment-to-population ratio for males declined steadily. The employment-to-population ratio for females rose quite steadily from 1976 to 1990, but fell in the early 1990s and rebounded in the late 1990s and early 2000s. It then crashed after the 2009 recession. The overall increase in female labour force activity was one of the largest social and economic changes in the twentieth century. The increase in the female employment-to-population ratio offset the fall in the male employment-to-population ratio over the whole time period.

There are a variety of reasons why the male employment-to-population ratio has been declining. Longer life expectancy creates a longer period of retirement and therefore, given the same retirement age, there are more retired people. There is a very slow movement toward earlier retirement in Canada. There is a longer period of postsecondary education for both men and women. All these factors lower the employment-to-population ratio over time.

The Labour Force Survey also calculates the number of hours worked per employed person. Figure 18–2 shows the **average hours** per week per employed worker in Canada. Again, the recessions stand out. Those who remained employed did work fewer hours. You will notice a slight decline in average hours of work for the period of the data (the scale of this diagram varies within a very small range—less than two hours). Although the labour input into production could rise if each worker in Canada worked a few more hours, this is very unlikely to be a large source of an increased labour input. As Canadians get richer, they are likely to want more leisure time, not less. Many people work part time by choice in order to have more time for family or schooling. These people do not want more hours of work.

We can write what we have learned as an equation:

$$\text{Total hours} = \text{Average hours per employee} \times \frac{\text{Number of employees}}{\text{Population}} \times \text{Population}$$

If we accept that the first two variables in the equation above (the employment-to-population ratio and the average hours worked per employed person) are very slow to change, then the labour input into the production process in Canada will grow only if the Canadian population grows. How can the total population of Canada grow?

## Natural Population Growth

In a closed economy—a country without international interaction—the identity

$$\text{Population change} = \text{Number of births} - \text{Number of deaths}$$

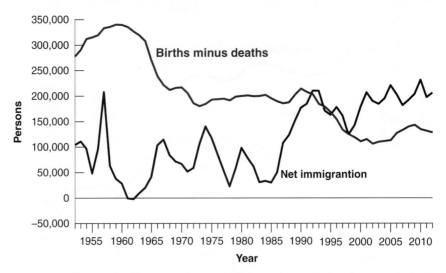

## FIGURE 18–3

**Sources of Population Growth in Canada, 1952–2012**

The source of population growth in Canada shifted dramatically over time. The bulge of the baby boom in the 1950s stands out as the period when births greatly exceeded deaths. Net immigration was relatively small and in fact was negative in 1961 and 1962. After 1990, as birth rates dropped, net immigration increased. Since 1996, population growth from net immigration has substantially exceeded natural population growth.

*Source:* Births, CANSIM II variable V62; Deaths, CANSIM Variable V77; Immigration and Emigration from CANSIM Table 051-0037.

completely describes population change. One of the few countries in the world that would look much like this equation would be North Korea. In North Korea, both immigration and emigration are very small. This equation describes only part of population growth in Canada. Figure 18–3 plots births minus deaths in Canada over the last half-century. The baby boom of the 1950s stands out. As the generation born in the late 1950s passed through the population structure, there were first more children, then more working-age adults, and finally there will be more retired and aged adults. The children of the baby boom create a small "echo" of this pattern. We are not primarily concerned with the consequences of the baby boom (fascinating though they are). We want to use Figure 18–3 to make the point that in the near term, **natural population growth** from the excess of births over deaths in Canada is declining. From 1989, natural population growth drops rapidly from 200,000 to 100,000 persons per year. In some countries, as their population ages and birth rates drop, natural population growth could become negative. Europe and Japan are also close to or at negative natural population growth. As these countries became richer and more females participated in the workforce, the number of births dropped below the number of deaths. A number of countries have attempted policies to increase birth rates—usually some combination of payments per child, extended parental leave programs, and the provision of more child care. In Canada, Quebec has travelled the furthest along this route. In 1997, the province began to provide $5 a day for child care. In 2005, Quebec began to pay nontaxable child benefits of $2100 for the first child, $1045 each for the second and third children, and $1600 for a fourth child up to a maximum of $5790. In 2006, Quebec replaced the federal parental leave policy with a more generous one. The number of births in Quebec did increase slightly. The reality is that net immigration will be the source of population growth in Canada for the foreseeable future.

## Immigration and Emigration in Canada

Canada is a nation of immigrants. Many of the users of this book are immigrants or the children of immigrants. Given the discussion above, it will not surprise you to learn that the growth in labour inputs in Canada now depends primarily on **net immigration**. Net immigration is the difference between the number of people moving to Canada from other countries, **immigration**, and the number of people leaving Canada to live in other countries, **emigration**. Table 18–1 fills in the values for the identity

Population change = Number of births − Number of deaths + Net immigration

The table shows one of several population projections made by Statistics Canada in 2012. This is a medium growth projection. Deaths begin to catch up to births as the population ages. Net immigration, immigrants minus emigrants, is a much larger component of population growth. Population is measured in millions, the remaining variables in thousands.

| Period | Population at Beginning | Births | Deaths | Immigrants | Emigrants |
|---|---|---|---|---|---|
| 2012/2013 | 34,921.90 | 404.7 | 254.9 | 263.1 | 47.8 |
| 2013/2014 | 35,317.50 | 409.1 | 258.7 | 266.3 | 48.1 |
| 2014/2015 | 35,711.70 | 413.2 | 262.6 | 269.5 | 48.3 |
| 2015/2016 | 36,103.90 | 416.9 | 266.4 | 272.7 | 48.6 |
| 2016/2017 | 36,493.80 | 420.2 | 270.3 | 275.9 | 48.8 |
| 2017/2018 | 36,881.00 | 422.9 | 274.2 | 279.0 | 49.1 |
| 2018/2019 | 37,264.80 | 425.2 | 278.2 | 282.2 | 49.4 |
| 2019/2020 | 37,644.60 | 427.0 | 282.2 | 285.3 | 49.6 |
| 2020/2021 | 38,025.10 | 428.3 | 286.4 | 288.4 | 49.9 |
| 2021/2022 | 38,405.50 | 429.1 | 290.5 | 291.5 | 50.1 |
| 2022/2023 | 38,785.50 | 429.3 | 294.8 | 294.6 | 50.4 |
| 2023/2024 | 39,164.30 | 429.2 | 299.3 | 297.8 | 50.6 |

Source: Statistics Canada, Population Projections for Canada, Provinces and Territories, Publication 91-520-XTable 3-1 Medium Growth. http://www.statcan.gc.ca/pub/91-520-x/2010001/t147-eng.htm.

as much as possible. The identity is the correct description of population change in Canada. Table 18–1 makes it clear that over the next decades net immigration will be the major source of population growth in Canada, as it has been in the recent past.

The dominant role of immigration in population and labour force growth in Canada leads to two macroeconomic questions: (1) Do immigrants cause unemployment? (2) How much immigration is the "right" amount?

First, it should be absolutely obvious that immigration cannot itself "cause" the unemployment rate to be higher. We have had massive net immigration in the last 40 years into Canada. Average unemployment rates have been more or less stable since 1970, while immigration rates have increased, both in absolute terms and relative to the population. Within Canada, the province of Alberta, which saw a substantial increase in immigration in the last decade, currently has the lowest, not the highest, unemployment rate. Common sense tells us that immigrants, like the native-born, have to be housed, fed, educated, and clothed. This is an increase in aggregate demand. Immigrants are productive and thus increase aggregate supply. Over the long term, immigration leads to equal increases in aggregate supply and aggregate demand. There are numerous studies that find that the unemployment rates of immigrants and native-born Canadians are similar. In fact, immigrants use Employment Insurance and other forms of social assistance less, not more, than do native-born Canadians. With a little thought, this fact may not be that surprising. Immigrants are, for the most part, persons with enough talents, ability, and courage to leave their own cultures and go to a new country. Such characteristics are likely to lead to economic success.

The second question asked was: How much net immigration is the "right" amount? This is a much harder question to answer. It is a cause of much social tension in some developed countries. It seems to cause less social tension in Canada. But how fast a society wants population growth to occur is not obvious. For example, most immigrants end up in one of Canada's three largest cities: Toronto, Vancouver, or Montreal. Do we want these cities to continue to grow into their surrounding agricultural areas? Are there congestion and other environmental consequences of further urban growth in these three cities? Is it possible to encourage immigrants to

In statistical studies, this is sometimes called sample-selection bias. You might think random samples of the native-born and immigrants are comparable. But these random samples draw on different pools of persons. The pool of immigrants has the characteristics of persons willing to leave their own cultures and go to another culture on a permanent basis. These are not going to be a random sample of persons from their countries of origin. The sample of the native-born will be much closer to a random sample of persons born in Canada. The only persons missing from the draw of the native-born will be those who left Canada, a relatively small group.

The other, very controversial way to add labour input to the Canadian economy is much more recent. There has always been a small temporary foreign workers program. These workers were covered under a Seasonal Agricultural Workers Program. They were brought in to harvest, plant, and generally do manual farm work that was no longer considered a desirable job by native-born Canadians or immigrants who arrived as permanent residents. The graph below shows how the temporary worker program has expanded since the year 2000 and particularly since 2006.

There are two lines on the graph. One line shows the number of temporary foreign workers present in Canada on December 1 of each year. You can see this number grew from about 50,000 in 1987 to 300,000 in 2011. Half that increase took place after 2006.

We know that the population of Canada and the labour force also increased over this period. The upper line in Figure 1 shows the temporary foreign work force as a percent of the labour force. This value rose from 0.5 percentage points in 1987 to 1.7 percentage points in 2011.

We need to be careful here. Figure 1 refers to the level of the temporary foreign workforce in Canada. This is different from the rate of growth of the population or the labour force. But the increase in the level of temporary foreign workers from 2002 to 2011 added significantly to the level of the labour force and, thus in a small way, to the growth rate of the labour force from 2002 to 2011.

The program has been very controversial. In terms of our labour market model in Chapter 9, we would argue that a large number of temporary foreign workers would reduce the bargaining power of labour and increase the bargaining power of employers. This would increase the markup and reduce the real wage. This would, all else equal, increase the unemployment rate. This is the analysis done by those who oppose the expansion of the temporary foreign workers program.

The President of the Alberta Federation of Labour, on April 29, 2013, is quoted as saying,

*"The temporary foreign worker program has to be scrapped,"* AFL president Gil McGowan said. *"Employers are clearly turning to it as a first choice so they can hire people who have fewer legal protections, can be paid less than their Canadian counterparts, and who can be kicked out of the country if they make a fuss."*[†]

The reasons for the program's rapid expansion after 2006 are unclear. The government's official statement is that:

*The Temporary Foreign Worker Program (TFWP) allows Canadian employers to hire foreign nationals to fill temporary labour and skill shortages when qualified Canadian citizens or permanent residents are not available.*[†]

The key is deciding that a qualified Canadian citizen or permanent resident is not available. This is done through a Labour

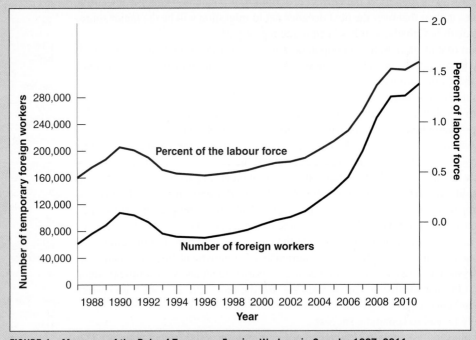

**FIGURE 1    Measures of the Role of Temporary Foreign Workers in Canada, 1987–2011**

*Source:* Statistics Canada CANSIM II Table 282-0002.

---

[†]Gil McGowan, President, Alberta Federation of Labour, "Businesses being given temporary foreign worker permits regardless of economic need," 29 April 2013
[†]http://www.cic.gc.ca/english/resources/publications/employers/temp-foreign-worker-program.asp

Market Opinion (LMO) issued by Human Resources and Skills Development Canada (HRSDC) on a case-by-case basis, based on an employer application. Clearly, in spite of relatively high unemployment rates after 2008, more permits for temporary foreign workers were issued.

Some changes were announced to the program in April 2013. These included a requirement that the temporary foreign workers be paid the prevailing wage. Previously employers had been allowed to pay 15% less than the prevailing wage. Employers will now have to pay fees to obtain the necessary LMO. The government claims that employers with temporary foreign workers will be required to have a plan in place to replace that worker in the future. Finally, there may be a provision that employers can require only either English or French as a language requirement for a job. It is unclear at the time of writing whether these changes will be vigorously enforced. What is clear is that the temporary foreign workers program allowed the labour force in Canada to be about 1 percentage point higher in 2011 than it would have been without the program.

*Sources:* The Minister's position on the Temporary Foreign Workers Program is found at http://www.cic.gc.ca/english/resources/publications/employers/temp-foreign-worker-program.asp. The Alberta Federation of Labour website is http://www.afl.org.

settle elsewhere? Most Canadians seem to recognize that if net immigration were zero, then the population of Canada would both fall and certainly become older on average. The discussion of old age pensions in Chapter 16 in the Focus box "Old Age Pensions and Capital Accumulation in Canada" told us that, without net immigration, fewer and fewer workers will be supporting the average retired person in the public pay-as-you-go pension arrangements that are already in place. This would be a problem.

On June 18, 2008, Parliament approved significant changes to the *Immigration and Refugee Protection Act*. The intent of the changes, which remain controversial, is to reduce a large backlog in applications to immigrate to Canada that had built up over several years. Under the previous rules, the immigration office was required to process applications in the order in which they arrived. Under the new system, the current Minister of Immigration may prioritize in a public way (published in the *Canada Gazette*) a different order for processing applications: "The new provisions will allow the Department to choose, from the new applications, those that best meet Canada's labour market needs. Under the current system, which was much less flexible, CIC (Citizenship and Immigration Canada) processed applications from skilled workers in the order in which they were received." Hence, specific types of skilled workers can be given priority in processing. The Minister has made use of these powers to change the composition of immigration. There has been a shift in the composition of immigrants away from family class immigrants (those reunifying with family members in Canada) to both economic migrants and a category of immigrants called "other." The Focus box "Temporary Foreign Workers in Canada" discusses another even more controversial change: the increase in the use of temporary foreign workers to augment the Canadian labour force. As shown in Table 18–1, net immigration will continue to be the primary source of growth in the Canadian labour force over the next decade.

There will be significant growth in *N*, whether measured as the total number of workers or as the total number of hours. Whatever the number of immigrants finally is, they need to be equipped with capital to work with. In the closed economy, capital can come from only a reduction in current consumption. In the open economy, new capital can come from two sources: a reduction in current consumption or from foreign borrowing. We investigate these sources next.

# 18-2 | Equipping Workers with Capital in an Open Economy

## A Closed Economy Review

Before we actually ask how we equip workers with capital in an open economy, we need to review the creation of new physical capital in a closed economy. If there is no government sector (we will add the government sector to this analysis in Chapter 25), then we wrote in Chapter 16 that:

$$I_t = S_t = Y_t - C_t \tag{18.1}$$

where $I_t$ is new capital formation, the amount of physical investment, $S_t$ is savings, $Y_t$ is total output, and $C_t$ is total consumption. The second equation to review:

$$K_{t+1} = (1 - \delta)K_t + I_t \tag{18.2}$$

kept track of the level of the capital stock at the beginning of period $t+1$, denoted $K_{t+1}$. The total capital stock in the country increases only if investment was large enough to replace the amount of capital depreciating (wearing out). $\delta$ is the depreciation rate. Using these two equations, we found the steady-state level of output, looked at the short-term and longer-term effects of changing the savings rate, and chose a value of the savings rate to maximize $C$ in the long run. While these are all interesting issues to address, we did not emphasize the most difficult issue these two equations raise: If you want more capital stock in the future, equation (18.2) says you must invest more today, and then equation (18.1) says that if you invest more today, you *must* consume less today. This is an unpleasant choice. No one wants to give up consumption. In the open economy, there is a little more freedom to choose. But that freedom does come at a cost.

## Consumption and Investment Choices in an Open Economy

When international trade is possible, equation (18.1) is rewritten as:

$$C_t + I_t = Y_t + Q_t - X_t = Y_t - NX_t \tag{18.3}$$

The total of consumption and investment in any period can now be different from the total amount of domestic production. In particular, this country can now increase investment in period $t$ and thus its capital stock in period $t+1$ *without* reducing consumption in period $t$. How? Rearrange equation (18.3) so that:

$$I_t = Y_t - C_t + Q_t - X_t = Y_t - C_t - NX_t$$

Suppose this country wants to increase investment and leave consumption unchanged. This can occur if net exports ($NX_t$) become more negative. To be absolutely clear on this vital point, let us consider a numerical example. Suppose we start with $Y_t = 100$, $C_t = 70$, and $I_t = 30$ and set both exports and imports to zero. We can then increase $I_t$ (investment) by \$10 and leave consumption unchanged only if this country imports the additional investment goods. The first lesson learned: If the use of goods and services ($C_t + I_t$) is greater than the production of goods ($Y_t$) in any period $t$, then net exports in that period must be negative. This sounds like a great situation; this country can now increase its future capital and hence its future production and not reduce its consumption today. But as we warned you before, there is a catch.

## The Accumulation of Foreign Debts in an Open Economy

The catch is quite straightforward. The foreign countries do not typically make a gift of the extra resources needed for the additional investment spending, which are the imports we use to install the new capital goods. Rather, they lend us those goods or they lend us the money to buy those goods. When you are lent money, the lender expects to be repaid and usually to be repaid with interest. Foreign lenders are no different from any other type of lender. To keep track of our loans from foreigners (and our loans to foreigners), we need one more equation and two more pieces of notation. $B_t^f$ is going to measure the amount of foreign bonds people in the domestic country hold at the beginning of period $t$. $B$ stands for bonds and $f$ for foreign. $B_t^f$ is positive if Canadians have net foreign assets that is, Canadians lent more then they borrow from abroad and is negative if Canadians have net foreign debts. We will see in the data that the units of $B_t^f$ can be quite complicated. We are simply going to measure them in units of real output (the same units used for $Y_t$ and its components). This once again sets the real exchange rate $\epsilon$ equal to 1 for simplicity. The equations below use bonds as a shorthand for all possible types of international financial instruments. We are going to have one interest rate on all loans made to or taken from foreigners with these bonds. That real interest rate is denoted $r$, and $r$ is not going to vary over time; $r$ is a real interest rate (a concept fully explored in the next chapter). For now

In writing equation (18.3), the real exchange rate $\epsilon$ is set equal to unity in every period. This means that the units we are using to measure domestic production are the same units we use to measure exports and imports. This saves some notation without changing the basic analysis. $Q_t$ is imports and $X_t$ is exports, $NX_t$ is net exports. ▶

Foreign aid is the giving of additional resources from one country to another. Foreign aid would allow additional consumption or investment without incurring foreign debts. That is the point of foreign aid. This equation ignores foreign aid. Foreign aid is a small part of providing additional resources. Most international transfers of resources take place through borrowing and lending, not gifts. Canadian taxpayers do make gifts to other countries through official international aid organizations. The private ▶ sector in Canada makes gifts to other countries through both Canadian nongovernmental organizations (NGOs), such as Mennonite Central Committee (MCC), and through international NGOs, such as UNICEF and OXFAM. The total value of gifts from Canada to other countries is quite small. The official goal for gifts from the Canadian taxpayer to other countries is 0.7% of GDP. This goal has not been achieved since it was set in 1995.

$r$ (in decimal form) means that if we lend one dollar of output to a foreigner in period $t$, they will repay $(1+r)$ dollars of output in period $t+1$. If we borrow one dollar of output in period $t$ from a foreigner in period $t$, then we will repay $(1+r)$ dollars of output in period $t+1$.

These are inflation-adjusted or real dollars throughout this chapter. We keep track of our net foreign assets (or our net foreign debts) using:

$$B_{t+1}^f - B_t^f = rB_t^f + Y_t - (C_t + I_t) \tag{18.4}$$

Equation (18.4) says that the money foreigners owe to us (our foreign assets) increases $(B_{t+1}^f - B_t^f$ is positive) when the sum of the interest we earn on our foreign assets $(rB_t^f)$ and our production $(Y_t)$ exceeds our use of resources $(C_t + I_t)$. Equation (18.4) is a version of Canada's international budget constraint.[1] The left-hand side of equation (18.4) is Canada's **current account balance**.

Equation (18.4) has a perfect analogy to your own finances. Think of yourself as a country (and everyone else is now the rest of the world). Start off your year in debt, so $B_t^f$ is negative. In this example, $B_t^f = -\$1500$; you have a debt outstanding on your credit card. Suppose this year, the sum of your consumption (the food you eat—denote this $C_t$ and set this equal to $\$9000$) and your investment (a stove you buy—denote this $I_t$ and set this equal to $\$500$) is exactly the earnings you make from your job ($Y_t$—your earnings from your job were $\$9500$). You might ask why we treat the stove purchase as a physical investment. A stove lasts through many years of productive use. A stove is used to produce other goods and services rather than being directly consumed. Thus, in this example, the stove stands in for physical investment. You are already in debt and must also pay the interest on existing debt—that is, $rB_t^f$ is negative in your version of equation (18.4). If the interest rate on your credit card is 10%, then $rB_t^f = 0.10 \times -\$1500 = -\$150$. Your assets at the beginning of period $t$ were negative. Since you spent exactly what you earned, you could not pay off any of your debts or the interest on your debt and, in fact, must borrow a bit more. The new borrowing is $rB_t^f$, which is used to "pay" the interest on your debt. Now you owe even more—the original debt plus the interest you did not pay. Your total financial assets at the end of the year will be negative $\$1650$. This is called "rolling over" your debt. You reborrowed the money you had owed at the beginning of the period, and you borrowed the interest you owed on that money. It is like having a credit card bill where you pay nothing on the bill, not even the minimum payment. The next month the bill has the same debt plus the interest that you did not pay last month, even when you did not use the card. Thus, your debt would rise by exactly the amount of the interest. In the numerical example above $B_{t+1}^f - B_t^f = rB_t^f$ because $Y_t$ was exactly equal to $C_t + I_t$.

Countries can "roll over" their debt as well. As long as the lenders are willing to allow the interest to be added to the debt outstanding, the country can use its entire production for consumption and investment. This is not typical, either for you or for a country. A lender usually wants the interest paid and perhaps some of the debt repaid, if for no other reason than to believe that some day all the debt will be repaid. There is a minimum payment on a credit card for this reason. Similarly, countries are expected to make a minimum payment on their foreign debts. It is very important for you and for a country to keep track of debts. How can we tell if a country experiences increasing or decreasing foreign debts?

We can rewrite equation (18.4) as:

$$B_{t+1}^f - B_t^f = rB_t^f + X_t - Q_t = rB_t^f + NX_t \tag{18.5}$$

using the identity $Y_t = C_t + I_t + X_t - Q_t$. This equation calculates a country's current account balance. We have seen a version of this equation in Chapter 6 in Table 6–3. In Table 6–3, we

---

[1] **DIGGING DEEPER.** There is no government spending or taxes in (18.4). This keeps an already complicated analysis a bit simpler. The role of the government in the current account is considered in Chapter 25.

If this is positive, this country could also be repaying net foreign debts—that is, both $B_{t+1}^f$ and $B_t^f$ are negative but $B_{t+1}^f$ is smaller in absolute value. Then less interest will be paid on net debt in the future.

used the middle portion of equation (18.5). Equation (18.5) presents the current account balance in a second way. On the far left, the current account balance is written as the change in the country's foreign assets. If this is positive, then this country could be acquiring foreign assets, that is, increasing its wealth in the form of foreign assets. These foreign assets earn interest and will allow higher consumption in the future. If the value of $B_{t+1}^f - B_t^f$ on the far left of (18.5) is negative, then either foreign assets become a smaller positive value or your foreign debts take on a more negative value (that would mean foreign debts are increasing). When a current account balance is negative, then either more of the future output of this country must be devoted to paying the interest on these debts and eventually repaying these debts or less interest will be earned in the future on that country's net foreign assets.

The middle and right sides of equation (18.5) are also the current account balance, written as it appeared in Table 6–3, as the sum of the trade balance (net exports) and the net value of investment income received and investment income paid. Hence, the change in a nation's foreign indebtedness is the sum of the trade balance and the investment income balance.

There is a third way to look at the accumulation of international debt. Rewriting (18.4) as

$$B_{t+1}^f - B_t^f = (rB_t^f + Y_t) - (C_t + I_t) = GNP_t - (C_t + I_t) \qquad (18.6)$$

GDP: total incomes (and production) of capital and labour located within a national border. GNP: total incomes from capital and labour earned by persons normally resident within a national border.

emphasizes the fact (as we said in Chapter 6) that GNP (gross national product) is slightly different from GDP (gross domestic product)—that is, $GNP_t = rB_t^f + GDP_t$. Most of the time, we do not get very excited about the difference between GDP and GNP because in studying the behaviour of GDP, we learn about employment, unemployment, and the difference between actual output and the natural rate of output as the main source of inflationary pressure. These are the variables we care most about. But the difference between GNP and GDP is precisely the net interest received from or paid to foreigners. If GNP is less than GDP, then your income available to consume or invest is less than your production because part of your production must be used to pay interest on existing debts. If we want to keep careful track of foreign debts, we must make the distinction between GNP and GDP.

The catch to using foreign resources to increase your capital stock without reducing consumption is now understood. If your income (GNP, *not* GDP) is less than your expenditures, including expenditures on new capital, you must borrow. The foreigners you borrow from expect to be repaid with interest. If your income (GNP, *not* GDP) is more than your expenditures, then you are able to lend, and you expect to be repaid by foreigners with interest. There is a huge amount of international borrowing and lending. Canada has been one of the largest participants in international financial markets over the past century. Canada has been a large-scale international borrower for most its existence as a nation.

## Canada's International Portfolio

Table 18–2 presents Canada's international portfolio as of the end of 2012. A portfolio is a collection of your assets and your debts. *International* refers to the debts you owe to foreigners and the debts foreigners owe to you. *International* also refers to the assets foreigners own in Canada and the assets Canadians own in other countries. Table 18–2 shows Canadians own some $1782.0 billion in foreign assets. $64.5 billion of those assets are called **official international reserves**. These particular assets are primarily bonds issued by the governments of other countries and owned by our federal government. These are the assets used for the foreign exchange market intervention we discussed in Chapter 14. As you can see, these assets are a relatively "small" amount of money. We have simplified the rest of the data and divided the remaining assets and liabilities into four other categories.

The largest category within Canadian assets is "Direct investment abroad"—equal to $711.6 billion. This category refers to a situation in which a corporation located in a foreign country has a controlling interest of its shares owned by Canadians. The usual situation is a foreign subsidiary of a Canadian firm; for example, Canadian Pacific Railways owns a variety of railway lines in the United States, and the Bank of Montreal owns a number of banks in the United States. A quick look at the lower half of Table 18–2 shows a large number of foreign

| TABLE 18–2 | Canada's International Investment Position, 2012 (in billions of Canadian dollars) | |
|---|---|---|
| **Foreign Assets of Canadians** | | **1782.0** |
| Direct investment abroad | | 711.6 |
| Portfolio foreign stocks | | 365.6 |
| Foreign bonds | | 166.6 |
| All other assets | | 473.7 |
| Official international reserves | | 64.5 |
| **Foreign Liabilities of Canadians** | | **2034.3** |
| Foreign direct investment in Canada | | 633.9 |
| Portfolio Canadian stocks | | 194.4 |
| Canadian bonds | | 763.3 |
| All other liabilities | | 442.7 |
| **Canada's Net International Investment Position** | | **−252.3** |

Source: Calculations by authors from CANSIM II Table 376-0141.

This table presents Canada's international assets, international debts, and net foreign assets at the end of 2012. It is updated annually by Statistics Canada.

firms also own controlling interest in Canadian firms (often as wholly owned subsidiaries). **Foreign direct investment** in Canada totals $633.9 billion. Foreign direct investment in Canada can be seen in nearly any industrial park in Canada, where a look at the names on the buildings tells you that at least one firm is foreign controlled. Direct investment is an important method through which new foreign capital enters Canada and Canadians provide capital to residents of other countries. Why is it so useful to have this form of foreign lending? The usual reason is that these firms are in a business where the most straightforward way to enter another country's market is to set up a subsidiary. This can occur if the product has specialized service needs, for example, heavy equipment built by multinational firms such as Caterpillar or Komatsu. This often occurs if the product or service is associated partly or entirely with patented information—the best way to ensure quality and retain absolute control of the information is to set up a subsidiary. Coca-Cola with its protected formula is an example of this type of foreign investment. Pharmaceutical firms also fall into this category as do various forms of copyrighted entertainment. Foreign direct investment can occur if the production processes within a firm are heavily integrated across borders. The most obvious example in Canada is the various foreign-owned automobile-manufacturing facilities. The individual plants in both Canada and the United States produce all versions of the particular model for all of North America. It is clear from the data in Table 18–2 that foreign direct investment is a huge part of international lending and borrowing.

The remaining categories of assets and liabilities fit into the general category **foreign portfolio investment**, where Canadians and nonresidents own assets outside their own countries as part of investment portfolios—that is, without voting control. These assets can be stocks or in the form of bonds or other loans. On the asset side, these are Canadian holdings of foreign stocks where Canadians do not have voting control of the foreign company in question. Canadians hold these stocks to receive their share of any profits these companies might earn. Canadians do choose to hold a lot of foreign equity in this form: $365.6 billion in 2012. Foreigners hold fewer Canadian shares without voting control: only $194.4 billion. This makes complete sense. Both Canadians and foreigners hold shares without control to diversify risk across stock markets. If times are bad in Canada, Canadians can hope that their foreign shares will have a high payoff. Foreigners want a similar performance from their holdings of Canadian shares. Because Canada is so small compared with the rest of the world, it makes sense that foreigners want only a relatively small holding of Canadian stocks for diversification purposes. The same logic suggests Canadians would want a lot of foreign stocks to diversify their portfolio across many countries.

Bonds are promises to pay money well into the future, conventionally more than one year into the future. Canadians own $166.6 billion in foreign bonds but owe foreigners $763.3 billion in the form of bonds. Canadian provincial governments and, to a lesser degree, the federal government sell bonds to foreigners.

You now realize that the real interest rate in equations (18.4) through (18.6) is a very complex weighted average of returns on all the financial instruments in Table 18–2. This will include interest rates on bank loans, bonds, dividends on shares, and capital gains.

Two categories are labelled "All other assets" and "All other liabilities." These financial instruments are mixtures of short-term bonds and bank loans as well as bank accounts—all financial instruments that pay a rate of interest. There are no voting rights attached to these financial instruments. You will notice that Canada owes a lot of international debt in this form—$442.7 billion at the end of 2012, and Canadians are also owed a substantial debt in this form—$473.7 billion. The last two categories (bonds and all other assets) are closest to the simple idea of net foreign debt in equations (18.4) through (18.6).

The bottom line in Table 18–2 presents Canada's **net international investment position**. Canadians owe $252.3 billion more to foreigners than foreigners owe to us. This is our net foreign debt. This means, with a population of 35 million, the average Canadian owed $7208 to the rest of the world at the end of 2012. This is the debt on which interest must be paid, and eventually, if Canadians want to, this debt may be repaid. Both the payment of interest and the repayment of principal involve a reduction in consumption in the future. Was it a good thing for Canadians to take on this debt in the past?

## When Is International Debt Good for an Economy?

Canada is not the only economy in the world with a significant international debt. In the past 20 years, the United States has moved from being a net international creditor to a net international debtor. We saw in Chapter 6 that Kuwait was a large lender to the rest of the world—that is, for Kuwait, $B_t^f$ is a large positive value. Many developing countries, including many of the former communist countries in transition to market economies, are taking on foreign debt. We have already seen the main reason for such activity. If a country wants to install some more physical capital and does not want to reduce consumption now, it must borrow

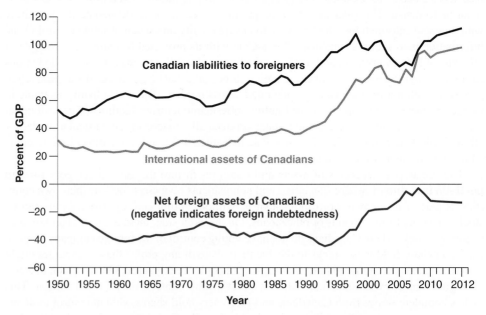

**FIGURE 18–4**

**Canada's International Debts and Assets 1950–2012**

Canada's international debts and assets, here measured relative to GDP, are both large. Both grew rapidly since 1990 as Canadians diversified into foreign assets and foreigners diversified into Canadian assets. Net foreign debt (the negative value of net foreign assets) has two peaks. An earlier peak, in 1961, was associated with large direct foreign investment in the Canadian economy. The later peak, in 1993, was associated with large government deficits, an issue further discussed in Chapter 25.

*Source: Total foreign assets,* using CANSIM II variable V235395; *total foreign debt,* using CANSIM II variable V235411; *net foreign debt,* using CANSIM II variable V235422; *nominal GDP* 1926–1960, using CANSIM II variable V500633, 1961–2007 using CANSIM II variable V646937.

FIGURE 18-5

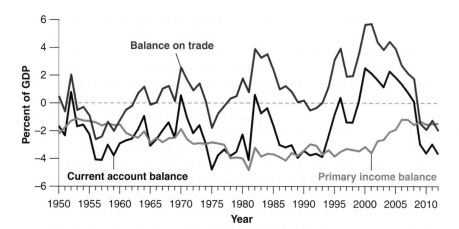

**Canada's Interaction with the Rest of the World**

The current account balance shows the change in Canada's net foreign debt. A negative value indicates an increase in net foreign debts. For most of the period after 1950, Canadians borrowed from the rest of the world. Only from 1999 to 2008 do we observe a series of consecutive years with a current account surplus. The negative investment income balance is the interest paid on Canada's foreign debts. It is the difference between GNP and GDP. Finally, the positive balance on trade in the majority of years in the data shows that Canada exports goods and services to other countries to pay the interest on Canada's foreign debts.

*Source:* 1950 to 1980: *Current account balance* CANSIM II variable V113713; *primary income balance* CANSIM II variable V113723; *balance on trade* CANSIM II variable, V113714; *nominal GDP* 1926–1960 CANSIM II variable V500633, 1961–1980 CANSIM II variable V646937. 1981 to 2012: *Current account balance* CANSIM II variable V61914609; *primary income balance* CANSIM II variable V61914683; *balance on trade* CANSIM II variable, V61914617; *nominal GDP* CANSIM II variable V62305783.

from the rest of the world to install the new physical capital. Equations (18.3) and (18.4) make this clear. Borrowing from the rest of the world is not a problem as long as the new capital installed is productive enough to pay the interest on the debt. This seems likely to be the case in many circumstances. First, if this is a country with a small amount of capital per worker, then the marginal product of capital will be high, and it will be relatively easy to pay the interest on the foreign loan. There will be many profitable opportunities for lending in a country that is short of capital. Second, many foreign loans are for specific projects, such as the development of a new mine, oilfield, or railway where the need for the new capital is well defined. In the appendix to this chapter, we look in more detail at how international debts can make a country better off. The analysis in the appendix makes precise the idea of an optimal amount of foreign borrowing. The precision comes with some complexity. We look at Canada's international debts in a broader sense below.

Figures 18–4 and 18–5 are different ways of answering the question: Is Canada's net foreign debt too large? Figure 18–4 looks at the size of Canada's debt relative to total production in Canada. This is like looking at the debts owed by your family relative to your family's income. If your family owes $10,000 but makes $100,000, there is no problem. If the debt is $100,000 and family income is $10,000 per year, there is a problem. Net foreign debt in Canada as a percent of GDP has two peaks, 41% in 1961 and 45% in 1993. These two peaks are probably different. The first peak followed very large foreign investments that enlarged Canada's physical capital stock in the 1950s. Specific projects in the 1950s included the oil and gas pipelines that crossed Canada from Alberta to Ontario as well as the building of the St. Lawrence Seaway. The peak in 1993 seems to be due to large public sector borrowing during the 1980s. We will discuss this issue further in Chapter 25 under the heading "The Twin Deficits." One startling aspect of Figure 18–4 is the enormous growth in both foreign assets and foreign debts after 1993. Canadians appear to be diversifying into foreign assets. Foreigners are diversifying into Canadian assets. This graph shows a clear effect of globalization in international financial markets. The second feature is a large fall in Canada's net foreign debts from 1993 until 2008. Net foreign debts are a mere 3% of GDP in 2008. However net foreign debts then rise rapidly to 13.4% of GDP at the end of 2012.

◄ The peaks are troughs in Figure 18–4 since debts are negative assets.

A second way to look at the data is found in Figure 18–5. The current account balance tells us if Canada's net foreign debt is increasing or decreasing. In almost every year from 1950 to 1995, Canada's current account balance has been negative. Why did Canada's debts as a percentage of GDP not grow very much? During the early period in which the debt was increasing, GDP or production, partly from the new capital, was also increasing quickly. Thus, for most of the period before 1975, net foreign debts did not grow faster than the ability to service that debt. The entirely negative line in Figure 18–5 is the percentage of GDP used to service Canada's net foreign debt. The value of this gap is, to recall Chapter 6, the difference between GDP and GNP. In the 1950s about 1.5% of GDP was used to pay the interest on Canada's debts. It is labelled the primary income balance. This number increased to 2.4% in the 1960s to 3% in the 1970s, and then to 4% in the 1980s. By the late 1980s, Canada's international debts were looking like a problem. A growing proportion of Canada's production was claimed by foreigners. However, the 1990s saw a sharp reversal (0.5% of GDP is about $5 billion), and an average of 3.4% of GDP was used to service foreign debt over that decade. In 2012, about 1.5 of GDP was used to pay interest on foreign debt. This change resulted from a dramatic swing in the current account balance from negative to positive in the late 1990s. From 1999 to 2008, Canadians repaid foreign debt or ran a current account surplus. However, the current account deficit was negative from 2009 to 2012 and very large. Canada's international debts were increasing again.

From this brief look at the data, it seems like international borrowing was clearly good for Canada in the 1950s. It allowed a large expansion of the Canadian capital stock and Canadian output without a large drop in consumption. There was a gradual decline in net foreign debts as a percentage of GDP throughout the 1960s and even into the 1970s. The period of the 1980s and early 1990s saw an expansion of foreign debts and an increase in the percentage of GDP used to service those debts. Canadians took on foreign debt from 1980 to 1998 without a proportional increase in output to service those debts. It is too early to tell if this is happening again from 2009 to 2012. This is a concern that we discuss further in Chapter 25.

There is absolutely no doubt that, over the history of Canada, borrowing from foreigners played a significant role in the creation of the Canadian capital stock. Many profitable investment opportunities were financed from abroad. The same story can be told for many other countries in the world.

## 18-3 | The Import and Export of Technology

### The Flows

We have presented evidence that Canada imports labour inputs from the rest of the world through net immigration. We have presented evidence that Canada's growth is partly due to the import of physical and associated financial capital from the rest of the world. Canada has frequently run current account deficits. Common sense tells us that the import of technology from the rest of the world is also an important part of the growth process in any country, and Canada is no exception. If a Canadian or a Canadian firm creates a new product, it often moves to export that product. If it does so in the form of a foreign subsidiary, it exports its technology to another country. This is only one form of the export of technology. However, it is also possible that a Canadian inventor registers a patent in another country and receives payments for the use of that idea. Similarly, foreign inventors will register patents and copyrights in Canada. Canadians do make payments to nonresidents for the rental of their technology.

The OECD presents some numbers of the **technology balance of payments**. These numbers for Canada are summarized in Table 18–3. They clearly do not cover all aspects of technology transfers. For example, if part of the profits remitted to a parent from a Canadian subsidiary are payments for the use of the parent's technology, this is a substantial undercounting. The OECD tries to capture licence fees and copyright fees paid across borders. The values in Table 18–3 are for 1995 and then 2004 to 2007. The first observation is that these numbers are very small relative to the values in Figure 18–5. In that figure, the primary income balance in 2012 is −1.5% of GDP, or about $27 billion. The values in Table 18–3 are

| TABLE | 18–3 | Canada's Technology Balance of Payments (millions of US dollars) | |
|---|---|---|---|
| Year | Receipts | | Payments |
| 1995 | 1283.1 | | 1007.7 |
| ... | ... | | ... |
| 2004 | 2805.5 | | 1174.5 |
| 2005 | 2652.3 | | 1207.3 |
| 2006 | 2776.9 | | 1420.2 |
| 2007 | 3066.8 | | 1315.5 |

*Source:* Tables 69 and 70, Main Science and Technology Indicators (MSTI), 2007 edition, OECD.

The OECD makes an attempt to calculate a balance of trade in technology. The numbers are difficult to interpret since much of the trade in technology comes in the form of foreign direct investment and the profit flows in both directions for technology firms operating across the border.

in millions of dollars. Thus the net balances here are in the order of $1 to 2 billion. In Table 18–3, Canada is a net exporter of technology by a relatively small amount. However, the transfer of technology across borders takes place in thousands of unmeasured ways: books, the Internet, education, conferences, subsidiaries, the migration of knowledgeable people, and probably many other ways we cannot even think of.

## Policy Implications of the Transfer of Technology

In Chapter 17, we discussed how the appropriability of research results is one determinant of the rate of technological progress and thus of growth. The argument is made that with a strong set of laws protecting the use of new innovations and the generation of monetary returns from intellectual property, there will be more new innovations. This is the justification for patent and copyright laws. There are always problems in the enforcement of such laws even within a country. How different does an innovation have to be before you are allowed a new patent? How much effort goes into the enforcement of copyright laws? Most of us have personal experience at the photocopying machine or with downloading material from the Internet. We know little effort is expended in enforcing copyright laws on individuals. But we also observe lawsuits filed for patent and copyright infringements at a corporate level.

Problems related to appropriability of ideas are magnified in the international setting. In the World Trade Organization (WTO), the organization that creates and enforces international trade agreements, payment across borders for the use of intellectual property has been one of the most difficult issues to settle. In particular, there have been huge problems with the piracy of software across international borders. There has been much concern about very poor countries making large payments for drugs that are needed to stave off the spread of AIDS (acquired immune deficiency syndrome) and stabilize the lives of AIDS sufferers. These drugs are developed in rich countries by private drug companies that view them as their corporate property and wish to be paid for their development costs. They are happy to put these drugs up for sale to poor countries, but the poor countries feel that they cannot afford the payments the companies want and want to pay a much smaller fee for the use of these drugs. They often want to make and use generic copies of these drugs. It is almost impossible to stop a poor country that is determined to use these drugs without paying licence fees. This issue remains very much unsettled in the WTO. Even in Canada, a rich country, drug patents have been a controversial issue. Until 1987, Canadian generic drug manufacturers were allowed to make generic copies of patented drugs after 10 years for a relatively small licensing fee. After 1987, the generic drug companies were forced to wait 17 years for the same opportunity. This did make new drugs created in other countries more expensive for Canadians. This change may also have created a stronger incentive for Canadian as well as foreign drug companies to develop new drugs. In the United States, there has been periodic pressure on Congress to shorten the period of monopoly granted to a new drug from 20 years to 10 years, the period of the pre-1987 law in Canada. Should such legislation ever be passed, Canada then might return to its pre-1987 drug patent laws to match those in the United States. These examples are among many where the need to consider the international aspect of intellectual property laws arises.

## 18-4 | Growth in the Open Economy: A Summary

This chapter has emphasized that growth in the open economy makes extensive use of international inputs. There has been substantial migration of labour among countries. In Canada's case, net immigration is the numerically dominant component of overall population growth. This is likely to be the case for nearly all developed countries in the next few decades. There have been enormous international capital flows. Canada is a net debtor because of previous inflows of foreign capital. This has not created severe problems in the Canadian economy where production has increased enough to pay the interest on the foreign loans. Finally, we know that technology and knowledge flow across international borders. We know that this flow is quite difficult to measure in any accurate way. However, it must be the case that in any open economy, knowledge from all sources, both foreign and domestic, is used to create economic progress.

### SUMMARY

- In an open economy, growth in total output can come from both domestic and international sources. More output requires more labour, more capital, or more technology. Any of the three inputs to production may come from the rest of the world.

- Labour inputs to the production process are best measured by total hours of work. Total hours of work are the product of average hours of work and the number of workers. The number of workers depends on both total population and the employment-to-population ratio. Neither the employment-to-population ratio nor average hours of work change rapidly over time. Thus, a larger population will be the major source of the growth in the labour input in Canada.

- In Canada, natural population growth, the excess of births over deaths, has declined steadily since the 1950s' baby boom. Net immigration, the excess of immigrants over emigrants, is the main source of population growth in Canada.

- Increasing the capital stock in either a closed or open economy means physical investment must be larger than depreciation. If a society wants more capital in a closed economy, current consumption must be reduced.

- In an open economy, more capital can be created without a reduction in current consumption by increasing foreign borrowing. A current account deficit (the term for foreign borrowing) increases your foreign debt and thus future payments of interest on that debt.

- Canada has engaged in extensive international borrowing since 1950. It appears that for the first 25 years after 1950, this international borrowing was used to increase Canada's physical capital stock and output. The situation after 1975 is more complicated. There are periods of increasing international debts without a decline and sometimes with an increase in the proportion of national production used to pay interest on that debt.

- There are substantial flows of technology across international borders. These flows create particular difficulties in international trade agreements as countries and companies try to enforce intellectual property laws across borders.

### KEY TERMS

- average hours, 355
- current account balance, 361
- employment-to-population ratio, 354
- emigration, 356
- foreign direct investment, 363
- foreign portfolio investment, 363

- immigration, 356
- natural population growth, 356
- net immigration, 356
- net international investment position, 364
- official international reserves, 362
- technology balance of payments, 366

## 1. TRUE/FALSE/UNCERTAIN

**a.** Total population in a country increases only if there is an excess of births over deaths.

**b.** Canadians owned no foreign assets in 2012.

**c.** Average hours of work in Canada have declined over the past decade.

**d.** In an open economy, the capital stock can be expanded without a decrease in consumption.

**e.** Payments across international borders for intellectual property are an important part of Canada's trade.

## 2. IMMIGRATION POLICY IN CANADA

Consider immigration policy in Canada in more detail by working with Table 18–1.

**a.** Is natural population growth in Canada expected to become negative in Table 18–1?

**b.** If the government decided to reduce total immigration by 50,000 persons per year starting in 2013/2014, estimate the population at the end of 2015/2016. What assumptions have you made to make your estimate?

**c.** The government changed immigration rules in 2008 so that a larger proportion of immigrants are in categories immediately needed by employers. What are the implications for Canada's employment-to-population ratio over time?

**d.** Use Figures 18–1 and 18–2 to consider the following. In 2012, Canadian residents worked 585,290,830 hours.

If 2013 through 2015 allow in an "extra" 50,000 immigrants per year and these emigrants work in the same proportions as Canadians, by what percentage does Canada's labour input rise? What complications exist for this calculation?

## 3. AN INCREASE IN CAPITAL AND INTERNATIONAL DEBTS

Fill in the missing values in Table 1, Question 3 below.

$CA_t$ is notation for the current account balance. All other notations are in the text. The stock variable $B_t^f$ is calculated at the end of the period using equation (18.4). The stock variable $K_t$ is calculated as of the beginning of the period using equation (18.2). At the end of period 1 (the beginning of period 2) $B_t^f$ is zero. $K_t$ equals 300 at the beginning of period 2. The interest rate earned on foreign assets or paid on foreign debt is 10%.

**a.** What is the value of the depreciation rate $\delta$? Why is the capital stock unchanged from year 4 to year 5?

**b.** What is the value of $B_t^f$ at the end of period 2? Is there a current account deficit in period 2? Explain the source of the current account deficit in year 3. Calculate net foreign debts at the end of year 3.

**c.** There is a sharp fall in consumption in year 5. What is the effect of that drop in consumption in the current account? What is the effect of that drop in consumption in this country's net foreign debts at the end of year 5?

## TABLE 1, QUESTION 3

| Year | $Y_t$ | $C_t$ | $I_t$ | $X_t$ | $Q_t$ | $CA_t$ | $B_t^f$ | Trade Balance | $K_t$ |
|------|-------|-------|-------|-------|-------|--------|---------|---------------|-------|
| 2 | 100 | 70 | 30 | 20 | 20 | | 0 | | 300 |
| 3 | 100 | 65 | 40 | | 25 | | −5 | | |
| 4 | 105 | 73 | 31 | 21 | 20 | | | | 310 |
| 5 | 105 | 68 | 31 | | 20 | | | | 310 |

## 4. THE INTERNATIONAL DEBTS OF THE UNITED STATES [WEB]

The international debts of the United States are of direct concern to Canadians. The United States is our largest trading partner. A very useful source of basic American economic data is the Appendix Tables to the *Economic Report of the President*. This can be accessed through any search engine under "economic report of the President." The statistical tables are even available as a spreadsheet.

**a.** Use the table titled "U.S. International Transactions," and find a decade in which there is only one current account surplus. From 1992 to 2012, there is an unbroken string of current account deficits. Explain what this string does to the U.S. international asset position. Explain why the column "balance on income" remains positive to 1998, while the current account balance is negative after 1992. What is the significance of the "balance on income" switching from positive to negative?

**b.** Find the table entitled "International investment position of the United States." This will list U.S. international assets and debts for approximately 10 years. According to this table, is the United States a net debtor to the rest of the world? What is the form of the largest U.S. foreign asset? What is the form of the largest U.S. foreign debt?

**c.** The first table in the *Economic Report of the President* usually presents GDP numbers. Calculate, for the years of net foreign debt available, the ratio of net international debts to U.S. GDP. Is the U.S. international debt becoming a problem? Why, or why not? Suppose that the U.S. national debt becomes a problem for U.S. policy makers. They want to reduce imports and increase exports. How would this have an impact on Canada?

---

# THE OPTIMAL AMOUNT OF FOREIGN BORROWING

This appendix uses a two-period framework to ask and answer the following question: How much international borrowing is optimal? This is a difficult question. It involves making the correct choice of physical investment and then the best choice of consumption over time. International financial markets are used to allow a country to expand its choice set and make the very best of its opportunities. Using the two-period analysis helps us see the nature of the best choice. We can also answer the question: "How much international borrowing is optimal?" when there are many periods of time. However, the mathematics required for the many-period problem is beyond the scope of this book. The key lessons can be learned from the two-period example below.

▲

*Optimal* means making the best decision from the set of available decisions.

## An Improvement Using Only International Borrowing and Lending

We will start our country at the beginning of period 1 without either foreign debts or foreign assets. In the notation of the body of the chapter, $B^f = 0$. The real interest rate available to our country on the international capital market is 7%. Figure 18A–1 shows what this country is able to do when only international borrowing and lending are used to make an improvement. This is our first step to understanding the optimal current account choice. We will then build gradually. On the horizontal axis is dollars in period 1, representing choices made *now*. On the vertical axis is dollars in period 2, representing choices made in the *future*. We will simply call these period 1 and period 2. This country,

▲

This material is very closely related to the material in Appendix A to Chapter 21. In Chapter 21, we use a similar two-period model to represent a multi-period consumption problem.

without any physical investment in period 1 (we add physical investment shortly), produces 50 dollars of output in period 1 and then 40 dollars of output in period 2. You could think of this country as Kuwait. We looked at Kuwait's balance of payments in Chapter 6. In Kuwait, oil reserves are falling over time so that existing wells will produce less in the second period. Kuwait expects its production (its GDP) to be lower in the second period. We start our analysis at point A in Figure 18A–1. If there is neither international

**An Improvement Using Only International Borrowing and Lending**

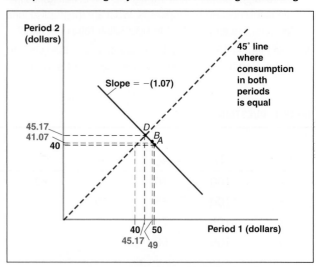

Without international lending and borrowing, consumption in period 1 must equal production in period 1, and consumption in period 2 must equal production in period 2. Point *A* with $50 of consumption in period 1 and $40 of consumption in period 2 represents this choice. Point *B* shows the effect of lending $1 to nonresidents in period 1 and consuming the repayment of that loan in addition to production in period 2. Point *D* shows the situation where consumption is equal in period 1 and period 2. The country lends $4.83 in period 1, thus reducing consumption in period 1 to $45.17. The loan is repaid with 7% interest in period 2, allowing period 2 consumption to rise to $40 + (1.07 × $4.83) = $45.17.

borrowing nor international lending and no physical investment in period 1, then point A must also represent the consumption choices in this country. Using equations and the notation from the body of the chapter, we write:

$$C_1 = Y_1 = 50 \text{ and } C_2 = Y_2 = 40$$

where $C$ is consumption and $Y$ is GDP or output. This choice says this country simply consumes its production in each period. Is there a better choice?

Appendix A to Chapter 21 introduces the concept of indifference curves, a concept you may have used in a microeconomics course. This concept helps identify a better choice. We could add indifference curves on consumption in period 1 and period 2 to Figure 18A–1. However, we will use a simpler idea here. We are going to state that if consumption can be made exactly equal between period 1 and period 2, then this society will be happier. We appeal to the idea that persons generally prefer a smoother path of consumption. We see households saving for retirement to smooth consumption. Most of us do not want to eat like a glutton one month and then starve the next month or be homeless one month and live in a palace the next month. We see Kuwait and other resource-rich societies saving today to build up their foreign assets. These assets enable future consumption to be equal to current consumption even after the oil runs out. Note that consumption in period 1 at point A is not equal to consumption in period 2 at point A. This is not the best choice for this society. We are going to consider two ways for this country to equalize consumption between period 1 and period 2. The first way involves lending dollars to the rest of the world in period 1 and then adding the repayment of those loans to consumption in period 2.

Figure 18A–1 first explores the idea of taking $1 from period 1 output and lending it to a nonresident. Starting from point A, consumption in period 1 is reduced to $49 at point B. This money is lent to a nonresident on the international capital market. That nonresident repays the $1 loan with 7% interest in period 2. Consumption in period 2 at point B is increased to $41.07, the $40 of income already available in period 2 and the repayment of the loan made to the nonresident in period 1. Point B is "better" than point A because consumption is now more equal. How much lending to nonresidents is required to equalize consumption across the two periods? We can solve the equation:

$$50 - L_1 = 40 + 1.07(L_1)$$

for the size of the period 1 loan (denoted $L_1$) that will equalize consumption in the two periods. The left side of the equation above is consumption in period 1, income minus the loan to the nonresident. The right side of the equation above is consumption in period 2, income plus the repayment of the loan made to the nonresident in period 1. Solving this equation yields $L_1 = \$4.83$. If this country saves $4.83 in period 1,

this reduces period 1 consumption to $50 − $4.83 = $45.17. When the loan made by this country to a nonresident is repaid in period 2 with interest, period 2 consumption rises to $40 + 1.07($4.83) = $45.17. In Figure 18A–1, this is a movement from point A to point D. D is a point of equal consumption. In our simplified model, equal consumption is the most desirable consumption choice. There is no reason for this country to save in period 2—this is a two-period model, and there is no further activity after the second period. This disadvantage of the two-period model ends if the problem is extended to a multi-period framework.

We have learned two important lessons. International lending and borrowing can be used to equalize consumption over time. International financial markets have allowed this country to be better off because consumption is now more equal than it would be without international financial markets. We can use the equations from the body of this chapter to note that this country has a current account surplus in period 1 in Figure 18A–1. The current account surplus is $Y_1 - C_1 = \$50 - \$45.17 = \$4.83$. There is no physical investment up to this point in the example. Physical investment is introduced immediately below.

### An Improvement in Well Being from Physical Investment Activity Only

Figure 18A–2 introduces the possibility of using physical investment to make consumption more equal across the two periods. Physical investment means taking some period 1 output and using it to install more physical capital in period 1 rather than consuming those resources in period 1. Consumption in period 1 must be reduced to allow that physical investment to take place. Most countries do have some physical investment opportunities. To continue with the Kuwait example, there may be new oilfields to discover and put into production. If more physical capital is installed in period 1, then there is more production in period 2. Investment in physical capital can also be used to equalize consumption because investment reduces consumption in period 1 and increases consumption in period 2.

Table 18A–1 shows how much extra production will occur in period 2 when different amounts of physical capital (measured in dollars) are installed in this country in period 1. This table shows that capital has decreasing returns. This assumption was also made in Chapter 15. The first dollar of new capital installed in period 1 increases period 2 output by $5. This is shown by moving from point A to point B in Figure 18A–2. The second dollar of new physical capital (a total of $2 of investment spending) increases output in period 2 by three more dollars, a movement from point B to point D in Figure 18A–2. At point D, consumption in period 1 equals consumption in period 2. Both are equal to $48. Figure 18A–2 is now a bit trickier to read. From point A, as more physical capital is installed, there is less consumption

**An Improvement Using Only Physical Investment**

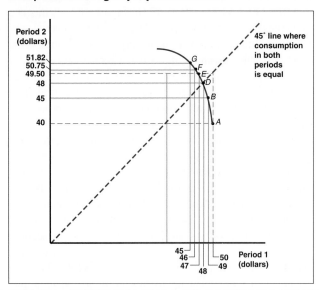

Without any physical investment in new capital in period 1 (and without international borrowing and lending), consumption in period 1 must equal production in period 1 and consumption in period 2 must equal production in period 2. Point A with $50 of consumption in period 1 and $40 of consumption in period 2 represents this choice. The first dollar invested in physical capital increases period 2 production and consumption by $5 while reducing period 1 consumption by only $1. This decision is represented in moving from point A to point B. If a second dollar is spent on physical investment in period 1, then consumption in period 1 is $48, but consumption and production in period 2 is also $48. This is the movement from point B to point D. Further investment in period 1 continues to increase production and consumption in period 2 but only at the cost of reduced consumption in period 1. Such a decision is represented in moving from point D to points E, F, or G.

in period 1. You are moving to the left from point A to keep track of the reduction in consumption. The distance left from point A measures the reduction in consumption from $50. The distance from the origin measures consumption in period 1. But there is more output and more consumption in period 2. Point D is the best choice for this country if the only available option to move consumption from period 1 to period 2 is physical investment in period 1.

We can compare Figures 18A–1 and 18A–2. Note that point D in Figure 18A–2 is clearly better than point D in Figure 18A–1. In Figure 18A–2, consumption in both periods is equal to $48. In Figure 18A–1, the equal consumption available in both periods is only $45.17. We can see why this is the case. The first dollar of investment into physical capital is much more productive (it earned $5) than the first dollar lent to foreigners (which earned only $1.07). Both returns are gross rates of return. The second dollar of physical investment is also more productive than a dollar lent to foreigners; it repays $3, the second dollar lent to foreigners pays only $1.07. For this country, it is better to use its first $2 on physical investment opportunities than it is to lend to nonresidents. The rate of return is higher.

Let us continue in Figure 18A–2 to use physical investment opportunities to try to generate changes in consumption opportunities. If we invest a third dollar in physical capital, then period 1 consumption is $47 and period 2 consumption is $49.5. This is point E. Moving from point D to point E still looks like a good rate of return on physical investment. One dollar invested in new capital yielded $1.50 in period 2 income, a gross rate of return of 1.5 or a net rate of return of 50%. But we have a problem! Consumption in the two periods becomes less equal in moving from point D to point E in Figure 18A–2. In moving from point E to point F, we invest an additional dollar (the fourth dollar) in physical capital to yield a gross return of $1.25 or a net return of 25%. This seems to create more

| TABLE 18A–1 | Investment and Consumption without International Borrowing | | | | | |
|---|---|---|---|---|---|---|
| Point in Figure 18A–2 | Production in Period 1 | Physical Investment in Period 1 | Consumption in Period 1* | Production in Period 2 | Marginal Product of Dollar of New Capital | Consumption in Period 2** |
| A | 50 | 0 | 50 | 40 | — | 40 |
| B | 50 | 1 | 49 | 45 | 5 | 45 |
| D | 50 | 2 | 48 | 48 | 3 | 48 |
| E | 50 | 3 | 47 | 49.5 | 1.5 | 49.5 |
| F | 50 | 4 | 46 | 50.75 | 1.25 | 50.75 |
| G | 50 | 5 | 45 | 51.82 | 1.07 | 51.82 |
| H | 50 | 6 | 44 | 52.82 | 1 | 52.82 |

*This consumption choice in period 1 reflects the fact that if investment is increased, then consumption must decrease.

**This consumption choice in period 2 reflects the fact that production in period 2 and consumption in period 2 are identical in the absence of international borrowing and lending.

of a problem as consumption in period 1 continues to fall and consumption in period 2 continues to rise. Finally, the fifth dollar of physical capital (moving from point $F$ to point $G$) yields a gross return of $1.07 or a net return of 7%. As we undertook more physical investment, at point $G$, with $5 invested in physical capital, then consumption becomes more unequal. At point $G$, period 1 consumption is only $45 (the $50 in period 1 income less the $5 invested in new physical capital) and period 2 consumption is $51.82 at point $G$. We have failed miserably to organize the country to have equal consumption in the two periods. The best we can do, if we are using only physical investment to equalize consumption, is point $D$. This is quite odd: There seem to be very good investment opportunities with very high rates of return at $E$ and $F$, 50% and 25%, respectively. These rates of return are much higher than the 7% rate of return on international investments available in Figure 18A–1. We return to this fact later.

We are trapped by equation (18.1), repeated:

$$I_t = S_t = Y_t - C_t \qquad (18.1)$$

Equation (18.1) says that only if we reduce consumption today can we increase investment and increase consumption tomorrow. Equation (18.1) must be true in a closed economy. But all is not lost. We are in an open economy. We learned that equation (18.3) can sidestep equation (18.1), repeated:

$$C_t + I_t = Y_t + Q_t - X_t = Y_t - NX_t \qquad (18.3)$$

Now, we can increase both consumption and investment in period 1 if we are willing to borrow from the rest of the world. Making use of international capital markets will allow us to exploit all good physical investment opportunities and equalize consumption. It will be the best of Figures 18A–1 and 18A–2.

### An Improvement Using Both Physical Investment and International Borrowing and Lending

The problem with point $G$ in Figure 18A–2 is that we have too much production and consumption in period 2 and too little consumption in period 1. This is the opposite problem to that faced at point $A$ in Figure 18A–1, where we had too much consumption in period 1 and not enough consumption in period 2. We found that lending to the rest of the world would solve the problem in Figure 18A–1. We use that insight to solve our new problem, that of too little consumption in period 1 and too much consumption in period 2 at point $G$ in Figure 18A–2. From point $G$, we need to borrow in period 1 and then repay the loan in period 2. How large a loan will exactly equalize consumption from point $G$ in Figure 18A–2? Let the value of the borrowing in period 1 be $L_G$. $L_G$ is the solution to the following equation:

$$51.82 - 1.07(L_G) = 50 - 5 + L_G$$

The left side of the equation above is consumption in period 2: production in period 2 minus the repayment of the loan. The right side is consumption in period 1: production minus investment plus the value of the loan. The two values of consumption are set equal. Solving yields $L_G = \$3.29$. Substituting that value finds $C_1 = C_2 = \$48.29$. This is marked as point $G^*$ on Figure 18A–3. This is the very best point this country can attain. How do we know this?

First, note that $G^*$ is better than either point $D$ in Figure 18A–1 or point $D$ in Figure 18A–2. International borrowing

An Improvement Using Both Physical Investment and International Borrowing and Lending: The Optimal Current Account Choice

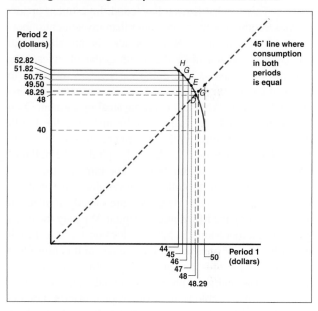

Without any physical investment in new capital in period 1 (and without international borrowing and lending), consumption in period 1 must equal production in period 1, and consumption in period 2 must equal production in period 2. Point $A$ represents this choice. The first dollar invested (point $A$ to point $B$) in physical capital increases period 2 production and consumption by $5 while reducing period 1 consumption only by $1. The second dollar is spent on physical investment in period 1, then without international borrowing and lending) consumption in both period 1 and period 2 would be $48. This is the movement from point $B$ to point $D$. Further investment in period 1 continues to increase production in period 2. The third, fourth, and fifth dollar of physical investment yield a return greater than or equal to the 7% cost of borrowing a dollar from a nonresident. Thus, if these physical investments take place, the economy moves through points $E$, $F$, and $G$. At $G$, consumption in period 1 and period 2 are not equal. However, if this economy borrows $3.29 in period 1 to move itself from point $G$ to point $G^*$, then consumption in the two periods is equalized at $48.29. This is the best equal-consumption point available; $3.29 is the optimal current account deficit.

and lending makes this country even better off. From point $G$, point $G^*$ is the largest amount of most equal consumption available, that is, $48.29 is larger than $48. We need to "prove" that $G$ in Figure 18A–3 is the best physical investment choice. There is a clear argument that this country should not invest in the sixth dollar of physical capital, that is, move period 2 production from point $G$ to point $H$ in either Figure 18A–3 or Table 18A–1. Why? One more dollar invested in physical capital from point $G$ to point $H$ yields a gross return of $1 or a net return of 0%. If the country took that dollar and lent that dollar to a foreigner instead of investing in more physical capital, that dollar would earn a gross return of $1.07 or a net return of 7%. Lending the extra dollar to a foreigner is better than an additional unit of physical investment. The physical investment from $G$ to $H$ is worse than simply lending on the international capital market. This is what Kuwait has found. Investment opportunities in other countries are better than investment opportunities in Kuwait itself. Now, consider the possibility that this country did not make the fourth dollar of investment into physical capital. That dollar earned 25% invested in physical capital but could earn only 7% invested on international markets. This is a good physical investment. You can borrow at 7% and make 25% by installing the fourth dollar of capital. Finally, the movement from $F$ to $G$, the fifth dollar of investment in physical capital, is the dollar of investment that yields exactly the same rate of return, 7%, that it would earn if the dollar had been placed in the international capital market. Here, you are exactly indifferent about installing the fifth dollar of capital. We play the usual game in microeconomics. Since it does no harm to install the fifth dollar of physical capital, we do so. It is now clear that the best plan for new physical investment is to invest until the gross marginal product of capital equals the gross rate of return available on the world capital market. Point $G$ is the best physical investment choice. It dominates both point $H$ and point $F$.

Now, consider the possibility that this country will lend a dollar to a foreigner from point $G$. This is completely silly. Such a loan would take the country away from point $G^*$ and make consumption in period 1 even lower and consumption in period 2 even higher. Borrowing $3.29 to move from $G$ to $G^*$ is the very best choice this country can make. $G^*$ in Figure 18A–3 is better than point $D$ in Figure 18A–2. At $G^*$, consumption in each period is $48.29. You

might not think that is very much of a difference. It is "only" 0.81% more consumption in each period. But 0.81% of GDP is quite a large number, and the second period in this model represents many future periods. The movement from point $D$ in Figure 18A–2 to point $G^*$ in Figure 18A–3 could be a substantial improvement. The source of the improvement is due to the fact that the international capital market allowed this country to borrow at a 7% rate of interest to invest in physical capital that produced a higher than 7% rate of return. This gap between the cost of borrowing and the return on physical capital allows a little more consumption in both periods.

### Putting the Analysis in the Language of the Current Account

The last step is to put the graphical analysis into the language of the current account. Using Figure 18A–3, in period 1 and working from points $G$ and $G^*$:

$$Y_1 = 50 \quad C_1 = 48.29 \quad I_1 = 5$$

Thus:

$$Q_1 = Y_1 - C_1 - I_1 = CA_1 = -3.29$$

The current account deficit in period 1 is simply the trade balance because there are no initial foreign assets or debts in this example. Imports are large enough to make up for the gap between the sum of consumption and investment ($C_1 + I_1$) and production ($Y_1$).

In period 2:

$$Y_2 = 51.82 \quad C_2 = 48.29 \quad I_2 = 0$$

There is no physical investment in period 2 because it makes no sense to install more capital to produce output in a nonexistent third period. This is a limitation of the two-period model. The current account surplus in period 2 is:

$$X_2 + rB_1^f = 3.53 + (0.07)(-3.29) = Y_2 - C_2 = 3.29$$

Since $B_1^f = -3.29$, we can use equation (18.4) and know that the value of net foreign debt at the end of period 2 is zero. Exports (the gap between production and consumption) are large enough in period 2 to fully repay the period 1 loan with interest. The current account surplus in period 2 is exactly the correct amount to repay the optimal current account deficit in period 1.

This appendix makes two points. First, with a world capital market there is an optimal amount of physical investment in an open economy. All physical investment opportunities

that yield a return higher than the cost of borrowing on the world market should be undertaken. They yield a profit and add to the country's consumption opportunities. Second, after an optimal physical investment plan is identified, a country has an optimal current account deficit as well. Given the best choice of physical investment using the rule above, a country can borrow and lend to generate a smooth or smoother consumption path. This will yield a clear value for the optimal current account deficit (or surplus) in period 1 and a plan to repay and service that debt in the future. This plan will create benefits from international borrowing and lending for all countries.

The appendix should close with both a cautionary note and a note of optimism. In the example above, the country involved repays its foreign debt smoothly. We often read of situations where this does not occur. Argentina and several other Latin American countries had difficulty repaying debts in the last decade, but there will be others because many other countries have had difficulty repaying or servicing foreign debts in the past. A failure to repay or service foreign debts is a fairly regular occurrence. The reasons are many and varied. There can be war or natural disaster. There can be fraud—it has been the case that promised physical investments in period 1 did not take place. Rather, the rulers of the country involved embezzled the international loan. There can be revolution and political turmoil. Sometimes, these events are combined. Although the international bankruptcies make the headlines, there are many years when countries do exactly what we have described in this chapter and in this appendix. They make use of international capital markets to borrow. This allows the installation of new physical capital and the creation of future output without large reductions in current consumption. Other countries, with poorer investment opportunities at home, are happy to lend to the countries in need of such loans. Loans are smoothly repaid. This process has gone on at a large scale for the past 250 or more years all over the world. It is not likely to stop anytime in the near future.

# Expectations

## The next four chapters look at the role of expectations in the macroeconomy.

### Chapter 19

Chapter 19 introduces two important tools. The first is the distinction between the real interest rate and the nominal interest rate. The second is the concept of expected present discounted value. The chapter ends by deriving and discussing the "Fisher hypothesis," the proposition that in the medium run, nominal interest rates fully reflect inflation and money growth.

### Chapter 20

Chapter 20 focuses on the role of expectations in financial markets. It first looks at the determination of bond prices and bond yields. It shows how we can learn about the course of expected future interest rates by looking at the yield curve. It then turns to stock prices, and shows how they depend on expected future dividends and interest rates. It discusses whether stock prices always reflect fundamentals or may instead contain bubbles or fads. A similar analysis is applied to housing markets and foreign exchange markets.

### Chapter 21

Chapter 21 focuses on the role of expectations in consumption and investment decisions. It argues that consumption depends partly on current income and partly on wealth defined as the sum of financial, housing, and human wealth—the expected present value of labour income. It argues that investment depends partly on current cash flow and partly on the expected present value of future profits.

### Chapter 22

Chapter 22 puts the pieces together and looks at the role of expectations in fluctuations. It modifies our previous description of goods market equilibrium (the *IS* relation) to reflect the effect of expectations on spending. It then revisits the effects of monetary and fiscal policies on output. It shows, in particular, that in contrast to the results derived in the core, a fiscal contraction may increase output, even in the short run.

# Expectations: The Basic Tools

## Expectations

The consumer considering whether to buy a new car must ask: Can I safely take a new car loan? How much of a wage raise can I expect over the next few years? How safe is my job?

The manager who observes an increase in current sales must ask: Is this a temporary boom that I should meet with the existing production capacity? Or does this upswing reflect a permanent increase in sales, in which case I should order new machines? How much additional profit can I expect if I buy a new machine?

The pension fund manager who observes a boom in the stock market must ask: Are stock prices going to increase further, or is the boom likely to fizzle? Does this increase in prices reflect expectations of higher profits by firms in the future? Do I share those expectations? Should I reallocate some of my funds between stocks and bonds?

These examples make it clear that many economic decisions depend not only on what is happening today, but also on expectations of what will happen in the future. Indeed, some decisions should depend very little on what is happening today. For example, why should an increase in sales today, if that increase is not accompanied by expectations of higher sales in the future, lead a firm to alter its investment plans? The new machines may not be in operation before sales have returned to normal. Till then, they might sit idle, gathering dust.

Until now, we have not paid much attention to the role of expectations in goods and financial markets. We have ignored them in our construction of both the *IS-LM* model and the aggregate demand component of the *AS-AD* model that builds on the *IS-LM* model. When looking at the goods market, we assumed that consumption depended on current income and that investment depended on current sales. When looking at financial markets, we lumped assets together and called them "bonds"; we then focused on the choice between bonds and money and ignored the choice between bonds and stocks, short-term bonds and long-term bonds, and so on. Only in the foreign exchange market did the expected exchange rate next year play a role. But if next year's expected exchange rate matters, so does the expectation of the exchange rate in the following year. We ignored this. We introduced these simplifications to build the intuition for the basic mechanisms at work. It is now time to think about the role and the determination of expectations in fluctuations. This is our task in this and the next three chapters.

In this chapter, we lay the groundwork by introducing two key concepts: The first is the distinction between the *nominal* and the *real* interest rates. The second is the concept of *expected present discounted value*. We then show, in the last two sections of the chapter, how the distinction between real and nominal interest rates sheds light on the relation between interest rates and inflation in the short run and the medium run. The next three chapters build on this groundwork. Chapter 20 looks at the role of expectations in financial markets. It looks in particular at the determination of the term structure of interest rates, the determination of stock prices, and the possibility of bubbles in housing markets. Chapter 21 looks at the role of expectations in consumption and investment decisions. Chapter 22 puts the pieces together: It extends the analysis of the *IS-LM* model we developed in the core to allow for the presence of expectations. It then takes another look at the role and the limits of policy in an economy in which expectations play a major role in affecting decisions.

## 19-1 | Nominal versus Real Interest Rates

In 1981, the *annual T-bill rate*—the interest rate on one-year government bonds—was 17.5%. In 2007, the annual T-bill rate was only 4.3%. Although most of us cannot borrow at the same interest rate as government can, the interest rates faced as consumers were also substantially lower in 2007 than in 1980. Borrowing was clearly much cheaper in 2007 than it was in 1981.

Or was it? In 1981, inflation was around 10%. In 2007, inflation was around 2%. This information would seem very relevant: The interest rate tells us how many dollars we will have to pay in the future in exchange for having one more dollar today. But we do not consume dollars; we consume goods. When we borrow, what we really want to know is how many goods we shall have to give up in the future in exchange for the goods we get today. Likewise, when we lend, we want to know how many goods—not how many dollars—we will get in the future for the goods we give up today. The presence of inflation makes the distinction important. What is the point of receiving high interest payments in the future if inflation between now and then is so high that we are able to buy only a few goods with the proceeds?

To examine this further, let us introduce two definitions. Let us refer to interest rates in terms of dollars (or, more generally, in units of the national currency) as **nominal interest rates**. The interest rates printed in the financial pages of newspapers are nominal interest rates. For example, when we say that the one-year T-bill rate is 4.3%, we mean that for every dollar that government borrows by issuing one-year T-bills, it promises to pay $1.043 a year from now. More generally, if the nominal interest rate for year $t$ is $i_t$, borrowing one dollar this year requires you to pay $1 + i_t$ dollars next year. This relation is represented in Figure 19–1(a): one dollar this year corresponds to $1 + i_t$ dollars next year.

Let us refer to interest rates expressed *in terms of a basket of goods* as **real interest rates**. Thus, if we denote the real interest rate for year $t$ by $r_t$, then, by definition, borrowing the equivalent of one basket of goods this year requires you to pay the equivalent of $1 + r_t$ baskets of goods next year. This relation is represented in Figure 19–1(b): 1 basket of goods this year corresponds to $1 + r_t$ baskets of goods next year.

◄ Annual T-bill rates in 2012 were 1.1%, even lower than in 2007. We return to that fact later. For now, comparing 1981 and 2007 makes the point we want to make more clearly.

Nominal interest rate: the interest rate in terms of dollars.

We will substitute "this year" for "today" and "next year" ◄ for "one year from today."

◄ Real interest rate: the interest rate in terms of a basket of goods.

### Computing the Real Interest Rate

Let us look at the relation between the nominal and the real interest rates. Suppose the nominal interest rate is $i_t$. What is the real interest rate $r_t$, and how can we construct it? To start, assume there is only one good in the economy, say, bread (we will add jam and other goods later). If you borrow enough to eat one more kilogram of bread this year, how much will you have to repay, in terms of kilograms of bread, next year?

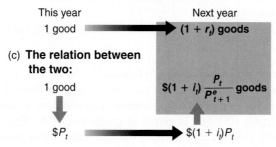

(a) Definition:
**The one-year nominal interest rate**

This year — $1  →  Next year — $(1 + i_t)$

(b) Definition:
**The one-year real interest rate**

This year — 1 good  →  Next year — $(1 + r_t)$ **goods**

(c) **The relation between the two:**

1 good  →  $\$(1 + i_t)\dfrac{P_t}{P^e_{t+1}}$ **goods**

$\$P_t$  →  $\$(1 + i_t)P_t$

**FIGURE 19–1**

**Nominal and Real Interest Rates**

Figure 19–1(c) helps us derive the answer.

- If the price of a kilogram of bread this year is $P_t$ dollars, to eat one more kilogram of bread, you must borrow $P_t$ dollars. This is represented by the arrow pointing down in Figure 19–1(c).
- Let $i_t$ be the one-year nominal interest rate, the interest rate in terms of dollars. If you borrow $P_t$ dollars, you will have to repay $(1 + i_t) P_t$ dollars next year. This is represented by the arrow from left to right at the bottom of Figure 19–1(c).
- What you care about is not dollars, but kilograms of bread. Thus, the last step involves converting dollars to kilograms of bread next year. Let $P_{t+1}^e$ be the price of bread you expect for next year. (The superscript "$e$" indicates this is an expectation: You do not know yet what the price of bread will be next year.) How much you expect to repay next year, in terms of kilograms of bread, is therefore equal to $(1 + i_t) P_t / P_{t+1}^e$. This is represented by the arrow pointing up in Figure 19–1(c).

Putting together parts (b) and (c) of Figure 19–1, it follows that one plus the one-year real interest rate, $r_t$, is defined by:

$$1 + r_t = (1 + i_t) \frac{P_t}{P_{t+1}^e} \qquad (19.1)$$

Two simple manipulations make it look friendlier.

Denote expected inflation by $\pi_t^e$. Given there is only one good—bread—the expected rate of inflation equals the expected change in the dollar price of bread between this year and next year, divided by the dollar price of bread this year:

$$\pi_t^e = \frac{(P_{t+1}^e - P_t)}{P_t} \qquad (19.2)$$

Add one to both sides in equation (19.2):

$$1 + \pi_t^e = 1 + \frac{(P_{t+1}^e - P_t)}{P_t}$$

Reorganize:

$$1 + \pi_t^e = \frac{P_{t+1}^e}{P_t}$$

Take the inverse on both sides:

$$\frac{1}{1 + \pi_t^e} = \frac{P_t}{P_{t+1}^e}$$

Replace in (19.1):

$$1 + r_t \equiv \frac{1 + i_t}{1 + \pi_t^e}$$

Using equation (19.2), rewrite $P_t / P_{t+1}^e$ in equation (19.1) as $1/(1 + \pi_t^e)$. Replace in (19.1) to get:

$$(1 + r_t) = \frac{1 + i_t}{1 + \pi_t^e} \qquad (19.3)$$

*One plus the real interest rate equals the ratio of one plus the nominal interest rate, divided by one plus the expected rate of inflation.*

Equation (19.3) gives us the *exact* definition of the real interest rate. However, when the nominal rate and expected inflation are not too large—say, less than 20% per year—a close approximation to this equation is given by the simpler relation:

$$r_t = i_t - \pi_t^e \qquad (19.4)$$

This approximation is derived in proposition 6, Appendix 2. To see how close the approximation is, suppose the nominal interest rate is 10% and expected inflation is 5%. Using the exact formula (19.3) gives $r_t = 4.8\%$. The approximation given by equation (19.4) is 5%, which is close enough. The approximation is not nearly as good when nominal interest rates and expected inflation are very high, say, equal to 100% and 80% respectively—the exact formula gives a real interest rate of 11%, whereas the approximation yields 20%.

Equation (19.4) is simple, and you should remember it. It says that *the real interest rate is (approximately) equal to the nominal interest rate minus expected inflation*. It has several implications:

- When expected inflation equals zero, the nominal and the real interest rates are equal.
- Because expected inflation is typically positive, the real interest rate is typically lower than the nominal interest rate.
- For a given nominal interest rate, the higher the expected rate of inflation, the lower the real interest rate.

The case where expected inflation happens to be equal to the nominal rate is worth looking at more closely. Suppose the nominal interest rate and expected inflation both equal 10%, and you are the borrower. For every dollar you borrow, you will have to repay $1.10 next year, but dollars will be worth 10% less in terms of goods next year. Thus, if you borrow the equivalent of one good, you will have to repay the equivalent of one good next year: The real cost of borrowing—the real interest rate—is equal to zero. Now, suppose you are the lender: For every dollar you lend, you will receive $1.10 next year. This looks attractive, but dollars next year will be worth 10% less in terms of goods. If you lend the equivalent of one good, you will get the equivalent of one good next year: Despite a 10% nominal interest rate, the real interest rate is equal to zero.

We have assumed so far that there was only one good, bread. But what we have done generalizes easily. All we need to do is to substitute the *price level*—the price of a basket of goods—for the price of bread. If we use the consumer price index (CPI) to measure the price level, the real interest rate tells us how much consumption we must give up next year in order to consume more today.

## Nominal and Real Interest Rates in Canada since 1975

Let us return to the question with which we started this section. We can now restate it as follows: Was the *real interest rate* lower in 2007 than it was in 1980? More generally, what has happened to the real interest rate in Canada since 1975?

The answer is given in Figure 19–2, which plots both nominal and real interest rates since 1975. For each year, the nominal interest rate is the one-year T-bill rate at the beginning of the year. To construct the real interest rate, we need a measure for expected inflation—more precisely, the rate of inflation expected as of the beginning of each year. The source line for Figure 19–2 gives details. Here, expected inflation in the next calendar year is the average forecast over a group of private-sector forecasters. These forecasters were surveyed by three different firms over the period 1975–2012.

Figure 19–2 shows how important the adjustment for expected inflation is. The nominal interest rate in 1981 was 17.5%. It fell to 5.9% in 2000 and to 4.3% in 2007. Both are annual averages of daily rates. However, the measure of the real rate of interest in Figure 19–2 fell from 6.9% in 1981 to 3.7% in 2000 to 2.3% in 2007. The much smaller decline in real rates follows from the fact that both inflation and expected inflation have steadily declined since the early 1980s.

We have answered the question we asked at the beginning of the section. Borrowing, in terms of the real interest rate, was cheaper in 2007 than in 1981. Let us now turn to the situation in January 2013, the last observation in Figure 19–2. In January 2011, the nominal interest

The real interest rate $(i - \pi^e)$ is based on expected inflation, not actual inflation. If actual inflation turns out to be different from expected inflation, the realized real interest rate $(i - \pi)$ will turn out to be different from the real interest rate.

To reflect this distinction, the real interest rate is sometimes called the *ex-ante* real interest rate ("*ex-ante*" means "before the fact"; here, before inflation is known), and the realized real interest rate is called the *ex-post* real interest rate ("*ex-post*" means "after the fact"; here, after inflation is known).

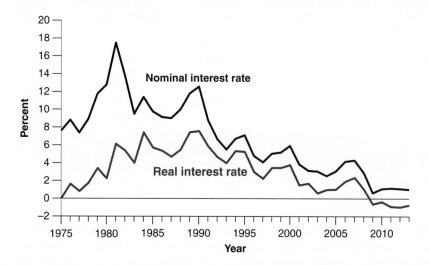

**Year**

*Sources:* The *nominal interest rate* plotted from 1975–1986 is the six-month T-bill rate using CANSIM II variable V122552; after 1987, the nominal interest rate is the one-year T-bill rate using CANSIM variable V122498. The *real rate* is the nominal rate minus expected inflation. In 1984–2000, expected inflation is the average next-year inflation rate from Consensus Forecast. In 1975–1983, expected inflation is the average next-year forecast from the Conference Board of Canada Survey of Forecasters. From 2001, expected inflation is the average forecast reported in the January issue of *The Economist* in that year.

**FIGURE 19–2**

**Nominal and Real T-Bill Rates in Canada, 1975–2012**

Although both nominal and real interest rates declined from peaks in 1980 and 1990, the decline in nominal interest rates has been much larger than the decline in expected inflation. Real interest rates have fallen since the 1990s. In the most recent years, expected inflation has been larger than the nominal interest rate and the real interest rate has been negative.

# FOCUS Why Deflation Can Be Very Bad: Deflation and the Real Interest Rate in the United States During the Great Depression

The Focus box "The Great Depression in North America" in Chapter 11 introduced you to the Great Depression, undoubtedly the central macroeconomic event of the 20th century and one that still haunts makers of policy. We saw that the period from 1929 to 1939 was, for North America, a period of unprecedented high unemployment.

The Great Depression has many elements in common with the current crisis: A large increase in asset prices before the crash—housing prices in this crisis, stock market prices in the Great Depression—and the amplification of the shock through failure in the banking system. As you can see by comparing the output growth and unemployment numbers in Table 1 to the numbers for the current crisis in Chapter 1, the increase in unemployment in the Great Depression was much larger then than in the current crisis. In this box, we shall focus on just one aspect of the Great Depression, the evolution of the nominal and the real interest rates and the dangers of deflation.

As you can see in the third column of the table, the Fed decreased the nominal interest rate, although it did this slowly. The nominal interest rate decreased from 5.3% in 1929 to 2.6% in 1933. Nominal interest rates did not quite hit the zero we saw in 2008 and 2009. They were low by historical standards. At the same time, as shown in the third column, the increase in unemployment led to a sharp decrease in inflation. Inflation, equal to zero in 1929, turned negative in 1930,

reaching −9.2% in 1931, and −10.8% in 1932. If we make the assumption that expected deflation was equal to actual deflation in the current year, we can construct a series for the real interest rate (there are no survey data on expected inflation in the Great Depression). This is done in the last column of the table and gives a hint for why output continued to decline until 1933. The real interest rate reached 12.3% in 1931, 14.8% in 1932, and still a very high 7.8% in 1933! In spite of low nominal interest rates, real interest rates were very high. It is no great surprise that, at those interest rates, both consumption and investment demand remained very low, and the depression got worse.

In 1933, the economy seemed to be in a **deflation trap**, with low activity leading to more deflation, a higher real interest rate, lower spending, and so on. Starting in 1934, however, deflation gave way to inflation, leading to a large decrease in the real interest rate, and the economy began to recover. Why, despite a very high unemployment rate, the U.S. economy was able to avoid further and further deflation remains a hotly debated issue in economics. Some point to a change in monetary policy, a very large increase in the money supply, leading to a change in inflation expectations. Others point to the policies of the New Deal, in particular the establishment of a minimum wage, thus limiting further wage decreases. Whatever the reason, this was the end of the deflation trap and the beginning of a long recovery.

| TABLE 1 | The Nominal Interest Rate, Inflation, and the Real Interest Rate, 1929–1933 | | | |
|---|---|---|---|---|
| Year | Unemployment Rate (%) | One-Year Nominal Interest Rate (%) | Inflation Rate (%) | One-Year Real Interest Rate (%) |
| 1929 | 3.2 | 5.3 | 0.0 | 5.3 |
| 1930 | 8.7 | 4.4 | −2.5 | 6.9 |
| 1931 | 15.9 | 3.1 | −9.2 | 12.3 |
| 1932 | 23.6 | 4.0 | −10.8 | 14.8 |
| 1933 | 24.9 | 2.6 | −5.2 | 7.8 |

See Focus box "The Great Depression in North America" in Chapter 11. One-year nominal interest rates in the United States from Lawrence H. Officer, "What Was the Interest Rate Then?" in *Measuring Net Worth*, 2011. http://www.measuringworth.com/datasets/interestrates/result.php

rate was a very low 1.025%. As we saw in Chapter 1 and Chapter 11, nominal interest rates around the world have been kept exceptionally low as central banks have tried to increase demand and reduce unemployment following the world recession in 2009. The measure of expected inflation in Canada for the year 2013 yet to happen, an average of the beliefs of the forecasters surveyed by *The Economist* magazine in December of 2012, was 1.8%. Using equation (19.4), the real interest rate was negative, equal to −0.775%. In fact, according to Figure 19–2, and using the methodology described above, real interest rates have been negative since 2009. The intent of these negative real interest rates is to stimulate spending.

We are now in a position to more clearly understand some comments made earlier in Chapter 11 and in Chapter 1. We indicated negative inflation can generate particular problems, especially if the economy is in a liquidity trap. Now that we have introduced the distinction between nominal and real interest rates, we can understand why. If nominal interest rates are at or near zero, the central bank cannot decrease the nominal interest rate further. Suppose, under the pressure of high unemployment, inflation decreases further and then turns into actual deflation—that is, inflation becomes negative. Then suppose that this situation persists and expected inflation becomes negative. Then the real interest rate would become positive and demand would fall. This would make it even harder for the economy to recover even though the central bank has cut the nominal interest rate to zero.

In Chapter 1, we saw that, except for the United States in 2009, actual inflation in North America remained positive throughout the crisis period. Even in the United States, actual inflation in 2009 was only a small negative value, –0.3%. In the data on expected inflation in Canada used to construct Figure 19–2, expected inflation remained positive from 2008 to 2013. However, it seems clear that the possibility of negative actual inflation and negative expected inflation was a real worry during the crisis in 2008 and 2009. The worry is not unfounded: As examined in the Focus box "Why Deflation Can Be Very Bad: Deflation and the Real Interest Rate in America During the Great Depression," it is clear that expected inflation was negative and real interest rates were large and positive in the Great Depression. More recently it is clear that expected inflation has been negative in Japan and the ensuing positive real interest rates with a zero nominal interest rate has played a role in the slow growth of the Japanese economy.

# 19-2 | Expected Present Discounted Values

Let us now turn to the second key concept we introduce in this chapter, that of expected present discounted value.

To see why this concept is helpful, let us return to the example of the manager considering whether to buy a new machine. On the one hand, buying and installing the machine involves a cost today. On the other, the machine allows for higher production, higher sales, and thus higher profits in the future. The question facing the manager is whether the value of these expected profits is higher than the cost of buying and installing the machine. This is where the concept of expected present discounted value comes in handy: The **expected present discounted value** of a sequence of future payments is the value today of this expected sequence of payments. Once the manager has computed the expected present discounted value of the sequence of profits, her problem becomes simple. If this value exceeds the initial cost, she should go ahead and buy the machine. If it does not, she should not.

As in the case of the real interest rate in section 19-1, the practical problem is that expected present discounted values are not directly observable. They must be constructed from information on the sequence of expected payments and interest rates. Let us first look at the mechanics of construction.

## Computing Expected Present Discounted Values

If the one-year nominal interest rate is $i_t$, lending one dollar this year yields $1 + i_t$ dollars next year. Equivalently, borrowing one dollar this year implies paying back $1 + i_t$ dollars next year. In that sense, one dollar this year is worth $1 + i_t$ dollars next year. This relation is represented graphically in Figure 19–3(a).

Turn the argument around and ask: One dollar *next year* is worth how many dollars this year? The answer, shown in Figure 19–3(b), is $1/(1 + i_t)$ dollars. Think of it this way: If you lend $1/(1 + i_t)$ dollars this year, you will receive $1/(1 + i_t) \times (1 + i_t) = 1$ dollar next year. Equivalently, if you borrow $1/(1 + i_t)$ dollars this year, you will have to repay exactly one dollar next year.

Thus, one dollar next year is worth $1/(1 + i_t)$ dollars this year. More formally, we say that $1/(1 + i_t)$ is the *present discounted value* of one dollar next year. The term "present" comes

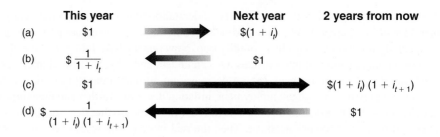

FIGURE 19–3

Computing Present
Discounted Values

This year | Next year | 2 years from now

(a)    $1    →    $(1 + $i_t$)

(b)    $\dfrac{1}{1 + i_t}$    ←    $1

(c)    $1    →    $(1 + $i_t$)(1 + $i_{t+1}$)

(d)    $\dfrac{1}{(1 + i_t)(1 + i_{t+1})}$    ←    $1

Discount rate: $i_t$
Discount factor: $1/(1 + i_t)$
If the discount rate goes
up, the discount factor goes
down.

from the fact that we are looking at the value of a payment next year in terms of dollars *today*. The term "discounted" comes from the fact that the value next year is discounted, with $1/(1 + i_t)$ being the **discount factor** (the one-year nominal interest rate, $i_t$, is sometimes called the **discount rate**). Note that because the nominal interest rate is always positive, the discount factor is always less than 1: A dollar next year is worth less than a dollar this year. The higher the nominal interest rate, the lower is the value this year of a dollar next year. If $i = 5\%$, the value this year of a dollar next year is $1/1.05 \approx 95$ cents. If $i = 10\%$, the value this year of a dollar next year is $1/1.10 \approx 91$ cents.

Now, apply the same logic to the value this year of a dollar two years from now. For the moment, assume that current and future one-year nominal interest rates are known with certainty. Let $i_t$ be the nominal interest rate for this year, and $i_{t+1}$ be the one-year nominal interest rate next year.

If you lend one dollar for two years, you will get $(1 + i_t)(1 + i_{t+1})$ dollars two years from now. Put another way, one dollar this year is worth $(1 + i_t)(1 + i_{t+1})$ dollars two years from now. This relation is represented in Figure 19–3(c).

What is one dollar two years from now worth this year? By the same logic as before, the answer is $1/[(1 + i_t)(1 + i_{t+1})]$ dollars: If you lend $1/[(1 + i_t)(1 + i_{t+1})]$ dollars this year, you will get exactly one dollar in two years. More formally, the *present discounted value of a dollar two years from now* is equal to $1/[(1 + i_t)(1 + i_{t+1})]$ dollars. This relation is shown in Figure 19–3(d). If, for example, the one-year nominal interest rate is the same this year and next, and equal to 5%, so $i_t = i_{t+1} = 5\%$, then the present value of a dollar in two years is equal to $1/(1.05)^2$ or about 91 cents this year.

**A General Formula.** Having gone through these steps, it is easy to derive the present discounted value for the general case.

Consider a sequence of payments in dollars, now and in the future. Assume for the moment that these future payments are known with certainty. Denote the current payment by $\$z_t$, the payment next year by $\$z_{t+1}$, the payment two years from now by $\$z_{t+2}$, and so on.

The present discounted value of this sequence of payments—the value in this year's dollars of the sequence of payments, which we shall call $\$V_t$—is given by:

$$\$V_t = \$z_t + \frac{1}{(1 + i_t)}\$z_{t+1} + \frac{1}{(1 + i_t)(1 + i_{t+1})}\$z_{t+2} + \cdots$$

Each payment in the future is multiplied by its respective discount factor. The more distant the payment, the smaller is the discount factor, and thus the smaller the value of the payment this year. In other words, future payments are discounted more heavily, so their present value is lower.

We have assumed so far that both future payments and future interest rates were known with certainty. Actual decisions, however, have to be based on expectations of future payments rather than on actual values for these payments. In our earlier example, the manager cannot be sure of how much profit the new machine will actually bring; nor can she be sure of what interest rates will be. The best she can do is to get the best forecasts she can, and then compute the *expected present discounted value* of profits, based on these forecasts.

How do we compute the expected present discounted value when future payments or interest rates are uncertain? Basically in the same way as before, but replacing the *known* future payments and *known* interest rates in the expression above by *expected* future payments and *expected* interest rates.[1] Formally, denote expected payments next year by $\$z_{t+1}^e$, expected payments two years from now by $\$z_{t+2}^e$, and so on. Similarly, denote the expected one-year nominal interest rate next year by $i_{t+1}^e$, and so on (the one-year nominal interest rate this year, $i_t$, is known today, so it does not need a superscript "*e*"). The expected present discounted value of this expected sequence of payments is given by:

$$\$V_t = \$z_t + \frac{1}{(1 + i_t)} \$z_{t+1}^e + \frac{1}{(1 + i_t)(1 + i_{t+1}^e)} \$z_{t+2}^e + \cdots \qquad (19.5)$$

"Expected present discounted value" is a heavy expression to carry; we will often use, for short, just **present value**. Also, it will be convenient to have a shorthand way of writing equations, such as equation (19.5). To denote the present value of an expected sequence for $\$z$, we will write $V(\$z_t)$, or just $V(\$z)$.

## Using Present Values: Examples

Equation (19.5) has two important implications:

- The present value depends positively on current and expected future payments. An increase in either $\$z$ or any future $\$z^e$ leads to an increase in the present value.

  ◀ $\$z$ or future $\$z^e\uparrow \Rightarrow V\uparrow$

- The present value depends negatively on current and expected future interest rates. An increase in either $i$ or in any future $i^e$ leads to a decrease in the present value.

  ◀ $i$ or future $i^e\uparrow \Rightarrow V\downarrow$

Equation (19.5) is not simple, however, and intuition for these effects is best built by going through some examples.

**Constant Interest Rates.** To focus on the effects of the sequence of payments on the present value, assume that interest rates are expected to be constant over time so that $i_t = i_{t+1}^e = \ldots$ and denote their common value by $i$. The present value formula—equation (19.5)—becomes:

$$\$V_t = \$z_t + \frac{1}{(1 + i)} \$z_{t+1}^e + \frac{1}{(1 + i)^2} \$z_{t+2}^e + \cdots \qquad (19.6)$$

In this case, the present value is a *weighted sum* of current and expected future payments: The weights decline *geometrically* through time. The weight on a payment this year is 1; the weight on the payment *n* years from now is $[1/(1 + i)]^n$. With a positive interest rate, the weights get closer and closer to zero as we look further and further into the future. For example, with an interest rate equal to 10%, the weight on a payment in 10 years is equal to $1/(1 + 0.10)^{10}$ = 0.386 so that a payment of \$1000 in 10 years is worth \$386 this year; the weight on a payment in 30 years is $1/(1 + 0.10)^{30}$ = 0.057 so that a payment of \$1000 in 30 years is worth only \$57 this year!

◀ The weights correspond to the terms of a geometric series. See geometric series in Appendix 2.

**Constant Interest Rates and Payments.** In some cases, the sequence of payments for which we want to compute the present value is simple. For example, a fixed-rate 30-year mortgage requires constant dollar payments over 30 years. Consider a sequence of equal payments—

[1]**DIGGING DEEPER.** This statement glosses over a difficult issue. If people dislike risk, the value of a risky payment, now or in the future, will be lower than that of a riskless payment, even if both have the same expected value. We will ignore this effect here, assuming implicitly that people in the economy are **risk neutral** (they are indifferent to risk). Studying what happens when people are **risk averse** (when they dislike risk) would take us too far afield. It would require a whole course, namely, a course in finance theory.

call them $z without a time index—over $n$ years including the current year. In this case, the present value formula in equation (19.6) simplifies to:

$$\$V_t = \$z \left[ 1 + \frac{1}{(1 + i)} + \cdots + \frac{1}{(1 + i)^{n-1}} \right]$$

Because the terms in the expression in brackets represent a geometric series, we can compute the sum of the series and get:

By now, geometric series should not hold any secret, and you should have no problem deriving this relation. But if you do, see Appendix 2.

$$\$V_t = \$z \frac{1 - [1/(1 + i)^n]}{1 - [1/(1 + i)]}$$

Suppose you have just won a million dollars in the lottery and have been presented with a two-metre-long $1,000,000 cheque on TV. Afterwards, you are told that to protect you from your worst spending instincts as well as from your many new "friends," the province will pay you the million dollars in equal yearly installments of $50,000 over the next 20 years. What is the present value of your prize? Taking, for example, an interest rate of 6%, the equation above gives $V = \$50,000\,(0.688)/(0.057) =$ or about $608,000. Not bad, but winning the prize did not make you a millionaire.

What is the present value if $i$ equals 4%? 8%? (Answers: $706,000; $530,000)

**Constant Interest Rates and Payments, Going on Forever.** Let us go one step further and assume that payments are not only constant, but also go on forever. Real world examples are harder to come by for this case, but one comes from nineteenth-century England, when government issued *consols*, bonds paying a fixed yearly amount forever. In Canada, the Canadian Pacific Railway issued similar consols for a period of time. These bonds were repurchased and retired by the company. Let $z be the constant payment. Assume that payments start next year rather than right away as in the previous example (this makes for simpler algebra). From equation (19.6), we have:

Many consols were bought back by the British government at the end of the nineteenth and early twentieth centuries. But some are still around.

$$\$V_t = \frac{1}{(1 + i)}\$z + \frac{1}{(1 + i)^2}\$z + \cdots$$

$$= \frac{1}{(1 + i)}\left[ 1 + \frac{1}{(1 + i)} + \cdots \right]\$z$$

where the second line follows by factoring out $1/(1 + i)$. The reason for factoring out $1/(1 + i)$ should be clear from looking at the term in brackets: It is an infinite geometric sum, so we can use the property of geometric sums to rewrite the present value as:

$$\$V_t = \frac{1}{1 + i}\frac{1}{(1 - [1/(1 + i)])}\$z$$

Or simplifying (the steps are given in the application of proposition 2 in Appendix 2):

$$\$V_t = \frac{\$z}{i}$$

The present value of a constant sequence of payments $z is equal to the ratio of $z to the interest rate $i$. If, for example, the interest rate is expected to be 5% forever, the present value of a consol that promises $10 per year forever equals $10/0.05 = $200. If the interest rate increases and is now expected to be 10% forever, the present value of the consol decreases to $10/0.10 = $100.

**Zero Interest Rates.** Because of discounting, computing present discounted values typically requires the use of a calculator. There is, however, a special case worth keeping in mind where computations simplify. This is the case where the interest rate is equal to zero. Because the interest rate is, in fact, positive, this is only an approximation, but it is a very useful one for back-of-the-envelope computations. The reason is obvious from equation (19.6): If $i = 0$, then $1/(1 + i)$ equals 1, and so does $1/(1 + i)^n$ for any power $n$. For that reason, the present discounted value of a sequence of expected payments at zero interest rate is then just the *sum* of those expected payments.

## Nominal versus Real Interest Rates, and Present Values

We have so far computed the present value of a sequence of dollar payments by using interest rates in terms of dollars—nominal interest rates. Specifically, we have written equation (19.5):

$$\$V_t = \$z_t + \frac{1}{(1 + i_t)} \$z^e_{t+1} + \frac{1}{(1 + i_t)(1 + i^e_{t+1})} \$z^e_{t+2} + \cdots$$

where $i_t$, $i^e_{t+1}$, ... is the sequence of current and expected future nominal interest rates, and $\$z_t$, $\$z^e_{t+1}$, $\$z^e_{t+2}$, ... is the sequence of current and expected future dollar payments.

Suppose we want to compute instead the present value of a sequence of *real* payments, that is, payments in terms of a basket of goods rather than in terms of dollars. Following the same logic as before, what we need to do is to use the right interest rates for this case, namely, interest rates in terms of the basket of goods—*real interest rates*. Specifically, we can write the present value of a sequence of real payments as:

$$V_t = z_t + \frac{1}{(1 + r_t)} z^e_{t+1} + \frac{1}{(1 + r_t)(1 + r^e_{t+1})} z^e_{t+2} + \cdots \tag{19.7}$$

where $r_t$, $r^e_{t+1}$, ... is the sequence of current and expected future real interest rates, $z_t$, $z^e_{t+1}$, $z^e_{t+2}$, ... is the sequence of current and expected future real payments, and $V_t \equiv \$V_t/P_t$ is the real present value of future payments.

These two ways of writing the present value are equivalent. That is, we can compute the present value as (1) the present value of the sequence of payments expressed in dollars, discounted using nominal interest rates, or (2) the present value of payments expressed in real terms, discounted using real interest rates.

Do we need both formulas? Yes. Which one is more helpful depends on the context. Take bonds, for example. Bonds typically are claims to a sequence of nominal payments over a period of years. For example, a 10-year bond may promise $50 a year for 10 years, plus a final payment of $1000 in the last year. So, when we look at the pricing of bonds in Chapter 20, we shall rely on equation (19.5) rather than on equation (19.7).

But sometimes, we have a better sense of future expected real values than of future expected dollar values. You may have little idea of what your dollar income will be in 20 years: Its value depends very much on what happens to inflation between now and then. But you may be confident that your nominal income will increase at least as much as inflation—equivalently, that your real income will not decrease. In this case, using equation (19.5), which requires you to form expectations of future dollar income, may be difficult; using equation (19.7), which requires you to form expectations of future real income, will be easier. For that reason, when we discuss consumption and investment decisions in Chapter 21, we will rely on equation (19.7) rather than on equation (19.5).

How bad an approximation it is depends on how far the interest rate is from zero. Go back to the lottery example. The sum of payments is $1,000,000. If the interest rate is 1%, the present value of payments is $911,000. The approximation is not too bad. If the interest rate is 2%, the expected present value is $834,000. The approximation quickly gets worse.

The proof that they are equivalent is given in the appendix to this chapter. Go through it to test your understanding of the two tools introduced in this chapter: real versus nominal rates, and expected present values.

# 19-3 | Nominal and Real Interest Rates, and the *IS-LM* Model

In the next three chapters, using the tools we have just developed, we will explore the role of expectations in determining activity. In the rest of this chapter, we take a first step, introducing the distinction between real and nominal interest rates in the *IS-LM* model, and then exploring the relation among money growth, inflation, and real and nominal interest rates.

In the *IS-LM* model we developed in the core (Chapter 5), the interest rate entered in two places: It affected investment in the *IS* relation, and it affected the choice between money and bonds in the *LM* relation. Which interest rate—nominal or real—were we talking about in each case?

Take the *IS* relation first. Our discussion earlier in this chapter should make it clear that in deciding how much investment to undertake, firms care about the *real interest rate*: Firms produce goods. They want to know how much they will have to repay, not in terms of dollars but in terms of goods. So, what belongs in the *IS* relation is the real interest rate. Let *r* denote the real interest rate. The *IS* relation therefore must be rewritten as:

We will ignore time subscripts here; they are not needed for the rest of the chapter.

$$Y = C(Y - T) + I(Y, r) + G$$

Investment spending, and thus the demand for goods, depends on the real interest rate.

Now, turn to the *LM* relation. In deriving the *LM* relation, we argued that the demand for money depends on the interest rate. Were we referring to the nominal interest rate or the real interest rate?

The answer is the *nominal interest rate*. Remember why the interest rate affects the demand for money. When thinking about whether to hold money or bonds, people take into account the opportunity cost of holding money rather than bonds—what they give up by holding money rather than bonds. Money pays a zero nominal interest rate. Bonds pay a nominal interest rate of *i*. Hence, the opportunity cost of holding money is equal to the difference between the two interest rates, $i - 0 = i$, which is just the nominal interest rate. Therefore, the *LM* relation is still given by:

$$\frac{M}{P} = YL(i)$$

Collecting the two equations and the relation between the real and the nominal interest rates, the extended *IS-LM* model is given by:

| IS: | $Y = C(Y - T) + I(Y, r) + G$ |
|---|---|
| LM: | $M/P = YL(i)$ |
| Real interest rate: | $r \approx i - \pi^e$ |

Note an immediate implication of these three equations. The interest rate directly affected by monetary policy (the interest rate that enters the *LM* equation) is the nominal interest rate. The interest rate that affects spending and output (the rate that enters the *IS* relation) is the real interest rate. The effects of monetary policy on output therefore depend on the relation between the movements in the nominal interest rate and the real interest rate. To explore this implication further, the next section looks at the effects of an increase in money growth on the nominal interest rate and the real interest rate, both in the short run and in the medium run.

Interest rate in the *IS* relation: Real interest rate, *r* Interest rate in the *LM* relation: Nominal interest rate, *i*

## 19-4 | Money Growth, Inflation, and Nominal and Real Interest Rates

*The Bank of Canada's decision to allow for higher money growth is the main factor behind the decline in interest rates in the last six months.*

(Imaginary quotation, circa 2001)

*The nomination of David Dodge as Governor of the Bank of Canada, perceived to be softer on inflation than an appointment from inside the Bank of Canada, has led financial markets to worry about higher money growth, higher inflation, and higher interest rates in the future.*

(Imaginary quotation, circa 2001)

These two quotations are made up, but they are composites of what was written at the time. Which one is correct? Does higher money growth lead to lower interest rates, or does it lead to higher interest rates? The answer is: Both are correct! There are two keys to this answer. The first is the distinction we just introduced between the real and the nominal interest rates. The second is the distinction we developed in the core between the short run and the medium run. As we shall see, the full answer is:

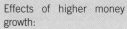

Effects of higher money growth:

| | Short Run | Medium Run |
|---|---|---|
| $i$ | ↓ | ↑ |
| $r$ | ↓ | — |

- Higher money growth leads to lower nominal interest rates in the short run but to higher nominal interest rates in the medium run.
- Higher money growth leads to lower real interest rates in the short run but has no effect on real interest rates in the medium run.

The purpose of this section is to develop this answer and draw its implications.

## Nominal and Real Interest Rates in the Short Run

To look at the short run, it is convenient to reduce the three equations we derived in the last section—the *IS* relation, the *LM* relation, and the relation between the real and the nominal interest rates—to two, by replacing the real interest rate in the *IS* relation by the nominal interest rate minus expected inflation. This gives

$$IS: \quad Y = C(Y - T) + I(Y, i - \pi^e) + G$$

$$LM: \quad M/P = Y L(i)$$

We could eliminate the nominal interest rate and keep the real interest rate. $r$ would enter the *IS* relation; $(r + \pi^e)$ would enter the *LM* relation. The graphical analysis would look a bit different, but the conclusions would be the same.

These two equations are the same as in Chapter 5, with just one difference: Spending in the *IS* relation depends on the real interest rate, which is equal to the nominal interest rate minus expected inflation.

The associated *IS* and *LM* curves are drawn in Figure 19–4, for given values of $P$, $M$, $\pi^e$, $G$, and $T$.

- For a given expected rate of inflation ($\pi^e$), the nominal interest rate and the real interest rate move together. Hence, a decrease in the nominal interest rate implies an equal decrease in the real interest rate, leading to an increase in spending and in output: The *IS* curve is downward sloping.
- The *LM* curve is upward sloping: An increase in output leads to an increase in the demand for money, putting pressure on the nominal interest rate.

If $r = i - \pi^e$, then
$$\Delta r = \Delta i - \Delta \pi^e.$$
If $\pi^e$ is constant,
$$\Delta \pi^e = 0,$$
so,
$$\Delta r = \Delta i.$$

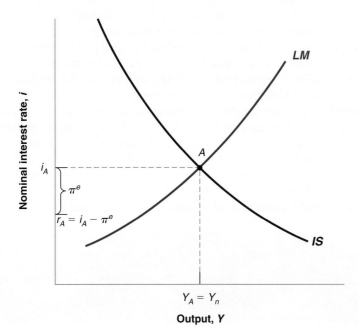

### FIGURE 19–4

**Equilibrium Output and Interest Rates**

The equilibrium level of output and the equilibrium nominal interest rate are given by the intersection of the *IS* and the *LM* curves. The real interest rate equals the nominal interest rate minus expected inflation.

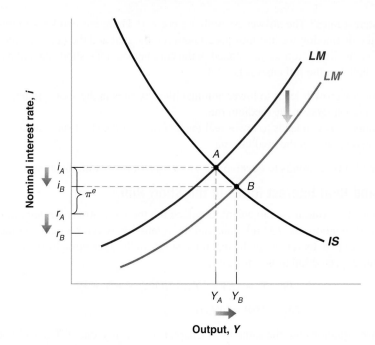

**FIGURE 19–5**

**The Short-Run Effects of an Increase in Money Growth**

An increase in money growth increases the real money stock in the short run. This increase in real money leads to an increase in output and a decrease in both the nominal and the real interest rates.

- The equilibrium is at the intersection of the *IS* and *LM* curves, point *A*, with output level $Y_A$, nominal interest rate $i_A$. Given the nominal interest rate $i_A$, the real interest rate $r_A$ is given by $r_A = i_A - \pi^e$.

Assume the economy initially is at the natural level of output, so $Y_A = Y_n$. Now, suppose that the central bank increases the rate of growth of money. What happens to output, to the nominal interest rate, and to the real interest rate in the short run?

One of the lessons from our analysis of monetary policy in the core is that in the short run, the faster increase in nominal money will not be matched by an equal increase in the price level. In other words, the higher rate of growth of nominal money will lead, in the short run, to an increase in the real money stock, (*M/P*). This is all we need to know for our purposes. What happens to output and to interest rates in the short run is shown in Figure 19–5.

The increase in the real money stock leads to a downward shift in the *LM* curve, from *LM* to *LM'*: For a given level of output, the increase in the real money stock leads to a decrease in the nominal interest rate. The *IS* curve does not shift: Given expected inflation, a given nominal interest rate corresponds to the same real interest rate and to the same level of spending and output. The equilibrium moves from *A* to *B*: Output is higher. The nominal interest rate is lower, and given expected inflation, so is the real interest rate.

To summarize: In the short run, the increase in nominal money growth leads to an increase in the real money stock. This increase in real money leads to an increase in output, and to a decrease in the nominal and the real interest rates.[2] Return to our first quotation: The goal of the Bank of Canada in the fall of 2001 and through 2002 was precisely to achieve this outcome. Worried that a slowdown in growth in the United States might lead to a recession in Canada, the Bank of Canada increased money growth in order to decrease the real interest rate, depreciate the real exchange rate (remember Chapters 6, 7, and 8), and increase output.

> In the short run, when the rate of money growth increases, *M/P* increases. Both *i* and *r* decrease.

[2]**DIGGING DEEPER.** Even in the short run, there may be a second effect at work—in addition to the increase in *M/P*. As money growth increases, so does inflation—although, initially, by less than money growth. As inflation increases, expected inflation may also increase. The implications of an increase in expected inflation are explored in problem 8 at the end of the chapter. In short, the increase in expected inflation leads to an even larger decrease in the real interest rate in the short run.

## Nominal and Real Interest Rates in the Medium Run

Turn now to the medium run. Suppose the central bank increases the rate of money growth permanently. What will happen to output, nominal interest rates, and real interest rates in the medium run?

To answer that question, we rely on two of the central propositions we derived in the core. The two propositions were derived in a model that did not make a distinction between real and nominal rates, but they still hold here:

- In the medium run, output returns to its natural level.

◀ In the medium run: $Y = Y_n$

    As we saw in Chapter 9, this is because in the medium run, the unemployment rate must return to the natural unemployment rate. The natural level of output is simply the level of output associated with the natural unemployment rate.

    Although we spent Chapters 15 to 18 looking at growth of output over time, we will, for simplicity, ignore output growth here. Thus, we will assume that $Y_n$, the natural level of output, is constant over time.

- In the medium run, the rate of inflation is equal to the rate of money growth minus the rate of growth of output.

    We derived this conclusion in Chapters 12 and 13. The intuition for it is simple: A growing level of output implies a growing level of transactions and thus a growing demand for real money. If output is growing at 3%, the real money stock must also grow at 3% per year. If the nominal money stock grows at a rate different from 3%, the difference must show up in inflation (or deflation). For example, if nominal money growth is 10%, then inflation must be equal to 7%.

    If, as we assume here, output growth is equal to zero, this proposition takes an even simpler form: In the medium run, the rate of inflation is equal to the rate of nominal money growth.

◀ In the medium run, (if $g_y = 0$) $\pi = g_M$

The implications of these two propositions for the behaviour of the real and the nominal interest rates in the medium run are then straightforward:

- Take the real interest rate first. For convenience, let us rewrite the *IS* equation:

$$Y = C(Y - T) + I(Y, r) + G$$

    One way of thinking about the *IS* relation is that it tells us, for given values of $G$ and $T$, what real interest rate, $r$, is needed to sustain a given level of spending, and so a given level of output, $Y$. If, for example, output is equal to its natural level $Y_n$, then, for given values of $G$ and $T$, the real interest rate must be such that:

$$Y_n = C(Y_n - T) + I(Y_n, r) + G$$

    By analogy with our use of the word "natural" to denote the level of output in the medium run, call this value of the real interest rate the *natural real interest rate*, and denote it by $r_n$. Then, our earlier proposition that in the medium run, output returns to its natural level, $Y_n$, has a direct implication: For given $G$ and $T$, in the medium run, the real interest rate returns to the natural interest rate, $r_n$. In other words, in the medium run, both output *and* the real interest rate are unaffected by the rate of money growth.

- Turn to the nominal interest rate. Recall the relation between the nominal and the real interest rate:

$$i = r + \pi^e$$

    We have just seen that in the medium run, the real interest rate equals the natural interest rate, $r_n$. This means:

$$i = r_n + \pi^e$$

In the medium run, expected inflation is equal to actual inflation (people do not have incorrect expectations of inflation forever), so:

$$i = r_n + \pi$$

In the medium run, inflation is equal to money growth (recall we are assuming that the rate of growth of output equals zero), so:

$$i = r_n + g_M$$

In words: In the medium run, an increase in money growth leads to an equal increase in the nominal interest rate.

To summarize: In the medium run, money growth does not affect the real interest rate but affects both inflation and the nominal interest rate one for one. A permanent increase in nominal money growth of, say, 10%, is eventually reflected in a 10% increase in the inflation rate and a 10% increase in the nominal interest rate—leaving the real interest rate unchanged.

The result that, in the medium run, nominal interest rates increase one for one with inflation is known as the **Fisher effect**, or the **Fisher hypothesis**, after Irving Fisher, an economist at Yale University, who first stated it at the beginning of the twentieth century. This result underlies the second quotation at the beginning of the section: If financial investors were, indeed, worried that nominating David Dodge, a governor from outside the Bank of Canada, in place of John Crow, would lead to higher money growth, they were right to expect higher nominal interest rates in the future.

Irving Fisher, *The Rate of Interest* (New York: Macmillan, 1906).

In this case, their fears turned out to be unfounded. The Bank of Canada remained committed to low inflation throughout the 1990s. In 2013, history repeated itself and the Bank of Canada governor was again appointed from outside in the person of Stephen Poloz.

## From the Short Run to the Medium Run

We have now shown how to reconcile the two quotes at the beginning of the section: An increase in monetary growth (a monetary expansion) is likely to lead to a *decrease* in nominal interest rates in the short run but to an *increase* in nominal interest rates in the medium run.

What happens between the short run and the medium run? A complete characterization of the movements of real and nominal interest rates over time would take us beyond what we can do here. But the basic features of the adjustment process are easy to describe.

In the short run, real and nominal interest rates go down. Why don't they stay down forever? As long as the real interest rate is below the natural real interest rate (the value corresponding to the natural level of output), output is higher than the natural level. Equivalently, unemployment is below the natural rate. From the Phillips curve relation, we know that as long as unemployment is below the natural rate, inflation increases.

In the short run: $i \downarrow r \downarrow$
$$r < r_n \Rightarrow Y > Y_n$$
$$Y > Y_n \Rightarrow u < u_n$$
$$u < u_n \Rightarrow \pi \uparrow$$

As inflation increases, it eventually becomes higher than nominal money growth, leading to negative real money growth. When real money growth turns negative, the nominal interest rate starts increasing. And, given expected inflation, so does the real interest rate.

Over time: $\pi \uparrow$
Eventually $\pi > g'_M$
$$g'_M - \pi < 0 \Rightarrow i \uparrow$$

In the medium run, the real interest rate increases back to its initial value. Output is then back to its natural level, unemployment is back to its natural rate, and inflation is no longer changing. As the real interest rate converges back to its initial value, the nominal interest rate converges to a new higher value, equal to the real interest rate plus the new, higher rate of nominal money growth.

In the medium run:
$$r = r_n$$
$$Y = Y_n,$$
$$u = u_n, \pi \text{ constant}$$
$$\pi = g'_M$$
$$i = r_n + g'_M$$

Figure 19–6 summarizes these results by showing the adjustment over time of the real and the nominal interest rates to an increase in nominal money growth from, say, 0% to 10%, starting at time $t$. Before time $t$, both interest rates are constant and equal to each other. The real interest rate is equal to $r_n$. The nominal interest rate is also equal to $r_n$ (as inflation and expected inflation are equal to zero).

At time $t$, the rate of money growth increases from 0% to 10%. The increase in the rate of nominal money growth leads, for some time, to an increase in real money and to a decrease in the nominal interest rate. As expected inflation increases, the decrease in the real interest rate is larger than the decrease of the nominal interest rate.

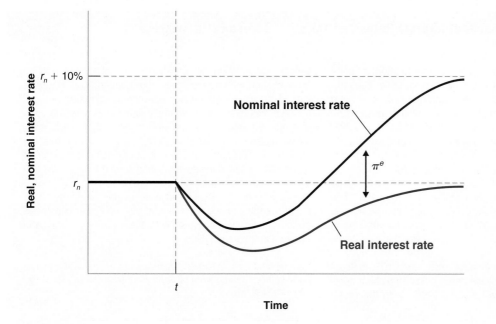

FIGURE 19-6

**The Adjustment of the Real and the Nominal Interest Rates to an Increase in Money Growth from 0% to 10%**

An increase in money growth leads initially to a decrease in both the real and the nominal interest rates. Over time, the real interest rate returns to its initial value. The nominal interest rate converges to a new higher value. This new higher value is equal to the initial value plus the increase in money growth.

Eventually, the nominal and the real interest rates start increasing. In the medium run, the real interest rate returns to its initial value. Inflation and expected inflation converge to the new rate of money growth, thus 10%. The nominal interest rate converges to a value equal to the real interest rate plus 10%.

## Evidence on the Fisher Hypothesis

There is plenty of evidence that a monetary expansion decreases nominal interest rates in the short run (see, for example, section 5-5). But how much evidence is there for the Fisher hypothesis, the proposition that in the medium run, increases in inflation lead to one-for-one increases in nominal interest rates?

Economists have tried to answer this question by looking at two types of evidence. The first is the relation between nominal interest rates and inflation *across countries*. Because the relation holds only in the medium run, we should not expect inflation and nominal interest rates to be close to each other in any one country at any one time, but the relation should hold on average. This approach is explored further in the Focus box "Nominal Interest Rates and Inflation across Latin America," which looks at Latin American countries in the early 1990s and finds substantial support for the Fisher hypothesis.

The second type of evidence is the relation between the nominal interest rate and inflation over time for one country. Again, the Fisher hypothesis does not suggest that the two should move together from year to year. But it does suggest that the long swings in inflation should eventually be reflected in similar swings in the nominal interest rate. To see these long swings, we need to look at as long a period of time as we can. Figure 19–7 looks at the nominal interest rate and inflation in Canada since 1950. The nominal interest rate is the one-to-three-year bond yield, and the inflation rate is the rate of change of the CPI.

Figure 19–7 has several interesting features.

● The steady increase in inflation from the early 1950s to the early 1980s was associated with a roughly parallel increase in the nominal interest rate. The decrease in inflation since the mid-1980s has been associated with a decrease in the nominal interest rate. These evolutions support the Fisher hypothesis.

Figure 1 plots nominal interest rates and inflation for eight Latin American countries (Argentina, Bolivia, Chile, Ecuador, Mexico, Peru, Uruguay, and Venezuela) for both 1992 and 1993. (Because the Brazilian numbers would dwarf those from other countries, they are not included here. In 1992, Brazil's inflation rate was 1008% and its nominal interest rate was 1560%. In 1993, inflation was 2140% and the nominal interest rate was 3240%.) The numbers for inflation refer to the rate of change of the consumer price index. The numbers for nominal interest rates refer to the "lending rate." The exact definition of this term varies with each country, but you can think of it as corresponding to the prime interest rate in Canada—the rate charged to borrowers with the best credit rating.

Note the wide range of inflation rates—from 10% to about 100%. This is precisely why we have chosen to present numbers from Latin America in the early 1990s. With this much

variation in inflation, we can learn a lot about the relation between nominal interest rates and inflation. And Figure 1, indeed, shows a clear relation between inflation and nominal interest rates. The line drawn in the figure plots what the nominal interest rate should be under the Fisher hypothesis, assuming an underlying real interest rate of 10% so that $i = 10\% + \pi$. The slope of the line is one: Under the Fisher hypothesis, a 1% increase in inflation should be reflected in a 1% increase in the nominal interest rate.

As you can see, the line fits well; roughly half of the points are above the line, the other half below. The Fisher hypothesis appears roughly consistent with the evidence from Latin America in the early 1990s.

*Source:* International Financial Statistics, International Monetary Fund (various issues). World Economic Outlook (1993). Used by permission of IMF.

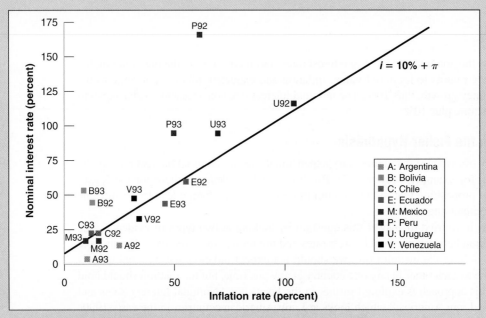

**FIGURE 1   Nominal Interest Rates and Inflation: Latin America, 1992 and 1993**

*Brazil is not shown; its four-digit nominal interest rate and inflation rate would be off the scale.*

- Evidence of the short-run effects that we discussed earlier is also easy to see. The nominal interest rate lagged behind the increase in inflation in the 1970s, whereas the disinflations of the early 1980s and early 1990s were associated with an initial *increase* in the nominal rate, followed by a much slower decline in the nominal interest rate than in inflation.
- There is a very sharp inflation spike in 1951. This spike underlines the "medium run" qualifier in the Fisher hypothesis. In 1951, inflation was high, over 10%, but short-lived, and it disappeared before it had time to be reflected in a higher nominal interest rate. It took sustained higher inflation to generate a higher nominal interest rate.

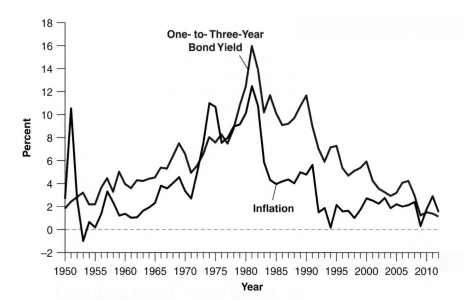

FIGURE   19–7

The One-to-Three-Year Yield
and Inflation, 1950–2012

The increase in inflation
from the 1950s to the early
1980s was associated with
an increase in the nominal
interest rate. The decrease
in inflation since 1982
has been associated with
a decrease in the nominal
interest rate.

*Source: Inflation* using
CANSIM II variable
V41690973; *nominal interest rate* using CANSIM II
variable V122558.

- We see again that inflation has been larger than the nominal interest rate in the last 4 years of Figure 19–7. Thus real interest rates have exceeded nominal interest rates.

More careful studies confirm our basic conclusion. The Fisher hypothesis that in the medium run increases in inflation are reflected in a higher nominal interest rate appears to fit the data quite well. But the adjustment may take a long time. The data confirm the speculation by Milton Friedman, which we quoted in Chapter 12, that it typically takes a "couple of decades" for nominal interest rates to reflect the higher inflation rate.

## SUMMARY

- The nominal interest rate tells us how many dollars one has to repay in the future in exchange for one dollar today.

- The real interest rate tells us how many goods one has to repay in the future in exchange for one good today.

- The real interest rate is approximately equal to the nominal interest rate minus expected inflation.

- The expected present discounted value of a sequence of payments is the value this year of the expected sequence of payments. It depends positively on current and future expected payments. It depends negatively on current and future expected interest rates.

- In discounting a sequence of current and expected future nominal payments, one should use current and expected future nominal interest rates. In discounting a sequence of current and expected future real payments, one should use current and expected future real interest rates.

- Investment decisions depend on the real interest rate. The choice between money and bonds depends on the nominal interest rate. Thus, the real interest rate enters the *IS* relation, whereas the nominal interest rate enters the *LM* relation.

- In the short run, an increase in money growth typically leads to a decrease of both the nominal interest rate and the real interest rate. In the medium run, an increase in money growth has no effect on the real interest rate and increases the nominal interest rate one for one.

- The proposition that, in the medium run, changes in inflation are reflected one for one in changes in the nominal interest rate is known as the Fisher effect, or the Fisher hypothesis. The empirical evidence suggests that although it takes a long time, changes in inflation are eventually reflected in changes in the nominal interest rate.

- deflation trap, 382
- discount factor, 384
- discount rate, 384
- expected present discounted value, 383
- Fisher effect, Fisher hypothesis, 392

- nominal interest rate, 379
- present value, 385
- real interest rate, 379
- risk averse, 385
- risk neutral, 385

## QUESTIONS AND PROBLEMS

### 1. TRUE/FALSE/UNCERTAIN

a. As long as inflation remains roughly constant, the movements in the real interest rate are equal to the movements in the nominal interest rate.

b. If inflation turns out to be higher than expected, then the realized real cost of borrowing turns out to be lower than expected.

c. Looking across countries, the real interest rate is likely to vary much less than the nominal interest rate.

d. The real interest rate is equal to the nominal interest rate divided by the price level.

e. In the medium run, the real interest rate is not affected by money growth.

f. The Fisher effect states that in the medium run, the nominal interest rate is not affected by money growth.

g. The experience of Latin American countries in the early 1990s supports the Fisher hypothesis.

h. The value today of a nominal payment in the future cannot be greater than the nominal payment itself.

i. The real value today of a real payment in the future cannot be greater than the real payment itself.

### 2. REAL AND NOMINAL INTEREST RATES: PART I

Explain whether you would use real payments and real interest rates or nominal payments and nominal interests rates to compute:

a. The present discounted value of the profits from purchasing a new machine.

b. The present value of a 20-year government bond.

c. Making the decision whether to buy a new car or lease a new car.

### 3. REAL AND NOMINAL INTEREST RATES: PART II

For each of the following, compute the real interest rate using the exact formula and the approximation formula.

a. $i = 4\%$; $\pi^e = 2\%$

b. $i = 15\%$; $\pi^e = 11\%$

c. $i = 54\%$; $\pi^e = 46\%$

### 4. REAL AND NOMINAL INTEREST RATES: PART III

a. Can the nominal interest rate ever be negative? Explain.

b. Can the real interest rate ever be negative? Under what circumstances? If so, why not just hold cash instead?

c. What are the effects of a negative real interest rate on borrowing and lending?

d. Find a recent issue of *The Economist* and look at the tables in the back ("Economic Indicators" and "Financial Indicators"). Use the three-month money-market rate as the nominal interest rate and the most recent three-month rate of change in consumer prices as the expected rate of inflation (both are expressed in annual terms). Which countries have the lowest nominal interest rates? Which countries have the lowest real interest rates? Are some of these real interest rates negative?

### 5. EARLY VERSUS LATE TAX CREDITS

You want to save $2000 today for retirement in 40 years. You have to choose between two plans:

i. Pay no taxes today, put the money in an interest-yielding account, and pay taxes equal to 25% of the total amount withdrawn at retirement. (This is similar to most RRSPs.)

ii. Pay taxes equivalent to 20% of the investment amount today, put the remainder in an interest-yielding account, and pay no taxes when you withdraw your funds at retirement.

**a.** What is the expected present discounted value of each of these options if the interest rate is 1%? 10%?

**b.** Which alternative would you pick in each case? Under what circumstances would you pick the other policy? (*Hint:* Think of the tax rates.) This is the structure of an RRSP in some countries, including Canada and the United States.

## 6. CONSOLS

The present value of an infinite stream of dollar payments of $z (that starts next year) is $z/i when the nominal interest rate, $i$, is constant. This formula gives the price of a consol. It also is a good approximation for the present discounted value of a stream of constant payments over long but not infinite periods. Let us examine how close the approximation is. Suppose that $i = 10\%$.

**a.** Let $z = 100$. What is the present value of the consol?

**b.** What is the expected present discounted value for a bond that pays $z over the next 10 years? 20 years? 30 years? 60 years? (*Hint:* Use the formula from Chapter 19, but remember to adjust for the first payment.)

**c.** Repeat the exercise with $i = 2\%$ and $i = 5\%$.

## 7. THE FISHER HYPOTHESIS

**a.** What is the Fisher hypothesis?

**b.** Does the experience of Latin American countries in the 1990s support or refute the Fisher hypothesis? Explain.

**c.** Look at the figure in the Focus box on Latin America. Note that the line drawn through the scatter of points does not go through the origin. Does the Fisher effect suggest that it should go through the origin? Explain.

**d.** "If the Fisher hypothesis is true, then changes in the growth rate of the money stock translate one for one into changes in $i$, and the real interest rate is left unchanged. Thus, there is no room for monetary policy to affect activity." Discuss.

## 8. THE SHORT-RUN EFFECTS OF AN INCREASE IN MONEY GROWTH REVISITED

When looking at the short run in section 19-4, we concentrated on the effects of higher nominal money growth on the real money stock. We saw how this led to higher output and lower nominal and real interest rates.

Starting from the analysis in the text (as summarized in Figure 19–5 Point B), assume that as a result of higher money growth, expected inflation increases by $\Delta\pi^e$.

**a.** Show the effect of the increase in $\pi^e$ on the *IS* curve. Explain in words.

**b.** Show the effect of the increase in $\pi^e$ on the *LM* curve. Explain in words.

**c.** Show the combined effects of the increase in the real money stock and of the increase in expected inflation on output and on the nominal interest rate. Could the nominal interest rate end up higher, not lower, than before the change in money growth? Why?

**d.** Even if what happens to the nominal interest rate is ambiguous, can you tell what happens to the real interest rate? (*Hint:* What happens to output? What does this imply for what happens to the real interest rate?)

---

### APPENDIX

# DERIVING THE EXPECTED PRESENT DISCOUNTED VALUE USING REAL OR NOMINAL INTEREST RATES

This appendix shows that the two ways of expressing present discounted values, equations (19.5) and (19.7), are equivalent.

Let us first rewrite these two equations.

Equation (19.5) gives the present value as the sum of current and future expected *nominal payments*, discounted using current and future expected *nominal interest rates*:

$$\$V_t = \$z_t + \frac{1}{1 + i_t}\$z_{t+1}^e$$

$$+ \frac{1}{(1 + i_t)(1 + i_{t+1}^e)}\$z_{t+2}^e + \cdots \quad (19.5)$$

Equation (19.7) gives the present value as the sum of current and future expected *real payments*, discounted using current and future expected *real interest rates*:

$$V_t = z_t + \frac{1}{1 + r_t}z_{t+1}^e$$

$$+ \frac{1}{(1 + r_t)(1 + r_{t+1}^e)}z_{t+2}^e + \cdots \quad (19.7)$$

Divide both sides of equation (19.5) by the current price level, $P_t$. The left side becomes $\$V_t/P_t = V_t$, the real present discounted value, the same as the left-hand side of equation (19.7).

Now, consider each term on the right of equation (19.5):

- The first becomes $\$z_t/P_t = z_t$, the current payment in real terms. This term is the same as the first term on the right of equation (19.7).

- The second is given by $[1/(1 + i_t)](\$z_{t+1}^e/P_t)$. Multiplying the numerator and the denominator by $P_{t+1}^e$, the price level expected for next year, gives:

$$\frac{1}{1 + i_t} \frac{P_{t+1}^e}{P_t} \frac{\$z_{t+1}^e}{P_{t+1}^e}$$

The third fraction, $\$z_{t+1}^e/P_{t+1}^e$, is the expected real payment at time $t+1$. Consider the second fraction. Note that $P_{t+1}^e/P_t$ can be rewritten as $1 + [(P_{t+1}^e - P_t)/P_t]$, thus, using the definition of expected inflation, as $(1 + \pi_t^e)$. This gives:

$$\frac{(1 + \pi_t^e)}{(1 + i_t)} z_{t+1}^e$$

Finally, using the definition of the real interest rate in equation (19.3), $[1 + r_t = (1 + i_t)/(1 + \pi_t^e)]$ gives:

$$\frac{1}{(1 + r_t)} z_{t+1}^e$$

This is the same as the second term on the right-hand side of equation (19.7).

- The same method applies to the other terms; make sure that you can derive the next one.

It follows that equations (19.5) and (19.7) are equivalent ways of stating and deriving the expected present discounted value of a sequence of payments.

# Financial Markets and Expectations

## Expectations

In our first look at financial markets in the core section (back in Chapter 4), we assumed there were only two assets, money and just one type of bond—so that we could easily focus on the choice between money and all other assets. We are now ready to relax this assumption. In this chapter, we look at the choices among nonmoney assets—between short-term and long-term bonds, between bonds and stocks, at houses—and take a brief look at the choice between foreign and domestic bonds.

    Section 20-1 looks at the determination of bond prices and the yield curve. It shows in particular how we can use the yield curve to infer what financial markets expect to happen to short-term interest rates in the future. Section 20-2 looks at the determination of stock prices. It shows how stock prices depend on current and expected future profits, as well as on current and expected future interest rates. It then discusses the relation between movements in stock prices and movements in economic activity. Section 20-3 looks at fads and bubbles in the stock market—episodes when stock prices appear to move for reasons unrelated to either profits or interest rates—and discusses their macroeconomic implications. Section 20-4 looks at the housing market. Houses are often the largest component of a household's portfolio. Finally, Section 20-5 applies these ideas to the fluctuations in the value of the Canadian dollar as determined in foreign exchange markets.

# 20-1 | Bond Prices and the Yield Curve

Bonds differ in two basic dimensions:

- **Default risk**, the risk that the issuer of the bond will not pay back the full amount promised by the bond.
- **Maturity**, the length of time over which it promises to make payments to the holder. A bond that promises to make one payment of $1000 in six months has a maturity of six months; a bond that promises $100 per year for the next 20 years and a final payment of $1000 at the end of those 20 years has a maturity of 20 years. Maturity is the more important dimension for our purposes, and we will focus on it here.

Bonds of different maturities each have a price and an associated interest rate called the *yield to maturity*, or simply the *yield*. By looking on any given day at the yields on bonds of different maturities, we can graphically trace the relation between yields and maturity. This relation is called the **yield curve**, or the **term structure of interest rates** (the word "term" is synonymous with maturity).

Figure 20–1 gives the term structure on Canadian government bonds in June 1990 and January 1997. The choice of the two dates is not accidental; why we chose them will be clear shortly.

Note the yield curve is upward sloping in January 1997. The three-month rate (the interest rate on a three-month T-bill) was only 2.9%, whereas the long-term rate (the interest rate on bonds with more than 10 years to maturity) was 7.4%. Note the yield curve in June 1990 slopes down. The three-month rate was 13.5%, and the long-term rate was 10.5%.

Why did the yield curve slope up in 1997 and down in 1990? What does a yield curve tell us about expectations in financial markets? To answer these questions, we proceed in two steps. First, we look at the relation among the *prices of bonds* of different maturities. Second, we show the relation among *yields of bonds* of different maturities and examine the determinants of the shape of the yield curve.

## Bond Prices as Present Values

Consider two bonds: a one-year bond that promises one payment of $100 in one year, and a two-year bond that promises one payment of $100 in two years. Let their prices today be $\$P_{1t}$ and $\$P_{2t}$, respectively. How will these two prices be determined?

Term structure ⇔ Yield curve

To find out what the term structure is at the time you read this chapter, simply search for a yield curve for Canada. There are slightly different ways to calculate a yield curve and you will have various choices. The basic shape will be the same.

Two steps: (1) the determination of bond prices, and (2) the determination of bond yields.

Note both bonds are *discount bonds* (see the Focus box).

---

**FIGURE 20–1**

**Canadian Yield Curves, June 1990 and January 1997**

In January 1997, the Canadian yield curve sloped upward. In June 1990, it sloped downward.

*Source:* Various benchmark bond and Treasury bill yields from CANSIM II Table 1760043 were used to construct these curves.

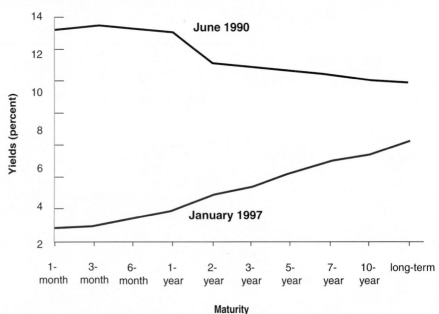

Understanding the basic vocabulary of financial markets will help make them less mysterious. Here is a basic vocabulary review.

- Bonds are issued by government to finance its deficit or by firms to finance their investment. If issued by government or by government agencies, the bonds are called **government bonds**. If issued by firms, they are called **corporate bonds**.

- In the United States and Canada, bonds are rated for their default risk (the risk they will not be repaid) by two private firms, the Standard and Poor's Corporation (S&P) and Moody's Investors Service. Moody's **bond ratings** range from *Aaa* for bonds with nearly no risk of default, such as Canadian federal government bonds, to *C* for bonds whose default risk is high. A lower rating typically implies that the bond has to pay a higher interest rate. The difference between the interest rate paid on a bond and the interest rate paid on the bond with the highest (best) rating is called the **risk premium**.

  Bonds with high default risk are known as **junk bonds**. Because they promised a very high interest rate, they became very popular with financial investors in the 1980s. After a few well-publicized defaults, they are less popular today.

- Bonds that promise a single payment at maturity are called **discount bonds**. The single payment is called the **face value** of the bond.

- Bonds that promise multiple payments before maturity and one payment at maturity are called **coupon bonds**. The payments before maturity are called **coupon payments**. The final payment is called the face value of the bond. The ratio of coupon payments to the face value is called the **coupon rate**. The **current yield** is the ratio of the coupon payment to the price of the bond.

  For example, a bond with coupon payments of $5 each year, a face value of $100, and a price of $80 has a coupon rate of 5% and a current yield of 6.25%.

From an economic viewpoint, neither the coupon rate nor the current yield are interesting measures. The correct measure of the interest rate on a bond is its *yield to maturity*, or simply *yield*; you can think of it as roughly the average annual interest rate paid by the bond over its life (we will define it more precisely later in this chapter).

- **Short-term**, **medium-term**, and **long-term bonds** typically refer to bonds with maturity of one year or less, one to 10 years, and 10 years or more, respectively.

- Government bonds range in maturity from a few days to 30 years. Bonds with a maturity of up to a year when they are issued are called Treasury bills, or T-bills. They are discount bonds, making only one payment at maturity. Federal government bonds with a maturity of one to 30 years when they are issued are called **Canada bonds**. These are coupon bonds. Provinces issue similar bonds.

- Bonds are typically nominal bonds: They promise a sequence of fixed nominal payments—payments in terms of domestic currency. However, there are other types of bonds. Among them are **indexed bonds**, bonds that promise not fixed nominal payments but rather payments adjusted for inflation. Instead of promising to pay, say, $100 in a year, a one-year indexed bond promises to pay $100(1 + \pi)$, where $\pi$ is the rate of inflation that will take place over the coming year. Because they protect bondholders against the risk of inflation, indexed bonds are popular in many countries. They play a particularly important role in the United Kingdom, where, over the last 20 years, people have increasingly used them to save for retirement. By holding long-term indexed bonds, they can make sure that the payments they receive when they retire will be protected from inflation. In Canada, indexed bonds are called **real return bonds**. Such bonds have been sold in Canada since 1991. They are used to help measure expected inflation. They are held mostly by pension plans that offer pensions that increase with the price level.

Take the *one-year bond* first. Let the current one-year nominal interest rate be $i_{1t}$. Note that we now denote the one-year interest rate in year $t$ by $i_{1t}$, rather than simply by $i_t$ as we did in earlier chapters. This is to make it easier to remember that it is the *one-year* interest rate.

The price of the one-year bond today is the present value of $100 next year. So:

$$\$P_{1t} = \frac{\$100}{1 + i_{1t}} \tag{20.1}$$

The price of a one-year bond varies inversely with the current one-year nominal interest rate. We already saw this relation in Chapter 4. Indeed, we saw that what actually is determined in the bond market is the price of one-year bonds, and the one-year interest rate is then inferred from the price according to equation (20.1). Reorganizing equation (20.1), it follows that if the price of one-year bonds is $\$P_{1t}$, then the current one-year interest rate equals $(\$100 - \$P_{1t})/\$P_{1t}$.

Turn now to the *two-year bond*. Its price is the present value of $100 in two years:

$$\$P_{2t} = \frac{\$100}{(1 + i_{1t})(1 + i^e_{t+1})} \tag{20.2}$$

where $i_{1t}$ denotes the one-year interest rate this year and $i^e_{t+1}$ denotes the one-year rate expected by financial markets for next year. The price of a two-year bond depends on both the current one-year rate and the one-year rate expected for next year.

In the same way, we could write the price of an $n$-year bond—a bond that promises to pay, say, $100 in $n$ years—as depending on the sequence of one-year rates expected by financial markets over the next $n$ years.

Before exploring further the implications of equations (20.1) and (20.2), let us look at an alternative derivation of equation (20.2) based on the notion of *arbitrage*. This alternative derivation will prove useful.

## Arbitrage and Bond Prices

In Chapter 6, we had a similar discussion about whether to hold a one-year bond denominated in Canadian dollars or a one-year bond denominated in American dollars.

Suppose you have the choice between holding one-year bonds or two-year bonds. You care about how much you will have one year from now. Which bonds should you hold?

- For every dollar you put in one-year bonds, you will get $(1 + i_{1t})$ dollars next year. This relation is represented in the first line of Figure 20–2.
- Because the price of a two-year bond is $\$P_{2t}$, every dollar you put in two-year bonds buys you $\$1/\$P_{2t}$ bonds today. When next year comes, the bond will have only one more year before maturity and thus will have become a one-year bond. Therefore, the price at which you can expect to sell it next year is $\$P^e_{1t+1}$, the expected price of a one-year bond next year. Thus, for every dollar you put in two-year bonds, you can expect to receive $(\$P^e_{1t+1}/\$P_{2t})$ dollars next year. This is represented in the second line of Figure 20–2.

Which bonds should you hold? Suppose that you, and other financial investors, care *only* about the expected return and choose to hold only the bond with the higher expected return.[1]

Under this assumption, and if there are positive amounts of one-year and two-year bonds in the economy, it follows that the two bonds must offer the same expected one-year return. To see why, suppose this condition were not satisfied. For example, suppose that the one-year return on one-year bonds were lower than the expected one-year return on two-year bonds. Nobody would want to hold the existing supply of one-year bonds, and the market for one-year bonds would not be in equilibrium. Only if the expected one-year return is the same will financial investors be willing to hold both one-year bonds and two-year bonds.

**FIGURE 20–2**

**Returns from Holding One-Year and Two-Year Bonds for One Year**

| | Year $t$ | Year $t + 1$ |
|---|---|---|
| One-year bonds | $1 ➡ | $1 $(1 + i_{1t})$ |
| Two-year bonds | $1 ➡ | $1 $\dfrac{\$P^e_{1t+1}}{\$P_{2t}}$ |

[1]**DIGGING DEEPER.** The return from holding one-year bonds for one year is known with certainty. The return from holding two-year bonds for one year depends on the price of one-year bonds next year and is therefore uncertain. The assumption that financial investors care only about expected return is another way of saying they are indifferent to risk—in other words, they are risk neutral. This is the same assumption we made to derive expected present discounted values in Chapter 19. In the context of the choice between bonds of different maturities, it is called the **expectations hypothesis**—to capture the notion that the choice depends on only expected returns.

If the two bonds offer the same expected one-year return, it follows from Figure 20–2 that:

$$1 + i_{1t} = \frac{\$P^e_{1t+1}}{\$P_{2t}} \qquad (20.3)$$

We use "arbitrage" to denote the proposition that the expected returns on two assets must be equal. Some economists reserve "arbitrage" for the narrower proposition that *riskless* profit opportunities do not go unexploited.

The left side gives the return per dollar from holding a one-year bond for one year; the right side gives the expected return per dollar from holding a two-year bond for one year. We will call such equations as (20.3)—equations that state that the expected returns on two assets have to be equal—**arbitrage** relations.

Rewrite equation (20.3) as:

$$\$P_{2t} = \frac{\$P^e_{1t+1}}{1 + i_{1t}} \qquad (20.4)$$

Arbitrage implies that the price of a two-year bond today is the present value of the expected price of the bond next year. This raises the question: What does the expected price of one-year bonds next year ($\$P^e_{1t+1}$) depend on?

The answer is straightforward. Just as the price of a one-year bond this year depends on this year's one-year interest rate, the price of a one-year bond next year will depend on the one-year interest rate next year. Writing equation (20.1) for next year (year $t + 1$) and denoting expectations in the usual way:

$$\$P^e_{1t+1} = \frac{\$100}{(1 + i^e_{1t+1})}$$

The price of the bond next year is expected to equal the final payment, $100, discounted by the one-year rate expected for next year.

Replacing $\$P^e_{1t+1}$ in equation (20.4) gives:

$$\$P_{2t} = \frac{\$100}{(1 + i_{1t})(1 + i^e_{1t+1})} \qquad (20.5)$$

The relation between arbitrage and present values: Arbitrage between bonds of different maturities implies that bond prices are equal to the expected present values of payments on these bonds.

This expression is the same as equation (20.2). What we have shown is that *arbitrage* between one- and two-year bonds implies that the price of the two-year bond is the *present value* of the payment in two years, namely, $100 discounted using current and next year's expected one-year rates. We could have used the same approach to derive the price of three-year bonds and so on; you may want to make sure you can do it. The relation between arbitrage and present value is important; we will use it again in this and later chapters.

## From Bond Prices to Bond Yields

We have derived bond prices. We now move to bond yields.

To begin, we need a definition of the yield to maturity. The **yield to maturity** on an $n$-year bond, or equivalently the $n$-**year interest rate**, is defined as that constant annual interest rate that makes the bond price today equal to the present value of future payments on the bond.

This definition is simpler than it sounds. For example, take the two-year bond we introduced earlier. Denote its yield by $i_{2t}$, where the subscript 2 reminds us that this is the yield to maturity on a two-year bond, or equivalently the two-year interest rate. This yield is defined as the constant annual interest rate that would make the present value of $100 in two years equal to the price of the bond today:

$$\$P_{2t} = \frac{\$100}{(1 + i_{2t})^2} \qquad (20.6)$$

$\$90 = \dfrac{\$100}{(1 + i_{2t})^2} \Rightarrow$

$(1 + i_{2t})^2 = \dfrac{\$100}{\$90} \Rightarrow$

$(1 + i_{2t}) = \sqrt{\dfrac{\$100}{\$90}} \Rightarrow$

$i_{2t} = 5.4\%$

Suppose the bond sells for $90 today. Then, the two-year rate $i_{2t}$ is given by $\sqrt{100/90} - 1$, or 5.4%. In other words, holding the bond for two years—until maturity—yields an interest rate of 5.4% per year.

What is the relation of the two-year rate to the current one-year rate and the expected one-year rate? To answer this question, we simply compare equation (20.6) with equation (20.5). Eliminating $\$P_{2t}$ between the two gives:

$$\frac{\$100}{(1 + i_{2t})^2} = \frac{\$100}{(1 + i_{1t})(1 + i^e_{1t+1})}$$

Rearranging:

$$(1 + i_{2t})^2 = (1 + i_{1t})(1 + i^e_{1t+1})$$

We used a similar approximation when we looked at the relation between nominal and real interest rates in Chapter 19. See proposition 3 in Appendix 2.

This gives the exact relation between the two-year rate and the current and expected one-year rates. A useful approximation to this relation is given by:

$$i_{2t} \approx \frac{1}{2}(i_{1t} + i^e_{1t+1}) \tag{20.7}$$

Equation (20.7) is intuitive and important. It says that the two-year rate is (approximately) the average of the current one-year rate and next year's expected one-year rate. The relation extends to interest rates on bonds of higher maturity. *The n-year rate is (approximately) equal to the average of current and expected one-year rates over this and the next (n − 1) years*:

$$i_{nt} \approx \frac{1}{n}(i_{1t} + i^e_{1t+1} + \cdots + i^e_{1t+n-1})$$

These relations give us the key we need to interpret the yield curve. *An upward-sloping yield curve tells us that financial markets expect short-term rates to increase in the future. A downward-sloping yield curve tells us that financial markets expect short-term interest rates to decrease in the future.*

An example will make this clear. Return to the January 1997 yield curve in Figure 20–1. We can infer from it what the financial markets expected the one-year interest rate to be one year hence—namely, in January 1998. To do so, multiply both sides of equation (20.7) by 2, and reorganize to get:

$$i^e_{1t+1} = 2i_{2t} - i_{1t} \tag{20.8}$$

In January 1997, $i_{1t}$ (the one-year rate, the interest rate for 1997) was 3.64%. The two-year rate was 4.44%. The expected one-year rate for January 1998 was therefore equal to $(2 \times 4.44\%) - 3.64\% = 5.24\%$, thus 1.6% above the January 1997 one-year rate.[2]

## The Yield Curve and Economic Activity

In Chapter 22, we will extend the *IS-LM* model to take explicitly into account what we have learned about the effects of expectations on decisions. For the moment, the basic *IS-LM* will do.

Why was the yield curve so steep in January 1997? Why did financial markets expect short-term interest rates to decrease in June 1990? To answer both questions, let us use the *IS-LM* we developed in the core (Chapter 5). Also, to concentrate on the difference between interest rates of different maturities, let us leave aside the distinction between nominal and real interest rates we introduced in Chapter 19. More specifically, let us assume that expected inflation is equal to zero so that real and nominal rates are the same. Figure 20–3 draws the *IS-LM*, with the (nominal) interest rate on the vertical axis and output on the horizontal axis.

[2]**DIGGING DEEPER.** Back to risk: Bonds of higher maturity are more risky to hold because if they are sold before maturity, variations in their price can lead to large gains or losses. Contrary to our assumption that people are indifferent to risk, participants in bond markets are, in fact, risk averse and require a risk premium for bonds of higher maturity. Thus, a mildly upward-sloping yield curve is more likely to reflect a risk premium that increases with maturity rather than expectations of higher short-term rates in the future. The computation in the text does not take this risk premium into account.

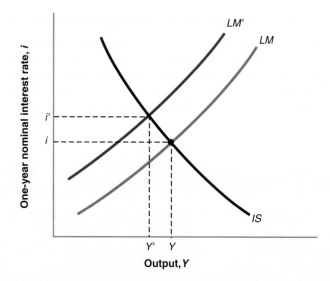

FIGURE 20-3

**On the Brink of the 1990–1991 Recession**

Tight money in the early 1990s led to above-average short-term interest rates.

In June 1990, the Canadian economy was slipping into a recession. The Bank of Canada, concerned about inflation, had made a concerted effort to constrain the money supply. We studied this episode in Chapter 13. In terms of Figure 20–3, monetary policy had shifted the *LM* curve from its usual position to *LM′*. Interest rates were driven up to *i′* in early 1990, but market participants expected that the recession would lead the Bank to return to a less restrictive policy stance and future interest rates would be lower. Canada experienced a deep and prolonged recession. Then as we saw in Chapter 5, there was a combination of tighter fiscal policy and looser monetary policy through the mid-1990s. As of June 1990, the negatively sloped yield curve said that financial markets correctly expected that interest rates were temporarily high and would fall in the future.

By early 1997, however, it looked as though the Canadian economy was on the verge of rapid growth. The U.S. economy was booming. The Bank of Canada was pleased with the low and stable rate of inflation and did its best to jump-start the economy. Look at Figure 20–4. Fiscal tightening in the Canadian economy since 1993 had left us with a leftward shift of the *IS* curve to *IS′*. The expansionary monetary policy of the Bank had shifted the *LM* curve to *LM′*. Market participants realized that these shifts would eventually end and that over time these curves would shift back to their usual levels and interest rates would return to *i*. The interest rate at *i″* looked lower than its future value. In January 1997 the yield curve had an upward slope.

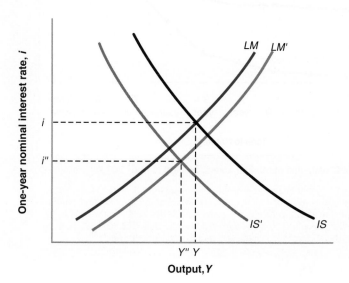

FIGURE 20-4

**The Expected Path of Recovery as of Early 1997**

The market expected the recovery to bring higher interest rates.

This section has covered a lot of ground. Let us briefly summarize the main points:

● Arbitrage between bonds of different maturities implies that the price of a bond is the present value of the payments on the bond, discounted using current and expected short-term interest rates. Thus, higher current or expected short-term interest rates lead to lower bond prices.

● The yield to maturity on a bond with a maturity of n years (or equivalently, the n-year rate) is approximately equal to the average of current and expected future one-year interest rates.

## FOCUS    The Yield Curve in Canada and the United States in 2013

Figure 1 shows the yield curve in Canada and in the United States from January to April of 2013. Consider the United States first. At the short end, the T-bill rate is nearly equal to zero: The United States is in a liquidity trap. The yield curve tells us that financial markets expect this to remain the case for the next three years: The one-year rate is equal to 0.15%, the two-year rate equal to 0.26%, the three-year rate is less than 0.38%. Only when we look at yields beyond 5 years to maturity are yields larger. In short: financial markets believe that the U.S. economy will remain weak, and thus the Fed will keep the nominal interest rate very low for a long time to come.

A commitment to very low interest rates is explicit in the policy statements of the Fed. To quote from the December 12, 2012, policy statement:

*". . . the Committee decided to keep the target range for the federal funds rate at 0 to 1/4 percent and currently anticipates that this exceptionally low range for the federal funds rate will be appropriate at least as long as the unemployment rate remains above 6-1/2 percent . . ."*

Financial markets appear to have taken this statement at face value and, with no prospect of the unemployment rate reaching 6.5% in the next three years, the yield curve reflects the Fed's policy statement.

The level of interest rates in Canada is higher than in the United States. The yield curve is flat at 1% out 3 years. The interpretation of the Canadian yield curve is that financial markets expect the Bank of Canada to keep interest rates constant at about 1% for the next 3 years.

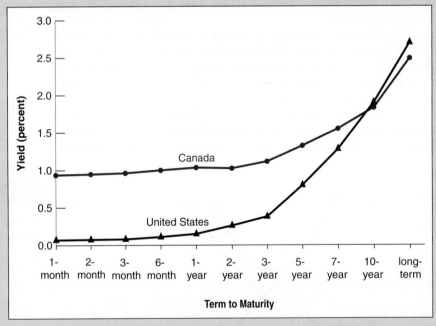

**FIGURE 1    Yield Curves in Canada and the United States, January to April 2013**

*Source:* Table & excerpt from 1 month to 1 year; Treasury Bill yields; from 2 years to long-term Government of Canada bond yields. Both as reported in CANSIM II Table 176-0043 and averaged over the first four months of 2013. United States yields from Series beginning with DGS, Federal Reserve Economic Database (FRED). Long-term yield for the United States is 20-year bond. 2-month yield for the United States is average of 1-month and 3-month yields.

- The slope of the yield curve tells us what financial markets expect to happen to short-term interest rates in the future. A downward-sloping yield curve implies that the market expects a decrease in short-term rates in the future; an upward-sloping yield curve implies that the markets expect an increase in short-term rates in the future. In the Focus box "The Yield Curve in Canada and the United States in 2013," we use this result to look at expected monetary policy in these two countries in 2013.

## 20-2 | The Stock Market and Movements in Stock Prices

We have so far focused on bonds. But while government finances itself primarily by issuing bonds, the same is not true of firms. Firms raise funds in two ways: through **debt finance**—bonds and loans—and through **equity finance**, through issues of **shares**—or stock, as shares are also called. Instead of paying predetermined amounts as bonds do, stocks pay **dividends** in an amount decided by the firm. Dividends are paid from the firm's profits. They are typically less than profits, as firms retain some of their profits to finance their investment. But dividends move with profits: When profits increase, so do dividends.

Our focus in this section is on the determination of stock prices. As a way of introducing the issues, Figure 20–5 shows the behaviour of an index of stock prices, the *Standard and Poor's/Toronto Stock Exchange Composite Index* from 1960 to 2012. Movements in the index measure movements in the average stock price of 300 large companies based in Canada. Many of the companies in the TSE 300 also list their shares on the stock exchanges in the United States, and many Canadians purchase shares listed on American stock exchanges. Two American stock price indexes are the *Standard and Poor's 500 Composite Index* (average prices of 500 large companies) and the *Dow Jones Industrial Index* (average prices of only 30 large industrial companies). Similar indexes exist for other countries. (The *Nikkei Index* reflects movements in stock prices in Tokyo, and the *FT* and *CAC* indexes reflect stock-price movements in London and Paris, respectively.)

Figure 20–5 plots two lines. One line, labelled nominal, gives the evolution of the index as publicly available, the number you see on your preferred screen if you follow the stock market. The index shows near constancy until 1980 and a rapid overall increase since. It rose from 2000 in 1980 to more than 14,000 in 2007.

This index, however, is nominal—that is, it gives the evolution of stock prices in terms of dollars. Of more interest to us is the evolution of the index in real terms (that is, adjusted for inflation). The evolution of that index, constructed by dividing the nominal index by the CPI for each year, is shown by the lower line in Figure 20–5. By construction, the CPI is equal to 1 in 2002, so the nominal and real indexes are equal by construction in 2002.

The plot of the real index shows a somewhat different picture. It shows a real stock price index that fluctuated in a relatively narrow range, from 3000 to 5000 over the whole period from 1960 until 1995. Then, from 1995 to 2000, real stock prices grew very rapidly so that a stock portfolio worth $100 in 1995 (index value 5000) was worth over $200 in 2000 (index value over 10,000). This doubling over five years is measured in constant dollars. Truly, these were amazing returns on holding stocks. After 2000, the real value (and the nominal value) of stocks moved a lot—both up and down. In 2012, the real value of the stock index was roughly its value in 2000. Between these years there were annual declines in the value of the stock market of 27,12,10,11,22 and 9 percentage points of its value. Since the total value of the stock market was roughly constant from 2000 to 2012, between other years, stock prices rose. Stock markets are very volatile.

Why do stock prices move so much over brief periods of time? While we do not offer a complete answer (if we could, we would be making our fortunes on the stock market, not teaching and researching macroeconomics), we ask in the next section how stock prices respond to changes in the economic environment and in macroeconomic policy.

FIGURE    20–5

**The Value of the Shares on the Toronto Stock Exchange in Nominal and Real Terms**

The value of equity fluctuates enormously, both over the long term and from year to year. The real value of the stock market fluctuated over a relatively small range. Since 1990, stock markets have seen an overall rise in real values punctuated by a number of sharp drops. The drop from the November 2007 peak to the February 2009 bottom over the course of the crisis was more than 1/3 of the peak value.

*Source:* Nominal value of shares on Toronto Stock Exchange CANSIM II variableV122620. Real value of shares is nominal value deflated by Consumer Price Index CANSIM II variable V41690973.

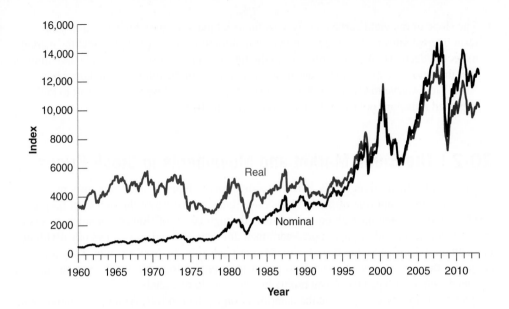

## Stock Prices as Present Values

What determines the price of a stock that promises a sequence of dividends in the future? By now, we are sure the material in Chapter 19 has become familiar, and you already know the answer: The stock price must equal the present value of future expected dividends.

Let $\$Q_t$ be the price of the stock. Let $\$D_t$ denote the dividend this year, $\$D_{t+1}^e$ the dividend expected for next year, $\$D_{t+2}^e$ the dividend expected for two years from now, and so on.

Suppose we look at the price of the stock just after the dividend has been paid this year—this price is known as the *ex-dividend price*—so that the first dividend to be paid after the purchase of the stock is next year's dividend. (This is just a matter of convention; alternatively, we could look at the price before this year's dividend has been paid.) The price of the stock is then given by:

$$\$Q_t = \frac{\$D_{t+1}^e}{1 + i_{1t}} + \frac{\$D_{t+2}^e}{(1 + i_{1t})(1 + i_{1t+1}^e)} + \cdots \tag{20.9}$$

The price of the stock is equal to the present value of the dividend next year, discounted using the current one-year interest rate, plus the present value of the dividend two years from now, discounted using both this year's one-year interest rate and next year's expected one-year interest rate, and so on.

As in the case of long-term bonds, the present value relation in equation (20.9) can be derived from arbitrage, from the assumption that the expected return per dollar from holding a stock for one year must be equal to the return from holding a one-year bond. The derivation is given in Appendix A at the end of this chapter. (Going through it will improve your understanding of the relation between arbitrage and present value, but it can be skipped.)[3]

---

[3]**DIGGING DEEPER.** Two complications: (1) The assumption we have maintained throughout this and the previous chapter that financial investors are risk neutral and require equal expected rates of returns on all assets is definitely not right here. Holding stocks for one year is much more risky than holding one-year bonds for one year, and historically, financial investors have required a *risk premium*—a higher expected rate of return—for holding stocks relative to bonds. How to modify both the arbitrage equation and the present value formula to take account of a risk premium is discussed in Appendix A at the end of this of this chapter. (2) That arbitrage implies that the price of a stock is the present value of dividends is true except in the presence of speculative bubbles, which we discuss in Section 20-3.

Equation (20.9) gives the stock price as the present value of *nominal* dividends, discounted by *nominal* interest rates. From Chapter 19, we know we can rewrite it to get the *real* stock price as the present value of *real* dividends, discounted by *real* interest rates. So, we can rewrite the real stock price as:

$$Q_t = \frac{D_{t+1}^e}{(1 + r_{1t})} + \frac{D_{t+2}^e}{(1 + r_{1t})(1 + r_{1t+1}^e)} + \cdots \qquad (20.10)$$

$Q_t$ and $D_t$, without a dollar sign, denote the real price and real dividends at time $t$. *The real stock price is the expected present value of future real dividends, discounted by the sequence of one-year real interest rates.*

This relation has two important implications. Higher expected future real dividends lead to a higher stock price. Higher current and expected future one-year real interest rates lead to a lower stock price. Let us now see what light this relation sheds on movements in the stock market.

The two equivalent ways of writing the stock price: The nominal stock price equals the expected present discounted value of future nominal dividends, discounted by current and future nominal interest rates. The real stock price equals the expected present discounted value of future real dividends, discounted by current and future real interest rates.

## The Stock Market and Economic Activity

Figure 20–5 showed the large movements in stock prices over the last 50 years. It is not unusual for the index to go up or down by large amounts within a year. In 1974, the stock market went down by 37% (in real terms); in 1983, it went up by 22%. From 2007 to 2008, the stock market fell by 12% and then fell a further 23% from 2008 to 2009. There were many days in the fall of 2008 with very large fluctuations in the value of the stock market in both directions. What causes these movements?

The first point to be made is that these movements are, for the most part, unpredictable. The reason is best understood by thinking in terms of the choice people have between stocks and bonds. If it were widely believed that a year from now, the price of a stock was going to be 20% higher than today's price, holding the stock for a year would be unusually attractive, much more attractive than holding short-term bonds. There would be a very large demand for the stock. Its price would increase *today* to the point where the expected return from holding the stock was back in line with the expected return on other assets. In other words, the expectation of a high stock price next year would lead to a high stock price today.

There is, indeed, a saying in economics that it is a sign of a well-functioning stock market that movements in stock prices are unpredictable. The saying is too extreme: A few financial investors may, indeed, have better information or simply be better at reading the future. If they are only a few, they may not buy enough of the stock to bid its price all the way up today. Thus, they may get large expected returns. But the basic idea is, nevertheless, right. The financial market gurus who regularly predict large imminent movements in the stock market over the next few months are quacks. Major movements in stock prices cannot be predicted.

You may have heard the proposition that stock prices follow a **random walk**. This is a technical term, but with a simple interpretation: Something—it can be a molecule, or the price of an asset—follows a random walk if each step it takes is as likely to be up as it is to be down. Its movements are therefore unpredictable.

If movements in the stock market cannot be predicted, if they are the result of news, where does this leave us? We can still do two things:

- We can do Monday-morning quarterbacking, looking back and identifying the news to which the market reacted.
- We can ask "what if" questions. For example, What would happen to the stock market if the Bank of Canada were to embark on a more expansionary policy or if consumers were to become more optimistic and increase spending?

Let us look at two "what if" questions. To do so, let us use the *IS-LM* model. To simplify things, let us assume, as we did earlier, that expected inflation equals zero so that real and nominal interest rates are equal.

**A Monetary Expansion and the Stock Market.** Suppose the economy is in a recession (output is below its natural level) and the Bank of Canada decides to adopt a more expansionary monetary policy. The increase in money shifts the *LM* curve down in Figure 20–6. Equilibrium output moves from A to A'. How will the stock market react? The answer depends on what the stock market expected monetary policy to be before the Bank of Canada's move.

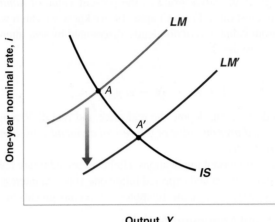

FIGURE 20-6

**An Expansionary Monetary Policy and the Stock Market**

A monetary expansion decreases the interest rate and increases output. What it does to the stock market depends on whether financial markets anticipated the monetary expansion.

If the stock market fully anticipated the expansionary policy, then the stock market will not react: Neither its expectations of future dividends nor its expectations of future interest rates are affected by a move it had already anticipated. Thus, in equation (20.9) nothing changes, and stock prices will remain the same.

Suppose, instead, that the Bank of Canada's move is at least partly unexpected. In that case, stock prices will increase. There are two reasons for this. First, a more expansionary monetary policy implies lower interest rates for some time. Second, a more expansionary monetary policy also implies higher output for some time (until the economy returns to the natural level of output), and so higher dividends. As equation (20.9) tells us, both lower interest rates and higher dividends, current and expected, will lead to an increase in stock prices.

**An Increase in Consumer Spending and the Stock Market.** Now, consider an unexpected shift of the *IS* curve to the right, resulting, for example, from stronger-than-expected consumer spending. As a result of the shift, equilibrium output in Figure 20–7(a) increases from *A* to *B*. Will stock prices go up? One is tempted to say yes: A stronger economy means higher profits and higher dividends for some time. But this answer is incomplete, for at least two reasons.

First, it ignores the effect of higher activity on interest rates: The movement along the *LM* curve from *A* to *B* also implies an increase in interest rates. Higher interest rates decrease stock prices. Which of the two effects—higher profits or higher interest rates—dominates? The answer depends on the slope of the *LM* curve. As drawn in Figure 20–7(b), a very steep *LM* curve implies large increases in interest rates, small increases in output, and so a fall in stock prices. As drawn in Figure 20–7(c), a very flat *LM* curve leads to small increases in interest rates, large increases in output, and so an increase in stock prices.

Second, it ignores the effect of the shift in the *IS* curve on the Bank of Canada's behaviour. In practice, this is the effect that financial investors often care about the most. When receiving the news of unexpectedly strong economic activity, the main question in the stock market is: How will the Canadian and American central banks react?

- Will the central bank accommodate the shift in the *IS* curve—that is, increase money supply in line with money demand to avoid an increase in the interest rate? This case is shown in Figure 20–7(d). **Accommodation** corresponds to a downward shift of the *LM* curve, from *LM* to *LM'*. In this case, the economy will go from point *A* to point *B'*. Stock prices will increase: Output is expected to be higher, and interest rates are not expected to increase.

- Will the central bank instead keep the same level of the money supply leaving the *LM* curve unchanged? This is the case we saw in Figure 20–7(a); the economy will go from *A*

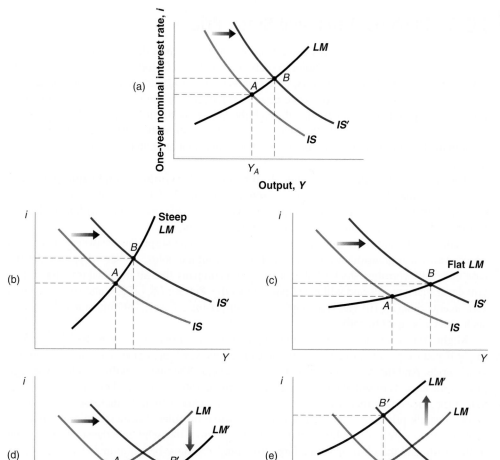

FIGURE 20-7

An Increase in Consumption Spending and the Stock Market

(a) The increase in consumption spending leads to a higher interest rate and a higher level of output. What happens to the stock market depends on the slope of the *LM* curve and on the central bank's behaviour. (b) Steep *LM* curve: The interest rate increases a lot, and output increases little. Stock prices go down. (c) Flat *LM* curve: The interest rate increases little, and output increases a lot. Stock prices go up. (d) The central bank accommodates: The interest rate does not increase, but output does. Stock prices go up. (e) The central bank decides to keep output constant: The interest rate increases, but output does not. Stock prices go down.

to $B$. As we saw earlier, what happens to stock prices is ambiguous. The economy will have higher profits, but the interest rate will be higher as well.

- Or will the central bank worry that an increase in output above $Y_A$ may lead to an increase in inflation? This will be the case if the economy is already close to the natural level of output, if $Y_A$ is close to $Y_n$. This case is shown in Figure 20–7(e). In this case, a further increase in output would lead to an increase in inflation, something that the central bank wants to avoid. The central bank decides to counteract the rightward shift of the *IS* curve with a monetary contraction, an upward shift of the *LM* curve from *LM* to *LM'* so that output does not change. In that case, stock prices will surely go down: There is no change in expected profits, but the interest rate is now likely to be higher for some time.

To summarize: Changes in output may or may not be associated with changes in stock prices in the same direction. Whether they are depends on (1) what the market expected in the first place, (2) the source of the shocks, and (3) how the market expects the central bank to react to the output change. Figure 20–7 with parts (a) though (e) is a warning about simplistic interpretations of the stock market and macroeconomic outcomes.

## 20-3 | Bubbles, Fads, and Stock Prices

Do all movements in stock prices come from news about future dividends or interest rates? Many economists doubt it. They point to such times as Black October in 1929, when the U.S. stock market fell by 23% in two days, or to October 19, 1987, when the Dow Jones index fell by 22.6% in a single day, or, to invoke more recent events, when stock markets in all countries moved up and down day by day through the fall of 2008. There was an amazing rise of Japanese stock prices in the 1980s, followed by a sharp fall in the 1990s. In each case, they point to the lack of obvious news, or at least news important enough to justify such enormous movements.

They argue that stock prices are not always equal to their **fundamental value**, defined as the present value of expected dividends given in equation (20.10), and that stocks are sometimes underpriced or overpriced. Overpricing eventually ends, sometimes with a crash as in October 1987, or with a long slide as has occurred in Japan.

Under what conditions can such mispricing occur? The surprising answer is that it can occur even when investors are rational and when arbitrage holds. To see why, consider the case of a truly worthless stock (that is, a stock of a company that all financial investors know will never make profits and will never pay dividends). Putting $D_{t+1}^e$, $D_{t+2}^e$, and so on, equal to zero in equation (20.10) yields a simple and unsurprising answer: The fundamental value of such a stock is equal to zero.

Might you, nevertheless, be willing to pay a positive price for such a stock? Yes. You might if you expect the price at which you can sell the stock next year to be higher than this year's price. And the same applies to a buyer next year: She may be willing to buy at a high price if she expects to sell at an even higher price in the following year. This process suggests that stock prices may increase just because investors expect them to increase. Such movements in stock prices are called **rational speculative bubbles**. Financial investors may be behaving rationally as the bubble inflates. Even those investors who hold the stock at the time of the crash, and therefore sustain a large loss, may also have been rational. They may have realized there was a chance of a crash but also a chance that the bubble would keep growing and they could sell at an even higher price.

> In a speculative bubble, the price of a stock is higher than its fundamental value. Investors are willing to pay a high price for the stock in anticipation of being able to resell the stock at an even higher price.

To make things simple, our example assumed the stock to be fundamentally worthless. But the argument is general and applies to stocks with a positive fundamental value as well. People might be willing to pay more than the fundamental value of a stock if they expect its price to increase more in the future. And the same argument applies to other assets, such as housing, gold, and paintings. Two such bubbles are described in the Focus box, "Famous Bubbles: From Tulipmania in Seventeenth-Century Holland to Russia in 1994."

> In the context of the U.S. stock market, Alan Greenspan has called it "irrational exuberance."

Are all deviations from fundamental values in financial markets rational bubbles? Probably not. Many financial investors are not rational. An increase in stock prices in the past, say, due to a succession of good news, often creates excessive optimism. If investors simply extrapolate from past returns to predict future returns, a stock may become "hot" (high priced) for no reason other than the fact that its price has increased in the past. Such deviations of stock prices from their fundamental value are called **fads**. We are all aware of the existence of fads outside of the stock market; there are good reasons to believe that they exist in the stock market as well.

How much of the movement in stock prices is due to movements in the fundamental value of stocks and how much is due to fads and bubbles? At any point in time, this question is very much on the minds of economists and investors. A peak in real stock prices in August 2000 is shown in Figure 20–5. However, at least some people—those who were selling their stocks—thought stock prices were about to fall. But it seems unlikely that those who bought in August 2000 expected prices to fall dramatically. Stock prices describe a transaction where a seller wants to sell, presumably believing the price will fall, and a purchaser wants to buy, presumably believing prices will rise. Both are comparing the stock price to a fundamental price and then adding their own belief about whether the actual price is at the fundamental price

FOCUS

**Famous Bubbles: From Tulipmania in Seventeenth-Century Holland to Russia in 1994**

### Tulipmania in Holland

In the seventeenth century, tulips became increasingly popular in western European gardens. A market developed in Holland for both rare and common forms of tulip bulbs.

The episode called the "tulip bubble" took place from 1634 to 1637. In 1634, the price of rare bulbs started increasing. The market went into a frenzy, with speculators buying tulip bulbs in anticipation of even higher prices later. The price of a bulb called "Admiral Van de Eyck," for example, increased from 1500 guineas in 1634 to 7500 guineas in 1637, the equivalent of the price of a house at the time. There are stories about a sailor mistakenly eating some bulbs, only to realize the cost of his "meal" later. In early 1637, prices increased faster.

**Anthony Claesz (1592–1635), *Tulips, Lilies, Irises, & Roses*. Around the time this painting was painted, some tulip bulbs in Holland were selling for the same price as a house.**

Even the price of more common bulbs skyrocketed, rising by a factor of up to 20 in January. But, in February 1637, prices collapsed. A few years later, bulbs were trading for roughly 10% of their value at the peak of the bubble.

### The MMM Pyramid in Russia

In 1994, a Russian "financier," Sergei Mavrody, created a company called MMM and proceeded to sell shares, promising shareholders a rate of return of at least 3000% per year!

The company was an instant success. The share price increased from 1600 rubles (then $1) in February to 105,000 rubles ($51) in July. And by July, according to company claims, the number of shareholders had increased to 10 million.

The trouble was that the company was not involved in any type of production and held no assets, except for its 140 offices in Russia. The shares were intrinsically worthless. The company's initial success was based on a standard pyramid scheme: MMM used the funds from the sale of new shares to pay the promised returns on the old shares. Despite repeated warnings by government officials, including Boris Yeltsin, that MMM was a scam and that the increase in the price of shares was a bubble, the promised returns were just too attractive to many Russian people, especially in the midst of a deep economic recession.

The scheme could work only as long as the number of new shareholders—and thus new funds to be distributed to existing shareholders—increased fast enough. By the end of July 1994, the company could no longer make good on its promises, and the scheme collapsed. The company closed. Mavrody tried to blackmail government into paying the shareholders, claiming that not doing so would trigger a revolution or a civil war. Government refused, leading many shareholders to be angry at government rather than at Mavrody. Later that year, Mavrody actually ran for Parliament, as a self-appointed defender of the shareholders who had lost their savings. He won!

*Source:* The account of "Tulipmania in Holland" is taken from Peter Garber, "Tulipmania," *Journal of Political Economy* 97 (3), June 1989: pp. 535–560. © 1989 University of Chicago Press. Used by permission of University of Chicago Press.

---

as well as their own belief that they will find a buyer in the future who will be willing to pay a higher price.

The general question about what determines stock prices is important for both finance and macroeconomics. The stock market is more than a sideshow. In the next chapter, we will see that not only are stock prices affected by economic activity, but also that, through investment and consumption decisions, stock prices may affect economic activity. Many economists look at the fall in stock prices at the beginning of the Great Depression and view that fall as one of the causes of the Great Depression. In Japan, the long slump of the 1990s was preceded by the bursting of a speculative bubble that ran through the 1980s. The more recent historical bubble appears to have been in residential real estate, primarily in the United States but also in other countries. The next section looks at residential housing markets in Canada and the United States between 1987 and 2012.

## 20-4 | Residential Housing Markets in North America, 1987–2012

Your house, or your parents' house, is often the most important asset in the household portfolio. By this point in the text, we should all be aware of the fall in American house prices in from 2007 to 2011. The total fall in real house prices in the United States, illustrated in Figure 20–8, was about 40%.

It is noteworthy that the increase in real housing prices in the United Sates began in 1996. In the decade between 1996 and 2006, real house prices doubled. As the decade progressed, houses looked like an asset that never fell in price. This ignored the historical evidence that real house prices in the United States had fallen by 25% from 1989 to 1996. Memories are apparently very short. What about Canada?

Canada experienced a similar fall in house prices from a 1989 peak to a 2000 trough. The size of the decline was, as in the United States, 25%, but the decline continued for four more years. The big run up in house prices started in Canada in 2002. Although Canadian house prices did fall slightly in 2009, they have resumed their relentless increase as of the time of writing in early 2013. As of 2012, real house prices in Canada are almost double their low in 1999. What might make house prices rise?

We have presented a model of real stock prices in equation (20.10). To remind you, that model said that the value of a stock was the present discounted value of real dividends, discounted at the sequence of real interest rates. Houses are not very different from stocks. Instead of paying dividends, a house can be rented and the owner of the house receives the rent. If you are buying a house to live in yourself, you can think of renting the house to yourself. You are saving the rent you would have paid to someone else. Either case leads to an expression parallel to equation (20.10) for houses:

$$Q_t^H = \frac{R_t^e}{(1 + r_{1t})} + \frac{R_{t+1}^e}{(1 + r_{1t})(1 + r_{1t+1}^e)} + \frac{R_{t+2}^e}{(1 + r_{1t})(1 + r_{1t+1}^e)(1 + r_{1t+2}^e)} + \cdots \quad (20.11)$$

Where $Q_t^H$ is the real price of the house and $R_t^e$ is the real rent the owner expects to earn on the house in period $t$. As in the model of stocks where the stock is valued *ex-dividend* this house

### FIGURE 20–8

**Real House Prices in Canada and the United States, 1987–2012**

Real house prices in the United States nearly doubled between 1996 and 2006. The subsequent bursting of the bubble was the key event in setting off the world economic crisis. Real house prices in Canada began to increase in 2000 and, with a brief decline during the world economic crisis, have continued to rise.

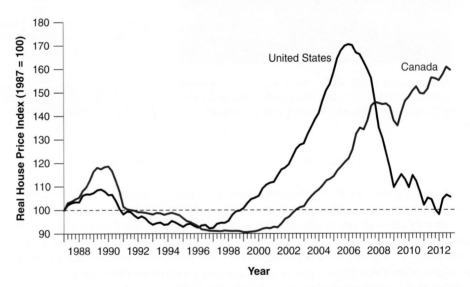

*Source:* United States: Case-Shiller national house price index deflated by Consumer Price Index, Series CPIAUSL, Federal Reserve Economic Database (FRED), http://research.stlouisfed.org/fred2/; Canada: From 1987 to February 1999, New Home Price Index, CANSIM II variable V53600422; From March 1999 to 2012, Teranet–National Bank Home Price Index for 11 cities. The two indexes are merged. Both nominal indexes are deflated by Consumer Price Index, CANSIM II variable V41690972.

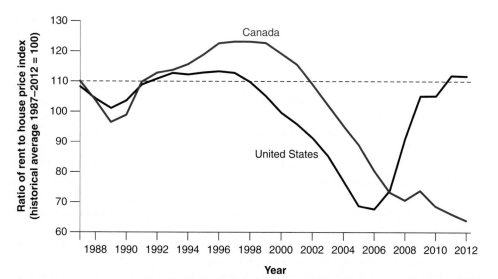

**FIGURE 20-9**

**Comparing Rents and Prices on Houses in Canada and the United States, 1987–2012**

A bubble occurs when the price of an asset departs far from its fundamental value. For a house, the return is the rent and the relevant measure of the bubble is the ratio of rent to price. If the value of the ratio of a rent index to a house price index is low, then either house prices are high or rents are low. In 2006, house prices were so high in the United States, that ratio went to its historical low. In Canada, as of 2012, that ratio is at its historical low.

*Source:* United States: Case-Shiller national house price index, rent component of Consumer Price Index, Series CUUR0000SEHA, Federal Reserve Economic Database (FRED), http://research. stlouoisfed.org/fred2/; Canada: 1987 to 1999 New Home Price Index, CANSIM II variable V53600422; 1999 to 2012; National Bank House Price Index, rent component of Consumer Price Index, CANSIM II variable V41693350.

is valued immediately after the rent is paid.[4] Thus the real price of a house should rise in two circumstances:

- If the expected stream of real rents were to rise
- If the interest rates used to discount the expected stream of real rents should fall

When we use only the two statements above we are applying the fundamentals model from section 20-3 to house prices. Is there an argument that houses, like stocks, can become involved in rational speculative bubbles?

The answer would seem to be yes. Figure 20–9 presents some evidence that housing prices in the United States and in Canada were (or are) involved in a rational speculative bubble. An index is created that looks at the ratio of rents to house prices. The average value of that index for the period from 1987 to 2012 is set equal to 100. You can see periods where rents are low relative to house prices in the late 1980s and period where rents are high relative to house prices in the early 1990s. If you compare Figure 20–9 to Figure 20–8, you will see that it is house prices that are moving. Rents do not rise or fall much over this period.

In Figure 20–9, the ratio of rents to house prices drops very rapidly after 1996 in the United States and after 2000 in Canada. Thus people are buying houses for higher and higher prices even though the rent they could earn from owning that house is not rising. The rental part of the return on owning a house is at historic lows in the United States in

---

[4]**DIGGING DEEPER.** An astute reader (or a student who is acting as a landlord) will realize there are at least two other simplifications in writing equation (20.11). The expected rent has to be interpreted as the rent net of property taxes to be paid as well as the rent net of money to be spent on maintenance—that is money spent to keep the house in the same condition as it was bought in. However, adding these factors would not change the basic analysis. Adding these items would simply complicate the notation.

2006 and in Canada in 2012. A reasonable question: Why were people willing to pay higher and higher prices for houses for much of this period in both Canada and the United States?

The only reasonable answer is that the purchasers of these houses believed that, even though the rental return on the house was low, the capital gain on owning the house would be large and would, in a sense, continue forever. This is a rational speculative bubble in action. As long as the house purchasers believed the value of the house they purchased would rise in value, it made sense to buy the house even though the savings on rent relative to the price of the house were low. Using Figure 20–9, there is evidence that the rent-to-price ratio was far lower than its previous historical low value in the United States as of 2006. This would predict a fall in house prices if house prices were to return to match the historical fundamentals. Such a fall in house prices did occur in the United States. Figure 20–9 suggests that the prices of houses in the United States have returned to their fundamental level. What about Canada?

Figure 20–9 makes it look easy to conclude that Canadian house prices, as of 2012, are due for a correction. For the rent-to-price ratio to return to its historic average, Canadian house prices must fall in the same way that American house prices fell. It is an important issue. As we shall see in the next chapter, if a large component of household wealth in Canada is in houses (and it is), then household wealth would fall if house prices fell. A large fall in house prices would almost certainly reduce aggregate demand in Canada. The Focus box "Are Canadian Houses Overpriced in 2013" looks at the evidence presented by *The Economist* news magazine on house prices in Canada and other countries.

## 20-5 | Exchange Rate Movements and Expectations*

We saw in Chapter 6 and again in Chapter 14 how the interest-parity condition led to a relation between the short-term domestic nominal interest rate and the foreign nominal interest rate on the one hand, and the current nominal exchange rate and the expected future nominal exchange rate on the other.

The same condition can be used to derive a relation between the long-term domestic real interest rate and the long-term foreign real interest rate on the one hand, and the current real exchange rate and the expected future real exchange rate on the other. This seems like a mouthful, but do not worry: It is simpler than it sounds. And this relation will provide us with a way of thinking about movements of the exchange rate.

### Real Interest Rates and the Real Exchange Rate

Consider, as in Chapter 6, the choice between one-year Canadian and one-year U.S. bonds. But instead of expressing the two rates of return in Canadian dollars as we did there, let us express both of them in terms of Canadian goods. Suppose you decide to invest the equivalent of one Canadian good, to "invest one Canadian good," for short, in what follows:

- Suppose you decide to hold Canadian bonds. Let $r_t$ be the one-year Canadian real interest rate, the interest rate on one-year Canadian bonds in terms of Canadian goods. By the definition of the real interest rate, you will get $(1 + r_t)$ Canadian goods next year. This is represented by the top line in Figure 20–10.
- Suppose you decide instead to hold U.S. bonds. This involves exchanging Canadian dollars for U.S. dollars, holding U.S. bonds for a year, and selling U.S. dollars for Canadian dollars a year from now.

---

*This material can be skipped without loss of continuity.

**Are Canadian Houses Overpriced in 2013?**

A sampling of headlines in the *Financial Post*, May 18, 2013, reads:

- Are Canadians putting too much faith in housing market?
- Flaherty dismisses worries over housing amid "healthy" correction
- What housing crisis? Many homeowners would be spared in a major correction.

These headlines tell you how much the housing market matters to Canadians. If house prices were to fall toward a historic norm, as indicated in Figure 20–9, then Canadians would feel less wealthy and consume less. There would be fewer new houses built. Aggregate demand would fall. But having house prices continue to rise might lead to an even larger bubble bursting later with even worse consequences. The meaning of the headline term "soft landing" is that house prices stabilize or fall very, very slowly and maybe grow very, very slowly—it is rather a vague term.

If we are in a bubble, then eventually house prices must fall. How do we know if we are in a bubble? Figure 20–9 gave one answer; look at the ratio of rents to house prices. If that ratio is low, house prices are predicted to fall. But there are other ways to ask if we are in a bubble. *The Economist* magazine publishes an evaluation of the magnitude of the overvaluation or undervaluation of houses around the world. It uses the ratio of

rents to prices (in a manner similar to Figure 20–9) and offers an analysis based on the ratio of prices to disposable income. The logic, very roughly, is that since the long-run ability to pay for a house depends on disposable income, these two values should stay in the same proportion. Table 1 shows the analysis for 8 countries.

Canada's 78 percent overvaluation based on *The Economist's* calculations of the ratio of rents to prices is the largest overvaluation in the table. The extent of the overvaluation based on the ratio of house prices to disposable income is also large. According to both calculations, Canadian house prices would be expected to fall after 2013. However, the prices of houses in Canada continued to rise in 2012. This data is part of the concern that Canada's housing market is in a bubble.

According to this table, house prices in America are undervalued and should rise. They did rise in 2012. In 5 of the 7 countries where houses were overvalued, prices fell.

*The Economist* began to produce this table in 2007. The last column of Table 1 gives you a sense of the volatility of house prices around the world since the crisis in 2007. We know house prices have fallen in the United States since 2007. But they also fell by large amounts in Britain, Spain, and Italy. House prices rose by large amounts in Canada, Australia, and Sweden. House prices did not change in France.

| TABLE | 1 | *The Economist* House–Price indicators, 2013 |

| Country | % Overvalued (+) or Undervalued(−1) based on | | % Change from 2012 to 2013 | % Increase in House Prices from Quarter 4, 2007 to 2013 |
|---------|-------------------|------------------------------|------------------|---------------------------------|
| | Ratio to Rents | Ratio to Disposable Income | | |
| Canada | 78 | 34 | 3.3 | 20.0 |
| France | 50 | 35 | −1.3 | 2.7 |
| Australia | 45 | 23 | 0.3 | 10.4 |
| Sweden | 31 | 18 | −2.6 | 8.1 |
| Britain | 21 | 12 | −0.9 | −11.2 |
| Spain | 19 | 21 | −9.3 | −24.3 |
| Italy | −1 | 12 | −4.0 | −11.3 |
| U.S. | −7 | −20 | 4.3 | −20.5 |

*Source: The Economist* house–price indicators, January 12, 2013.

Let $\epsilon_t$ be the real exchange rate, the relative price of U.S. goods in terms of Canadian goods. A real exchange rate of $\epsilon_t$ means you get $(1/\epsilon_t)$ U.S. goods for every Canadian good you invest.

Let $r_i^*$ be the one-year U.S. real interest rate, the interest rate on one-year U.S. bonds in terms of U.S. goods. Let the expected real exchange rate a year from now be $\epsilon_{t+1}^e$. Then, for every Canadian good you invest in one-year U.S. bonds, you can expect to get $(1/\epsilon_t)(1 + r_i^*)$ $\epsilon_{t+1}^e$ Canadian goods next year. The three steps involved in the transaction are represented in the bottom part of Figure 20–10.

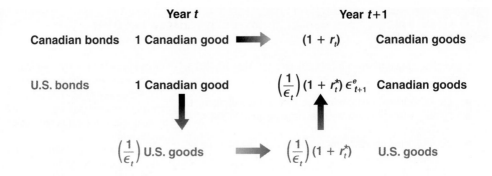

**FIGURE 20–10**

Expected Returns, in Terms
of Canadian Goods, from
Holding Canadian or U.S.
Bonds

If we assume that expected returns expressed in the same units (here, Canadian goods) must be equal in equilibrium (the interest-parity condition), the following condition must hold:

$$(1 + r_t) = \left(\frac{1}{\epsilon_t}\right)(1 + r_t^*)(\epsilon_{t+1}^e) \qquad (20.12)$$

This equation gives us a relation between the domestic and the foreign real interest rates on the one hand, and the current and expected future real exchange rates on the other.

You may wonder whether this differs from the condition derived in terms of nominal interest rates and nominal exchange rates, contained in equation (6.2). The answer is no. The two conditions are equivalent, and we can derive one from the other. (It is presented as an exercise at the end of this chapter. The derivation is not much fun, but it is good practice and a useful way of brushing up on the relation between nominal and real interest rates, and nominal and real exchange rates.)

The basic reason they are equivalent is that the interest-parity condition states that the expected returns *when expressed in common units*—whatever these units are, as long as they are common—must be equal. Until now, we took the common unit to be the Canadian dollar. Here, we take the common unit to be a Canadian good (or to be very precise, the bundle of goods used to define the Canadian dollar price index in the real exchange rate).

## Long-Term Real Interest Rates and the Real Exchange Rate

We have just looked at the choice of holding domestic versus foreign bonds *for one year*. But we can apply the same logic to the choice of holding domestic and foreign bonds *for many years*. Suppose you decide to invest the equivalent of one Canadian good—to invest one Canadian good, for short—for n years in either n-year Canadian bonds or n-year U.S. bonds (think of n as, say, 10 years).

- Suppose you decide to hold n-year Canadian bonds. Let $r_{nt}$ be the n-year Canadian real interest rate. Recall that by the definition of an n-year interest rate, $r_{nt}$ is the average annual interest rate you can expect to get if you hold the n-year bond for n years. So, by the definition of the n-year real interest rate, you can expect to get $(1 + r_{nt})^n$ goods in n years. This is represented in the top line of Figure 20–11.
- Now, suppose you decide to hold n-year U.S. bonds instead. Let $\epsilon_t$ be the real exchange rate. Let $r_{nt}^*$ be the n-year U.S. real interest rate. Let the expected real exchange rate n years from now be $\epsilon_{t+n}^e$. Then, for every Canadian good you invest in n-year U.S. bonds, you can expect to get $(1/\epsilon_t)(1 + r_{nt}^*)^n \epsilon_{t+n}^e$ Canadian goods in n years. This set of steps is represented in the bottom part of Figure 20–11.

If we assume again that expected returns have to be the same, then the following condition must hold:

$$(1 + r_{nt})^n = \left(\frac{1}{\epsilon_t}\right)(1 + r_{nt}^*)^n(\epsilon_{t+n}^e) \qquad (20.13)$$

FIGURE 20–11

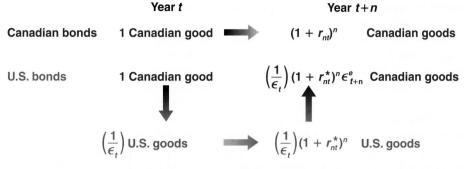

A good approximation (derived as an application of proposition 5 in Appendix 2 at the end of the book) is given by:

$$n\, r_{nt} = n\, r_{nt}^* + \frac{(\epsilon_{t+n}^e - \epsilon_t)}{\epsilon_t}$$

Rewriting the equation so that the current exchange rate is on the left:

$$\epsilon_t = \frac{\epsilon_{t+n}^e}{1 + n(r_{nt} - r_{nt}^*)} \tag{20.14}$$

This relation says that the real exchange rate today depends on the expected future real exchange rate *n* years from now and on the differential between *n*-year domestic and foreign real interest rates. Let us look at it more closely.

## The Real Exchange Rate, Trade, and Interest Rate Differentials

The first determinant of the current real exchange rate in equation (20.14) is the expected future real exchange rate, $\epsilon_{t+n}^e$. If we take the number of years, *n*, to be large, we can think of $\epsilon_{t+n}^e$ as the exchange rate that financial market participants expect to prevail in the *medium run* or the *long run*. For simplicity, we will now call it the *long-run real exchange rate*.

How should we think of the long-run real exchange rate? In the long run, we can assume the current account will be roughly balanced. No country can run a current account deficit each and every year, if there were a current account deficit every year, foreign debt would increase without limit. Just as a person cannot have unlimited personal debt because lenders will stop lending to him, a country faces a similar limit on its total foreign debt. Similarly, a country does not want its foreign assets to increase forever. Eventually, the foreign assets should be used for consumption purposes. Most individuals do not want to keep working to accumulate personal wealth forever; they want to eventually retire and spend most of their assets on an enjoyable retirement. If the current account is to be zero, then the trade balance is negative for a country with positive foreign assets. Kuwait was the example in Chapter 6. In Canada's case, our existing foreign assets are negative—that is, we are indebted to foreigners. For a zero current account balance, our long-run real exchange rate must generate a trade surplus equal to the difference between GDP and GNP.[5]

The second determinant of the current real exchange rate is the difference between domestic and foreign long-term real interest rates. *An increase in the domestic long-term real interest rate over the foreign long-term real interest rate leads to a decrease in the real exchange rate—a real appreciation.* We focused on this mechanism when discussing a similar relation

---

[5]**DIGGING DEEPER.** This is not quite right. An increase in population or productivity may allow a constant ratio of foreign debt to GDP, while the current account remains in deficit. We ignore growth in population and technology above.

between the nominal interest rate and the nominal exchange rate in Chapter 8. Let us go through its logic again.

Suppose the long-term domestic real interest rate goes up, making domestic bonds more attractive than foreign bonds. As investors try to shift out of foreign bonds into domestic bonds, they sell foreign currency and buy domestic currency so that the domestic currency appreciates. Because the exchange rate is expected to return eventually to its long-run value, the more the domestic currency appreciates today, the more it is expected to depreciate in the future. Therefore, the domestic currency appreciates today to the point at which the expected future depreciation exactly offsets the fact that the long-term domestic real interest rate is higher than the long-term foreign real interest rate. At that point, financial investors are again indifferent to holding domestic bonds or holding foreign bonds.

We now have a way of thinking about exchange rate movements. Let us use this approach first to look at the movements of the Canadian dollar in the 1990s and then, more generally, to look at the effects of monetary policy and the relation between interest rates and exchange rates.

## The Canadian Dollar from 1998 to 2012

Remember the large movements in the Canadian dollar from 1998 to 2012, a real depreciation, followed by a substantial real appreciation after 2001. In light of the theory we just developed, we can ask: Were these movements due more to movements in long-term real interest rates in Canada relative to the United States or more to movements in the long-run real exchange rate?

Note from equation (20.14) that if the long-run real exchange rate were constant, there would be an exact negative relation between the difference between the domestic and the foreign long-term real interest rates ($r_{nt} - r_{nt}^*$), and the real exchange rate, $\epsilon_t$.

This statement suggests the following approach to interpreting movements in the real exchange rate: Construct for each year the difference between the long-term domestic real interest rate and the foreign long-term real interest rate. Then, plot the real exchange rate against this difference. If the two series move closely together, differences in long-term real interest rates must be the dominant factor in explaining movements in the real exchange rate. If they do not, changes in the long-run real exchange rate must play an important role.

Figure 20–12 implements this approach. It focuses on the bilateral real exchange rate between the United States and Canada from 1998 to 2012. As we saw in Chapter 6, movements in this bilateral real exchange rate are the movements that matter to Canada.

We introduced inflation-indexed bonds in Focus box "The Vocabulary of Bond Markets" earlier in the chapter.

The real exchange rate is defined and constructed in the same way as in Figure 6–6. It is given by ($E_t P_t^*/P_t$), where $E_t$ is the Canadian dollar/U.S. dollar exchange rate, and $P_t$ and $P_t^*$ are the GDP deflators in Canada and the United States, respectively. The evolution of the real exchange rate is given by the upper line in the figure. It is measured on the scale at the right of the figure.

The gap between the long-term Canadian and U.S. real interest rate for each year using yields on inflation-indexed bonds is plotted in Figure 20–12. The lower line in the figure plots the difference between the U.S. and the Canadian real interest rates. This difference is measured in percentage points on the scale at the left of the figure.

Equation (20.14) says that if Canada has a higher real interest rate than the United States, then for the same value of the expected long-term real exchange rate, the Canadian real exchange rate should appreciate (remember—this means the real exchange rate index takes on a smaller value). If Canada has a lower real interest rate than the United States, equation (20.14) says that the Canadian real exchange rate should depreciate when the expected value of the long-run real exchange rate is constant.

It is difficult to see this pattern in the data shown in Figure 20–12. Often when Canadian real interest rates are below American real interest rates, the level of the real exchange rate in Canada is a small number—that is, its value has appreciated, not depreciated. This is true from 1998 to 2002.

In the latter part of this period, from 2005 to 2012, Canadian real interest rates are usually about 0.4 percentage points lower than U.S. real rates, and the Canadian dollar appreciates in

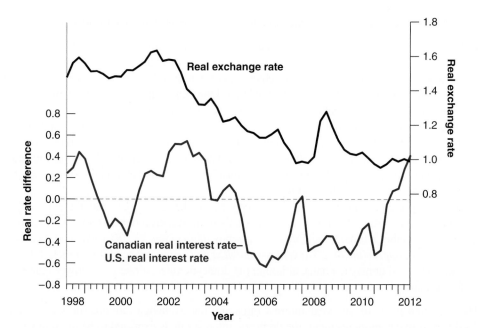

FIGURE 20-12

**The Real Exchange Rate and the Difference Between Long-Term Real Interest Rates in Canada and the United States**

When Canadian real interest rates are lower than American real interest rates, equation (20.14) predicts a real depreciation. Similarly, when Canadian real interest rates are higher than American real interest rates, equation (20.15) predicts a real appreciation. There is modest evidence supporting this simplified model of real exchange rate movements.

*Source:* Real exchange rate—see Figure 6–6. Real interest rate in the United States, Series WTP30A28, Federal Reserve Economic Database (FRED), http://research.stlouoisfed.org/fred2/; Real interest rate in Canada, CANSIM II variable V122553. Both real rates are real yields on inflation-indexed bonds.

real terms in most of these years. The lower interest rate in Canada is offset by a real appreciation and, in this sense, real returns equalize. The relationship is not tight.

Does equation (20.14), in terms of the interest rate gap—its denominator—ever act as a very useful practical tool to look at long-term real exchange rate movements? In 2007 there is quite a sharp movement of the interest rate differential toward zero and a simultaneous appreciation of the Canadian real exchange rate. That fits equation (20.14). But such points are not common in the data.

We have to accept that the main insight from equation (20.14) is one we have seen before. Movements in exchange rates are a complicated mixture of changes in the expected long-run value of the real exchange rate and changes in the interest-rate differential. It is difficult to untangle the two types of changes in practice.

## Monetary Policy, Interest Rates, and Exchange Rates

Let us now return to how monetary policy works in an open economy with flexible exchange rates. Let us start with a blatantly unrealistic case. It is easier to analyze, and it provides a good base on which to build a more realistic discussion.

Assume there is no inflation, here or abroad, current or expected; we do not need to distinguish between nominal and real interest rates or between nominal and real exchange rates. Suppose further that initially, domestic and foreign interest rates are expected to be constant and equal to each other.

Now, suppose the central bank unexpectedly announces that in order to increase output, it has decided to decrease interest rates. The central bank announces that one-year interest rates will be 2 percentage points lower for each of the next five years, after which they will return to normal. Financial markets fully believe this announcement.

What happens at the time of the announcement? Short-term interest rates go down by 2 percentage points, and so do rates on bonds with maturities less than or equal to five years. Yields on bonds with longer maturity go down, but by less.

What is the effect on the exchange rate today? To answer, work backwards in time.

- Start five years in the future. The exchange rate five years from now depends on what is expected to happen to interest rates thereafter, as well as on the long-run exchange rate. Because the announcement does not change expectations of interest rates beyond the first five years and presumably does not change the long-run exchange rate either, there is no change in the expected real exchange rate five years from now.
- What happens between today and five years hence? The interest-parity condition tells us that for each of the next five years, there must be an expected appreciation of the domestic currency of 2% per year so that the expected rates of return on holding domestic and foreign bonds are equal. That means there must be an expected cumulative appreciation of $5 \times 2\% = 10\%$ over the next five years.
- As the expected exchange rate five years hence is unchanged, to generate the expected appreciation of 10% over the next five years there must therefore be a depreciation today of 10%. In other words, if the domestic currency *depreciates by 10% today* and then is expected to *appreciate by 2% a year for the next five years*, financial investors will be willing to hold domestic bonds, although the domestic interest rate is 2% lower than the foreign interest rate.

The expected paths of one-year interest rates and the exchange rate are shown in Figure 20–13. Before the announcement, the domestic interest rate is expected to be the same as the foreign interest rate forever. After the announcement, the domestic interest rate is expected to be 2 percentage points lower than the foreign interest rate for five years. The effect of the announcement is an increase in the exchange rate of 10% at the time of the announcement (a 10% depreciation), followed by a decrease of 2% a year (an expected appreciation of 2% a

FIGURE 20–13

**The Effects of Monetary Policy on the Interest Rate and the Exchange Rate**

A decrease in interest rates expected to last for five years leads to a depreciation today, followed by expected appreciation over the next five years.

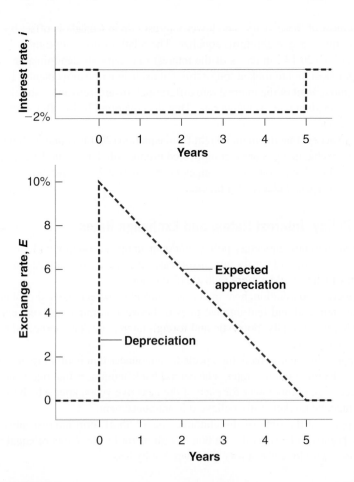

year) over the next five years. Note how much the exchange rate initially moves and over-shoots its long-run value—increasing first, only to decrease back to its initial value five years later. For that reason, this exchange rate adjustment is often referred to as **overshooting**.

This result is an important one. When, in the early 1970s, countries moved from fixed to flexible exchange rates, the large fluctuations in exchange rates that followed came as a sur-prise to most economists. For a long time, these fluctuations were thought to be the result of irrational speculation in foreign exchange markets. It was not until the mid-1970s that econo-mists realized that these large movements could be explained, as we have done here, by the rational reaction of financial markets to differences in future interest rates.

## Policy and Expectations

In the example we just looked at, we dismissed many complications. We assumed, in par-ticular, that the central bank announced what it was going to do over the next five years and that financial markets fully believed the announcement. In practice, this is not the way things happen.

When the central bank cuts interest rates, financial markets have to assess whether this action signals a major shift in monetary policy and is just the first of many such cuts or whether this cut is just a temporary movement in interest rates. Announcements by the central bank itself may not be very useful: The central bank itself may not know what it will do in the future. Typically, it will be reacting to early signals, which may be reversed later. Financial markets also have to assess how foreign central banks will react, whether they will stay put or follow suit and cut their interest rates.

To summarize: How a change in the short-term interest rate affects the exchange rate is more complex than it appeared in Chapter 6. The response of the exchange rate depends very much on the effect of the change in the interest rate on expectations of future domestic and foreign interest rates. Sometimes, a small decrease in short-term interest rates may convince markets that monetary policy has substantially changed, resulting in a large decrease in long-term interest rates and a large depreciation. But if markets anticipated a large cut and the central bank announces a smaller cut than was anticipated, the effect may actually be an appreciation, not a depreciation.

- Arbitrage among bonds of different maturities implies that the price of a bond is the present value of the payments on the bond, discounted using current and expected short-term interest rates. Hence, higher current or ex-pected short-term interest rates lead to lower bond prices.

- The yield to maturity on a bond with a maturity of $n$ years (or equivalently, the $n$-year interest rate) is approximately equal to the average of current and expected future one-year interest rates over this and the next $n - 1$ years.

- The slope of the yield curve (equivalently, the term struc-ture) tells us what financial markets expect to happen to short-term interest rates in the future. A downward-sloping yield curve implies that the markets expect a decrease in short-term rates; an upward-sloping yield curve implies that the markets expect an increase in short-term rates.

- The fundamental value of a stock is the present value of expected future real dividends, discounted using current

and future expected one-year real interest rates. In the absence of bubbles or fads, the price of a stock is equal to its fundamental value.

- An increase in expected dividends leads to an increase in the fundamental value of stocks; an increase in cur-rent and expected one-year interest rates leads to a decrease in the fundamental value.

- Changes in output may or may not be associated with changes in stock prices in the same direction. Whether they are depends on (1) what the markets expected in the first place, (2) the source of the shocks, and (3) how the markets expect the central bank to react to the output change.

- Stock prices can be subject to bubbles or fads that lead a stock price to differ from its fundamental value. Bubbles are episodes when financial investors buy a stock for a price higher than its fundamental value in an-ticipation of reselling the stock at an even higher price.

"Fad" is a general term for times when, for reasons of fashion or overoptimism, financial investors are willing to pay more than the fundamental value of the stock.

- House prices can also be subject to bubbles or fads that lead a house price to differ from its fundamental value. The fundamental value of a house should be the present discounted value of its rent (net of expenses to run the house such as property taxes and maintenance).

- The real exchange rate today depends both on the long-run real exchange rate and on the difference between domestic and foreign long-term real interest rates. An increase in the domestic long-term real interest rate over the corresponding foreign interest rate leads to a real appreciation and a decrease leads to a real depreciation.

- Movements in Canadian interest rates relative to U.S. interest rates explain some of the movements in the Canadian real exchange rate since 1998. However, the trend real appreciation over the whole period likely reflects an overall decline in Canada's foreign debt as a percent of GDP.

- When account is taken of expectations, changes in monetary policy may lead to large variations in the exchange rate. An increase in interest rates leads to a large initial appreciation, followed by a slow depreciation over time. This large initial movement of the exchange rate is known as overshooting.

## QUESTIONS AND PROBLEMS

### 1. TRUE/FALSE/UNCERTAIN

a. Junk bonds are bonds nobody wants to hold.

b. The price of a one-year bond decreases when the nominal one-year interest rate increases.

c. Given the Fisher hypothesis (see Chapter 19), an upward-sloping yield curve may indicate that financial markets are worried about inflation in the future.

d. Long-term interest rates typically move more than short-term interest rates.

e. An equal increase in expected inflation and nominal interest rates at all maturities should have no effect on the stock market.

f. A monetary expansion will lead to an upward-sloping yield curve.

g. A rational investor should never pay a positive price for a stock that will never pay dividends.

h. The strong performance of the U.S. stock market of the 1990s reflects the strong performance of the U.S. economy.

### 2. THE YIELD TO MATURITY

Determine the yield to maturity of each of the following bonds:

a. A discount bond with a face value of $1000, a maturity of three years, and a price of $800.

b. A discount bond with a face value of $1000, a maturity of four years, and a price of $800.

c. A discount bond with a face value of $1000, a maturity of four years, and a price of $850.

### 3. THE YIELD CURVE

Suppose that the interest rate this year is 5% and financial markets expect the interest rate to increase by 0.5 percentage point each year for the following three years. Determine the yield to maturity on a:

a. one-year bond.

b. two-year bond.

c. three-year bond.

### 4. THE EQUITY PREMIUM, DIVIDENDS, AND STOCK PRICES

A share is expected to pay a dividend of $1000 next year, and the real value of dividend payments is expected to increase by 3% per year forever after. Determine the current price of the stock if the real interest rate is expected to remain constant at:

a. 5%.

b. 8%.

Now, suppose that people require a risk premium to hold stocks (as described in the first appendix to this chapter).

c. Repeat (a) and (b) with the required risk premium at 8%.

d. Repeat (a) and (b) with the required risk premium at 4%.

e. What happens to stock prices if the risk premium decreases? Explain in words.

### 5. MACROECONOMICS AND STOCK PRICES

Using the *IS-LM* model, determine the impact of each of the following on stock prices. If the effect is ambiguous, explain what additional information would be needed to reach a conclusion.

a. An unexpected expansionary monetary policy with no change in fiscal policy.

b. A fully expected expansionary monetary policy with no change in fiscal policy.

c. A fully expected expansionary monetary policy with expansionary fiscal policy.

### 6. EXPANSIONARY MONETARY POLICY AND THE YIELD CURVE

In the previous chapter, we examined the effects of an increase in the growth rate of money on interest rates and inflation.

a. Draw the path of the nominal interest rate following an increase in growth rate of money.

Suppose that the lowest point in the path is reached after one year and that the long-run value is achieved after three years.

b. Draw the yield curve, just after the increase in the growth rate of money, one year later, and three years later.

### 7. WORKING WITH THE DECISION TO BUY A HOUSE

This problem helps you use and think about the fundamental equation that values a house, equation (20.11).

a. Suppose that real rent on a house is expected to be $600 per month forever and that one-year interest rates are expected to be constant at 3%. Calculate the value of a house using expression (20.11). *Hint:* Use proposition 2 in Appendix 2.

b. Now reduce interest rates to 2% and recalculate the value of the same house when net rent does not change. What do you think about Figure 20–8, given this result?

c. Now suppose your university is expected to grow and rents in the areas nearest the university are expected to increase to $900 per month. Explain the effect on house prices. Real interest rates are expected to remain at 3%.

d. Suppose you, as a student representative on the university governance committee, know before others that the university is planning to expand. You understand that rents, while expected to remain at $600 per month for the next five years, will eventually rise to $900 per month as the university grows. You are offered a house near the university at $240,000. Should you buy it?

### 8. DERIVING THE INTEREST-PARITY CONDITION IN TERMS OF REAL INTEREST RATES

This problem helps you derive equation (20.11) in the text. Start from the interest-parity condition:

$$(1 + i_t) = (1 + i_t^*)\frac{E_{t+1}^e}{E_t}$$

Recall the definition of the (domestic) real interest rate:

$$(1 + r_t) = \frac{1 + i_t}{1 + \pi_t^e}$$

where $\pi_t^e = (P_{t+1}^e - P_t)/P_t$ is the expected rate of inflation. Similarly, the foreign real interest rate is given by:

$$(1 + r_t^*) = \frac{1 + i_t^*}{1 + \pi_t^{*e}}$$

where $\pi_t^{*e} = (P_{t+1}^{*e} - P_t^*)/P_t^*$ is the expected foreign rate of inflation. Recall that the real exchange rate is defined as:

$$\epsilon_t = E_t P_t^*/P_t$$

So the expected real exchange rate is given by:

$$\epsilon_{t+1}^e = E_{t+1} P_{t+1}^{*e}/P_{t+1}^e$$

Derive equation (20.11) in the text. (*Hint:* Use the two interest rate relations to eliminate nominal interest rates in the interest-parity condition. Then, rewrite to get from nominal exchange rates to real exchange rates.)

## 9. EXPECTED NOMINAL AND REAL DEPRECIATIONS

Assume that the nominal interest rate on 10-year bonds is 10% at home and 6% abroad. Further, assume inflation is expected to be 6% at home and 3% abroad.

a. What is the expected annual real depreciation consistent with interest parity?

b. What is the expected annual nominal depreciation consistent with interest parity?

c. If you expected a nominal appreciation of the domestic currency over the next 10 years, which bond would you purchase?

### FURTHER READING

There are many bad books written about the stock market. A good one, and one that is fun to read, is Burton Malkiel, *A Random Walk Down Wall Street*, 10th ed. (New York: Norton, 2011).

An account of historical bubbles is given by Peter Garber in "Famous First Bubbles," *Journal of Economic Perspectives* 4 (2), Spring 1990: pp. 35–54.

## APPENDIX A

# ARBITRAGE AND STOCK PRICES

This appendix shows that in the absence of rational speculative bubbles, arbitrage between stocks and bonds implies that the price of a stock is equal to the expected present value of dividends.

Suppose you face the choice of investing either in one-year bonds or in stocks for a year. What should you choose?

Suppose you decide to hold one-year bonds. Then, for every dollar you put in one-year bonds, you will get $(1 + i_{1t})$ dollars next year. This payoff is represented in the upper line of Figure 20A–1.

Suppose, instead, you decide to hold stocks for a year. This implies buying a stock today, receiving a dividend next year, and then selling the stock. As the price of a stock is $\$Q_t$, every dollar you put in stocks buys you $\$1/\$Q_t$ stocks. And for each stock you buy, you expect to receive $(\$D^e_{t+1} + \$Q^e_{t+1})$, the sum of the expected dividend and the stock price next year. So, for every dollar you put in stocks, you expect to receive $(\$D^e_{t+1} + \$Q^e_{t+1})/\$Q_t$ dollars next year. This payoff is represented in the lower line of Figure 20A–1.

Let us use the same arbitrage argument we used for bonds earlier. If financial investors care only about expected rates of return, then equilibrium requires that the expected rate of return from holding stocks for one year be the same as the rate of return on one-year bonds:

$$\frac{(\$D^e_{t+1} + \$Q^e_{t+1})}{\$Q_t} = 1 + i_{1t}$$

Rewrite this equation as:

$$\$Q_t = \frac{\$D^e_{t+1}}{(1 + i_{1t})} + \frac{\$Q^e_{t+1}}{(1 + i_{1t})} \qquad (20.A1)$$

Arbitrage implies that the price of the stock today must be equal to the present value of the expected dividend plus the present value of the expected stock price next year.

The next step is to think about what determines $\$Q^e_{t+1}$, the expected stock price next year. Next year, financial investors will again face the choice between stocks and one-year bonds. Thus, the same arbitrage relation will hold. Writing the previous equation, but now for time $t+1$, and taking expectations into account gives:

$$\$Q^e_{t+1} = \frac{\$D^e_{t+2}}{(1 + i^e_{1t+1})} + \frac{\$Q^e_{t+2}}{(1 + i^e_{1t+1})}$$

The expected price next year is simply the present value next year of the sum of the expected dividend and price two years from now. Replacing the expected price $\$Q^e_{t+1}$ in equation (20A.1) gives:

$$\$Q_t = \frac{\$D^e_{t+1}}{(1 + i_{1t})} + \frac{\$D^e_{t+2}}{(1 + i_{1t})(1 + i^e_{1t+1})} + \frac{\$Q^e_{t+2}}{(1 + i_{1t})(1 + i^e_{1t+1})}$$

The stock price is the present value of the expected dividend next year plus the present value of the expected dividend two years from now plus the expected price two years from now.

If we replace the expected price in two years as the present value of the expected price and dividends in three years, and so on for $n$ years, we get:

$$\$Q_t = \frac{\$D^e_{t+1}}{(1 + i_{1t})} + \cdots + \frac{\$D^e_{t+n}}{(1 + i_{1t})\cdots(1 + i^e_{1t+n-1})} + \frac{\$Q^e_{t+n}}{(1 + i_{1t})\cdots(1 + i^e_{1t+n-1})}$$

**FIGURE 20A-1**

**Returns from Holding One-Year Bonds or Stocks for One Year**

| | Year $t$ | Year $t+1$ |
|---|---|---|
| One-year bonds | $1 | $1 $(1 + i_{1t})$ |
| Stocks | $1 | $1 $\dfrac{\$D^e_{t+1} + \$Q^e_{t+1}}{\$Q_t}$ |

Look at the last term, which is the present value of the expected price in $n$ years. As long as people do not expect the stock price to explode in the future, then, as we keep replacing $Q^e_{t+n}$, and $n$ increases, this term will go to zero. To see why, suppose the interest rate is constant and equal to $i$, and people expect the price of the stock to converge to some value, call it $\$\overline{Q}$ in the far future. Then, the last term becomes $\$\overline{Q}/(1 + i)^n$. If the interest rate is positive, the term goes to zero as $n$ becomes large.* The previous expression reduces to equation (20.9) in the text: The price today is the present value of expected future dividends.

### An Extension to the Present Value Formula to Take Risk into Account

If people perceive stocks as more risky than bonds, and people dislike risk, they will require a risk premium to hold stocks rather than bonds. In the case of shares, this risk premium is called the **equity premium**. Denote it by $\theta$ (the Greek lowercase letter theta). If $\theta$ is, for example, 5%, then people will hold stocks only if the expected rate of return on stocks exceeds the expected rate of return on short-term bonds by 5 percentage points a year.

In that case, the arbitrage equation between stocks and bonds becomes:

$$\frac{\$D^e_{t+1} + \$Q^e_{t+1}}{\$Q_t} = 1 + i_{1t} + \theta$$

The only change is the presence of $\theta$ on the right side of the equation. Going through the same steps as above, the stock price equals:

$$\$Q_t = \frac{\$D^e_{t+1}}{(1 + i_{1t} + \theta)} + \cdots$$

$$+ \frac{\$D^e_{t+n}}{(1 + i_{1t} + \theta) \cdots (1 + i^e_{1t+n-1} + \theta)} + \cdots$$

The stock price is still equal to the present value of expected future dividends. But the discount rate here equals the interest rate plus the equity premium. Note that the higher the premium, the lower is the stock price. Over the last 100 years in the United States, the average equity premium has been equal to roughly 5%. But (in contrast to our assumption above) it is not constant. The equity premium appears, for example, to have decreased since the early 1950s, from around 7% to less than 3% today. Variations in the equity premium are another source of fluctuations in stock prices.

---

**APPENDIX B**

# THE REAL EXCHANGE RATE, AND DOMESTIC AND FOREIGN REAL INTEREST RATES

This appendix derives equation (20.13), a relation between real exchange rates and real interest rates.

### Deriving the Real Interest-Parity Condition

Start from the nominal interest-parity condition, equation in Chapter 6:

$$(1 + i_t) = (1 + i^*_t)\frac{(E_t)}{E^e_{t+1}}$$

Recall the definition of the real interest rate from Chapter 19, equation (19.3):

$$(1 + r_t) \equiv \frac{(1 + i_t)}{(1 + \pi^e_t)}$$

where $\pi^e_t \equiv (P^e_{t+1} - P_t)/P_t$ is the expected rate of inflation. Similarly, the foreign real interest rate is given by:

$$(1 + r^*_t) \equiv \frac{(1 + i^*_t)}{(1 + \pi^{*e}_t)}$$

where $\pi^{*e}_t \equiv (P^{*e}_{t+1} - P^*_t)/P^*_t$ is the expected foreign rate of inflation.

---

*DIGGING DEEPER. When prices are subject to rational bubbles as discussed in Section 20-3, the condition that the expected stock price does not explode is not satisfied. When there are bubbles, the stock price need not be equal to the present value of expected dividends.

Use these two relations to eliminate nominal interest rates in the interest-parity condition, so:

$$(1 + r_t) = (1 + r_t^*)\left[\frac{E_t\,(1 + \pi_t^{*e})}{E_{t+1}^e(1 + \pi_t^e)}\right] \qquad (20.\text{A}1)$$

Note from the definition of inflation that $(1 + \pi_t^e) = P_{t+1}^e/P_t$ and, similarly, $(1 + \pi_t^{*e}) = P_{t+1}^{*e}/P_t^*$.

Using these two relations in the term in brackets gives:

$$\frac{E_t\,(1 + \pi_t^{*e})}{E_{t+1}^e\,(1 + \pi_t^e)} = \frac{E_t P_{t+1}^{*e} P_t}{E_{t+1}^e P_t^* P_{t+1}^e}$$

Reorganizing terms:

$$\frac{E_t P_{t+1}^{*e} P_t}{E_{t+1}^e P_t^* P_{t+1}^e} = \frac{E_t P_t/P_t^*}{E_{t+1}^e P_{t+1}^e/P_{t+1}^{*e}}$$

Using the definition of the real exchange rate:

$$\frac{E_t P_t/P_t^*}{E_{t+1}^e P_{t+1}^e/P_{t+1}^{*e}} = \frac{\epsilon_t}{\epsilon_{t+1}^e}$$

Replacing in equation (20.A1) gives:

$$(1 + r_t) = (1 + r_t^*)\frac{\epsilon_t}{\epsilon_{t+1}^e}$$

Or, equivalently:

$$\epsilon_t = \frac{1 + r_t}{1 + r_t^*}\epsilon_{t+1}^e \qquad (20.\text{A}2)$$

The real exchange rate today depends on the domestic and foreign real interest rates this year and the expected future real exchange rate next year. This equation corresponds to equation (20.12) in the text, but now in terms of the real rather than nominal exchange and interest rates.

## Solving the Real Interest-Parity Condition Forward

The next step is to solve equation (20.A2) forward, in the same way we did for equation (20.4) in the text. The equation above implies that the real exchange rate in year $t+1$ is given by:

$$\epsilon_{t+1} = \frac{1 + r_{t+1}}{1 + r_{t+1}^*}\epsilon_{t+2}^e$$

Taking expectations, as of year $t$:

$$\epsilon_{t+1}^e = \frac{1 + r_{t+1}^e}{1 + r_{t+1}^{*e}}\epsilon_{t+2}^e$$

Replacing in the previous relation:

$$\epsilon_t = \frac{(1 + r_t)(1 + r_{t+1}^e)}{(1 + r_t^*)(1 + r_{t+1}^{*e})}\epsilon_{t+2}^e$$

Solving for $\epsilon_{t+2}^e$ and so on gives:

$$\epsilon_t = \frac{(1 + r_t)(1 + r_{t+1}^e)\cdots(1 + r_{t+n}^e)}{(1 + r_t^*)(1 + r_{t+1}^{*e})\cdots(1 + r_{t+n}^{*e})}\epsilon_{t+n}^e$$

This relation gives the current real exchange rate as a function of current and expected future domestic real interest rates, of current and expected future foreign real interest rates, and of the expected real exchange rate in year $t+n$.

The advantage of this relation over the relation we derived in the text between the nominal exchange rate and nominal interest rates, equation (6.2), is that it is typically easier to predict the future real exchange rate than to predict the future nominal exchange rate. If, for example, the economy suffers from a large trade deficit, we may be fairly confident that there will have to be a real depreciation—that $\epsilon_{t+n}^e$ will have to be higher. Whether there will be a nominal depreciation—what happens to $E_{t+n}^e$—is harder to tell. That depends on what happens to inflation, both at home and abroad, over the next $n$ years.

# Expectations, Consumption, and Investment

## Expectations

Having looked at the role of expectations in financial markets, we now turn to their role in determining the two main components of spending—consumption and investment. This description of consumption and investment will be the main building block of the expanded *IS-LM* model we will develop in Chapter 22.

Section 21-1 looks at consumption and shows how consumption decisions depend not only on current income, but also on expected future income as well as on financial wealth. Section 21-2 turns to investment and shows how investment decisions depend on current and expected profits and current and expected interest rates. Section 21-3 takes a brief look at the history and determinants of investment in new housing. Finally, section 21-4 looks at the movements of consumption and investment over time and shows how we can interpret them in light of the theories developed in this chapter.

## 21-1 | Consumption

How do people decide how much to consume and how much to save? In our first pass at the answer in the core section (Chapter 3), we made the simple assumption that consumption and saving depended on current income. By now, you do not need to be convinced that they depend on much more, particularly on expectations of the future. We now explore how those expectations affect the consumption decision.

The theory of consumption on which this section is based was developed independently in the 1950s by Milton Friedman of the University of Chicago, who called it the **permanent income theory of consumption**, and by Franco Modigliani, of the Massachusetts Institute of Technology (MIT), who called it the **life cycle theory of consumption**. Each chose his label carefully. Friedman's "permanent income" emphasized that consumers look beyond current income. Modigliani's "life cycle" emphasized that consumers' natural planning horizon is their entire lifetime.

The behaviour of aggregate consumption has remained a hot area of research ever since, for two reasons. The first is simply the sheer size of consumption in GDP and therefore the need to understand movements in consumption. The second is the increasing availability of large surveys of individual consumers, such as the Panel Study of Income Dynamics described in the Focus box "Up Close and Personal: Learning from Panel Data Sets." These surveys, which were not available when Friedman and Modigliani developed their theories, have allowed economists to steadily improve their understanding of how consumers actually behave. What follows summarizes what we know today.

> Friedman received the Nobel prize in economics in 1976 and Modigliani in 1985.

### The Very Foresighted Consumer

Let us start with an assumption that will surely—and rightly—strike you as extreme but will serve as a convenient benchmark. We will call it the theory of the *very foresighted consumer*. How would a very foresighted consumer decide how much to consume? He would proceed in two steps.

---

## FOCUS    Up Close and Personal: Learning from Panel Data Sets

**Panel data sets** are data sets that give the value of one or more variables for many individuals or many firms over time. We described one such survey, the *Labour Force Survey*, in Chapter 9. Another is the Panel Study of Income Dynamics, or PSID. This data is available only in the United States. Canada has a panel data set for income and unemployment called SLID (Survey of Labour Income Dynamics), which tracks individuals for as long as six years. But SLID asks only about labour market experiences and not about consumption. In any case, as part of the cutback in the activities of Statistics Canada under the Conservative government, the SLID was cancelled in 2012.

The PSID was started in 1968, with approximately 4800 families. Interviews of these families have been conducted every year since and are still continuing. The survey has grown as new individuals have joined the original families, either by marriage or by birth. Each year, the survey asks people about their income, wage rate, number of hours worked, health, and food consumption. (The focus on food consumption is because one of the survey's initial aims was to better understand the living conditions of poor families. The survey would be more

useful if it asked about all of consumption rather than food consumption. Unfortunately, it does not.)

By using over 30 years of information about individuals and about extended families, the survey has allowed economists to ask and answer questions for which there was previously only anecdotal evidence. Among the many questions for which the PSID has been used in the recent past are the following:

● How much does (food) consumption respond to transitory movements in income? For example, to the loss of income from becoming unemployed?
● How much risk-sharing is there within families? For example, when a family member becomes sick or unemployed, how much help does he or she get from other family members?
● How much do people care about staying geographically close to their families? When somebody becomes unemployed, for example, how does the probability that he will migrate to another city depend on how many family members live in the city in which he currently lives?

---

- First, he would add up the value of the stocks and bonds he owns, the value of his chequing and savings accounts, the value of the house he owns minus the mortgage still due, and so on. This would give him a notion of his financial wealth and his **housing wealth**.

    He would also estimate what his after-tax labour income was likely to be over his working life and compute the present value of expected after-tax labour income. This would give him an estimate of what economists call his **human wealth**—to contrast it with his **nonhuman wealth**, defined as the sum of financial and housing wealth.

- Adding his human and nonhuman wealth, he would have an estimate of his **total wealth**. He would then decide how much to spend out of this total wealth. A reasonable assumption is that he would decide to spend a proportion of total wealth such as to maintain roughly the same level of consumption each year throughout his life. If that level of consumption was higher than his current income, he would then borrow the difference. If it was lower than his current income, he would instead save the difference.

With a slight abuse of language, we will use "housing wealth" to refer not only to housing but also to the other goods that the consumer may own, from cars to paintings and so on.

Human wealth (= Present value of expected after-tax labour income) + Non-human wealth (= Housing wealth + Financial wealth) = Total wealth

Let us write this formally. What we have described is a consumption decision of the form:

$$C_t = C \, (\text{Total wealth}_t) \qquad (21.1)$$

where $C_t$ is consumption, and (total wealth$_t$) is the sum of nonhuman wealth (financial plus housing wealth) and human wealth (the expected present value of after-tax labour income).

This description contains much truth: Like the foresighted consumer, we surely do think about our wealth and our expected future labour income in deciding how much to consume today. But one cannot help thinking that it assumes too much computation and foresight on the part of the typical consumer.

To get a better sense of what the description implies and what is wrong with it, let us apply this decision process to the problem facing a typical university student.

Because we are all consumers, we can use introspection as a way of checking on the plausibility of a particular theory. Alas, introspection is not without potential pitfalls: Economists perhaps do not think like other people. . . .

## An Example

Let us assume you are 21 years old, with three more years of university before you take your first job. Some of you may be in debt today, having borrowed to go to university; some of you may own a car and a few other worldly possessions. For simplicity, let us assume your debt and your possessions roughly offset each other so that your nonhuman wealth is equal to zero. Your only wealth is your human wealth, the present value of your expected after-tax labour income.

Based on what we know today, you can expect your starting salary in three years to be around $40,000 (in year 2000 dollars) and to increase by an average of 3% a year in real terms, until your retirement at age 60. About 25% of your income will go to taxes.

You are welcome to use your own numbers, and see where the computation takes you.

Building on what we saw in Chapter 19, let us compute the present value of your labour income as the value of *real* expected after-tax labour income, discounted using *real* interest rates (equation (19.7)). Let $Y_{Lt}$ denote real labour income in year $t$. Let $T_t$ denote real taxes (net of transfers). Let $V(Y_{Lt}^e - T_t^e)$ denote your human wealth, that is, the expected present value of your after-tax labour income. To make the computation simple, assume the real interest rate equals zero. The expected present value is simply the sum of expected after-tax labour income over your working life and is therefore given by:

$$V(Y_{Lt}^e - T_t^e) = 0.75[1 + (1.03) + (1.03)^2 + \cdots + (1.03)^{36}](\$40,000)$$

The first term (0.75) comes from the fact that because of taxes you keep only 75% of what you earn. The second term $[1 + (1.03) + (1.03)^2 + \cdots + (1.03)^{36}]$ reflects the fact that you expect your real income to increase by 3% a year for 37 years (you will start earning income at age 24 and work until age 60). The third term ($40,000) is the initial level of labour income, in year 2000 dollars. Using the properties of geometric series to solve for the sum in brackets gives:

$$V(Y_{Lt}^e - T_t^e) = 0.75(66.2)(\$40,000) = \$1,986,000$$

Your wealth today, the expected value of your lifetime after-tax labour income, is around $2 million.

How much should you consume? You can expect to live about 16 years after retirement, so your expected remaining life today is 56 years. If you want to consume the same amount every year, the constant level of consumption that you can afford equals your total wealth divided by your expected remaining life, or \$1,986,000/56 = \$35,464 a year. Given that your income until you get your first job is equal to zero, this implies borrowing \$35,464 a year for the next three years and starting to save when you get your first job.

## Toward a More Realistic Description

The computation of what consumption level you can sustain is made easier by our assumption that the real interest rate equals zero. In this case, if you consume one fewer good today, you can consume exactly one more good next year, and the condition you must satisfy is simply that the sum of consumption over your lifetime is equal to your wealth. If you want to consume a constant amount each year, then, to find how much you can consume each year, you need to divide your wealth by the remaining number of years in your life.

Your first reaction to this computation may be that this is a stark and slightly sinister way of summarizing your life prospects. Your second reaction may be that while you agree with most of the ingredients that went into the computation, you surely do not intend to borrow \$35,464 × 3 = \$106,392 over the next three years.

1. You may not want to plan for constant consumption over your lifetime and may be quite happy with deferring higher consumption until later. Student life usually does not leave much time for expensive activities. You may want to defer memberships in golf clubs and trips to the Galapagos islands to later in life. You also have to think about the additional expenses that will come with having children, sending them to nursery school, summer camp, postsecondary education, and so on.

2. You may find that the amount of computation and foresight involved in the computation we just went through far exceeds the amount you use in your own decisions. You may never have thought until now about exactly how much income you are going to make, and for how many years. You may feel that most consumption decisions are made in a simpler, less forward-looking fashion.

3. The computation of total wealth is based on forecasts of what can reasonably be expected to happen. But things can turn out better or worse. What happens if you are unlucky and you become unemployed or sick? How will you pay back what you borrowed? You may well want to be prudent, making sure that you can adequately survive even the worst outcomes and thus borrow much less than \$106,392.

4. Even if you decided to borrow \$106,392, you are likely to find the bank from which you try to borrow that amount to be unreceptive. Why? The bank may worry that you are taking on a commitment you will not be able to afford if times turn bad and that you may not be able or willing to repay the loan.

These reasons, all good ones, imply that to characterize consumers' actual behaviour, we must modify the description we gave earlier. The last three reasons in particular suggest consumption depends not only on total wealth but also on current income.

Take the second reason. You may, because it is a simple rule, decide to let your consumption follow your income and not think about what your wealth might be. In that case, consumption will depend on current income, not on your wealth. Now, take the third reason. It implies that a safe rule may be to consume no more than your current income. This way, you do not run the risk of accumulating debt that you could not repay if times were to turn bad. Or take the fourth reason. It implies that you may have little choice anyway. Even if you wanted to consume more than your current income, you may be unable to do so because no bank will make you a loan.

If we want to allow for a direct effect of current income on consumption, what measure of current income should we use? A convenient variable is after-tax labour income, introduced earlier when defining human wealth. This leads to a consumption function of the form:

$$C_t = C(\text{Total wealth}_t, Y_{Lt} - T_t) \tag{21.2}$$
$$( \quad + \quad , \quad + \quad )$$

The plus sign under "Total wealth" indicates that an increase in total wealth increases consumption. The same holds for $Y_{Lt} - T_t$.

In words: *Consumption is an increasing function of total wealth and of current after-tax labour income. Total wealth is the sum of nonhuman wealth—(financial wealth plus housing wealth) and of human wealth—(the present value of expected after-tax labour income).*

The practical issue then becomes how much consumption depends on total wealth (and thus on expectations of future income) and how much on current income. Some consumers, especially those who have temporarily low income and poor access to credit, are likely to consume their current income regardless of what they expect will happen to them in the future. A worker who becomes unemployed and has no financial wealth may have a hard time borrowing to maintain her level of consumption, even if she is fairly confident that she will soon find another job. Consumers who are richer and have easier access to credit are more likely to give more weight to the expected future and to try to maintain roughly constant consumption through time.

The relative importance of wealth and income on consumption can be settled only by looking at the empirical evidence. This is not easy to do, and the Focus box "How Much Do Expectations Matter? Looking for Natural Experiments" explains why. But even if some details still need to be filled in, the basic evidence is clear and unsurprising: Both total wealth and current income affect consumption.

Tiff Macklem of the Bank of Canada did an exhaustive study of consumption in Canada as part of the Bank's research effort to model behaviour in the Canadian economy. This study

◀ How expectations of higher output in the future affect consumption today:

Future output ↑ ⟹
Future labour income ↑ ⟹
Human wealth ↑ ⟹
Consumption today ↑

Future output ↑ ⟹
Future dividends ↑ ⟹
Stock prices ↑ ⟹
Nonhuman wealth ↑ ⟹
Consumption today ↑

---

# FOCUS    How Much Do Expectations Matter? Looking for Natural Experiments

How much does consumption depend on current income versus expected future income? This is not an easy question to answer because, most of the time, expectations of future income move very much with current income. If we get promoted and receive a raise, not only does our current income go up, but, typically, so does the income we can expect to receive in future years. Whether or not we are very foresighted, our consumption will typically move closely with our current income.

What can economists do to disentangle the effects of current income versus future income? They must look for times and events where current income and expected future income move in different ways and then look at what happens to consumption. Such events are called **natural experiments**: "experiments" in the sense that, like laboratory experiments, these events allow us to test a theory or to get a better estimate of an important parameter; and "natural" meaning that, unlike researchers in the physical sciences, economists typically cannot run experiments themselves. They must rely on experiments given by nature—or, as we will see in our second example below, created by policy makers.

Here are three examples from recent research on consumption:

## (1) Retirement

Retirement implies a large, predictable change in labour income: Labour income drops to zero. By looking at how people save for retirement, we can, in principle, find out whether, when, and by how much people take into account the predictable decline in their future labour income.

A recent U.S. study, based on a panel data set called the *Survey of Income and Program Participation*, sheds some light

on retirement behaviour. Table 1, taken from the study, shows the mean level and the composition of total wealth for people between 65 and 69 years in 1991.

A mean wealth of $313,807 is substantial (U.S. per capita personal disposable income was $16,205 in 1991), suggesting an image of forward-looking individuals making careful saving decisions and retiring with enough wealth to enjoy a comfortable retirement.

A closer look at the table, and at differences between individuals, suggests two caveats.

● The largest component of wealth is the present value of Social Security benefits, an amount over which workers have no control. Indeed, one of the main motivations behind the introduction of the Social Security program in the United States was to make sure people contributed to their retirement, whether or not they would have done so on their own. The third largest component is an employer-provided pension—another component over which workers have limited control. The only components that clearly reflect individual saving decisions (personal retirement assets + other financial assets) account only for $53,010, or about 17% of total wealth. Thus, one also can read the evidence as suggesting that people save enough for retirement because they are forced to, through social security and other contributions.

● The numbers in the table are averages and hide substantial differences across individuals. The same study shows that most people retire with little more than their Social Security pensions. More generally, studies

*(continued)*

---

of retirement saving give the following picture: Most people appear to give little thought to retirement saving until some time during their 40s. At that point, many start saving for retirement. But many also save little and rely mostly on Social Security benefits when they retire.

## (2) Announced tax cuts

In 1981, the Reagan administration designed a fiscal package with phased-in tax cuts over 1981 to 1983. Income tax rates were to be reduced in three steps: 5% in 1981, 10% in 1982, and 8% in 1983, implying a cumulative reduction of 23%, a very large amount, indeed. Congress passed the package in July 1981, and it became law in August 1981.

This period of U.S. history provides us with a natural experiment. The experiment is a change in expected future after-tax labour income coming from an anticipated decrease in taxes. And the question we want to answer is simple: Did consumers react in 1981 to the expected decrease in taxes in 1982 and 1983, and if so, by how much?

This is exactly the question asked by James Poterba, from Massachusetts Institute of Technology (MIT), in a 1988 article. Using econometrics, Poterba looked for evidence of an unusual increase in consumption, given disposable income, in the summer of 1981 (the time when Congress passed the package). He found no evidence of such an increase.

Is this conclusive evidence that consumers do not take into account changes in expected future income in their consumption decision? Not necessarily. There are at least two alternative interpretations of the facts. People may have believed that Congress would change its mind, leading them to take a wait-and-see attitude and wait for the actual decreases in taxes to adjust their consumption. Or maybe people do not take into account expected changes in taxes but take into account other expected changes in their income (say, an expected promotion or the coming of retirement). These arguments cannot be dismissed. But what can be safely said is that the evidence from that particular natural experiment does not provide evidence for a strong effect of expected future tax changes on consumption.

Canada had a recent experience with announced income tax cuts. In an *Economic Statement* (October 18, 2000) just prior to the federal election of November 27, 2000, Finance Minister Paul Martin promised to substantially reduce federal income taxes over the next five years. Mr. Martin's party was expected to win the election and did. In 2001, when economic growth slowed in both Canada and the United States, the tax cuts in 2001 and those promised in future years were credited with maintaining strong consumer demand. However, without a panel data set, such as the PSID, further testing of this hypothesis is difficult.

## (3) The effects of changes in the value of houses on consumption

A key macroeconomic concern in the last decade has been the effect of increases in house prices on consumption. The mechanism is quite clear, as the value of houses rises relative to the overall price level, consumers feel wealthier and consume more. Banks are very willing to allow consumers to borrow against the value of their house in the form of mortgage-backed lines of credit. We saw in Chapter 20 an enormous rise and fall in the price of houses in the United States. We saw a rise, but not yet a fall, in the price of houses in Canada. The macroeconomic question is whether consumers responded to the increase in wealth by increasing consumption. The way to test this hypothesis is to ask whether consumption rose more in countries and states where house prices increased more. That is precisely what Karl Case, John Quigley, and Robert Shiller did. They studied 14 countries and a panel of U.S. states during the 1980s and 1990s. More recently, Katya Kartashova and Ben Tomlin asked the same question in Canada and found non-housing consumption was associated with house price increases across regions in Canada. These two papers are part of a much larger literature. The conclusion from the literature is that there is a large effect of housing wealth on consumption. As housing prices fall, we would predict a decline in consumption. This is exactly what occurred in 2008 and 2009 in the United States. If Canadian house prices were to fall significantly, we would expect consumption to fall as well.

*Sources: On the Reagan tax cuts:* James Poterba, "Are Consumers Forward Looking? Evidence from Fiscal Experiments," *American Economic Review* 78 (2), May 1988: pp. 413–418.

*On the increases in real estate prices:* Karl E. Case, John N. Quigley, and Robert J. Shiller, "Comparing Wealth Effects: The Stock Market versus the Housing Market," *Advances in Macroeconomics* 5 (1), Article 1, 2005.

| TABLE 1 | Mean Wealth of People in the United States, Age 65–69, in 1991 (in 1991 Dollars) |
|---|---|
| Social Security pension | $ 99,682 |
| Employer-provided pension | 62,305 |
| Personal retirement assets | 10,992 |
| Other financial assets | 42,018 |
| Home equity | 64,955 |
| Other equity | 33,855 |
| Total | $313,807 |

*Source:* Venti and Wise, Table A1. (The first two items are expected present values of future payments.)

has been updated several times by researchers at the Bank of Canada. The conclusion: Canadian consumption fits equation (21.2)—fluctuations in both wealth and in current disposable income after taxes explain fluctuations in consumption.

## Putting Things Together: Current Income, Expectations, and Consumption

Let us go back to what motivates this chapter, the importance of expectations in the determination of spending. Note first that with consumption behaviour described by equation (21.2), expectations affect consumption in two ways:

- They affect it directly through human wealth: To compute their human wealth, consumers have to form their own expectations of future labour income, real interest rates, and taxes.
- They affect it indirectly, through nonhuman wealth—stocks, bonds, housing. Consumers do not need to do any computation here and can take the value of these assets as a given. But as we saw in Chapter 20, the computation is, in effect, done for them by financial markets. The price of their stocks, for example, depends itself on expectations of future dividends and interest rates.

This dependence of consumption on expectations has, in turn, two main implications.

First, *consumption is likely to respond less than one for one to fluctuations in current income*. In thinking about how much they should consume, consumers look at more than current income. If they conclude that a decrease in income is permanent, they may decrease consumption one for one with the decrease in income. But if they conclude that the decrease in current income is transitory, they will adjust their consumption by less. In a recession, consumption adjusts less than one for one to decreases in income. This is because consumers know that recessions typically do not last for more than a few quarters and that the economy will eventually return to its natural output level. The same is true during expansions. Faced with an unusually rapid increase in income, consumers are unlikely to increase consumption by as much. They are likely to assume that the boom is transitory and that things will return to normal.

Second, *consumption may move even if current income does not change*. The election of a charismatic leader who articulates the vision of an exciting future may lead people to become more optimistic about the future in general and about their own future income in particular, leading them to increase consumption even if their current income does not change. We know that "consumer confidence" appears in the news as a key economic variable. It measures optimism about future income prospects among households. Optimistic consumers increase their consumption, and pessimistic consumers decrease their consumption and can even "cause" a recession.

> Go back to the two consumption functions we used in the core:
> Looking at the short run (Chapter 3), we assumed $C = c_0 + c_1 Y$. (Ignore taxes for simplicity here.) This implied that when output increased, consumption increased less than proportionately ($C/Y$ goes down). This was appropriate, as our focus was on output fluctuations—on transitory movements in output.
> Looking at the long run (Chapter 16), we assumed that $S = sY$, or, equivalently, $C = (1 - s)Y$. This implied that when output increases, consumption increases proportionately ($C/Y$ is constant). This was appropriate, as our focus was on permanent—long-run—movements in output.

> What does this suggest happens to the saving rate in a recession?

# 21-2 | Investment

How do firms make investment decisions? In our first pass at the answer in the core (Chapter 5), we took investment to depend on the current interest rate and the current level of sales. We improved on that answer in Chapter 19 by pointing out that what mattered was the real interest rate, not the nominal interest rate. It is clear that these answers underplayed the role of expectations. We will now look at their role more closely.

Think of the decision by a firm about buying a new machine. What will matter is the present value of profits the firm expects from having this machine, compared with the cost of buying the machine. If the present value exceeds the cost, the firm should buy the machine—that is, invest; if the present value is less than the cost, then the firm should not buy the machine—that is, not invest. This, in a nutshell, is the theory of investment. Let us look at it in more detail.

## Investment and Expectations of Profit

Let us go through the steps a firm must take to determine whether to buy a new machine. (Although we refer to a machine, the same reasoning applies to the other components of investment—the building of a new factory, the renovation of an office complex, and so on.)

1. To compute the present value of expected profits, the firm first must estimate how long the machine will last. Most machines are like cars: They can last nearly forever, but as time passes, they become more and more expensive to maintain and less and less reliable.

If the firm has a large number of machines, we can think of $\delta$ as the proportion of machines that die every year. If the firm starts the year with $K$ working machines and ▶ does not buy new ones, it has only $K(1 - \delta)$ machines left one year later, and so on.

   Let us assume a machine loses its usefulness at rate $\delta$ (the Greek lowercase letter delta) per year. A machine that is new this year is worth only $(1 - \delta)$ machines next year, $(1 - \delta)^2$ machines in two years, and so on. The *depreciation rate*, $\delta$, measures how much usefulness the machine loses from one year to the next. What are reasonable values for $\delta$? This is a question that the statisticians in charge of computing how the capital stock changes over time have had to answer. On the basis of their studies of depreciation of specific machines and buildings, they use numbers between 4 and 15% per year for machines and between 2 and 4% per year for buildings and factories. There are direct, if imperfect, measures of the Canadian physical capital in the National Balance Sheets.

2. The firm must then compute the present value of expected profits. To capture the fact that it takes some time to put machines in place (and even more time to build a factory or an office building), let us assume that a machine bought in year $t$ becomes operational—and starts depreciating—only one year later, in year $t+1$.

   Denote profit per machine in real terms by $\Pi$ (this is an uppercase pi as opposed to the lowercase pi, which we use to denote inflation). If the firm purchases a machine in year $t$, the machine generates its first expected profit in year $t+1$; denote this expected profit by $\Pi^e_{t+1}$. The present value, in year $t$, of this expected profit in year $t+1$, is given by

$$\frac{1}{1 + r_t} \Pi^e_{t+1}$$

This computation is represented by the arrow pointing left in the upper line of Figure 21–1. Because we are measuring profit in real terms, we are using real interest rates to discount future profits. This is one of the lessons we learned in Chapter 19.

Denote expected profit per machine in year $t+2$ by $\Pi^e_{t+2}$. Because of depreciation, only $(1 - \delta)$ of the machine bought in year $t$ is left in year $t+2$, so the expected profit from the machine is equal to $(1 - \delta) \Pi^e_{t+2}$. The present value of this expected profit as of year $t$ is equal to:

$$\frac{1}{(1 + r_t)(1 + r^e_{t+1})} (1 - \delta)\Pi^e_{t+2}$$

This computation is represented by the arrow pointing left in the lower line of Figure 21–1.

The same reasoning applies to expected profit in following years. Putting the pieces together gives us *the present value of expected profits* from buying the machine in year $t$—call it $V(\Pi^e_t)$:

$$V(\Pi^e_t) = \frac{1}{1 + r_t} \Pi^e_{t+1} + \frac{1}{(1 + r_t)(1 + r^e_{t+1})} (1 - \delta)\Pi^e_{t+2} + \cdots \qquad (21.3)$$

---

**FIGURE  21–1**

**Computing the Present Value of Expected Profits**

| Present Value in Year $t$ | Expected Profit in: Year $t+1$ | Year $t+2$ ... |
|---|---|---|
| $\dfrac{1}{1 + r_t} \Pi^e_{t+1}$ | ⬅ $\Pi^e_{t+1}$ | |
| $\dfrac{1}{(1 + r_t)(1 + r^e_{t+1})} (1 - \delta)\Pi^e_{t+2}$ | ⬅ | $(1 - \delta)\Pi^e_{t+2}$ |

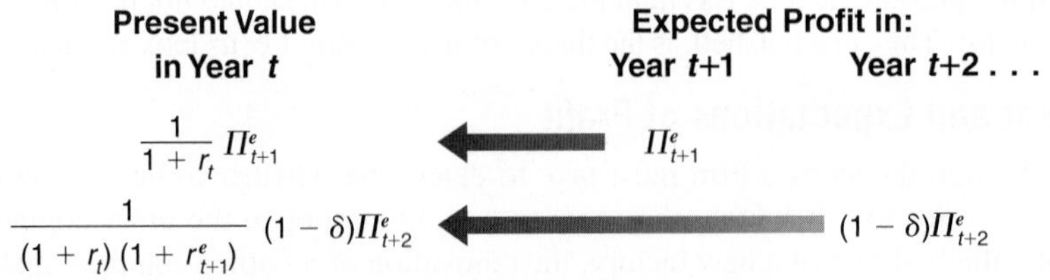

The expected present value is equal to the discounted value of expected profit next year plus the discounted value of expected profit two years from now (taking into account the depreciation of the machine) and so on.

3. The firm must then decide whether to buy the machine. This decision depends on the relation between the present value of expected profits and the price of the machine. To simplify notation, let us assume that the real price of a machine—that is, the machine's price in terms of the basket of goods produced in the economy—equals one. What the firm must then do is compare the present value of profits to one.

If the present value is less than one, the firm should not buy the machine: If it did, it would be paying more for the machine than it expects to get back in profits later. If the present value exceeds one, the firm has an incentive to buy the new machine.

Let us now jump from this one-firm, one-machine example to investment in the economy as a whole. Let $I_t$ denote aggregate investment. Denote profit per machine, or more generally profit per unit of capital (where capital includes machines, factories, office buildings, and so on), for the economy as a whole by $\Pi_t$. Denote the expected present value of profit per unit of capital by $V(\Pi_t^e)$, defined as in equation (21.3). Our discussion suggests an investment function of the form:

$$I_t = I(V(\Pi_t^e)) \qquad (21.4)$$
$$(\,+\,)$$

In words: Investment depends positively on the expected present value of future profits (per unit of capital). The higher the current or expected profits, the higher the expected present value and the higher the level of investment is; the higher the current or expected real interest rates, the lower the expected present value, and thus the lower the level of investment.

If the present value computation the firm has to make strikes you as quite similar to the present value computation we saw in Chapter 20 for the fundamental value of a stock, you are right. This relation was first explored by James Tobin, from Yale University, who argued that there should indeed be a tight relation between investment and the value of the stock market. His argument and the evidence are presented in the Focus box "Investment and the Stock Market."

Tobin received the Nobel prize in economics in 1981.

## A Convenient Special Case

Before exploring further implications and extensions of equation (21.4), it is useful to go through a special case, where the relation among investment, profit, and interest rates becomes very simple.

Suppose firms expect both future profits (per unit of capital) and future interest rates to remain at the same level as today so that $\Pi_{t+1}^e = \Pi_{t+2}^e = \cdots = \Pi_t$, and $r_{t+1}^e = r_{t+2}^e = \cdots = r_t$. Under these assumptions, equation (21.3) becomes:

$$V(\Pi_t^e) = \frac{\Pi_t}{r_t + \delta} \qquad (21.5)$$

(The derivation is given in appendix B of this chapter.) The present value of expected profits is simply the ratio of profit to the sum of the real interest rate and the depreciation rate.

Replacing (21.5) in equation (21.4), investment is:

$$I_t = I\left(\frac{\Pi_t}{r_t + \delta}\right) \qquad (21.6)$$

Look more closely at the fraction in parentheses. The denominator—the sum of the real interest rate and the depreciation rate—is called the **user cost** or the **rental cost of capital**. To see why, suppose the firm, instead of buying the machine, rented it by the year from a rental agency. How much would the rental agency charge? Even if the machine did not depreciate, the agency would have to charge as rent an interest rate equal to $r_t$ times the price of the

Such arrangements exist: Many firms lease cars and trucks from leasing companies.

Suppose a firm has 100 machines and 100 shares outstanding—one share per machine. Suppose the price per share is $2, and the purchase price of a machine is only $1. Obviously the firm should invest—buy a new machine—and finance it by issuing a share: Each machine costs the firm $1 to purchase, but stock market participants are willing to pay $2 for a share corresponding to this machine when it is installed in the firm.

This is an example of a more general argument made by Tobin that there should be a tight relation between the stock market and investment. When deciding whether or not to invest, he argued, firms might not need to go through the type of complicated computation you saw in the text. In effect, the stock price tells firms how much the stock market values each unit of capital already in place. The firm then has a simple problem: Compare the purchase price of an additional unit of capital to the price the stock market is willing to pay for it. *If the stock market value exceeds the purchase price, the firm should buy the machine; otherwise, it should not.*

Tobin then constructed a variable corresponding to the value of a unit of capital in place relative to its purchase price and looked at how closely it moved with investment. He used the symbol "q" to denote the variable, and the variable has become known as **Tobin's q.** Its construction is as follows.

1. Take the total value of U.S. corporations, as assessed by financial markets. That is, compute the sum of their stock market value (the price of a share times the number of shares). Compute also the total value of their bonds outstanding (firms finance themselves not only through stocks but also through bonds). Add together the value of stocks and bonds. Subtract the firms' financial assets, the value of the cash, bank accounts, and any bonds the firms might hold.

2. Divide this total value by the value of the capital stock of U.S. corporations at replacement cost (the price firms would have to pay to replace their machines, their plants, and so on).

The ratio gives us, in effect, the value of a unit of capital in place relative to its current purchase price. This ratio is *Tobin's q.* Intuitively, the higher q, the higher the value of capital relative to its current purchase price, and the higher investment should be. (In the example at the start of the box, Tobin's q is equal to 2, so the firm should definitely invest.)

How tight is the relation between Tobin's q and investment? The answer is given in Figure 1, which plots two variables for each year from 1960 to 2010 for the United States.

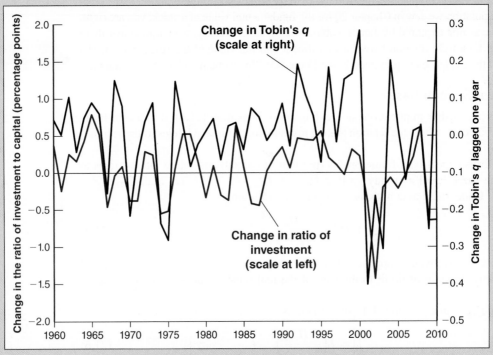

**FIGURE 1    Tobin's *q* versus the Ratio of Investment to Capital. Annual Rates of Change, since 1960**

*Source:* Flow of Funds Accounts Nonfarm Nonfinancial Corporate Business. Investment (line 12, Table F102). Capital measured by Nonfinancial assets (line 2, Table B102). Numerator of q: Market value of Equity (line 35) + [Financial Liabilities (line 21) − (Financial Assets (Total assets (line 1) − Nonfinancial assets (line 2))] all Table B102. Denominator of q: Nonfinancial assets (line 2, Table B102).

Measured on the left vertical axis is the change in the ratio of investment to capital.

Measured on the right vertical axis is the change of Tobin's q. This variable has been lagged once. For 1987, for example, the figure shows the change in the ratio of investment to capital for 1987, and the change in Tobin's q for 1986—that is, a year earlier. The reason for presenting the two variables this way is that the strongest relation in the data appears to be between investment this year and Tobin's q last year. Put another way, movements in investment this year are more closely associated with movements in the stock market last year rather than with movements in the stock market this year; a plausible explanation is that it takes time for firms to make investment decisions, build new factories, and so on.

The figure shows that there is a clear relation between Tobin's q and investment. This is not because firms blindly follow the signals from the stock market, but because investment decisions and stock market prices depend very much on the same factors—expected future profits and expected future interest rates.

machine (we have assumed the price of a machine to be 1 in real terms, so $r_t$ times 1 is just $r_t$): The agency has to get at least as much from buying and then renting the machine as it would from, say, buying bonds. In addition, the rental agency would have to charge for depreciation, $\delta$ times the price of the machine, 1. The rent would therefore be equal to $(r_t + \delta)$. Even though firms typically do not rent their machines, $(r_t + \delta)$ still captures the implicit cost—sometimes called the *shadow cost*—to the firm of using the machine for one year.

The investment function given by equation (21.6) then has a simple interpretation: *Investment depends on the ratio of profit to the user cost*. The higher the profit compared with the user cost, the higher the level of investment is; the higher the real interest rate, the higher the user cost and the lower the level of investment.

This relation among profit, the real interest rate, and investment relies on a strong simplifying assumption: The future is expected to be the same as the present. It is nevertheless a useful relation to remember, and a relation macroeconomists keep handy in their toolbox. ◀

## Current versus Expected Profits

Let us now return to the general case. Equations (21.3) and (21.4) imply that investment should be forward looking and depend primarily on *expected future profits*. (Under our assumption that new capital starts being operational only one year after purchase, current profit does not even appear in equation (21.3).) One striking empirical fact about investment, however, is how it moves with fluctuations in *current profit*.

This relation is shown in Figure 21–2, which plots investment and profit between 1981 and 2012 for the Canadian economy. Investment is measured as *investment in nonresidential*

If the future is expected to be the same as the present, investment depends on the ratio of profit to the user cost—the sum of the real interest rate and the depreciation rate.

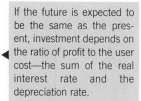

Profit ↑ ⟹ Investment ↑
Real interest rate ↑
⟹ Investment ↓

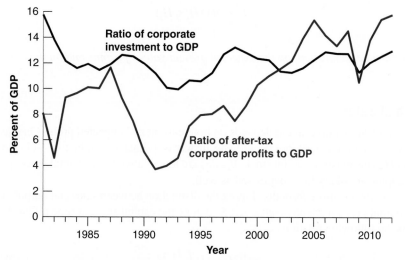

**FIGURE 21-2**

**Corporate Investment and Corporate Profits in Canada, 1981–2012**

There is a clear relation between corporate profits and corporate investment— when profits rise, investment rises and when profits fall, investment falls. More recently, although corporate profits have increased rapidly as a percent of GDP, investment has not increased as rapidly.

*Source:* After-tax corporate profits, CANSIM II variable V62306729; Corporate investment is the sum of CAMSIM II variables V62305767, V62305768, V62305769. Both variables are expressed as a percent of GDP, CANSIM II variable V62305783.

*structures and equipment*. Profit is constructed as the ratio of the sum of *after-tax profits of corporations* divided by GDP. After-tax profits are total profits of corporations and government business enterprises minus direct taxes paid by corporations. Figure 21–2 shows that this measure of after-tax profit varies substantially as a percent of GDP. The 1981–1982, 1990–1991, and 2008–2009 recessions coincide with very sharp reductions in profits.

The positive relation between investment, also as a percentage of GDP, and current profit is clear in Figure 21–2. Is this relation inconsistent with the theory we have just developed, which holds that investment should be related to the present value of expected future profits rather than to current profit? It need not be: If firms expect future profits to move very much like current profit, then the present value of profits will move very much like current profit, and so will investment.

Economists who have looked at the question more closely have concluded, however, that the effect of current profit on investment is stronger than the theory we have developed so far would predict. (How they have gathered some of the evidence is described in the Focus box "Profitability versus Cash Flow.") On the one hand, some firms with highly profitable investment projects but low current profit appear to be investing too little. On the other hand, some firms that have high current profit sometimes appear to invest in projects of doubtful profitability. In short, current profit appears to affect investment, even after controlling for the expected present value of profits.

Why does current profit play a role in the investment decision? The answer lies in our discussion in section 21-1 of why consumption also depends directly on current income. Many of the reasons we used to explain the behaviour of consumers also apply to firms:

1. If its current profit is low, a firm that wants to buy new machines can get the funds it needs only by borrowing. It may be reluctant to borrow: Although expected profits may look good, things may turn bad, leaving the firm unable to repay the debt. But if current profit is high, the firm may be able to finance its investment by retaining some of its earnings and without having to borrow. The bottom line is that higher current profit may lead the firm to invest more.

2. Even if the firm wants to invest, it may find it difficult to borrow. Potential lenders may not be convinced the project is as good as the firm says, and they may worry the firm will be unable to repay. If the firm has large current profits, it does not have to borrow and so does not need to convince potential lenders. It can proceed and invest as it pleases and is more likely to do so.

In summary, to fit the investment behaviour we observe, the investment equation is better written as:

$$I_t = I(V(\Pi_t^e), \Pi_t) \qquad (21.7)$$

$$( \quad + \quad , \quad + )$$

*Investment depends both on the expected present value of profits and on the current level of profit.*

## Profit and Sales

We have argued that investment depends on both current and expected profit. One last step is to ask: What, in turn, determines profit? The answer is: primarily two factors—(1) the level of sales, and (2) the existing capital stock. If sales are low relative to the capital stock, profits per unit of capital are likely to be depressed as well.

Let us write this more formally. Ignore the distinction between sales and output, and let $Y_t$ denote output or, equivalently, sales. Let $K_t$ denote the capital stock at time $t$. Our discussion suggests the following relation:

$$\Pi_t = \Pi \left( \frac{Y_t}{K_t} \right) \qquad (21.8)$$

$$( + )$$

## FOCUS    Profitability versus Cash Flow

How much does investment depend on the expected present value of profits, and how much does it depend on current profit? Economists often refer to the question as the relative importance of **profitability** (the expected present discounted value of profits) versus **cash flow** (current profit, the net flow of cash the firm is receiving) in investment decisions.

The difficulty in answering this question is similar to the problem of identifying the relative importance of current and expected future incomes on consumption—a problem we discussed in the first Focus box in this chapter: Most of the time, cash flow and profitability are likely to move together. Firms that do well typically have both large cash flows and good future prospects. Firms that suffer losses often also have poor future prospects.

As in the case for consumption, the best way to isolate the effects of cash flow and profitability is to identify times or events when cash flow and profitability move in different directions and then look at what happens to investment. This is the approach taken by Owen Lamont, an economist at the University of Chicago. An example will help you understand Lamont's strategy.

Think of two firms, A and B. A is involved only in steel production. B is composed of two parts, one part steel production, the other part petroleum exploration.

Suppose there is a sharp drop in the price of oil, leading to losses in oil exploration. This shock decreases firm B's cash flow. If the losses in oil exploration are large enough to offset the profits from steel production, firm B may show an overall loss.

The question we can now ask is: As a result of the decrease in the price of oil, will firm B invest less in its steel operation than firm A does? If only *profitability* in steel production matters, there is no reason for firm B to invest less in its steel operation than firm A does. But if current *cash flow* also matters, the fact that firm B has a lower cash flow may prevent it from investing as much as firm A does in its steel operation. Looking at investment in the steel operations of the two firms can tell us how much investment depends on cash flow versus profitability.

This is the empirical strategy followed by Lamont. He focuses on what happened in 1986 when the price of oil in the United States dropped by 50%, leading to large losses in oil-related activities. He then looks at whether firms that had substantial oil activities cut investment in their non–oil activities relatively more than other firms in the same non–oil activities. He concludes that they did. He finds that for every $1 decrease in cash flow due to the decrease in the price of oil, investment spending in non-oil activities was reduced by 10 to 20 cents. In short, current cash flow matters.

Huntley Schaller, from Carleton University, uses another strategy to estimate the impact of cash flows on Canadian investment. He compares firms that belong to a tightly knit web of corporate directorships, a sort of Canadian analogue to the Japanese Keiretsu, with those that are large, independent, and on their own. He estimates that $1 of after-tax cash flow can have very different impacts on the investment decisions of the two kinds of firms. For firms that are members of an industrial group, the increase may be as little as 5 cents, while for firms that are largely on their own, the impact may be as large as 60 cents.

The issue of cash flow and corporate investment came alive in 2012 when Governor Mark Carney of the Bank of Canada pointed out that Canadian corporations had "dead money." The Governor meant that, as corporate profits had increased, corporations accumulated cash and did not increase physical investment spending as much as they had in the past. Figure 21–2 actually shows that as profits rose at the end of the recession in 2009, business investment did not rise very much. This is modest support for the "dead money" observation. The more challenging question: Why has investment not recovered as vigorously as in past years?

*Sources:* Owen Lamont, "Cash Flow and Investment: Evidence from Internal Capital Markets," *Journal of Finance* 52 (1), March 1997: 83–109.

A general review of studies along these lines is given by R. Glenn Hubbard, "Capital-Market Imperfections and Investment," *Journal of Economic Literature* 36 (1), March 1995: pp. 193–225.

Huntley Schaller, "Asymmetric Information, Liquidity Constraints and Canadian Investment," *Canadian Journal of Economics* 26 (3), August 1993: pp. 552–574.

---

Profit per unit of capital is an increasing function of the ratio of sales to the capital stock: given the capital stock, the higher the sales, the higher the profit; given sales, the higher the capital stock, the lower the profit.

How does this relation hold in practice? Figure 21–3 plots yearly changes in profit per unit of capital and changes in the ratio of output to capital since 1982. As in Figure 21–2, profit is defined as after-tax profits now divided by total corporate sector assets in structures and machinery and equipment. The ratio of output to capital is constructed as the ratio of GDP to total assets of corporations and government business enterprises.

The figure shows a relation between changes in profit and changes in the ratio of output to capital. Given that most of the year-to-year changes in the ratio of output to capital come from movements in output (capital moves slowly over time; even large swings in investment lead

FIGURE    21–3

**Changes in the Ratio of After-Tax Profit to Capital and Changes in the Ratio of Output to Capital, 1982–2012**

The ratio of profit to capital and the ratio of output to capital do move together over time.

*Source:* After-tax profits, CANSIM II variable V62306729. Capital of corporate sector sum of CANSIM II variables V52229143 and V52229100. Output is GDP CANSIM II variable V62305783.

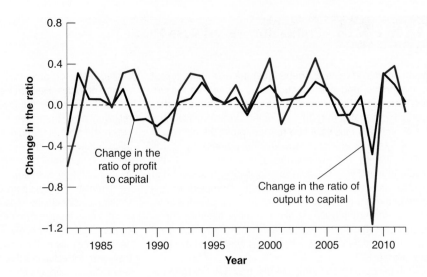

to slow changes in capital), we can state the relation as follows: Profit decreases in recessions and increases in expansions.

Why is this relation between output and profit relevant here? Because it implies a link between *current output* and *expected output* on the one hand and *investment* on the other. For example, the anticipation of a long, sustained economic expansion leads firms to expect high profits, now and for some time in the future. These expectations, in turn, lead to higher investment. The effect of current and expected output on investment, together with the effect of investment back on demand and output, will play a crucial role when we return to the determination of output in Chapter 22.

High expected output ⇒ High expected profit ⇒ ▶ High investment today.

## 21-3 | Investment Spending on New Houses

The components of aggregate demand in 2012 were presented in Table 3–1 (Chapter 3). Expenditures on new residential housing are treated as part of investment. Residential housing construction was about one-third of all investment in 2012. It makes sense to treat the building of a new house as an addition to the nation's capital stock. The new house will produce a stream of accommodation services over many years. You could place a monetary value on those housing services by renting the house and discounting the expected future stream of rents.

If we modified equation (21.3) and replaced the stream of expected profits from buying the machine with the stream of expected rents (after maintenance costs and taxes) from building a house, we would have an expression for the value of a house. You would build a new house when the present values of the expected rents exceed the cost of building the house. When interest rates are low, then the present value of the expected rents is higher and more new houses will be built.

There is a simpler way to think of the decision of an individual family to build a new house. Suppose they have some money saved for a down payment. The rest of the house purchase must be financed with a mortgage loan. If the mortgage interest rate is lower, the monthly payment on the mortgage will be lower. Lower interest rates make it more likely the family will build a new house. This is what we concluded above.

The second important aspect of the family's decision to build the new home is to ask: Will the home rise or fall in value? When they have to move, will they make or lose money when they sell their house? It is difficult to know what is in the mind of the family but we start with

**FIGURE    21–4**

**Residential Housing Investment, 1987–2012**

Residential housing investment varied from 4% to 7% of GDP since 1987. Since the year 2000, the combination of low real interest rates and a continuous increase in the real price of houses has led to increases in residential housing investment as a share of GDP.

*Source:* Real house price index—see Figure 20–8. Residential investment CANSIM II variable V62305765; GDP CANSIM II variable V62305783.

the assumption that proved useful in earlier chapters: the family's expectation of future price increases depends partly on what has just been observed, perhaps over a number of recent years.

Figure 21–4 puts the second idea into practice. On the left-hand axis is residential housing investment as a percent of GDP. This percent varies from a low of 4% to a high of 7%. Housing investment is both important to the economy and quite variable over time. The right-hand axis is the real house price index from Figure 20–8. It is quite clear that fewer new houses are built after periods when real house prices have been falling. When the level of real house prices began to increase steadily after the year 2000, a much larger proportion of GDP was devoted to building new houses. It is very plausible that families deciding to build new houses believed their investment would increase in value as they had in the recent past. If you recall Figure 19–2, the period after the year 2000 and especially the period after 2008 was also a period of unprecedented low, even negative real interest rates. For both reasons, Canadians have decided to build a large number of new homes since the year 2000.

## 21-4 | The Volatility of Consumption and Investment

You surely will have noticed the similarities between our treatment of consumption and of investment behaviour in sections 21-1 and 21-2:

- Whether consumers perceive current movements in income to be transitory or permanent affects their consumption decisions.
- In the same way, whether firms perceive current movements in sales to be transitory or permanent affects their investment decisions. The less they expect a current increase in sales to last, the less they revise their assessment of the present value of profits, and thus the less likely they are to buy new machines or build new factories. This is why, for example, the boom in sales that happens every year over Christmas does not lead to a boom in investment every year in December. Firms understand that this boom is transitory.

In North America, retail sales are, on average, 24% higher in December than in other months. In France and Italy, sales are 60% higher in December. (These numbers and other facts about such seasonal cycles come from J. Joseph Beaulieu and Jeffrey Miron, "A Cross Country Comparison of Seasonal Cycles and Business Cycles," *Economic Journal* 102 (413), July 1992: pp. 772–778.)

But there are also important differences between consumption and investment decisions:

- The theory of consumption we developed implies that when faced with an increase in income consumers perceive as permanent, they respond with *at most* an equal increase in consumption. The permanent nature of the increase in income implies that they can afford to increase consumption now and in the future by the same amount as the increase in income. Increasing consumption more than one for one would require cuts in consumption later, and there is no reason for consumers to want to plan consumption this way.

- Now, consider the behaviour of firms faced with an increase in sales they believe to be permanent. The present value of expected profits increases, leading to an increase in investment. In contrast to consumption, there is no implication that the increase in investment should be no greater than the increase in sales. Rather, once a firm has decided that an increase in sales justifies the purchase of a new machine or the building of a new factory, it may want to proceed quickly, leading to a large but short-lived increase in investment spending. This increase may exceed the increase in sales.

  More concretely, take a firm that has a ratio of capital to its annual sales of, say, three. An increase in sales of $10 million this year, if expected to be permanent, requires the firm to spend $30 million on additional capital if it wants to maintain the same ratio of capital to output. If the firm buys the additional capital right away, the increase in investment spending this year will be equal to *three times* the increase in sales. Once the capital stock has adjusted, the firm will return to its normal pattern of investment. This example is extreme because firms are unlikely to adjust their capital stock right away. But even if they do adjust their capital stock more slowly, say, over a few years, the increase in investment may still exceed the increase in sales for a while.

  We can tell the same story in terms of equation (21.8). As we make no distinction here between output and sales, the initial increase in sales leads to an equal increase in output, $Y$, so that $Y/K$ (the ratio of the firm's output to its existing capital stock) also increases. The result is higher profit, which leads the firm to undertake more investment. Over time, the higher level of investment leads to a higher capital stock, $K$, so that $Y/K$ decreases, returning to normal. Profit per unit of capital returns to normal, and so does investment. Thus, in response to a permanent increase in sales, investment may increase a lot initially and then return to normal over time.

These differences suggest that investment should be more volatile than consumption. How much more volatile? The answer from the data is given in Figure 21–5, which plots yearly rates of change in household consumption and corporate investment since 1982. To make the figure easier to interpret, both rates of change are plotted as deviations from the average rate of change so that they are, on average, equal to zero.

You can see two things in the figure:

- Consumption and investment usually move together: Recessions, for example, are typically associated with decreases in *both* investment and consumption. Given our discussion, which has emphasized that consumption and investment depend largely on the same determinants, this should not come as a surprise.

- Investment is, indeed, much more volatile than consumption. Relative movements in investment range from $-22$ to $+15\%$, whereas relative movements in consumption range only from $-6$ to $+2\%$.

- Another way of stating the same fact is that whereas the level of investment is much smaller than the level of consumption (recall that investment accounts for about 15% of GDP versus about 60% for consumption) the range of changes in the level of investment from one year to the next is roughly the same as the range of changes in the level of consumption from one year to the next. Both components contribute roughly equally to fluctuations in output over time.

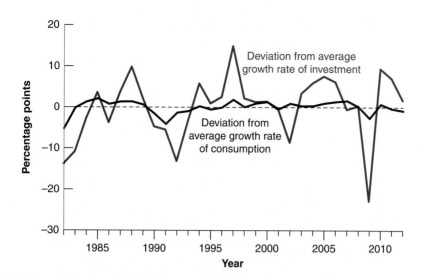

FIGURE 21–5

**The Relative Variability of Consumption and Investment in Canada, 1982–2012**

Relative movements in consumption are much smaller than relative movements in investment.

*Source:* Real business investment, sum of CANSIM II variables V62305736, V62305737, V62305738; Real household consumption, CANSIM II variable V62305724.

## SUMMARY

- Consumption depends on both current income and wealth. Wealth is the sum of nonhuman wealth (financial and housing wealth) and human wealth (the present value of expected after-tax labour income).

- The response of consumption to changes in income depends on whether consumers perceive these changes as transitory or permanent.

- Consumption is likely to respond less than one for one to movements in income, and consumption may move even if current income does not change.

- Investment depends on both current profit and the present value of expected future profits.

- Under the simplifying assumption that firms expect profits and interest rates to be the same in the future as they are today, we can think of investment as depending on the ratio of profit to the user cost of capital, where the user cost is the sum of the real interest rate and the depreciation rate.

- Movements in profit are closely related to movements in output. Hence, we can think of investment as depending indirectly on current and future expected output movements. Firms that anticipate a long output expansion, and thus a long sequence of high profits, will invest. Movements in output that are not expected to last will have a small effect on investment.

- An important part of investment is spending on building new houses. More new houses are built when interest rates are low and when real house prices have been increasing, and presumably are expected to continue to increase.

- Investment is much more volatile than consumption.

## KEY TERMS

- cash flow, 441
- housing wealth, 431
- human wealth, 431
- life cycle theory of consumption, 430
- natural experiment, 433
- nonhuman wealth, 431

- panel data set, 430
- permanent income theory of consumption, 430
- profitability, 441
- Tobin's $q$, 438
- total wealth, 431
- user cost or rental cost of capital, 437

## QUESTIONS AND PROBLEMS

**1. TRUE/FALSE/UNCERTAIN**

**a.** For the typical university student, human wealth and nonhuman wealth are approximately equal.

**b.** Events such as retirement and announced tax cuts do not suggest that expectations of future income are major factors affecting consumption.

c. Buildings and factories depreciate much faster than machines do.

d. A high value for Tobin's $q$ indicates the stock market believes that capital is overvalued and thus investment should be lower.

e. Economists have found that the effect of current profit on investment can be fully explained by the effect of current profit on expectations of future profits.

f. Data from the past three decades suggest that corporate profits are closely tied to the business cycle.

g. Changes in consumption and investment are typically of the same sign and are roughly of the same magnitude.

h. The construction of new houses is a large part of investment spending.

i. The percent of GDP spent building new houses does not vary much over time.

## 2. PDV COMPUTATIONS AND RETIREMENT

A consumer has nonhuman wealth equal to $100,000. She earns $40,000 this year and expects her salary to rise by 5% in real terms each year for the following two years. She will then retire. The real interest rate is equal to 0% and is expected to remain at 0% in the future. Labour income is taxed at the rate of 25%.

a. What is this consumer's human wealth?

b. What is her total wealth?

c. If she expects to live for another seven years after retirement and wants her consumption to remain the same (in real terms) every year from now on, how much can she consume this year?

d. If she were given a bonus of $20,000 in the current year only, with all future salary payments remaining as stated earlier, by how much could she increase consumption now and in the future?

e. Now, suppose that at retirement, the Canada Pension Plan will start paying each year benefits equal to 60% of the consumer's earnings during her last working year. (Assume benefits are not taxed.) How much can she consume this year (and still maintain constant consumption)?

## 3. INVESTMENT DECISIONS IN THE PRETZEL INDUSTRY

A pretzel manufacturer is considering buying a pretzel-making machine that costs $100,000. The machine will depreciate by 8% per year. It will generate real profits equal to $18,000 next year, $18,000 (1–0.08%) two years from now (that is, the same real profits, but adjusted for depreciation),

$18,000 (1–0.08%)$^2$ three years from now, and so on. Determine whether the manufacturer should buy the machine if the real interest rate is assumed to remain constant at:

a. 5%.　　　　b. 10%.　　　c. 15%.

## 4. INVESTING IN EDUCATION

Suppose that at age 22, you have just finished university and have been offered a starting salary of $40,000. Your salary will remain constant in real terms. However, you have also enrolled in a professional school. The school takes two years to complete, and upon graduation, you expect your starting salary to be 10% higher in real terms and remain constant in real terms thereafter. The tax rate on labour income is 40%.

a. If the real interest rate is zero and you expect to retire at age 60 (that is, if you do not go to professional school, you expect to work for 38 years in total), what is the maximum you should be willing to pay in tuition to attend this professional school?

b. What should you pay in tuition for professional school if you expect to pay 30% of your income in taxes?

## 5. WEALTH ACCUMULATION

Suppose that every consumer is born with zero financial wealth and lives through three periods: youth, middle age, and retirement age. Consumers work in the first two periods and retire in the last one. Their income is $5 in the first period, $25 in the second, and $0 in the last one. Inflation and expected inflation are zero, and the real interest rate is also zero.

a. What is the present discounted value of future labour income at the beginning of life? What is the highest sustainable level of consumption such that consumption is equal in all three periods?

b. For each age group, what is the amount of saving that allows consumers to maintain the constant level of consumption you found in (a)? (*Hint:* Saving can be a negative number, if the consumer needs to borrow in order to maintain a certain level of consumption.)

c. Suppose there are $N$ people born each period. What is the total saving? (*Hint:* Compute the total amount saved by the generations that save and subtract the total amount dissaved by the generations that dissave.) Explain.

d. What is the total financial wealth in the economy? (*Hint:* Compute the financial wealth of people at the beginning of the first period of life, the second period of life, and the third period of life. Remember that people can be in debt, so financial wealth can be negative. Add them up.)

Suppose now that restrictions on borrowing do not allow young consumers to borrow. At each age group, consumers once again compute their total wealth and then determine their desired level of consumption as the highest level that allows their consumption to be equal in all three periods. However, if that is greater than their income plus their financial wealth, then they are constrained to consuming exactly their income plus their financial wealth.

**e.** Derive consumption in each period of life. Explain the difference from your answer to (a).

**f.** Derive total saving. Explain the difference, if any, from your answer to (c).

**g.** Derive total financial wealth. Explain the difference from your answer to (d).

**h.** "Financial liberalization may be good for people, but it is bad for overall capital accumulation." Discuss.

## 6. THE BUILDING OF NEW HOUSES

Suppose a family is trying to decide whether to build a new house. They find a lot that costs $120,000 and learn that building the house will cost $180,000. They have $40,000 saved to make a down payment.

**a.** Ignoring various other costs (legal fees, taxes, and the like), what is the size of mortgage required for this family to purchase this house?

**b.** Use a search engine to find a mortgage calculator and retrieve the monthly payment for this mortgage when the mortgage interest rate is 4% and the period of amortization (the length of time to repay the entire mortgage) is 25 years.

Use a search engine to find a mortgage calculator and retrieve the monthly payment for this mortgage when the mortgage interest rate is 6% and the period of amortization (the length of time to repay the entire mortgage) is 25 years.

Explain the effect of interest rates on the decision to purchase the house.

**c.** Suppose the family expects they will have to move in five years. They will sell this house and pay off the remaining mortgage. They have two expectations about the price of houses: when they are pessimistic they believe that house prices will fall by 1% each year for the next five years; when they are optimistic they believe that house prices will rise by 3% for the next five years. How much more money will they have in five years if the optimistic projection is correct? How does their belief about house price affect their decision to build the house?

## 7. MOVEMENTS IN CONSUMPTION AND INVESTMENT

For this exercise, you will need annual data on real consumption and real investment. Many of you will have access to the CANSIM II database from Statistics Canada. Retrieve to a spreadsheet (1) personal expenditure on goods and services (2) spending by firms on nonresidential structure and machinery. Both variables should be measured in constant dollars. Use your spreadsheet to carry out the following exercises:

**a.** On average, how much bigger is consumption than this measure of investment?

**b.** Compute the change in the levels of consumption and investment from one year to the next, and graph them for the period 1982–2012. Are the year-to-year changes in consumption and investment of the same magnitude?

**c.** What do your answers in (a) and (b) imply about the volatility of consumption and investment? Is this implication consistent with Figure 21–5?

**d.** There are two major recessions fully within the data, 1990–1991 and 2008–2009. Using your graph from part (b), which component played the largest role in each of these recessions—consumption or investment? Is this consistent with what we have learned so far about these recessions?

## FURTHER READING

A technical description of how wealth, disposable income, and consumption interact in Canada is found in Tiff Macklem, "Wealth, Disposable Income and Consumption: Some Evidence for Canada," *Bank of Canada Working Paper*, November 1994. This paper can be found, along with many others, at the Bank of Canada website (www.bankofcanada.ca).

# USING GRAPHS TO ILLUSTRATE CONSUMPTION DECISIONS WHEN EXPECTATIONS ARE IMPORTANT[1]

It is useful to represent the material in section 21-1 using graphs. Many of us are visual in our learning strategy. Using graphs, the consumer has only two periods in his planning horizon. We will call these periods 1 and 2; you can think of these two periods as the present and the future. With only two periods, we can apply the methods familiar to many students of a microeconomics course. We start with the choices available to the consumer when making consumption decisions over time. These are the consumer's budget lines. We then add indifference curves to this diagram; these curves represent how the consumer compares different points available for consumption. Finally, we address various macroeconomic events already discussed in section 21-1.

## What Choices Are Available to the Consumer?

In the text, we denoted after-tax labour income in period $t$ as $Y_{Lt} - T_t$. In period 1, this is known to the consumer and denoted $Y_{L1} - T_1$. In period 2, as of period 1, you expect after-tax labour income of $Y^e_{L2} - T^e_2$. Both are measured in real dollars. Real dollars represent baskets of goods that a consumer can buy. Taxes in both periods are usually zero in this appendix. For simplicity, we will measure everything in dollars where these are understood to represent baskets of goods consumers can buy. In the two-period case, there is one real interest rate, denoted $r$. Thus, if you lend \$1 (1 basket of goods) in period 1, you receive \$$(1 + r)$ (baskets of goods) in period 2. If you borrow \$1 in period 1, you repay \$$(1 + r)$ in period 2. Borrowing and lending rates are frequently different in the marketplace. For our purposes, this distinction is not important.

Figure 21A–1 shows a consumer with \$40 of after-tax labour income in period 1 and \$60 of expected after-tax labour income in period 2. This consumer expects an increase in labour income from now to the future—that is, an increase in after-tax income from period 1 to period 2. We will assume this consumer has no nonhuman wealth (later, we relax this assumption). The real interest rate is 7% from period 1 to period 2. The two incomes are marked as point $A$ on Figure 21A–1. What consumption choices can the consumer make from point $A$?

One choice is simply to consume the incomes in the period in which they are earned. Consumption would be \$40 in period 1 and \$60 in period 2. This is point $A$ on the diagram. This is not the only choice available to this consumer.

## FIGURE 21A–1

**Consumption Choices in the Two-Period Model**

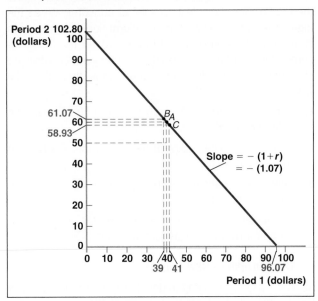

Point $A$ represents the after-tax labour income measured in real terms. This consumer earns \$40 in period 1 and expects to earn \$60 in period 2. The real interest rate, paid on loans and earned on savings, is 7%. The budget line shows how the consumer can save to reduce period 1 consumption and increase period 2 consumption. This is a movement from point $A$ to point $B$. The budget line also shows how the consumer can borrow to increase period 1 consumption but only at the cost of reduced period 2 consumption. This is a movement from point $A$ to point $C$.

He can certainly save \$1 of income in period 1. This means he consumes only \$39 in period 1 but is then able to consume \$61.07 in period 2. The \$1 he saved in period 1 earns 7 cents in interest and increases his consumption by \$1.07. He can also consume the principal on his savings in period 2. This is point $B$. He could save \$2 in period 1 and consume $2 \times (1.07) = \$2.14$ more in period 2. Note that the slope of the budget line is $-(1.07)$ or $-(1 + r)$, where the interest rate is written in decimal form. Thus, if the consumer makes the unlikely decision to consume nothing in period 1, the maximum possible consumption in period 2 is \$60 + $(1.07) \times \$40 = \$102.8$. This is the intercept of the vertical axis. The more interesting intercept is the intercept on the horizontal axis. From point $A$, the consumer could consume one more dollar in period 1. But he must borrow that dollar. If he borrows a dollar and increases consumption to \$41, then he must repay that dollar with interest, and consumption in the second period is reduced \$60 − $((1.07) \times \$1) = \$58.93$. This is point $C$ on the diagram. If he wants \$42 of consumption in period 1, then he must borrow $2 in period 1 and repay $2 × 1.07 = $2.14 in period 2. This leaves only $60 − $2.14 = $57.86 to consume in period 2. What is the maximum amount this consumer could consume in period 1? Suppose he promises a lender to repay a loan with all $60 of expected period 2 income. He cannot borrow $60 in period 1, as the lender would also want interest on the loan. The maximum amount he can borrow in period 1 is $60 divided by 1.07, or $56.07. The horizontal intercept, the maximum consumption possible in period 1 is:

$$\$40 + \$60/1.07 = \$40 + \$56.07 = \$96.07$$

This is an exact two-period representation of the expression (20.1) on page 401 in section 21-1, where the interest rate is positive and there are only two periods needed to calculate this person's human wealth. The more general formula is:

$$\text{Human wealth} = Y_{L1} + Y^e_{L2}/(1 + r) \quad (21A.1)$$

Human wealth is the present discounted value of expected after-tax labour income. Human wealth has a visual representation as the maximum consumption available in period 1 (using only after-tax labour income), where consumption in period 2 is zero. This concept generalizes so that wealth is the maximum consumption in the current period, consumption in period 1, when you plan to have zero consumption in all future periods. To fully generalize the concept, we also need to add nonhuman wealth to the diagram.

Adding nonhuman wealth to the diagram is quite straightforward. Suppose the nonhuman wealth of this consumer is $20, perhaps a bond or a mutual fund. It is denoted $F_1$, the subscript indicating this is nonhuman (financial) wealth in period 1. In Figure 21A–2, point $A$ is at $60 of consumption in period 2 and at $60 of consumption in period 1. Point $A$ is our label for a point where there is no lending or borrowing based on after-tax labour incomes. Why? If our consumer chooses to consume $60 in period 1, this uses $40 of after-tax labour income and the $20 of financial wealth. This exhausts his financial wealth. He has no debts and no assets entering period 2 and simply consumes all his after-tax labour income in period 2. We now use the same method as above to represent variation around point $A$.

Suppose that our consumer chooses to consume only $59 in period 1. Then, the $1 not consumed remains in financial wealth and earns 7% interest. Consumption in period 2 can rise to $60 + $1.07, marked as point $B$. Suppose that our consumer wants more than $60 of consumption in period 1. Point $C$ shows $61 of consumption in period 1. To obtain that much consumption in period 1, our consumer spends all his after-tax labour income, all his financial wealth, and borrows $1. That dollar must be repaid with interest so consumption in period 2 at point $C$ must be $60 − $1.07 or $58.93. We have now learned the slope of the choice line, the budget line, remains at −1.07

**Financial Wealth and Consumption Choices in the Two-Period Model**

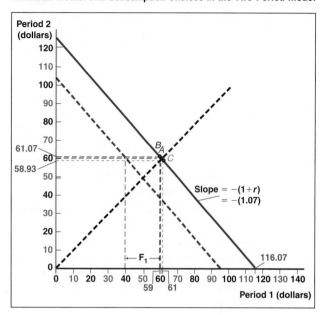

If the consumer above has financial wealth in period 1 equal to $20, then his consumption choices are enlarged. The budget line moves out horizontally by the amount of financial wealth.

or −(1 + r). What is the value of the horizontal intercept, the maximum possible consumption in period 1 if consumption in period 2 is zero? It is:

$$\$20 + \$40 + \$60/1.07 = \$116.07$$

Using the formula developed above and calling this intercept "wealth" because it is the maximum consumption available in period 1, we write:

$$\text{Wealth} = \text{Nonhuman wealth} + \text{Human wealth}$$

or in symbols:

$$W_1 = F_1 + Y_{L1} + Y^e_{L2}/(1 + r) \quad (21A.2)$$

If you substitute the values in the example above into the formula, you should get $116.07. Now that we have a graphical representation of the choices available to our consumer, we need a way to represent the choice actually made. Equation 21A.2 is the equation for the *budget line*. This line is the maximum amount of consumption available in period 2 for each choice of consumption in period 1 (or vice versa). With the budget line, we use another tool from microeconomics: indifference curves.

▲

Budget line: In a diagram of consumer choice, the budget line represents the choices available to the consumer. For a given value of consumption in period 1, the budget line is the largest value of consumption available in period 2.

## Representing Choices Using Indifference Curves

In Figure 21A–3, three indifference curves have been drawn. Each represents combinations of consumption in period 1 and period 2 where our consumer is indifferent—that is, does not have a preference among the points that are on the same indifference curve. Points *A*, *B*, *D*, and *E* are four such points on the middle curve in the figure. Moving from *A* to *B*, our consumer willingly gives up $1 of consumption in period 1 to receive $1.07 of consumption in period 2 and is equally happy. The slope of the indifference curve is $-1.07$. If consumers tend to prefer relatively equal amounts of consumption in both periods, then the indifference curves are "bowed in" to the origin. This is shown along the middle indifference curve by using two more points, points *D* and *E*. Note that this is a place where the consumer has a lot of period 1 consumption and not much period 2 consumption at point *D*. Thus, to move from *D* to *E*, one more dollar of period 1 consumption will occur only if very little (in the diagram only $0.30) period 2 consumption is lost. Another way to

say this is that the negative slope of the indifference curve is steepest where period 1 consumption is relatively low and flattest where period 1 consumption is relatively high. The slope is negative throughout. In order to be just as happy (indifferent), if you give up consumption in period 1, you require more consumption in period 2. An indifference curve that is further from the origin is one where the consumer is better off—that is, has more consumption in both periods. Moving from either point *A* or point *B* to point *C* is clearly an improvement, there is more consumption in both periods. An indifference curve where all points are worse is closer to the origin than the middle indifference curve. We think of an infinite number of *indifference curves* (although we drew only three) so that the consumer can rank every point in the diagram.

▲

Indifference curve: In the diagram of consumer choice, an indifference curve represents combinations of consumption in period 1 and consumption in period 2 that the consumer likes equally. Moving along an indifference curve does not increase or reduce the well being of the consumer. If the consumption of both goods increases, the well being of the consumer must improve and move the consumer to a higher indifference curve.

## FIGURE 21A–3

**Indifference Curves in the Two-Period Model**

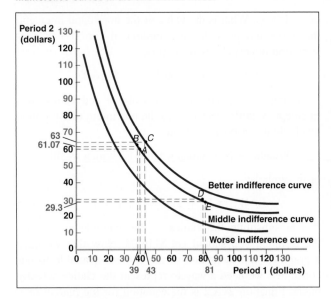

Indifference curves are combinations of points where the consumer is equally happy with either of the consumption choices. Along the middle indifference curve, the consumer finds points *A* and *B* equally satisfactory. Along the same curve, the consumer finds points *D* and *E* equally satisfactory. The "bowed to the origin shape" and the negative slope along a line implies that consumers generally prefer more equal consumption. Finally, any point on the indifference curve with the point *C* (a point clearly better than either point *A* or point *B* because there are more of both goods) are superior to all the points on the middle indifference curve.

There is a useful special case of indifference curves. These are drawn in Figure 21A–4. These are right-angled indifference curves, where the right angle passes through the 45° line. These "curves" say that this consumer strongly prefers equal consumption in the two periods, so much so that this consumer is *only* better off if he gets more consumption in both periods—that is, point *B* is better than point *A*, but point *C*, where there is more consumption in period 1 but the same amount of consumption in period 2 as at point *A*, is, from the point-of-view of this rather peculiar consumer, just the same as point *A*. These are quite silly indifference curves; most of us would think point *C* is clearly better than point *A*. At *C*, we have more consumption in period 1 than at point *A* and the same amount of period 2 consumption as at point *A*. But we actually used this kind of indifference curve in section 21-1 when we found "the constant level of consumption that you can afford" as the best choice. Using these peculiar indifference curves means that if equal consumption in each period of your life is a choice available, this is the choice that will be made. The case of equal consumption in all periods of your life is a choice where an algebraic solution is particularly easy. We will make this assumption when it is useful. We can put together the indifference curves for either the general case or the special case with the budget line to determine the consumer's choices. Then, we can conduct a series of macroeconomic experiments.

**Peculiar Indifference Curves**

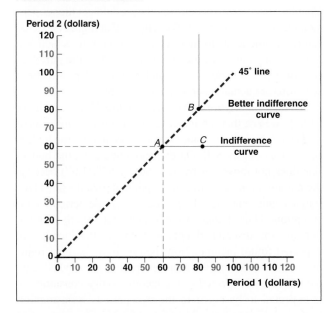

These indifference curves will lead consumers to always (if at all possible) choose equal consumption in both periods. These are useful in getting analytical solutions to our consumer problem. They are not very realistic; most of us would actually like point *C* better than point *A*, not the same as point *A*.

**The Best Consumption Choice Using General Indifference Curves**

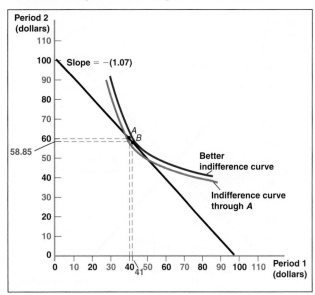

From point *A*, the consumer borrows. This increases period 1 consumption and reduces period 2 consumption. However, the activity of borrowing moves the consumer to an indifference curve that represents a higher level of well being; borrowing makes the consumer better off. Point *B* is on a better indifference curve than point *A*.

## Making the Best Available Choice

The general case is illustrated in Figure 21A–5. Using our first budget constraint from Figure 21A–1 (after-tax labour income in period 1 = $40, after-tax labour income in period 2 = $60, zero nonhuman wealth, real interest rate = 7%), if the consumer neither borrows nor lends, then consumption in period 1 is $40 and consumption in period 2 is $60. This is unlikely to be the best choice because if at all possible, most of us prefer fairly equal consumption across the periods of our life. Most people, for example, your parents, are saving for retirement. They are reducing consumption now and moving consumption to the future when after-tax labour income will be lower. Persons who win large lottery prizes usually spread the spending of their winnings over the rest of their lifetime. In Figure 21A–5, this desire to have more equal consumption is revealed. At point *A*, the slope of the indifference curve is clearly shown as −1.15. This consumer will give up, from point *A*, $1.15 of consumption in period 2 to get $1 more of consumption in period 1 and be just as happy. The cost to this consumer (the slope of the budget line) of an extra dollar of consumption in period 1 is $1.07 of consumption in period 2. When this consumer actually gives up $1.07 in period 2 consumption, he is able to move to an indifference curve that is

farther from the origin. Thus, this consumer will borrow from point *A* because the action of borrowing moves him to a higher indifference curve at *B*. At point *B* the slope of the indifference curve and the slope of the budget line are both −1.07, and this is the highest indifference curve this consumer can attain. This consumer borrowed in period 1 and repaid the loan in period 2 in order to make his consumption more equal between the two periods. Note that consumption in period 1 can be higher because the relatively high expected after-tax labour income in period 2 allows this consumer to borrow and then repay the loan.

Figure 21A–6 reworks this problem for the right-angle indifference curves in Figure 21A–4. These are convenient indifference curves because we know these curves will lead to our consumer choosing exactly equal consumption in the two periods. We also add financial wealth in period 1 to the problem. The best available consumption choice solves the equation:

$$C_1 + C_2^e/(1 + r) = [(2 + r)/(1 + r)]C$$
$$= F_1 + (Y_{L1} + Y_{L2}^e/(1 + r)) \qquad (21A.3)$$

so that:

$$C = [((1 + r)/(2 + r))] [F_1 + (Y_{L1} + Y_{L2}^e/(1 + r))] \qquad (21A.4)$$

**The Solution When Consumption Is Equal in Each Period**

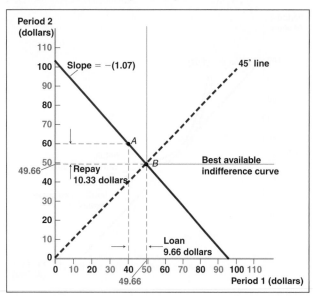

The right-angle indifference curve in Figure 21A–4 allows the analytical solution to the consumer's problem illustrated in this figure. Equal consumption means the choice made is along the 45° line. The consumer borrows in period 1 and repays the loan in period 2. The size of the loan is just enough to equalize consumption.

$C$ is the choice of consumption in both periods. This is an exact formula in the two-period case for the words in section 21-1—that is, that consumption could be written as a function of wealth:

$$\text{Consumption} = C(\text{Total wealth})$$
$$= [((1 + r)/(2 + r))] \times \text{Total wealth}$$

If we solve this for the following values: $F_1 = 0$; $r = 0.07$; $Y_{L1} = 40$; $Y^e_{L2} = 60$, then $C_1 = C_2 = C = 49.66$. A loan of $9.66 is taken out in period 1 and $1.07 \times \$9.66 = \$10.33$ is repaid in period 2. This is illustrated in Figure 21A–6. You might notice that when the interest rate is zero, this formula says consume half your wealth in period 1 and half your wealth in period 2. We used this result in section 21-1. We are now going to use graphs and this formula to consider the various macroeconomic events already considered in section 21-1.

### Higher Expected Future Income

Let us start from Figure 21A–1. Suppose that expected after-tax labour income in period 2 increases from $60 to $80. This is represented in Figure 21A–7 by a shift out in the budget line. The original budget line is dotted. An increase in expected future after-tax labour income could occur because of an expected tax cut, an increase in "consumer"

confidence" (you believe your income will increase as a recession comes to an end), or the introduction of the Canada Pension Plan in the 1960s. In that plan, discussed in Chapter 16, consumers believed they would get higher pension income on retirement. We will see that higher expected future income leads to more consumption now, which is a lower saving rate now, the effect predicted by the introduction of a pay-as-you-go national pension plan. All these scenarios are actual macroeconomic events.

Comparing Figure 21A–7 with Figure 21A–1 or Figure 21A–6, we see that the increase in expected future income moves the budget line out. On the vertical axis, the budget line moves out by $20. On the horizontal axis, the budget line does not move out by $20, but by $20/(1.07) because the maximum increase in consumption in period 1 must take into account repaying a loan used to increase period 1 consumption. Thus, human wealth and total wealth increase only by the discounted present value of the increase in expected future income. Nonetheless, if we assume right-angle indifference curves represent preferences and allocate the increase in expected future income so that consumption is expected to be equal in the two periods, consumption in period 1 rises from $49.66 to $59.32. To arrange this

**The Effect of an Increase in Expected Future Income**

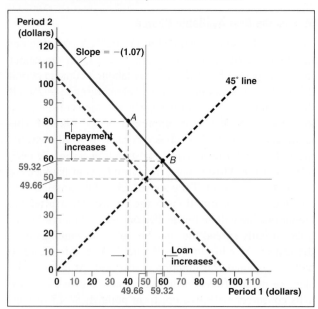

An increase in expected future income in period 2 will lead to an increase in consumption in period 1. This requires even more borrowing in period 1 and a larger loan repayment in period 2. The consumer is acting to equalize consumption across the two periods in this example using the right-angled indifference curves. The borrowing leads to a higher level of well being for the typical consumer.

increase in period 1 consumption, this consumer must borrow even more in period 1. We have learned two crucial facts. Consumption today will rise if income is expected to rise in the future. We have also learned that consumption today will not rise by the full increase in expected future income.

## The Effect of a Change in Nonhuman Wealth

We will use the same special case to explore the effect of a decrease in financial or nonhuman wealth. We will start from Figure 21A–2 and construct Figure 21A–8. In Figure 21A–2, our consumer had $40 of after-tax income in period 1, $60 of after-tax income expected in period 2, and $20 of financial wealth in period 1. Point A was the point where there was neither lending nor borrowing in period 1. It happens to be the point of equal consumption and, for the family of right-angled indifference curves, the best choice available. Suppose there is a stock-market crash so that as stock values fall, nonhuman wealth falls from $20 to $10. This will shift in the budget line by $10. The original budget line is dotted. Total wealth will also fall by $10. But

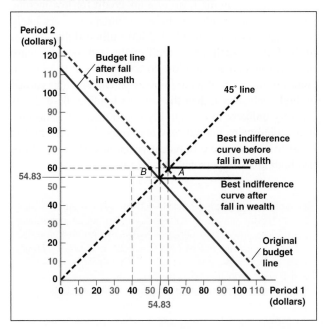

FIGURE 21A–8

**The Effect of a Reduction in Financial Wealth**

There are large fluctuations in financial wealth as stock prices and housing prices move. This figure explores the effect of such fluctuations on period 1 consumption. When financial wealth falls, so does period 1 consumption. The decrease in consumption is less than the decrease in financial wealth. Consumers try to maintain equal consumption in the two periods of their lives. If the second period represents a large number of future periods, then the effect of a fall in financial wealth on period 1 consumption may be quite small.

consumption in period 1 will not fall by $10. Using equation 21A–4, we find that consumption in both period 1 and period 2 (they are always equal) falls from $60.00 to $54.83. Our consumer, faced with a decline in financial wealth, acts such that consumption remains constant over the two periods. Note that this plan still requires our consumer to borrow $4.83 in period 1, repay $1.07 × $4.83 = $5.17 in period 2, and consume $60 − $5.17 = $54.83 in period 2.

This exercise teaches us a second important lesson. Fluctuations in financial wealth should lead to fluctuations in consumption, but not on a one-for-one basis. If we take period 2 to represent many future periods together, a large change in financial wealth may have only a small effect on consumption in period 1.

## When Our Consumer Cannot Borrow against Future Income

It is frequently the case that a consumer cannot borrow against her future after-tax labour income. Most loans to consumers that are of any size (that is beyond the loan in a credit card balance) are backed by some kind of physical collateral. Furthermore, the value of the loan is usually less than the value of the physical collateral. Buying a car requires a substantial down payment so that the balance of the loan is less than the resale value of the car. In this case, the lender is protected against the borrower losing his job or having a car accident. Purchasing a house requires a down payment so that the mortgage outstanding is less likely to exceed the value of the home. This arrangement puts the risk of house price fluctuations onto the borrower, not the lender. You or your friend may have a student loan outstanding. A student loan is truly a loan against expected future after-tax labour income. However, this loan market does not work without government intervention. Government steps in and guarantees at least the principal on your student loan. The bank or other lender has no other guarantee that you will not simply leave for a world tour after graduation and refuse to repay your loan. Thus, there are many persons in society who cannot borrow against future income and have no significant financial wealth available for current consumption.[2] The two-period diagram is very helpful in representing this situation.

Figure 21A–9 illustrates the following case: After-tax income in period 1 is quite low, only $25; but expected after-tax income in period 2 is much higher, $80. Current financial wealth is zero. This may be similar to your plans after graduation. Clearly, this consumer would like to be

---

[2]Many middle-aged persons do have significant financial wealth in the form of a future pension. However, this form of financial wealth cannot be reduced for current consumption. Many of you will find that quite early in your career, you will be required to join a pension plan. This forces you to have positive financial wealth even at a time in your life when you might not choose to be saving.

**The Two-Period Model When the Consumer Cannot Borrow against Expected Future After-Tax Labour Income**

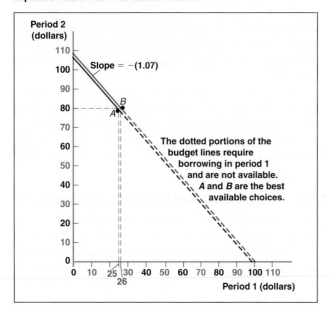

The dotted portions of the budget lines require borrowing in period 1 and are not available. A and B are the best available choices.

Many consumers cannot easily borrow against after-tax expected future income. If expected future income is high and current income low and the consumer cannot borrow against high expected future income (a common situation for many in society), then the best consumption plan available is to consume all period 1 income in period 1 and all period 2 income in period 2. The budget line is truncated so that it is possible only to increase period 2 consumption. Period 1 consumption cannot be increased. If one more dollar of period 1 income becomes available, then it will all be spent. This is illustrated in moving from point A to point B. This consumer's marginal propensity to consume out of additional period 1 income is 1.

able to borrow against expected after-tax labour income with nearly any shape of indifference curve you would draw. For equal expected consumption in the two periods with our usual 7% interest rate, this would require a loan of $26.57 in period 1. This loan would be in excess of our consumer's period 1 income, and unless the bank shared this person's knowledge and optimism about her future income, in all likelihood, this loan would be refused. While a small

loan might be granted, perhaps at a prohibitive rate, to keep the analysis simple, assume no loan is available to this consumer in period 1. In Figure 21A–9, this means while the consumer can save from her period 1 income and increase her consumption in period 2, she cannot borrow to increase the period 1 consumption. The dotted portion of the budget line is no longer available to her. The best choice available to this consumer is to consume all the period 1 income in period 1 and all the period 2 income in period 2. She can do no better. Many of us have been or are in exactly this situation. Why is this situation important to macroeconomists?

The consumer in Figure 21A–9, if given one additional dollar in period 1 income, will consume all that additional dollar in period 1. In Chapter 3, we made the argument that the average person in society, if given an extra dollar of after-tax income, will consume part of that extra dollar and save part of that extra dollar. This analysis tells us that some people in society, those who would like to borrow but cannot, will, in fact, consume all the extra dollars in income as consumption. This is illustrated in Figure 21A–9. This analysis tells us that the marginal propensity to consume in a society depends partly on the proportion of consumers who are *liquidity constrained*.

The concept of a liquidity-constrained consumer has very important practical implications. Who in society actually gets an increase in after-tax labour income matters! If a tax cut comes in the form of a tax credit for low-income parents of young children, these consumers are very likely to be liquidity constrained. A $500 million dollar tax cut in the form of such a tax credit might lead to an increase in aggregate demand of close to $500 million. If a tax cut comes in the form of a cut in taxes on capital gains earned on high-tech shares, then the persons holding these shares are very unlikely to be liquidity constrained. A $500 million capital gains tax cut may lead only to a $100 million boost in consumption. In recent years, in Canada, we have had both kinds of personal income tax reductions.

▲

Liquidity constrained: A liquidity-constrained consumer would like to borrow against future labour income but cannot obtain such a loan. The consequence of being liquidity constrained is: If such a consumer receives an extra dollar of after-tax income now, he increases consumption by one full dollar. Equivalently, if a liquidity constrained consumer expects to receive more income in the future, consumption now is not affected.

## SUMMARY

This appendix explores the use of graphs to illustrate consumption decisions when expectations matter. The graphs clarify the definition of wealth—wealth is consumption in period 1 of your life when consumption in all other periods is zero. The graphs show that an increase in expected

future income will increase consumption immediately. A reduction in financial wealth will reduce consumption immediately. Both effects are smaller than the change in expected income or the change in financial wealth respectively. Both effects occur because consumers try to equalize consumption between periods. Finally, the graphs illustrate the behaviour of a liquidity-constrained consumer. Such a consumer would like to borrow but cannot borrow. If he receives one extra dollar of after-tax income now, he increases consumption by one dollar immediately. These consumers play an important role in the transmission of aggregate demand changes.

## QUESTIONS AND PROBLEMS

### 1. TRUE/FALSE/UNCERTAIN

**a.** An increase in expected future after-tax labour income in period 2 usually leads to an increase in consumption in period 1.

**b.** An increase in period 1 after-tax labour income never leads to an equal increase in period 1 consumption.

**c.** An increase in the real interest rate must reduce human wealth and thus period 1 consumption.

**d.** An increase in financial wealth leads to an increase in period 1 consumption.

### 2. WHEN BORROWING AND LENDING RATES DIFFER

Start from Figure 21A–1. After-tax labour income in period 1 is $40 and after-tax labour income in period 2 is $60. Draw the budget line when the consumer can borrow at 10% but receives only 7% return on his savings from period 1 to period 2.

**a.** For the case of the right-angled indifference curves, work out the amount of borrowing when consumption is equal in period 1 and period 2.

**b.** Suppose there is more competition in the banking industry and the borrowing rate falls to 8%. Calculate the effect on period 1 consumption.

### 3. WHEN CONSUMERS ARE IMPATIENT

The case where consumption is equal in the two periods is an extreme case. Many of us are impatient and want our fun now. We can represent this by saying the period 1 consumption is always 5% larger than period 2 consumption.

**a.** Draw the right-angled indifference curves that are consistent with period 1 consumption being 5% higher than period 2 consumption.

**b.** For the case where the borrowing and lending rate are both equal to 7%, create the appropriate consumption function for period 1 consumption:

$$C_1 = C(\text{Total wealth}) = \alpha \times \text{Total wealth}$$

**c.** How does the value of the parameter $\alpha$ compare with its value in equation (21A.4)?

**d.** If a society becomes even more impatient, in the way suggested above, what happens to the value of the marginal propensity to consume out of period 1 after-tax labour income?

## APPENDIX B

# DERIVATION OF THE EXPECTED PRESENT VALUE OF PROFITS WHEN FUTURE PROFITS AND INTEREST RATES ARE EXPECTED TO BE THE SAME AS TODAY

We saw that the expected present value of profits is given by:

$$V(\Pi_t^e) = \frac{1}{1 + r_t} \Pi_{t+1}^e$$

$$+ \frac{1}{(1 + r_t)(1 + r_{t+1}^e)} (1 - \delta)\Pi_{t+2}^e + \cdots \quad (21\text{B}.1)$$

If firms expect both future profits (per unit of capital) and future interest rates to remain at the same level as today so that $\Pi_{t+1}^e = \Pi_{t+2}^e = \cdots = \Pi_t$, and $r_{t+1}^e = r_{t+2}^e = \cdots = r_t$, the equation becomes:

$$V(\Pi_t^e) = \frac{1}{1 + r_t} \Pi_t + \frac{1}{(1 + r_t)^2} (1 - \delta)\Pi_t + \cdots$$

Factoring out $[1/(1 + r_t)]\Pi_t$:

$$V(\Pi_t^e) = \frac{1}{1 + r_t} \Pi_t \left( 1 + \frac{1 - \delta}{1 + r_t} + \cdots \right)$$

The term in parentheses in this equation is a geometric series, a series of the form $1 + x + x^2 + \cdots$ where $x$ equals $(1 - \delta)/(1 + r_t)$. Thus, its sum is given by $1/(1 - x) = (1 + r_t)/(r_t + \delta)$. Replacing it in the equation above, we get:

$$V(\Pi_t^e) = \frac{1}{1 + r_t} \Pi_t \left( \frac{1 + r_t}{r_t + \delta} \right)$$

Simplifying gives the equation we use in the text:

$$V(\Pi_t^e) = \frac{\Pi_t}{(r_t + \delta)} \quad (21\text{B}.2)$$

# Expectations, Output, and Policy

## Expectations

In Chapter 20, we saw how expectations affected the determination of bond and stock prices. In Chapter 21, we saw how expectations affected consumption and investment decisions. Now, in this chapter, we put the pieces together and take another look at the effects of monetary and fiscal policies.

Section 22-1 draws the major implication of what we have learned, namely, that expectations of both future income and future interest rates affect current spending and therefore affect current output. Section 22-2 looks at monetary policy. It shows how the effects of monetary policy depend crucially on how expectations respond to policy: Monetary policy affects only the current interest rate. What happens to spending and output then depends on how changes in the current interest rate lead people and firms to change their expectations of future interest rates and of future income and, by implication, lead them to change their investment and consumption decisions. Section 22-3 turns to fiscal policy. It shows that in sharp contrast to the simple model we discussed in the core, a fiscal contraction may, under the right circumstances, lead to an increase in output, even in the short run. Again, how expectations respond to policy is at the centre of the story.

## 22-1 | Expectations and Decisions: Taking Stock

Let us start by reviewing what we have learned and discuss how we should modify the characterization of goods and financial markets—the *IS-LM* model—we developed in the core.

### Expectations and the *IS* Relation

The theme of Chapter 21 was that both consumption and investment decisions very much depend on expectations of future income and interest rates. The channels through which expectations affect consumption and investment spending are summarized in Figure 22–1.

A model that gave a detailed treatment of consumption and investment along the lines shown in Figure 22–1 could be very complicated, and although this can be done—and, indeed, is done in the large empirical models that macroeconomists build to understand the economy and analyze policy—this is not the place to try. We want to capture the essence of what we have learned so far—the dependence of consumption and investment on expectations of the future—without getting lost in the details.

To do so, we make a major simplification that we also made in the appendix to Chapter 21. We reduce the present and the future to only two periods: (1) a *current* period, which you can think of as the current year, and (2) a *future* period, which you can think of as all future years lumped together. This way we do not have to keep track of expectations about each ◀ future year.

> This way of dividing time between "today" and "later" is the way many of us organize our own lives: Think of "things to do today" versus "things that can wait."

Having made this assumption, how should we then write the *IS* relation for the current period? Let us go back to the *IS* relation we wrote down before thinking about the role of ◀ expectations in consumption and investment decisions:

> This is the equation we saw in Chapter 19, where we introduced the distinction between real and nominal interest rates.

$$Y = C(Y - T) + I(Y, r) + G$$

Goods-market equilibrium requires that output be equal to aggregate spending—the sum of consumption spending, investment spending, and government spending. Before we introduce expectations into this equation, it will prove convenient to rewrite it in more compact form, but without changing its content. Let us define:

$$A(Y, T, r) \equiv C(Y - T) + I(Y, r)$$

where *A* stands for **aggregate private spending**, or, simply, *private spending*. With this nota- ◀ tion we can rewrite the *IS* relation as:

> The reason for doing so is to regroup the two components of demand, *C* and *I*, which both depend on expectations. We continue to treat *G*, government spending, as exogenous—unexplained within our model.

$$Y = A(Y, T, r) + G \qquad (22.1)$$
$$(+, -, -)$$

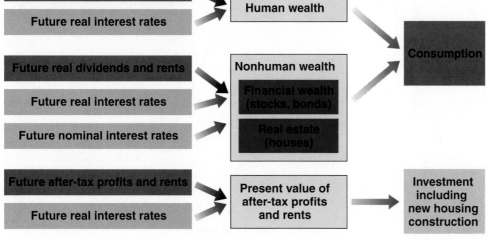

### FIGURE 22-1

**Expectations and Spending: The Channels**

Expectations affect consumption and investment decisions, both directly and through asset values.

The properties of aggregate private spending, $A$, follow from the properties of consumption and investment that we laid down in earlier chapters:

- Aggregate private spending is an increasing function of income, $Y$: Higher income (equivalently, output) increases consumption and investment.
- It is a decreasing function of taxes, $T$: Higher taxes decrease consumption.
- It is a decreasing function of the real interest rate, $r$: A higher real interest rate decreases investment, including investment in new houses.

All we have done so far is simplify notation. Now, we need to extend equation (22.1) to reflect the role of expectations. The natural extension is to allow spending to depend not only on current variables, but also on their expected values in the future period, thus:

$$Y = A(Y, T, r, Y'^e, T'^e, r'^e) + G \qquad (22.2)$$
$$(+, -, -, +, -, -)$$

Notation: Primes stand for values of the variables in the future period. The superscript "$e$" stands for "expected." ▶

Primes denote future values and the superscript "$e$" denotes an expectation, where $Y'^e$, $T'^e$, and $r'^e$ denote expected future income, expected future taxes, and the expected future real interest rate, respectively. The notation is a bit heavy, but what it captures is straightforward:

$Y$ or $Y'^e \uparrow \Rightarrow A \uparrow$
$T$ or $T'^e \uparrow \Rightarrow A \downarrow$
$r$ or $r'^e \uparrow \Rightarrow A \downarrow$

▶
- Increases in either current or expected future income increase private spending.
- Increases in either current or expected future taxes decrease private spending.
- Increases in either the current or expected future real interest rate decrease private spending.

With goods-market equilibrium now given by equation (22.2), Figure 22–2 shows the new *IS* curve. As usual, to draw the curve, we take all variables other than current output, $Y$, and the current real interest rate, $r$, as given. Thus, the *IS* curve is drawn for given values of current and future expected taxes, $T$ and $T'^e$, for given values of expected future output, $Y'^e$, and for given values of the expected future real interest rate, $r'^e$.

The new *IS* curve is still downward sloping, and the reason is the same as before: A decrease in the current real interest rate leads to an increase in spending, which leads, through a multiplier effect, to an increase in output. We can say more, however: The new *IS* curve is much steeper than the *IS* curve we drew in earlier chapters. Put another way, a large decrease in the current interest rate is likely to have only a small effect on equilibrium output.

## FIGURE 22–2

**The New *IS* Curve**

Given expectations, a decrease in the real interest rate leads to a small increase in output. Increases in government spending, or in expected future output, shift the *IS* curve to the right. Increases in taxes, in expected future taxes, or in the expected future real interest rate shift the *IS* curve to the left.

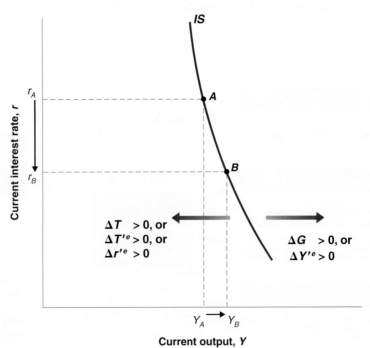

To see why, take point $A$ on the $IS$ curve in Figure 22–2, and consider the effects of a decrease in the real interest rate. The effect of the decrease in the real interest rate on output depends on the strength of two effects: (1) the effect of the real interest rate on spending, given income, and (2) the size of the multiplier. Let us examine each one.

- A decrease in the current real interest rate, *given unchanged expectations of the future real interest rate*, does not have much effect on spending. We saw why in the previous chapters: A change in only the current real interest rate does not lead to large changes in present values and so does not lead to large changes in spending. For example, firms are not likely to change their investment plans very much in response to a decrease in the current real interest rate if they do not expect future real interest rates to be lower as well.

  *In terms of derivatives, $A_r$ is small (in absolute value).*

- The multiplier is likely to be small. Recall that the size of the multiplier depends on the size of the effect of a change in current income (output) on spending. But a change in current income, *given unchanged expectations of future income*, is unlikely to have a large effect on spending. The reason is that changes in income that are not expected to last have only a limited effect on both consumption and investment. Consumers who expect their income to be higher only for a year will increase consumption, but by much less than the increase in income. Firms expecting sales to be higher only for a year are unlikely to change their investment plans very much.

  *In terms of derivatives, $A_Y$ is small.*

Putting things together, a large decrease in the current real interest rate, from $r_A$ to $r_B$ in Figure 22–2, leads to only a small increase in output, from $Y_A$ to $Y_B$. The $IS$ curve, which goes through points $A$ and $B$, is steeply downward sloping.

Changes in current taxes ($T$) or in government spending ($G$) shift the $IS$ curve. An increase in current government spending increases spending at a given interest rate, shifting the $IS$ curve to the right; an increase in taxes shifts the $IS$ curve to the left. These shifts are represented in Figure 22–2.

Changes in expected future variables also shift the $IS$ curve. An increase in expected future output, $Y'^e$, shifts the $IS$ curve to the right: Higher expected future income leads consumers to feel wealthier and consume more. Higher expected future output implies higher expected profits, leading firms to invest more. Higher expected future income would encourage households to build new homes. By a similar argument, an increase in expected future taxes leads consumers to decrease current spending and shifts the $IS$ curve to the left. And an increase in the expected future real interest rate decreases current spending, shifting the $IS$ curve to the left. These shifts are also represented in Figure 22–2. Figure 22-2 does not show all possible shift factors in the new IS curve. A current tax cut, for example, would shift the curve to the right.

## The *LM* Relation Revisited

The *LM* relation we derived in Chapter 4 and have used until now was given by:

$$\frac{M}{P} = Y L(i) \tag{22.3}$$

where $M/P$ is the supply of money and $Y L(i)$ is the demand for money. Equilibrium in financial markets requires that the supply of money be equal to the demand for money. The demand for money depends on real income and on the short-term nominal interest rate—the opportunity cost of holding money. We derived this demand for money before thinking about expectations. Now that we have, the question is: Should we modify equation (22.3)? The answer—we are sure this will be good news—is no.

Think of your own demand for money. How much money you want to hold today depends on your *current* level of transactions, not on the level of transactions you expect next year or the year after; there will be time to adjust your money balances to your transaction level if it changes in the future. And the opportunity cost of holding money today depends on the *current* nominal interest rate, not on the expected nominal interest rate next year or the year after. If short-term interest rates were to increase in the future, increasing the opportunity cost of holding money, the time to reduce your money balances would not be now.

So, in contrast to the consumption decision, the decision about how much money to hold is myopic, depending primarily on current income and the current short-term nominal interest rate. We can still think of the demand for money as depending on the current level of output and the current nominal interest rate and use equation (22.3) to describe the determination of the nominal interest rate in the current period.

To summarize: We have seen that expectations about the future play a major role in spending decisions. This implies that expectations enter the *IS* relation: Private spending depends not only on current output and the current real interest rate, but also on expected future output and the expected future real interest rate. In contrast, the decision about how much money to hold is largely myopic: The two variables entering the *LM* relation are still current income and the current nominal interest rate.

## 22-2 | Monetary Policy, Expectations, and Output

In the basic *IS-LM* model, there was only one interest rate, *i*, which entered both the *IS* relation and the *LM* relation. When the Bank of Canada expanded the money supply, "the" interest rate went down and spending increased. From the previous three chapters, we have learned that there are, in fact, many interest rates and that we must keep two distinctions in mind:

● The distinction between the nominal interest rate and the real interest rate
● The distinction between current and expected future interest rates

The interest rate that enters the *LM* relation, and thus the interest rate that the Bank of Canada affects directly, is the *current nominal interest rate*. In contrast, spending in the *IS* relation depends on both *current and expected future real interest rates*. Economists sometimes state this distinction even more starkly by saying that although the Bank of Canada controls the *short-term nominal interest rate*, what matters for spending and output is the *long-term real interest rate*.

Let us look at this more closely. Recall from Chapter 19 that the real interest rate is approximately equal to the nominal interest rate minus expected current inflation—inflation expected, as of today, for the current period:

$$r = i - \pi^e$$

Similarly, the expected future real interest rate is approximately equal to the expected future nominal interest rate minus expected future inflation—inflation expected, as of today, for the future period.

$$r'^e = i'^e - \pi'^e$$

When the Bank of Canada increases money supply, therefore decreasing the current nominal interest rate, *i*, the effect on the current and the expected future real interest rates depends on two factors:

● Whether the increase in money supply leads financial markets to revise their expectations of the future nominal interest rate, $i'^e$, as well.
● Whether the increase in money supply leads financial markets to revise their expectations of current and future inflation, $\pi^e$ and $\pi'^e$. If, for example, the change in money leads them to expect more inflation in the future, the expected future real interest rate, $r'^e$, will decrease by more than the expected future nominal interest rate, $i'^e$.

For the moment, we will leave aside the second factor, the role of changing expectations of inflation, and focus on the first, the role of changing expectations of the future nominal interest rate. Thus, we will assume that expected current and future inflation are both equal to zero $\pi^e = \pi^{e'} = 0$. In this case, we need not distinguish between the nominal and the real interest rates, as they are equal, and we can use the same letter to denote both.

We explored the role of changing expectations of inflation on the relation between the nominal interest rate and the real interest rate in Chapter 19. Leaving changes in expected inflation aside will keep the analysis simpler here. You have, however, all the elements you need to think through what would happen if we also allowed expectations of current inflation and future inflation to adjust in response to an increase in money supply. How would these expectations adjust? Would this lead to a larger or a smaller effect on output in the current period?

Let $r$ and $r'^e$ denote the current and expected future real (and nominal) interest rates. With this simplification, we can rewrite the $IS$ and $LM$ relations in equations (22.2) and (22.3) as:

$$IS: \quad Y = A(Y, T, r, Y'^e, T'^e, r'^e) + G \qquad (22.4)$$

$$LM: \quad \frac{M}{P} = Y L(r) \qquad (22.5)$$

The $IS$ relation is unchanged. The $LM$ relation is now in terms of the real interest rate, which, here, is equal to the nominal interest rate.

The corresponding $IS$ and $LM$ curves are drawn in Figure 22–3(a). The vertical axis measures the current interest rate, $r$; the horizontal axis measures current output, $Y$. The $IS$ curve is downward sloping and steep. We saw the reason earlier: For given expectations, a change in the current interest rate has a limited effect on spending, and the multiplier is small. The $LM$ curve is upward sloping. An increase in income leads to an increase in the demand for money; given the supply of money, the result is an increase in the interest rate.

There is no need in this case to distinguish here between real and nominal interest rates: Given zero expected inflation, they are the same.

Now, suppose that at point $A$, the economy is in a recession, and the Bank of Canada decides to increase the money supply. Assume for the moment this expansionary monetary policy does not change expectations of either the future interest rate or future output. In Figure 22–3(b),

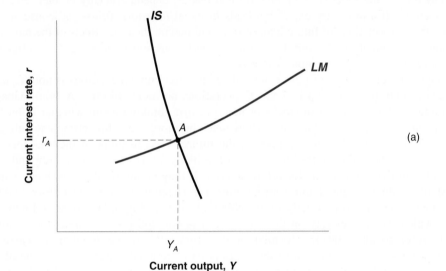

(a)

(b)

**FIGURE 22–3**

**The Effects of an Expansionary Monetary Policy**

(a) The equilibrium is determined by the intersection of the $IS$ and the $LM$ curves. (b) The effects of monetary policy on output depend very much on whether and how monetary policy affects expectations.

LM shifts down to LM". (Because we already use primes to denote future values of the variables, we will use double primes [such as in LM"] to denote shifts in curves in this chapter.) The equilibrium moves from point A to point B, with higher output and a lower interest rate. The steep IS curve, however, implies that the increase in money has only a small effect on output: Changes in the current interest rate, unaccompanied by changes in expectations, have only a small effect on spending and, in turn, on output.

But is it reasonable to assume that expectations are unaffected by an expansionary monetary policy? Is it not likely that as the Bank of Canada decreases the current interest rate, financial markets anticipate lower interest rates in the future as well, along with higher future output stimulated by this lower future interest rate? What happens if they do? At a given current interest rate, prospects of a lower future interest rate and of higher future output both increase spending and output; they shift the IS curve to the right, from IS to IS". The new equilibrium is given by point C. Thus, although the direct effect of the expansion in money on output is limited, the full effect, once changes in expectations are taken into account, is much larger.

To summarize: We have just learned something important. The effects of monetary policy (of any type of macroeconomic policy for that matter) depend crucially on their effect on expectations. If a monetary expansion leads financial investors, firms, and consumers to revise their expectations of future interest rates and output, then the effects of the monetary expansion on output may be very large. But if expectations remain unchanged, the effects of the monetary expansion on output will be small.

Saying that the effect of policy depends on its effect on expectations is not the same as saying that anything can happen. Expectations are not arbitrary. A fund manager deciding whether to invest in stocks or bonds, a firm thinking about whether to build a new plant, a consumer thinking about how much he should save for retirement—all give a lot of thought to what may happen in the future. We can think of them as forming expectations about the future by assessing the likely course of future policy and then working out the implications for future activity. If they do not do it themselves—surely most of us do not spend our time solving macroeconomic models before making decisions—they do so indirectly by watching TV and reading newsletters and newspapers, which themselves rely on the forecasts of public and private forecasters. Economists refer to expectations formed in this forward-looking manner as **rational expectations**. The introduction of the assumption of rational expectations is one of the most important developments in macroeconomics in the last 25 years and is discussed further in the Focus box "Rational Expectations."

The Focus box "The Liquidity Trap, Quantitative Easing, and the Role of Expectations" adds to the monetary policy mix. Here it is explicit that policy at hand directly affects expectations of inflation and, indeed, does not work unless it affects expectations of inflation. It will not surprise students to learn this becomes particularly important in the case of the liquidity trap.

We could go back and think about the implications of rational expectations in the case of the monetary expansion we have just studied. It will be more fun to do this in the context of a change in fiscal policy, and this is what we now turn to.

## 22-3 | Deficit Reduction, Expectations, and Output

Recall the conclusions we reached in the core about the effects of a budget deficit reduction:

- In the medium run and the long run, a budget deficit reduction is likely to be beneficial for the economy. In the medium run, a lower budget deficit leads to higher investment. In the long run, higher investment translates into higher output.
- In the short run, however, unless it is offset by a monetary expansion, a reduction of the budget deficit leads to a reduction in spending, and thus to a contraction in output.

Given expectations, an increase in money supply leads to a shift in the LM and a movement down the steep IS. This leads to a large decrease in r, and a small increase in Y.

If the increase in money supply leads to an increase in $Y^e$ and a decrease in $r^e$, the IS curve shifts to the right, leading to a larger increase in Y.

See section 10-5 for the analysis of short- and medium-run effects, and section 16-2 for the analysis of long-run effects—through the effect on the saving rate and, in turn, on capital accumulation.

Most macroeconomists today routinely solve their models under the assumption of rational expectations. But this was not always the case. Indeed the two decades after 1970 in macroeconomics are often labelled the "rational expectations" revolution.

The importance of expectations is an old theme in macro-economics. But until the early 1970s, macroeconomists thought of expectations in one of two ways:

1. One was as **animal spirits** (from an expression Keynes introduced in the *General Theory* to refer to movements in investment that could not be explained by movements in current variables): Shifts in expectations were considered important but largely unexplained.

2. The other was as simple: backward-looking rules. For example, people were often assumed to have **adaptive expectations** (an assumption we used in Chapter 10 and Chapter 13), to assume that if their income had grown fast in the past it would continue to do so in the future, to revise their expectations of future inflation upward if they had underpredicted in the past, and so on.

In the early 1970s, a group of macroeconomists led by Robert Lucas and Thomas Sargent argued that these assumptions did not do justice to the way people form expectations. (Lucas received the Nobel prize in 1995 for his work on expectations.) They argued that in thinking about the effects of alternative policies, economists should assume that people have rational expectations, that people look to the future and do the best job they can in predicting it. This is not the same as assuming that people know the future but rather that they use the information they have in the best possible way.

Using the popular macroeconomic models of the time, Lucas and Sargent showed how replacing traditional assumptions about expectations formation with the assumption of rational expectations would fundamentally alter the results. We saw, for example, in Chapter 13 how Lucas challenged the notion that disinflation necessarily required an increase in unemployment for some time. Under rational expectations, he argued, a credible disinflation policy might decrease inflation without any increase in unemployment. More generally, Lucas and Sargent's research showed the need for a complete rethinking of macroeconomic models under the assumption of rational expectations, and this is what has happened since.

Most macroeconomists today use the assumption of rational expectations as a working assumption in their models and in their analyses of policy. This is not because they believe that people always have rational expectations. Surely, there are times when people, firms, or financial market participants lose sight of reality and become too optimistic or too pessimistic. Recall the discussion of bubbles in Chapter 20. The events of the crisis have made it clear that economists need to pay more attention to these events. However we also saw that it may be difficult to be sure whether a bubble exists.

In thinking about the likely effects of a particular economic policy, the best assumption to make seems to be that financial markets, people, and firms will do the best they can to work out its implications. Designing a policy on the assumption that people will make systematic mistakes in responding to it is unwise.

So, why did it take several decades following 1970 for rational expectations to become a standard assumption in macroeconomics? Largely because of technical problems. Under rational expectations, what happens today depends on expectations of what will happen in the future. But what happens in the future depends on what happens today. The success of Lucas and Sargent in convincing most macroeconomists to use rational expectations comes not only from the strength of their case, but also from showing how it could actually be done. Much progress has been made since in developing solution methods for larger and larger models. Today, several large macroeconometric models are solved under rational expectations. (We presented a simulation from such a model in Chapter 10. We will see another example in Chapter 23.)

---

It is this adverse short-run effect that—in addition to the unpopularity of increases in taxes or reductions in transfers or in other government programs—has often deterred governments from tackling their budget deficit: Why take the risk of a recession now for benefits that will accrue only in the future?

In the past 10 years, however, a number of economists have questioned this conclusion and have argued that a deficit reduction may actually increase output even in the *short run*. Their basic argument is simple: If people take into account the future beneficial effects of deficit reduction, their expectations about the future may improve enough to lead to an increase rather than a decrease in current spending and so an increase in current output. This section presents their argument formally. The Focus box "Can a Budget Deficit Reduction Lead to an Output Expansion? Some Evidence from Ireland and Other Countries" reviews some of the supporting evidence on this proposition and, to be fair, finds the results for Ireland are *not* the usual result. The evidence is that most "austerity" programs have involved a period of slower growth or a recession. This is, of course, the situation we have focused on in previous chapters.

> The term "austerity" is in common use to describe any program of fiscal consolidation where spending is reduced, transfers are reduced, or taxes are increased as a government tries to reduce its deficit.

The scope for conventional monetary policy, namely a reduction in the nominal short-term interest rate, simply disappeared in several major economies after 2008. From the end of 2008 through 2013, the nominal short-term interest rate was close to zero in the United States. In Japan, interest rates have been less than half a percent since 2000 and, as of 2013, were once again at zero. Both economies are in a liquidity trap. This has led the Fed and, more recently, the Bank of Japan to explore unconventional policies. These policies come by the name of "quantitative easing" or "credit easing." These policies can be thought of an attempt to alter expectations in two ways. We look at them more closely here.

First, the semantics: Economists typically refer to "quantitative easing" to denote operations in which, when the interest rate is already zero and the economy is in the liquidity trap, the central bank continues to increase the money supply through open market operations, either by buying more T-bills or by buying longer-maturity government bonds. The purpose of quantitative easing is to increase the money supply even when interest rates cannot be lowered further. Economists apply the term "credit easing" to operations in which the central bank buys a specific type of asset; for example, mortgage-backed securities, or even stocks. The focus is then not so much on the increase in the money supply, but on the effects of the price or the interest rate on the specific asset being bought. Both types of policies go under the name of "unconventional" monetary policy.

Why should such operations have any effect? We have seen that once the interest rate is zero, monetary policy cannot reduce the current interest rate any further. As both bonds and money paid the same nominal interest rate, namely zero, people willingly held more money and fewer bonds in response to an open market operation, leaving the nominal interest rate unchanged and equal to zero. Economists have identified three channels through which quantitative or credit easing may affect the economy:

- Arbitrage may not hold. Investors may, for example, think that an asset is so risky that they do not want to hold it at all. Or, and this happened during the crisis, investors may be short of funds and may have to sell the asset, even if they want to keep it. In this case, by doing credit easing, (i.e., by buying the asset), the central bank can replace these investors, increase the price of the asset, and decrease the associated interest rate. Or, to take another example, if banks, for the reasons we saw in Chapter 11, suddenly lose some of their funding and are forced in turn to ration loans and turn down some borrowers, the central bank may be able to finance some of the borrowers. In short, when arbitrage fails, credit easing can work.
- Quantitative easing may affect expectations of future nominal interest rates. As this chapter makes clear, given inflation expectations, what matters is not so much the current nominal interest rate as the future nominal interest rates. If the increase in the money supply is taken as a signal by markets that the central bank will continue to follow a very expansionary monetary policy in the future, and thus keep nominal interest rates low for a long time,

this will increase spending today. The Focus box in Chapter 20 "The Yield Curve in Canada and the United States in 2013" showed that the policy may have been effective in the United States in 2013.

- Quantitative easing may affect expectations of inflation. In the strange world of the liquidity trap, higher expected inflation is good, as it leads to lower current and future expected real interest rates. Thus, if the large increase in the money supply leads people to expect more inflation in the future, this will also increase spending today. On January 22, 2013, a Joint Statement from the government in Japan and the Bank of Japan formally increased the target for inflation in Japan from 1% to 2% as measured by the Consumer Price Index.

None of these channels is a sure thing. The first is more likely to work during the acute phase of a crisis, when perceptions of risk are high and some investors have to sell assets in a hurry. The other two work through expectations and are far from mechanical. If expectations of either future nominal interest rates or of inflation do not move, easing will have no effect on spending, and in turn no effect on output.

What does the evidence suggest? To answer, we can look at what has happened in the United States during the crisis. Once the room for conventional monetary policy was exhausted, the Fed decided to use both credit and quantitative easing. In November 2008, it started a program known as **Quantitative Easing I, or QEI**, in which it purchased large amounts of mortgage-backed securities. (A more appropriate name for the program would be Credit Easing I, as the purpose was clearly to decrease the interest rate on those particular assets, assets that private investors no longer wanted to hold.) In August 2010, in what is known as **Quantitative Easing II, or QEII**, the Fed started purchasing long-term government bonds, further increasing the money supply. Figure 1 shows the size and the composition of the assets held by the Fed since 2007. There are three zones. The Fed purchased large amounts of mortgage-backed securities and a few other assets. These are labeled "Credit market interventions." The Fed purchased large amounts of long-term government bonds, labeled "Government securities excluding T-bills." The Fed made direct loans to bank and non-bank financial institutions during the acute phase of the crisis. These are labeled "Liquidity facilities." You can see how, as a result of these purchases, central bank money has more than tripled in size, from roughly 6% of GDP in 2007 to nearly 20% of GDP in 2011! Has this massive increase had an effect on interest rates, either on MBS or on long-term bonds? Most of the research concludes that it has, but that the effects have been relatively modest, perhaps on the order of a decrease of 0.5% for the interest rate on long-term bonds. The effect on inflation expectations is harder to assess, but the good news is that expected inflation has remained positive, avoiding the deflation spiral that took place during the Great Depression (see the Focus box "Why Deflation Can Be Very Bad: Deflation and the Real Interest Rate in America During the Great Depression" in Chapter 19). There is, of course, no evidence on the policy change in Japan that started in 2013.

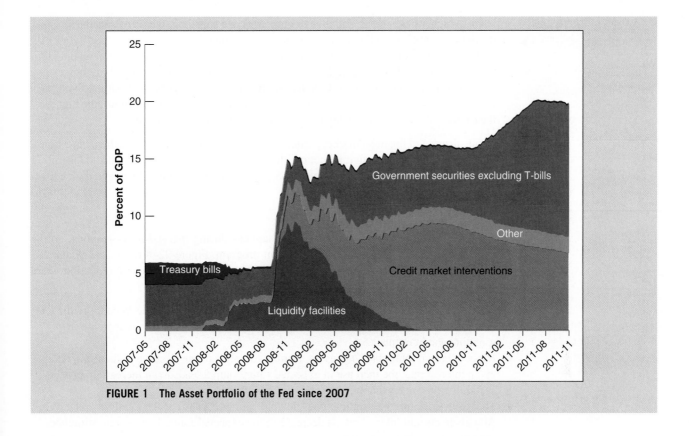

25 ─

20 ─

**Percent of GDP**

15 ─

Government securities excluding T-bills

10 ─

Other

5 ─

Treasury bills

Credit market interventions

Liquidity facilities

0 ─

2007-05 2007-08 2007-11 2008-02 2008-05 2008-08 2008-11 2009-02 2009-05 2009-08 2009-11 2010-02 2010-05 2010-08 2010-11 2011-02 2011-05 2011-08 2011-11

**FIGURE 1    The Asset Portfolio of the Fed since 2007**

Assume the economy is described by equation (22.4) for the *IS* relation and equation (22.5) for the *LM* relation. Now, suppose that government announces a program to reduce the deficit, through decreases both in current spending, $G$, and in future spending, $G'^e$. What will happen to output during *this period*? Is it even possible that output could rise this period?

## The Role of Expectations about the Future

Suppose first that expectations of future output ($Y'^e$) and of the future interest rate ($r'^e$) do not change. Then we get the standard answer, the decrease in government spending in the current period leads to a shift in the *IS* curve to the left, and thus to a decrease in equilibrium output. The crucial question therefore is: What happens to expectations? To answer, let us go back to what we learned in the core about the effects of a deficit reduction in the medium run and the long run:

● In the medium run, a deficit reduction has no effect on output. It leads, however, to a lower interest rate and to higher investment. These were two of the main lessons of Chapter 10. Let us review the logic behind each one.

   Recall that when we look at the medium run, we ignore the effects of capital accumulation on output. Thus, in the medium run, the natural level of output depends on the level of productivity (taken as given) and on the natural level of employment. The natural level of employment depends on the natural rate of unemployment. If spending by government on goods and services does not affect the natural rate of unemployment—and there is no obvious reason why it should—then changes in spending will not affect the natural level of output. Thus, deficit reduction has no effect on the level of output in the medium run.

   Now, recall that output must be equal to spending, which itself is the sum of public and private spending. Given that output is unchanged and that public spending is lower, private spending must be higher. This requires a lower interest rate: A lower interest rate

In the medium run: Y does not change, $I\uparrow$

In the long run, $I\uparrow \Rightarrow K\uparrow \Rightarrow Y\uparrow$

leads to higher investment, and thus to higher private spending, which offsets the decrease in public spending and leaves output unchanged.

- In the long run—that is, taking into account the effects of capital accumulation on output—higher investment leads to a higher capital stock, and thus to a higher level of output.

This was the main lesson of Chapter 16: the higher the proportion of output saved (or invested, as the two must be equal for the goods market to be in equilibrium), the higher the capital stock, and thus the higher the level of output in the long run.

If people, firms, and financial market participants have rational expectations, then, in response to the announcement of a deficit reduction, they will expect these developments to take place in the future. Thus, they will revise their expectation of future output ($Y'^e$) up and their expectation of the future interest rate ($r'^e$) down.

## Back to the Current Period

We can now return to the question of what happens during *this period* in response to the announcement and start of the deficit reduction program. Figure 22–4 draws the *IS* and *LM* curves for the current period. In response to the announcement of the deficit reduction, there are now three factors shifting the *IS* curve:

- Current government spending ($G$) goes down, leading to a shift of the *IS* curve to the left. At a given interest rate, the decrease in government spending leads to a decrease in spending and in output.
- Expected future output ($Y'^e$) goes up, leading to a shift of the *IS* curve to the right. At a given interest rate, the increase in expected future output leads to an increase in private spending, thus increasing output.
- The expected future interest rate goes down, leading to a shift of the *IS* curve to the right. At a given current interest rate, a decrease in the expected future interest rate stimulates spending and increases output.

What is the net effect of these three shifts in the *IS* curve? Can the effect of expectations on consumption and investment spending offset the decrease in government spending? Without much more information about the exact form of the *IS* and *LM* relations and about the details of the deficit reduction program, we cannot tell which shifts will dominate and whether output will go up or down. But our theoretical analysis tells us that both cases are possible, that output may go up in response to the deficit reduction. And it gives us a few hints about when this might happen.

**FIGURE  22–4**

**The Effects of Deficit Reduction on Current Output**

When account is taken of its effect on expectations, the decrease in government spending need not lead to a decrease in output.

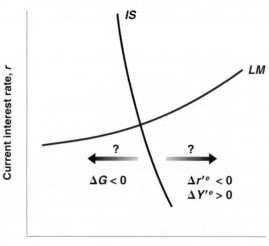

**Can a Budget Deficit Reduction Lead to an Output Expansion? Some Evidence from Ireland and Other Countries**

Nearly every advanced economy faces a significant budget deficit, many due to the aftermath of the crisis and some due to a long-term imbalance between spending and taxation. We look at these issues more in Chapters 23 and 25. In this box we consider the question: Is there any evidence that an **austerity** program that reduces the deficit can increase output in the current period, that is, in the short run? One very interesting example is Ireland, a country that went through two deficit reduction programs in the 1980s. After we look at Ireland, we will look at more general and more important evidence.

1. The first Irish deficit-reduction program started in 1982. In 1981, the budget deficit was 13% of GDP. Government debt, the result of the accumulation of current and past deficits, was 77% of GDP, a very high level. The Irish government clearly had to regain control of its finances. Over the next three years, it embarked on a program of deficit reduction based mostly on tax increases. This was an ambitious program: Had output continued to grow at its normal growth rate, the program would have reduced the deficit by 5% of GDP.

   The results were dismal. As shown in line 2 of Table 1, output growth was low in 1982, and negative in 1983. Low output growth went with a major increase in the unemployment rate, from 9.5% in 1981 to 15% in 1984 (line 3). Because of low output growth, tax revenues—which depend on the level of economic activity—were lower than anticipated. The actual deficit reduction from 1981 to 1984, shown in line 1, was only 3.5% of GDP. The debt-to-GDP ratio continued to rise and was 97% in 1984.

2. A second attempt to reduce Irish budget deficits was made starting in February 1987. At the time, things were still very bad. The 1986 deficit was 10.7% of GDP; debt stood at 116% of GDP, a record high in Europe at the time. This new program of deficit reduction was different from the first. It was focused more on reducing the role of government and cutting government spending than on increasing taxes. The tax increases in the program were

achieved through a tax reform that widened the tax base—increasing the number of households paying taxes—rather than through an increase in the marginal tax rate. The program was again very ambitious: Had output grown at its normal rate, the reduction in the deficit would have been 6.4% of GDP.

The results of the second program could not have been more different from the results of the first. 1987 to 1989 were years of strong growth, with average GDP growth exceeding 5%. The unemployment rate was reduced by almost 2%. Because of strong output growth, tax revenues were higher than anticipated, and the deficit was reduced by nearly 9% of GDP.

A number of economists have argued that the striking difference between the results of the two programs can be traced to the different reaction of expectations in each case. The first program, they argue, focused on tax increases and did not change what many people saw as too large a role of government in the economy. The second program, with its focus on cuts in spending and on tax reform, had a much more positive impact on expectations, and so a positive impact on spending and output.

Are these economists right? One variable, the household saving rate—defined as disposable income minus consumption, divided by disposable income—strongly suggests that expectations were different in these two periods. To interpret the behaviour of the saving rate, recall the lessons from Chapter 21 about consumption behaviour. When disposable income grows unusually slowly or goes down—as it does in a recession—consumption typically slows down or declines by less than disposable income because people expect things to improve in the future. Put another way, when the growth of disposable income is unusually low, the saving rate typically comes down. Now look (in line 4) at what happened from 1981 to 1984: Despite low growth throughout the period and a recession in 1983, the household saving rate actually increased slightly during the period. Put another way, people reduced their consumption by more than the reduction in their disposable income: They were very pessimistic about the future.

| TABLE | 1 | Fiscal and Other Macroeconomic Indicators, Ireland, 1981–1984 and 1986–1989 | | | | | | | |
|---|---|---|---|---|---|---|---|---|---|
| | | 1981 | 1982 | 1983 | 1984 | 1986 | 1987 | 1988 | 1989 |
| 1. Budget deficit (% of GDP) | | −13.0 | −13.4 | −11.4 | −9.5 | −10.7 | −8.6 | −4.5 | −1.8 |
| 2. Output growth rate (%) | | 3.3 | 2.3 | −0.2 | 4.4 | −0.4 | 4.7 | 5.2 | 5.8 |
| 3. Unemployment rate (%) | | 9.5 | 11.0 | 13.5 | 15.0 | 17.1 | 16.9 | 16.3 | 15.1 |
| 4. Household saving rate (% of disposable income) | | 17.9 | 19.6 | 18.1 | 18.4 | 15.7 | 12.9 | 11.0 | 12.6 |

*Source: OECD Economic Outlook, June 1998.*

(continued)

Now look at the period 1986 to 1989. During that period, economic growth was unusually strong. By the same argument as in the previous paragraph, we would have expected consumption to increase less strongly, and thus the saving rate to increase. Instead, the saving rate dropped sharply, from 15.7% in 1986 to 12.6% in 1989. Consumers must have become much more optimistic about the future to increase their consumption by more than the increase in their disposable income.

The next question is whether this difference in the adjustment of expectations over the two episodes can be attributed fully to the differences in the two fiscal programs. The answer is surely no. Ireland was changing in many ways at the time of the second fiscal program. Productivity was increasing much faster than real wages, reducing the cost of labour for firms. Attracted by tax breaks, low labour costs, and an educated labour force, many foreign firms were relocating to Ireland and building new plants: These factors played a major role in the expansion of the late 1980s. Irish growth was then very strong, usually more than 5% per year from 1990 to the time of the crisis in 2007. Surely, this long expansion is due to many factors. Nevertheless, the change in fiscal policy in 1987 probably played an important role in convincing people, firms—including foreign firms—and financial markets that the government was regaining control of its finances. And the fact remains that the substantial deficit reduction of 1987–1989 was accompanied by a strong output expansion, not by the recession predicted by the basic *IS-LM* model.

Is Ireland the usual case? The International Monetary Fund studied austerity programs in 15 countries over 29 years. The strong conclusion is that the case of Ireland was unusual. A fiscal consolidation equal to 1 percent of GDP—for example a 0.5% increase in taxes and a 0.5% decrease in spending, typically reduced GDP by 0.5% after two years. There is a wide range of experiences that suggests, as in Ireland, the exact details of the fiscal program and the situation in which the fiscal program is carried out matter a lot. Given the discussion in the chapter of the important role of expectations, this conclusion is not surprising.

What factors matter the most? The ability to lower interest rates and depreciate the currency during the austerity program can offset much of the impact of the program. This result should remind you of the Focus box "The Martin-Theissen Policy Mix" in Chapter 5. The second factor that matters is quite consistent with the Irish experience. Deficit reduction programs that focus on expenditure reduction seem to have smaller impact on GDP growth than deficit reduction programs that focus on tax increases. As in the Irish case, consumers who expect their taxes to remain high in the future may decide to consume less today. Before you jump to a conclusion that it is obvious that government spending should be reduced rather than taxes raised, note that the decision to reduce government expenditures to reduce the deficit does involve choosing specific government programs that will no longer be in place. Thus you may see reductions in government spending on health, education, the environment, defence or infrastructure. What government programs to reduce is another whole discussion in economics!

### FURTHER READING

For a more systematic look at whether and when fiscal consolidations have been expansionary (and a mostly negative answer), see "Will It Hurt? Macroeconomic Effects of Fiscal Consolidation," Chapter 3, *World Economic Outlook*, International Monetary Fund, October 2010.

Note that the smaller the decrease in current government spending ($G$), the smaller is the adverse effect on spending today. Note also that the larger the decrease in expected future government spending ($G'^e$), the larger is the effect on expected future output and interest rates, and thus the larger the favourable effect on spending today. This suggests that **backloading** (the tilting of the deficit reduction toward the future), with small cuts today and larger cuts in the future, is more likely to lead to an increase in output.

On the other hand, backloading raises other issues. If government announces the need for painful cuts in spending but then defers the required measures to some time in the future, its credibility—the perceived probability that government will actually do what it has promised—may well decrease. Government must perform a delicate balancing act: There have to be enough cuts in the current period to show a commitment to deficit reduction and enough cuts left to the future to reduce the adverse effects on the economy in the short run.

More generally, our analysis suggests that anything in a deficit reduction program that improves expectations of how the future will look is likely to make the short-run effects of deficit reduction less painful. Let us give two examples.

Measures that are perceived by firms and financial markets as reducing some of the existing distortions in the economy may improve expectations and make it more likely that output increases in the short run. Take, for example, unemployment benefits. We saw in Chapter 9 that lower unemployment benefits lead to a decline in the natural rate of unemployment, and thus a higher natural level of output. Thus, a reform of the social insurance system, which includes a reduction in the generosity of unemployment benefits, is likely to have two effects on spending, and thus on output in the short run. The first is the adverse effect on the consumption of the unemployed: Lower unemployment benefits will reduce their income and their consumption. The second is a positive effect on spending through expectations: The anticipation of a lower unemployment rate and of a higher level of output in the future may lead to both higher consumption and higher investment. If the second effect dominates, the effect may be an increase in overall spending, increasing output not only in the medium run, but also in the short run.

◄ An important caveat: Even if a reduction in unemployment benefits increases output, this surely does not imply that unemployment benefits should be eliminated. Even if aggregate income goes up, we must worry about distribution effects: The consumption of the unemployed goes down, and the pain associated with being unemployed goes up.

Another example is that of an economy where government has, in effect, lost control of its budget: Government spending is high, tax revenues are low, and the deficit is very large. In such an environment, a credible deficit reduction program is also more likely to increase output in the short run. Before the announcement of the program, people may have expected major political and economic trouble in the future. The announcement of a program of deficit reduction may well reassure people that government has regained control and that the future is less bleak than they anticipated. This decrease in pessimism about the future may lead to an increase in spending and output, even if taxes are increased as part of the deficit reduction program.

◄ As we will see in Chapter 25, a very large deficit occasionally leads to very high inflation.

To summarize: A program of deficit reduction may increase output even in the short run. Whether it does depends on many factors, in particular:

- The credibility of the program: Will spending be cut or taxes increased in the future as announced?
- The timing of the program: How large are spending cuts in the future relative to current spending cuts?
- The composition of the program: Does the program remove some of the distortions in the economy?
- The state of government finances in the first place: How large is the initial deficit? Is this a "last chance" program? What will happen if it fails?

◄ Note how far we are from the results of Chapter 3, where by choosing spending and taxes wisely, government could achieve any level of output it wanted. Here, even the direction of the effect of a deficit reduction on output may be hard to predict.

This gives you a sense of both the importance of expectations in determining the outcome and of the difficulty of predicting the effects of fiscal policy in such a context.

## SUMMARY

- Spending in the goods market depends on current and expected future output and on the current and the expected future real interest rate. Changes in expected future output or in the expected future real interest rate lead to changes in spending and in output today.

- By implication, the effects of any policy on spending and output depend on whether and how policy affects expectations of future output and the real interest rate.

- The assumption of rational expectations is that people, firms, and participants in financial markets form expectations of the future by assessing the course of future expected policy and then working out the implications for future output, interest rates, and so on. Although it is clear that most people do not go through this exercise themselves, we can think of them doing so indirectly by

watching TV and reading newspapers, which in turn rely on the predictions of public and private forecasters.

- Although there surely are cases where people, firms, or financial investors do not have rational expectations, the assumption seems to be the best benchmark to evaluate the potential effects of alternative policies. Designing a policy on the assumption that people will make systematic mistakes in responding to it is surely unwise.

- Changes in money supply affect the short-term nominal interest rate. Spending, however, depends on the current and the expected future real interest rates. Thus, the effect of monetary policy on activity depends crucially on whether and how changes in the short-term nominal interest rate lead to changes in the current and the expected future real interest rate.

- When account is taken of its effect on expectations, a budget deficit reduction may lead to an increase rather than a decrease in output. This is because expectations of higher output and lower interest rates may more than offset the direct effect of the deficit reduction on spending.
- When the evidence on the effect of budget deficit reduction on output is studied across many countries, the usual case is that a budget deficit reduction does lead to less aggregate demand and a reduction in output. However, there are rare cases where, within a country, the expectations effect appears to dominate and a budget deficit reduction is accompanied by an increase in output in the short run.

## KEY TERMS

- adaptive expectations, 463
- aggregate private spending, 457
- animal spirits, 463
- austerity, 467
- backloading, 468
- quantitative easing I (QEI), 464
- quantitative easing II (QEII), 464
- rational expectations, 462

## QUESTIONS AND PROBLEMS

### 1. TRUE/FALSE/UNCERTAIN

a. Changes in expected future one-year real interest rates have a much larger effect on spending than changes in the current one-year real interest rate.

b. The introduction of expectations implies that the *IS* curve is still downward sloping but is now much flatter.

c. Current real money demand is inversely related to the future nominal interest rate.

d. The rational expectations assumption implies that consumers take into account the effects of future fiscal policy on output.

e. Future monetary policy affects future economic activity but not current economic activity.

f. Depending on its effect on expectations, a fiscal contraction may actually lead to an economic expansion.

g. The very different effects of Ireland's deficit reduction programs in 1982 and in 1987 provide strong evidence against the hypothesis that deficit reduction can lead to an expansion of output in the short run.

### 2. POLICY EXPERIMENTS

For each of the following, determine whether the *IS* curve, the *LM* curve, neither curve, or both curves shift. In each case, assume that expected current inflation and future inflation are equal to zero and that no other exogenous variable is changing.

a. A decrease in the expected future real interest rate.

b. A steeper yield curve.

c. An increase in the current money supply.

d. An increase in the expected future money supply.

e. An increase in expected future taxes.

f. A decrease in expected future income.

### 3. RATIONAL EXPECTATIONS

"The rational expectations assumption is unrealistic, because it essentially amounts to the assumption that every consumer has perfect knowledge of the economy." Discuss this statement.

### 4. FISCAL POLICY

A new prime minister, who promised during her campaign that she would cut taxes, has just been elected. People trust that she will keep her promise but that the tax cuts will be implemented only in the future. Determine the impact of the election result on current output, the current interest rate, and current private spending under each of the following assumptions. (In each case, indicate what you think will happen to $Y^e$, $r^e$, and $T'^e$, and then how these changes in expectations affect output today. You can ignore any long-run effects on capital accumulation and output in the long run.)

a. The Bank of Canada will not change its policy.

b. The Bank of Canada will act to prevent any change in future output.

c. The Bank of Canada will act to prevent any increase in the future interest rate.

### 5. PAUL MARTIN'S DEFICIT REDUCTION PLAN

When the Liberals were elected in 1993, the federal deficit in fiscal year 1992–1993 was $40.4 billion. Finance

Minister Paul Martin toured Canada making it clear that the federal deficit would be reduced.

**a.** What does deficit reduction imply for output in the medium run and the long run? What are the advantages of reducing the deficit?

In February 1995, Finance Minister Martin committed to deficit reductions. The projected maximum deficits: 1994–1995, $37.9 billion; 1995–1996, $32.7 billion; 1996–1997, $24.3 billion. Deficits would be even lower if tax revenues grew faster than expected.

**b.** Why was the deficit reduction package backloaded? Are there any advantages and disadvantages to this approach?

From 1994 through 1997, the Canadian dollar depreciated.

**c.** Explain why the Bank of Canada might allow the Canadian dollar to depreciate in the short run, while the federal government was reducing the deficit.

## 6. PAUL MARTIN'S DEFICIT REDUCTION PLAN (CONTINUED)

**a.** Go to the website of the Bank of Canada (www.bankofcanada.ca) under "Rates and Statistics," "Selected Historical Interest Rates." Using the three-month Treasury Bill Auction, the five-year Government of Canada Benchmark Bond Yield, and the Long-term Government of Canada Benchmark Bond Yield, plot the yield curve for January 1993 and January 1996. Does the yield curve reveal a change in expectations in financial markets from 1993 to 1996?

**b.** Figure 9–2 shows Canada's unemployment rate. Did unemployment rise or fall after 1993? Did the economy go into a recession as the deficit was reduced?

**c.** Go to the Statistics Canada website (www.statcan.gc.ca). Under "Canadian Statistics/Government/Revenues, Expenditures and Debt/Federal general government revenue and expenditure," you can find a report of the federal deficit in the last five fiscal years. Use the table entitled "Fiscal Transactions percent of GDP" in Fiscal Reference Tables. What happened to the federal deficit from 1993–1994 to 1997–1998? Was Mr. Martin's plan to stabilize the deficit successful?

**d.** Are there any reasons to think that factors other than the deficit reduction package may have helped reduce the deficit in the 1990s? (*Hint:* Look at the growth rate of real GDP in the late 1990s relative to the early 1990s.)

# Back to Policy

Nearly every chapter of this book has looked at the role of policy. The next three chapters put it all together.

## Chapter 23

Chapter 23 asks two questions: Given the uncertainty about the effects of macroeconomic policies, would it be better not to use policy at all? And even if policy potentially can be useful, can we trust policy makers to carry out the right policy? Bottom line: Uncertainty limits the role of policy; policy makers do not always do the right thing. But with the right institutions, policy can help and should be used.

## Chapter 24

Chapter 24 looks at monetary policy. It reviews what we have learned, chapter by chapter, and then focuses on two issues. The first is the optimal rate of inflation: High inflation is bad, but how low a rate of inflation should the central bank aim for? The second is the design of policy: What is the role of the measured money supply? Given a target rate of inflation, how much should the central bank be willing to deviate from the target to stabilize output? The chapter includes a description of the way monetary policy is conducted in Canada today. Finally, we make some comments on how the world economic crisis changed the way in which monetary policy is conducted.

## Chapter 25

Chapter 25 looks at fiscal policy. Again, it reviews what we have learned and then looks more closely at the mechanics of debt, taxes, and spending implied by the government budget constraint. We look at the cyclically adjusted budget balance. We consider the dangers of very high debts and the possibility of hyperinflation. The relation between the government's deficit and the current account deficit is considered. We close with a study of federal fiscal policy in Canada over the last 20 years.

# Should Policy Makers Be Restrained?

## Back to Policy

A recurrent theme of this book has been that macroeconomic policy has an important role to play. The right mix of fiscal and monetary policies can, we have argued, help a country out of a recession without increasing inflation. Better macroeconomic policies can stimulate investment and capital accumulation and affect long-term growth.

The collapse of housing prices in the United States, and the issues with bankruptcies and near-bankruptcies of various financial institutions, led to a substantial fall in private sector aggregate demand in 2009, not just in the United States but throughout the world. A series of policy actions were taken were intended to minimize the short-run macroeconomic consequences of the financial market events. We have looked at these actions throughout this book.

In the United States there was a significant fiscal stimulus: both spending increases and tax cuts. On October 8, 2008, there was a coordinated reduction in interest rates in the countries using the euro as well as in Britain, the United States, and Canada. Interest rates remained low for many years after 2008. Also, in the fall of 2008, there was an agreement to extend fiscal stimulus across those same countries. Canada joined the stimulus, somewhat reluctantly and belatedly, with the implementation of substantial fiscal stimulus for 2009 and 2010 announced in the January 2009 Budget.

However, the choice to undertake activist macroeconomic policy is clearly at odds with much of the macroeconomic analysis prior to the world economic crisis. This analysis suggests that policy makers should be restrained; that is, the question posed by the title of this chapter is to be answered strongly in the affirmative. Two types of restraints are often proposed.

The usual restraint on fiscal policy is a law requiring a balanced budget. Such a law was passed by a Social Credit government in British Columbia in 1991 and was immediately repealed by the New Democrat government that followed. The current and very prominent federal fiscal policy objective in Canada, as of this writing in 2013, is a return to a balanced budget at the federal level. In a Throne Speech presented October 2013, just as this book goes to print, the federal Conservatives are planning to enact some type of balanced budget law. There are few details at this time.

Monetary policy rules have also been very popular. Some central banks are constrained by law to having only one goal for policy: price stability. Should the Bank of Canada face a similar constraint? For a brief period during the drafting of the Charlottetown Accord (the 1992 attempt to reform the Canadian constitution), a proposal was made to incorporate the goal of price stability for the operation of the Bank of Canada directly into the Canadian constitution. The proposal (and the Charlottetown Accord itself) was not implemented. In the crisis atmosphere in the autumn of 2008, it seems like all rules governing the behaviour of central banks and the regulation of financial markets were tossed in the trash and policy was made on the fly. Would it have been better in 2008 to have restraints on monetary and fiscal policy? Would it be better in general to have restraints on monetary and fiscal policy?

Arguments for restraints on policy fall in two general categories:

1. Policy makers may have good intentions, but they end up doing more harm than good.
2. Policy makers do what is best for themselves, which is not necessarily what is best for the country.

The argument against a rigid policy rule is simply that it is not possible to write a policy rule that covers all possible circumstances.

This chapter develops and examines these arguments in the context of macroeconomic policy in general. Chapters 24 and 25 then examine monetary policy and fiscal policy in more detail.

## 23-1 | Uncertainty and Policy

One aspect of the first argument in favour of policy restraints is that those who know little should do little. The argument has two parts: First, macroeconomists and, by implication, the policy makers who rely on their advice know little; and, second, they should therefore do little.

### How Much Do Macroeconomists Actually Know?

Macroeconomists are like doctors treating cancer. They know a lot, but there is also a lot they do not know.

Take an economy with high unemployment, where the central bank is considering the use of monetary policy to increase economic activity. Think of the sequence of links between an increase in money and an increase in output—all the questions the central bank faces when deciding whether and by how much to increase money supply:

- Is the current high rate of unemployment a sign that unemployment is above the natural rate or a sign that the natural rate has increased (see Chapter 9)? If the economy is too close to the natural rate, is there a risk that monetary expansion will lead to a decrease in unemployment below the natural rate and an increase in inflation (Chapters 12 and 13)?
- By how much will the change in money supply decrease the short-term interest rate (Chapter 4)? What will be the effect of the decrease in the short-term interest rate on the long-term interest rate (Chapter 20)? By how much will stock prices increase (Chapter 20)? By how much will the currency depreciate (Chapters 8, 14, and 20)?
- How long will it take for lower long-term interest rates and higher stock prices to affect investment and consumption spending (Chapter 21)? How long will it take for the J-curve effects to work themselves out and for the trade balance to improve (Chapter 7)? What is the danger that the effects come too late, when the economy has already recovered?
- How will the proposed policy affect expectations of future output and future interest rates (Chapter 22)?

When assessing these questions, central banks—or macroeconomic policy makers, in general—do not operate in a vacuum. They rely, in particular, on macroeconometric models. The equations in these models give estimates of how these individual links have looked in the past. But different models give different answers. This is because they have different structures, different lists of equations, and different lists of variables.

Figure 23–1 uses a Bank of Canada study that compares the predictions of 11 different macroeconometric models of the Canadian economy to various changes in the model's policy variable. Figure 23–1 traces out the predictions for real GDP in each model, following a temporary increase in short-term interest rates. (You may recall seeing this same diagram in Chapter 5.) The increase in interest rates is 1% for one quarter, then 0.75% in the next quarter, 0.5% in the third quarter, and 0.25% in the fourth quarter. The diagram shows that real GDP does fall in response to the increase in interest rates. That was the point made in Chapter 5: The *IS-*

FIGURE  23-1

**The Responses of Output to a Temporary Increase in Short-Term Interest Rates on GDP: 11 Predictions from 11 Models of the Canadian Economy**

These graphs show the response of output (in percentage points) to a policy of increasing the short-term nominal interest rate by 1 percentage point for one quarter, 0.75 percentage points in the next quarter, 0.5 percentage points in the third quarter, and 0.25 percentage points in the fourth quarter. The increase in interest rates ends in the fifth quarter. This represents a temporary tightening of monetary policy in the Canadian economy. There is a wide variation in the predicted response of the economy to tighter monetary policy across the 11 models.

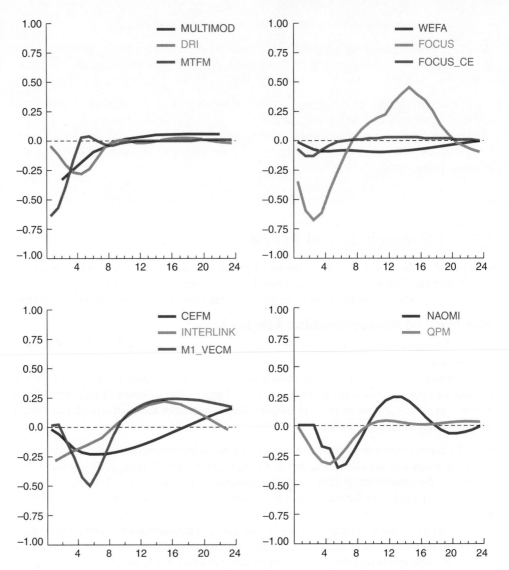

*Source:* Figure 6ca in Denise Coté, John Kusczak, Jean-Paul Lam, Ying Liu, and Pierre St. Amant, "A Comparison of Twelve Macroeconomic Models of the Canadian Economy," *Bank of Canada Technical Report*, No. 94, April 2003.

*LM* model does generate the correct picture of the behaviour of the economy in the short run. But the size of the fall in real GDP and the timing of the fall in real GDP are not the same in all the models. In some models the fall is immediate. In others, the peak reduction in real GDP is more than four quarters (the time units are quarter years) after the initial interest rate surge. In some models there is a "rebound": After the period of slower real GDP growth, there a period of faster GDP growth. In some models, GDP returns smoothly to its normal level. In short, the Bank of Canada faces considerable uncertainty about the exact effects of policy.

## Should Uncertainty Lead Policy Makers to Do Less?

Should uncertainty about the effects of policy lead policy makers to do less? In general, the answer is yes. Consider the following example, which builds on the simulation we just looked at.

Suppose that the Canadian economy is in recession. The unemployment rate is 10.0%, and the Bank of Canada is considering using monetary policy to expand output. To concentrate on uncertainty about the effects of policy, let us assume that the Bank of Canada knows everything else for certain. On the basis of its forecasts, it *knows* that without changes in monetary policy, unemployment will still be 10.0% next year. It knows that the natural rate of unemployment is 8.0%, and therefore the unemployment rate is 2 percentage points above the natural rate. And it knows, from Okun's law, that 1% more output growth for a year leads to a reduction in the unemployment rate of 0.4%.

Under these assumptions, the Bank of Canada knows that if it could achieve 5% more output growth over the coming year, the unemployment rate a year from now would be lower by 0.4 times 5% = 2%, thus down to its natural rate of 8.0%. By how much should the Bank of Canada reduce the interest rate?

Taking the average one-year-out response of GDP to the change in interest rates in Figure 23–1 and assuming that interest rate increases and declines are exact opposites, then the initial 1% increase in interest rates appears, on average, to reduce real GDP in the fourth quarter after the interest rate increase by somewhere between 0.25 and 0.50%. Let us assume the exact number is 0.4%; that is, the increase in interest rates that starts with 1 percentage point and then is gradually ended as described in the previous section leads to a 0.4% reduction in real GDP one year later. Thus, a decrease in interest rates of 1 percentage point should increase GDP growth by 0.4 percentage points.

Suppose the Bank of Canada takes this calculation to hold as the exact truth about the economy. What they should do is straightforward. To return the unemployment rate to its natural rate in one year requires 5% more output growth. Thus to increase real GDP growth by the required 5% requires an initial decrease in interest rates of 5% divided by 0.4 or a initial 12.5% reduction in the nominal interest rate. Then the short-term interest rate is returned to its path as described above—that is, in the second quarter, short rates are 9.375% lower than they would have been, in the third quarter rates are 6.25% lower, and in the fourth quarter rates are a mere 3.125% lower. If the economy's response is the average of the 12 models, this activist monetary policy of reducing interest rates will return the economy to the natural rate of unemployment in one year.

The proposed policy is an enormous reduction in the short-term interest rate. We have already seen that short-term interest rates are between 0 and 2% in many countries, including Canada. Such large reductions in the nominal interest rate would hit the zero lower bound on nominal interest rates and the economy would be in the liquidity trap.

And even if it were possible to reduce interest rates by the required 12.5 percentage points, it might not be desirable. Suppose that instead of an increase of real GDP of 0.4% per 1 percentage point cut in interest rates, the actual increase in real GDP were 0.6%. This would be within the range of the 12 models. Then GDP growth would increase not by 5% but by 7.5%. The unemployment rate would then fall not by the desired 1% but by more. Using the estimate of Okun's Law from Chapter 13, unemployment would fall by 3 percentage points, not 2 percentage points as desired. Finally, using the expectations-augmented Phillips curve, the rate of inflation would then rise by 0.4 times 3.00 or 1.2 percentage points. If the unemployment rate had fallen by only 2 percentage points, then inflation would have increased by only 0.8 percentage points. As we will learn in the next chapter, the Bank of Canada has an inflation target of between 1 and 3% per year. Thus, risking an additional increase in inflation of 0.4 percentage points induces some risk of breaching the inflation target.

The conclusions that follow from Figure 23–1 are fairly clear. When there is a range of possible responses of the economy to a cut in interest rates and the Bank of Canada is uncertain about the effects of cuts, smaller cuts will be preferred over larger cuts in most situations. Uncertainty does not mean policy is never carried out; it simply reduces the size of policy actions taken in any given situation.

## Uncertainty and Restraints on Policy Makers

Let us summarize what we have learned so far. There is substantial uncertainty about the effects of macroeconomic policies. This uncertainty should lead policy makers to be more cautious, to use less active policies. Policies should be aimed broadly at avoiding prolonged

In the real world, of course, the Bank of Canada does not know any of these things with certainty. It can only make forecasts. It does not know the exact value of the natural rate, or the exact coefficient in Okun's law. ◀ Introducing these sources of uncertainty would reinforce our basic conclusion.

recessions, slowing down booms, and avoiding inflationary pressure. The higher the unemployment or inflation, the more active the policies should be. But they should stop well short of **fine tuning**, of trying to achieve constant unemployment or constant output growth.

These conclusions would have been controversial 20 years ago. Back then, there was a heated debate between two groups of economists. One group, headed by Milton Friedman from Chicago, argued that because of long and variable lags, activist policy was likely to do more harm than good. The other group, headed by Franco Modigliani from Massachusetts Institute of Technology (MIT), had just built the first generation of large macroeconometric models and believed that economists' knowledge of the economy was becoming good enough to allow increasingly fine tuning the economy. Today, most economists recognize that there is substantial uncertainty about the effects of policy. They also accept the implication that this uncertainty should lead to less active policies.

Note that what we have developed so far is an argument for *self-restraint by* policy makers, not for *restraints on* policy makers. If policy makers understand the implications of uncertainty—and there is no reason to think they do not—they will, on their own, follow less active policies. There is no reason to impose further restraints, such as the requirement that money growth be constant or that the budget be balanced. Let us now turn to arguments for restraints on policy makers.

Friedman and Modigliani are the same two economists who independently developed the modern theory of consumption (Chapter 21).

## 23-2 | Expectations and Policy

One reason the effects of macroeconomic policy are uncertain is the interaction of policy and expectations. How a policy works, and sometimes whether it works at all, depends not only on how it affects current variables but also on how it affects expectations about the future (the main theme of Chapter 22). However, the importance of expectations for policy goes beyond uncertainty about the effects of policy. This brings us to a discussion of games.

Until the 1970s, macroeconomic policy was seen in the same way as the control of a complicated machine. Methods of **optimal control**, developed initially to control and guide rockets, were increasingly being used to design macroeconomic policy. Economists no longer think this way. It has become clear that the economy is fundamentally different from a machine, even a very complex one. Unlike a machine, the economy is composed of people and firms that try to anticipate what policy makers will do, and they react not only to current policy, but also to expectations of future policy. Hence, macroeconomic policy must be thought of as a **game** between policy makers and the economy. So, when thinking about policy, what we need is not **optimal control theory** but rather **game theory**.

Let us clarify semantics. When economists say "game," they do not mean "entertainment," they mean **strategic interactions** between **players**. In the context of macroeconomic policy, the players are the policy makers and "the economy"—more concretely, the people and the firms in the economy. The strategic interactions are clear: What people and firms do depends on what they expect policy makers to do. In turn, what policy makers do depends on what is happening in the economy.

Game theory has given economists many insights, often explaining how some apparently strange behaviour makes sense when one understands the nature of the game being played. One of these insights is particularly important for our discussion of restraints here: Sometimes you can do better in a game by giving up some of your options. To see why, let us start with an example from outside economics: governments' policies concerning hijackers.

Game theory is an important tool in all branches of economics. The 1994 Nobel prize in economics was awarded to the three game theorists John Nash from Princeton, John Harsanyi from Berkeley, and Reinhard Selten from Germany. You may have seen the film about John Nash, *A Beautiful Mind*.

### Hostage Takings and Negotiations

Most governments have a stated policy that they will not negotiate with hostage takers. The reason for this stated policy is clear: to deter hostage taking by making it not worthwhile to take hostages.

Suppose, despite the stated policy, someone is taken hostage. Now that the hostage taking has taken place anyway, why not negotiate? Whatever compensation the hostage takers demand is likely to be less costly than the alternative—the likelihood that the hostage will be killed or much blood will be shed in a possibly unsuccessful rescue attempt. So, the best policy would appear to be: Announce that you will not negotiate, but if a hostage taking happens, negotiate nevertheless.

Upon reflection, it is clear this would, in fact, be a very bad policy. The decisions of hostage takers do not depend on the stated policy but on what they expect will actually happen if they take a hostage. If they know that negotiations will actually take place, they will rightly consider the stated policy as irrelevant. And hostage takings will take place.

So, what is the best policy? Despite the fact that once a hostage taking has occurred and negotiations typically lead to a better outcome, the best policy is for governments to commit *not* to negotiate. The possibility of repeated hostage-takings and repeated negotiations is more real once the government agrees to negotiate once. By giving up the option to negotiate, they are likely to prevent hostage takings in the first place.

Let us now turn to a macroeconomic example, based on the relation between inflation and unemployment. As you will see, exactly the same logic is involved.

## Inflation and Unemployment Revisited

Recall the relation between inflation and unemployment we derived in Chapter 12 (equation (12.7), with the time indexes omitted):

$$\pi = \pi^e - \alpha(u - u_n) \tag{23.1}$$

Inflation ($\pi$) depends on expected inflation ($\pi^e$) as embodied in wages set in labour contracts and on the difference between the actual unemployment rate and the natural unemployment rate ($u - u_n$). The coefficient $\alpha$ captures the effect of unemployment on inflation, given expected inflation: When unemployment is above the natural rate, inflation is lower than expected; when it is below the natural rate, inflation is higher than expected.

Suppose the Bank of Canada announces it will follow a monetary policy consistent with zero inflation. On the assumption that wage setters believe the announcement, expected inflation ($\pi^e$) as embodied in wage contracts is equal to zero, and the Bank of Canada faces the following relation:

$$\pi = -\alpha(u - u_n) \tag{23.2}$$

If the Bank of Canada follows through on its announced policy of zero inflation, expected and actual inflation will both be equal to zero, and unemployment will be equal to the natural rate.

Zero inflation and unemployment equal to the natural rate is not a bad outcome. But it would seem that the Bank of Canada can actually do even better. Recall from Chapter 12 that $\alpha$ was a critical parameter. In Canada, we estimated $\alpha$ as 0.4. So, equation (23.2) implies that by accepting just 1% inflation, the Bank of Canada can achieve an unemployment rate of 0.4 percentage point below the natural rate. Suppose that the Bank of Canada—and everybody else in the economy—finds the trade-off attractive and decides to decrease unemployment by 0.4 percentage point in exchange for an inflation rate of 1%. In Chapter 2, we saw that an extra 0.4% of inflation in a year does not seem very costly, particularly when compared to an extra 1 percentage point of unemployment. This is reconfirmed in Chapter 24 where we look at the costs of inflation in more detail. This incentive to deviate from the announced policy once the other player has moved—in this case, once wage setters have set the wage—is known in game theory as the **time inconsistency** of optimal policy. In our example, the Bank of Canada can improve the outcome for this period by deviating from its announced policy of zero inflation: By accepting some inflation, it can achieve a substantial reduction in unemployment.

Unfortunately, this is not the end of the story. Seeing that the Bank of Canada has increased money by more than it announced it would, wage setters are likely to wise up and begin to expect positive inflation of 1%. If the Bank of Canada still wants to achieve an unemployment

A refresher: Given labour market conditions and given their expectations of what prices will be, firms and workers set nominal wages. Given the nominal wages they have to pay, firms then set prices. Thus, prices depend on expected prices and labour market conditions. Equivalently, price inflation depends on expected price inflation and labour market conditions. This is what is captured in equation (23.1).

For simplicity, we assume that the Bank of Canada can choose the rate of inflation exactly. In doing so, we ignore uncertainty about the effects of policy (the topic of section 23-1, but not a central issue here).

The natural rate of unemployment, despite its name, has no claim to being natural or best in any sense (see Chapters 9, 10 and 11). It may be perfectly reasonable for the Bank of Canada and everyone else in the economy to prefer an unemployment rate lower than the natural rate.

rate 0.4 percentage point below the natural rate, it now has to accept 2% inflation. However, if it does, wage setters are likely to increase their expectations of inflation further, and so on.

The eventual outcome is likely to be high inflation. Because wage setters understand the Bank of Canada's motives, expected inflation catches up with actual inflation, and the Bank of Canada will eventually be unsuccessful in its attempt to achieve unemployment below the natural rate. In short, attempts by the Bank of Canada to make things better lead, in the end, to things being worse. The economy ends up with the *same unemployment rate* as would have prevailed if the Bank of Canada had followed its announced policy, but with *much higher inflation*.

How relevant is this example? Very relevant. Reread Chapter 12. We can see the history of the Phillips curve and the increase in inflation in the 1970s around the world as coming precisely from central bank attempts to maintain unemployment below the natural rate, leading to higher and higher expected and actual inflation. In that light, the shift of the original Phillips curve can be seen as the adjustment of wage setters' expectations to the central bank's behaviour.

So, what is the best policy in this case? It is for the Bank of Canada to make a credible commitment that it will not try to decrease unemployment below the natural rate. By giving up the option of deviating from its announced policy, the Bank of Canada can achieve unemployment equal to the natural rate and zero inflation. The analogy with the hostage-taking example is clear: By credibly committing not to do something that would appear desirable at the time, policy makers can achieve a better outcome: no hostage takings in our earlier example, no inflation here.

## Establishing Credibility

How can a central bank credibly commit not to deviate from its announced policy?

One way to establish its credibility is for the central bank to give up—or to be stripped, by law, of—its policy-making power. For example, the mandate of the bank can be defined by law in terms of a simple rule, such as setting money growth at 0% forever.

Such a law surely takes care of the problem of time inconsistency. But such a tight restraint comes close to throwing the baby out with the bathwater. We want to prevent the central bank from pursuing too high a rate of money growth in an attempt to lower unemployment below the natural rate. But—subject to the restrictions discussed in section 23-1—we still want the central bank to be able to expand money supply and lower interest rates when unemployment is far above the natural rate, and contract money supply and raise interest rates when unemployment is far below the natural rate. Such actions become impossible under a constant-money-growth rule. There are, indeed, better ways to deal with time inconsistency. In the case of monetary policy, our discussion suggests a way this can be done:

1. Make the central bank independent. Appointing central bankers for longer terms and making it harder to fire them will make them more likely to resist political pressure to decrease unemployment below the natural rate.

    Figure 23–2 provides the evidence that central bank independence matters. The vertical axis gives the average annual inflation rate in 18 OECD countries for the period 1960 to 1990. The sample ends in 1990. In 1990, the countries in the European Union linked their currencies directly to the Deutschmark and then after 1999 adopted the euro. You learned in Chapter 14 that once a country fixes the value of the nominal exchange rate to that of its principal trading partner, it adopts the inflation rate of that partner in the medium run. That is exactly what these European countries did after 1990; they "borrowed" the low inflation rate in Germany. However, prior to that time, they did have flexible exchange rates and the option to have their own inflation rate. The 18 countries had widely varying inflation rates between 1960 and 1990. The horizontal axis of the graph represents the values of an index of central bank independence. Points are assigned to aspects of the legislation enabling the central bank to operate. More points are given if the central bank is more independent. For example, does the government of

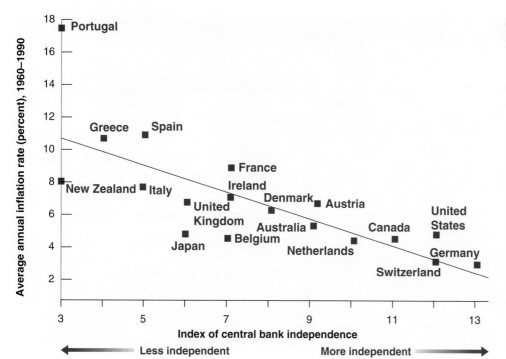

**FIGURE 23-2**

**Inflation and Central Bank Independence, 1960–1990**

Across the OECD countries, the higher the degree of central bank independence, the lower is the rate of inflation.

*Source:* Vittorio Grilli, Donato Masciandaro, and Guido Tabellini, "Political and Monetary Institutions and Public Financial Policies in the Industrial Countries," *Economic Policy* 6(3), October 1991: pp. 341–392. © Wiley-Blackwell UK. Used by permission of the publisher.

the day have the legislative power to fire the central bank governor? If the government has this power, the point score is lower. A high point score indicates a more independent central bank. In Figure 23–2, the regression line shows that the more independent central banks did deliver the lowest inflation rates—evidence that supports the time inconsistency model outlined earlier.

In fact, the evidence presented in Figure 23-2 and other studies was considered so strong that many countries rewrote their legislation that governed their central bank. New Zealand changed its central bank to be fully independent. In the most famous example, British Prime Minister Tony Blair's first act on taking office in 1997 was to transfer the power to set short-term interest rates from the Chancellor of the Exchequer (the British Minister of Finance) to a committee headed by the Governor of the Bank of England. This was a dramatic change.

2. A second strategy is to choose a "conservative" central banker, somebody who dislikes inflation and is unwilling to accept more inflation in exchange for less unemployment when unemployment is at the natural rate. When the economy is at the natural rate, such a central banker simply will not be tempted to embark on a monetary expansion. Thus, the problem of time inconsistency will disappear altogether.

Appointing as the head of the central bank someone who does not have the same preferences as the general public might seem like a solution that only a game theorist would devise. However, it has occurred. In fact, Israel has twice appointed professors of monetary economics: Michael Bruno in 1996 and, more recently, Stanley Fischer in 2006. These appointments are clearly designed to be nonpolitical appointments. In 1996 inflation in Israel was about 10% per year and by the end of Bruno's term it had fallen to 2%.

3. A third strategy to establish credibility has been to make central banks more "transparent." In this context a transparent bank reveals to the public as much as possible concerning the information that the central bank uses to make its decisions and the process by which the decisions are made. In Britain the votes of each member of the committee to raise, lower, or leave interest rates unchanged are released to the public. Some banks

In the summer of 1994, President Clinton appointed Alan Blinder, an economist from Princeton, vice-chairman (in effect, second in command) of the Federal Reserve Board, the American central bank. A few weeks later Blinder, speaking at an economic conference, indicated his belief that the Fed has both the responsibility and the ability, when unemployment is high, to use monetary policy to help the economy recover. This statement was badly received. Bond prices fell, and most newspapers ran editorials critical of Blinder.

Why was the reaction of markets and newspapers so negative? It was surely not that Blinder was wrong. There is no doubt that monetary policy can and should help the economy out of a recession. Indeed, the Federal Reserve Bank Act of 1978 requires the Fed to pursue full employment as well as low inflation.

The reaction was negative because, in terms of the argument we developed in the text, Blinder revealed by his words that he was not a conservative central banker; he cared about unemployment as well as inflation. With the unemployment rate at the time equal to 6.1%, close to what was thought to be the natural rate of unemployment at the time, markets interpreted Blinder's statements as suggesting that he might want to decrease unemployment below the natural rate. Interest rates increased because of higher expected inflation—bond prices decreased.

The moral of the story: Whatever views central bankers may hold, they should try to look and sound conservative. This is why, for example, many heads of central banks are reluctant to admit, at least in public, the existence of any trade-off between unemployment and inflation, even in the short run.

You occasionally will read that a central bank governor has "spoken like a true central banker." The expression is taken to mean that it is practically impossible to infer any actual meaning from the statement he or she just made. The only exception is for the central banker to be clear that that more inflation is bad and more inflation will not happen under his or her watch.

release the forecasts made by the central bank's forecasting department that are used in these meetings.

The argument is that more transparency will stabilize inflation and inflation expectations as wage setters and financial market operators understand why the central bank is taking (or not taking) policy action.

Figure 23–3 presents some evidence on transparency and inflation. As in Figure 23–3, the index is constructed by awarding points for actions taken to increase transparency: the higher the index, the more transparent the central bank. There is a weak relationship where more transparency is associated with less inflation. The relationship is weak because at the same value of the transparency index, either 0.6, 0.7, or 0.8, inflation varies widely. Transparency does not seem to be as important as independence, or perhaps as important as being a "conservative" central banker. The Focus box "Was Alan Blinder Wrong in Speaking the Truth?" looks at a specific incident where it appears that a central banker was too transparent. However, the Bank of Canada, as we shall see in Chapter 24, has taken a number of steps to be more transparent over the last decade. Inflation targeting, which started in 1991 in Canada, can be thought of as both a more transparent and a more independent policy making situation.

## Time Inconsistency and Restraints on Policy Makers

Let us summarize what we have learned in this section: We have examined arguments for putting restraints on policy makers, based on the issue of time inconsistency. We have looked at the case of monetary policy. But similar issues arise in the context of fiscal policy as well, for example, in the case of debt repudiation, an issue we will discuss in Chapter 25.

When issues of time inconsistency are relevant, tight restraints on policy makers—such as a fixed-money-growth rule in the case of monetary policy—can provide a coarse solution. But the solution may have large costs if it prevents the use of macroeconomic policy altogether. Better ways typically involve designing better institutions (such as an independent central bank) that can reduce the problem of time inconsistency without eliminating monetary policy as a macroeconomic policy tool.

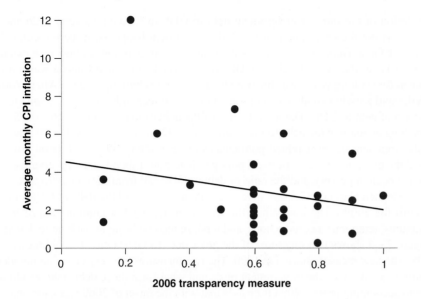

**Average Inflation and Transparency, All Countries**

This figure shows a weak relationship between central banks that are more transparent—that is, spend more effort explaining the reasons for the monetary policy in place—and a lower rate of average inflation between July 2003 and July 2006.

*Source*: Figure 3 in Christopher Crowe and Ellen E. Meade, "The Evolution of Central Bank Governance around the World," *Journal of Economic Perspectives* 21 (4), 2007: pp. 69–90. © IMF. Printed by permission.

## 23-3 | Politics and Policy

We have assumed so far that policy makers are *benevolent*—that they try to do what is best for the economy. However, much public discussion challenges that assumption: Politicians or policy makers, the argument goes, do what is best for themselves, and this is not always what is best for the country.

You may have heard the arguments: Politicians avoid hard decisions, they pander to the electorate, partisan politics leads to gridlock, and nothing ever gets done. Discussing the flaws of democracy goes far beyond the scope of this book. What we can do here is review briefly how these arguments apply to macroeconomic policy, then look at the empirical evidence, and see what light it sheds on the issue of policy restraints.

### Games between Policy Makers and Voters

Many macroeconomic measures involve trading off short-run losses against long-run gains—or, symmetrically, short-run gains against long-run losses.

Take, for example, tax cuts. By definition, tax cuts lead to lower taxes today. They are also likely to lead to an increase in activity, and so to an increase in pretax income, for some time. But unless they are matched by equal decreases in government spending, they lead to a larger budget deficit and to the need for an increase in taxes in the future. If voters are shortsighted, the temptation for politicians to cut taxes may prove irresistible. Politics may lead to systematic deficits, at least until the level of government debt has become so high that politicians are scared into action. ◀

Now, move on from taxes to macroeconomic policy in general. Again, suppose that voters are shortsighted. If the politicians' main goal is to please voters and get re-elected, what better policy than to expand aggregate demand before an election, leading to higher growth and lower unemployment? True, growth in excess of the normal growth rate cannot be sustained, and eventually the economy must return to the normal level of output: Higher growth must be followed by lower growth later. But with the right timing and shortsighted voters, higher ◀ growth can win the elections. Thus, we might expect a clear **political business cycle**, with higher growth, on average, before elections than after elections.

The arguments we have just laid out are familiar; in one form or another, you surely have heard them before. And their logic is convincing. So it may come as a surprise that they do not fit the facts very well.

For example, our discussion of taxes might lead you to expect that budget deficits and high government debt have always been and will always be with us. Figure 23–4, which gives

The tax cuts both decrease tax rates and increase activity. But they also lead to a long sequence of deficits, which may take considerable time to eliminate. We will look at the relation between current and future taxes more formally when we examine the implications of the government budget constraint in Chapter 25.

From Okun's law, output growth in excess of normal growth leads to a decline in the unemployment rate below the natural rate. In the medium run, we know that the unemployment rate must increase back to the natural rate. This, in turn, requires output growth below normal growth for some time. (See Chapter 13, in particular, Table 13–1).

the evolution of the ratio of government debt to GDP in Canada between 1926 and 2012, shows this is not the case. The first two buildups in debt happened in very special circumstances. The Great Depression, with a large reduction in both output and tax revenue, led to a sharp increase in the ratio of debt to GDP. World War II, in which Canada was a principal combatant for six long years, was financed by an enormous buildup of debt. After World War II ended, rapid growth in real GDP and some fairly significant inflation led to a long reduction in the ratio of debt to GDP. The lowest value of the debt ratio is seen in 1976, 30.9%.

The long increase in the debt-to-GDP ratio from 1976 to 1996, a period of 20 years, seems to fit the argument of shortsighted politicians well. But after 1996, the Liberal government reversed the previous 20 years of fiscal policy (where both Liberal and Conservative governments had been in power), and the ratio of debt to GDP fell from 75% in 1996 to about 40% in 2006. Stephen Harper's Conservatives were then elected and the debt-to-GDP ratio stabilized until the 2009 recession. When the recession occurred, a combination of increased expenditures, temporary tax reductions, and a fall in income brought back large deficits.

Figure 23–4 shows two measures of the gross debt-to-GDP ratio. The old measure stops in 2008. The new measure started in 1990. The two measures are very close but not identical. Measuring exactly what the government owes and what form those debts take would lead us deep into accounting issues. What is clear is that with the onset of 2009 recession and the following years of large deficits, the debt-to-GDP ratio began to rise again.

## The Political Business Cycle

The relation between the deficit, debt, and GDP is explored in detail in Chapter 25. ▶

Chapter 25 will examine alternative—and empirically more successful—explanations for the evolution of government debt, both over time and across countries.

The broader historical record suggests that by itself, a short-sighted political business cycle does not explain much of the past evolution of deficits and debt.

Let us return to the political-business-cycle argument that policy makers try to get high output growth before the elections so that they will be re-elected. We can look only at the American evidence on this point. An American president knows, when he (or she) is elected, exactly when the next election will occur. Election dates are fixed in advance, and thus an American president could try to generate an economic boom just before the next election. To date, only Ontario and British Columbia have experimented with fixed election dates. We cannot distinguish between booms "caused" by an upcoming election and elections that are "caused" by a previous boom. At the federal level, the October 2008 election called by

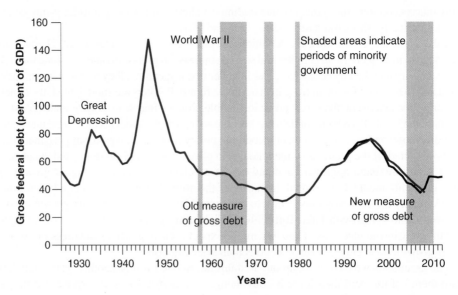

### FIGURE 23–4

**The Evolution of the Ratio of Gross Federal Debt to GDP, 1926–2012**

The ratio of federal debt to GDP has moved a lot since 1926. There are three peaks. The Great Depression years saw GDP fall and the debt-to-GDP ratio rise. World War II saw a very large increase in GDP but an even larger increase in debt and deficits to finance the war. From 1970 to 1997, in peacetime, persisitent deficits under Liberal and Conservative governments saw debt grow. This was reversed in 1997 and reversed again in 2009.

*Source:* Old measure of gross debt: Gross federal debt using CANSIM II variable V151537; nominal GDP using CANSIM II variables V500633 and V646925. New measure of gross debt: CANSIM II variable V6269805. The two measures are similar but not identical.

Prime Minister Stephen Harper violated, at least in a sense, the Conservatives' own legislation to have four years between federal elections. Some thought Harper called the election one year early precisely to avoid the expected recession since house prices in the United States and the rest of the world had already begun to collapse. In the United States, if the political business cycle were important, we would expect to see faster growth before elections than after elections. There is very weak evidence for this effect. In the United States, real economic growth is slightly higher in the fourth year of a presidential term than in the first year. The difference in growth rates is small.

## Games between Policy Makers

Another line of argument focuses not on games between politicians and voters, but rather on games between political parties. For example, take the issue of budget deficit reduction in Canada. When first elected, the Conservative government of Brian Mulroney had a clear mandate to reduce the deficit. It did not succeed in reducing the deficit. Some of its failure was part of the normal electoral and political process. Deficit reductions involve making painful decisions, either reducing spending or raising taxes. But other factors seemed to be at work as well. Some of the Conservatives were small "c" conservatives from Western Canada who clearly wanted less government spending. Some of the Conservatives were Quebec nationalists who did not want less government spending. Each side of this rather uneasy coalition wanted to set government's priorities. Perhaps as a result, the issue was not resolved. Each side on the issue may have simply hoped the other side would give up first.

Game theorists refer to these situations as **wars of attrition**. The hope that the other side will give in leads to long and often costly delays. Such wars of attrition are endemic in fiscal policy. Deficit reduction often takes place long after it would be best.

Figure 23–4 allows us to explore one more aspect of deficits and debt as the outcome of a political game. It is sometimes suggested that when there is a minority government it is more difficult to increase taxes and more difficult to reduce spending. Spending increases may be needed to keep all the parties happier and the government in power. If this were the case, we would expect to see the debt-to-GDP ratio rise more during minority governments. The shaded years in Figure 23–4 correspond to years when Canada had a federal minority government of either party. There is no obvious pattern where the debt-to-GDP ratio rises in the shaded years; in fact, it looks to be the opposite.

> Wars of attrition are not limited to fiscal policy: You may remember strikes in both basketball and baseball where all or part of the season was cancelled because owners and players could not reach an agreement.

## Back to a Balanced-Budget Law

Let us end this chapter with one of the issues we started with, the cases for and against a balanced-budget law. Most economists do not favour balanced-budget laws. Their arguments are presented below.

**The Case against a Balanced-Budget Law.** A balanced-budget law might (only might) eliminate the problem of deficits. In virtually every balanced-budget law actually agreed to, there are many loopholes, and the actual consequences, if any, of breaking the law are quite trivial. The Focus box "The Stability and Growth Pact (SGP): A Short History" presents the attempt by Europe to sign an international treaty within the euro currency union to enforce a reduction in deficits in member countries. A reasonable conclusion: this attempt failed spectacularly.

In failing, the SGP joins most or all other balanced budget laws on the dust heap of history. The province of Ontario passed the following balanced-budget law in 1999: the members of the Cabinet can plan a deficit of up to 1% of GDP only if they plan to run an equal or greater surplus in the following year. However, the law does not apply if there has been a natural disaster, a war, or a decline in revenue for any reason other than a reduction in a statutory tax rate. This last condition, of course, creates a loophole the size of a jetliner. Ontario has run many deficits since 1999.

The Maastricht treaty, negotiated by the countries of the European Union in 1991, set a number of convergence criteria that countries had to meet in order to qualify to join the euro area (see the Focus box "The Euro: A Short History" in Chapter 14). Among the convergence criteria (you can think of these as budget rules) were two restrictions on fiscal policy: First, the budget deficit had to be below 3% in all member countries. Second, the ratio of national debt to GDP had to be below 60%, or at least "approaching this value at a satisfactory pace." That second phrase should immediately tell you how hard it is to write rules about fiscal policy.

In 1997, would-be members of the euro area agreed to make some of these restrictions permanent. The **Stability and Growth Pact** (SGP), signed in 1997, required members of the euro area to adhere to the following fiscal rules:

● Countries committed to balance their budgets in the medium run. They were to present programs to the European authorities, specifying their objectives for the current and following three years in order to show how they were making progress to this goal.

● Countries were to avoid excessive deficits, except under exceptional circumstances. Following the Maastricht treaty criteria, excessive deficits were defined as deficits in excess of 3% of GDP. Exceptional circumstances were defined as a decline of GDP larger than 2%.

● Sanctions were to be imposed on countries that ran excessive deficits. These sanctions could range from 0.2 to 0.5% of GDP—so, for a country like France, up to roughly 10 billion dollars!

Figure 1 plots the evolution of budget deficits since 1990 for the euro area as a whole. Note how, from 1993 to 2000, budget balances went from a deficit of 5.8% of euro area GDP to a surplus of 0.1%. The performance of some of the member countries was particularly impressive: Greece reduced its deficit from 13.4% of GDP to a reported 1.4% of GDP (it was discovered in 2004 that the Greek government had cheated in reporting its deficit numbers and that the actual improvement, although impressive, was less than reported; the deficit for 2000 is now estimated to have been 4.1%); Italy's deficit went from 10.1% of GDP in 1993 to only 0.9% of GDP in 2000.

Was the improvement entirely due to the SGP rules? The answer is almost certainly no. The decrease in nominal interest rates, which decreased the interest payments on the debt, and the strong expansion of the late 1990s both played important roles. But, again as in the United States, the fiscal rules also played a significant role: The carrot—the right to become a member of the euro area—was attractive enough to lead a number of countries to take tough measures to reduce their deficits.

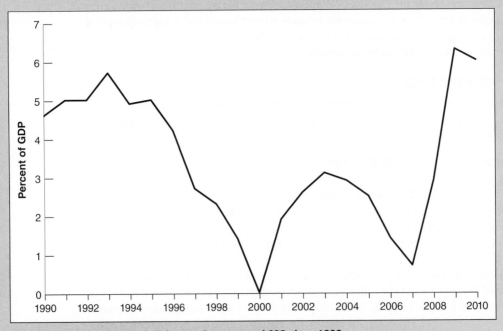

**FIGURE 1   Euro Area Budget Deficits as a Percentage of GDP since 1990**

*Source:* Eurostat, General Government Deficit/Surplus, http://app/eurostat.ec.europa.eu

Things turned around, however, after 2000. From 2000 on, deficits started increasing. The first country to break the limit was Portugal in 2001, with a deficit of 4.4%. The next two countries were France and Germany, both with deficits in excess of 3% of GDP in 2002. Italy soon followed. In each case, the government of the country decided it was more important to avoid a fiscal contraction that could lead to even slower output growth than to satisfy the rules of the SGP.

Faced with clear "excessive deficits" (and without the excuse of exceptional circumstances because output growth in each these countries was low but positive), European authorities found themselves in a quandary. Starting the excessive deficit procedure against Portugal, a small country, might have been politically feasible, although it is doubtful that Portugal would have ever been willing to pay any fine. Starting the same procedure against the two largest members of the euro area, France and Germany, proved politically impossible. After an internal fight between the two main European authorities, the European Commission and the European Council—the European Commission wanted to proceed with the excessive deficit procedure, while the European Council, which represents the states, did not—the procedure was suspended.

The crisis made it clear that the initial rules were too inflexible. Romano Prodi, the head of the European Commission, admitted to that much: In an interview in October 2002, he stated, "I know very well that the Stability Pact is stupid, like all decisions that are rigid." And the attitudes of both France and Germany showed that the threat to impose large fines on countries with excessive deficits was simply not credible.

For two years, the European Commission explored ways to improve the rules so as to make them more flexible and, by implication, more credible. In 2005, a new, revised SGP was adopted. It kept the 3% deficit and 60% debt numbers as thresholds but allowed for more flexibility in deviating from the rules. Growth no longer had to be less than zero for the rules to be suspended. Exceptions were also made if the deficit came from structural reforms, or from public investment. Fines were gone, and the plan was to rely on early public warnings as well as on peer pressure from other euro area countries.

For a while, deficits as a percent of GDP declined, largely due to strong growth. But the crisis, and the associated sharp decrease in revenues, led again to a sharp increase in budget deficits. In 2010, 23 out of 27 EU countries stood in violation of the 3% deficit limit, and it was clear that the rules had to be reconsidered. In March 2011 a new set of rules, known as the **Euro Plus Pact**, was adopted. It requires member countries to translate the SGP rules into national legislation, either through a constitutional amendment or a framework law. Whether or not these new rules work any better than the initial pact remains to be seen.

Beyond their impracticality—that is, that they are difficult to write and difficult to enforce—the main argument against a balanced-budget law is that in times when there is a large fall in private demand, you actually want to run a deficit to increase total demand. For Canada, this clearly happened in 2009 and 2010. Exports to the United States fell. Deficits were increased to offset part of the effects of the lost exports. It is clear the recession would have been larger in Canada if we had had an enforceable balanced budget law.

A second argument against a balanced budget law is simpler. Any rule that a legislature may impose upon itself can be undone with a subsequent vote whenever needed. Proponents of these laws do recognize that fact. They argue the law is useful in any case because of the increased political cost of the action to actually repeal the balanced-budget law. It brings the issue of the budget deficit and increased debt directly in front of the public.

Finally, it is hard to argue balanced-budget laws are actually needed to reduce a deficit and stabilize debt. After all, Figure 23–4 shows that the Canadian federal government under the Liberals stabilized and reduced the national debt after 1997 without a balanced-budget law. Similarly the Conservatives are expecting to balance the budget and stabilize the national debt by 2015-2016 without the aid of a balanced budget law. This has happened in other countries and sub-national jurisdictions.

**The Case for a Balanced-Budget Law.** To a few economists, a balanced-budget law is potentially useful. These economists are typically more skeptical of the usefulness of macroeconomic policy as a tool to stabilize output. Thus, a balanced-budget law may prevent any policy, including a bad policy. They are willing to give up fiscal policy as a macroeconomic instrument and if a balanced budget law makes that more likely to happen, that is a good thing.

The second argument for a balanced-budget law might be to force a more intelligent discussion around the introduction of a new government spending initiative. If the balanced-budget law were in place and taken seriously, a discussion of a new spending initiative should be accompanied by an explicit discussion of how to raise the revenue to pay for the initiative. This might be a microeconomic argument for a balanced budget law. No political party could propose a new program without proposing a way to pay for a new program.

- There is substantial uncertainty about the effects of macroeconomic policies. This uncertainty should lead policy makers to be more cautious and to use less active policies. Policies must be broadly aimed at avoiding prolonged recessions, slowing down booms, and avoiding inflationary pressure. The higher the level of unemployment or inflation, the more active the policies should be. But they should stop short of fine tuning, of trying to maintain constant unemployment or constant output growth.

- Using macroeconomic policy to control the economy is fundamentally different from controlling a machine. Unlike a machine, the economy is composed of people and firms that try to anticipate what policy makers will do and react not only to current policy but also to expectations of future policy. In this sense, macroeconomic policy can be thought of as a game between policy makers and the economy.

- When playing a game, it is sometimes better for a player to give up some of his options. For example, when a hostage taking occurs, it is best to negotiate with hostage takers. But a government that credibly commits to not negotiating with hostage takers—that gives up the option of negotiation—is actually more likely to deter hostage takings in the first place.

- The same argument applies to various aspects of macroeconomic policy. By credibly committing to not using

monetary policy to decrease unemployment below its natural rate, a central bank can alleviate fears that money growth will be high and, in the process, decrease both expected and actual inflation. When issues of time inconsistency are relevant, tight restraints on policy makers—such as a fixed-money-growth rule in the case of monetary policy—can, indeed, provide a coarse solution. But the solution may have large costs if it prevents the use of macroeconomic policy altogether. Better methods typically involve designing better institutions (such as an independent central bank) that can reduce the problem of time inconsistency without eliminating monetary policy as a macroeconomic policy tool.

- Another argument for putting restraints on policy makers is that they may play games either with the public or among themselves, and these games may lead to undesirable outcomes. Politicians may try to fool a short-sighted electorate by choosing policies with short-run benefits but large long-term costs—for example, large budget deficits. Political parties may delay painful decisions, hoping that the other party will make the adjustment and take the blame. These problems exist, although they are less prevalent than is usually perceived. In such cases, tight restraints on policy, such as a law to balance the budget, provide a partial solution. However, the evidence is that balanced-budget laws are ineffective and easily sidestepped in practice.

- Euro Plus Pact, 487
- fine tuning, 478
- game, 478
- game theory, 478
- optimal control, 478
- optimal control theory, 478

- players, 478
- political business cycle, 483
- Stability and Growth Pact, 486
- strategic interactions, 478
- time inconsistency, 479
- war of attrition, 485

**1. TRUE/FALSE/UNCERTAIN**

**a.** There is so much uncertainty about the effects of monetary policy that we would be better off not using it.

**b.** Elect a Liberal government if you want low unemployment.

**c.** There is clear evidence of political business cycles in the United States: increases in economic activity just before elections and lower economic activity after elections.

**d.** Balanced-budget laws are effective in reducing budget deficits.

**e.** You should never negotiate with hostage takers.

**f.** Once a central bank announces a target inflation rate, it has no incentive to deviate from the target.

**2. TIME CONSISTENCY**

Has the problem of "time consistency" ever arisen in your personal life? Who were the players in that "game"?

## 3. DESIGNING POLICY TO WIN ELECTIONS

You are an advisor to a newly elected prime minister. She will face new elections four years from now. Inflation last year was 3%, and the unemployment rate was equal to the natural rate. The Phillips curve is given by:

$$\pi_t = \pi_{t-1} - \alpha(u_t - u_n)$$

a. Assume you can use fiscal and monetary policies to achieve any unemployment rate you want for each of the next four years. Write a short memo to the prime minister indicating what unemployment and inflation rates she should try to achieve.

b. How would you change the content of your memo if the Phillips curve is given by:

$$\pi_t = \pi_t^e - \alpha(u_t - u_n)$$

and the evidence is that people form rational expectations?

## 4. THE NEW ZEALAND EXAMPLE

New Zealand rewrote the charter of its central bank in the early 1990s to make steady, low inflation its only goal. Why would New Zealand want to do this?

## 5. LIBERALS AND CONSERVATIVES

There are two parties: the Liberals, who care a lot more about unemployment than about inflation, and the Conservatives, who care a lot more about inflation than about unemployment.

The Phillips curve is given by:

$$\pi_t = \pi_t^e - \alpha(u_t - u_n)$$

where $\pi_t^e$ denotes expectations held in year $t - 1$ for inflation in year $t$.

There are elections at the end of this year. Liberals and Conservatives have an equal chance of winning and being in power next year.

a. Describe how people will form expectations of inflation for next year.

b. Given these expectations, describe what happens to inflation and unemployment next year if the Liberals win.

c. Given these expectations, describe what happens to inflation and unemployment next year if the Conservatives win.

d. Suppose now that everybody expects Liberals to win the elections. Suppose the Liberals indeed win. What happens to inflation and unemployment next year? Explain.

## 6. CUTTING THE BUDGET: THE PRISONER'S DILEMMA

Suppose there is a budget deficit in the United States. It can be reduced by cutting defence spending or by cutting welfare programs or by cutting both.

The Democrats have to decide whether to support cuts in welfare programs. The Republicans have to decide whether to support cuts in defence spending. Each party has to decide what to do, without knowing the decision of the other party.

The possible outcomes can be represented in Table 1, Question 6.

To understand how to read this table, look at the bottom-left corner. If Democrats vote for welfare cuts, and Republicans vote against cuts in defence spending, the outcome is that the Republicans are very happy and the Democrats are unhappy. The Republicans get 3 (a high positive number), and the Democrats get −2. Make sure you understand each of the four outcomes.

### TABLE 1, QUESTION 6

| | | Welfare cuts | |
| --- | --- | --- | --- |
| | | Yes | No |
| Defence | Yes | (R = 1, D = 1) | (R = −2, D = 3) |
| cuts | No | (R = 3, D = −2) | (R = −1, D = −1) |

a. If the Republicans decide to cut defence spending, what is the best response of the Democrats? Given this response, how much will the Republicans get?

b. If the Republicans decide not to cut defence spending, what is the best response of the Democrats? Given this response, how much will the Republicans get?

c. What will the Republicans do? What will the Democrats do? Will the budget deficit be reduced? Why, or why not? (This is an example of a game known as the prisoner's dilemma in game theory.) Is there a way to improve the outcome?

---

### FURTHER READING

A leading proponent of the view that governments misbehave and should be tightly restrained is James Buchanan, from George Mason University. Buchanan received the Nobel prize in 1986 for his work on public choice. Read his book co-authored with Richard Wagner, *Democracy in Deficit: The Political Legacy of Lord Keynes* (New York: Academic Press, 1977).

A text specific to the issues raised in this chapter is Alan Drazen's *Political Economy in Macroeconomics* (Princeton University Press, 2001).

For an interpretation of the increase in inflation of time inconsistency, see Henry Chappell and Rob McGregor, "Did Time Consistency Contribute to the Great Inflation?," *Economics and Politics 16,* November 2004: pp. 233–251.

# Monetary Policy: A Summing Up

## Back to Policy

Nearly every chapter has had something to say about monetary policy. This chapter puts it all together and ties up the remaining loose ends. The chapter explores two basic issues in some detail:

1. The optimal inflation rate. There is no question that very high inflation is costly. But how low should inflation be? Should central banks aim for an average inflation rate of, say, 2% or 4%, aim for price stability, or even aim for deflation (negative inflation)?
2. The design of monetary policy. Once the central bank has decided what rate of inflation it wants to achieve, how should it design monetary policy? Given that it directly controls money growth, should it announce a target rate for money growth? Or should it announce a target rate of inflation and try to hit it as best as it can? Should it target the inflation rate or a price level at some point in the future, and why is that different? In the short run, how much should it be willing to deviate from whatever target it has announced if, say, the economy goes into recession? How much does the exchange rate matter for monetary policy?

   As part of exploring these issues, the chapter looks at what the Canadian central bank—the Bank of Canada—actually does, how it designs and carries out monetary policy, and how well it has done in the recent past. We close with some notes on how the world economic crisis has changed monetary policy.

# 24-1 | What We Have Learned about Monetary Policy

- In Chapter 4, we looked at the determination of money demand and money supply and the effects of monetary policy on the interest rate. We saw how an increase in money supply (achieved through an open market operation) leads to a decrease in the interest rate. We also saw that a central bank may choose to announce a target for the interest rate and then manipulate the money supply, or in a more complicated presentation of the banking system, manipulate the monetary base to achieve the target interest rate.

- In Chapter 5, we looked at the short-run effects of monetary policy on output. We saw how an increase in money leads, through a decrease in the interest rate, to an increase in spending and to an increase in output.

- In Chapter 8, we looked at the effects of monetary policy in an economy with open goods and financial markets. We saw how, in an open economy, monetary policy affects spending and output not only through interest rates, but also through the exchange rate. An increase in money leads to both a decrease in the interest rate and a depreciation of the exchange rate. The changes in both interest rate and exchange rate increase spending and output.

- In Chapter 10, we looked at the effects of changes in money on output and prices, not only in the short run, but also in the medium run. We saw that in the medium run, money is neutral: Changes in money are fully reflected in changes in prices.

- In Chapter 11, we looked two specific situations in which monetary policy gets more complicated. In the liquidity trap, conventional monetary policy is ineffective. The interest rate cannot be lowered below zero. If there is a supply shock, monetary policy cannot prevent a decline in output in the medium run.

- In Chapter 12, we had a first look at the relation among money growth, inflation, and unemployment. We saw that in the medium run, increases in money growth is reflected one for one in an increase in inflation, leaving the unemployment rate unaffected.

- In Chapter 13, we looked at alternative disinflation strategies. On the basis of the Canadian disinflations in the early 1980s and early 1990s and other disinflations around the world, we concluded that disinflations typically come at a cost of higher unemployment for some time.

- In Chapter 14, we discussed the pros and cons of different monetary policy regimes, of flexible versus fixed exchange rates. We discussed the pros and cons of adopting a common currency, such as the euro.

- In Chapter 19, we introduced a distinction between the nominal interest rate and the real interest rate. We saw how higher money growth leads to a lower nominal interest rate in the short run but to a higher nominal interest rate—and an unchanged real interest rate—in the medium run.

- In Chapter 22, we returned to the short-run effects of monetary policy on output, taking into account the effects of monetary policy on expectations. We saw that monetary policy affects the short-term nominal interest rate, but that spending depends primarily on both current and expected future short-term real interest rates. We saw how, as a result, the effects of monetary policy on output depend on how expectations respond to policy.

- In Chapter 23, we looked at the problems facing macroeconomic policy in general and monetary policy in particular. We saw that uncertainty about the effects of policy should lead to more cautious policies. We saw that even well-intentioned policy makers may sometimes not do what is best and that there is a case for restraints on policy makers. We also looked at the case for making the central bank independent and appointing a conservative central banker.

In this chapter, we first look at the choice of the optimal inflation rate. Then we think about how to conduct monetary policy in theory. There are some useful and interesting details concerning how the Bank of Canada actually conducts monetary policy in Canada today. Finally, we return to the world economic crisis of 2008 and 2009 and look at how that crisis changed the conduct of monetary policy.

## 24-2 | The Optimal Inflation Rate

Table 24–1 shows that inflation has steadily gone down in rich countries since the early 1980s. In 2005, average inflation in the OECD was 2.2%, down from 10.5% in 1981. The 30 countries in the OECD saw a decline in average inflation from 2.2% in 2005 to 1.2% in 2010; 27 of the 30 OECD countries had inflation less than 5% in 2010; and 22 of the 30 countries had inflation between 1 and 3%. The three countries with inflation above 5% in 2010: Australia (5.1%); Luxembourg (5.3%); and Turkey (6.45%).

Does this imply that most central banks have now achieved the best possible inflation outcome? Or should they aim for an even lower inflation rate, perhaps 0%? The answer depends on the costs and benefits of inflation.

### The Costs of Inflation

"Hyperinflation" is a term that refers to a very high inflation rate, frequently defined as inflation of more than 50% per month. The causes of hyperinflation are discussed in Chapter 25.

It is quite clear that very high inflation (sometimes called hyperinflation), say, 50% a month or more, can thoroughly disrupt economic activity. The debate in the OECD countries today, however, is not about the costs of inflation rates of 10% a month or more. Inflation of 10% a month is still a very high and disruptive rate of inflation. Rather, it centres on the advantages of, say, 0% versus 2% or 4% inflation a year. Within that range, economists identify four main costs of inflation: shoe-leather costs, tax distortions, money illusion, and inflation variability.

In the medium run, the real interest rate is not affected by inflation. Thus, an increase in inflation is reflected one for one in an increase in the nominal interest rate (Chapter 19).

**Shoe-Leather Costs.** In the medium run, a higher inflation rate leads to a higher nominal interest rate, and thus to a higher opportunity cost of holding money. As a result, people decrease their money balances by making trips to the bank more often—hence the expression **shoe-leather costs**. These trips would be avoided if inflation were lower, and people could be doing other things instead, working more or enjoying more leisure.

During hyperinflations, shoe-leather costs can become quite large. But their importance in times of moderate inflation is limited. If an inflation rate of 4% leads people to go to the bank one more time every month or to do one more transaction between their money market fund and their chequing account every month, this hardly qualifies as a major cost of inflation.

**Tax Distortions.** The second cost of inflation comes from the interaction between the tax system and inflation. Consider, for example, the taxation of capital gains. Taxes on capital gains are typically based on the change in the dollar price of the asset between the time it was purchased and the time it is sold: this implies that the higher the rate of inflation, the higher the tax. An example will make this clear.

| TABLE 24–1 | Inflation Rates in the OECD, 1981–2010 | | | | | |
|---|---|---|---|---|---|---|
| Year | 1981 | 1985 | 1990 | 1995 | 2005 | 2010 |
| OECD average[1] | 10.5% | 6.5% | 5.9% | 5.1% | 2.2% | 1.2% |
| Number of countries with inflation below 5%[2] | 2 | 10 | 15 | 21 | 28 | 27 |

[1]Average of GDP deflator inflation rates, using relative GDPs measured at PPP prices as weights.

[2]Out of 30 countries.

Suppose that inflation has been running at $\pi$ a year for the last 10 years. Suppose that you bought a cottage for $50,000 ten years ago, and you are selling it today for $50,000 times $(1 + \pi)^{10}$—so its real value is unchanged. If the capital-gains tax is 30%, the *effective tax rate* on the sale of your cottage—defined as the ratio of the tax you pay to the price for which you sell your house—is:

$$(30\%) \frac{50{,}000(1 + \pi)^{10} - 50{,}000}{50{,}000(1 + \pi)^{10}}$$

◀ The numerator of the fraction equals the sale price minus the purchase price. The denominator is the sale price.

Because you are selling your cottage for the same real price for which you bought it, your real capital gain is zero, and you should not be paying any tax. Indeed, if $\pi = 0$—if there has been no inflation—then the effective tax rate is 0%. But if $\pi = 4\%$, then the effective tax rate is 9.7%: Despite the fact that your real capital gain is zero, you end up paying a high tax. In Canadian tax law, your principal residence (but not a second residence) is exempt from capital-gains tax partly for this very reason.

The problems extend beyond capital-gains taxes on cottages. There are inflation-induced capital gains on shares as well. Although the real rate of return on an asset is the real interest rate, not the nominal interest rate, income for the purpose of income taxation includes nominal interest payments, not real interest payments. Or, to take yet another example, the income levels corresponding to different income-tax rates may not increase automatically with inflation. As a result, people could be pushed into higher tax brackets as their nominal income—but not necessarily their real income—increased over time, an effect known as *bracket creep*. Bracket creep was removed from the Canadian tax system from 1974 to 1986. In 1986, tax brackets were increased only by inflation in excess of 3% in each year. Economists C.G. Ruggieri, D. Van Wart, and R. Howard at the Alberta Treasury estimated that between 1986 and 1993, federal and provincial governments took in 2% more of GDP because of the cumulative effects of bracket creep. In 1999, Finance Minister Paul Martin announced that for federal income taxes, brackets would be fully indexed for inflation and bracket creep would end.

◀ Some economists argue that the costs of bracket creep were, in fact, much larger. As tax revenues steadily increased, there was little pressure on government to control spending. The result, they argue, was an increase in the size of government in the 1960s and 1970s far beyond what would have been desirable.

You may argue this cost is not a cost of inflation per se but rather the result of a badly designed tax system. In the example of the cottage we just discussed, government could eliminate the problem if it *indexed* the purchase price to the price level—that is, it adjusted the purchase price for inflation since the time of purchase—and computed the tax on the difference between the sale price and the adjusted purchase price. Under that computation, there would be no capital gains and therefore no capital-gains tax to pay. But because tax codes rarely allow for such systematic adjustment, the inflation rate matters and leads to distortions.

**Money Illusion.** The third cost comes from *money illusion*, the notion that people appear to make systematic mistakes in assessing nominal versus real changes. Many computations that would be simple under price stability become more complicated when there is inflation. In comparing their income this year to their income in the past, people have to keep track of the history of inflation. In choosing between different assets or deciding how much to consume or save, they have to keep track of the difference between the real interest rate and the nominal interest rate. Casual evidence suggests that many people find these computations difficult and often fail to make the relevant distinctions. Economists and psychologists have gathered more formal evidence, and it suggests that inflation often leads people and firms to make incorrect decisions (see the Focus box "Money Illusion"). If this is the case, then a simple solution is to have no inflation.

**Inflation Variability.** The last cost comes from the fact that higher inflation is typically associated with *more variable inflation*. And more variable inflation means that financial assets such as bonds, which promise fixed nominal payments in the future, become riskier.

Take a bond that pays $1000 in 10 years. With constant inflation over the next 10 years, the real value of the bond in 10 years is known with certainty. But with variable inflation, the

There is a lot of anecdotal evidence that many people fail to adjust properly for inflation in their financial computations. Recently, economists and psychologists have started looking at money illusion more closely. In a recent study, two psychologists, Eldar Shafir from Princeton and Amos Tversky from Stanford, and one economist, Peter Diamond from MIT, designed a survey aimed at finding how prevalent money illusion is and what causes it. Among the many questions they asked of people in various groups (people at Newark International Airport, people at two New Jersey shopping malls, and a group of Princeton undergraduates) is the following:

Suppose Adam, Ben, and Carl each received an inheritance of $200,000 and each used it immediately to purchase a house. Suppose each sold his house one year after buying it. Economic conditions were, however, different in each case:

- During the time Adam owned the house, there was a 25% deflation—the prices of all goods and services decreased by approximately 25%. A year after Adam bought the house, he sold it for $154,000 (23% less than what he had paid).
- During the time Ben owned the house, there was no inflation or deflation—the prices of all goods and services did not change significantly during the year. A year after Ben bought the house, he sold it for $198,000 (1% less than what he had paid).
- During the time Carl owned the house, there was a 25% inflation—the prices of all goods and services increased by approximately 25%. A year after Carl bought the house, he sold it for $246,000 (23% more than what he had paid).

Please rank Adam, Ben, and Carl in terms of the success of their house transactions. Assign "1" to the person who made the best deal and "3" to the person who made the worst deal.

In nominal terms, Carl clearly made the best deal, followed by Ben, followed by Adam. But what is relevant is how they did in real terms—adjusting for inflation. In real terms, the ranking is reversed: Adam, with a 2% real gain, made the best deal, followed by Ben (with a 1% loss), followed by Carl (with a 2% loss).

The survey's answers were the following:

| Rank | Adam | Ben | Carl |
| --- | --- | --- | --- |
| 1st | 37% | 15% | 48% |
| 2nd | 10% | 74% | 16% |
| 3rd | 53% | 11% | 36% |

Carl was ranked first by 48% of the respondents, and Adam was ranked third by 53% of the respondents. These answers suggest that money illusion is very prevalent. In other words, people (even Princeton undergraduates) have a hard time adjusting for inflation.

*Source:* Eldar Shafir, Peter Diamond, Amos Tversky, "Money Illusion", Quarterly Journal of Economics, 1 997 1 1 2(2): pp. 341–374. p. 522: " Money Illusion" by Eldar Shafir, Peter Diamond, and Amos Tversky from the *Quarterly Journal Of Economics*, 1 997 (No. 2): 341–374. Copyright © 1997 Oxford University Press. Reprinted by permission of the publisher.

real value of $1000 in 10 years becomes uncertain. Saving for retirement becomes more difficult. For those who have invested in bonds, lower inflation than expected means a better retirement; but higher inflation may mean poverty. This is one of the reasons retirees, for whom part of income is fixed in dollar terms, typically worry more about inflation than other groups in the population.

You may argue, as in the case of taxes, that these costs are not due to inflation per se but rather to the financial markets' inability to provide assets that protect their holders against inflation. Rather than issuing only nominal bonds (bonds that promise a fixed nominal amount in the future), governments or firms could also issue *indexed bonds*—bonds that promise a nominal amount adjusted for inflation so that people do not have to worry about the real value of the bond when they retire. Indeed, as we saw in Chapter 20, several governments have now introduced such bonds. Indexed bonds now play an important role in the United Kingdom, where, over the last 20 years, people increasingly have used them to save for retirement. Canada has a small market in indexed federal government bonds. Indexed bonds were introduced in the United States only in 1997. They account for only a small proportion of U.S. government bonds at this point. We used returns on Canadian and American indexed bonds to construct Figure 20–12.

## The Benefits of Inflation

Inflation is actually not all bad. One can identify three benefits of inflation: (1) seignorage, (2) the option of negative real interest rates for macroeconomic policy, and (3) (somewhat paradoxically) the use of the interaction between money illusion and inflation in facilitating real wage adjustments.

**Seignorage.** Money creation—the ultimate source of inflation—is one of the ways in which government can finance its spending. Put another way, money creation is an alternative to borrowing from the public or raising taxes.

Typically, government does not "create" money to pay for its spending. Rather, it issues and sells bonds and spends the proceeds. But if the bonds are bought by the central bank, which then creates money to pay for them, the result is the same: Other things being equal, the revenues from money creation—that is, *seignorage*—allow government to borrow less from the public or to lower taxes.

How large is seignorage in practice? Its importance in the OECD economies today, and for the range of inflation rates we are considering, is limited. Take the case of Canada: The ratio of the monetary base—the money issued by the Bank of Canada (see Chapter 4)—to GDP is about 4%. An increase in money growth of 4% per year (which eventually leads to a 4% increase in inflation) would therefore lead to an increase in seignorage of 4% $\times$ 4%, or 0.16% of GDP. This is a small amount of revenues to get in exchange for 4% more inflation. ◄ This amount of revenue is not relevant in the discussion of inflation between 0% and 4%.

Let $H$ denote the monetary base. Then:
$$\frac{Seignorage}{Y} = \frac{\Delta H}{PY}$$
$$= \frac{\Delta H}{H} \frac{H}{PY}$$
$\Delta H/H$: Rate of growth of the monetary base
$H/PY$: Ratio of the monetary base to (nominal) GDP

**The Option of Negative Real Interest Rates.** This argument follows from our discussion of the liquidity trap in Chapter 11. A numerical example will help here.

- Consider two economies, both with a *natural real interest rate* equal to 2%.
- In the first economy, the central bank maintains an average inflation rate of 4%, so the nominal interest rate is on average equal to 2% + 4% = 6%.
- In the second economy, the central bank maintains an average inflation rate of 0%, so the nominal interest rate is on average equal to 2% + 0% = 2%.
- Suppose both economies are hit by a similar adverse shock, which leads, at a given real interest rate, to a decrease in spending and a decrease in output in the short run.
- In the first economy, the central bank can decrease the nominal interest rate from 6% to 0% before it hits the liquidity trap; thus there is a decrease of 6%. Under the assumption that expected inflation does not change immediately and remains equal to 4%, the real interest rate decreases from 2% to −4%. This is likely to have a strong positive effect on spending and help the economy recover.
- In the second economy, the central bank can only decrease the nominal interest rate from 2% to 0%, a decrease of 2%. Under the assumption that expected inflation does not change right away and remains equal to 0%, the real interest rate decreases only by 2%, from 2% to 0%. This small decrease in the real interest rate may not increase spending by very much.

In short, an economy with a higher average inflation rate has more room to use monetary policy to fight a recession. An economy with a low average inflation rate may find itself unable to use monetary policy to return output to the natural level of output. As we saw in Chapter 11, this possibility is far from being just theoretical. Many countries today find themselves in the liquidity trap, unable to decrease interest rates further. The question is whether this should lead the country to choose slightly higher average inflation in the future. Some economists argue that the current crisis is an exceptional event, that it is unlikely that countries will face a liquidity trap again in the future, and so there is no need to adopt a higher average inflation rate. Others argue that the problems faced by a country in a liquidity trap are so serious that we should avoid taking the risk that it happens again, and that a higher rate of inflation is in fact justified. This debate is far from settled.

**Money Illusion Revisited.** Paradoxically, the presence of money illusion provides at least one argument for having a positive inflation rate.

To see why, consider two situations. In the first, inflation is 4% and somebody's wage increases by 1% in dollar terms. In the second, inflation is 0%, and the wage is decreased by

3% in dollar terms. Both lead to the same decrease in the real wage, namely, 3%. There is some evidence, however, that many people will accept the real wage cut more easily in the first case than in the second.

Why is this example relevant to our discussion? The constant process of change that characterizes modern economies means some workers must sometimes take a real pay cut. Thus, the argument goes, the presence of inflation allows for these downward real-wage adjustments more easily than no inflation. This argument is plausible. Economists have not established its importance; but because so many economies now have very low inflation, we soon may be in a position to test it.

## The Optimal Inflation Rate: The Current Debate

A fight between metaphors: Because inflation makes these real wage adjustments easier to achieve, some economists say inflation "greases the wheels" of the economy. Others, emphasizing the adverse effects of inflation on relative prices, say that inflation instead "puts sand" in the economy.

At this stage, most central banks in richer countries have an inflation target of about 2%. They are, however, being challenged on two fronts. Some economists want to achieve price stability—that is, 0% inflation. Others want, instead, a higher target rate of inflation, say 4%.

Those who want to aim for 0% make the point that 0% is a very different target rate from all others: It corresponds to price stability. This is desirable in itself. Knowing the price level will be roughly the same in 10 or 20 years as it is today simplifies a number of complicated decisions and eliminates the scope for money illusion. Also, given the time consistency problem facing central banks (discussed in Chapter 23), credibility and simplicity of the target inflation rate are important. Some economists and some central bankers believe price stability—that is, a 0% target—can achieve these goals better than a target inflation rate of 2%. So far, however, no central bank has actually adopted a 0% inflation target.

This reasoning is sometimes known as the "slippery slope" argument.

Those who want to aim for a higher rate argue that it is essential not to fall in the liquidity trap in the future, and that, for these purposes, a higher target rate of inflation, say 4%, would be helpful. Their argument has gained little support among central bankers. They argue that if central banks increase their target from its current value of 2% to 4%, people may start anticipating that the target will soon become 5%, then 6%, and so on, and inflation expectations will no longer be anchored. Thus, they see it as important to keep current target levels.

The debate goes on. For the time being, most central banks appear to be aiming for low but positive inflation—that is, inflation rates of about 2%.

## The Optimal Rate of Inflation: The Canadian Debate

It may seem that the discussion of the optimal rate of inflation takes place only in theory. In Canada, this debate was active between 1988 and 1994, and the debate continues today in a slightly different form. John Crow was appointed Governor of the Bank of Canada in 1987. In February of 1988, in a speech at the University of Alberta as part of the Hanson Lecture series, he announced that the role of the Bank of Canada was to conduct monetary policy "so as to achieve a pace of monetary expansion that promotes stability in the value of money." The intent of this statement was clear: Zero or close-to-zero inflation was to be the Bank's objective while he was Governor.

There was a volume of papers on the issue, *Zero Inflation: The Goal of Price Stability* edited by Richard G. Lipsey, (Toronto: C.D. Howe Institute, March 1990). This volume contains contributions from most of Canada's prominent macroeconomists. The volume was generally supportive of the move to a lower inflation rate.

Later in the Hanson Lecture and in subsequent speeches, Crow made clear statements as to why price stability was to be the Bank's goal. He believed lower inflation and eventually zero inflation would promote predictability in the inflation rate: "In my view, the notion of a high yet stable rate of inflation is simply unrealistic." Crow also believed that the lower and more predictable rate of inflation would increase real output growth: "Because inflation creates distortions, output will be higher over time in conditions of price stability than in those of inflation." (All quotations are from the Hanson Lecture, reprinted in the *Bank of Canada Review*, February 1988, pp. 3–17.) But the benefits of zero inflation were and are very much in dispute.

Three arguments were also made that measured inflation rates should not be driven to zero—that is, that price stability was not the best goal for monetary policy. First, it is widely known among economists that inflation as measured by the percent change in a consumer price index is overstated by somewhere between 1 and 2%—that is, when measured inflation is 1%, actual inflation may actually be zero. Thus, a policy to produce price stability as zero measured inflation may actually produce falling prices. The central bank needs to explain this issue carefully so that the public understands measured inflation of 1% is price stability. The other two arguments against measured price stability do not depend on the details of the construction of price indexes. They are also the arguments we made earlier, that two important prices may contain important nominal downward rigidities. One price is the money wage. If workers strongly resist cuts in their money wages, a small positive inflation rate may allow real wages to fall as needed to allow for more effective adjustment in labour markets. The second price with an important rigidity is the nominal interest rate, which cannot fall below zero. It could be useful to have a negative real interest rate at times.

It was not until February 27, 1991, that the time horizon for the achievement of lower (but not zero) inflation was specified. On that day, for the first time in Canadian history, a time path (a series of targets) for inflation was specified and this time path was specified jointly by the Department of Finance and the Bank of Canada. The path was very specific: Reduce inflation to 3% or less by the end of 1992, 2.5% or less by the middle of 1994, and 2% or less by the end of 1995, with "further progress to price stability thereafter." The **inflation target** above was defined within a band of plus or minus 1 percentage point. The "further progress" statement was crucial because it assumed that, once inflation of 2% was achieved, there would be a further reduction in inflation. This document makes sense only if you believe the optimal rate of inflation is less than 2%—or why else would you continue to reduce inflation?

In October 1993, the Liberals won the federal election, an election in which the 1990–1991 recession had been a major policy issue. The Liberals had criticized the Conservative government and the Bank of Canada during the course of the election. The Liberal leader, Jean Chrétien, denounced the Bank of Canada as "obsessed with inflation." After the Liberal election victory, Prime Minister Chrétien and new Finance Minister Paul Martin had to decide whether to reappoint John Crow as Governor. Crow's term expired February 1, 1994. Crow had made it clear that he believed in a further reduction in inflation as specified in the 1991 agreement and in the Hanson Lecture. What did the new Liberal government want?

The desires of the new government became clear when Paul Martin announced that John Crow would not be reappointed. Then in February 1994, a new inflation target agreement between the government and the Bank set the inflation target at 2% within a band of 1 to 3% for the next four years. Agreements with the same target rate of inflation—that is, 2%—were announced in 1998, in 2001, in 2006, and again in 2011. The essential part of the 2011 agreement reads:

- *The target will continue to be defined in terms of the 12-month rate of change in the total CPI.*
- *The inflation target will continue to be the 2 per cent mid-point of the 1 to 3 per cent inflation-control range.*
- *The agreement will run for another five-year period, ending 31 December 2016.*

*The Bank will continue its research into potential improvements in the monetary policy framework. Before the end of 2016, the Government and the Bank will review the experience over the period and the results of the research and determine the appropriate target for the years ahead.*

What are the potential improvements to inflation targeting that need more research? The subtle differences between different ways in which inflation might be targeted are illustrated in Table 24–2 over a five-year horizon, a horizon similar to the current inflation agreement.

The first row is an exaggerated picture of the "perfect path," in which the price level never changes and inflation is always zero. The path is not realistic. In a similar sense, the second path where inflation is always 2% each and every year is not realistic. How could the Bank set an exact inflation target and hit it each period? Given a variety of unexpected events in the economy, such a path is not possible.

In particular, such an exact path would have great difficulty with any kind of unexpected changes in the prices of goods that compose consumer price indexes. You know that gas

In *Shooting the Hippo: Death by Deficit and Other Canadian Myths* (see Further Readings), Linda McQuaig does not draw a flattering portrait of the decision making at the Bank of Canada. Chapter 3 is entitled "John Crow and the Politics of Obsession." Paul Krugman makes similar points in his book *The Age of Diminished Expectations,* where he states, "As far as economic analysis can tell us, a steady inflation rate of 4 or 5% does very little harm." John Crow would not have agreed.

| TABLE 24–2 | Examples of Inflation Rates and Price Paths for Different Inflation Target Agreements | | | | | |
|---|---|---|---|---|---|---|
| **Type of Policy** | **2011** | **2012** | **2013** | **2014** | **2015** | **2016** |
| Zero inflation each year | 100 (0%) | 100 (0%) | 100 (0%) | 100 (0%) | 100 (0%) | 100 (0%) |
| Exactly 2% inflation each year | 100 | 102 (2%) | 104.04 (2%) | 106.12 (2%) | 108.24 (2%) | 110.40 (2%) |
| An average of 2% inflation over the period | 100 | 103 (3%) | 105.06 (2%) | 106.11 (1%) | 107.17 (1%) | 110.38 (2%) |
| Inflation always in the target range of 1 to 3% | 100 | 103 (3%) | 106.09 (3%) | 108.21 (2%) | 110.37 (2%) | 112.58 (2%) |
| Variable inflation with an average of zero | 100 | 102 (2%) | 99.96 (−2%) | 100.95 (1%) | 99.95 (−1%) | 99.95 (0%) |

This table shows how the price level would evolve when the Bank of Canada follows different inflation targeting agreements. The first two rows present totally unrealistic agreements in which the Bank of Canada exactly hits a target of either 0 or 2% inflation each year. The next agreements are more interesting. In the third row, the average rate of inflation is equal to 2% over the agreement. In the fourth row, inflation always remains within the 1 to 3% band. In the fifth row, the agreement sees policy averaging a zero rate of inflation but not necessarily achieving zero inflation in each year.

prices enter the consumer price index and the price of gas rises and falls with world oil prices. If no prices other than oil prices changed, then inflation would seem to rise and fall. Thus, there are very good reasons to specify the desired inflation path as a band.

The second row of Table 24–2 shows inflation at exactly 2% each year in each of the 5 years. The target is hit each and every year exactly.

The third row shows an inflation rate that varies, but averages 2% over the five periods. In some years inflation is greater than 2% and in other years inflation is less than 2%. First, notice that this policy "works" in the sense that in the policy with exactly 2% inflation each year the price level in 2016 is 110.40 and in the policy with the average rate of inflation equal to 2%, the price level in 2016 is 110.38. The price level in 2016 in rows 2 and 3 are identical for practical purposes. A pensioner with a fixed nominal pension in 2016 has the same purchasing power under both policies. The subtle difference between the two policies is that, to operate the second policy during the periods of disinflation going from 3 to 2 to 1% between 2011 and 2014, unemployment would be rising and, as inflation increased, unemployment would be falling. In order to achieve average inflation of 2%, some variability in unemployment is required as the Bank actively manages the economy to average 2% inflation over the 5 years.

There is less or perhaps even no implicit management of the economy in the fourth row of Table 24–2. Here, inflation is 3% for 2012 and 2013. The Bank simply says that as long as inflation is within the target bounds, no policy action is needed. Then inflation falls to 2% for the remaining three years. Again there is no active policy action. But the price level in 2016 is higher under this policy: 112.58 instead of 110.4. The pensioner with the fixed nominal pension is worse off. The policy described in the fourth row of Table 24–2 is an inflation target policy with a range, *but*—and it is an important *but*—this is not a policy that requires the average value of inflation to be 2% for the five years of the agreement. Rather, the policy requires inflation to stay within the 1 to 3% range in each year of the five-year agreement.

Finally, the fifth row asks what would happen if the target path required an average inflation rate of zero over the five years. If there are any periods when inflation is positive, there also must be periods when inflation is negative. This is called deflation and we discussed one problem with deflation earlier: When inflation is negative, even a very low nominal interest rate, perhaps even a zero interest rate, is a positive real interest rate and would reduce aggregate demand. There is also an argument that deflation can lead to a deflationary spiral. As consumers see prices falling, they may come to believe prices will fall further. This leads them to put off purchases, which reduces aggregate demand, increases unemployment, and further reduces inflation, which is already negative, to a more negative number. We have discussed the consequences of deflation in Japan and the experience of deflation in the Great Depression of the 1930s. Both experiences suggest deflation is associated with low growth and high unemployment and is to be avoided by policy makers. Many of the policy actions taken during the autumn of 2008 were to ward off the threat of deflation as house prices and oil prices were falling.

In Canada, we have a record of six inflation target agreements: 1991, 1994, 1998, 2001, 2006, and 2011. The last four agreements opted for a plan where inflation was always in the target range of 1 to 3%. Looking again at the current agreement, it says: *"The inflation target will continue to be the 2 per cent mid-point of the 1 to 3 per cent inflation-control range."* From this language, we cannot tell if the agreement intends that the average rate of inflation over the five years will be 2% or whether the rate of inflation will fall between 1 and 3% in all five years of the agreement. By comparing the second and third rows of Table 24–2, we can see these are not the same policy. Since the agreement did not explicitly write the policy as an average rate of inflation over five years rather than inflation between 1 and 3% in each of the five years, it is reasonable to believe that the Bank and the government prefer the slightly more vague versions of the agreement where different interpretations of policy success are possible.

# 24-3 | The Design of Monetary Policy

Once a central bank has decided what rate of inflation it wants to achieve, it still faces two issues, one seemingly settled and one very much unsettled:

- Should the central bank announce a target rate for money growth (which it controls), or should it announce a target for inflation (which is what it cares about, but does not control directly)? This issue appears to be settled in favour of announcing a target for inflation rather than money growth. In this section, we will understand why this is the case.
- Having chosen to announce a target for inflation, how closely should the central bank try to meet that target for inflation and over what time horizon? For example, in the short run, how much weight should it put on meeting the target versus getting the economy out of a recession?

## Money Growth and Inflation Revisited

Consider the following two propositions: (1) In the medium run and the long run, inflation is determined by the growth rate of the money stock. (2) The central bank controls the growth rate of the money stock.

Together, the two propositions suggest a simple rule for monetary policy: Compute the growth rate of the money stock consistent with the desired rate of inflation, and announce this growth rate as the target. By meeting its money growth target, the central bank will then achieve its desired rate of inflation.

> Setting a money growth target was strongly advocated by, among others, Milton Friedman in the late 1960s. In the early 1970s, the Bank of Canada and other central banks did have a money growth target.

As appealing as this rule sounds, it runs into a serious problem: It does not work! The central bank does not exactly control the growth rate of money. If we return to Chapters 4 and 11, we remember that money is primarily deposits in chartered banks and that those deposits represent decisions of many customers to take out loans, and decisions by bank managers to issue loans. Life is just not quite as simple as the theory suggests.

Money growth and inflation do broadly move together. If money growth is high, inflation will also be high; and if money growth is low, inflation will be low. But the relation is not tight enough that by choosing a rate of money growth, the central bank can achieve precisely its desired rate of inflation.

You can see this proposition is shown in Figure 24–1, which plots three-year averages of the inflation rate (using the CPI as the price index) against three-year averages of the growth rate of two different measures of the growth rate on the money supply in Canada: a measure

FIGURE 24-1

**Money Growth and Inflation—Three-Year Averages**

There is a very broad relationship in that, when inflation fell in stages from 10% to 5% to 2%, money growth did decline. But this relationship is weak even over the medium term and is of very limited use for setting central bank policy on a year-by-year basis.

*Source:* M1+, CANSIM II variable V37258; M2+, CANSIM II variable V41552798; Inflation CANSIM II variable V41690973.

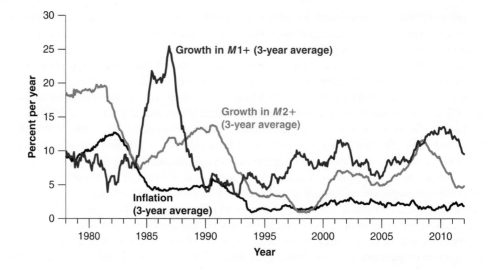

From Chapter 5, equation (5.3) (the *LM* equation): The real money supply (the left side) must be equal to the real demand for money (the right side):

$$\frac{M}{P} = YL(i)$$

If, as a result of the introduction of cell phones that can undertake transactions, the real demand for money halves, then:

$$\frac{M}{P} = \frac{1}{2}YL(i)$$

For a given level of output and a given interest rate, *M/P* must also halve. If the central bank does not adjust *M*, this implies that *P* must double. This would make the relation between the growth in *M* and the growth in *P* weaker—as in Figure 24–1.

called **M1+(gross)** and a measure called **M2+(gross)**. M1+ is the measure of money where most deposits at banks pay little or no interest. M2+ includes some bank deposits that pay higher rates of interest as well as some mutual funds and deposits at life insurance companies.

The reason for using three-year averages should be clear: In the short run, changes in money growth affect mostly output, not inflation. It is only in the medium run that a relation between money growth and inflation should emerge. Taking three-year averages of both money and inflation is a way of looking for the presence of such a medium-run relation. Although interpretation of Figure 24–1 is subjective, Figure 24–1 shows that in Canada, since 1975, the relation between M1+ growth and inflation has not been very tight.

Why is there no tight relation between money growth and inflation? The answer is because of *shifts in the demand for money*. An example will help here. Suppose, as is already happening in places like Kenya, your phone takes on the ability to make payments directly from your bank account. Your phone already has the ability to switch money instantly and easily from a bank account that pays a bit more interest to a bank account that can be used to make payments from the phone. You may be able to take this new technology and keep slightly more of your assets in a bank account that pays interest and slightly fewer assets in a bank account that pays little or no interest. Many of us now carry almost no currency in our pockets.

All of these changes will move around the ratio of money to income at a given interest rate. Money is some total of currency held by the public as well as the total balance in specific sets of accounts in banks. In periods of rapid technological change, this ratio will and has moved.

The reason the demand for money shifts over time goes beyond the introduction of new payment technologies. To more fully understand why the demand for money shifts, we must challenge an assumption we have maintained until now, namely, that there was a sharp distinction between money and other assets. In fact, there are many financial assets that are close to money. They cannot be used for transactions—at least not without substantial restrictions—but they can be exchanged for money at little cost. In other words, they are very **liquid**; this makes them potentially attractive substitutes for money. Shifts between money and these assets are the main factor behind shifts in the demand for money.

Take, for example, *money market funds*. Money market funds are financial intermediaries that hold as assets short-maturity securities (typically, Treasury bills) and have deposits (or shares, as they are called) as liabilities.

The presence of shifts between money and other liquid assets have led central banks to construct measures that include not only money, but also other liquid assets. These aggregates are called **monetary aggregates**, and typically come under the names similar to those we have already seen $M0$, $M1$, $M2$, $M3$, and so on. **$M2+$**—which is also sometimes called **broad money**—includes $M1+$ (currency and chequable deposits), plus all chequable notice deposits and personal term deposits. $M1+$ is as close as Canada gets to a measure of money that represents money easily used in transactions.

The construction of $M2$ and other monetary aggregates would appear to offer a solution to our earlier inflation targeting problem. If most of the shifts in the demand for money are between $M1+$ and other assets within $M2+$, the demand for $M2+$ should be more stable than the demand for $M1+$, so there should be a tighter relation between $M2$ growth and inflation than between $M1+$ growth and inflation. Thus, the central bank should target growth in $M2+$.

Figure 24–1 does show a closer relation between growth in $M2+$ and inflation over the medium term. But it is not perfect. The solution to the instability in the relation between money growth and inflation was the adoption of an inflation target.

## Inflation Targeting

In most countries, central banks have defined as their primary goal the achievement of a low inflation rate, both in the short run and in the medium run. This is known as *inflation targeting*.

- Trying to achieve a given inflation target *in the medium run* would seem (and indeed is) a clear improvement over trying to achieve a nominal money growth target. After all, in the medium run, the primary goal of monetary policy is to achieve a given rate of inflation. Better to have an inflation rate as the target than nominal money growth as a target, which, as we have seen, may not lead to the desired rate of inflation.
- Trying to achieve a given inflation target *in the short run* would appear to be much more controversial. Focusing exclusively on inflation would seem to eliminate any role monetary policy could play in reducing output fluctuations. But, in fact, this is not necessarily the case.

To see why, return to the Phillips curve relation among inflation, $\pi_t$, lagged inflation, $\pi_{t-1}$, and the deviation of the unemployment rate, $u_t$ from the natural rate of unemployment, $u_n$ (equation (12.8)):

$$\pi_t = \pi_{t-1} - \alpha(u_t - u_n)$$

Let the inflation rate target be $\pi^*$. Suppose the central bank could achieve its inflation target exactly in every period. Then the relation would become:

$$\pi^* = \pi^* - \alpha(u_t - u_n)$$

The unemployment rate $u_t$ would always equal $u_n$, the natural rate of unemployment; by implication, output would always be equal to the natural level of output. In effect, inflation targeting would lead the central bank to act in such a way as to eliminate all deviations of output from its natural level.

The intuition: If the central bank saw that an adverse demand shock were going to lead to a recession, it would know that, absent a monetary expansion, the economy would experience a decline in inflation below the target rate of inflation. To maintain stable inflation, the central bank would then rely on a monetary expansion to avoid the recession. The converse would apply to a favourable demand shock: Fearing an increase in inflation above the target rate, the central bank would rely on a monetary contraction to slow the economy and keep output at the natural level of output. As a result of this active monetary policy, output would remain at the natural level of output all the time.

The result we have just derived—that inflation targeting eliminates deviations of output from its natural level—is too strong, however, for two reasons:

**1.** The central bank cannot always achieve the rate of inflation it wants in the short run. So suppose that, for example, the central bank was not able to achieve its desired rate of

First to adopt inflation targeting was New Zealand in 1990, which set a target range for inflation of 0 to 2%. Next was Canada in 1991, setting a target range for inflation of 1 to 3%. Since then, some form of inflation targeting has been adopted by, among others, the United Kingdom, Sweden, Israel, and Spain. The euro area countries, whose monetary policy is set by the European Central Bank, have an inflation target of "below 2%." As of January 2012, the United States, the last major holdout, adopted a formal inflation target.

$$0 = -\alpha(u_t - u_n)$$
$$\Rightarrow u_t = u_n.$$

inflation last year, so $\pi_{t-1}$ is higher than $\pi^*$. Then it is not clear that the central bank should try to hit its target this year and achieve $\pi_t = \pi^*$: The Phillips curve relation implies that such a decrease in inflation would require a potentially large increase in unemployment.

2. Like all other macroeconomic relations, the Phillips curve relation above does not hold exactly. It will happen that, for example, inflation increases even when unemployment is at the natural rate of unemployment. In this case, the central bank will face a more difficult choice: whether to keep unemployment at the natural rate and allow inflation to increase, or to increase unemployment above the natural rate to keep inflation in check.

These qualifications are important, but the basic point remains: Inflation targeting makes good sense in the medium run and allows for monetary policy to stabilize output close to its natural level in the short run.

## Interest Rate Rules

Recall from Chapter 19 that, in the medium run, the real interest rate is equal to the natural real interest rate, so the nominal interest rate moves one for one with the inflation *rate*. If $r_n = 2\%$ and the target inflation rate $\pi^* = 4\%$, then the target nominal interest rate $i^* = 2\% + 4\% = 6\%$. If the target inflation rate $\pi^*$ is 0%, then $i^* = 2\% + 0\% = 2\%$

Given the discussion so far, the question now is how to achieve the inflation target. Inflation is clearly not under the direct control of the central bank. In answer to this question, John Taylor, from Stanford University, argued in the 1990s that, since the central bank affects spending through the interest rate, the central bank should think directly in terms of the choice of an interest rate rather than a rate of nominal money growth. He then suggested a rule that the central bank should follow to set the interest rate. This rule, which is now known as the **Taylor rule**, goes as follows:

- Let $\pi_t$ be the rate of inflation and $\pi^*$ be the target rate of inflation.
- Let $i_t$ be the nominal interest rate controlled by the central bank and $i^*$ be the target nominal interest rate—the nominal interest rate associated with the target rate of inflation, $\pi^*$, in the medium run.
- Let $u_t$ be the unemployment rate and $u_n$ be the natural unemployment rate.

Think of the central bank as choosing the nominal interest rate, $i$. (Recall from Chapter 4 that, through open market operations, and ignoring the liquidity trap, the central bank can achieve any short-term nominal interest rate that it wants by manipulating the balances of chartered banks at the Bank of Canada.) Then, Taylor argued, the central bank should use the following rule:

$$i_t = i^* + a(\pi_t - \pi^*) - b(u_t - u_n)$$

where $a$ and $b$ are positive coefficients.

Let's look at what the rule says:

- If inflation is equal to target inflation ($\pi_t = \pi^*$) and the unemployment rate is equal to the natural rate of unemployment ($u_t = u_n$), then the central bank should set the nominal interest rate, $i_t$, equal to its target value, $i^*$. This way, the economy can stay on the same path, with inflation equal to the target inflation rate and unemployment equal to the natural rate of unemployment.
- If inflation is higher than the target ($\pi_t > \pi^*$), the central bank should increase the nominal interest rate, $i_t$, above $i^*$. This higher interest rate will increase unemployment, and this increase in unemployment will lead to a decrease in inflation. The coefficient $a$ should therefore reflect how much the central bank cares about inflation. The higher $a$ is, the more the central bank will increase the interest rate in response to inflation, the more the economy will slow down, the more unemployment will increase, and the faster inflation will return to the target inflation rate. In any case, Taylor pointed out, $a$ should be larger than one. Why? Because what matters for spending is the real interest rate, not the nominal interest rate. When inflation increases, the central bank, if it wants to decrease spending and output, must increase the *real* interest rate. In other words, it must increase the nominal interest rate more than one for one with inflation.

- If unemployment is higher than the natural rate of unemployment ($u_t > u_n$), the central bank should decrease the nominal interest rate. The lower nominal interest rate will increase output, leading to a decrease in unemployment. The coefficient $b$ should reflect how much the central bank cares about unemployment. The higher $b$ is, the more the central bank will be willing to deviate from target inflation to keep unemployment close to the natural rate of unemployment.

In stating this rule, Taylor did not argue that it should be followed blindly: Many other events, such as an exchange rate crisis or the need to change the composition of spending on goods, and thus the mix between monetary policy and fiscal policy, justify changing the nominal interest rate for other reasons than those included in the rule. But, he argued, the rule provided a useful way of thinking about monetary policy: Once the central bank has chosen a target rate of inflation, it should try to achieve it by adjusting the nominal interest rate. The rule it should follow should take into account not only current inflation, but also current unemployment.

Since it was first introduced, the Taylor rule has generated a lot of interest, both from researchers and from central banks:

- Interestingly, researchers looking at the behaviour of both the Fed in the United States and the Bundesbank in Germany have found that, although neither of these two central banks thought of itself as following the Taylor rule, this rule actually described their behaviour fairly well over the last 15–20 years before the crisis.
- Other researchers have explored whether it is possible to improve on this simple rule: for example, whether the nominal interest rate should be allowed to respond not only to current inflation, but also to expected future inflation.
- Yet other researchers have discussed whether central banks should adopt an explicit interest rate rule and follow it closely, or whether they should use the rule more informally, and feel free to deviate from the rule when appropriate.
- In general, most central banks have now shifted from thinking in terms of nominal money growth to thinking in terms of an interest rate rule. Whatever happens to nominal money growth as a result of following such a nominal interest rate rule is increasingly seen as less important or even unimportant, both by the central banks and by financial markets.

◀ The European Central Bank continues to place some importance on growth in monetary aggregates.

## 24-4 | The Bank of Canada in Action

Let us end this chapter by looking at how the Bank of Canada actually designs and carries out monetary policy.

◀ The Bank of Canada's website (www.bankofcanada. ca) gives a lot of information about how the Bank of Canada is organized and what it does.

### The Bank's Mandate

The Bank was formed in 1935. The **Bank of Canada Act** has been amended many times since then, but the preamble still gives the Bank the responsibility *to regulate credit and currency in the best interests of the economic life of the nation, to control and protect the external value of the national monetary unit and to mitigate by its influence fluctuations in the general level of production, trade, prices, and employment, so far as may be possible within the scope of monetary action, and generally to promote the economic and financial welfare of Canada.*

◀ A brief (and very reasonable) history of the Bank is available on its webpage.

Such a vague mandate leaves a lot of room for interpretation. What are the best interests of the nation? Should the Bank focus on obtaining stable income growth and high employment, low and stable inflation, some particular value for the Canadian dollar, low interest rates, or some undetermined combination of all? Since its founding, the Bank has, at one time or another, focused on each of these goals. The Bank has, since 1988, chosen to focus mostly on controlling inflation. The Bank has adopted this position because it argues that providing price stability is the best thing it can do to encourage a well-functioning economy. The Bank of Canada, at least in its policy announcements, seems to roughly follow a Taylor rule. How does it set interest rates in practice?

## The Instruments of Monetary Policy

In Chapter 4, we emphasized the link between money and reserves so that the supply of money equalled the demand for money (equation (4.11)). Using the equality of the demand and supply of money in equilibrium, equation (4.11) is written as:

$$\frac{1}{c + \theta(1 - c)} = \frac{M}{H} \tag{24.1}$$

$M$ is money supply, the sum of currency and chequable deposits. $H$ is the monetary base—the sum of currency and reserves held by banks. In some countries, such as the United States, and Canada before 1994, banks must hold reserves that equal a certain fraction of their deposits. In Canada, since 1994, reserves (the commercial banks' deposits at the Bank of Canada) are not held to meet legal requirements but to facilitate the clearing of cheques and other transfers between commercial banks; that is why they are often called **settlement balances**. The parameter $c$ is the ratio of currency to chequable deposits; $\theta$ denotes the ratio of settlement balances held by commercial banks to chequable deposits. The expression $1/[c + \theta (1 - c)]$ is called the money multiplier. Monetary policy directly changes $H$, the quantity of high-powered money.

Only a small number of financial institutions in Canada hold deposits ($H$) at the Bank of Canada. Strictly speaking, we should refer to them as "direct clearers" rather than banks, but we will stick with the simpler label. Every night, transfers drawn on these banks are matched up, and the balance is settled by transferring deposits at the Bank of Canada. For example, suppose bank A holds claims, such as cheques drawn on bank B, of $10 billion, while bank B holds claims on bank A of $11 billion. The difference of $1 billion is paid by transferring that amount from bank A's account held at the Bank of Canada to the account held by bank B. Deposits at the Bank of Canada pay only a low rate of interest, 50 basis points less than the Bank Rate. So, the banks have an incentive to minimize these balances. What if bank A doesn't have enough in its account to cover this transfer? It can borrow the necessary amount from either the Bank of Canada or from another commercial bank that has extra money in its account. These loans are for one day only or "overnight." The Bank of Canada fixes a band of 50 basis points (one-half of 1%) for such overnight loans. The Bank of Canada announces it will make overnight loans at the highest interest rate in that band. This interest rate is called the Bank Rate. Thus, the overnight rate on one-day loans between the commercial banks is never higher than the Bank Rate because any commercial bank offered a loan by another commercial bank at a rate higher than the Bank Rate will choose to borrow from the Bank of Canada instead because its rate is lower. Thus, the Bank of Canada effectively sets a maximum interest rate in the large market for overnight loans.

From March 1980 to February 1996, the Bank Rate was set equal to the average interest rate, established at the auction of three-month Government of Canada Treasury bills, plus 25 basis points. The new definition of the Bank Rate went into effect February 22, 1996. ▶

On the Bank of Canada webpage, both the **target for the overnight rate** (25 basis points less than the Bank Rate) and the Bank Rate are posted. Changes in the target for the overnight rate and thus in the Bank Rate are announced using a predetermined schedule, about every four to six weeks. Figure 24–2 shows the target overnight rate between 1996 and 2012.

In a world of perfect certainty, it would not matter if the Bank of Canada fixed the level of reserves to achieve a given market-clearing interest rate in the overnight market or if it fixed the market-clearing interest rate to obtain a given level of reserves. In practice, because of uncertainties in the links between its actions and the subsequent path of output and prices, the Bank follows the second strategy. Having determined a desired path for the target overnight rate, often just called the overnight rate target or even the target rate (following a procedure to be described below), the Bank of Canada then adjusts reserves in order to keep the overnight interest rate in its band. The main tool in managing reserves is transfers of federal government accounts. The federal government maintains fairly large cash balances to finance its activities. These balances are held in accounts at the Bank of Canada and at private banks. Managing these balances provides an effective way to change the supply of reserves. For example, a

FIGURE 24–2

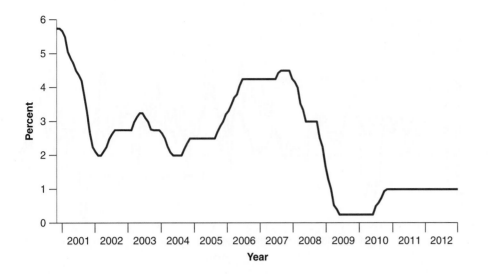

**The Target Overnight Interest Rate in Canada, 1996–2012**

Approximately eight times a year, the Bank of Canada sets a target for the overnight interest rate. The decision to change or not to change the rate is accompanied by a press release explaining the decision. This interest rate is the main instrument of monetary policy in Canada.

*Source:* CANSIM II variable V39079.

transfer of $1 billion from government's account at the Bank of Canada to bank A creates an increase of $1 billion in the reserves held by bank A. An opposite transfer reduces reserves. Thus the Bank of Canada can keep the overnight loan rate at its target rate.

Thus, although we talked about using open market operations in Chapter 4 to change high-powered money, transfers between deposits of the federal government at chartered banks and the Bank of Canada change high-powered money in an equivalent way.

## The Practice of Policy

How does the Bank decide what policy to follow?

Because the actions of the monetary authority feed into the growth of nominal income and prices with long and variable lags, the Bank of Canada needs to keep its sights on what it expects will happen to the economy six months to several years ahead. The Bank goes through a cycle. Each time the target for the overnight interest rate needs to be announced, the Bank's staff prepares forecasts and simulations of the effects of different monetary policies. A path for the overnight interest rate is sketched out for the next few years that will generate inflation consistent with the Bank's goals. Within this cycle, the Bank frequently updates its estimates of the path of the economy and reassesses its desired path for the target rate.

Information about the path of short-term interest rates plays a role. If short-term rates are lower than what the Bank expected, it is often a signal that aggregate demand in the economy has not grown as quickly as the Bank had forecast. The Bank takes this as a signal that it should reduce the target rate in order to stimulate growth in aggregate demand. Because of the importance of international trade, the Bank also keeps an eye on the exchange rate; it views sharp declines in the exchange rate as stimulating aggregate demand and as a potential signal to raise the target rate. Of course, both interest rates and the exchange rate can move in response to shocks that have no consequence for inflation. The Bank tries to use a variety of information sources to isolate the source of the shocks that appear and to determine if any response is warranted.

Since November 2000, the Bank of Canada has preset a schedule, one year ahead, for the announcement of policy decisions with respect to interest rate changes. A press release explaining the reasons behind the decision to raise, lower, or maintain the interest rate is part of any announcement. A committee of senior Bank of Canada officials makes the interest rate decision, with the Governor playing the central role on the committee. It is thought that a preset schedule is a better way to operate monetary policy in Canada. In particular, having a Canadian schedule that is distinct from a similar schedule in the United States is a useful way to emphasize the separation of Canadian and American monetary policies under a flexible exchange rate and with a distinct inflation target as the focus of Canadian monetary policy.

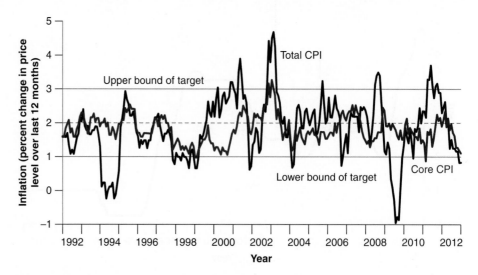

**FIGURE 24–3**

**Inflation in Canada, 1993–2012**

Here we compare two measures of annual inflation (the increase in the price level over the previous 12 months) to the target for inflation between 1993 and 2012. You already know about the total CPI. Core CPI is a price index that excludes volatile components. In this period, average total CPI inflation was 1.93% and average core CPI inflation was 1.82%. Using either measure, the inflation targets were met on average but not in each month.

*Source:* Consumer Price Index using CANSIM II variable V41690973; core Consumer Price Index using CANSIM II variable V41693242.

## The Role of Target Ranges for Inflation

Since 1991, the Bank of Canada has announced explicit targets for the rate of inflation. The target was set at 3% for 1992 and was reduced slowly to 2% in 1995, where it has remained since. In fact, the Bank announces a range that is its target, plus or minus 1%. How close has the Bank come to hitting its inflation target? The answer is given in Figure 24–3, which plots the rate of inflation for each year since 1993 and gives the Bank's target range since 1992. The Bank also presents inflation using a measure of the CPI that excludes volatile components, such as food, energy, and the effect of indirect taxes. This is called **core inflation**. Both measures appear in Figure 24–3.

Why should the Bank announce a range for inflation and use two measures?

1. The target reminds people of the long-term goal of monetary policy to keep inflation low—that is, at 2%.
2. The range indicates that part of the goal of monetary policy is to keep inflation low *and* stable—that is, near 2%. The range is fairly narrow.
3. The addition of the core inflation measure allows the Bank to point out times where energy or food price increases are lifting total CPI inflation beyond the bands while the remainder of prices are well-behaved.

The announcement and interpretation of total inflation and core inflation work in conjunction with the announcements of changes in interest rates, specifically the target overnight interest rate illustrated in Figure 24–2. Consider the two figures together but remember that Figure 24–2 starts in 1996 and Figure 24–3 starts in 1993.

The Bank moves interest rates to keep inflation within the bands. Thus in 1996 when inflation was low and declining, the Bank was cutting interest rates. However in 2000, there were sharp interest rate cuts while total inflation was rising but core inflation was falling. What is missing from this analysis is the rise in unemployment in 2001. The Bank combined low core inflation and slower economic growth to explain that it was appropriate to cut interest rates. Thus, the Bank does not look only at inflation in its interest rate decisions.

Both core and total inflation were rising over 2004 and 2005. At this time unemployment was declining, and you can see the Bank increasing interest rates to keep inflation on target.

We finally reach the period from 2008 to the present. Figure 24–2 shows the sharp cut in interest rates in 2008—the cut of interest rates to zero. There was certainly no problem with high inflation. In fact, the great worry was the establishment of negative inflation and, even worse, negative expected inflation. Figure 24–3 does show the broader CPI measure with negative inflation over several consecutive months.

The Bank of Canada was also partly co-operating with other countries in making a choice to sharply reduce interest rates. We know from Chapters 6 and 8 that if the Bank of Canada had not reduced interest rates in conjunction with the other countries, the Canadian dollar would have appreciated and the recession would have been made worse in Canada.

After 2010, with both measures of inflation mostly within the target zone, the Bank of Canada raised the target interest rate to 1% in the last half of 2011. It has remained at 1% to the time of writing in 2013.

## The Exchange Rate

The Bank of Canada is not likely to agree that the behaviour of the exchange rate should fall under the overall assessment of monetary policy in this chapter. The reasoning: When you have an inflation target and the inflation target has been achieved, policy is successful. However, if you review the mandate of the Bank of Canada, it includes the statements that the Bank is to "control and protect the external value of the national monetary unit" and to "generally promote the economic and financial welfare of Canada." Either statement could suggest that thinking about the exchange rate as one of Canada's most important prices is part of the Bank's policy mandate. The Bank, however, does make it clear that the value of the Canadian dollar is not its primary responsibility. Is this a valid argument?

◄ The modern term for the "external value of the national monetary unit" is the exchange rate.

Figure 24–4 presents the nominal value of the Canadian dollar (the exchange rate) between 1993 and 2012, the period of inflation targeting. You may need to review Chapters 6, 7, and 8. There is a large depreciation to 2002 and, as discussed in Chapter 7, a large increase in net exports. There is a large appreciation from 2002 to 2012. We showed this is associated with a fall in the share of net exports. To consider this a good outcome for the Canadian economy, you would make the argument that since inflation remained on target and the economy was at the natural rate of output, this reallocation of jobs and people took place very gradually while the economy remained at or near full employment.

It is difficult to make the argument that Canada was at full employment in 2008, 2009, and 2010. The depreciation and then appreciation of the Canadian dollar over that period is hard to explain. The depreciation would have increased net exports, at least by reducing Canadian trips to the United States to shop. However, the depreciation and subsequent appreciation were so

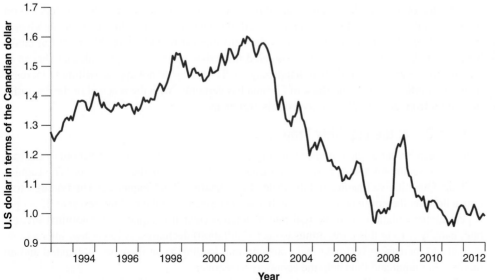

**FIGURE 24–4**

**The Exchange Rate in Canadian Dollars per U.S. Dollar, 1993–2012**

As noted in Chapters 6 and 7, the early part of this period saw a large nominal (and real) depreciation of the Canadian dollar. Then after 2002 to 2008, there was a substantial trend appreciation of the Canadian dollar. There is a strange and hard to explain sharp depreciation, then appreciation, of the Canadian dollar from 2008 to 2010.

*Source:* CANSIM II variable V37426.

In September 2011, Switzerland, which like Canada is a trading country, decided to fix the Swiss franc at 1.2 francs per euro. ▶ This was done to prevent the Swiss franc from appreciating further and further reducing Swiss net exports.

short and sharp that, given the lags we discussed in Chapter 7, it seems unlikely this was crucial. However the trend appreciation since 2002 clearly reduced net exports. Many argue the relatively high value of the Canadian dollar has slowed the recovery of the Canadian economy to full employment. However, there is no serious suggestion that Canada adopt a fixed exchange rate and prevent a further appreciation of the Canadian dollar as of the time of writing.

# 24-5 | Challenges from the Crisis

Until 2007, most central banks believed that inflation targeting provided them with a solid framework for monetary policy. This was certainly true for the Bank of Canada. In most countries, inflation was stable, and output fluctuations were smaller than they had been in the past. The crisis has presented them with two challenges:

- The liquidity trap has prevented them from decreasing the interest rate as much as they wanted.
- It has become clear that stable inflation is not, by itself, a guarantee of macroeconomic stability: The crisis can clearly be traced to problems in the housing and in the financial sectors that built up long before 2007.

Let's take each challenge from the crisis in turn.

## The Liquidity Trap

See, in particular, Chapter 11 on the liquidity trap, in Chapter 22 the Focus box "The Liquidity Trap, Quantitative Easing, and the Role of Expectations," and the discussion of optimal inflation earlier in this ▶ chapter.

When an economy falls into the liquidity trap, conventional monetary policy (namely, the use of the nominal interest rate) can no longer be used. This raises three issues: first, whether economies can avoid falling into the trap in the first place; second, whether and how they can get out of the trap; and third, if an economy is in the trap, whether there are unconventional monetary policy tools available. We have already discussed these issues at various points in the book. What follows puts things together.

## Avoiding Falling into the Liquidity Trap

A way of dealing with the liquidity trap is simply to avoid falling into it! One way to do so is to have higher average inflation. We discussed this argument in section 24-2. The higher the average inflation, the higher the average nominal interest rate is, and the more room the central bank has to decrease the nominal interest rate in response to an adverse shock before falling in the liquidity trap.

Whether or not this should lead central banks to adopt a higher target inflation depends on the probability that, once this crisis has passed, the economy will be hit again by an adverse shock so large that the central bank hits the zero interest bound again. Most central banks have concluded that the shocks that triggered this crisis were so exceptional, that shocks of this magnitude are very unlikely to happen again. Thus, they do not appear willing to increase their target inflation rate. The Bank of Canada has certainly, with the renewal of the 2% inflation target from 2011 to 2016, rejected this argument.

## Getting Out of the Liquidity Trap

In the strange world of the liquidity trap, higher expected inflation can help get out of the trap and help the economy recover. We went through the argument in the Focus box "The Liquidity Trap, Quantitative Easing, and the Role of Expectations" in Chapter 22: The liquidity trap puts a floor on the nominal interest rate, but not necessarily on the real interest rate. If people expect higher inflation, then the real rate of interest (which is equal to the nominal interest rate, namely zero in this case, minus expected inflation) decreases. A lower real interest rate is likely to increase investment and consumption, leading to an increase in demand and an increase in output and thus help the economy to recover.

This is one of the reasons why, before the crisis, most central banks did not worry much about the liquidity trap. Even if they could not decrease the nominal interest rate, they thought they could decrease the real interest rate by increasing inflation expectations. The issue, however, is how to actually get people to expect higher inflation. There is a circular aspect to the reasoning: If people indeed increase their inflation expectations, the economy will indeed recover, unemployment will decrease, and, from the Phillips curve relation, lower unemployment and higher expected inflation are likely to lead to higher inflation, validating the initial increase in expected inflation. But if expectations of inflation do not increase in the first place, neither will the real rate, activity, nor inflation.

One of the ways that central banks have tried to affect inflation expectations during the crisis has been their use of *quantitative easing*, a large increase in the money stock. One of the arguments given by proponents of quantitative easing was that people, seeing large increases in the money supply, would expect more inflation. Has it worked? So far, the evidence is mixed at best. There is not much evidence that quantitative easing, which has now been used in a number of countries (in particular, the United States, the United Kingdom, and Japan) has had much effect on inflation expectations.

To summarize: While unconventional monetary policy tools can help, they do not work as reliably as does conventional monetary policy, namely movements in the short-term nominal interest rate. Even taking unconventional monetary policy tools into account, being in the liquidity trap considerably reduces the scope of monetary policy.

## Macro-Prudential Regulation

Before the crisis, central bankers did not ignore bubbles. Indeed, starting in the mid-2000s, the Fed became worried about the increase in housing prices. Certainly since 2010, both the Bank of Canada and the Minister of Finance have been vocal about the rising price of houses in Canada. However central banks have found it hard to intervene in a bubble, for a number of reasons. First, they have found it difficult to assess whether the price increases reflect increases in fundamentals (for example, low interest rates) or reflect a bubble (i.e., increases in prices above what were justified by fundamentals). Second, they worried that an increase in the interest rate, while it might indeed stop the increase in housing prices, would also slow down the whole economy and trigger a recession. Third, they thought that, even if the increase in housing prices was indeed a bubble, and the bubble were to burst and lead to a decrease in housing prices later, they could counter the adverse effects on demand through an appropriate decrease in the interest rate. Fourth, policies that are deliberately intended to slow the housing market, both by reducing the volume of sales and the price of houses, are not very politically popular. Finance Minister Flaherty has taken a number of steps to slow the Canadian housing market—mostly by raising down payments and shortening mortgage terms. These have been criticized by real estate agents and home builders as too draconian.

For a discussion of bubbles versus fundamentals, see Chapter 19.

The crisis has forced the regulatory authorities in all countries to reconsider the regulation of financial institutions. As we saw throughout this book, and especially in Chapter 11, housing price declines combined with the buildup of risk in the U.S. financial system led to a major financial and macroeconomic crisis in the world.

As a result, a broad consensus is emerging, along two lines:

- It is risky to wait. Even if there is doubt about whether an increase in asset prices reflects fundamentals or a bubble, it may be better to do something than not: Better to stand for a while in the way of a fundamental increase and turn out to be wrong, than to let a bubble build up and burst, with major adverse macroeconomic effects. The same applies to buildups of financial risk; for example, excessive bank leverage. Better to prevent high leverage, at the risk of decreasing bank credit, than allow it to build up, increasing the risk of a financial crisis.
- To deal with bubbles, credit booms, or dangerous behaviour in the financial system, the interest rate is not the right policy instrument. It is too blunt a tool, affecting the whole economy rather than resolving the problem at hand. The right instruments are **macro-prudential tools**, rules that are aimed directly at borrowers, or lenders, or banks and other financial institutions, as the case may require.

What form might some of the macro-prudential tools take? Some tools may be aimed at borrowers:

- Suppose the central bank is worried about what it perceives to be an excessive increase in housing prices. It can tighten conditions under which borrowers can obtain mortgages. A measure used in many countries is a ceiling on the size of the loan borrowers can take relative to the value of the house they buy, a measure known as the maximum **loan-to-value ratio**, or maximum **LTV**. Reducing the maximum loan-to-value ratio is likely to decrease demand and thus slow down the price increase. (The Focus box "LTV Ratios and Housing Price Increases from 2000 to 2007" examines the relation between maximum LTVs and housing price increases in the period leading up to the crisis.)
- The authority that regulates mortgage lending can take a variety of steps. The minimum down payments as a percentage of the purchase price can be increased. The maximum term of the mortgage can be shortened. The maximum percentage of household income that can be devoted to the service of the mortgage can be reduced.

Some tools may be aimed at lenders, such as banks or foreign investors:

- Suppose the central bank is worried about an increase in bank leverage. We saw why this should be a concern in Chapter 11: High leverage was one of the main reasons why housing price declines led to the financial crisis. The central bank can impose minimum capital ratios so as to limit leverage. These may take various forms (for example, a minimum value for the ratio of capital to all assets, or a minimum value for the ratio of capital to risk weighted assets, with more risky assets having a higher weight). In fact, in a series of agreements known as **Basel II** and **Basel III**, many countries have agreed to impose the same minima on their banks. A more difficult and unresolved issue is whether and how such capital ratios should be adjusted over time as a function of economic and financial conditions (whether, for example, they should be increased if there appears to be excessive credit growth).

Go back to Chapter 11 for a refresher on the relation between leverage and capital ratios.

While there is large agreement that the use of such *macro-prudential* tools is desirable, many questions remain:

- In many cases, we do not know how well these tools work (for example, how much a decrease in the maximum LTV ratio affects the demand for housing, or whether foreign investors can find ways of avoiding capital controls).
- There are likely to be complex interactions between the traditional monetary policy tools and these macro-prudential tools. For example, there is some evidence that very low interest rates lead to excessive risk taking, be it by investors or by financial institutions. If this is the case, a central bank that decides, for macroeconomic reasons, to lower interest rates may have to use various macro-prudential tools to offset the potential increase in risk taking. Again, we know very little about how to correctly go about this.
- The question arises of whether macro-prudential tools should be, together with traditional monetary policy tools, under the control of the central bank or under the control of a separate authority. The argument for having the central bank in charge of both monetary and macro-prudential tools is that these tools interact, and thus only one centralized authority can use them in the right way. The argument against it is the worry that such a consolidation of tools may give too much power to an independent central bank.

At this stage, some countries have taken one route, while others have taken another. In the United Kingdom, the central bank has been given power over both monetary and macro-prudential tools. The United States is sorting through and implementing legislation that is intended to improve financial market regulation.

The Canadian regulatory framework is, as usual, complicated. Some financial institutions are regulated by the provinces. However the regulation of larger national financial institutions is shared by the minister of finance and the Bank of Canada. The Canadian regulatory framework was always tighter than the American framework, before the crisis and really for the last

Is it the case that countries that had more stringent restrictions on borrowing had lower housing price increases from 2000 to 2007? The answer is given in Figure 1. The figure, taken from an IMF study, shows the evidence for 21 countries for which the data could be obtained.

The horizontal axis plots the maximum loan-to-value (LTV) ratio on new mortgages across countries. This maximum is not necessarily a legal maximum, but may be a guideline, or a limit over which additional requirements, such as mortgage insurance, may be asked of the borrower. A ratio of 100% means that a borrower may be able to get a loan equal to the value of the house. Actual values vary from 60% in South Korea; to 100% in a large number of countries, including the United States; to 125% in The Netherlands. The vertical axis plots the increase in the nominal price of housing from 2000 to 2007 (measuring the real price increase would lead to a very similar picture). The figure also plots the regression line, the line that best fits the set of observations.

The figure suggests two conclusions:

The first is that there indeed appears to be a positive relation between the LTV ratio and the housing price increase. South Korea and Hong Kong, which imposed low LTV ratios, had smaller housing price increases. Spain and the United Kingdom, with much higher ratios, had much larger price increases.

The second is that the relation is far from tight. This should not come as a surprise, as surely many other factors played a role in the increase in housing prices. But, even controlling for other factors, it is difficult to identify with much confidence the precise effect of the LTV ratio. Looking forward, we shall have to learn a lot more about how an LTV-based regulatory tool might work before it can be used as a reliable macroprudential tool.

*Source:* Christopher Crowe, Giovanni Dell'Ariccia, Deniz Igan, and Pau Rabanal, "Policies for Macrofinancial Stability: Options to Deal with Real Estate Booms," Staff Discussion Note, International Monetary Fund, February 2011.

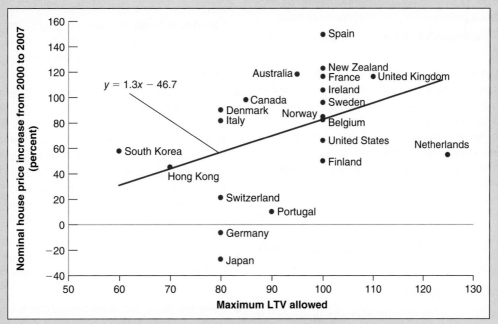

**FIGURE 1    Maximum LTV Ratios and Housing Price Increases, 2000–2007**

20 years or more. Tighter regulation did not actually make the large Canadian banks particularly happy. Banks would have preferred looser regulation that would have allowed higher profits and more risk taking. However, as we came to understand in Chapter 11, when the crisis came, a tighter and less risky regulatory environment led Canadian banks to face less risk on the down side as well. Canadian banks and Canadian bank regulators gained a partly deserved and partly undeserved world reputation for excellent regulation.

To summarize: The crisis has shown that macroeconomic stability requires the use not only of traditional monetary instruments, but also of macro-prudential tools. How best to use them is one of the challenges facing macroeconomic policy makers today.

Bank of Canada Governor Mark Carney was hired away from the Bank of Canada to the Bank of England at a reported pay packet of £874,000 pounds per year, a very large increase over his Bank of Canada salary.

## On the Optimal Rate of Inflation

- Inflation is down to very low levels in most OECD countries. One question facing central banks is whether they should try to achieve zero inflation—that is, price stability. A second question is whether the central bank should set a target for the price level several periods out. Then to hit that target, a period of higher inflation must be followed by a period of lower inflation.

- The main arguments for zero inflation are the following:
  - Inflation, together with an imperfectly indexed tax system, leads to tax distortions.
  - Because of money illusion, inflation leads people and firms to make incorrect decisions.
  - Higher inflation typically comes with higher inflation variability, creating more uncertainty and making it more difficult for people and firms to make the right decisions about the future.
  - As a target, price stability has a simplicity and a credibility that a positive inflation target does not have.

- There are also arguments for maintaining low but positive inflation.
  - Revenues from money growth (seignorage) allow for lower taxes elsewhere. However, this argument is quantitatively unimportant when comparing inflation rates of 0% and, say, 4%.
  - Positive actual and expected inflation allow the central bank to achieve negative real interest rates, an option that can be useful when fighting a recession.
  - Positive inflation allows firms to achieve real wage cuts when needed without requiring nominal wage cuts.
  - A further decrease from the current positive rate of inflation to zero would imply an increase in unemployment for some time, and this transition cost may exceed whatever benefits come from zero inflation.

## On the Design of Monetary Policy

- Once a central bank has decided what rate of inflation it wants to achieve, it faces two issues. First, should it choose a target for money growth or for inflation? Second, how closely should it try to meet the target?

- Because of shifts in the demand for money, the relation between $M1+$ growth and inflation is not tight. Thus, targeting $M1+$ growth could lead to large movements in inflation.

- Growth rates of monetary aggregates that include money and other liquid assets, such as $M2+$, move slightly more closely with inflation. But the relation is still not very tight. And more importantly, these larger aggregates are not under the control of the central bank.

- These problems have led several central banks to shift to inflation targeting. The issue then is how close the central bank should try to stay to the target.

- The Taylor rule gives a useful way of thinking about how the central bank should operate. The central bank should move its interest rate in response to two main factors: the deviation of the inflation rate from its target and the deviation of the unemployment rate from the natural rate. A central bank that follows this rule will stabilize activity and achieve its target inflation rate in the medium run.

## On the Bank of Canada

- The Bank of Canada was founded in 1935 *"to regulate credit and currency in the best interests of the economic life of the nation."* The Bank influences the level of short-term interest rates by controlling reserves. Since 1994 (and in practice for several years before that), these reserves have been deposits held to settle transfers between the direct clearers. The main instrument of monetary policy is the transfer of federal government balances between the Bank and the direct clearers.

- The Bank sketches out the path for its target overnight interest rate that will allow it to hit its inflation targets approximately six months to several years ahead. Within the six-month cycle, the Bank constantly monitors its assumptions and forecasts. On a week-to-week basis, the Bank pays particular attention to the movements in short-term interest rates and the multilateral exchange rate. Unexpected movements in these variables sometimes prompt a change in the Bank Rate.

- It is legitimate to ask if the Bank of Canada should have paid more attention to the exchange rate in the last two decades.

- Every few years, the Bank announces a target range for inflation. Since 1995, the target has been 2% with a band of ±1%.

- The Bank has done a good job of hitting its inflation targets since 1992, although inflation has sometimes fallen below the target range.

- The world economic crisis of 2008 and 2009 has led central banks to look for ways to avoid entering a liquidity trap and ways to exit a liquidity trap once in one.

- The world economic crisis of 2008 and 2009 has led central banks to consider various types of macro-prudential regulations. These are designed to keep financial institutions less risky.

- *Bank of Canada Act*, 503
- Basel II, 510
- Basel III, 510
- broad money, or *M2+*, 501
- core inflation, 506
- inflation target, 497
- liquid, 500
- loan-to-value (LTV) ratio, 510

- macro-prudential tools, 509
- *M1+*(gross), 500
- *M2+*(gross), 500
- monetary aggregate, 500
- settlement balances, 504
- shoe-leather costs, 492
- target for the overnight rate, 504
- Taylor rule, 502

## QUESTIONS AND PROBLEMS

### 1. TRUE/FALSE/UNCERTAIN

**a.** The most important argument for a positive rate of inflation in the OECD countries is seignorage.

**b.** The Bank of Canada should target *M2* growth.

**c.** Fighting inflation should be the Bank's only purpose.

**d.** Announcing target ranges for money growth would limit the flexibility and therefore the usefulness of monetary policy.

**e.** We would do just as well if we replaced the governor of the Bank of Canada with the Taylor rule.

**f.** The higher the inflation rate, the higher is the effective tax rate on income.

**g.** No major trading country has fixed its exchange rate since the world economic crisis in 2009.

### 2. MONEY DEMAND SHIFTS

How would each of the following affect the demand for *M1+* and *M2+*?

**a.** Banks reduce penalties on early withdrawal from time deposits.

**b.** It becomes possible to use your phone to make payments directly from an interest-earning term deposit.

**c.** Government legislates a tax on all ATM transactions.

**d.** The federal government decides to impose a tax on all transactions in short-term government securities.

### 3. NOMINAL INTEREST RATES, INFLATION, AND TAXES

Suppose you have a mortgage of $50,000. Consider two cases:

**i.** Expected inflation is 0%; the nominal interest rate on your mortgage is 4%.

**ii.** Expected inflation is 10%; the nominal interest rate on your mortgage is 14%.

**a.** What is the real interest rate you are paying on your mortgage in each case?

**b.** Suppose that you can deduct nominal mortgage interest payments from your income before paying the income tax (as is the case in the United States). Assume that the tax rate is 25%. Thus, for each dollar you pay in mortgage interest, you pay 25 cents less in taxes, in effect getting a subsidy from government for your mortgage costs. Compute, in each case, the real interest rate you are paying on your mortgage, taking into account this subsidy.

**c.** "In Canada, inflation is good for homeowners." Discuss this statement.

### 4. *M2+* AND *M1+*

Suppose that *M1+* growth is very high but *M2+* growth is equal to zero. Should you worry about inflation? Explain.

### 5. MONETARY POLICY IN ACTION

Using equation (24.1), show three ways in which monetary policy can decrease the interest rate, given the level of output. In each case, explain how it works.

### 6. NEGATIVE REAL INTEREST RATES

"The worry that with deflation real interest rates cannot be negative is misplaced. Fiscal policy can decrease the cost of borrowing as much as it wants, by offering subsidies to borrowers." Discuss this statement.

### 7. THE BANK OF CANADA

Access the website of the Bank of Canada (www.bankofcanada.ca).

**a.** Find the most recent targeting agreement and identify the target for inflation.

**b.** Read the most recent press release concerning a change in interest rates and ask, "Does the Bank seem to be more worried about a slowdown in growth or a pickup in the pace of inflation?"

**c.** What is happening to the target interest rate?

## 8. INFLATION TARGETS AND THE TAYLOR RULE

Many countries around the world have set explicit inflation targets for the central bank. Suppose the inflation target is $\pi^*$ and the Phillips curve looks like the one described in the chapter:

$$\pi_t = \pi_{t-1} + \alpha(u_t - u_n)$$

**a.** If the central bank is able to keep the inflation rate equal to the target inflation rate every period, does this imply that there will be dramatic fluctuations in unemployment?

**b.** Given your answer to (a), should all countries adopt inflation targets?

**c.** Explain how the Taylor rule implements an inflation target both directly and indirectly.

| | |
|---|---|
| | |

**FURTHER READING**

For evidence of nominal wage rigidity and the scope for inflation to facilitate real wage adjustments, see the results of a survey of managers by Alan Blinder and Don Choi, in "A Shred of Evidence on Theories of Wage Rigidity," *Quarterly Journal of Economics 105*, 1990: pp. 1003–1016.

For a discussion of the pros and cons of low inflation, look at George Akerlof, William Dickens, and George Perry, "The Macroeconomics of Low Inflation," *Brookings Papers on Economic Activity*, Vol. 1, 1996.

For more details on how the Bank of Canada operates, download "The Transmission of Monetary Policy in Canada" from the Bank of Canada's website. It contains articles from the *Bank of Canada Review* that outline the details of monetary policy during the first half of the 1990s.

It is a measure of the controversial nature of the 1990s disinflations in both Canada and the United States that books that dealt with the optimal rate of inflation and other macroeconomic issues became bestsellers. In Canada, Linda McQuaig's *Shooting the Hippo: Death by Deficit and Other Canadian Myths* (Viking Press, 1995) is popular. In the United States, Paul Krugman's book *The Age of Diminished Expectations* (The MIT Press, 1992) dealt with similar issues. Both books are nontechnical and lively.

"Modern Central Banking," written by Stanley Fischer for the 300th anniversary of the Bank of England, published in *The Future of Central Banking*, edited by Forrest Capie, Stanley Fischer, Charles Goodhart, and Norbert Schnadt (Cambridge: Cambridge University Press, 1995), provides a very interesting discussion of the current issues in central banking. Read also "What Central Bankers Could Learn from Academics—and Vice Versa," by Alan Blinder, in *Journal of Economic Perspectives 11 (2)*, Spring 1997: pp. 3–19.

On inflation targeting, read "Inflation Targeting: A New Framework for Monetary Policy?" by Ben Bernanke and Frederic Mishkin, in *Journal of Economic Perspectives 11 (2)*, Spring 1997: pp. 97–116.

For more on the Taylor rule, read John Taylor, "Discretion versus Policy Rules in Practice," in *Carnegie Rochester Conference Series on Public Policy 39* (Amsterdam: North-Holland, 1993), pp. 195–214.

A Bank of Canada conference volume, *Issues in Inflation Targeting*, was published in 2006. A series of papers on the C.D. Howe website posted in 2008 discuss whether zero inflation or a 2% average inflation path is a better policy after 2011. The paper by Christopher Ragan, "The Road Ahead for Canadian Inflation Targeting," is a nontechnical summary. Finally, David E.W. Laidler and William B.P. Robson's book *Two Percent Target: Canadian Monetary Policy since 1991* (C.D. Howe Institute, Policy Study 37, 2004) contains a detailed history of Canadian monetary policy from 1991 to 2004.

# Fiscal Policy: A Summing Up

At the time of writing, fiscal policy is very much the centre of current policy discussions. In most advanced economies, the recent crisis has led to large budget deficits and a large increase in government debts. In Greece, there are ongoing negotiations between the government and its creditors on how much debt will be repaid. The problem goes beyond Greece. In a number of countries, investors have started worrying about whether debt can indeed be repaid and are asking for higher interest rates to compensate for the risk of default. This calls for governments to reduce deficits by a large amount, stabilize the debt, and reassure investors. At the same time, however, the recovery is weak and a fiscal contraction is likely to slow it down further, at least in the short run. Thus, governments face a difficult choice: Reduce deficits rapidly and reassure markets that they will pay their debt, at the risk of lower growth or even a recession; or reduce deficits more slowly in order to avoid further slowing the recovery, at the risk of not convincing investors that debt will be stabilized.

The purpose of this chapter is to review what we have learned about fiscal policy so far; to explore in more depth the dynamics of deficits and debt; and to shed light on the problems associated with high public debt and large budget deficits. We then apply what we have learned to the Canadian situation since 1993.

**Section 25-1** takes stock of what we have learned about fiscal policy in this book so far.

**Section 25-2** looks more closely at the government budget constraint and examines its implications for the relation between budget deficits, the interest rate, the growth rate, and government debt.

**Section 25-3** introduces an important concept: the cyclically adjusted budget balance. Because revenue falls in a recession and outlays rise in a recession, the actual budget deficit can be a very misleading measure of the government's longer-run fiscal plans and its short-run fiscal choices. The cyclically adjusted budget balance, if implemented and used correctly, provides more reliable information about a country's long-run fiscal stance and its short-run fiscal choices.

**Section 25-4** discusses the dangers associated with high government debt, from higher taxes, to higher interest rates, to default, and to high inflation.

**Section 25-5** looks specifically at the dangers of large government deficits in an open economy. It addresses the proposition that a large government deficit is frequently associated with a large current account deficit.

**Section 25-6** closes the discussion by studying four episodes of fiscal policy in Canada since 1993. Two we have seen briefly before: the successful reduction of Canadian deficits without a recession in the 1990s and the use of fiscal policy to reduce the size of the 2009 recession in Canada. Two are new: the brief interlude of tax cutting and expenditure increases from 2006 to 2008 and the plans after the 2009 recession to achieve a balanced budget.

# 25-1 | Fiscal Policy: What We Have Learned

We have looked at fiscal policy in a variety of places throughout the book.

- In Chapter 3, we looked at the role of government spending and taxes in determining demand and output in the short run. We saw how in the short run, increases in government spending and decreases in taxes both increase output.

- In Chapter 5, we looked at the short-run effects of fiscal policy on output and the interest rate. We saw how a fiscal contraction leads to decreases in both output and the interest rate. We also saw how fiscal and monetary policies can be used to affect both the level and the composition of output.

- In Chapter 7, we looked at the effects of fiscal policy when the economy is open to trade. We saw how fiscal policy affects both output and the trade balance and examined the relation between budget deficits and trade deficits. We saw how fiscal policy and exchange-rate adjustments can be used to affect both the level and the composition of output. Multipliers on fiscal stimulus packages are much smaller in an open economy.

- In Chapter 8, we looked at the role of fiscal policy in an economy with open goods and financial markets. We saw how, in the presence of international capital mobility, the effects of fiscal policy depend on the exchange-rate regime. Fiscal policy has a much stronger effect on output under fixed exchange rates than under flexible exchange rates.

- In Chapter 10, we looked at the effects of fiscal policy in the short run and the medium run. We saw that in the medium run (taking the capital stock as given), changes in fiscal policy have no effect on output and are simply reflected in a different composition of spending.

- In Chapter 11, we looked at the need to use fiscal policy to increase aggregate demand when the economy is in the liquidity trap. Here fiscal policy can increase output when conventional monetary policy is ineffective.

- In Chapter 16, we looked at how saving and thus budget deficits affect the level of capital accumulation and the level of output in the long run. We saw how once capital accumulation is taken into account, larger deficits decrease capital accumulation, leading to a lower level of output in the long run.

- In Chapter 22, we looked at the short-run effects of fiscal policy, taking into account not only its direct effects through taxes and government spending, but also its effects on expectations. We saw how the effects of a deficit reduction on output depend on expectations of future fiscal and monetary policies. We also saw how a deficit reduction may, in some circumstances, be expansionary, even in the short run.

- In Chapter 23, we looked at the problems facing fiscal policy makers, from uncertainty about the effects of policy to issues of time consistency and credibility. We briefly discussed the pros and cons of restraints on the conduct of fiscal policy, such as a law or agreement of some type to balance the budget. We saw these agreements are rarely effective.

Do not confuse the words "deficit" and "debt." (Many journalists and politicians do.) Debt is a stock, what government owes as a result of past deficits. The deficit is a flow, how much government borrows in a given year.

Fiscal policy is the central issue facing advanced economies today. Table 25–1 presents the numbers on deficits for all levels of government in four OECD countries: Canada, the United States, Germany, and Italy, as well as the OECD as a whole. Table 25–2 presents similar numbers on total government debt. Before we look in detail at these tables, there are three important general remarks. The numbers are presented as a percent of GDP. This is the right way to compare countries.

The data are presented for **general government**. This means that all levels of government are added together within a country. This is important because countries have many levels of government and the different levels of government play different roles in different countries. In Canada, provinces provide health, education, welfare, and a significant part of the justice system. In other countries, a federal or local government might provide all or part of such services. The only sensible way to compare across countries is to combine the different levels of government.

| TABLE 25–1 | General Government Budget Balances after the World Recession (surplus (+) or deficit (−) as a percent of GDP) | | | | | | | |
|---|---|---|---|---|---|---|---|---|
| | **2006** | **2007** | **2008** | **2009** | **2010** | **2011** | **2012** | **2013** |
| Canada | 1.8 | 1.5 | −0.3 | −4.8 | −5.2 | −4.0 | −2.6 | −2.3 |
| United States | −2.2 | −2.9 | −6.6 | −11.9 | −11.4 | −10.2 | −8.7 | −5.4 |
| Germany | −1.7 | 0.2 | −0.1 | −3.1 | −4.2 | −0.8 | 0.2 | −0.2 |
| Italy | −3.4 | −1.6 | −2.7 | −5.4 | −4.3 | −3.7 | −2.9 | −3.0 |
| Total OECD | −2.2 | −2.9 | −6.6 | −10.8 | −10.0 | −7.9 | −6.5 | −7.1 |

*Source:* General government financial balance; OECD Economic Outlook 93 database, extract May 2013. Years 2012 and 2013 are projections. "General government" refers to all levels of government. In Canada, general government is the combination of federal, provincial, and local governments.

The tables use data constructed by the Organisation for Economic Co-operation and Development (OECD). The OECD does a great deal of work to make the general government data as comparable as possible across member countries. The reality is that national and provincial numbers are often, shall we say, modified in presentation for political purposes (we will see a clear example later in Canada) and we need to depend partly on the work done by more impartial international agencies to find comparable and clear numbers.

> The International Monetary Fund (IMF) presents similar numbers for its member countries. Canada belongs to both groups.

Table 25–1 shows that, from 2008 to 2009, OECD governments experienced a very sharp increase in their deficits. We saw in Chapter 7 that this was partly by international agreement. The G20 countries (who overlap with the OECD) agreed to cut taxes or increase spending at the same time. We know that as the recession hit all these countries, revenues for governments would fall and outlays, especially on payments to the unemployed would rise. Canada's fiscal stimulus from 2008 to 2009 seems quite in line with those of the other three countries in Table 25–1 and the OECD as a whole. The reduction in Canada's overall government deficit also seems similar to that in the OECD as a whole—from a peak of 5.2% of GDP in 2010 to a projected 2.3% of GDP in 2013. The fiscal path in Canada is similar to that for the OECD as a whole, a drop in the deficit of 2.9 percentage points of GDP from 2010 to 2013.

Table 25–2 shows the percent of total GDP owed in the form of gross financial liabilities by all levels of governments. This is called the **debt-to-GDP ratio** or the **debt ratio**. All 5 rows show a sharp increase in the debt ratio after the recession of 2009. This is, of course, the result of the large deficits as well as a fall in GDP (the denominator of the ratio) from 2008 to 2009 in some countries.

In Canada and Germany, the level of indebtedness is expected to level off at between 80 and 90 percent of GDP (the difference here between 85 and 88 is unimportant.) In the United States and in Italy as well as in the total of the OECD the ratio of debt to GDP continues to grow. To understand why this is happening, we turn to the government budget constraint.

| TABLE 25–2 | General Government Gross Financial Liabilities after the World Recession (percent of GDP) | | | | | | | |
|---|---|---|---|---|---|---|---|---|
| | **2006** | **2007** | **2008** | **2009** | **2010** | **2011** | **2012** | **2013** |
| Canada | 68.6 | 65.0 | 69.2 | 81.5 | 83.0 | 83.4 | 85.5 | 85.2 |
| United States | 65.8 | 66.3 | 75.3 | 88.8 | 97.9 | 102.3 | 106.3 | 109.1 |
| Germany | 69.8 | 65.6 | 69.9 | 77.5 | 86.1 | 86.3 | 89.2 | 87.9 |
| Italy | 119.0 | 114.4 | 116.9 | 130.1 | 128.9 | 122.0 | 140.2 | 143.6 |
| Total OECD | 75.9 | 74.3 | 80.9 | 92.3 | 96.9 | 103.5 | 108.8 | 111.9 |

*Source:* General government gross financial liabilities: OECD Economic Outlook 93 database, extract May 2013. Years 2012 and 2013 are projections.

# 25-2 | The Government Budget Constraint

Where does government debt come from? Suppose that, starting from a balanced budget, government cuts taxes, creating a deficit. What will happen to debt over time? Will government need to increase taxes later? If so, by how much?

To answer these questions, we must start with the definition of the budget deficit. We can write the budget deficit in year $t$ as:

$$\text{Deficit}_t = rB_{t-1} + G_t - T_t \tag{25.1}$$

All variables in the government budget constraint are measured in real terms. $B_{t-1}$ is government debt at the end of year $t-1$, or equivalently, at the beginning of year $t$; $r$ is the real interest rate, which we will take to be constant here. Thus, $rB_{t-1}$ equals the real interest payments on the existing government debt. $G_t$ is government spending on goods and services during year $t$. $T_t$ is taxes minus transfers during year $t$. In words: The budget deficit equals spending, including interest payments on the debt, minus taxes net of transfers.

Note two characteristics of equation (25.1):

- We measure interest payments as real interest payments (the product of the *real* interest rate times existing debt) rather than as actual interest payments (the product of the nominal interest rate times existing debt). As we discuss in the Focus box "Inflation Accounting and the Measurement of Deficits," this is the correct way of measuring interest payments. However, official measures of the deficit include actual (nominal) interest payments and are therefore incorrect. The correct measure of the deficit is sometimes called the **inflation-adjusted deficit**. If both the debt and inflation are low, the gap between the inflation-adjusted deficit and the reported deficit is small. But this is not always the case.

- For consistency with our definition of $G$ as spending on goods and services earlier, $G$ does not include transfer payments. Transfers are instead subtracted from taxes so that $T$ stands for taxes minus transfers. Official measures of government spending add transfers to spending on goods and services and define revenues as taxes, not taxes net of transfers. These are only accounting conventions. Whether transfers are added to spending or subtracted from taxes makes a difference to the measurement of $G$ and $T$ but clearly does not affect the measure of the deficit.

The **government budget constraint** then simply states that the *change in government debt during year t* is equal to the *deficit during year t*:

$$B_t - B_{t-1} = \text{deficit}_t$$

If government runs a deficit, government debt increases. If government runs a surplus, government debt decreases.

Using the definition of the **deficit**, we can rewrite the government budget constraint as:

$$B_t - B_{t-1} = rB_{t-1} + G_t - T_t \tag{25.2}$$

The government budget constraint links the change in debt to the initial level of debt (which affects interest payments) and to current government spending and taxes.

It is often convenient to decompose the deficit into the sum of two terms:

- Interest payments on the debt.
- The difference between spending and taxes. This second term is called the **primary deficit** (equivalently $T_t - G_t$, is called the **primary surplus**).

Using this decomposition, we can rewrite equation (25.2) as:

$$\underbrace{B_t - B_{t-1}}_{\text{Change in the debt}} = \underbrace{rB_{t-1}}_{\text{Interest payments}} + \underbrace{G_t - T_t}_{\text{Primary deficit}}$$

Let $G$ denote spending on goods and services, $Tr$ denotes transfers, and $Tax$ denotes total taxes. Then,

$$\text{Deficit} = G + Tr - Tax$$

This can be rewritten in two (equivalent) ways:

$$\text{Deficit} = G = (Tax - Tr)$$

The deficit is equal to spending on goods and services, minus net taxes—total taxes minus transfers. This is the way we write it in the text:

$$\text{Deficit} = (G + Tr) - Tax$$

The deficit is equal to total spending—spending on goods and services plus transfers—minus total taxes. This is the way government reports spending and revenues.

Or, moving to the right and reorganizing:

$$B_t = (1+r)B_{t-1} + \overbrace{G_t - T_t}^{\text{Primary deficit}} \tag{25.3}$$

Debt at the end of year $t$ equals $(1+r)$ times debt at the end of year $t-1$, plus the primary deficit during year $t$, $(G_t - T_t)$. This relation will prove very useful in what follows.

## Current versus Future Taxes

Let us look at the implications of a one-year decrease in taxes for the path of debt and future taxes. Start from a situation where, until year 1, government has balanced its budget, so that debt is equal to zero. During year 1, government decreases taxes by 1 for 1 year. Thus, debt at the end of year 1, $B_1$, is equal to 1. What happens thereafter? Let us consider different cases.

**Full Repayment in Year 2.** Suppose that government decides to repay the debt fully during year 2. From equation (25.3), the budget constraint for year 2 is given by:

$$B_2 = (1 + r) B_1 + (G_2 - T_2)$$

If the debt is fully repaid during year 2, then debt at the end of year 2 is equal to zero: $B_2 = 0$. Replacing $B_1$ by 1 and $B_2$ by 0 in the preceding equation gives:

$$T_2 - G_2 = (1 + r)$$

---

**FOCUS**  **Inflation Accounting and the Measurement of Deficits**

Official measures of the budget deficit are constructed as nominal interest payments on the nominal level of debt, in this box also denoted $B$ to total $iB$, plus spending on goods and services, $G$, minus taxes net of transfers, $T$ (we have dropped the time indexes, which are not needed here):

Official measure of the deficit $= iB + G - T$

This is an accurate measure of the *change in nominal debt* over the year. If it is positive, government is spending more than it receives and must therefore issue new debt. If it is negative, government buys debt back.

But it is not an accurate measure of the *change in real debt*, the change in how much government owes, expressed in terms of goods rather than dollars. To see why not, suppose the official measure of the deficit is equal to zero, so government neither issues nor buys back debt, and the amount of nominal debt remains the same. Suppose inflation is positive and equal to 10%. Then, at the end of the year, the real value of the debt has decreased by 10%. If we define—as we should—the real deficit as the change in the real value of the debt of government, government is, in fact, running a budget surplus equal to 10% times the initial level of debt.

More generally, if $B$ is nominal debt and $\pi$ is inflation, the official measure of the deficit overstates the correct measure by an amount equal to $\pi B$. Put another way, the correct measure of the real deficit in a given year is obtained by subtracting $\pi B$ from the official measure:

Correct measure of the real deficit $= iB + G - T - \pi B$
$$= (i - \pi)B + G - T$$
$$= rB + G - T$$

where $r = i - \pi$ is the real interest rate. The correct measure of the real deficit is thus equal to real interest payments plus government spending minus taxes net of transfers, all measured in the same dollars. (Note that $r$ is equal here to the nominal interest rate minus *actual* inflation and should more accurately be called the "realized real interest rate," to distinguish it from the real interest rate, which is equal to the nominal interest rate minus *expected* inflation.)

The difference between the official and correct measures of the deficit equals $\pi B$. So, the higher the rate of inflation, $\pi$, or the higher the level of debt, $B$, the more inaccurate the official measure is. In countries in which both inflation and debt are high, the official measure may record a very large budget deficit, when, in fact, real government debt is actually decreasing.

Figure 1 plots the official measure and an inflation-adjusted measure of the federal budget deficit in Canada from 1970 to 2012. Each year the deficits are measured as a percent of GDP. The official measure shows a substantially higher deficit (and a smaller surplus) in all years. There is positive debt outstanding in all years and inflation is positive in all years. From 1970 to 1975, although the actual deficit is positive, the inflation-adjusted deficit is negative. These are years of high inflation. With lower inflation after 1993, the two measures become more similar.

*(continued)*

---

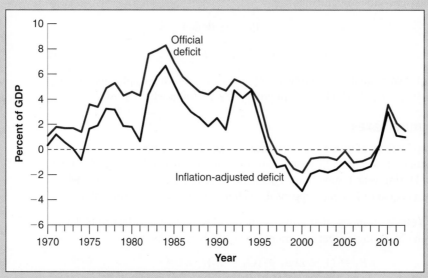

**FIGURE 1** Official and Inflation-Adjusted Federal Deficit in Canada, 1970–2012

*Source:* Table 2. Fiscal Reference Tables, 2012. Inflation calculated using the Consumer Price Index, CANSIM II variable V41690973.

To repay the debt fully during year 2, government must run a primary surplus equal to $(1 + r)$. It can do so in one of two ways: a decrease in spending or an increase in taxes. We will assume here and in what follows that the adjustment comes through taxes so that the path of spending is unaffected. It follows that the decrease in taxes by 1 below normal during year 1 must be offset by an increase in taxes by $(1 + r)$ above normal during year 2. The path of taxes and debt corresponding to this case is given in Figure 25–1(a) (assuming a value for $r$ of 10%). The black bars represent taxes during each year—as deviations from their initial level, and the green lines represent the level of debt at the end of each year.

> Full repayment in year 2:
> $T_1 \downarrow$ by 1
>
> $\Rightarrow T_2 \uparrow$ by $(1 + r)$

**Full Repayment in Year $t$.** Now, suppose that government decides to wait until year $t$ to increase taxes and repay the debt. So, from year 2 to year $t-1$, the primary deficit is equal to zero. Let us work out what this implies for the level of debt at the beginning of year $t$ (equivalently, the end of year $t-1$).

During year 2, the primary deficit is zero. So, from equation (25.3), debt at the end of year 2 is:

$$B_2 = (1 + r) B_1 + 0 = (1 + r)$$

where the second equality follows from the fact that $B_1 = 1$.

With the primary deficit still equal to zero during year 3, debt at the end of year 3 is:

$$B_3 = (1 + r) B_2 + 0 = (1 + r)(1 + r) = (1 + r)^2$$

Solving for debt at the end of year 4 and so on, it is clear that as long as government keeps a primary deficit equal to zero, debt grows at a rate equal to the interest rate, and thus debt at the end of year $t-1$ is given by:

$$B_{t-1} = (1 + r)^{t-2} \tag{25.4}$$

Despite the fact that taxes are cut only in year 1, debt keeps increasing over time, at a rate equal to the interest rate. The reason: Although the primary deficit is equal to zero, debt is now positive, and so are interest payments on the debt. Each year, government must issue more debt to pay the interest on existing debt.

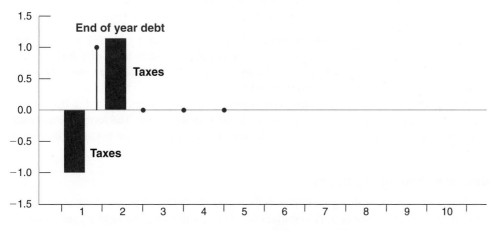

(a) **Debt reimbursement in year 2**

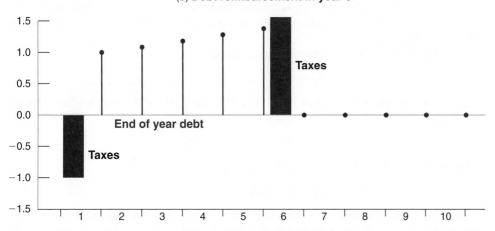

(b) **Debt reimbursement in year 6**

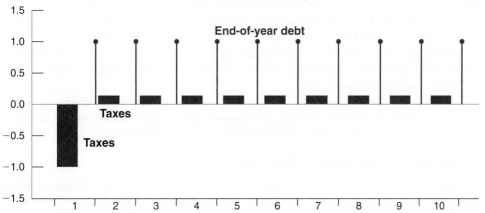

(c) **Debt stabilization in year 2**

**FIGURE 25–1**

**Tax Cuts, Debt Repayment, and Debt Stabilization**

(a) If debt is fully repaid during year 2, the decrease in
taxes of 1 in year 1 requires
an increase in taxes equal to
$(1 + r)$ in year 2. (b) If debt
is fully repaid during year $t$,
the decrease in taxes of 1 in
year 1 requires an increase
in taxes equal to $(1 + r)^{t-1}$
during year $t$. In this case,
$t = 60$. (c) If debt is stabilized
from year 2 on, then taxes
must be permanently higher
by $r$ from year 2 on.

In year $t$, the year in which government decides to repay the debt, the budget constraint is:

$$B_t = (1 + r) B_{t-1} + (G_t - T_t)$$

If debt is fully repaid during year $t$, then $B_t$ (debt at the end of year $t$) is zero. Replacing $B_t$
by zero, and $B_{t-1}$ by its expression from equation (25.4), gives:

$$0 = (1 + r)(1 + r)^{t-2} + (G_t - T_t)$$

Add exponents:
$(1 + r)(1 + r)^{t-2} =$
$(1 + r)^{t-1}$ (see Appendix 2).

Reorganizing and bringing $G_t - T_t$ to the right implies:

$$T_t - G_t = (1 + r)^{t-1}$$

To pay back the debt, government must run a primary surplus equal to $(1 + r)^{t-1}$ during year $t$. If the adjustment is done through taxes, the initial decrease in taxes of 1 during year 1 leads to an increase in taxes of $(1 + r)^{t-1}$ during year $t$. The path of taxes and debt corresponding to this case is given in Figure 25–1(b).

Full repayment in year $t$:
$T_1 \downarrow$ by 1
$\Rightarrow T_t \uparrow$ by $(1 + r)^{t-1}$

This example yields our first basic conclusion. If spending is unchanged, a decrease in taxes must eventually be offset by an increase in taxes in the future. The longer government waits to increase taxes or the higher the real interest rate, the higher the eventual increase in taxes.

## Debt and Primary Surpluses

We have assumed so far that government fully repays the debt. Let us now look at what happens to taxes if government only stabilizes the debt. (Stabilizing the debt means changing taxes or spending so that debt remains constant.)

Suppose that government decides to stabilize the debt from year 2 on. Stabilizing the debt from year 2 on means that debt at the end of year 2 and thereafter remains at the same level as at the end of year 1.

From equation (25.3), the budget constraint for year 2 is:

$$B_2 = (1 + r)B_1 + (G_2 - T_2)$$

Under our assumption that debt is stabilized in year 2, $B_2 = B_1 = 1$. Replacing in the preceding equation:

$$1 = (1 + r) + (G_2 - T_2)$$

Bringing $G_2 - T_2$ to the left side and reorganizing:

$$T_2 - G_2 = (1 + r) - 1 = r$$

To avoid a further increase in debt during year 1, government must run a primary surplus equal to real interest payments on the existing debt. It must do so in following years as well: Each year, the primary surplus must be sufficient to cover interest payments and thus to leave the debt level unchanged. The path of taxes and debt is shown in Figure 25–1(c): Debt remains at 1 from year 1 on. Taxes are permanently higher from year 1 on, by an amount equal to $r$; equivalently, from year 1 on, government runs a primary surplus equal to $r$.

Stabilizing the debt from year 2 on:
$T_1 \downarrow$ by 1
$\Rightarrow T_2, T_3, \ldots \uparrow$ by $r$

The logic of this argument extends directly to the case where government waits until year $t$ to stabilize. Whenever government stabilizes, it must from then on run a primary surplus sufficient to pay interest on the debt.

This example yields our second basic conclusion. The legacy of past deficits is higher government debt. To stabilize the debt, government must eliminate the deficit. To do so, it must run a primary surplus equal to the interest payments on the existing debt.

## The Evolution of the Debt-to-GDP Ratio

We have focused so far on the evolution of the level of debt. But in an economy in which output grows over time, it makes more sense to focus instead on the ratio of debt to output. This formulation also allows a comparison between countries as in Tables 25–1 and 25–2. To see how this change in focus modifies our conclusions, we need to go from equation (25.3) to an equation that gives the evolution of the debt-to-GDP ratio—the debt ratio. Table 25–2 presented data on the debt ratio for four countries and the OECD as a whole.

To do this, first divide both sides of equation (25.3) by real output, $Y_t$, to get:

$$\frac{B_t}{Y_t} = (1 + r)\frac{B_{t-1}}{Y_t} + \frac{G_t - T_t}{Y_t}$$

Next, rewrite $B_{t-1}/Y_t$, as $(B_t/Y_{t-1})(Y_{t-1}/Y_t)$ (in other words, multiply top and bottom by $Y_{t-1}$):

$$\frac{B_t}{Y_t} = (1 + r)\left(\frac{Y_{t-1}}{Y_t}\right)\frac{B_{t-1}}{Y_{t-1}} + \frac{G_t - T_t}{Y_t}$$

Start from:
$$Y_t = (1 + g)Y_{t-1}.$$
Divide both sides by:
$$Y_t$$
to get:
$$1 = (1 + g)Y_{t-1}/Y_t.$$
Reorganize to get:
$$Y_{t-1}/Y_t = 1/(1 + g)$$

We are nearly where we want to be: All the terms in the equation are now in terms of ratios to GDP$_t$ ($Y_t$). We can simplify further. Assume that output growth is constant, and denote the growth rate of output by $g$, so $Y_{t-1}/Y_t$ can be written as $1/(1 + g)$. Use the approximation $(1 + r)/(1 + g) = 1 + r - g$. We can then rewrite the equation as:

This approximation is derived as proposition 6 in Appendix 2 at the end of the book.

$$\frac{B_t}{Y_t} = (1 + r - g)\frac{B_{t-1}}{Y_{t-1}} + \frac{G_t - T_t}{Y_t}$$

Finally, move $B_{t-1}/Y_{t-1}$ to the left to get:

$$\frac{B_t}{Y_t} - \frac{B_{t-1}}{Y_{t-1}} = (r - g)\frac{B_{t-1}}{Y_{t-1}} + \frac{G_t - T_t}{Y_t} \qquad (25.5)$$

*The change in the debt ratio is equal to the sum of two terms. The first is the difference between the real interest rate and the growth rate times the initial debt ratio. The second is the ratio of the primary deficit to GDP.*

Compare equation (25.5), which gives the evolution of the ratio of debt to GDP, with equation (25.2), which gives the evolution of debt itself. The difference is the presence of $r - g$ with equation (25.5) compared to $r$ in equation (25.2). The reason for the difference is extremely important: Suppose the primary deficit is zero. Debt will then increase at a rate equal to the real interest rate, $r$. But if GDP is growing as well, the ratio of debt to GDP will grow more slowly; it will grow at a rate equal to the real interest rate minus the growth rate of output, $r - g$.

Figure 23–4 showed the evolution of the debt-to-GDP ratio for the Canadian federal government from 1926 to 2012. Equation (25.5) shows that the more the debt-to-GDP ratio increases,

- the higher the real interest rate.
- the lower the growth rate of output.
- the higher the initial debt ratio.
- the higher the ratio of the primary deficit to GDP.

The effects of all four factors can be seen in Figure 23–4. The debt-to-GDP ratio rose rapidly during the Great Depression when GDP fell. During World War II, there was a very large primary deficit to pay for the war effort. In the long period after World War II, real interest rates were low (in fact, they were negative as we shall see later) and growth in real output was high so that even though the debt-to-GDP ratio peaked at over 140% at the end of World War II, it fell rapidly. Finally, from about the mid-1970s until 1993 was a period when Canada had large deficits, which are seen in Figure 1 in the Focus box "Inflation Accounting and the Measurement of Deficits." After 1997, deficits turned into surpluses until the 2009 recession. After 2009, slow (even negative) growth in output and large deficits set the debt ratio growing again.

Tables 25–1 and 25–2 show the same factors at play in all OECD countries after 2006. The recession, negative GDP growth, increased the debt ratio. Large deficits were incurred from 2009 to 2011 as fiscal policy was used to increase demand. Finally, although we cannot see it in the tables, the debt ratios would have risen even more had nominal interest rates not been at record lows, even zero in the United States. Real interest rates, as we saw in Chapter 19, were slightly negative. The debt ratio appears to be stabilizing in Germany and Canada. In Canada and in Germany, there has been enough positive output growth and a sufficiently low primary deficit to stabilize the debt ratio.

The picture for the OECD in total and for both the United States and Italy is less cheerful. Remember that the United States is by far the largest economy in the OECD total. The U.S.

budget deficit is still very large, although it is declining. At the federal level in the United States, the Democrats and Republicans are simply unable to come up with a plan to reduce a very large federal deficit. The Republicans want all deficit reduction from expenditure reduction, the Democrats want a mixture of spending reduction and significant tax increases. In Italy and in much of the rest of Europe, debt ratios are forecast to rise in 2013. Europe is forecast to go into a second recession in 2013—with negative or zero growth in many countries including Italy. Low or zero growth in combination with continued large deficits, using equation (25.5), will inexorably lead to further increases in the debt ratio.

## 25-3 | Deficits, Output Stabilization, and the Cyclically Adjusted Budget Balance

We have seen throughout the book that fiscal policy—increases in spending or a decrease in the tax rate—is used for the stabilization of output. In this section, we look at a complicated measurement question: How do we know if a government has made fiscal changes that are intended to stabilize output?

The problem we face is that using the actual deficit to measure a government's fiscal intervention is very misleading. At the simplest level, if output falls and the government does nothing—that is, makes no changes to tax rates and no changes to expenditure—the fall in revenue associated with the fall in output would either reduce a surplus or increase an existing deficit. The actual government deficit would suggest a policy intervention had occurred. But no policy intervention occurred—the government changed neither expenditures nor tax rates.

To help assess whether fiscal policy is only being used to stabilize the economy, economists have constructed measures that tell them what the deficit would be, under existing tax and spending rules, if output were at its natural level. Such measures come under many names. Two common names are the **full-employment deficit** or the **structural deficit**. We will use **cyclically adjusted budget balance (CABB)**, the term used by Canada's Department of Finance. Such a measure gives a simple benchmark by which to judge the direction of fiscal policy: If the actual deficit is large but the cyclically adjusted budget balance is equal to zero, then current fiscal policy is consistent with no systematic increase in the level of nominal debt over time. Debt will increase as long as output is below its natural level; but if output returns to its natural level, the deficit will disappear.

This does not imply that the goal should be to maintain the CABB equal to zero at all times. In a recession and wanting to stabilize output, government may want to run a deficit large enough that even the CABB is negative. In that case, the fact that the CABB is negative also provides a clear warning: The return of output to its natural level is not enough to move the deficit to zero. The level of debt will continue to rise and, if the economy is not growing fast enough or the interest rate on the debt is too high, the government will have to take specific measures to decrease the deficit at some point in the future or the debt ratio will grow.

The theory underlying the cyclically adjusted budget balance is clear. The practice has proven tricky. To understand these issues, we need to look at how measures of the cyclically adjusted deficit are constructed. Construction requires two steps. First, establish how much lower the deficit would be if output were, say, 1% higher. Second, assess how far away output is from its natural level.

The first step is straightforward. A reliable rule of thumb is that a 1% decrease in output leads automatically to an increase in the deficit of 0.5% of GDP in most countries. This increase occurs because most taxes are proportional to output, whereas most government spending does not depend as much on the level of output. The portions of government outlays that do depend on output—employment insurance payments and welfare payments—rise as output falls. That means that a decrease in output, which leads to a decrease in revenues and a small increase in spending, naturally leads to a larger deficit. If output is, say, 5% below its natural level, the deficit as a ratio to GDP will be about 2.5% larger than it would be if output

If you return to equation (25.5), you will note that even if the CABB is zero, the debt ratio could either rise or fall depending on the interest rate and the growth rate of real GDP.

Somewhere in the federal budget documents under a heading like "Sensitivity of the Budget Balance to Economic Shocks" you would find the sensitivity of the federal budget balance to a reduction in GDP growth.

were at its natural level. (This effect of activity on the deficit has been called an **automatic stabilizer**: A recession naturally generates a deficit, and therefore an automatic fiscal expansion that partly counteracts the recession.)

The second step is more difficult. Recall from Chapter 9 that the natural level of output is the output level that would be produced if the economy were operating at the natural rate of unemployment. You have to estimate the natural rate of unemployment and equivalently the natural level of output. By now you know that various methods could be used and different methods would lead to different final estimates.

Suppose you have a deficit of $5B and current output is $90B. If you estimate the natural level of output to be $100B and use the rule of thumb above, a return to the natural level of output would generate $5B in tax revenues and completely wipe out the deficit. The CABB is zero in this example. But if you estimate that the natural level of output is $110B, the CABB is not zero but rather is a surplus of $5B. The larger the estimate is of potential output, the larger the CABB surplus (or the smaller the CABB deficit). The accuracy of the estimate of the gap between current output and the natural level of output is crucial in making a good estimate of the CABB.

This got European countries in trouble in the 1980s. They constantly underestimated the natural level of unemployment and thus overestimated the natural level of output. Fiscal plans were made assuming deficits would go away when full employment was reached in the medium term. This did not happen and deficits persisted. As a result, most of the decade was characterized by high deficits and a large increase in debt-to-GDP ratios. The dangers of high debt-to-GDP ratios are discussed in the next section.

The more recent presentations of the CABB of the Canadian federal government added a third step, one not usually part of the calculation of the CABB either in Canada or in any other country. The government decided that that some portion of its real expenditures (the G in the usual equation) could be re-labelled as cyclical—that is, temporary—for only as long as the economy is away from full employment. At that point, presumably that spending would end since it is no longer needed for stimulus purposes and the government would no longer undertake this spending. The spending is the "fault" of the cycle. This methodology reduced the CABB considerably in 2009 and 2010. The Focus box "What Is Canada's Cyclically Adjusted Budget Balance?" shows that this methodology, at least as followed in Department of Finance reports made in 2010 and 2011, was highly flawed. Department of Finance measures of the CABB for the federal government were presented in an inconsistent way in 2010, 2011, and 2012.

## FOCUS   What Is Canada's Federal Cyclically Adjusted Budget Balance?

The short answer: our federal government has not given us a reliable and clear answer to this question. The cyclically adjusted budget balance (CABB) is an important number and an important concept. It recognizes that government outlays and especially government revenue sources are sensitive to the distance the economy is from the natural level of output. We know the actual deficit will be larger when output is low. Tax revenues will be smaller. Outlays, especially outlays on payments to the unemployed and payments to those on social assistance, will be larger.

The actual value of the CABB provides two useful pieces of information. The change in the CABB from one year to the next tells us if fiscal policy is being used to actively stabilize the economy. If the CABB becomes more negative, policy has become more stimulative—that is, spending has increased or

taxes have been reduced. The second useful piece of information in the CABB refers to long-term fiscal sustainability. A large negative CABB says even if the economy were at full employment, the ratio of debt to GDP is more likely to increase. Equation (25.5) tells us if the primary surplus is less than the difference between the real interest rate on the debt and the growth rate of GDP multiplied by the current debt ratio, the debt ratio will rise. Given that both pieces of information are important, it would seem to be important to calculate the CABB carefully and clearly.

Table 1 shows that in Canada, the federal Department of Finance has not presented clear or consistent information about the CABB since 2010. Each year in October, the Department of Finance publishes the Fiscal Reference Tables (FRT). Each October, a series purported to represent the CABB is

*(continued)*

presented. Table 1 is constructed from the FRT reports published in 2010, 2011, and 2012.

The usual interpretation of the CABB is that if the economy were at the natural level of output, the deficit would take on the CABB value. The *change* in the CABB reflects information on the change in the fiscal stimulus. The *level* of the CABB reflects information on how far the economy is from the natural level of output.

Focus on the year 2009, the recession year. The actual deficit was huge, 3.4% of GDP. This was a very large change from the small deficit, 0.4% of GDP in 2008. Was the actual deficit the result of a fiscal stimulus package?

When the government reported in October 2010, the answer was a tentative yes. The CABB swung from a surplus of 0.5% of GDP in 2008 to a CABB of 0.0% of GDP in 2009. The fiscal stimulus was half a percent of GDP from 2008 to 2009.

When the government reported in October 2011, the answer was a flat out no. The CABB moved from 0.0 in 2008 to a surplus of 0.6 in 2009. Thus according to the 2011 presentation of the 2009 CABB, the fiscal stimulus was negative; fiscal policy was actually tighter in 2009 than in 2008.

Finally when the government reported to Canadians in October 2012, we received different information again! The fiscal stimulus that had already taken place in the past, as reported in 2012, was back on: the CABB moved from a reported 0 in 2008 to −0.7 in 2009. Thus the information about fiscal stimulus from 2008 to 2009 from the change in the CABB varied considerably with the year of reporting.

What about the information in the level of the CABB? Again focus on 2009. The actual deficit: 3.4% of GDP. The CABB of zero as reported in October 2010 would normally be interpreted as saying, if the economy had been at full employment in 2009, there would have been no deficit. The value 0.6 reported in 2011 would be interpreted that, if the economy had been at full employment in 2009, there would have been a surplus. In 2012, rather than the CABB balance or the CABB surplus reported in the two previous years, the October 2012 report stated that if the economy had been at full employment in 2009, there would still have been a deficit. The swings in the reported value of the 2009 CABB from 2010 to 2011 to 2012 make no sense.

How does the government explain these numbers? To quote the footnotes to Table 46 in 2010, "For 2009, temporary counter-cyclical fiscal measures are included in the cyclical component of the balance and therefore excluded from the cyclically-adjusted budgetary balance." This is a strange new concept of the CABB.

One supposes that, when reporting in 2010, enough spending in 2009 was simply declared to be cyclical until the CABB in 2009 was zero. The entire deficit was declared to be cyclical. The same pronouncement was made in October 2011 about the 2010 deficit of 2.0% of GDP. The entire deficit was again cyclical. The assertion: this government would never operate with a deficit except as part of countercyclical fiscal policy.

The government then had a change of heart in October 2012. In the 2012 FRT, the government announced that the CABB in 2009, 2010, and 2011 had actually been negative— that is, even if Canada were at full employment, there would have been deficits of 0.7% in 2009, 0.7% in 2010, and 0.8% of GDP in 2011. The only logical interpretation: tax revenues even at full employment were not sufficient to cover outlays at full employment. The political conclusion: when the government wanted to blame the entire deficit on the recession, it did so in 2010 and 2011. When the government wanted to justify expenditure cuts in 2012 to balance the budget, the CABB mysteriously became negative.

We can only conclude that the government is not providing enough information to create a useful measure of the CABB. Neither the change in the CABB from year to year nor its level in a given year has been consistently and usefully reported. The Parliamentary Budget Officer writes, in what can only be considered an understatement (structural balance is yet another term for the CABB):

*"While Parliamentarians benefit from reviewing Finance Canada's historical estimates of the Government's structural balance on a Public Accounts basis, they would benefit further by receiving information regarding Finance Canada's projections of the Government's structural balance over the medium term as well as regarding Finance Canada's methodology and assumptions used to construct its estimates and projections."*

*Sources* The Parliamentary Budget Officer, Page 24, *Economic and Fiscal Outlook*, April 29, 2013

In other, less polite words, Finance Canada's information on the CABB as provided to Parliament is not very useful!

| TABLE | 1 | Measures of the Federal Cyclically Adjusted Budget Balance from the 2010, 2011, and 2012 Issues of the Fiscal Reference Tables (percent of potential GDP) | | | | | | |
|---|---|---|---|---|---|---|---|---|
| Source | Table | Variable | 2006 | 2007 | 2008 | 2009 | 2010 | 2011 |
| FRT 2012 | Table 17[1] | Actual Balance | 1.0 | 0.6 | −0.4 | −3.4 | −2.0 | −1.5 |
| FRT 2010 | Table 46[2] | CABB | 0.9 | 0.7 | 0.5 | 0.0 | NA | NA |
| FRT 2011 | Table 46[2] | CABB | 0.5 | 0.8 | 0.0 | 0.6 | 0.0 | NA |
| FRT 2012 | Table 17[1] | CABB | 0.7 | 0.3 | 0.0 | −0.7 | −0.7 | −0.8 |

1. Fiscal year measure. 2. Calendar year measure. Fiscal year 2006–07 aligned to calendar year 2006.

| TABLE 25–3 | General Government Primary Cyclically Adjusted Budget Balances (percent of GDP) | | | | | | | |
|---|---|---|---|---|---|---|---|---|
| | **2006** | **2007** | **2008** | **2009** | **2010** | **2011** | **2012** | **2013** |
| Canada | 1.6 | 1.2 | −0.9 | −3.0 | −4.0 | −3.3 | −2.5 | −2.0 |
| United States | −1.4 | −2.0 | −5.0 | −8.8 | −8.1 | −6.8 | −5.5 | −3.3 |
| Germany | 1.0 | 2.0 | 1.4 | 0.6 | −1.4 | 0.8 | 1.5 | 1.3 |
| Italy | −0.1 | 1.5 | 1.2 | 0.5 | 1.6 | 2.3 | 4.4 | 5.0 |
| Total OECD | −0.6 | −0.9 | −2.7 | −5.8 | −5.3 | −4.0 | −3.3 | −2.0 |

*Source:* General government cyclically adjusted primary balance: OECD Economic Outlook 93 database, extract May 2013. Years 2012 and 2013 are projections.

Table 25–3 presents more useful OECD values for the CABB for all governments in Canada and three other countries. These are the primary deficits or surpluses that would occur at full employment. These more useful and accurate numbers can be used in two ways.

*Primary surpluses or deficits appear in equation (25.5).*

The change between years measures the size of the fiscal stimulus. For example, in Canada from 2008 to 2009, the primary CABB moved from −0.9 to −3.0. This was the stimulus spending and temporary tax cuts in the much-advertised Economic Action Plan as well as deficit spending by provincial and municipal partners. Was Canada's plan big or small? Doing the same calculation for the other three countries shows that from 2008 to 2009, Canada's stimulus was half the size of the American stimulus but larger than the stimulus in Germany or Italy.

*The OECD also presents cyclically adjusted tax revenue and cyclically adjusted outlays as separate pieces of information. This allows the reader to consider the role of outlay changes and tax revenue changes in the business cycle and how they might vary across countries.*

The CABB plays a second equally important role. We imagine that the economy has returned to the natural level of output. Then we can ask, using equation (25.5), if the primary deficit at the natural level of output as a ratio of GDP is small enough to stabilize the debt ratio. This is a useful piece of information that is simply not given by the actual deficit. After the planned reduction in government spending as of 2013, the OECD calculated Canada's primary cyclically adjusted deficit at 2% of GDP. Then, using equation (25.5), the difference between the real interest rate and the growth rate must be at least 2 percentage points so that the debt-to-GDP ratio remains stable. Is this likely? It is actually hard to say. A growth rate of real GDP of 2% per year seems possible. The current real interest rate is negative or close to zero. So there is no issue as long as the real interest rate stays low. But if the real interest rate were to increase substantially, the possibility we consider in the next section, Canada's all-government debt ratio could increase very quickly.

For Germany and Italy, the cyclically adjusted primary balance is forecast to be a surplus in 2013. Thus, at reasonable growth rates of real GDP and reasonable interest rates, the debt ratio should fall. The United States seems to be in the most trouble. The primary deficit, even at full employment, is forecast at 3.3% of GDP. Thus, even at a zero real rate of interest, to stabilize the debt ratio, output in the United States must grow at 3.3% per year. This seems very unlikely.

## 25-4 | The Dangers of Very High Debt: High Debt, Default Risk, and Vicious Circles

Suppose that, for good or bad reasons, large deficits have led to a high debt ratio. What should the government do then? Simply trying to stabilize the debt at this high level is unwise: The lesson from history is that a very high debt has two outcomes: it can lead to vicious circles or it creates an incentive for inflation and even hyperinflation. Let's look at each more closely.

Return to equation (25.5):

$$\frac{B_t}{Y_t} - \frac{B_{t-1}}{Y_{t-1}} = (r - g)\frac{B_{t-1}}{Y_{t-1}} + \frac{(G_t - T_t)}{Y_t}$$

Take a country with a high debt ratio, say, 100%. Suppose the real interest rate is 3% and the growth rate is 2%. The first term on the right is $(3\% - 2\%)$ times $100\% = 1\%$ of GDP. Suppose further that the government is running a primary surplus of 1%, thus just enough to keep the debt ratio constant (the right side of the equation equals $(3\% - 2\%)$ times $100\% + (-1\%) = 0\%$).

Now suppose financial investors start to worry that the government may not be able to fully repay the debt. They ask for a higher interest rate to compensate for what they perceive as a higher risk of default on the debt. But this in turn makes it more difficult for the government to stabilize the debt. Suppose, for example, that the interest rate increases from 3% to, say, 8%. Then, just to stabilize the debt, the government needs to run a primary surplus of 6% (the right side of the equation is then equal to $(8\% - 2\%) \times 100 + (-6 = 0)$. Suppose that, in response to the increase in the interest rate, the government indeed takes measures to increase the primary surplus to 6%. The spending cuts or tax increases that are needed are likely to prove politically costly, potentially generating more political uncertainty, a higher risk of default, and thus a further increase in the interest rate. Also, the sharp fiscal contraction is likely to lead to a recession, decreasing the growth rate. Both the increase in the real interest rate and the decrease in growth further increase $(r - g)$, requiring an even larger surplus to stabilize the debt. At some point, the government may become unable to increase the primary surplus sufficiently, and the debt ratio starts increasing, leading financial markets to become even more worried and require an even higher interest rate. Increases in the interest rate and increases in the debt ratio feed on each other. The **vicious circle** can result in a debt explosion.

In short, the higher the ratio of debt to GDP, the larger the potential for catastrophic debt dynamics. Even if the fear that the government may not fully repay the debt was initially unfounded, it can easily become self-fulfilling. The increased interest the government must pay on its debt can lead the government to lose control of its budget and lead to an increase in debt to a level such that the government is unable to repay the debt, thus validating the initial fears.

The lesson is clear. When a government inherits a high debt ratio, it should aim at decreasing it over time. As equation (25.5) made clear, it can achieve this through a combination of primary surpluses, high growth rates, and low real interest rates.

This is far from an abstract issue. Investors' worries about default risk are affecting interest rates in a number of countries in Europe. Greece, Italy, and Spain, all countries with high debt ratios, have been considered candidates for a vicious circle. As interest rates rise on debt issued by these countries, the higher interest rates make it more difficult for these countries to stabilize the debt ratio.

We can now turn to the next question: What if a government does not succeed in stabilizing the debt, and debt and interest rates explode? Then, historically, one of two things happens: Either the government explicitly defaults on its debt, or the government relies increasingly on money finance, which typically leads to very high inflation. Let's look at each outcome in turn.

## Debt Default

At some point, when a government finds itself facing very high interest rates, it may decide to default. Default is often partial, and creditors take what is known as a **haircut**: A haircut of 30%, for example, means that creditors receive only 70% of what they were owed. Default also comes under many names, many of them euphemisms—probably to make the prospects more appealing (or less unappealing) to creditors. It is called **debt restructuring**, or **debt rescheduling** (when interest payments are deferred rather than cancelled), or, quite ironically, private sector involvement (the private sector, i.e., the creditors, are asked to *get involved*, i.e., to accept a haircut). It may be unilaterally imposed by the government, or it may be the result of a negotiation with creditors: Creditors, knowing that they will not be fully repaid in any case, may prefer to work out a deal with the government. Greece is indeed involved in negotiations with its creditors, with haircuts around 50%.

When debt is very high, default would seem like an appealing solution: Having a lower level of debt after default reduces the size of the required fiscal consolidation and thus makes it more credible. It lowers required taxes, potentially allowing higher growth. But default comes with very high costs. If debt is held, for example, by pension funds, the retirees may suffer very much from the default. If it is held by banks, then banks may go bankrupt, with major adverse effects on the economy. If debt is held instead mostly by foreigners, then the country's reputation may be lost, and it may be very difficult for the government to borrow abroad for a long time. So, in general, and rightly so, governments are very reluctant to default on their debt. The alternative is money finance of the debt, assuming that the government can require the central bank to purchase some or all of the debt issued by the government.

## Money Finance

Most of the time, fiscal and monetary policies proceed independently. The government finances its deficit through borrowing. The central bank chooses the supply of money so as to achieve its objective (for example, low inflation). But, when the fiscal situation is bad, either because deficits are large or debt is high, and the interest rate faced by the government is high, it becomes increasingly tempting for the government to want to finance itself through money finance, that is, by selling bonds directly to the central bank in return for central bank money. Central bank money could take the form of deposits of commercial banks at the central bank or the form of issues of new currency. It does not matter which form it takes. The key is that fiscal policy then determines the behaviour of the money supply, a case known as **fiscal dominance**.

Governments do not literally finance themselves through money creation. As we saw in Chapter 4, it is the central bank that creates money. But when the central bank finds itself in the fiscal dominance situation, the central bank must do what the government tells it to do. The government issues new bonds and tells the central bank to buy them. The central bank then pays the government with the money it creates, and the government uses that money to finance its deficit. This process is called **debt monetization**.

For a refresher on central bank money, see section 4-3.

How large a deficit can a government finance through such money creation? Let $H$ be the amount of central bank money in the economy. (We shall refer to central bank money simply as "money" in what follows.) Let $\Delta H$ be money creation—that is, the change in the nominal money stock from one month to the next. (When you look at the numbers below, you will understand why we use the month rather than, say, the year, as the unit of time.) The revenue, in real terms (that is, in terms of goods), that the government generates by creating an amount of money equal to $\Delta H$ is therefore $\Delta H/P$—money creation during the period divided by the price level. This revenue from money creation is called **seignorage**.

The word is revealing: The right to issue money was a precious source of revenue for the "seigneurs" of the past: They could buy the goods they wanted by issuing their own money and using it to pay for the goods.

We can summarize what we have just learned by writing

$$\text{seignorage} = \frac{\Delta H}{P}$$

Seignorage is equal to money creation divided by the price level. To see what rate of (central bank) nominal money growth is required to generate a given amount of seignorage, we can rewrite $\Delta H/P$ as

$$\frac{\Delta H}{P} = \frac{\Delta H}{H}\frac{H}{P}$$

In words: We can think of seignorage ($\Delta H/P$) as the product of the rate of nominal money growth ($\Delta H/H$) and the real money stock ($H/P$). Replacing this expression in the previous equation gives

$$\text{seignorage} = \frac{\Delta H}{H}\frac{H}{P}$$

This gives us a relation between seignorage, the rate of nominal money growth, and real money balances. To think about relevant magnitudes, it is convenient to take one more step and divide both sides of the equation by monthly GDP, $Y$, to get:

$$\frac{\text{seignorage}}{Y} = \frac{\Delta H}{H}\left(\frac{H/P}{Y}\right) \tag{25.6}$$

Suppose the government is running a budget deficit equal to 10% of GDP and decides to finance it through seignorage, so $(\text{deficit}/Y) = (\text{seignorage}/Y) = 10\%$. The average ratio of central bank money to monthly GDP in advanced countries is roughly equal to 1, so choose $(H/P)/Y = 1$. This implies that nominal money growth must satisfy:

$$\frac{\Delta H}{H} \times 1 = 10\% \implies \frac{\Delta H}{H} = 10\%$$

To finance a deficit of 10% of GDP through seignorage, given a ratio of central bank money to monthly GDP of 1, the monthly growth rate of nominal money must be equal to 10%.

This is surely a very high rate of money growth, but one might conclude that this is an acceptable price to pay to finance the deficit. Unfortunately, this conclusion would be wrong. As money growth increases, inflation is likely to follow. And very high inflation is likely to lead people to want to reduce their demand for real money, and in turn the demand for central bank money measured in real terms. In other words, as the government increases $\Delta H/H$, $H/P$ is likely to decrease. As it does so, the government needs to increase the rate of money growth further to achieve the same level of revenues. But higher money growth leads to further inflation, a further decrease in $H/P$, and the need for further money growth. Soon, high inflation is likely to turn into **hyperinflation**, the term that economists use for very high inflation— typically inflation in excess of 30% per month.

Hungary has the distinction of having had not one, but two, hyperinflations, one after World War I and one after World War II.

This scenario has been replayed many times in the past. You may have heard of the hyperinflation that existed in post-World War I Germany, a hyperinflation often associated with the rise of Adolf Hitler to power. In 1913, the value of all currency circulating in Germany was 6 billion marks. Ten years later, in October 1923, 6 billion marks was barely enough to buy a one-kilo loaf of rye bread in Berlin. A month later, the price of the same loaf of bread had increased to 428 billion marks. But the German hyperinflation is not the only, nor indeed even the fastest, hyperinflation since 1922.

A recent study defined a hyperinflation as starting when the monthly inflation rate hits 50% and ending when the monthly inflation rate drops below 50% and stays there for one full year. Using that definition, the study documented 56 hyperinflations between 1922 and 2012. The most rapid increase in prices was in Hungary in 1945 where it took 15 hours for prices to double at the peak. (In the German hyperinflation of 1922 it took 1.41 days.) More recently there have been hyperinflations in Zimbabwe (2007), Yugoslavia (1992), Serbia (1992), Armenia (1993), and Turkmenistan (1992).

It will come as no surprise that hyperinflations have enormous economic costs:

- The transaction system works less and less well. One famous example of inefficient exchange occurred in Germany at the end of its hyperinflation: People actually had to use wheelbarrows to cart around the huge amounts of currency they needed for their daily transactions.

A joke heard in Israel during the high inflation of the 1980s: "Why is it cheaper to take the taxi rather than the bus? Because in the bus, you have to pay the fare at the beginning of the ride. In the taxi, you pay only at the end."

- Price signals become less and less useful: Because prices change so often, it is difficult for consumers and producers to assess the relative prices of goods and to make informed decisions. The evidence shows that the higher the rate of inflation, the higher the variation in the relative prices of different goods. Thus the price system, which is crucial to the functioning of a market economy, also becomes less and less efficient.

- Swings in the inflation rate become larger. It becomes harder to predict what inflation will be in the near future, whether it will be, say, 500% or 1000% over the next year. Borrowing at a given nominal interest rate becomes more and more of a gamble. If we borrow at, say, 1000% for a year, we may end up paying a real interest rate of 500% or 0%: a large difference! The result is that borrowing and lending typically come to a stop in the final months of hyperinflation, leading to a large decline in investment.

We are discussing here the costs of very high inflation. In Chapter 24, we saw the discussion today in OECD countries is about the costs of, say, 4% inflation versus 0%.

So, as inflation becomes very high, output falls. There is typically an increasing consensus that it should be stopped. In the usual case, the currency is reformed or the country adopts a foreign currency as its currency. This prevents further monetization of the debt and inflation stops. The government via the central bank no longer has recourse to money finance. Inflation stops, but not before the economy has suffered substantial costs.

How likely is such a scenario to play again in the future? We hope that, in an advanced economy, the central bank would refuse to monetize the government's debts. Much depends on the relationship between the government and the central bank. To the extent that central banks have become more independent, the danger is lower than in the past. But it cannot be excluded.

## More Subtle Use of Inflation to Reduce High Levels of Debt

It cannot be denied that inflation will, if it is unexpected (and perhaps even if it is not unexpected) reduce the debt ratio. Return once again to equation (25.5):

This is an equation you cannot see too many times!

$$\frac{B_t}{Y_t} - \frac{B_{t-1}}{Y_{t-1}} = (r - g)\frac{B_{t-1}}{Y_{t-1}} + \frac{(G_t - T_t)}{Y_t}$$

Look at the term $(r - g)$. If inflation is large and unexpected, then the real interest rate paid on the government's debt could be negative. If growth is positive then the term $(r - g)$ is doubly negative and the debt ratio falls rapidly. The Focus box "How Countries Decreased Their Debt Ratios after World War II" makes it clear that both unexpected inflation and rapid economic growth played a huge role in Canada and other countries in reducing war debts after World War II.

Suppose that the inflation is expected and that, according to the Fisher equation, the nominal interest rate fully adjusts and the real interest rate remains unchanged. Could inflation still help reduce the debt ratio? We looked at this issue indirectly in Chapter 24. We noted that many taxes were not fully indexed for inflation and that some inflation could raise tax rates. We noted that while it may be difficult to reduce the nominal wages of workers, if there is some inflation, government may successfully reduce real wages of the workers they employ, either because of money illusion or simply because it is politically possible to freeze nominal wages. Both mechanisms seem to be important in practice.

See section 19-4.

See section 24-2.

---

## FOCUS    How Countries Decreased Their Debt Ratios after World War II

After World War II, many countries had very high debt ratios, often in excess of 100% of GDP. Yet, two or three decades later, the debt ratios were much lower, often below 50%. How did they do it? The answer is given in Table 1.

Table 1 looks at four countries: Australia, Canada, New Zealand, and the United Kingdom. Column 1 gives the period during which debt ratios decreased. The first year is either 1945 or 1946. The last year is the year in which the debt ratio reached its lowest point; the period of adjustment varies from 13 years in Canada, to 30 years in the United Kingdom. Column 2 gives debt ratios at the start and at the end of the period. The most striking numbers here are those for the United Kingdom: an initial debt ratio of 270% of GDP in 1946 and an impressive decline, down to 47% in 1974.

To interpret the numbers in the table, go back to equation (25.5). It tells us that there are two, not mutually exclusive, ways in which a country can reduce its debt ratio. The first is through high primary surpluses. Suppose, for example, that $(r - g)$ was equal to 0. Then the decrease in the debt ratio over some period would just be the sum of the ratios of primary surpluses to GDP over the period. The second is through a low $(r - g)$, so either through low real interest rates or through high growth, or both.

*(continued)*

| TABLE | 1 | Changes in Debt Ratios Following World War II | | | | |
|---|---|---|---|---|---|---|
| | 1 | 2 | 3 | 4 | 5 | 6 |
| Country | Start/End Year | Start/End Debt Ratio | Primary Balance | Growth Rate | Real Interest Rate | Inflation Rate |
| Australia | 1946–1963 | 92–29 | 1.1 | 4.6 | –2.3 | 5.7 |
| Canada | 1945–1957 | 115–59 | 3.6 | 4.3 | –1.4 | 4.0 |
| New Zealand | 1946–1974 | 148–41 | 2.3 | 3.9 | –2.9 | 4.9 |
| United Kingdom | 1946–1975 | 270–47 | 2.1 | 2.6 | –1.5 | 5.5 |

Columns 2 and 3: Percent of GDP. Columns 4 to 6: Percent.

*Source:* S.M.A. Abbas et al., "Historical Patterns and Dynamics of Public Debt: Evidence from a New Database," *IMF Economic Review* 2011 59 (November): pp. 717–742.

With this in mind, columns 3 to 5 give first the average ratio of the primary balance to GDP, then the average growth rate of GDP, and the average real interest rate over the relevant period.

Look first at primary balances in column 3. Note how all four countries indeed ran primary surpluses on average over the period. But note also that these primary surpluses account only for a small part of the decline in the debt ratio. Look, for example, at the United Kingdom. The sum of the ratios of the primary surpluses to GDP over the period is equal to 2.1% times 30 = 63% of GDP, so accounting for less than a third of the decline in the debt ratio, 223% (270 – 47) of GDP.

Now look at the growth rates and the real interest rates in columns 4 and 5. Note how high growth rates and how low real interest rates were during the period. Take Australia, for example.

The average value of $(r - g)$ during the period was –6.9% (–2.3% – 4.6%). This implies that, even if the primary balance had been equal to zero, the debt ratio would have declined each year by 6.9%. In other words, the decline in debt was not mainly the result of primary surpluses, but the result of sustained high growth and sustained negative real interest rates.

This leads to a final question: Why were real interest rates so low? The answer is given in column 6. During the period, average inflation was relatively high. This inflation, combined with consistently low nominal interest rates, is what accounts for the negative real interest rates. Put another way, a large part of the decrease in debt ratios was achieved by paying bond holders a negative real return on their bonds for many years.

## 25-5 | The Twin Deficits

To consider our last problem associated with a large government deficit, we need to return to the open economy. Many economists argue there is a link between the current account deficit (discussed in Chapters 6 and 18) and the government deficit. These are sometimes called the **twin deficits**.

We begin by reminding ourselves that all of GDP ($Y_t$) created in a country must go somewhere. Thus, in a year:

$$Y_t = C_t + I_t + G_t + X_t - Q_t$$

In the language of Chapters 6 and 7, the real exchange rate is set at a value of one.

Remember $X_t$ is exports and $Q_t$ is imports. We neglect real exchange rate effects and measure everything in units of domestic output. Rearranging the equation above by subtracting and adding $T_t$ yields:

$$(Y_t - T_t - C_t) + (T_t - G_t) = I_t + (X_t - Q_t)$$

Finally, we add $rB_t^f$ to both sides and label the items in parentheses as:

$$(rB_t^f + Y_t - T_t - C_t) + (T_t - G_t) = I_t + (rB_t^f + X_t - Q_t)$$

Private sector saving    Primary government surplus    Investment    Current account surplus where $r$ is the real interest rate paid or earned on net foreign assets, denoted $B^f_t$ as in Chapter 18. Two groups in society engage in saving on the left-hand side. The private sector saves by not consuming part of Gross National Product (GNP $= rB^f_t - Y_t$) after it has paid its taxes net of transfers, $T_t$. The public or government sector runs a primary surplus if $T_t - G_t$ is positive or a primary deficit if $T_t - G_t$ is negative. The right-hand side shows that society can save in one of two forms. New physical capital ($I_t$) can be installed. Society can accumulate more net foreign assets or repay foreign debts if the item in parentheses labelled current account surplus is positive.

The "twin deficits" observation notes that if government runs a primary deficit *and* the private sector does not increase its savings by the same amount, the sum of new investment and the current account surplus must fall. In practice, both are likely to fall somewhat. But in a very open economy, such as Canada's, it seems very likely that a government deficit will lead to a current account deficit very quickly. Why?

Suppose that you are a Canadian with some savings. If you see a profitable investment opportunity, $I_t$ will be positive. You would choose to save and build a new factory. Now, government runs a deficit and needs to borrow. The government sells you a bond which you buy with your savings. You no longer have the savings to build your new factory but the

◀ The statement that private savings will not increase when the government increases its primary deficit is the statement that Ricardian equivalence does not hold. See Focus box "Is Fiscal Policy Neutral in the Short Run?"

## FOCUS  Is Fiscal Policy Neutral in the Short Run?

A few economists make an argument that fiscal policy is neutral in the short run. They mean that a tax cut will not increase aggregate demand or output in the short run. In this extreme view, neither a deficit nor government debt has an effect on economic activity. They simply do not matter!

This argument is known as the **Ricardian equivalence** proposition. David Ricardo, a nineteenth-century English economist, was the first to articulate its logic. His argument was further developed and given prominence in the 1970s by Robert Barro, then at Chicago, now at Harvard University. For this reason, the argument is also known as the **Ricardo–Barro proposition**.

The best way to understand the proposition's logic is to use the example of tax changes from section 25-2. Suppose that government decreases taxes by 1 this year. And at the same time, it announces that to repay the debt, it will increase taxes by $(1 + r)$ next year.

What will be the effect of the initial tax cut on consumption? A plausible answer is that it will have no effect at all. Why? Because consumers realize that the tax cut is not much of a gift: Lower taxes this year are exactly offset, in present value, by higher taxes next year. Put another way, their human wealth—the present value of after-tax labour income—is unaffected. Current taxes go down by 1, but the present value of next year's taxes goes up by $(1 + r)/(1 + r) = 1$, and the net effect of the two changes is exactly equal to zero.

We can look at the same result another way, by looking at saving rather than consumption. To say that consumers do not change consumption in response to the tax cut is the same as saying that *private saving increases one for one with the deficit*. Thus, the Ricardian equivalence proposition says that if a government finances a given path of spending through deficits, private saving will increase one for one with the decrease in public saving, leaving total saving unchanged.

How seriously should you take the Ricardian equivalence proposition? Most economists would answer, "Seriously, but not seriously enough to think that deficits and debt are irrelevant." A major theme of this book has been that expectations matter, that consumption decisions depend not only on current income, but also on future income. If it were widely believed that a tax cut this year is going to be followed by an offsetting increase in taxes *next year*, the effect on consumption probably would be small. Many consumers would save most or all the tax cut in anticipation of higher taxes next year. (Replace "year" with "month" or "week" and the argument becomes even more convincing.)

Tax cuts rarely come, however, with the announcement of tax increases a year later. Consumers have to guess when and how taxes will eventually be increased. But insofar as future tax increases appear more distant and their timing more uncertain, consumers are more likely to ignore them. This may be the case because they expect to retire before taxes go up or, more likely, because they just do not think that far into the future.

In addition and importantly, liquidity-constrained consumers (see Chapter 21) who receive a larger government transfer with the increased deficit will spend it. It is clear there are many liquidity-constrained consumers.

Finally, if Ricardian equivalence were true, the twin deficits should not be observed. This is simply not the case. Open economies with large government deficits do run current account deficits.

So, it is safe to conclude that budget deficits have an important effect on activity. In the short run, larger deficits are likely to lead to higher demand and higher output. In the long run, higher government debt lowers capital accumulation and thus lowers output. In the open economy, large government deficits lead to current account deficits.

**FIGURE 25–2**

**The Twin Deficits**

There is a relation between the primary surplus of all governments in Canada and the current account balance. When governments run primary deficits or smaller primary surpluses, they add to Canada's international debts.

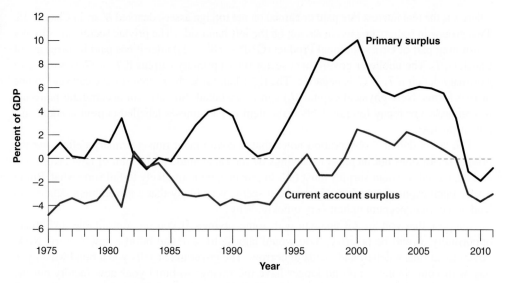

*Source:* Current account balance see Figure 18–5; Primary surplus: all governments, Table 46, Fiscal Reference Tables 2012 minus Interest on the Public Debt, Table 34, Fiscal Reference Tables 2012.

profitable opportunity to build the new factory still exists. You simply take out a loan from a foreigner (thus running a current account deficit) and continue to hold the government bond. The additional government borrowing "crowded" you into the international financial market. In a simpler scenario, one that also occurs in Canada, government may sell its bonds directly to foreigners. This is the favoured route of many Canadian provinces but not the usual route taken by the federal government. In either case, because total private sector saving did not expand as the government sector went into deficit, the most likely result of an increased government deficit is an increased current account deficit. In this world, investment remains the same, consumption increases, and the current account deficit rises when the government runs a primary deficit. These are the "twin deficits."

Figure 25–2 shows some evidence that larger primary deficits for all governments in Canada are associated with a larger current account deficit. As the primary deficits turned to primary surpluses, the current account moved into surplus in the late 1990s and early 2000s. When government again operated with primary deficits after 2009, the current account went into deficit.

Are the "twin deficits" a problem? It really depends, as it did in Chapter 18, on why government is borrowing. We argued in Chapter 18 that international borrowing is a useful source of physical capital when it is used to increase future production, which then repays the international loan. There is no reason why public sector primary deficits could not be used to build new public sector capital, roads, airports, and other infrastructure. It may even pay to borrow for education. However, the argument above does not avoid repaying the foreign loan. And if the foreign loan is not used to increase future production, then a higher current account deficit today does mean larger repayments of foreign debt in the future. A government deficit, in contributing to a current account deficit, can reduce the welfare of future generations in this way.

## 25-6 | Fiscal Policy in Canada since 1993

Fiscal policy in Canada since 1993 can be divided into four periods of time. First: from 1993 to 2006, under Liberal governments, there was a successful effort to reduce a very large deficit and reduce the level of debt. It is not an exaggeration to see this period as an example of a successful **fiscal consolidation** or a successful **austerity** program. Second: the Conservatives, when first elected in 2006, cut taxes in 2006 and 2008 without cutting spending. A surplus turned into a balanced budget. Third: the U.S. recession of

2008 and 2009 had a strong negative effect on the Canadian economy. Output fell and would have fallen more had the Conservative government not eventually responded with a period of temporary fiscal stimulus in 2009 and 2010. Fourth: the period from 2011 and beyond is expected to be a period of small tax increases and substantial spending cuts. The Conservatives' goal is to go into the next federal election on October 2015 with a balanced federal budget.If the federal budget is balanced or in surplus, the Conservatives will offer an election platform of further significant tax reductions. We will look at each period in more detail.

## Period One: Fiscal Consolidation in Canada 1993–2006

After the Liberal election victory in October 1993, new Finance Minister Paul Martin had to formulate both a short-term plan and a long-term plan for federal fiscal policy. Large federal deficits over the past 20 years had left the federal government deeply in debt. In addition, throughout the 1970s and 1980s foreign debts of all Canadians, both government and private, had skyrocketed. What fiscal plan could successfully lead Canada out of the twin deficits?

In 1993, the year of Paul Martin's appointment, the peacetime national debt of Canada staggers the mind. Figure 23–4 shows the steady increase in federal national debt (ignoring the provinces) peaking at 75 percent of Canada's GDP in 1996.

◀ In fact, other measures indicate that the federal government may owe even more money. The federal government owes money in the form of future pensions promised to its employees. It owes money in the form of guarantees on bonds issued by agencies of the federal government.

Martin's first problem was to convince Canadians that the deficit and the debt were serious problems. He toured the country explaining this to Canadians. What effect does such a large national debt have on the Canadian economy?

First, we saw in our analysis of long-run growth in a closed economy that if there is a higher national debt, the physical capital stock could be lower. This effect may be small in Canada's open economy where borrowers can access capital markets in the rest of the word (see Chapter 18).

Second, the existence of such a large federal debt puts a severe constraint on federal fiscal choices. The interest on the federal debt must be paid, or government must declare bankruptcy. To service the debt, the required primary surplus means higher taxes at the same level of government services. Less tax revenue is available for other government spending—health care, education, and transportation, for example.

Third, if you increase tax rates to service a higher debt, you may increase the costs of taxes. By costs of taxes, we do not mean the taxes themselves. We mean the welfare costs to society of the distortions associated with tax collection. The direct costs of tax collection are the costs of hiring the tax collectors, the taxpayers filling in forms, and the enforcement of tax laws. While these costs are significant, they will be incurred at any level of taxation, that is, at either a high tax rate or a low tax rate. The welfare costs of tax distortions may increase when tax rates are higher.

Here are several examples of tax distortions. Suppose that there is an increase in the income tax rate and Canadians respond by working less and taking more time off as holidays. This would reduce total GDP. We could look at this reduction in production as a result of a tax distortion. But part of the tax distortion is offset by the enjoyment of the extra holiday time. Any other tax creates a similar distortion. If gasoline is taxed more heavily, then Canadians would drive a little less. If a payroll is taxed, then employers will hire fewer new workers. If there is a general increase in the sales tax rate, then Canadians consume less and save a little more. All taxes create some kind of distortion, a change in the decision made by you or me, whether as households or firms. When more interest on the national debt increases tax rates, these distortions increase. This is a cost of the national debt, even if all the national debt is entirely held by residents of Canada.

Fourth, we note that not all the national debt is held by Canadians. We saw in Figure 25–2 that Canada's foreign debts increased when Canadian governments run a deficit. This is a clear-cut reduction in the welfare of Canadians when the national debt is held by foreigners.

An additional issue can arise if foreigners hold a large part of Canadian debt. This is closely related to our discussion of vicious circles as part of the dangers of very high debt. If the debt gets very large, foreigners may require a higher interest rate on all types of bonds issued by Canadians. Was this a problem for Canada in 1993?

In 1993, an editorial in *The Wall Street Journal* took note of Canada's large foreign and national debt, suggesting to its readers that this debt was getting riskier and should be held only at a higher interest rate. With a headline "Bankrupt Canada?"

> *Mexico isn't the only U.S. neighbor flirting with the financial abyss. Turn around and check out Canada, which has now become an honorary member of the Third World in the unmanageability of its debt problem. If dramatic action isn't taken in next month's federal budget, it's not inconceivable that Canada could hit the debt wall. . . .*
>
> *Canada has the second-highest ratio of debt to GDP of any industrialized country, only Italy surpasses it. But Italy finances most of its debt through domestic borrowing, while Canada ran a $30 billion-dollar balance-of-payments deficit last year. About 40 percent of Canada's provincial debt is held by foreigners. They should worry that 35 percent of all federal revenues now go to service the debt.*

(*The Wall Street Journal*, January 12, 1993)

Source: "Bankrupt Canada?" Wall Street Journal, Eastern edition [New York, N.Y] 12 Jan 1995: A14.

It seemed that the combination of domestic and foreign factors made Canadians ready in 1994 to tackle the issue of the federal deficit. How could this be done?

## The Liberal Record

In Paul Martin's initial budget in February 1994, the strongest possible language concerning Canada's fiscal situation was used to indicate deficit reduction was the highest policy priority:

> *This means making fundamental changes to our unemployment insurance system.*
>
> *It means overhauling the structure of federal–provincial transfers for social programs. . . .*
>
> *It is now time for the government to get its fiscal house in order. For years governments have been promising more than they can deliver and delivering more than they can afford. That has to end. We are ending it. The actions taken in this budget will reduce the deficit from $45.7 billion this year to $39.7 billion in 1994–95 and $32.7 billion the year after.*

(The Budget Speech, February 1994, p. 2)

Source: The Budget Speech, The Honourable Paul Martin, P.C., M.P. Minister of Finance, February 22, 1994, Department of Finance Canada.

It is fair to say that Martin and Prime Minister Jean Chrétien delivered. Table 25–4 shows how the Liberal government turned a deficit of 3.7% of GDP into a string of surpluses that generated a dramatic fall in the debt-to-GDP ratio. Canada's fiscal house was put in order. How was it done?

Table 25–4 measures federal government expenses and revenues in the most sensible way—that is, as a percent of GDP. This also lets us use equation (25.5), the central equation in this chapter, in the analysis. Otherwise, numbers such as $39.7 billion simply overwhelm and become meaningless. You can see that over the period of Liberal government, program spending as a percent of GDP fell from 14.9% to a low of 12.1% and then increased to 12.8%. Budgetary revenues rose as a percent of GDP over this period, beginning at 17.3% of GDP, peaking at 18.2% of GDP, and then falling to 16.2% of GDP. The large primary surplus over this period meant, using equation (25.5), that the debt-to-GDP ratio fell. As the debt-to-GDP ratio fell, the percent of GDP needed to service the government's debt fell dramatically, from

| TABLE | 25–4 | The Liberal Fiscal Record, 1995–2006 |

| Fiscal Year | Program Expenses (% GDP) | Budgetary Revenues (% GDP) | Public Debt Charges (% GDP) | Budgetary Surplus (+) or Deficit (−) (% GDP) |
|---|---|---|---|---|
| 1994–1995 | 16.0 | 17.0 | 5.7 | −4.8 |
| 1995–1996 | 14.9 | 17.3 | 6.1 | −3.7 |
| 1996–1997 | 13.3 | 17.9 | 5.6 | −1.0 |
| 1997–1998 | 13.0 | 18.2 | 4.9 | 0.3 |
| 1998–1999 | 12.7 | 18.1 | 4.7 | 0.7 |
| 1999–2000 | 12.1 | 18.0 | 4.4 | 1.5 |
| 2000–2001 | 12.1 | 18.1 | 4.1 | 1.9 |
| 2001–2002 | 12.3 | 16.6 | 3.6 | 0.7 |
| 2002–2003 | 12.7 | 16.5 | 3.2 | 0.6 |
| 2003–2004 | 12.7 | 16.4 | 2.9 | 0.8 |
| 2004–2005 | 13.7 | 16.4 | 2.6 | 0.1 |
| 2005–2006 | 12.8 | 16.2 | 2.5 | 0.9 |

The table presents federal government outlays, revenues, interest on the debt, and the consequent surplus or deficit for the decade of federal budgets associated with Prime Minster Jean Chrétien and Finance Minister Paul Martin. All values are shown as a percent of GDP.

*Source:* Table 2, *Fiscal Reference Tables*, 2008.

6.1% to 2.5% of GDP. To put this in perspective, as of fiscal year 1995–1996, 35% of federal revenue (6.1/17.3) was spent to service the federal debt. By the end of the Liberal time in office, only about 15% of federal revenue (2.5/16.2) was spent to service the federal debt.

It is interesting to look at the expenditure reductions undertaken by the Liberal government. Figure 25–3 illustrates, again as a percent of GDP, the components of federal spending. The actions of the Liberal government are found to the left of the vertical line.

The first thing to do is to add the vertical distance for the two lines related to transfers. One is entitled **transfers to other levels of government**, the other **transfers to persons**. The

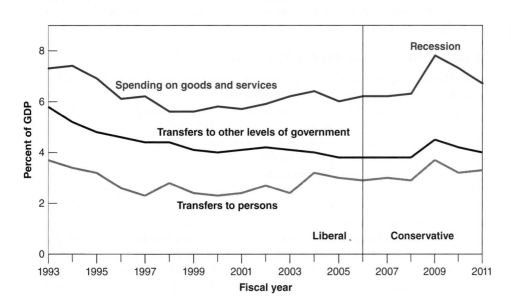

| FIGURE | 25–3 |

**Federal Government Spending in Canada, 1993–2011**

Federal government spending is measured as a percent of GDP. There are three categories: spending on goods and services; transfers to persons; and transfers to other levels of government. Total transfers exceed spending on goods and services.

*Source:* Table 8, Fiscal Reference Tables, 2012.

terms are self-explanatory. You can see that the major activity of the federal government is to transfer cash. How do we know this? The vertical sum of these two lines representing the two transfers always exceeds the vertical line representing goods and services. The federal government in Canada does not really buy much in the way of goods and services. The heavy lifting—spending on education and health—is done by the provinces.

Once you understand that transfers are more than one-half of federal government expenditure, it will not surprise you that when the Liberals cut federal expenditures, as seen by the area to the left of the vertical line in Figure 25–3 the cuts were in transfers to persons and transfers to other levels of government (the provinces). Over the time of the Liberal governments, total transfers to persons fell by about 2 full percent of GDP. How large is this decline? Nominal GDP in Canada in 2006 was about $1500 billion and 2% of $1500 is $30 billion. For convenience, assume Canada's population in 2006 was about 30 million (to make the arithmetic easy) so that federal transfers for each Canadian (man, woman, and child) had fallen relative to fiscal year 1993–1994 by $1000. Since payments to the elderly and to relatively poor families with children actually rose, the bulk of the reduced spending was reductions in unemployment benefits. Some of that spending fell because the unemployment rate fell steadily over this period.

Figure 25–3 also gives insight into the rocky path of federal–provincial relationships under the Chrétien government. You can see that the period opened with a sharp drop in federal transfers to the provinces, a drop of more than1% of GDP. Transfers to other levels of government stabilized by the end of the period but did not recover their original proportion of GDP.

Having looked at the expenditure side of the federal budget, let us turn in Table 25–4 to the revenue side. The Liberals did increase total taxes between 1995–1996 and 1997–1998. Tax revenue peaked at 18.2% of GDP and remained at or above 18% of GDP for the next three fiscal years. The Liberals were a high-tax government until 2000–2001. The high taxes and the reduction in expenditures swung the federal government into massive surpluses that peaked at 1.9% of GDP. The 2001–2002 fiscal year saw a dramatic shift in fiscal policy.

First program expenses rose slightly, mostly as small increases in transfers to the provinces, as the Liberal governments tried to restore federal–provincial peace. You can also see that between fiscal years 2000–2001 and 2005–2006, the Liberal federal government reduced tax revenue by nearly 2% of GDP. These were mostly reductions in personal income taxes over a number of years. There were reductions in rates, changes in brackets, and an important modification of the treatment of inflation in federal income tax so that "bracket creep" would no longer take place. The largest difference between the fiscal policies of the Liberal government after 2001–2002 and the subsequent Conservative government was the choice of which tax to reduce, not whether to reduce taxes.

## The Conservative Fiscal Record from 2006 to 2009

Stephen Harper campaigned on a promise to reduce the Goods and Services Tax (the GST) by 1 percentage point for two consecutive budget years.

In the first Conservative Budget, presented May 2, 2006, the first cut in the GST rate from 7% to 6% was duly announced to take effect July 1, 2006. The Fiscal Update of November 2007 announced that as of January 1, 2008, the GST rate would be reduced to 5%. The Conservatives kept their promise to reduce the GST.

The two GST reductions and a wide variety of other smaller tax cuts reduced federal budgetary revenues from 16.3% of GDP in 2006–2007 to an estimated 14.7% in 2008–2009. About half of the 1.6 percentage point reduction in federal revenue was associated with the GST cut.

The Conservatives, in spite of some rhetoric that they would also reduce program expenses, did no such thing. In the last year of the Liberal government, 2005–2006 program expenses were 12.8% of GDP. In the first two years of the Conservative government, program expenses actually rose to 13% of GDP. Figure 25–3 shows that this increase in federal government spending was neither an increase in transfers to persons nor in transfers to the provinces. Other components of federal spending grew slightly faster than GDP over the first Conservative years.

The upshot of Conservative activity on the fiscal side between 2006 and 2008 was a movement of the federal government from a surplus of about 1% of GDP to a small deficit of 0.4% of GDP in the fiscal year 2008–2009. Part of the 2008–2009 deficit was undoubtedly associated with a decline in economic activity in late 2008 and early 2009. It is most likely that the budget would have been roughly balanced had the recession not begun but, given the way the cyclically adjusted deficit was presented by the government in 2010 and 2011 (see again the Focus box "What Is Canada's Federal Cyclically Adjusted Budget Balance?"), we may never know. The data reported as of 2012, but not in 2010 or 2011, suggest that even had we had no recession, Conservative tax cuts would have created a deficit at full employment. But the recession did occur and makes a fascinating narrative for Canadian fiscal policy!

## The Implementation of Countercyclical Fiscal Policy, 2009–2011

The Conservatives were re-elected with another minority government in October 2008. The federal government provides economic information to Parliament twice a year. There is a formal Budget each spring with some information about tax and expenditure plans for the upcoming fiscal years. There is a fall Economic Statement or Update. In November 2008, Finance Minister Flaherty duly presented such a statement. An uproar and, depending on your viewpoint, a mini-constitutional crisis emerged.

The projections presented by the Conservatives in November 2008 are found in Table 25–5 on the left-hand (non-italic) values. As of November 2008, the world economic situation was bad and everyone knew it was bad (except apparently Mr. Flaherty). In the United States, housing prices had continued their downward trend. A large number of financial institutions in the United States and other countries had failed or had been bailed out by the U.S. and other governments in early fall 2008. Stock markets around the world had fallen in value by 40 to 60 percentage points. A particular issue for Canada was a precipitous drop in the prices of oil and other commodities that Canada produces and exports in large quantities. The collapse in auto sales reduced economic activity in southern Ontario. As a result of these events, the forecast of real GDP growth in 2009 of 2.4% in Canada made in the February 2008 Budget was revised downwards by Finance Minister Flaherty to 0.3% in the November Statement. Most observers viewed the use of a positive forecast of real economic growth in Canada over 2009 as a wildly optimistic forecast by Minister Flaherty. Minister Flaherty proposed ◄ reductions in government spending to maintain budget balance in the face of slower economic growth. For this and other reasons, in the week following the Economic and Fiscal Statement, the three opposition parties planned to defeat the government because the Economic Statement did not, in their view, contain sufficient recognition of the changed economic circumstances and the U.S. recession. A formal coalition of the Liberal and New Democratic parties was formed to create a new government with cabinet seats shared between the two parties. The Bloc Quebecois agreed to vote non-confidence against the Conservatives over the Economic Statement and to vote confidence in the proposed coalition government. Faced with certain defeat in the House of Commons, Prime Minister Stephen Harper asked the Governor General to prorogue Parliament to prevent a vote of non-confidence from taking place. The Governor General agreed, and Parliament was prorogued to January 26, 2009.

The Harper government introduced a new Budget on January 27, 2009, for approval by the House of Commons. Table 25–5 shows how drastically Conservative economic plans were altered in the two months between November 27, 2008, and January 27, 2009. The November Statement projected a balanced budget in all years from 2008–2009 through 2011–2012, with a small surplus in 2012–2013. The November projection depended, as already noted, on Canada avoiding any consequences of the U.S. recession and continuing with positive but slower economic growth. Such a rosy economic forecast preserved the level of federal revenues.

The OECD's forecast for Canadian economic growth, publicly released in November 2008 and almost certainly available to Minister Flaherty, was for economic growth in Canada of −0.5% in 2009.

TABLE 25-5 **The Implementation of Countercyclical Fiscal Policy in January 2009**

| Fiscal Year | Program Expenses (% GDP) | | Budgetary Revenues (% GDP) | | Public Debt Charges (% GDP) | | Budgetary Surplus(+) or Deficit (−) (% GDP) | |
|---|---|---|---|---|---|---|---|---|
| 2006–2007 Actual | 13.0 | | 16.3 | | 2.3 | | 1.0 | |
| 2007–2008 Actual | 13.0 | | 15.8 | | 2.2 | | 0.6 | |
| **Projections** | **Nov. 2008** | **Jan. 2009** | **Nov. 2008** | **Jan. 2009** | **Nov. 2008** | **Jan. 2009** | **Nov. 2008** | **Jan. 2009** |
| 2008–2009 | 12.9 | 12.9 | 14.9 | 14.7 | 2.0 | 1.9 | 0.0 | −0.1 |
| 2009–2010 | 13.4 | 14.7 | 15.4 | 14.4 | 2.0 | 2.0 | 0.0 | −2.2 |
| 2010–2011 | 13.3 | 14.5 | 15.3 | 14.7 | 2.0 | 2.0 | 0.0 | −1.8 |
| 2011–2012 | 13.1 | 13.6 | 15.2 | 15.0 | 2.1 | 2.1 | 0.0 | −0.7 |
| 2012–2013 | 13.0 | 13.3 | 15.2 | 15.0 | 2.0 | 2.0 | 0.2 | −0.3 |

The table presents federal government outlays, revenues, interest on the debt, and the consequent surplus or deficit for the period associated with Prime Minster Stephen Harper and Finance Minister Jim Flaherty. All values are shown as a percent of GDP. The period includes two years of actual data for fiscal year 2006–2007 and 2007–2008, then two sets of projected data. One set of projected data is from the fall Economic Update presented November 27, 2008. The other very different set of projected data is from Budget 2009, presented two months later on January 27, 2009.

*Source*: Table 2, *Fiscal Reference Tables*, 2008; The Economic and Fiscal Statement, November 27, 2008; Budget 2009, January 27, 2009.

The January 2009 Budget forecast a growth rate for Canadian real GDP in 2009 of −0.8%, a negative value. The growth forecast for 2009 had been reduced by 1.1% from the forecast of only two months previously. Negative GDP growth would, in itself, reduce revenues and increase spending. In fact, the calculations in the Budget state that a 1 percentage point shortfall in real GDP growth reduces federal budgetary revenues by $2.7 billion and increases expenditures, primarily employment insurance benefits, by $400 million. Thus, the Canadian federal government would go into deficit even if no further policy actions were taken. This type of change is the automatic stabilizer mentioned in the chapter. In this situation the cyclically adjusted budget balance would be zero while the actual deficit would be positive. However the January 2009 Budget contained very significant changes in fiscal policy. The Budget was entitled the "Economic Action Plan."

The goal of the changes in fiscal policy was to increase demand for domestic goods, demand that would replace lost demand for exports to the United States. You can divide government's measures into their effects on $C$, $I$, and $G$ in the framework where $Y = C + I + G + XQ$. It is important to recognize that $G$ includes the construction of physical capital to be owned by the government, often called **infrastructure**.

There was a very large temporary program to build infrastructure in the public sector: roads, bridges, and buildings. The stated two-year cost of the proposed program to the federal government was $12 billion. However, the program required matching funds by provinces, municipalities, and other partners such as universities and colleges. There was a smaller $2 billion program to build social housing, again in conjunction with the provinces. In both programs, there were important issues about obtaining rapid provincial co-operation and getting the project done in 2009 and 2010 when aggregate demand was still low. Figure 25–3 shows the increase in federal spending on goods and services.

A variety of programs were designed to increase consumer spending, $C$. There was a small permanent cut in income taxes. There was a temporary increase in transfers associated

The branding was apparently so successful that every year since, the Budget has been entitled Economic Action Plan and has been accompanied by a flood of advertising paid for by the Department of Finance. The purpose of the advertising is a matter of opinion and controversy.

with extending in length the time period for the receipt of employment insurance benefits. Although home renovations could also be considered an investment in the housing stock, consumers who spent between $1000 and $10,000 on a home renovation between January 27, 2009, and February 1, 2010, could receive a tax subsidy on that building project. It is very clear this temporary tax credit did stimulate home renovations.

In terms of government action to stimulate investment by the business sector ($I$), the Budget had fewer options. We saw in Chapter 21 that $I$ depends on current and expected future profits and on the current cash flow of corporations. Given the expected reduction of demand in 2009, all these factors point to a reduction in $I$, not an increase in $I$. The fall in commodity and oil prices made investments in these sectors less attractive. The Budget did contain proposals to spend some funds helping specific industries and communities most hard hit by the recession, but details were not very clear.

Table 25–5 shows the overall effects of all these changes on the federal budget. Program expenses were projected to rise during 2009–2010 by 1.8 percentage points of GDP, an enormous increase. Program expenses remained high in the next fiscal year and then fell very slowly but never returned to their 2008–2009 level. The Conservatives became a big-spending government as of January 2009. Second, tax revenues fell in 2009–2010 by a full percentage point of GDP. This was partly because GDP fell, but it was also due to the income tax reductions and the temporary tax credits discussed above. Tax revenues remained at 15% of GDP in the end years of the projection. Finally, since expenditures rose and tax revenues fell, the deficit returned. Indeed the forecast deficit for 2009–2010 was 2.2% of GDP or $33.7 billion followed by a deficit of $29.8 billion in 2010–2011. Deficits were expected to continue to 2012–2013 as of January 2009.

Thus there was a slight increase in the debt-to-GDP ratio and a slight increase in the percent of GDP used to pay public debt charges. This debt and deficit path bears no resemblance to the balanced budgets of the November Economic Statement. It was a complete U-turn in two months.

The January 27 Budget was supported by the Liberal party under its new leader, Michael Ignatieff, and the Conservatives remained in power.

It is fairly clear that the fiscal changes announced and implemented in the January 2009 Budget did alleviate the effects of the world recession in Canada.

The reduction in GDP and the increase in unemployment lasted a shorter period of time than in the previous two Canadian recessions. The decline in output was larger than in the 1990–91 recession but smaller than the 1982 recession (see Focus box "Recessions in Canada since 1981" in Chapter 3.)

> The really interesting question: Had the Conservatives had a majority in the fall of 2008, would they have proceeded with the plan in the November Economic Update to balance the budget even as GDP fell? We will never know.

The goal of the 2009 Economic Action Plan was probably not to avoid a recession altogether but to make any recession smaller and less painful. This likely occurred. In Chapters 3, 21, and 23 we talked about some of the challenges of making good fiscal policy decisions in the short run. The decision needs to be timely—that is, the fiscal stimulus has to arrive at the same time as the downturn. You have to be certain there is a negative adverse shock—that is, that forecast reduction in aggregate demand is certain enough to happen that fiscal stimulus is needed. Uncertainty about the coming recession cannot be allowed to paralyze a decision. The proposed change in fiscal policy has to be effective—that is, actually increase aggregate demand. This was the case: the infrastructure did get built and home renovations were done. The fiscal stimulus cannot be too large or the economy may be stimulated beyond the natural level of output. That clearly did not occur. The fiscal stimulus needs to be temporary—that is, the tax cut needs to end or the spending needs to end when the need for stimulus ends. Certainly the Conservatives planned to and did withdraw the stimulus as soon as possible. The home renovation tax credit ended as scheduled. Infrastructure programs were wound down. Most economists would judge that the fiscal stimulus did alleviate some of the effects of the U.S. recession on Canada. The Conservatives certainly took credit for the Economic Action Plan and its results and won the 2011 election with a majority government. What occurred next in Canadian fiscal policy?

# The Fiscal Plan under a Majority Government, 2011–2015

The Budget of March 21, 2011, the first Conservative Budget with a majority government, and the second Conservative majority Budget of March 21, 2013, laid out Conservative plans to 2015–16—that is, to the next election date. The plan is simple: balance the budget by 2015–2016!

In the 2011 election, the Conservative campaigned partly on their reputation as good economic managers—that the Economic Action Plan of 2009 had alleviated the worst of the recession, and that Canada had come through the recession with less damage than other countries. The comparisons were mostly with the United States. They promised the budget would be balanced by the 2015 election. They promised, if the budget were balanced in 2015, that after that election they would offer two large personal income tax changes. Neither change would reduce income tax rates. Both would see some families and some individuals have the ability to move a portion of their income so it would face lower tax rates and reduce their overall tax burden.

One very significant tax change would move Canada toward a family unit of income taxation. If a family with two earners had children under the age of 18, the higher-income parent could split her income and move some income to the lower-income parent. The income moved would then face a lower tax rate. Family income splitting is a very popular idea. If the Conservatives can present a balanced budget or a budget in surplus by 2015–16, they have promised to implement family-income splitting for adults with children under 18. This promise will beat at the heart of the next Conservative election campaign. It is a costly election promise; most estimates set the reduction in tax revenue at $2–3 billion per year.

The second proposed tax change is to further enlarge the annual amount of savings Canadians can shield in Tax-Free Savings Accounts per year from $5500 to $10,000. This would also reduce income tax revenues quite significantly over time as more and more interest income escapes taxation.

Given the political imperative to produce a balanced budget in time for an election in the fall of 2015, it is not surprising that the Conservatives hope that plans made in 2012 and 2013 produce a balanced budget by 2015. Table 25–6 shows us the plan from the 2013 Budget documents. The planned deficit falls from 1.5% of GDP in 2011–12 to zero in 2015–16. The Budget sets both transfers to persons and transfers to other levels of governments at a fixed percent of GDP throughout this period. The signal is that any changes within these programs will increase spending only as a nominal GDP grows.

If transfers do not change as a percent of GDP, the entire reduction in outlays as a percent of GDP must fall on goods and services spending. The required reduction is 0.9% of GDP. The Budget estimates that nominal GDP in 2015 will be $2058 billion; 0.9% of $2058 billion is $18.5 billion. Even as of June 2013, we still do not have a clear idea what program expenditures will be reduced. The Parliamentary Budget Officer has gone to court to try and force the government to place more detailed information on spending plans before Parliament. At the moment, it is fair to say that Canadians are waiting for more information.

> If one parent earns $80,000 and the other parent earns $30,000, family income splitting allows each parent to be taxed as though each earned $55,000. This changes their income tax brackets and reduces overall taxes.

> Suppose an individual has $10,000 in a GIC earning 3%. The $300 in annual interest from the GIC is taxable. If the tax rate is 30%, the owner of the GIC pays $90 a year in taxes. If the GIC is placed in a tax-free savings account, no taxes are paid on the interest.

> What we do know is that federal civil servants will be fewer in number, will face wage restraint, and will be expected to contribute more of their wages to fund their pensions. That much is clear from the budget documents. The details of these changes in the working conditions of federal civil servants remain to be negotiated.

| TABLE 25–6 The Conservative Fiscal Plan in the 2013 Budget | | | | | |
|---|---|---|---|---|---|
| Year | 2011–12 | 2012–13 | 2013–14 | 2014–15 | 2015–16 |
| Budgetary revenue | 14.1 | 14.0 | 14.2 | 14.4 | 14.5 |
| Public debt charges | 1.8 | 1.6 | 1.6 | 1.6 | 1.6 |
| Program expenses | 13.8 | 13.8 | 13.6 | 13.2 | 12.9 |
| Transfers to persons | 3.9 | 3.9 | 3.9 | 3.9 | 3.9 |
| Transfers to other governments | 3.2 | 3.2 | 3.2 | 3.2 | 3.2 |
| Goods and services | 6.7 | 6.7 | 6.4 | 6.0 | 5.8 |
| Budget balance | −1.5 | −1.4 | −1.0 | −0.3 | 0.0 |

*Source:* Budget, March 21, 2013. Economic Action Plan 2013.

Now let's do some more arithmetic. The federal deficit needs to fall by 1.5% of GDP from 2011–12 to 2015–16. The government has told us that total outlays will fall by 1.1% of GDP. The Budget also reports that the outlays that pay interest on the public debt will fall by 0.2% of GDP from 2011 to 2015 (Table 25–6) and non-interest outlays (these are called Program Expenses) will fall by 0.9% of GDP. To achieve budget balance by 2015, federal revenues must also rise by 0.4% of GDP. The proportion of GDP collected as taxes is projected to rise. Most people would call this an increase in tax rates. What tax rates are going to rise?

It is actually very difficult to ascertain in the Conservative plans where the additional tax revenue of 0.4% of GDP is going to come from in order to balance the Budget; 0.4% of GDP is roughly $8 billion in 2015. A lot of the increased revenue appears to come from a significant increase in Employment Insurance premiums of 5 cents per $100 in insurable earnings in each of 2013, 2014, and 2015 in March 2013 Budget. This may not sound like much of a tax increase, but all employees pay EI premiums and there are millions of employees. The March 2013 Budget says this is 0.1% of nominal GDP. It would appear the increase in EI premiums accounts for about one-quarter of the proposed increase in tax rates. These planned increases in EI premiums were then ◀ cancelled in September 2013. This revenue source is no longer part of the long-term budget plan.

There are some Conservatives who argue that, because EI payments are a premium for insurance against being unemployed, they are not a tax.

A second, much smaller, identified revenue increase in the 2013 Budget is that in the fiscal year 2015–16, the government expects to raise 333 million additional dollars in tariff revenue. Tariffs are taxes on imports. A group of countries, including China, India, and Korea, whose products when imported to Canada received lower tariffs, will face higher tariffs in 2015. These countries are considered to no longer need a lower tariff rate intended to help lower-income developing countries. The tariff increases are labelled by the government as "modernization of Canada's General Preferential Tariff regime." The Budget uses the oddest terminology and labels the tariff revenue increases as "annual savings." It is very unclear who is saving this money. Canadian consumers will pay higher tariffs on imports from those countries. However $333 million is a tiny percent (perhaps 0.02% of GDP). The tariff revenue increases and EI premium increases simply do not add up to the 0.4% of GDP revenue increases needed to balance the budget by 2015.

The remainder of the needed revenue to be raised in the 2013 Budget is associated with something the Conservatives call a combination (depending on the year and item) of "Tax Fairness" and "Closing Tax Loopholes." A quotation from the 2013 Budget (p. 271), is typical of the language used in the Budgets of 2011, 2012, and 2013:

> *In total, actions in Economic Action Plan 2013 to close tax loopholes and improve the fairness and integrity of the tax system will provide about $315 million in savings in 2013–14, rising to over $1.2 billion in 2017–18, or a total of $4.4 billion over the next five years.*

> Source: Budget Plan: Jobs, Growth and Long-term Prosperity-Economic Action Plan 2013, Government of Canada

The "savings" (once again, it is not clear who is doing the saving) are tax increases as the tax base is rearranged and redefined and the Canada Revenue Agency apparently constantly improves its ability to capture revenue at existing tax rates. There were similar revenue enhancing measures announced in the Economic Action Plans of 2010, 2011, and 2012. The total additional revenue from "Tax Fairness" and "Closing Tax Loopholes" is about $3.5 billion in 2015 (Economic Action Plan 2013, p. 298).

The federal spending cuts and tax increases will act to reduce aggregate demand in Canada. The Cyclically Adjusted Budget Balance for all governments in Canada (Table 25–3) is forecast to move from −3.3% of GDP in 2011 to −2.0% of GDP in 2013. From 2011 to 2015, as discussed above, the federal government plans to reduce expenditures by 1.1% of GDP and raise taxes by 0.4% of GDP. These numbers suggest a modest tightening of fiscal policy in Canada between 2011 and 2015, a mini-austerity program. The effect of that mini-austerity program on aggregate demand and output will unfold as this book is read over the next several years. Whether Canada makes a return to full employment from 2011 to 2015 depends partly on whether the other components of aggregate demand increase to offset the reduction in aggregate demand from the public sector.

- The recessions around the world in 2009 increased government deficits in the OECD. Part of the increase was due to the fall in GDP. Part of the increase was due to the use of fiscal stimulus to reduce the magnitude of the recession. All OECD countries saw a significant increase in their national debts.

- The government budget constraint gives the evolution of government debt as a function of spending and taxes. One way of expressing the constraint is that the change in debt (the deficit) is equal to the primary deficit plus interest payments on the debt. The primary deficit is the difference between government spending on goods and services, $G$, and taxes net of transfers, $T$.

- If government spending is unchanged, a decrease in taxes must be offset by an increase in taxes in the future. The longer the government waits to increase taxes or the higher the real interest rate, the higher is the eventual increase in taxes.

- The legacy of past deficits is higher debt. To stabilize the debt, government must eliminate the deficit. To do so, it must run a primary surplus equal to the interest payments on the existing debt. Thus a large debt requires higher taxes to service the debt.

- To stabilize the economy, government may choose to run deficits during recessions and surpluses during booms. The cyclically adjusted budget balance (CABB) deficit tells what the budget balance would be, under existing tax and spending rules, if output were at its natural level. It can be a useful tool to understand whether fiscal policy is being changed to stabilize the economy. It can also be a useful tool to understand if fiscal policy is sustainable in the long run. Reporting of the CABB for Canada by the Department of Finance in 2009, 2010, and 2011 was confusing.

- A very large public debt can be dangerous. It can lead to a vicious circle if the interest rate on the debt increases, which then increases the deficit further. In extreme cases, a very high debt and deficit can lead to hyperinflation.

- An increase in the government deficit leads to an increase in the current account deficit. In an open economy, part of the increase in government borrowing increases foreign borrowing.

- Under the Ricardian equivalence proposition, a larger deficit leads to an equal increase in private saving. Thus, deficits have no effect on demand, output, or the current account balance. The accumulation of debt does not affect capital accumulation or international debts. In reality, Ricardian equivalence fails, and larger deficits lead to higher demand and higher output in the short run. The accumulation of debt leads to lower capital accumulation, and thus to lower output in the long run. The accumulation of government debt is usually associated with the accumulation of foreign debt.

- The Liberal governments between 1995 and 2005 did succeed in stabilizing and then reducing the debt-to-GDP ratio in Canada. Taxes were first increased and then reduced. Spending was permanently reduced as a percentage of GDP. The federal government ran surpluses for nine consecutive years.

- The Conservative governments in 2006, 2007, and 2008 reduced taxes as a percentage of GDP. Spending as a percentage of GDP did not fall over this period. The federal surplus turned into a deficit.

- The Economic and Fiscal Statement presented on November 27, 2008, included a forecast of positive economic growth for Canada in 2009 and suggested economic stimulus was not necessary. The Conservative government faced defeat by a coalition of the Liberals and the New Democrats (with the support of the Bloc Québecois) and prorogued Parliament to avoid a non-confidence vote over the Economic Statement. On January 27, 2009, the Conservatives presented a Budget that projected negative economic growth in Canada for 2009. An argument was made for a large increase in government spending and large reductions in taxes to offset the expected recession. This Budget passed with the support of the Liberals. A fiscal stimulus was used in 2009 and 2010 to mitigate part of the effects of the U.S. recession on Canada.

- The Conservative governments in 2012 and 2013 presented Budget plans that increase taxes as a percent of GDP by 0.4% and cut total spending as a percent of GDP by 1.1% between 2011 and 2015. The goal is a balanced budget or a budget surplus by 2015.

- austerity, 534
- automatic stabilizer, 525
- cyclically adjusted budget balance (CABB), 524
- debt monetization, 529

- debt rescheduling, 528
- debt restructuring, 528
- debt-to-GDP ratio, or debt ratio, 517
- deficit, 518

## QUESTIONS & PROBLEMS

### 1. TRUE/FALSE/UNCERTAIN

**a.** The best way to measure the government deficit is as a percent of GDP.

**b.** Government can never have a negative debt position.

**c.** The recession decreased the budget deficit in most OECD countries.

**d.** If Ricardian equivalence holds, an increase in taxes will affect neither consumption nor saving nor the current account.

**e.** The ratio of debt to GDP cannot exceed 100%. If it did, more than GDP would be needed to pay interest on the debt.

**f.** There were no episodes of hyperinflation in the 1990s. Hyperinflation occurred only after World War I and World War II.

### 2. BUDGET NUMBERS

Consider an economy where the official budget deficit is 4% of GDP; the debt-to-GDP ratio is 100%; the nominal interest rate is 10%; and the inflation rate is 7%.

**a.** What is the primary deficit/surplus?

**b.** What is the inflation-adjusted deficit/surplus?

**c.** Use the rule of thumb in the text that a 1% decline in output leads to an increase in the deficit of half of 1%. If you are told that the Cyclically Adjusted Budget Balance in this country is $-2\%$ of GDP, how far is this economy below the natural level of output?

**d.** Suppose that the unemployment rate is equal to the natural rate. Suppose that the normal growth rate is 2%. Is the debt-to-GDP ratio going up or down?

**e.** If things continue as in (d), what will be the debt-to-GDP ratio in 10 years?

### 3. ASSUME THAT THE DEMAND FOR CENTRAL BANK MONEY TAKES THE FORM

$$\frac{H}{P} = Y[1 - (r + \pi^e)]$$

*where* $Y = 1000$ *and* $r = 0.1$.

**a.** Assume that, in the short run, $\pi^e$ is constant and equal to 25%. Calculate the amount of seignorage for each annual rate of money growth, $\Delta H/H$, listed below.

**i.** 25%

**ii.** 50%

**iii.** 75%

**b.** In the medium run, $\pi^e = \pi = \Delta H/H$. Compute the amount of seignorage associated with the three rates of annual money growth in part (a). Explain why the answers differ from those in part (a).

### 4. THE TWIN DEFICITS

**a.** Identify and name the following terms

**i.** $r B^f_t + Y_t$

**ii.** $r B^f_t + Y_t - T_t$

**iii.** $r B^f_t + Y_t - T_t - C_t$

**iv.** $T_t - G_t$

**v.** $r B^f_t + X_t - Q_t$

**b.** In an open economy, why might private investment, $I_t$, remain unchanged when the government cuts taxes?

**c.** In an open economy, why might consumption, $C_t$, change when the government cuts taxes?

**d.** If the government cuts taxes and consumption rises while investment remains unchanged, what must happen to the current account deficit?

**e.** We have ignored any short-run effects of a tax cut in the analysis above; that is, we have left $Y_t$, unchanged. If the tax cut increases $Y_t$ in the short run, what other effects will the tax cut have on the current account deficit?

**f.** The back page of *The Economist* has a set of data entitled "Trade, exchange rates, budget balances and interest rates." Find the five largest negative budget balances. How many of these countries have a negative current account balance? Find the five largest positive budget balances. How many of these countries have a positive current account balance?

**5. CONSIDER AN ECONOMY CHARACTERIZED BY THE FOLLOWING FACTS:**

**i.** The debt-to-GDP ratio is 40%.

**ii.** The primary deficit is 4% of GDP.

**iii.** The normal growth rate is 3%.

**iv.** The real interest rate is 3%.

**a.** Using your favourite spreadsheet software, compute the debt-to-GDP ratio in 10 years, assuming that the primary deficit stays at 4% of GDP each year; the economy grows at the normal growth rate in each year; and the real interest rate is constant, at 3%.

**b.** Suppose the real interest rate increases to 5%, but everything else remains as in part (a). Compute the debt-to-GDP ratio in 10 years.

**c.** Suppose the normal growth rate falls to 1%, and the economy grows at the normal growth rate each year. Everything else remains as in part (a). Calculate the debt-to-GDP ratio in 10 years. Compare your answer to part (b).

**d.** Return to the assumptions of part (a). Suppose policymakers decide that a debt-to-GDP ratio of more than 50% is dangerous. Verify that reducing the primary deficit to 1% immediately, and that maintaining this deficit for 10 years, will produce a debt-to-GDP ratio of 50% in 10 years. Thereafter, what value of the primary deficit will be required to maintain the debt-to-GDP ratio of 50%?

**e.** Continuing with part (d), suppose policy makers wait five years before changing fiscal policy. For five years, the primary deficit remains at 4% of GDP. What is the debt-to-GDP ratio in five years? Suppose that after five years, policy makers decide to reduce the debt-to-GDP ratio to 50%. In years 6 through 10, what constant value of the primary deficit will produce a debt-to-GDP ratio of 50% at the end of year 10?

**f.** Suppose that policy makers carry out the policy in either parts (d) or (e). If these policies reduce the growth rate of output for a while, how will this affect the size of the reduction in the primary deficit required to achieve a debt-to-GDP ratio of 50% in 10 years?

**g.** Which policy—the one in part (d) or the one in part (e)—do you think is more dangerous to the stability of the economy?

## FURTHER READINGS

The website of the federal Department of Finance contains a vast amount of information on federal fiscal policy in Canada. Unfortunately, as we have seen, some of that information is misinformation and presented in a highly partisan way. You even have to read critically and carefully, through some of the data reported in the Fiscal Reference Tables.

The same can be said about the website for the Centre of Policy Alternatives, which presents a left-wing view of fiscal policy in Canada. Their annual "Shadow Budgets" offer an alternative view of the role of government.

There are a number of sources for less partisan material. The Parliamentary Budget Officer (PBO) was set up in 2006 as one of the Conservative election promises. It was to parallel non-partisan economic analysis units in other countries, most notably the highly respected Congressional Budget Office in the United States. However the Canadian PBO has been under-resourced and has had many of its requests for the information necessary to do its job rejected

by the government that created it. Its future is not clear. The C.D. Howe Institute produces useful analyses of the budget stance of the Canadian federal government each year.

At the time of writing, there are a number of Canadian economists who participate as bloggers on Canadian economic issues. Stephen Gordon of Laval University writes very good columns for *Maclean's*. Kevin Milligan at the University of British Columbia comments, particularly on public finance issues. *The Globe and Mail* presents a column called "Economy Lab" that has worthwhile contributions from a number of economists in Canada.

Two international organizations, the OECD and the IMF, whose publications we have used in this chapter produce annual fiscal reports on member countries and material that is specific to Canada. These usually amalgamate all levels of government to make data more comparable across countries.

# Epilogue: The Story of Macroeconomics

We have spent 25 chapters presenting the framework that most economists use to think about macroeconomic issues, the major conclusions they draw, and the issues on which they disagree. How this framework has been built over time is a fascinating story. It is the story we want to tell in this chapter.

**Section 26-1** starts at the beginning of modern macroeconomics—with Keynes and the Great Depression.

**Section 26-2** turns to the *neoclassical synthesis*, a synthesis of Keynes's ideas with those of earlier economists—a synthesis that dominated macroeconomics until the early 1970s.

**Section 26-3** describes the *rational expectations critique*, the strong attack on the neoclassical synthesis that led to a complete overhaul of macroeconomics starting in the 1970s.

**Section 26-4** gives you a sense of the main lines of research in macroeconomics up to the recent crisis.

**Section 26-5** takes a first pass at assessing the effects of the recent crisis on macroeconomics.

**John Maynard Keynes**

Corbis

## 26-1 | Keynes and the Great Depression

The history of modern macroeconomics starts in 1936, with the publication of Keynes's *General Theory of Employment, Interest, and Money*. As he was writing the *General Theory*, Keynes confided to a friend: "I believe myself to be writing a book on economic theory which will largely revolutionize—not, I suppose at once but in the course of the next ten years, the way the world thinks about economic problems."

Keynes was right. The book's timing was one of the reasons for its immediate success. The Great Depression was not only an economic catastrophe, but also an intellectual failure for the economists working on **business cycle theory**—as macroeconomics was then called. Few economists had a coherent explanation for the Depression, either for its depth or for its length. The economic measures taken by the Roosevelt administration as part of the New Deal had been based on instinct rather than on economic theory. The *General Theory* offered an interpretation of events, an intellectual framework, and a clear argument for government intervention.

The *General Theory* emphasized **effective demand**—what we now call *aggregate demand*. In the short run, Keynes argued, effective demand determines output. Even if output eventually returns to its natural level, the process is slow at best. One of Keynes's most famous quotes is: "In the long run, we are all dead."

In the process of deriving effective demand, Keynes introduced many of the building blocks of modern macroeconomics:

- The relation of consumption to income, and the multiplier, which explains how shocks to demand can be amplified and lead to larger shifts in output
- **Liquidity preference** (the term Keynes gave to the demand for money), which explains how monetary policy can affect interest rates and aggregate demand
- The importance of expectations in affecting consumption and investment, and the idea that *animal spirits* (shifts in expectations) are a major factor behind shifts in demand and output.

The *General Theory* was more than a treatise for economists. It offered clear policy implications, and they were in tune with the times: Waiting for the economy to recover by itself was irresponsible. In the midst of a depression, trying to balance the budget was not only stupid; it was dangerous. Active use of fiscal policy was essential to return the country to high employment.

## 26-2 | The Neoclassical Synthesis

Within a few years, the *General Theory* had transformed macroeconomics. Not everyone was converted, and few agreed with it all. But most discussions became organized around it.

By the early 1950s, a large consensus had emerged, based on an integration of many of Keynes's ideas and the ideas of earlier economists. This consensus was called the **neoclassical synthesis**. To quote from Paul Samuelson, in the 1955 edition of his textbook *Economics*—the first modern economics textbook:

> "In recent years, 90 per cent of American economists have stopped being 'Keynesian economists' or 'Anti-Keynesian economists.' Instead, they have worked toward a synthesis of whatever is valuable in older economics and in modern theories of income determination. The result might be called neo-classical economics and is accepted, in its broad outlines, by all but about five per cent of extreme left-wing and right-wing writers."

*Source:* "Economics", Paul Samuelson, 1955, McGraw-Hill

The neoclassical synthesis was to remain the dominant view for another 20 years. Progress was astonishing, leading many to call the period from the early 1940s to the early 1970s the golden age of macroeconomics.

**Paul Samuelson**

Oliver Blanchard

## Progress on All Fronts

The first order of business after the publication of the *General Theory* was to formalize mathematically what Keynes meant. While Keynes knew mathematics, he had avoided using it in the *General Theory*. One result was endless controversies about what Keynes meant and whether there were logical flaws in some of his arguments.

**The *IS-LM* Model.** A number of formalizations of Keynes's ideas were offered. The most influential one was the *IS-LM* model, developed by John Hicks and Alvin Hansen in the 1930s and early 1940s. The initial version of the *IS-LM* model—which was actually very close to the version presented in Chapter 5 of this book—was criticized for emasculating many of Keynes's insights: Expectations played no role, and the adjustment of prices and wages was altogether absent. Yet the *IS-LM* model provided a basis from which to start building, and as such it was immensely successful. Discussions became organized around the slopes of the *IS* and *LM* curves, what variables were missing from the two relations, what equations for prices and wages should be added to the model, and so on.

Franco Modigliani

**Theories of Consumption, Investment, and Money Demand.** Keynes had emphasized the importance of consumption and investment behaviour, and of the choice between money and other financial assets. Major progress was soon made along all three fronts.

In the 1950s, Franco Modigliani (then at Carnegie Mellon, later at MIT) and Milton Friedman (at the University of Chicago) independently developed the theory of consumption we saw in Chapter 21. Both insisted on the importance of expectations in determining current consumption decisions.

James Tobin

James Tobin, from Yale, developed the theory of investment, based on the relation between the present value of profits and investment. The theory was further developed and tested by Dale Jorgenson, from Harvard. You saw this theory in Chapter 21.

Tobin also developed the theory of the demand for money and, more generally, the theory of the choice between different assets based on liquidity, return, and risk. His work has become the basis not only for an improved treatment of financial markets in macroeconomics, but also for finance theory in general.

**Growth Theory.** In parallel with the work on fluctuations, there was a renewed focus on growth. In contrast to the stagnation in the pre–World War II era, most countries were experiencing rapid growth in the 1950s and 1960s. Even if they experienced fluctuations, their standard of living was increasing rapidly. The growth model developed by MIT's Robert Solow in 1956, which we saw in Chapters 16 and 17, provided a framework to think about the determinants of growth. It was followed by an explosion of work on the roles saving and technological progress play in determining growth.

Robert Solow

**Macroeconometric Models.** All these contributions were integrated in larger and larger macroeconometric models. The first U.S. macroeconometric model, developed by Lawrence Klein from the University of Pennsylvania in the early 1950s, was an extended *IS* relation, with 16 equations. With the development of the National Income and Product Accounts (making available better data) and the development of econometrics and of computers, the models quickly grew in size. The most impressive effort was the construction of the MPS model (MPS stands for MIT-Penn-SSRC, for the two universities and the research institution—the Social Science Research Council—involved in its construction), developed during the 1960s by a group led by Modigliani. Its structure was an expanded version of the *IS-LM* model, plus a Phillips curve mechanism. But its components—consumption, investment, and money demand—all reflected the tremendous theoretical and empirical progress made since Keynes.

## Keynesians versus Monetarists

With such rapid progress, many macroeconomists—those who defined themselves as **Keynesians**—came to believe that the future was bright. The nature of fluctuations was

Lawrence Klein

**Milton Friedman**

becoming increasingly well understood; the development of models allowed policy decisions to be made more effectively. The time when the economy could be fine-tuned, and recessions all but eliminated, seemed not far in the future.

This optimism was met with skepticism by a small but influential minority, the **monetarists**. The intellectual leader of the monetarists was Milton Friedman. Although Friedman saw much progress being made—and was himself the father of one of the major contributions to macroeconomics, the theory of consumption—he did not share in the general enthusiasm. He believed that the understanding of the economy remained very limited. He questioned the motives of governments as well as the notion that they actually knew enough to improve macroeconomic outcomes.

In the 1960s, debates between "Keynesians" and "monetarists" dominated the economic headlines. The debates centred around three issues: (1) the effectiveness of monetary policy versus fiscal policy, (2) the Phillips curve, and (3) the role of policy.

**Monetary Policy versus Fiscal Policy.** Keynes had emphasized *fiscal* rather than *monetary* policy as the key to fighting recessions. And this had remained the prevailing wisdom. The *IS* curve, many argued, was quite steep: Changes in the interest rate had little effect on demand and output. Thus, monetary policy did not work very well. Fiscal policy, which affects demand directly, could affect output faster and more reliably.

Friedman strongly challenged this conclusion. In their 1963 book *A Monetary History of the United States, 1867–1960*, Friedman and Anna Schwartz painstakingly reviewed the evidence on monetary policy and the relation between money and output in the United States over a century. Their conclusion was not only that monetary policy was very powerful, but that movements in money did explain most of the fluctuations in output. They interpreted the Great Depression as the result of a major mistake in monetary policy, a decrease in the money supply due to bank failures—a decrease that the Fed could have avoided by increasing the monetary base, but had not.

Friedman and Schwartz's challenge was followed by a vigorous debate and by intense research on the respective effects of fiscal policy and monetary policy. In the end, a consensus was reached. Both fiscal policy and monetary policy clearly affected the economy. And if policy makers cared about not only the level but also the composition of output, the best policy was typically a mix of the two.

**The Phillips Curve.** The second debate focused on the Phillips curve. The Phillips curve was not part of the initial Keynesian model. But because it provided such a convenient (and apparently reliable) way of explaining the movement of wages and prices over time, it had become part of the neoclassical synthesis. In the 1960s, based on the empirical evidence up until then, many Keynesian economists believed that there was a reliable trade-off between unemployment and inflation, even in the long run.

Milton Friedman and Edmund Phelps (from Columbia University) strongly disagreed. They argued that the existence of such a long-run trade-off flew in the face of basic economic theory. They argued that the apparent trade-off would quickly vanish if policy makers actually tried to exploit it—that is, if they tried to achieve low unemployment by accepting higher inflation. As we saw in Chapter 8 when we studied the evolution of the Phillips curve, Friedman and Phelps were definitely right. By the mid-1970s, the consensus was indeed that there was no long-run trade-off between inflation and unemployment.

**Edmund Phelps**

**The Role of Policy.** The third debate centred on the role of policy. Skeptical that economists knew enough to stabilize output and that policy makers could be trusted to do the right thing, Friedman argued for the use of simple rules, such as steady money growth (a rule we discussed in Chapter 24). Here is what he said in 1958:

"A steady rate of growth in the money supply will not mean perfect stability even though it would prevent the kind of wide fluctuations that we have experienced from time to time in the past. It is tempting to try to go farther and to use monetary changes to offset other factors making for expansion and contraction . . . The available evidence casts grave doubts on the possibility of producing any fine adjustments in economic activity by fine adjustments in monetary policy—at least in the present state of knowledge. There are thus serious limitations to the possibility of a discretionary monetary policy and much danger that such a policy may make matters worse rather than better.

Political pressures to 'do something' in the face of either relatively mild price rises or relatively mild price and employment declines are clearly very strong indeed in the existing state of public attitudes. The main moral to be drawn from the two preceding points is that yielding to these pressures may frequently do more harm than good."

*Source:* "The Supply of Money and Changes in Prices and Output," Testimony to Congress, 1958.

As we saw in Chapter 23, this debate on the role of macroeconomic policy has not been settled. The nature of the arguments has changed a bit, but the debate continues today.

# 26-3 | The Rational Expectations Critique

**Robert Lucas**

Despite the battles between Keynesians and monetarists, macroeconomics at around 1970 looked like a successful and mature field. It appeared to successfully explain events and guide policy choices. Most debates were framed within a common intellectual framework. But within a few years, the field was in crisis. The crisis had two sources.

One was events. By the mid-1970s, most countries were experiencing *stagflation*, a word created at the time to denote the simultaneous existence of high unemployment and high inflation. Macroeconomists had not predicted stagflation. After the fact and after a few years of research, a convincing explanation was provided, based on the effects of adverse supply shocks on both prices and output. (We discussed the effects of such shocks in Chapter 11.) But it was too late to undo the damage to the discipline's image.

The other source was ideas. In the early 1970s, a small group of economists—Robert Lucas from Chicago; Thomas Sargent, then from Minnesota and now at New York University; and Robert Barro, then from Chicago and now at Harvard—led a strong attack against mainstream macroeconomics. They did not mince words. In a 1978 paper, Lucas and Sargent stated:

"That the predictions [of Keynesian economics] were wildly incorrect, and that the doctrine on which they were based was fundamentally flawed, are now simple matters of fact, involving no subtleties in economic theory. The task which faces contemporary students of the business cycle is that of sorting through the wreckage, determining what features of that remarkable intellectual event called the Keynesian Revolution can be salvaged and put to good use, and which others must be discarded."

*Source:* Lucas and Sargent (1978) "After Keynesian Economics," in After the Phillips Curve: Persistence of High In?ation and High Unemployment [Boston: Federal Reserve Bank of Boston, 1978].

**Thomas Sargent**

## The Three Implications of Rational Expectations

Lucas and Sargent's main argument was that Keynesian economics had ignored the full implications of the effect of expectations on behaviour. The way to proceed, they argued, was to assume that people formed expectations as rationally as they could, based on the information they had. Thinking of people as having *rational expectations* had three major implications, all highly damaging to Keynesian macroeconomics.

**The Lucas Critique.** The first implication was that existing macroeconomic models could not be used to help design policy. Although these models recognized that expectations affect behaviour, they did not incorporate expectations explicitly. All variables were assumed to depend on current and past values of other variables, including policy variables. Thus, what the models captured was the set of relations between economic variables as they had held in the past, under past policies. Were these policies to change, Lucas argued, the way people formed expectations would change as well, making estimated relations—and, by implication, simulations generated using existing macroeconometric models—poor guides to what would happen under these new policies. This critique of macroeconometric models became known as the Lucas critique. To take again the history of the Phillips curve as an example, the data

**Robert Barro**

up to the early 1970s had suggested a trade-off between unemployment and inflation. As policy makers tried to exploit that trade-off, it disappeared.

**Rational Expectations and the Phillips Curve.** The second implication was that when rational expectations were introduced in Keynesian models, these models actually delivered very un-Keynesian conclusions. For example, the models implied that deviations of output from its natural level were short lived, much more so than Keynesian economists claimed.

This argument was based on a reexamination of the aggregate supply relation. In Keynesian models, the slow return of output to the natural level of output came from the slow adjustment of prices and wages through the Phillips curve mechanism. An increase in money, for example, led first to higher output and to lower unemployment. Lower unemployment then led to higher nominal wages and to higher prices. The adjustment continued until wages and prices had increased in the same proportion as nominal money, until unemployment and output were both back at their natural levels.

But this adjustment, Lucas pointed out, was highly dependent on wage setters' backward-looking expectations of inflation. In the MPS model, for example, wages responded only to current and past inflation and to current unemployment. But once the assumption was made that wage setters had rational expectations, the adjustment was likely to be much faster. Changes in money, to the extent that they were anticipated, might have no effect on output: For example, anticipating an increase in money of 5% over the coming year, wage setters would increase the nominal wages set in contracts for the coming year by 5%. Firms would in turn increase prices by 5%. The result would be no change in the real money stock, and no change in demand or output.

Within the logic of the Keynesian models, Lucas therefore argued, only *unanticipated changes in money* should affect output. Predictable movements in money should have no effect on activity. More generally, if wage setters had rational expectations, shifts in demand were likely to have effects on output for only as long as nominal wages were set—a year or so. Even on its own terms, the Keynesian model did not deliver a convincing theory of the long-lasting effects of demand on output.

**Optimal Control versus Game Theory.** The third implication was that if people and firms had rational expectations, it was wrong to think of policy as the control of a complicated but passive system. Rather, the right way was to think of policy as a game between policy makers and the economy. The right tool was not *optimal control*, but *game theory*. And game theory led to a different vision of policy. A striking example was the issue of *time inconsistency* discussed by Finn Kydland (then at Carnegie Mellon, now at UC Santa Barbara) and Edward Prescott (then at Carnegie Mellon, now at Arizona State University), an issue that we discussed in Chapter 23: Good intentions on the part of policy makers could actually lead to disaster.

To summarize: When rational expectations were introduced, Keynesian models could not be used to determine policy; Keynesian models could not explain long-lasting deviations of output from the natural level of output; the theory of policy had to be redesigned, using the tools of game theory.

## The Integration of Rational Expectations

As you might have guessed from the tone of Lucas and Sargent's quote, the intellectual atmosphere in macroeconomics was tense in the early 1970s. But within a few years, a process of integration (of ideas, not people, because tempers remained high) had begun, and it was to dominate the 1970s and the 1980s.

Fairly quickly, the idea that rational expectations was the right working assumption gained wide acceptance. This was not because macroeconomists believed that people, firms, and participants in financial markets always form expectations rationally. But rational expectations appeared to be a natural benchmark, at least until economists had made more progress in understanding whether, when, and how actual expectations systematically differ from rational expectations.

Work then started on the challenges raised by Lucas and Sargent.

**The Implications of Rational Expectations.** First, there was a systematic exploration of the role and implications of rational expectations in goods markets, in financial markets, and in labour markets. Much of what was discovered has been presented in this book. For example:

Robert Hall

- Robert Hall, then from MIT and now at Stanford, showed that if consumers are very foresighted (in the sense defined in Chapter 21), then changes in consumption should be unpredictable: The best forecast of consumption next year would be consumption this year! Put another way, changes in consumption should be very hard to predict. This result came as a surprise to most macroeconomists at the time, but it is in fact based on a simple intuition: If consumers are very foresighted, they will change their consumption only when they learn something new about the future. But, by definition, such news cannot be predicted. This consumption behaviour, known as the **random walk of consumption**, became the benchmark in consumption research thereafter.

- Rudiger Dornbusch from MIT showed that the large swings in exchange rates under flexible exchange rates, which had previously been thought of as the result of speculation by irrational investors, were fully consistent with rationality. His argument—which we saw in Chapter 20—was that changes in monetary policy can lead to long-lasting changes in nominal interest rates; changes in current and expected nominal interest rates lead in turn to large changes in the exchange rate. Dornbusch's model, known as the *overshooting* model of exchange rates, became the benchmark in discussions of exchange rate movements.

Rudiger Dornbusch

**Wage and Price Setting.** Second, there was a systematic exploration of the determination of wages and prices, going far beyond the Phillips curve relation. Two important contributions were made by Stanley Fischer, then at MIT, now governor of the Central Bank of Israel, and John Taylor, then from Columbia University and now at Stanford. Both showed that the adjustment of prices and wages in response to changes in unemployment can be slow *even under rational expectations*.

Fischer and Taylor pointed out an important characteristic of both wage and price setting, the **staggering** of wage and price decisions. In contrast to the simple story we told earlier, where all wages and prices increased simultaneously in anticipation of an increase in money, actual wage and price decisions are staggered over time. So there is not one sudden synchronized adjustment of all wages and prices to an increase in money. Rather, the adjustment is likely to be slow, with wages and prices adjusting to the new level of money through a process of leapfrogging over time. Fischer and Taylor thus showed that the second issue raised by the rational-expectations critique could be resolved, that a slow return of output to the natural level of output can be consistent with rational expectations in the labour market.

Stanley Fischer

**The Theory of Policy.** Third, thinking about policy in terms of game theory led to an explosion of research on the nature of the games being played, not only between policy makers and the economy but also between policy makers—between political parties, or between the central bank and the government, or between governments of different countries. One of the major achievements of this research was the development of a more rigorous way of thinking about fuzzy notions such as "credibility," "reputation," and "commitment." At the same time, there was a distinct shift in focus from "what governments should do" to "what governments actually do," an increasing awareness of the political constraints that economists should take into account when advising policy makers.

In short: By the end of the 1980s, the challenges raised by the rational-expectations critique had led to a complete overhaul of macroeconomics. The basic structure had been extended to take into account the implications of rational expectations, or, more generally, of forward-looking behaviour by people and firms. As we have seen, these themes have played a central role in this book.

John Taylor

## 26-4 | Developments in Macroeconomics Up to the 2009 Crisis

From the late 1980s to the crisis, three groups dominated the research headlines: the new classicals, the new Keynesians, and the new growth theorists. (Note the generous use of the word "new." Unlike producers of laundry detergents, economists stop short of using "new and improved." But the subliminal message is the same.)

### New Classical Economics and Real Business Cycle Theory

Giuseppe Aresu/Associated Press

**Edward Prescott**

The rational-expectations critique was more than just a critique of Keynesian economics. It also offered its own interpretation of fluctuations. Lucas argued that instead of relying on imperfections in labour markets, on the slow adjustment of wages and prices, and so on to explain fluctuations, macroeconomists should see how far they could go in explaining fluctuations as the effects of shocks in competitive markets with fully flexible prices and wages.

This research agenda was taken up by the **new classicals**. The intellectual leader is Edward Prescott, and the models he and his followers developed are known as **real business cycle (RBC)** models. Their approach was based on two premises.

The first was methodological. Lucas had argued that, in order to avoid earlier pitfalls, macroeconomic models should be constructed from explicit microfoundations (i.e., utility maximization by workers, profit maximization by firms, and rational expectations). Before the development of computers, this was hard, if not impossible, to achieve: Models constructed in this way would have been too complex to solve analytically. Indeed, much of the art of macroeconomics was in finding simple shortcuts to capture the essence of a model while keeping the model simple enough to solve (it still remains the art of writing a good textbook). The development of computing power made it possible to solve such models numerically, and an important contribution of RBC theory was the development of more and more powerful numerical methods of solution, which allowed for the development of richer and richer models.

The second approach was conceptual. Until the 1970s, most fluctuations had been seen as the result of imperfections, of deviations of actual output from a slowly moving natural level of output. Following up on Lucas's suggestion, Prescott argued in a series of influential contributions that fluctuations could indeed be interpreted as coming from the effects of technological shocks in competitive markets with fully flexible prices and wages. In other words, he argued that movements in actual output could be seen as movements in—rather than as deviations from—the natural level of output. As new discoveries are made, he argued, productivity increases, leading to an increase in output. The increase in productivity leads to an increase in the wage, which makes it more attractive to work, which leads workers to work more. Productivity increases therefore lead to increases in both output and employment, just as we observe in the real world. Fluctuations are desirable features of the economy, not something policy makers should try to reduce.

Not surprisingly, this radical view of fluctuations was criticized on many fronts. As we discussed in Chapter 17, technological progress is the result of many innovations, each taking a long time to diffuse throughout the economy. It is hard to see how this process could generate anything like the large short-run fluctuations in output that we observe in practice. It is also hard to think of recessions as times of technological *regress*, times in which productivity and output both go down. Finally, as we have seen, there is strong evidence that changes in money, which have no effect on output in RBC models, in fact have strong effects on output in the real world. Still, the conceptual RBC approach proved influential and useful. It made an important point—that not all fluctuations in output are deviations of output from its natural level, but movements in the natural level itself.

### New Keynesian Economics

The term **new Keynesians** denotes a loosely connected group of researchers who shared a common belief that the synthesis that emerged in response to the rational-expectations critique was basically correct. But they also shared the belief that much remained to be learned about the nature of imperfections in different markets and about the implications of those imperfections for macroeconomic fluctuations.

There was further work on the nature of **nominal rigidities**. As we saw earlier in this chapter, Fischer and Taylor had shown that with staggering of wage or price decisions, output can deviate from its natural level for a long time. This conclusion raised a number of questions: If staggering of decisions is responsible, at least in part, for fluctuations, why don't wage setters/price setters synchronize decisions? Why aren't prices and wages adjusted more often? Why aren't all prices and all wages changed, say, on the first day of each week? In tackling these issues, George Akerlof (from Berkeley) and N. Gregory Mankiw (from Harvard University) derived a surprising and important result, often referred to as the **menu cost** explanation of output fluctuations:

Each wage setter or price setter is largely indifferent as to when and how often he changes his own wage or price (for a retailer, changing the prices on the shelf every day versus every week does not make much of a difference to the store's overall profits). Therefore, even small costs of changing prices—like the costs involved in printing a new menu, for example—can lead to infrequent and staggered price adjustment. This staggering leads to slow adjustment of the price level and to large aggregate output fluctuations in response to movements in aggregate demand. In short, decisions that do not matter much at the individual level (how often to change prices or wages) lead to large aggregate effects (slow adjustment of the price level, and shifts in aggregate demand that have a large effect on output).

Another line of research focused on the imperfections in the labour market. We discussed in Chapter 9 the notion of *efficiency wages*—the idea that wages, if perceived by workers as being too low, may lead to shirking by workers on the job, to problems of morale within the firm, to difficulties in recruiting or keeping good workers, and so on. One influential researcher in this area was Akerlof, who explored the role of "norms," the rules that develop in any organization—in this case, the firm—to assess what is fair or unfair. This research led him and others to explore issues previously left to research in sociology and psychology, and to examine their macroeconomic implications. In another direction, Peter Diamond (from MIT), Dale Mortensen (from Cornell), and Christopher Pissarides (from the London School of Economics) looked at the labour market as the market characterized by constant reallocation, large flows, and bargaining between workers and firms, a characterization that has proven extremely useful and that we relied upon in Chapter 9.

Yet another line of research, which turned out to be important when the crisis took place, explored the role of imperfections in credit markets. Most macro models assumed that monetary policy worked through interest rates, and that firms could borrow as much as they wanted at the market interest rate. In practice, many firms can borrow only from banks. And banks often turn down potential borrowers, despite the willingness of these borrowers to pay the interest rate charged by the bank. Why this happens, and how it affects our view of how monetary policy works, was the focus of research by, in particular, Ben Bernanke (then from Princeton, and now the Chairman of the Fed) and Mark Gertler (from New York University).

George Akerlof

Ben Bernanke

## New Growth Theory

After being one of the most active topics of research in the 1960s, growth theory had gone into an intellectual slump. Since the late 1980s however, growth theory has made a strong comeback. The set of new contributions went under the name of **new growth theory**.

Two economists, Robert Lucas (the same Lucas who spearheaded the rational-expectations critique) and Paul Romer, then from Berkeley, now at New York University, played an important role in defining the issues. When growth theory faded in the late 1960s, two major issues were left largely unresolved. One issue was the role of increasing returns to scale—whether, say, doubling capital and labour can actually cause output to more than double. The other was the determinants of technological progress. These are the two major issues on which new growth theory concentrated.

Paul Romer

**Philippe Aghion**

**Peter Howitt**

**Andrei Shleifer**

**Daron Acemoglu**

The discussions of the effects of R&D on technological progress in Chapter 17 very modestly reflects some of this work but there was much more to be said. An important contribution here was the work of Philippe Aghion (from Harvard University) and Peter Howitt (from Brown University), who developed a theme first explored by Joseph Schumpeter in the 1930s, the notion that growth is a process of *creative destruction* in which new products are constantly introduced, making old ones obsolete. Institutions that slow this process of reallocation (for example, by making it harder to create new firms or by making it more expensive for firms to lay off workers) may slow down the rate of technological progress and thus decrease growth.

Research also tried to identify the precise role of specific institutions in determining growth. Andrei Shleifer (from Harvard University) explored the role of different legal systems in affecting the organization of the economy, from financial markets to labour markets, and, through these channels, the effects of legal systems on growth. Daron Acemoglu (from MIT) explored how to go from correlations between institutions and growth—democratic countries are on average richer—to causality from institutions to growth: Does the correlation tell us that democracy leads to higher output per person, or does it tell us that higher output per person leads to democracy, or that some other factor leads to both more democracy and higher output per person? Examining the history of former colonies, Acemoglu argued that their growth performance has been shaped by the type of institutions put in place by their colonizers, thus showing a strong causal role of institutions in economic performance.

## Toward an Integration

In the 1980s and 1990s, discussions between these three groups, and in particular between "new classicals" and "new Keynesians," were often heated. New Keynesians would accuse new classicals of relying on an implausible explanation of fluctuations and ignoring obvious imperfections; new classicals would in turn point to the ad hoc nature of some of the new Keynesian models. From the outside—and indeed sometimes from the inside—macroeconomics looked like a battlefield rather than a research field.

By the 2000s however, a synthesis appeared to be emerging. Methodologically, it built on the RBC approach and its careful description of the optimization problems of people and firms. Conceptually, it recognized the potential importance, emphasized by the RBC and the new growth theory, of changes in the pace of technological progress. But it also allowed for many of the imperfections emphasized by the New Keynesians, from the role of bargaining in the determination of wages, to the role of imperfect information in credit and financial markets, to the role of nominal rigidities in creating a role for aggregate demand to affect output. There was no convergence on a single model or on a single list of important imperfections, but there was broad agreement on the framework and on the way to proceed.

A good example of this convergence was the work of Michael Woodford (from Columbia) and Jordi Gali (from Pompeu Fabra in Catalonia). Woodford, Gali, and a number of coauthors developed a model, known as the *new Keynesian model*, that embodies utility and profit maximization, rational expectations, and nominal rigidities. You can think of it as a high-tech version of the model that was presented in Chapter 22. This model proved extremely useful and influential in the redesign of monetary policy—from the focus on inflation targeting to the reliance on interest rate rules—that we described in Chapters 4 and 24. It led to the development of a class of larger models that build on its simple structure but allow for a longer menu of imperfections and thus must be solved numerically. These models, which are now standard work horses in most central banks, are known as "**dynamic stochastic general equilibrium**," or *DSGE*, models.

# 26-5 | First Lessons for Macroeconomics after the Crisis

Just at the time at which a new synthesis appeared to be in sight and macroeconomists felt that they had the tools to understand the economy and design policy, the crisis started, and, at the time of writing this chapter, is still continuing. We saw in Section 26-1 how the Great

Depression had led to a dramatic reassessment of macroeconomics and started the Keynesian revolution. You may ask: Will this crisis have the same effect on macroeconomics, leading yet to another revolution? It is too early to say, but our guess is: probably not.

There is no question that the crisis reflects a major intellectual failure on the part of macroeconomics. The failure was in not realizing that such a large crisis could happen, that the characteristics of the economy were such that a relatively small shock, in this case the decrease in U.S. housing prices, could lead to a major financial and macroeconomic global crisis. The source of the failure was a lack of focus on the role of the financial institutions in the economy. (To be fair, a few macroeconomists who were looking more closely at the financial system sounded the alarm; best known among them Nouriel Roubini, from New York University, and the economists at the Bank for International Settlements in Basel, whose job it is to follow financial developments closely.)

By and large, the financial system and the complex role of banks and other financial institutions in the intermediation of funds between lenders and borrowers was ignored in most macroeconomic models. There were exceptions. Work by Doug Diamond (from Chicago) and Philip Dybvig (from Washington University in Saint Louis) in the 1980s had clarified the nature of bank runs (which we examined in Chapter 4): Illiquid assets and liquid liabilities created a risk of runs even for solvent banks. The problem could only be avoided by the provision of liquidity by the central bank if and when needed. Work by Bengt Holmström and Jean Tirole (both from MIT) had shown that liquidity issues were endemic to a modern economy. Not only banks, but firms could well find themselves in a position where they were solvent, but illiquid, unable to raise the additional cash to finish a project or unable to repay investors when they wanted repayment. An important paper by Andrei Shleifer called "The Limits of Arbitrage" had shown that, after a decline in an asset price below its fundamental value, investors might not be able to take advantage of the arbitrage opportunity; indeed they may themselves be forced to sell the asset, leading to a further decline in the price and a further deviation from fundamentals. Behavioural economists (for example, Richard Thaler, from Chicago) had pointed to the way in which individuals differ from the rational individual model typically used in economics, and had drawn implications for financial markets.

Thus, most of the elements needed to understand the crisis were available. Much of the work, however, was carried out outside macroeconomics, in finance or corporate finance. The elements were not integrated in a consistent macroeconomic model, and their interactions were poorly understood. Leverage, complexity, and liquidity, the factors which, as we saw in Chapter 11, combined to create the crisis, were nearly fully absent from the macroeconomic models used by central banks.

Several years after the beginning of the crisis, things have changed dramatically. Not surprisingly, researchers have turned their attention to the financial system and the nature of macro financial linkages. Further work is taking place on the various pieces, and these pieces are starting to be integrated into the large macroeconomic models. The lessons for policy are also being drawn, be it on the use of **macro-prudential** tools or the dangers of very high public debt. There is still a long way to go, but, in the end, our macroeconomic models will be richer, with a better understanding of the financial system. Yet, we must be realistic: If history is any guide, the economy will be hit by yet another type of shock we have not thought about.

The lessons from the crisis probably go beyond adding the financial sector to macroeconomic models and analysis. The Great Depression had, rightly, led most economists to question the macroeconomic properties of a market economy and to suggest a larger role for government intervention. The crisis is raising similar questions. Both the new classical and new Keynesian models had in common the belief that, in the medium run at least, the economy naturally returned to its natural level. The new classicals took the extreme position that output was always at its natural level. The new Keynesians took the view that, in the short run, output would likely deviate from its natural level. But they maintained that, eventually,

Michael Woodford

Oliver Blanchard

Jordi Gali

Oliver Blanchard

Bengt Holmström

Oliver Blanchard

Jean Tirole

Antoine Devouard/Redux Pictures

in the medium run, natural forces would return the economy to the natural level. The Great Depression and the long slump in Japan were well known; they were seen however as aberrations and thought to be caused by substantial policy mistakes that could have been avoided. Many economists today believe that this optimism was excessive. After three years in the liquidity trap, it is clear that the usual adjustment mechanism—namely, a decrease in interest rates in response to low output—is not operational. It is also clear that the room for policy, be it monetary policy or fiscal policy is also more limited than previously thought.

If there is a consensus, it might be that with respect to small shocks and normal fluctuations, the adjustment process works; but that, in response to large, exceptional shocks, the normal adjustment process may fail, the room for policy may be limited, and it may take a long time for the economy to repair itself. For the moment, the priority is for researchers is to better understand what has happened, and for policy makers to use, as best they can, the monetary and fiscal policy tools they have, to steer the world economy back to health.

## SUMMARY

- The history of modern macroeconomics starts in 1936, with the publication of Keynes's *General Theory of Employment, Interest, and Money*. Keynes's contribution was formalized in the *IS-LM* model by John Hicks and Alvin Hansen in the 1930s and early 1940s.

- The period from the early 1940s to the early 1970s can be called the golden age of macroeconomics. Among the major developments were the development of the theories of consumption, investment, money demand, and portfolio choice; the development of growth theory; and the development of large macroeconometric models.

- The main debate during the 1960s was between Keynesians and monetarists. Keynesians believed developments in macroeconomic theory allowed for better control of the economy. Monetarists, led by Milton Friedman, were more skeptical of the ability of governments to help stabilize the economy.

- In the 1970s, macroeconomics experienced a crisis. There were two reasons. One was the appearance of stagflation, which came as a surprise to most economists. The other was a theoretical attack led by Robert Lucas. Lucas and his followers showed that when rational expectations were introduced, (1) Keynesian models could not be used to determine policy, (2) Keynesian models could not explain long-lasting deviations of output from its natural level, and (3) the theory of policy needed to be redesigned using the tools of game theory.

- Much of the 1970s and 1980s was spent integrating rational expectations into macroeconomics. As is reflected in this book, macroeconomists are now much more aware of the role of expectations in determining the effects of shocks and policy and of the complexity of policy than they were two decades ago.

- Recent research in macroeconomic theory, up to the crisis, proceeded along three lines. New classical economists explored the extent to which fluctuations can be explained as movements in the natural level of output, as opposed to movements away from the natural level of output. New Keynesian economists explored more formally the role of market imperfections in fluctuations. New growth theorists explored the determinants of technological progress. These lines were increasingly overlapping, and, on the eve of the crisis, a new synthesis appeared to be emerging.

- The crisis reflects a major intellectual failure on the part of macroeconomics: the failure to understand the macroeconomic importance of the financial system. While many of the elements needed to understand the crisis had been developed before the crisis, they were not central to macroeconomic thinking and were not integrated in large macroeconomic models. Much research is now focused on macro-financial linkages.

- The crisis has also raised a larger issue about the adjustment process through which output returns to its natural level. If there is a consensus, it might be that with respect to small shocks and normal fluctuations, the adjustment process works, and policy can accelerate this return; but that, in response to large, exceptional shocks, the normal adjustment process may fail, the room for policy may be limited, and it may take a long time for the economy to repair itself.

## FURTHER READING

- Two classics are J. M. Keynes, *The General Theory of Employment, Interest, and Money* (Macmillan Press, 1936), and Milton Friedman and Anna Schwartz, *A Monetary History of the United States, 1867–1960* (Princeton University Press, 1963). Warning: The first makes for hard reading, and the second is a heavy volume.

- For an account of macroeconomics in textbooks since the 1940s, read Paul Samuelson's, "Credo of a Lucky Textbook Author," *Journal of Economic Perspectives* 11, Spring 1997: pp. 153–160.

- In the introduction to *Studies in Business Cycle Theory* (MIT Press, 1981), Robert Lucas develops his approach to macroeconomics and gives a guide to his contributions.

- The paper that launched real business cycle theory is Edward Prescott, "Theory Ahead of Business Cycle Measurement," *Federal Reserve Bank of Minneapolis Quarterly Review* 10 (4), Fall 1986: pp. 9–22. It is not easy reading.

- For more on new Keynesian economics, read David Romer, "The New Keynesian Synthesis," *Journal of Economic Perspectives* 7, Winter 1993: pp. 5–22.

- For more on new growth theory, read Paul Romer, "The Origins of Endogenous Growth," *Journal of Economic Perspectives* 8, Winter 1994: pp. 3–22.

- For a detailed look at the history of macroeconomic ideas, with in-depth interviews of most of the major researchers, read Brian Snowdon and Howard Vane, *Modern Macroeconomics: Its Origins, Development and Current State* (Edward Elgar, 2005).

- For two points of view on the state of macroeconomics pre-crisis, read V. V. Chari and Patrick Kehoe, "Macroeconomics in Practice: How Theory Is Shaping Policy," *Journal of Economic Perspectives* 20 (4), 2006: pp. 3–28; and N. Greg Mankiw, "The Macroeconomist as Scientist and Engineer," *Journal of Economic Perspectives* 20 (4), 2006: pp. 29–46.

- For a skeptical view of financial markets and the contributions of Thaler and Shleifer among others, read *The Myth of the Rational Market. A History of Risk, Reward, and Delusion on Wall Street* by Justin Fox (HarperCollins, 2009).

- For an assessment of macroeconomic policy post-crisis, read *In the Wake of the Crisis: Leading Economists Reassess Economic Policy*, edited by Olivier Blanchard et al (MIT Press, 2012).

If you want to learn more about macroeconomic issues and theory:

- Most economics journals are heavy on mathematics and are hard to read. But a few make an effort to be more friendly. The *Journal of Economic Perspectives,* in particular, has nontechnical articles on current economic research and issues. The *Brookings Papers on Economic Activity*, published twice a year, analyze current macroeconomic problems. So does *Economic Policy*, published in Europe, which focuses more on European issues.

- Most regional Federal Reserve Banks also publish reviews with easy-to-read articles; these reviews are available free of charge. Among these are the *Economic Review* published by the Cleveland Fed, the *Economic Review* published by the Kansas City Fed, the *New England Economic Review* published by the Boston Fed, and the *Quarterly Review* published by the Minneapolis Fed.

- More advanced treatments of current macroeconomic theory—roughly at the level of a first graduate course in macroeconomics—are given by David Romer, *Advanced Macroeconomics* (McGraw-Hill, fourth edition, 2011) and by Olivier Blanchard and Stanley Fischer, *Lectures on Macroeconomics* (MIT Press, 1989).

# APPENDICES

## Appendix 1: An Introduction to Canada's System of National Accounts

This appendix introduces the basic structure of Canada's System of National Accounts. Canada's national accounts underwent a major revision in the fall of 2012. This revision produced consistent data back to 1981. This is the reason that much (not all) of the data presented in this book goes back to 1981. The revisions in 2012 were carried out partly to recognize the importance of the non-profit sector and partly to make Canada's national accounts more comparable to those in other countries.

The basic measure of aggregate economic activity is Gross Domestic Product or GDP. The System of National Accounts is organized around two decompositions of GDP. One looks at income: Who receives what? The other looks at expenditures: What is produced and who buys it?

### The Expenditure Side

Table A1–1 looks at the expenditure side of the national accounts, at who buys what. The table has three main blocks: consumption, investment, and the foreign sector. You may ask: Where did the government sector go? In the 2012 treatment of the national accounts, the government sector is found consuming in the consumption block, and investing in the investment block. Having a clear separation between consumption and investment facilitates measuring the contribution of capital to economic growth. It does make it more difficult to locate the activities of the government sector.

- Three economic units consume. Total consumption, $1,408,997 M, is by far the largest component of GDP, 77%. But remember this calculation includes both direct household consumption (line 2) and government consumption (line 8) as well as the production of non-profits (line 7).

- The clear separation of non-profit institutions from the business sector is another new element of Canada's national accounts. Here the production of

---

**TABLE A1–1** GDP: The Expenditure Side, 2012 (Millions of Dollars)

| | | | |
|---|---:|---:|---:|
| CONSUMPTION | | | |
| Final consumption expenditure: | | 1,408,997 | (1) |
| Household final consumption expenditure | | 986,268 | (2) |
| Durable goods | 119,260 | | (3) |
| Semi-durable goods | 70,978 | | (4) |
| Non-durable goods | 250,666 | | (5) |
| Services | 545,364 | | (6) |
| Non-profit institutions serving household Final consumption expenditure | | 28,052 | (7) |
| General governments final consumption expenditure | | 394,677 | (8) |
| INVESTMENT | | | |
| Gross fixed capital formation | | 436,758 | (9) |
| Business gross fixed capital formation | | 360,167 | (10) |
| Residential structures | 126,008 | | (11) |
| Nonresidential structures | 116,077 | | (12) |
| Machinery and equipment | 80,093 | | (13) |
| Intellectual property products | 37,989 | | (14) |
| Non-profit institutions serving household's gross fixed capital formation | | 1,885 | (15) |
| General government's gross fixed capital formation | | 74,706 | (16) |
| Investment in inventories | | 7,983 | (17) |
| THE FOREIGN SECTOR | | | |
| Exports | | 545,827 | (18) |
| Imports | | 582,271 | (19) |
| Statistical discrepancy | | 310 | (20) |
| Gross domestic product at market prices | | 1,817,604 | (21) |

*Source:* Statistics Canada, Gross domestic product, expenditure-based, CANSIM Table 380-0064.

some non-profit institutions is treated as producing goods consumed by society. These non-profits produce goods and services for free to consumers. Examples would be churches, food banks, other social service organizations, and political parties. The total consumption of this type, called **non-profit institutions serving household final consumption expenditure**, is $28,052 M (line 7). A non-profit that produces goods for sale—a credit union is an example—is treated as a business.

- The government sector, including all levels of government (that is the meaning of the term *general*), also produces a great deal of output. This is formally called **general government's final consumption expenditure**. This value, $394,677 M (line 8) is large, 21.7% of GDP. This item would include the salaries of government sector employees, police, firefighters, teachers, and all other civil servants. These are government purchases of labour that are producing public services.

- Households are the largest consumers. **Household final consumption expenditure**, direct consumption by households, $986,268M (line 2), is 54% of GDP. This consumption is divided into four categories (lines 3 to 6): **durable goods**; **semi-durable goods**; **non-durable goods**; and **services**. Durable good purchases include the purchases of new cars.

The same three economic units (households, government, and non-profits) invest, that is, spend resources on the creation of new capital that leads to future production. Total investment, $436,758 M (line 9), is 24% of GDP. It is the fourth sector, the business sector, that creates the largest amount of new capital.

- The business sector invests a total of $360,167 M (line 10), which is more than 80% of total investment. **Business gross fixed capital formation** (more simply **business investment**) has two categories that we would think of as traditional investment by the business sector: **nonresidential structures** (line 12) and **machinery and equipment** (line 13). The former is new buildings—think of stores and factories. The latter is the equipment to go into the new buildings—think of machines and computers. The revised national accounts now separate out a third component of investment by the business sector, investment labelled **intellectual property products**, $37,989 M (line 14). This is spending on research and development of new ideas to be used in the future to increase production. In that sense, they are logically part of investment.

- New purchases of **residential structures** are included in business gross fixed capital formation. This is the building of new homes, both rental homes and owner-occupied homes. The logic of including housing being built for rental as a business sector investment seems clear—businesses build apartments and rent them for profit. The logic of including new homes built by households for their own occupation treats households for this purpose (and this purpose only) as a business. Households are treated as though they are building a new home to rent to themselves.

- The non-profit sector undertakes a very small amount of investment, $1,885 M (line 15).

- The government sector undertakes a very large amount of investment, $74,706 M (line 16). **General government's gross fixed capital formation** includes the building of new physical capital owned by the general government sector: roads, buildings, as well as the furniture and equipment within those buildings. It also includes direct research and development spending that develops new intellectual property within the government sector.

The sum of consumption and investment, whether by the private sector or by government, is the total amount of goods and services *demanded* by households, governments and businesses resident within Canada's borders. But GDP is the total value of final goods and services *produced* within Canada's borders. To move from demand to production requires two further adjustments, one minor and the other major.

- The minor adjustment is **investment in inventories** (line17). Firms could sell more than they produce in a given year if inventory falls. If that were the case, this item would be negative and firms would draw down inventory. Production (GDP) would be less than demand. In 2012, this item is positive. Firms produced more than they sold in 2012 and inventories increased. This item is a small percentage of GDP, only 0.4 percentage points. But it must be included to provide an accurate measure of production rather than a measure of demand.

- The major adjustment in the measurement of production considers the foreign sector. A great deal of production in Canada is exported. In 2012, **exports** were $545,827 M (line 18) or 30% of GDP. These are goods not included in total domestic demand as measured by the sum of consumption and investment. Exports are added to domestic demand to measure production.

- However it is equally important that much of domestic demand is met by goods and services imported from other countries. Thus imports, $582,271 M (line 19) are subtracted from the total of consumption,

| | | |
|---|---:|---:|
| Compensation of employees | 916,505 | (1) |
|     Wages and salaries | 795,032 | (2) |
|     Employer's social contributions | 121,473 | (3) |
| Gross operating surplus | 502,989 | (4) |
|     Net operating surplus: corporations | 259,460 | (5) |
|     Consumption of fixed capital: corporations | 181,991 | (6) |
|     Consumption of fixed capital: general governments and non-profit institutions serving households | 61,538 | (7) |
| Gross mixed income | 212,313 | (8) |
|     Net mixed income | 160,138 | (9) |
|     Consumption of fixed capital: unincorporated business | 52,175 | (10) |
| Taxes less subsidies on production | 77,062 | (11) |
| Taxes less subsidies on products and imports | 109,046 | (12) |
| Statistical discrepancy | −311 | (13) |
| Gross domestic product at market prices | 1,817,604 | (14) |

*Source:* Statistics Canada, Gross domestic product, income based, CANSIM Table 380-0063.

investment and exports to finish the calculation of total production within Canada's borders.

GDP should be the sum of consumption (line 1); investment (line 9); investment in inventories (line17) and exports (line 18) minus imports (line19). That sum is $1,817,294 M. This is $310 M (line 20) less than GDP (line 21). The difference between the total production measured by expenditure and the level of GDP is the **statistical discrepancy**. As the name suggests, this is added to (or subtracted from) the measure of total expenditure on goods produced in Canada from the expenditure side to allow a more exact measure of total production. To clearly understand where the statistical discrepancy comes from, we must look at measuring GDP as a total of all incomes earned.

## The Income Side

As emphasized in Chapter 2, GDP can also be measured using the sum of all incomes earned in the production of goods and services. When sales and purchases of intermediate goods are removed, the incomes earned by all units in society must equal the value of final goods and services produced in that society. The income side of the national accounts follows through this logic to generate a second measure of GDP. The income side of the national accounts is presented in Table A1-2. However, parts of this process are not as transparent as the expenditure side of the national accounts. There are three measures of incomes earned and a very large adjustment for taxes.

- **Compensation of employees** is by far the largest component of incomes. The goal of this category is to measure incomes that can clearly be attributed to labour as a factor of production. Total compensation of employees is $916,505 M (line 1), 50% of GDP. **Wages and salaries** dominate total compensation. Wages and salaries are measured before taxes are subtracted. **Employer's social contributions** are included as compensation of employees. Employers make contributions to various social insurance plans operated by the government. The Canada and Quebec Pension Plan as well as the Employment Insurance system would be the most prominent examples. The argument is that these plans generate benefits to employees and thus such payments by employers should be included in compensation.

- The second category of incomes earned from production within Canada is the **gross operating surplus** (line 4). The total of this item is $502,989 M or 27.6% of GDP. The goal of this category is to measure all of the incomes that can be clearly attributed to capital as a factor of production.

- A great deal of capital is owned by the corporate sector. This capital earns profits, called **net operating surplus: corporations** that total $259,460 M (line 5) in 2012. In this category, some of these profits are paid out as interest, some are paid out as dividends and some are retained within the corporations. The income that is earned by that capital after the deduction of compensation of employees and after the deduction of **consumption of fixed capital: corporations** (line 6) is $259,460 M (line 5). Why is the consumption of fixed capital by corporations treated as a separate item? Conceptually, we would like to know how much income and production is attributed to capital wearing out with use.

- In a similar way, the national accounts measure the amount of production that can be attributed to capital wearing out when the capital is owned by either the government sector or the non-profit sector (line 7). Conceptually this is the spending needed by these combined sectors that would keep the level of their capital stock unchanged.

- The first two components of the income side of the national accounts work with incomes that can either be clearly attributed to labour—(the income of employees), or clearly attributed to capital—(corporate profits and depreciation). But there is a very large unincorporated business sector. The most useful way to think of this sector is that it is the small business sector. In fact it would include any form of business enterprise that is not incorporated. The issue for the national accounts is that the income earned in this sector clearly mixes up the return to capital owned in this sector and return to labour by the people who work in this sector. Here is a simple example: A farm earns income that is clearly a mixture of payment for the farmer's time and the farmer's capital. This is the origin of the term "mixed." The terminology simply makes it clear that although we have a good estimate of the total income of this sector, we are not able to clearly distinguish between the payments to labour and the payments to capital within some sectors of the economy.

- **Gross mixed income** $212,313 M (line 8) is the sum of **net mixed income** (line 9) and **consumption of fixed capital: unincorporated business** (line 10). Line 10 represents the wearing out of capital in the unincorporated business sector. Finally, we need two major adjustments to move from the total of incomes earned in production to the value of final goods and services sold, the definition of GDP from the expenditure side. The incomes measured above include taxes that will be paid on those incomes—that is, they are incomes before taxes are deducted. But there are many taxes that are levied as production and sales take place. These taxes are included in the sale price and thus included in GDP when measured by the value of final goods and services sold. Taxes can be negative if they are subsidies. A subsidy would reduce the price of the good or service; tax increases the price of goods.

- The item **taxes less subsidies on production** (line 11) is the value of taxes paid in the course of production when such taxes do not vary with the quantity or value of production. Property taxes are a prominent example.

- The item **taxes less subsidies on products and imports** (line 12) is the value of taxes paid in the course of production when such taxes vary with the quantity and value of production. Sales taxes and taxes on tobacco and alcohol would fall into this category.

If we were to add all of the income of labour and capital—that is, lines (1), (4), and (8) as well as all taxes less subsidies, lines (11) and (12), we should get the same measure of GDP found in Table A1–1. The value of final goods and services purchased, which we calculated in Table A1–1 to be $1,817,915, does not equal $1,818,028 M, the sum of lines (1), (4), (8), (11), and (12) in Table A1–2. The two measures of GDP are not equal. It would actually be surprising if they were equal since they are constructed from different records and surveys. The gap between the measure in Tables A1–1 and A1–2 is $621 M. In 2012, the level of GDP calculated from adding together incomes is larger than the level of GDP calculated by adding up total expenditures (in some years the level of GDP from the sum of incomes could be less than the measure of GDP from the sum of expenditures). The difference is split in half. $311 M is subtracted from the measure of GDP calculated from incomes in Table A1–2 and $310 M is added to the measure of GDP calculated in Table A1–1. The half is chosen to be an integer number. These final adjustments, both called a statistical discrepancy, are approximately equal in value and opposite in sign. The statistical discrepancy entries mean that the measure of GDP from the income side and the measure of GDP from the expenditure side take the same value.

## A Warning

National accounts give an internally consistent description of aggregate activity. But underlying these accounts are many choices about what to include and what not to include, where to put some types of income or spending, and so on. Here are three examples:

- Work within the home is not counted in GDP. Thus, to take an extreme example, if two women decide to babysit each other's child and pay each other for the babysitting services, measured GDP will go up, while true GDP clearly does not change. The solution would be to count work within the home in GDP, in the same way that we impute a consumption value for owner-occupied housing. But so far, this has not been done.

- The purchase of a house is treated as an investment, and housing services are then treated as part of consumption. Contrast this with the treatment of automobiles. Despite the fact that automobiles provide services for a long time—although not as long a time as houses do—purchases of automobiles are not treated as investment. They are treated as consumption and appear in the national accounts only in the year in which they are bought.
- Physical investment and education are treated asymmetrically. Firms' purchases of machines are treated as investment. The purchase of education is treated as consumption of education services. But education is clearly, in part, an investment: People acquire it, in part, to increase their future income.

The list could go on and on. However, the purpose of these examples is not to make you conclude that the system of national accounts is wrong. Most of the choices we just saw were made for good reasons, often because of data availability or for simplicity of treatment. Rather, the point is that to use the national accounts in the best way, you should understand not only their logic but also the choices made in constructing a national accounts system and thus the limitations placed on their use.

## KEY TERMS

- business gross fixed capital formation, A2
- business investment, A2
- compensation of employees, A3
- consumption of fixed capital: corporations, A3
- consumption of fixed capital: unincorporated business, A3
- durable goods, A2
- employer's social contributions, A3
- exports, A2
- general government's final consumption expenditure, A2
- general government's gross fixed capital formation, A2
- gross mixed income, A3
- gross operating surplus, A3
- household final consumption expenditure, A2

- intellectual property products, A2
- investment in inventories, A2
- machinery and equipment, A2
- net mixed income, A3
- net operating surplus: corporations, A3
- non-durable goods, A2
- non-profit institutions serving household final consumption expenditure, A2
- nonresidential structures, A2
- residential structures, A2
- semi-durable goods, A2
- services, A2
- statistical discrepancy, A3
- taxes less subsidies on production, A4
- taxes less subsidies on products and imports, A4
- wages and salaries, A3

## FURTHER READING

An overview of the System of National Accounts is found at http://www.statcan.gc.ca/nea-cen/about-apropos/index-eng.htm. There is a much needed glossary of all terms used in the System of National Accounts in Canada at http://www.statcan.gc.ca/nea-cen/gloss/index-eng.htm.

## Appendix 2:
## A Math Refresher

This appendix presents the mathematical tools and the mathematical results that are used in the book.

## Geometric Series

**Definition.** A geometric series is a sum of numbers of the form:

$$1 + x + x^2 + \cdots + x^n$$

where $x$ is a number that may be greater or smaller than one, and $x^n$ denotes $x$ to the power $n$—that is, $x$ times itself $n$ times.

Examples of such series are:

- The sum of spending in each round of the multiplier (Chapter 3). If $c$ is the marginal propensity to consume, then the sum of increases in spending after $n$ rounds is given by:

$$1 + c + c^2 + \cdots + c^{n-1}$$

- The present discounted value of a sequence of payments of 1 each year for $n$ years (Chapter 19), when the interest rate is equal to $i$:

$$1 + \frac{1}{1+i} + \frac{1}{(1+i)^2} + \cdots + \frac{1}{(1+i)^{n-1}}$$

We usually have two questions we want to answer when encountering such a series. The first one is what the sum is. The second is whether the sum explodes as we let $n$ increase, or reaches a finite limit. The following propositions tell you what you need to know to answer these questions.

Proposition 1 tells you how to compute the sum:

**Proposition 1:**

$$1 + x + x^2 + \cdots + x^n = \frac{1 - x^{n+1}}{1 - x} \quad (A.1)$$

The proof is as follows. Multiply the sum by $(1 - x)$, and use the fact that $x^a x^b = x^{a+b}$ (that is: one has to add exponents when multiplying):

$$
\begin{aligned}
(1 + x + x^2 &+ \cdots + x^n)(1 - x) \\
&= 1 + x + x^2 + \cdots + x^n \\
&\quad - x - x^2 - \cdots - x^n - x^{n+1} \\
&= 1 \qquad\qquad\qquad\qquad - x^{n+1}
\end{aligned}
$$

All the terms on the right, except for the first and the last, cancel. Dividing both sides by $(1 - x)$ gives equation (A.1).

This formula can be used for any $x$ and any $n$. If, for example, $x$ is 0.9 and $n$ is 10, then the sum is equal to 6.86. If $x$ is 1.2 and $n$ is 10, then the sum is equal to 32.15.

Proposition 2 tells you what happens as $n$ gets large:

**Proposition 2:** If $x$ is less than 1, the sum goes to $1/(1 - x)$ as $n$ gets large. If $x$ is equal to or greater than one, the sum explodes as $n$ gets large.

The proof is as follows: If $x$ is less than 1, then $x^n$ goes to zero as $n$ gets large. Thus, from equation (A.1), the sum goes to $1/(1 - x)$. The difference between $n$ and $n+1$ when $n$ is large is not important here. If $x$ is greater than 1, then $x^n$ becomes larger and larger as $n$ increases, $1 - x^n$ becomes a larger and larger negative number, and the ratio $(1 - x^n)/(1 - x)$ becomes a larger and larger positive number. Thus, the sum explodes as $n$ gets large.

*Application from Chapter 19*: Consider the present value of a payment of \$1 forever, starting next year, when the interest rate is equal to $i$. The present value is given by:

$$\frac{1}{(1 + i)} + \frac{1}{(1 + i)^2} + \cdots \quad (A.2)$$

Factoring out $1/(1 + i)$, rewrite this present value as:

$$\frac{1}{(1 + i)}\left[1 + \frac{1}{(1 + i)} + \cdots\right]$$

The term in brackets is a geometric series, with $x = 1/(1 + i)$. As the interest rate $i$ is positive, $x$ is less than 1. Applying proposition 2, when $n$ gets large, the term in brackets is thus equal to:

$$\frac{1}{1 - \dfrac{1}{(1 + i)}} = \frac{(1 + i)}{(1 + i - 1)} = \frac{(1 + i)}{i}$$

Replacing the term in brackets in the previous equation by $(1 + i)/i$ gives:

$$\frac{1}{(1 + i)}\left[\frac{(1 + i)}{i}\right] = \frac{1}{i}$$

The present value of a sequence of payments of \$1 a year forever, starting next year, is thus equal to 1 over the interest rate. If $i$ is equal to 5%, the present value is equal to \$20.

## Useful Approximations

Throughout the book, we use several approximations that make computations easier. These approximations are most reliable when the variables $x$, $y$, $z$ below are small, say, between 0 and 10%. The numerical examples in propositions 3 through 10 that follow are based on the values $x = 0.05$ and $y = 0.03$.

## Proposition 3:

$$(1 + x)(1 + y) \approx (1 + x + y) \qquad \text{(A.3)}$$

The proof is as follows: Expanding $(1 + x)(1 + y)$ gives $(1 + x)(1 + y) = 1 + x + y + xy$. If $x$ and $y$ are small, then the product $xy$ is very small and can be ignored as an approximation (for example, if $x = 0.05$ and $y = 0.03$, then $xy = 0.0015$). So $(1 + x)(1 + y)$ is approximately equal to $(1 + x + y)$.

For the values $x$ and $y$ above, for example, the approximation gives 1.08 compared to an exact value of 1.0815.

*Application from Chapter 6*: Arbitrage between domestic and foreign bonds leads to the following relation:

$$(1 + i_t) = (1 + i_t^*) \left( 1 + \frac{(E_{t+1}^e - E_t)}{E_t} \right)$$

Using proposition 3 on the right-hand side of the equation gives:

$$(1 + i_t^*) \left( 1 + \frac{(E_{t+1}^e - E_t)}{E_t} \right)$$

$$\approx \left( 1 + i_t^* + \frac{(E_{t+1}^e - E_t)}{E_t} \right)$$

Replacing in the arbitrage equation gives:

$$(1 + i_t) \approx \left( 1 + i_t^* + \frac{(E_{t+1}^e - E_t)}{E_t} \right)$$

Subtracting 1 from both sides gives:

$$i_t \approx i_t^* + \frac{(E_{t+1}^e - E_t)}{E_t}$$

The domestic interest rate is approximately equal to the foreign interest rate plus the expected rate of depreciation of the domestic currency.

## Proposition 4:

$$(1 + x)^2 \approx 1 + 2x \qquad \text{(A.4)}$$

The proof follows directly from proposition 3, with $y = x$. For the value of $x = 0.05$, the approximation gives 1.10, compared with an exact value of 1.1025.

*Application from Chapter 20*: From arbitrage, the relation between the two-year interest rate and the current and expected one-year rates is given by:

$$(1 + i_{2t})^2 = (1 + i_{1t})(1 + i_{1t+1}^e)$$

Using proposition 4 for the left-hand side of the equation gives:

$$(1 + i_{2t})^2 \approx 1 + 2\, i_{2t}$$

Using proposition 3 for the right-hand side of the equation gives:

$$(1 + i_{1t})(1 + i_{1t+1}^e) \approx 1 + i_{1t} + i_{1t+1}^e$$

Replacing in the original relation gives:

$$1 + 2\, i_{2t} = 1 + i_{1t} + i_{1t+1}^e$$

Or, reorganizing:

$$i_{2t} = \frac{(i_{1t} + i_{1t+1}^e)}{2}$$

The two-year rate is approximately equal to the average of the current and expected one-year rates.

## Proposition 5:

$$(1 + x)^n \approx 1 + nx \qquad \text{(A.5)}$$

The proof follows by repeated application of propositions 3 and 4. For example, $(1 + x)^3 = (1 + x)^2(1 + x) \approx (1 + 2x)(1 + x)$ by proposition 4, $\approx (1 + 2x + x) = 1 + 3x$ by proposition 3.

The approximation becomes worse as $n$ increases, however. For example, for $x = 0.05$ and $n = 5$, the approximation gives 1.25, compared to an exact value of 1.2763. For $n = 10$, the approximation gives 1.50, compared to an exact value of 1.63.

*Application*: In Chapter 20, we saw that arbitrage between $n$-year Canadian bonds and $n$-year American bonds implies:

$$(1 + r_{nt})^n = \left( \frac{1}{\epsilon_t} \right)(1 + r_{nt}^*)^n (\epsilon_{t+n}^e)$$

From proposition 5, it follows that:

$$(1 + r_{nt})^n \approx (1 + nr_{nt})$$

and:

$$(1 + r_{nt}^*)^n \approx (1 + nr_{nt}^*)$$

Note also that we can rewrite the two terms in $\epsilon$ on the right in the arbitrage equation as:

$$\frac{\epsilon_{t+n}^e}{\epsilon_t} = 1 + \frac{(\epsilon_{t+n}^e - \epsilon_t)}{\epsilon_t}$$

Replacing these three expressions in the arbitrage relation gives:

$$(1 + nr_{nt}) \approx (1 + nr_{nt}^*)\left( 1 + \frac{(\epsilon_{t+n}^e - \epsilon_t)}{\epsilon_t} \right)$$

From proposition 3, it follows that:

$$(1 + nr_{nt}) \approx \left(1 + nr_{nt}^* + \frac{(\epsilon_{t+n}^e - \epsilon_t)}{\epsilon_t}\right)$$

Or, simplifying:

$$n(r_{nt} - r_{nt}^*) \approx \frac{(\epsilon_{t+n}^e - \epsilon_t)}{\epsilon_t}$$

The expected rate of real dollar depreciation over the next $n$ years is approximately equal to $n$ times the difference between the $n$th year Canadian and American real interest rates.

**Proposition 6:**

$$\frac{(1 + x)}{(1 + y)} \approx (1 + x - y) \qquad (A.6)$$

The proof is as follows: Consider the product of $(1 + x - y)(1 + y)$. Expanding this product gives $(1 + x - y)(1 + y) = 1 + x + xy - y^2$. If both $x$ and $y$ are small, then $xy$ and $y^2$ are very small, so $(1 + x - y)(1 + y) \approx (1 + x)$. Dividing both sides of this approximation by $(1 + y)$ gives the proposition above.

For the values of $x = 0.05$ and $y = 0.03$, the approximation gives 1.02, while the correct value is 1.019.

*Application from Chapter 19*: The real interest rate is defined by:

$$(1 + r_t) \equiv \frac{(1 + i_t)}{(1 + \pi_t^e)}$$

Using proposition 6 gives:

$$(1 + r_t) \approx (1 + i_t - \pi_t^e)$$

Simplifying:

$$r_t \approx i_t - \pi_t^e$$

This gives us the approximation we use at many points in the book: The real interest rate is approximately equal to the nominal interest rate minus expected inflation.

These approximations are also very convenient when dealing with *growth rates*. Define the rate of growth of $x$ by $g_x \equiv \Delta x/x$, and similarly for $z$, $g_z$ and for $y$, $g_y$. The numerical examples below are based on the values $g_x = 0.05$ and $g_y = 0.03$.

**Proposition 7:** If $z = xy$, then:

$$g_z \approx g_x + g_y \qquad (A.7)$$

The proof is as follows. Let $\Delta z$ be the increase in $z$ when $x$ increases by $\Delta x$ and $y$ increases by $\Delta y$. Then, by definition:

$$z + \Delta z = (x + \Delta x)(y + \Delta y)$$

Divide both sides by $z$ so that:

$$\frac{(z + \Delta z)}{z} = \frac{(x + \Delta x)}{x} \frac{(y + \Delta y)}{y}$$

where we have used on the right-hand side the fact that dividing by $z$ is the same as dividing by $xy$. Simplifying gives:

$$\left(1 + \frac{\Delta z}{z}\right) = \left(1 + \frac{\Delta x}{x}\right)\left(1 + \frac{\Delta y}{y}\right)$$

Or, equivalently:

$$(1 + g_z) = (1 + g_x)(1 + g_y)$$

From proposition 3, $(1 + g_z) \approx (1 + g_x + g_y)$, or, equivalently, $g_z \approx g_x + g_y$.

For the values of $g_x$ and $g_y$ above, the approximation gives $g_z = 8\%$, while the correct value is 8.15%.

*Application from Chapter 17*: Let a production function be of the form $Y = NA$, where $Y$ is production, $N$ is employment, and $A$ is productivity. Denoting the growth rates of $Y$, $N$, and $A$ by $g_Y$, $g_N$, and $g_A$ respectively, proposition 7 implies $g_Y \approx g_N + g_A$: The rate of output growth is approximately equal to the rate of employment growth plus the rate of productivity growth.

**Proposition 8:** If $z = x/y$, then:

$$g_z \approx g_x - g_y \qquad (A.8)$$

The proof is as follows: Let $\Delta z$ be the increase in $z$, when $x$ increases by $\Delta x$ and $y$ increases by $\Delta y$. Then, by definition:

$$z + \Delta z = \frac{x + \Delta x}{y + \Delta y}$$

Dividing both sides by $z$ and using the fact that $z = x/y$ gives:

$$1 + \Delta z/z = \frac{1 + (\Delta x/x)}{1 + (\Delta y/y)}$$

Or, substituting:

$$1 + g_z = \frac{1 + g_x}{1 + g_y}$$

From proposition 6, $(1 + g_z) \approx (1 + g_x - g_y)$, or, equivalently, $g_z \approx g_x - g_y$.

For the values of $g_x = 0.05$ and $g_y = 0.03$, the approximation gives $g_z = 2\%$, while the correct value is 1.9%.

*Application from Chapter 12:* The real money supply is $M/P$. The rate of growth of the real money supply is $g_M - \pi$, where $g_M$ is the rate of growth of the money supply and $\pi$ is the rate of inflation. The rate of growth of the real money supply is equal to the rate of growth of the nominal money supply minus the rate of inflation.

## Functions

We use functions informally in the book, as a way of denoting how a variable depends on one or more other variables.

In some cases, we look at how a variable $Y$ moves with a variable $X$. We write this relation as:

$$Y = f(X)$$
$$+$$

A plus sign below $X$ indicates a positive relation: An increase in $X$ leads to an increase in $Y$. A minus sign indicates a negative relation: An increase in $X$ leads instead to a decrease in $Y$.

In some cases, we allow the variable $Y$ to depend on more than one variable. For example, we allow $Y$ to depend on $X$ and $Z$:

$$Y = f(X, Z)$$
$$(+, -)$$

The signs indicate that an increase in $X$ leads to an increase in $Y$ holding the value of $Z$ constant, and that an increase in $Z$ leads to a decrease in $Y$ holding the value of $X$ constant.

An example of such a function is the investment function in Chapter 5:

$$I = I(Y, i)$$
$$(+, -)$$

This equation says that investment, $I$, increases with production, $Y$, and decreases with the interest rate, $i$.

In some cases, it is reasonable to assume that the relation between two or more variables is a linear relation. A given increase in $X$ always leads to the same increase in $Y$. In that case, the function is given by:

$$Y = a + bX$$

The parameter $a$ is called the **intercept**: It gives the value of $Y$ when $X$ is equal to zero. The parameter $b$ is called the **slope**: It tells us by how much $Y$ increases when $X$ increases by one.

The simplest linear relation is the relation $Y = X$, which is represented by the 45-degree line and has a slope of one. Another example of a linear relation is the consumption function introduced in Chapter 3:

$$C = c_0 + c_1 Y_D$$

where $C$ is consumption and $Y_D$ is disposable income. The parameter $c_0$ tells us what consumption would be if disposable income were equal to zero. The parameter $c_1$ tells us by how much consumption increases when income increases by 1 unit; $c_1$ is called the propensity to consume.

## KEY TERMS

- intercept, A9
- slope, A9

# Appendix 3:
# An Introduction to Econometrics

How do we know that consumption depends on disposable income? How do we know the value of the propensity to consume? To answer these questions and, more generally, to estimate behavioural relations and find out the values of the relevant parameters, economists use *econometrics*—the set of statistical techniques designed for use in economics. Econometrics can get fairly mathematical, but the basic principles behind econometric techniques are simple. This appendix shows you these basic principles.

To do so, we will use as an example the consumption function introduced in Chapter 3, and we will concentrate on estimating $c_1$, the propensity to consume out of disposable income.

## Changes in Consumption and Changes in Disposable Income

The propensity to consume tells us by how much consumption changes for a given change in disposable income. A natural first step is simply to plot changes in consumption versus changes in disposable income and see how the relation between the two looks. This is done in Figure A3–1.

The vertical axis in Figure A3–1 measures the annual change in consumption minus the average annual change in consumption since 1982. More precisely, let

$C_t$ denote consumption in year $t$. Let $\Delta C_t$ denote $C_t - C_{t-1}$, the change in consumption from year $t-1$ to year $t$. Let $\overline{\Delta C}$ denote the average annual change in consumption since 1982. The variable measured on the vertical axis is constructed as $\Delta C_t - \overline{\Delta C}$. A positive value of the variable represents an increase in consumption larger than average, a negative value represents an increase in consumption smaller than average.

Similarly, the horizontal axis measures the annual change in disposable income, minus the average annual change in disposable income since 1982, $\Delta Y_{Dt} - \overline{\Delta Y_D}$.

A particular square in the figure gives the deviations of the change in consumption and disposable income from their respective means for a particular year between 1982 and 2012. In 1991, for example, the change in consumption was lower than average by \$23 billion, and the change in disposable income was also lower than average by \$23 billion dollars. (For our purposes, it is not important to know which year each square refers to, just what the set of points in the diagram looks like. So, except for 1991, the years are not indicated in Figure A3–1.)

Figure A3–1 suggests two main conclusions:

- First, there is a clearly positive relation between changes in consumption and changes in disposable income. Most of the points lie in the upper-right and lower-left quadrants of the figure: When disposable income increases by more than average, consumption also typically increases by more than average; when

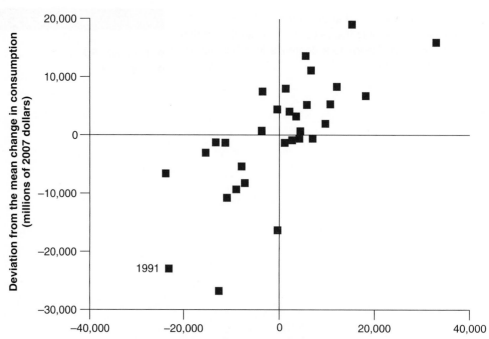

**FIGURE  A3–1**

**Changes in Consumption versus Changes in Disposable Income, 1982–2012**

There is a clearly positive relation between changes in consumption and changes in disposable income.

*Source:* CANSIM II variable V3860062: Real consumption expenditures in 2002 dollars; Real Personal Disposable Income is CANSIM II variable V498186 deflated with the Implicit Chain Price Index for Personal Expenditures on Consumer Goods and Services CANSIM II variable V3860230.

Deviation from the mean change in consumption (millions of 2007 dollars)

1991

Deviation from the mean change in personal disposable income (millions of 2007 dollars)

disposable income increases by less than average, typically so does consumption.

- Second, the relation between the two variables is good but not perfect. In particular, there are three points in the upper-left quadrant: These are years where a smaller-than-average change in disposable income was associated with a larger-than-average change in consumption.

Econometrics allows us to state these two conclusions more precisely and to get an estimate of the propensity to consume. Using an econometrics software package, we can find the line that fits the cloud of points in Figure A3–1 best. This line-fitting process is called **ordinary least squares (OLS)**. (The term "least squares" comes from the fact that the line has the property that it minimizes the sum of the squared distances of the points to the line—thus it gives the "least" "squares." The word "ordinary" comes from the fact that this is the simplest method used in econometrics.) The estimated equation corresponding to the line is called a **regression**, and the line itself is called the **regression line**.

In our case, the estimated equation is given by:

$$(\Delta C_t - \overline{\Delta C}) = 0.61(\Delta Y_{Dt} - \overline{\Delta Y_D}) + \text{residual}$$
$$\overline{R}^2 = 0.53 \quad (A3.1)$$

The regression line corresponding to this estimated equation is drawn in Figure A3–2. Equation (A3.1) reports two important numbers (econometrics packages give more information than reported above; a typical printout, together with further explanations, is given in the Focus box "A Guide to Understanding Econometric Results"):

- The first is the estimated propensity to consume. The equation tells us that an increase in disposable income of $1 billion above normal is typically associated with an increase in consumption of $0.61 billion above normal. In other words, the estimated propensity to consume is 0.61. It is positive but smaller than 1.

- The second important number is $\overline{R}^2$, which is a measure of how well the regression line fits.

   Having estimated the effect of disposable income on consumption, we can decompose the change in consumption for each year into that part that is due to the change in disposable income—the first term on the right in equation (A3.1)—and the rest, which is called the **residual**. For example, the residual for 1991 is indicated in Figure A3–2 by the vertical distance from the point representing 1991 to the regression line.

   If all the points in Figure A3–2 were exactly on the estimated line, all residuals would be equal to zero; all changes in consumption would be explained by changes in disposable income. As you can see, however, this is not the case. $\overline{R}^2$ is a statistic that tells us how well the line fits. $\overline{R}^2$ is always between 0 and 1.

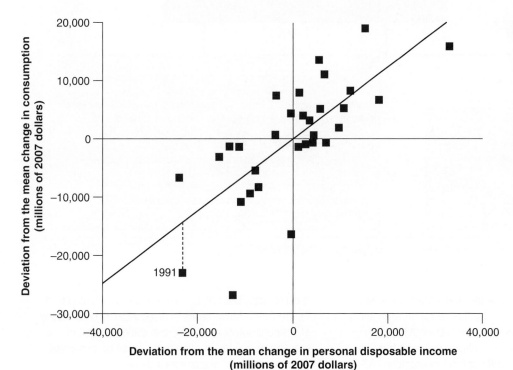

**FIGURE A3–2**

**Changes in Consumption and Changes in Disposable Income: The Regression Line**

The regression line is the line that fits the scatter of points best.

*Source:* See Figure A3–1.

In your readings, you may run across results of estimation using econometrics. Here is a guide, which uses the slightly simplified, but otherwise untouched, computer output for the equation (A3.1):

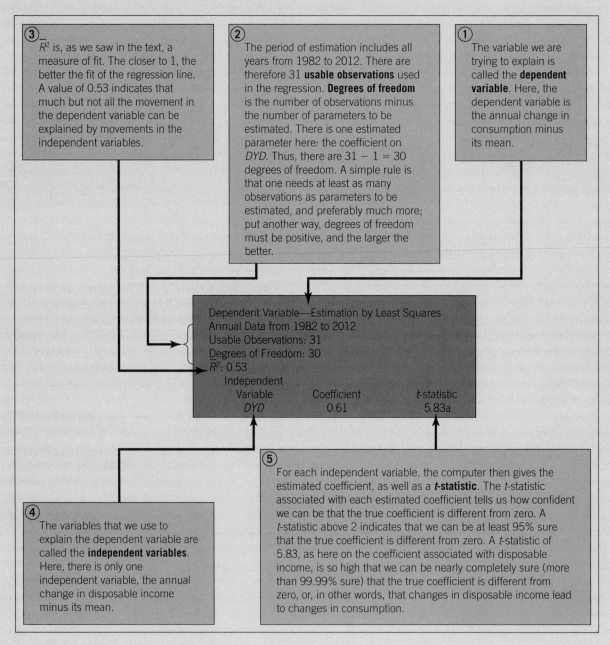

③ $\overline{R}^2$ is, as we saw in the text, a measure of fit. The closer to 1, the better the fit of the regression line. A value of 0.53 indicates that much but not all the movement in the dependent variable can be explained by movements in the independent variables.

② The period of estimation includes all years from 1982 to 2012. There are therefore 31 **usable observations** used in the regression. **Degrees of freedom** is the number of observations minus the number of parameters to be estimated. There is one estimated parameter here: the coefficient on *DYD*. Thus, there are $31 - 1 = 30$ degrees of freedom. A simple rule is that one needs at least as many observations as parameters to be estimated, and preferably much more; put another way, degrees of freedom must be positive, and the larger the better.

① The variable we are trying to explain is called the **dependent variable**. Here, the dependent variable is the annual change in consumption minus its mean.

Dependent Variable—Estimation by Least Squares
Annual Data from 1982 to 2012
Usable Observations: 31
Degrees of Freedom: 30
$\overline{R}^2$: 0.53

| Independent Variable | Coefficient | t-statistic |
|---|---|---|
| *DYD* | 0.61 | 5.83a |

④ The variables that we use to explain the dependent variable are called the **independent variables**. Here, there is only one independent variable, the annual change in disposable income minus its mean.

⑤ For each independent variable, the computer then gives the estimated coefficient, as well as a **t-statistic**. The t-statistic associated with each estimated coefficient tells us how confident we can be that the true coefficient is different from zero. A t-statistic above 2 indicates that we can be at least 95% sure that the true coefficient is different from zero. A t-statistic of 5.83, as here on the coefficient associated with disposable income, is so high that we can be nearly completely sure (more than 99.99% sure) that the true coefficient is different from zero, or, in other words, that changes in disposable income lead to changes in consumption.

A value of 1 would imply that the relation between the two variables is perfect, that all points are exactly on the regression line. A value of 0 would imply that the computer can see no relation between the two variables. The value of $\overline{R}^2$ of 0.53 in equation (A3.1) is quite high, but not 1. It confirms the message from Figure A3–2: Movements in disposable income clearly affect consumption, but there is still quite a bit of movement in consumption that cannot be explained by movements in disposable income.

## Correlation versus Causality

What we have established so far is that consumption and disposable income typically move together. More formally, we have seen that there is a positive **correlation**—the technical term for "co-relation"—between annual changes in consumption and annual changes in disposable income. And we have interpreted this relation as showing **causality**—that an increase in disposable income causes an increase in consumption.

We need to think again about this interpretation. A positive relation between consumption and disposable income may reflect the effect of disposable income on consumption. But it may also reflect the effect of consumption on disposable income. Indeed, the model we developed in Chapter 3 tells us that if, for any reason, consumers decide to spend more, then output, thus income, and, in turn, disposable income will increase. If part of the relation between consumption and disposable income comes from the effect of consumption on disposable income, interpreting equation (A3.1) as telling us about the effect of disposable income on consumption is not right.

An example will help here: Suppose that consumption does not depend on disposable income so that the true value of $c_1$ is equal to zero. (This is not very realistic, but it will make the point most clearly.) So, draw the consumption function as a horizontal line (a line with a slope of zero) in Figure A3–3. Next, suppose that disposable income is equal to $Y_D$ so that the initial combination of consumption and disposable income is given by point $A$.

Now, suppose that because of improved confidence, consumers increase their consumption so that the consumption line shifts up. If demand affects output, then income, and, in turn, disposable income increase so that the new combination of consumption and disposable income will be given by, say, point $B$. If, instead, consumers become more pessimistic, the consumption line shifts down, and so does output, leading to a combination of consumption and disposable income given by point $D$.

If we look at that economy, we observe points $A$, $B$, and $D$. If, as we did earlier, we then draw the best-fitting line through these points, we estimate an upward-sloping line, such as $CC'$, and so estimate a positive value for the propensity to consume, $c_1$. Remember, however, that the true value of $c_1$ is zero. Why do we get the wrong answer—a positive value for $c_1$ when the true value is zero? That is because we interpret the positive relation between disposable income and consumption as showing the effect of disposable income on consumption, where, in fact, the relation reflects the effect of consumption on disposable income: Higher consumption leads to higher demand, higher output, and so higher disposable income.

There is an important lesson here: *the difference between correlation and causality*. The fact that two variables move together does not imply that movements in the first variable cause movements in the second variable. Perhaps the causality runs the other way: Movements in the second variable cause movements in the first variable. Or perhaps, as is likely to be the case here, the causality runs both ways: Disposable income affects consumption, *and* consumption affects disposable income.

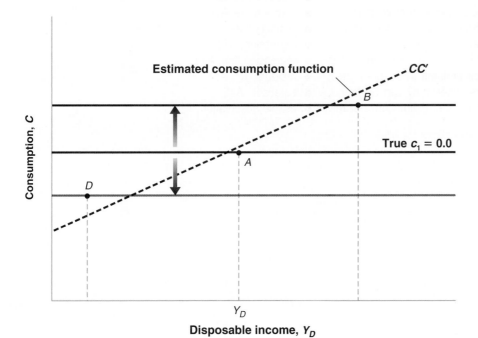

**FIGURE    A3–3**

**A Misleading Regression**

The relation between disposable income and consumption comes from the effect of consumption on income rather than from the effect of income on consumption.

Is there a way out of the correlation-versus-causality problem? If we are interested—and we are—in the effect of disposable income on consumption, can we still learn that from those data? The answer is yes, but only by using more information.

Suppose that we *knew* that a specific change in disposable income was not caused by a change in consumption. Then, by looking at the reaction of consumption to *this* change in disposable income, we could learn how consumption responds to disposable income; we could estimate the propensity to consume.

This answer would seem to simply assume away the problem: How can we know that a change in disposable income is not due to a change in consumption? In fact, sometimes, we can. Suppose, for example, that government embarks on a major increase in defence spending, leading to an increase in demand and, in turn, an increase in output. In that case, if we see both disposable income and consumption increase, we can safely assume that the movement in consumption reflects the effect of disposable income on consumption and thus estimate the propensity to consume.

This example suggests a general strategy:

- Find exogenous variables—that is, variables that affect disposable income but are not, in turn, affected by it.

- Look at the change in consumption in response not to all changes in disposable income—as we did in our earlier regression—but to those changes in disposable income that can be explained by changes in these exogenous variables.

By doing so, we can be confident that what we are estimating is the effect of disposable income on consumption, and not the other way around.

The problem of finding such exogenous variables is known as the **identification problem** in econometrics. These exogenous variables, when they can be found, are called **instruments**. Methods of estimation that rely on the use of such instruments are called **instrumental variable methods**.

When equation (A3.1) is estimated using an instrumental variable method (using changes in lagged U.S. real GDP and changes in lagged exports to the United States as instruments), the estimated equation becomes:

$$(\Delta C_t - \overline{\Delta C}) = 0.57(\Delta Y_{Dt} - \overline{\Delta Y_D}) + \text{residual (A3.2)}$$

Note that the coefficient on disposable income, 0.57, is fairly close to the coefficient 0.61 in equation (A3.1). Our earlier estimate in equation (A3.1) reflected not only the effect of disposable income on consumption, but also the effect of consumption back on disposable income. The use of instruments eliminates this second effect. We would conclude, in Canada's case, that the second effect is quite small.

This short introduction to econometrics is no substitute for a course in econometrics. But it gives you a sense of how economists use data to estimate relations and parameters and to identify causal relations between economic variables.

## KEY TERMS

- causality, A13
- correlation, A13
- degrees of freedom, A12
- dependent variable, A12
- identification problem, A14
- independent variable, A12
- instrumental variable methods, A14
- instruments, A14
- ordinary least squares (OLS), A11
- regression, A11
- regression line, A11
- residual, $\overline{R}^2$, A11
- *t*-statistic, A12
- usable observation, A12

# Appendix 4:
# Symbols Used in This Book

| Symbol | Term | Introduced in Chapter |
|---|---|---|
| $(\ )^d$ | Superscript $^d$ means demanded | |
| $(\ )^e$ | Superscript $^e$ means expected | |
| $(\ )^s$ | Superscript $^s$ means supply | |
| $A$ | Aggregate private spending | 22 |
| | *Also:* labour productivity/state of technology | 9, 17 |
| $\alpha$ | Effect of unemployment rate on inflation rate, given expected inflation | 12 |
| $B$ | Bonds | 4 |
| $B^f$ | Net foreign assets | 18 |
| $\beta$ | Effect of an increase in output growth on the unemployment rate | 13 |
| $C$ | Consumption | 3 |
| $CA$ | Current account balance | 18 |
| $CU$ | Currency | 4 |
| $c$ | Proportion of money held as currency | 4 |
| $c_0$ | Consumption when disposable income equals zero | 3 |
| $c_1$ | Propensity to consume | 3 |
| $D$ | Chequable deposits | 4 |
| | *Also:* real dividend on a stock | 20 |
| $\$D$ | Nominal dividend on a stock | 20 |
| $\delta$ | Depreciation rate | 16 |
| $E$ | Nominal exchange rate (price of foreign currency in terms of domestic currency) | 6 |
| $\bar{E}$ | Fixed nominal exchange rate | 8 |
| $E^e$ | Expected future exchange rate | 6 |
| $\epsilon$ | Real exchange rate | 6 |
| $G$ | Government spending | 3 |
| $g_A$ | Growth rate of technological progress | 17 |
| $g_K$ | Growth rate of capital | 17 |
| $g_M$ | Growth rate of nominal money | 13 |
| $g_N$ | Growth rate of population | 17 |
| $g$ | Growth rate of output | 13 |
| $\bar{g}_y$ | Normal rate of growth of output | 13 |
| $H$ | High-powered money/monetary base/central bank money | 4 |
| | *Also:* human capital | 16 |
| $I$ | Investment | 3 |
| $\bar{I}$ | Investment, taken as exogenous | 3 |
| $I_S$ | Inventory investment | 3 |
| $i$ | Nominal interest rate | 4 |
| $i_1$ | One-year nominal interest rate | 20 |
| $i_2$ | Two-year nominal interest rate | 20 |
| $i^*$ | Foreign nominal interest rate | 6 |
| $K$ | Capital stock | 15 |
| $L$ | Labour force | 2 |
| $M$ | Money stock (nominal) | 4 |

| Symbol | Term | Introduced in Chapter |
|---|---|---|
| $M^d$ | Money demand (nominal) | 4 |
| $M^s$ | Money supply (nominal) | 4 |
| $m$ | Markup of prices over wages | 9 |
| $N$ | Employment | 2 |
| $N_n$ | Natural level of employment | 9 |
| $NX$ | Net exports | 7 |
| $P$ | GDP deflator/CPI/price level | 2 |
| $P^*$ | Foreign price level | 6 |
| $\pi$ | Inflation | 2 |
| $\Pi$ | Profit per unit of capital | 21 |
| $Q$ | Imports | 3 |
| | *Also:* real stock price | 20 |
| $Q^H$ | Real house price | 20 |
| $\$Q$ | Nominal stock price | 20 |
| $R$ | Bank reserves | 4 |
| $R^e$ | Expected real rent on a house | 20 |
| $r$ | Real interest rate | 19 |
| $S$ | Private saving | 3 |
| $s$ | Private saving rate | 16 |
| $T$ | Net taxes (taxes paid by consumers minus transfers) | 3 |
| $Tr$ | Government transfers | 26 |
| $\theta$ | Reserve ratio of banks | 4 |
| $U$ | Unemployment | 2 |
| $u$ | Unemployment rate | 2 |
| $u_n$ | Natural rate of unemployment | 9 |
| $V$ | Present value of a sequence of real payments z | 19 |
| $\$V$ | Present value of a sequence of nominal payments $z | 19 |
| $W$ | Nominal wage | 9 |
| $Y$ | Real GDP/output/supply of goods | 2 |
| $\$Y$ | Nominal GDP | 2 |
| $Y_D$ | Disposable income | 3 |
| $Y_L$ | Labour income | 21 |
| $Y_n$ | Natural level of output | 9 |
| $Y^*$ | Foreign output | 7 |
| $X$ | Exports | 3 |
| $Z$ | Demand for goods | 3 |
| $z$ | Factors that affect the wage, given unemployment | 9 |
| | *Also:* real payment from an asset | 19 |
| $\$z$ | Nominal payment from an asset | 19 |

# GLOSSARY

**above the line, below the line**   In the balance of payments, the items in the *current account* are above the line drawn to divide them from the items in the *capital account,* which appear below the line.

**accelerationist Phillips curve**   See *modified Phillips curve.*

**accommodation**   A change in the money supply by the central bank to maintain a constant interest rate in the face of changes in money demand or in spending.

**accommodative monetary policy**   A situation in which, as economic output increases with a expansionary fiscal policy, the monetary authority increases the money supply and prevents interest rates from increasing.

**adaptive expectations**   A backward-looking method of forming expectations by adjusting for past mistakes.

**adjusted nominal money growth**   Nominal money growth minus normal output growth.

**aggregate demand relation**   The demand for output at a given price level. It is derived from equilibrium in goods and financial markets.

**aggregate output**   Total amount of output produced in the economy.

**aggregate private spending**   The sum of all non-government spending. Also called *private spending.*

**aggregate production function**   The relation between the quantity of aggregate output produced and the quantities of inputs used in production.

**aggregate supply relation**   The price level at which firms are willing to supply a given level of output. It is derived from equilibrium in the labour market.

**American Recovery and Reinvestment Act**   The Act of Congress that cut taxes and increased spending by the U.S. federal government in response to the 2008 economic crisis.

**animal spirits**   A term introduced by Keynes to refer to movements in investment that could not be explained by movements in current variables.

**anticipated money**   Movements in nominal money that could have been predicted based on the information available at some time in the past.

**appreciation**   An increase in the price of the domestic currency in terms of a foreign currency. Corresponds to a decrease in the exchange rate.

**appropriability (of research results)**   The extent to which firms benefit from the results of their research and development efforts.

**arbitrage**   The proposition that the expected rates of return on two financial assets must be equal. Also called *risky arbitrage* to distinguish it from *riskless arbitrage,* the proposition that the actual rates of return on two financial assets must be the same.

**austerity**   A generic term for fiscal policies that are intended to reduce a deficit—some combination of tax increases; cuts in transfers and cuts in spending.

**automatic stabilizer**   The fact that a decrease in output leads, under given tax and spending rules, to an increase in the budget deficit. This increase in the budget deficit in turn increases demand and thus stabilizes output.

**autonomous spending**   That component of the demand for goods that does not depend on the level of output.

**average hours**   The average hours per week worked by Canadians who are employed either full time or part time.

**backloading**   A policy choice to reduce a deficit over time where, in announcing a multi-year deficit reduction program, most of the reduction takes place in years further into the future.

**balance of payments**   A set of accounts that summarizes a country's transactions with the rest of the world.

**balanced budget**   A budget in which taxes are equal to government spending.

**balanced growth**   The situation in which output, capital, and effective labour all grow at the same rate.

**bands (for exchange rates)**   The limits within which the exchange rate is allowed to move under a fixed exchange rate system.

**Bank of Canada**   Canada's central bank.

***Bank of Canada Act***   The Act of Parliament that describes the responsibilities and structure of the Bank of Canada.

**Bank Rate**   The top of the 50 basis point target band for the overnight rate as set by the Bank of Canada.

**bank run**   Simultaneous attempts by depositors to withdraw their funds from a bank.

**bargaining power**   The relative strength of each side in a negotiation or a dispute.

**base year**   When constructing real GDP by evaluating quantities in different years using a given set of prices, the year to which this given set of prices corresponds.

**Basel I, Basel II:**   Agreements (associated with the city of Basel in Switzerland) where a group of richer countries agree to impose similar and larger capital ratios on commercial banks.

**behavioural equation**   An equation that captures some aspect of behaviour.

**bilateral real exchange rate**   The real exchange rate between two countries.

**bond**   A financial asset that promises a stream of known payments over some period of time.

**bond rating**   The assessment of a bond based on its default risk.

**brain drain**   A term used to describe the emigration of highly educated workers from one country to another.

**broad money**   See *M2+.*

**budget deficit**   When the excess of government expenditures (outlays) over government revenues is expressed as a positive number.

**business cycle theory**   The study of macroeconomic fluctuations.

**business cycles**   See *output fluctuations.*

**business gross fixed capital formation**   Installation of new physical capital by the corporate sector

**business investment**   A shorter name for *business gross fixed capital formation.*

**Canada bond**   A bond issued by the Canadian federal government with a maturity of 1 to 30 years.

**Canada Deposit Insurance Corporation (CDIC)**   The agency of the federal government that implements deposit insurance in the broader banking sector.

**Canada Pension Plan (CPP)**   One of the ways in which the federal government provides pensions to elderly persons in Canada. The CPP is partly a pay-as-you-go plan and partly a funded plan. The Quebec Pension Plan (QPP) is the equivalent plan for Quebecers.

**capital account**   In the balance of payments, a summary of a country's asset transactions with the rest of the world.

**capital accumulation**   Increase in the capital stock.

**capital consumption allowances**   The estimated amount of the economic depreciation (wearing out) of corporate and public sector capital.

**capital controls**   Restrictions on the foreign assets domestic residents can hold and on the domestic assets foreigners can hold.

**capital depreciation**   See *capital consumption allowances.*

**capital ratio**   Ratio of the capital of a bank to its assets.

**cash flow**   The net flow of cash a firm is receiving.

**causality**   A relation between cause and effect.

**central bank money**   Money issued by the central bank. Also known as the *monetary base* and *high-powered money.*

**central parity**   The reference value of the exchange rate around which the exchange rate is allowed to move under a fixed exchange rate system. The centre of the *band.*

**changes in business inventories**   In the national income and product accounts, the change in the physical volume of inventories held by businesses.

**chequable deposits**   Deposits at banks and other financial institutions against which cheques can be written.

**Cobb–Douglas production function**   A frequently used functional relationship among output, capital input, and labour input where there are constant returns to scale.

**collateral**   The asset pledged in order to get a loan. In case of default, the asset goes to the lender.

**collateralized debt obligation (CDO)**   Security based on an underlying portfolio of assets.

**collective bargaining**   Bargaining about wages between firms and unions.

**common currency area**   A group of geographic units whose economics share the same currency.

**compensation of employees**   The sum of payments made directly to employees—wages and salaries—and employer's social contributions.

**confidence band**   When estimating the dynamic effect of one variable on another, the range of values where we can be confident the true dynamic effect lies.

**constant returns to scale** The proposition that a proportional increase (or decrease) of all inputs leads to the same proportional increase (or decrease) in output.

**consumer price index (CPI)** The cost of a given list of goods and services consumed by a typical consumer.

**consumption (C)** Goods and services purchased by consumers.

**consumption function** A function that relates consumption to its determinants.

**consumption of fixed capital: corporations** The estimated amount of the economic depreciation (wearing out) of corporate sector capital.

**consumption of fixed capital: unincorporated business** The estimated amount of the economic depreciation (wearing out) of capital in the unincorporated business sector.

**contractionary open market operation** An open market operation in which the central bank sells bonds to decrease the money supply.

**convergence** The tendency for countries with lower output per capita to grow faster, leading to convergence of output per capita across countries.

**coordination (of macroeconomic policies between two countries)** The joint design of macroeconomic policies to improve the economic situation in the two countries.

**Core inflation** a measure of inflation that excludes the effects of food and energy prices as well as changes in indirect tax rates.

**corporate bond** A bond issued by a corporation.

**corporate profits** In the national income and product accounts, firms' revenues minus costs (including interest payments) and minus depreciation.

**correlation** A measure of the way two variables move together. A positive correlation indicates that the two variables tend to move in the same direction. A negative correlation indicates that the two variables tend to move in opposite directions. A correlation of zero indicates that there is no apparent relation between the two variables.

**cost of living index** The average price of a consumption bundle.

**coupon bond** A bond that promises multiple payments before maturity and one payment at maturity.

**coupon payments** The payments before maturity on a coupon bond.

**coupon rate** The ratio of the coupon payment to the face value of a coupon bond.

**crawling peg** An exchange rate mechanism in which the exchange rate is allowed to move over time according to a pre-specified formula.

**credibility** The degree to which people and markets believe that a policy announcement will actually be implemented and followed through.

**credit channel** The channel through which monetary policy works by affecting the amount of loans made by banks to firms.

**currency** Coins and bills.

**currency board** An exchange rate system in which: (i) the central bank stands ready to buy or sell foreign currency at the official exchange rate; (ii) the central bank cannot engage in open market operations, that is buying or selling government bonds.

**current account** In the balance of payments, the summary of a country's payments to and from the rest of the world.

**current account balance** The change in a country's net foreign assets or debts.

**current yield** The ratio of the coupon payment to the price of a coupon bond.

**cyclically adjusted budget balance (CABB)** A measure of what the government budget balance would be under existing tax and spending rules, if output were at its natural level. Also called the *structural budget deficit, full-employment deficit, cyclically adjusted deficit, standardized employment deficit.*

**debt finance** Financing based on loans or the issuance of bonds.

**debt monetization** The printing of money to finance a deficit.

**debt ratio** See *debt-to-GDP ratio.*

**debt repudiation** A unilateral decision by a debtor not to repay its debt.

**debt rescheduling** A situation in which, as debts were to come due, they could not be repaid. The terms of repayment for the debts are changed—either the time of repayment is put off to the future, the amount of debt owed is reduced, or the interest rate is lowered, or all three. Also called *debt restructuring.*

**debt restructuring** see debt rescheduling.

**debt-to-GDP ratio** The ratio of total government debt to gross domestic product. Also called simply the *debt ratio.*

**decreasing returns to capital** The property that increases in capital lead to smaller and smaller increases in output as the level of capital increases.

**decreasing returns to labour** The property that increases in labour lead to smaller and smaller increases in output as the level of labour increases.

**default risk** The risk that the issuer of a bond will not pay back the full amount promised by the bond.

**deficit** See *budget deficit.*

**deflation** Negative inflation.

**deflation trap** A situation in which low economic activity leads to deflation and then expected deflation which, at the same nominal interest rate, is a higher real interest rate which further lowers economic activity.

**degrees of freedom** The number of usable observations in a *regression* minus the number of parameters to be estimated.

**demand deposit** A bank account that allows depositors to write cheques or get cash on demand, up to an amount equal to the account balance.

**demand for domestic goods** The demand for domestic goods by people, firms, and governments, both domestic and foreign. Equal to the domestic demand for goods plus net exports.

**Department of Finance** The ministry of the federal government responsible for the broad outline of fiscal policy in Canada. The Minister of Finance is usually the federal politician most closely linked to presentation of the federal budget.

**dependent variable** A variable whose value is determined by one or more other variables.

**deposit insurance** A government program that provides insurance for depositors against the financial failure of the bank where the deposits are held. The banks must pay a premium for this service and follow some regulations about the distributions of their loans.

**depreciation** A decrease in the price of the domestic currency in terms of a foreign currency. Corresponds to an increase in the exchange rate.

**depreciation rate** A measure of how much usefulness a piece of capital loses from one period to the next.

**depression** A deep and long-lasting recession.

**devaluation** An increase in the exchange rate in a fixed exchange-rate system.

**discount bond** A bond that promises a single payment at maturity.

**discount factor** The value today of a dollar (or other national currency unit) at some time in the future.

**discount rate** The interest rate used to discount a sequence of future payments. Equal to the nominal interest rate when discounting future nominal payments, to the real interest rate when discounting future real payments.

**discouraged worker** A person who has given up looking for employment.

**disinflation** A decrease in inflation.

**disposable income (Y_D)** The income that remains once consumers have received transfers from the government and paid their taxes.

**dividends** The portion of a corporation's profits that the firm pays out each period to shareholders.

**dollar GDP** See *nominal GDP.*

**dollarization** The use of U.S. dollars in domestic transactions in a country other than the United States.

**domestic demand for goods** The sum of consumption, investment, and government spending.

**dual labour market** A labour market that combines a *primary labour market* and a *secondary labour market.*

**durable goods** Commodities that can be stored and have an average life of at least three years.

**duration of unemployment** The period of time during which a worker is unemployed.

**dynamics** Movements of one or more economic variables over time.

**dynamic stochastic general equilibrium** Macro models derived from optimization by firms, consumers, and workers.

**Easterlin paradox** an initial finding by economist Richard Easterlin that in rich countries increases in income per capita did not lead to increases in happiness.

**econometrics** Statistical methods applied to economics.

**effective demand** Synonym for *aggregate demand.*

**effective labour** The number of workers in an economy times the state of technology.

**effective real exchange rate** See *multilateral exchange rate.*

**efficiency wage** The wage at which a worker is performing a job most efficiently or productively.

**efficiency wage theories**   These theories of wage determination link an increase in the wage paid to workers to an increase in the efficiency or productivity.

**employer's social contributions**   Payments made by employers on behalf of employees to social programs.

**Emigration**   number of people leaving Canada to live permanently in another country.

**Employment Insurance**   This is the federal program that provides benefits to workers who become unemployed through layoffs or financial failures of firms. It also provides maternity, paternity, and adoption benefit. Also called Unemployment Insurance in the past.

**employment rate**   The percentage of the population that could work that are employed.

**employment-to-population ratio**   This is the employment rate in ratio form: the proportion of the population over 15 years of age and able to work that are employed.

**endogenous variable**   A variable that depends on other variables in a model and is thus explained within the model.

**equilibrium**   The equality between demand and supply.

**equilibrium condition**   The condition that supply be equal to demand.

**equilibrium in the goods market**   The condition that the supply of goods be equal to the demand for goods.

**equity finance**   Financing based on the issuance of shares.

**equity premium**   Risk premium required by investors to hold stocks rather than short-term bonds.

**euro**   The new European currency that replaced national currencies in 12 countries in 2002.

**euro area**   The 17 countries, as of 2013, that replaced national currencies with the euro.

**Euro Plus Pact**   A set of rules created in 2011 to apply to national fiscal policies in countries using the euro. The rules are intended to reduce deficits and debt.

**European Central Bank (ECB)**   The central bank, located in Frankfurt, in charge of determining monetary policy in the euro zone.

**European Monetary System (EMS)**   A fixed exchange rate system in place in most of the countries of the European Union, from 1978 to 1999.

**European Union (EU)**   The 27 countries, as of 2013, that form an economic zone in Europe where people and goods move freely. Formerly called the European Community.

**exchange rate mechanism (ERM)**   The rules that determined the bands within which the member countries of the European Monetary System had to maintain their bilateral exchange rate.

**exogenous variable**   A variable that is not explained within a model but rather is taken as given.

**expansion**   A period of positive GDP growth.

**expansionary open market operation**   An open market operation in which the central bank buys bonds to increase the money supply.

**expectations hypothesis**   The hypothesis that financial investors are risk neutral, which implies expected returns on all financial assets have to be equal.

**expectations-augmented Phillips curve**   See *modified Phillips curve*.

**expected present discounted value**   The value today of an expected sequence of future payments. Also called *present discounted value* or *present value*.

**exports ($X$)**   The purchases of domestic goods and services by foreigners.

**face value (on a bond)**   The single payment at maturity promised by a discount bond.

**fad**   A period of time during which, for reasons of fashion or overoptimism, financial investors are willing to pay more than the fundamental value of a stock.

**federal funds rate**   The interest rate determined by equilibrium in the federal funds market. The interest rate affected most directly by changes in monetary policy.

**Federal Open Market Committee (FOMC)**   A committee composed of the seven governors of the Fed, plus five District Bank presidents. The FOMC directs the activities of the *Open Market Desk*.

**Federal Reserve Bank (the Fed)**   The U.S. central bank.

**fertility of research**   The degree to which spending on research and development translates into new ideas and new products.

**financial account**   In the balance of payments, a summary of a country's asset transactions with the rest of the world.

**financial intermediary**   A financial institution that receives funds from people and/or firms, and uses these funds to make loans or buy financial assets.

**financial investment**   The purchase of financial assets.

**financial markets**   The markets in which financial assets are bought and sold.

**financial wealth**   The value of all one's financial assets minus all financial liabilities. Sometimes called *wealth* for short.

**fine tuning**   A macroeconomic policy aimed at precisely hitting a given target, such as constant unemployment or constant output growth.

**fire sale prices**   Very low asset prices, reflecting the need for sellers to sell, and the absence of sufficient buyers, because of liquidity constraints.

**fiscal consolidation**   See *fiscal contraction*.

**fiscal contraction**   A policy aimed at reducing the budget deficit through a decrease in government spending or an increase in taxation. Also called *fiscal consolidation* or *austerity*.

**fiscal dominance**   A situation in which fiscal policy and fiscal needs drive the behaviour of the money supply and central bank.

**fiscal expansion**   An increase in government spending or a decrease in taxation, which leads to an increase in the budget deficit.

**fiscal policy**   A government's choice of taxes and spending.

**fiscal year**   An accounting period of 12 months. In Canada, the fiscal year of most provincial governments and the federal government runs from April 1 of one calendar year to March 31 of the next calendar year. Thus, fiscal year 2002–2003 refers to the period from April 1, 2002, to March 31, 2003. Corporations and other accounting units also declare fiscal years, which need not correspond to calendar years.

**Fisher effect**   The proposition that in the long run an increase in nominal money growth is reflected in an identical increase in both the nominal interest rate and the inflation rate, leaving the real interest rate unchanged. Also called *Fisher hypothesis*.

**Fisher hypothesis**   See *Fisher effect*.

**fixed exchange rate**   An exchange rate between the currencies of two or more countries that is fixed at some level and adjusted only infrequently.

**fixed investment**   See *investment (I)*.

**flexible exchange rate**   See *floating exchange rate*.

**float**   The exchange rate is said to float when it is determined in the foreign exchange market, without central bank intervention.

**floating exchange rate**   An exchange rate determined in the foreign-exchange market without central bank intervention.

**flow**   A variable that can be expressed as a quantity per unit of time (such as income).

**foreign direct investment**   The purchase of existing firms or the development of new firms by foreign investors.

**foreign exchange**   Foreign currency; all currencies other than the domestic currency of a given country.

**foreign-exchange reserves**   Foreign assets held by the central bank.

**foreign portfolio investment**   Foreign portfolio investment is foreign holdings of Canadian stocks without majority control of the firms. It also includes foreign holdings of bank loans to Canadians or bonds issued by Canadians.

**four tigers**   The four Asian economies of Singapore, Taiwan, Hong Kong, and South Korea.

**full-employment deficit**   See *cyclically adjusted deficit*.

**fully funded old age security system**   Retirement system in which the contributions of current workers are invested in financial assets, with the proceeds (principal and interest) given back to the workers when they retire.

**fundamental value (of a stock)**   The present value of expected dividends.

**G-8**   The eight major economic powers in the world: the United States, Japan, France, Germany, the United Kingdom, Italy, Russia, and Canada.

**game**   *Strategic interactions* between *players*.

**game theory**   The prediction of outcomes from *games*.

**GDP adjusted for inflation**   See *real GDP*.

**GDP deflator**   The ratio of nominal GDP to real GDP; a measure of the overall price level. Gives the average price of the final goods produced in the economy.

**GDP growth**   The growth rate of real GDP in year $t$; equal to $(Y_t - Y_{t-1})/Y_{t-1}$.

**GDP in 2007 dollars**   See *real GDP*.

**GDP in constant dollars**   See *real GDP*.

**GDP in current dollars**   See *nominal GDP*.

**GDP in terms of goods**   See *real GDP*.

**general equilibrium**   A situation in which there is equilibrium in all markets (goods, financial, and labour).

**general government**   A term for the government sector that includes all levels of government: federal, provincial, and local.

**general government's final consumption expenditure**   Consumption expenditure on goods and services by all levels of government.

**general government's gross fixed capital formation**   Expenditure on capital goods by all levels of government.

**geometric series**   A mathematical sequence in which the ratio of one term to the preceding term remains the same. A sequence of the form $1 + c + c^2 + \cdots + c^n$.

**gold standard**   A system in which a country fixed the price of its currency in terms of gold and stood ready to exchange gold for currency at the stated parity.

**golden-rule level of capital**   The level of capital at which long-run consumption is maximized.

**government bond**   A bond issued by a government or a government agency.

**government budget constraint**   The budget constraint faced by the government. The constraint implies that an excess of spending over revenues must be financed by borrowing, and thus leads to an increase in debt.

**government spending ($G$)**   The sum of general government's final consumption expenditure and general government's gross fixed capital formation.

**government transfers**   Payments made by the government to individuals that are not in exchange for goods or services. Example: Canada Pension Plan payments or welfare payments.

**Great Depression**   The severe worldwide depression of the 1930s.

**gross domestic product (GDP)**   A measure of aggregate output in the national income accounts. (The market value of the goods and services produced by labour and property located in Canada.)

**gross mixed income**   Total incomes generated in the unincorporated business sector.

**gross national product (GNP)**   Income accruing to factors of production, both labour and capital, owned by Canadian residents.

**gross operating surplus**   The sum of incomes accruing to capital in the corporate, government, and non-profit sectors.

**growth**   The steady increase in aggregate output over time.

**Guaranteed Income Supplement (GIS)**   This is a major federal government program of transfers to the elderly who are also poor and have no other support. Your income must fall below a certain threshold to receive the GIS.

**haircut**   The loss on the value of debt experienced by the owner of the debt as a result of debt rescheduling or debt restructuring.

**hedonic pricing**   An approach to calculating real GDP that treats goods as providing a collection of characteristics, each with an implicit price.

**high-powered money**   See *central bank money.*

**hires**   Workers newly employed by firms.

**household final consumption expenditure**   Goods and services purchased by consumers.

**housing wealth**   The value of the housing stock.

**human capital**   The set of skills possessed by the workers in an economy.

**human wealth**   The labour-income component of wealth.

**hyperinflation**   Very high inflation.

**identification problem**   In econometrics, the problem of finding whether correlation between variables $X$ and $Y$ indicates a causal relation from $X$ to $Y$, or from $Y$ to $X$, or both. This problem is solved by finding exogenous variables, called *instruments*, that affect $X$ and do not affect $Y$ directly, or affect $Y$ and do not affect $X$ directly.

**identity**   An equation that holds by definition, denoted by the sign $\equiv$.

**illiquidity**   A situation in which financial markets do not allow the sale of securities that are usually liquid, that is, easily sold for cash.

**Immigration**   number of people permanently moving to Canada from other countries

**imports ($Q$)**   The purchases of foreign goods and services by domestic consumers, firms, and the government.

**income**   The flow of revenue from work, rental income, interest, and dividends.

**independent variable**   A variable that is taken as given in a relation or in a model.

**index number**   A number, such as the GDP deflator, that has no natural level and is thus set to equal some value (typically 1 or 100) in a given period.

**indexed bond**   A bond that promises payments adjusted for inflation. These are also called *real return bonds.*

**indirect taxes**   Taxes on goods and services, primarily sales taxes.

**Industrial policy**   a term used to describes government policies, tax reductions, subsidies to direct government investment in a specific sector of the economy to encourage growth

**inflation**   A sustained rise in the general level of prices.

**inflation rate**   The rate at which the price level increases over time.

**inflation targeting**   The conduct of monetary policy so as to achieve a given inflation rate over time.

**inflation targets**   If a central bank uses inflation targets it sets a public target, usually a band, for the desired rate of inflation. In Canada, the inflation target is 1 to 3%.

**inflation tax**   The product of the rate of inflation and real money balances.

**inflation-adjusted deficit**   The correct economic measure of the budget deficit: the sum of the *primary deficit* and real interest payments.

**Infrastructure**   A term referring to capital owned by the government

**instrumental variable methods**   In econometrics, methods of estimation that use *instruments* to estimate causal relations between different variables.

**instruments**   In econometrics, the exogenous variables that allow the identification problem to be solved.

**intellectual property products**   Investment spending to develop intellectual property; also called *research and development spending.*

**intercept**   In a linear relation between two variables, the value of the first variable when the second variable is equal to zero.

**interest parity condition**   See *uncovered interest parity relation.*

**intermediate good**   A good used in the production of a final good.

**International Monetary Fund (IMF)**   The principal international economic organization. Publishes *World Economic Outlook* annually and *International Financial Statistics (IFS)* monthly.

**inventory investment ($I_S$)**   The difference between production and sales.

**investment ($I$)**   Purchases of new houses and apartments by people, and purchases of new capital goods (machines and plants) by firms and the non-profit sector.

**investment in inventories**   The difference between production and sales.

**investment income**   In the current account, income received by domestic residents from their holdings of foreign assets.

**IS curve**   A downward-sloping curve relating output to the interest rate. The curve corresponding to the *IS relation,* the equilibrium condition for the goods market.

**IS relation**   An equilibrium condition stating that the demand for goods must be equal to the supply of goods, or equivalently that investment must be equal to saving. The equilibrium condition for the goods market.

**J-curve**   A curve depicting the initial deterioration in the trade balance caused by a real depreciation, followed by an improvement in the trade balance.

**junior securities**   Securities that, if bankruptcy of the issuer occurs, are paid after senior securities.

**junk bond**   A bond with a high risk of default.

**Keynesians**   Term used in a variety of ways intended to convey that the person or persons discussed places particular emphasis on the macroeconomic framework proposed by John Maynard Keynes.

**labour force**   The sum of those employed and those unemployed.

**Labour Force Survey (LFS)**   A large monthly survey of Canadian households used in particular to compute the unemployment rate.

**labour hoarding**   The practice of retaining workers during a period of low product demand rather than laying them off.

**labour in efficiency units**   See *effective labour.*

**labour productivity**   The ratio of output to the number of workers.

**layoffs**   Workers who lose their jobs either temporarily or permanently.

**leverage ratio**   Ratio of the assets of the bank to its capital (the inverse of the capital ratio).

**Libor rate**   Rate at which banks lend to each other.

**life cycle theory of consumption**   The theory of consumption, developed initially by Franco Modigliani, that emphasizes that the planning horizon of consumers is their lifetimes.

**linear relation**   A relation between two variables such that a one-unit increase in one variable always leads to an increase of $n$ units in the other variable.

**liquid** An asset is "liquid" when it can be sold for cash quickly and without significant transactions costs. Thus, a Treasury bill is very liquid. A house is not a liquid asset: Although it can be converted into cash, it may take some time and involve large transactions costs. Assets vary in their liquidity.

**liquid asset** An asset that can be sold easily and at little cost.

**liquidity facilities** A mechanism set up in the 2008 crisis to allow commercial banks to borrow directly from the central bank—often with a lower quality of collateral than previously required for such loans.

**liquidity preference** The term introduced by Keynes to denote the demand for money.

**liquidity trap** The case where nominal interest rates are close to zero, and monetary policy cannot therefore decrease them further.

**LM curve** An upward-sloping curve relating the interest rate to output. The curve corresponding to the *LM relation,* the equilibrium condition for financial markets.

**LM relation** An equilibrium condition stating that the demand for money must be equal to the supply of money. The equilibrium condition for financial markets.

**loan-to-value (LTV) ratio** The size of a loan on a house relative to the value of the house.

**logarithmic scale** A scale in which the same proportional increase represents the same distance on the scale so that a variable that grows at a constant rate is represented by a straight line.

**long run** A period of time extending over decades.

**long-term bond** A bond with maturity of 10 years or more.

**Lucas critique** The proposition, put forth by Robert Lucas, that existing relations between economic variables may change when policy changes. An example is the apparent trade-off between inflation and unemployment, which may disappear if policy makers try to exploit it.

**M1** The sum of currency, traveller's cheques, and chequable deposits—assets that can be used directly in transactions. Also called *narrow money* and *denoted M1+ or M1+(gross)*

**M2** M1 plus money market mutual fund shares, money market and savings deposits, and time deposits. Also called *broad money,* sometimes *denoted M2+ or M2+(gross).*

**Maastricht treaty** A treaty signed in 1991 that defined the steps involved in the transition to a common currency for the European Union.

**machinery and equipment** Investment in new machinery and equipment by the incorporated business sector.

**macro-prudential tools** A set of regulations imposed on the commercial banking sector intended to help stabilize the macroeconomy.

**macroeconomics** The study of aggregate economic variables, such as production for the economy as a whole, or the average price of goods.

**marginal propensity to import** The effect on imports from an additional dollar in income.

**market for overnight funds** This is the financial market in which banks and other financial institutions lend money to each other for one day "overnight."

**Marshall–Lerner condition** The condition under which a real depreciation leads to an increase in net exports.

**maturity** The length of time over which a financial asset (typically a bond) promises to make payments to the holder.

**medium run** A period of time between the *short run* and the *long run.*

**medium-term bond** A bond with maturity of one to 10 years.

**menu cost** The cost of changing a price.

**merchandise trade** Exports and imports of goods.

**microeconomics** The study of production and prices in specific markets.

**models of endogenous growth** Models in which accumulation of physical and human capital can sustain growth even in the absence of technological progress.

**modified Phillips curve** The curve that plots the change in the inflation rate against the unemployment rate. Also called an *expectations–augmented Phillips curve* or an *accelerationist Phillips curve.*

**monetarism, monetarists** A group of economists in the 1960s, led by Milton Friedman, who argued that monetary policy had powerful effects on activity.

**monetary aggregate** The market value of a sum of liquid assets. *M1* is a monetary aggregate that includes only the most liquid assets.

**monetary base** See *central bank money.*

**monetary contraction** A change in monetary policy that leads to an increase in the interest rate. Also called *monetary tightening.*

**monetary expansion** A change in monetary policy that leads to a decrease in the interest rate.

**monetary–fiscal policy mix** The combination of monetary and fiscal policies in effect at a given time.

**monetary tightening** See *monetary contraction.*

**money** Those financial assets that can be used directly to buy goods.

**money growth rate** The rate of growth of the money stock.

**money market funds** Financial institutions that receive funds from people and use them to buy short-term bonds.

**money multiplier** The increase in the money supply resulting from a one-dollar increase in central bank money.

**mortgage-backed security (MBS)** A security (or bond) issued on which the interest to be paid is derived from a group of pooled mortgages.

**mortgage lender** Any financial institution that lends money as a mortgage; a loan for which property is the collateral.

**multilateral real exchange rate** The real exchange rate between a country and its trading partners, computed as a weighted average of bilateral real exchange rates. Also called the *trade-weighted real exchange rate* or *effective real exchange rate* or *the multilateral exchange rate.*

**multiplier** The ratio of the change in an *endogenous variable* to the change in an *exogenous variable* (for example, the ratio of the change in output to a change in autonomous spending).

**Mundell–Fleming model** A model of simultaneous equilibrium in both goods and financial markets for an open economy.

**national income and expenditure accounts** The system of accounts used to describe the evolution of the sum, the composition, and the distribution of aggregate output.

**natural experiment** A real-world event that can be used to test an economic theory.

**natural level of employment** The level of employment that prevails when unemployment is equal to its natural rate.

**natural level of output** The level of production that prevails when employment is equal to its natural level.

**natural population growth** The excess of births over deaths in a given period of time.

**natural rate of unemployment** The unemployment rate at which price and wage decisions are consistent.

**neoclassical synthesis** A consensus in macroeconomics, developed in the early 1950s, based on an integration of Keynes's ideas and the ideas of earlier economists.

**net capital flows** Capital flows from the rest of the world to the domestic economy minus capital flows to the rest of the world from the domestic economy.

**net exports (X − Q)** The difference between exports and imports. Also called the *trade balance.*

**net immigration** Immigration minus emigration in a given period of time.

**net international investment position** A measure of Canada's net foreign assets or debts.

**net investment income** Receipts of factor income from abroad minus payments of factor income to nonresidents. This item measures service payments or Canada's net foreign debts.

**net mixed income** Total incomes earned by the unincorporated business sector after subtracting capital consumption allowances accruing to capital owned by that sector.

**net operating surplus: corporations** Total profits earned by the incorporated business sector after subtracting capital consumption allowances accruing to capital owned by that sector.

**net transfers paid** In the current account, the value of transfers to other countries paid less the value of transfers received from other countries.

**neutrality of money** The proposition that an increase in nominal money has no effect on output or the interest rate but is reflected entirely in a proportional increase in the price level.

**new classicals** A group of economists who interpret fluctuations as the effects of shocks in competitive markets with fully flexible prices and wages.

**new growth theory** Recent developments in growth theory that explore the determinants of technological progress and the role of increasing returns to scale in growth.

**new Keynesians** A group of economists who believe in the importance of nominal rigidities in fluctuations, and are exploring the role of market imperfections in explaining fluctuations.

**Nikkei index** An index of the nominal value of stocks in Japan.

**nominal exchange rate**   The price of foreign currency in terms of domestic currency. The number of units of domestic currency you can get for one unit of foreign currency.

**nominal GDP**   The sum of the quantities of final goods produced in an economy times their current price. Also known as *dollar GDP* and *GDP in current dollars.*

**nominal interest rate**   Interest rate in terms of the national currency (in terms of dollars in Canada). Tells us how many dollars one has to repay in the future in exchange for one dollar today.

**nominal rigidities**   The slow adjustment of nominal wages and prices to changes in economic activity.

**nonaccelerating inflation rate of unemployment (NAIRU)**   The unemployment rate at which inflation neither decreases nor increases. See *natural rate of unemployment.*

**non-durable goods**   Commodities that can be stored but have an average life of less than three years.

**non-human wealth**   The financial and housing component of wealth.

**non-profit institutions serving household final consumption expenditure**   The part of household consumption produced in the non-profit sector.

**nonresidential investment**   The purchase of new capital goods by firms: *structures* and *producer durable equipment.*

**nonresidential structures**   Investment in new buildings by the incorporated business sector.

**normal growth rate**   The rate of output growth needed to maintain a constant unemployment rate.

**North American Free Trade Agreement (NAFTA)**   An agreement signed by the United States, Canada, and Mexico in which the three countries agreed to establish all North America as a free-trade zone.

**not in the labour force**   Number of people who are neither employed nor looking for employment.

***n*-year interest rate**   See *yield to maturity.*

**official international reserves**   Holdings of foreign assets by the federal government. These are held to allow intervention in foreign exchange markets.

**Okun's law**   The relation between GDP growth and the change in the unemployment rate.

**Old Age Security (OAS)**   A major federal program that transfers funds to older Canadians. Every Canadian over the age of 65 receives an OAS payment. Higher-income older Canadians repay a portion of this payment through their income taxes.

**open market operation**   The purchase or sale of government bonds by the central bank for the purpose of increasing or decreasing the money supply.

**openness in factor markets**   The opportunity for firms to choose where to locate production and for workers to choose where to work and whether or not to migrate.

**openness in financial markets**   The opportunity for financial investors to choose between domestic and foreign financial assets.

**openness in goods markets**   The opportunity for consumers and firms to choose between domestic and foreign goods.

**optimal control**   The control of a system (a machine, a rocket, an economy) by means of mathematical methods.

**optimal control theory**   The set of mathematical methods used for *optimal control.*

**optimal currency area**   Two regions that share the same currency are a currency union or currency area. If they are in an optimal currency area, then they either experience similar economic shocks or share complete labour mobility.

**ordinary least squares**   A statistical method to find the best fitting relation between two or more variables.

**Organisation for Economic Co-operation and Development (OECD)**   An international organization that collects and studies economic data for many countries. Most of the world's rich countries belong to the OECD.

**Organization of Petroleum Exporting Countries (OPEC)**   A group of countries who export petroleum and make a joint decision on total production of petroleum within their group. In the 1970s this group controlled a large proportion of world petroleum production.

**output fluctuations**   Movements in output around its trend.

**output per capita**   A country's gross domestic product divided by its population.

**overnight interest rate**   The interest rate charged for lending and borrowing overnight.

**overshooting**   The large movement in the exchange rate triggered by a monetary expansion or contraction.

**panel data set**   A data set that gives the values of one or more variables for many individuals or many firms over some period of time.

**paradox of saving**   The result that an attempt by people to save more may lead both to a decline in output and to unchanged saving.

**parameter**   A coefficient in a behavioural equation.

**participation rate**   The ratio of the labour force to the noninstitutional civilian population.

**patent**   The legal right granted to a person or firm to exclude anyone else from the production or use of a new product or technique for a certain period of time.

**pay-as-you-go social security system**   Retirement system in which the contributions of current workers are used to pay benefits to retirees.

**peg**   The exchange rate to which a country commits under a fixed exchange rate system.

**perfect capital mobility**   The situation where there are no regulatory controls or barriers placed on the purchase of assets across international borders.

**permanent income theory of consumption**   The theory of consumption, developed by Milton Friedman, that emphasizes that people make consumption decisions based not on current income, but on their notion of permanent income.

**Phillips curve**   The curve that plots the relation between (1) movements in inflation and (2) unemployment. The original Phillips curve captured the relation between the inflation rate and the unemployment rate. The modified *Phillips curve* captures the relation between (1) the change in the inflation rate and (2) the unemployment rate.

**players**   The participants in a *game.* Depending on the context, players may be people, firms, governments, and so on.

**point-year of excess unemployment**   A difference between the actual unemployment rate and the natural unemployment rate of one percentage point for one year.

**policy mix**   See *monetary–fiscal policy mix.*

**political business cycle**   Fluctuations in economic activity caused by the manipulation of the economy for electoral gain.

**present value**   See *expected present discounted value.*

**price level**   The general level of prices in an economy.

**price-setting relation**   The relation between the price chosen by firms, the nominal wage, and the markup.

**primary deficit**   Government spending, excluding interest payments on the debt, minus government revenues. (The negative of the *primary surplus.*)

**primary income balance**   The difference between earnings on foreign assets and payments on foreign debts.

**primary income paid**   Part of Gross Domestic Product, incomes earned within a national border, is generated by assets owned by non-residents. The largest component is interest and dividends on assets within a domestic country owned by non-residents. A smaller component is labour income earned by non-residents temporarily working within the domestic country and sending income abroad.

**primary income received**   Countries earn part of their Gross National Product on assets located beyond their borders. The largest component is investment income, interest and dividends on foreign assets. A smaller component is labour income earned by domestic residents temporarily working abroad and sending income back home.

**primary labour market**   A labour market where jobs are good, wages are high, and turnover is low. Contrast to the *secondary labour market.*

**primary surplus**   Government revenues minus government spending, excluding interest payments on the debt.

**private saving (*S*)**   Saving by consumers. The value of consumers' disposable income minus their consumption.

**production function**   The relation between the quantity of output and the quantities of inputs used in production.

**profitability**   The expected present discounted value of profits.

**propagation mechanism**   The dynamic effects of a *shock* on output and its components.

**propensity to consume ($c_1$)**   The effect of an additional dollar of disposable income on consumption. Also called *marginal propensity to consume.*

**propensity to save**   The effect of an additional dollar of disposable income on saving (equal to one minus the propensity to consume). Also called *marginal propensity to save.*

**public saving (*T–G*)**   Saving by the government; equal to government revenues minus government spending. Also called the *budget surplus.* (A *budget deficit* represents public dissaving.)

**purchasing power** Income in terms of goods.

**purchasing power parity (PPP)** A method of adjustment used to allow for international comparisons of GDP.

**quantitative easing I (QEI), quantative easing II (QEII)** The actions taken by the Federal Reserve during the crisis to increase the money supply even when the interest rate was already zero.

**Quebec Pension Plan (QPP)** The major way in which the Quebec government provides pensions to elderly persons in Quebec. The QPP is partly a pay-as-you-go plan and partly a funded plan. The Canada Pension Plan (CPP) is the equivalent plan for the rest of Canada.

**quits** Workers who leave their jobs in search of better alternatives.

**quotas** Restrictions on the quantities of goods that can be imported.

$\overline{R}^2$ A measure of fit, between zero and one, from a *regression*. An $\overline{R}^2$ of zero implies that there is no apparent relation between the variables under consideration. An $\overline{R}^2$ of 1 implies a perfect fit: All the *residuals* are equal to zero.

**random walk** The path of a variable whose changes over time are unpredictable.

**random walk of consumption** The proposition that if consumers are foresighted, changes in their consumption should be unpredictable.

**rate of growth of multifactor productivity** See *Solow residual.*

**rating agencies** Private sector firms in financial markets that offer opinions on the quality of securities issued by firms and governments.

**rational expectations** The formation of expectations based on rational forecasts, rather than on simple extrapolations of the past.

**rational speculative bubble** An increase in stock prices based on the rational expectation of further increases in prices in the future.

**real appreciation** An increase in the relative price of domestic goods in terms of foreign goods. A decrease in the real exchange rate.

**real business cycle (RBC) models** Economic models that assume that output is always at its natural level. Thus all output fluctuations are movements of the natural level of output, as opposed to movements away from the natural level of output.

**real depreciation** A decrease in the relative price of domestic goods in terms of foreign goods. An increase in the real exchange rate.

**real exchange rate** The relative price of foreign goods in terms of domestic goods.

**real GDP** A measure of aggregate output. The sum of quantities produced in an economy times their price in a base year. Also known as *GDP in terms of goods, GDP in constant dollars, GDP adjusted for inflation.* The current measure of real GDP in Canada is called *GDP in (chained) 1997 dollars.*

**real GDP in chained (2007) dollars** See *real GDP.*

**real interest rate** Interest rate in terms of goods. Tells us how many goods one has to repay in the future in exchange for one good today.

**real oil price** The price of crude oil expressed in constant dollars.

**real return bond** A bond issued by the federal government that pays a real rate of interest and repays a principal that is indexed to the Consumer Price Index.

**realignment** Adjustment of parities in a fixed exchange-rate system.

**recession** A period of negative GDP growth. Usually refers to at least two consecutive quarters of negative GDP growth.

**reference week** The particular week in the month when the Labour Force Survey is taken.

**regression** The output of *ordinary least squares.* Gives the equation corresponding to the estimated relation between variables, together with information about the degree of fit and the importance of the different variables.

**regression line** The best-fitting line corresponding to the equation obtained by using *ordinary least squares.*

**rental cost of capital** See *user cost of capital.*

**research and development (R&D)** Spending aimed at discovering and developing new ideas and products.

**reservation wage** The wage that would make a worker indifferent to working or becoming unemployed.

**reserve ratio** The ratio of bank reserves to chequable deposits.

**reserves** These are deposits held by chartered banks and other financial institutions at the Bank of Canada. It is another term for *settlement balances.*

**residential investment** The purchase of new homes and apartments by people.

**residential structures** Investment in the building of new homes.

**residual** The difference between the actual value of a variable and the value implied by the *regression line.* Small residuals indicate a good fit.

**revaluation** A decrease in the exchange rate in a fixed exchange-rate system.

**Ricardian equivalence** The proposition that neither government deficits nor government debt have an effect on economic activity. Also called the *Ricardo–Barro proposition.*

**Ricardo–Barro proposition** See *Ricardian equivalence.*

**risk averse** A person is risk averse if he/she prefers to receive a given amount for sure to an uncertain amount with the same expected value.

**risk neutral** A person is risk neutral if he/she is indifferent between receiving a given amount for sure or an uncertain amount with the same expected value.

**risk premium** The difference between the interest rate paid on a bond and the interest rate paid on a given bond with the highest rating.

**sacrifice ratio** The number of point-years of excess unemployment needed to achieve a decrease in inflation of 1%.

**safe haven** An expression used to describe a country where assets earn a lower rate of return than in another country because they are perceived as less risky.

**saving** The sum of private and public saving, denoted by *S.*

**saving rate** The proportion of income that is saved.

**savings** The accumulated value of past saving. Also called *wealth.*

**scatter diagram** A graphic presentation that plots the value of one variable against the value of another variable.

**secondary income balance** The net of tranfers received from the rest of word and transfers made to the rest of the world in the balance of payments.

**secondary labour market** A labour market where jobs are poor, wages are low, and turnover is high. Contrast to the *primary labour market.*

**securitization** The issuance of securities, based on an underlying portfolio of assets, such as mortgages, or commercial paper.

**seignorage** The revenues from the creation of money.

**semi-durable goods** Purchases by households of semi-durable goods for consumption. Examples include apparel and furniture.

**senior securities** Securities that, if bankruptcy of the issuer occurs, are paid before junior securities.

**separations** Workers who are leaving or losing their jobs.

**services** Commodities that cannot be stored and thus must be consumed at the place and time of purchase.

**settlement balances** These are deposits held by chartered banks and other financial institutions at the Bank of Canada. It is another term for *reserves.*

**shadow banking system** The set of non-bank financial institutions, from SIVs to hedge funds.

**share** A financial asset issued by a firm that promises to pay a sequence of payments, called dividends, in the future. Also called *stock.*

**shocks** Movements in the factors that affect aggregate demand and/or aggregate supply.

**shoe-leather costs** The costs of going to the bank to take money out of a chequing account.

**short run** A period of time extending over a few years at most.

**short-term bond** A bond with maturity of one year or less.

**slope** In a linear relation between two variables, the amount by which the first variable increases when the second increases by one unit.

**slump** A long period of no growth.

**Solow residual** The excess of actual output growth over what can be accounted for by the growth in capital and labour.

**solvency** The situation in which the value of the bank's capital is positive.

**Stability and Growth Pact** An agreement signed by some European countries in 1997 to limit budget deficits and the ratio of debt to GDP.

**stabilization program** A government program aimed at stabilizing the economy (typically stopping high inflation).

**stagflation** The combination of stagnation and inflation.

**staggering of wage decisions** The fact that different wages are adjusted at different times, making it impossible to achieve a synchronized decrease in nominal wage inflation.

**standardized employment deficit**   See *cyclically adjusted budget balance (CABB)*.

**state of technology**   The degree of technological development in a country or industry.

**statistical discrepancy**   A difference between two numbers that should be equal, based on differences in sources or methods of construction.

**Statistics Canada**   The federal government agency that collects and publishes statistics that describe the economic and social activities of Canadians.

**steady state**   In an economy without technological progress, the state of the economy where output and capital per worker are no longer changing. In an economy with technological progress, the state of the economy where output and capital per effective worker are no longer changing.

**stock**   A variable that can be expressed as a quantity at a point in time (such as wealth). Also a synonym for *share*.

**stocks**   An alternative term for *inventories*.

**strategic interactions**   An environment in which the actions of one player depend on and affect the actions of another player.

**structural deficit**   See *cyclically adjusted budget balance (CABB)*.

**structural rate of unemployment**   See *natural rate of unemployment*.

**structured investment vehicle (SIV)**   Financial intermediaries set up by banks. SIVs borrow from investors, typically in the form of short-term debt, and invest in securities.

**subprime mortgages**   Mortgages with a higher risk of default by the borrower.

**subprimes**   See *subprime mortgages*.

**sudden stops**   A situation in which there is a sudden reduction in the willingness of investors to purchase securities denominated in the currency of a country.

**supply shock**   An unexpected macroeconomic event that reduces the level of the natural rate of output and increases the level of the natural rate of unemployment.

**target for the overnight rate**   The Bank of Canada announces a target range for the overnight funds rates and acts to keep the actual overnight funds rate within the bounds of their announced target.

**target interest rate**   See *target for the overnight rate*.

**tariffs**   Taxes on imported goods.

**taxes less subsidies on production**   The value of taxes paid in the course of production when such taxes do not vary with the quantity or value of production.

**taxes less subsidies on products and imports**   The value of taxes paid in the course of production when such taxes vary with the quantity and value of production.

**Taylor rule**   A rule, suggested by John Taylor, telling a central bank how to adjust the nominal interest rate in response to deviations of inflation from its target, and of the unemployment rate from the natural rate.

**T-bill**   See *Treasury bill*.

**technological catch-up**   A situation in which a country increases the level of technology in production by using technology developed in other countries.

**technological frontier**   A situation in which a country is using the highest available level of technology and *technological catch-up* is not possible.

**technological progress**   An improvement in the state of technology.

**technology balance of payments**   An estimate of the value of exports of technology minus the value of imports of technology.

**technology gap**   The differences between states of technology across countries.

**TED spread**   The difference between the interbank lending rate and the treasury bill rate in the United States.

**term structure of interest rates**   See *yield curve*.

**time inconsistency**   In game theory, the incentive for one player to deviate from his previously announced course of action once the other player has moved.

**Tobin's $q$**   The ratio of the value of the capital stock, computed by adding the stock market value of firms and the debt of firms, to the replacement cost of capital.

**total wealth**   The sum of human wealth and nonhuman wealth.

**toxic assets**   Assets held by banks in the crisis that were of little value.

**trade balance**   The difference between exports and imports. Also called *net exports*.

**trade deficit**   A negative trade balance; that is, imports exceed exports.

**trade surplus**   A positive trade balance; that is, exports exceed imports.

**trade-weighted real exchange rate**   See *multilateral real exchange rate*.

**transfers**   See *government transfers*.

**transfers to other levels of government**   Monetary transfers from one level of government to another.

**transfers to persons**   Transfers of money from a government to a person.

**transfers to the provinces**   Federal government tax revenues that are given to the provinces.

**Treasury bill**   A government bond with a maturity of up to one year. Both the U.S. and Canadian governments issue such bills. Also called the *T-bill*.

**Troubled Asset Relief Program (TARP)**   Part of the U.S. response to the financial crisis in 2008 was both the purchase of assets from banks and the direct purchase of shares in banks to help maintain bank liquidity.

**$t$-statistic**   A statistic associated with an estimated coefficient in a regression that indicates the level of confidence that the true coefficient differs from zero.

**twin deficits**   A positive relationship sometimes observed in which a large government debt is associated with a large current account or trade deficit.

**unanticipated money**   Movements in nominal money that could not have been predicted based on the information available at some time in the past.

**uncovered interest parity relation**   An arbitrage relation stating that domestic and foreign bonds must have the same expected rate of return, expressed in terms of the domestic currency.

**underwater mortgage**   The situation in which the value of the mortgage on a property exceeds the value of the property.

**Unemployment Insurance**   See *Employment Insurance*.

**unemployment rate**   The ratio of the number of unemployed to the labour force.

**usable observation**   An observation for which the values of all the variables under consideration are available for *regression* purposes.

**user cost of capital**   The cost of using capital over a year, or a given period of time. The sum of the real interest rate and the depreciation rate. Also called the *rental cost of capital*.

**value added**   The value a firm adds in the production process, equal to the value of its production minus the value of the intermediate inputs it uses in production.

**velocity**   The ratio of nominal income to money; the number of transactions for a given quantity of money, or the rate at which money changes hands.

**vicious circle**   A situation in which, with a large amount of government debt outstanding, the debt is perceived to become more risky and the interest rate on the debt rises. The consequent increase in interest payments then increases the deficit and the debt.

**wage indexation**   A rule that automatically increases wages in response to an increase in prices.

**wage-price spiral**   The mechanism by which increases in wages lead to increases in prices, which lead in turn to further increases in wages, and so on.

**wage-setting relation**   The relation between the wage chosen by wage setters and the unemployment rate.

**wages and salaries**   Payments to persons who work.

**war of attrition**   Occurs when both parties to an argument hold their ground, hoping that the other party will give in.

**wealth**   See *financial wealth*.

**wholesale funding**   Bank issue of short-term debt to create funds to re-lend in place of attracting deposits to lend.

**yield curve**   The relation between yield and maturity for bonds of different maturities. Also called the *term structure of interest rates*.

**yield to maturity**   The constant interest rate that makes the price of an *n*-year bond today equal to the present value of future payments. Also called the *n-year interest rate*.

# INDEX

Note: bold-faced page references identify definitions; *f* following a page reference indicates a figure or photo; *t* following a page reference indicates a table; and *n* following a page reference indicates a footnote